UNIVERSITY CASEBOOK SERIES®

FAMILY PROPERTY LAW

CASES AND MATERIALS ON WILLS, TRUSTS, AND ESTATES

NINTH EDITION

THOMAS P. GALLANIS
Allison and Dorothy Rouse Chair in Law, George Mason University
Visiting Professor of Law and Charles J. Merriam Scholar,
University of Chicago
Chair Visiting Professor of Law, Shanghai Jiao Tong University

FOUNDATION
PRESS

University Casebook Series is a trademark registered in the U.S. Patent and Trademark Office.

© 1991, 1997, 2002 FOUNDATION PRESS
© 2006, 2011 THOMSON REUTERS/FOUNDATION PRESS
© 2014, 2019, 2020 LEG, Inc. d/b/a West Academic
© 2024 LEG, Inc. d/b/a West Academic
        860 Blue Gentian Road, Suite 350
        Eagan, MN 55121
        1-877-888-1330

Published in the United States of America

ISBN: 979-8-88786-406-8

Preface

This book concerns the transmission of family wealth, a process wherein the law of the family intersects with the law of property. Disputes involving family property often pit one family member against another. To be sure, the transmission of family property often occurs quietly, privately, and harmoniously. But not always. In this book, we shall encounter intensely personal disputes—siblings against siblings; children of a prior marriage against their surviving stepparent; aunt or uncle against niece or nephew. We can safely imagine the aftermath of the dispute, with strained or even severed family relationships. In reading the cases reprinted herein, do not overlook the human dimension. Family property law affects not only the wealth but also the emotional lives of human beings.

Once a static area, family property law has entered a reform phase as it responds to a variety of social and legal developments. These developments include: changing notions of family and society; the acceptance of a partnership theory for assessing the financial aspects of a marriage; a growing recognition that the traditional rules and doctrines advertised as giving effect to intention can work to undermine it; and the need to reshape the law of donative transfers into a unity, thus departing from the traditional approach in which one set of rules governs wills and another set of rules governs other property arrangements such as life insurance, pension benefits, and revocable trusts.

The casebook centers on the Uniform Probate Code (UPC) and the Uniform Trust Code (UTC). The UPC was promulgated in 1969 and was substantially revised in 1990, again in 2008, and again in 2019, with further amendments in 2021. The UTC was promulgated in 2000 and is the first effort ever to produce a comprehensive uniform act on trusts. The UPC and UTC will influence family property law deep into this century.

The book is divided into four parts. Part I covers the essential core of a standard three-credit course in trusts and estates: the policy basis of inheritance and the changing character of intergenerational wealth transfer; intestate succession; the requirements for executing and revoking wills; the rise of will substitutes, including joint accounts, joint tenancies, life insurance, pension accounts, and revocable trusts; spousal protection and community property; the creation and termination of trusts; trust administration and the powers and duties of trustees; support, discretionary, and spendthrift trusts; trust modification and termination; and the particular rules applicable to charitable trusts. Part I also contains a chapter on the Changing American Family, which addresses the implications of the changing definitions of family for intestacy and constructional law.

Part II contains the materials for a two-credit advanced course ("Trusts & Estates II") for students who have already taken the basic course. Here we explore substantive provisions of wills and trust instruments, with concentrated attention given to recurring construction problems and pitfalls in drafting, powers of appointment, the classification (and consequences of classification) of estates and future interests, and the impact of rules of policy restricting the disposition of property, including the rule against perpetuities. Instructors offering the basic course as four credits, rather than three, may wish to add one or more of these topics.

Part III explores two further topics: elder law and federal transfer taxation. Instructors offering the basic course as four credits, rather than three, may wish to include one or both of these topics.

Part IV, titled "Looking to the Future," offers thought-provoking materials that can appropriately be covered in the last day or two of a basic or advanced course. The chapter invites students to think about the policy implications of the tools of the estate planner, and how these tools may change in future decades.

Code Book. The casebook is meant to be used with a companion code book (selected by the instructor) that contains the UPC, the UTC, and other relevant uniform acts. The casebook itself references but does not reproduce these uniform acts. Much is to be gained by studying the statutory text and official comments in the context of a code or act as a whole. One such code book is Thomas P. Gallanis, *Uniform Trust and Estate Statutes* (Foundation Press).

Editorial Conventions. This casebook adheres to the customary convention of omitting footnotes from cases and other extracted sources without disclosure. Also omitted are citations within cases without the customary disclosure by way of ellipses. For the most part, citations to precedent within court opinions are omitted except where the citation identifies quoted passages. The book uses ellipses to disclose deletion of substantive material.

Acknowledgments. First and foremost, I want to record my gratitude to all of the prior authors of *Family Property Law*: Professors Richard Wellman (d. 2005) of the University of Michigan Law School and the University of Georgia School of Law, Lawrence Waggoner of the University of Michigan Law School, Gregory Alexander of the Cornell University Law School, and Mary Louise Fellows of the University of Minnesota Law School. I had the special pleasure of working with Larry, Greg, and Mary Lou on the third and fourth editions and am grateful to them for entrusting me with the editions beginning with the fifth. I am also grateful to two authors on other books that served as predecessors to *Family Property Law*. These books are *Family Property Settlements* and *Trusts and Succession*, authored by Professors Olin L. Browder, Jr. (d. 2007) and George E. Palmer (d. 1994), both of the University of Michigan Law School. The work of all of these authors continues to benefit *Family Property Law*.

Preface

It is a pleasure to thank the University of Iowa College of Law and the Antonin Scalia Law School of George Mason University for research support and research assistance. The student research assistants who have provided invaluable help on this Ninth Edition are Kaitlin Chen, Conor Martini, Austin Quinn, and Robert Ryu.

THOMAS P. GALLANIS

January 2024

Summary of Contents

Table of Contents

Table of Contents

Page

Table of Contents

Table of Abbreviations

Am. L. Prop. . . . . American Law of Property (A. James Casner ed. 1952)

Atkinson on Wills . . . . Thomas E. Atkinson,
Handbook of the Law of Wills (2d ed. 1953)

Bogert on Trusts . . . . George G. Bogert & George T. Bogert,
Law of Trusts and Trustees (2d ed. 1984-88,
3d ed. led by Amy Morris Hess, 2000-present)

Gray on Perpetuities . . . . John Chipman Gray,
The Rule Against Perpetuities (4th ed. 1942)

IRC . . . . Internal Revenue Code

Palmer on Restitution . . . . George E. Palmer, Law of Restitution (1978)

Page on Wills . . . . W. Page, Law of Wills
(W. Bowe & D.Parker rev. eds. 1959-82)

Restatement 3d of Property . . . . Restatement (Third) of Property: Wills and
Other Donative Transfers

Restatement 2d of Property . . . . Restatement (Second) of Property:
Donative Transfers

Restatement of Property . . . . Restatement of Property

Restatement 3d of Trusts . . . . Restatement (Third) of Trusts

Restatement 2d of Trusts . . . . Restatement (Second) of Trusts

Restatement of Trusts . . . . Restatement of Trusts

Scott on Trusts . . . . Austin W. Scott, Law of Trusts
(William F. Fratcher ed. 4th ed. 1987-89)

Scott & Ascher on Trusts . . . . Austin W. Scott & Mark L. Ascher,
Scott and Ascher on Trusts (5th ed. 2006-2010,
6th ed. 2019-present)

Simes & Smith on Future Interests . . . . Lewis M. Simes & Allan F. Smith,
Law of Future Interests (2d ed. 1956)

Table of Abbreviations

UPC. . . . . Uniform Probate Code

UTC. . . . . Uniform Trust Code

Table of Cases

The principal cases are in italic. Other cases are in roman.
References are to pages.

Table of Cases

Table of Cases

Table of Cases

Permissions

I acknowledge with thanks the following authors and publishers who have given permission to reproduce extracts from their copyrighted works.

Permissions

Ramo, Roberta Cooper, Musings of a Family Lawyer, 22 Prob. Law. 1 (1996). Reprinted by permission of the author.

Rein-Francovich, Jan E., An Ounce of Prevention: Grounds for Upsetting Wills and Will Substitutes, 20 Gonz. L. Rev. 1 (1984/1985). Reprinted by permission of the author and the Gonzaga Law Review.

Simes, Lewis M., The Policy Against Perpetuities, 103 U. Pa. L. Rev. 707 (1955). Reprinted by permission of the University of Pennsylvania Law Review.

Uniform Acts and Codes are reprinted by permission of the Uniform Law Commission.

U.S. Trust Company, Living Will, in Practical Drafting–Will and Trust Provisions. Reprinted by permission of the U.S. Trust Company.

Van Dolson, Randall D., Medicaid Eligibility Rules and Trusts for Disabled Children, 133 Trusts and Estates 51 (1994). Reprinted by permission of the author and Intertec Publishing Company.

Waggoner, Lawrence W., The Uniform Probate Code's Elective Share: Time for a Reassessment, 37 U. Mich. J.L. Reform 1 (2003). Copyright © 2003 by Lawrence W. Waggoner. Reprinted by permission of the author.

UNIVERSITY CASEBOOK SERIES®

FAMILY PROPERTY LAW

CASES AND MATERIALS ON WILLS, TRUSTS, AND ESTATES

NINTH EDITION

PART ONE
THE CORE THREE-CREDIT COURSE

Chapter 1

Introduction

"If there is any rule that requires a property book to be dull, it has been our aim to violate it."

– A. James Casner & W. Barton Leach[1]

PART A. THE FAMILY PROPERTY LAWYER

FAMILY PROPERTY LAW is an unconventional title for a classroom book on wills and trusts. We chose the title to emphasize the relationship between the family and the transmission of wealth. The law of succession plays a crucial role in the creation and maintenance of families. Family law plays an equally crucial role in wealth transmission.

The connection between family and property was the centerpiece of a lecture delivered by Roberta Cooper Ramo in 1996, when she was the President of the American Bar Association. Here is an extract from her lecture, presented to the American College of Trust and Estate Counsel and titled *Musings of a Family Lawyer*, 22 Prob. Law. 1, 11-13 (1996):

> We [trust and estate lawyers]... [wrongly] allow those who specialize in the dissolution of families to take the name "family law" or "family lawyer." In fact, it is trust and estate lawyers, especially in these days of enormously complicated relationships, who look after and usually represent the entire family, with all of the difficult ethical challenges and disclosures and explanation that true fact requires. What you and I do is listen to the desires, to the wishes, to the hopes, to the terrors and to the facts of the life and the death of members of a family unit as they define it. Which is very often beyond what the law allows and these days includes relationships for which there is no legal standing—for example, gay or lesbian partners, relationships between men and women, between friends, sisters, brothers, aunts, uncles, cousins, business partners and, most difficult often, between parents and their children. And we figure out, within the bounds of the law and the continually changing tax systems and our imaginations, how we can take the assets of that group that thinks of itself as a family and magnify those assets to provide for those people that our client or clients loves or feels some obligation to care for over the lives of many generations.
>
> But the best of us do more.... We ask terrible questions about children and grandchildren. We know everything. We bring comfort with our reality and clarity for these complicated times. We talk to people who know they are dying, we anguish when our clients sometimes do not know who they really are and who no longer recognize us....

---

1. A. James Casner & W. Barton Leach, Cases and Text on Property 8 (1951).

We know something more sensitive than our clients' secrets. We are entrusted, we family lawyers, to make their dreams come true. Our practice is focused on both life and death. We have longer lives these days in America but perhaps with less quality of life and much more need for financial security and help. Death is always complicated because of the difficulty in planning in a financial way and because now we have serial relationships and we need to care for people in each of the layers of our clients' lives.... Also it is our job, our duty, our professional obligation to help with literal questions of death and when and how it should be allowed to come.

Through the joint exploration of property and family, this book strives to present the social and legal foundations of family property law.

———

INTERNET REFERENCES. Estate planning is on the Internet. The home page for the American Bar Association's Section of Real Property, Trust and Estate Law is www.americanbar.org/groups/real_property_trust_estate/. The home page for the American College of Trust and Estate Counsel is www.actec.org.

If you are interested in seeing the wills of famous people, such as Elvis Presley, Frank Sinatra, Clark Gable, Princess Diana, Walt Disney, and many others, see www.truetrust.com/Famous_Wills_and_Trusts/Famous_Wills_and_Trusts2.html.

PART B. THE PROBATE/NONPROBATE DISTINCTION

"What's in a name? that which we call a rose
By any other name would smell as sweet."
– Juliet, daughter of Capulet[2]

You probably already know that one way to transmit property at death is by writing a will. The court-supervised process of determining whether a will is valid is called "probate," from the Latin *probare*, meaning "to prove." The court in which this occurs is typically called a "probate court." The same court also oversees a related process: the administration of the decedent's estate. Indeed, the relationship between "probate" and "administration" is so close that, in informal usage, the two terms are used synonymously.

What you may not have realized is that there are ways to transmit property at death that need not involve a court process at all. Rather than using a will, the owner of property can instead use a "will substitute" to arrange for a "nonprobate transfer." Put simply, a nonprobate transfer occurs outside of probate; it does not require any court process. The owner of property merely designates one or more beneficiaries to receive the property at the owner's death. A formal definition of a nonprobate transfer appears in section 7.1 of the Restatement 3d of Property, which defines a

---

2. W. Shakespeare, Romeo and Juliet, act 2, scene 2, lines 45-46.

will substitute as "an arrangement respecting property or contract rights that is established during the donor's life, under which (1) the right to possession or enjoyment of the property or to a contractual payment shifts outside of probate to the donee at the donor's death; and (2) substantial lifetime rights of dominion, control, possession, or enjoyment are retained by the donor." One example of a will substitute is life insurance. The owner of the life insurance policy can designate a beneficiary to receive the proceeds upon the owner's death. The proceeds are paid directly from the insurance company to the beneficiary, without involving the probate court. To learn more about the rise of will substitutes, read the following extract.

John H. Langbein, The Nonprobate Revolution and the Future of the Law of Succession
97 Harv. L. Rev. 1108, 1108-09, 1113-25 (1984)

The law of wills and the rules of descent no longer govern succession to most of the property of most decedents. Increasingly, probate bears to the actual practice of succession about the relation that bankruptcy bears to enterprise: it is an indispensable institution, but hardly one that everybody need use....

I. THE WILL SUBSTITUTES

Four main will substitutes constitute the core of the nonprobate system: life insurance, pension accounts, joint accounts, and revocable trusts. When properly created, each is functionally indistinguishable from a will—each reserves to the owner complete lifetime dominion, including the power to name and to change beneficiaries until death. These devices I shall call "pure" will substitutes, in contradistinction to "imperfect" will substitutes (primarily joint tenancies), which more closely resemble completed lifetime transfers. The four pure will substitutes may also be described as mass will substitutes: they are marketed by financial intermediaries using standard form instruments with fill-in-the-blank beneficiary designations....

Although the revocable trust is the fundamental device that the estate-planning bar employs to fit the carriage trade with highly individuated instruments, the revocable trust also keeps company with the mass will substitutes. Standard-form revocable trusts with fill-in-the-blank beneficiary designations are widely offered in the banking industry and were at one time aggressively promoted in the mutual fund industry. The Totten trust, an especially common variant, is simply a deposit account in which the beneficiary designation is thinly camouflaged under language of trust. The depositor names himself trustee for the beneficiary, but retains lifetime dominion and the power to revoke.... Either by declaration of trust or by transfer to a third-party trustee, the appropriate trust terms can replicate the incidents of a will. The owner who retains both the equitable life interest and the power to alter and revoke the beneficiary designation has used the trust form to achieve the effect of testation. Only nomenclature distinguishes the remainder interest created by such a trust from the mere expectancy arising under a will. Under either the trust or the will, the interest of the beneficiaries is both revocable and ambulatory....

The "pure" will substitutes are not the only instruments of the nonprobate revolution; "imperfect" will substitutes—most prominent among them the common-law joint tenancy—also serve to transfer property at death without probate. Joint tenancies in real estate and in securities are quite common; joint tenancies in automobiles and other vehicles are also fairly widespread. Because they ordinarily effect lifetime transfers, joint tenancies are "imperfect" rather than "pure" will substitutes. When the owner of a house, a car, a boat, or a block of IBM common stock arranges to take title jointly, his cotenant acquires an interest that is no longer revocable and ambulatory. Under the governing recording act or stock transfer act, both cotenants must ordinarily join in any subsequent transfer. Yet like the pure will substitutes, joint tenancy arrangements allow the survivor to obtain marketable title without probate: under joint tenancy, a death certificate rather than a probate decree suffices to transfer title....

II. THE HIDDEN CAUSES OF THE NONPROBATE REVOLUTION

The will substitutes differ from the ordinary "last will and testament" in three main ways. First, most will substitutes—but not all—are asset-specific: each deals with a single type of property, be it life insurance proceeds, a bank balance, mutual fund shares, or whatever. Second, property that passes through a will substitute avoids probate. A financial intermediary ordinarily takes the place of the probate court in effecting the transfer. Third, the formal requirements of the Wills Act—attestation and so forth—do not govern will substitutes and are not complied with. Of these differences, only probate avoidance is a significant advantage that transferors might consciously seek.... The probate system has earned a lamentable reputation for expense, delay, clumsiness, makework, and worse. In various jurisdictions, especially the dozen-odd that have adopted or imitated the simplified procedures of the Uniform Probate Code of 1969 ("[original] UPC"), the intensity of hostility to probate may have abated a little. There are, however, intrinsic limits to the potential of probate reform. As Richard Wellman, the principal draftsman of the [original] UPC, forthrightly declared: "The assumption that administration of an estate requires a judicial proceeding is as doubtful as it is costly." Because the Anglo-American procedural tradition is preoccupied with adversarial and litigational values, the decision to organize any function as a judicial proceeding is inconsistent with the interests that ordinary people regard as paramount when they think about the transmission of their property at death: dispatch, simplicity, inexpensiveness, privacy. As long as probate reform still calls for probate, it will not go far enough for the tastes of many transferors, who view probate as little more than a tax imposed for the benefit of court functionaries and lawyers.

The puzzle in the story of the nonprobate revolution is not that transferors should have sought to avoid probate, but rather that other persons whose interests probate was meant to serve—above all, creditors—should have allowed the protections of the probate system to slip away from them. Probate performs three essential functions: (1) making property owned at death marketable again (title-clearing); (2) paying off the decedent's debts (creditor protection); and (3) implementing the decedent's donative intent respecting the property that remains once the claims of creditors have been discharged (distribution).... Although the will substitutes are not well suited to clearing title and protecting creditors, a series of changes in the nature of wealth and in the business practices of creditors has diminished the importance of these functions....

The probate court is empowered to transfer title to a decedent's real property and thereby to restore it to marketability under the recording system. The cautious procedures of probate administration have seemed especially appropriate for realty, because the values tend to be large and the financing complex. In theory, the probate court should exercise a similar title-clearing function for all personalty, down to the sugar bowl and the pajamas, because only a court decree can perfect a successor's title in any item of personalty. Of course, ordinary practice quite belies the theory. Beyond the realm of vehicles and registered securities, which are covered by recording systems and thus resemble realty in some of the mechanics of transfer, formal evidence of title is not required to render personalty usable and marketable.

The preoccupation of probate procedure with the transfer of title to single-tenancy real estate reflects the wealth patterns of the small-farm, small-enterprise economy of the nineteenth century that shaped our probate tradition.... Promissory instruments—stocks, bonds, mutual funds, bank deposits, and pension and insurance rights—are the dominant component of today's private wealth. Together with public promises (that is, government transfer payments) these instruments of financial intermediation eclipse realty and tangible personalty.

The instruments of financial intermediation depend upon an underlying administrative capacity that is without counterpart in the realm of realty and tangible personalty. Financial intermediation is, as the term signifies, intrinsically administrative.... Once a bureaucracy appropriate to such tasks is in operation, only a scant adaptation is necessary to extend its functions and procedures to include the transfer of account balances on death. The probate system nonetheless backstops the practice of financial intermediaries in important ways. The standard form instruments of the nonprobate system all but invariably name the transferor's probate estate as the ultimate contingent beneficiary. If, therefore, the named beneficiaries predecease the transferor or cannot be identified, the financial intermediary remits the fund to probate distribution. Messy heirship determinations are foisted off onto the courts. Likewise, if the proper course of distribution is for some reason doubtful, or if contest threatens, financial intermediaries can force the probate (or other) courts to decide the matter.... In this way the nonprobate system rides "piggyback" on the probate system.... In the nonprobate system, genuine disputes still reach the courts, but routine administration does not....

The other set of changes that underlie the nonprobate revolution concerns another great mission of probate: discharging the decedent's debts. Many of the details of American probate procedure, as well as much of its larger structure, would not exist but for the need to identify and pay off creditors. These procedures are indispensable, but—and here I am asserting a proposition that has not been adequately understood—only for the most exceptional cases. In general, *creditors do not need or use probate.*

I have undertaken to verify this point within the retail and consumer credit industry. Without mounting a systematic empirical study, I have tried to inquire broadly among credit officers and credit information specialists and their lawyers. Among those I interviewed, I found unanimity both on the central proposition that probate plays an inconsequential role in the collection of decedents' debts, and on the reasons why.

In the vast majority of cases, survivors pay off decedents' debts voluntarily and rapidly....

Creditors know that survivors behave in this way, and they rely upon voluntary notice from survivors as their primary means of learning about a debtor's death.... In the remainder of cases, which usually involve unmarried decedents, the creditor commonly discovers the death when the account becomes delinquent and collections personnel begin making inquiries. None of the large retail creditors with whom I spoke made any effort to take advantage of the formal notice-of-death procedures contained in the probate codes for their protection, nor did they have anyone assigned to read newspaper obituaries or inspect official death registers....

Creditor protection is also intertwined with a variant of the principal will substitute, life insurance. So-called credit life insurance typically discharges an insured's account balance at death....

Toward the upper end of the scale of consumer debt, where we encounter automobile finance, we find a different mode of creditor protection, the security interest.... This leverage over survivors ordinarily leads to out-of-court settlement of such debts.... When this formidable battery of out-of-court payment and collection practices fails to clear a debt, the creditor protection system of probate may also be unavailing. Although the safeguards of notice, court filings, hearings, adjudication, and so forth are meant to protect creditors, they are often self-defeating, because they make probate proceedings too expensive to be cost effective for collecting routine debts. Account balances are often so small that collection costs would exceed the likely recovery even if nonlawyers handled most of the filings and subsequent steps.

Nonetheless, creditors do use probate. The large creditors with whom I spoke were prepared to go to probate to attempt to collect debts of several thousand dollars when preliminary investigation by credit information agencies or in-house personnel revealed the likelihood of substantial assets in a probate estate. None seemed concerned to trace nonprobate assets....

In the late twentieth century, creditor protection and probate have largely parted company. Had this development been otherwise, the rise of the will substitutes could not have occurred. If creditors had continued to rely significantly upon probate for the payment of decedents' debts, creditors' interests would have constituted an impossible obstacle to the nonprobate revolution. For—make no mistake about it—the will substitutes do impair the mechanism by which probate protects creditors.

Even though the substantive law governing most of the major will substitutes usually recognizes the priority of creditors' claims over the claims of gratuitous transferees (life insurance is sometimes an exception), the decentralized procedures of the nonprobate system materially disadvantage creditors.

Notes and Questions

1. *Probate Administration.* The purpose of this Note is to give you a general sense of the process and of the responsibilities of the decedent's *personal representative* (p.r.). Any discussion of probate administration quickly becomes complicated because the probate laws are not uniform and the practices in local probate offices are diverse. Nevertheless, a general description of the probate process is possible. If a decedent dies without a valid will or if the decedent's will fails to name an executor, the court, in accordance with statutory direction, will name an administrator for the probate estate. If the will names an executor who is willing and able to serve, that person will act as the p.r. of the probate estate. Executors and administrators have the same responsibilities. They are fiduciaries who are entrusted with the probate property of decedents. They are accorded powers that they must exercise on behalf of those persons who have claims to the probate estates of decedents—beneficiaries and creditors. In preparation for beginning the probate administration process, the p.r. should consult with the family and assist, as requested, with funeral arrangements. The p.r. should also ascertain surviving kin and obtain their addresses, notify the decedent's bank, employer, insurer, and annuity obligor of the decedent's death, identify and protect the decedent's moveable assets, and review records for business contracts, property transactions, debts, and credits. The p.r. is responsible for locating the decedent's will and obtaining copies of the decedent's death certificate.

Upon collecting this information and notifying the appropriate persons, the p.r. should file a petition for probate of the will and obtain court appointment as p.r. The will should be probated in the county in which the decedent was domiciled at death. If real property is located in another jurisdiction, the p.r. will also have to seek ancillary administration in that jurisdiction. The p.r. should arrange for probate bonds, if necessary, and give required notices to creditors of the estate.

A p.r.'s next responsibility is to collect, protect, inventory, and appraise all probate assets. All estate cash and checks payable to the decedent should be deposited in the p.r.'s estate account. This would include collecting and depositing insurance proceeds that are payable to the estate as well as any sums owed to the decedent. In addition, a p.r. is responsible for taking possession, storing, or otherwise securing tangible personal assets. Sometimes it is necessary to prepare an inventory of estate assets for court filing and to arrange for appraisal of estate assets as may be required by the court or dictated by federal and state tax rules. The p.r. should set up a record system to identify probate and nonprobate assets passing at death to surviving joint tenants and death beneficiaries. This information will be required for reporting on state inheritance and federal estate tax returns. Finally, the p.r. has a responsibility to investigate business arrangements that may require attention and make appropriate protective and managerial arrangements.

The p.r. must also consider all estate claims presented to him or her or to the court, by gathering the necessary information needed to reject or allow each of the claims. The United States Supreme Court held in Tulsa Professional Collection Services, Inc. v. Pope, 485 U.S. 478 (1988), that the due process clause requires that creditors of the decedent who are known to, or reasonably ascertainable by, the p.r. must be given actual notice of court proceedings serving to bar creditors' claims. The Court held that notice by publication is insufficient.

The p.r. should discharge undisputed and minor obligations as soon as possible. In making these decisions, the p.r. should consider the amount of all known claims against an estate and an estate's liquidity. The p.r. is responsible for making sure that all taxes are paid and paid in a timely fashion. The p.r. must obtain all the information necessary to file necessary tax returns pertaining to federal and state income and transfer taxes. In addition to discharging claims, the p.r. should consider the other cash demands on the estate. These would include payments for family allowances, which are statutorily provided (see Chapter 8), administrative expenses, and legacies. The p.r. must make decisions about how needed cash may be best raised and what assets, if any, need to be liquidated. The p.r. must also make investment decisions, taking into consideration market conditions as well as the circumstances of estate beneficiaries. The p.r. has the responsibility for managing and investing the probate assets prudently pending distribution.

Finally, the p.r. must determine the respective rights of estate beneficiaries. The p.r. must prepare an accounting of receipts and disbursements. This accounting must indicate whether the receipts and disbursements are related to income or principal. The p.r. must also prepare a distribution plan for the court and obtain approval from the beneficiaries of the plan. The p.r. should consider whether to make partial distributions in cash or in kind. Those decisions will be influenced by tax consequences for the estate and for the affected beneficiaries. A final distribution will occur from the estate upon the issuance of an order by the court or upon the receipt by the p.r. of a release from the beneficiaries.

For an analysis and critique of probate administration, see John H. Martin, Reconfiguring Estate Settlement, 94 Minn. L. Rev. 42 (2009). For an empirical study examining the operation of the probate system in one California county, see David Horton, In Partial Defense of Probate: Evidence from Alameda County, California, 103 Geo. L.J. 605 (2015).

2. *Creditors' Claims*. Professor Langbein writes that creditors do not rely much on probate administration to secure discharge of debts owed them. His analysis, however, focuses exclusively on voluntary creditors. What about persons who have tort claims or claims for child support against the decedent? Do you think property passing by will substitutes, such as life-insurance proceeds and the funds on deposit in joint bank accounts, should be beyond the reach of creditors? The question of

creditors' rights to reach nonprobate property is discussed in Chapter 7. We shall see that the rights of creditors to reach nonprobate property are frequently determined by statute and depend on the type of will substitute involved.

3. *The Right of Publicity*. Although descendibility is clear for most property interests, it has been disputed with regard to the right of publicity. The right of publicity is the legal recognition of a person's interest in his or her own name, signature, likeness, or other indicia of identity. See Restatement 3d of Unfair Competition §46 (1995). The importance of the question whether heirs can control the use of a person's identity after the person's death has grown in recent years as digital technology has increased the opportunities for commercial use of deceased celebrities. Although the majority of jurisdictions that have considered this issue by statute or by court-made law recognize the right of publicity to be descendible, most limit the duration of the right. These jurisdictions vary a great deal in the length of time that they recognize post-mortem publicity rights. See, e.g., Cal. Civil Code §3344.1(g) (70 years); Ind. Code §32-36-1-8 (100 years); Va. Code Ann. §8.01-40(B) (20 years). On the estate-tax consequences of a descendible right of publicity, see the exchanges between Mitchell Gans, Bridget Crawford and Jonathan Blattmachr, on the one hand, and Joshua Tate, on the other, in 117 Yale L.J. Pocket Part 203 (2008), 118 Yale L.J. Pocket Part 38 (2008), and 118 Yale L.J. Pocket Part 50 (2008). For a high-profile case involving the taxation and valuation of Michael Jackson's image and likeness, see Estate of Jackson, T.C. Memo. 2021-48.

It is possible for heirs to register a person's name or likeness as a trademark after the person's death. See, e.g., Pirone v. MacMillan, Inc., 894 F.2d 579 (2d Cir. 1990) (after Babe Ruth's death, his daughters registered the name "Babe Ruth" as a trademark); Estate of Presley v. Russen, 513 F.Supp. 1339 (D. N.J. 1981).[3]

4. *"Digital" Assets*. What happens at death to a person's "digital" assets, such as a Facebook account or an online bank account? Some service providers have policies covering what happens when an individual dies, but many others do not. The Uniform Law Commission has promulgated a uniform act to address these issues. The original Uniform Fiduciary Access to Digital Assets Act was promulgated in 2014, but this version swiftly encountered strong opposition from service providers and their lobbyists. A Revised Uniform Fiduciary Access to Digital Assets Act was promulgated in 2015. Perhaps the most notable difference between the two versions is that the original act created a presumption that the decedent had granted "lawful consent" for access by a fiduciary—such as the decedent's executor or trustee—to the decedent's digital assets. The revised act creates no such presumption. Instead, a fiduciary (or non-fiduciary) has access to a decedent's digital assets only if the decedent expressly granted such consent in a will, trust, power of attorney, or other

---

3. In the United Kingdom, trademark registration has been refused for "Diana, Princess of Wales," "Elvis," "Elvis Presley," "Jane Austen," and "Tarzan." See 2000 WL 33148951 ("Diana, Princess of Wales"); 1999 WL 250121 ("Elvis," "Elvis Presley"); 1999 WL 33210361 ("Jane Austen"); 1970 WL 29546 ("Tarzan").

record or by means of "online tool" created by the service provider. In the absence of such an express grant of authority, the terms-of-service agreement with the online provider is controlling. For a discussion of the original and revised acts, see Suzanne Brown Walsh, Benjamin Orzeske & Turney P. Berry, You Can't Always Get What You Want: Understanding the Revised Uniform Fiduciary Access to Digital Assets Act, Tr. & Est. 25 (Nov. 2015). As this edition of the casebook goes to press, the revised uniform act has been enacted in more than forty-five states.

5. *The Will/Will Substitute Distinction.* Professor Langbein writes that "[t]he owner who retains both the equitable life interest and the power to alter and revoke the beneficiary designation has used the trust form to achieve the effect of testation. Only nomenclature distinguishes the remainder interest created by such a trust from the mere expectancy arising under a will." Langbein, above, at 1113. That passage was probably confusing when you read it, because it seems to say that what the law calls a will and what the law calls a revocable trust have the same substantive consequences. If that is so, why distinguish the two instruments at all? The answer is that family property law is in a transitional stage, moving toward the elimination of the will/will substitute distinction. The twentieth-century nonprobate revolution has significantly affected family property law. On many important issues, wills and will substitutes are treated alike. For example, statutory protections of spouses provide that nonprobate as well as probate property is reachable by disinherited spouses. See Chapter 8. Similarly, the federal and state income and transfer tax laws encompass property passing by wills and will substitutes. See Chapter 19. Full integration of the law of wills and will substitutes, however, is not yet complete. Many legal consequences still turn on whether an instrument is labeled a will or a will substitute. For example, statutes typically provide that a devise (in a will) to one's spouse is revoked upon divorce. Many of these statutes, however, fail to extend the revocation-on-divorce rule to will substitutes. But see Uniform Probate Code §2-804. Throughout the study of family property law, the will/will substitute distinction requires the following inquiries: Does this rule apply only to wills? Should the rule, or a variant of it, apply to will substitutes? A still further question is: Does, or should, the rule apply to *all* donative transfers, including lifetime transfers that are not will substitutes, such as irrevocable lifetime trusts?

Problem

Of the following assets, which would be subject to probate administration at G's death, assuming that G died first, survived by A?

Which of the assets would be subject to probate administration at G's death if A died first, survived by G?

(1) Car: Title in G

(2) Bank accounts:

Checking account: Joint title in G and A

Savings account: Title in G

(3) LMN Mutual Fund: Title in G and A as equal tenants in common

(4) Certificate of Deposit: G and A as joint owners with right of survivorship

(5) Series EE U.S. Savings Bonds: Title in G, payable on death to A

(6) Home: Title in G and A as joint tenants with right of survivorship

(7) Group term life insurance on life of G with A named as beneficiary

(8) Qualified pension plan provided to G by G's employer with A named as beneficiary in case of death before retirement.

PART C. DONATIVE FREEDOM

"We owe respect to the living; to the dead, we owe only truth."[4]

1. Cultural Tradition: Donative Freedom v. Competing Interests

The Restatement 3d of Property introduces its subject by stating that "[t]he organizing principle of the American law of donative transfers is freedom of disposition."[5] Freedom of disposition, or donative freedom, encompasses several distinct yet related ideas—the right to give your property away during life and to pass it on at death, the right to choose who gets it, the right to choose the form in which they get it, and the right to give another person the right to make those choices even after your death. Donative freedom has a strong cultural tradition in Anglo-American law.[6]

Is freedom of disposition socially and economically justified? As Professor Edward Halbach asked: "What justifications are there for the private transmission of wealth from generation to generation? And how do we rationalize allowing only some individuals, selected by accident of birth, to enjoy significant comforts and power they have not earned?"[7] Therein lies the dilemma: The idea of freedom of disposition focuses on the right of the donor to transmit the wealth that he or she earned, but that right must be balanced against the right of the recipient to receive wealth that he or she did not earn. From the standpoint of the donor, the ability to pass property at death and choose who gets it plays a part in motivating industry, creativity, entrepreneurship, saving, and investment.

---

4. La Critique de L'Oedipie, Lettre Première in Oeuvres Complètes de Voltaire 15 n.1 (Moland ed. 1877) (editor's note).

5. Restatement 3d of Property at 3.

6. See Ronald Chester, Inheritance In American Legal Thought, in Inheritance and Wealth in America 23, 23-32 (Robert K. Miller, Jr. & Stephen J. McNamee eds. 1998).

7. Edward C. Halbach, Jr., An Introduction to Death, Taxes and Family Property, in Death, Taxes and Family Property 4-5 (Edward C. Halbach, Jr., ed. 1977).

From the standpoint of the recipient, the following extract from Ronald Kessler's book, The Season: Inside Palm Beach and America's Richest Society 6, 284 (1999), suggests some of the detrimental economic and social consequences resulting from inherited fortunes:

> With only 9,800 residents, Palm Beach is inherently a very small town .... Here, on $5 billion worth of real estate, live some of the richest people in the world.... For the heirs of old wealth, Palm Beach offers a synthetic society that reveres lineage and breeding rather than accomplishment....
>
> .... People brought up without the need to struggle bypass life's learning processes.... Existing on inherited funds, their sole decision each day is where they should go for lunch and dinner.... Inherently weak, they are susceptible to the constant pressure to drink. Many become alcoholics.

See also, Busman Heir Admits He Was Boat Playboy, Chicago Sun-Times, June 4, 1973 (describing Stuart Holzman, who "spent 10 years driving a bus" in order to fulfill a condition of employment in his uncle's will; but once Stuart inherited the family fortune, he "indulged himself in a $45,000 shopping spree ... scattering $100 bills in his wake as he roared away with bikini-clad girls in three speedboats").

Donative freedom would seem, on the one hand, to be consistent with the philosophy of liberal individualism, which profoundly influences the relationship between the government and its citizens within the United States. On the other hand, to permit large transmissions of wealth would seem to contradict the foundation on which our capitalist democracy was built and the basic tenets of liberal individualism itself. Once the focus shifts from the donor to the recipient, vestiges of a class system become all too apparent. Acquiring significant amounts of family wealth by gift or by will is difficult to reconcile with liberal individualism's commitment to equality and its rejection of status by birthright.

Disparity in inheritance on an individual basis can contribute to disparity in wealth even among persons with equal incomes, education, health, and marital status.[8] It is the consequence of wealth and its effect on inequality in American society that Deborah C. Malamud explores in her article Class-Based Affirmative Action:

---

8. Lester Thurow offers these comments about how large fortunes are made:

> Large instantaneous fortunes are created when the financial markets capitalize new above-average rate of return investments to yield average rate of return financial investments. It is this process of capitalizing disequilibrium returns that generates rapid fortunes.... To become very rich one must generate or select a situation in which an above-average rate of return is about to be capitalized....
>
> Once great wealth has been created, the holder diversifies his portfolio and after that is subject to diversification and to earning the market rate of return. Because most holders of wealth eventually diversify their portfolios, great fortunes remain even after the underlying disequilibrium in the real capital markets disappears....
>
> Once created, large fortunes maintain themselves through being able to diversify and through inheritance.

Lester C. Thurow, Generating Inequality: Mechanisms of Distribution in the U.S. Economy 149 (1975).

Lessons and Caveats, 74 Tex. L. Rev. 1847, 1871-72 (1996):

> Wealth is distributed far less equally than income in American society. Wealth barriers are strongly resistant to intergenerational mobility, and inequality in wealth has greatly increased in the United States since the mid-1970s. Wealth has a major impact on life chances, in that it diminishes the dependency of an individual's economic well-being upon occupation, income, educational attainment, or any of the other conventionally measured elements of relative economic position. Even the expectation of future wealth is highly significant in assessing an individual's economic circumstances. For example, a recent college graduate who expects to inherit wealth in the near future can accept a "meaningful" low-paying job in social services, the humanities, or the arts and can even create the appearance that he is living on his salary. But he knows that if he ever wants to buy a house, he need not save in advance for a down payment (an obstacle that would be insurmountable for nonwealthy people of his income); he knows that he need not save money for retirement, limit himself to jobs that provide health benefits, or worry that his choices will render him unable to afford to raise children. Wealth is thus a source of personal economic freedom in a broader sense: it is the freedom to take risks, to make mistakes, to be cushioned from market forces. To fail to consider wealth is to understate the extent both of economic inequality in the United States and of its intergenerational transmission.

Issues of freedom of disposition have repeatedly arisen in public in the context of the debate over the federal estate and generation skipping transfer taxes (see Chapter 19). One commentator argued: "Th[e] instinct to leave your own money to your own children cannot be called selfish. Sociobiologists, in fact, would call it altruistic, for in their view the willingness of an organism—usually a gene—to sacrifice so that its offspring flourishes is the very definition of altruism. Whether or not one agrees with them, repeal of the estate tax taps into very strong family feelings."[9] Another commentator argued, however: "[T]he real danger is that if [estate] taxes are eliminated, the historic and unique character of American society and culture will be placed in jeopardy. From the start, we have been a nation struggling to balance two competing values: freedom and equality.... Individuals [are] entitled to personal wealth and property as the legitimate fruit of labor and reason. Entitlement by birth, however, [is] not inherently healthy; it [is] the distinguishing feature of an aristocratic society.... [T]he wealthiest Americans—those worth tens of millions to many billions—should not be allowed to pass on every penny of these riches to their children."[10]

The issue is broader than the current transfer tax debate, however, because the present taxes only partially redress social inequality. Professor Anne Alstott has offered the thought-provoking proposal that a tax regime truly committed to equality of opportunity would combine lifetime inheritance taxation on private transfers with

---

9. Alan Wolfe, The Moral Sense in Estate Tax Repeal, N.Y. Times, July 24, 2000, at A23.

10. Leon Botstein, America's Stake in the Estate Tax, N.Y. Times, July 23, 2000, §4, at 15.

a government-provided "universal, public inheritance ... to every person." See Anne L. Alstott, Equal Opportunity and Inheritance Taxation, 121 Harv. L. Rev. 469 (2007). See also Anne L. Alstott, Family Values and the Law of Inheritance, 7 Socioeconomic Review 145 (2009); Anne L. Alstott, Family Values, Inheritance Law, Inheritance Taxation 63 Tax. L. Rev. 123 (2009).

2. Constitutional Protection?

Although donative freedom has a strong cultural tradition in Anglo-American law, it is not considered to be constitutionally protected against all forms of interference or limitation. Indeed, donative freedom is not completely unfettered in American law.[11] The Supreme Court has upheld the constitutionality of the federal transfer tax laws (see Chapter 19), which curtail to some extent the right during life or at death to transmit your property above a certain amount. See New York Trust Co. v. Eisner, 256 U.S. 345 (1921) (federal estate tax); Bromley v. McCaughn, 280 U.S. 124 (1929) (federal gift tax). If you are married, state elective share law (see Chapter 8) curtails to some extent the right to choose who gets your property at death, by giving a surviving spouse a right to a portion of the decedent-spouse's estate. The Rule Against Perpetuities and other rules (see Chapter 17) restrict the right to choose the form in which beneficiaries receive the property. In Irving Trust Co. v. Day, 314 U.S. 556 (1942), the Supreme Court held that the Fourteenth Amendment does not prohibit a state from granting the decedent's surviving spouse the right to an elective share in the decedent's estate and requiring that any waiver of that elective share right be in writing and "duly acknowledged." Writing for the Court in that case, Justice Jackson stated:

> Rights of succession to the property of a deceased, whether by will or by intestacy, are of statutory creation, and the dead hand rules succession only by sufferance. *Nothing in the Federal Constitution forbids the legislature of a state to limit, condition, or even abolish the power of testamentary disposition over property within its jurisdiction.* Expectations or hopes of succession, whether testate or intestate, to the property of a living person, do not vest until the death of that person.

Id. at 562 (emphasis added). See Daniel J. Kornstein, Inheritance: A Constitutional Right?, 36 Rutgers L. Rev. 741 (1984).

The view of the Court in *Irving Trust* was that "the dead hand rules succession only by sufferance." Does that view accurately describe the current state of the constitutional law? Consider the following case and the notes following it.

---

11. Because the restrictions on donative freedom are fairly modest, the Restatement 3d of Property states that "[p]roperty owners have the *nearly* unrestricted right to dispose of their property as they please." Restatement 3d of Property §10.1 comment a (emphasis added).

Hodel v. Irving
481 U.S. 704 (1987)

Justice O'CONNOR delivered the opinion of the Court.

The question presented is whether the original version of the "escheat" provision of the Indian Land Consolidation Act of 1983 effected a "taking" of appellees' decedents' property without just compensation.

I

Towards the end of the 19th century, Congress enacted a series of land Acts which divided the communal reservations of Indian tribes into individual allotments for Indians and unallotted lands for non-Indian settlement. This legislation seems to have been in part animated by a desire to force Indians to abandon their nomadic ways in order to "speed the Indians' assimilation into American society," and in part a result of pressure to free new lands for further white settlement. ... Until 1910, the lands of deceased allottees passed to their heirs "according to the laws of the State or Territory" where the land was located, and after 1910, allottees were permitted to dispose of their interests by will in accordance with regulations promulgated by the Secretary of the Interior. Those regulations generally served to protect Indian ownership of the allotted lands.

The policy of allotment of Indian lands quickly proved disastrous for the Indians. Cash generated by land sales to whites was quickly dissipated, and the Indians, rather than farming the land themselves, evolved into petty landlords, leasing their allotted lands to white ranchers and farmers and living off the meager rentals. The failure of the allotment program became even clearer as successive generations came to hold the allotted lands. Thus 40-, 80-, and 160-acre parcels became splintered into multiple undivided interests in land, with some parcels having hundreds, and many parcels having dozens, of owners. Because the land was held in trust and often could not be alienated or partitioned, the fractionation problem grew and grew over time.

...In 1960, both the House and the Senate undertook comprehensive studies of the problem. These studies indicated that one-half of the approximately 12 million acres of allotted trust lands were held in fractionated ownership, with over 3 million acres held by more than six heirs to a parcel. Further hearings were held in 1966, but not until the Indian Land Consolidation Act of 1983 did the Congress take action to ameliorate the problem of fractionated ownership of Indian lands.

Section 207 of the Indian Land Consolidation Act—the escheat provision at issue in this case—provided:

> No undivided fractional interest in any tract of trust or restricted land within a tribe's reservation or otherwise subjected to a tribe's jurisdiction shall descendent [sic] by intestacy or devise but shall escheat to that tribe if such interest represents 2 per centum or less of the total acreage in such tract and has earned to its owner less than $100 in the preceding year before it is due to escheat.

Congress made no provision for the payment of compensation to the owners of the interests covered by §207. The statute was signed into law on January 12, 1983, and became effective immediately.

The three appellees—Mary Irving, Patrick Pumpkin Seed, and Eileen Bissonette—are enrolled members of the Oglala Sioux Tribe. They are, or represent, heirs or devisees of members of the Tribe who died in March, April, and June 1983. Eileen Bissonette's decedent, Mary Poor Bear-Little Hoop Cross, purported to will all her property, including property subject to §207, to her five minor children in whose name Bissonette claims the property. Chester Irving, Charles Leroy Pumpkin Seed, and Edgar Pumpkin Seed all died intestate. At the time of their deaths, the four decedents owned 41 fractional interests subject to the provisions of §207. The Irving estate lost two interests whose value together was approximately $100; the Bureau of Indian Affairs placed total values of approximately $2,700 on the 26 escheatable interests in the Cross estate and $1,816 on the 13 escheatable interests in the Pumpkin Seed estates. But for §207, this property would have passed, in the ordinary course, to appellees or those they represent.

Appellees filed suit in the United States District Court for the District of South Dakota, claiming that §207 resulted in a taking of property without just compensation in violation of the Fifth Amendment. The District Court concluded that the statute was constitutional. It held that appellees had no vested interest in the property of the decedents prior to their deaths and that Congress had plenary authority to abolish the power of testamentary disposition of Indian property and to alter the rules of intestate succession.

The Court of Appeals for the Eighth Circuit reversed. Although it agreed that appellees had no vested rights in the decedents' property, it concluded that their decedents had a right, derived from the original Sioux allotment statute, to control disposition of their property at death. The Court of Appeals held that appellees had standing to invoke that right and that the taking of that right without compensation to decedents' estates violated the Fifth Amendment.

II

[A discussion of standing is omitted.]

III

The Congress, acting pursuant to its broad authority to regulate the descent and devise of Indian trust lands, enacted §207 as a means of ameliorating, over time, the problem of extreme fractionation of certain Indian lands. By forbidding the passing on at death of small, undivided interests in Indian lands, Congress hoped that future generations of Indians would be able to make more productive use of the Indians' ancestral lands. We agree with the Government that encouraging the consolidation of Indian lands is a public purpose of high order. The fractionation problem on Indian reservations is extraordinary and may call for dramatic action to encourage consolidation. The Sisseton-Wahpeton Sioux Tribe, appearing as amicus curiae in support of the Secretary of the Interior, is a quintessential victim of fractionation. Forty-acre tracts on the Sisseton-Wahpeton Lake Traverse Reservation, leasing for about $1,000 annually, are commonly subdivided into hundreds of undivided interests, many of which generate only pennies a year in rent. The average tract has 196 owners and the average owner undivided interests in 14 tracts. The administrative headache this represents can be fathomed by examining Tract 1305, dubbed "one of the most fractionated parcels of land in the world." Tract 1305 is 40 acres and produces $1,080 in income annually. It is valued at $8,000. It has 439 owners, one-third of whom receive less than $.05 in annual rent and two-thirds of whom receive less than $1. The largest interest holder receives $82.85 annually. The common denominator used to compute fractional interests in the property is 3,394,923,840,000. The smallest heir receives $.01 every 177 years. If the tract were sold (assuming the 439 owners could agree) for its estimated $8,000 value, he would be entitled to $.000418. The administrative costs of handling this tract are estimated by the Bureau of Indian Affairs at $17,560 annually....

There is no question that the relative economic impact of §207 upon the owners of these property rights can be substantial. Section 207 provides for the escheat of small undivided property interests that are unproductive during the year preceding the owner's death. Even if we accept the Government's assertion that the income generated by such parcels may be properly thought of as de minimis, their value may not be. While the Irving estate lost two interests whose value together was only approximately $100, the Bureau of Indian Affairs placed total values of approximately $2,700 and $1,816 on the escheatable interests in the Cross and Pumpkin Seed estates. These are not trivial sums.... Of course, the whole of appellees' decedents' property interests were not taken by §207. Appellees' decedents retained full beneficial use of the property during their lifetimes as well as the right to convey it inter vivos. There is no question, however, that the right to pass on valuable property to one's heirs is itself a valuable right....

...In one form or another, the right to pass on property—to one's family in particular—has been part of the Anglo-American legal system since feudal times. The fact that it may be possible for the owners of these interests to effectively control disposition upon death through complex inter vivos transactions such as revocable trusts is simply not an adequate substitute for the rights taken, given the nature of the property. Even the United States concedes that total abrogation of the right to pass property is unprecedented and likely unconstitutional. Moreover, this statute effectively abolishes both descent and devise of these property interests even when the passing of the property to the heir might result in consolidation of property—as for instance when the heir already owns another undivided interest in the property. Since the escheatable interests are not, as the United States argues, necessarily de minimis, nor, as it also argues, does the availability of inter vivos transfer obviate the need for descent and devise, a total abrogation of these rights cannot be upheld.

... The judgment of the Court of Appeals is
Affirmed.

Notes

1. *Amendments to the Act.* In 1984, while *Irving* was pending in the Court of Appeals, Congress amended §207 prospectively in three significant ways. First, the amended act provided that the land must be shown to be incapable of earning $100 in any one of the five years following the death of the decedent. Second, the amended act permitted the decedent to devise the land to any other owner of land subject to §207, the aim being to consolidate the fractions. Third, the amended act provided that the escheat provision could be overriden by a tribal solution for preventing further descent or fractionation of the escheatable interests if approved by the Secretary of the Interior.

2. *Babbitt v. Youpee.* In an 8-to-1 decision, the U.S. Supreme Court in Babbitt v. Youpee, 519 U.S. 234 (1997), held the amended act unconstitutional. The case was brought by the children of William Youpee, who had died leaving a will. His will devised his several undivided interests in allotted lands to his children, who were enrolled tribal members. He devised each interest to a single descendant and therefore did not further fractionate ownership. The Court considered the amendments to §207 and held, in an opinion written by Justice Ginsburg, that they did not cure the constitutional infirmities identified in *Irving*:

> Congress' creation of an ever-so-slight class of individuals equipped to receive fractional interests by devise does not suffice, under a fair reading of *Irving*, to rehabilitate the measure. Amended §207 severely restricts the right of an individual to direct the descent of his property. Allowing a decedent to leave an interest only to a current owner in the same parcel shrinks drastically the universe of possible successors. And, as the Ninth Circuit observed, the "very limited group [of permissible devisees] is unlikely to contain any lineal descendants.'...
>
> The United States also contends that amended §207 satisfies the Constitution's demand because it does not diminish the owner's right to use or enjoy property during his lifetime, and does not affect the right to transfer property at death through non-probate means. These arguments did not persuade us in *Irving* and they are not more persuasive today.

519 U.S. at 244-245. The Court's treatment of the takings issue as applied to American Indian law is disquieting. What is particularly pernicious about *Irving* and *Youpee* is that the Court chose to raise to the level of constitutional protection an individual property owner's right to devise when presented with cases involving property owners who objected to a statute designed to further collective tribal ownership. For a further discussion of why the Supreme Court's protection of the valuable property-held interest of descendibility inappropriately interfered with routine legislative attempts to develop "anti-fragmentation mechanisms," see Michael A. Heller, The Boundaries of Private Property, 108 Yale L.J. 1163, 1213-17 (1999).

Having applied the Anglo-American tradition to decide the constitutionality of §207 and later amendments to it, the court left outstanding the question of what remains of the philosophical and historical tradition of "the dead hand rules succession only by sufferance." Professor Ronald Chester addresses this issue in Essay: Is the Right to Devise Property Constitutionally Protected?—The Strange Case of *Hodel v. Irving*, 24 Sw. U. L. Rev. 1195, 1208-09 (1995):

> Justice O'Connor viturally ignores the route left open to the affected Indians under the Act—that of will substitutes.... Thus, depending on local law, property-holders can transfer a remainder away, reserving a life estate and general power of appointment; transfer into a joint tenancy, with the property passing automatically to the survivor; establish a revocable trust; or put a payable-on-death beneficiary on a deed or a contract....
>
> ...*Hodel v. Irving* is not technically saying that the complete abrogation of the rights of descent and devise is in itself unconstitutional. What the Court is saying is that "complete abolition of both descent and devise of a particular class of property *may* be a taking" in circumstances such as those in *Irving*, where the Court felt alternative means of passing property at death were not realistically available....
>
> Thus, the apparent damage that *Hodel v. Irving* does to the centuries-old positivist position of *Irving v. Day*, may, upon further reflection, be minor....

4. *The Uniform Partition of Heirs Property Act.* Excessive fractionation of land affects more than tribal land. As land descends, especially by intestate succession, the land is owned by more co-tenants, each having smaller fractional interests. Any co-tenant may file a lawsuit seeking partition of the property. The partition may result in a sale at auction, often below the market value. To help remedy the problem, the Uniform Law Commission promulgated the Uniform Partition of Heirs Property Act in 2010. The Act applies to "heirs property," defined in §2(5) as

> real property held in tenancy in common which satisfies all of the following requirements as of the filing of a partition action:
>
> (A) there is no agreement in a record binding all the cotenants which governs the partition of the property;
>
> (B) one or more of the cotenants acquired title from a relative, whether living or deceased; and
>
> (C) Any of the following applies:
>
>> (i) 20 percent or more of the interests are held by cotenants who are relatives;
>>
>> (ii) 20 percent or more of the interests are held by an individual who acquired title from a relative, whether living or deceased; or
>>
>> (iii) 20 percent or more of the cotenants are relatives.

If property is heirs property and a partition action is filed, the Act applies. It provides rules for determining the fair market value of the property (in §6); a procedure by which a co-tenant, other than the one who filed the partition action, may buy-out the other interests (in §7); a preference for partition in kind rather than partition by sale (in §§8 and 9); and, if there is to be a partition by sale, procedures for conducting the sale that are designed to maximize the likelihood that the sale realizes the property's market value (in §10). As this edition of the casebook goes to press, the Act has been enacted in more than 20 states.

3. Limits on the Dead Hand?

Shapira v. Union National Bank
315 N.E.2d 825 (Ohio Ct. Com. Pl. 1974)

HENDERSON, Judge.

This is an action for a declaratory judgment and the construction of the will of David Shapira, M.D., who died April 13, 1973, a resident of this county. By agreement of the parties, the case has been submitted upon the pleadings and the exhibit. The portions of the will in controversy are as follows:

> Item VIII. All the rest, residue and remainder of my estate, real and personal, of every kind and description and wheresoever situated, which I may own or have the right to dispose of at the time of my decease, I give, devise and bequeath to my three (3) beloved children, to wit: Ruth Shapira Aharoni, of Tel Aviv, Israel, or wherever she may reside at the time of my death; to my son Daniel Jacob Shapira, and to my son Mark Benjamin Simon Shapira in equal shares, with the following qualifications: . . .
>
> (b) My son Daniel Jacob Shapira should receive his share of the bequest only if he is married at the time of my death to a Jewish girl whose both parents were Jewish. In the event that at the time of my death he is not married to a Jewish girl whose both parents were Jewish, then his share of this bequest should be kept by my executor for a period of not longer than seven (7) years and if my said son Daniel Jacob gets married within the seven year period to a Jewish girl whose both parents were Jewish, my executor is hereby instructed to turn over his share of my bequest to him. In the event, however, that my said son Daniel Jacob is unmarried within the seven (7) years after my death to a Jewish girl whose both parents were Jewish, or if he is married to a non Jewish girl, then his share of my estate, as provided in item 8 above should go to The State of Israel, absolutely.

The provision for the testator's other son Mark, is conditioned substantially similarly. Daniel Jacob Shapira, the plaintiff, alleges that the condition upon his inheritance is unconstitutional, contrary to public policy and unenforceable because of its unreasonableness, and that he should be given his bequest free of the restriction. Daniel is 21 years of age, unmarried and a student at Youngstown State University.

CONSTITUTIONALITY

Plaintiff's argument that the condition in question violates constitutional safeguards is based upon the premise that the right to marry is protected by the Fourteenth Amendment to the Constitution of the United States. Meyer v. Nebraska (1923); Skinner v. Oklahoma (1942); Loving v. Virginia (1967). In Meyer v. Nebraska, holding unconstitutional a state statute prohibiting the teaching of languages other than English, the court stated that the Fourteenth Amendment denotes the right to marry among other basic rights. In *Skinner v. Oklahoma*, holding unconstitutional a state statute providing for the sterilization of certain habitual criminals, the court stated that marriage and procreation are fundamental to the very existence and survival of the race. In *Loving v. Virginia*, the court held unconstitutional as violative of the Equal Protection and Due Process Clauses of the Fourteenth Amendment an antimiscegenation statute under which a black person and a white person were convicted for marrying. In its opinion the United States Supreme Court made the following statements:

> There can be no doubt that restricting the freedom to marry solely because of racial classifications violates the central meaning of the Equal Protection Clause.
>
> ...The freedom to marry has long been recognized as one of the vital personal rights essential to the orderly pursuit of happiness by free men. ...
>
> Marriage is one of the 'basic civil rights of man,' fundamental to our very existence and survival.... The Fourteenth Amendment requires that the freedom of choice to marry not be restricted by invidious racial discriminations. Under our Constitution, the freedom to marry, or not marry, a person of another race resides with the individual and cannot be infringed by the State.

From the foregoing, it appears clear, as plaintiff contends, that the right to marry is constitutionally protected from restrictive state legislative action. Plaintiff submits, then, that under the doctrine of Shelley v. Kraemer (1948), the constitutional protection of the Fourteenth Amendment is extended from direct state legislative action to the enforcement by state judicial proceedings of private provisions restricting the right to marry. Plaintiff contends that a judgment of this court upholding the condition restricting marriage would, under Shelley v. Kraemer, constitute state action prohibited by the Fourteenth Amendment as much as a state statute.

In Shelley v. Kraemer the United States Supreme Court held that the action of the states to which the Fourteenth Amendment has reference includes action of state courts and state judicial officials. Prior to this decision the court had invalidated city ordinances which denied blacks the right to live in white neighborhoods. In Shelley v. Kraemer owners of neighboring properties sought to enjoin blacks from occupying properties which they had bought, but which were subjected to privately executed restrictions against use or occupation by any persons except those of the Caucasian race. Chief Justice Vinson noted, in the course of his opinion at page 13: 'These are cases in which the purposes of the agreements were secured only by judicial enforcement by state courts of the restrictive terms of the agreements.'

In the case at bar, this court is not being asked to enforce any restriction upon Daniel Jacob Shapira's constitutional right to marry. Rather, this court is being asked to enforce the testator's restriction upon his son's inheritance. If the facts and circumstances of this case were such that the aid of this court were sought to enjoin Daniel's marrying a non-Jewish girl, then the doctrine of Shelley v. Kraemer would be applicable, but not, it is believed, upon the facts as they are.

Counsel for plaintiff asserts, however, that his position with respect to the applicability of Shelley v. Kraemer to this case is fortified by two later decisions of the United States Supreme Court: Evans v. Newton (1966) and Pennsylvania v. Board of Directors of City Trusts of the City of Philadelphia (1957)....

Both of [these cases] involved restrictive actions by state governing agencies, in one case with respect to a park, in the other case with respect to a college. Although both the park and college were founded upon testamentary gifts, the state action struck down by the court was not the judicial completion of the gifts, but rather the subsequent enforcement of the racial restrictions by the public management.

Basically, the right to receive property by will is a creature of the law, and is not a natural right or one guaranteed or protected by either the Ohio or the United States constitution. It is a fundamental rule of law in Ohio that a testator may legally entirely disinherit his children. This would seem to demonstrate that, from a constitutional standpoint, a testator may restrict a child's inheritance. The court concludes, therefore, that the upholding and enforcement of the provisions of Dr. Shapira's will conditioning the bequests to his sons upon their marrying Jewish girls does not offend the Constitution of Ohio or of the United States.

PUBLIC POLICY

The condition that Daniel's share should be 'turned over to him if he should marry a Jewish girl whose both parents were Jewish' constitutes a partial restraint upon marriage. If the condition were that the beneficiary not marry anyone, the restraint would be general or total, and, at least in the case of a first marriage, would be held to be contrary to public policy and void. A partial restraint of marriage which imposes only reasonable restrictions is valid, and not contrary to public policy. The great weight of authority in the United States is that gifts conditioned upon the beneficiary's marrying within a particular religious class or faith are reasonable.

Plaintiff contends, however, that in Ohio a condition such as the one in this case is void as against the public policy of this state.... There can be no question about the soundness of plaintiff's position that the public policy of Ohio favors freedom of religion . . . .

Counsel contends that if 'Dr. David Shapira, during his life, had tried to impose upon his son those restrictions set out in his Will he would have violated the public policy of Ohio... [and that] public policy is equally violated by the restrictions Dr. Shapira has placed on his son by his Will.' This would be true, by analogy, if Dr. Shapira, in his lifetime, had tried to force his son to marry a Jewish girl as the condition of a completed gift. But it is not true that if Dr. Shapira had agreed to make his son an inter-vivos gift if he married a Jewish girl within seven years, that his son could have forced him to make the gift free of the condition....

The only [relevant case] cited by plaintiff's counsel [is] ...Maddox v. Maddox (1854). The testator in this case willed a remainder to his niece if she remain a member of the Society of Friends. When the niece arrived at a marriageable age there were but five or six unmarried men of the society in the neighborhood in which she lived. She married a non-member and thus lost her own membership. The court held the condition to be an unreasonable restraint upon marriage and void, and that there being no gift over upon breach of the condition, the condition was in terrorem, and did not avoid the bequest. It can be seen that while the court considered the testamentary condition to be a restraint upon marriage, it was primarily one in restraint of religious faith. The court said that with the small number of eligible bachelors in the area the condition would have operated as a virtual prohibition of the niece's marrying, and that she could not be expected to 'go abroad' in search of a helpmate or to be subjected to the chance of being sought after by a stranger....

In arguing for the applicability of the Maddox v. Maddox test of reasonableness to the case at bar, counsel for the plaintiff asserts that the number of eligible Jewish females in this county would be an extremely small minority of the total population especially as compared with the comparatively much greater number in New York, whence have come many of the cases comprising the weight of authority upholding the validity of such clauses. There are no census figures in evidence. While this court could probably take judicial notice of the fact that the Jewish community is a minor, though important segment of our total local population, nevertheless the court is by no means justified in judicial knowledge that there is an insufficient number of eligible young ladies of Jewish parentage in this area from which Daniel would have a reasonable latitude of choice. And of course, Daniel is not at all confined in his choice to residents of this county, which is a very different circumstance in this day of travel by plane and freeway and communication by telephone, from the horse and buggy days of the 1854 Maddox v. Maddox decision. Consequently, the decision does not appear to be an appropriate yardstick of reasonableness under modern living conditions....

Finally, counsel urges that the Shapira condition tends to pressure Daniel, by the reward of money, to marry within seven years without opportunity for mature reflection, and jeopardizes his college education. It seems to the court, on the contrary, that the seven year time limit would be a most reasonable grace period, and one which would give the son ample opportunity for exhaustive reflection and fulfillment of the condition without constraint or oppression. Daniel is no more being 'blackmailed into a marriage by immediate financial gain,' as suggested by counsel, than would be the beneficiary of a living gift or conveyance upon consideration of a future marriage--an arrangement which has long been sanctioned by the courts of this state. Thompson v. Thompson (1867).

In the opinion of this court, the provision made by the testator for the benefit of the State of Israel upon breach or failure of the condition is most significant.... [because] it demonstrates the depth of the testator's conviction. His purpose was not merely a negative one designed to punish his son for not carrying out his wishes. His unmistakable testamentary plan was that his possessions be used to encourage the preservation of the Jewish faith and blood, hopefully through his sons, but, if not, then through the State of Israel. Whether this judgment was wise is not for this court to determine. But it is the duty of this court to honor the testator's intention within the limitations of law and of public policy. The prerogative granted to a testator by the laws of this state to dispose of his estate according to his conscience is entitled to as much judicial protection and enforcement as the prerogative of a beneficiary to receive an inheritance.

It is the conclusion of this court that public policy should not, and does not preclude the fulfillment of Dr. Shapira's purpose, and that in accordance with the weight of authority in this country, the conditions contained in his will are reasonable restrictions upon marriage, and valid.

Notes and Questions

1. *Analytical Framework.* The Restatement 2d of Property §6.2 provides in pertinent part:

> An otherwise effective restriction in a donative transfer designed to prevent the acquisition or retention of an interest in the event of some, but not all, first marriages of the transferee is valid if, and only if, under the circumstances, the restraint does not unreasonably limit the transferee's opportunity to marry....
>
> Comment a. ....The restraint unreasonably limits the transferee's opportunity to marry if a marriage permitted by the restraint is not likely to occur.
>
> Comment c. ...If marriage within the permitted sphere would be so contrary to [the transferee's] beliefs that it is unlikely that such marriage will ever occur, the restraint is general and invalid. By the same token, if the religious beliefs of the transferee do not stand in the way of such marriage, but the number of persons eligible for marriage to the transferee is negligible, the restraint is again general in effect and therefore invalid.

2. *Economic Analysis.* Consider the viewpoint of Richard A. Posner, Economic Analysis of Law 548 (7th ed. 2007):

> Suppose a man leaves money to his son in trust, the trust to fail however if the son does not marry a woman of the Jewish faith by the time he is 25 years old. The judicial approach in such cases is to refuse to enforce the condition if it is unreasonable. In the case just put it might make a difference whether the son was 18 or 24 at the time of the bequest and how large the Jewish population was in the place where he lived.
>
> This approach may seem wholly devoid of an economic foundation, and admittedly the criterion of reasonableness is here an unilluminating one. Consider, however, the possibilities for modification that would exist if the gift were inter vivos rather than testamentary. As the deadline approached, the son might come to his father and persuade him that a diligent search had revealed no marriageable Jewish girl who would accept him. The father might be persuaded to grant an extension or otherwise relax the condition. If the father is dead, this kind of 'recontracting' is impossible....

3. *Policy.* Should courts enforce conditions such as the one in Dr. Shapira's will? Why or why not?

4. *Daniel's Perspective.* What if Daniel had converted to another religion? What if he wanted to postpone marriage until after earning a Ph.D.? What if he were gay?

5. *A Gendered Phenomenon?* For evidence suggesting that "male testators tend to set more conditions than females," see Daphna Hacker, The Gendered Dimensions of Inheritance: Empirical Food for Legal Thought, 7 J. Empir. Legal Stud. 322, 335 (2010) (discussing an earlier study).

6. *Application to Will Substitutes?* Marcille Borcherding created a revocable trust providing that the share of her son Robert should be distributed to him outright at her death if he was then unmarried but that, if he was then married, the share should remain in trust. Robert sued, claiming that the provision was an invalid restraint on marriage. The Indiana Supreme Court upheld the provision on the ground that the state's statutory prohibition on marriage restraints referred only to "devises." See Rotert v. Stiles, 174 N.E.3d 1067 (Ind. 2021).

EXTERNAL REFERENCES. Martin D. Begleiter, Taming the "Unruly Horse" of Public Policy in Wills and Trusts, 26 Quinnipiac Prob. L. J. 125 (2012); Matthew Harding, Some Arguments Against Discriminatory Gifts and Trusts, 31 Oxford J. Legal Stud. 303 (2011); Ronald J. Scalise Jr., Public Policy and Antisocial Testators, 32 Cardozo L. Rev. 1315 (2011); Palma Joy Strand, Inheriting Inequality: Wealth, Race, and the Laws of Succession, 89 Or. L. Rev. 453 (2010).

PART D. TERMINOLOGY

"Words, words, words; I'm so sick of words.
I get words all day through, first from him, now from you."
– Eliza Doolittle to Freddy Eynsford-Hill[12]

Family property law uses a specialized terminology when identifying the principal actors involved in wealth transmission and their activities and documents. To be sure, some of the new legal terms you will encounter are ambiguous and have led to litigation requiring courts to interpret the meaning of a disposition found in a will or other type of document. They will be significant sources of discussion in the chapters that follow. Many of the terms, however, have well-accepted meanings, and it is those that we introduce you to here.

A person dying without a valid will has died *intestate*. A person who dies with a valid will is said to have died *testate* and is called the *testator* or *testatrix*. Older legal jargon distinguishes between the testator (if a man) and the testatrix (if a woman). This gendered grammar serves no legal purpose. In our text, as in the Uniform Probate Code (UPC or Code) and most state statutes, we refer to all persons who died with a valid will as the testator. The term "testatrix" still occasionally shows up in court opinions, however. We have not used our editing pen to change the term in the excerpts of opinions included in the book.

When a decedent's will fails to dispose of all of his or her property, it is usually said that the decedent has died *partially intestate*, rather than *partially testate*. Whether a person dies partially or fully intestate, intestate property is distributed in accordance with intestate succession statutes. We examine these in Chapter 2 but

---

12. My Fair Lady (Warner Brothers 1964).

offer a few words here. The American statutes on intestate succession are derived in part from two sources in English law: the common-law canons of descent, which determined inheritance of land, and the English Statute of Distribution 1670, 22 Car. 2, ch. 10, which governed succession to personal property. The separate treatment of land and personal property in the English law of intestate succession gave rise to a special terminology. Inheritance of land was called *descent*. In fact, the word *inheritance* itself was reserved for intestate succession to land. Those who took land by intestacy were called *heirs*. Succession to personal property was often called *distribution* because of the fact that title to personal property passed to the personal representative, who made distribution to those entitled to share in an intestate's personal property after paying the debts and any other claims against the estate. As a consequence, statutes on intestate succession were (and still are) called *statutes of descent and distribution.* Those who took personal property by intestacy were called *distributees* or *next of kin.*

The history is somewhat the same in testate succession. In older usage, a disposition of land by will was a *devise*, and the one to whom the land was given was a *devisee*. A disposition of personal property was a *legacy* or *bequest*, and the recipient was a *legatee*. Today the words are commonly used interchangeably, especially devisee and legatee. UPC §1-201 defines the word "devise," when it appears in the Code, as "a testamentary disposition of real or personal property." We have gone along with this newer usage and in this book we usually refer to testamentary dispositions of land or personal property as "devises" and the recipients as "devisees."

Although the rules for intestate succession to real and personal property have major points of difference in a few American jurisdictions, and minor ones in some others, the tendency from an early time in our legal history has been to eliminate such differences. Today, in well over two-thirds of the states, there is a single pattern of inheritance without regard to the nature of the property.

One important difference, however, remains in most states. In accordance with the traditions of English law, title to and the right of possession of land pass directly to the heirs, whereas title to and the right of possession of personal property pass to the *administrator*, a fiduciary who is now often called the *personal representative (p.r.).* The same difference appears in the law of wills. Title to and possession of land disposed of by will vests in the devisee, whereas title to and possession of personal property goes to the personal representative, the *executor*, where the will names an executor. Where there is legislation on the point, however, title to both real and personal property usually passes directly to the heirs or devisees, subject to a right of possession in the personal representative for purposes of properly administering the estate. See, e.g., UPC §§3-101, 3-709. The old difference in concept can still be found in some states where they require the personal representative first to use the personal property found in the estate to pay estate creditors before using the real property. With the modern tendency to eliminate differences between succession of real and personal property, the old terminology is disappearing. Lawyers now often use the words "inheritance," "heirs," and "next of kin" without regard to the character of the estate. Nevertheless, disregard of the older usage is still dangerous as long as there is some reason for differentiating between real and personal property. For example, testators sometimes make devises to their own or somebody else's "heirs" or "next of kin." A devise of real property to "next of kin," or a devise of personal property to "heirs," may be ambiguous if the applicable law contains a different pattern for succession for real and personal property.

PART E. SOURCES OF FAMILY PROPERTY LAW

1. Restatements

Throughout this book, you will find frequent references to the Restatements of Property and to the Restatements of Trusts. These Restatements are central to family property law. The Restatement Third of Property: Wills and Other Donative Transfers (referred to herein as the Restatement 3d of Property) was finished in 2011.[13] The Restatement Third of Trusts (referred to herein as the Restatement 3d of Trusts) was finished in 2012.[14]

The previous editions of these Restatements greatly influenced the development of family property law during the twentieth century. The Restatement 3d of Property and the Restatement 3d of Trusts will be influential in the twenty-first century.

The Restatements are issued in the name of the American Law Institute (ALI or Institute) and are formulated through an extensive deliberative process.

Harry Kyriakodis (ALI Librarian), What Law Students Should Know About the American Law Institute
Copyright © 1996 by Harry Kyriakodis and the American Law Institute.
The American Law Institute [ALI] was organized in 1923 as a result of a study reporting that the two chief defects in American law were its uncertainty and its complexity. Produced by a group of prominent judges, lawyers, and law professors, the study called for the formation of a new organization whose mission would be to improve the law and its administration. According to the Institute's Certificate of Incorporation, its purpose is "to promote the clarification and simplification of the law and its better adaptation to social needs, to secure the better administration of justice, and to encourage and carry on scholarly and scientific legal work."

---

13. Lawrence W. Waggoner of the University of Michigan was the Reporter and John H. Langbein of Yale University was the Associate Reporter for the Restatement 3d of Property.

14. Edward C. Halbach, Jr. of the University of California at Berkeley was the Reporter and Thomas P. Gallanis then of the University of Iowa and Randall Roth of the University of Hawaii were Associate Reporters for the final volume of the Restatement 3d of Trusts.

To this end, the Institute undertook to formulate a comprehensive series of Restatements of the common law. Between 1923 and 1944, Restatements were developed for Agency, Conflict of Laws, Contracts, Judgments, Property, Restitution, Security, Torts, and Trusts. In 1952, ALI started the Second series of Restatements, which included new editions of the original Restatements plus new subjects, including Foreign Relations Law and Landlord and Tenant Law. The Third Restatement series, now in progress, includes projects on the Law Governing Lawyers; Torts (Apportionment of Liability and Products Liability); Trusts; and Property ([Wills and Other] Donative Transfers, Mortgages, and Servitudes)....

A project is undertaken by ALI only after careful consideration by its officers and Council (its governing body). A legal scholar with expertise in the field is designated the project's "Reporter." The Reporter submits drafts of "black-letter" text and explicating commentary to a carefully constituted group of Advisers. With most recent projects, drafts are also reviewed by a larger Members Consultative Group consisting of ALI members with particular interest in the subject. If approved by the Council, tentative and proposed final drafts are presented to the membership during an Annual Meeting of the Institute, where members may approve the drafts or recommit them for further revision or reconsideration. Over a period of years, this careful and deliberative process eventually produces the official text of an ALI Restatement ....

Members of The American Law Institute are selected on the basis of professional achievement and demonstrated interest in the improvement of the law. The Institute's membership consists of eminent federal and state judges, distinguished lawyers, and respected law professors. Elected membership is currently limited to 3000, which includes some members in foreign countries. The Chief Justice of the United States, Associate Justices of the Supreme Court, Chief Judges of the U.S. Court of Appeals, and chief justices of the highest state courts are ex officio members of the Institute, as are deans of law schools that are members of the Association of American Law Schools. The influence of the Institute's work is widespread, and many ALI publications have been accorded an authority greater than that of any legal treatise. This is largely due to the care with which the work is produced, the quality of the personnel involved in each project and in the ALI Council and membership, and the degree and deliberative consideration each draft is given. Over the years, there have been over 130,000 published court decisions citing the Restatements of the Law ....

2. Uniform Trusts and Estates Acts

Uniform Probate Code. For statutory law, this book centers on the Uniform Probate Code (UPC) and the Uniform Trust Code (UTC). The UPC was originally promulgated by the Uniform Law Commission[15] (ULC) in 1969. Richard V.

---

15. Short for the National Conference of Commissioners on Uniform State Laws.

Wellman, then of the University of Michigan and later of the University of Georgia, was the Chief Reporter. The UPC has had a profound effect on American law. The UPC was the first effort, ever, at comprehensive codification of the law of estates and probate. Its major divisions cover the substantive and procedural law of intestacy, wills, donative transfers, guardianship, conservatorship, and estate and trust administration.

The UPC is not a static Code. The UPC, like other uniform acts in the field of trusts and estates, is constantly monitored by a supervisory body called the Joint Editorial Board for Uniform Trust and Estate Acts (JEB). The JEB is composed of nine members—three from the ULC, three from the American Bar Association's Section on Real Property, Trust and Estate Law, and three from the American College of Trust and Estate Counsel. Seven of these nine members (including the chair, Bruce M. Stone of the Goldman Felcoski & Stone firm in Florida) are practitioners of national reputation; two (David M. English of the University of Missouri and Nancy A. McLaughlin of the University of Utah) are professors. There are, in addition, an Executive Director (Thomas P. Gallanis of George Mason University) and two liaison members (Mary Louise Fellows of the University of Minnesota and Robert H. Sitkoff of Harvard University).

Throughout the forty-plus years after the UPC's origination, the JEB has, with the approval of the ULC, revised a section here and there to eliminate unintended consequences and, in some cases, to reflect changed policy choices. But the supervisory process took a dynamic turn starting in the mid-1980s. The heightened activity culminated, in 1989, and again in 1998, in a thoroughly revised Article VI, dealing with multiple-party accounts and related areas, and, in 1990 and again in 2008, in a dramatically revised Article II, the core substantive article of the UPC. Lawrence W. Waggoner of the University of Michigan—a long-standing participant in the JEB, now emeritus—was the Reporter for these Article II revisions. In 2019, Article II was again revised substantially, with further amendments in 2021. The co-Reporters for the 2019 and 2021 revisions were Mary Louise Fellows and Thomas P. Gallanis.

We believe that the current version of the UPC will influence American family property law for many decades. At the same time, you must bear in mind that the earlier versions of the UPC or non-UPC law still constitutes the law in many states. The UPC revisions are so comprehensive that it will take significant periods of study before large numbers of states will move to enact them. Thus, in this book, we principally focus on the current version of the UPC, making references to former versions or non-UPC law as necessary.

Uniform Trust Code. In 2000, the ULC approved the Uniform Trust Code (UTC), which is the first comprehensive uniform codification of the law of trusts. The Reporter for the UTC was David M. English of the University of Missouri. Although a number of prior uniform acts related to trusts, the importance of trusts in family estate planning, as well as the incompleteness of those acts, led to a recognition of the need for a uniform act that more comprehensively addressed trust-law issues. The initial model for the UTC was Division 9 of the California Probate Code, which contains an extensive trust statute. It was also drafted in close coordination with the preparation of the Restatement 3d of Trusts. As it does for the UPC, the JEB monitors the UTC and recommends updates to the UTC as necessary. Because we believe that the UTC will influence the development of trust law during this century, we focus on its provisions throughout the trust chapters of this book.

Primary Statutory References. This book is meant to be used with a statute book containing the UPC, the UTC, and various other uniform laws that are germane to family property law. There is more than one such book available.

The casebook and the statute book are integrated by the freestanding captions in the casebook denominated Primary Statutory References. These Primary Statutory References direct you to the central statutory material reproduced in the statute book that you should examine in conjunction with the topic you are about to study.

———

INTERNET REFERENCES. The home page for the American Law Institute is www.ali.org. The home page for the Uniform Law Commission is www.uniformlaws.org, which has links to the text of uniform laws, lists of enacting states, and drafts of uniform laws in process.

EXTERNAL REFERENCES. Mary Louise Fellows & Thomas P. Gallanis, The Uniform Probate Code's New Intestacy and Class Gift Provisions, 46 ACTEC L.J. 127 (2021); Thomas P. Gallanis, Trusts & Estates: Teaching Uniform Law, 58 St. Louis U. L.J. 671 (2014); John H. Langbein, Major Reforms of the Property Restatement and the Uniform Probate Code: Reformation, Harmless Error, and Nonprobate Transfers, 38 ACTEC L.J. 1 (2012); Lawrence W. Waggoner, What's in the Third and Final Volume of the New Restatement of Property that Estate Planners Should Know About, 38 ACTEC L.J. 23 (2012); John H. Langbein, Why Did Trust Law Become Statute Law in the United States?, 58 Ala. L. Rev. 1069 (2007).

Chapter 2

Intestate Succession

PART A. INTRODUCTION

Primary Statutory Reference: *UPC §2-104*

Who Is Likely to Die Intestate? Empirical research has demonstrated that age and wealth are good predictors of will-making. The older and wealthier you are, the more likely you are to have a will. Conversely, those without a will tend to be young, hence considered unlikely to die soon. Having children is also a good predictor of will-making. Most of the people without a will do not have children. See Mary Louise Fellows et al., Public Attitudes About Property Distribution at Death and Intestate Succession Laws in the United States, 1978 Am. B. Found. Res. J. 319 (hereinafter referred to as the 1978 Survey). Besides age, income, and child-rearing, what additional factors might explain why people do or do not make wills? See Alyssa A. DiRusso, Testacy and Intestacy: The Dynamics of Wills and Demographic Status, 23 Quin. Prob. L.J. 36 (2009); John M. Astrachan, Why People Don't Make Wills, 118 Tr. & Est. 45 (Apr. 1979). One article suggests that intestacy rates would be lower if lawyers did a better job of marketing their will-drafting services. See Michael R. McCunney & Alyssa A. DiRusso, Marketing Wills, 16 Elder L.J. 33 (2008).

Of course, even for people who die intestate, intestacy is often not the prevailing form of family property transfer. Many decedents die having provided for the disposition of at least some of their property through a will substitute, such as a joint tenancy with right of survivorship or a life insurance contract.[1]

Historical Roots of Intestacy Rules. The intestacy rules of modern America have their roots in medieval England. Under the English canons of descent (which developed from customary rules), only persons related by blood to the decedent could be heirs. Blood relatives were divided into three groups: descendants (or "issue"), ancestors, and collaterals.

According to the English canons, the intestate's land was inherited by his surviving descendant(s). The canons provided that (1) a male descendant should be preferred to a female descendant and (2) among male descendants, the eldest should

---

1. In addition, a state's intestacy statute may not apply to every property interest found in the decedent's probate estate. For example, California's statute on the right of publicity includes its own distribution scheme if the decedent fails to transfer the right during life or by will. See Cal. Civ. Code §3344.1(d). For further discussion of the right of publicity, see Chapter 1.

take the entire estate (a rule called primogeniture). In a society such as England's, which was dominated by a landed male aristocracy, one purpose of primogeniture was to preserve the large family estates in the male line. Primogeniture was abolished by the Administration of Estates Act 1925, 15 & 16 Geo. 5, ch. 23, §45.

The English Statute of Distribution 1670, which governed succession to personal property, followed neither of these rules and basically codified well-established customary rules dividing personal property equally among the decedent's children, with a portion for a surviving wife. See 22 & 23 Car. 2, ch. 10 (1670) (with Americanized spelling):

> Provided always and be it enacted by the authority aforesaid that ... every ... person who by this Act is enabled to make distribution of the surplusage of the estate of any person dying intestate shall distribute the whole surplusage of such estate or estates in manner and form following, that is to say, one third part of the said surplusage to the wife of the intestate, and all the residue by equal portions to and amongst the children of such persons dying intestate, and such persons as legally represent such children in case any of the said children be then dead.... And in case there be no children nor any legal representatives of them, then one [half] of the said estate is to be allotted to the wife of the intestate, the residue of the said estate to be distributed equally to every of the next of kindred of the intestate who are in equal degree and those who legally represent them.

If an intestate died without leaving a living descendant, his land passed to collateral heirs; ancestors were completely excluded from inheriting land. The exclusion of ancestors was not followed either by the English Statute of Distribution or in any U.S. jurisdiction.

In America, rejection of the preference for males to females and of primogeniture among male descendants began during the colonial period. Reform of intestacy law, including the elimination of primogeniture in virtually all of the states in favor of a rule treating children equally, reflected the influence of the political tradition of republicanism that animated the Revolution. The preambles to the Revolutionary and post-Revolutionary acts governing inheritance expressed the republican abhorrence of aristocracy, family dynasties, and large estates.[2] This ideology co-existed uneasily with the commitment to individual rights of ownership. The conflict between individual freedom of disposition and the prevention of dynastic wealth is one of the recurrent themes in American succession law.

Policy Bases of Intestate Succession; Default versus Mandatory Rules. What objectives should guide policymakers in developing a system for succession of

---

2. See, e.g., 2 Laws of the State of Delaware, ch. 53 (Samuel & James Adams pub. 1797); 1 Public Acts of the General Assembly of North Carolina, ch. 22 (James Iredell ed., Francis Xavier Martin rev. 1804). For further discussions of the relationship between early American inheritance law and republican political ideology, see Gregory S. Alexander, Time and Property in the American Republican Legal Culture, 66 N.Y.U. L. Rev. 273 (1991); Stanley N. Katz, Republicanism and the Law of Inheritance in the American Revolutionary Era, 76 Mich. L. Rev. 1 (1977).

property upon the death of a person who lacked a valid will or will substitute? The rationale that today is commonly ascribed to intestacy laws is expressed in the following passage from the court's opinion in King v. Riffee, 309 S.E.2d 85, 87-88 (W. Va. 1983):

> Our laws concerning intestate succession are designed to effect the orderly distribution of property for decedents who lack either the foresight or the diligence to make wills. The purpose of these statutes ... is to provide a distribution of real and personal property that approximates what decedents would have done if they had made a will. Spouses and children enjoy a favored position under the laws of intestate succession because, on statistical average, they are the natural objects of most people's bounty.

The rules of intestacy are *default rules*, not mandatory rules. They apply only where the decedent has not effectively provided otherwise, as by writing a valid will. The distinction between default and mandatory rules has been described as follows:

> Default rules, also called background rules, gap fillers, or rules of construction are rules of law that yield to the contrary intention of the people they are designed to regulate. Mandatory rules, in contrast, are rules that cannot be altered by an expression of contrary intention. By way of illustration: the speed limit on a highway is a mandatory rule because it cannot be changed by an individual driver's whim; however the requirement under some probate codes that beneficiaries must survive [the decedent] by 120 hours is a default rule that can be trumped by a contrary provision in the testator's will.

Thomas P. Gallanis, Default Rules, Mandatory Rules, and the Movement for Same-Sex Equality, 60 Ohio St. L.J. 1513, 1515 (1999). Mandatory rules defeat intention for reasons of overriding policy. Default rules in family property law, in contrast, are designed to effectuate intention, or presumed intention.

Default rules also do more. In the 1978 Survey, discussed above, at 324, the authors suggest that effectuating probable intentions of decedents is not the only objective of intestacy statutes:

> The alternative ... rationale for adopting a particular distributive pattern in an intestacy statute is that it serves society's interests. There are four identifiable community aims: (1) to protect the financially dependent family; (2) to avoid complicating property titles and excessive subdivision of property; (3) to promote and encourage the nuclear family; and (4) to encourage the accumulation of property by individuals. If society's well-being requires a distributive pattern different from the determined wishes of intestate decedents, the decedents' wishes should be subordinated.

To this list, we would add another objective: to produce a pattern of distribution that the recipients believe is fair and thus does not produce disharmony within the surviving family members or disdain for the legal system.

Requirement of Survival. Only persons who survive the decedent are entitled to succeed to the decedent's property by testate or intestate succession. See Restatement 3d of Property §1.2. Unless altered by statute, survival by only an instant is sufficient. On occasion, decedents and their devisees or heirs die in circumstances—such as an automobile or airplane accident—in which it is impossible to determine the order of deaths. To meet this problem, almost all states had passed a statute identical to or closely patterned after the original Uniform Simultaneous Death Act (1953) (USDA), §1 of which provides:

> *§1. No Sufficient Evidence of Survivorship.* Where the title to property or the devolution thereof depends upon priority of death and there is no sufficient evidence that the persons have died otherwise than simultaneously, the property of each person shall be disposed of as if he had survived....

Why does the USDA presume that the testator or intestate survived the other? Dissatisfied with the USDA, the original UPC provided that "any individual who fails to survive the decedent by 120 hours is deemed to have predeceased the decedent." Current UPC §2-104 embraces the 120-hour rule but goes further by requiring that survival by 120 hours be established "by clear and convincing evidence." See also UPC §2-702 (adopting the 120-hour requirement of survival for all donative dispositions, including wills and life insurance, and for joint tenancies and joint accounts with a survivorship feature). In 1991, the Uniform Law Commission revised the USDA to adopt the UPC's 120-hour requirement of survival.

Notes and Problems

1. *Simultaneous Deaths.* A and B, a young married couple with no children, were tragically killed in an automobile accident. Both died intestate. They were both survived by their parents. There was no sufficient evidence that they died otherwise than simultaneously. Under the original USDA quoted above, who inherits A's estate and who inherits B's estate?

2. *Near Simultaneous Deaths.* Assume the same facts as in Problem 1, except that the evidence establishes that B outlived A, but by less than five hours. Under the original USDA quoted above, who inherits A's estate and who inherits B's estate? Under UPC §2-104, who inherits A's estate and who inherits B's estate?

3. *Requirement of Survival for a Specified Period.* In will drafting, it is not unusual to specify a required period of survival.[3] John F. Kennedy, Jr., and his wife, Carolyn Bessette-Kennedy, died on July 16, 1999, in the crash of a private airplane piloted by John Kennedy. They were both in their mid-thirties and had no children. In disposing of his tangible property, John's will required a 30-day survival period:

---

3. Princess Diana's will provided that "[a]ny person who does not survive me by at least three months shall be deemed to have predeceased me ...." Jerry Garcia's will devised one-third of his estate to his wife, Deborah Koons, provided she "survives me for sixty (60) days ...."

I, JOHN F. KENNEDY, JR., of New York, New York, make this my last will, hereby revoking all earlier wills and codicils....

FIRST: I give all my tangible personal property (as distinguished from money, securities and the like), wherever located, other than my scrimshaw set previously owned by my father, to my wife, Carolyn Bessette-Kennedy, if she is living on the thirtieth day after my death, or if not, by right of representation to my then living issue, or if none, by right of representation to the then living issue of my sister, Caroline Kennedy Schlossberg, or if none, to my said sister, Caroline, if she is then living. If I am survived by issue, I leave this scrimshaw set to said wife, Carolyn, if she is then living, or if not, by right of representation, to my then living issue. If I am not survived by issue, I give said scrimshaw set to my nephew John B. K. Schlossberg, if he is then living, or if not, by right of representation to the then living issue of my said sister, Caroline, or if none, to my said sister Caroline, if she is then living. I hope that whoever receives my tangible personal property will dispose of certain items of it in accordance with my wishes however made known ....

Definition of Death. The Uniform Determination of Death Act (1980) defines death as follows:

> *Section 1. [Determination of Death.]* An individual who has sustained either (1) irreversible cessation of circulatory and respiratory functions, or (2) irreversible cessation of all functions of the entire brain, including the brain stem, is dead. A determination of death must be made in accordance with accepted medical standards.

In 1991, the Uniform Law Commission incorporated the Uniform Determination of Death Act into §1-107 of the UPC and the revised USDA.

The definition of death is crucially important for determining when organ retrieval should take place. Both the legal and medical communities have had to face the difficult policy questions raised by the dual goals of maximizing the availability of organs and preserving the rights and interests of patients and their families. Although ethicists have engaged in significant debate concerning a legal and medical definition that uses two different criteria for determining death, the Act has achieved widespread adoption. For further discussion of the question of determining death and its relationship to organ donation, see James M. DuBois, Non-Heart-Beating Organ Donation: A Defense of the Required Determination of Death, 27 J.L. Med. & Ethics 126 (1999); Jerry Menikoff, Doubts about Death: The Silence of the Institute of Medicine, 26 J.L. Med. & Ethics 157 (1998); John T. Potts, Jr. et al., Commentary: Clear Thinking and Open Discussion Guide IOM's Report on Organ Donation, 26 J.L. Med. & Ethics 166 (1998).

Relatives in Gestation at the Decedent's Death. For purposes of intestacy and for purposes of devises of any present interest in property, persons who are born after the decedent's death typically are not eligible to receive the decedent's property.[4] However, the common law treats persons in gestation at the decedent's death as if they were alive at the decedent's death if they subsequently are born alive. This principle is codified in some states and in the UPC. See UPC §2-104.

In administering this principle, there is precedent suggesting a rebuttable presumption that the date of conception was nine months prior to the date of birth. See, e.g., Equitable Trust Co. v. McComb, 168 A. 203, 207 (Del. Ch. 1933); In re Wells, 221 N.Y.S. 714, 724 (Sur. Ct. 1927). To be entitled to share in the decedent's estate, a child in gestation at the decedent's death must be born alive and probably must be born viable. See, e.g., Ebbs v. Smith, 394 N.E.2d 1034 (1979). Under UPC §2-104(a)(2), the child must survive birth by at least 120 hours.

Posthumous Conception. The UPC provides inheritance and other rights to children conceived after the death of a parent if the embryo is in utero not later than 36 months, or the child is born not later than 45 months, after the parent's death. This topic is discussed in Chapter 3.

PART B. GENERAL PATTERNS OF INTESTATE SUCCESSION

1. Spouse

Primary Statutory Reference: *UPC §2-102*

One of the major concerns in intestacy law is the appropriate share for the decedent's surviving spouse. Consideration of the spousal share requires an evaluation of other relatives' claims to the estate. Under most state statutes, the surviving spouse inherits the entire estate if the decedent leaves no surviving descendants or parents. That is to say, most states give priority to the claims of the surviving spouse over those of siblings, grandparents, and any other collateral relatives or ancestors.

If the decedent leaves descendants, the surviving spouse may have to share part of the estate with them in some states. This is so even when some or all of the descendants are adults with adequate means of support and when the surviving spouse is in far greater financial need. That financial need may result from the spouse's dependency on a limited, fixed income or because of health concerns or both. It is also so even when some or all of the decedent's descendants are minors, in which case any portion the minors inherit must be placed in what frequently can be a cumbersome and expensive conservatorship. See Part B.2.c below.

---

4. Some exceptions to this rule can arise with regard to devises made to a class of persons. See Chapter 16.

If the decedent leaves no descendants but leaves a parent or parents, the spouse may have to share the estate with the parent or parents in some states. This result might seem appropriate if the parent or parents have financial need and/or the couple have not been married very long. It seems more problematic if the parents are financially self-sufficient.

What seems clear is that family circumstances vary too much to think that any intestacy statute could be designed to achieve a fair result in every case. Moreover, a complex set of rules can add administration costs, as well as lead to public confusion and misunderstanding. See Part C.2 below, considering the question whether courts should be given discretionary powers in intestate succession. What also seems clear is that the question of fairness demands consideration not only of the decedent's likely intent, but also a consideration of the decedent's duties and obligations to family members.

Discerning Decedent's Intent from Will Substitutes? If a decedent dies intestate but with one or more will substitutes, can the beneficiary designations of the will substitutes be used to inform us of the decedent's intent regarding the disposition of the intestate estate? For a preliminary analysis, see Mary Louise Fellows, E. Gary Spitko & Charles Q. Strohm, An Empirical Assessment of the Potential for Will Substitutes to Improve State Intestacy Statutes, 85 Ind. L.J. 409 (2010).

Original Uniform Probate Code. As originally promulgated in 1969, §2-102 of the UPC granted the decedent's surviving spouse the entire intestate estate if the decedent left neither surviving descendants nor surviving parents. If either a descendant or a parent survived the decedent, the surviving spouse received the first $50,000 plus one-half of the remaining balance of the estate. If one or more of the decedent's descendants were not the surviving spouse's descendants, the UPC did not give the spouse priority on the first $50,000. Instead, it limited the spouse's share to one-half of the intestate estate.

The use of the lump-sum-plus-a-fraction-of-the-remaining-balance device enabled the UPC to pay (or appear to pay) a proper obeisance to tradition while assuring the spouse the entire estate in the modest estates of $50,000 and under, and assuring the spouse the bulk of the estate if it did not have an appreciably greater value than $50,000. In a $100,000 estate, for example, the spouse's share was $75,000, with $25,000 going to the decedent's descendants or parents. In a $150,000 estate, the spouse took $100,000, with $50,000 going to the descendants or parents.

Non-Uniform Legislation. Contrasted with the intestacy patterns generally in effect when the UPC was promulgated in 1969, the surviving spouse's share granted by the UPC was quite generous. The UPC became a catalyst for legislatures to reconsider the share passing to the spouse. Currently, most non-UPC states now provide that the spouse receive a significant portion of the intestate estate both when the decedent is survived by descendants and when the decedent is not survived by descendants, but is survived by one or more parents.

Public Attitudes. Except perhaps for the wealthy, whose behavior should have very little relevance to the proper design of an intestacy law, studies have identified a strong social preference to give the entire estate to the surviving spouse, even when the decedent has surviving children or parents.[5]

These empirical studies confirm that the UPC was aligned more closely with public attitudes than the non-UPC laws in effect at the time. Although the UPC retained the traditional approach of splitting the estate between the spouse and the descendant or parent, it used the lump-sum-plus-a-fraction device to make an actual split less likely, and made the spouse's share greater than 50 percent when a split did occur.

Uniform Probate Code. The current UPC makes significant revisions to the spouse's intestate share. Section 2-102 continues to favor the surviving spouse but also attempts to adjust the share of the spouse to take account of our multiple-marriage society, in which the traditional marriage lasting a lifetime is on the decline.

Problems

1. D married S, and together they had three children, A, B, and C. Under the UPC, who is or are D's heir(s)?

2. Assume the same facts as in Problem 1, except that D died—survived by S, A, B, and C—with a will leaving all of his property to his children in equal shares. Under the UPC, who is or are D's heir(s)? Why might the heir(s) matter?

3. Assume the same facts as in Problem 2, except that D's net probate estate was valued at $100,000, and D also owned $1 million in life insurance, with S named as the beneficiary. Does this change anything? If so, what?

4. D died intestate with a net probate estate valued at $350,000, survived by his spouse, S. In the following cases, what is S's intestate share under UPC §2-102? Where does the rest of the estate go? See UPC §2-103. (For purposes of these problems, ignore the provision, added in 2008, in UPC §1-109 incorporating an

---

5. See, e.g., Mary Louise Fellows et al., Public Attitudes about Property Distribution at Death and Intestate Succession Laws in the United States, 1978 Am. B. Found. Res. J. 319, 351-54, 358-64, 366-68; Contemporary Studies Project, A Comparison of Iowans' Dispositive Preferences with Selected Provisions of the Iowa and [Original] Uniform Probate Codes, 63 Iowa L. Rev. 1041, 1089 (1978); Marvin B. Sussman et al., The Family and Inheritance 86-87, 89-90, 143-45 (1970); Olin L. Browder, Jr., Recent Patterns of Testate Succession in the United States and England, 67 Mich. L. Rev. 1303, 1307-09 (1969); Allison Dunham, The Method, Process and Frequency of Wealth Transmission at Death, 30 U. Chi. L. Rev. 241, 252-53 (1963); U.K. Law Comm'n, Family Law: Distribution on Intestacy (No. 187) app. C, at 36-37, 40-45 (1989). But see Daphna Hacker, The Gendered Dimensions of Inheritance: Empirical Food for Legal Thought, 7 J. Empir. Legal Stud. 322, 334 (2010) (discussing conflicting evidence on the question whether "women prefer allocation where the interests of their children are well-protected, while men prefer to give the surviving spouse freedom to use the resources as she or he wishes").

automatic cost-of-living adjustment.)

(a) D and S had three joint children, A, B and C, all of whom survived D.

(b) An investigative reporter discovers that S is not A's mother.

(c) The reporter discovers instead that S had an additional three children, not with D, who survived D.

EXTERNAL REFERENCES. John W. Fisher, II & Scott A. Curnutte, Reforming the Law of Intestate Succession and Elective Shares: New Solutions to Age-Old Problems, 93 W. Va. L. Rev. 61 (1990); Martin L. Fried, The Uniform Probate Code: Intestate Succession and Related Matters, 55 Alb. L. Rev. 927 (1992); Lawrence W. Waggoner, Spousal Rights in Our Multiple-Marriage Society: The Revised Uniform Probate Code, 26 Real Prop. Prob. & Tr. J. 683 (1992).

2. Descendants

Primary Statutory References: *UPC §§2-103, 2-106, 2-708*

a. Descendants' Share

In the absence of a surviving spouse, all states—UPC and non-UPC states alike—give the entire estate to the decedent's descendants, *i.e.*, to the decedent's children and descendants of deceased children. The descendants, if there are any, inherit to the exclusion of the decedent's ancestors, such as parents and grandparents, and to the exclusion of collateral relatives, such as brothers and sisters.

When a decedent dies leaving a surviving spouse as well as descendants, the descendants' share is determined in accordance with the applicable distribution patterns outlined in the section on "Spouse" above.

b. Representation Among Descendants

Any share that goes to the decedent's descendants is divided among them by representation.[6] The term "descendants" (or "issue") indicates a multiple-generation class, which includes not only children, but also grandchildren, great-grandchildren, and so on through the descending line.

To explore the idea of representation, we give you G, a 78-year-old widow who has just died, leaving some married surviving children in their late forties or early fifties, a somewhat greater number of surviving grandchildren in their twenties or

---

6. The idea of taking by representation is traceable to the canons of descent, which provided that lineal descendants should represent their deceased ancestors in inheritance. The idea of taking by representation also was carried over into the Statute of Distribution. In one form or another, representation appears in all the American statutes.

early thirties, a few of whom are married with young children.[7]

G's four-generation family is depicted in the chart below, except that the chart does not show the descendants' spouses, G's ancestors, or G's collateral relatives. The parenthetical figures show each survivor's age.

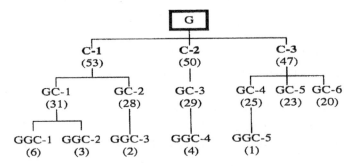

One of the principal features of representation is that the property is divided among the living persons who are nearest to the decedent in each descending line. A descendant is not an eligible taker if he or she has a living ancestor who is also a descendant of the decedent. Consequently, the only descendants who share in G's estate are C-1, C-2, and C-3. In all states, each child takes a 1/3 share. G's grandchildren and great-grandchildren take nothing. The spouses of descendants do not share in the decedent's estate.

What happens if one or more of G's children predeceased G? Here, the answer is not the same in all states. The result differs depending on which system of representation the state has chosen. There are four main systems of representation. We give you their names now and explain them in the next paragraphs: (1) strict per stirpes, (2) modified per stirpes, (3) the system of the original (pre-1990) UPC, and (4) the system of the current UPC.

Strict Per Stirpes System. The strict per stirpes system was used by the common law under the canons of descent for land,[8] and a minority of states in this country prescribe it for intestate succession of both land and personal property.[9]

---

7. Many people now live long enough to have grown grandchildren and young great-grandchildren. See Here Come the Great-Grandparents, N.Y. Times, Nov. 2, 2006, at G1.

We made all persons with children married in the hypothetical to avoid issues regarding the law's treatment of children whose parents are not married to each other. We address those and other status questions in Chapter 3. For now, the purpose of the hypothetical is to help you understand the concept of representation and the different representational systems found in the intestacy statutes around the country.

8. See 2 William Blackstone, Commentaries *218.

9. See, e.g., Fla. Stat. §732.104; Ga. Code §53-2-1; Ill. Rev. Stat. ch. 755, §5/2-1; Va. Code Ann. §64.2-202. Tennessee, which otherwise has adopted the original UPC's general pattern of intestacy, continues to use per stirpes. Tenn. Code §31-2-106. Minnesota and South Dakota, which have

The strict per stirpes system operates in three steps:

Step One: Divide the estate into primary shares at the generation nearest to the decedent (*i.e.*, at the children generation). This primary-share generation is often described by the courts as the generation at which the "stocks" or "roots" or "stirpes" are determined. The number of primary shares is equal to the number of children alive at the decedent's death plus the number of children who predeceased the decedent leaving descendants who survived the decedent. Any deceased children who have no living descendants are disregarded in determining the number of primary shares. The number of primary shares is determined at the children generation even if no children survive the decedent.

Step Two: Allocate the primary shares. One share goes to each living member of the children generation, if any. One share also goes to the descendants of each deceased child with living descendants.

Step Three: Divide and subdivide each primary share allocated to the living descendants of a deceased child. Each of these primary shares is divided and subdivided among the deceased child's descendants.

In the chart above, suppose that G was survived by all descendants except the children (C-1, C-2, and C-3). Under the strict per stirpes system, G's intestate estate would be distributed as follows: 1/6 each to GC-1 and GC-2 (representing C-1); 1/3 to GC-3 (representing C-2); and 1/9 each to GC-4, GC-5, and GC-6 (representing C-3).

Modified Per Stirpes. With the exception of the first step, the modified per stirpes system is identical to the strict per stirpes system. *Step One* in this system is to divide the estate into primary shares at the generation nearest to the decedent *that contains at least one living member*. Thus, if *all* of the decedent's children are dead but at least one grandchild is alive, the primary shares are determined at the grandchildren generation rather than at the children generation.

In the chart above, if G was survived by all descendants except the children (C-1, C-2, and C-3), G's intestate estate would be distributed under the modified per stirpes system as follows: 1/6 to each of the grandchildren (GC-1 through GC-6).

This system is sometimes called "per capita *with representation*," a term that really means per capita at the nearest generation with a living member, with descendants of deceased members of that generation taking by representation. Because the second and third steps in this system and in the per stirpes system are the same, this system is sometimes called "modified per stirpes." Indeed, it is

---

otherwise adopted the UPC's general pattern of intestacy, continue to use per stirpes. Minn. Stat. §524.2-106 (adopting the per-stirpes system for the descendants of the decedent, the per-capita-with-representation system for the descendants of the decedent's parents, and per capita without representation for the descendants of the decedent's grandparents); S.D. Codified Laws §29A-2-106.

sometimes employed under the statutory term "per stirpes."[10]

Original Uniform Probate Code System. As promulgated in 1969, UPC §2-106 adopted a variation of the modified per stirpes system. Although the statutory language could have been drafted more clearly, §2-106 was meant to codify *Step One* of the modified per stirpes system, meaning that the primary-share generation is the nearest generation to the decedent containing at least one living member.[11]

The UPC, from 1969 until 1990, departed from the modified per stirpes system at *Step Three*. Under this original version of §2-106, each share allocated to the descendants of a deceased member of the primary-share generation was divided and subdivided "in the same manner." The same manner required that a primary share be subdivided at the next generation to the deceased descendant containing *at least one living member*.

In the chart above, suppose that G is predeceased by C-1, GC-1, and GC-2, with all others surviving. Under the original UPC, C-1's 1/3 primary share is brought down to the next generation with at least one living member: the generation of GGC-1, GGC-2, and GGC-3. The share is divided equally among GGC-1, GGC-2, and GGC-3, giving each 1/9. Under the modified per stirpes system, in contrast, C-1's primary share would be subdivided at the (deceased) grandchildren generation, giving GGC-1 and GGC-2 a 1/12 share each and GGC-3 a 1/6 share.

Current Uniform Probate Code—Per Capita at Each Generation. As revised in 1990, UPC §2-106 now adopts a system of representation known as "per capita at each generation." This system assures equality among members of the same generation whose parents predeceased them.

The system can be described by the following three operational steps:

Step One: Divide the estate into primary shares at the nearest generation to the decedent containing at least one living member. The number of primary shares is the number of living persons in that generation plus the number of deceased persons in that generation who have living descendants.

Step Two: Allocate one primary share to each living member of the primary-share generation.

Step Three: Combine the remaining primary shares, if any, into a single share and assume that the descendants already allocated a share (and their descendants) predeceased the decedent. Then distribute that single share among the decedent's descendants in accordance with Step One.

---

10. See, e.g., Ark. Code Ann. §28-9-205; Ohio Rev. Code Ann. §§2105.06, .12, .13, as interpreted in Kraemer v. Hook, 152 N.E.2d 430 (Ohio 1958).

11. The statutory phrase "surviving heirs in the nearest degree of kinship" would have made this point more clearly had it said "surviving heirs in the nearest degree of kinship that contains one or more surviving heirs."

To see how it accomplishes the desired result, suppose that C-2 and C-3 predeceased G, with all others surviving.

Both the original and current versions of UPC §2-106 give a 1/3 share to C-1. Under the original version, however, the four grandchildren do not receive equal shares. GC-3 represents C-2 and gets a full 1/3 share. The other three represent C-3 and each takes a 1/9 share. Under the current UPC, equality among the four grandchildren is achieved. GC-3, GC-4, GC-5, and GC-6 each receives a 1/6 share.

This system consistently results in "horizontal equality," (*i.e.*, equality among members of the same generation) as distinguished from the "vertical equality" (*i.e.*, equality among children's families) consistently accomplished by the per stirpes system.

Problem

A has died intestate. A's family is charted below. Descendants who survived A are in bold italics. Under each of the four systems of representation, who is entitled to what shares of A's estate?

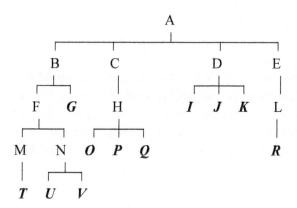

Use of the Various Systems of Representation in Planning. Wills and trusts frequently rely on multiple-generation class gifts. For example: "to A for life, remainder to A's descendants who survive A." Good drafting supplements this disposition by designating which system of representation the testator or grantor of the trust wants used. What system should be used in the absence of an express designation?[12] See, for example, UPC §2-708.

_____

12. Recall that the will of John F. Kennedy, Jr., provided that his issue were to take "by right of representation." Kennedy's will did not define "representation," but N.Y. Est. Powers & Trust Law §2-1.2 provides that in instruments executed on or after Sept. 1, 1992, issue take by representation as defined in §1-2.16. That section defines "by representation" as meaning the UPC system of

Many lawyers' documents use strict per stirpes: "to A for life, remainder to A's descendants who survive A, per stirpes." Although the strict per stirpes system has a commonly understood meaning, some courts have held that the phrase "per stirpes" invokes the modified per stirpes system. See, e.g., Kraemer v. Hook, 152 N.E.2d 430 (Ohio 1958). Therefore, the use of the term "per stirpes" without further clarification risks litigation over the term's meaning. See UPC §2-709 for a statutory rule of construction defining "per stirpes." In the absence of such a statutory rule of construction, it is good practice to insert a clause in the will or trust that defines the term.[13] It is essential to be clear about whether the initial division into primary shares is to be made at the children generation of A, even when no member of that generation is living, or whether the initial division into primary shares is to be made at the nearest generation to A that contains at least one living member.

Litigation has arisen in a number of cases over the use of phrases such as "to my brothers and sisters, per stirpes," or "to my nieces and nephews, per stirpes." See, e.g., Hartford Nat'l Bank & Trust Co. v. Thrall, 440 A.2d 200 (Conn. 1981); Bennett v. Lloyd, 267 S.E.2d 3 (Ga. 1980); Will of Griffin, 411 So.2d 766 (Miss. 1982); Wachovia Bank & Trust Co. v. Livengood, 294 S.E.2d 319 (N.C. 1982).

And then there are drafting gems such as these: "to Joe Thomas Russell, per stirpes" (Schroeder v. Gebhart, 825 So.2d 442 (Fla. Dist. Ct. App. 2002)); "to my wife, Jessie E. Walters, per stirpes" (Estate of Walters, 519 N.E.2d 1270 (Ind. Ct. App. 1988)); "[t]o Bernice Mesick, if she survives me, per stirpes" (Estate of Johnson, No. C6-98-1883, 1999 WL 118639 (Minn. Ct. App. Mar. 9, 1999)); "to my nephew, Sergio Pastorino, per stirpes" (Estate of Herceg, 193 Misc.2d 201, 747 N.Y.S.2d 901 (Sur. Ct. 2002)). An empirical study of 230 wills probated in 2015 in Sussex County, New Jersey, found that 44—nearly 20 percent—contained a devise to a named individual "per stirpes." David Horton & Reid Kress Weisbord, Boilerplate and Default Rules in Wills Law: An Empirical Analysis, 103 Iowa L. Rev. 663, 694 (2018).

Despite lawyers' preference for strict per stirpes, empirical research has indicated that, if asked, most clients would prefer the horizontal equality accomplished by the current UPC. See Raymond H. Young, Meaning of "Issue" and "Descendants,"13 ACTEC Notes 225 (1988). Why do you suppose this discrepancy exists? How would you pose the representation question to a client?

---

representation (known as "per capita at each generation").

13. For examples of litigation that could have been avoided by a definitional clause, see Rhodes v. First Alabama Bank, 699 So.2d 204 (Ala. Civ. App. 1997) (litigating meaning of "to the descendants of my other children per stirpes"); Trust Estate of Dwight, 909 P.2d 561 (Haw. 1995) (litigating meaning of "to such of the issue of my said adopted children as shall then be living in equal shares per stirpes").

c. Guardianships/Conservatorships for Minors and Incapacitated Adults

Because minors and incapacitated adults lack competence, they must depend on others for care and property management. All states have judicial procedures for appointing persons to perform these functions. In non-UPC states, the laws providing protective proceedings contemplate two types of guardians: guardian of the person, a fiduciary who is judicially charged with the care and custody of the minor or incapacitated adult; and guardian of the property (or estate)—sometimes called a "conservator"—a fiduciary who is responsible for managing assets that a minor or incapacitated adult owns.

One of the major estate planning concerns of parents with minor children is to designate a particular person, usually a close friend or relative, to act as guardian of the child's person (and who will typically also serve as guardian, or conservator, of the child's property). The need arises if both parents die, together or separately, before the child reaches the age of majority. The need also arises when a minor child is reared by a single parent and that parent dies. In most states, a guardian may be designated by a will. Uniform law allows a parent to appoint a guardian by will "or other record." Uniform Guardianship, Conservatorship, and Other Protective Arrangements Act §206(b)(1). This phrase includes durable powers of attorney, trust instruments, and specific documents for guardianship appointments. If the parents die intestate, they often have no say over who will be appointed guardian of their minor child or children. There must be a court proceeding, and the court will appoint a guardian from a list of available relatives. For parents with minor children, the opportunity to name a guardian for their children is a primary motivating factor for them to seek legal advice and execute a will.

Procedures and Powers. Procedures for appointment of the guardian, both of the person and of the property, have often been slow and expensive. Even after appointment, further judicial proceedings can be needed, increasing the delay and cost of guardianship. This is especially so for guardianship of the ward's property. If there are multiple children, separate guardianships have to be obtained for each child, even though the same person is usually appointed guardian for each child. The guardian does not have title to the ward's property. Rather, the guardian is merely custodian of the property with limited powers. These powers are defined by statute, and historically statutes defined the powers inadequately, both in the sense of uncertainty of meaning and in the failure to grant certain important powers, particularly concerning investment of protected property. These deficiencies made it necessary in many instances for the guardian to obtain court authorization for actions in dealing with the ward's property, generating expenses that diminish the ward's assets. Required accounting and bonds further depleted the wealth available to the ward.

Many states have reformed their guardianship laws to ameliorate some of these problems. The Uniform Law Commission promulgated a Uniform Guardianship and

Protective Proceedings Act (1987), which was revised in 1997. The revised version was incorporated into the UPC as Article V. In 2017, the Uniform Law Commission promulgated a further revision, called the Uniform Guardianship, Conservatorship, and Other Protective Arrangements Act. This new act will soon be incorporated into the UPC as Article V, replacing the 1997 version. Under the 1997 and 2017 acts, the person who is appointed conservator is accorded powers, duties, and liabilities comparable to those of a trustee. Under both statutory schemes, the conservator also receives substantial management powers that are exercisable without court order.

Avoiding Conservatorship. Some devices are available to avoid the problems associated with property guardianships or conservatorships, but they require pre-death planning. For minors, these devices include a trust created during the parent's life or at death in the parent's will. The creation of a trust and consideration of a variety of the provisions it might contain are the subject of Chapters 9 through 11. An alternative device is the creation of a custodianship through a lifetime transfer to minors under the Uniform Gifts to Minors Act (1966) or lifetime or testamentary transfers to minors under the newer Uniform Transfers to Minors Act (1986) (UTMA). Under the UTMA, the custodian has substantial discretionary powers free of court supervision and for that reason is preferable to a conservatorship. The UTMA is most useful for relatively small gifts, while trusts are preferable if large amounts of property are involved. For incapacitated adults, other devices are available, including durable powers of attorney and statutory custodial trusts. See Chapter 18.

3. Ancestors and Collaterals

Primary Statutory References: *UPC §§2-103, 2-106, 2-107, 2-114*

a. Parents and Their Descendants

Parents. The decedent's parents and their descendants inherit to the exclusion of more remote ancestors and their descendants.[14] The decedent's parents and their descendants inherit, however, only if the decedent leaves no surviving descendants. Under UPC §§2-102 and 2-103, parents of decedents with large estates inherit if the decedent leaves a surviving spouse but no descendants. The parents take one-fourth of that part of the probate estate, if any, that exceeds $300,000. (For purpose of the preceding sentence, the inflation adjustment in UPC §1-109 is ignored.)

---

14. Under the English canons of descent, as condensed by Blackstone, an intestate's land "shall linearly descend to the issue of the person who last died seized, *in infinitum*; but shall never linearly ascend." 2 William Blackstone, Commentaries *208. Legal historians have not provided an adequate explanation for the preclusion of ancestors from inheriting land. The English Statute of Distribution allowed ancestors to inherit, as does every U.S. jurisdiction.

If the decedent leaves neither a surviving spouse nor surviving descendants, the decedent's parents inherit to the exclusion of the decedent's surviving siblings or their descendants under most intestacy statutes. This also was the rule under the pre-2019 version of UPC §2-103. The 2019/2021 revision of the UPC responds to modern society by taking into account blended families not only with respect to the share passing to the surviving spouse under §2-102 but also the share passing to the decedent's surviving parent or parents under §2-103(d) and (e). See Problems 3 and 4 on pp. 48-49.

The parent-child relationship is unique among familial relationships because of the physical, emotional, and financial vulnerability of children while they are minors. The law and society place primary responsibility for the safety and well-being of minor children on their parents. If the parents fail to meet those responsibilities, should they be allowed to inherit from their child's intestate estate? This question has gained some public attention when minor children have died accidentally, and parents, who had previously abandoned them, claim a share of their estates, which include damages from a wrongful death suit.

The issue of "worthy parents" is not necessarily limited, however, to situations in which the child dies while a minor and the estate includes property as a result of a child's wrongful death. UPC §2-114(a) provides that a parent is barred from inheriting from or through a child if "the parent's parental rights were terminated and not judicially reestablished" or if "there is clear and convincing evidence that immediately before the child's death the parental rights of the parent could have been terminated... on the basis of nonsupport, abandonment, abuse, neglect, or other actions or inactions of the parent toward the child."

UPC §2-114(c), added in 2019, is explicit that the termination of parental rights does not affect the right of the child or a descendant of the child to inherit from or through the parent.

Ancestral Property. At common law, land returned to the branch of the family from which the decedent inherited it. See 2 William Blackstone, Commentaries *220. Some type of ancestral-property rule persists in only a few states.[15] Neither the original UPC nor the current UPC contains an ancestral-property rule.

More Than Two Parents. In some states, a child can have more than two parents. The Uniform Parentage Act (2017) also opens the door to this possibility. In 2019, the UPC was revised to cover the possibility that a decedent might have more than two parents. We discuss this further in Chapter 3.

---

15. See Ky. Rev. Stat. §391.020 (applying only to real estate with different consequences depending on whether the decedent's parent who made the gift is alive and whether the decedent is a minor); Nev. Rev. Stat. §134.070-.080 (applying to both real and personal property that has been inherited by a child who dies as a minor and unmarried).

Descendants of Parents. Under both the pre-2019 and current versions of UPC §2-103, if none of the decedent's parents survives, the descendants of the decedent's parents inherit by representation. See, e.g., current UPC §2-103(f). Under the current version of UPC §2-103(d) and (e), some descendants of the decedent's deceased parents can inherit even if one or more of the decedent's parents is alive, unless the descendants of a deceased parent are the same as the descendants of a living parent and vice versa.

If descendants of parents do inherit, they do so "by representation." The system of representation employed in the jurisdiction most likely will be the same system employed in the jurisdiction for representation among the decedent's own descendants. UPC §2-106 applies the per-capita-at-each-generation system. But see Minn. Stat. §524.2-106 (described in note 9).

Relatives of the "Half Blood." A widely adopted rule is that relatives of the half blood are treated the same as relatives of the whole blood. This rule is codified in most states. If, for example, the decedent's father has children from a prior relationship, those children will be the decedent's half siblings. They inherit as if they were full siblings.

In the modern era, the term "half blood" is outdated. The rule of equal treatment applies also, for example, to persons who are adopted by a common ancestor. If, for example, a decedent's mother has an adopted son from a prior relationship, he also will be decedent's half brother. UPC §2-107 was revised in 2019 to remove the references to blood. As revised, §2-107 provides: "An heir inherits without regard to how many common ancestors in the same generation the heir shares with the decedent."

Relatives by Marriage (Affinity). Relatives of the decedent's spouse, such as the spouse's parents, siblings, or descendants of siblings, and spouses of the decedent's relatives, such as daughters- and sons-in-law, are relatives by marriage (sometimes called relatives by affinity). Nearly all jurisdictions exclude them from inheriting under their intestacy statutes. See Chapter 3, discussing stepchildren.

Problems

1. G died intestate with a net probate estate of $500,000. She was survived by her husband H and her mother M. How will G's estate be distributed under the current UPC?

2. C, a fourteen year old child, was regularly left home alone by his parents without minimal food, clothing, or heat. During a bungled attempt to kidnap him, C died intestate. Under the current UPC, what do his parents inherit?

3. D had two parents, P1 and P2. P1 also had one other child, A. P2 also had one other child, B. D died intestate, predeceased by P2 and survived by P1, A, and B. Under the pre-2019 UPC and the current UPC, how will D's estate be distributed?

4. Same facts as in Problem 3 except that A and B were the children of P1 and P2. Under the current UPC, how will D's estate be distributed?

5. H1 and W were married and had two children, A and B. After H1 died, W married H2, and together they had a child, C. B then married S. W then died, followed by A, who died intestate. Under the current UPC, how will A's estate be distributed?

6. A's family chart is provided below. A died intestate. Family members who survived A are indicated in bold italics. Under the current UPC, how will A's estate be distributed?

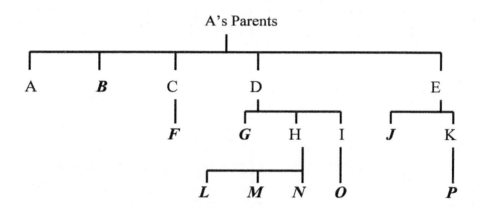

b. More Remote Ancestors and Collaterals

Parentelic System. To summarize the preceding description of intestacy statutes, excepting the discussion of the share passing to the surviving spouse, we have identified the first two steps of the "parentelic system." A parentela consists of an ancestor and that ancestor's surviving descendants. The parentelic system of inheritance is based on a preference for persons who are in the nearest parentela to the decedent. Thus, the parentelic system provides that the first parentela (the decedent's own surviving descendants) inherits first; if that parentela contains no surviving members, the second parentela (the decedent's parents and their descendants) inherit next; and so on.

This procedure—going, step by step, up the ladder of ancestral seniority—can theoretically continue forever, but no state does that. Under the UPC, the parentelic system is carried through the third parentela (grandparents and their descendants).

The Table of Consanguinity, on p. 50, illustrates the parentelic system. Each column represents a parentela.

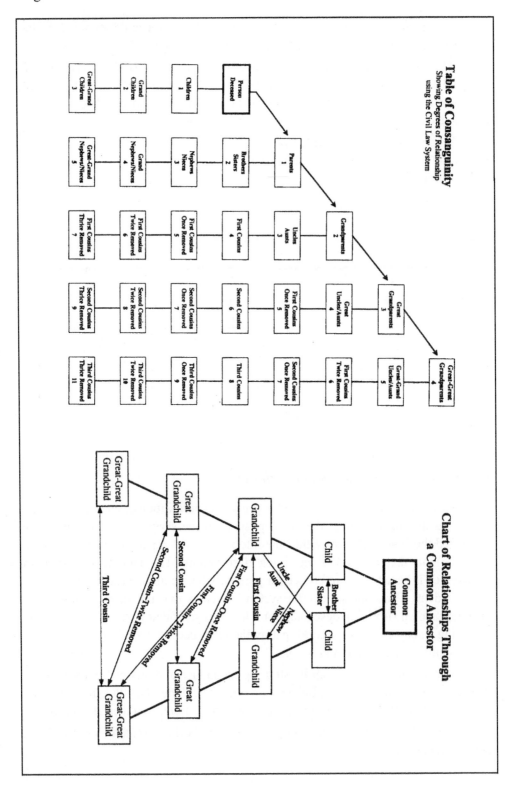

Under the pre-2019 version of UPC §2-103, the estate was divided into paternal and maternal halves (if there was at least one grandparent or descendant of a grandparent in each half).

This approach is outdated, for three reasons. First, the decedent's parents might be of the same sex, thereby making references to "paternal" and "maternal" grandparents inapplicable. Second, the per-capita-at-each-generation system of representation should apply also to grandparents (and their descendants). Third, the decedent might have more than two parents and/or more than two sets of grandparents. To illustrate the operation of current UPC §2-103(g) and (h), consider the following problems.

Problems

How will G's intestate estate be distributed under the current UPC?

1. G was survived only by three grandparents: GP1 and GP2 are the parents of G's predeceased father; GP3 is the parent of G's predeceased mother. How does this result differ from the result under the pre-2019 UPC?

2. G's grandparent GP1 had a daughter (G's aunt), A. G's grandparent GP2 had a son (G's uncle), B. A and B are not siblings. G was survived by only by GP1, A, and B. (This fact-pattern does not invite analysis under the pre-2019 UPC because you are not given information on whether the survivors are on G's paternal side, maternal side, or both.)

3. Same facts as in Problem 2 except that A and B are the children of GP1 and GP2 (and thus are siblings).

Nearest Kindred—Determining Degrees of Kinship. Some American statutes (but not the UPC) provide that, if no member of any of the specifically designated parentela survives the intestate, the estate passes to the intestate's "nearest kindred" or "next of kin." The degrees of kinship are given on the Table of Consanguinity. (They are the numerals in the boxes.) By way of example, the decedent's nephew or niece is related to the decedent in the third degree. This type of distribution is *nonrepresentational.* Relatives take in their own right, not as representatives of deceased ancestors. Each heir takes an equal share, because all the relatives who are entitled to participate in the estate will be in the same degree.

The Civil-Law Method. The method for computing degrees of kinship used in American law often relies on the English judges' interpretation of "next of kindred in equal degree" found in the Statute of Distribution. They applied the civil-law method of computing degrees, which consists of counting generations under the following formula: count the number of generations (1) up from the intestate to the intestate's ancestor who is also an ancestor of the collateral relative and (2) down from that common ancestor to the collateral relative. The total of these two figures constitutes the degree of kinship for each collateral relative. See 4 Richard Burn, Ecclesiastical Law 538-43 (9th ed. 1842). Under this formula, a sister or brother is related to the decedent in the second degree, a niece or nephew is related in the third degree, and an aunt or uncle is also related in the third degree. Many American statutes explicitly provide that degrees shall be computed according to the method of the civil law. When the statute has been silent, most courts have used this method.

The Modified Civil-Law Method. Under a fairly widespread statutory modification of the civil-law method, when there are two or more collateral relatives in equal degree who claim through different common ancestors, those claiming through the ancestor nearest to the decedent take to the exclusion of the others. Is this system any different from the parentelic scheme?

The Current UPC—Per Capita at Each Generation Consistently. The pre-2019 UPC, which divided the intestate estate into maternal and paternal halves, did not apply the per-capita-at-each-generation system of representation consistently. In contrast, the current UPC does apply the system consistently. For illustrations, see Problem 1 on p. 51 and Problem (a) below.

Limitations on Inheritance. Both the English canons of descent and the Statute of Distribution provided for inheritance by any blood relative no matter how remote the relationship. Through the first half of the twentieth century, nearly all U.S. jurisdictions adopted the same rule. This rule of unlimited inheritance, however, makes probate administration more complex. It increases the potential number of problems concerning proof of heirship under the intestacy statutes, and, even if the decedent dies with a will, it requires that all remote relatives be identified and located so that they might have the opportunity to contest any wills offered for probate.

The increased administrative costs are hard to justify when the potential takers of the probate estate are distant relatives with whom the decedent had no personal or social ties—so-called "laughing heirs."

Following the approach of the Model Probate Code published in 1946 as the product of a research effort by the University of Michigan Law School in cooperation with a committee of the American Bar Association, the original and current versions of the UPC abandon the rule of unlimited inheritance. See UPC §§2-103, 2-105. See also Problem (b) below.

Problems

G died intestate, survived only by the following relatives. In each case, how will G's estate be distributed under the pre-2019 UPC and the current UPC?

(a) D (G's first cousin on G's mother's side) and by E and F (G's first cousins on G's father's side).

(b) Two relatives, both of whom are on G's mother's side: R (the first cousin of G's mother) and S (the grandson of G's first cousin). What if, instead, G was survived only by R?

PART C. REARRANGING INTESTATE SUCCESSION

1. Agreements, Settlements, and Disclaimers

Primary Statutory References: *UPC §§2-1106, 3-912*

Uniform Disclaimer of Property Interests Act

The intestacy statutes make it appear that decedents' estates must be distributed in accordance with the statutory rules unless the decedent executes a will. The statutes also make it appear that heirs have no power to vary an intestacy statute's operation. Neither is precisely true.

DePaoli v. Commissioner of Internal Revenue
62 F.3d 1259 (10th Cir. 1995)

JENKINS, Senior District Judge.

This case arises out of the taxpayers' efforts to escape estate taxes by disclaiming a testamentary transfer of property. The Tax Court held the purported disclaimer invalid for estate tax purposes, subjecting the taxpayers to liability not only for estate taxes but also for a gift tax and an addition to tax under §6651(a)(1) of the Internal Revenue Code. The taxpayers appeal. We have jurisdiction under I.R.C. §7482(a)(1) and reverse.

I. BACKGROUND

Quinto DePaoli, Sr., a resident of New Mexico, died in 1987. He was survived by his wife, Soila DePaoli, and his only son, Quinto DePaoli, Jr. Quinto Senior's will left his entire estate to Quinto Junior. The will was formally probated on December 30, 1987. On July 21, 1988, shortly before the estate tax return was due, Soila and Quinto Junior moved to have the probated will set aside. They claimed that the original will had been destroyed, that the will admitted to probate was actually a duplicate copy and that Quinto Senior had intended to make a new will leaving Quinto Junior the greatest amount he could receive without any tax liability (namely, $600,000) and leaving the bulk of the estate to Soila but that he had died before he could execute the new will. Quinto Junior acknowledged that he could claim a substantial part of the estate but agreed to receive only $600,000 to settle the will contest. The probate court granted the motion and ordered the estate distributed accordingly.

The federal estate tax return filed for Quinto Senior's estate indicated that the entire estate passed to Soila, less certain expenses and a $600,000 bequest to Quinto Junior. The bequest to Soila was classified as a deductible bequest to a surviving spouse. The return indicated that no property passed to the surviving spouse as a result of a qualified disclaimer under I.R.C. §2518(b),[16] and no written disclaimer was attached to the return. The return indicated that no tax was due, since the tax on the $600,000 taxable estate was within the unified credit available to the estate.

The Commissioner denied the entire marital deduction on the grounds that Quinto Senior's will, as probated, bequeathed all his property to his son and the agreement between Quinto Junior and Soila was invalid. The Commissioner also determined that the agreement between Quinto Junior and Soila constituted a taxable gift for gift tax purposes and assessed an addition to tax against Quinto Junior under I.R.C. §6651(a)(1) for failing to file a gift tax return.

The Tax Court upheld the Commissioner's determinations. The court held that Quinto Junior's agreement to forego all but $600,000 of his father's estate did not entitle the estate to the marital deduction because the portion of the estate passing to Soila passed to her from Quinto Junior and not from Quinto Senior. The court further held that the property passing to Soila constituted a taxable gift from Quinto Junior, making Quinto Junior liable for the federal gift tax. Finally, the court held that Quinto Junior's failure to file a gift tax return was not "due to reasonable cause" and that Quinto Junior was therefore liable for an addition to tax under I.R.C. §6651(a)(1). The Tax Court concluded that the deficiency in estate tax due was $1,633,250, the deficiency in gift tax due was $1,297,750 and the addition to tax was $324,438. Quinto Junior, the estate, and Quinto Senior's personal representatives (Soila and Rachel Craig) appealed.

II. DISCUSSION

The appellants claim that the Tax Court erred by denying the estate a marital deduction. They claim that, as a result of Quinto Junior's disclaimer of his property rights under Quinto Senior's will, Quinto Senior's property passed to his surviving spouse (Soila) as a matter of law and was therefore properly deducted...

Estate taxes are imposed on the value of a decedent's taxable estate. In determining the value of the taxable estate, the value of property that passes to a surviving spouse is deducted. If property passes from a decedent to someone other

---

16. "For purposes of [I.R.C. §2518](a), the term "qualified disclaimer" means an irrevocable and unqualified refusal by a person to accept an interest in property but only if—

(1) such refusal is in writing,

(2) such writing is received by the transferor of the interest, his legal representative, or the holder of the legal title to the property to which the interest relates not later than the date which is 9 months after the later of—

(A) the day on which the transfer creating the interest in such person is made, or

(B) the day on which such person attains age 21,

(3) such person has not accepted the interest or any of its benefits, and

(4) as a result of such refusal, the interest passes without any direction on the part of the person making the disclaimer and passes either—

(A) to the spouse of the decedent, or

(B) to a person other than the person making the disclaimer."

than the surviving spouse and that person makes a "qualified" disclaimer that results in the surviving spouse being entitled to the property, the disclaimed interest is treated as passing directly from the decedent to the surviving spouse and therefore qualifies for the marital deduction.

To qualify, a disclaimer must meet certain requirements, chief of which, for purposes of this appeal, is that, as a result of the disclaimer, the interest passes to the surviving spouse "without any direction on the part of the person making the disclaimer." I.R.C. §2518(b)(4). The Tax Court held that Quinto Junior's agreement to forego all but $600,000 of his father's estate was not a qualified disclaimer because his interest would not have passed to Soila without his direction.[17]

The requirement that the disclaimed property pass without any direction from the person making the disclaimer means that the disclaimer must result in a valid passing of the disclaimed interest to the surviving spouse by operation of state law. Federal law does not prescribe rules for the passing of disclaimed property interests, so any disclaimed property passing other than by operation of state law must be at the direction of the disclaimant. Under New Mexico law, unless the decedent indicates otherwise in his will, any disclaimed property passes as if the disclaimant had predeceased the decedent. Under New Mexico's antilapse statute, if a devisee who is related to the testator by kinship is treated as if he had predeceased the testator, the devisee's "issue" who survive the testator by 120 hours "take in place of" the devisee. Thus, if Quinto Junior had "issue," his disclaimer would not have caused the disclaimed property to pass to his stepmother, Soila, by operation of law and therefore would not have been a qualified disclaimer under I.R.C. §2518(b) entitling the estate to the marital deduction.

Quinto Junior has never been married but has two illegitimate children--Thomas Derrick DePaoli and Christopher Noel Contreras DePaoli. Derrick was five years old at the time of Quinto Senior's death, and Christopher was four. The Tax Court concluded that the property Quinto Junior disclaimed would not have passed to Soila absent his agreement that Soila take the property but would have passed to Derrick and Christopher. The petitioners claim that Quinto Junior's illegitimate children were not his "issue" within the meaning of the antilapse statute and therefore would not have taken in his place as a result of his disclaimer....

Quinto Junior's tax returns do not show on their face that he intended his

---

17. The Commissioner does not claim and the Tax Court did not hold that the disclaimer failed to meet the requirements for a valid disclaimer under New Mexico law. The Tax Court doubted whether Quinto Junior intended to make a qualified disclaimer under federal law when he entered into the settlement agreement with Soila, since the estate tax return did not indicate that any property passed to Soila as a result of a qualified disclaimer. The court called the argument "patently an afterthought with weak factual support." However, the Commissioner concedes that the Tax Court did not reject the taxpayers' claim on that ground. It held only that the disclaimer was not a qualified disclaimer under I.R.C. §2518(b)(4) because it directed that the disclaimed property pass to Soila. It is only that issue that we need address.

illegitimate children to be his heirs, that is, to inherit from him under New Mexico's intestate succession statutes. Consequently, they were not his "issue" within the meaning of the antilapse statute.... Therefore, when Quinto Junior disclaimed an interest in his father's estate, that interest passed to his stepmother, Soila, by operation of law, making the disclaimer a "qualified disclaimer" within the meaning of I.R.C. §2518(b). Because the property passing to Soila, the surviving spouse, passed as a result of a qualified disclaimer, the estate properly claimed the marital deduction. Moreover, because the property is deemed to have passed directly from Quinto Senior to Soila, the disclaimer did not make Quinto Junior liable for the federal gift tax. Finally, because Quinto Junior was not required to file a gift tax return as a result of the disclaimer, he is not liable for the addition to tax under I.R.C. §6651(a)(1) for failing to file a gift tax return.

We recognize that the parties' settlement, which provided the basis for their disclaimer argument, may be nothing more than a blatant attempt to avoid paying estate taxes. However, neither the probate court nor the Tax Court found anything wrong with the disclaimer other than its purported direction that the estate pass to Soila. The validity of the disclaimer is not properly before us. We have concluded that the effect of the disclaimer under the unique New Mexico probate statutes in effect at the time was to cause the estate to pass to Soila regardless of any direction on the part of Quinto Junior, thus making the estate eligible for the marital deduction under federal law. There is nothing wrong with trying to escape tax liability if the law allows a taxpayer to do so. We believe in this case the law allowed the estate to claim the marital deduction. That does not mean that the petitioners can successfully escape taxation altogether. It simply means that the Commissioner may have to wait until Soila dies to collect taxes on the estate.

REVERSED.

Notes and Questions

1. *Agreement Among the Heirs.* If an intestate's heirs are not satisfied with the distribution under the intestacy statute, they normally can divide up the decedent's assets in a different way. UPC §3-912 contains a provision authorizing private agreements among successors. Would this section have resolved the DePaolis' tax difficulties?

2. *Problem of Unascertained Heirs or Heirs Who Lack Capacity.* If all the successors are competent adults, any agreement among the successors will be enforced. In many situations, however, successors include minors and/or persons who lack capacity to enter into agreements. UPC §1-403, which was amended in 1997, provides (in the absence of a conflict of interest) for conservators to represent the protected persons whose estates they control, for trustees to represent trust beneficiaries, for parents to represent their minor children under certain conditions, and for the appointment of guardians ad litem to represent the interests of unborn

and unascertained parties. It only applies, however, to "formal proceedings" and "judicially supervised settlements."

That limitation is a substantial one because formal judicial proceedings can result in delays and considerable expense. The challenge is whether a statute could be designed to allow issues arising under intestacy, wills, and trusts to be resolved by agreement without court approval. The key to the effectiveness and fairness of such a statute is to identify those instances in which minors or other persons under a disability, unborns, or unascertained parties can be represented adequately by others who have similar, and not conflicting, interests. If their interests cannot be adequately represented by others, the statute would have to provide for the appointment of a special representative who could negotiate on their behalf. Article 3 of the Uniform Trust Code (UTC) establishes criteria permitting representation of trust beneficiaries by fiduciaries (personal representatives, guardians, and conservators) and parents. See UTC §303. It also permits an otherwise unrepresented "minor, incapacitated, or unborn individual, or a person whose identity or location is unknown and not reasonably ascertainable" to be represented "by another having a substantially identical interest with respect to the particular question or dispute." UTC §304. Representation can only occur if there is no conflict of interest between the representative and the person represented. Article 3 only applies to trusts. The Joint Editorial Board for Uniform Trust and Estate Acts is considering how it might extend the UTC's approach to nonjudicial settlements to issues concerning intestacy and wills.

3. *Settlements Accepted by the IRS.* Treasury Regulation (Treas. Reg.) §20.2056(c)-2(d)(2) provides:

> If as a result of the controversy involving the decedent's will, or involving any bequest or devise thereunder, a property interest is assigned or surrendered to the surviving spouse, the interest so acquired will be regarded as having "passed from the decedent to his surviving spouse" only if the assignment or surrender is a bona fide recognition of enforceable rights of the surviving spouse in the decedent's estate. Such a bona fide recognition will be presumed where the assignment or surrender was pursuant to a decision of a local court upon the merits in an adversary proceeding following a genuine and active contest....

Would this provision have resolved the DePaolis' tax difficulties?

4. *Disclaimers under State Law.* A disclaimer, sometimes called a renunciation, is the refusal to accept gratuitously transferred property. For lifetime transfers, the right to disclaim frequently is expressed in terms of the donee's nonacceptance of a gift. The acceptance requirement for a completed gift and the right to disclaim an inheritance or a devise are conceptually the same—both reflect a policy that ownership cannot be forced upon a transferee. The common law, which originated the disclaimer doctrine, broadly protected a transferee's right to "just say no." The courts adopted a relation-back doctrine, under which a disclaimer was considered to

relate back to the date of the transfer and operate as a nonacceptance. Under relation back, all claims of creditors and governmental taxing authorities seeking to attribute ownership rights to the disclaimant were ineffective. The only exception at common law was that heirs could not prevent title from passing to them by intestate succession.[18]

The breadth of the relation-back doctrine led to the growing popularity of disclaimers. Disclaimers have now become a matter of statutory law in most jurisdictions. In 1999, the Uniform Law Commission promulgated the Uniform Disclaimer of Property Interests Act (UDPIA), which updates and replaces a number of uniform disclaimer acts dating back to 1973. In 2002, the Uniform Law Commission incorporated the UDPIA into the UPC as Part 11 of Article II (UPC §§2-1101 to 2-1117), replacing the UPC's original disclaimer provision contained in §2-801. The UDPIA specifies the time when a disclaimer becomes effective and provides that a disclaimer "is not a transfer, assignment, or release." See UPC §2-1105(e), (f).

Although disclaimer statutes increase the formalities for accomplishing a disclaimer, they should not be interpreted as reflecting dissatisfaction with the common law. On the contrary, these statutes are designed to make disclaimers more useful to beneficiaries through regularization. Perhaps the clearest proof of legislative approval of the right to disclaim is the statutory extension to property passing by intestacy and to new types of nontestamentary transfers.

5. *Federal Disclaimer Legislation.* Disclaimers are a significant component of post-mortem estate planning. With federal tax savings a major motivating factor when a beneficiary considers a disclaimer, qualification under the federal statute inevitably becomes of primary importance.[19]

Under IRC §§2518 and 2046, a disclaimant incurs no federal transfer tax consequences if the disclaimer meets the IRC's definition of a "qualified disclaimer." Generally speaking, a qualified disclaimer must be "irrevocable and unqualified;" in writing and filed within nine months of the later of the time of the transfer or the disclaimant's twenty-first birthday; the disclaimant must not have accepted the interest or any of its benefits; and the interest must pass, without direction by the disclaimant, to either the transferor's spouse or a person other than the disclaimant.

---

18. See, e.g., Watson v. Watson, 13 Conn. 83 (1839); Coomes v. Finegan, 7 N.W.2d 729 (Iowa 1943). The theory was that intestate succession could not be refused because it arises by operation of law. See Christian M. Lauritzen, II, Only God Can Make an Heir, 48 Nw. U.L. Rev. 568 (1953).

19. Beneficiaries have instituted malpractice claims for failure of attorneys to advise them on tax savings available through disclaimer. See, e.g., Linck v. Barokas & Martin, 667 P.2d 171 (Alaska 1983) (recognizing negligence claim); Barner v. Sheldon, 678 A.2d 717 (N.J. Super. Ct. App. Div. 1996) (refusing to recognize negligence claim).

The enactment of these federal provisions has diminished the significance of the state law requirements. State disclaimer statutes are now playing secondary roles as spoilers and facilitators of the federal tax law. A state's disclaimer law may affect the manner of obtaining qualification of a disclaimer for tax purposes if it contains more restrictive rules than the federal statute. In a few situations, a more restrictive requirement can prevent a disclaimer from being "qualified" for federal tax purposes.[20] State laws also indirectly affect federal taxation because they control the devolution of disclaimed property. By selecting devolution patterns that most frequently coincide with the disclaimant's dispositive intent, the state can remove a potential disincentive to disclaim and encourage its citizens to take advantage of tax-saving opportunities.

6. *Creditors' Rights.* The prevailing view in the United States is that a beneficiary can disclaim an interest to prevent creditors from reaching the property. Creditors' rights may be defeated even if the disclaimer would otherwise qualify as a fraudulent conveyance. See, e.g., Tompkins State Bank v. Niles, 537 N.E.2d 274 (Ill. 1989); Frances Slocum Bank & Trust Co. v. Estate of Martin, 666 N.E.2d 411 (Ind. Ct. App. 1996). The courts reason that, in the absence of explicit statutory direction to the contrary, the relation-back theory should apply and the disclaimer should be effective as against creditors.[21] In Drye v. United States, 528 U.S. 49 (1999), however, the Court held that a disclaimer of a son's right to take his mother's estate by intestacy was ineffective to defeat a tax lien against the disclaimant.

The appropriate treatment of disclaimers under the Federal Bankruptcy Code turns on the timing of the disclaimer. Disclaimers arise in two contexts under the Code. The first context concerns fraudulent conveyances. The Code creates a federal fraudulent conveyance statute. 11 U.S.C. §548(a). This provision permits a bankruptcy trustee "to avoid any transfer... of an interest of the debtor in property... made or incurred on or within two years before the date of the filing of the petition... if the debtor... received less than a reasonably equivalent value in exchange for such transfer...." Section 548 presents the issue of whether a pre-petition disclaimer should be effective as against creditors. The second context concerns the inclusion in the bankruptcy estate of inheritances that occur within 180 days after a petition for bankruptcy relief has been filed. 11 U.S.C. §541(a)(5). This provision raises the

---

20. IRC §2518(c)(3) provides that if the beneficiary transfers the property or interest to the person or persons who would have taken the property had the disclaimer been effective under local law, the disclaimer will qualify for federal tax purposes. Although this rule eliminates reliance on local law in the majority of disclaimer cases, it remains inadequate for interests that are not transferable. That can happen if the interest is subject to a spendthrift provision. See Chapter 11. The problem can also arise if local law does not permit a personal representative of a beneficiary who is dead or incompetent to make a disclaimer or a gratuitous transfer. But see UPC §2-1114 (providing that any disclaimer that is qualified for tax purposes is a valid disclaimer under the Act).

21. For examples of statutes protecting creditors' rights against disclaimers, see Fla. Stat. §739.402(2); Mass. Laws ch. 190B, §2-801(h)(2).

issue of whether a disclaimer of an inheritance, which occurs within 180 days of a bankruptcy petition, is an unauthorized post-petition transfer under 11 U.S.C. §549(a).

In both contexts, the crucial question of statutory interpretation would seem to be whether a disclaimer should constitute a "transfer" under federal bankruptcy law. See Douglass G. Boshkoff, Bankruptcy in the Seventh Circuit: 1991, 25 Ind. L. Rev. 981, 983 (1992); Gregory M. McCoskey, Death and Debtors: What Every Probate Lawyer Should Know About Bankruptcy, 34 Real Prop. Prob. & Tr. J. 669, 684-90 (2000). The courts, however, have not approached disclaimer issues in this way. In Jones v. Atchison (In re Atchison), 101 B.R. 556 (Bankr. S.D. Ill. 1989), aff'd, 925 F.2d 209 (7th Cir.), cert. denied, 502 U.S. 860 (1991), a case arising out of Illinois, the Seventh Circuit held that a pre-petition disclaimer was effective. It reasoned that the relation-back theory embraced by the applicable state law prevented the debtor from having a property interest to transfer. Accord Simpson v. Penner (In re Simpson), 36 F.3d 450 (5th Cir. 1994) (per curiam).

In a case also arising out of Illinois, Williams v. Chenoweth (In re Chenoweth), 132 B.R. 161 (Bankr. S.D. Ill. 1991), aff'd, 143 B.R. 527 (S.D. Ill. 1992), aff'd, 3 F.3d 1111 (7th Cir. 1993), the bankruptcy court held that a post-petition disclaimer violated §549 and the Seventh Circuit affirmed.[22] The bankruptcy court distinguished *Atchison* by reasoning that "[t]he 'entitled to acquire' language of § 541(a)(5)(A) results in a much broader definition of property of the estate for testamentary interests arising after bankruptcy and manifests Congress' intent to capture such interests for the trustee and the bankruptcy estate." 132 B.R. at 164. For other cases holding that post-petition disclaimers are avoidable, see In re Gilroy, 235 B.R. 512 (Bankr. D. Mass. 1999); Cornelius v. Cornell (In re Cornell), 95 B.R. 219 (Bankr. W.D. Okla. 1989); Geekie v. Watson (In re Watson), 65 B.R. 9 (Bankr. C.D. Ill. 1986); Flanigan v. Lewis (In re Lewis), 45 B.R. 27 (Bankr. W.D. Mo. 1984). See Adam J. Hirsch, Inheritance and Bankruptcy: The Meaning of the "Fresh Start," 45 Hastings L.J. 175, 183 n. 25 (1994) (reviewing the case law in this area).

An issue closely associated with creditors' rights concerns the effect of a disclaimer on eligibility for public assistance and Medicaid benefits. The prevailing view is that a disclaimer causes a loss of eligibility for public assistance. See, e.g., Troy v. Hart, 697 A.2d 113 (Md. Ct. Spec. App.), cert. denied, 700 A.2d 1215 (Md. 1997); Molloy v. Bane, 631 N.Y.S.2d 910 (App. Div. 1995); see also Hinschberger v. Griggs County Soc. Serv., 499 N.W.2d 876 (N.D. 1993) (denying medical

---

22. Should §541(a)(5) apply if a testator conditions a devise on her not dying during the 180 days following the commencement of the devisee's bankruptcy case? The court in In re McGuire, 209 B.R. 580 (Bankr. D. Mass. 1997), presented with similar facts held the condition effective for bankruptcy purposes and that the property subject to the conditional devise did not become part of the bankruptcy estate. This case suggests interesting estate planning strategies for preventing creditors from reaching property intended for a debtor.

assistance benefits to a claimant based on his release for less than adequate consideration of his rights to his wife's estate, including his right to an elective share and family allowance); Tannler v. Wisconsin Dep't of Health & Soc. Serv., 564 N.W.2d 735 (Wis. 1997) (terminating Medicaid eligibility for surviving spouse's failure to make spousal election). Contra, e.g., Estate of Kirk, 591 N.W.2d 630 (Iowa 1999).

7. *Disposition of Disclaimed Property.* If the testamentary or nontestamentary instrument provides for an alternative disposition in the event of a disclaimer, that alternative disposition controls. See, e.g, Estate of Devlin, 259 N.Y.S.2d 531 (Sur. Ct. 1964); UPC §2-1106(b)(2). In the absence of an alternative disposition, a disclaimed interest passes as provided by the disclaimer statute or by the common law. In general, for property passing by will or by intestacy, the statutes apply the fiction that the disclaimant predeceased the decedent. See UPC §2-1106(b)(3). For property passing by a nontestamentary instrument, they apply the fiction that the disclaimant predeceased the date that the instrument became effective.

8. *Representation Revisited.* Can a disclaimer be used to manipulate shares under the various systems of representation? Notice the difference between a disclaimer statute that provides that the decedent's "estate" devolves as if the disclaimant predeceased the decedent and one that provides that the "disclaimed interest" devolves as if the disclaimant predeceased the decedent.

How does the language of UPC §2-1106(b)(3)(C) handle this problem?

Problems

1. G died intestate, a resident of a jurisdiction governed by UPC Article II, Part 1. G was survived by her son, A, and by three granddaughters, X, Y, and Z. X and Y are A's children. Z is the child of a predeceased son, B. A disclaimed all his interest in his mother's estate. What result under a statute providing that the decedent's "estate" devolves as if the disclaimant predeceased the decedent? Under a statute providing that the "disclaimed interest" devolves as if the disclaimant predeceased the decedent? Under UPC §2-1106(b)(3)(C)?

2. In Problem 1, suppose that A predeceased G but B survived G. B disclaimed. What result under these various statutes?

INTERNAL REFERENCE. For the effect of disclaimers by present-interest beneficiaries on remainder interests, see Chapter 15.

EXTERNAL REFERENCES. Ronald A. Brand & William P. LaPiana, Disclaimers in Estate Planning: A Guide to Their Effective Use (1990); Adam J. Hirsch, The Problem of the Insolvent Heir, 74 Cornell L. Rev. 587 (1989); John H. Martin, Perspectives on Federal Disclaimer Legislation, 46 U. Chi. L. Rev. 316 (1979).

2. *Formality versus Discretion in Intestate Succession*

If the decedent's heirs can voluntarily rearrange intestacy patterns of distribution, should the courts have a power to vary the shares on the petition of one or more parties in interest? Under American law, as under the English canons of descent and the Statute of Distribution, intestate shares are determined mechanically. A surviving spouse's share, for example, is determined solely by reference to the decedent's other surviving relatives (or, under the UPC, by reference also to the surviving spouse's descendants). Traditional legislation does not authorize a court to inquire into the harmony or disharmony in the marital relationship. It does not allow for inquiry into the surviving spouse's contribution to the decedent's wealth.[23] It does not allow for any inquiry into the surviving spouse's needs, such as might be determined by the extent of the survivor's own assets and earning power.[24] All these issues are deemed irrelevant. In this sense, the current American law of intestate succession can be characterized as having a high degree of formality.

Although the UPC is path-breaking in important ways, it does not break with tradition on this point. The basic statutory scheme of the UPC still looks to the decedent's surviving relatives to determine the share of any particular relative. Put differently, the UPC determines the shares passing to a relative by applying mechanical factors relating to the existence of a surviving spouse, descendants, and other relatives based on fixed parent-child relationships. No judicial discretion was introduced into the statutory scheme.

The American reliance on fixed rules contrasts with the position of English law, which permits courts to alter the intestate shares or the provisions of the decedent's will in order to provide "reasonable financial provision" for certain persons related to, or dependent on, the decedent. See the Inheritance (Provision for Family and Dependants) Act 1975, with its subsequent amendments. This approach, known as TFM (or Testator's Family Maintenance), prevails in many common-law countries.

The question of formality versus discretion will come up again in several other areas of succession law. At this point, it will be useful for you to begin thinking about the reasons for and against discretion and formality and about whether the cogency of these reasons varies from one context to another.

---

23. See Chapter 8, discussing the relevance of the length of the marriage for determining the spouse's share. See also Ark. Stat. §28-9-214(2) (permitting a spouse of a childless decedent to receive the entire estate only if the decedent and spouse were married for three years or more).

24. Such information is relevant, however, under family allowance statutes that are in effect in most states. We study these statutes in Chapter 8, but at this point we need to bear in mind that they permit a judge to make a discretionary support allowance out of certain assets of the estate for the needs of the surviving spouse and children during the period of estate administration. In practice, these discretionary allowances often consume a substantial portion or all of a small estate.

EXTERNAL REFERENCES. Rosalind F. Atherton, Family Provision Legislation in Common Law Jurisdictions, in International Academy of Estate and Trust Law: Selected Papers 1997-1999, at 681 (Rosalind F. Atherton ed. 2001); S. M. Cretney, Reform of Intestacy: The Best We Can Do?, 111 Law Q. Rev. 77 (1995); Frances H. Foster, Linking Support and Inheritance: A New Model from China, 1999 Wis. L. Rev. 1199; Mary Ann Glendon, Fixed Rules and Discretion in Contemporary Family Law and Succession Law, 60 Tul. L. Rev. 1165 (1986).

PART D. ALTERING INTESTATE SUCCESSION BY MEANS OTHER THAN TESTAMENTARY DISPOSITION

In Part C, we learned that the heirs are not bound by the distributive pattern of the intestacy statute. What means are available to the decedent for altering the intestacy statute? The most obvious means is to make a valid will disposing of the decedent's entire estate. This is the topic of Chapter 4. Short of that, the decedent can alter the intestacy scheme by making an advancement, entering into a contractual agreement with a potential heir, and possibly by executing a so-called negative will.

1. Advancements and Related Doctrines

Primary Statutory Reference: *UPC §2-109*

Advancements. An advancement is a gift made during life to a family member that has the effect of reducing the share of the probate estate that the donee receives by intestate succession upon the donor's death intestate.[25] The primary purpose of the advancements doctrine is to further the intestacy statute's distribution pattern assuring equal treatment among the decedent's children. By taking into account lifetime parental gifts to children, for example, the advancement doctrine achieves more equal sharing by the children of their parent's wealth when the parent dies without a will.

Most jurisdictions originally modeled their advancement statutes upon the English Statute of Distribution, which provided only the manner for accounting for these lifetime gifts. The English courts apparently treated all gifts made during the life of the decedent as advancements, except gifts of small sums or gifts made for the purpose of maintenance or in satisfaction of the decedent's support obligation. Proof of whether a gift fell within one of the exceptions to the rule rested on objective evidence of the nature or purpose of the gift. See, e.g., Taylor v. Taylor, 20 L.R.-Eq.

---

25. See Chapter 6 for discussion of the related doctrine of satisfaction, having to do with gifts made to satisfy will devises.

155 (1875); Boyd v. Boyd, 4 L.R.-Eq. 305 (1867).

American statutes, following the English Statute of Distribution, made no attempt to define an advancement or to provide guidelines on the type of transfers to be treated as advancements. Unlike their English counterparts, however, the American courts generally refused to adopt any objective tests to identify advancements.[26] Instead, they interpreted the advancement statutes as authorizing an inquiry to determine if the decedent's specific intent was to make an advancement rather than an absolute gift. See, e.g., Holland v. Bonner, 218 S.W. 665 (Ark. 1920); Bulkeley v. Noble, 19 Mass. (2 Pick.) 337 (1824). Predictably, this judicial inquiry created a significant number of cases involving factual disputes that were made difficult by the inevitable unreliability of the evidence admitted to show the decedent's intent.

Disenchantment with the operation of the advancements doctrine led a number of nineteenth-century legislatures to restrict advancements to gifts accompanied by a writing expressing the decedent's intent to make an advancement. The general rule is that a decedent can avoid the operation of the intestacy statute only by executing a will. Why should a writing that does not meet the will formality requirements be sufficient to vary the intestacy law by having a gift treated as an advancement?

All American jurisdictions have statutes providing for advancements. See Restatement 3d of Property §2.6, Statutory Note. Two common features of the statutes are that they expand the class of advancees beyond the decedent's children to include all of the decedent's heirs, and they require written evidence of an intent to make an advancement. See UPC §2-109.

Releases and Assignments. Presumptive heirs (or devisees) can *release* their expectancy interests to the decedent. Presumptive heirs (or devisees) can also *assign* their expectancy interests to third persons—or to other presumptive heirs; see Rector v. Tatham, 196 P.3d 364 (Kan. 2008). Contracts to release or assign expectancy interests are only enforceable in equity and only if the heir (or devisee) receives fair consideration. If releasors or assignors predecease the decedent, should their descendants be bound by their ancestor's dealings?

Should a release apply to devises in a will executed subsequent to the contract of release? In Ware v. Corwell, 465 S.E.2d 809 (Va. 1996), the court held that a release by a daughter to her mother prevented the daughter from taking under her mother's will, even though the will was executed subsequent to the release agreement. As a result of this holding the testator's son inherited the mother's estate to the exclusion of his sister. Two facts make the result in *Ware* not surprising. First, the release by its written terms applied to subsequently executed wills. Second, it was executed by

---

26. South Carolina is the only state in which the courts have held that the specific intent of the decedent is irrelevant. The objective circumstances surrounding the gift, such as the amount or purpose of the gift, are considered to determine if a court should treat a particular gift as an advancement. See, e.g., Heyward v. Middleton, 43 S.E. 956 (S.C. 1903); Rees v. Rees, 11 Rich. Eq. 86 (S.C. 1859); McCaw v. Blewit, 2 McCord Eq. 90 (S.C. 1827).

the daughter and mother, as well as the son, as part of a settlement agreement over a dispute of ownership. The settlement agreement thus operated as an assignment by the mother's daughter to her son, as well as a release by the daughter to her mother. *Ware* serves as a warning to attorneys to ask their clients about prior transfers and agreements and consider how they should be taken into account in the estate plan.

Problems

1. G paid for his elder daughter, D, to attend medical school, costing $100,000. Later, G died intestate, survived only by D and D's younger sister, E. Did G made an advancement to D?

2. Assume the same facts as in Problem 1, except that G paid the tuition each term by check. On the memo line of the check, he wrote: "This is an advancement against D's share of my intestate estate." Later, he died intestate, survived only by D's younger sister, E, and by D's son, X. Who inherits what share(s) of G's estate under the UPC?

3. Assume the same facts as in Problem 2, except that G is survived only by D and E. G's intestate estate is worth $500,000. Who gets how much?

4. Isaac had two sons, Esau and Jacob. While Isaac was still alive, Esau sold his interest in Isaac's estate to Jacob for a meal of bread and lentils. (See Genesis 25:33-34.) Would this be enforceable under modern American law?

EXTERNAL REFERENCE. Mary Louise Fellows, Concealing Legislative Reform in the Common-Law Tradition: The Advancements Doctrine and The Uniform Probate Code, 37 Vand. L. Rev. 671 (1984).

2. Negative Wills

Primary Statutory Reference: *UPC §2-101(b)*

Waring v. Loring
504 N.E.2d 644 (Mass. Sup. Ct. 1987)

LYNCH, Justice....

The parties have stipulated to the following facts. The testator, Frank Peabody, died on September 28, 1918. He was survived by his wife, Gertrude Peabody, and his daughter, Amelia Peabody. His will, which was executed in 1915, was admitted to probate by the Suffolk County Probate Court on October 17, 1918. After providing substantial bequests to various individuals and organizations, Frank Peabody left the bulk of his property for the benefit of his wife and daughter. In accordance with these provisions, Gertrude received certain real and tangible personal property, and a life interest in a trust funded with one-half of Frank

Peabody's residuary estate. Amelia received the remainder of that trust and other substantial real and personal property, including a life interest in a second trust funded with the other half of the residuary estate. It is the principal of this second trust that is at issue in this proceeding.

On Amelia's death, the trust principal was to be paid to her issue by right of representation. In 1984, however, Amelia died without issue. Frank Peabody's will provided in paragraph seventh that in such case the trustees were to pay several legacies, and then distribute any balance among Frank Peabody's partners at Kidder, Peabody & Company, who were living both at his death and at the date of distribution. As none of Frank Peabody's partners at Kidder, Peabody & Company survived Amelia, and the will contained no further affirmative provision for disposition of the trust remainder, the balance of the trust is not disposed of by Frank Peabody's will.

Under the Massachusetts statute of descent and distribution in effect at Frank Peabody's death, Gertrude, as surviving widow, would receive one-third of the intestate property, and Amelia, as sole issue, would receive two-thirds.

The executors of Amelia's estate oppose distribution in accordance with this statute, however, on the ground that Gertrude's right to share in intestate property is precluded by paragraph ninth of Frank Peabody's will, which provides in its entirety as follows. "NINTH: The provisions of this will for the benefit of my wife, Gertrude Peabody, are in lieu of dower and of all her statutory rights in or to any part of my estate."...

We do not feel compelled to regard those statutory rights that are referred to in paragraph ninth of the will as including the widow's share in case of an intestacy arising from a failed disposition. Intestacy rights in the Commonwealth are statutory rights. However, in the context of paragraph ninth, considering what the testator must have had in mind by reason of that language, we decline to read the term "statutory rights" as including intestate rights....

Because we decline to read the terms of paragraph ninth as including intestate rights, we remand the case with instructions that Gertrude's estate is entitled to share in the property undisposed of by the will of Frank Peabody, in accordance with the statute of descent and distribution in effect at the time of the testator's death.

So ordered.

WILKINS, Justice (dissenting)....

Paragraph ninth of the will says that "[t]he provisions of this will for the benefit of my wife, Gertrude Peabody, are in lieu of dower and of all her statutory rights in or to any part of my estate." The right of Mrs. Peabody to take an intestate share of her husband's estate is a statutory right. We should give effect to the language as written. There is no reason to strain to read some limitation into it. It seems most reasonable to give effect to the provisions of the will so far as possible even when resorting to the statute governing intestate distribution. The suggestion that, once there is an intestacy, the will must be ignored is without logical support and is contrary to our cases, before today.

The remainder of the trust share held for the life of Amelia Peabody should be given in its entirety to Amelia's estate.

Notes and Questions

1. *Majority View.* Under prevailing court-made law in the United States, which relied on early English decisions, an intent to disinherit expressed in a will has no effect on the right of an heir to inherit any intestate portion of the estate. See Cook v. Seeman, 858 S.W.2d 114 (Ark. 1993). English courts subsequently recognized negative wills as long as the testator left at least one heir to succeed to the property. See In re Wynn, [1984] 1 W.L.R. 237 (Ch. 1983); Lett v. Randall, 107 Rev. Rep. 26 (Ch. 1855); Bund v. Green, 12 Ch. D. 819 (1879).

2. *Uniform Probate Code and Restatement Third.* The distinction between a testamentary provision directing that a devisee receive property and one directing that a devisee *not* receive property makes little sense if the purpose of a will is to provide the means of avoiding the effect of intestacy statutes and of achieving the testator's donative intent. UPC §2-101(b) reverses the prevailing common-law rule because that rule "defeats a testator's intent for no sufficient reason."[27] UPC §2-101(b) comment. Restatement 3d of Property §2.7 also authorizes negative wills, contrary to the prevailing common-law rule. Under the UPC, if a testator writes a will that disinherits an heir, the heir is presumed to have disclaimed. The distribution of the presumed disclaimed share is therefore governed by UPC Article II, Part 11 (the UDPIA).

3. *Waring.* How would *Waring* be decided under the UPC?

4. *Estate of Jetter.* UPC §2-101(b) does not impose any qualification on the right of a testator to disinherit the testator's heirs. Nevertheless, the South Dakota Supreme Court in Estate of Jetter, 570 N.W.2d 26 (S.D. 1997), appeal after remand, 590 N.W.2d 254 (S.D. 1999), interpreted S.D. Codified Laws §29A-2-101(b), which is the UPC provision, as adopting the English rule. After devising his entire estate to his brother, the testator stated in his will, "I have intentionally omitted all of my heirs ... who are not specifically mentioned herein, and I hereby generally and

---

27. See Martin D. Begleiter, Article II of the Uniform Probate Code and the Malpractice Revolution, 59 Tenn. L. Rev. 101, 114 (1991) (explaining how the UPC provision "should prevent any malpractice action based on a person who decedent desired would take nothing by intestacy").

Before the promulgation of §2-101(b), New York had been the only state to overrule the common law. It alters the statutory definition of a will to include a direction by a testator as to how property "shall not be disposed of." N.Y. Est. Powers & Trusts Law §1-2.19. If a testator disinherits an heir in a will, the effect of the New York statute is to treat the heir as having predeceased the testator for purposes of applying the intestacy statute. See, e.g., Cairo's Estate, 312 N.Y.S.2d 925 (App. Div. 1970), aff'd per curiam, 272 N.E.2d 574 (N.Y. 1971).

specifically disinherit each and all persons whomsoever claiming to be my heirs-at-law ...." 570 N.W.2d at 27. The court erroneously held that the disinheritance clause was ineffective because the statute did not authorize a clause disinheriting *all* of the testator's heirs when it resulted in an escheat.[28] The Restatement 3d of Property § 2.7 comment a takes a position opposite to *Jetter*, stating that "[t]he class to be disinherited need not be limited to a group constituting some but not all of the testator's heirs." Accord Estate of Walter, 97 P.3d 188 (Colo. Ct. App. 2003); Estate of Melton, 272 P.3d 668 (Nev. 2012).

5. *Estate of Samuelson*. Interpreting a statute identical to UPC §2-101, the North Dakota Supreme Court held that a provision in the testator's will stating that he "intentionally failed to provide" for his half-sister precluded her "from taking by both testate and intestate succession." Estate of Samuelson, 757 N.W.2d 44, 48 (N.D. 2008).

EXTERNAL REFERENCES. J. Andrew Heaton, Note, The Intestate Claims of Heirs Excluded by Will: Should "Negative Wills" Be Enforced?, 52 U. Chi. L. Rev. 177 (1985); Frederic S. Schwartz, Models of the Will and Negative Disinheritance, 48 Mercer L. Rev. 1137 (1997); Annot., Effect of Will Provision Cutting off Heir or Next of Kin, or Restricting Him to Provision Made, to Exclude Him from Distribution of Intestate Property, 100 A.L.R.2d 325 (1965).

---

28. In Julia M. Melius, Note, Was South Dakota Deprived of $3.2 Million? Intestacy, Escheat, and the Statutory Power to Disinherit in the Estate of Jetter, 44 S.D. L. Rev. 49 (1999), the author concluded that "[t]he correct decision [in *Jetter*] would have allowed not only Jetter, but all future testators, to control the disposition of their intestate properties. Instead, under an erroneous application of the new statutory provisions in South Dakota, the court chose to follow the 'English Rule.'"

Chapter 3

The Changing American Family

The structure of the American family is undergoing profound change. The traditional "Leave It to Beaver" family, consisting of a wage-earning husband, a stay-at-home wife, and two or three joint children, has not disappeared, but it is no longer the only prominent pattern. Approximately 51 percent of all married couples now have both spouses in the labor force.[1] Divorce and remarriage rates are higher than in the years before 1970,[2] and many married couples have children from prior marriages. Many families are headed by single parents, overwhelmingly mothers.[3] Unmarried opposite- and same-sex couples, including some with children, are increasingly prevalent. This chapter reflects on how family property law is responding to different family arrangements. We begin with the law of intestate succession. We then turn to the law governing the interpretation of donative documents such as wills, nonprobate beneficiary designations, and trust instruments.

PART A. INTESTATE SUCCESSION

In Chapter 2, we saw that intestacy statutes, such as UPC §§2-102 and 2-103, provide inheritance rights to the decedent's surviving "spouse" and "descendants," among others. Who is a "spouse" for purposes of intestate succession? Who is a "descendant"? These are the questions that we address in this Part.

1. Who Is a "Spouse"?

"[H]anging and marriage, you know, go by destiny."
– George Farquhar[4]

Marriage. Marriage creates a spousal relationship between the two persons who are married to each other. The rights accruing to a surviving spouse in probate law are based on that spousal status. These rights include the right to a share of the estate

---

1. U.S. Census Bureau, America's Families and Living Arrangements: 2022, tbl. FG1 (2022).

2. In the 1950s and 1960s, the divorce rate never exceeded 2.6 per 1000 women. U.S. Census Bureau, Statistical Abstract of the United States: 1999, tbl. 91. In a report issued on July 13, 2023, the Census Bureau reported that the divorce rate in 2021 was 6.9 per 1000 women, which was a drop from the 2011 divorce rate of 9.7 per 1,000 women. See https://www.census.gov/library/stories/2023/07/marriage-divorce-rates.html.

3. U.S. Census Bureau, America's Families and Living Arrangements: 2022, tbl. C3 (2022).

4. George Farquhar, The Recruiting Officer, act 3, scene 2.

if the decedent dies intestate. States also provide a surviving spouse other statutory rights, such as a family allowance, protection against intentional disinheritance (traditionally referred to as an "elective share"), and protection against unintentional disinheritance by a premarital will that the decedent failed to revise after the marriage. In most states, these and other similar rights accrue only to the person who was married to the decedent when the decedent died. In the United States, marriage is available to opposite-sex and same-sex couples equally. See Obergefell v. Hodges, 135 S.Ct. 2584 (2015).

Divorce, Separation, Misconduct. If the decedent's marriage is dissolved by divorce or annulment, the decedent's former spouse loses the status of surviving spouse. Likewise, if the decedent's marriage is void because it was bigamous, incestuous, or preceded by an invalid divorce decree, the decedent's would-be spouse does not have the status of surviving spouse. But what if the decedent's divorce or annulment is itself invalid? Or what if the decedent and decedent's spouse separate but do not divorce? Or what if a divorce suit is pending but not final at the time of the decedent's death? Some, but not all, of the questions that may arise are addressed by UPC §2-802.

Holmes v. Fentress
1980 WL 353651 (Ohio App. 1980)

MOYER, Judge. This matter is before us on plaintiffs' appeal from a decision of the Probate Court of Franklin County, Ohio, granting summary judgment to defendant. The judgment declared that defendant qualified as the surviving spouse of the decedent Harold Carlin for purposes of intestate succession.

Harold Carlin, also known as Harold Frederick Neff (prior to his name change in 1944), and defendant Marie Geissinger were married in Detroit, Michigan, in 1926. In 1935 defendant filed suit for divorce. Without her knowledge, the divorce action was dismissed in 1936. Both defendant and the decedent believed they had been legally divorced and both parties subsequently married other spouses. Harold Carlin's second wife predeceased him.

On November 7, 1974, Harold Carlin executed a will naming his "dear friend, Marie D. Geissinger" as his sole beneficiary. A short time later, on February 25, 1975, Carlin was declared mentally incompetent. He died on November 16, 1978, leaving no children and, to his knowledge, no wife. Carlin was survived by the plaintiffs, his sister Marie E. Holmes, and two brothers, Bernarr Neff and Ralph Neff. He was also survived by a niece, Donna Fentress, the daughter of a deceased brother. Plaintiffs filed a complaint to contest the will which had been admitted to probate in December of 1978. They claimed to be the heirs at law of their deceased brother. They further allege that the decedent lacked testamentary capacity when he executed the purported will, that defendant exerted undue influence upon the testator when he executed his will, and that the defendant perpetrated fraud against the decedent in the execution of his will. In addition, the plaintiffs allege that defendant had waived her right to take from the decedent as his surviving spouse.

The court, finding no genuine issue of fact, sustained defendants' motion for summary judgment. In sustaining the judgment the court stated the material facts to be:

1. The decedent, Harold Carlin, and the defendant, Marie D. Geissinger, were married at Detroit, Michigan, on September 22, 1926.

2. The marriage relationship was still valid and subsisting at the death of Harold Carlin.

3. Marie D. Geissinger was the sole beneficiary under the will of the decedent, Harold Carlin; and under the statute of the descent and distribution, she is also the surviving spouse and sole heir at law of Harold Carlin.

The court also found plaintiffs lacked standing to contest the will and dismissed the action.

Plaintiffs raise the following four assignments of error in support of their appeal:....

III. The court erred in finding that Geissinger was the surviving spouse of Harold Carlin and sole heir at law, because there is a genuine issue raised as to Geissinger's credibility whether she did or did not divorce Carlin.

IV. The trial court erred in its finding that Geissinger is the sole heir at law of Harold Carlin and thus entitled to his intestate estate because she has by her sworn oath, sworn testimony, and actions waived her rights and is estopped from asserting rights that derive from her marriage to Harold Carlin....

Plaintiffs' assertion in their third assignment of error, that Ms. Geissinger was not a credible witness, is apparently based on the conflict between her testimony in legal proceedings in 1976 that she had been divorced from Harold Carlin, and her claim in the proceedings before us that she is his surviving spouse.

While it is true that issues of credibility are not properly resolved by summary judgment..., we do not find that any issue of credibility is raised in this case. It has been established that prior to 1979 all the parties to this action believed that Harold Carlin and Marie Geissinger had been divorced. It is manifestly clear that the divorce referred to by Ms. Geissinger was the action filed in Franklin County in 1935, and subsequently dismissed. The only indication in the record that any other divorce had been referred to is a statement by counsel for plaintiffs that he was searching the records in another state for possible evidence of a divorce there. That statement is insufficient to create a substantial issue of the credibility of Ms. Geissinger. Plaintiffs' third assignment of error is overruled.

Plaintiffs' final assignment of error submits that, even if Ms. Geissinger was Harold Carlin's surviving spouse, she is precluded by waiver or estoppel from asserting her rights to inherit. The equitable appeal of that argument has some merit.

Plaintiffs argue that, because Ms. Geissinger believes she was divorced from Harold Carlin and acted consistently with that belief for over 40 years, she is precluded from now claiming the statutory rights of the surviving spouse. That is the rule in some jurisdictions.... However, that is not the rule in Ohio. ...

A waiver is generally defined as an intentional relinquishment of a known right. It may derive from an express waiver or from conduct. Myers v. Hoops (1956), 74 Ohio Law Abs. 280. It is undisputed that Ms. Geissinger did not know that she was still married to the decedent. Thus, she could not have relinquished a known right. She could not terminate her marriage merely by stating that she was divorced and by believing that she had been divorced. She could not waive her right to inherit property from her husband without knowing that she had a right to inherit.

The basis for plaintiffs' claim of estoppel appears to be that Ms. Geissinger's long-standing posture as the ex-spouse of Harold Carlin somehow induced plaintiffs to take in and care for the decedent. For estoppel to apply, the party to be estopped must himself have a complete knowledge of the facts. It has been adequately demonstrated that Ms. Geissinger shared the same mistake of fact about the divorce as the other parties. Further, there is no indication that plaintiffs took in and cared for Harold Carlin in reliance on the belief that he would die intestate, leaving them as his sole heirs at law. Thus, no basis for estoppel exists. Plaintiffs' fourth assignment of error is overruled.

While we recognize the apparent paradoxical nature of the result of this case, we are bound by the law of Ohio in reviewing the record before us. The trial court did not err in applying that law to the facts of this case.

For the foregoing reasons the judgment of the Common Pleas Court of Franklin County, Probate Division, is affirmed.

Notes and Question

1. *Question.* How would *Holmes* have been decided under the UPC?

2. *UPC §2-802.* UPC §2-802 addresses some but not all status questions. Note that §2-802 is not framed as a definition of "spouse." Instead, it gives a list of situations in which a person is *not* a surviving spouse. The most obvious of these is the case in which the marriage ended by valid divorce or annulment. The others are cases in which the survivor obtained or consented to a final decree or judgment of divorce or annulment, even though the decree later proves to have been invalid; in which the survivor, following an invalid decree obtained by the decedent, participated in a marriage ceremony with a third individual; and in which the survivor was a party to a valid proceeding purporting to terminate all marital property rights.

3. *Other Grounds for Loss of Status as Surviving Spouse.* A few states, by statute, go further than UPC §2-802 and bar the surviving spouse from taking as an heir for

desertion or adultery.[5] Legislation in some other states extends the bar to persons convicted of a felony for conduct constituting physical or financial abuse. See, e.g., Or. Rev. Stat. §112.455 et seq. Courts also may interpret physical and emotional abuse of one's spouse as constructive abandonment. See, e.g., In re Jellech, 854 S.W.2d 828 (Mo. Ct. App. 1993) (applying a Missouri statute to deny a husband a right to the decedent's estate based on evidence that his "abusive conduct, in conjunction with the evidence of his other actions, was such that... decedent could not reasonably have been expected to live with [the husband]").

———

Common-Law Marriage. Most states have abolished common-law marriage by statute. Negative judicial and legislative reaction to the concept of common-law marriage grew during the late nineteenth century. One criticism of the concept was that the informality of common-law marriages made them highly vulnerable to fraud and perjury.[6] See, e.g., Wagner's Estate, 159 A.2d 495 (1960). Another was that common-law marriage undermined the sanctity of marriage. See, e.g., Sorensen v. Sorensen, 100 N.W. 930, 932 (Neb. 1904). See generally Michael Grossberg, Governing the Hearth: Law and the Family in Nineteenth-Century America (1985).

Only eight states (Colorado, Iowa, Kansas, Montana, Oklahoma, Rhode Island, Texas, and Utah) and the District of Columbia still authorize common-law marriages.[7] The requirements necessary to establish a common-law marriage differ from state to state but can be summarized as follows:

> The jurisdictions which recognize common law marriages all require that the parties presently agree to enter into the relationship of husband and wife. Most jurisdictions also require cohabitation, or actually and openly living together as husband and wife.... Some jurisdictions further require that the parties hold themselves out to the world as husband

---

5. See, e.g., Ky. Rev. Stat. §392.090; Mo. Rev. Stat. §474.140; N.H. Rev. Stat. §560:19; N.Y. Est. Powers & Trusts Law §5-1.2(a)(5), (6); N.C. Gen. Stat. §31A-1(a)(3), (b); 20 Pa. Cons. Stat. §2106 (a); Va. Code §64.2-308(A).

6. Dan Barry, No Catastrophe Is Off-Limits to Fraud, N.Y. Times, Jan. 5, 2003: "If all humanity had responded to the World Trade Center collapse with generosity and respect for the dead, the earth might have spun from its axis. Fear not, though: scores of people rose to the occasion, scamming, conning and lying to claim their undeserved share of the relief intended for the truly victimized.... [For example,] Namor Young, who combined details of two ex-boyfriends to conjure a missing common-law husband. When Michael Young went off to work at the trade center, she said, he had a goatee, a couple of tattoos—including a 'Namor' on his belly—and a souvenir lighter from Atlantic City. Oh, and he was left-handed. And his blood type was O-positive. Ms. Young collected more than $53,000 in aid before being caught, convicted and sentenced to prison."

7. *Colorado*: See In re Marriage of Hogsett v. Neale, 478 P.3d 713 (Colo. 2021) (revising the test for common-law marriage).
Iowa: But see Iowa Code §595.11 (valid marriage but aiders and abetters required to pay $50 cash to state).

and wife, and acquire a reputation as a married couple. However, other jurisdictions hold that cohabitation and reputation are not requirements of a valid common law marriage, but solely matters of evidence.

Under all of these definitions, evidence that the parties have stated "We're not married, we're just living together" will destroy the claim of a common law marriage.

Sol Lovas, When Is a Family Not a Family? Inheritance and the Taxation of Inheritance Within the Non-Traditional Family, 24 Idaho L. Rev. 353, 361 (1987). New Hampshire has codified a statutory version of common-law marriage applicable only on death.[8]

In 2015, Probate Judge Guy Herman of Travis County, Texas, became the first judge in the U.S. to recognize a same-sex common-law marriage. See Lauren McGaughy, In a First, Texas Court Recognizes Same-Sex Common Law Marriage, Houston Chronicle, Sept. 16, 2015. See also LaFleur v. Pyfer, 479 P.3d 869 (Colo. 2021), recognizing a same-sex common-law marriage created before same-sex marriage was legal.

The Restatement 3d of Property §2.2 comment f provides that a common-law spouse is a spouse for purposes of intestate succession in states recognizing common-law marriage.

————

Putative Spouses. The purpose of the putative spouse doctrine is to protect the financial and property interests of a person who enters into a marriage believing in good faith that it is a valid marriage. It is largely controlled by statute in the United States.

One such statute is §209 of the Model Marriage and Divorce Act (1973) (MMDA), which provides that a putative spouse "acquires the rights conferred upon a legal spouse."[9] A putative spouse is defined in §209 as "[a]ny person who has

---

8. N.H. Rev. Stat. §457:39.

9. Section 209 goes on to declare:

If there is a legal spouse or other putative spouses, rights acquired by a putative spouse do not supersede the rights of the legal spouse or those acquired by other putative spouses, but the court shall apportion property, maintenance, and support rights among the claimants as appropriate in the circumstances and in the interests of justice.

The Official Comment accompanying §209 further explains:

It is possible for a person to have more than one putative spouse at the same time, since good faith is the test. In addition, a putative spouse and a legal spouse may be able to claim from a single estate or from other funds legally available to a spouse. A common situation of the latter type might involve a bigamous marriage in which the second spouse was never married or had been divorced. In such cases, the court is instructed to apportion property and the other financial incidents of marriage between the legal and the putative spouse, or among putative spouses. A fair and efficient apportionment standard is likely to be the length of time each spouse cohabited with the common partner.

cohabited with another to whom he is not legally married in the good faith belief that he was married to that person."[10]

The MMDA has been enacted only in six states: Arizona, Colorado, Georgia, Minnesota, Montana, and Washington.

The UPC says nothing about putative spouses. It neither confers rights upon nor explicitly denies rights to putative spouses. Courts in a UPC state are free to adopt the putative spouse doctrine (or not to adopt it), and legislatures can enact both the UPC and the MMDA if they wish.

The Restatement 3d of Property §2.2 comment e provides that "[u]nless precluded by applicable statute, a putative spouse is treated as a legal spouse for purposes of intestacy."

Unmarried Partners. In modern America, fewer than half of the nation's households (46.8%) are comprised of married couples. See U.S. Census Bureau, America's Families and Living Arrangements: 2022, tbl. H1 (2022). The Census Bureau reported approximately 9.9 million unmarried opposite-sex couples (in 2022) and 498,300 unmarried same-sex couples (in 2021) sharing living arrangements.

Not surprisingly, most of the litigation involving unmarried partnerships arises in the context of a dissolution during life. Claims arising at death are less common because, if the partners remain devoted to each other, the deceased partner probably provided for the survivor by will or other parts of an estate plan. Therefore, it is unusual for a surviving partner to claim legal rights to a share of a decedent's estate. When these claims do arise, however, they typically invoke theories based on contract or on status, or both.

Problem

Read the following materials. Compare and contrast the contractual approach to unmarried partners in *Estate of Quarg* with the status-based approach in the American Law Institute's Principles of the Law of Family Dissolution. What does the contractual approach do well, and what does it do poorly? Are there advantages to a status-based approach? Are there difficulties?

Some states had adopted the putative spouse doctrine by statute before the promulgation of the MMDA. See, e.g, Cal. Fam. Code §2251; Wis. Stat. §765.24; see also 42 U.S.C. §416(h)(1)(B) (adopting the putative spouse doctrine for purposes of qualifying for benefits under the Social Security Act)

10. California courts have used the putative spouse doctrine to recognize a claim for an intestate share by an unmarried cohabitor. See, e.g., Estate of Leslie, 689 P.2d 133 (Cal. 1984). California courts have also applied the doctrine to a claim for other spousal rights, such as rights under an omitted spouse statute. See, e.g., Estate of Sax, 263 Cal. Rptr. 190 (Ct. App. 1989).

Estate of Quarg
938 A.2d 193 (N.J. Super. Ct. 2008)

LINTNER, P.J.A.D.   Defendant Barbara Quarg (Barbara) appeals from a judgment of the Chancery Division, Probate Part, imposing a constructive trust on the surviving spouse's share of the intestate estate of Robert Quarg, in favor of plaintiff, Francine Levy Quarg (Francine). We remand for further proceedings, as modified by us, to determine whether Francine's allegations establish an implied contractual right to the proceeds of Robert's estate....

The following are the undisputed facts presented to the Chancery judge on stipulation by the parties. Barbara and Robert were married on September 29, 1956. On December 24, 1957, Barbara gave birth to twins, Robert and Patricia Quarg. Barbara and Robert lived together until October 1958, when Barbara took the children and left the marital residence. Barbara and Robert never again lived as husband and wife but they never divorced.

The only legal proceedings that took place between them were for visitation and child support, which occurred in New York in 1959-1960. When Robert visited the children, Barbara made herself scarce to avoid having words with him. Robert's visitations with the children ended by 1968. From 1969 to 2004, the only contact Barbara had with Robert was one meeting to discuss an issue regarding their son. They also had three brief unplanned encounters. Barbara visited Robert in hospice nine days before his death.

Francine met Robert in 1961. They began a relationship shortly thereafter and Robert moved in with Francine. On November 13, 1962, a son, Jonathan, was born to the couple. Both Francine and Jonathan took Robert's surname. The couple lived together continuously from 1961 until Robert entered a hospital in 2004, just weeks before his death. During that time period, they bought a home together, which was deeded to them as husband and wife. They also listed themselves as husband and wife on health insurance applications and also in all other respects held themselves out as husband and wife.

Robert died intestate on December 8, 2004. His estate was valued at $345,568.63, of which $226,068.63 was personal property and $119,500 was real property. Letters of Administration were initially granted to Robert's daughter, Patricia. On June 29, 2005, Jonathan and Francine filed a Verified Complaint and Order to Show Cause seeking to establish a legal parent-child relationship between Jonathan and Robert.

In the [third] count of the complaint,... Francine asserted that she and Robert lived as unmarried cohabitants for more than four decades, during which they had formed an "intimate relationship founded on mutual trust, dependence and raised expectations." She sought to share in Robert's estate, claiming that if Barbara is permitted to inherit as surviving spouse, Francine would be "unjustly impoverished" and Barbara "unjustly enriched."...

On December 19, 2006, the judge issued her opinion from the bench. She found that the intestacy statutes create a "statutory will ... case law ... militate[d] against [Barbara's] entitlement to any interest, either by way of intestacy taking or elective-share." The judge relied, in part, on the decision in Carr v. Carr, 120 N.J. 336, 576 A.2d 872 (1990), for the principle that spouses may acquire an interest in marital property by virtue of their mutual efforts during marriage that contribute to the creation, acquisition, and preservation of such property. She then reasoned that Barbara did not play a role in the joint enterprise with Robert nor did she establish that the assets accumulated were for her benefit. As to Francine, the judge recognized that, while not qualifying as Robert's statutory wife or registered domestic partner, Francine was his "partner, caregiver, builder of dreams and assets," thus entitling her the equitable remedy of a constructive trust establishing her share in Robert's estate.

On appeal, Barbara argues that she is entitled to receive one-half of Robert's estate under the applicable provisions of N.J.S.A. 3B:5-3d, which sets the intestate share of a surviving spouse at one-half if there is surviving issue, one or more of whom are not issue of the surviving spouse. Barbara also argues that N.J.S.A. 3B:8-1 does not apply because the elective share statute protects spouses who are disinherited by will by providing for an elective share. She maintains that the judge erred in fashioning a constructive trust. She asserts that the facts in Carr are not analogous because the plaintiff in Carr, although in the process of obtaining a divorce, was still married to the decedent and seeking equitable distribution at the time of his death. Barbara further argues that the cases that permit unmarried cohabitants to collect equitable distribution deal with the palimony rights between unmarried couples.

We agree with Barbara that the probate statutes do not afford Francine a remedy under the circumstances of this case. However, we part company with her contention that Francine's factual allegations do not warrant judicial intervention. We do so for slightly different reasons than those expressed by the Chancery judge.... Viewing Francine's allegations together with the circumstances presented we are compelled to remand for further proceedings based upon implied contract.

We begin our analysis with the Court's decision in Kozlowski v. Kozlowski, 80 N.J. 378, 390-91, 403 A.2d 902 (1979). Kozlowski dealt with a non-married plaintiff seeking palimony from the defendant, her male partner. Kozlowski, supra, 80 N.J. at 380. In Kozlowski, the defendant expressly promised to support his female partner for the rest of her life. However, the Court noted that it is of "no legal consequence" whether the promise is expressed or implied, stating:

> The only difference is in the nature of the proof of the agreement. Parties entering this type of relationship usually do not record their understanding in specific legalese. Rather, as here, the terms of their agreement are to be found in their respective versions of the

agreement, and their acts and conduct in the light of the subject matter and the surrounding circumstances.

In his concurring opinion, Justice Pashman agreed with the majority that a promise to provide for a life partner may be expressed or implied, with intent being discernable from the couple's "conduct and actions interpreted in light of all the surrounding circumstances." Id. at 390 (Pashman, J., concurring). However, he went one step further, pointing out that in the absence of agreement a court could look to quantum meruit or its equitable remedies, including constructive and resulting trusts, to ensure that one party to a relationship is not unjustly enriched and the other unjustly impoverished. Id. at 390-91 (Pashman, J., concurring).

In Carr, supra, 120 N.J. at 399-40, the husband died while the wife's divorce case was pending. The Court fashioned an equitable constructive trust remedy for the wife because her husband's death extinguished her divorce case along with her claim for equitable distribution, and she was not afforded a remedy under the elective share provision of the probate code. Id. at 351. The Court recognized that the wife's seventeen-year marriage was a joint enterprise, which contributed to the acquisition of marital property that would otherwise entitle her to equitable distribution had her husband not died. Id. at 347-50. The Court remanded the matter to permit an evidential showing "to avoid ... unjust enrichment that would occur if the marital property devolving to Mr. Carr's estate included the share beneficially belonging to Mrs. Carr." Id. at 353-54.

Quoting from Justice Pashman's concurring opinion in Kozlowski, the Carr Court noted that a constructive trust was an appropriate remedy because "courts may presume that the parties 'intended to deal fairly with one another [and will] employ the doctrine of quantum meruit, or equitable remedies such as constructive or resulting trusts' in order to ensure that one party has not been unjustly enriched, and the other unjustly impoverished, on account of their dealings." Id. at 352 (quoting Kozlowski, supra, 80 N.J. at 390-91 (Pashman, J., concurring)).

The circumstances in In re Estate of Roccamonte, 174 N.J. 381, 808 A.2d 838 (2002), are somewhat similar to those before us. In Roccamonte, the plaintiff brought suit against her partner's estate, seeking a lump-sum award for her lifetime. The couple had lived together for more than twenty-five years even though the decedent never divorced his wife. Id. at 386. The decedent had promised the plaintiff that he would see to it that she was provided for during her life. He died without a will. Id. at 387.

Applying the same rationale to a probate action as it did in Kozlowski, the Roccamonte Court reaffirmed the principle that where an unmarried adult partner is induced to cohabit in a marital-like relationship by a promise of support, that promise will be enforced by the court whether it is oral or written, implied or express, or inferable from the parties' acts and conduct rather than by what they said. Id. at 389. Noting the right to support does not come from the relationship, but instead from contract, the court fashioned the same contractual remedy, as it did in Kozlowski, namely, a one-time lump sum in an amount equal to the present value of the reasonable future support the decedent has promised to provide. Id. at 390....

The Court in Roccamonte reached its decision based upon concepts of implied contract, despite the previous reference in Carr to Justice Pashman's concurrence in Kozlowski. It did not adopt the use of quantum meruit (a quasi contract imposed by law without reference to the parties' intent; see, e.g., Kopin v. Orange Prods., Inc., 297 N.J.Super. 353, 366, 688 A.2d 130 (App.Div.), certif. denied, 694 A.2d 194 (1997)) nor apply equitable concepts of constructive trust used by the Chancery judge in rendering her decision here....

As previously pointed out, one of the components of Francine's complaint alleged that she would become unjustly impoverished if she did not share in Robert's estate. More importantly, as the surviving partner, after more than forty years of living with Robert as married, Francine asserts that the relationship was "founded on mutual trust, dependency and raised expectations." In our view, such allegations bespeak an implied promise by Robert not to leave Francine impoverished, but rather, to see to it, as best he could, that she survived with adequate provisions during the remainder of her life.

Because such a promise can be reasonably inferred from Robert's and Francine's conduct and actions, when viewed together with the lengthy period of living as husband and wife, we remand the matter to the Chancery Division for a plenary hearing, if necessary, to determine whether Francine can establish an enforceable implied promise as detailed in Roccamonte....

The matter is remanded for further proceedings in accordance with this opinion....

Notes

1. *Express Contract Required?* Some jurisdictions have taken the position that only an express contract concerning property division upon dissolution of a unmarried partnership is enforceable. They do not recognize an implied contract. See, e.g., Levar v. Elkins, 604 P.2d 602 (Alaska 1980); Morone v. Morone, 413 N.E.2d 1154 (N.Y. 1980) (unmarried partners who cohabitate). Cf. Moors v. Hall, 143 A.D.2d (N.Y.App. Div. 1988), in which the court recognized an implied contract between unmarried partners who did not cohabitate.

2. *Express Written Contract Required?* Should only express *written* contracts be enforceable? The Uniform Premarital Agreement Act §2 (1983) provides that a premarital agreement is enforceable only if it is in writing. The Uniform Premarital and Marital Agreements Act §6 (2012) requires a premarital or marital agreement to be "in a record and signed by both parties." The American Law Institute's Principles of the Law of Family Dissolution (PLFD) provides certain rights automatically to unmarried partners who meet the document's definitions, but if the

partners wish to alter the remedies available under the PLFD, they must do so in a written agreement signed by both parties. See PLFD §§7.01(2)(a),[11] 7.04(1).

Recognition of Unmarried Partnerships by the American Law Institute. As mentioned above, the American Law Institute has promulgated The Principles of the Law of Family Dissolution (PLFD). Chapter 6 of the PLFD concerns unmarried partners. Professor Ira Mark Ellman, the chief reporter, has summarized the approach of Chapter 6 as follows:

> Chapter 6's treatment of domestic partners does not adopt the contractual approach most often associated with the California Supreme Court's decision in *Marvin v. Marvin*, but instead follows more recent trends that treat persons as having entered a relationship with legal significance when they live together and share a life together for a sufficient period of time.... Under the formulation adopted by the Institute, parties who live together with their common child, for the required minimum time period, are deemed domestic partners. The required time period is left for the adopting jurisdiction to choose, but the commentary suggests that a two-year period would be reasonable. Unrelated parties who do not have a common child are presumed to be domestic partners if they share a common household for a separately-established minimum period, the commentary suggesting a three-year period as a reasonable choice. The resulting presumption is rebuttable by evidence that the parties did not "share a life together as a couple," a defined phrase that is elaborated upon in the commentary. Parties may also be treated as domestic partners if one of them shows that they shared a common household and a life together for a "significant period of time," even if that time is less than the minimum periods set in the other provisions. Once parties are considered domestic partners, the dissolution of their relationship triggers property and compensatory payment (alimony) remedies that overlap almost entirely with those available at the dissolution of marriage. It should be noted that Chapter 6 addresses only the legal claims that the domestic partners have against one another at the dissolution of their relationship. Nothing in the chapter requires third parties, such as employers or government agencies, to accord any special treatment of the domestic partners. The relationship of third parties to married couples, or unmarried domestic partners, is not within the scope of the ALI's Family Dissolution project. Chapter 6 makes no distinction between opposite-sex and same-sex couples, incorporating both within its rules.

---

11. Comment b to §7.01 provides:

   b. Scope. ...This chapter also applies to agreements between domestic partners that would avoid, alter, or augment legal consequences that would otherwise arise under Chapter 6 when their relationship ends. This chapter is not intended, however, to govern contracts between nonmarital partners in jurisdictions that do not follow the principles such as those in Chapter 6. That is because the chapter is designed for agreements that vary otherwise applicable legal norms, such as those that govern the obligations of married couples at divorce, or that govern nonmarital couples who acquire legal obligations to one another by operation of law, as under Chapter 6. This chapter is not intended to govern agreements between persons who have no obligations to one another except as they may create by their agreement. The requirements of this Chapter also do not govern contracts concerning financial claims that one spouse may have at the other's death. Such contracts are covered by the Restatement Third, Property (Wills and Other Donative Transfers).

Ira Mark Ellman, ALI Family Law Report, Sept. 11, 2000 (available at www.ssrn.com, abstract no. 241418). For a dissenting view, see David Westfall, Forcing Incidents of Marriage on Unmarried Cohabitants: The American Law Institute's *Principles of Family Dissolution*, 76 Notre Dame L. Rev. 1467 (2001).

The Restatement 3d of Property §2.2 comment g states:

> g. *Domestic partner....* To the extent that a domestic partner is treated [by the PLFD] as having the status of a spouse, conferring rights on such a partner on the dissolution of the relationship, the domestic partner who remains in that relationship with the decedent until the decedent's death should be treated as a legal spouse for purposes of intestacy.

The Need for Legislative Solutions. Very few states provide inheritance rights to unmarried partners. For a survey of state law, see Carlyn S. McCaffrey, The Property Rights of Unmarried Cohabitants in the USA, 24 Tr. & Trustees 97 (2017). Many legal scholars have urged state legislatures and the Uniform Law Commission to recognize and protect the property interests of unmarried partners based on their status. For articles in this vein, see Thomas P. Gallanis, Inheritance Rights for Domestic Partners, 79 Tul. L. Rev. 55 (2004); Susan N. Gary, Adapting Intestacy Laws to Changing Families, 18 Law & Ineq. 1 (2000); E. Gary Spitko, The Expressive Function of Succession Law and the Merits of Non-Marital Inclusion, 41 Ariz. L. Rev. 1063 (1999).

In 2021, the Uniform Law Commission promulgated the Uniform Cohabitants' Economic Remedies Act (UCERA). The scope of UCERA is modest. It does not create new rights for an unmarried cohabitant but merely enables a cohabitant to enforce contractual or equitable rights arising from the cohabitant's contributions to the relationship. The term "contributions to the relationship" is defined in §2(3) to mean contributions "that benefit the other cohabitant, both cohabitants, or the cohabitants' relationship, in the form of efforts, activities, services, or property." The definition of the term explicitly excludes "sexual relations."

Related Estate Planning Issues. All fifty states and the District of Columbia permit an individual to designate someone (a proxy) to make health-care decisions when that individual is incapacitated. For an example of a health-care proxy statute, see the Uniform Health-Care Decisions Act (2023) (UHCDA), discussed in Chapter 18. If an individual fails to make a designation, the statutes typically identify a class of persons who may serve as surrogate decision-makers. The UHCDA proritizes the individual's "spouse [or domestic partner]"; then an adult child or parent; then the individual's "cohabitant." The term "cohabitant" is defined as "each of two individuals who have been living together as a couple for at least one year after each became an adult or was emancipated and who are not married to each other[or are not [domestic partners] with each other]."

2. Who Is a "Descendant"?

Primary Statutory References: *UPA §§201, 613(c) (2017)*

Finding a satisfactory meaning of the term "descendant" is surprisingly vexing. The question of who qualifies as a descendant is treated as a status question in the sense that the inheritance rights of the decedent's descendants are linked to the identification of legally recognized parent-child relationships. A decedent's grandchild *is* a grandchild because the decedent is a parent of a child who in turn is a parent of the grandchild.

Here we examine the circumstances under which the law does or should recognize a parent-child relationship for purposes of intestate succession.

In 2017, the Uniform Law Commission approved a new, comprehensive Uniform Parentage Act, known as the UPA (2017). For an overview of the Act by its principal drafter, see Courtney C. Joslin, Nurturing Parenthood Through the UPA (2017), Yale L. J. Forum (Jan. 7, 2018).

One provision of the UPA (2017) must be mentioned straightaway: the UPA (2017) opens the door to the possibility that a child may have more than two parents. Section 613(c), Alternative B, provides in pertinent part: "The court may adjudicate a child to have more than two parents under this [act] if the court finds that failure to recognize more than two parents would be detrimental to the child."

In 2019, the UPC was amended to conform to the UPA (2017), with some further amendments approved in 2021. For a discussion of the UPC amendments, see Mary Louise Fellows & Thomas P. Gallanis, The Uniform Probate Code's New Intestacy and Class Gift Provisions, 46 ACTEC L.J. 127 (2021). In the following pages, we discuss the UPA (2017) and the UPC revisions.

Primary Statutory References: *UPC §§2-103, 2-114 to 2-119*

Adoption. Adoption as a social institution has undergone substantial change within the past half century. Unknown to the English common law, which exhibited a strong preoccupation with blood ties,[12] adoption is now a widely accepted method of creating a parent-child relationship. See, e.g., UPA §201(4) (2017).

In all U.S. states, either by statute or judicial decision, adopted children inherit from their adoptive parents. Moreover, UPC §2-118 and most non-UPC statutes treat

-----

12. The English aversion to adoption was transplanted to the American colonies, but diminished availability of alternatives helped to facilitate the recognition of adoption in the mid-19th century. Following enactment of the first adoption acts between 1849 and 1850, the remaining states quickly authorized adoption, by statute or case law. See Michael Grossberg, Governing the Hearth (1985).

adopted persons as children of their adoptive parents for *all* inheritance purposes. In other words, they allow a child not only to inherit *from* but also *through* the adoptive parent and allow adoptive family members to inherit from or through the adopted child.

There is less agreement, however, on inheritance by adopted children from their *previous* parents and from ancestors and collateral relatives of their previous parents.

Estates of Donnelly
502 P.2d 1163 (Wash. 1973)

NEILL, J. May an adopted child inherit from her natural grandparents? Both the trial court and the Court of Appeals... answered "yes." We granted review... and disagree. In speaking of heirs and inheritance, we refer to the devolution of property by law in intestacy and not by testamentary or other voluntary disposition.

John J. and Lily Donnelly, husband and wife, had two children, a daughter, Kathleen M., now Kathleen M. Kelly, and a son, John J., Jr. The son had one child, Jean Louise Donnelly, born October 28, 1945. Jean Louise's father, John J. Donnelly, Jr., died on July 9, 1946, less than a year after her birth. Her mother, Faith Louise Donnelly, married Richard Roger Hansen on April 22, 1948. By a decree entered August 11, 1948, Jean Louise was adopted by her step-father with the written consent of her natural mother. She lived with her mother and adoptive father as their child and kept the name Hansen until her marriage to Donald J. Iverson....

Lily Donnelly, the grandmother, died October 7, 1964, leaving a will in which she named but left nothing to her two children. All of her property she left to her husband....

John J. Donnelly, Sr., the grandfather, died September 15, 1970, leaving a will dated October 16, 1932, in which he left his entire estate to his wife, Lily, who had predeceased him. He, too, named but left nothing to his two children, and made no provision for disposition of his property in event his wife predeceased him. His daughter, Kathleen M. Kelly, as administratrix with wills annexed of the estates of her parents, brought this petition to determine heirship and for a declaration that Jean Louise Iverson, the granddaughter, take nothing and that she, Kathleen M. Kelly, the daughter, be adjudged the sole heir of her mother and father, Lily and John J. Donnelly, Sr., to the exclusion of Jean Louise Iverson, her niece and their granddaughter.

The trial court decided that each was an heir. It concluded that Jean Louise Iverson, daughter of John J. Donnelly, Jr., and granddaughter of his father, John J. Donnelly, Sr., should inherit one-half of the latter's estate and that Kathleen M. Kelly, daughter of John J. Donnelly, Sr., should inherit the other half of the estate.

Kathleen M. Kelly, the daughter of decedent, appealed to the Court of Appeals which affirmed, and now to this court. With the issue recognized to be close and of general importance, we granted review....

As the trial court in its memorandum opinion and the Court of Appeals noted, the issue is whether RCW 11.04.085, which says that an adopted child shall not be deemed an heir of his natural parents, cuts off the inheritance from the natural grandparents as well. The Court of Appeals put the question precisely...:

> In Washington, may a natural granddaughter inherit from her intestate grandparents, notwithstanding her adoption by her stepfather after the death of her natural father, the son of the decedent grandparents?

The sole beneficiary under his will having predeceased him, John J. Donnelly, Sr., died intestate. His estate would thus pass by the statutes governing intestacy according to RCW 11.04.015, which says:

> The net estate of a person dying intestate... shall be distributed as follows:....
>
> (2) ...the entire net estate if there is no surviving spouse, shall descend and be distributed...
>
> (a) To the *issue* of the intestate; if they are all in the same degree of kinship to the intestate, they shall take equally, or if of unequal degree, then those of more remote degree shall take by representation.
>
> (Italics ours.)

Issue "includes all the lawful lineal descendants of the ancestor." RCW 11.02.005(4). A descendant is one "who is descended from another; a person who proceeds from the body of another, such as a child, grandchild." Black's Law Dictionary 530 (Rev. 4th ed. 1968). Thus, both the daughter and granddaughter are descendants and issue of John J. Donnelly, Sr. The daughter under the descent and distribution statutes would take as the most immediate descendant, and the granddaughter being of more remote degree would take by representation as the sole issue of her deceased father who stood in the same degree of kinship to John J. Donnelly, Sr., as did Kathleen M. Kelly. RCW 11.04.015.

RCW 11.02.005(3) states:

> [E]ach share of a deceased person in the nearest degree shall be divided among those of his issue who survive the intestate and have no ancestor then living who is in the line of relationship between them and the intestate, those more remote in degree taking together the share which their ancestor would have taken had he survived the intestate.

Thus, a statutory right to inherit one-half of the grandfather's estate is vested in Jean Louise Iverson, the granddaughter, unless that right is divested by operation of RCW 11.04.085, which declares that an adopted child is not to be considered an heir of his natural parents:

> A lawfully adopted child shall not be considered an "heir" of his natural parents for purposes of this title.

When the question of the right of an adopted child to inherit from his natural parents came before us, the intent of the legislature was clear from the literal language of the statute. We held that RCW 11.04.085 prevents an adopted child from taking a share of the natural parent's estate by intestate succession. However, reference to the literal language of RCW 11.04.085 does not answer the instant question, *i.e.*, whether, by declaring that an adopted child shall not take from his natural parent, the legislature also intended to remove the adopted child's capacity to represent the natural parent and thereby take from the natural grandparent.

The purpose of statutory interpretation is to ascertain and give effect to the intent of the legislature. To decide whether RCW 11.04.085 also severs the right of the adopted child to inherit from a remote ancestor, we must first determine why the legislature terminated the rights of inheritance with respect to the natural parent....

The legislature has addressed itself to the inheritance rights of adopted children in both the probate and domestic relations titles of RCW .... For example, RCW 26.32.140 also directly affects the inheritance rights of an adopted child:

> By a decree of adoption the natural parents shall be divested of all legal rights and obligations in respect to the child, and *the child* shall be free from all legal obligations of obedience and maintenance in respect to them, and *shall be* to all intents and purposes, and for all legal incidents, *the child, legal heir, and lawful issue of his or her adopter or adopters, entitled to all rights and privileges, including the right of inheritance* and the right to take under testamentary disposition, and subject to all the obligations of a child of the adopter or adopters begotten in lawful wedlock.
> (Italics ours.)

Since RCW 11.04.085 and RCW 26.32.140 each delimit the inheritance rights of an adopted child, the two statutes must be read in pari materia....

It is clear that: (1) the adopted child cannot take from his natural parent because he is no longer an "heir" (RCW 11.04.085); and, (2) the adopted child enjoys complete inheritance rights from the adoptive parent, as if he were the natural child of the adoptive parent (RCW 26.32.140). Both statutes are in harmony with the fundamental spirit of our adoption laws—*i.e.*, that for all purposes the adopted child shall be treated as a "child of the adopter... begotten in lawful wedlock."

Legislative intent is to be ascertained from the statutory text as a whole, interpreted in terms of the general object and purpose of the legislation.

The question at bench should, therefore, be decided in the context of the broad legislative objective of giving the adopted child a "fresh start" by treating him as the natural child of the adoptive parent, and severing all ties with the past. We believe it clearly follows that the legislature intended to remove an adopted child from his natural bloodline for purposes of intestate succession.

The trial court and Court of Appeals, however, held that although an adopted child may not take *from* a natural parent dying intestate, the same child may take *through* the natural parent, by representation, if the natural parent dies before the natural grandparent. Little supportive reasoning is offered for this inconsistent result. In reaching its conclusion, the Court of Appeals reasoned that consanguineal ties are so fundamental that an explicit expression of legislative intent is required to deprive an adopted child of the bounty which would normally be his by reason of the "intuitive impulses" generated by the blood relationship. The Court of Appeals reasoned that had the legislature desired to remove an adopted child from its natural bloodline, it could have used the word "kin" in place of the word "parents" in RCW 11.04.085. Thus, since RCW 11.04.085 does not specify that an adopted child may not take from an intestate natural grandparent, this capacity is not lost....

The legislative policy of providing a "clean slate" to the adopted child permeates our scheme of adoption. The natural grandparents are not entitled to notice of any hearing on the matter of adoption. RCW 26.32.080. RCW 26.32.150 provides that, unless otherwise requested by the adopted, all records of the adoption proceeding shall be sealed and not open to inspection. Pursuant to RCW 26.32.120, a decree for adoption shall provide: (1) for the issuance of a certificate of birth for the adopted child, containing such information as the court may deem proper; and (2) that the records of the registrar shall be secret. RCW 70.58.210 declares that the new birth certificate shall bear the new name of the child and the names of the adoptive parents of the child, but shall make no reference to the adoption of the child. Thus, the natural grandparents have no assurance that they will know the new name or residence of the adopted child. Indeed, in the usual "out of family" adoption situation the administrator of a deceased natural grandparent's estate will be unable to locate—much less to identify—the post-adoption grandchild.

The consistent theme of the relevant legislation is that the new family of the adopted child is to be treated as his natural family. The only conclusion consistent with the spirit of our overlapping adoption and inheritance statutes is that RCW 11.04.085 was intended to transfer all rights of inheritance out of the natural family upon adoption and place them entirely within the adopted family.

Respondent suggests it is most probable that the legislature never considered the problem of inheritance by adopted persons from their remote natural kin when it passed RCW 11.04.085. Thus, respondent contends that the word "parents" should be strictly construed. We disagree....

The broad legislative purpose underlying our statutes relating to adopted children is consistent only with the inference that RCW 11.04.085 was intended to remove respondent, an adopted child, from her natural bloodline for inheritance purposes. If the adopted child cannot take from her natural father, she should not represent him and take from his father.

The chain of inheritance was broken by respondent's adoption. Reversed.

HAMILTON, C.J., and STAFFORD, WRIGHT and UTTER, JJ., concur.

[The dissenting opinion of HALE, J., in which FINLEY, HUNTER, and ROSELLINI, JJ., concurred, is omitted.]

Notes and Questions

1. *Uniform Probate Code.* How would *Donnelly* have been decided under the pre-2019 UPC? Under the current UPC?

2. *Adult Adoption?* Can a person be adopted as an adult? In most states, the answer is yes. The topic is discussed below on p. 100. For a discussion of the inheritance consequences of adult adoption, see Richard C. Ausness, Planned Parenthood: Adult Adoption and the Right of Adoptees to Inherit, 41 ACTEC L. J. 241 (2015/2016).

3. *Unmarried Partners and Adoption.* For unmarried couples that have children, or that want to have children, there are obstacles when both partners seek to be recognized as parents of the child. The reason is that many of the state statutes regulating adoption rely on marital status. Second-parent adoption is the term used to refer to an adoption by the unmarried partner of the child's existing parent. The availability of second-parent adoption depends on the law of each state.

The Uniform Adoption Act (UAA), promulgated by the Uniform Law Commission in 1994, is a legislative attempt to facilitate joint parenting arrangements between unmarried couples. UAA §4-102 addresses the question of second-parent adoptions by providing:

> (b) For good cause shown, a court may allow an individual who does not [qualify as a stepparent], but has the consent of the custodial parent of a minor to file a petition for adoption under this [article]. A petition allowed under this subsection must be treated as if the petitioner were a stepparent.

The UAA thus avoids defining a cohabitating partner and leaves it to the courts to determine whether "good cause" is shown to warrant treating a petitioning cohabitating partner as a stepparent.

———

Primary Statutory References: *UPC §§2-118, 2-119; UPA §609 (2017)*

De Facto Parentage. A legally recognized parent-child relationship can be created without a formal adoption. One such method is by an adjudication of de facto parentage. Section 609 of the UPA (2017) provides in pertinent part:

> ... the court shall adjudicate the individual who claims to be a de facto parent to be a parent of the child if the individual demonstrates by clear-and-convincing evidence that:
>
> (1) the individual resided with the child as a regular member of the child's household for a significant period;
>
> (2) the individual engaged in consistent caretaking of the child;

(3) the individual undertook full and permanent responsibilities of a parent of the child without expectation of financial compensation;

(4) the individual held out the child as the individual's child;

(5) the individual established a bonded and dependent relationship with the child which is parental in nature;

(6) another parent of the child fostered or supported the bonded and dependent relationship required under paragraph (5); and

(7) continuing the relationship between the individual and the child is in the best interest of the child.

Professor Courtney Joslin, the principal drafter of the UPA (2017), explains this provision as follows:

> ...[T]he UPA (2017) includes an entirely new method of establishing parentage—the de facto parent provision. Most states today extend some protection to functional, nonbiological parents. Some states do this through a holding-out provision. But even more states recognize and protect functional parent-child relationships under equitable doctrines. The UPA (2017) incorporates this trend in the law in a particularly robust way. Under [§]609, persons alleging themselves to be "de facto parents"—that is, parents in fact—can be recognized as legal parents who stand in parity with any other legal parents, including genetic parents, for all purposes. This new method of establishing parentage based on function is written in gender-neutral terms and applies equally to men and women.

Joslin, Nurturing Parenthood, Yale L.J. Forum at 601-602.

The UPC was revised in 2019 to recognize de facto parentage for inheritance purposes and to maintain the connection between the de facto child and the child's previous parents. See UPC §§2-118(b), 2-119(c).

Problems

1. A and B were unmarried cohabitants. With A's consent, B commenced a proceeding on the basis of de facto parentage to be adjudicated a second parent of A's four-year-old child, X. The court adjudicated B on that basis to be a parent of X. After the adjudication, A, B, and X died intestate in that order, each surviving the predeceased individual(s) by more than 120 hours. X was survived only by A's parent, P. With respect to the intestate estates of A and B, did X have the right to inherit? With respect to the intestate estate of X, does P have the right to inherit?

2. A and B were married and had a child, X. When X was four years old, A and B divorced, and B married C. When X was twelve years old, C commenced, with the consent of A and B, a proceeding on the basis of de facto parentage to be adjudicated a parent of X. The court did not terminate the parental rights of A or B when it adjudicated C to be a parent of X. Later, X died intestate, survived only by A, B, and C. Who inherits X's intestate estate?

Primary Statutory References: *UPC §§2-103(j), 2-118, 2-122*

Stepchildren and Foster Children. Unless adopted or adjudicated a de facto child, a stepchild usually is not entitled to inherit from stepparents or the stepparents' relatives. The UPC, however, gives inheritance rights, as a last resort before escheat, to some stepchildren, namely the children of the decedent's predeceased spouses. See UPC §2-103(j).

Consistent with the traditional rule on stepchildren, foster children are not entitled in most states nor under the UPC to inherit from members of their foster families.

In California, however, stepchildren or foster children (and their descendants) are entitled to inherit from or through their stepparents or foster parents if "the relationship of parent and child" began "during the person's minority and continued throughout the [parties'] joint lifetimes" and if "it is established by clear and convincing evidence that the foster parent or stepparent would have adopted the person but for a legal barrier." Cal. Prob. Code §6454. The California statute has generated considerable litigation. Several cases have required the courts to interpret the phrase "but for a legal barrier." The California courts have also been required to address the question of what constitutes a continuous relationship.

"Equitable Adoption" of Foster Children. Foster children who have not been formally adopted by their foster parents may nevertheless obtain inheritance rights under a doctrine called "equitable adoption." Courts also refer to this doctrine as "virtual adoption," "de facto adoption," or "adoption by estoppel." Courts in over half the states have recognized such a doctrine,[13] but a number of jurisdictions have rejected it. The strongest factual situation presented for applying the doctrine is where the foster parents expressly contracted to adopt the child but failed to complete the adoption procedures. Even if the child cannot prove an express contract, courts have implied a contract under certain circumstances.

The cases are divided on whether an equitable adoption only qualifies the child to inherit from the child's foster parents or grants the child full status as a child of the foster parents for other purposes.[14]

---

13. A recent state recognizing the doctrine is Illinois. See DeHart v. DeHart, 986 N.E.2d 85 (Ill. 2013). A recent state rejecting the doctrine is Wyoming. Estate of Scherer, 336 P.3d 129 (Wyo. 2014).

14. For cases granting full status, see First Nat'l Bank v. Phillips, 344 S.E.2d 201 (W. Va. 1985) (allowed an equitably adopted child to inherit from a foster parent's other child); Foster v. Cheek, 96 S.E.2d 545 (Ga. 1957) (allowed an equitably adopted child to receive insurance benefits providing for a "child" on a policy insuring a foster parent); Bower v. Landa, 371 P.2d 657 (Nev. 1962) (allowed a suit under a wrongful death statute for the death of a foster parent); Estate of Radovich, 308 P.2d 14 (Cal. 1957) (an equitably adopted child had a right to favorable state inheritance tax treatment).
Contra, e.g., Reynolds v. Los Angeles, 222 Cal. Rptr. 517 (Ct. App. 1986) (denied a foster father the right to pursue a wrongful death action upon the accidental death of his equitably adopted son); In re Estate of Jenkins, 904 P.2d 1316 (Colo. 1995) (en banc) (denied an equitably adopted child the right to take under the testamentary trust of his foster grandfather); First National Bank v. People, 516 P.2d

California grants a foster child a right of inheritance if the child would have been adopted "but for a legal barrier" (see above). But California also continues to recognize the need for the doctrine of equitable adoption. See Cal. Prob. Code §6455 ("Nothing in this chapter affects or limits application of the judicial doctrine of equitable adoption for the benefit of the child or the child's issue.").

The UPC does not codify the doctrine of equitable adoption. See UPC §2-122.

Problems

1. A and B were married and had a child, X. When X was seventeen years old, A and B divorced, and B married C. Later, A and B died, followed by C, who died intestate. C was survived only by X and by C's parent, P. Under the current UPC, who inherits C's intestate estate?

2. Same facts as Problem 1 except that C was survived only by X. Under the current UPC, who inherits C's intestate estate?

EXTERNAL REFERENCE. Michael J. Higdon, When Informal Adoption Meets Intestate Succession: The Cultural Myopia of the Equitable Adoption Doctrine, 43 Wake Forest L. Rev. 223 (2008).

———

Primary Statutory References: *UPC §2-117, UPA §202 (2017)*

Children of Parents Not Married to Each Other. Historically, the common law labeled a nonmarital child as "filius nullius"—the child of no one. Such a child formally lacked the right to inherit from or through either parent. The law in practice, however, was more complicated. Church courts and, later, common-law courts enforced a father's duty to support his children born out of wedlock, thus indicating some willingness to recognize the parent-child relationship between nonmarital children and their biological parents. See Richard H. Helmholz, Support

---

639 (Colo. 1973) (denied favorable inheritance tax treatment to an equitably adopted child); Board of Education v. Browning, 635 A.2d 373 (Md. 1994) (denied an equitably adopted child the right to inherit from the foster parent's sister); McGarvey v. State, 533 A.2d 690 (Md. 1987) (denied favorable inheritance tax treatment to an equitably adopted child); Estate of Riggs, 440 N.Y.S.2d 450 (Sur. Ct. 1981) (denied family members of a foster parent the right to inherit from an equitably adopted child).

Courts have held that the doctrine has no effect on the child's right to inherit from the child's biological parents. See, e.g., Kupec v. Cooper, 593 So. 2d 1176 (Fla. Dist. Ct. App. 1992); Gardner v. Hancock, 924 S.W.2d 857 (Mo. Ct. App. 1996). Courts have also held that the doctrine is not available to a person who claims to have been equitably adopted as an adult. See, e.g., Miller v. Paczier, 591 So. 2d 321 (Fla. Dist. Ct. App. 1991).

See generally Annot., Modern Status of Law as to Equitable Adoption or Adoption by Estoppel, 122 ALR5th 205 (originally published in 2004).

Orders, Church Courts, and the Rule of Filius Nullius: A Reassessment of the Common Law, 63 Va. L. Rev. 431 (1977).

The UPC reverses the common law. Individuals inherit from and through their parents regardless of their parents' marital status. UPC §2-117. The UPA (2017) embraces the same rule for parentage generally: "A parent-child relationship extends equally to every child and parent, regardless of the marital status of the parent." UPA §202 (2017).

For discussion, see Paula A. Monopoli, Toward Equality: Nonmarital Children and the Uniform Probate Code, 45 U. Mich. J. L. Ref. 995 (2012).

Problem

A and B were unmarried partners with a child, X. A died, survived only by B and X. Under the current UPC, who inherits A's intestate estate?

———

Primary Statutory References: *UPC §§2-104, 2-120, 2-121*

Children by Assisted Reproduction. Medical technology allows for the conception of a child by means other than sexual intercourse. The development of assisted reproductive technologies challenges traditional notions of family, kinship, and parenting with far-reaching social and legal implications.[15] One commentator underscores the complex issues we face:

> We now live in an era where a child may have as many as five different "parents." These include a sperm donor, an egg donor, a surrogate or gestational host, and two nonbiologically related individuals who intend to raise the child. Indeed, the process of procreation itself has become so fragmented by the variety and combinations of collaborative-reproductive methods that there are a total of sixteen different reproductive combinations, in addition to traditional conception and childbirth. This total is the product of varying the source of the male gametes (whether by husband or third-party donor), the source of the female gametes (whether by wife or third-party egg donor), the location of fertilization (whether in the wife, the laboratory, or the surrogate host), and the site of gestation (either in the wife or the surrogate). [John Lawrence Hill, What Does It Mean to

———

15. Courts are beginning to grapple with the right to determine the disposition of frozen embryos when the parties, usually after divorce, disagree. In J.B. v. M.B., 783 A.2d 707 (N.J. 2001), the court adopted the rule that an agreement entered into when in vitro fertilization is begun is enforceable, "subject to the right of either party to change his or her mind about disposition up to the point of use or destruction of any stored preembryos." Accord, Speranza v. Repro Lab Inc., 875 N.Y.S.2d 449 (App. Div. 2009), rejecting the parents' request to use their dead son's sperm, because the agreement signed by the son when he deposited the sperm specified that the sperm would be destroyed in the event of his death; Estate of Kievernagel, 83 Cal.Rptr.3d 311 (Cal. App. 2008), rejecting the surviving wife's request to use her dead husband's sperm, because the deposit agreement indicated that the sperm would be discarded upon his death.

Be a "Parent"? The Claims of Biology as the Basis for Parental Rights, 66 N.Y.U. L. Rev. 353, 355 (1991).]

The UPA (2017) contains detailed provisions on parent-child relationships arising from assisted reproduction. Article 7 of the UPA (2017) applies to assisted reproduction that does not involve a surrogacy agreement. Article 8 of the UPA (2017) applies to assisted reproduction involving a surrogacy agreement.

In 2019, UPC §§2-120 and 2-121 were revised to incorporate these UPA provisions by reference. In other words, for UPC purposes, Articles 7 and 8 of the UPA (2017) will determine parent-child relationships arising from assisted reproduction. The one exception is that the UPC uses its own rules on time-limits for posthumous assisted reproduction.

UPC §2-104 provides that inheritance rights are granted only to individuals who are living at the decedent's death or who are "deemed to be living at the decedent's death." To consider how this provision might apply in the context of posthumous assisted reproduction, read the following paragraphs.

Inheritance Rights and Posthumous Reproduction. In general, existing statutes relating to inheritance laws were not designed to address the question of a child born from a posthumous pregnancy. For example, children born from a posthumous pregnancy would not qualify as heirs of their decedent fathers or mothers under statutes codifying the common law regarding children in gestation. They only apply to children in gestation before the decedent's death.

The Restatement 3d of Property §2.5 comment *l* takes a broader view, articulating the position that, "to inherit from the decedent, a child produced from genetic material of the decedent by assisted reproductive technology must be born within a reasonable time after the decedent's death in circumstances indicating that the decedent would have approved of the child's right to inherit." See also Estate of Kolacy, 753 A.2d 1257 (N.J. Super. Ct. Ch. Div. 2000) ("Given that [the] general legislative intent [is to enable children to inherit property from their parents], it seems to me that once we establish, as we have in this case, that a child is indeed the offspring of a decedent, we should routinely grant that child the legal status of being an heir of the decedent, unless doing so would unfairly intrude on the rights of other persons or would cause serious problems in terms of the orderly administration of estates.").

The question often arises in litigation over Social Security benefits, a context in which the federal government looks to state inheritance and family law. See, e.g., Astrue v. Capato, 132 S.Ct. 2021 (2012) (denying benefits under Florida law); Vernoff v. Astrue, 568 F.3d 1102 (9th Cir. 2009) (denying benefits under California law); Beeler v. Astrue, 651 F.3d 954 (2011) (denying benefits under Iowa law); Finley v. Astrue, 270 S.W.3d 849 (Ark. 2008) (denying benefits under Arkansas law); Khabbaz v. Commissioner, 930 A.2d 1180 (N.H. 2007) (denying benefits under New Hampshire law); Gillett-Netting v. Barnhart, 371 F.3d 593 (9th Cir.

2004) (granting benefits under Arizona law); Woodward v. Commissioner, 760 N.E.2d 257 (Mass. 2002) (granting benefits under Massachusetts law). Sometimes a federal court will certify the question of inheritance law to the relevant state supreme court. See, e.g., Amen v. Astrue, 822 N.W.2d 419 (Neb. 2012); Burns v. Astrue, 289 P.3d 551 (Utah 2012).

The UPC provides that, for purposes of intestate succession, a child born from a posthumous pregnancy who is born alive and survives for 120 hours is treated as if it had been in gestation at the parent's death if *either* the embryo is in utero not later than 36 months after the parent's death *or* the child is born not later than 45 months after the parent's death. The UPC commentary explains the rationale for the 36- and 45-month periods:

> The 36-month period is designed to allow for a period of grieving, time to decide whether to go forward with assisted reproduction, and the possibility of initial unsuccessful attempts to achieve a pregnancy.... If the assisted-reproduction procedure is performed in a medical facility, the date when the embryo is in utero will ordinarily be made evident by medical records. In some cases, however, the procedure is not performed in a medical facility, so such evidence may be lacking. Providing an alternative of birth within 45 months is designed to provide certainty in such cases. ...

Problem

A is a soldier scheduled to be deployed to an area of armed conflict. Before deployment, he deposits his sperm at a clinic so that his long-time girlfriend, B, can use it in the event of his death. A is killed in action. One year later, B uses the sperm in a medical facility and succeeds in becoming pregnant. Nine months thereafter, she gives birth to X. Of whom is X a child for purposes of intestate succession under the current UPC?

PART B. CLASS GIFTS IN DONATIVE DOCUMENTS

1. Who Is a "Descendant"?

Primary Statutory References: *UPC §§2-701, 2-705, 8-101(b)(5)*

Wills, trusts, and other donative documents commonly include gifts to classes of persons, such as "to A's children" or "to A's descendants." Do these terms include adopted or de facto or nonmarital children and descendants? What about children or descendants produced by assisted reproduction?

The drafting lawyer should expressly address these questions in the instrument. If the instrument fails to indicate the donor's intent one way or the other, the law must provide an answer. Intestacy statutes are not controlling in these circumstances, but they are often used as guides to what the donor likely intended and to public policy. The answers are found in "rules of construction"—also known as default rules.

The Restatement 3d of Property §11.3 comment a provides that rules of construction "are devices that *attribute* intention to *individual* donors in particular circumstances on the basis of *common* intention. [They] are rebuttable upon a finding of a different intention. If there is no finding of a different intention... the meaning of the ambiguous portion of the document is controlled by the rule of construction.... Rules of construction... therefore operate as special-purpose presumptions in the law of donative transfers."

In the materials that follow, we examine some of the constructional rules governing class gifts to children and descendants.

EXTERNAL REFERENCE. Lawrence W. Waggoner, Class Gifts under the Restatement (Third) of Property, 33 Ohio N. U. L. Rev. 993 (2007).

————

Primary Statutory References: *UPC §§2-118, 2-119, 2-705*

Adopted Children. Courts and statutes usually treat an adopted child as a member of the class if the donor of the class gift adopted that child. See UPC §2-705; Restatement 3d of Property §14.5(1). The more difficult situation arises where someone other than the donor adopted the child. Suppose, for example, that Alice makes a gift to her "nieces and nephews," and Alice's brother adopts a daughter. According to the so-called "stranger-to-the-adoption" doctrine developed by the courts, Alice is presumed *not* to have intended to have her adopted niece share in the class gift. Alice is a stranger to the adoption and, the common law presumed, did not want her donative plans affected by it. Warren Buffett, for example, told his son's adopted daughter that she was not "legally or emotionally" a part of his family. See Michelle Nichols, Documentary on Wealth Gap Divides Buffett Family, Reuters, February 21, 2008.

UPC §2-705(d) abrogates the stranger-to-the-adoption doctrine if (1) the parent, a relative of the parent, or the spouse or surviving spouse of the parent performed functions customarily performed by a parent before the child reached the age of majority, or (2) the parent intended to perform such functions but was prevented from doing so by death or incapacity, if the intent is proved by clear and convincing evidence.

Ohio Citizens Bank, below, tells the story of one state's struggle to dislodge the stranger-to-the-adoption doctrine and raises the question whether laws that change or expand the rights of adopted children should apply to documents in existence on the effective date of the statute or only to documents executed subsequently.

Ohio Citizens Bank v. Mills
543 N.E.2d 1206 (Ohio 1989)

The facts, and procedural background, of this case are as follows. On September 21, 1944, Charles H. Breyman created an inter vivos trust which provided for the ultimate distribution of the trust assets to his "living grandchildren and to the living children of each deceased grandchild" upon the death of his daughter, Marie Breyman Mills. He also permitted his daughter to postpone the time of distribution beyond her death until after the death of her son, Robert E. Mills, Breyman's grandson. Prior to her death in 1973, Marie Breyman Mills did exercise the power of extension and postponed the distribution of the trust assets until 1985, the date of Robert E. Mills' death. Charles Breyman died in 1945. In 1957, Robert E. Mills married Esther K. Mills. Five years thereafter, Robert E. Mills adopted his wife's children from her previous two marriages, Roxanne Mills Pugh and Judith Lynne Muth. Later, [after Esther's death in 1963,[16]] Robert E. Mills remarried, and from that marriage emanated one natural child, Robert David Mills, appellant herein.

Following the death of Robert E. Mills in 1985, the trustee commenced a trust construction action to determine the beneficiaries of the Breyman trust. Named as defendants in that action were appellant, Robert David Mills, the natural child of Robert E. Mills, appellees, Roxanne Mills Pugh and Judith Lynne Muth, the adopted children of Robert E. Mills, and Elva Marie Bonser, an alleged illegitimate child of Robert E. Mills.

The matter was submitted to the trial court upon the stipulated facts and the parties' cross-motions for summary judgment. In two separate entries, the trial court entered judgment against Elva Marie Bonser and appellees Pugh and Muth, respectively. In the latter entry, the trial court relied upon the law in effect at the time Breyman created his trust and the "stranger to the adoption" doctrine to determine that Breyman did not intend to include adopted children in the designated class of trust beneficiaries. The court found as a matter of law that appellees are not beneficiaries of the Breyman trust.

Upon appeal by Pugh and Muth, the appellate court applied the adoption statute in effect at the time of review to determine that Breyman did intend to include adopted persons and reversed the decision of the trial court.

This cause is now before this court....

HOLMES, J. The issue presented for our consideration is whether R.C. 3107.15(A)(2), which in effect abrogated the common-law "stranger to the adoption" doctrine, may be applied in construing wills or trust documents created prior to the effective date of such statute. We answer such query in the negative, and accordingly reverse the court of appeals....

---

16. Reported by the appellate court. Ed.

Various presumptions or rules of construction have been historically utilized by the courts in this area of the law. One of these presumptive rules is that of "stranger to the adoption," with which we deal herein. Such rule basically is to the effect that there is a presumption that a testator or settlor intended to include a child adopted by him within a generally stated class, but where the testator or settlor is a stranger to an adoption of another, such as where the adoption takes place after the testator's death, it will be presumed that he did not intend the adopted child to be included within the designated class, unless a contrary intention clearly appears.

The courts also must look to the circumstances surrounding the execution of the will or trust. The most important factor here would be the time of the adoption in relation to the execution of the will or trust, or to the death of the testator or settlor. If the facts show that the adoption took place within the lifetime of the testator or settlor, and he knew about and approved of such adoption, the adopted child may well be included within the class.

Also, of course, reviewing courts must look to the various statutes regulating the rights of an adopted child, including the current statutes and the legislative history of such statutes. Specifically, when construing an inter vivos trust, as here, a court should determine the intent of the settlor in light of the law existing at the time of the creation of the trust, since an inter vivos trust speaks from the date of its creation—not the date upon which the assets are distributed. In construing the words used by a settlor, it is a well-established presumption that the testator or settlor was acquainted with the relevant then-existing statutes, their judicial interpretation and the effect they might have on the devolution of his estate. In 1944, when Charles Breyman created the inter vivos trust at issue, the "stranger to the adoption" doctrine was recognized, and he set forth no provisions in the trust contrary to the presumption that adopted children were not included in a gift to "living children of each deceased grandchild."

However, appellees argue, and the court of appeals agreed, that the "stranger to the adoption" doctrine is no longer a rule of construction in Ohio, by virtue of R.C. 3107.15(A)(2), which "places adopted children on the same footing as natural children." That statute, effective January 1, 1977, provides:

> (A) A final decree of adoption and an interlocutory order of adoption that has become final, issued by a court of this state, shall have the following effects as to all matters within the jurisdiction or before a court of this state:...
>
> (2) To create the relationship of parent and child between petitioner and the adopted person, as if the adopted person were a legitimate blood descendant of the petitioner, for all purposes including inheritance and applicability of statutes, documents, and instruments, whether executed before or after the adoption is decreed, which do not expressly exclude an adopted person from their operation or effect.

The timeliness of the applicability of an adoption statute such as R.C. 3107.15, as it relates to the beneficiary rights of adopted children, is an important consideration for a reviewing court, and goes directly to the question of what law governs, in point of time. While the general rule, as stated above, is that the law existing at the time an inter vivos trust is executed is the law which applies, a subsequent legislative enactment which changes the rights of inheritance of adopted persons may apply, depending on the intent of the General Assembly.

In this regard, a statute will not be applied retrospectively unless a contrary intention clearly appears. Where a statute is to be applied prior to its effective date in such a manner as to entirely abrogate a longstanding common-law rule, the General Assembly must clearly state its intention in order to do so.

The adoption statute construed here, R.C. 3107.15, does not specifically state that it should apply retrospectively to all existing wills, but only that it shall apply to instruments, "whether executed before or after *the adoption is decreed.*" (Emphasis added.) Although the presumption embodied in the "stranger to the adoption" doctrine may no longer be applied subsequent to the effective date of the statute, the application of this doctrine has not been totally abrogated by the statutory change. The doctrine may still be utilized in the interpretation of certain wills and trust instruments executed prior to such effective date, January 1, 1977.

Reasonably interpreted, and given the absence of an express intention to apply its provisions retrospectively, R.C. 3107.15(A)(2) shall be applied prospectively, and subsequent to its effective date, January 1, 1977, to those documents, statutes, and instruments, whether executed before or after an adoption is decreed, which do not expressly exclude the adopted person from the law's or instruments' operation and effect. Provisions of an inter vivos trust shall continue to be governed by the law existing at the time of its creation, absent a contrary expression of intent within the trust instrument itself....

Finally, appellees argue that, in any event, the adoption statute in effect at the time Charles Breyman created his trust also abrogated the "stranger to the adoption" doctrine. We are unpersuaded, since appellees' arguments reflect an erroneous reading of the legislative history of the adoption statute and of our cases construing such legislative changes.

Prior to 1932 the rights of adopted persons were set forth in G.C. 8030. That section provided, in pertinent part, as follows:

> ... and the child shall be invested with every legal right, privilege, obligation and relation in respect to education, maintenance and the rights of inheritance to real estate, or to the distribution of personal estate on the death of such adopting parent or parents as if born to them in lawful wedlock; provided, such child shall not be capable of inheriting property expressly limited to the heirs of the body of the adopting parent or parents....

In construing this statute, this court held that adopted children were enabled to inherit from but not through their adopting parents. The "stranger to the adoption" doctrine was a valid rule of construction.

The adoption statute was expanded with the enactment of G.C. 10512-19, effective January 1, 1932. That section added the following language to the prior statute after the limitation to the heirs of the body:

> ... but shall be capable of inheriting property expressly limited by will[17] or by operation of law to the child or children, heirs or heirs at law, or next of kin, of the adopting parent or parents, or to a class including any of the foregoing....

We interpreted these provisions to overrule prior law and allow adopted children to inherit both from as well as through their parents. When G.C. 10512-19 was renumbered G.C. 10512-23 upon the establishment of Ohio's "Adoption Code", effective January 1, 1944, no substantive changes were made to the relevant provisions above. Thus, the law existing at the time of the execution of the Charles Breyman trust was restricted to the rights of inheritance of adopted children, by will or intestate succession, and did not speak to trust instruments. The law existing at this time also recognized the "stranger to the adoption" doctrine.

With the enactment of G.C. 8004-13, effective August 28, 1951, the rights of adopted persons were further expanded by omitting the inheritance rights stated above at G.C. 10512-19 and in lieu thereof adding the following provision:

> ... For all purposes under the laws of this state, including without limitation all laws and wills governing inheritance of and succession to real or personal property and the taxation of such inheritance and succession, a legally adopted child shall have the same status and rights, and shall bear the same legal relationship to the adopting parents as if born to them in lawful wedlock and not born to the natural parents; provided:
>
> (A) Such adopted child shall not be capable of inheriting or succeeding to property expressly limited to heirs of the body of the adopting parent or parents....

This provision, by its express language, was still not made specifically applicable to trust instruments.

G.C. 8004-13 remained basically unchanged as R.C. 3107.13 until 1972, when two significant changes were made. R.C. 3107.13 was amended effective January 26, 1972 to read, in pertinent part, as follows:

> ... For all purposes under the laws of this state, including without limitation all laws, wills, and trust instruments governing inheritance of and succession to real or personal property and the taxation of an estate, a legally adopted child shall have the same status and rights, and shall bear the same legal relationship to the adopting parents as if born to them in lawful wedlock and not born to the natural parents; provided:

---

17. In Dollar Savings & Tr. Co. v. Turner, 529 N.E.2d 1261 (Ohio 1988), the Ohio Supreme Court applied the antilapse statute, Ohio Rev. Code Ann. §2107.52, to a revocable inter vivos trust, even though the terms of the statute applied only to wills. The Ohio legislature responded by amending Ohio Rev. Code §2107.01 to provide that the term "will" in the antilapse and other statutes "does not include inter vivos trusts or other instruments that have not been admitted to probate." The intent of the amendment was "to supersede" *Dollar Savings*. 1992 Ohio Laws 427 §3. Ed.

(A) Such adopted child shall not be capable of inheriting or succeeding to property expressly limited to heirs of the body of the adopting parents....

Unless an express intention to the contrary appears in a will or trust instrument, "child," "children," "issue," "grandchild," or "grandchildren," includes a legally adopted child, for the purpose of inheritance to, through, or from the adopting parents of such child, irrespective of when such will was executed or such trust was created.

The provisions of the amended statute for the first time made the right to inherit under the adoption statutes applicable to trust instruments. These revisions also provided that when the term "children" is used in a trust instrument, such term includes a legally adopted child irrespective of when the trust was created.

Thus, it was only after 1972 that the "stranger to the adoption" doctrine began to be eroded. The final expansion of the rights of adopted children came with the enactment of current R.C. 3107.15, effective in 1977. This section removed the limitation prohibiting adopted children from inheriting property limited to "heirs of the body" and, thus, although prospectively, fully accorded adopted children the same rights of inheritance as natural born children. The abrogation of the "stranger to the adoption" doctrine has been a slow, deliberate process, and had not yet begun when Charles Breyman executed his trust in 1944.

Accordingly, based upon the law existing in 1944, we conclude that the presumption embodied in the "stranger to the adoption" doctrine is applicable to the Charles Breyman trust, consistent with the grantor's intent. Such intent was to include only natural children in the distribution of assets of his trust estate. The judgment of the court of appeals is reversed, and the judgment of the trial court is reinstated.

Judgment reversed.

MOYER, C.J., and SWEENEY, DOUGLAS, WRIGHT, HERBERT R. BROWN and EVANS, J., concur.

Notes and Questions

1. *Ohio Legislation—Response to Mills*. Effective May 30, 1996, the Ohio legislature amended Ohio Rev. Code §3107.15 to provide that a final decree of adoption creates a parent-child relationship "for all purposes including inheritance and applicability of statutes, documents, and instruments, whether executed before or after the adoption is decreed, and whether executed or created before or after [the effective date of this amendment], which do not expressly exclude an adopted person from their operation or effect." For discussion, see Fifth Third Bank v. Crosley, 669 N.E.2d 904 (Ohio Misc. 1996).

2. *Uniform Probate Code*. Had the UPC governed in *Mills*, the outcome would have been different. Section 8-101(b)(5) provides that "any rule of construction or presumption provided in the Code applies to instruments executed... before the [Code's] effective date unless there is a clear indication of a contrary intent." Thus,

UPC §2-705, which abrogates the stranger-to-the-adoption rule for all governing instruments, not merely for wills, applies. Under §2-705(d)(1), Roxanne and Judith would have been included in the class gift because Robert E. Mills likely performed parental functions while they were minors and, even if he did not, his spouse did so. Thus, Roxanne and Judith would have been included in the class gift, and each would have taken a one-third share. Robert David Mills would have received only one-third of the corpus, not all of it.

3. *Policy of Pre-Effective Date Application.* As a matter of legislative policy, should changes in statutory rules of construction be restricted to documents executed after the statute's effective date? What justifications are there for the approach of the UPC and the current Ohio statute of extending application of its constructional rule abrogating the stranger-to-the-adoption doctrine to documents executed before the statute's effective date?

Will of Hoffman, below on p. 105, demonstrates that a change in a common-law rule of construction often applies to documents executed before the court's decision. Is the case for application to pre-effective date documents stronger for common-law changes in rules of construction than it is for statutory changes in rules of construction?

4. *Remainder Interest to "Heirs."* If the remainder interest created by Charles Breyman's trust had been in favor of Robert E. Mills's "heirs" rather than his "children," the predominant rule of construction is that Robert's heirs should be determined by reference to the intestacy statute in existence at Robert's death, not the statute in existence when Charles executed his trust.[18] See In re Dodge Testamentary Trust, 330 N.W.2d 72 (Mich. Ct. App. 1982) (set forth in Chapter 16); UPC §2-711; Restatement 3d of Property §16.1.

Adoption of Adults. Adoption statutes generally permit adoptions of adults.[19] An adoption of an adult devisee may be useful in preventing an anticipated will contest. By removing the testator's disappointed collateral relatives as heirs, the adoption prevents them from having standing to contest the will. See, e.g., Collamore v. Learned, 50 N.E. 518 (Mass. 1898).[20] Will this planning technique work under the UPC? See UPC §§2-118, 2-119. What further implications arising out of the adoption should be considered before an attorney advises a client to enter into an

---

18. But cf. Society Nat'l Bank v. Jacobson, 560 N.E.2d 217 (Ohio 1990).

19. A most extraordinary use of adult adoptions was posed in a biography of Huntington Hartford, heir to the A. & P. fortune. Wishing to rid himself of his first wife, he is reported to have suggested that his mother adopt her and make her his sister! Lisa R. Gubernick, Squandered Fortune (1991).

20. But see Adoption of Sewall, 51 Cal. Rptr. 367 (Ct. App. 1966) (allowing disappointed collateral heir to attack adoption decree for fraud and undue influence).

adult adoption? See UPC §§2-118, 2-119; Uniform Adoption Act (UAA) §§1-102, 1-105, 5-101, 5-102 (1994).

Can or should an adoption of an adult be used to qualify a person as a member of a class for purposes of sharing in a class gift? Will this technique work under the UPC? See UPC §§2-701, 2-705. In the absence of clarifying legislation or language in the governing instrument,[21] courts have differed on whether to treat the adult as an adopted child for purposes of construing the dispositive instrument.

Adoption of a Spouse or Unmarried Partner. The Uniform Adoption Act expressly prohibits the adoption of a spouse. UAA §5-101(a)(1). In the absence of a statute prohibiting adoptions of spouses, the question arises whether the adopted spouse should be treated as a member of the class eligible to share in the class gifts other than those found in the adopting parent's donative documents. In Minary v. Citizens Fidelity Bank & Trust Co., 419 S.W.2d 340, 343-44 (Ky. 1967), a wife who was adopted by her husband under the state's adoption statute was not treated as a child for purposes of determining the takers of a class gift to heirs found in her mother-in-law's will.[22] The court focused on the question of achieving the testator's likely intent and did not address the question of the absence of a parent-child relationship between the husband and wife:

> It is of paramount importance that man be permitted to pass on his property at his death to those who represent the natural objects of his bounty.... [Our adoption] statutes should not be given a construction that does violence to the above rule....

Accord, In re Belgard's Trust, 829 P.2d 457 (Colo. Ct. App. 1991) (court recognized the wife's right to inherit from her husband as his child through the intestacy statute but denied her the right to be included in a class gift to her husband's children in a trust created by the husband's mother; court did not focus on husband-wife relationship but the fact that the adoption was of an adult).

Although the reasons for the adoptions may have been different than for adoptions of spouses, petitions for adoption of same-sex partners have also been controversial. In Adoption of Swanson, 623 A.2d 1095 (Del. 1993), Richard Sorrels, age 66, petitioned to adopt James Swanson, age 51, his lifetime partner. The purpose of the adoption was "to formalize the close emotional relationship that had existed between them for many years and to facilitate their estate planning," including preventing claims against their respective estates by family members and reducing inheritance tax liability under Delaware law. The court recognized that the adoption statute

---

21. It is not unusual to find form books for wills and trusts that define class gift terms as including an adopted child "only if the individual was adopted under the age of 18 at the date of adoption." See, e.g., Mich. Will Manual p. XVI-22 (1990).

22. A challenge to the validity of the adoption was dismissed for lack of jurisdiction. See Minary v. Minary, 395 S.W.2d 588 (Ky. 1965).

confers discretion on the family court to approve adult adoptions and that it would be against public policy to foster an incestuous relationship. It nevertheless held that

> where, as here, the petition contemplates an adoption that is not only within the scope of the statute, but which is also widely recognized as a proper exercise of the authority granted by the statute, we can divine no reason why this petition should be denied.
>
> Since the primary object of statutory construction is to reach a result in conformity with legislative policy, once that policy is determined we need only test the construction by the rules of reasonableness and conformity with that policy. In this case, our construction of the statute—permitting the adoption of one adult by another for economic reasons—is consistent with a policy promoting limited judicial inquiry into the purposes or motives behind such a relationship.

In contrast, in a 4-2 decision, the New York Court of Appeals in Adoption of Robert Paul P., 471 N.E.2d 424, 425-27 (N.Y. 1984), denied the petition of a gay man to adopt his partner:

> [A]doption in New York, as explicitly defined in Section 110 of the Domestic Relations Law, is "the legal proceeding whereby a person takes another person into the *relation of child* and thereby acquires the rights and incurs the responsibilities of *parent*." (Emphasis supplied.) It is plainly not a quasi-matrimonial vehicle to provide nonmarried partners with a legal imprimatur for their sexual relationship, be it heterosexual or homosexual.... Moreover, any such sexual intimacy is utterly repugnant to the relationship between child and parent in our society, and only a patently incongruous application of our adoption laws—wholly inconsistent with the underlying public policy of providing a parent-child relationship for the welfare of the child...—would permit the employment of adoption as the legal formalization of an adult relationship between sexual partners under the guise of parent and child....
>
> While there are no special restrictions on adult adoptions under the provisions of the Domestic Relations Law, the Legislature could not have intended that the statute be employed "to arrive at an unreasonable or absurd result."... Such would be the result if the Domestic Relations Law were interpreted to permit one lover, homosexual or heterosexual, to adopt the other and enjoy the sanction of the law on their feigned union as parent and child.
>
> The comment to UAA §5-101 indicates that the drafters favor the approach adopted in *Robert Paul P.* The comment includes a cite to the case and the statement that "[i]f a relationship other than that of parent and child is intended, the adoption may be denied."

If adoption of domestic partners is allowed, questions about whether the adopted adult should be treated as a member of a class eligible to share in a class gift found in donative documents executed by someone other than the adoptive parent will have to be addressed. Cf. First Nat'l Bank of Dubuque, v. Mackey, 338 N.W.2d 361 (Iowa 1983) (settlor's daughter adopted her "friend" with whom she "shared an apartment" when she was 58 and the friend was 44; the daughter's purpose in adopting her friend was to make her friend the sole beneficiary of the trust; the court held that she should not be included as a member of the class named in the trust absent evidence that the adopted adult had an *in loco parentis* relationship with the adopter).

Pam Belluck & Alison Leigh Cowan, Partner Adopted by an Heiress Stakes Her Claim
N.Y. Times, Mar. 19, 2007

On an island liberally sprinkled with the affluent and well-connected members of such clans as Bush, du Pont, Rockefeller and Cabot, the Watson family [descendants of Thomas Watson, the founder of IBM] occupies a special place....

Recently, though, the Watson name has surfaced in a different context, a most unusual lawsuit. It concerns Olive F. Watson, 59, granddaughter of the I.B.M. founder and daughter of Thomas J. Watson Jr., the company's longtime chief executive; and Patricia Ann Spado, 59, her former lesbian partner of 14 years.

In 1991, Ms. Watson, then 43, adopted Ms. Spado, then 44, under a Maine law that allows one adult to adopt another. The reason, Ms. Spado has contended in court documents, was to allow Ms. Spado to qualify as an heir to Ms. Watson's estate.

But less than a year after the adoption, Ms. Watson and Ms. Spado broke up. Then in 2004, Ms. Watson's mother died, leaving multimillion-dollar trusts established by her husband to be divided among their 18 grandchildren.

Re-enter Ms. Spado with a claim....

Problems

1.   When G was 50 years old, he created an irrevocable inter vivos trust, directing the trustee to pay the income to G's mother M for life and, on M's death, to distribute the trust property "to G's children who survive M." When G created the trust, he had two children, A and B. When G reached 60, he decided that he would like to have his wife, W, share in the distribution of the trust property on M's death. He therefore adopted his wife, who was 40 years old at the time of the adoption. This spousal adoption was permitted under state law. Later, M died, survived by G, A, B, and W. Under the current UPC, who is entitled to the trust property? Would the result change if W were not G's wife but instead G's domestic partner or lover?

2. G's will devised property in trust, directing the trustee to pay the income to G's daughter D for life and, on D's death, to distribute the property "to D's children." After G's death, D and her husband H1 applied for and were granted a divorce. D and H1 had one child, C1. The divorce decree granted custody of C1 to D. Later, D married a widower, H2, who had a 17-year-old child, C2, from his former marriage. After her marriage to H2, D adopted C2 (who was then 18 years old), and H2, with the consent of H1, adopted C1. Later, D died, survived by H1, H2, C1 and C2. Under the current UPC, who is entitled to the trust property?

———

Primary Statutory References: *UPC §§2-118, 2-119, 2-705*

De Facto Parentage. Should class gifts to "children" or "descendants" be construed to include children of de facto parents? UPC §2-705 answers this question in the affirmative, but with the same limitations as in the case of adoption if the de facto parent is not the transferor.

Problem

Same facts as Problem 2 above, except that, instead of adopting C2, D successfully petitioned to be adjudicated a parent of C2 on the basis of de facto parentage. Under the current UPC, who is entitled to the trust property?

———

Primary Statutory Reference: *UPC §2-705*

Stepchildren and Foster Children. Usually courts do not construe class gifts to include stepchildren. See Restatement 3d of Property §14.1 comment k. California, however, applies a constructional rule that includes as a member of a class eligible to share in class gifts some stepchildren and foster children (or their issue when appropriate to the class). See Cal. Prob. Code §21115. The statute incorporates California's intestacy rule, see Cal. Prob. Code §6454, which recognizes a parent-child relationship if it begins during the stepchild's or foster child's minority and continues throughout the parent and child's joint lifetimes and if it is established by clear and convincing evidence that the stepparent or foster parent would have adopted the child but for a legal barrier.

Courts have refused to extend the doctrine of equitable adoption to presume that an equitably adopted child should be treated as a member of class in a donative instrument executed by a member of the foster parent's kindred. See, e.g., Matter of Estate of Jenkins, 904 P.2d 1316 (Colo. 1995) (en banc).

Problem

Same facts as Problem 2 above, except that D neither adopted C2 nor petitioned to be adjudicated a parent of C2 on the basis of de facto parentage. Under the current UPC, who is entitled to the trust property?

———

Children of Parents Not Married to Each Other. Should nonmarital children be included in class gifts? Consider the following case.

Will of Hoffman
385 N.Y.S.2d 49 (App. Div. 1976)

BIRNS, J.... Mary Hoffman, the testatrix died in 1951. Her will established a trust for the benefit of her two cousins and provided that when the first of the two should die, his one-half share of the income should be paid for the remainder of the trust term "to his issue."

One cousin is still living; the other died in 1965, survived by a daughter and a son named Stephen. Stephen died in 1972 leaving two children, the infants represented by respondent-appellant herein. Stephen never married the mother of these children nor was an order of filiation entered. The Surrogate, however, determined that the two children were indeed the children of Stephen.

Relying on precedent, the Surrogate ruled that ... the term "issue" as used in the will meant lawful issue only, and absent an intention to the contrary it could not be assumed that the testatrix intended illegitimate descendants as the object of her bounty.

In this court, as she did below, respondent-appellant asserted that inasmuch as the word "issue" in the provision of the will under consideration was not qualified by the word "lawful," the question of legitimacy was not in decedent's mind when she made her will. In addition, the change in conventional attitudes towards illegitimates, as reflected in statutes and decisions, would warrant a construction of the word "issue" as including illegitimates, in the absence of contrary intent to exclude them.

Petitioner-respondent emphasizes that under settled case law, where the word "issue" appears in a will it will be interpreted to mean only lawful descendants in the absence of clear evidence of a contrary intent of a testator.

We recognize that precedents do hold that in the absence of an express intent to the contrary by a testator, the word "issue" presumes lawful issue and not illegitimate offspring. This presumption has its roots in an earlier society where there was no sense of injustice in the teaching that the sins of the fathers were to be visited upon their children and succeeding generations....

Because of changes in societal attitudes and recent developments in constitutional law, we are of the opinion that, to the extent that precedents require this burden to be placed upon illegitimate claimants under a will, the law is not only outmoded, but discriminatory and should be rejected. We would reverse....

Apparently the precise question before us has never been decided by the Court of Appeals or this court....

Our statutes do provide continuing evidence of legislative concern for illegitimate children....

While nothing in the [Estates, Powers, and Trusts Law] provides that illegitimate children are "issue" for the purposes of taking under a will, rights of illegitimates to share in the estates of their kin are expanding. In fact, present attitudes appear to reject an inferior social or legal status for illegitimates.

[Many] statutes, state and federal,... demonstrate significant changes in societal attitudes vis-a-vis illegitimate children, each of which was directed toward the elimination of disadvantages, legal and social, suffered by illegitimates. This parade of legislation was well underway, when in 1950, the testatrix executed the will before us.

The question raised is whether social and statutory changes require a reconsideration of the rule which presumed an intent by testatrix to exclude illegitimate descendants in sharing under her will.

Certainly, it cannot be said, as a matter of fact, that the testatrix was aware of these changes in societal attitudes as evidenced by the legislation referred to, or aware of community attitudes towards premarital sex or sex without marriage. Nor can it be said with any degree of assurance that at the time she executed her will she was provided with an explanation of the word "issue" which appeared on the type-written pages of that document. It is just as likely that the word "issue" in her mind had a meaning no different from "progeny" or "offspring".

The will itself supports the conclusion that the bequest to her cousins was of paramount concern in establishing the trust. It is most unlikely that she gave any more than passing thought to the children who now, 25 years after her death, claim under her will, particularly as to whether or not they would be legitimate.

The presumed intent of the testator with which all the precedents are concerned, although represented as rebuttable, is in fact, in most cases irrebuttable. The passage of time has made it impossible to establish that the testatrix did not intend to exclude illegitimate descendants from sharing under her will....

To continue to rely upon these precedents and then declare that in using the word "issue" in her will, testatrix intended only lawful issue and not illegitimates is to attribute to her a frame of mind not at all supported by the facts. We recognize that the testatrix should possess the broadest freedom of choice in making known the objects of her bounty, and that it is the duty of the court to ascertain the testatrix's intent. Nevertheless, the court should not under the guise of determining the testatrix's intent substitute its own preference as to the legatees who shall take under the will. There should be a demonstrable relation between judicial interpretation of a will and the testatrix's actual frame of mind....

We have been instructed that "[t]hat court best serves the law which recognizes that the rules of law which grew up in a remote generation may, in the fullness of experience be found to serve another generation badly, and which discards the old rule when it finds that another rule of law represents what should be according to the established and settled judgment of society, and no considerable property rights have become vested in reliance upon the old rule. It is thus great writers upon the common law have discovered the source and method of its growth, and in its growth found its health and life. It is not and it should not be stationary. Change of this character should not be left to the Legislature."

The Court of Appeals has stated, just recently: "... from the earliest times the doctrine of *stare decisis* did not require a strict adherence to precedent in every instance...."

There are cases also where "the rule of adherence to precedent though it ought not be abandoned, ought to be in some degree relaxed." In the case before us, we are of the opinion that rigid adherence to precedent will produce a result not warranted by facts but rather by adherence to an anachronistic rule.

Therefore we reject the rule that where the word "issue," standing alone, appears in a will, it will be interpreted to include within its meaning only lawful descendants. We hold that the word "issue" should be construed to refer to legitimate and illegitimate descendants alike in the absence of an express qualification by the testatrix.

Further justification for our decision today can be found in expanding concepts of the Equal Protection Clause (U.S. Constitution, 14th Amendment). To construe "issue" in a will as excluding illegitimate children otherwise entitled to inherit thereunder, is, as stated before, nothing more than the substitution of judicial preference for a testator's intent. Such preference, under the guise of judicial construction, we believe, is state action. (See Shelley v. Kraemer, 334 U.S. 1.) State action is proscribed if it promotes discrimination based upon an unconstitutional classification....

In holding that illegitimates are covered by the Equal Protection Clause, the Supreme Court of the United States [in Weber v. Aetna Casualty & Surety Co., 406 U.S. 164] struck down as discriminatory a statute which provided that illegitimate children did not have the same right to share in the death benefits under a Louisiana workmen's compensation statute as did legitimate children....

Because of the expanding concept of equal protection we should not adhere rigidly to the rules enunciated in the cases cited as precedents herein. To do so would require us to hold that illegitimates enjoyed a lesser status than legitimate children before the law in cases such as the one before us.

In rejecting archaism, we do no more in this appeal than hold that the word "issue" as used by testatrix in her will should have no meaning other than that ordinarily and customarily imputed to persons in its usage in the absence of any manifestation of an intent to the contrary.... Accordingly, the law will not be required to discriminate against children labeled illegitimate through no fault of their own.... All concur.

Notes and Questions

1. *New York Legislation.* As amended in 1990, New York legislation codifies the *Hoffman* rule by providing that, "[u]nless the creator expresses a contrary intention,... a nonmarital child is the child of a mother and is the child of a father if

the child is entitled to inherit from such father under section 4-1.2 of this chapter [set forth above on page 97]." N.Y. Est. Powers & Trusts Law §2-1.3.[23]

2. *Rules of Construction Regarding Nonmarital Children.* The law is moving away from the traditional constructional rule that children of unmarried parents are presumptively *excluded* from membership under class-gift terminology. The rule of construction that should replace the traditional rule is more controversial. Is it to be the opposite rule, as the *Hoffman* court held and the New York legislation provides, under which nonmarital children are presumptively *included* under class-gift terminology? Is some intermediate rule more appropriate, under which children of unmarried parents are included in some circumstances, but excluded in others? Keep in mind that rules of construction supply *presumptive* meaning to the language in a private instrument, such as a will or trust. Transferors are not bound by a rule of construction. Well-drafted documents expressly address whether nonmarital children are intended to be takers of gifts made to classes of beneficiaries. The function of the rule of construction is to reflect the likely intent of transferors who are silent.

For the UPC's rules, see UPC §2-705(b) and (d). See also UPC §2-117.

3. *Adopted-Out Nonmarital Children.* Suppose a nonmarital child is later adopted. Under what circumstances should the child be considered a "child" of the previous parents for purposes of a class gift? The UPC's rules are in UPC §§2-119, 2-705.

Problems

1. G's will devised property in trust, directing the trustee to pay income to G's son S for life and, on S's death, to distribute the property "to S's children." S was the father of two children, C1 and C2. C1 was born out of wedlock, and S as a single parent reared C1. Later, S married W and together they had a child, C2. For purposes of the class gift created by G, who are S's children under the current UPC?

2. What if, instead, C1 had been reared by C1's mother as a single parent?

———

Primary Statutory References: *UPC §§2-120, 2-121, 2-705*

Children by Assisted Reproduction. How should the law treat children conceived by assisted reproduction for purposes of interpreting class gifts? Consider the following materials.

---

23. This statute only applies to wills of persons dying on and after September 1, 1991, and to lifetime instruments previously executed that on that date were subject to the grantor's power to revoke or amend, and to all lifetime instruments executed on or after that date.

Restatement 3d of Property

§14.8 Child of Assisted Reproduction: Non-Surrogacy. Unless the language or circumstances establish that the transferor had a different intention, a child of assisted reproduction whose birth mother is not acting as a surrogate for an intended parent or parents is treated for class-gift purposes as a child of:

(1) the child's birth mother; and

(2) another person, if any, who consented to assisted reproduction by the birth mother with intent to be treated as the child's other parent. Consent to assisted reproduction by the birth mother with intent to be treated as the child's other parent is established if the person:

(A) signed a writing or other record, before or after the child's birth, exhibiting intent, in light of all the facts and circumstances, to be treated as the child's other parent; or

(B) in the absence of a signed writing or other record that satisfies paragraph (2)(A):

(i) functioned as the child's other parent within a reasonable time after the child's birth;

(ii) intended to function as the child's other parent within a reasonable time after the child's birth but was prevented from doing so by an event such as death or incapacity; or

(iii) intended to be treated as the other parent of a posthumously conceived child, but only if that intent is established by clear and convincing evidence.

In re Martin B.
841 N.Y.S.2d 207 (Sur. Ct. 2007)

ROTH, J. This uncontested application for advice and direction in connection with seven trust agreements executed on December 31, 1969, by Martin B. (the Grantor) illustrates one of the new challenges that the law of trusts must address as a result of advances in biotechnology. Specifically, the novel question posed is whether, for these instruments, the terms "issue" and "descendants" include children conceived by means of in vitro fertilization with the cryopreserved semen of the Grantor's son who had died several years prior to such conception.

The relevant facts are briefly stated. Grantor (who was a life income beneficiary of the trusts) died on July 9, 2001, survived by his wife Abigail and their son Lindsay (who has two adult children), but predeceased by his son James, who died of Hodgkins Lymphoma on January 13, 2001. James, however, after learning of his illness, deposited a sample of his semen at a laboratory with instructions that it be cryopreserved and that, in the event of his death, it be held subject to the directions of his wife Nancy. Although at his death James had no children, three years later Nancy underwent in vitro fertilization with his cryopreserved semen and gave birth on October 15, 2004, to a boy (James Mitchell). Almost two years later, on August

14, 2006, after using the same procedure, she gave birth to another boy (Warren). It is undisputed that these infants, although conceived after the death of James, are the products of his semen....

All seven instruments give the trustees discretion to sprinkle principal to, and among, Grantor's "issue" during Abigail's life. The instruments also provide that at Abigail's death the principal is to be distributed as she directs under her special testamentary power to appoint to Grantor's "issue" or "descendants" (or to certain other "eligible" appointees). In the absence of such exercise, the principal is to be distributed to or for the benefit of "issue" surviving at the time of such disposition (James's issue, in the case of certain trusts, and Grantor's issue, in the case of certain other trusts). The trustees have brought this proceeding because under such instruments they are authorized to sprinkle principal to decedent's "issue" and "descendants" and thus need to know whether James's children qualify as members of such classes.

The question thus raised is whether the two infant boys are "descendants" and "issue" for purposes of such provisions although they were conceived several years after the death of James....

We turn first to the laws of the governing jurisdictions.[24] At present, the right of a posthumous child to inherit (EPTL 4-1.1[c] [in intestacy]) or as an after-born child under a will (EPTL 5-3.2 [under a will]) is limited to a child conceived during the decedent's lifetime. Indeed, a recent amendment to section 5-3.2 (effective July 26, 2006) was specifically intended to make it clear that a post-conceived child is excluded from sharing in the parent's estate as an "after-born" (absent some provision in the will to the contrary, EPTL 5-3.2[b]). Such limitation was intended to ensure certainty in identifying persons interested in an estate and finality in its distribution (see Sponsor's Mem., Bill Jacket L. 2006, ch. 249). It, however, is by its terms applicable only to wills and to "after-borns" who are children of the testators themselves and not children of third parties (see Turano, Practice Commentaries, McKinney's Cons. Laws of N.Y., Book 17B, EPTL 5-3.2, at 275). Moreover, the concerns related to winding up a decedent's estate differ from those related to identifying whether a class disposition to a grantor's issue includes a child conceived after the father's death but before the disposition became effective.

With respect to future interests, both the District of Columbia and New York have statutes which ostensibly bear upon the status of a post-conceived child. In the D.C. Code, the one statutory reference to posthumous children appears in section 704 of title 42 which in relevant part provides that, "[w]here a future estate shall be limited to heirs, or issue, or children, posthumous children shall be entitled to take in the same manner as if living at the death of their parent...." New York has a very similar

---

24. One of the trusts was expressly governed by the law of New York. The other trusts were governed by the law of the District of Columbia. Ed.

statute, which provides in relevant part that, "[w]here a future estate is limited to children, distributees, heirs or issue, posthumous children are entitled to take in the same manner as if living at the death of their ancestors" (EPTL 6-5.7). In addition, EPTL 2-1.3(2) provides that a posthumous child may share as a member of a class if such child was conceived before the disposition became effective.

Each of the above statutes read literally would allow post-conceived children—who are indisputably "posthumous"—to claim benefits as biological offspring. But such statutes were enacted long before anyone anticipated that children could be conceived after the death of the biological parent. In other words, the respective legislatures presumably contemplated that such provisions would apply only to children en ventre sa mere (see e.g. Turano, Practice Commentaries, McKinney's Cons. Laws of N.Y., Book 17B, EPTL 6-5.7, at 176)....

...On the one hand, certainty and finality are critical to the public interests in the orderly administration of estates. On the other hand, the human desire to have children, albeit by biotechnology, deserves respect, as do the rights of the children born as a result of such scientific advances. To achieve such balance, the [existing] statutes [on posthumous conception in other states], for example, require written consent to the use of genetic material after death and establish a cut-off date by which the child must be conceived. It is noted parenthetically that in this regard an affidavit has been submitted here stating that all of James's cryopreserved sperm has been destroyed, thereby closing the class of his children.

Finally, we turn to the instruments presently before the court. Although it cannot be said that in 1969 the Grantor contemplated that his "issue" or "descendants" would include children who were conceived after his son's death, the absence of specific intent should not necessarily preclude a determination that such children are members of the class of issue. Indeed, it is noted that the Restatement of Property suggests that "[u]nless the language or circumstances indicate that the transferor had a different intention, a child of assisted reproduction [be] treated for class-gift purposes as a child of a person who consented to function as a parent to the child and who functioned in that capacity or was prevented from doing so by an event such as death or incapacity" (Restatement [Third] of Property [Wills and Other Donative Transfers] 14.8 [Tentative Draft No. 4, 2004]).

The rationale of the Restatement ... should be applied here, namely, if an individual considers a child to be his or her own, society through its laws should do so as well. It is noted that a similar rationale was endorsed by our State's highest court with respect to the beneficial interests of adopted children (Matter of Park, 15 N.Y.2d 413, 260 N.Y.S.2d 169, 207 N.E.2d 859). Accordingly, in the instant case, these post-conceived infants should be treated as part of their father's family for all purposes. Simply put, where a governing instrument is silent, children born of this new biotechnology with the consent of their parent are entitled to the same rights "for all purposes as those of a natural child" (id., at 418, 260 N.Y.S.2d 169, 207 N.E.2d 859).

Although James probably assumed that any children born as a result of the use of his preserved semen would share in his family's trusts, his intention is not controlling here. For purposes of determining the beneficiaries of these trusts, the controlling factor is the Grantor's intent as gleaned from a reading of the trust agreements (see, Matter of Fabbri, 2 N.Y.2d 236, 159 N.Y.S.2d 184, 140 N.E.2d 269; Matter of Larkin, 9 N.Y.2d 88, 211 N.Y.S.2d 175, 172 N.E.2d 555; Jewell v. Graham, 24 F.2d 257, 57 App.D.C. 391; O'Connell v. Riggs National Bank, 475 A.2d 405). Such instruments provide that, upon the death of the Grantor's wife, the trust fund would benefit his sons and their families equally. In view of such overall dispositive scheme, a sympathetic reading of these instruments warrants the conclusion that the Grantor intended all members of his bloodline to receive their share.

Based upon all of the foregoing, it is concluded that James Mitchell and Warren are "issue" and "descendants" for all purposes of these trusts.

As can be seen from all of the above, there is a need for comprehensive legislation to resolve the issues raised by advances in biotechnology. Accordingly, copies of this decision are being sent to the respective Chairs of the Judiciary Committees of the New York State Senate and Assembly.

Decree signed.

Question

Would the same result be reached under the current UPC?

2. Who Is a "Spouse"?

Primary Statutory References: *UPC §§2-705, 8-101(b)(5)*

Suppose that, in the 1950s, a settlor created a trust designed to last for 90 years, giving the trustee discretion to make distributions of the trust income from time to time in the trustee's discretion among the settlor's then-living "descendants and their spouses." In 2018, the settlor's granddaughter G married her same-sex partner, P. Is P a permissible beneficiary of trust income?

After the U.S. Supreme Court's decision recognizing same-sex marriage in Obergefell v. Hodges, 576 U.S. 644 (2015), the issue is bound to arise: How should a fiduciary or a court interpret the word "spouse" or "spouses" in a donative document executed before the advent of same-sex marriage?

Questions

Should P be a permissible beneficiary of trust income? Why or why not? What result under the current UPC?

EXTERNAL REFERENCES. Mary Louise Fellows & Thomas P. Gallanis, The Uniform Probate Code's New Intestacy and Class Gift Provisions, 46 ACTEC L.J. 127 (2021); Lee-ford Tritt, The Stranger-to-the-Marriage Doctrine, 2019 Wis. L. Rev. 373 (2019).

Chapter 4

Execution of Wills

"Where there's a will there's relations."
– Jill Paton Walsh & Dorothy L. Sayers[1]

Intestate succession is a default regime that operates in the absence of a valid will. However, intestacy has not always operated as a default regime. It was once mandatory law. In medieval England, property owners were deprived of the right to make a will. To be sure, the power to dispose of personal property by will was recognized early. The ecclesiastical courts asserted jurisdiction over succession to personal property on death and encouraged bequests for religious and charitable purposes, as well as for the decedent's family. During the Anglo-Saxon period, both men and women could dispose of land at death, but recognition of testamentary transfers ceased within about a century after the Norman Conquest. The gift of land by will "stood condemned," Maitland wrote, "because it is a death-bed gift, wrung from a man in his agony. In the interest of honesty, in the interest of the lay state, a boundary must be maintained against ecclesiastical greed and the other-worldliness of dying men." 2 Frederick Pollock & Frederic W. Maitland, History of English Law 328 (2d ed. 1898). The church courts never gained jurisdiction over succession to land, and the king's courts were not concerned with seeing that a man atoned for his wrongs by devoting a portion of his property to pious objects.

Land passed by inheritance to the eldest son. Nevertheless, landowners sought means to make provision at death for their other children, for pious uses, and perhaps for a general freedom of testamentary disposition. This became possible after the Court of Chancery, administering equity, began to enforce uses in the early part of the fifteenth century. A landowner would transfer land to ("enfeoff") X, to hold to the use of the feoffor for life and then to such uses as the feoffor might appoint in his will. The Chancellor recognized the will appointing the use (for it was not a disposition of legal title to land) and compelled X to carry out the use.

One of the purposes of the Statute of Uses 1536 (27 Hen. 8, ch. 10) was to eliminate testamentary disposition of land by way of use. The preamble to the statute condemned "wills and testaments, sometimes made by nude parolx and words, sometimes by signs and tokens, and sometimes by writing, and for the most part made by such persons as be visited with sickness, in their extreme agonies and pains, or at such time as they have scantly had any good memory or remembrance." But the demand for power of testation was strong, and four years later, in 1540, Parliament

---

1. Jill Paton Walsh & Dorothy L. Sayers, A Presumption of Death 285 (2002)(a new mystery featuring Lord Peter Wimsey and Harriet Vane).

enacted the first English Statute of Wills, permitting testamentary disposition of land (with certain limitations that are important only to the student of the history of feudalism).

Probate Procedure. Procedurally, the determination about whether a particular decedent left a valid will is made in a proceeding in which the instrument is *offered* for probate by the *proponent*. If the instrument is found to be valid, it is *admitted to probate* as the decedent's last will. This procedure developed early in English law for wills of personal property, but not for wills of real property, even after wills of land were authorized by statute in 1540. The ecclesiastical courts assumed jurisdiction over wills of personal property but not of land. Until a probate court was established in England in the mid-nineteenth century and given jurisdiction over the probate of all wills, there was no direct means of establishing the validity of a will of land. Instead, validity was usually put in issue by an action in ejectment or trespass brought to try the title to land.

Nearly everywhere in this country, some court is given jurisdiction to probate wills, whether the property involved is real or personal or both. In many states, there are separate probate courts, although they may go by other names, such as surrogates' courts in New York or orphans' courts in Pennsylvania. In other states, the court of general jurisdiction, such as a circuit or county court, exercises probate jurisdiction. Although there are many local differences in the jurisdiction of probate courts, in general they perform more functions than evaluating the validity of wills. Probate courts appoint executors and administrators and exercise supervision over these personal representatives in the administration of decedents' estates, regardless of whether the decedents died testate or intestate. The appointment of a personal representative—called an "executor" if nominated in a will, otherwise called an "administrator"—is traditionally described as the grant of *letters testamentary* or *letters of administration*.

The process of probate varies significantly from jurisdiction to jurisdiction within the United States. Here, only a few general comments will be offered.

American probate courts have traditionally tended to exercise a style of supervision over decedents' estates that is overly formal. A fully adjudicated distribution order is probably unnecessary in most cases. Most estates pass without controversy to a sole surviving heir or a small group of adults who are eager to expedite estate settlement. Nevertheless, personal representatives could not, under traditional probate rules, shortcut mandatory closing procedures. The resulting costs and delays help to explain the popularity of the will substitutes we shall study in Chapter 7.

The Uniform Probate Code was originally drafted in 1969 in response to widely publicized criticisms of typical probate systems. See Richard V. Wellman, The Uniform Probate Code: A Possible Answer to Probate Avoidance, 44 Ind. L.J. 191 (1969). Article III of the UPC, covering probate of wills and administration of decedents' estates, was designed to permit estates of all sizes and asset mixes to be settled with as little procedure as possible. Article IV, devoted to estates located in two or more jurisdictions, permits personal representatives appointed in the decedent's domicile to unify estates[2] for administration purposes merely by filing copies of the domiciliary probate and appointment orders in the local probate office, thereby gaining the powers of a locally appointed personal representative.

Under the UPC, probate jurisdiction is assigned to a court that has the stature of a trial court of general jurisdiction, in terms of the qualifications of the judge, the finality of its orders, and the range of matters it may consider. The UPC establishes the office of "registrar," to be occupied by an official who is empowered to probate wills and open estates in "informal" (nonadjudicative) proceedings. Informal proceedings do not involve advance notice to interested persons, a hearing, or the presentation of testimony. The registrar responds to a detailed application for probate by an interested person.

An estate is opened by the appointment of a personal representative. Whether the estate is testate or intestate, the personal representative's powers are the same. Persons interested in the estate may request "formal" (adjudicated) proceedings as an alternative to informal probate.

In the absence of binding court orders, estates are settled and titles cleared through UPC limitations and purchaser-protection provisions. Under UPC §3-108, wills must be probated or contested, and estates must be opened, within three years after death. Section 3-803 provides that claims against an estate are barred no later than one year after the decedent's death. Purchasers and other third persons who assist or deal with a personal representative for value and in good faith are protected by §3-714.

The view underlying UPC procedures is that the court's role should be "wholly passive until some interested person invokes its power to secure resolution of a matter" and that the court "should refrain from intruding into family affairs unless relief is requested, and limit its relief to that sought." General Comment to UPC Article III. Informal procedures are preferred to formal court process and supervision. The UPC even provides for administration without a personal

---

2. Non-uniform probate laws tend to force separate administrations in each state where land or other assets belonging to the decedent may be located. Succession to land is governed by the law of the situs, meaning that local probate procedures are virtually unavoidable in each state where the decedent owned land. Succession to personal and intangible assets is controlled by the law of the decedent's domicile, but procedural rules protect local creditors, and possessors and controllers of out-of-state assets of a decedent may insist on local appointment of an administrator to whom they can make safe payment or delivery. Enactment of Articles III and IV of the UPC by the situs state means that the domiciliary personal representatives from other states can avoid local administrations in the UPC state by filing copies of letters of authority from the decedent's domicile and copies of duly probated wills with a probate office at the location of the assets. Following these steps, a personal representative can give marketable title by deed in a sale or distribution without court involvement. For a brief discussion of ancillary administrations with and without the UPC, see Richard V. Wellman, How the Uniform Probate Code Deals with Estates that Cross State Lines, 5 Real Prop., Prob. & Tr. J. 159 (1970).

representative in the case of a small estate consisting entirely of personalty. See UPC §§3-1201 to -1202.

Statutory Formalities for a Valid Will. The typical statutory formalities for a valid will are that the will must be: (1) in *writing*; (2) *signed* by the testator; and (3) *attested* by credible witnesses. The details of two of these requirements—signature and attestation—vary considerably from state to state. These variations are largely attributable to the fact that, before the widespread adoption of the UPC, American statutes were—and still are in non-UPC states—largely copied from one or the other (or, in some cases, partly from both) of two English statutes: the Statute of Frauds 1677 and the Wills Act 1837.

> ***Statute of Frauds 1677, §5.***[3] [A]ll devises and bequests of any lands ... shall be in writing and signed by the party so devising the same or by some other person in his presence and by his express directions and shall be attested and subscribed in the presence of the said devisor by three or four credible witnesses or else they shall be utterly void and of none effect.

> ***Wills Act 1837, §9.***[4] [N]o will shall be valid unless it shall be in writing and executed in manner hereinafter mentioned; (that is to say,) it shall be signed at the foot or end thereof by the testator, or by some other person in his presence and by his direction; and such signature shall be made or acknowledged by the testator in the presence of two or more witnesses present at the same time, and such witnesses shall attest and subscribe the will in the presence of the testator, but no form of attestation shall be necessary.

The later English statute, the Wills Act 1837, increased rather than decreased the statutory formalities. Before the promulgation of the UPC in 1969, most American states had opted for a statute modeled on the Statute of Frauds provision with its relatively fewer formal requirements. The UPC reduced the formalities still further in order to validate the will whenever possible. Accordingly, UPC §2-502 originally required a will to be in writing, signed by the testator, and signed by two persons who witnessed either the testator's act of signing or the testator's acknowledgment either of the testator's own signature or of the will.

Uniform Probate Code. The current version of UPC §2-502 generally continues the original set of formalities. It takes two further steps, however, in the direction of upholding wills whenever responsibly possible. One of these steps is codified at §2-502(a)(3)(B), which validates a will that has been notarized rather than attested. We examine this innovation at p. 147. The second step is codified at §2-503, containing a harmless-error rule under which a will that was not executed in conformity with §2-502 is valid if the proponent can establish by clear and convincing evidence that

---

3. Statute of Frauds 1677, 29 Car. 2, ch. 3.

4. Wills Act 1837, 7 Wm. 4 & 1 Vict., ch. 26.

the decedent intended the proffered document to constitute the decedent's will. (Section 3.3 of the Restatement 3d of Property sets forth a similar harmless-error rule.) This innovation is discussed at pp. 129-130.

Military Wills. Congress has made available an alternative set of formalities for military wills, called "military testamentary instruments":

10 U.S.C. §1044d. Military testamentary instruments: requirement for recognition by States.

(a) *Testamentary Instruments to Be Given Legal Effect.* A military testamentary instrument—

(1) is exempt from any requirement of form, formality, or recording before probate that is provided for testamentary instruments under the laws of a State; and

(2) has the same legal effect as a testamentary instrument prepared and executed in accordance with the laws of the State in which it is presented for probate.

(b) *Military Testamentary Instruments.* For purposes of this section, a military testamentary instrument is an instrument that is prepared with testamentary intent in accordance with regulations prescribed under this section and that—

(1) is executed in accordance with subsection (c) by (or on behalf of) a person, as a testator, who is eligible for military legal assistance;

(2) makes a disposition of property of the testator; and

(3) takes effect upon the death of the testator.

(c) *Requirements for Execution of Military Testamentary Instruments.* An instrument is valid as a military testamentary instrument only if—

(1) the instrument is executed by the testator (or, if the testator is unable to execute the instrument personally, the instrument is executed in the presence of, by the direction of, and on behalf of the testator);

(2) the execution of the instrument is notarized by—

(A) a military legal assistance counsel;

(B) a person who is authorized to act as a notary under section 1044a of this title who—

(i) is not an attorney; and

(ii) is supervised by a military legal assistance counsel; or

(C) a State-licensed notary employed by a military department or the Coast Guard who is supervised by a military legal assistance counsel;

(3) the instrument is executed in the presence of at least two disinterested witnesses (in addition to the presiding attorney), each of whom attests to witnessing the testator's execution of the instrument by signing it; and

(4) the instrument is executed in accordance with such additional requirements as may be provided in regulations prescribed under this section.

PART A. FORMALITIES OF EXECUTION: THE PROPONENT'S CASE

As indicated above, most non-UPC statutes in this country prescribe formalities for the execution of a will modeled on one or the other of the English statutes. In the majority of non-UPC states, the legislation is based on the Statute of Frauds 1677, except that only two witnesses are required.[5] Some states have added requirements not found in the English statutes, such as the requirement that a will be "published," which is interpreted to require the testator to declare to the witnesses that the document is the testator's will.[6]

In addition to wills executed with the standard formalities, a substantial number of states also recognize the validity of wills executed with fewer formalities. Here we are principally speaking of *holographic wills.* The formalities prescribed for a valid holographic will are that the will must be written in the handwriting of the testator and signed, and, in some states, that it must be dated. We discuss holographic wills later in this chapter.

Purpose of the Statutory Formalities. The Restatement 3d of Property states that the purpose of the statutory formalities "is to determine whether the decedent adopted the document as his or her will." To this end, the Restatement states that the statutory formalities serve four functions—evidentiary, cautionary, protective, and channeling:

> The evidentiary function requires solid evidence of the existence and content of the decedent's directions. The cautionary function requires some indication that the decedent arrived at these directions with adequate awareness. The protective function attempts to assure that the contents and the execution of the will were the product of the decedent's free choice. The channeling function is meant to facilitate a substantial degree of standardization in the organization, language, and content of most wills, so that they can be prepared and administered in a fairly routine manner.[7]

The Restatement further states that "[t]he formalities are meant to facilitate [an] intent-serving purpose, not to be ends in themselves." As we shall see, however, many courts seem to view the formalities as ends in themselves.

---

5. Three witnesses were once required in a few states, principally in New England.

6. The Statutory Note to Restatement 3d of Property §3.1 lists Arkansas, Indiana, Iowa, Louisiana, New York, Oklahoma, Pennsylvania, and Tennessee as states that require a will to be "published." California requires that the witnesses understand that the instrument is the testator's will. See Cal. Prob. Code §6110.

7. Restatement 3d of Property §3.3 comment a. The channeling function might seem to encourage the use of formal language, to the exclusion of messages of personal sentiment. Should wills contain personal messages to the decedent's surviving family? See Daphna Hacker, Soulless Wills, 35 Law & Soc. Inquiry 957 (2010).

Strict-Compliance Approach. The traditional judicial approach to the statutory formalities has been one of requiring strict compliance. Writing in 1975, Professor John Langbein observed:

> The law of wills is notorious for its harsh and relentless formalism. The Wills Act prescribes a particular set of formalities for executing one's testament. The most minute defect in formal compliance is held to void the will, no matter how abundant the evidence that the defect was inconsequential. Probate courts do not speak of harmless error in the execution of wills. To be sure, there is considerable diversity and contradiction in the cases interpreting what acts constitute compliance with what formalities. But once a formal defect is found, Anglo-American courts have been unanimous in concluding that the attempted will fails.

John H. Langbein, Substantial Compliance With the Wills Act, 88 Harv. L. Rev. 489 (1975).

The strict-compliance approach is epitomized by the English case of In re Groffman, [1969] 2 All E.R. 108 (P.), in which the judge, Sir Jocelyn Simon, conceded that he would gladly uphold the validity of the will "if I could consistently with my judicial duty," but because of a minor defect in the execution ceremony, "I am bound to pronounce against this will."

The Reform Movement. The strict-compliance approach still persists, but it is also coming under increasing scrutiny and, as a result of a new reform movement, which we will observe in the ensuing materials, has begun to give way in some jurisdictions. The reform movement has been spearheaded by Professor Langbein's scholarship, by the Uniform Probate Code, and by the Restatement 3d of Property. See pp. 129-130. Such an abrupt change in attitude never develops in a straight line, however. It sometimes only shows up in a dissenting opinion, and sometimes does not show up at all.

1. Attested (or Notarized) Wills

Primary Statutory References: *UPC §§2-502, 2-503*

The Preferred Method for Executing a Valid Will. As indicated earlier, the statutes differ among the states as to various details of formality. Differences in the statutes create a potential for invalidity even if the testator complies with the formality requirements of the state in which the will is executed or where the testator is domiciled. If the testator changes domicile or if the testator owns real property in other states, the common-law rules of conflict-of-laws potentially could lead to the will being held partially or totally invalid. Most states, however, have enacted statutes that recognize a will executed outside the state. UPC §2-506, for example, recognizes a will executed outside the state in accordance with either the law of the place of execution or of the testator's domicile. See Restatement 3d of Property, Statutory Note to §3.1 (describing variations in choice-of-law statutes); Jeffrey A.

Schoenblum, Multijurisdictional Estates and Article II of the Uniform Probate Code, 55 Alb. L. Rev. 1291 (1992) (analyzing UPC §2-506).

The presence of the common-law rules and the lack of uniformity within the choice-of-law statutes suggest the advisability of complying with the maximum formalities called for by the law of any state.

Attestation Clauses. An attestation clause is located immediately below the line for the testator's signature. A typical attestation clause provides:

> The foregoing instrument, consisting of ___ typewritten pages, including this page, was signed, published and declared by the above named testator to be his [her] last will, in the presence of us; we, in his [her] presence, at his [her] request, and in the presence of each other, have subscribed our names as witnesses; and we declare that at the time of the execution of this instrument the testator, according to our best knowledge and belief, was of sound mind and under no constraint.

Dated at _____, _____, this ____ day of _____, _____.

_____	_____
Witness	Address
_____	_____
Witness	Address
_____	_____
Witness	Address

With the possible exception of the "notarial will" in Louisiana,[8] no state requires the use of an attestation clause as a prerequisite to validity. Nevertheless, lawyers routinely use one because it raises a rebuttable presumption that the events recited therein actually occurred. See Restatement 3d of Property §3.1 comment q. In most states, the presumption is regarded as a presumption of fact. That means the presumption remains operative and is entitled to evidentiary weight notwithstanding the introduction of contrary evidence. See, e.g., Estate of Clark, 603 N.W.2d 290 (Mich. Ct. App. 1999); Jackson v. Patton, 952 S.W.2d 404 (Tenn. 1997); see also Estate of Johnson, 780 P.2d 692 (Okla. 1989) (holding will invalid where testimony of witnesses persuasively contradicted attestation clause). Even if the witnesses' testimony contradicts the events recited in the attestation clause, the presumption of regularity continues as long as the testimony is insufficient to show that the testator failed to comply with the statutory formalities. See Estate of Ross, 969 S.W.2d 398 (Tenn. Ct. App. 1997), appeal denied (Tenn. 1998).

On occasion, a will, regular on its face but without an attestation clause, has been denied probate when the witnesses could not recall whether the required procedures

---

8. See La. Civ. Code art. 1577 which requires the witnesses and a notary, in the presence of the testator and each other, to sign a declaration stating in effect that "the testator has declared or signified that this instrument is his testament and has signed it at the end and on each other separate page."

had been followed. For example, in Young v. Young, 313 N.E.2d 593 (Ill. App. Ct. 1974), the court said, "where the purported will does not contain an attestation clause, the proponent of the will has the burden of proving its proper execution by other evidence.... The [proponent] has furnished no such evidence."

Lawyer Liability for Invalid Execution. A lawyer who supervises the execution of a will may be liable to the intended devisees if the lawyer caused the will to be invalidly executed. See Martin D. Begleiter, First Let's Sue All the Lawyers—What Will We Get: Damages for Estate Planning Malpractice, 51 Hastings L.J. 325 (2000); John R. Price, Duties of Estate Planners to Nonclients: Identifying, Anticipating and Avoiding the Problems, 37 S. Tex. L. Rev. 1063 (1996).

In In re Grant, 936 P.2d 1360 (Kan. 1997), the court censured a lawyer for altering a will after the death of the decedent to conceal the fact that the will had been invalidly executed.

Should a lawyer be liable to a potential beneficiary of a will if the decedent dies before the lawyer completes preparation of the will or arranges for its execution? American courts typically find the lawyer not liable. See Radovich v. Locke-Paddon, 41 Cal. Rptr. 2d 573 (Ct. App. 1995); Krawczyk v. Stingle, 543 A.2d 733 (Conn. 1988); Gregg v. Lindsay, 649 A.2d 935 (Pa. Super. Ct. 1994), appeal denied, 661 A.2d 874 (Pa. 1995). See also Michael G. Desmarais, Is the "Backover Defense" Now Viable in a Legal Malpractice Action for Negligent Estate Planning?, 22 ACTEC Notes 348 (1997) (critiquing *Radovich*).

Contrast the English case of White v. Jones, [1993] 3 All E.R. 481 (C.A.), where the English Court of Appeal, Civil Division, held lawyers liable to the devisees named in the testator's letter to his solicitor giving directions regarding the preparation of a new will. Although the requested will was a simple will, preparation of it was unreasonably delayed.

a. The Signature Requirement

All American statutes, including §2-502 of the Uniform Probate Code, require the testator to sign the will. The UPC and many non-UPC statutes qualify the signature requirement by the rule that, if the testator does not sign the will, someone else can sign the testator's name if it is done in the presence and at the direction of the testator. A further requirement, sometimes imposed by non-UPC statutes, is that persons who sign for testators must also sign their own names and sometimes also give their addresses. See Restatement 3d of Property, Statutory Note to §3.1.

Estate of McKellar, below, considered the validity of a will under a statute modeled on the English Statute of Frauds 1677.

Estate of McKellar
380 So.2d 1273 (Miss. 1980)

BROOM, J. Execution and attestation of a purported Last Will and Testament are at issue in this case appealed from the Chancery Court of Lauderdale County. In that court Tiny Bell filed for probate a document said to be Greta Meador McKellar's true Last Will and Testament. The matter was contested and after hearing testimony the lower court found that the document was statutorily deficient and therefore invalid....

The purported Last Will and Testament of Greta Meador McKellar (McKellar herein) is a five-page instrument [completely written out in McKellar's own handwriting and] dated August 23, 1977. McKellar died March 29, 1979.... According to the document at issue, several beneficiaries of McKellar's purported Will were persons not her heirs at law. Her heirs at law were stated to be Tiny Bell, named by the lower court as her administratrix, Nell Thrash and Jacqueline Field.

First paragraph of the purported Will is in the following language:

To Whom it May Concern
I, Greta Meador McKellar, being of sound mind and body, declare this to be my last Will and testimony [sic] concerning my real and personal property....

The document consists of five pages (four sheets of paper), the last of which is on the reverse side of page 1. Near the bottom of the last page, being page No. 5, is the following:

The following have witness [sic] my writing of this five page will—
Luciana Brewer
Lucille Jay
Douglas Watkins.

Nowhere on the instrument except in the opening paragraph does McKellar's purported signature appear.

Testimony adduced to the lower court included the three people whose names appear at the end of the document as witnesses. Douglas Watkins testified that she[9] took the deceased McKellar to the hospital, and that while a patient in the hospital, McKellar called Watkins to her room and said, "Sign this." Watkins did not see McKellar write any part of the document; nor did she see McKellar sign her name, nor hear McKellar acknowledge signing the document. According to Watkins, McKellar did not tell her what the document was.

Another witness to the instrument, Luciane [sic] Brewer, stated that McKellar called her to McKellar's hospital room where McKellar handed Brewer one page to

---

9. Note to students: Douglas Watkins is female. Ed.

sign. She testified that in all McKellar had four or five pieces of paper, and that when she (Brewer) signed it, she saw no other names on the paper. Brewer's further testimony was that McKellar discussed the contents of the instrument with her but did not state that McKellar told her that McKellar had signed the instrument. Brewer did not read the instrument.

Lucille Jay testified that McKellar asked her to come to McKellar's room where McKellar said, "This is my Last Will and Testimony [sic]...." Jay stated that when she signed the instrument as a witness, she did not examine it but that Mrs. Brewer had already signed it when she, Jay, signed it.

The witness Watkins kept the controversial document until the day after the funeral when she opened the envelope containing the document.

The chancellor in his opinion held that the

> [P]urported will was not signed by the purported testatrix as is required by law and the cases in this jurisdiction. It is the opinion of this Court that the statements made to the witnesses by the purported testatrix did not carry with it any words signifying that the purported testatrix had signed the will.

Upon this record we cannot say that the decree against the purported Will was manifestly wrong or that the chancellor's finding was contrary to the law or the evidence. Careful analysis of the testimony establishes that none of the witnesses who testified stated that they saw or read or heard the entire document. None of the pages of the document except near the bottom of page five was signed by a witness, and McKellar's purported signature was at the top of page one. No testimony is in the record that any of the witnesses saw or observed McKellar either affix her signature on the document or heard her acknowledge that she had previously or at any time signed or affixed her signature to the document.

Under the case law of this state, the execution of a Will is a statutory privilege and not a constitutional or common law right. We have held many times that the intention of a testator is the paramount issue in the construction of Wills but one's intention does not become important nor the object of search by a court until there is first established a Will executed according to statutory requirements. Wilson v. Polite, 218 So. 2d 843 (Miss. 1969). *Wilson* dealt with a purported Will wherein the testatrix did not sign (subscribe) at the bottom. Accordingly we held it not to be a valid holographic Will. In *Wilson*, there were no attesting witnesses to the purported Will, and it could not be valid as a non-holographic Will so it was a nullity. *Wilson* made the following pronouncement concerning a non-holographic or attested Will (the type now at issue):

> [T]he name of the testator may be written at any place on the instrument, so long as it is declared to be his signature, and the instrument is published and signed in the presence of the witnesses.

Our statute applicable here is Mississippi Code Annotated §91-5-1 (1972) which states in pertinent part that:

> [S]uch last will and testament, or codicil, be signed by the testator or testatrix, or by some other person in his or her presence and by his or her express direction. Moreover, if not wholly written and subscribed by himself or herself, it shall be attested by two (2) or more credible witnesses in the presence of the testator or testatrix....

Upon this record we cannot say that the Will was properly executed ... and therefore the lower court must be affirmed. Affirmed.

PATTERSON, C.J., SMITH and ROBERTSON, P.JJ., and SUGG, WALKER, LEE, BOWLING and COOPER, JJ., concur.

Notes and Questions

1. *Questions*. What formal defect caused Greta McKellar's will to fail? To what do you attribute the court's picky attitude? Was it because the court suspected that Greta's will was an unreliable expression of her true wishes?

2. *"Signature" in the Exordium?* When Greta McKellar wrote her name in the exordium, was she signing her will? The Restatement 3d of Property §3.1 comment j states:

> *j. Testator's signature....* To be a signature, the testator must write his or her name with the intent of adopting the document as his or her own. A signature provides evidence of finality, and serves to distinguish the final will from a preliminary draft, an incomplete document, or scribbled thoughts about how the will might take shape in the future. The testator's handwritten name in freestanding form at the end of the document unquestionably satisfies the signature requirement. The testator's handwritten name in freestanding form at any other place on the document raises an inference that the testator "signed" the document.
>
> A person's name written in his or her own handwriting is not necessarily a signature. If the testator's name is not written in freestanding form, then there should be other evidence that the testator adopted the document as his or her will in order to count the handwritten name as a signature.

Courts going as far back as Lemayne v. Stanley, 3 Lev. 1, 83 Eng. Rep. 545 (K.B. 1681), have accepted a handwritten name in the exordium as the testator's signature, given other evidence of finality. See Philip Mechem, The Rule in *Lemayne v. Stanley*, 29 Mich. L. Rev. 685 (1931). Without additional evidence of finality, most courts have been unwilling to treat the decedent's handwritten name in the exordium as a signature (see, e.g., Estate of Erickson, 806 P.2d 1186 (Utah 1991)), and some courts have been unwilling to do so even with additional evidence of finality (see Estate of Wedeberg, 589 N.E.2d 1000 (Ill. App. Ct.), appeal denied, 602 N.E.2d 453 (Ill. 1992)).

3. *Attestation Without Knowledge?* The report in *McKellar* tells us that the witness Watkins was instructed to "sign this" but did not know what she was signing. Does the witness's lack of knowledge matter? Was Greta McKellar's will properly attested? See Estate of Griffith, 30 So.3d 1190, 1194 (Miss. 2010) (holding that "an attesting witness must have some knowledge that the document being signed is, in fact, the testator's last will and testament").

———

Position of the Testator's Signature. Unlike the English Statute of Frauds 1677 and the Uniform Probate Code, the English Wills Act 1837 requires the testator to sign "at the foot or end" of the will.[10]

In this country, a few states follow the English Wills Act and require the testator's signature to be at the end of the will.[11]

For cases in which the will failed because the testator did not meet the statutory sign-at-the-end requirement, see, e.g., Sears v. Sears, 82 N.E. 1067 (Ohio 1907) (concerning a decedent who, using a printed will form, failed to sign her name on the indicated dotted line but did write her name in the attestation clause below the signature line); Estate of Proley, 422 A.2d 136 (Pa. 1980) (concerning a decedent who, using a printed will form designed to be folded over, wrote her name on the back portion on a blank line below the printed words "Will of ....").

The Restatement 3d of Property §3.1 comment *l* provides: "Depending on the facts and circumstances, [provisions of a will that appear below the testator's signature] might be given effect under the harmless-error doctrine (see §3.3),[12] but if not, their existence does not invalidate the will and prevent the provisions appearing above the testator's signature from being given effect."[13]

———

10. The rigidity of this requirement, or at least of its interpretation, was relaxed somewhat by an amendment in 1852 that permitted, *inter alia*, a signature "so placed at or after, or following, or under, or beside or opposite to the end of the will, that it shall be apparent on the face of the will that the testator intended to give effect by such his signature to the writing signed as his will...." 15 & 16 Vict., ch. 24.

11. The "sign-at-the-end" statutes are listed in Restatement 3d of Property, Statutory Note to §3.1.

12. The harmless-error doctrine of Restatement 3d of Property §3.3 is set forth below p. 129. Ed.

13. In Winters' Will, 98 N.Y.S.2d 312 (App. Div. 1950), aff'd without opinion, 98 N.E.2d 477 (N.Y. 1951), the court held a will invalid where the decedent and the proper number of attesting witnesses signed their names underneath the dispositive provisions of the instrument but above a clause naming certain persons as executors. N.Y. Est. Powers & Trusts Law §3-2.1(a)(1)(A) was subsequently amended to provide that the material above (but not below) the signature can be given effect. See Estate of Mergenthaler, 474 N.Y.S.2d 253 (Sur. Ct. 1984) (invalidating the residuary devise because a four-page will had been improperly stapled and paginated prior to execution, resulting in the testator signing page three rather than page four).

The Sign-First Requirement. Most courts assume that the testator must sign the will before the witnesses sign. See, e.g., Burns v. Adamson, 854 S.W.2d 723 (Ark. 1993); Wheat v. Wheat, 244 A.2d 359 (Conn. 1968). By substantial authority, however, the exact order of signing is not critical if the testator and the witnesses sign as part of a "single (or continuous) transaction." See, e.g., Bain v. Hill, 639 So. 2d 178 (Fla. Dist. Ct. App. 1994); Waldrep v. Goodwin, 195 S.E.2d 432 (Ga. 1973); Hopson v. Ewing, 353 S.W.2d 203 (Ky. 1962); Restatement 3d of Property §3.1 comment m. A few courts have rejected the single-transaction idea. See, e.g., Barnes v. Chase, 94 N.E. 694 (Mass. 1911); Marshall v. Mason, 57 N.E. 340 (Mass. 1900); Estate of Hartung, 145 A.2d 798 (N.J. Super. Ct. App. Div. 1958).

Suppose a testator signs her will *before* the witnesses arrive. After the witnesses arrive, she asks them to sign her will as witnesses and tells them that she already signed it. But, she folds the paper in such a way that the witnesses never see her signature. If the case were governed by a statute modeled on the English Statute of Frauds 1677, the will would probably be valid. See Betts v. Lonas, 172 F.2d 759 (D.C. Cir. 1948).

But would the will be valid if the case were governed by a statute modeled on the English Wills Act 1837, which requires that the testator's "signature shall be made or acknowledged by the testator in the presence of" the witnesses? See Hudson v. Parker, 1 Rob. Ecc. 14, 25, 163 Eng. Rep. 948, 952 (P. Ct. 1844), where the court said:

> What is the plain meaning of acknowledging a signature in the presence of witnesses?—what do the words import but this?—"Here is my name written, I acknowledge that name so written to have been written by me; bear witness;" how is it possible that the witnesses should swear that any signature was acknowledged unless they saw it?

Accord Patten v. Patten, 558 P.2d 659 (Mont. 1976) (will invalid). But see Norton v. Georgia Railroad Bank & Trust Co., 285 S.E.2d 910 (Ga. 1982), where the court held that a testator's acknowledgment of his signature to the witnesses "need not be explicit, but may be inferred from conduct." A witness testified that he was not in the house when the testator signed the will. The witness later entered the living room and sat at a table "right by" the testator and across from the lawyer who drafted the will. The lawyer asked the witness to witness the instrument, and the witness signed it in the presence of the testator. The court held that the testator's conduct was a sufficient acknowledgment of his signature to the witness.

Crossed Wills. H and W go to a lawyer for simple wills. At their request, the lawyer prepares a will for W devising her entire estate to H if H survives her, and if not, to the couple's children, A and B. The lawyer also prepares a will for H devising his entire estate to W if she survives him, and if not, to A and B. When W and H go to the lawyer's office to sign the wills, the lawyer confuses the wills and gives W's will to H to sign and H's will to W to sign. The mistake is not discovered until W dies, survived by H, A, and B. Does W have a valid will? In Estate of Pavlinko, 148 A.2d 528 (Pa. 1959), the court held that the will signed by H "could not [be] probated as [W's] will, because it was not signed by [her] ... [and that the will signed by W] is a meaningless nullity." But see In re Snide, 418 N.E.2d 656 (N.Y. 1981), described in Chapter 13.

Restatement 3d of Property

§3.3 Excusing Harmless Errors. A harmless error in executing a will may be excused if the proponent establishes by clear and convincing evidence that the decedent adopted the document as his or her will.

....

[Comment] b. Excusing harmless errors. In applying [the harmless-error rule] to particular cases, a hierarchy of sorts has been found to emerge among the formalities. The requirement of a writing is so fundamental to the purpose of the execution formalities that it cannot be excused as harmless under the principle of this Restatement. Only a harmless error in executing a *document* can be excused under this Restatement.

Among the defects in execution that can be excused, the lack of a signature is the hardest to excuse. An unsigned will raises a serious but not insuperable doubt about whether the testator adopted the document as his or her will. A particularly attractive case for excusing the lack of the testator's signature is a crossed will case, in which, by mistake, a wife signs her husband's will and the husband signs his wife's will. Because attestation makes a more modest contribution to the purpose of the formalities, defects in compliance with attestation procedures are more easily excused.

Notes

1. *The First Reform Movement—Substantial Compliance.* In 1975, Professor John Langbein wrote an influential law review article, arguing that "the insistent formalism of the law of wills is mistaken and needless" and that "the familiar concept of substantial compliance should now be applied to the Wills Act." As he explained, "The finding of a formal defect should not lead to automatic invalidity, but to a further inquiry: does the noncomplying document express the decedent's testamentary intent, and does its form sufficiently approximate Wills Act formality to enable the court to conclude that it serves the purposes of the Wills Act?" John H. Langbein, Substantial Compliance with the Wills Act, 88 Harv. L. Rev. 489, 489 (1975).

The Restatement Second of Property §33.1 comment g adopted the substantial compliance approach: "In the absence of a legislative corrective..., the court should apply a rule of substantial compliance, under which a will is found validly executed if the document was executed in substantial compliance with the statutory formalities and if the proponent establishes by clear and convincing evidence that the decedent intended the document to constitute his or her will."

For an example of judicial adoption of the substantial compliance approach, see Will of Ranney, 589 A.2d 1339 (N.J. 1991).[14] However, for examples of the potential restrictiveness of a doctrine requiring *substantial* compliance, see Estate of Voeller, 534 N.W.2d 24 (N.D. 1995) (refusing to validate a codicil under a substantial compliance approach when one of the two witnesses present at the execution of the codicil failed to sign); Estate of Leavey, 202 P.3d 99 (Kan.App. 2009) (declining to validate a will when one witness attested properly and one witness initialed each page, on the ground that the second witness's failure to attest properly was not a "slight or trifling departure" from the statutory requirements); Pomar v. Hash, 2017 WL 639416 (Va. 2017) (holding that a will lacking the signature of a second witness does not satisfy substantial compliance).

2. *The Current Reform Movement—The Harmless-Error Rule.* The harmless-error rule of the Restatement 3d of Property and of UPC §2-503 is quite similar to statutes in effect in Israel,[15] several Australian states (Australian Capital Territory, New South Wales, Northern Territory, Queensland, South Australia, Tasmania, Victoria, and Western Australia),[16] and several Canadian provinces (Manitoba, New Brunswick, Prince Edward Island, Quebec, and Saskatchewan).[17]

During the last several years in the United States, California, Colorado, D.C., Hawaii, Michigan, Minnesota, Montana, New Jersey, Ohio, Oregon, South Dakota, Utah, and Virginia have adopted statutes modeled on UPC §2-503.[18]

---

14. New Jersey subsequently enacted the harmless-error rule of UPC §2-503. See N.J. Stat. §3B:3-3.

15. Israel Succession Law, 5725-1965, in Ministry of Justice, 19 Laws of the State of Israel 62, ch. 3, §25 (1965).

16. Australian Capital Territory Wills Act §11A; New South Wales Succession Act §8; Queensland Succession Act of 1981, §18; South Australia, Wills Act 1946, as amended by Wills (Miscellaneous) Amendment Act 1994, §12; Tasmanian Wills Act §10; Victoria Wills Act 1997 §9; Western Australia Wills Act 1970, §32. On the harmless-error rule in Australia, see Rosalind Atherton, Dispensing with Wills Formality in Australia: The Problem of the Draft Will in the Tranquil Revolution, (1994) Austl. Prop. L.J. 68; John H. Langbein, Excusing Harmless Errors in the Execution of Wills: A Report on Australia's Tranquil Revolution in Probate Law, 87 Colum. L. Rev. 1, 4 (1987); Stephanie Lester, Admitting Defective Wills to Probate, Twenty Years Later: New Evidence for the Adoption of the Harmless-Error Rule, 42 Real Prop. Prob. & Tr. J. 577 (2007); P. Vines, When is the Testator's Intention the Requisite Intention under the Dispensing Power?, (1995) Austl. Prop. L.J. 152.

17. Manitoba Statutes 1982-83-84, c. 31, Wills Act, §23; New Brunswick Wills Act §35.1; Prince Edward Island Probate Act §70; Quebec Civ. Code §714; Saskatchewan Wills Act 1996, §37. A harmless-error rule is also adopted in the Uniform Wills Act of Canada §19 (1988).

18. Cal. Prob. Code §6110(c)(2); Colo. Rev. Stat. §15-11-503; D.C. Code §18-906; Haw. Rev. Stat. §560:2-503; Mich. Comp. Laws §700.2503; Minn. Stat. §524.2-503; Mont. Code §72-2-523; N.J. Stat. §3B:3-3; Ohio Rev. Code §2107.24; Or. Rev. Stat. §112.238; S.D. Codified Laws §29A-2-503; Utah Code §75-2-503; Va. Code §64.1-49.1.

Problem

Theodore W. Dwight, the founder of the modern Columbia Law School, had neglected to make a will until he was near death. After giving instructions for the preparation of his will, he had the draft brought to his bedside on the morning of June 18, 1892. Witnesses were present as the will execution began. Dwight wrote "Theodore W. Dwi" and part of the letter "g" when he suddenly died.[19] What result under strict compliance? Under substantial compliance? Under UPC §2-503?

———

Unsigned Will. In Dalk v. Allen, 774 So.2d 787 (Fla. Dist. Ct. App. 2000), review granted, 789 So.2d 343 (Fla. 2001), Christel McPeak went to her attorney's office to sign her will and other estate planning documents. There were eight documents requiring her signature: four duplicate originals of the "Living Will and Designation of Health Care Surrogate," three duplicate originals of the "Durable Power of Attorney" and the original "Will." Christel reviewed all of the documents and expressed to her attorney that they met with her approval and complied with her wishes. The court then found:

9. On March 20, 1998 each of the duplicate original Living Wills and Powers of Attorney were fully executed, witnessed, and, in the case of the Powers of Attorney, notarized.

10. On March 20, 1998 the "Last Will and Testament of Christel D. McPeak" was witnessed and notarized in the presence of Mrs. McPeak and in the presence of Attorney Baker, Jemma Baker and Anne Dick. However, due to confusion in circulation of multiple original documents for signature and mistake, that document was not physically signed by Mrs. McPeak.

11. Nevertheless, during the joint meeting for signature of documents, Mrs. McPeak did declare in the presence of witnesses and the notary the "Last Will and Testament of Christel D. McPeak", necessarily including the typed signature affixed thereon, to be her Last Will and Testament.

The court held that Christel McPeak's will was invalid:

It is clear from the record and the trial court's findings of fact, that the absence of a signature resulted from a mistake. The decedent apparently intended to sign the will, but

———

For support of the harmless-error rule, see Bruce H. Mann, Formalities and Formalism in the Uniform Probate Code, 142 U. Pa. L. Rev. 1033 (1994). For criticism of the harmless-error rule, see Lloyd Bonfield, Reforming the Requirements for Due Execution of Wills: Some Guidance from the Past, 70 Tul. L. Rev. 1893 (1996); Melanie B. Leslie, The Myth of Testamentary Freedom, 38 Ariz. L. Rev. 235 (1996); C. Douglas Miller, Will Formality, Judicial Formalism, and Legislative Reform: An Examination of the New Uniform Probate Code "Harmless Error" Rule and the Movement Toward Amorphism (Pts. 1 & 2), 43 Fla. L. Rev. 167 (1991), 43 Fla. L. Rev. 599 (1991).

19. See Samuel F. Howard & Julius Geobel, Jr., A History of the School of Law: Columbia University 132 (1955).

clearly she did not. While we recognize that her intentions, as expressed in the purported will, may have been thwarted by operation of the statute, nevertheless the will is not entitled to probate for lack of her signature.

The court did, however, certify to the Florida Supreme Court the following question: "May a constructive trust be imposed over the assets of an estate in favor of a beneficiary named in an invalidly executed will, where the invalidity is the result of a mistake in its execution, and the invalid will expresses the clear intention of the decedent to dispose of her assets in the manner expressed therein?" The certification was based on Estate of Tolin (set forth in Chapter 5), a case in which the Florida Supreme Court had held that a constructive trust could be imposed to correct a unilateral mistake in attempting to revoke a codicil.

In Allen v. Dalk, 826 So.2d 245 (Fla. 2002), the Florida Supreme Court "answer[ed] the certified question in the negative [and] decline[d] the invitation to extend the *Tolin* case beyond its facts." The concurring opinion of ANSTEAD, C.J., offered the opinion that "even under section 2-503 of the Uniform Probate Code ... it is doubtful that an unsigned will would be given any effect." Do you agree? Cf. Estate of Hall, p. 147.

For cases holding that an unsigned will can be admitted to probate under statutes mirroring UPC §2-503, see Estate of Attia, 895 N.W.2d 564 (Mich. App. 2016); Will and Codicil of Macool, 3 A.3d 1258, 1266 (N.J. Super. 2010).

Digitized Scan of Handwritten Signature. In Taylor v. Holt, 134 S.W.3d 830 (Tenn. Ct. App. 2003), the testator, Steve Godfrey, prepared a one-page will on his computer. Godfrey asked two neighbors to act as witnesses to the will. In the presence of both neighbors, Godfrey affixed a digitized scan of his handwritten signature at the end of the document. Godfrey then printed the document. Each neighbor then signed their names below Godfrey's and dated the document next to their respective signatures.

In the document, Godfrey devised everything he owned to a person identified only as Doris. Godfrey died approximately one week later. Doris Holt, whom the court described as Godfrey's "girlfriend," lived with Godfrey at the time of his death.

The court affirmed the decision of the trial court upholding the will, relying on a statute that provides that the term "signature" "includes a mark... or any other symbol or methodology executed or adopted by a party with intention to authenticate a writing or record...." The court analyzed the case as follows:

> In the case at hand, Deceased did make a mark that was intended to operate as his signature. Deceased made a mark by using his computer to affix his computer generated signature, and, as indicated by the affidavits of both witnesses, this was done in the presence of the witnesses. The computer generated signature made by Deceased falls into the category of "any other symbol or methodology executed or adopted by a party with intention to authenticate a writing or record," and, if made in the presence of two attesting witnesses, as it was in this case, is sufficient to constitute proper execution of a will.

Further, we note that Deceased simply used a computer rather than an ink pen as the tool to make his signature, and, therefore, complied with [the Tennessee will-execution statute] by signing the will himself.

b. The Attestation Requirement

Primary Statutory References: *UPC §§2-502, 2-503, 2-505*

Estate of Peters
526 A.2d 1005 (N.J. 1987)

[Conrad Peters died on March 28, 1985. His wife, Marie, predeceased him by slightly more than five days. Conrad and Marie had no children by their marriage, but Marie had a son, Joseph Skrok, by a prior marriage. Marie's will devised her entire estate to Conrad if he survived her (which he did), but if not, to Joseph. Conrad's will devised his entire estate to Marie if she survived him (which she did not), but if not, to Joseph.

At Marie's request, her sister-in-law, Sophia M. Gall, an insurance agent and notary public, prepared the wills for Marie and Conrad. About two years before he died, Conrad suffered a stroke that put him into the hospital. The stroke affected him physically but not mentally. Marie, Sophia, and Sophia's husband (Marie's brother), came to Conrad's hospital room with Conrad's will. Sophia read the provisions of the will to Conrad, who then assented to it and signed it. None of the individuals who witnessed Conrad's signing of the will signed the will as witness, the apparent intention being to await the arrival of two of Sophia's employees, Mary Gall and Kristen Spock.

Later in the afternoon, after Mary and Kristen arrived, Sophia reviewed the will briefly with Conrad, who, in the presence of Mary and Kristen, indicated his approval and acknowledged his signature, Sophia then signed the will as a notary, but neither Mary nor Kristen placed her signature on the will. Sophia then folded the will and handed it to Marie. When Conrad died fifteen months later, the two witnesses, Mary and Kristen, had still not signed the will.

Joseph Skrok presented Conrad's will for probate. Its validity was disputed by the State of New Jersey, which would succeed to Conrad's estate if his will was invalid. Conrad left no surviving blood relatives.

At the probate proceeding, Sophia testified as to why the two intended witnesses never signed the will:

As I say, just because of the emotional aspect of the whole situation, my sister-in-law was there, my husband, her brother was there, myself and the two girls. There were six of us. The other patients had visitors. It got to be kind of—I don't know how to explain it, just the situation, and the girls were in a hurry to get back to the office, because they had to leave the office, I honestly think in their minds, when they saw me sign the will, they thought that is why they were there. And we folded up the will, gave it [to] my sister-in-law. It was just that type of situation.

The trial court found the will validly executed, by treating Sophia's signature as notary as the valid signature of a witness and by allowing one of the other witnesses to sign the will. The Appellate Division reversed.]

HANDLER, J. ....The operative statute governing the validity of the execution of a will is N.J.S.A. §3B:3-2. The statute prescribes the formalities necessary for the proper execution of a will. It requires (1) that the will be in writing and (2) that it be signed by the testator (or by someone in his presence and at his direction). It also requires that a will be signed by at least two persons who witnessed either (a) the signing or (b) the testator's acknowledgment of his signature or of the will....

Wills are solely the creatures of positive law. "The right to make a will is derived from the statute." A. Clapp, 5 New Jersey Practice, Wills and Administration §41, at 173 (3d ed. 1982). . . . Historically, courts have held that, as statutory creations, wills must adhere to the requirements prescribed by the statute. Failure to comply with the statutory requirements has long resulted in a will being declared invalid, no matter how accurately the document may have reflected the wishes of the testator.

This policy of construing the wills statute's formalities strictly came to be criticized for producing inequitable results and for encouraging, in effect, the circumvention of the wills statutes through such means as conveyances in joint tenancy, revocable trusts, tentative or "Totten" trusts, and cash value life insurance policies.... The perception of inequitable results, coupled with the decline of wills, relative to other instruments, as means of devising property after death, led the National Conference of Commissioners of Uniform State Laws and the American Bar Association, in August 1969, to propose adoption of the [original] Uniform Probate Code. The Code's approach was not to encourage courts to abandon their strict construction of the formalities prescribed, but rather to reduce the number and refine the scope of those formalities so that, if strict construction were employed, "inequities" in individual cases would occur less frequently and would be justified by the importance of the interests protected by the formal requirements that were retained....

A second approach to reform was proposed in 1975 by Professor John Langbein, in "Substantial Compliance With the Wills Act," [88 Harv. L. Rev. 489 (1975)]. According to Professor Langbein, "finding of a formal defect should lead not to automatic invalidity, but to a further inquiry: does the noncomplying document express the decedent's testamentary intent, and does its form sufficiently approximate Wills Act formality to enable the court to conclude that it serves the purposes of the Wills Act?" Id....

The current statute, a variant of the [original] Uniform Probate Code, constitutes a significant statutory change from its predecessor with respect to how a will must be witnessed. In accordance with the [original] Uniform Probate Code, the thrust of the change is to reduce the number of formalities entailed in the witnessing of the execution of a will and, in doing so, to ease the difficulty of complying with the formalities that are prescribed for witnesses....

Plaintiff argues that the repeal of N.J.S A. §3A:3-2 and the elimination of the requirement that the witness sign in the presence of the testator indicate that the Legislature intended that a witness could sign a will as a subscribing witness at any time after the testator has signed or acknowledged the will, even after the testator's death. Plaintiff points to the lack of any other restrictions in the statute relating to when witnesses may sign a will. Plaintiff thus argues that the procedure employed here was within the contemplation of the statute. In the alternative, plaintiff argues that, in the absence of any allegation of fraud, the will should be validated as in substantial compliance with the statute. We treat first the argument that the procedure involved here—allowing the witness to sign the will some eighteen months after the will was witnessed, where the testator had died with the will unsigned by witnesses some fifteen months after the will was witnessed—complies with the statute.

It cannot be overemphasized that the Legislature, in reforming the Wills statute, did not dispense with the requirement that the execution of a will be witnessed. Indeed, it is arguable that as the number of formalities have been reduced, those retained by the Legislature have assumed even greater importance, and demand at least the degree of scrupulous adherence required under the former statute.

It is generally acknowledged that witnesses serve two functions, which can be characterized as "observatory" and "signatory." The current statute clearly requires the fulfillment of both functions; a testamentary writing proffered as a will, in the statute's terms, "shall be *signed* by at least two persons each of whom *witnesses* either the signing or the testator's acknowledgment of the signature or of the will."

The observatory function consists of the actual witnessing—the direct and purposeful observation—of the testator's signature to or acknowledgment of the will. It entails more than physical presence or a casual or general awareness of the will's execution by the testator; the witnessing of a will is a concomitant condition and an integral part of the execution of the will.

The signatory function consists of the signing of the will by the persons who were witnesses. The signatory function may not have the same substantive significance as the observatory function, but it is not simply a ministerial or precatory requirement. While perhaps complementary to the observatory function, it is nonetheless a necessary element of the witnessing requirement. The witness' signature has significance as an evidentiary requirement or probative element, serving both to demonstrate and to confirm the fulfillment of the observatory function by the witnesses. There is nothing, therefore, to suggest that in retaining the requirement that a will's execution be witnessed, the Legislature meant to imply that either witnessing function is dispensable. The statutory policy to reduce the required formalities to a minimum should not, in our view, be construed to sanction relaxation of the formalities the statute retained.

Resolution of the issue of when the witnesses must sign the will in relation to their observations of the execution of the will by the testator follows from the purpose of the requirement that the will be signed. Because, as noted, the signatory function serves an evidentiary purpose, the signatures of the witnesses would lose probative worth and tend to fail of this purpose if the witnesses were permitted to sign at a time remote from their required observations as witnesses. Consequently, because the witnessing requirement of the statute consists of the dual acts of observation and signature, it is sensible to infer that both acts should occur either contemporaneously with or in close succession to one another.

We are thus satisfied that it would be unreasonable to construe the statute as placing no time limit on the requirement of obtaining two witnesses' signatures. By implication, the statute requires that the signatures of witnesses be affixed to a will within a reasonable period of time from the execution of the will.

The requirement of subscription within a reasonable time follows also from the consistent policy of this state that execution formalities are substantive requirements, and, therefore, that execution defects are substantive. Because the purpose of execution formalities is to prevent fraud and undue influence, they have consistently been held by our courts to be substantive requirements. The fact that the Legislature has reduced the number of execution formalities required does not diminish the significance of the formalities it retained; if anything, in our view, their significance is heightened. What this Court stated in Hale's Will, supra, 21 N.J. at 297, 121 A.2d 511, is no less true under the reformed statute: the purpose of execution formalities is to "forestall[] fraud by the living upon the dead [to] discourage imposition on the unwary...."

Given our conclusion that the witnesses must sign within a reasonable time from observation, the question is whether the time period involved here—in which the testator died with the will still unsigned by witnesses fifteen months after the will was witnessed—is reasonable. Two factors in this case affect our determination of reasonableness: (1) the fact that the witness signed after the testator's death; and (2) the fact that some eighteen months passed between the observatory and signatory functions of the witness. While there have been no New Jersey cases addressing the issue of whether a witness may sign a will after the testator's death, the problem has been treated in other jurisdictions. In Estate of Flicker, 215 Neb. 495, 339 N.W.2d 914, 915 (1983), the Nebraska Supreme Court observed that the purpose of the witnessing requirement is to prevent fraud or mistake, and that permitting witnesses to sign after the testator's death "would erode the efficacy of [this] safeguard...." Thus, "[the witnesses'] signatures are the last acts in the ceremony required by the statute. By its terms, the statute requires a witness to sign." See also Matter of Estate of Mikeska, 140 Mich. App. 116, 362 N.W.2d 906, 910 (1985) ("We agree with the holding in *Flicker*, as well as with the rationale"); Rogers v. Rogers, 71 Or. App.

133, 691 P.2d 114 (1984) (a will, as an ambulatory instrument, takes effect at the time of the testator's death; failure to comply with the formalities of execution by the time the testator has died results in an invalid will).

In this case, the Appellate Division declined to adopt a bright-line rule under N.J.S.A. §3B:3-2 requiring witnesses' signatures before the death of the testator. It expressly left open the question raised by Leo's Will, 12 Ha. Supp. 61 (Fla. Dade Co. Cir. Ct. 1958), concerning the validity of a will where a testator has died moments after execution, but before the witnesses have had an opportunity to sign. We endorse this conclusion. There may indeed be cases in which the affixation of witnesses' signatures after the testator's death would be reasonable, particularly if the witnesses were somehow precluded from signing before the testator died. This case, however, does not present such a situation. Even if one accepts the testimony that the emotional trauma of the moment prevented the witnesses from signing the will while the testator was hospitalized, there is simply no adequate explanation of the failure to have obtained their signatures in the extended fifteen-month interval prior to his death. If the Legislature's retention of the signing requirement is to be at all effectual, signing must occur within a reasonable time of observation to assure that the signature attests to what was actually observed, and not to what is vaguely remembered. While this requirement does not necessarily entail subscription prior to the testator's death, the interval here between the observation and the testator's death was simply too long for subscription after death to have been reasonably within the contemplation of the statute.

Plaintiff argues in the alternative, however, that even if compliance with execution formalities was defective, this Court should validate the will in the absence of any allegation of fraud because it was in "substantial compliance" with the statute. Thus, given the historical trend toward liberalization of the wills statute described above, and the policy favoring validation of wills that "meet the minimal formalities of the statute," the ultimate question raised by this case is how courts should construe wills that fail to satisfy even the "minimal formalities" retained in the statute.

As Professor Langbein has explained, "[t]he substantial compliance doctrine would permit defective compliance with . . . ceremonials to be evaluated purposively. It would permit the proponents to prove that in the circumstances of the case the testator executed the will with finality and that the execution is adequately evidenced notwithstanding the defect." Langbein, "Substantial Compliance with the Wills Act," supra, at 521. The doctrine has been criticized, however, because it reduces predictability of wills:

> The argument in favor of the implementation of the substantial compliance doctrine is that, while it lacks the predictability of the [original] U.P.C., it does insist upon a higher degree of formality yet with the understanding that where the failure to comply with any formality is shown, proof may be received to demonstrate that the function of the formality has still been met. . . . The problem is that wills are unlike the world of contract where the

demands of business often necessitate informality. . . Wills are more often made without such demands of time pressure. The testator has every opportunity to comply with formality requirements.

A second problem is the ambiguity of "substantial compliance." ... Does it mean that some formalities are more important than others and that substantial compliance involves completion of only the important formalities?

[Nelson and Starck, "Formalities and Formalism: A Critical Look at the Execution of Wills," 6 Pepperdine L. Rev. 331, 355 (1979).]

In addition, the doctrine's reliability has been questioned because of its emphasis upon evidence of testamentary intention and the recollection of distant, indistinct events. Irmiston, "Formalities and Wills: A Plea for Caution," American/Australian/New Zealand Law: Parallels and Contrasts, A.B.A., 72, 74 (1980). This has led to rejection of the doctrine in some states, where it has been found to "lead to confusion and uncertainty," Hopkins v. Hopkins, 708 S.W.2d 31, 32 (Tex. Ct. App. 1986).

The ....New Jersey courts have generally rejected a rule of substantial compliance....

To [adopt a substantial-compliance doctrine] on the facts of this case would, in our view, effectively vitiate the statutory requirement that witnesses sign the will.[20] We continue to believe that, as a general proposition, strict, if not literal, adherence to statutory requirements is required in order to validate a will, and that the statutory requirements must be satisfied regardless of the possibility of fraud in any particular case.

Accordingly, for the reasons stated, the judgment below is affirmed.

Notes and Questions

1. *Signature Requirement.* Nearly all statutes require two witnesses to "sign" the will.[21] For cases treating a witness's handwritten name appearing in the body of a will as a signature, see Mossler v. Johnson, 565 S.W.2d 952 (Tex. Civ. App. 1978); Robinson v. Ward, 387 S.E.2d 735 (Va. 1990).

2. *Reasonable Time.* What is the probative value of the witnesses' signatures and why is that value lost of the witnesses don't sign at or within a "reasonable" time after the execution ceremony? How is "reasonableness" to be determined?

---

20. We are unwilling to foreclose consideration of the substantial compliance doctrine in a case where there is no question of fraud, and where, unlike this case, there has been a clear attempt to comply with a statutory formality but compliance is deficient. In this case, however, the statutory formalities contemplate at a minimum witnessing by two persons; the treatment of a notary's signature as that of a witness does not compensate for the absence of the signature of a second witness.

21. A notable exception is Pennsylvania, which does not require the witnesses to sign the will (see 20 Pa. Cons. Stat. Ann. § 2502).

3. *Uniform Probate Code.* The 1990 revisions to UPC §2-502 introduced a reasonable-time standard for signing by the witnesses, but because of the harmless-error rule of §2-503, the failure of the witnesses to sign the will within a reasonable time is not necessarily fatal to the validity of the will.

4. *Attestation After the Testator's Death.* The comment to UPC §2-502 explains that "the reasonable-time requirement could be satisfied even if the witnesses sign after the testator's death." In contrast, the California Supreme Court adopted "the bright line rule that witnesses' signatures should be affixed to the document at least by the time it becomes operative, the death of the testator." Estate of Saueressig, 136 P.3d 201, 205 (Cal. 2006). *Saueressig*, however, is no longer good law on this point, thanks to the enactment, effective January 1, 2009, of a harmless-error rule in Cal. Prob. Code §6110(c)(2).

———

Presence Requirement. Non-UPC statutes commonly prescribe that the witnesses must sign the will "in the presence of" the testator. In these states, signing by the witnesses outside of the presence of the testator, followed or preceded by an acknowledgment of the signature in the testator's presence, is generally not permitted. See, e.g., Chase v. Kittredge, 93 Mass. (11 Allen) 49 (1865); Estate of Fischer, 886 A.2d 996 (N.H. 2005); see also Atkinson on Wills § 72, at 344; Annot., What Constitutes the Presence of the Testator in the Witnessing of His Will, 75 A.L.R.2d 318 (1961); Price v. Abate, 9 So.3d 37 (Fla.App. 2009)(bizarrely relying on the definition of "presence" used in the state's statute criminalizing lewd and lascivious acts in the presence of a child). But see, e.g., Wade v. Wade, 195 S.E. 339 (W. Va. 1938) (a witness's acknowledgment and identification of his signature were equivalent to an actual signing of his name in the presence of the testator and the other witness).

Statutes modeled on the English Wills Act 1837 commonly impose additional signing-in-the-presence-of requirements: They require that the *testator* sign (or acknowledge the signature) "in the presence of" the *witnesses* and that the *witnesses* sign "in the presence of" *each other*.[22] The "presence" requirement has proved to be troublesome, in part because of the narrow meaning many courts have given to the word.

Stevens v. Casdorph
508 S.E.2d 610 (W. Va. 1998)

PER CURIAM:...

---

22. The English Wills Act did not literally require the witnesses to sign in the presence of each other. It required the testator to sign or acknowledge the signature in the presence of the witnesses present at the same time. The witnesses were then required to sign in the presence of the testator.

I. Factual Background. On May 28, 1996, the Casdorphs took Mr. Homer Haskell Miller to Shawnee Bank in Dunbar, West Virginia, so that he could execute his will.[23] Once at the bank, Mr. Miller asked Debra Pauley, a bank employee and public notary, to witness the execution of his will. After Mr. Miller signed the will, Ms. Pauley took the will to two other bank employees, Judith Waldron and Reba McGinn, for the purpose of having each of them sign the will as witnesses. Both Ms. Waldron and Ms. McGinn signed the will. However, Ms. Waldron and Ms. McGinn testified during their depositions that they did not actually see Mr. Miller place his signature on the will. Further, it is undisputed that Mr. Miller did not accompany Ms. Pauley to the separate work areas of Ms. Waldron and Ms. McGinn.

Mr. Miller died on July 28, 1996. The last will and testament of Mr. Miller, which named Mr. Paul Casdorph[24] as executor, left the bulk of his estate to the Casdorphs.[25] The Stevenses, nieces of Mr. Miller, filed the instant action to set aside the will. The Stevenses asserted in their complaint that Mr. Miller's will was not executed according to the requirements set forth in W.Va.Code §41-1-3 (1995).[26] After some discovery, all parties moved for summary judgment. The circuit court denied the Stevenses' motion for summary judgment, but granted the Casdorphs' cross motion for summary judgment. From this ruling, the Stevenses appeal to this Court.

II. Standard of Review. This Court has held that "[a] circuit court's entry of summary judgment is reviewed de novo." Syl. pt. 1, Painter v. Peavy, 192 W.Va. 189, 451 S.E.2d 755 (1994)....

III. Discussion. The Stevenses' contention is simple. They argue that all evidence indicates that Mr. Miller's will was not properly executed. Therefore, the will should be voided. The procedural requirements at issue are contained in W.Va.Code §41-1-3 (1997). The statute reads:

> No will shall be valid unless it be in writing and signed by the testator, or by some other person in his presence and by his direction, in such manner as to make it manifest that the name is intended as a signature; and moreover, unless it be wholly in the handwriting of the testator, *the signature shall be made or the will acknowledged by him in the presence of at least two competent witnesses, present at the same time; and such witnesses shall subscribe the will in the presence of the testator, and of each other,* but no form of attestation shall be necessary. (Emphasis added.)

The relevant requirements of the above statute calls for a testator to sign his/her

---

23. Mr. Miller was elderly and confined to a wheelchair.

24. Paul Casdorph was a nephew of Mr. Miller.

25. Mr. Miller's probated estate exceeded $400,000.00. The will devised $80,000.00 to Frank Paul Smith, a nephew of Mr. Miller. The remainder of the estate was left to the Casdorphs.

26. As heirs, the Stevenses would be entitled to recover from Mr. Miller's estate under the intestate laws if his will is set aside as invalidly executed.

will or acknowledge such will in the presence of at least two witnesses at the same time, and such witnesses must sign the will in the presence of the testator and each other. In the instant proceeding the Stevenses assert, and the evidence supports, that Ms. McGinn and Ms. Waldron did not actually witness Mr. Miller signing his will. Mr. Miller made no acknowledgment of his signature on the will to either Ms. McGinn or Ms. Waldron. Likewise, Mr. Miller did not observe Ms. McGinn and Ms. Waldron sign his will as witnesses. Additionally, neither Ms. McGinn nor Ms. Waldron acknowledged to Mr. Miller that their signatures were on the will. It is also undisputed that Ms. McGinn and Ms. Waldron did not actually witness each other sign the will, nor did they acknowledge to each other that they had signed Mr. Miller's will. Despite the evidentiary lack of compliance with W.Va.Code § 41-1-3, the Casdorphs' argue that there was substantial compliance with the statute's requirements, insofar as everyone involved with the will knew what was occurring. The trial court found that there was substantial compliance with the statute because everyone knew why Mr. Miller was at the bank. The trial court further concluded there was no evidence of fraud, coercion or undue influence. Based upon the foregoing, the trial court concluded that the will should not be voided even though the technical aspects of W.Va.Code § 41-1-3 were not followed.

Our analysis begins by noting that "[t]he law favors testacy over intestacy." Syl. pt. 8, Teubert's Estate, 171 W.Va. 226, 298 S.E.2d 456 (1982). However, we clearly held in syllabus point 1 of Black v. Maxwell, 131 W.Va. 247, 46 S.E.2d 804 (1948), that "[t]estamentary intent and a written instrument, executed in the manner provided by [W.Va.Code §41-1-3], existing concurrently, are essential to the creation of a valid will." *Black* establishes that mere intent by a testator to execute a written will is insufficient. The actual execution of a written will must also comply with the dictates of W.Va.Code § 41-1-3. The Casdorphs seek to have this Court establish an exception to the technical requirements of the statute. In Wade v. Wade, 119 W.Va. 596, 195 S.E. 339 (1938), this Court permitted a narrow exception to the stringent requirements of the W.Va.Code §41-1-3....

Wade stands for the proposition that if a witness acknowledges his/her signature on a will in the physical presence of the other subscribing witness and the testator, then the will is properly witnessed within the terms of W.Va.Code §41-1-3. In this case, none of the parties signed or acknowledged their signatures in the presence of each other. This case meets neither the narrow exception of *Wade* nor the specific provisions of W.Va.Code §41-1-3.

IV. Conclusion. In view of the foregoing, we grant the relief sought in this appeal and reverse the circuit court's order granting the Casdorphs' cross-motion for summary judgment.

REVERSED.

WORKMAN, J., dissenting: The majority once more takes a very technocratic approach to the law, slavishly worshiping form over substance. In so doing, they not only create a harsh and inequitable result wholly contrary to the indisputable intent of Mr. Homer Haskell Miller, but also a rule of law that is against the spirit and intent of our whole body of law relating to the making of wills.

There is absolutely no claim of incapacity or fraud or undue influence, nor any allegation by any party that Mr. Miller did not consciously, intentionally, and with full legal capacity convey his property as specified in his will. The challenge to the will is based solely upon the allegation that Mr. Miller did not comply with the requirement of West Virginia Code 41-1-3 that the signature shall be made or the will acknowledged by the testator in the presence of at least two competent witnesses, present at the same time. The lower court, in its very thorough findings of fact, indicated that Mr. Miller had been transported to the bank by his nephew Mr. Casdorph and the nephew's wife. Mr. Miller, disabled and confined to a wheelchair, was a shareholder in the Shawnee Bank in Dunbar, West Virginia, with whom all those present were personally familiar. When Mr. Miller executed his will in the bank lobby, the typed will was placed on Ms. Pauley's desk, and Mr. Miller instructed Ms. Pauley that he wished to have his will signed, witnessed, and acknowledged. After Mr. Miller's signature had been placed upon the will with Ms. Pauley watching, Ms. Pauley walked the will over to the tellers' area in the same small lobby of the bank. Ms. Pauley explained that Mr. Miller wanted Ms. Waldron to sign the will as a witness. The same process was used to obtain the signature of Ms. McGinn. Sitting in his wheelchair, Mr. Miller did not move from Ms. Pauley's desk during the process of obtaining the witness signatures. The lower court concluded that the will was valid and that Ms. Waldron and Ms. McGinn signed and acknowledged the will "in the presence" of Mr. Miller.

In Wade v. Wade, 119 W.Va. 596, 195 S.E. 339 (1938), we addressed the validity of a will challenged for such technicalities and observed that "a narrow, rigid construction of the statute should not be allowed to stand in the way of right and justice, or be permitted to defeat a testator's disposition of his property." 119 W.Va. at 599, 195 S.E. at 340-341. We upheld the validity of the challenged will in *Wade*, noting that "each case must rest on its own facts and circumstances to which the court must look to determine whether there was a subscribing by the witnesses in the presence of the testator; that substantial compliance with the statute is all that is required...." Id. at 599, 195 S.E. at 340. A contrary result, we emphasized, "would be based on illiberal and inflexible construction of the statute, giving preeminence to letter and not to spirit, and resulting in the thwarting of the intentions of testators even under circumstances where no possibility of fraud or impropriety exists." Id. at 600, 195 S.E. at 341.

The majority's conclusion is precisely what was envisioned and forewarned in 1938 by the drafters of the *Wade* opinion: illiberal and inflexible construction, giving preeminence to the letter of the law and ignoring the spirit of the entire body of testamentary law, resulting in the thwarting of Mr. Miller's unequivocal wishes....

The majority strains the logical definition of "in the presence" as used in the operative statute. The legal concept of "presence" in this context encompasses far more than simply watching the signing of the will, which is the technical, narrow interpretation of the word apparently relied upon by the majority. Where the attestation of the will by the witnesses occurred within the same room as the testator, there is, at the very minimum, prima facie evidence that the attestation occurred within the "presence" of the testator. See 20 Michie's Jurisprudence, Wills §34 (1993); Annotation, What Constitutes the Presence of the Testator in the Witnessing of His Will, 75 A.L.R.2d 318 (1961)....

The majority embraces the line of least resistance. The easy, most convenient answer is to say that the formal, technical requirements have not been met and that the will is therefore invalid. End of inquiry. Yet that result is patently absurd. That manner of statutory application is inconsistent with the underlying purposes of the statute. Where a statute is enacted to protect and sanctify the execution of a will to prevent substitution or fraud, this Court's application of that statute should further such underlying policy, not impede it. When, in our efforts to strictly apply legislative language, we abandon common sense and reason in favor of technicalities, we are the ones committing the injustice.

I am authorized to state that Justice MAYNARD joins in this dissent.

Notes and Questions

1. *Line-of-Vision Test.* The prevailing interpretation of the "presence" requirement is that the witness must have signed within the testator's "line of vision." The line-of-vision test requires at a minimum "that the testator, without changing his position, might have seen the will being attested; it is not necessary that he actually saw it." See Newton v. Palmour, 266 S.E.2d 208 (Ga. 1980); Estate of Ross, 969 S.W.2d 398 (Tenn. Ct. App. 1997), appeal denied (1998). One court even held that the will failed because the testator, ill in bed, could only see the backs of the witnesses as they signed, not their hands or the paper on which they wrote. Presence, the court said, means "'within view'; and it follows, that the thing to be seen, or to be within the power of the party to see, is the very act of subscribing by the witness." Graham v. Graham, 32 N.C. 219 (1849). The line-of-vision test also would not be met if a witness signs a will while on the telephone with the testator who is across town in his home affirming his intent to execute a will and have the witness sign it as a witness. Will of Jefferson, 349 So. 2d 1032 (Miss. 1977). Suppose the testator is blind. Under the line-of-vision test, what result? See, e.g., Welch v. Kirby, 255 F. 451 (8th Cir. 1918) (will upheld).

2. *Conscious-Presence Test.* A respectable number of courts, and now the Restatement 3d of Property §3.1 comment p, have interpreted the "presence" requirement more liberally. They have adopted the "conscious-presence" test, which recognizes that a person can sense the presence of another without seeing the other person. "If [the witnesses] are so near at hand that they are within the range of any

of [the testator's] senses, so that he knows what is going on, the [presence] requirement has been met." See, e.g., Demaris' Estate, 110 P.2d 571 (Or. 1941).

3. *Uniform Probate Code.* Instead of codifying the conscious-presence test, the original UPC largely dispensed with the "presence" requirement. The current version of UPC §2-502 substantially carries forward this approach. The only place the "presence" requirement is retained is where testators direct someone else to sign for them. Section 2-502 of the original UPC required that person to sign the testator's name "in the testator's presence." The current version requires the person to sign the testator's name "in the testator's *conscious* presence." (emphasis added).

The UPC does not require the *witnesses* to sign in the presence of the testator or in the presence of each other. It requires the witnesses to "witness" the testator's act of signing the will or "witness" the testator's act of acknowledging either the signature or the will. Presumably, the "witnessing" requirement means that they must observe the act. See Estate of Allcott, 912 P.2d 671 (Idaho Ct. App. 1995) (concerning two witnesses who did not witness the testator signing her will, acknowledging her signature, or acknowledging her will). The requirement would not be satisfied by showing simply that the act took place within their line of sight.

In Stevens v. Casdorph, would Homer Miller's will have been validly executed under UPC §2-502? Under the harmless-error rule of UPC §2-503 or Restatement 3d of Property §3.3?

———

Competency of Attesting Witnesses. The English Statute of Frauds 1677 required the witnesses to be "credible." In this country, most non-UPC statutes require the witnesses to be either "credible" or "competent." Today in almost all states the conviction of a crime no longer makes a person an incompetent witness to a will. See Page on Wills §19.82. Mental incompetency, whether from mental deficiency, extreme intoxication, or the influence of drugs, remains a ground of disqualification as a witness. See id. §19.83. Insofar as age is concerned, a few states specifically provide by statute a minimum age, such as eighteen, for attesting witnesses. See, e.g., Ark. Code §28-25-102(a); Idaho Code §15-2-505; see also Norton v. Hinson, 989 S.W.2d 535 (Ark. 1999) (rejecting harmless-error rule and holding decedent's will invalid because attesting witness was not 18 years old as required by statute). More commonly, however, no age is specified in the statute, and the cases usually allow minors who are old enough to observe, remember, and relate the facts occurring at the execution ceremony to be valid witnesses. See, e.g., Estate of Dejmal, 289 N.W.2d 813 (Wis. 1980); Atkinson on Wills §65, at 320 (though noting that some states do keep minimum age requirements below the age of majority); Page on Wills §19.81 (thought noting that there is some authority declaring a person under age 14 prima facie incompetent to be a witness).

Interested Witnesses—Disqualified at Common Law. The Statute of Frauds 1677 was construed to disqualify a witness who was a devisee under the will and, therefore, presumably interested in sustaining the will. At that time, a person who had an interest in the outcome of litigation was disqualified from testifying as a witness because of that interest. (Parties to a lawsuit could not testify in their own behalf.) In construing the Statute of Frauds, the courts carried over this incapacity of the "testimonial" witness to the attesting witness. See Alvin E. Evans, The Competency of Testamentary Witnesses, 25 Mich. L. Rev. 238 (1927). The result was that a will wholly failed where one of the necessary attesting witnesses was also a devisee.

Purging Statutes. After a time, it came to be thought in England that the invalidity of the entire will was unnecessarily harsh on the other devisees. To remedy the situation, a statute—sometimes referred to as a "purging statute"—was passed in 1752 that provided that the disposition to the attesting witness should be void, but the witness should "be admitted as a witness to the execution of such will." 25 Geo. 2, ch. 6, §1. By eliminating the witness's interest, the witness was made "credible" and the will was saved.

In this country, as indicated above, most non-UPC statutes require attesting witnesses to be either "credible" or "competent." See Restatement 2d of Property, Statutory Note to §33.1. Whichever word is used, the devise of a beneficial interest is usually regarded as disqualifying the witness, unless there is a purging statute similar to the English statute of 1752.

Almost all non-UPC states have purging-type legislation. Most American purging statutes go on to provide a partial exception for a devisee who is also an heir of the testator or a devisee under the testator's prior will.[27] Under this partial exception, heirs or devisees who are necessary witnesses forfeit only the portions of their devises that exceed the amount they would have taken by intestacy or under prior wills if the wills in question were invalid. Suppose, for example, that G's will devised $10,000 to X. X served as an attesting witness to G's will. G's prior will, which was not witnessed by X and which was revoked by the subsequent will, devised $8,000 to X. Under the heir/devisee exception, X forfeits $2,000 of the $10,000 devise contained in G's subsequent will. Are witnesses who are devised less than what they would have taken if the wills they witnessed were invalid "interested" witnesses? See Sparhawk v. Sparhawk, 92 Mass. 155 (1865), and other cases cited in Atkinson on Wills §65, at 315 n.48.

Devise to Spouse of a Witness. The common-law disqualification of a witness who had an interest in the outcome of litigation extended also to the witness's

---

27. One court interpreted a purging statute to have the heir/devisee exception, though the statute expressed no such exception. See Manoukian v. Tomasian, 237 F.2d 211 (D.C. Cir. 1956), cert. denied, 352 U.S. 1026 (1957). (The position is now codified in D.C. Code §18-104.) But see, e.g., Rosenbloom v. Kokofsky, 369 N.E.2d 1142 (Mass. 1977) (refusing to adopt the exception).

spouse; and this same notion was applied in England to hold that the spouse of a devisee was not a credible witness to a will. Moreover, the 1752 statute did not save the will, because it invalidated a devise only to the attesting witness. The situation was remedied in the English Wills Act 1837 by invalidating a devise to the spouse of an attesting witness as well as to the witness. See 7 Wm. 4 & 1 Vict., ch. 26, §15.[28]

In this country, the purging statutes in about eight states expressly cover a devise to the spouse of an attesting witness. The spouse rule has survived constitutional challenge. See Dorfman v. Allen, 434 N.E.2d 1012 (Mass. 1982).

In the absence of an express provision in the purging statute voiding all or a portion of a devise to the spouse of an attesting witness, a number of decisions have held that spouses of devisees are not "interested" witnesses. See, e.g., Estate of Harrison, 738 P.2d 964 (Okla. Ct. App. 1987); Estate of Livingston, 999 S.W.2d 874 (Tex. App. 1999).

Time When Competency is Required. The competency or incompetency of the witness is determined when the will is executed. Thus, in Estate of Parsons, 163 Cal. Rptr. 70 (Ct. App. 1980), the court held that a witness who disclaimed her devise was not made disinterested.[29]

Uniform Probate Code—Interest of Attesting Witness Not Disqualifying. UPC §2-505 charted a new course on the treatment of interested witnesses. Under §2-505, interested witnesses are not disqualified as attesting witnesses and they do not forfeit any portion of their devises. Close to 40 percent of the states now follow this rule. See Restatement 3d of Property, Statutory Note to §3.1. The rationale of the UPC drafters was that disregarding the interest of the witnesses simplifies the law, prevents unjust results for homemade wills in which family members innocently serve as witnesses, and does not appreciably increase the opportunity for fraud or undue influence. See the comment to UPC §2-505.

---

28. The same history appears in some of our states, though with a surprising time lag. Thus Illinois and New Hampshire enacted statutes at a fairly early date modeled on the English legislation of 1752. In 1892, the New Hampshire court held that the spouse of a devisee was not a competent witness to the will, that the statute did not apply to the devise, and that the will was not therefore properly executed. See Kittredge v. Hodgman, 32 A. 158 (N.H. 1892). In 1909, the same decision was reached in Illinois. See Fearn v. Postlethwaite, 88 N.E. 1057 (Ill. 1909). In 1911, each state amended its statute so as to invalidate not only a devise to an attesting witness but also a devise to the witness's spouse.

29. California subsequently changed its rule by adopting a modified version of the UPC. Under Cal. Prob. Code §6112, "any person generally competent to be a witness may act as a witness to a will," but "the fact that the will makes a devise to a witness [who is a necessary witness] creates a presumption that the witness procured the devise by duress, menace, fraud, or undue influence."

c. Notarization as an Alternative to Attestation

Primary Statutory References: *UPC §2-502(a)(3)(B) (added in 2008)*

Estate of Hall
51 P.3d 1134 (Mont. 2002)

JUSTICE JIM REGNIER delivered the Opinion of the Court. Sandra Kay Ault appeals from the Findings of Fact, Conclusions of Law and Order of the Eighth Judicial District Court, Cascade County. We affirm.

The following issue is dispositive of this appeal: Did the District Court err in admitting the Joint Will to formal probate?

Background. James Mylen Hall ("Jim") died on October 23, 1998. At the time of his death, he was 75 years old and lived in Cascade County, Montana. His wife, Betty Lou Hall ("Betty"), and two daughters from a previous marriage, Sandra Kay Ault ("Sandra") and Charlotte Rae Hall ("Charlotte"), survived him.

Jim first executed a will on April 18, 1984 (the "Original Will"). Approximately thirteen years later, Jim and Betty's attorney, Ross Cannon, transmitted to them a draft of a joint will (the "Joint Will"). On June 4, 1997, Jim and Betty met at Cannon's office to discuss the draft. After making several changes, Jim and Betty apparently agreed on the terms of the Joint Will. Jim and Betty were prepared to execute the Joint Will once Cannon sent them a final version.

At the conclusion of the meeting, however, Jim asked Cannon if the draft could stand as a will until Cannon sent them a final version. Cannon said that it would be valid if Jim and Betty executed the draft and he notarized it. Betty testified that no one else was in the office at the time to serve as an attesting witness. Jim and Betty, therefore, proceeded to sign the Joint Will and Cannon notarized it without anyone else present.

When they returned home from the meeting, Jim apparently told Betty to tear up the Original Will, which Betty did. After Jim's death, Betty applied to informally probate the Joint Will. Sandra objected to the informal probate and requested formal probate of the Original Will.

On August 9, 2001, Judge McKittrick heard the will contest. He issued the Order admitting the Joint Will to probate on August 27, 2001. Sandra appealed....

Discussion. Did the District Court err in admitting the Joint Will to formal probate?

In contested cases, the proponent of a will must establish that the testator duly executed the will. For a will to be valid, two people typically must witness the testator signing the will and then sign the will themselves. *See* §72-2-522(1)(c), MCA [pre-2008 UPC §2-502(a)(3)]. If two individuals do not properly witness the document, §72-2-523, MCA [UPC §2-503], provides that the document may still be treated as if it had been executed under certain circumstances. One such circumstance is if the proponent of the document establishes by clear and convincing evidence that the decedent intended the document to be the decedent's will. *See* § 72-2-523, MCA; *[Estate of] Brooks,* 279 Mont. [516] at 522, 927 P.2d [1024] at 1027.

Sandra urges this Court not to use §72-2-523, MCA, "to circumvent the statute requiring two witnesses to the execution of a will." Jim and Betty's failure to use witnesses, according to Sandra, was not an innocent omission on their part. She also expresses concern that the improperly witnessed Joint Will materially altered a long-standing agreement to divide the property. She primarily argues, however, that the Joint Will should be invalid as a matter of law because no one properly witnessed it.

Sandra's numerous arguments about why the will was improperly witnessed are irrelevant to this appeal. Neither party disputes that no witnesses were present at the execution of Jim and Betty's Joint Will as required by §72-2-522, MCA. In the absence of attesting witnesses, §72-2-523, MCA, affords a means of validating a will for which the Montana Legislature expressly provides. The only question before this Court, therefore, is whether the District Court erred in concluding that Jim intended the Joint Will to be his will under §72-2-523, MCA. We conclude that the court did not err.

The District Court made several findings of fact that supported its conclusion. In particular, it noted that the Joint Will specifically revoked all previous wills and codicils made by either Jim or Betty. Furthermore, the court found that, after they had executed the Joint Will, Jim directed Betty to destroy the Original Will.

Sandra does not dispute any of the court's factual findings. She argues only that Betty testified that she and Jim had not executed the will even after they had signed it. In making this argument, she points to the following testimony:

> Question: Do you know if [Jim] gave [Sandra and Charlotte] a copy of the new will?
> Answer: I don't believe he did, no.
> Question: Do you know why?
> Answer: Well, I guess because we didn't have the completed draft without all the scribbles on it.
> Question: So he thought that will was not good yet?
> Answer: No, he was sure it was good, but he didn't give it to the girls. And we didn't give it to my son. We didn't give it to anybody.
> Question: Why?
> Answer: Because it wasn't completely finished the way Ross was going to finish it.

This testimony may suggest that Betty believed that the Joint Will was not in a final form because of "all the scribbles on it." Nevertheless, she immediately goes on to state that she believed the will was good. When asked if it were Jim's and her intent for the Joint Will to stand as a will until they executed another one, she responded, "Yes, it was." The court could reasonably interpret this testimony to mean that Jim and Betty expected the Joint Will to stand as a will until Cannon provided one in a cleaner, more final form. Sandra points to no other evidence that suggests that Jim did not intend for the Joint Will to be his will.

For these reasons, we conclude that the District Court did not err in admitting the Joint Will into final probate. Because Jim directed Betty to destroy the Original Will, we also conclude that the District Court did not err in finding that these acts were acts of revocation of the Original Will under §72-2-527, MCA.

AFFIRMED.

Lawrence W. Waggoner, The UPC Authorizes Notarized Wills
34 ACTEC J. 83, 84-86 (2008)

....The 2008 UPC amendments introduced another new concept in will execution: the notarized will. Under this concept, a will that is in writing, signed by the testator, and notarized is validly executed. Notarization is an option only, and not required. A will is still validly executed under the UPC if it is attested by two witnesses who witnessed the testator's act of signing or acknowledging the signature or the will. The rebuttable presumption that the events recited in an attestation clause occurred is now codified [see UPC §3-406], and the self-proving affidavit procedure is also still authorized [see UPC §2-504].

What is the rationale for recognizing notarized wills? The will-execution formalities are thought to serve several functions—evidentiary, cautionary (ceremonial), channeling, and protective. A notarized will would seem to serve all of these functions. The danger that a notarized will would not reliably represent the decedent's wishes seems minimal. A notarized will would almost always be upheld under the UPC's harmless-error rule. Treating a notarized will as validly executed would allow such a will to be upheld without the need to satisfy the clear and convincing standard of proof, and would be especially beneficial in states that have not enacted a harmless-error rule.

The UPC and many non-UPC states authorize holographic wills. One of the reasons for validating a holographic will is that the larger handwriting sample yields greater assurance of the identity of the maker of the document than a mere signature. In the case of a notarized will, the notarial seal serves the same function, because one of the notary's principal duties is to verify the identity of the person signing the document.[30]

---

30. See, e.g., Uniform Law on Notarial Acts §2(a) (1985), which provides: "In taking an acknowledgment, the notarial officer must determine, either from personal knowledge or from satisfactory evidence, that the person appearing before the officer and making the acknowledgment is the person whose true signature is on the instrument." See also the website of the National Notary Association <http://www.nationalnotary.org>. [The Uniform Law on Notarial Acts (1985) has since been updated and is now the Uniform Law on Notarial Acts (2010). Section 5(a) in the new Act, which

The American notary does not serve the same function as the notary in the European civil-law countries. The civil-law notary supervises the execution of an "authenticated will," in which the notary is a quasi-judicial officer who determines whether the testator has mental capacity and is free of duress and undue influence.[31] Compliance with the American execution formalities does no such thing: A validly executed will is still subject to contest on grounds of lack of capacity, undue influence, duress, fraud, or forgery.[32]

Allowing notarization as an optional method of execution can benefit practice. Cases have begun to emerge in which the supervising attorney, with the client and all witnesses present, circulates one or more estate-planning documents for signature, and fails to notice that the client or, in the case of the will, one of the witnesses has unintentionally neglected to sign one of the documents.[33] Such an omission often, but not always, arises when the attorney prepares multiple estate-planning documents—a will, a durable power of attorney, a health-care power of attorney, and perhaps a revocable trust.[34] It is common practice, and sometimes required by state law, that the documents other than the will be notarized.[35] It would reduce confusion and chance for error if all of the documents could be executed with the same formality.

---

corresponds to Section 2(a) of the old Act, is substantially the same. Ed.]

31. *See* Nigel P. Ready, Brooke's Notary (12th ed. 2009); Nicole M. Reina, Protecting Testamentary Freedom in the United States by Introducing Into Law the Concept of the French Notaire, 19 N.Y.L. Sch. J. Hum. Rts. 427 (2003); Pedro A. Malavet, The Foreign Notarial Legal Services Monopoly: Why Should We Care?, 31 J. Marshall L. Rev. 945 (1998); Aloysius A. Leopold & Gerry W. Beyer, Ante-Mortem Probate: A Viable Alternative, 43 Ark. L. Rev. 131, 150-52 (1990); John H. Langbein, Living Probate: The Conservatorship Model, 77 Mich. L. Rev. 63, 64-66 (1978).

32. See Restatement 3d of Property §§8.1 to 8.5 (2003). This is true even in Louisiana, the only American civil-law state. Although the website of the Louisiana Notary Association describes the Louisiana notary as a civil-law notary (*see* <http://www.lna.org>), and although Louisiana's notarial testament requires two competent attesting witnesses and notarization (see La. Civ. Code Ann. art. 1577), a notarial testament is still subject to contest on the grounds of lack of capacity, undue influence, duress, fraud, or forgery (see La. Civ. Code Ann. arts. 1470-1484).

33. If the testator neglects to sign, the harmless-error rule might or might not save it. Compare Estate of Denner, 2006 WL 510530 at *4 (N.J. Super. Ct. Ch. Div. Feb. 28, 2006), with Fisher v. Barnes (In re Estate of Dancer), 13 P.3d 1231 (Colo. Ct. App. 2000); Allen v. Dalk, 826 So.2d 245 (Fla. 2002) (dictum in concurring opinion). In the case of an ERISA unsigned change-of-beneficiary form, compare Davis v. Combes, 294 F.3d 931 (7th Cir. 2002), with BankAmerica Pension Plan v. McMath, 206 F.3d 821 (9th Cir. 2000).

34. See, e.g., Dalk v. Allen, 774 So.2d 787 (Fla. Dist. Ct. App. 2000); Sisson v. Park Street Baptist Church, 24 E.T.R.2d 18 (Ont. Gen. Div. 1998).

35. Under the Employee Retirement Income Security Act of 1974 (ERISA), as amended by the Retirement Equity Act of 1984 (REAct), ERISA grants a surviving spouse certain rights to ERISA-covered pension plans. The spouse can waive those rights, but the waiver must be witnessed by a plan representative or a notary public. See 29 U.S.C. §1055(c)(2)(A); I.R.C. §417(a)(2)(A).

For a variety of reasons, some individuals avoid professional advice and attempt to execute wills on their own. As long as it is clear that the decedent adopted the document as his or her will, the law has no reason to deny validity on the ground of defective execution. The harmless-error rule is one curative measure for this problem. Allowing notarization as an optional method of execution is another. The public is accustomed to thinking that a document is made "legal" by getting it notarized. To some, this conception is mistakenly but understandably carried over to executing a will.[36] A testator who goes to the trouble of going to a bank or even a package or photocopy store[37] to get a home-drawn will notarized shows as much of a deliberate purpose to make the will final and valid as asking a couple of individuals to sign as witnesses. In effect, the UPC as amended treats the notary as the equivalent of two attesting witnesses. The case law invalidating a notarized will after death arises from the decedent's ignorance of the statutory requirements, not in response to evidence raising doubt that the will truly represents the decedent's wishes.[38]

What about the possibility of wrongdoing? To be sure, someone could forge a relative's will and, using fake identification, perhaps succeed in getting it notarized. That danger is also present, however, in the case of an attested will in which, under the UPC and many non-UPC statutes, the attesting witnesses need not know the testator and need not be disinterested. [See UPC §2-505.] A fraudulent will, whether attested or notarized, would typically be challenged by the decedent's disappointed relatives. The law has long relied upon the courts to identify such cases and rule accordingly.[39]

Question

If *Estate of Hall* were decided under the current UPC, would the court need to use the harmless-error rule?

---

36. The lawyer supervising the execution ceremony in Dalk v. Allen, above p. 131, had the will notarized. Chief Justice Warren Burger had his home-drawn will witnessed and notarized.

37. A California statute provides that "[a]t least one person involved in the management of a professional photocopier shall be required to hold a current commission from the Secretary of State as a notary public in this state." Cal. Bus. & Prof. Code §22454.

38. See, e.g., Estate of Saueressig, 136 P.3d 201 (Cal. 2006); Orrell v. Cochran, 695 S.W.2d 552 (Tex. 1985).

39. Proof of fraud or forgery affecting the acknowledgment would invalidate a notarized will. See UPC §3-406.

d. The Writing Requirement (and Electronic Wills)

Primary Statutory References: *Uniform Electronic Wills Act*

The Uniform Probate Code is typical in that it requires a will to be in writing. The Restatement 3d of Property §3.1 comment i provides that:

> *i. The writing requirement....* The requirement of a writing does not require that the will be written on sheets of paper, but it does require a medium that allows the markings to be detected. A will, for example, scratched in the paint on the fender of a car would be in writing, but one "written" by waving a finger in the air would not be.

Video or Audio Recording? A videotape or audio tape recording is not recognized as a writing and cannot operate as the will itself. See Estate of Reed, 672 P.2d 829 (Wyo. 1983) (court rejected a proffered tape recording as a holographic will). Videotapes have been admitted into evidence, however, for the purpose of proving a testator's testamentary capacity and freedom from undue influence.[40] On the advantages and potential problems of video recording, see Gerry W. Beyer, Video-Recording the Will Execution Ceremony, Estate Planning Studies (April 2010), available at http://ssrn.com/abstract=1609462.

Electronic Wills. Should the law allow electronic wills? Consider the following case.

In re Estate of Castro
Ct. of Com. Pleas, Prob. Div., Lorain Co., Ohio, No. 2013ES00140 (June 19, 2013)

WALTHER, J. This matter came before the Court upon the Application to Probate Will and Application for Authority to Administer Estate filed by Miguel Castro. Hearing was held before the Court on June 18, 2013.

This case concerns the creation and introduction on an electronic will. It appears to he a case of first impression in the State of Ohio.

The facts are as follows:

In late December 2012, Javier Castro presented at Mercy Regional Medical Center in Lorain, Ohio. He was told by medical personnel that he would need a blood transfusion. For religious reasons, he declined to consent to the blood transfusion. He understood that failure to receive the blood transfusion would ultimately result in his death.

On December 30, 2012, Javier had a discussion with two of his brothers, Miguel Castro and Albie Castro, about preparing a will. Because they did not have any paper

---

40. See, e.g., Geduldig v. Posner, 743 A.2d 247 (Md. Ct. Spec. App. 1999); Estate of Burack, 607 N.Y.S.2d 711 (App. Div. 1994); Estate of Kessler, 977 P.2d 591 (Wash. Ct. App. 1999); Ind. Code §29-1-5-3(c).

or pencil, Albie suggested that the will be written on his Samsung Galaxy tablet. The Court is aware that a "tablet", is a one-piece mobile computer. Tablets typically have a touchscreen, with finger or stylus pen gestures replacing the conventional computer mouse. Albie had owned the tablet for a couple of months prior to the date in question. Albie's Samsung Galaxy tablet has a program or application called "S Note" that allows someone to "write" on the tablet with the stylus pen. The program then allows the writing to be preserved or saved exactly as the person has written it.

Miguel and Albie both testified that Javier would say what he wanted in the will and Miguel would handwrite what Javier had said using the stylus. Miguel and Albie both testified that each section would be read back to Javier and that the whole document was also read back to Javier. Testimony was had that Javier, Miguel and Albie had discussions concerning each and every paragraph in the will. Before he could sign the will, Javier was transported to the Cleveland Clinic in Cleveland, Ohio.

Miguel testified that later that same date, at the Cleveland Clinic, Javier signed the Will on the tablet in his presence. Albie also testified that Javier signed the will in his presence. Oscar DeLeon, nephew of Javier, arrived shortly thereafter and became the third witness to the will.

Oscar testified that he did not see Javier sign the will, rather Javier acknowledged in his presence that he had signed the will on the tablet.

After the will was executed, Albie retained possession of the tablet that contained the will. Albie testified that the tablet is password protected and has been in his continuous possession since December 30, 2012. Miguel and Albie testified that the will has not be altered in any way since it was signed by Javier on December 30, 2012. Both testified that the paper copy of the will presented to the Court on February 11, 2013 is an exact duplicate of the will in the tablet that was prepared and signed on December 30, 2012.

Javier, Miguel, Albie and Oscar were all over 18 years of age on December 30, 2012.

Miguel, Albie and Oscar all testified that on December 30, 2012, Javier was of sound mind and memory and under no restraint. Specifically, testimony was had that Javier knew who his family members were, who his heirs were and what was the extent of his assets.

Dina Cristin Cintron, niece of Javier, testified that Javier told her that he had signed the will on the Samsung Galaxy notebook. Similar testimony was also received from Marelisa Leverknight and. Steve Leverknight, that Javier told them he had signed the will on the tablet and that it contained his wishes.

Javier died on January 30, 2013.

On February 11, 2013, the Application to Probate Will and Application for Authority to Administer Estate were filed by Miguel Castro. On that same date, Miguel also presented a copy of a will purported to be signed by Javier. The will consists of three pages. The first two pages indicate that the will is the last will and testament of Javier Castro and has eleven numbered paragraphs. The eleven numbered paragraphs contain the naming of Miguel as Executor, dispositions of Javier's property along with instructions to the Executor. The copy of the will has a green background, with lines and black writing. It looks like a green legal pad.

The third page contains the signature of Javier Castro along with the signatures of Miguel, Albie and Oscar.

If the will were to be declared invalid, Javier's estate would pass by intestate succession under R.C. 2105.06. Javier had no lineal descendents. In this case, Benjamin Castro Sr. and Maria Castro, Javier's father and mother, respectively, would inherit his estate. Benjamin Castro Sr. and Maria Castro did not personally appear at the hearing on June 18, 2013. Instead, Attorney Deanne Robison appeared on behalf of Mr. and Mrs. Castro and stated that they did not contest the admittance of the will. Attorney Robison further stated that if the will were to be declared invalid, her clients would still distribute the assets according to Javier's wishes as stated in the will. ...

... R.C. 2107.03 provides the method for making a will. It states in part:

> Except oral wills, every will shall he in writing, but may be handwritten or typewritten. The will shall be signed at the end by the testator or by some other person in the testator's conscious presence and at the testator's express direction. The will shall be attested and subscribed in the conscious presence of the testator, by two or more competent witnesses, who saw the testator subscribe, or heard the testator acknowledge the testator's signature.

The questions for the Court are as follows:

1) Is this a "writing" and was the will "signed" and,

2) Has sufficient evidence been presented that this is the last will and testament of Javier Castro.

R.C. 2107.03 requires only that the will be in "writing". It does not require that the writing be on any particular medium. Nowhere else in Chapter 21 is "writing" defined. Although not necessarily controlling, R.C. 2913.01(F) is instructive on the definition of a "writing". It provides: "'Writing' means any computer software, document, letter, memorandum, note, paper, plate, data, film, or other thing having in or upon it any written, typewritten, or printed matter, and any token, stamp, seal, credit card, badge, trademark, label, or other symbol of value, right, privilege, license, or identification." If the Court were to apply this definition of a writing to R.C. 2107.03, the document on the Samsung Galaxy tablet would qualify as a "writing". The writing in this contains of the stylus marks made on the tablet and saved by the application software. I believe that the document prepared on December 30, 2012 on Albie's Samsung Galaxy tablet constitutes a "writing" under R.C. 2107.03. To rule otherwise would put restrictions on the meaning of "writing" that the General Assembly never stated.

The tablet application also captured the signature of Javier. The signature is a graphical image of Javier's handwritten signature that was stored by electronic means on the tablet.

Similarly, I believe that this qualifies as Javier's signature under R.C. 2107.03. Thus, the writing was "signed" at the end by Javier.

Evidence was presented by six witnesses that Javier had stated that the document he signed on the tablet were his wishes and that it was his last will and testament. Testimony was elicited from all six witnesses that Javier never subsequently expressed any desire or intention to revoke, amend or cancel the will.

As stated above, R.C. 2107.03 provides in part: "The will shall be attested and subscribed in the conscious presence of the testator, by two or more competent witnesses, who saw the testator subscribe, or heard the testator acknowledge the testator's signature." This will contained no attestation clause. Rather it merely contains the signature of the three men who testified that they witnessed the will.

R.C. 2107.24 provides:

> If a document that is executed that purports to be a will is not executed in compliance with the requirements of section 2107.03 of the Revised Code, that document shall be treated as if it had been executed as a will in compliance with the requirements of that section if a probate court, after holding a hearing, finds that the proponent of the document as a purported. will has established, by clear and convincing evidence, all of the following:
> (1) The decedent prepared the document or caused the document to be prepared.
> (2) The decedent signed the document and intended the document to constitute the decedent's will.
> (3) The decedent signed the document under division (A)(2) of this section in the conscious presence of two or more witnesses. As used in division (A)(3) of this section, "conscious presence" means within the range of any of the witnesses' senses, excluding the sense of sight or sound that is sensed by telephonic,electronic, or other distant communication.

The Court finds by clear and convincing evidence that Javier signed the will; that he intended the document to be his last will and testament; and that the will was signed in the presence of two or more witnesses. Therefore, all three subsections of R.C. 2017.24 have been proven. ...

The Court finds that the document signed on December 30, 2012 on the Samsung Galaxy tablet is the last will and testament of Javier Castro and should be admitted to probate.

IT IS SO ORDERED.

Notes and Questions

1. Did Javier Castro's will fail to comply with Ohio Revised Code §2107.03?

2. *Harmless Error as an Alternative to Electronic Will Legislation?* Another judicial decision using the harmless-error rule to validate an electronic will is In re Estate of Horton v. Jones, 925 N.W.2d 207 (Mich.App. 2018). Duane Horton committed suicide, leaving a handwritten journal entry stating in pertinent part: "My final note, my farewell is on my phone. The app should be open. If not look on evernote...." A typed electronic note was found, with Horton's full name typed at the end of the note. One paragraph in the note stated:

> Have my uncle go through my stuff, pick out the stuff that belonged to my dad and/or grandma, and take it. If there is something he doesn't want, feel free to keep it and do with it what you will. My gun (aside from the shotgun that belonged to my dad) are your's [sic] to do with what you will. Make sure my car goes to Jody if at all possible. If at all possible, make sure that my trust fund goes to my half-sister Sheila, and only her. Not my mother. All my other stuff is you're [sic] do whatever you want with. I do ask that anything you well [sic], you give 10% of the money to the church, 50% to my sister Sheila, and the remaining 40% is your's [sic] to do whatever you want with.

The trial court held that the electronic note did not satisfy the statutory requirements for will execution but nevertheless admitted the note to probate under the state's version of UPC §2-503. The appellate court affirmed.

In light of *Castro* and *Horton*, what are the advantages and disadvantages of relying on the harmless-error rule to handle electronic wills?

3. *The Advent of Electronic Will Legislation.* Nevada was the first U.S. state to enact a statute authorizing electronic wills. See Nev. Rev. Stat. §133.085. Under this statute, an electronic will must be created and maintained in an electronic record; contain the date and the electronic signature of the testator; include at least one authentication characteristic of the testator;[41] and be created and stored in such a manner that only one authoritative copy exists. The authoritative copy must be maintained and controlled by the testator or a custodian designated by the testator in the electronic will.

4. *The Uniform Electronic Wills Act.* In 2019, the Uniform Law Commission approved the Uniform Electronic Wills Act. The Act requires an electronic will to be (1) a record that is readable as text at the time of signing, (2) signed by the testator or another individual in the testator's physical presence and by the testator's direction, and (3) either attested by two witnesses or acknowledged by the testator before a notary public. See §5(a). The Act also has a harmless-error rule. See §6, bracketed as optional.

---

41. The statute defines "authentication characteristic" as a characteristic of a certain person that is unique to that person and that is capable of measurement and recognition in an electronic record as a biological aspect of or physical act performed by that person. Such a characteristic may consist of a fingerprint, a retinal scan, voice recognition, facial recognition, video recording, a digitized signature or other commercially reasonable authentication using a unique characteristic of the person.

5. *Remote Attestation or Notarization?* Must the witnesses or the notary be in the testator's physical presence, or can the attestation or notarization be done remotely, for example by webcam? The Uniform Electronic Wills Act contains bracketed language authorizing the witnesses or the notary to be in the "electronic presence" of the testator. See §5(a)(3). "Electronic presence" is defined in §2(2) as "the relationship of two or more individuals in different locations communicating in real time to the same extent as if the two individuals were physically present in the same location." What are the advantages and dangers of remote attestation or notarization?

6. *Electronic Wills, Remote Attestation, and the Choice of Law.* Can a resident of a UPC state, physically present in that state, execute an electronic will remotely, with the witnesses located in a different state that has enacted the Uniform Electronic Wills Act and its bracketed provisions on remote attestation? See UPC §2-506.

7. *Other Electronic Estate Planning Documents.* In 2022, the Uniform Law Commission approved the Uniform Electronic Estate Planning Documents Act, which authorizes the use of electronic documents and electronic signatures on "non-testamentary estate planning documents." Examples of such documents include trust instruments, powers of attorney, health-care proxies, disclaimers, or "any other record intended to carry out an individual's intent regarding property or health care while incapacitated or on death" other than a will. See §102(5).

e. Self-Proved Wills

Primary Statutory References: *UPC §§2-504, 3-406*

A majority of the states authorize wills executed with attesting witnesses to be made self-proved. See Restatement 3d of Property, Statutory Note to §3.1. A self-proved will is a will for which the testator and the witnesses have executed an affidavit before a notary public or similar officer detailing the procedures followed in the execution of the testator's will. The effect of a self-proved will varies among jurisdictions. In some jurisdictions, a self-proved will conclusively establishes that all formalities have been met. The UPC conclusively presumes that all the signature requirements have been satisfied and creates a rebuttable presumption that all other requirements have been satisfied.

A self-proved will also serves to eliminate the need for the witnesses to testify upon the filing of the will to prove its authenticity. The current UPC carries forward the self-proved will provisions found in the former versions of UPC §2-504(a) and (b) without substantive amendment. See also UPC §3-406, detailing the effect of having a self-proved will.

The genius of the idea of the self-proved will is that it was not set up in the statutes as a requirement but rather as an option. In the hands of certain courts, however, it has turned out to have unfortunate consequences. Cases have arisen in which the testator or the witnesses, through confusion or through misdirection by lawyers or others assisting the parties during the execution procedure, have only signed the self-proving affidavit and not the will itself. Most courts have upheld such wills. See, e.g., Estate of McKay, 802 P.2d 443 (Ariz. Ct. App. 1990); Will of Carter, 565 A.2d 933 (Del. 1989); Hickox v. Wilson, 496 S.E.2d 711 (Ga. 1998); Estate of Dellinger v. First Source Bank, 793 N.E.2d 1041 (Ind. 2003); Estate of Benson, 1996 WL 118367 (Minn. Ct. App. Mar. 19, 1996) (unpublished opinion); Hampton Roads Seventh-Day Adventist Church v. Stevens, 657 S.E.2d 80 (Va. 2008). But see, e.g., Estate of Chastain, 401 S.W.3d 612 (Tenn. 2012) (denying probate).

The 1990 revision to the UPC added a new subsection (c) to §2-504 to respond to this potential execution mistake by providing that, if necessary to prove a will's due execution, a signature affixed to a self-proving affidavit will be considered to be a signature affixed to the will. For further discussion of self-proving affidavits, see Bruce H. Mann, Self-Proving Affidavits and Formalism in Wills Adjudication, 63 Wash. U. L.Q. 39 (1985); Annot., 1 A.L.R. 5th 965 (1992).

Military Wills. The federal statute providing an alternative set of formalities for military wills (see p. 119) authorizes a self-proving affidavit. The use of a self-proving affidavit provides prima facie evidence that the will was executed in compliance with the formalities. See 10 U.S.C. §1044d(d).

Electronic Wills. The Uniform Electronic Wills Act contains provisions to make an electronic will self-proved. See §8 of that Act.

———

INTERNET REFERENCES. To the surprise of virtually no one, you can now order up a custom-prepared will online. See www.legalzoom.com. Other sites include www.nolo.com and uslegalwills.com.

In Unauthorized Practice of Law Committee v. Parsons Technology, Inc., 1999 WL 47235 (N.D. Tex. 1999), the court granted summary judgment in favor of the Unauthorized Practice of Law Committee of the Texas State Bar and issued an order permanently enjoining Parsons Technology, Inc. from selling and distributing its software programs, Quicken Family Lawyer Version 8.0 and Quicken Family Lawyer '99, within the state of Texas. In Unauthorized Practice of Law Committee v. Parsons Technology, Inc., 179 F.3d 956 (5th Cir. 1999), the Fifth Circuit Court of Appeals vacated the injunction and judgment in favor of the plaintiff because after the district court decision the Texas Legislature enacted an amendment to its unauthorized-practice-of-law statute providing that "the 'practice of law' does not include the design, creation, publication, distribution, display, or sale ... [of] computer software, or similar products if the products clearly and conspicuously state that the products are not a substitute for the advice of an attorney," effective immediately. H.B. 1507, 76th Leg., Reg. Sess. (Tex. 1999).

f. Statutory Wills

The term "statutory will" refers to two distinct concepts, the California Statutory Will and the Uniform Statutory Will Act. Both, however, have a feature in common, which is that they offer state-sponsored patterns of property distribution that differ from the state-directed pattern of property distribution under the intestacy law.

Both the California Statutory Will and the Uniform Statutory Will Act require that the will be executed in accordance with the state's rule for executing an attested will. The will forms supplied to the public under the California Statutory Will legislation provide explicit directions to the testator for the procedures required for valid execution. For discussion of statutory wills and consideration of ways to improve their effectiveness, see Gerry W. Beyer, Statutory Fill-In-the-Blank Will Forms, Prob. & Prop., Nov.-Dec. 1996, at 26; Gerry W. Beyer, Statutory Fill-in Will Forms—the First Decade: Theoretical Constructs and Empirical Findings, 72 Or. L. Rev. 769 (1993); Gerry W. Beyer, Statutory Will Methodologies— Incorporated Forms vs. Fill-In Forms: Rivalry or Peaceful Coexistence?, 94 Dick. L. Rev. 231 (1990); Theresa A. Bruno, The Deployment Will, 47 A.F. L. Rev. 211 (1999); Herbert T. Krimmel, A Criticism of the California Statutory Will, 19 W. St. U. L. Rev. 77 (1991).

California Statutory Will. The California statutory will is a state-sponsored will form. Cal. Prob. Code §§6200-6243. The form is available online at http://www.calbar.ca.gov/portals/0/documents/publications/Will-Form.pdf. Other states that have enacted the California Statutory Will include Maine, Michigan, and Wisconsin.

Uniform Statutory Will Act (1984). Rather than offer a state-sponsored set of will forms, the Uniform Statutory Will Act follows a different approach, called the incorporation-by-reference approach. The dispositive provisions are set forth in the statute rather than in the will. The testator adopts (incorporates by reference) the statutory pattern by executing a will that states that all or a specified portion of the testator's estate is to be disposed of in accordance with the enacting state's Uniform Statutory Will Act. Only Massachusetts and New Mexico have adopted the Uniform Statutory Will Act. The Uniform Law Commission no longer promotes it as a recommended act.

2. Wills Neither Attested nor Notarized

Primary Statutory References: *UPC §§2-502(b), 2-502(c), 2-503*

Wills valid, in at least some jurisdictions, that are neither attested nor notarized fall into two categories: holographic wills and nuncupative wills. By far, most of the litigation arises in connection with holographic wills.

Nuncupative Wills. A minority of states, by statute, allow personal property (often with a maximum limit on value), and in a few instances real property, to pass under nuncupative (oral) wills. "Soldiers in active military service" and "mariners or sailors at sea" traditionally have been able to make such wills. See Statute of Frauds 1677, 29 Car. 2, ch. 3, §§19-21, 23; Wills Act 1837, 7 Wm. 4 & 1 Vict., ch. 26, §11. Cf. Military Wills, p. 119.

Some states allow persons in their "last illness"—"one so violent that the testator has not the time, opportunity, or means to make a written will in legal form"—to make oral wills, provided certain requirements are met. The testator must: (1) be dying and know it; (2) express orally the intent to make an oral will; and (3) call upon "competent" witnesses (usually at least two) to witness that the spoken words are testator's last will. The witnesses must put into writing their testimony within a prescribed time after the act, and generally the nuncupative act must take place within the testator's home, unless the testator was "surprised" by the "last illness" while on a journey.[42]

Nothing in the Uniform Probate Code recognizes nuncupative wills.

Holographic Wills. A holographic will is one that is written entirely or materially in the handwriting of the testator. Although holographic wills were not authorized in England (unless properly attested), a majority of American jurisdictions now statutorily recognize their validity. All of the statutes require that the testator sign the will and all of them dispense with witnesses to the execution. A few, however, contain a provision concerning the number of witnesses needed to prove the testator's handwriting. A number of the statutes also require that the will be dated. A few require that the will be signed "at the end."

Under statutes such as the California provision in effect in *Estate of Black*, below, courts have sometimes validated a holographic will containing some nonholographic matter under one of two theories—the *intent theory* or the *surplusage theory*. Both theories recognize that words or marks on a sheet of paper that are not in the testator's handwriting do not necessarily disqualify the handwritten portion as a holographic will. Under the intent theory, words or marks not intended by the testator to be part of the will need not be in the testator's handwriting. Under the surplusage theory, the portions of the document in the testator's handwriting are given effect as a holographic will if they make sense as a will standing alone, without regard to the portions of the document not in the testator's handwriting. The Restatement 3d of Property §3.2 comment b adopts the surplusage theory, but also provides that a jurisdiction committed to the intent theory should adopt a presumption that any portion that is surplusage—any portion not essential for the

---

42. See Restatement 3d of Property, Statutory Note to §3.2; Atkinson on Wills §§76-78; Page on Wills §§20.13-20.31; Kevin R. Natale, Note, A Survey, Analysis, and Evaluation of Holographic Will Statutes, 17 Hofstra L. Rev. 159 (1988).

handwritten provisions to make sense as a will—was not intended by the testator to be part of the will.

Estate of Black
641 P.2d 754 (Cal. 1982)

RICHARDSON, J. Appellant Gene Ray Bouch appeals from the denial of probate of the holographic will of Frances B. Black, deceased, who died on September 6, 1977, a resident of Long Beach, California. [See p. 162 for] a copy of the instrument, which purported to leave the bulk of her estate to appellant and his family.... It may be seen from an examination that the instrument was handwritten on three pages of a partially preprinted stationer's form. It is conceded by all parties that all of the handwriting, including the date and her name, is that of the testatrix. Probate was denied because of her incorporation of some of the printed language on the stationer's form. Having found that none of the incorporated material is either material to the substance of the will or essential to its validity as a testamentary disposition, we conclude that the trial court erred in rejecting the holograph ....

Testatrix used three copies of a stationer's form, which form obviously was intended to be used for a one-page will. In appropriate blank spaces in the exordium clause at the top of each page, and in her own handwriting, testatrix inserted her signature and the place of her domicile. Other printed language on each page of the form relating to residuary gifts, the appointment of an executor, attesting witnesses and a testimonium clause generally was either stricken or ignored by testatrix. At the bottom of her third and last page, however, following all of the dispositive provisions of the will, she inserted in the appropriate spaces of the preprinted form the name and gender of her executor. And although she dated the holograph entirely in her own hand at the top of the first page of her will, she also utilized pertinent blanks to insert the date of the instrument at the end of the last page and to identify the city and state in which she executed it.

Using virtually all of the remaining space on each of the three pages, testatrix expressed in her own handwriting a detailed testamentary disposition of her estate, including specific devises and legacies to individuals and a charitable institution and a bequest of her residuary estate. As noted, no handwriting of any other person appears on any of the three pages.

Probate was denied to the holograph apparently because testatrix was seen to have "incorporated" the indicated preprinted portions of the form "as part of her will," in violation of the presumed, implied prohibition of Probate Code section 53, which provides:

> A holographic will is one that is entirely written, dated and signed by the hand of the testator himself. It is subject to no other form, and need not be witnessed. No address, date or other matter written, printed or stamped upon the document, which is not incorporated in the provisions which are in the handwriting of the decedent, shall be considered as any part of the will.

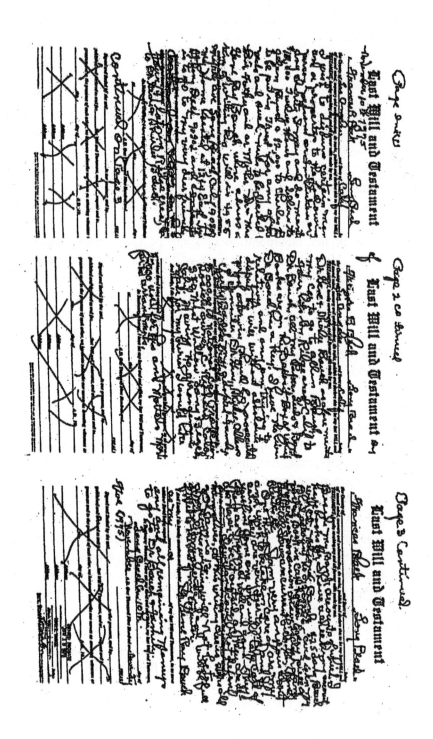

Where, as here, there is no conflict in the evidence, "the validity of the holographic instrument must be determined entirely by reference to the applicable statutes and principles of law." (Estate of Baker, 59 Cal. 2d 680, 683, 381 P.2d 913, 31 Cal. Rptr. 33 (1963)) Unanimously in *Baker*, we stressed that "The policy of the law is toward a construction favoring validity, in determining whether a will has been executed in conformity with statutory requirements." (Ibid.) Moreover, we affirmed "the tendency of both the courts and the Legislature ... toward greater liberality in accepting a writing as an holographic will...." (Ibid.) "*Substantial compliance with the statute, and not absolute precision is all that is required....*" (Id., at p. 685,....)

... In construing section 53 we bear in mind the primary legislative purpose of the holographic will statute which was identified by us in Estate of Dreyfus (1917) 175 Cal. 417, 418-419, 165 P. 941, as the prevention of "fraudulent will-making and disposition of property" by virtue of the recognized difficulty of forging an entire handwritten instrument. After reviewing the legislative history of the statute in Dreyfus we had "no doubt that (the holographic provision) owes its origin to the fact that a successful counterfeit of another's handwriting is exceedingly difficult, and that, therefore, the requirement that it should be in the testator's handwriting would afford protection against a forgery of this character." (Id., at p. 419, 165 P. 941.) ... An overly technical application of the holographic will statute to handwritten testamentary dispositions, which generally are made by persons without legal training, would seriously limit the effectiveness of the legislative decision to authorize holographic wills ....

Read literally, section 53 requires only that a holographic will be "written, dated and signed" by the hand of testatrix, and that printed matter not incorporated in the handwritten provisions not be considered as any part of the will.... Frances Black's will fully satisfies the requirements of the statute. There is no question as to the authorship or authenticity of the handwritten document before us. To reiterate: There is no handwriting on any page of the holograph which is not admittedly that of testatrix. The will is dated both at its beginning and partially at its end in the handwriting of testatrix. She wrote her name on each page and we deem this a sufficient "signature." On each of the first two pages she referred to the instrument as her "will," and on the last page she expressed the hope that "this writing" would be given legal effect. The completeness and integrity of the testamentary disposition written in her own handwriting, in our view, is itself evidence of her intent to authenticate the document as her last will and testament by affixing her signature at the top of each page. We have repeatedly said that "It is settled in California that the signature need not be located at the end (of a holographic will) but may appear in another part of the document, provided the testator wrote his name there with the intention of authenticating or executing the instrument as his will." (Estate of Bloch 39 Cal. 2d 570, 572-573, 248 P.2d 21 (1952)).

No sound purpose or policy is served by invalidating a holograph where every statutorily required element of the will is concededly expressed in the testatrix' own handwriting and through the laws of intestacy to the daughter of her predeceased husband by a former marriage—in fact, a stranger to her—thereby excluding those whom she described in the holograph as "my very dear friends" and "my adopted family" and the charity which was apparently close to her heart and which she specifically wished to benefit. The resulting frustration and defeat of her testamentary plan would be directly contrary to our *Baker* reasoning and would serve neither valid public policy nor common sense.

The order appealed from is reversed.

[The dissenting opinion of MOSK, J., is omitted.]

Notes

1. *First-Generation Holographic Will Statutes.* Section 53 of the California Probate Code was a first-generation holographic-will statute. The essential characteristic of the first-generation holographic-will statute is that it requires a holographic will to be *entirely* written, signed, and dated in the testator's handwriting. Under this type of statute, most courts have held wills like that in *Black* invalid. See, e.g., Wolcott's Estate, 180 P. 169 (Utah 1919). Contra, e.g., Fairweather v. Nord, 388 S.W.2d 122 (Ky. 1965); Estate of Teubert, 298 S.E.2d 456 (W. Va. 1982). For a collection of cases on the subject, see Annot., Requirement That Holographic Will, or its Material Provisions, Be Entirely in Testator's Handwriting, 37 A.L.R.4th 528.

2. *Second-Generation Holographic Will Statutes.* The original UPC established the second-generation holographic will statute. Original UPC §2-503 retained the signature requirement, deleted the requirement that the will be dated, and replaced the requirement that the will be "entirely" in the handwriting of the testator with the requirement that the "material provisions" be in the testator's handwriting. After *Black* was decided, the California legislature replaced its holographic will statute with a provision nearly identical to original UPC §2-503. Cal. Prob. Code §6111(a).

Second-generation holographic will statutes have generated litigation about whether nonhandwritten portions of the document can be used to establish testamentary intent.

Estate of Johnson, 630 P.2d 1039, 1040-41 (Ariz. Ct. App. 1981), was decided under original UPC §2-503. The decedent, Arnold H. Johnson, died on January 28, 1978, at the age of 79. He was survived by six children. A printed will form was presented for probate. The italicized portions shown below were in the decedent's handwriting. In part, the will reads:

THE LAST WILL AND TESTAMENT
I *Arnold H. Johnson* a resident of *Mesa Arizona of Maricopa* County, State of Arizona, being of sound and disposing mind and memory, do make, publish and declare this my last

WILL AND TESTAMENT, hereby revoking and making null and void any and all other last Wills and Testaments heretofore by me made....

Second—I give devise and bequeath to *My six living children as follows*

To John M. Johnson 1/8 of my Estate

Helen Marchese	*1/8*
Sharon Clements	*1/8*
Mirriam Jennings	*1/8*
Mary D. Korman	*1/8*
A. David Johnson	*1/8*

To W.V. Grant, Souls Harbor Church

3200 W. Davis Dallas Texas   *1/8*

To Barton Lee McLain	)
and Marie Gansels	)
Address 901 E. Broadway Phoenix	) *1/8*
~~*Az*~~ *Mesa*	)

The trial court denied Probate of this document, and on appeal the appellate court affirmed, saying in part:

> Initially it is to be noted that Arizona has adopted the [original] Uniform Probate Code, the holographic will provisions being contained in §2-503 ....
>
> The statutory requirement that the material provisions be drawn in the testator's own handwriting requires that the handwritten portion clearly express a *testamentary* intent.... In our opinion, the only words which establish this requisite testamentary intent on the part of the decedent are found in the *printed* portion of the form....

Johnson would seem no longer to be good law after the decision of Estate of Muder, 765 P.2d 997, 1000 (Ariz. 1988), reversing 751 P.2d 986 (Ariz. Ct. App. 1988). The court said:

> We hold that a testator who uses a preprinted form, and *in his own handwriting* fills in the blanks by designating his beneficiaries and apportioning his estate among them and signs it, has created a valid holographic will. Such handwritten provisions may draw testamentary context from both the printed and the handwritten language on the form. We see no need to ignore the preprinted words when the testator clearly did not, and the statute does not require us to do so.

Estate of Foxley, 575 N.W.2d 150 (Neb. 1998), was decided under a holographic will statute similar to the original UPC's holographic will statute.[43] Eileen C. Foxley

---

43. Neb. Rev. Stat. §30-2328 provides: "An instrument which purports to be testamentary in nature but does not comply with [the statute relating to attested wills] is valid as a holographic will, whether or not witnessed, if the signature, the material provisions, and an indication of the date of signing are in the handwriting of the testator and, in the absence of such indication of date, if such instrument is

executed a valid will on February 8, 1985. When she executed the will, she had six daughters and two sons. The will divided the bulk of her estate among her six daughters in equal shares. In December 1993, one of the daughters, Jane F. Jones, died and was survived by her only son, Hogan. The evidence at trial indicated that Foxley did not want her grandson, Hogan, to participate in her estate because she believed that he had abused his mother (Foxley's daughter).

Foxley died in October 1994. Upon her death, two of her daughters found a folder containing the original will and a photocopy of the will in the den of Foxley's home. Foxley had made handwritten alterations on the photocopy of the will. In its original form, Article I provided:

> My only children are William C. Foxley, Sarah F. Gross, John C. Foxley, Winifred F. Wells, Elizabeth F. Leach, Sheila F. Radford, Mary Ann Pirotte and Jane F. Jones.

Foxley had lined through "Jane F. Jones" and had written in her own handwriting: "her share to be divided to between 5 daughters. E.F. 1-7-94."

In its original form, Article III provided:

> I hereby give, devise and bequeath all of the rest of my proper [*sic*] to my six (6) daughters in equal shares.

Foxley had lined through "six" and had written "5" below "(6)."

The trial court found that Foxley had substantially complied with the requirements of a holographic codicil and admitted the photocopy and original will to probate. The Court of Appeals affirmed, finding that Foxley's signature, the material provisions, and an indication of the date of signing were in her handwriting and that she had clearly demonstrated her intentions by her spoken words, her writings, and her actions.

The Supreme Court of Nebraska reversed. The court held that the holographic codicil was invalid because the "handwritten words, standing alone, do not evidence a clear testamentary intent." The court also held that the handwritten portions, "[w]hen read on their own without reference to the original will,... cannot be understood (575 N.W.2d at 155):

> The statement "her share to be divided to between 5 daughters" does not express testamentary intent and is not clear without a handwritten reference to which daughter is to be excluded. Similarly, the line through "Jane F. Jones" is not sufficient because that line has no meaning unless read in conjunction with the typewritten names. Without the requisite testamentary intent, Foxley's handwritten words cannot be deemed material provisions.

---

the only such instrument or contains no inconsistency with any like instrument or if such date is determinable from the contents of such instrument, from extrinsic circumstances, or from any other evidence."

The result was that one-sixth of Mrs. Foxley's estate went to her grandson under the Nebraska antilapse statute.

The Reporter's Note to Restatement 3d of Property §3.2 said this of *Foxley*: "By refusing to treat the nonhandwritten portions of the original, attested will as extrinsic evidence that can be considered in determining testamentary intent and the meaning of the handwritten codicil, the court reached a manifestly unjust result."

The Uniform Law Commission has similarly criticized *Foxley* in the Comment to UPC §2-502(c).

3. *Third-Generation Holographic Will Statute.* The *Johnson* case and the lower appellate court decision in the *Muder* case prompted the drafters of the UPC to amend the original UPC's holographic will statute. Under the current version of UPC §2-502(b) and (c), only the "material portions of the document" need be in the testator's handwriting and portions of the document that are not in the testator's handwriting, along with other extrinsic evidence, can be used to establish testamentary intent.[44]

4. *Misreading of the UPC?* In treating the printed portion of a holographic will written on a preprinted will form as extrinsic evidence, have the courts misread the UPC? The Restatement 3d of Property §3.2 comment c points out that under the original and current UPC, "the nonholographic material on a preprinted will form is part of the holographic will, not extrinsic evidence."

EXTERNAL REFERENCE. Stephen Clowney, In Their Own Hand: An Analysis of Holographic Wills and Homemade Willmaking, 43 Real Prop., Tr. & Est. J. 27 (2008).

PART B. GROUNDS OF CONTEST: THE CONTESTANT'S CASE

1. Testamentary Intent

Primary Statutory Reference: *UPC §2-502(c)*

To be a will, the document must be executed with testamentary intent. At common law, extrinsic evidence can be used to establish testamentary intent if the nature of the document is ambiguous. See, e.g., Kauffman's Estate, 76 A.2d 414 (Pa. 1950). The question of the admissibility of extrinsic evidence arises most often with respect to holographic wills. UPC §2-502(c) and Restatement 3d of Property §§3.1 and 3.2

---

44. Arizona and California have enacted a similar provision regarding extrinsic evidence. Ariz. Rev. Stat. §14-2502(B); Cal. Prob. Code §6111.5.

provide that extrinsic evidence is admissible, whether or not the nature of the document is ambiguous.

Restatement 3d of Property

§3.1, Comment g. Testamentary intent. To be a will, the document must be executed with testamentary intent, i.e., the decedent must intend the document to be a will or to become operative at the decedent's death. Whether the decedent executed a document with testamentary intent is a question of fact on which evidence of intention may be considered. A clear, unambiguous expression of testamentary intent in the document raises a strong (but not irrebuttable) presumption that the document was executed with testamentary intent. The presumption is rebuttable only by clear and convincing evidence.

§3.2, Comment c. Testamentary intent—holographic wills. Holographic wills as well as attested wills must be executed with testamentary intent. See § 3.1 comment g. Testamentary intent need not be shown from the face of the will, but can be established by extrinsic evidence. Extrinsic evidence can also be used to establish the meaning of a holographic will.

Estate of Kuralt
981 P.2d 771 (Mont. 1999)

LEAPHART, J. On July 4, 1997, Charles Kuralt died in a hospital in New York City. His widow, Suzanna "Petie" Baird Kuralt, thereafter filed a petition in the state courts of New York for probate of his estate. On September 15, 1997, Petie, as the Domiciliary Foreign Personal Representative of the Estate of Charles Kuralt, secured Montana counsel ..., seeking to probate certain real and personal property owned by Mr. Kuralt in Madison County, Montana.

On September 30, 1997, Appellant Patricia Elizabeth Shannon, an intimate companion of Mr. Kuralt for nearly thirty years, ... challenged the application of Mr. Kuralt's New York will to the real and personal property in Madison County. In part, the basis for Shannon's petition was a letter, dated June 18, 1997, which she had received from Mr. Kuralt shortly before his death indicating that he intended Shannon to "inherit" 90 acres along the Big Hole River. Shannon claimed that the letter constituted a valid holographic will that entitled her to Mr. Kuralt's real property in Madison County and, therefore, that the property should not be allowed to pass under the antecedent terms of Mr. Kuralt's New York will.

The Estate ... [argued in response] that Mr. Kuralt's June 18, 1997 letter expressed, at most, only a future intent to make a will, but not a present testamentary intent to devise the Montana property to Shannon.[45]

Notwithstanding the Estate's pending motion for summary judgment, the evidentiary hearing on Shannon's petition began on March 3, 1998, with the presentation of Shannon's case in chief. Thus, on March 3 and 4, 1998, the District Court heard "extrinsic evidence" bearing upon Mr. Kuralt's intent in writing the letter of June 18, 1997. This evidence showed, *inter alia*, that Mr. Kuralt had already transferred 20 acres of his land along the Big Hole River to Shannon in 1997, and that although that transaction had been structured as a "sale," it had been in substance a gift because Mr. Kuralt had secretly supplied the $80,000 in purchase money to Shannon before the ostensible transfer took place. Further, this extrinsic evidence suggested that, prior to Mr. Kuralt's fatal illness, Mr. Kuralt and Shannon had planned to transfer the remaining 90 acres of Mr. Kuralt's property along the Big Hole River in the same manner—as a sham "sale"-gift transaction—in the fall of 1998.

...[T]he District Court ... agreed with the Estate's position and held that the June 18, 1997 letter "clearly contemplates a separate testamentary instrument not yet in existence to accomplish the transfer of the Montana property." Shannon appeals from the order of the District Court granting partial summary judgment to the Estate. We reverse the District Court and remand for trial because there are genuine issues of material fact.

Issues Presented. There are two issues on appeal:

(1.) Was the District Court correct in concluding that summary judgment was appropriate because the evidence raised no genuine issues of material fact?

(2.) Did the District Court err in concluding that the letter of June 18, 1997, was not a valid holographic will because it expressed no present testamentary intent?

Factual Background. Mr. Kuralt and Shannon first met in 1968 in Reno, Nevada, when Mr. Kuralt brought his CBS show "On the Road" to Reno to cover the creation and dedication of the "Pat Baker Park," a project which Shannon had spearheaded. During that weekend, Mr. Kuralt, a married man, invited Shannon to dinner. Thus began a protracted personal relationship between Mr. Kuralt and Shannon, lasting nearly thirty years until Mr. Kuralt's untimely death on July 4, 1997. Mr. Kuralt and Shannon took pains over the years to keep their relationship secret, and were so successful in doing so that even though his wife, Petie, knew that Mr. Kuralt owned property in Montana, she was unaware, prior to Mr. Kuralt's death, of his relationship with Shannon.

---

45. It is undisputed in this case that Mr. Kuralt's letter of June 18, 1997, meets the threshold formal requirements for a valid holographic will: Mr. Kuralt was of sound mind and sufficient age at the time that he wrote the letter, and the letter is entirely in Mr. Kuralt's handwriting and was signed by him. See §§ 72-2-521 and -522(2), MCA. Thus, the only issue in dispute here is the question of whether Mr. Kuralt possessed the requisite testamentary intent in writing the letter.

From 1968 to 1978, Shannon and Mr. Kuralt saw each other every two-to-three weeks for several days at a time. Indeed, Mr. Kuralt maintained close contact by telephone and mail, and spent a majority of his non-working time with Shannon during this ten-year period. Although Mr. Kuralt and Shannon spent less time together over the remaining twenty years of their relationship, they maintained meaningful personal and financial ties. The couple regularly vacationed together, frequently traveling around the United States, as well as Europe.

Mr. Kuralt also established close, personal relationships with Shannon's three children, acting as a surrogate father and providing them with emotional and material support which continued into their adult lives. For example, Mr. Kuralt paid the entire tuition for Shannon's eldest daughter to attend law school and for Shannon's son to attend graduate school. Over the years, in fact, Mr. Kuralt was the "primary source of support" for Shannon and her children, providing them with substantial sums of money on a regular basis—usually $5,000 to $8,000 per month....

On May 3, 1989, Mr. Kuralt executed a holographic will, which stated as follows:

May 3, 1989

In the event of my death, I bequeath to Patricia Elizabeth Shannon all my interest in land, buildings, furnishings and personal belongings on Burma Road, Twin Bridges, Montana.

Charles Kuralt

34 Bank St.

New York, N.Y. 10014

Mr. Kuralt mailed a copy of this holographic will to Shannon.

However, Mr. Kuralt thereafter executed a formal will, on May 4, 1994, in New York City. In this will, Mr. Kuralt proclaimed: "I, CHARLES KURALT, a resident of the City, County and State of New York, declare this to be my Last Will and Testament and revoke all my prior wills and codicils." With respect to real property owned by Mr. Kuralt, the will provided:

> TWO: I devise all my real property (including any condominium) which is used by me as a residence or for vacation purposes, together with the buildings and improvements thereon, if any, to my wife, PETIE, if she shall survive me.
>
> ....
>
> FIVE: All the residue and remainder of my property and estate, real and personal, of whatever nature and wherever situate, including any property not effectively disposed of by the foregoing provisions of this Will, but excluding any property over which I have any power of appointment or disposal which power I hereby expressly do not exercise (hereinafter referred to as my "residuary estate"), I dispose of as follows: [the will then proceeds to gift the entire residuary estate outright to Petie, except for a credit shelter trust

benefitting the Kuralts' two children].[46]

The will makes no specific mention of the description or location of any of the real property, in Montana or elsewhere, that had been owned by Mr. Kuralt. The beneficiaries ... are his wife, Petie, and the Kuralts' two children; neither Shannon nor her children are named as beneficiaries....

On April 9, 1997, Mr. Kuralt deeded his interest in the original 20-acre parcel with the cabin along the Big Hole River to Shannon. Although Shannon ostensibly "paid" Mr. Kuralt $80,000 for this parcel, those funds in fact came from Mr. Kuralt, who, some time earlier, had begun sending Shannon installments of money to accumulate the necessary "purchase" price. It appears that Mr. Kuralt and Shannon dressed this gift up as a sale so as to keep their long-standing personal relationship a secret. After the filing of the deed to the 20-acre parcel, Shannon sent Mr. Kuralt, at his request, a blank buy-sell real estate form. Apparently, Mr. Kuralt's intent was to deed the additional 90 acres along the Big Hole River to Shannon. At Shannon's behest, however, Mr. Kuralt and Shannon agreed that this transfer should be accomplished in much the same manner as they had previously negotiated the "sale" of the 20-acre parcel with the cabin—by Mr. Kuralt providing the purchase money so that the gift-transaction could be disguised as a sale. They further agreed that the transaction would be consummated in September of 1997 when Shannon, her son, and Mr. Kuralt had agreed to meet at the Montana cabin.

Tragically, Mr. Kuralt became suddenly ill and entered a New York hospital on June 18, 1997. On that same date, Mr. Kuralt wrote a letter to Shannon in which he expressed grave concern for his health and arguably sought to devise the remainder of the Montana property to Shannon:

June 18, 1997

Dear Pat—

Something is terribly wrong with me and they can't figure out what. After cat-scans and a variety of cardiograms, they agree it's not lung cancer or heart trouble or blood clot. So they're putting me in the hospital today to concentrate on infectious diseases. I am getting worse, barely able to get out of bed, but still have high hopes for recovery ... if only I can get a diagnosis! Curiouser and curiouser! I'll keep you informed.

I'll have the lawyer visit the hospital to be sure you inherit[47] the rest of the place in MT. if it comes to that.

I send love to you & [your youngest daughter,] Shannon. Hope things are better there!

Love,

C.

---

46. A "credit shelter trust" is a frequently used planning technique for saving transfer taxes. Ed.

47. In the original letter, Kuralt underlined the word "inherit." Ed.

Enclosed with this letter were two checks made payable to Shannon—one for $8,000 and the other for $9,000. After this letter was mailed, Mr. Kuralt did not have any formal testamentary document drawn up devising the 90-acres of Montana property to Shannon. Thus, Shannon sought to probate the letter of June 18, 1997, as a valid holographic codicil to Mr. Kuralt's formal 1994 will, a claim which the District Court rejected ....

Discussion. (1.) Was the District Court correct in concluding that summary judgment was appropriate because the evidence raised no genuine issues of material fact?...

When drawing all reasonable inferences in favor of Shannon, as the party opposing summary judgment, we conclude that the extrinsic evidence raises a genuine issue of material fact as to whether Mr. Kuralt intended to gift, rather than sell, the remaining 90 acres of his Madison County property to Shannon. The plain language of the letter of June 18, 1997, indicates, as Shannon points out, that Mr. Kuralt desired that Shannon "inherit" all of his property along the Big Hole River. While other language in the letter—"I'll have the lawyer visit the hospital ... if it comes to that"—might suggest, as the Estate argues and as the District Court concluded, that Mr. Kuralt was contemplating a separate testamentary instrument not yet in existence, it is far from certain that that is the result Mr. Kuralt intended by the letter....

We hold that, because there is a genuine issue of material fact, the District Court erred in granting judgment as a matter of law. Accordingly, we reverse the court's grant of summary judgment and remand, for trial, the factual question of whether, in light of the extrinsic evidence, Mr. Kuralt intended the letter of June 18, 1997, to effect a testamentary disposition of the 90 acres in Madison County to Shannon.

Our holding obviates the need for this Court to reach the second issue on appeal. We note, however, that the parties spend a good deal of energy arguing, with respect to the second issue on appeal, whether extrinsic evidence on testamentary intent may be considered in any will dispute or only in those cases in which the alleged testamentary document is ambiguous as to intent. While we do not express any opinion with respect to the second issue on appeal, as we do not reach that issue herein, we deem it necessary, for purposes of guiding these proceedings on remand, to address the evidentiary question of whether a court may admit extrinsic evidence only when the alleged testamentary document is ambiguous as to intent.

In arguing to the District Court that extrinsic evidence may be admitted regardless of ambiguity, Shannon relied principally upon § 72-2-522, MCA,[48] which states in relevant part: "*Intent that the document constitute the testator's will may be established by extrinsic evidence*, including, for holographic wills, portions of the

---

48. Mont. Code Ann. §72-2-522 is the same as UPC §2-502(c), except that the Montana enactment substituted the word "may" for "can." Ed.

document that are not in the testator's handwriting." Section 72-2-522(3), MCA (emphasis added). The language of that statute does not admit of any exception or qualification, but clearly permits a court to discretionarily admit extrinsic evidence bearing on testamentary intent in any will dispute. As a practical matter, a court will generally turn to extrinsic evidence when the alleged testamentary document is ambiguous as to intent; however, a court "may" admit extrinsic evidence in any will dispute where that evidence is helpful in ascertaining testamentary intent or lack thereof....

We do not disagree with the Estate's position that "[e]xtrinsic evidence is not admissible to supply testamentary intent when such intent is clearly absent on the face of the writing."... We are of the opinion, however, that Mr. Kuralt's letter of June 18, 1997, does not reveal a clear lack of testamentary intent. The letter suggests, as previously noted, that Mr. Kuralt desired Shannon to "inherit" the remainder of his property along the Big Hole River. Of course, as the parties dispute, other language in the letter raises the question of whether that expression of Mr. Kuralt's desire embodies merely an intent to perform an act in the future (i.e., prospective intent to draft a formal codicil to his Last Will), rather than a present, testamentary intent to dispose of his property (i.e., intent that the very letter constitute a valid holographic codicil to his Last Will).

However, when viewed in light of the extrinsic evidence, which shows not only the history of gift-giving by Mr. Kuralt to Shannon and her children but also that Mr. Kuralt wrote the letter in dispute under circumstances of dire health, the question of whether that letter contains the necessary *animus testandi* becomes an issue suitable for resolution by the trier of fact. Because Mr. Kuralt's letter is unclear as to testamentary intent, the District Court properly admitted extrinsic evidence bearing upon Mr. Kuralt's intent in the summary judgment proceeding. The court should, therefore, also admit all extrinsic evidence relevant to the question of Mr. Kuralt's testamentary intent when the issue goes to trial.

In sum, we reverse the District Court's grant of summary judgment to the Estate because there are genuine issues of material fact which preclude judgment as a matter of law. Accordingly, we remand for trial the question of whether Mr. Kuralt's June 18, 1997, letter evinces testamentary intent. In resolving that question at trial, the District Court shall admit, for the benefit of the trier of fact, extrinsic evidence germane to the question of testamentary intent.

REVERSED AND REMANDED.

WILLIAM E. HUNT, SR., JIM REGNIER, and JAMES C. NELSON, JJ., concur.

CHIEF JUSTICE J.A. TURNAGE dissenting.

I respectfully dissent and would affirm the District Court holding that the June 18, 1997 letter "clearly contemplates a separate testamentary instrument not yet in existence to accomplish the transfer of the Montana property."

Section 72-2-523, MCA, requires that a document or writing added upon a document can only constitute a decedent's will if the proponent establishes by clear and convincing evidence that the decedent intended the document or writing to constitute, in this case, decedent's holographic codicil.

The letter of June 18, 1997, and the record in this case does not meet the standard of clear and convincing evidence.

The June 18, 1997 letter, as set forth in the majority opinion, contains this—and only this—language relating to the question of a holographic will: "I'll have the lawyer visit the hospital to be sure you inherit the rest of the place in MT. if it comes to that." That language clearly indicates that decedent Kuralt did not intend the letter to operate as a holographic will but, rather, expressed his intent that at a future date he would have a lawyer visit him in the hospital to be sure that Patricia Shannon would, by a document thereafter to be executed, inherit "the rest of the place in MT." Such language is precatory and expresses only a desire or wish. It certainly does not constitute imperative, direct terms of bequest.

Notes and Question

1. *Result on Remand.* On remand, the trial court found that Charles Kuralt's letter of June 18, 1997, was written with testamentary intent:

> This Court's careful review of the disputed letter, when considered with extrinsic evidence, leads this Court to conclude Kuralt intended, by the very letter, to dispose of his remaining Montana property to Shannon through inheritance. Prior to Kuralt's admission to the hospital, it is clear he intended to transfer the Montana property to Shannon via gift or sham real estate transactions. However, all of that changed when Kuralt accepted the fact his medical condition was serious and undiagnosed....
>
> [The sentence] "I'll have the lawyer visit the hospital to be sure you <u>inherit</u> the rest of the place in MT. if it comes to that" (emphasis in original) ... together with extrinsic evidence specifically informs Shannon that "you inherit the rest of the place in Montana."

Estate of Kuralt, No. DP-29-1997-3609 (Mont. Dist. Ct., March 22, 2000).

In Estate of Kuralt, 15 P.3d 931, 934 (Mont. 2000), the Supreme Court of Montana affirmed the judgment of the trial court, saying:

> The record supports the District Court's finding that the June 18, 1997 letter expressed Kuralt's intent to effect a posthumous transfer of his Montana property to Shannon....
>
> The District Court focused on the last few months of Kuralt's life to find that the letter demonstrated his testamentary intent. The conveyance of the 20-acre parcel for no real consideration and extrinsic evidence that Kuralt intended to convey the remainder of the Montana property to Shannon in a similar fashion provides substantial factual support for the District Court's determination that Kuralt intended that Shannon have the rest of the Montana property.
>
> The June 18, 1997 letter expressed Kuralt's desire that Shannon inherit the remainder of the Montana property. That Kuralt wrote the letter in extremis is supported by the fact

that he died two weeks later. Although Kuralt intended to transfer the remaining land to Shannon, he was reluctant to consult a lawyer to formalize his intent because he wanted to keep their relationship secret. Finally, the use of the term "inherit" underlined by Kuralt reflected his intention to make a posthumous disposition of the property. Therefore, the District Court's findings are supported by substantial evidence and are not clearly erroneous. Accordingly, we conclude that the District Court did not err when it found that the letter dated June 18, 1997 expressed a present testamentary intent to transfer property in Madison County to Elizabeth Shannon.

2. Contrast *Kuralt* with Edmundson v. Estate of Fountain, 189 S.W.3d 427 (Ark. 2004). The Supreme Court of Arkansas affirmed a lower court decision denying probate to a handwritten document in the following form:

> Last Will Jan. 1 1997
> Kay Edmonston
> 160 acre farm & contents rema[in]ing
> 37 head of cattle at this time
> 1972 truck
> Wayne Fountain
> cattle on Wayne's Farm
> Fiddle
> Shirley Washington
> 200.00
> E.W. Fountain
> 200.00
> Nell Harris
> 200.00
> */s/ Oral W. Fountain*
> Witness.
> */s/ Ricky Smithson*
> */s/ Justin McAlister*

Kay, Wayne, Shirley, E.W., and Nell, were the decedent's five children. The court found that the handwriting was that of the decedent, but that the document was not valid as a will because it lacked testamentary intent: "[W]here testamentary intent cannot be ascertained from the face of the document, extrinsic evidence may not be admitted." Moreover, the court said that the title "Last Will" "does not cure the defective nature of this document" because the document lacks "any language indicating that Fountain intended to give or leave certain property to each of her children." The court held inadmissible the testimony of the decedent's sister, who testified that the decedent told her she had made a will, and the testimony of the attesting witnesses, who testified that they knew the document was her will.

3. *Question*. How does the approach to extrinsic evidence in UPC §2-502(c) compare to the approach in *Kuralt* or *Edmundson*? See also Uniform Electronic Wills Act §5(b).

———

Use of Extrinsic Evidence to Show Lack of Testamentary Intent: Sham Will. The question of testamentary intent can also arise in the context of an attested will. Should a court allow extrinsic evidence to show that a decedent lacked the requisite testamentary intent even though the proffered document is by all appearances a properly executed attested will? In Lister v. Smith, 3 Sw. & Tr. 282, 288-89 164 Eng. Rep. 1282, 1285 (P. Ct. 1863), the testator executed a codicil to his will, but extrinsic evidence was presented and the jury found that he never intended the codicil to be operative. His purpose in executing the codicil was to force a member of his family to give up a house that she occupied; the codicil revoked a bequest to the woman's daughter. The court held the evidence admissible, saying:

> The momentous consequences of permitting parol evidence ... to outweigh the sanction of a solemn act are obvious. It has a tendency to place all wills at the mercy of a parol story that the testator did not mean what he said. On the other hand, if the fact is plainly and conclusively made out; that the paper which appears to be the record of a testamentary act, was in reality the offspring of a jest, or the result of a contrivance to effect some collateral object, and never seriously intended as a disposition of property, it is not reasonable that the Court should turn it into an effective instrument. And such no doubt is the law. There must be the *animus testandi*.... But here I must remark that the Court ought not, I think, to permit the fact to be taken as established, unless the evidence is very cogent and conclusive.

See also Vickery v. Vickery, 170 So. 745 (Fla. 1936) (denying probate to a will, regular on its face, when the evidence showed that the decedent executed it to satisfy a requirement for initiation into a Masonic order); Fleming v. Morrison, 72 N.E. 499 (Mass. 1904) (denying probate to a will, regular on its face, when the evidence showed that the decedent had told the drafting lawyer that it was a "fake" will made for the purpose of inducing Mary Fleming, who was named as the sole devisee in the purported will, to have sex with him). Cases are collected in Annot., Admissibility of Extrinsic Evidence Upon Issue of Testamentary Intent, 21 A.L.R.2d 319.

Conditional Wills. When persons are about to enter into life-threatening situations, do the wills they execute in contemplation of this imminent danger remain valid if they survive? Would it make a difference if the life-threatening activity is described in the will as the reason for executing the will? In Eaton v. Brown, 193 U.S. 411, 414-15 (1904), the decedent, Caroline Holley, wrote a will stating, "I am going on a Journey and may not ever return. And if I do not, this is my last request." She went on to make a specific devise to a church and leave the residuary of her estate to her adopted son. She returned to her home after her trip and died several months later.

Justice Holmes delivered the opinion of the Court, ordering that the will be admitted to probate. He reasoned that,

> [s]he was thinking of the possibility of death or she would not have made a will. But that possibility at that moment took the specific shape of not returning from her journey, and so she wrote "if I do not return," before giving her last commands. We need not consider whether, if the will had nothing to qualify these words, it would be impossible to get away from the condition. But the two gifts are both of a kind that indicates an abiding and unconditioned intent,—one to a church, the other to a person whom she called her adopted son. The unlikelihood of such a condition being attached to such gifts may be considered. And then she goes on to say that all that she has is her own hard earnings and that proposes to leave it to whom she pleases. This last sentence of self-justification evidently is correlated to and imports an unqualified disposition of property; not a disposition having reference to a special state of facts by which alone it is justified and to which it is confined. If her failure to return from the journey had been the condition of her bounty,—an hypothesis which is to the last degree improbable in the absence of explanation,—it is not to be believed that when she came to explain her will she would not have explained it with reference to the extraordinary contingency upon which she made it depend instead of going on to give a reason which, on the face of it, has reference to an unconditioned gift.

Eaton exemplifies the general attitude of the courts, which is to resolve doubts in favor of validity. See, e.g., Estate of Mallett, 873 P.2d 715 (Ariz. Ct. App. 1994) (holding that a holographic will that stated that "if I should expire from this operation; I wish my wife ... should inhert [sic] everything" was not a conditional will, but instead expressed the testator's inducement for writing the will); Albright v. Albright, 901 S.W.2d 144 (Mo. Ct. App. 1995) (rejecting the allegation that the will was conditional on residuary devisee being a minor at the time of the testator's death). Decisions denying probate to wills because the stated conditions fail do occur from time to time. See, e.g., Estate of Blankenship, 518 S.E.2d 615 (S.C. Ct. App. 1999), in which a husband and wife executed a joint will. The will stated that "in the event we should die simultaneously or within a short time of each other," we devise our property to all our children except our daughter, Anne. The wife died three years after her husband, and the court held that her will was "clearly and unambiguously conditional."

2. Testamentary Capacity

Primary Statutory References: *UPC §§2-501, 5-411*

a. Age Requirement

Probate codes commonly establish a minimum age for the execution of a will. UPC §2-501 and almost all non-UPC statutes set 18 as the minimum age. See Restatement 3d of Property §8.2, Reporter's Note.

The age requirement is purely a physical requirement and, as illustrated by Estate of Teel, 483 P.2d 603 (Ariz. Ct. App. 1971), can be over-inclusive and under-inclusive as compared with its purpose of assuring that only a person of mature judgment can execute a will. In *Teel*, the decedent, Marvin Teel, was approximately 54 years of age when he executed his will, but he was developmentally disabled and possessed the mental capacity of a 10- to 12-year-old. The will was upheld.

b. Mental Requirement

"Serve the nuts. I mean, serve the guests the nuts."
– Nora Charles (Myrna Loy) in the madcap mystery The Thin Man[49]

Mental Deficiency. UPC §2-501 not only requires a person to be at least 18 years old when executing a will, but also requires the person to be "of sound mind." It is usually thought that the mental capacity needed to execute a will is not as high as that needed to make an irrevocable lifetime gift. Why not? The Restatement 3d of Property sets forth the generally accepted standards for mental capacity to make (or revoke) various types of donative transfers:

§8.1 Requirement of Mental Capacity

(a) A person must have mental capacity in order to make or revoke a donative transfer.

(b) If the donative transfer is in the form of a will, a revocable will substitute, or a revocable gift, the testator or donor must be capable of knowing and understanding in a general way the nature and extent of his or her property, the natural objects of his or her bounty, and the disposition that he or she is making of that property, and must also be capable of relating these elements to one another and forming an orderly desire regarding the disposition of the property.

(c) If the donative transfer is in the form of an irrevocable gift, the donor must have the mental capacity necessary to make or revoke a will and must also be capable of understanding the effect that the gift may have on the future financial security of the donor and of anyone who may be dependent on the donor.

The definition of mental capacity relates to mental *ability*, not actual knowledge. In Williams v. Vollman, 738 S.W.2d 849 (Ky. Ct. App. 1987), an elderly testator was held competent to execute a will at a time when his wife and one of his daughters were deceased, but he was unaware of their deaths because the news was kept from him for fear that it would weaken his resolve to live. The test, the court said, "does not require that the testator have actual knowledge of the objects of his bounty." The test only requires that he have "sufficient mind to know the objects of his bounty."

The California statute, below, is unusual in its detail.

---

49. The Thin Man (MGM 1934).

California Probate Code

§811. Deficits in mental functions.

(a) A determination that a person is of unsound mind or lacks the capacity to make a decision or do a certain act, including, but not limited to, the incapacity to contract, to make a conveyance, to marry, to make medical decisions, to execute wills, or to execute trusts, shall be supported by evidence of a deficit in at least one of the following mental functions, subject to subdivision (b), and evidence of a correlation between the deficit or deficits and the decision or acts in question:

(1) *Alertness and attention, including, but not limited to, the following*:

(A) Level of arousal or consciousness.

(B) Orientation to time, place, person, and situation.

(C) Ability to attend and concentrate.

(2) *Information processing, including, but not limited to, the following*:

(A) Short- and long-term memory, including immediate recall.

(B) Ability to understand or communicate with others, either verbally or otherwise.

(C) Recognition of familiar objects and familiar persons.

(D) Ability to understand and appreciate quantities.

(E) Ability to reason using abstract concepts.

(F) Ability to plan, organize, and carry out actions in one's own rational self-interest.

(G) Ability to reason logically.

(3) *Thought processes*. Deficits in these functions may be demonstrated by the presence of the following:

(A) Severely disorganized thinking.

(B) Hallucinations.

(C) Delusions.

(D) Uncontrollable, repetitive, or intrusive thoughts.

(4) *Ability to modulate mood and affect*. Deficits in this ability may be demonstrated by the presence of a pervasive and persistent or recurrent state of euphoria, anger, anxiety, fear, panic, depression, hopelessness or despair, helplessness, apathy or indifference, that is inappropriate in degree to the individual's circumstances.

(b) A deficit in the mental functions listed above may be considered only if the deficit, by itself or in combination with one or more other mental function deficits, significantly impairs the person's ability to understand and appreciate the consequences of his or her actions with regard to the type of act or decision in question.

(c) In determining whether a person suffers from a deficit in mental function so substantial that the person lacks the capacity to do a certain act, the court may take into consideration the frequency, severity, and duration of periods of impairment.

(d) The mere diagnosis of a mental or physical disorder shall not be sufficient in and of itself to support a determination that a person is of unsound mind or lacks the capacity to do a certain act.

Fletcher v. DeLoach
360 So.2d 316 (Ala. 1978)

TORBERT, C.J. The appellant, Mary Elizabeth DeLoach Fletcher, is the proponent of Ada B. Padgett's last will and testament, which was executed on April 15, 1970. [T]he testatrix died on October 31, 1975.... The appellees, a son and granddaughter of the testatrix, contested the probate of said will[,] and moved that the contest of the will be transferred to circuit court for a trial by jury. See sections 43-1-70, 43-1-78, Code of Alabama 1975. The probate judge ordered the transfer of the cause to circuit court for trial by jury on April 2, 1976.

The trial ... judge, after hearing the evidence, ruled that the will had been properly executed and that there was no evidence of undue influence or fraud in the case. Therefore, the only issue submitted to the jury was whether the testatrix possessed testamentary capacity at the time she executed the will of April 15, 1970. The jury found for the appellees (contestants) on the issue of testamentary capacity, and the trial judge ordered that Mrs. Fletcher was not entitled to have the will probated.

Mrs. Fletcher filed a motion for new trial ..., alleging that the testimony and the evidence failed to support the jury's verdict. The trial judge denied this motion.... Mrs. Fletcher appeals from the denial of her motion for a new trial and from the jury verdict on a similar ground—whether the contestants satisfied their burden to prove the testatrix's lack of testamentary capacity. We hold that there was evidence before the jury which would tend to show that the testatrix lacked testamentary capacity at the time she executed the will of April 15, 1970, and we therefore refuse to overturn the verdict of the jury where it has not been shown to be clearly wrong and unjust.

The testatrix must have testamentary capacity in order to execute a valid will; I.e., she must have

> mind and memory sufficient to recall and remember the property she was about to bequeath, and the objects of her bounty, and the disposition which she wished to make—to know and understand the nature and consequences of the business to be performed, and to discern the simple and obvious relation of its elements to each other....

Knox v. Knox, 95 Ala. 495, 503, 11 So. 125, 128 (1892). However, since it is presumed that every person has the capacity to make a will, the contestant has the burden to prove a lack of testamentary capacity.... Unless the contestant presents evidence that the testatrix suffered from a permanent type of insanity prior to the execution of the will (which was not shown in this case), the contestant's burden of proof is met when the jury is reasonably satisfied from the evidence that the testatrix did not have testamentary capacity at the time she executed the will.

When mental capacity is at issue, the factual inquiry must necessarily be of the broadest range.... Thus, evidence offered as to the mental and physical condition of the testatrix, either before or immediately after execution of the will, is admissible since it tends to indicate her condition when the will was signed. Likewise, testimony regarding the testatrix's "conversations, deportment, acts, and appearance" has been found to be competent on the issue of testamentary capacity. Batson v. Batson, [117 So. 10, 15 (1928)].

Also relevant to this issue is the character of the testamentary scheme; i.e., the reasonableness of the distributions made by the testatrix in her will. It is permissible for the jury to examine the will to see if its provisions are "just and reasonable, and consonant with the state of the (testatrix's) family relations," since this would reflect on her capacity to recall the natural objects of her bounty. Fountain v. Brown, [38 Ala. 72, 74 (1861)]. This court, in Councill v. Mayhew, 172 Ala. 295, 55 So. 314 (1911), has stated that:

> An *unequal* disposition of property per se raises no presumption ... of testamentary incapacity, nor is it per se unnatural; but the unequal treatment of those who ostensibly have equal claims upon the testator's bounty, or the preference of one to the exclusion of another, may under the circumstances of a particular case, be deemed *unnatural*. In such a case, an *unnatural* disposition is a fact to be ascertained and considered by the jury [on the issue of testamentary capacity].

The pecuniary condition of the testatrix's heirs, when considered in the light of an unnatural disposition of property, would also reflect on the character of the will and would therefore be admissible.

There was sufficient evidence presented in this case for the jury to find that the testatrix lacked testamentary capacity when she signed her will on April 15, 1970. The testimony indicated that the testatrix became quite depressed after her eldest son died in January of 1970, and there was also evidence presented that she was disoriented when she went to Florida with relatives both before and after April 15, 1970. The evidence indicated a noticeable decline in the testatrix's attention to her appearance and to the cleanliness of her clothing immediately prior to the execution of the will.

The fact that the 1970 will left all of the estate to Mrs. Fletcher, the testatrix's daughter, thus making no provision for her son or granddaughter, could be evidence of an unnatural disposition of her property, and could be considered by the jury on the issue of testamentary capacity. This feature of the 1970 will is significant in that the 1970 instrument revoked the testatrix's prior will of 1959, which provided for the equal disposition of her estate among her three children.

The unnatural disposition manifested by the 1970 will and the pecuniary condition of the testatrix's heirs in 1970 (which did not show a great disparity between Mrs. Fletcher's financial condition and that of the testatrix's son and granddaughter), when considered with the evidence of the mental and physical condition of the testatrix before and after the execution of the will, supports the jury's verdict that the testatrix lacked testamentary capacity. In cases of this nature, the verdict of the jury cannot be overturned unless shown to be clearly wrong and unjust. The refusal of the trial judge to grant the appellant-proponent's motion for new trial strengthens this presumption in favor of the verdict. After a careful consideration of the record in this case, we feel that the jury's verdict is not clearly wrong and unjust, and the judgment entered in favor of the contestants is hereby affirmed.

BLOODWORTH, FAULKNER, ALMON and EMBRY, JJ., concur.

Notes

1. Contrast Selb's Estate, 190 P.2d 277 (Cal. Ct. App. 1948), in which the court stated: "It has been held over and over in this state that old age, feebleness, forgetfulness, filthy personal habits, personal eccentricities, failure to recognize old friends or relatives, physical disability, absent-mindedness and mental confusion do not furnish grounds for holding that a testator lacked testamentary capacity."

2. *Malpractice/Professional Responsibility.* Is a drafting attorney liable in malpractice for failing to investigate a client's capacity to execute a will? See Martin D. Begleiter, The Gambler Breaks Even: Legal Malpractice in Complicated Estate Planning Cases, 20 Ga. St. U. L. Rev. 277, 314-24 (2003).

The American College of Trust and Estate Counsel (ACTEC) Commentaries on the Model Rules of Professional Conduct provide that a lawyer "generally should not prepare a will, trust agreement or other dispositive instrument for a client whom the lawyer reasonably believes lacks the requisite capacity.... On the other hand, because of the importance of testamentary freedom, the lawyer may properly assist clients whose testamentary capacity appears to be borderline.... In [such] cases..., the lawyer should take steps to document and preserve evidence regarding the client's testamentary capacity and the facts and circumstances involved." ACTEC Commentaries on the Model Rules of Professional Conduct 167-168 (6th ed. 2023).

For a helpful guide to determining whether a client has the requisite capacity, see Assessment of Older Adults with Diminished Capacity: A Handbook for Lawyers (2005) (http://www.apa.org/pi/aging/resources/guides/diminished-capacity.pdf).

———

The Lucid Interval. The Restatement 3d of Property sets forth the well-accepted lucid-interval principle as follows:

§8.1, comment m. Lucid interval. A person who is mentally incapacitated part of the time but who has lucid intervals during which he or she meets the standard for mental capacity ... can, in the absence of an adjudication or statute that has contrary effect, make a valid will or a valid inter vivos donative transfer, provided such will or transfer is made during a lucid interval.

In Lucero v. Lucero, 884 P.2d 527, 530, 533-34 (N.M. Ct. App. 1994), one of eight children, Patricio Lucero, who was favored in a previous will, contested the subsequent will executed by Carolina M. Lucero on the grounds of testamentary incapacity. Carolina was under a conservatorship at the time she executed the second will and was diagnosed as having senile dementia and cortical atrophy. The court nevertheless upheld the district court's finding that the decedent had sufficient capacity based on a finding that it was executed during a lucid interval.

> In spite of her medical diagnosis, Mrs. Lucero enjoyed numerous lucid intervals. In July 1988 Mrs. Lucero attended a branding at the neighboring ranch owned by her daughter .... Mrs. Lucero participated in the activities and engaged in normal conversations dealing with ranching. The testimony indicated that, although her mental status did vary, Mrs. Lucero visited with family members in person and by telephone both prior to and after the time she executed her will in August 1988, and at such times she recognized family members and engaged in appropriate conversations....
>
> Numerous courts interpreting the UPC have found that generally senile, confused, or even mentally ill testators may possess sufficient capacity to execute a will during lucid moments....
>
> The UPC specifically provides that the appointment of a temporary conservator shall not be evidence of incapacity.[50] In the present case the district court found the record and findings in Mrs. Lucero's conservatorship proceedings created a rebuttable presumption that she lacked testamentary capacity. However, the district court found that presumption of a lack of testamentary capacity was overcome by "clear and convincing evidence that the decedent knew and recognized her issue, understood and acknowledged the general nature, character and extent of her estate and specifically requested the preparation of the Last Will and Testament at issue herein." There is substantial evidence in the record to support this finding.

See also Bye v. Mattingly, 975 S.W.2d 451 (Ky. 1998) (upholding validity of will, which the decedent's housekeeper who would take under a prior will challenged, based on the lucid interval doctrine notwithstanding that the decedent had been diagnosed with Alzheimer's disease and under a conservatorship); Baun v. Estate of Kramlich, 667 N.W.2d 672 (S.D. 2003).

---

50. The court cited N.M. Stat. §45-5-408D. The current uniform law is the Uniform Guardianship, Conservatorship, and Other Protective Arrangements Act (2017), which is in the process of being incorporated into the UPC. The Act does not use the terms "capacity" or "incapacity." Rather, it calls on a court "to make particularized findings about the adult's individual needs." §301 cmt. The Act emphasizes that the standard for appointing a conservator (of property) is not the same as the standard for appointing a guardian (of the person). See §401 cmt.

Authority of Conservator to Make a Will for a Protected Person. Courts have doubted that they have the power to authorize a conservator to make, amend, or revoke a will for a protected person unless a statute expressly authorizes that power. Such a power in the court is expressly authorized in the Uniform Guardianship, Conservatorship, and Other Protective Arrangements Act (2017) §414, which also requires the conservator to give notice before exercising the court-approved power.

Insane Delusion/Monomania/Partial Insanity. An insane delusion, sometimes called monomania or partial insanity, is a belief to which the testator adheres against all evidence and reason. "The subject-matter of the insane delusion must have no foundation in fact, and must spring from a diseased condition of mind. It does not mean merely a mistaken conclusion from a given state of facts, nor a mistaken belief of a sane mind as to the existence of facts." Dibble v. Currier, 83 S.E. 949 (Ga. 1914). Accord Jackson v. Austin, 1999 WL 760974 (Ark. Ct. App. Sept. 22, 1999) (upholding will) (unpublished opinion); Breeden v. Stone, 992 P.2d 1167 (Colo. 2000) (en banc) (upholding will).

In an article written by a lawyer and a physician, the authors state that DSM-IV-TR (the standard classification of mental illnesses used by mental health professionals) defines a delusion as follows:

> A false belief based upon [an] incorrect inference about external reality that is firmly sustained despite what almost everyone else believes and despite what constitutes incontrovertible and obvious proof or evidence to the contrary, that is not ordinarily held by other members of the person's culture or subculture. When a false belief involves a value judgment, it is regarded as a delusion only when the judgment is so extreme as to defy credibility. [Adam F. Streisand & James Edward Spar, A Lawyer's Guide to Diminishing Capacity and Effective Use of Medical Experts in Contemporaneous and Retrospective Evaluations, 33 ACTEC J. 180, 187 (2008).]

An insane delusion does not necessarily affect the validity of the will. As the North Dakota court stated in Kingdon v. Sybrant, 158 N.W.2d 863 (N.D. 1968): "[I]t is not sufficient to establish that the testator was the victim of [an insane] delusion, but the evidence must go further and establish that the will itself was the product of that delusion and that the testator devised his property in a way which, except for that delusion, he would not have done."

In Estate of Koch, 259 N.W.2d 655 (N.D. 1977), Chris and Elizabeth Koch were married in 1940 and divorced in 1974. They had five children. Chris died in 1976. In the 1960s, Chris came to believe that Elizabeth "was bad," that she "never did anything," and "was running around with other men." Chris expressed the view that no one cared for him and demonstrated suicidal tendencies. Doctors recommended psychiatric treatment, but Chris only agreed to being admitted to a medical ward of the hospital for about a week. A few years later, he suffered a heart attack and was hospitalized for over a month. Following this episode, his children noticed further deterioration of his mind and came to believe that he was sick mentally as well as physically. Chris continued to accuse Elizabeth of being unfaithful and of being an alcoholic. In 1973, Chris did undergo psychiatric care at various institutions. In that same year, Chris's two eldest daughters signed a petition to have him committed. The mental health board determined that Chris should not be committed. Shortly after the hearing, Chris wrote letters to two of his children telling them never to come home again. At a subsequent divorce hearing held in 1973, three of the children testified on behalf of their mother.

In March 1974, Chris executed a will devising all of his property to his brother. Between 1974 and his death in 1976, Chris spent some time with each of his children, but efforts at reconciliation with Elizabeth failed. During this period, Chris was able to function well in society, and his neighbors thought he was mentally competent. Indeed, they had no knowledge of his mental problems and suicidal tendencies. Chris told several people that his children had sided with their mother, Elizabeth, at the commitment and divorce proceedings, and that he thought the commitment proceeding was commenced to get his money.

The court held that Chris's 1974 will was invalid, saying: "[D]ecedent's feelings toward his children were produced by beliefs held by the decedent which were unfounded in fact and ... these beliefs were the reason the decedent excluded his natural objects of bounty from his will."

Questions. Did Chris Koch hold beliefs toward his children that were unfounded in fact? How well does the law of testamentary capacity work? How might it be improved?

Jan Ellen Rein-Francovich, An Ounce of Prevention: Grounds for Upsetting Wills and Will Substitutes
20 Gonz. L. Rev. 1, 64-68 (1984/1985)

Two common situations seem to invite a will contest. One is the so-called unnatural will scenario in which the testator either treats his children unequally or disowns his nuclear family in favor of a charity or a friend. The second is the stepparent scenario where the testator favors a spouse of his later years at the expense of his children by a prior marriage. In either case, the disappointed members of the family may become convinced that the decedent would not have made such a disposition had he not been either unbalanced or unduly pressured by the favored beneficiaries. Gifts between unpopular types of unmarried cohabitants (e.g., same sex friends; older woman-younger man) seem particularly vulnerable. Wills made by infirm or mentally impaired testators also invite contest.

It is not enough for a lawyer faced with such a situation to draft a technically perfect instrument. If it reasonably appears that the testator has capacity and he cannot be dissuaded from making the suspicious disposition, the lawyer who drafts a will which strongly suggests the possibility of a contest has a duty to take special precautions to ensure that the desired donative plan will survive the testator's death....

No-contest clauses are frequently inserted to discourage will contests. Such clauses (also called *in terrorem* or forfeiture clauses) purport to deprive any legatee or devisee who brings contest from taking his gift under the will. Although this device can be effective, in many cases it is of limited utility in discouraging contests. First, a potential contestant cannot be deterred by such a proviso unless the will leaves him a substantial gift. Second, many courts refuse to enforce such clauses when it appears that the contest was brought in good faith and on probable cause. This salutary exception is made out of concern that the device might otherwise be used by unscrupulous schemers as a weapon to secure the fruits of their misdeeds from challenge by scaring off those worthy contestants who should be encouraged to dispute a truly fishy-smelling will.

Several commentators have suggested the use of will substitute arrangements, particularly the revocable inter vivos trust. The theory is that lifetime transfers are "more resistant" to capacity and undue influence challenges even though the substantive capacity standard is higher for lifetime transactions than for wills. Of course, the effectiveness of this strategy depends on the type of will substitute employed and the atmosphere in which it is arranged.... Even trust agreements have been successfully challenged, particularly those drafted by an attorney selected by one of the major remainder beneficiaries and executed by an enfeebled, dependent settlor with no business experience. This suggests that lifetime property arrangements made by vulnerable transferors fare no better than wills executed by vulnerable testators. One also suspects the converse—that wills made by strong minded and active testators fare no worse than will substitutes arranged by strong minded and active settlors—also holds true.

Even if the devices and tactics just described are employed, the lawyer will want to take the precautions traditionally relied on by the estate planning bar to protect the donative plan. These center around the preparation and execution of the will itself.

All preliminary conferences with the testator should be held out of the presence of the prospective beneficiaries. Because even irregular wills tend to stand where a rational basis for the disposition is shown, it is a good idea to build a record of the reasons for the apparently unnatural will. The testator should be warned of the irregularity of the proposed plan and asked to explain his reasons for desiring such a disposition. The true reason should always be given because a fabricated explanation made to spare the feelings of an excluded heir may arm the potential contestant with a factual basis for claiming that the disposition was the product of an insane delusion. It may sometimes be desirable to include a statement of such reasons, albeit not necessarily in the will itself. Whether in the will or in a separate document, this memorialization should always be done in measured, factual terms, "without the use of extreme or bitter language." This is because hysterical language decreases the testator's credibility and also leaves the estate vulnerable to a suit for testamentary libel....

[L]ay testimony that the testator knew what he was doing often prevails over medical evidence of incapacity. This suggests that a carefully orchestrated execution ceremony is of prime importance. Too many lawyers select as witnesses anyone who happens to be around (usually secretaries) or, worse yet, send the client off with the will to have it witnessed on his own. The will should be attested by more than the minimum number of witnesses required by statute. Some of the persons selected should be acquainted with the testator (e.g., testator's neighbor, banker or clergyman) but all should be completely disinterested. Ample time should be allowed for the witnesses to chat with the testator and to form an opinion regarding the testator's capacity on that day. Some lawyers have employed psychiatrists to render an opinion at some stage of the proceedings. This strategy may backfire by suggesting that those who were advising the testator entertained doubts as to his capacity. In special cases it may be desirable to make a videotape or sound recording of the testator's conversation with the witnesses and the execution ceremony itself. This might serve to deter disgruntled relatives from bringing a contest or, if a contest is brought anyway, might permit the triers of fact to form their own impression of the testator's mental state.

Notes

1. No-Contest Clauses. UPC §§2-517 and 3-905, and Restatement 3d of Property §8.5, provide that no-contest clauses are unenforceable if probable cause exists for instituting the proceedings.[51] For judicial approval of this approach, see, e.g., Parker v. Benoist, 160 So.3d 198 (Miss. 2015). For criticism by some scholars, see Martin D. Begleiter, Anti-Contest Clauses: When You Care Enough to Send the Final Threat, 26 Ariz. St. L.J. 629 (1994); Dawn Koren, Note, No-Contest Clauses: Settlement Offers from the Grave, 12 Prob. L.J. 173 (1995). See also Jo Ann Engelhardt, In Terrorem Inter Vivos: Terra Incognita, 26 Real Prop. Prob. & Tr. J. 535 (1991) (advocating use of in terrorem clauses in lifetime trusts); Ronald R. Volkmer, The Continuing Saga of the Status of No-Contest Clauses, Estate Planning 45-47 (March 2010).

2. Revocable Trusts. One protection against contest that revocable trusts enjoy is that, unlike wills, potential contestants who are not beneficiaries of the trust are not ordinarily required to receive notice of the trust or its impending distribution at the settlor's death.

---

51. For the meaning of probable cause, see Estate of Shumway v. Gavette, 9 P.3d 1062 (Ariz. 2000); Restatement 3d of Property §8.5 comment c. Comment c provides:

Probable cause exists when, at the time of instituting the proceeding, there was evidence that would lead a reasonable person, properly informed and advised, to conclude that there was a substantial likelihood that the challenge would be successful. A factor that bears on the existence of probable cause is whether the beneficiary relied upon the advice of independent legal counsel sought in good faith after a full disclosure of the facts. The mere fact that the person mounting the challenge was represented by counsel is not controlling, however, since the institution of a legal proceeding challenging a donative transfer normally involves representation by legal counsel.

———

Strike Suits. Will contests inevitably involve consideration of complex familial relationships and sometimes difficult medical judgments. The demanding factual circumstances surrounding will executions that arise in many of the cases make it difficult to assess how well the law achieves the goal of furthering testamentary freedom by protecting testators from themselves. The excerpt from Professor Langbein's article, below, provides additional reasons for concern. The public's interest in having open access to courts must be weighed against assuring that the judicial process is not used as a coercive weapon.

For the proposition that a tort action for malicious prosecution can be brought against a contestant and the contestant's attorney for bringing an unsuccessful will contest on several grounds, some of which but not all were brought without probable cause, see Crowley v. Katleman, 881 P.2d 1083 (Cal. 1994). The court said that the policy favoring open access to the judicial system "becomes counterproductive... when it operates to promote litigation that is groundless and motivated by malice...."

For further discussion of nonfinancial motivations of contestants and the effect of changes in family structure, divorce, and remarriage, see Jeffrey P. Rosenfeld, Will Contests: Legacies of Aging and Social Change, in Inheritance and Wealth in America 173 (Robert K. Miller, Jr. & Stephen J. McNamee eds. 1998).

John H. Langbein, Living Probate: The Conservatorship Model
77 Mich. L. Rev. 63, 64-66 (1978)

Although we do not have comparative data directly on point, the impression is widespread that [will contests alleging testamentary incapacity] occur[] more frequently in the United States than on the Continent or in England. We may point to several factors that bear upon the differential:

(1) In civil law countries, children as well as the spouse have a forced share entitlement in the estate of a parent. The disinherited child, who is the typical plaintiff in American testamentary capacity litigation, is unknown to European law. The European parent can leave his heir disgruntled with the statutory minimum, but that share will often be large enough by comparison with the potential winnings from litigation to deaden the incentive to contest.

(2) Many Americans jurisdictions permit will contests on the question of capacity to be tried to a jury, which may be more disposed to work equity for the disinherited than to obey the directions of an eccentric decedent who is in any event beyond suffering. Civil jury trial has disappeared from English estate law; it was never known on the Continent.

(3) American law is unique among Western civil procedural systems in failing to charge a losing plaintiff with the attorney fees and other costs incurred by a defendant in the course of resisting the plaintiff's unjustified claim. In testamentary

capacity litigation the American rule has the effect of requiring decedents' estates to subsidize the depredations of contestants. Put differently, the American rule diminishes the magnitude of a contestant's potential loss, which diminishes his disincentive to litigate an improbable claim.

(4) Civil law systems provide for the so-called authenticated will, which is executed before a quasi-judicial officer called the notary. This is not the only means of making a valid will in European countries, and because it is costly it is not widely used. But the notarial procedure does permit a testator who fears a post-mortem contest to generate during his lifetime and have preserved with the will evidence of exceptional quality regarding, *inter alia*, his capacity. The notary before whom the testator executes his will is not a judge; he does not adjudicate capacity. But he is a legally qualified and experienced officer of the state who is obliged to satisfy himself of the testator's capacity as a precondition for receiving or transcribing the testament. The authenticated will is, therefore, extremely difficult for contestants to set aside for want of capacity in post-mortem proceedings....

A major reason that the impact of capacity litigation in America is so difficult to measure is that most of it is directed towards provoking pretrial settlements, typically for a fraction of what the contestants could be entitled to receive if they were to defeat the will. Especially when such tactics succeed, they do not leave traces in the law reports. Thus, the odor of the strike suit hangs heavily over this field. The beneficiaries named in the will are likely to be either charitable organizations whom the testator preferred to his relatives, or else those of his relatives and friends whom he loved most and who are most likely to want to spare his reputation from a capacity suit. They are typically put to the choice of defending a lawsuit in which a skilled plaintiff's lawyer will present evidence to a jury at a public trial touching every eccentricity that might cast doubt upon the testator's condition, or compromising the suit, thereby overriding the disposition desired by the testator and rewarding the contestants for threatening to besmirch his name.

INTERNET REFERENCE. For a website advertising the services of a physician who provides "expert services and litigation support" on questions of capacity and undue influence, see http://www.bennettblummd.com.

3. Undue Influence/Duress

Restatement 3d of Property

§8.3 Undue Influence, Duress, or Fraud

(a) A donative transfer is invalid to the extent that it was procured by undue influence, duress, or fraud.

(b) A donative transfer is procured by undue influence if the wrongdoer exerted such influence over the donor that it overcame the donor's free will and caused the donor to make a donative transfer that the donor would not otherwise have made.

(c) A donative transfer is procured by duress if the wrongdoer threatened to perform or did perform a wrongful act that coerced the donor into making a donative transfer that the donor would not otherwise have made.

(d) A donative transfer is procured by fraud if the wrongdoer knowingly or recklessly made a false representation to the donor about a material fact that was intended to and did lead the donor to make a donative transfer that the donor would not otherwise have made.

———

A contestant is not likely to discover direct evidence of undue influence/duress. The contestant's case usually must be based on circumstantial evidence. When cases are such that direct evidence of the truth is unavailable, the law generally responds by establishing presumptions. It is usually accepted that a presumption of undue influence arises if the alleged wrongdoer was in a confidential relationship with the donor and there were suspicious circumstances surrounding the preparation, formulation, or execution of the donative transfer. See, e.g., Estate of Laughter, 23 So.3d 1055 (Miss. 2009). Although there is disagreement about the matter, the Restatement 3d of Property provides that the effect of the presumption is to shift to the proponent the burden of going forward with the evidence, not the burden of persuasion. See Restatement 3d of Property §8.3 comment f. Accord Krueger v. Ary, 205 P.3d 1150 (Colo. 2009). On the definitions of "confidential relationship" and "suspicious circumstances," the commentary to Restatement 3d of Property §8.3 gives the following guidance:

> [Comment] g. *Confidential relationship—fiduciary, reliant, or dominant-subservient.* Traditionally, the single term "confidential relationship" has been used to describe a relationship that gives rise to a presumption of undue influence if coupled with suspicious circumstances. When examined more closely, the term "confidential relationship" embraces three sometimes distinct relationships—fiduciary, reliant, or dominant-subservient. For purposes of clarity, this Restatement refers to these relationships separately, although any one of them can be called "confidential" and give rise to a presumption of undue influence.
>
> A fiduciary relationship is one in which the confidential relationship arises from a settled category of fiduciary obligation. Some fiduciary relationships are between the donor and a hired professional. For example, an attorney is in a fiduciary relationship with his or her client, an institutional trustee is in a fiduciary relationship with the beneficiaries of the trust, and an institutional guardian or conservator is in a fiduciary relationship with his or her ward or protected person. Other fiduciary relationships are not necessarily between the donor and a hired professional. For example, an agent under a power of attorney is in a fiduciary relationship with his or her principal, but the donor's agent under a power of attorney frequently is a close family member or trusted friend who receives no fee for acting as agent. So also an individual trustee, guardian, or conservator might be a close family member or a trusted friend who might not receive a fee for acting in that capacity.

Whether a reliant relationship exists is a question of fact. The contestant must establish that there was a relationship based on special trust and confidence, for example, that the donor was accustomed to be guided by the judgment or advice of the alleged wrongdoer or was justified in placing confidence in the belief that the alleged wrongdoer would act in the interest of the donor. Examples might include the relationship between a financial adviser and customer or between a doctor and patient.

Whether a dominant-subservient relationship exists is a question of fact. The contestant must establish that the donor was subservient to the alleged wrongdoer's dominant influence. Such a relationship might exist between a hired caregiver and an ill or feeble donor or between an adult child and an ill or feeble parent.

In a particular case, these three relationships might overlap. That is, the alleged wrongdoer might be in a fiduciary, reliant, and dominant-subservient relationship with the donor. In another case, however, the relationships might not overlap. For example, an ill or feeble donor might be suspicious of the motives of a hired caregiver, but still be in a subservient relationship with that person, feeling that "I must do what he or she says."

[Comment] h. Suspicious circumstances. The existence of a confidential relationship is not sufficient to raise a presumption of undue influence. There must also be suspicious circumstances surrounding the preparation, execution, or formulation of the donative transfer. Suspicious circumstances raise an inference of an abuse of the confidential relationship between the alleged wrongdoer and the donor.

In evaluating whether suspicious circumstances are present, all relevant factors may be considered, including: (1) the extent to which the donor was in a weakened condition, physically, mentally, or both, and therefore susceptible to undue influence; (2) the extent to which the alleged wrongdoer participated in the preparation or procurement of the will or will substitute; (3) whether the donor received independent advice from an attorney or from other competent and disinterested advisors in preparing the will or will substitute; (4) whether the will or will substitute was prepared in secrecy or in haste; (5) whether the donor's attitude toward others had changed by reason of his or her relationship with the alleged wrongdoer; (6) whether there is a decided discrepancy between a new and previous wills or will substitutes of the donor; (7) whether there was a continuity of purpose running through former wills or will substitutes indicating a settled intent in the disposition of his or her property; and (8) whether the disposition of the property is such that a reasonable person would regard it as unnatural, unjust, or unfair, for example, whether the disposition abruptly and without apparent reason disinherited a faithful and deserving family member.

Lipper v. Weslow
369 S.W.2d 698 (Tex. Ct. Civ. App. 1963)

McDonald, Chief Justice.

This is a contest of the will of Mrs. Sophie Block, on the ground of undue influence. Plaintiffs, Julian Weslow, Jr., Julia Weslow Fortson and Alice Weslow Sale, are the 3 grandchildren of Mrs. Block by a deceased son; defendants are Mrs. Block's 2 surviving children, G. Frank Lipper and Irene Lipper Dover (half brother and half sister of plaintiffs' deceased father). (The will left the estate of testatrix to her 2 children, defendants herein; and left nothing to her grandchildren by the deceased son, plaintiffs herein). Trial was to a jury, which found that Mrs. Block's will, signed by her on January 30, 1956, was procured by undue influence on the part of the proponent, Frank Lipper. The trial court entered judgment on the verdict, setting aside the will.

Defendants appeal, contending there is no evidence, or insufficient evidence, to support the finding that the will was procured by undue influence.

Testatrix was married 3 times. Of her first marriage she had one son, Julian Weslow, (who died in 1949), who was father of plaintiffs herein. After the death of her first husband testatrix married a Mr. Lipper. Defendants are the 2 children of their marriage. After Mr. Lipper's death, testatrix married Max Block. There were no children born of this marriage. Max Block died several months after the death of testatrix.

On 30 January, 1956, Sophie Block executed the will in controversy. Such will was prepared by defendant, Frank Lipper, an attorney, one of the beneficiaries of the will, and Independent Executor of the will. The will was witnessed by 2 former business associates of Mr. Block. Pertinent provisions of the will are summarized as follows:

"That I, Mrs. Sophie Block,... do make, publish and declare this my last will and testament, hereby revoking all other wills by me heretofore made."

1, 2, 3 and 4.

(Provide for payment of debts; for burial in Beth Israel Cemetery; and for minor bequests to a servant, and to an old folks' home.)

5.

(Devises the bulk of testatrix's estate to her 2 children, Mrs. Irene Lipper Dover and Frank Lipper (defendants herein), share and share alike).

6.

States that $7000 previously advanced to Mrs. Irene Lipper Dover, and $9300 previously advanced to Frank Lipper be taken into consideration in the final settlement of the estate; and cancels such amounts "that I gave or advanced to my deceased son, Julian."

7.

Appoints G. Frank Lipper Independent Executor of the estate without bond.

8.

Provides that if any legatee contests testatrix's will or the will of her husband, Max Block, that they forfeit all benefits under the will.

9.

"My son, Julian A. Weslow, died on August 6, 1949, and I want to explain why I have not provided anything under this will for my daughter-in-law, Bernice Weslow, widow of my deceased son, Julian, and her children, Julian A. Weslow, Jr., Alice Weslow Sale, and Julia Weslow Fortson, and I want to go into sufficient detail in explaining my relationship in past years with my said son's widow and his children, before mentioned, and it is my desire to record such relationship so that there will be no question as to my feelings in the matter or any thought or suggestion that my children, Irene Lipper Dover and G. Frank Lipper, or my husband, Max, may have influenced me in any manner in the execution of this will. During the time that my said son, Julian, was living, the attitude of his wife, Bernice, was at times, pleasant and friendly, but the majority of the years when my said son, Julian, was living, her attitude towards me and my husband, Max, was unfriendly and frequently months would pass when she was not in my home and I did not hear from her. When my said son, Julian, was living he was treated the same as I treated my other children; and, my husband, Max, and I gave to each of our children a home and various sums of money from time to time to help in taking care of medical expenses, other unusual expenses, as well as outright gifts. Since my said son Julian's death, his widow, Bernice, and all of her children have shown a most unfriendly and distant attitude towards me, my husband, Max, and my 2 children G. Frank Lipper and Irene Lipper Dover, which attitude I cannot reconcile as I have shown them many kindnesses since they have been members of my family, and their continued unfriendly attitude towards me, my husband, Max, and my said children has hurt me deeply in my declining years, for my life would have been much happier if they had shown a disposition to want to be a part of the family and enter into a normal family relationship that usually exists with a daughter-in-law and grandchildren and great grandchildren. I have not seen my grandson, Julian A. Weslow, Jr. in several years, neither have I heard from him. My granddaughter, Alice Weslow Sale, I have not seen in several years and I have not heard from her, but I heard a report some months ago that she was now living in California and has since married William G. Sale. My granddaughter, Julia Weslow Fortson, wife of Ben Fortson, I have not seen in several years and I was told that she had a child born to her sometime in December 1952, and I have not seen the child or heard from my said granddaughter, Julia, up to this writing, and was informed by a friend that Julia has had another child recently and is now living in Louisiana, having moved from Houston; and needless to say, my said daughter-in-law, Bernice, widow of my deceased son, Julian, I have not seen in several years as she has taken little or no interest in me or my husband, Max, since the death of my son, Julian, with the exception that Christmas a year ago, if I remember correctly, she sent some flowers, which I acknowledged, and I believe she had sent some greeting cards on some occasions prior to that time. My said daughter-in-law, Bernice Weslow, has expressed to me, on several occasions, an intense hatred for my son, G. Frank Lipper, and my daughter, Irene Lipper Dover, which I cannot understand, as my said children have always shown her and her children every consideration when possible, and have expressed a desire to be friendly with her, and them. My said children, G. Frank Lipper, and Irene Lipper Dover, have at all times been attentive to me and my husband, Max, especially during the past few years when we have not been well. I will be 82 years old in June of this year and my husband, Max, will be 80 years of age in October of this year, and we have both been in failing health for the past few years and rarely leave our home, and appreciate any attention that is given us, and my husband, Max, and I cannot understand the unfriendly and distant attitude of Bernice Weslow, widow of my said son, Julian, and his children, before mentioned."

10.

(Concerns personal belongings already disposed of.)

"In Testimony Whereof, I have hereunto signed my name....

"(S) Sophie Block" (Here follows attestation clause and signature of the 2 witnesses.)

The record reflects that the will in question was executed 22 days before testatrix died at the age of 81 years. By its terms, it disinherits the children of testatrix's son, who died in 1949. Defendant Frank Lipper gets a larger share than would have been the case if the plaintiffs were not disinherited. Defendant Lipper is a lawyer, and is admittedly the scrivener of the will. There is evidence that defendant Lipper bore malice against his dead half brother. He lived next door to testatrix, and had a key to her house. The will was not read to testatrix prior to the time she signed same, and she had no discussion with anyone at the time she executed it. There is evidence that the recitations in the will that Bernice Weslow and her children were unfriendly, and never came about testatrix, were untrue. There is also evidence that the Weslows sent testatrix greeting cards and flowers from 1946 through 1954, more times than stated in the will.

Plaintiffs offered no direct evidence pertaining to the making and execution of the will on January 30, 1956 and admittedly rely upon circumstantial evidence of undue influence to support the verdict.

All of the evidence is that testatrix was of sound mind at the time of the execution of the will; that she was a person of strong will; that she was in good physical health for her age; and that she was in fact physically active to the day of her death.

Mrs. Weslow's husband died in 1949; and after 1952 the Weslows came about testatrix less often than before. The witness Lyda Friberg, who worked at the home of testatrix from 1949 to 1952, testified that in 1952 she had a conversation with Bernice Weslow in which Mrs. Weslow told her if her children didn't get their inheritance she would "sue them through every court in the Union"; that she told testatrix about this conversation, and that testatrix told her "she would have those wills fixed up so there would be no court business", and that she wasn't going to "leave them (the Weslows), a dime." The foregoing was prior to the execution of the will on January 30, 1956.

Subsequent to the execution of the will, testatrix had a conversation with her sister, Mrs. Levy. Mrs. Levy testified:

> Q. Who did she say she was leaving her property to?
>
> A. She was leaving it to her son and daughter.
>
> Q. What else did she say about the rest of her kin, if anything?
>
> A. Well she said that Julian's children had been very ugly to her; that they never showed her any attention whatever; they married and she didn't know they were married; they had children and they didn't let her know. After Julian passed away, she never saw any of the family at all. They never came to see her.
>
> Q. Did she make any statement?
>
> A. Yes she did. When she passed away, she didn't want to leave them anything; that they did nothing for her when she was living.

Shortly before she passed away, testatrix told Mrs. Augusta Roos that she was going to leave her property to her 2 children, and further:

Q. Did she give any reason for it?

A. Yes. She said that Bernice had never been very nice to her and the children never were over."

Again, subsequent to the making of her will, testatrix talked with Effie Landry, her maid. Mrs. Landry testified:

Q. Did Mrs. Block on any occasion ever tell you anything about what was contained in her will?

A. Yes.

Q. What did she tell you about that?

A. She said she wasn't leaving the Weslow children anything.

The only question presented is whether there is any evidence of undue influence. The test of undue influence is whether such control was exercised over the mind of the testatrix as to overcome her free agency and free will and to substitute the will of another so as to cause the testatrix to do what she would not otherwise have done but for such control.

The evidence here establishes that testatrix was 81 years of age at the time of the execution of her will; that her son, defendant Lipper, who is a lawyer, wrote the will for her upon her instruction; that defendant Lipper bore malice against his deceased half brother (father of plaintiffs); that defendant Lipper lived next door to his mother and had a key to her home; that the will as written gave defendant Lipper a larger share of testatrix's estate than he would otherwise have received; that while testatrix had no discussion with anyone at the time she executed the will, she told the witness Friberg, prior to executing the will, that she was not going to leave anything to the Weslows; and subsequent to the execution of the will she told the witnesses Mrs. Levy, Mrs. Roos, and Mrs. Landry that she had not left the Weslows anything, and the reason why. The will likewise states the reasons for testatrix's action. The testatrix, although 81 years of age, was of sound mind and strong will; and in excellent physical health. There is evidence that the recitations in testatrix's will about the number of times the Weslows sent cards and flowers were incorrect, to the extent that cards and flowers were in fact sent oftener than such will recites.

The contestants established a confidential relationship, the opportunity, and perhaps a motive for undue influence by defendant Lipper. Proof of this type simply sets the stage. Contestants must go forward and prove in some fashion that the will as written resulted from the defendant Lipper substituting his mind and will for that of the testatrix. Here the will and the circumstances might raise suspicion, but it does not supply proof of the vital facts of undue influence–the substitution of a plan of testamentary disposition by another as the will of the testatrix.

All of the evidence reflected that testatrix, although 81 years of age, was of sound mind; of strong will; and in excellent physical condition. Moreover, subsequent to the execution of the will she told 3 disinterested witnesses what she had done with her property in her will, and the reason therefor. A person of sound mind has the legal right to dispose of his property as he wishes, with the burden on those attacking the disposition to prove that it was the product of undue influence.

Testatrix's will did make an unnatural disposition of her property in the sense that it preferred her 2 children over the grandchildren by a deceased son. However, the record contains an explanation from testatrix herself as to why she chose to do such. She had a right to do as she did, whether we think she was justified or not.

Plaintiffs contend that the record supports an inference that testatrix failed to receive the cards and flowers sent to her, or in the alternative that she failed to know she received same, due to conduct of defendant Lipper. Here again, defendant Lipper had the opportunity to prevent testatrix from receiving cards or flowers from the Weslows, but we think there is no evidence of probative force to support the conclusion that he in fact did such. Moreover, the will itself reflected that some cards and flowers were in fact received by the testatrix, the dispute in this particular area going to the number of times that such were sent, rather than to the fact that any were sent.

We conclude there is no evidence of probative force to support the verdict of the jury. The cause is reversed and rendered for defendants.

Notes and Question

1. *Lawyer Named as Beneficiary of the Will.* Rules of professional responsibility generally forbid lawyers from naming themselves as beneficiaries in wills that they draft. Consider, as an example, Iowa Rule 32:1.8(c), essentially the same as ABA Model Rule of Professional Conduct (MRPC) 1.8(c):

Rule 1.8: Conflict of Interest: Current Clients: Specific Rules ....

(c) A lawyer shall not solicit any substantial gift from a client, including a testamentary gift, or prepare on behalf of a client an instrument giving the lawyer or a person related to the lawyer any substantial gift unless the lawyer or other recipient of the gift is related to the client. For purposes of this paragraph, related persons include a spouse, child, sibling, grandchild, parent, grandparent or other relative or individual with whom the lawyer or the client maintains a close, familial relationship.

Comment ....

Gifts to Lawyers

[6] A lawyer may accept a gift from a client, if the transaction meets general standards of fairness. For example, a simple gift such as a present given at a holiday or as a token of appreciation is permitted. If a client offers the lawyer a more substantial gift, paragraph (c) does not prohibit the lawyer from accepting it, although such a gift may be voidable by the client under the doctrine of undue influence, which treats client gifts as presumptively fraudulent. In any event, due to concerns about overreaching and imposition on clients, a lawyer may not suggest that a substantial gift be made to the lawyer or for the lawyer's benefit, except where the lawyer is related to the client as set forth in paragraph (c).

[7] If effectuation of a substantial gift requires preparing a legal instrument such as a will or conveyance the client should have the detached advice that another lawyer can provide.

The sole exception to this rule is where the client is a relative of the donee.

In the following cases, the attorney was suspended from the practice of law for violating the state's version of MRPC Rule 1.8(c): In re Polevoy, 980 P.2d 985 (Colo. 1999); In re McCann, 669 A.2d 49 (Del. 1995); Florida Bar v. Anderson, 638 So.2d 29 (Fla. 1994); Attorney Grievance Commission of Maryland v. Brooke, 821 A.2d 414 (Md. 2003); In re Watson, 733 N.E.2d 934 (Ind. 2000); Kalled's Case, 607 A.2d 613 (N.H. 1992); Disciplinary Counsel v. Bandy, 690 N.E.2d 1280 (Ohio 1998); In re Gillingham, 896 P.2d 656 (Wash. 1995); see also In re Vitko, 519 N.W.2d 206 (Minn. 1994) (ordering that attorney with prior disciplinary violations be disbarred for violation of Minnesota's Rule 1.8(c) despite absence of actual harm to testator).

The American College of Trust and Estate Counsel (ACTEC) has issued Commentaries on the Model Rules of Professional Conduct to provide guidance to estate planning lawyers. With respect to Rule 1.8(c), the Commentaries state:

> MRPC 1.8 generally prohibits a lawyer from soliciting a substantial gift from a client, including a testamentary gift, or preparing for a client an instrument that gives the lawyer or a person related to the lawyer a substantial gift. Under MRPC 1.8(c), a lawyer may properly prepare a will or other document that includes a substantial benefit for the lawyer or a person related to the lawyer if the lawyer or other recipient is related to the client.... [However,] the lawyer should exercise special care if the proposed gift to the lawyer or a related person is disproportionately large in relation to the gift the client proposes to make to others who are equally related.

ACTEC Commentaries on the Model Rules of Professional Conduct 133 (6th ed. 2023).

2. *Question.* Did G. Frank Lipper violate the MRPC or the ACTEC Commentaries?

3. *Lawyer Named as a Fiduciary in the Will.* Comment [8] to Iowa Rule 32:1.8 (MRPC 1.8) addresses the issue of a lawyer named as the client's personal representative or trustee:

> [8] [Rule 1.8] does not prohibit a lawyer from seeking to have the lawyer or a partner or associate of the lawyer named as executor of the client's estate or to another potentially lucrative fiduciary position. Nevertheless, such appointments will be subject to the general conflict of interest provision in [Rule 1.7] when there is a significant risk that the lawyer's interest in obtaining the appointment will materially limit the lawyer's independent professional judgment in advising the client concerning the choice of an executor or other fiduciary. In obtaining the client's informed consent to the conflict, the lawyer should advise the client concerning the nature and extent of the lawyer's financial interest in the appointment, as well as the availability of alternative candidates for the position.

See also Report of the Special Study Committee on Professional Responsibility, Preparation of Wills and Trusts that Name Drafting Lawyer as Fiduciary, 28 Real

Prop. Prob. & Tr. J. 803, 808-13 (1994). The Restatement of the Law Governing Lawyers also gives little guidance in this area. Most ethics committees and the few courts that have considered the issue view the practice as permissible, although some decisions contain a strong note of caution. See N.Y. Sur. Ct. R. §1850.6 (for wills naming lawyers as fiduciaries, affidavits are required by the testators indicating they understood lawyers would be entitled to fees and the reasons for nominating the lawyers; a failure to submit an affidavit warrants a hearing to determine whether an appointment was the product of undue influence); Joseph W. deFuria, Jr., A Matter of Ethics Ignored: The Attorney-Draftsman as Testamentary Fiduciary, 36 Kan. L. Rev. 275, 285-92 (1988) (detailed discussion of the authorities). But see Discipline of Martin, 506 N.W.2d 101 (S.D. 1993) (suspending lawyer for two years for misconduct, which included among other infractions naming himself as executor and trustee when that resulted in him being able to manage his own heavy debt to the estate).

For further discussion of this issue, see Paula A. Monopoli, American Probate ch. 2 (2003); A.B.A. Section of Real Prop. Prob. & Tr. L., Developments Regarding the Professional Responsibility of the Estate Planning Lawyer: The Effect of the Model Rules of Professional Conduct, 22 Real Prop. Prob. & Tr. J. 1 (1987); Frank Coolidge, New Avenue for Lawyers Boasts Old Tradition, 128 Tr. & Est. 20 (1989); deFuria, supra; Gerald P. Johnston, An Ethical Analysis of Common Estate Planning Practices—Is Good Business Bad Ethics?, 45 Ohio St. L.J. 57, 86-101 (1984); Edward D. Spurgeon & Mary J. Ciccarello, The Lawyer in Other Fiduciary Roles: Policy and Ethical Considerations, 62 Fordham L. Rev. 1357 (1994); Robert A. Stein & Ian G. Fierstein, The Role of the Attorney in Estate Administration, 68 Minn. L. Rev. 1107 (1984).

4. *Testamentary Appointment of Lawyer.* A provision in a will directing that the drafting lawyer be hired to represent the personal representative is usually held not binding on the personal representative. Clients have a right to hire their own lawyers, and in these cases, the client is the personal representative. See, e.g., Estate of Sieben, 128 N.W.2d 443 (Wis. 1964).

Suppose, in an effort to defeat the nonbinding effect of such an appointment, lawyers use the following provision for wills they draft:

> I hereby nominate X to be my personal representative subject to the condition that X agrees to employ [the drafting lawyer] as the lawyer for my estate; if X refuses, then Y is to be my personal representative, subject to the same condition; if both X and Y refuse, then the court is to appoint a personal representative who will agree to retain [the drafting lawyer].

Should the courts enforce this provision? Compare Estate of Deardoff, 461 N.E.2d 1292 (Ohio 1984) (provision held not enforceable) with Estate of Devroy, 325 N.W.2d 345 (Wis. 1982) (provision held enforceable). Binding or not, of course, Professor Johnston points out the practical effect of the testamentary appointment.

[I]t is still likely that the specified attorney will be retained, since the [personal representative] and members of the testator's family generally want to carry out the desires of the decedent. This, too, can be deceptive when the testator had no preference in the matter, and simply acceded to the provision inserted by the drafting attorney in the belief that it was routine boilerplate.

Johnston, above, at 106. See also Jean F. Powers, Testamentary Designations of Attorneys and Other Employees, 20 Golden Gate U. L. Rev. 261 (1990).

5. *Expenses of Defending a Will Contest.* UPC §3-720 provides that a personal representative who defends or prosecutes any proceeding in good faith, whether successful or not, is entitled to receive from the estate all necessary expenses and disbursements, including reasonable attorneys' fees.

6. *Commonwealth Variation of Wills Legislation.* Several Commonwealth jurisdictions have enacted legislation authorizing the court to vary the terms of a testator's will. The British Columbia Wills Variation Act, S.B.C. 1996 c.490, provided:

> §2. Despite any law or statute to the contrary, if a testator dies leaving a will that does not, in the court's opinion, make adequate provision for the proper maintenance and support of the testator's spouse or children, the court may, in its discretion, in any action by or on behalf of the spouse or children, order that the provision that it thinks adequate, just and equitable in the circumstances be made out of the testator's estate for the spouse or children.

The current version of this statute is substantially the same: the British Columbia Wills, Estates and Succession Act, S.B.C. 2009, c. 13, §20.

In Tataryn v. Tataryn Estate, [1994] 2 S.C.R. 807 (Can. 1994), Alex and Mary Tataryn, residents of British Columbia, were married for 43 years. Mr. and Mrs. Tataryn were industrious and frugal. Through their joint efforts, they amassed an estate valued at $315,265, which was held in Mr. Tataryn's name at the time of his death. The Tataryns had two sons, John and Edward. From the time John was six years of age, his father disliked him. Over the years, Mr. Tataryn's dislike of his eldest son grew in intensity. Nevertheless, Mrs. Tataryn "stuck up" for John.

Mr. Tataryn did not wish to leave anything to John. He feared that if he left any of his estate to his wife in her own right, she would pass it on to John. He made a will leaving his wife a life estate in the matrimonial house. In addition, Mrs. Tataryn was made the beneficiary of a discretionary trust of the income from the residue of the estate, with the second son Edward as trustee. He was to apply the income in his discretion for her benefit, and was also given the power to encroach upon the capital of the estate. After her death, everything was to go to Edward. He left nothing to John. Alex Tataryn explained in cl. 4 of his will why he did this:

I HAVE PURPOSELY excluded my son, JOHN ALEXANDER TATARYN, from any share of my Estate and purposely provided for my wife by the trust as set out above for the following reason: My wife Mary and my older son John have acted in various ways to disrupt my attempts to establish harmony in the family. Since JOHN was 12 years old he has been a difficult child for me to raise. He has turned against me and totally ignored me for the last 15 years of his life. He has been abusive to the point of profanity; he has been extremely inconsiderate and has made no effort to reconcile his differences with me. He has never been open to discussion with a view to establishing ourselves in unity. My son EDWARD is respectable and I commend him for his warm attitude towards me, his honesty, and his co-operation with me.

The Supreme Court of Canada rewrote the testator's will so that Mrs. Tataryn received title to the matrimonial home, a life interest in the rental property, and the entire residue of the estate after payment of the immediate gifts to the sons. Each son received an immediate gift of $10,000. Upon the death of Mrs. Tataryn, John received a right to one-third of the rental property and Edward received a right to two-thirds. Costs were to be paid from the estate. The court grounded its decision on the following analysis:

> The testator's first obligation was to provide maintenance for Mrs. Tataryn. But his legal obligation did not stop there. The marriage was a long one. Mrs. Tataryn had worked hard and contributed much to the assets she and her husband acquired. There are no factors, such as incompetence, negating her entitlement. Under the Divorce Act and the Family Relations Act she would have been entitled to maintenance and a share in the family assets had the parties separated. At a minimum, she must be given this much upon the death of her spouse.

> I turn next to the moral claims on the testator. The highest moral claim arises from the fact that Mrs. Tataryn has outlived her husband and must be provided for in the "extra years" which fate has accorded her. This is not a legal claim in the sense of a claim which the law would have enforced during the testator's lifetime. It is, however, a moral claim of a high order on the facts of this case. Mr. and Mrs. Tataryn regarded their estate as being there to provide for their old age. It cannot be just and equitable to deprive Mrs. Tataryn of that benefit simply because her husband died first. To confine her to such sums as her son may see fit to give her, as the testator proposed, fails to recognize her deserved and desirable independence and constitutes inadequate recognition of her moral claim.

> The remaining moral claims on the testator are those of the two grown and independent sons. The testator gave nothing to one, everything to the other, subject to his provision of money to Mrs. Tataryn. The moral claims of the sons cannot be put very high. There is no evidence that either contributed much to the estate.

> The "legal claims" of Mrs. Tataryn entitle her to at least half the estate and arguably to additional maintenance. Additionally, her "moral claim" to the funds set aside for old age is strong. These claims indicate that an "adequate, just and equitable" provision for her requires giving her the bulk of the estate. The moral claim of the sons is adequately met by the immediate gift of $10,000 awarded by the trial judge to each of them and a residuary interest in a portion of the property upon the death of Mrs. Tataryn.

For a discussion of the British Columbia legislation, see Ronald Chester, Disinheritance and the American Child: An Alternative from British Columbia, 1998 Utah L. Rev. 1.

Devises to Spouses and Domestic Partners. Courts recognize that spouses exert influence over one another regarding their estate plans. The courts, however, consider a spouse of a decedent to be a natural object and, therefore, they generally refuse to find undue influence when the spouse is the primary or sole beneficiary of the decedent's will. See, e.g., Estate of Mowdy, 973 P.2d 345 (Okla. Ct. App. 1998), cert. denied (1999) (upholding will contested by decedent's children against their stepmother).

Do courts consider a domestic partner to be a natural object of the testator's bounty? For much of the twentieth century, this was a difficult issue. In Lamborn v. Kirkpatrick, 50 P.2d 542, 544 (Colo. 1935), the court invalidated the will of a childless widower that his partner wrote for him as she sat at his bedside twelve days before his death. The will, which devised over half of the decedent's estate to his partner, was contested by the decedent's sister on the ground of undue influence. Rather than using the fact of cohabitation as a reason not to find undue influence, the court used it as a basis for finding it.

> We deem it proper to attach to illicit cohabitation... [a] moral basis for requiring an affirmative showing against the existence of undue influence from one who is shown to be guilty of illicit cohabitation.... The unlawful intimacy of this meretricious relation between a testator and a beneficiary who is not related to him by blood or marriage usually assumes a clandestine form and, after the testator's death, would almost invariably render such undue influence as results therefrom incapable of proof except by the aid of the presumption....

Accord Will of Kaufmann, 205 N.E.2d 864 (N.Y. 1965) (holding invalid a will that had left the decedent's entire estate to his domestic partner).

Fortunately, society's attitudes have changed for the better toward domestic partners. See, e.g., Evans v. May, 923 S.W.2d 712, 715 (Tex. Ct. App. 1996) (declining to hold that the devisee's "30-year relationship as the decedent's 'lifemate' constitutes undue influence as a matter of law").

The Restatement 3d of Property §8.3 comment f states:

> *f. Presumption of undue influence....* [A] testator's domestic partner as defined in §6.03 of the [ALI's] Principles of the Law of Family Dissolution: Analysis and Recommendations[, discussed in Chapter 3 -Ed.] is as much a natural object of the testator's bounty as a donor's spouse. So also is any other relationship entitling the donor's unmarried partner to intestacy rights under applicable law, such as a civil union relationship or a relationship based on the partners' signed reciprocal beneficiary designation. A testator's decision to leave a substantial devise or even the bulk or all of his or her estate to his or her unmarried partner is no more a basis for invalidating a will on the ground of undue influence than a similar dispositive plan favoring the testator's surviving spouse. The dispositive plan in either case is not considered unnatural and thus to invalidate it on the ground of undue influence requires strong evidence that the will was not the result of the testator's free and independent judgment.

EXTERNAL REFERENCES. Among the many articles on undue influence are Ronald Scalise, Undue Influence and the Law of Wills: A Comparative Analysis, 19 Duke J. Comp. & Int'l L. 41 (2008); Jeffrey G. Sherman, Can Religious Influence Ever Be "Undue" Influence?, 73 Brook. L. Rev. 579 (2008); Carla Spivack, Why the Testamentary Doctrine of Undue Influence Should Be Abolished, 58 Kan. L. Rev. 245 (2010). See also Lawrence A. Frolik, The Biological Roots of the Undue Influence Doctrine: What's Love Got to Do With It?, 57 U. Pitt. L. Rev. 841 (1996); Ray D. Madoff, Unmasking Undue Influence, 81 Minn. L. Rev. 571 (1997).

4. Fraud/Forgery

As applied to wills and succession, the concept of fraud is similar to the common-law tort action for deceit. See Atkinson on Wills §56. A testator can be defrauded in a variety of ways. *Fraud in the execution* occurs when a testator is defrauded about the nature or contents of the document he or she is signing. Another type of fraud is called *fraud in the inducement*. This type of fraud occurs when a testator is intentionally misled into forming a testamentary intention that he or she would not otherwise have formed.

Latham v. Father Divine
85 N.E. 2d 168 (N.Y.Ct.App. 1949)

DESMOND, Judge.

The amended complaint herein has, in response to a motion under rule 106 of the Rules of Civil Practice, been dismissed for insufficiency. Its principal allegations are these: plaintiffs are first cousins, but not distributees, of Mary Sheldon Lyon, who died in October 1946, leaving a will, executed in 1943, which gave almost her whole estate to defendant Father Divine, leader of a religious cult, and to two corporate defendants in some way connected with that cult, and to an individual defendant (Patience Budd) said to be one of Father Divine's active followers; that said will has been, after a contest instituted by distributees, probated under a compromise agreement with the distributees, by the terms of which agreement, to which plaintiffs were not parties, the defendants just above referred to will receive a large sum from the estate; that after the making of said will, decedent on several occasions expressed 'a desire and a determination to revoke the said will, and to execute a new will by which the plaintiffs would receive a substantial portion of the estate', 'that shortly prior to the death of the deceased she had certain attorneys draft a new will in which the plaintiffs were named as legatees for a very substantial amount, totalling approximately $350,000'; that 'by reason of the said false representations, the said undue influence and the said physical force' certain of the defendants 'prevented the deceased from executing the said new Will'; that, shortly before decedent's death, decedent again expressed her determination to execute the proposed new will which favored plaintiffs, and that defendants 'thereupon conspired to kill, and did kill, the deceased by means of a surgical operation performed by a doctor engaged by the defendants without the consent or knowledge of any of the relatives of the deceased.'

Nothing is better settled than that, on such a motion as this, all the averments of the attacked pleading are taken as true. For present purposes, then, we have a case where one possessed of a large property and having already made a will leaving it to certain persons, expressed an intent to make a new testament to contain legacies to other persons, attempted to carry out that intention by having a new will drawn which contained a large legacy to those others, but was, by means of misrepresentations, undue influence, force, and indeed, murder, prevented, by the beneficiaries named in the existing will, from signing the new one. Plaintiffs say that those facts, if proven, would entitle them to a judicial declaration, which their prayer for judgment demands, that defendants, taking under the already probated will, hold what they have so taken as constructive trustees for plaintiffs, whom decedent wished to, tried to, and was kept from, benefiting.

We find in New York no decision directly answering the question as to whether or not the allegations above summarized state a case for relief in equity. But reliable texts, and cases elsewhere, answer it in the affirmative. Leading writers ... state the law of the subject to be about as it is expressed in comment i under section 184 of the Restatement of the Law of Restitution: 'Preventing revocation of will and making new will. Where a devisee or legatee under a will already executed prevents the testator by fraud, duress or undue influence from revoking the will and executing a new will in favor of another or from making a codicil, so that the testator dies leaving the original will in force, the devisee or legatee holds the property thus acquired upon a constructive trust for the intended devisee or legatee.'...

While there is no New York case decreeing a constructive trust on the exact facts alleged here, there are several decisions in this court which, we think, suggest such a result and none which forbids it.... A constructive trust will be erected whenever necessary to satisfy the demands of justice. Since a constructive trust is merely 'the formula through which the conscience of equity finds expression,' its applicability is limited only by the inventiveness of men who find new ways to enrich themselves unjustly by grasping what should not belong to them. Nothing short of true and complete justice satisfies equity, and, always assuming these allegations to be true, there seems no way of achieving total justice except by the procedure used here....

Nor do we agree that anything in the Decedent Estate Law or the Statute of Frauds stands in the way of recovery herein. This is not a proceeding to probate or establish the will which plaintiffs say testatrix was prevented from signing, nor is it an attempt to accomplish a revocation of the earlier will.... The will Mary Sheldon Lyon did sign has been probated and plaintiffs are not contesting, but proceeding on, that probate, trying to reach property which has effectively passed thereunder. Nor is this a suit to enforce an agreement to make a will or create a trust or any other promise by decedent. This complaint does not say that decedent or defendants, promised plaintiffs anything or that defendants made any promise to decedent. The story is, simply, that defendants by force and fraud, kept the testatrix from making a will in favor of plaintiffs. We cannot say, as matter of law, that no constructive trust can arise therefrom....

This suit cannot be defeated by any argument that to give plaintiffs judgment would be to annul those provisions of the Statute of Wills requiring due execution by the testator. Such a contention, if valid, would have required the dismissal in a number of the suits herein cited. The answer is in *Ahrens v. Jones*, 169 N.Y. 555, 561: "The trust does not act directly upon the will by modifying the gift, for the law requires wills to be wholly in writing; but it acts upon the gift itself as it reaches the possession of the legatee, or as soon as he is entitled to receive it. The theory is that the will has full effect by passing an absolute legacy to the legatee, and that the equity, in order to defeat fraud, raises a trust in favor of those intended to be benefited by the testator, and compels the legatee, as a trustee ex maleficio, to turn over the gift to them."

The judgment of the Appellate Division, insofar as it dismissed the complaint herein, should be reversed, and the order of Special Term affirmed, with costs in this court and in the Appellate Division.

LOUGHRAN, C. J., and CONWAY and FULD, JJ., concur with DESMOND, J.

LEWIS and DYE, JJ., dissent and vote for affirmance upon the grounds stated by VAUGHAN, J., writing for the Appellate Division.

5. *Constructive Trust and Other Remedies*

Constructive Trust as a Remedy for Wrongful Conduct. For centuries, Anglo-American courts, both law and equity, have been working out relief in wrongful-conduct situations to prevent unjust enrichment by ordering restitution of the benefit to the one at whose expense it was obtained.

The law courts developed a remedy usually called *quasi-contract*. For example, if the defendant steals the plaintiff's goods and sells them, the plaintiff, suing in quasi-contract, may recover a money judgment for the amount realized on the sale. The action developed out of the common-law action of assumpsit, which was used to recover for breach of express contract. In the theft case, there was, of course, no express contract by which the defendant was to pay over the proceeds to the plaintiff, but the court treated the situation as though there were and allowed the plaintiff to make use of assumpsit. Although the history is somewhat more complicated than this, the process is illustrative of a tendency of lawyers (as well as other people) to make use of the familiar instead of developing a new set of ideas and techniques to meet the demands of the situations facing them. This development occurred in the law courts, and quasi-contract remains today a strictly legal remedy, seeking a money judgment.

While the law judges were working out quasi-contract, Chancery was developing its own remedies to prevent unjust enrichment, the principal one being *constructive trust*. If the defendant steals the plaintiff's money and uses the money to buy land, the plaintiff may sue in equity for a decree ordering the defendant to transfer title to the land to the plaintiff. The equity court treats the defendant as though the defendant were a trustee of the land for the benefit of the plaintiff. There is, of course, no express trust any more than there was an express contract in the first case.[52] The equity judge is giving relief to prevent unjust enrichment and is making use of a familiar idea for this purpose by "constructing" a trust. Unlike the law court's judgment in quasi-contract, this is not a money judgment but rather a judgment for specific restitution, requiring, that is, the transfer of title to a specific asset. The remedy is wholly in the province of equity.

If a wrongful act prevents a testator from making a will or a particular devise, courts have held that constructive trust relief is available to protect "disappointed hopes and unrealized expectations." See, e.g., Latham v. Father Divine, above.

A claim for constructive relief based on the wrongful acts can be asserted against innocent beneficiaries. The case of Pope v. Garrett, 211 S.W.2d 559, 561-62 (Tex. 1948), is typical on this point. Some days before her death, Carrie Simons requested a friend and neighbor, Thomas Green, to prepare a will for her, leaving all of her property to Claytonia Garrett. Simons and Garrett were unrelated. Green prepared the will as requested and read it to Simons. Simons then declared it to be her will and prepared to sign her name to it. Present in the room during this time were Garrett, the Reverend Preacher, Jewell Benson (a friend of Garrett), and several others, including Simons's sister, Lillie Clay Smith, and Simons's niece, Evelyn Jones. As Simons was about to sign the will, Smith and Jones—"by physical force or by creating a disturbance"—prevented her from carrying out her intention. Shortly after this incident, Simons suffered a severe hemorrhage, lapsed into a semi-comatose condition, and remained in that condition until her death a few days later. The court held that Garrett was entitled to the imposition of a constructive trust in her favor:

> Shall the trust in favor of Claytonia Garrett extend to the interests of the heirs who had no part in the wrongful acts? From the viewpoint of those heirs, it seems that they should be permitted to retain and enjoy the interests that vested in them as heirs, no will having been executed, and they not being responsible for the failure of Carrie Simons to execute it. On the other hand, from the viewpoint of Claytonia Garrett, it appears that a court of equity should extend the trust to all of the interests in the property in order that complete relief may be afforded her and that none of the heirs may profit as the result of the wrongful acts....

---

52. Later, we will study the express trust, which is frequently used by transferors in disposing of their wealth. See Chapters 9 to 12.

Accord White v. Mulvania, 575 S.W.2d 184 (Mo. 1978); Rogers v. Rogers, 473 N.E.2d 226 (N.Y. 1984); UPC §1-106; Palmer on Restitution §20.17.

Would Carrie Simons's will have been valid under the harmless-error rule of UPC §2-503 or Restatement 3d of Property §3.3?

Tortious Interference with an Inheritance. A person who—by undue influence, duress, fraud, or other tortious conduct—causes a decedent to divert property from one who would otherwise have received it through gift, devise, or intestate succession may be liable for damages in tort for wrongful interference with inheritance or gift. It is a relatively new theory of tort liability. See, e.g., Marshall v. Marshall, 275 B.R. 5 (C.D. Cal. 2002);[53] Henshall v. Lowe, 657 So. 2d 6 (Fla. Dist. Ct. App. 1995); Nemeth v. Banhalmi, 466 N.E.2d 977 (Ill. App. Ct. 1984); Doughty v. Morris, 871 P.2d 380 (N.M. Ct. App. 1994); Bohannon v. Wachovia Bank & Trust Co., 188 S.E. 390 (N.C. 1936); Restatement 2d of Torts §774B (1979); see also

---

53. In the *Marshall* case, the late Vickie Lynn Marshall, also known as Anna Nicole Smith, *Playboy* 1993 Playmate of the Year, and later a model for "Guess?" jeans, was 26 years old when she married J. Howard Marshall II, age 89, and said to be one of the richest persons in Texas. J. Howard, a lawyer, was once a member of the Yale Law School faculty, where he is thought to have taught trusts and estates! He and Vickie Lynn were married in June 1994; he died in August 1995.

In a probate proceeding in Texas, Vickie claimed that Howard had orally promised to leave her half of his estate. While the matter was pending, she filed for federal bankruptcy protection in California. In the course of the bankruptcy proceeding, she claimed that Howard's son, Pierce, had tortiously interfered with her expectancy of an inter vivos gift or a devise from Howard. The bankruptcy court agreed, awarding her $474 million against Pierce. After this judgment was entered, she filed in the Texas probate court a voluntary nonsuit of her claims against Pierce. The Texas court ultimately held that Vickie had no claim against Howard's estate. Pierce also appealed the bankruptcy court's decision to the federal district court in California, which vacated the bankruptcy court judgment but entered its own judgment for Vickie. She was awarded compensatory damages of $44 million a like amount in punitive damages against Pierce. Applying Texas law, the federal district court found that "[e]vidence of [the son's] tortious conduct was legion. Acting in concert with [an attorney], they backdated documents, altered documents, destroyed documents, suborned falsified notary statements, presented documents to J. Howard under false pretenses, and committed perjury."

In In re Vickie Lynn Marshall, 392 F.3d 1118 (9th Cir. 2004), however, the Ninth Circuit reversed, holding "that all federal courts... are bound by the probate exception to federal court jurisdiction and that [federal courts] are required to refrain from deciding state law probate matters...." In consequence, she was bound by the Texas proceeding that awarded her nothing.

In Marshall v. Marshall, 547 U.S. 293 (2006), the Supreme Court reversed and remanded. The Court held that the probate exception is limited to "the probate or annulment of a will and the administration of a decedent's estate; it also precludes federal courts from endeavoring to dispose of property that is in the custody of a state probate court." The exception "does not bar federal courts from adjudicating matters outside those confines and otherwise within federal jurisdiction." Justice Stevens concurred in part and concurred in the judgment. Stevens argued that there is no probate exception "that outs a federal court of jurisdiction it otherwise possesses."

In June 2006, Howard's son, E. Pierce Marshall, died unexpectedly at age 67. In February 2007, Anna Nicole Smith died at age 39, after collapsing at a hotel in Florida.

In March 2010, the Ninth Circuit held that the federal district court should have given preclusive effect to the Texas probate court's factual findings and legal conclusions. The Ninth Circuit reversed the district court's judgment and remanded with instructions for the district court to enter judgment in favor of Pierce. See In re Marshall, 600 F.3d 1037 (9th Cir. 2010).

Allen v. Hall, 974 P.2d 199 (Or. 1999) (en banc) (relying on tort of intentional interference with prospective economic advantage). Contra Labonte v. Giordano, 687 N.E.2d 1253 (Mass. 1997); Economopoulos v. Kolaitis, 528 S.E.2d 714 (Va. 2000). Courts have allowed these actions to be brought before the death of the testator. See, e.g., Carlton v. Carlton, 575 So. 2d 239 (Fla. Dist. Ct. App. 1991); Harmon v. Harmon, 404 A.2d 1020 (Me. 1979).

For actions brought after the testator's death, courts have held that a tort action for wrongful interference with inheritance will lie only if the claim for wrongful conduct could not have been asserted as part of the proceedings to admit a will to probate or in a will contest. See, e.g., Robinson v. First State Bank of Monticello, 454 N.E.2d 288 (Ill. 1983); see also, e.g., Estate of Knowlson, 562 N.E.2d 277 (Ill. App. Ct. 1990) (concluding that summary judgment in favor of defendant was prematurely granted because the unavailability of probate relief remains speculative until contests over prior wills are resolved). Some courts, however, permit a plaintiff to bring the tort action at the same time as the will contest. See, e.g., Estate of Roeseler, 679 N.E.2d 393 (Ill. App. Ct. 1997).

Unlike for a will contest, consequential and punitive damages are available under a tortious interference claim. Even if a will contestant prevails, he or she can bring a subsequent tort action seeking punitive damages based on attorney's fees incurred during the will contest. Another major difference is that the presumptions for validity and higher standards of proof that probate law has developed in furtherance of testamentary freedom are inapplicable in a tort suit. For further discussion of this tort, see John C.P. Goldberg & Robert H. Sitkoff, Torts & Estates: Remedying Wrongful Interference with Inheritance, 65 Stan. L. Rev. 335 (2013) (arguing that the tort should be repudiated as conceptually and practically unsound); M. Read Moore, At the Frontier of Probate Litigation: Intentional Interference with the Right to Inherit, Prob. & Prop., Nov.-Dec. 1993, at 6; Annot., Action for Tortious Interference with Bequest as Precluded by Will Contest Remedy, 18 A.L.R. 5th 211; Nita Ledford, Note, Intentional Interference with Inheritance, 30 Real Prop. Prob. & Tr. J. 325 (1995).

Living Probate. An 1883 Michigan statute unsuccessfully attempted to grant testators an option to "prove" or "validate" their wills while they were still alive.[54] The statute permitted the testator to petition the county probate court, which would then notify the presumptive heirs and others named by the testator of a hearing, at which the testator's testamentary capacity and freedom from fraud or undue influence would be determined. If these were established, the probate court would decree the validity of the will. Appeals from the decree and the testator's right to revoke or alter the will were expressly provided for by the statute. The Michigan

---

54. The Michigan statute is reprinted in Howard P. Fink, Ante-Mortem Probate Revisited: Can An Idea Have A Life After Death?, 37 Ohio St. L.J. 264, 268 n.8 (1976).

Supreme Court, however, held that the statute authorized a proceeding beyond the scope of judicial power and declared it unconstitutional. See Lloyd v. Wayne Circuit Judge, 23 N.W. 28 (Mich. 1885). It ought to be noted that, when *Lloyd* was decided, declaratory judgments were unknown to the law.

Between this early unsuccessful attempt in 1883 and the year 2009, only three states, Arkansas, North Dakota, and Ohio, had resurrected the idea of living probate. The Ohio statute generated some use but was repealed as of March 2019. In 2010, Alaska became the fourth state to allow pre-mortem probate. See Alaska Code §13.12.530 et seq.

Considerable literature exists advocating various forms of living probate. See, e.g., Gregory S. Alexander, The Conservatorship Model: A Modification, 77 Mich. L. Rev. 86 (1978); Gregory S. Alexander & Albert M. Pearson, Alternative Models of Ante-Mortem Probate and Procedural Due Process Limitations of Succession, 78 Mich. L. Rev. 89 (1979) (advocating an "administrative model," in which a guardian ad litem would conduct an independent investigation and report to the court; the court would hold a hearing and issue a binding judgment, without notice to affected persons); David F. Cavers, Ante Mortem Probate: An Essay in Preventive Law, 1 U. Chi. L. Rev. 440 (1934) (suggesting the appointment of a probate officer to determine the validity of a testator's will based on affidavits of the will drafter and disinterested witnesses as well as interviews of them and the testator); Howard P. Fink, Ante-Mortem Probate Revisited: Can An Idea Have A Life After Death?, 37 Ohio St. L.J. 264 (1976) (advocating a "contest model" of living probate, in which all affected persons would be notified and given an opportunity to contest the validity of the will in an adversarial proceeding; the court would then issue a declaratory judgment as to testamentary capacity, undue influence, and compliance with formalities of execution; this is the model that has been enacted in Arkansas, North Dakota, and Ohio); John H. Langbein, Living Probate: The Conservatorship Model, above p. 188 (advocating a "conservatorship model," in which all affected persons would be represented in an adversarial proceeding by a guardian ad litem); Aloysius A. Leopold & Gerry W. Beyer, Ante-Mortem Probate: A Viable Alternative, 43 Ark. L. Rev. 131 (1990) (advocating some form of ante-mortem probate); see also Gerry W. Beyer, Pre-Mortem Probate, Prob. & Prop., July-Aug. 1993, at 6.

Mary Louise Fellows argued in The Case Against Living Probate, 78 Mich. L. Rev. 1066, 1080 (1980), that the living-probate proposals are seriously flawed:

> First, the proposals will fail to achieve their own stated objectives of improving the evidence available during probate and assuring testators that their dispository schemes will be carried out. Second, all three proposals [i.e., the "contest," "conservatorship," and "administrative" models] make the testator pay a high price for these ephemeral advantages. Finally, and perhaps most important, all three proposals are unfair to presumptive takers, and under the Administrative Model that unfairness may rise to the level of a constitutional due process violation.

Settlement of Will Contests/Alternative Dispute Resolution. Will contests frequently end by settlement, not trial. See Jeffrey A. Schoenblum, Will Contests—An Empirical Study, 22 Real Prop. Prob. & Tr. J. 607, 618-24 (1987). Interest is also growing in using mediation to resolve will contests. See Lela P. Love & Stewart E. Sterk, Leaving More than Money: Mediation Clauses in Estate Planning Documents, 65 Wash. & Lee L. Rev. 539 (2008); Ronald Chester, Less Law, But More Justice?: Jury Trials and Mediation as Means of Resolving Will Contests, 37 Duq. L. Rev. 173 (1999); Susan N. Gary, Mediating Probate Disputes, Prob. & Prop., July-Aug. 1999, at 11; Robert N. Sacks, Mediation: An Effective Method to Resolve Estate and Trust Disputes, 27 Est. Plan. 210 (2000); E. Gary Spitko, Judge Not: In Defense of Minority-Culture Arbitration, 77 Wash. U. L.Q. 1065 (1999); E. Gary Spitko, Gone But Not Conforming: Protecting the Abhorrent Testator from Majoritarian Cultural Norms through Minority-Culture Arbitration, 49 Case W. Res. L. Rev. 275 (1999); see also Chapter 2 (discussing settlements and their potential tax consequences).

The Seward Johnson Case. In a highly publicized case, the children of Seward Johnson charged that their father's will was a product of undue influence by Seward's third wife, Basia (pronounced BAH-sha), a Polish immigrant who came to the United States with $200 in her pocket and shortly after arriving in this country landed a job as a maid in the Johnson household. Seward Johnson, some forty years older than Basia, was an heir to the Johnson & Johnson pharmaceuticals fortune. The case settled before the jury came to a verdict, resulting in $40 million of the approximately $400 million estate being paid to the children. The estate also paid approximately $25 million of legal fees for all the parties. See Barbara Goldsmith, Johnson v. Johnson (1987); David Margolick, Undue Influence: The Epic Battle for the Johnson & Johnson Fortune (1993). Legal experts agree that the children's lawsuit was weak, but more importantly that Johnson's lawyers should have taken steps during the planning process to reduce the risk of contest.[55] See John L. Carroll & Brian K. Carroll, Avoiding the Will Contest, Prob. & Prop., May-June 1994, at 61; John H. Langbein, Will Contests, 103 Yale L.J. 2039, 2045-47 (1994).

---

55. Before her death in 2013, Basia was listed in *Forbes* as having a net worth of $3.3 billion. The source of her fortune was listed as "Johnson & Johnson." See Forbes, The 400 Richest Americans (Special Report, September 19, 2012).

PART C. UNATTESTED DOCUMENTS AND EVENTS— INCORPORATION BY REFERENCE, INDEPENDENT SIGNIFICANCE, AND RELATED DOCTRINES

Primary Statutory References: *UPC §§2-510, -512, -513*

Integration. Wills frequently are composed of multiple pages. No state requires each sheet of paper of a multiple-page will to be separately executed. Writings contained on separate pieces of paper can be effective as parts of a single document. The process of integrating separate papers into one will, however, like the process of integrating separate papers into one contract under the Statute of Frauds, involves some proof of intention that the parts be considered together—proof that would be supplied, for example, by relation of sense or by physical attachment.

Occasionally, a court suggests that either relation of sense or physical attachment is essential to integration, see, e.g., Seiter's Estate, 108 A. 614 (Pa. 1919), but the actual decisions tend strongly to support the view that any evidence will suffice so long as the court is satisfied that at the time of execution the separate papers were present and regarded by the testator as parts of the will. See, e.g., Cole v. Webb, 295 S.W. 1035 (Ky. 1927); Estate of Beale, 113 N.W.2d 380 (Wis. 1962); see also Estate of Benson, 1996 WL 118367 (Minn. Ct. App. Mar. 19, 1996) (unpublished opinion) (relying on doctrine to validate will when witnesses signed self-proving affidavit); Annot., Validity of Will Written on Disconnected Sheets, 38 A.L.R.2d 477.

Incorporation by Reference. In most jurisdictions, unattested papers—papers that were not present when the will was executed—can be regarded as part of the will by incorporation. See Atkinson on Wills §80; Alvin E. Evans, Nontestamentary Acts and Incorporation by Reference, 16 U. Chi. L. Rev. 635 (1949); Alvin E. Evans, Incorporation by Reference, Integration, and Non-Testamentary Act, 25 Colum. L. Rev. 879 (1925).

Restatement 3d of Property

§3.4 Republication by Codicil. A will is treated as if it were executed when its most recent codicil was executed, whether or not the codicil expressly republishes the prior will, unless the effect of so treating it would be inconsistent with the testator's intent.

§3.5 Integration of Multiple Pages or Writings Into a Single Will. To be treated as part of a will, a page or other writing must be present when the will is executed and must be intended to be part of the will.

§3.6 Incorporation by Reference. A writing that is not valid as a will but is in existence when a will is executed may be incorporated by reference into the will if the will manifests an intent to incorporate the writing and the writing to be incorporated is identified with reasonable certainty.

Simon v. Grayson
102 P.2d 1081 (Cal. 1940)

WASTE, C.J. The question presented for determination upon this appeal involves the construction and effect to be given a provision in a will purporting to incorporate a letter by reference. Respondent's claim to certain of the estate's funds is based upon the terms of the letter. The appellants, who are residuary legatees under the will, contend that the attempted incorporation by reference was ineffectual. The facts, which were presented to the trial court upon agreed statement, are as follows:

S. M. Seeligsohn died in 1935. His safe deposit box was found to contain among other things, a will and codicil and a letter addressed to his executors. The will, which was dated March 25, 1932, contained a provision in paragraph four, leaving $6,000 to his executors

> to be paid by them in certain amounts to certain persons as shall be directed by me in a letter that will be found in my effects and which said letter will be addressed to Martin E. Simon and Arthur W. Green (the executors) and will be dated March 25, 1932.

Paragraph four also provided that any one having an interest in the will "shall not inquire into the application of said moneys" and that the executors "shall not be accountable to any person whomsoever for the payment and/or application of said sum ... this provision ... is in no sense a trust."

The letter found in the testator's safe deposit box was dated July 3, 1933, and stated:

> In paragraph VIII of my will I have left you $6,000—to be paid to the persons named in a letter and this letter is also mentioned in said paragraph. I direct that after my death you shall pay said $6,000 as follows: To Mrs. Esther Cohn, 1755 Van Ness Ave. San Francisco, Calif. the sum of $4,000— ... If any of the said persons cannot be found by you within six months after my death, or if any of the said persons shall predecease me, the sum directed to be paid to such persons ... shall be paid by you to my heirs as described in paragraph IX of my said Will....

This letter was written, dated and signed entirely in the handwriting of the testator. No letter dated March 25, 1932, was found among his effects.

The codicil to the will was executed November 25, 1933. It made no changes in paragraph IV of the will and contained no reference to the letter, but recited, "Except as expressly modified by this Codicil, my Will of March 25th 1932 shall remain in full force and effect."....

It is settled law ... that a testator may incorporate an extrinsic document into his will, provided the document is in existence at the time and provided, further, that the reference to it in the will clearly identifies it, or renders it capable of identification by extrinsic proof. An attempt to incorporate a future document is ineffectual, because a testator cannot be permitted to create for himself the power to dispose of his property without complying with the formalities required in making a will.

In the case at bar the letter presumably was not in existence when the will was executed, for the letter bore a date subsequent to the date of the will. However, the letter was in existence at the time the codicil to the will was executed. The respondent points out that under the law the execution of a codicil has the effect of republishing the will which it modifies, and argues from this that Seeligsohn's letter was an "existing document" within the incorporation rule.... The principle of republication thus applied is unquestionably sound. In revising his scheme of testamentary disposition by codicil a testator presumably reviews and reaffirms those portions of his will which remain unaffected. In substance, the will is re-executed as of that time. Therefore, the testator's execution of the codicil in the present case must be taken as confirming the incorporation of the letter then in existence, provided the letter can be satisfactorily identified as the one referred to in the will. And this is true, notwithstanding the codicil made no reference to the letter and recited that the will should remain in full force "except as expressly modified by this codicil", for the letter, if properly incorporated, would be an integral part of the republished will.

We are also of the opinion that the trial court did not err in concluding that the letter found with the will was the letter referred to in the will. Conceding the contrary force of the discrepancy in dates, the evidence of identity was, nevertheless, sufficient to overcome the effect of that factor. The ... informal document [need not] be identified with exact precision; it is enough that the descriptive words and extrinsic circumstances combine to produce a reasonable certainty that the document in question is the one referred to by the testator in his will. Here the letter was found in the safe deposit box with the will. It was addressed to the executors, as the will stated it would be. No other letter was found. Moreover, the letter is conceded to have been written by the testator, and its terms conform unmistakably to the letter described in the will. It identifies itself as the letter mentioned in the will and deals with the identical subject matter referred to in that portion of the will. All these circumstances leave no doubt that the letter of July 3, 1933, is the one that the testator intended to incorporate in paragraph four of his will....

The judgment is AFFIRMED.

SHENK, CARTER, CURTIS, and GIBSON, JJ., concur.

Notes and Question

1. *Incorporation by Reference—Recognition of the Doctrine.* A few states—notably Connecticut, Louisiana, and New York[56]—refuse to recognize the doctrine of incorporation by reference. In Hatheway v. Smith, 65 A. 1058 (Conn.

---

56. But see Matter of Fowles, 118 N.E. 611 (N.Y. 1918); N.Y. Est. Powers & Trusts Law §8-1.1(b) (permitting incorporation by reference into a charitable trust of a resolution, deed of trust, or declaration of trust made by a corporation formed for charitable purposes, provided the incorporated document is recorded).

1907), the Connecticut court reasoned that "the only power, given by [the statute of wills,] is that of disposing of ... property by means of a writing containing in itself language by which the subject and object of the testamentary gift intended is therein expressed."[57]

2. *Incorporation Into Holographic Wills*. The decisions are divided on the question whether a valid holographic will can effectively incorporate a writing that is not in the testator's handwriting. For cases upholding incorporation, see Plumel's Estate, 90 P. 192 (Cal. 1907); Johnson v. Johnson, 279 P.2d 928 (Okla. 1954). For cases rejecting incorporation, see Hewes v. Hewes, 71 So. 4 (Miss. 1916); Hinson v. Hinson, 280 S.W.2d 731 (Tex. 1955). The Restatement 3d of Property §3.6 comment f takes the position that incorporation "does not affect the holographic character of the will."

A typewritten signed document is not valid as a holographic will. See, e.g., Estate of McCune, 2004 WL 348925 (Cal. Ct. App. 2004) (not certified for publication). Would a will that is entirely written and signed in the testator's handwriting be valid as a holographic will if its only terms were a statement that "I hereby incorporate the typewritten document stapled to this holographic will"?

In Allen v. Maddock, 11 Moore P.C. 427, 14 Eng. Rep. 757 (P.C. 1858), Anne Foote attempted to execute a will, but it was invalid because it was attested by only one witness. Five years later, on her deathbed, she duly executed a codicil, which stated that it was "a codicil to my last will and testament." No other reference to the will was contained in the codicil, which merely disposed of a small amount of property to Anne's servant, Eliza. The court allowed the invalid will to be

---

57. The rejection of incorporation by reference in Connecticut was presaged by a decision some three years earlier, in a case involving William Jennings Bryan. Bryan, a self-styled candidate of the ordinary American, lost three presidential elections as the nominee of the Democratic Party. He opposed the gold standard and delivered the famous "Cross of Gold" speech at the 1896 Democratic Party national convention. A religious fundamentalist, he fought against the teaching of evolution in the public schools and helped prosecute the teacher, John Scopes, in the famous 1925 Scopes Trial in Tennessee.

Appeal of Bryan, 58 A. 748 (Conn. 1904), involved the will of Philo S. Bennett. Bennett's will devised $50,000 to Bennett's wife, Grace Imogene Bennett, "in trust, however, for the purposes set forth in a sealed letter which will be found with this will."

In connection with the execution of the will, Bennett, with Bryan's help, prepared a letter to Mrs. Bennett directing her to pay the $50,000 to Bryan. Bennett's letter explained that he believed the welfare of the nation depended upon the triumph of the political principles for which Bryan stood and that he wished to help Bryan financially, "so that he may be more free to devote himself to his chosen field." The letter was enclosed in a sealed envelope addressed to Mrs. Bennett. Both the will and the envelope were placed in the testator's safe deposit box, where they remained until after his death. Mrs. Bennett refused to honor the letter, largely because Bennett's will, which Bryan had helped prepare, left $20,000 to Bennett's female companion.

Bryan sued to enforce the letter but was unsuccessful. The court did not then pass on whether it would recognize the doctrine of incorporation by reference, but placed its decision on the ground that the requirements of a valid incorporation were not satisfied. In its view, the will did not contain "any clear, explicit, unambiguous reference to any specific document as one existing and known to the testator at the time his will was executed."

incorporated into the codicil, holding that the will was entitled to probate along with the codicil.

———

Republication. Republication of a will by codicil is usually thought of as the equivalent of *re-execution* of the will. This idea did not originate as a device to subvert the incorporation-by-reference requirement that only documents in existence when the will was executed can be incorporated. Instead, it originated as a device to subvert a different rule—the rule that a will could not dispose of land acquired after the will was executed.

From an early time, a will could bequeath after-acquired personal property, but it was not until the Wills Act 1837, see p. 118, that English law permitted a will to operate on after-acquired land. The church courts had jurisdiction over wills of personal property and borrowed from Roman law the concept that a will could dispose of after-acquired chattels. But general power of testation over land was first given by the Statute of Wills 1540, 32 Hen. 8, ch. 1, which enabled any person who should "have" any land to dispose of it "by last will and testament...." This language was soon construed as allowing disposition only of land owned by the testator when the will was executed. See Brett v. Rigden, 1 Plow. 340, 344, 75 Eng. Rep. 516, 523 (C.P. 1567); 7 William S. Holdsworth, History of English Law 365 (1926); 2 Frederick Pollock & Frederic W. Maitland, A History of English Law 315 (2d ed. 1898).

By §3 of the Wills Act 1837, the old rule as to land was changed in England so as to permit a person to dispose by will of "all real estate and all personal estate which he shall be entitled to, either at law or in equity, at the time of his death." In this country, the old rule as to after-acquired land has been everywhere eliminated; in most states, this has been accomplished by statute. See, e.g., UPC §2-602.

Acts Having Independent Significance. All jurisdictions give effect to devises that identify the property or the devisee by reference to acts and facts that have *independent* significance. The independent significance doctrine has been codified in some states. See UPC §2-512; Restatement 3d of Property, Statutory Note to §3.7. The Restatement 3d of Property formulates the doctrine as follows:

§3.7 *Independent Significance.* The meaning of a dispositive or other provision in a will may be supplied or affected by an external circumstance referred to in the will, unless the external circumstance has no significance apart from its effect upon the will.

One of the earliest applications of the independent significance doctrine occurred in Stubbs v. Sargon, 3 My. & Cr. 507, 511, 40 Eng. Rep. 1022, 1024 (Ch. 1838). The testator devised the premises in Little Queen Street to trustees to pay the rents to the testator's sister, Mary Innell, during her life, and after her decease, in trust to dispose of and divide the same unto and amongst the testator's partners who were in copartnership with her at the time of her death. The Chancellor upheld the devise, saying:

> In the present case, the disposition is complete. The devisee, indeed, is to be ascertained by a description contained in the will; but such is the case with many unquestionable devises. A devise to a second or third son, perhaps unborn at the time—many contingent devises—all shifting clauses—are instances of devises to devisees who are to be ascertained by future events and contingencies; but such persons may be ascertained, not only by future natural events and contingencies, but by acts of third persons.

The Chancellor's decision affirmed a decision by the Master of the Rolls, 2 Keen 255, 269, 48 Eng. Rep. 626, 632 (1837), who gave this explanation of the doctrine of independent significance:

> [If] the description be such as to distinguish the devisee from every other person, it seems sufficient without entering into the consideration of the question, whether the description was acquired by the devisee after the date of the will, or by the testator's own act in the ordinary course of his affairs, or in the management of his property, and I think that a devise to such person as may be the testator's partners or the disponees of his business may be good.

Examples of the many decisions approving references to circumstances having significance apart from their impact on the testamentary disposition include Dennis v. Holsapple, 47 N.E. 631 (Ind. 1897) (devise of all of my property to "[w]hoever shall take good care of me and maintain, nurse, clothe and furnish me with proper medical treatment"); Gaff v. Cornwallis, 106 N.E. 860 (Mass. 1914) (devise of "the contents, if any, of a drawer in said safe"); Brown v. Clothey, 79 N.E. 269 (Mass. 1906) (devise by a manufacturer of a product "which I may leave on hand at my decease"); Creamer v. Harris, 106 N.E. 967 (Ohio 1914) (devise "to Sadie Harris... one bureau and contents..."); Reinheimer's Estate, 108 A. 412 (Pa. 1919) (devise to "the party... who may be farming my farm and taking care of me at my death").

In In re Robson, [1891] 2 Ch. 559, a devise of the testator's desk "with the contents thereof" was held to pass title to money found therein and debts due the testator evidenced by notes contained in the desk. A key in the desk unlocked a separate tin box containing securities. The court held that the devisee was not entitled to the contents of the box. Many of the cases noted above involved similar questions of intention.

The will of another person is not a testamentary act of the decedent and therefore has independent significance. Thus, a will directing that property be distributed in accordance with the will of another person is effective even if the will of the other person was executed later. In re Tipler, 10 S.W.3d 244, 246, 249-50 (Tenn. Ct. App. 1998), appeal denied (Tenn. 1999) adopts this view. Gladys S. Tipler's 1982 attested will left most of her estate to her husband, James, upon the condition that he survive her. The will did not address the possibility that he might predecease her. Two days later, she executed a holographic codicil stating:

Should my husband predecesse [sic] *me I hereby declair* [sic] *that his last Will and testament upon his death is our agreement here to four* [sic] *made between us .... With the exception Mr. Tipler or myself can elect to make any changes as we desire depending upon which one predeceasest* [sic] *the other. If no changes are made by either of us this will be our last Will and testament.*

Gladys's husband executed his will in 1990 and died six months later. Gladys died in 1994. Her heirs challenged the validity of the codicil, arguing first that the "codicil should not be enforced because it referred to a document not yet in existence." Second they argued that Tennessee law requires all material provisions of a holographic will to be in the testator's handwriting and that the husband's will was not in Gladys Tipler's handwriting. The court held:

> [T]he doctrine of facts of independent significance is applicable in this case to permit Testatrix' codicil to refer to Husband's will, provided the document is a valid holographic codicil. To determine whether the holograph contains all material provisions in Testatrix' handwriting, the trial court properly considered Testatrix' intent.... Since Testatrix wanted her estate to go to whomever Husband wished, the codicil contained all material provisions in Testatrix' handwriting, even though it stated only that her estate should go to the beneficiaries under Husband's will and did not specifically name beneficiaries.

An example of an act having *no* independent significance apart from its effect on the will is the designation of one or more devisees in an *unattested* writing to be prepared *by the testator* after the will's execution. Thus, a devise "to the persons I name in a separate [unattested] letter to be prepared by me on a future date" is invalid, unless authorized by statute (or unless enforceable as a secret trust, on which see Chapter 9). We now turn to an example of a statute authorizing such a reference to an unattested writing.

Reference to Unattested Writing. UPC §2-513 introduced a new idea into American probate law. As part of its policy of effectuating a testator's intent by reducing formalities, the UPC permits a testator to dispose of tangible personal property without having to meet the requirements of the doctrines of incorporation by reference or acts having independent significance. Under the pre-1990 version of §2-513, a handwritten document or a signed writing was sufficient so long as the will referred to it. Under the current version, only a signed writing is authorized. Under either version, the writing can be executed before or after the will was written and modified at any time.

This idea has proven to be popular, and many states have enacted a provision similar or identical to either the former or current version of §2-513. See Jones v. Ellison, 15 S.W.3d 710 (Ark. Ct. App. 2000) (holding that under a statute based on the former version of the UPC, a note found in the testator's jewelry box was sufficient to demonstrate her intent to give the devisee the items found in jewelry box).

Problem

G's will devised her antique desk to her granddaughter, A. It also contained the following clause:

> I might leave a written statement or list disposing of items of tangible personal property. If I do and if my written statement or list is found and is identified as such by my Personal Representative no later than 30 days after the probate of this will, then my written statement or list is to be given effect to the extent authorized by law and is to take precedence over any contrary devise or devises of the same item or items of property in this will.

After G's death last month, G's will was discovered in the top drawer of her antique desk. In the same drawer was a piece of paper in G's handwriting, dated about a year after the date of execution of her will that says: "Antique desk to granddaughter, B."

Under the pre-1990 version of UPC §2-513, who is entitled to G's antique desk, A or B, if the handwritten document is unsigned? What would be the result if the current version of UPC §2-513 applies? Do your answers change if the handwritten document is signed by G?

PART D. JOINT REPRESENTATION IN ESTATE PLANNING

"But I'm always true to you, darlin', in my fashion.
Yes, I'm always true to you, darlin', in my way."
– Lois, in the musical Kiss Me, Kate[58]

Lawyers frequently represent both spouses when designing an estate plan for a married couple. The joint representation occurs either because the spouses ask for joint representation in view of their shared mutual estate-planning goals and their desire to avoid unnecessary legal fees, or because their lawyer encourages joint representation to ensure that the plans are compatible in meeting the couple's needs. Lawyers are well aware, however, that joint representation carries the risk that neither spouse "will receive the representation a single individual might receive under the same circumstances." Nevertheless, many of them conclude that "family needs, tax incentives, and the very nature of marriage often make separate counseling unnecessary, and indeed, inappropriate." Report of the ABA Special Study Committee on Professional Responsibility, Comments and Recommendations on the Lawyer's Duties in Representing Husband and Wife, 28 Real Prop. Prob. & Tr. J. 765, 770 (1994).

---

58. Always True to You (In My Fashion), from Kiss Me, Kate (1948) (lyrics and music by Cole Porter).

Problem

You are the estate planning lawyer for Harold and Wendy, a married couple with substantial assets. Harold and Wendy each have executed a will providing for the surviving spouse for life, with the assets then passing to their then-living descendants by representation. Wendy informs you that she has separately executed a codicil, prepared by another law firm, making a substantial devise to her secret lover. With this information, what can you do? What must you do? What, if anything, should you have done differently from the beginning of the representation? Consider the following materials.

Iowa Rules (tracking the ABA Model Rules of Professional Conduct)

Rule 32:1.6 [MRPC 1.6] Confidentiality of Information

(a) A lawyer shall not reveal information relating to the representation of a client unless the client gives informed consent, the disclosure is impliedly authorized in order to carry out the representation or the disclosure is permitted by paragraph (b)....

(b) A lawyer may reveal information relating to the representation of a client to the extent the lawyer reasonably believes necessary:...

(2) to prevent the client from committing a crime or fraud that is reasonably certain to result in substantial injury to the financial interests or property of another and in furtherance of which the client has used or is using the lawyer's services;

(3) to prevent, mitigate or rectify substantial injury to the financial interests or property of another that is reasonably certain to result or has resulted from the client's commission of a crime or fraud in furtherance of which the client has used the lawyer's services;....

Rule 32:1.7 [MRPC 1.7] Conflict of Interest: Current Clients

(a) Except as provided in paragraph (b), a lawyer shall not represent a client if the representation involves a concurrent conflict of interest. A concurrent conflict of interest exists if:

(1) the representation of one client will be directly adverse to another client; or

(2) there is a significant risk that the representation of one or more clients will be materially limited by the lawyer's responsibilities to another client, a former client or a third person or by a personal interest of the lawyer.

(b) Notwithstanding the existence of a concurrent conflict of interest under paragraph (a), a lawyer may represent a client if:

(1) the lawyer reasonably believes that the lawyer will be able to provide competent and diligent representation to each affected client;

(2) the representation is not prohibited by law;

(3) the representation does not involve the assertion of a claim by one client against another client represented by the lawyer in the same litigation or other

proceeding before a tribunal; and

(4) each affected client gives informed consent, confirmed in writing....

Florida Advisory Opinion 95-4 (May 30, 1997)

In a joint representation between husband and wife in estate planning, an attorney is not required to discuss issues regarding confidentiality at the outset of representation. The attorney may not reveal confidential information to the wife when the husband tells the attorney that he wishes to provide for a beneficiary that is unknown to the wife. The attorney must withdraw from the representation of both husband and wife because of the conflict presented when the attorney must maintain the husband's separate confidences regarding the joint representation....

Situation Presented. Lawyer has represented Husband and Wife for many years in a range of personal matters, including estate planning. Husband and Wife have substantial individual assets, and they also own substantial jointly-held property. Recently, Lawyer prepared new updated wills that Husband and Wife signed. Like their previous wills, the new wills primarily benefit the survivor of them for his or her life, with beneficial disposition at the death of the survivor being made equally to their children (none of whom were born by prior marriage)....

Several months after the execution of the new wills, Husband confers separately with Lawyer. Husband reveals to Lawyer that he has just executed a codicil (prepared by another law firm) that makes substantial beneficial disposition to a woman with whom Husband has been having an extra-marital relationship. Husband tells Lawyer that Wife knows about neither the relationship nor the new codicil, as to which Husband asks Lawyer to advise him regarding Wife's rights of election in the event she were to survive Husband. Lawyer tells Husband that Lawyer cannot under the circumstances advise him regarding same. Lawyer tells Husband that Lawyer will have to consider Lawyer's ethical duties under the circumstances. Lawyer tells Husband that, after consideration, Lawyer may determine to withdraw from representing Husband and Wife. Lawyer further tells Husband that, after consideration, Lawyer may determine to disclose to Wife the substance of Husband's revelation if Husband does not do so himself.

Issues Presented. The following ethical questions have been asked by the RPPTL Professionalism Committee:

1. Prior to Husband's recent disclosure, did Lawyer owe any ethical duty to counsel Husband and Wife concerning any separate confidence which either Husband or Wife might wish for Lawyer to withhold from the other?

2. Assuming that Husband does not make disclosure of the information [referred to in Issue 1.] to Wife:

a) Is Lawyer required to reveal voluntarily the information to Wife?

b) May Lawyer in Lawyer's discretion determine whether or not to reveal the information to the Wife? If so, what are the relevant factors which Lawyer may or should consider?

c) If Lawyer does not reveal the information to Wife, is Lawyer required to withdraw from the representation? If so, what explanation, if any, should Lawyer give to Wife?

3. May Lawyer continue to represent Husband alone if Lawyer notifies Wife that Lawyer is withdrawing from the joint representation and will no longer represent Wife? If so, is disclosure to Wife necessary in order to obtain her informed consent to Lawyer's continued representation of Husband?

4. Assuming that adequate disclosure is made to Wife, may Lawyer continue to represent both Husband and Wife if they both wish for Lawyer to do so?

The RPPTL Professionalism Committee views Lawyer's representation of Husband and Wife as a "joint representation." The committee concurs in this view ....

Discussion. From the inception of the representation until Husband's communication to Lawyer of the information concerning the codicil and the extra-marital relationship (hereinafter the "separate confidence"), there was no objective indication that the interests of Husband and Wife diverged, nor did it objectively appear to Lawyer that any such divergence of interests was reasonably likely to arise. Such situations involving joint representation of Husband and Wife do not present a conflict of interests and, therefore, do not trigger the conflict of interest disclosure-and-consent requirements of Rules 4-1.7(a) and 4-1.7(b), Rules Regulating The Florida Bar.[59]

In view of the conclusions reached in the remainder of this opinion, we conclude that, under the facts presented, Lawyer was not ethically obligated to discuss with Husband and Wife Lawyer's obligations with regard to separate confidences. While such a discussion is not ethically required, in some situations it may help prevent the type of occurrence that is the subject of this opinion.

We now turn to the central issue presented, which is the application of the confidentiality rule in a situation where confidentiality was not discussed at the outset of the joint representation.... In the situation presented, however, Lawyer's duty of communication to Wife appears to conflict with Lawyer's duty of confidentiality to Husband. Thus, the key question for our decision is: Which duty must give way? We conclude that, under the facts presented, Lawyer's duty of confidentiality must take precedence. Consequently, if Husband fails to disclose (or

---

59. It is important to recognize, however, that some spouses do not share identical goals in common matters, including estate planning. For example, one spouse may wish to make a Will providing substantial beneficial disposition for charity but the other spouse does not. Or, either or both of them may have children by a prior marriage for whom they may wish to make different beneficial provisions. Given the conflict of interest typically inherent in those types of situations, in such situations the attorney should review with the married couple the relevant conflict of interest considerations and obtain the spouses informed consent to the joint representation.

give Lawyer permission to disclose) the subject information to Wife, Lawyer is not ethically required to disclose the information to Wife and does not have discretion to reveal the information. To the contrary, Lawyer's ethical obligation of confidentiality to Husband prohibits Lawyer from disclosing the information to Wife....

It has been argued in some commentaries that the usual rule of lawyer- client confidentiality does not apply in a joint representation and that the lawyer should have the discretion to determine whether the lawyer should disclose the separate confidence to the non-communicating client. This discretionary approach is advanced in the Restatement, sec. 112 comment i. This result is also favored by the American College of Trusts and Estates in its Commentaries on the Model Rules of Professional Conduct (2d ed. 1995) (hereinafter the "ACTEC Commentaries"). [Same in the Commentaries (6th ed. 2023) at 88. Ed.] The Restatement itself acknowledges that no case law supports the discretionary approach. Nor do the ACTEC Commentaries cite any supporting authority for this proposition.

The committee rejects the concept of discretion in this important area. Florida lawyers must have an unambiguous rule governing their conduct in situations of this nature. We conclude that Lawyer owes duties of confidentiality to both Husband and Wife, regardless of whether they are being represented jointly. Accordingly, under the facts presented Lawyer is ethically precluded from disclosing the separate confidence to Wife without Husband's consent....

The committee further concludes that Lawyer must withdraw from the joint representation under the facts presented. An adversity of interests concerning the joint representation has arisen. This creates a conflict of interest. Many conflicts can be cured by obtaining the fully informed consent of the affected clients. Rule 4-1.7. Some conflicts, however, are of such a nature that it is not reasonable for a lawyer to request consent to continue the representation. The Comment to Rule 4-1.7 provides in pertinent part:

> A client may consent to representation notwithstanding a conflict. However, as indicated in subdivision (a)(1) with respect to representation directly adverse to a client and subdivision (b)(1) with respect to material limitations on representation of a client, when a disinterested lawyer would conclude that the client should not agree to the representation under the circumstances, the lawyer involved cannot properly ask for such agreement or provide representation on the basis of the client's consent.

In the situation presented, the conflict that has arisen is of an [sic] personal and, quite likely, emotionally-charged nature. Lawyer's continued representation of both Husband and Wife in estate planning matters presumably would no longer be tenable. Rule 4-1.16 thus requires Lawyer's withdrawal from representation of both Husband and Wife in this matter.

In withdrawing from the representation, Lawyer should inform Wife and Husband that a conflict of interest has arisen that precludes Lawyer's continued representation of Wife and Husband in these matters. Lawyer may also advise both Wife and Husband that each should retain separate counsel. As discussed above, however, Lawyer may not disclose the separate confidence to Wife. The committee recognizes that a sudden withdrawal by Lawyer almost certainly will raise suspicions on the part of Wife. This may even alert Wife to the substance of the separate confidence. Regardless of whether such surmising by Wife occurs when Lawyer gives notice of withdrawal, Lawyer nevertheless has complied with the Rules of Professional Conduct and has not violated Lawyer's duties to Husband.

Notes and Questions

1. *Joint Representation.* The Advisory Opinion analyzes the lawyer's representation of the spouses as a joint representation. What are the advantages and disadvantages of joint representation?

2. *Completely Separate Representation.* An alternative to joint representation is completely separate representation, meaning that each client is represented by his or her own lawyer. What are the advantages and disadvantages of completely separate representation?

3. *Separate Representation by the Same Lawyer?* Professor Jeffrey Pennell has advocated separate representation of multiple clients by the same lawyer. See, e.g., Jeffrey Pennell, Professional Responsibility: Reforms Are Needed to Accommodate Estate Planning and Family Counseling, 25 U. Miami Inst. Est. Plan. ch. 18 (1991). Under this approach, the clients agree that the lawyer will not disclose information about one client to the other(s) without permission. This approach is authorized in at least one jurisdiction, New York, see N.Y. State Bar Ass'n. Comm. on Prof. Ethics, Op. 761 (2003), but it has been heavily criticized by commentators. See, e.g., Geoffrey C. Hazard, Jr., Conflict of Interest in Estate Planning for Husband and Wife, 20 Prob. Law. 1, 13 (1994) ("Let me put the point bluntly. The concept of 'separate representation' is a legal and ethical oxymoron."); Teresa Stanton Collett, The Promise and Peril of Multiple Representation, 16 Rev. Litig. 567, 578 (1997). The American College of Trust and Estate Counsel (ACTEC) Commentaries on the Model Rules of Professional Conduct urge lawyers who undertake separate representation to do so "with care because of the stress it necessarily places on the lawyer's duties of impartiality and loyalty and the extent to which it may limit the lawyer's ability to advise each of the clients adequately." ACTEC Commentaries on the Model Rules of Professional Conduct 87 (6th ed. 2023).

4. *A v. B.* Disclosure questions can arise in situations other than one where one spouse separately confides to the lawyer representing both spouses. The manner a lawyer learns information about one spouse that might be material to the other spouse may justify different disclosure obligations, because one spouse did not communicate anything to the lawyer with an expectation that it would be kept confidential.

In A. v. B., 726 A.2d 924 (N.J. 1999), a law firm jointly represented spouses in the drafting and execution of wills in which they devised their respective estates to each other. The estate plans contemplated the possibility that the surviving spouse could ultimately devise the decedent spouse's estate to lineal descendants who were not lineal descendants of the decedent spouse. At the commencement of the representation, each spouse signed a letter explaining the possible conflicts of interest between the spouses and that information provided by one spouse could become available to the other. By signing the letter, each spouse "consented to and waived any conflicts arising from the firm's joint representation." The letter did not contain an express waiver of confidentiality.[60]

Because of a clerical error, the law firm had accepted representation of a mother bringing a paternity action against the husband. DNA evidence ultimately proved paternity, but issues remained concerning child support. Once the firm recognized the conflict of interest, it withdrew from its representation of the mother. After the firm encouraged the husband to inform his wife of the existence of the child, it stated that if he did not do so, it would. The firm believed that it was obligated to inform the wife "that her current estate plan may devise a portion of her assets through her spouse to the child." The husband took procedural actions in the paternity action to prevent the firm's disclosure.

The court analyzed the facts as presenting a conflict between a lawyer's duty of confidentiality and a lawyer's duty to inform clients of material facts. The court explicitly distinguished the hypothetical case set forth in Advisory Opinion 95-4 on three grounds: (1) the permissible disclosure rules differed, (2) the firm learned about the husband's paternity from a third party and not from the husband himself, and (3) the spouses had signed an agreement indicating their intent to share all information with each other.

The court concluded, under the New Jersey Rules of Professional Conduct, that the law firm was permitted to disclose the fact of the nonmarital child to the wife. It based its decision on a broad interpretation of the term "fraudulent act" that is found in the Rules. The court concluded that the husband's deliberate omission of the existence of the nonmarital child constituted a fraud on his wife.

EXTERNAL REFERENCE: For an excellent primer, see John R. Price, In Honor of Professor John Gaubatz: The Fundamentals of Ethically Representing Multiple Clients in Estate Planning, 62 U. Miami L. Rev. 735 (2008).

---

60. See ACTEC, Engagement Letters: A Guide for Practitioners (2d ed. 2007). This publication can be found at www.actec.org/documents/misc/actecengagementletters-2nded.pdf.

PART E. CONTRACTS TO DEVISE

Primary Statutory Reference: *UPC §2-514*

Claims that a decedent promised to devise property in return for certain services arise in a variety of contexts. In many states the Statute of Frauds prevents enforcement of oral promises to devise either in an action at law for breach of contract damages or in equity for specific performance. Despite non-enforceability of an oral contract to devise, though, the disappointed promisee may bring an action in quantum meruit to recover from the promisor's estate the value of any benefit for services rendered to the promisor.

Green v. Richmond
337 N.E.2d 691 (Mass. 1975)

HENNESSEY, J. This is an appeal by the defendant from a judgment rendered against him as the personal representative of the estate of Maxwell Evans Richmond (the decedent). The action was in the nature of quantum meruit and sought recovery for services rendered by the plaintiff in reliance on the decedent's oral promise to leave a will bequeathing his entire estate to her.

A jury trial in the Superior Court resulted in a verdict for the plaintiff in the amount of $1,350,000....

The facts are as follows: The plaintiff testified that she met the decedent in November, 1962, and shortly thereafter accepted his proposal of marriage. She was thirty-six years of age at the time, divorced, and had a fifteen-year old son; she was then employed as a secretary. The decedent was a wealthy, forty-nine year old bachelor whose holdings included licenses to operate three radio stations. Later the plaintiff became a stockbroker, earning about $20,000 a year.

About a year after they met, in October, 1963, the decedent stated that he had a "mental hangup" about marriage and asked to be released from the engagement; he said, however, that if the plaintiff would agree to "stay" with him, he would bequeath his entire estate to her at his death. The plaintiff agreed. There was other evidence directly corroborating the agreement. During the eight-year period between October, 1963, when bargain was made, and October, 1971, when the decedent died, there was evidence that the decedent, on several occasions, made statements to the plaintiff and other persons which could be found to be an acknowledgment by him of the original agreement. The last such occasion was on July 26, 1971, about three months before his death.

There was also evidence from which it could be found that the plaintiff kept her part of the agreement in reliance on the decedent's promise. There was detailed evidence of many services, of a social and domestic as well as of a business nature, performed by the plaintiff for the decedent over the eight-year period. There was evidence of many instances of sexual intercourse between the plaintiff and the decedent. The decedent died in October, 1971. The inventory value of his estate, which the judge permitted to be shown in evidence, was approximately $7,232,000.

1. It is clear that the oral agreement involved a promise to make a will, and as such was not binding. G.L. c. 259, §5. Nevertheless, if the oral agreement were legal and not contrary to public policy, the plaintiff could recover the fair value of her services.

We consider first the defendant's argument that a verdict should have been directed in his favor on the ground that the contract was illegal. The argument offered is that as matter of law the agreement included sexual intercourse or cohabitation as part of the consideration, and that such a contract will not be enforced as against public policy. Further, the argument is that even if the agreement did not expressly include illicit terms, the unlawful performance of the bargain precludes recovery. We conclude that there was no error in the denial of a directed verdict because these issues were properly submitted to the jury under appropriate instructions, and the jury obviously reached conclusions favorable to the plaintiff.[61]

The defendant ... argues that sexual intercourse was within the scope of the agreement and that the plaintiff therefore can recover nothing for her services; that additionally, or in the alternative, the plaintiff's performance in an illegal manner, by indulging in sexual intercourse, entitles her to no compensation, since her illegal performance was serious and not merely incidental to the agreement; that the illegality of the agreement and the illegality of the performance thereof were established as matter of law by the plaintiff's admissions on the witness stand at the trial, which the defendant argues were binding on her since there was no other evidence more favorable to her as to these issues; and that a directed verdict for the defendant was therefore required....

The judge, in denying the defendant's motion for a directed verdict, submitted to the jury the issue of illegality, both as to the content of the agreement and the nature of the plaintiff's performance. There was no error.... Where the evidence is disputed as to the terms or performance of an oral agreement, or the meaning of words used by the parties, the matter should be left to the jury. In this case there was disputed evidence, some of which was sufficiently favorable to the plaintiff to warrant submission of the issues to the jury.

Thus, the plaintiff's testimony as to the terms of the contract contained no reference to sexual intercourse as follows, viz.;

> He said he couldn't lose me, either, and then he said, "I have been thinking about something, and I want you to listen to me." He said: "I have been looking for you all my life. You're the perfect woman for me." He said: "If you will agree to stay with me without

---

61. It could persuasively be argued that only naive persons would conclude that sexual intercourse was not central to the arrangement between the parties. Nevertheless that reasoning is not relevant, since the evidence as summarized, infra, warranted the submission of the issues to the jury.

marriage, you will be happy. I will see that your life will be happy. There's only one thing you won't have. You won't have the emotional security a woman has when she knows she is married, but I will make it up to you. I am going to make my will out right away. Everything I have when I die will be yours. I owe nothing to anyone else."

The defendant contends, however, that other evidence particularly admissions by the plaintiff, required a conclusion that the contract included an agreement for sexual intercourse. The plaintiff had testified of many instances of sexual relations with the decedent. However, on this issue as well as on the related issue of illegality of performance, there was other evidence, including other testimony from the plaintiff, which was more favorable to the plaintiff. Therefore the issue was for the jury's consideration. From the totality of the evidence the jury were warranted in inferring that the illicit relations were no part of the contract, and were no more than an incidental part of the plaintiff's performance.

Thus, inferences favorable to the plaintiff were supported by the evidence. For example, the plaintiff testified that, throughout their relationship, she maintained her own apartment and paid all her own household bills; that the decedent bought her no expensive gifts, furs, cars, jewelry or diamonds and made no contribution to her son's tuition at college; that she did not even accompany him on his annual vacations, customarily taken at Christmastime, until 1966 or 1967, because she felt that she owed it to her son to be home with him during his Christmas vacations from school; and that the decedent, with the plaintiff's knowledge, took another woman with him when the plaintiff could not accompany him on his annual vacation.

Further, the witness Norman Solomon, who shared the decedent's apartment, testified that he never saw the plaintiff or any trace of her at the former residences of the decedent and that the decedent slept in his own apartment every night. The witness recalled only one time when he saw the plaintiff at the decedent's last residence. Solomon further testified that the decedent "traveled a lot with ... (a certain woman)," both before and after 1962, and "they made many trips together." Solomon quoted the plaintiff as saying, on one occasion, that both she and the decedent were free to "see" whomever of the opposite sex they might want to see.

A female witness, the "certain woman" referred to, supra, called by the defendant, testified that she took trips with the decedent each year between 1954 and 1958, inclusive. During the summer of 1963, she stayed at the defendant's apartment for about ten days. In 1964, she went on a trip to Jamaica with the decedent. In 1965, she went to St. Thomas and Puerto Rico with him. In 1967, she spent a week in Bermuda with him and then spent the entire summer at his apartment in Boston. Over the 1968 New Year's holiday, she went on a thirteen-day cruise with the decedent and, later in that year, went to St. Thomas with him. In 1969, she spent about a week with him at his summer residence in Marblehead and, in November of that year, the two of them went together to Florida for a week.

From all of this evidence the jury were justified in concluding that the sexual aspect of the relationship between the plaintiff and the decedent was no part of the bargain between the two, and no more than incidental to their relationship.

The defendant also argues that if the inventory of the probate estate had been excluded from evidence, as the defendant contends that it should have been, there would have been no evidence before the jury as to the value of the plaintiff's services. For this additional reason, the defendant says, there should have been a directed verdict for the defendant. There is no merit to this contention. Of the many and varied services as to which the plaintiff presented evidence, at least some of them were of such a routine and ordinary nature as to make their fair value a matter of common knowledge for the jury's consideration.

It follows from all that we have said that there was no error in the judge's denial of the defendant's motion for a directed verdict.

2. We turn now to the second issue argued by the defendant, viz.: that it was error to admit in evidence, over the objection and exception of the defendant, the Probate Court inventory showing the value of the estate. Actually there are two related questions raised here: (1) whether evidence as to the value of the estate is admissible and (2) if such evidence is admissible whether the probate inventory is an appropriate form of proof.

We consider first the question of the admissibility of the value of the estate. There is a divergence of opinion in other jurisdictions on the issue whether evidence of the contract terms, including value bargained for, shall be admitted as evidence of the value of the services sought by an action in quantum meruit. This divergence also exists with respect to the narrower question before us, i.e., whether the value of the decedent's estate was properly admitted as evidence of the value of the services rendered by the plaintiff on the basis that the value of the estate is the "price" put on the services by one of the contracting parties. There is precedent in somewhat similar Massachusetts cases for the admission of such evidence and the judge here undoubtedly relied on those decisions in making his rulings. We conclude that those decisions are controlling in the instant case and that the value of the estate was admissible in evidence.

There is substantial authority both judicial and scholarly which favors admissibility. Professor Corbin is emphatic as to the admissibility of this evidence:

> No one doubts, however, that the contract price or rate agreed upon by the parties is admissible in evidence to show what is the reasonable value of the performance that the defendant has received.

Corbin, Contracts, §1113 (1964). The annotation in 21 A.L.R.3d 9, 18 (1968) is further supportive of admissibility, noting that there is "considerable authority" for admitting the contract price terms as evidence of the value of the services, under the theory that it is an admission against interest and is evidence of the general making and performance of the contract. The annotation further cites authority for admitting the contract price terms although the contract is not enforceable as violative of the statute of frauds, in cases where the promise, as here, is to transfer an estate in consideration of services, and concludes that many courts have admitted the value of the estate in these cases....

We conclude that in the instant case appropriate proof of the value of the decedent's estate was admissible in evidence, and should be admitted at any subsequent retrial of the case.[62] Much of the reasoning advanced in favor of a directed verdict should receive consideration by the judge as substance for cautionary instructions to the jury against misuse of the evidence.

3. We turn now to a consideration of whether the probate inventory was an appropriate form of proof of the value of the estate, and whether, if it was not, it was error to admit the inventory in evidence in this case. We conclude that it was error.

The asset value was shown on the inventory as approximately $7,232,000. We have no way of knowing whether this amount accurately, or even remotely, represents the net value of the estate. We take notice that taxes, debts and other appropriate charges will substantially reduce this gross value. We assume that the inventory amount shown had some basis in fact, but the value of an estate is not shown by a list of its assets alone.... [I]n the special circumstances of this case we conclude that a preliminary showing of reliability was required before the amount of the inventory, which may or may not have been reflective of the value of the estate, was disclosed to the jury....

We conclude, therefore, that the judgment should be reversed and the case remanded to the Superior Court for a new trial limited to the issue of damages.

So ordered.

Notes and Questions

1. *Enforceability of the Contract.* If Maxwell Evans had made his promise to leave his entire estate to Bernyce Green in a signed letter to her, would she have been able to recover damages for breach of contract from his estate? Consider the following observations:

> Where there is a contract to devise or bequeath and the promisee fully performs on his part, if the promisor dies without fulfilling his obligation an ordinary action at law for breach of contract will lie. The action is for breach of contract by the deceased and should be brought against the personal representative in the same way as any other contract claim against the estate. The claim is assignable and may be enforced in the name of the assignee. Ordinarily the measure of damages will be the value of the thing promised by the promisor.

---

62. An interesting issue has been suggested: As of what date should the value of the estate be shown? Is it the date of the agreement or the date of the death? In the instant case the issue is not pressed, presumably because there was evidence that the decedent renewed his promise just a few months before his death.

Where the thing promised is a specific sum of money or a specific item of property the amount of damages is easily determined. If the promise is to give the entire estate or a fractional part thereof an action at law is hardly the appropriate remedy, but if that remedy is entertained the value of the thing promised is still the measure of damages. The difficulty here is with the remedy itself. Before the amount of damages can be fixed the net value of the estate must be ascertained. Since a jury is not a satisfactory body to supervise an estate accounting the law court should decline jurisdiction and transfer the case to equity where the parties will find a forum more adapted to their needs....

Recovery in quantum meruit such as is described above should not be confused with an action for damages for breach of the contract where an entirely different measure of damages is demanded. However, recovery in quantum meruit cannot be had unless the contract, even though oral, is proved.

Bertel M. Sparks, Contracts to Make Wills 136-40 (1956).

2. *Subsequent Development in Massachusetts.* The Supreme Judicial Court of Massachusetts held in Wilcox v. Trautz, 693 N.E.2d 141, 146 (Mass. 1998), that sex as part of the contract does not render the contract unenforceable as long as sexual services do not "constitute the only, or dominant, consideration for the agreement...."

3. *Quantum Meruit Recovery by Unmarried Cohabitors.* Even without an explicit oral promise to devise all or part of the estate in return for services, a surviving cohabitor may have a claim in quantum meruit against the other's estate for the value of services rendered the decedent in the expectation of compensation. See, e.g., Estate of Zent, 459 N.W.2d 795 (N.D. 1990); Suggs v. Norris, 364 S.E.2d 159 (N.C. Ct. App. 1988).

4. One newsworthy lawsuit concerning alleged oral promises to make a devise involved the estate of Doris Duke, the late billionaire heir of James B. Duke, the founder of American Tobacco Co. In 1988, Ms. Duke, who had no biological children, adopted Chandi Gail Heffner, a Hare Krishna follower with whom Duke shared interests in dance, animals, and Eastern philosophy. The two later had a falling-out, and Heffner was not named in Duke's will (a will contested on other grounds). Heffner sued the Duke estate for breach of an alleged oral promise to provide for her in the style to which she had become accustomed. The suit was settled, and Heffner received more than $65 million from the Duke estate. See George James, More Than $65 Million For Adopted Duke Daughter, N.Y. Times, Dec. 30, 1995, at 35.

Chapter 5

Revocation of Wills

A will is an inherently revocable document.[1] The methods of revoking a will by a subsequent instrument or by act are codified in all U.S. jurisdictions and are the subjects of Parts A and B of this Chapter. Part C covers situations in which a change in the testator's circumstances revokes a will. Parts D and E explore fact-patterns in which a will that was previously revoked is nevertheless given effect at the testator's death. Part F explores the validity and effect of a contract not to revoke a will.

PART A. REVOCATION BY SUBSEQUENT WILL

Primary Statutory Reference: *UPC §2-507*

All revocation statutes authorize a testator to revoke a will by validly executing a subsequent will that contains an express revocation clause.[2] See, e.g., UPC §2-507(a)(1). A will drafted by a lawyer typically contains an express revocation clause, such as "this will revokes all my prior wills and codicils."

The UPC permits revocation by a subsequent will that contains only a revocation clause. Both the UPC and the Restatement 3d of Property define the term "will" as including a testamentary instrument that merely revokes another will. See UPC §1-201(57); Restatement 3d of Property §3.1 comment a. A testator obtaining legal advice is unlikely to execute an instrument that only revokes a previous will, because lawyers typically advise a client to replace one will with another.

The UPC and non-UPC revocation statutes also provide that, in the absence of an express revocation clause, a previous will is revoked by an "inconsistent" subsequent will. See UPC §2-507(a)(1); see also Restatement 3d of Property §4.1 comment d.

Revocation by inconsistency (also called *implied revocation*) typically occurs when a testator, without the aid of an attorney, executes a will that does not include an express revocation clause. When a testator dies with two or more wills, and the latest one does not expressly revoke the previous ones, litigation can arise about whether the testator intended the subsequent will to replace the previous wills in whole or in part or merely to supplement them. This was the question in Gilbert v. Gilbert.

---

1. But see Part F of this Chapter on the validity and effect of a contract not to revoke a will.

2. Most courts hold that a holographic will can revoke a formal, attested will, even in a jurisdiction in which the statute provides that a will can be revoked only by an instrument executed with the same formalities as the revoked will. Cases are collected in Annot., Revocation of Witnessed Will by Holographic Will or Codicil, Where Statute Requires Revocation by Instrument of Equal Formality as Will, 49 A.L.R.3d 1223.

Gilbert v. Gilbert

652 S.W.2d 663 (Ky. Ct. App. 1983)

PAXTON, J. This is an appeal from a judgment of the Jefferson Circuit Court determining that a holographic instrument, consisting of two writings folded together inside a sealed envelope, was a codicil instead of a second and superseding will. Appellees are a brother of the testator, a niece and three nephews of the testator, and two beneficiaries unrelated to the testator. Appellants are the testator's sisters and remaining brothers.

Frank Gilbert died testate on June 5, 1979. Two writings were offered for probate: an eight-page typewritten instrument, prepared by an attorney, dated April 2, 1976, and the holographic instrument dated December 8, 1978. The "codicil" was written on the back of a business card and on the back of one of Frank's pay stubs. The card and stub were found folded together in a sealed envelope. On the back of the business card, Frank wrote: "12/8/78 Jim and Margaret I have appro $50,000.00 in Safe. See Buzz if anything happens [signed] Frank Gilbert". On the back of the pay stub, Frank wrote: "Jim & Margaret $20,000.00 the Rest divided Equally the other Living Survivors Bro. & Sisters [signed] Frank Gilbert 12/8/78". Written on the envelope is the following: "This day 12/8/1978 I gave to Jim and Margaret this card which I Stated what to do". "Jim and Margaret" are James Gilbert (one of the appellees) and Margaret Gilbert, brother and sister-in-law, respectively, of Frank Gilbert, the testator. The typewritten instrument and the holographic instrument were admitted to probate on September 4, 1979, the holographic instrument being admitted as a codicil.

Appellants subsequently brought a will contest action in Jefferson Circuit Court seeking to have the holographic instrument interpreted as a second and superseding will. After a hearing, the circuit court entered a judgment construing the second instrument as a codicil affecting only the money Frank kept in his employer's safe. This appeal is from that judgment. We affirm.

Appellants argue ... [that] the separate holographic writings should have been construed as a second and superseding will instead of a codicil.... This interpretation would eliminate James Gilbert from sharing in any portion of his brother's estate, except the $20,000.00 bequeathed to him and his wife, Margaret, in the "codicil". Appellees argue, of course, that the "codicil" pertains only to the money in the safe and that James takes both his share under the typewritten will and one-half of the first $20,000.00 of the money in the safe pursuant to the terms of the "codicil"....

The second instrument was probated as a codicil, but because it does not refer to the typewritten will, we prefer to characterize it as a second will. A testator can have more than one will effective at the same time, each distributing part of the estate. In such a case the subsequent wills "perform the office of codicils". Muller v. Muller, 108 Ky. 511, 516, 56 S.W. 802, 803 (1900). We believe that to be the situation in this case: the second will serves as a codicil because it does not contain a revocation clause and only distributes part of the residuary estate.

The holographic will does not revoke the typewritten one. We think it is very unlikely that Frank intended to supplant the elaborate distribution of his estate contained in the eight-page typewritten will with a single phrase scratched out on the back of a pay stub. Furthermore, there is no revocation clause in the second will and Kentucky courts have consistently held that one testamentary instrument revokes another only if it is the clear intent of the testator to do so, and even then the revocation is only to the extent necessary. The second will in this case need only re-distribute part of the residue.

We must resolve Frank's intent by looking at the four corners of the two wills, and harmonizing any conflicting provisions to give effect to every provision of each instrument. Here, it is easy to harmonize the two instruments. The only way to give effect to every provision of both instruments is to adopt the trial court's interpretation, to-wit: the two holographic writings comprise a second will that distributes only the money Frank kept in his employer's safe. It was not inconsistent for him to distribute, by a second will, a portion of his estate that would have passed under the residuary clause of the first will.

The judgment of the Jefferson Circuit Court is affirmed. All concur.

Notes

1. *Non-Uniform Probate Code Law.* Most non-UPC statutes fail to elaborate on how to determine whether a subsequent will is sufficiently inconsistent with an earlier will to revoke it in whole or in part. The Restatement 3d of Property formulates the following principle:

> §4.1, [Comment] d, Revocation by inconsistency.... If the later will makes a complete disposition of the testator's estate, it is presumed that the testator intended the later will to replace the earlier will.... Unless the presumption is rebutted by clear and convincing evidence, the earlier will is revoked and only the later will is operative on the testator's death.
>
> If the later will does not make a complete disposition of the testator's estate, it is presumed that the testator intended the later will to supplement rather than replace the earlier will. If this presumption is not rebutted by clear and convincing evidence, the later will revokes the earlier will only to the extent that the later will is inconsistent with the earlier will. Each will is fully operative on the testator's death to the extent that they are not inconsistent.

2. *Uniform Probate Code.* The Restatement's formulation is expressly adopted in UPC §2-507.

3. *Electronic Wills.* Can an electronic will revoke a prior paper will? Can an electronic will be revoked by a later will by inconsistency? See the Uniform Electronic Wills Act §7(a) and §7(b)(1).

4. *Will of Chief Justice Burger.* A year before his death on June 25, 1995, retired Chief Justice Burger prepared and executed the following will. He previously had

a fully attested will prepared by an attorney. His wife, Elvera, predeceased him, an event that may have prompted the making of the new will. Their two children, Margaret and Wade, survived him. Did the following will revoke the earlier will?

LAST WILL AND TESTAMENT
OF
WARREN E. BURGER[3]

I hereby make and declare the following to be my last will and testament.

1. My executors will first pay all claims against my estate;
2. The remainder of my estate will be distributed as follows: one-third to my daughter, Margaret Elizabeth Burger Rose and two-thirds to my son, Wade A. Burger;
3. I designate and appoint as executors of this will, Wade A. Burger and J. Michael Luttig.

IN WITNESS WHEREOF, I have hereunto set my hand to this my Last Will and Testament this *9th* day of June, 1994.

/s/ Warren E. Burger
WARREN E. BURGER

We hereby certify that in our presence on the date written above WARREN E. BURGER signed the foregoing instrument and declared it to be his Last Will and Testament and that at this request in his presence and in the presence of each other we have signed our names below as witnesses.

/s/ Nathaniel E. Brady residing at *120 'F' St., NW Washington, DC*
/s/ Alice M. Khu   residing at *3041 Meeting St. Falls Church, VA*

SWORN TO AND SUBSCRIBED BEFORE ME THIS *9*[th] DAY OF *June*, 19*94*.

Constance Y. Ferguson
NOTARY PUBLIC

CONSTANCE Y. FERGUSON
Notary Public District of Columbia
My Commission Expires January 31, 1999

Problems

Five years before her death, G executed Will #1, devising her antique desk to A, $20,000 to B, and the residue of her estate to C. Two years later, A died, and G executed Will #2, devising her antique desk to A's husband X, $10,000 to B, and the residue of her estate to C. Will #2 neither contained an express revocation provision nor referred to Will #1. At G's death, her net probate estate consisted of her antique desk (worth $10,000) and other property (worth $90,000).

1. Under the UPC, how should G's estate be divided among X, B, and C?

2. Would your answers change if Will #2 had not contained a provision devising the residue of the estate to C?

3. Should extrinsic evidence be admissible in determining the extent to which Will #1 is impliedly revoked by Will #2?

---

3. Italicized portions in handwriting. Ed.

PART B. REVOCATION BY UNATTESTED REVOCATORY ACT

Primary Statutory Reference: UPC §2-507

The English Statute of Frauds 1677, §6, 29 Car. 2, ch. 3, permitted revocation of a will by "burning, canceling, tearing or obliterating the same." The UPC and nearly all non-UPC statutes have a somewhat similar provision.[4]

That the statutes recognize revocation by act to the document exemplifies how the law can be molded by the practices of the people whose affairs it regulates. One reason for recognizing revocation by burning, tearing, etc. is the fact that many people choose this method of revoking their wills.[5]

The law treats a will as revoked because its maker *intended* to revoke it. Just as the law requires a writing to furnish reliable evidence of an intent to make a will, the law also insists upon reliable evidence of a manifestation of intent to revoke. In the main, reliable evidence consists either of another duly executed writing (revocation by instrument) or of some act to the instrument that tends of itself to suggest that the testator meant to revoke the will or some part of it.

Among the prescribed methods of revoking by act, most of the litigation has concerned cancellation. Cancellation occurs when the testator has crossed out or marked through the document or part of it or has written on the document words such as "canceled" or "null and void."

EXTERNAL REFERENCE. Verner F. Chaffin, Execution, Revocation, and Revalidation of Wills: A Critique of Existing Statutory Formalities, 11 Ga. L. Rev. 297 (1977).

---

4. Some statutory lists are less comprehensive than the one contained in the English statute. See, e.g., Goode v. Estate of Hoover, 828 S.W.2d 558 (Tex. Ct. App. 1992) (holding the original will valid under a statute that included only acts of destruction or cancellation when the attempted revocatory act consisted of removal and substitution of the first page of the will). UPC §2-507(a)(2) and many non-UPC statutes include "destroying."

5. "The old law enabled a man to revoke his will by canceling it, and such was the habit of Englishmen." Edward B. Sugden (later Lord St. Leonards), Speech in the House of Commons upon the Law of Wills Bill 32 (1838). Sir Edward Sugden was criticizing the failure of the Wills Act of 1837 to include "canceling" as a method of revoking a will by act to the document. He suggested "a few simple rules by which we ought to be governed in the alterations of our law of property," one of which was: "Run not counter to the habits of the people."

Kronauge v. Stoecklein[6]
293 N.E.2d 320 (Ohio Ct. App. 1972)

CRAWFORD, J. Plaintiffs, the appellants herein, are the heirs at law of Helen L. White, deceased. Defendants are her executor and the beneficiaries under her will, the principal beneficiary being Jennifer L. Jones aka Jennifer L. Manson.

The will of Helen L. White was executed on October 4, 1968. It was drawn upon the stationery of her attorney, Robert J. Stoecklein, who was also one of the witnesses to the will. She never spoke to him thereafter about changing or revoking the will.

On the otherwise blank margin of the will, in the handwriting of the testatrix, but not touching any of the writing in the will, appear these words:

> *This will is void. We have never heard or seen Jennifer Jones or did she come to Jess' funeral so I do not leave her anything*
> *April 17, 1971*

Plaintiffs brought this action to contest the will. Defendants filed a motion for summary judgment. The facts upon the motion were stipulated.

The court sustained the motion and entered judgment for the defendants, the appellees and proponents of the will. Plaintiffs, the appellants and contestants, have appealed.

The parties agree that the single question before us on appeal is whether the writing on the margin revoked the will.

There is no inherent or common-law right to dispose of one's property by will. Such right depends upon statute. The law is quite specific as to the formalities required to make a valid will, or to revoke it. R.C. §2107.33 provides the exclusive methods of revoking a will. These must be strictly complied with in order to make the revocation effective.

R.C. §2107.33 reads:

> A will shall be revoked by the testator by tearing, canceling, obliterating, or destroying such will with the intention of revoking it, or by some person in such testator's presence, or by such testator's express written direction, or by some other written will or codicil, executed as prescribed by sections 2107.01 to 2107.62, inclusive, of the Revised Code, or by some other writing which is signed, attested, and subscribed in the manner provided by

---

6. In connection with this case, it is helpful to know the provisions of the Ohio Wills Act (Ohio Rev. Code §2107.03) that governed the formalities of Helen White's will:

Except oral wills, every last will and testament shall be in writing, but may be handwritten or typewritten. Such will shall be signed at the end by the party making it, or by some other person in such party's presence and at his express direction, and be attested and subscribed in the presence of such party, by two or more competent witnesses, who saw the testator subscribe, or heard him acknowledge his signature.

such sections....

The intent of the testatrix here is not questioned.

It is conceivable that a writing might be so placed over the text of the instrument as to constitute [a cancellation]. Such is not the case here, where the writing does not touch any part of the wording in the will itself. It must therefore be classified as a writing which is not a canceling; and, of course, the writing does not purport to be "signed, attested and subscribed in the manner provided by such sections." (R.C. §§2107.01 to 2107.62.)....

Judgment affirmed.

SHERER, P.J. and KERNS, J., concur.

Notes, Questions, and Problem

1. *Invalid as a Revocation by Cancellation; Valid as a Revocation by Subsequent Will*. As the court suggested in the *Kronauge* case, a statement of cancellation, if properly executed, can be given effect as a revocation by subsequent will, regardless of whether the statement of cancellation touches any of the words on the will. See, e.g., Kehr's Estate, 95 A.2d 647 (Pa. 1953). Doubtless this is most likely to occur in jurisdictions that recognize holographic wills. See, e.g., Estate of Nielson, 165 Cal. Rptr. 319 (Ct. App. 1980); Estate of Langan, 668 P.2d 481 (Or. Ct. App. 1983).

2. *Touching of the Words*. No touching of the words is required for revocation by burning or tearing. See, e.g., Crampton v. Osborn, 201 S.W.2d 336 (Mo. 1947) (tearing); White v. Casten, 46 N.C. 197 (1853) (burning).

In contrast, most authority is consistent with the *Kronauge* proposition that words of cancellation in the margin or on the back of the will fail to revoke a will by cancellation. See, e.g., Noesen v. Erkenswick, 131 N.E. 622 (Ill. 1921); Yont v. Eads, 57 N.E.2d 531 (Mass. 1944); Thompson v. Royall, 175 S.E. 748 (Va. 1934). Contra Warner v. Warner's Estate, 37 Vt. 356 (1864).

In Kroll v. Nehmer, 705 A.2d 716, 716, 723 (Md. 1998), the court simply assumed, without discussion, that a testator effectively revoked her 1985 will by writing on the back of the will the words "VOID—NEW WILL DRAWN UP 6-28-90." See also Estate of Dickson, 590 So.2d 471 (Fla. Dist. Ct. App. 1991), in which the court held that words of cancellation that touched the notarial seal of the self-proving affidavit attached to the will qualified as a sufficient act revoking the will.

UPC §2-507(a)(2) eliminates the distinction between revocation by cancellation and revocation by burning or tearing. Regardless of the type of revocatory act, a touching of the words on the will is not required. The position of the UPC is supported by the Restatement 3d of Property §4.1 comment g.

3. *Problem*. On his deathbed, G crumpled up his will and threw it into a wastebasket, from which it was retrieved after his death. Was the will revoked? In SouthTrust Bank of Alabama N.A. v. Winter, 689 So.2d 69 (Ala. Civ. App. 1996),

the testator placed her will and a codicil in a paper sack in a hallway closet area that the testator referred to commonly as "trash alley." The court held that "as a matter of law, the mere placement of the will in the paper sack did not 'materially and permanently destroy the efficacy of the document.' Accordingly, placing the will in the paper sack was not an act of cancellation or abandonment and did not constitute a revocation of the will." (quoting Board of Trustees v. Calhoun, 514 So. 2d 895 (Ala. 1987)).

———

Revocatory Act Performed by Another. Like most probate code provisions on revocation, UPC §2-507 authorizes the performance of a revocatory act not only by the testator, but also by another person. The execution analogue of this procedure is the procedure under which someone other than the testator signs the testator's name. See Chapter 4. Not surprisingly, the question of whether the other person's act was done in the testator's "presence" arises in this context just as it did in the will execution context.

Consider, for example, the case of Estate of Bancker, 232 So. 2d 431 (Fla. Dist. Ct. App.), cert. denied, 238 So. 2d 111 (Fla. 1970). Adrian G. Bancker died in 1967, survived by his wife, three children, and a stepdaughter. Shortly before his death, Adrian became dissatisfied with the attorney who prepared his 1966 will and who was named alternate executor. For the purpose of reviving a former will,[7] Adrian directed his wife, stepdaughter, and her husband to destroy the 1966 will. Adrian remained in bed while they went into another room, removed the will from a wall safe, and destroyed it by tearing it into pieces and flushing them down a toilet. The court held that the 1966 will was not revoked, saying:

> [The Florida] statute specifically provides the revocation must be made in the presence of the testator. Under this statute, such revocation must take place in the physical and mental presence of the testator. The requirements for a valid revocation of a will must be strictly observed.

Would the outcome of the *Bancker* case have been different if the case had been governed by UPC §2-507?

If a testator telephones her attorney who has custody of her will and directs the attorney to destroy it, would the will be revoked under UPC §2-507? Would it matter whether the will was destroyed while the testator was on the telephone? Could the harmless-error rule of either UPC §2-503 or the Restatement 3d of Property §3.3 apply if the evidence clearly and convincingly shows that the testator intended to

---

7. In order to revive a former will in Florida, the testator must reexecute the former will or execute a codicil republishing the former will. See Fla. Stat. §§732.508(1), 732.511. Was the fact that the testator in *Bancker* did neither relevant to the outcome of the case?

revoke the will?[8] See Estate of O'Donnell, 803 S.W.2d 530 (Ark. 1991), overruled on other grounds by Edmundson v. Estate of Fountain, 189 S.W.3d 427 (Ark. 2004).

Ineffective Attempt to Revoke. If a testator intends to revoke a will by act to the document and the will is not destroyed by physical act because another person fraudulently intervened to prevent the destruction, the will remains effective. Without the physical act, an intent to revoke is insufficient to revoke a will. The courts, however, provide a remedy for any wrongful interference with an attempt to revoke, and aim to effectuate a testator's intent through the imposition of a constructive trust. See Chapter 4. See, e.g., Brazil v. Silva, 185 P. 174 (Cal. 1919) (the related case of Estate of Silva, 145 P. 1015 (Cal. 1915) had held the will revocation ineffective and directed the contestants to seek relief in equity); White v. Mulvania, 575 S.W.2d 184 (Mo. 1978).

Historically, the law of wills has limited the constructive trust remedy to situations in which a third party has wrongfully interfered with an attempt to execute or revoke a will.

Estate of Tolin
622 So. 2d 988 (Fla. 1993)

[On November 7, 1984, Alexander Tolin executed a will that devised the residue of his estate to his friend, Adair Creaig. The will was prepared by his attorney, Steven Fine, and executed in the attorney's office. The original will was retained by the attorney and a blue-backed photocopy of the original executed will was given to Mr. Tolin. On July 14, 1989, Alexander Tolin executed a codicil that changed the residuary beneficiary from Adair Creaig to Broward Art Guild, Inc. This codicil was also prepared by his attorney, Steven Fine, at the attorney's office. Again, the attorney retained the original in his office and gave Mr. Tolin a blue-backed photocopy of the original executed codicil.

Alexander Tolin died on October 14, 1990. Approximately six months before his death, Mr. Tolin advised his neighbor, Ed Weinstein, a retired New York attorney, that he had made a mistake and that he wished to revoke the codicil and reinstate Adair Creaig as the residuary beneficiary. Mr. Weinstein advised him that he could accomplish his purpose by tearing up the original codicil. At a meeting at which Mr. Tolin and Mr. Weinstein were present, Mr. Tolin handed Mr. Weinstein a blue-backed document, which he represented was his original codicil. Mr. Weinstein looked at the document. It appeared to him to be the original codicil and he handed it back to Mr. Tolin. Mr. Tolin then tore it up and destroyed it. It is not disputed that this document was torn up and destroyed with the intent and for the purpose of revocation.

---

8. Although the black letter of §3.3 only addresses harmless errors in executing a will, comment c to § 3.3 provides that "[t]he harmless-error rule established in this section applies ... also to the validity of attempts to revoke a will ...."

However, soon following Mr. Tolin's death, Mr. Weinstein spoke with Steven Fine and discovered for the first time that Mr. Fine had in his possession the original will and codicil. The document that Mr. Tolin tore up was actually the blue-backed photocopy that Mr. Fine had given to Mr. Tolin at the time of its execution. It is undisputed that this was an exact copy of the fully executed original codicil and was in all respects identical to the original except for the original signatures.

Steven Fine, the personal representative, petitioned the circuit court to admit the will and codicil to probate. He also filed a motion to determine the validity of the codicil. Additionally, Creaig filed a petition seeking revocation of the codicil. The circuit court entered an order revoking probate of the codicil and reinstating the provisions of the will.

On appeal, the district court reversed and held that destroying an unsigned copy of a will or codicil, even one containing a photo image of the original signature, is insufficient to revoke the original will or codicil. On rehearing, the district court certified the question raised by this case as one of great public importance, and the Supreme Court accepted jurisdiction.]

HARDING, J. The primary rule of construction in construing a will is ascertaining and giving effect to the testator's intent. Additionally, it is well settled that strict compliance with the will statutes is required in order to effectuate a revocation of a will or codicil. Estate of Dickson, 590 So.2d 471, 472 (Fla. 3d DCA 1991); Estate of Bancker, 232 So.2d 431, 433 (Fla. 4th DCA), cert. denied, 238 So.2d 111 (Fla.1970). Section 732.506 provides the procedure for revoking a will or codicil by physical act. Section 732.506 provides that

> [a] will or codicil is revoked by the testator, or by some other person in [the testator's] presence and at [the testator's] direction, by burning, tearing, canceling, defacing, obliterating, or destroying it with the intent, and for the purpose, of revocation.

.... Because the testator destroyed a copy of the codicil rather than the original codicil, his attempted revocation was ineffective.

The next issue we address is whether a constructive trust should properly be imposed when a testator fails to effectively revoke a codicil because of a mistake of fact which prevented the testator from fulfilling the requirements of section 732.506. A constructive trust is properly imposed when, as a result of a mistake in a transaction, one party is unjustly enriched at the expense of another. Wadlington v. Edwards, 92 So.2d 629 (Fla.1957). Although this equitable remedy is usually limited to circumstances in which fraud or a breach of confidence has occurred, it is proper in cases in which one party has benefitted by the mistake of another at the expense of a third party. Holmes v. Holmes, 463 So.2d 578 (Fla. 1st DCA 1985).

In the instant case, ... [i]t is clear that the testator's intent to revoke the codicil was frustrated by his mistake in destroying a copy of the codicil rather than the original. Further, the Broward Art Guild has benefitted from the testator's mistake at the expense of Creaig. Thus, we find that a constructive trust is appropriate under these unique and undisputed facts.

This case shows the importance of distinguishing an original document from a copy. The facts in the instant case show that the testator's mistake in destroying a copy of the codicil, rather than the original, was caused by the high quality of the copy, which made it indistinguishable from the original. As technology advances, the determination of whether an instrument is an original or a copy may become more difficult. Thus, it is advisable for attorneys preparing documents, such as wills and codicils, to consider designating which documents are copies. Such a designation would have aided in the disposition of this case.

Accordingly, we approve the holding of the district court that the testator's destruction of a copy of a codicil is not an effective revocation of the codicil. However, we remand the case to the district court with directions that upon remand to the trial court, a constructive trust shall be imposed on the assets conveyed by the codicil for Creaig's benefit.

It is so ordered.

OVERTON, SHAW and GRIMES, JJ., concur.

MCDONALD, J., concurs in result only with an opinion, in which BARKETT, C.J., and KOGAN, J., concur.

MCDONALD, Justice, concurring in result only.

Under the unique facts of this I conclude that the testator effectively revoked his codicil. I thus agree with the trial judge and the dissent in the case under review. The effect of the majority opinion is to accomplish the result of a revoked codicil. While I quarrel with the route it took, the majority reaches the correct destination and I therefore concur in the result.

BARKETT, C.J., and KOGAN, J., concur.

Notes

1. *Revocation under UPC or Restatement?* Under the UPC, would Alexander Tolin's 1989 codicil have been revoked? See §§2-507(a)(2), 2-503. Under the harmless-error rule of Restatement 3d of Property §3.3 (see Chapter 4)?

2. *Revocation of Electronic Will by Act.* What are the requirements for revoking an electronic will by act? Must the revocatory act be performed on the original of the electronic will, or can the revocatory act be performed on a copy? See the Uniform Electronic Wills Act §7(b)(2) and the accompanying Comment.

3. *Future of Constructive Trust Remedy in Florida and Elsewhere.* In Allen v. Dalk, 826 So.2d 245 (Fla. 2002), a testator, in a law office execution ceremony in which she signed multiple estate planning documents, somehow failed to sign one of the documents—her will. The Florida Supreme Court "decline[d] ... to extend [the] *Tolin* [case] beyond its facts," holding that the beneficiaries of the invalid will

were not entitled to a constructive trust in their favor. See Chapter 4.

The principle of *Tolin* is that the constructive trust remedy "is proper in cases in which one party has benefited by the mistake of another at the expense of a third party."[9] If this principle is sound, why should it not be extended beyond the facts of *Tolin*?

The Restatement 3d of Property §4.1 comment f supports the imposition of a constructive trust in cases like *Tolin*, and the Restatement 3d of Restitution and Unjust Enrichment §11 and the Restatement 3d of Trusts §16 support the imposition of a constructive trust or other equitable remedy to correct a unilateral mistake in connection with a donative transfer. Accord, Nelson v. Nelson, 205 P.3d 715 (Kan. 2009). But see Estate of Charitou, 595 N.Y.S. 308 (Sur. Ct. 1993), where the court on facts similar to *Tolin* rejected the imposition of a constructive trust because of the absence of wrongdoing. For further discussion of mistake and judicial reformation to prevent unjust enrichment resulting from mistake, see Chapter 13.

————

Presumption of Intent to Revoke. If a will contestant proves that the testator had custody of the will, a will that is found physically mutilated is presumed to be revoked. See, e.g., Estate of Bakhaus, 102 N.E.2d 818 (Ill. 1951).

As demonstrated in *Estate of May* below, the presumption is rebuttable. "Moreover, the presumption regarding a mutilated will must be tempered when the act is a blemish that could easily have occurred accidentally, such as a small tear across a corner or a singe mark that could have been caused by a dropped cigarette ash. Although insignificant acts such as these are technically sufficient as revocatory acts..., they must be shown to have been done by the testator with the intent to revoke." Restatement 3d of Property §4.1 comment j.

Estate of May
220 N.W.2d 388 (S.D. 1974)

DUNN, J.... The decedent lived alone on a farm a few miles from Parker, South Dakota. He executed a document on December 28, 1967 entirely in his own handwriting purporting to dispose of his property upon his death. There was no question raised of undue influence or of testamentary capacity. The decedent told Victor Brandt on at least two occasions that he did have a will, the last time being approximately three days before his death. On February 14, 1973 John R. May died in Turner County, South Dakota.

---

9. For another case in which the court reached the same conclusion, see Smithberg v. Illinois Municipal Retirement Fund, 735 N.E.2d 560, 565 (Ill. 2000), where the court said: "Although some form of wrongdoing is generally required for the imposition of a constructive trust, wrongdoing is not always a necessary element. For example, a constructive trust may be imposed in the case of mistake, although no wrongdoing is involved."

Mrs. Eva Christensen, respondent and a sister of the deceased, searched the decedent's home and bank boxes thoroughly after his death but could find no will. Mrs. Christensen, the sheriff of Turner County and others went through the papers of the deceased in his home; some papers were destroyed and others piled into boxes and stored in a rented barn near the home of a niece, Eva Brandt. Later, Mrs. Brandt found the contested will with the papers moved to the barn and in a box of documents which also contained current receipts, bills, bank statements and current business records of the deceased.

The document purporting to be a Holographic Will is hereby set out in full, showing where it was cut out of the book on the right margin, and where it was torn on the left margin.

There is no evidence to show what happened to the document[10] from the date it was

---

10. Note to students: Below is a transcription of the document. Ed.
December 28, 1967
[T]his is my will
[m]y doctor bills must be
that medicare does not
my hospital bills
Esther [his sister] gets $1200.00
Eva [his sister] gets $1200.00
Laura's [his deceased sister's] two (2) adopted girls

executed to the date it was found. It came from decedent's home and the inference would be that it was in decedent's possession at least until the date of his death. All of the witnesses testified that decedent's home was a mess with important documents as well as worthless scraps of paper piled around the house without any system or order. In the light of these facts the trial court ruled that the Holographic Will had been torn and obliterated by the decedent during his lifetime with the intent and for the purpose of revoking the same in accordance with SDCL 29-3-1 which states:

> Except in the cases in this chapter mentioned, no written will, nor any part thereof, can be revoked or altered, otherwise than:
> (1) By a written will or other writing of the testator, declaring such revocation or alteration, and executed with the same formalities with which a will should be executed by such testator; or
> (2) By being burnt, torn, canceled, obliterated, or destroyed, with the intent and for the purpose of revoking the same, by the testator himself, or by some person in his presence and by his direction.

In considering this statute we should also refer to SDCL 29-3-3:

> A revocation by obliteration on the face of the will may be partial or total, and is complete if the material part is so obliterated as to show an intention to revoke;....

As there was no extrinsic evidence that decedent intended to destroy the will, the trial court of necessity in reaching its decision had to rely on the presumption generally set out in 57 Am. Jur., Wills, §550, which reads as follows:

> It is generally agreed that if a will produced for probate, which is shown to have been in the custody of the testator after its execution, was found among the testator's effects after his death, in ... a state of mutilation, ... it will be presumed, in the absence of evidence to the contrary, that such act was performed by the testator with the intention of revoking the

---

$600.00
$600.00
[t]hey onnerd mother's will
passed away, the will
made was not dated
hold.
[brot]her Ed May did not
[m]other's will, so He gets $1.00
of what I have goes to
[S]DA [Seventh-day Adventist] Conference at Pierre, So. D.
who ever is president
[?] at that time can be
point the administrator.
would like the broom
[factor]y and supplies to go into our
/s/ John R. May
Parker So. Dak.

instrument.... Whatever presumption arises from acts of cancellation or mutilation is rebuttable, but the burden of the rebuttal rests upon the proponent.

Proponent of the will rebuts this presumption by evidence that the decedent told Victor Brandt (husband of Eva Brandt, niece of decedent) that he had a will on two different occasions, the last time being some three days before his death. This testimony was corroborated by Mrs. Brandt to the extent that her husband had advised her of decedent's statements at the time that they were made. No other will was ever found. Mrs. Brandt would be an heir of the decedent if the will was not upheld and would take nothing under the will. Accordingly, the testimony of the Brandts on this subject is most credible and convincing and any presumption of intent to revoke the will arising from the tearing while in the possession of the decedent was effectively rebutted. In Fleming v. Fleming, 367 Ill. 97, 10 N.E.2d 641, it is stated:

> Any act of tearing of the paper on which the will is written, however slight, is an act of tearing within the meaning of this statute if done with intent to revoke the will, but it is likewise true that no act of tearing or cutting, unless it be with the intention to revoke the will, accomplishes such purpose. The intent with which the act is done governs....

Thus the trial court's finding No. 6, that the will had been revoked "by tearing and obliterating same with the intent of revoking" is clearly erroneous under the evidence as there was no actual evidence of an intent to revoke, and the presumption of intent arising from the tearing was effectively rebutted.... [The court addresses the question of the proper disposition of the decedent's property under the will.]

It is concluded that the opponents of the will have not established that the Holographic Will executed by the testator on December 28, 1967 was ever revoked "By being burnt, torn, canceled, obliterated or destroyed with the intent and for the purpose of revoking the same...." The presumption of intent to revoke arising from the torn document has been rebutted and the will effectively provides for the disposition of decedent's property. Every effort should be made by the courts to uphold a will that has been validly executed. As the only evidence here on earth to indicate decedent's desires as to the disposal of his property upon his death, the Holographic Will should have been upheld.

Judgment reversed. All Justices concur.

———

Lost or Destroyed Wills. What happens if the decedent is known to have executed a will, but it cannot be found after death? If the will remained in the decedent's possession after execution, there are many decisions that presume that the decedent destroyed the will with intent to revoke. See Atkinson on Wills §101, at 553; Annots., Sufficiency of Evidence of Nonrevocation of Lost Will Not Shown to Have Been Inaccessible to Testator—Modern Cases, 70 A.L.R.4th 323.

Concerning this presumption, the Supreme Court of Iowa, in Estate of Crozier, 232 N.W.2d 554 (Iowa 1975), remarked:

> There is good reason why the burden of proof on the part of a lost will proponent [where the will was traced to the testator's possession] should not be prohibitive. "Wills are carelessly lost and misplaced and a reasonable opportunity should be given to establish such a will. Likewise wills are sometimes suppressed or destroyed for an ulterior purpose. The defeat of that purpose ought not be made too difficult or impossible."

Crozier went on to hold, however, that the presumption is rebuttable only by clear and convincing evidence. See also Estate of Mitchell, 623 So. 2d 274 (Miss. 1993) (reversing the lower court that gave a jury instruction that the presumption could be rebutted "by a preponderance of the evidence" and holding that the proponents of the will had to rebut the presumption by "clear and convincing proof"); Barnett v. Oliver, 2000 WL 286715 (Tenn. Ct. App. Feb. 17, 2000), quoting Shrum v. Powell, 604 S.W.2d 869 (Tenn. Ct. App. 1980) (holding that the proponent met its burden of showing by "'the clearest and most stringent evidence'" that the decedent did not revoke his will).

The Restatement 3d of Property §4.1 comment j requires a lower standard of proof to rebut the presumption. It provides that "the presumption [that the testator destroyed the will or performed some other revocatory act on it with intent to revoke] is not such a strong one that clear and convincing evidence is required to rebut it." The reason is that there can be other plausible reasons for the will's absence: the will might have been "accidentally destroyed or lost," or it might have been "wrongfully destroyed or suppressed by someone dissatisfied with its terms." Restatement 3d of Property §4.1 comment j. Accord Estate of Beauregard, 921 N.E.2d 954 (Mass. 2010) (relying on the Restatement 3d); Estate of Conley, 753 N.W.2d 384 (N.D. 2008); Estate of Glover, 744 S.W.2d 939 (Tex. 1988).

The Supreme Court of Mississippi in Estate of Leggett, 584 So. 2d 400 (Miss. 1991), quoted Jarman's Treatise on Wills with approval, and took the position that the amount of evidence needed to rebut the presumption depended on the nature of the testator's situation that might suggest either the likelihood or unlikelihood that the testator intended to revoke the will.

Wills Executed in Duplicate. To execute a will in duplicate means that the formal procedures for executing a will were performed on two copies of the same will. The effect of duplicate execution is that the testator has two identical wills. If a will is executed in duplicate, an act of revocation performed with revocatory intent on one of the duplicates also revokes the other duplicate. This rule is sometimes codified, as in Cal. Prob. Code §6121.

The presumption of revocation becomes a source of special difficulty for wills that are executed in duplicate. If one executed copy is retained by the testator and the other executed copy is retained by the testator's lawyer or delivered to another person (for example, the personal representative), and the copy retained by the testator cannot be found after death, courts have held that there is a presumption of destruction with intent to revoke. See, e.g., Horton v. Burch, 471 S.E.2d 879 (Ga. 1996); Estate of Fowler, 681 N.E.2d 739 (Ind. Ct. App. 1997), transfer denied, 698 N.E.2d 1186 (Ind. 1998). Yet, the fact that an executed copy of the will was safely in the custody of the lawyer or another might cause the testator to be careless with the retained executed copy. In these circumstances especially, the presumption rests on uncertain ground and its application could lead to a denial of probate in a case where the testator had no revocatory intent.

On occasion, courts have found the existence of duplicate wills sufficient to conclude that the will remains unrevoked. In Stiles v. Brown, 380 So. 2d 792 (Ala. 1980), for example, revocation of the will of Claude Stiles was avoided where Stiles' lawyer, James T. Tatum, Jr., twice gave Stiles the legal advice that "if he, Mr. Stiles, desired to revoke [the will], he would have to destroy both the duplicate original in his own possession and the one Mr. Tatum had in his possession." Although Stiles's copy could not be found after his death, the fact that Stiles had made no effort to destroy the duplicate retained by Tatum was considered strong evidence in rebutting the presumption of revocation.

Equally uncertain are the situations in which both executed copies were retained by the testator, but only one can be found after death. Courts have held that the presumption of revocation applies to these situations also. See, e.g., Phinizee v. Alexander, 49 So.2d 250 (Miss. 1950); Mittelstaedt's Will, 112 N.Y.S.2d 166 (App. Div. 1952), appeal dismissed, 109 N.E.2d 86 (N.Y. 1952). In Etgen v. Corboy, 337 S.E.2d 286, 291 (Va. 1985), however, the court held that:

> [W]here duplicate originals of a formally attested will are in the possession of the testator from the time of execution until discovery among his effects after death and one version is altered while the other is in its original condition, then neither will is entitled to a presumption that it is the true will of the testator. In such a situation, the proponents of the different versions of the will must prove that their version is the true will.

Leading writers on wills preach against duplicate execution. See, e.g., John R. Price & Samuel A. Donaldson, Price on Contemporary Estate Planning §4.33 at 4076 (2022). See also Atkinson on Wills §86. Retention by the lawyer or another of a conformed or photostatic copy of the executed will is, of course, quite another matter and highly recommended.[11]

Proof of Lost or Destroyed Wills. Rebutting the presumption of revocation is not the only barrier to probating a lost or destroyed will. About half of the states, including those that have enacted the UPC, require the will's contents and due

---

11. A copy of a will is conformed "if it has been clearly marked as a 'copy,' with the date and the names of the testator and witnesses inserted, preferably typed rather than printed or handwritten (e.g., */s/ Thomas T. Testator, /s/ Wilma W. Witness*)." Gerald P. Johnston, An Ethical Analysis of Common Estate Planning Practices—Is Good Business Bad Ethics?, 45 Ohio St. L.J. 57, 131 n.473 (1984).

execution to be proved by clear and convincing evidence.[12] See, e.g., White v. Brennan's Administrator, 212 S.W.2d 299, 3 A.L.R.2d 943 (Ky. 1948) (holding evidence sufficient); Estate of Shaughnessy, 648 P.2d 427 (Wash. 1982) (holding evidence insufficient).

Restrictive Lost Will Statutes. A few states place further conditions on the probate of a lost or destroyed will. One type of restrictive statute is Ark. Code Ann. §28-40-302, which provides:

> No will of any testator shall be allowed to be proved as a lost or destroyed will, unless:
>
> (1) The provisions are clearly and distinctly proved by at least two (2) witnesses, a correct copy or draft being deemed equivalent to one (1) witness; and
>
> (2) The will is:
>
> (A) Proved to have been in existence at the time of the death of the testator; or
>
> (B) Shown to have been fraudulently destroyed in the lifetime of the testator.[13]

This statute, like many others we study in this course, poses a dilemma for the courts. Taken literally, and applied strictly, the statute seems to impede rather than promote donative freedom. The statutory requirement that the will be "in existence at the time of death of the testator" or "have been fraudulently destroyed" would seem to mean that a court cannot probate an unrevoked lost will, even when the will's proponents can prove its contents. In such situations, many courts have interpreted the statutory language in such a way as to render it meaningless. The most popular approach has been to interpret "existence" to mean "legal existence." A will is in "legal existence" if it has not been revoked. Another approach has been to interpret the "fraudulently destroyed" part of the statutory language to include constructive as well as actual fraud. Are these interpretations of the statute supportable?

Fraud. If a person obtains access to a testator's will and wrongfully destroys it, the will is not revoked. The act to the document is ineffective because it is not accompanied by the testator's intent to revoke. Sadly, perpetrators of this type of fraud are difficult to catch. One *was* caught in Estate of Legeas, 258 Cal. Rptr. 858, 861-63 (Ct. App.), vacating 256 Cal. Rptr. 117 (Ct. App. 1989). Margaret Legeas's

---

12. The UPC does not contain an explicit provision imposing special requirements of proof in formal testacy proceedings seeking probate of lost or destroyed wills. Hence, the general rules of evidence control proof.

The Code does make it clear, however, that lost or destroyed wills must be established in formal rather than informal probate proceedings. See UPC §3-303 comment. Furthermore, the Code specifies that in formal proceedings the petition to establish a lost or destroyed will must "state the contents of the will, and indicate that it is lost, destroyed, or otherwise unavailable." UPC §3-402. The Code also makes it clear that the petition must request an order finding the will valid. UPC §3-405 governs the court's response to the petition, indicating that the judge may, but need not, "require proof of the matters necessary to support the order sought."

13. See also Nev. Rev. Stat. §136.240(3); Okla. Stat. tit. 58, §82; Wyo. Stat. §2-6-207.

1970 will devised $20,000 to "my beloved friend, attorney and advisor, Timothy J. McInerney," nominated him as executor, and gave him the power to distribute the residue of the estate "to each of my legatees named or otherwise referred to hereinbefore, and in such amounts as my Executor ... shall in his sole discretion determine, and to such charities as he shall, in his sole discretion, select."

Between 1970 and 1983, the close friendship between Mrs. Legeas and the McInerneys cooled. Mrs. Legeas felt that Mr. McInerney had unduly profited from a joint business venture and from his handling of the estate of Mrs. Legeas's husband. Mrs. Legeas was annoyed by "lovey-dovey" telephone calls from Mr. McInerney, whom she found intimidating and with whom she wished to avoid personal contact. Her feelings were the same with respect to Mrs. McInerney, although less intense. Mrs. Legeas' antagonism towards Mr. McInerney progressed from distrust to fear and outright hatred. In 1979, Mrs. Leagus executed a new will that omitted any mention of the McInerneys. Up to 1983, Mrs. Legeas concealed from the McInerneys knowledge that she had executed the 1979 will.

By May of 1983, Mrs. Legeas' physical condition had deteriorated to the point that her priest, Father Heneghan, had her placed in a nursing home. In August of that year, Mrs. McInerney initiated conservatorship proceedings and was appointed temporary conservator of the person and estate of Mrs. Legeas. Later that month, Mrs. McInerney, in collecting certain assets of the estate, such as passbooks, certificates of deposit, and stock certificates, discovered the 1979 will in one of Mrs. Legeas' safety deposit boxes. Surprised at its provisions, Mrs. McInerney put it into her purse. She later claimed that she had given it to Mrs. Legeas, who subsequently told the McInerney's that she had torn it up.

Mrs. Legeas died in 1984 at age 83, leaving an estate of $500,000. In a jury trial in probate court, which consolidated several actions, the jury returned a special verdict finding that the 1970 will had been revoked and that the 1979 will had been fraudulently destroyed. The jury also returned a general verdict finding Mr. and Mrs. McInheney liable for compensatory damages of $182,616.60 (representing attorneys' fees in the actions) and further finding Mr. McInerney liable for punitive damages of $150,000. On appeal, the Court of Appeal affirmed and stated:

> The area of transfers from a decedent's estate has proven to be a fertile breeding ground for fraud. Courts have condemned fraud in a constellation of contexts. Its reported manifestations have been organized by commentators into these categories: (1) in inducing or preventing an inter vivos conveyance; (2) in the procuring of the execution of a will; (3) in the prevention of the execution of a will; (4) in causing the revocation or alteration of a will; (5) in the prevention of the revocation or alteration of a will; and (6) in the destruction, concealment, or spoliation of a will. Our concern is with the last grouping.
>
> Judicial aversion to testamentary-related fraud is not a recent phenomenon. The common law of Britain permitted equitable relief to recover a bequest which had been frustrated by the destruction or concealment of a will.... Traditional equitable remedies such as the imposition of a constructive trust were, however, deemed inadequate for complete redress.

Beginning in 1834, the courts of eight states have explicitly recognized an independent tort action for damages caused in the intentional destruction, concealment, or spoliation of a will....

We believe it is fitting to augment these expressions of disapproving policy with a tort action for damages resulting from the fraudulent destruction, concealment, or spoliation of a will.

Safeguarding of Clients' Wills. After death, UPC §2-516 imposes a duty on any person who has custody of a will to deliver it upon the request of an "interested person" (which is defined in UPC §1-201(23)), to a person able to secure its probate or, if none is known, to an appropriate court. Section 2-516 also provides that a person is liable for damages for a failure to deliver a will.

Considering the practical and legal issues that arise when a will that was in the possession of the testator cannot be found after death, the obvious question is how best to safeguard a will. The practice of many attorneys is to offer safekeeping of the will in the law firm's vault. Is this practice ethical? A preliminary report of an ABA Committee concluded that it was:

> The opinion of the committee is that the practice [of attorney safekeeping] ought to be regarded as ethical, assuming the attorney provides safekeeping merely as an accommodation and makes it clear that his safekeeping is only an alternative to safekeeping by the client, by the fiduciary-designate, or by the county clerk (where authorized by statute). The general theme of the ethics opinions is that attorney safekeeping is permissible if the testator expressly requests it but, if the attorney initiates the safekeeping, the prominent case of *State v. Gulbankian* [196 N.W.2d 733 (1972)] indicates that he may be subject to disciplinary sanction for solicitation. Further, retention of the will by the attorney may also be deemed to increase his risk of malpractice exposure for failure to inform the client of changes in the law.

ABA Committee Report, Developments Regarding the Professional Responsibility of the Estate Planning Lawyer: The Effect of the Model Rules of Professional Conduct, 22 Real Prop. Prob. & Tr. J. 1, 28 (1987). See also Price & Donaldson, above p. 247, at 4076 (suggesting attorney safekeeping permissible "if requested by the client to do so"). Contrast Johnston, above at note 11, at 124-33, who suggests that the practice of attorney-retention requires devisees or the executor to retrieve the will from the drafting attorney, thereby creating an appearance of soliciting probate administration business.

Attorneys are starting to rethink the practice of attorney-retention. The practice raises practical problems. Over time, especially as law firms merge or break apart and as clients relocate, the firm and the client may lose track of each other. Some firms have documents in their vaults that date back several decades. Anxious to avoid responsibility for safekeeping of wills of lost clients, some firms have begun the process of trying to locate those one-time clients to return the originals to them, a task that the firms report is more difficult than they originally thought.

One alternative to attorney-retention is for the attorney to keep a photocopy, preferably a conformed copy, but deliver the original to the client upon execution. Another alternative, where available, is to use the procedure authorized by UPC §2-515, under which the testator or the testator's agent can deposit a will with a court for safekeeping.

Is There a Duty to Probate a Will? Must an unrevoked will be probated? Although any "interested person" can petition for probate of a will, the personal representative normally files the petition. If not, the self-interest of one or more of the devisees named in the will will typically prompt the filing of a petition.

If, however, the affected parties wish to suppress the will and divide up the decedent's assets in a different way, they normally can do so. See Annot., Family Settlement of Testator's Estate, 29 A.L.R.3d 8. UPC §3-912 authorizes private agreements among successors. See UPC §1-201(49) (defining "successors"). Such an agreement does not need the consent of the executor. Successors have the power to direct the executor not to probate the will and, if they do so, the executor loses standing to proceed. See UPC §3-720 comment. See Chapter 2 for discussions of problems of obtaining agreement of unascertained or incapacitated successors, potential adverse tax consequences, and disclaimers as an alternative to successors' agreements.

Partial Revocation by Revocatory Act. The English Statute of Frauds 1677 provided that no devise "nor any clause thereof" should be revoked except in the manner specified, including various acts to the document. Under the Wills Act of 1837 the comparable language was "no will... or any part thereof." The English courts construed the word "clause" in the Statute of Frauds to mean "part," see Swinton v. Bailey, L.R. 4 App. Cas. 70, 85 (1878), and the same construction seems to have been taken for granted under American statutes based on the Statute of Frauds. See Patrick v. Patrick, 649 A.2d 1204 (Md. Ct. Spec. App. 1994); Brown v. Brown, 74 S.E. 135 (S.C. 1912). Section 2-507 of the UPC allows a will "or any part thereof" to be revoked by revocatory act. Similar provisions appear in most non-UPC statutes. In all, or almost all, of these states, partial revocation by revocatory act seems to be recognized.

By necessity, a partial revocation by act to the document—if valid—has a double effect: it deprives someone of property and gives that property to someone else. Therefore, unless authorized by statute, courts have not recognized a partial revocation by act. See, e.g., Law v. Law, 3 So. 752 (Ala. 1888); Miles' Appeal, 36 A. 39 (Conn. 1896); Horst v. Horst, 920 N.E. 441 (Ohio Ct. App. 2009). Contra, e.g., Bigelow v. Gillott, 123 Mass. 102 (1877). This is true only of revocation by act to the document. Partial revocation by subsequent will is authorized throughout the United States. See Restatement 3d of Property §4.1 comment c.

In a state that does not allow partial revocation by act to the document, the result is that the will is probated as originally written. Complications arise, however, if the portion of the will that the testator attempted to eliminate cannot be read, and its contents cannot be established by other evidence. This was the circumstance presented to the court in Hansel v. Head, 706 So.2d 1142 (Ala. 1997), in which the testators of a joint will obliterated the name of one member of a class that was to receive a devise of cash assets. It addressed the statutory dilemma as follows:

> On the one hand, it is clear that we should give effect to the testators' intent with respect to the disposal of their property. On the other hand, it is also clear that we may not give effect to their intent to revoke that portion of the bequest that it obliterated, but that we should, if possible, enforce the will in its original form.
>
> When the obliterated portion of a will is undiscernible, the question becomes one more of evidence than of intent. When the question concerning a portion of a will is a lack of evidence, the remainder of the will should be upheld.... Here, the evidence is sufficient as to all but one legacy. The will itself exists....
>
> The attempted revocation of a portion of a will not material to the overall testamentary plan allows the will to be admitted to probate with the property that would have passed by the obliterated portion passing by intestacy. In this case, the obliteration of the name of one member of the class that is to receive one-half of the Heads' net cash assets is not material to the testators' overall testamentary plan. Thus, we hold that the will should be admitted to probate and the share allocable to the person whose name was obliterated should be disposed of through intestacy.

But see, e.g., Johannes' Estate, 227 P.2d 148 (Kan. 1951) (denying probate entirely).

In Wyoming, the court qualified partial revocation, limiting validity only to one in which "the testamentary scheme [after the partial revocation] is basically the same as before." Seeley v. Estate of Seeley, 627 P.2d 1357 (Wyo. 1981). In *Seeley,* the testator cut a provision out of her will that granted her son an option to purchase certain property, leaving the rest of the dispository plan unchanged. The court held the partial revocation valid.

In Dodson v. Walton, 597 S.W.2d 814 (Ark. 1980), the Arkansas court adopted a similar rule by limiting the effect of an interlineation or obliteration of part of a will to cases in which it "does not change the testamentary disposition provided for in the will." If it does operate to make such a change, the attempted partial revocation is ineffective and the will as originally drawn is to be given effect. In *Dodson,* the testator's will had devised her estate to six named persons who were to share equally. Subsequent to executing her will, she canceled the name of one of the devisees with the intent of excluding him from taking. The court held the partial revocation void and probated the will as originally executed. Justice Stroud dissented from the majority opinion in *Dodson* because it limited partial revocations only to wills containing no residuary clause or to some other provisions unrelated to property dispositions, such as the naming of an executor. Accord Estate of Malloy, 949 P.2d 804 (Wash. 1998) (en banc); see also Patrick v. Patrick, supra, (permitting some changes to the residuary clause, but not if the revocation "changes the character of the will").

The Restatement 3d of Property disapproves of the approach taken by the courts in *Seeley* and *Dodson*:

> *Restatement 3d of Property §4.1, [Comment] i. Partial revocation by act....* Even when partial revocation by act is authorized by statute, there still remains a measure of resistance to the practice. Although these statutes are held to permit revocation by act of a complete devise, it has sometimes been held that a partial revocation by act is ineffective if its purpose and effect would be to rearrange the shares within a single devise or otherwise to rewrite the terms of the will by deleting selected words.
>
> This Restatement disapproves any distinction between revocation of a complete devise and rearranging shares within a single devise or otherwise rewriting the terms of the will by deleting selected words. It is a classic example of a distinction without a difference.... In authorizing revocation of a will "or *any* part thereof" by act, the legislature has not limited the authorization to revocation of a complete devise. The legislature not only granted broad approval of deleting words but of the natural consequence of doing so—giving effect to the will as if the deleted words were not present.

Effect on a Codicil of a Revocation of the Will. The English Wills Act 1837 provided:

> *7 Wm. 4 & 1 Vict., ch. 26, §20:* That no will or codicil, or any part thereof, shall be revoked otherwise than ... by another will or codicil executed in manner herein-before required, or by some writing declaring an intention to revoke the same, and executed in the manner in which a will is herein-before required to be executed, or by the burning, tearing, or otherwise destroying the same by the testator, or by some person in his presence and by his direction, with the intention of revoking the same.

In Goods of Turner, L.R. 2 P. & D. 403 (1872), the court interpreted the statutory phrase "no will *or codicil* ... shall be revoked otherwise than by ...." to mean that a codicil can be revoked by act only if the act is performed on the codicil. An act performed on the will can revoke the will but not the codicil. This position became generally accepted in English law.

In the United States, courts have taken a different approach. The question usually turns on the relation between the dispositive provisions of the will and codicil, summed up in the following statement of a New York court:

> If they are necessarily interdependent or so inter-involved as to be incapable of separate existence, the revocation of the will ipso facto revokes the codicil, otherwise not.

Francis' Will, 132 N.Y.S. 695 (Sur. Ct. 1911). Accord Halpern's Estate, 224 N.Y.S.2d 58 (Sur. Ct. 1962); Ayres' Will, 43 N.E.2d 918 (Ohio Ct. App. 1940).

The Restatement 3d of Property separates the question of revocation from the issue of construction when it states:

> *§4.1, [Comment] n. Revocation of will by act—effect on codicil.* The revocation of a will by act does not revoke a codicil to the will. If the codicil depends on the revoked will for its meaning, however, the codicil may have no effect as a matter of construction.

Suppose a testator who has both a will and a subsequent codicil performs a revocatory act on the codicil but performs no revocatory act on the will itself. What issue does this raise? Does the revocation of the codicil revoke the will? See Estate of Hering, 166 Cal. Rptr. 298 (Ct. App. 1980) (discussed below on p. 266).

EXTERNAL REFERENCE. Annot., Sufficiency of Evidence of Nonrevocation of Lost Will Where Codicil Survives, 84 A.L.R.4th 531 (1991).

PART C. REVOCATION BY CHANGES IN CIRCUMSTANCES—MARRIAGE, DIVORCE, REMARRIAGE

Primary Statutory References: *UPC §2-804*

Restatement 3d of Property

§4.1 Revocation of Wills.... (b) The dissolution of the testator's marriage is a change in circumstance that presumptively revokes any provision in the testator's will in favor of his or her former spouse. Neither marriage nor marriage followed by birth of issue is a change in circumstance that revokes a will or any part of a will.

———

Between the time that a testator executes a will and dies, the testator's family circumstances can change dramatically.[14] The purpose of this Part is to explore how the law does, and should, treat a will that a testator executed without considering the possibility of subsequent marriage, divorce, or remarriage. The legal issues take on a greater urgency in view of the changing American family profile. The increasing incidences of divorce and remarriage heighten the likelihood that a testator's family circumstances will change after executing a will. If the law is to reflect the economic and social context in which it operates and is likely to continue to operate, it must incorporate changing family patterns into the law of will revocation.

Related to the issue of remarriage, of course, is the question of stepchildren. The *Spencer* case, below, is a case of remarriage by a widower. The case involves the common dispute pitting a decedent's children by a prior marriage against the decedent's second spouse. As Jane Bryant Quinn noted, "[When older people remarry, y]our friends will be enchanted, but don't be surprised if your children aren't. It's usually not the 'pater' they worry about but the patrimony." Jane Bryant Quinn, Making the Most of Your Money Now 84 (rev. ed. 2009).

---

14. For further discussion of changes in circumstances that occur between the time that a testator executes a will and dies, see Chapter 6, which considers changes in a testator's property and changes in the circumstances of a testator's devisees, and Chapter 8, which considers the unintentional disinheritance of a surviving spouse and children.

Automatic Revocation of Premarital Wills. At common law, a premarital will of a woman was revoked upon marriage and a premarital will of a man was revoked upon marriage and birth of issue. The will was revoked as soon as the operative event or events occurred. The fact that the spouse or the spouse and the couple's issue predeceased the testator was accorded no legal significance. See 1 Thomas Jarman, A Treatise on Wills 152 (2d Am. ed. 1849).

At one time in this country, more than half the states had a statute similar to the now-repealed Hawaii statute that was applicable in the *Spencer* case, below. Some of these statutes provided for revocation upon marriage alone, others for revocation upon marriage and birth of issue. A few states still have marriage-revocation statutes.[15] As we shall see in Chapter 8, modern probate codes invoke other means to protect the testator's new spouse and children against unintended disinheritance.

Estate of Spencer
591 P.2d 611 (Haw. 1979)

OGATA, J. Contestants-appellants (hereinafter appellants), who are children of the deceased testator, appeal from an Order Denying Motion for Declaratory Judgment and from an Order of Probate entered by the court below. The question presented to us on this appeal is whether a will in which the testator gives and bequeaths his entire estate to a woman by her maiden name, is revoked by the subsequent marriage of the testator to that woman by operation of HRS §536-11 (1975 Supp.).[16] This section provided the following:

> *By marriage.* If, after the making of a will, the testator or testatrix marries and no provision is made in the will for such contingency, such marriage shall operate as a revocation of the will, and the will shall not be revived by the death of the (testator's) or testatrix's spouse.

We hold that the statute operated to revoke the will and reverse the orders entered by the court below.

The facts in this case are not in dispute. On October 17, 1974, the testator, Robert Stafford Spencer (hereinafter "testator"), then a widower, executed a will in which he left his entire estate to "Sandra Jean Cantwell, of 361 Laleihoku Street, Wailuku, County of Maui, State of Hawaii." On December 28, 1974, testator married Sandra

---

15. Those states are Georgia, Kansas, Maryland, Nevada, Oregon, and Rhode Island. An Alabama statute that preserved the common-law distinction between a man's and a woman's premarital will, providing for the revocation of a woman's, but not a man's, will upon subsequent marriage alone, was held unconstitutional in Parker v. Hall, 362 So.2d 875 (Ala. 1978).

16. HRS §536-11 (1975 Supp.) was the applicable statute when the will was made and at the time of the testator's subsequent marriage. It was repealed by the [original] Uniform Probate Code, effective July 1, 1977. The [original] Uniform Probate Code provides for revocation of a will by divorce or annulment only and does not provide for revocation of a will by subsequent marriage.

Jean Cantwell (hereinafter "appellee"). On January 10, 1975, the testator died, leaving as survivors, the appellee, his wife, and two children by a prior marriage, who are the parties involved in this dispute.

Appellee filed in the court below a petition for probate of the will executed on October 17, 1974. Appellants thereafter filed an appearance and contest of will, and about two weeks later, filed a motion for declaratory judgment requesting the court to declare that the will submitted for probate had been revoked by the subsequent marriage of their father to Sandra Jean Cantwell, the sole beneficiary. At the hearing on the motion, appellee, over objection by appellants, was permitted to introduce evidence that tended to indicate that, at the time testator executed his will, he intended to marry Sandra Jean Cantwell. This evidence showed that prior to the marriage, on August 21, 1974, testator had designated the testamentary beneficiary as the beneficiary of his interest in the State Employees' Retirement System, under the designation of "Sandra Tarlton Spencer," and had referred to her on such form as his wife; and, that on September 3, 1974, the parties had met with the Reverend Winkler to set a date for their marriage. Upon these facts, the court below found that the testator's will was not revoked by operation of HRS §536-11 (1975 Supp.). The order denying the motion for declaratory judgment further stated:

> The Court further finds that HRS §536-11 does not automatically revoke a will made prior to marriage where such will names as beneficiary a person who later becomes the spouse of the testator, where there is clear evidence that the testator and such person intended to marry, even though there is no express provision in the will stating that it was providing for the contingency of such marriage;

HRS §536-11 (1975 Supp.) must be given effect according to its plain and obvious meaning. We have said that this court is bound by the plain, clear and unambiguous language of a statute unless the literal construction would produce an absurd and unjust result and would be clearly inconsistent with the purposes and policies of the statute.... We think the language used in HRS §536-11 (1975 Supp.) is explicitly clear and unambiguous, and the literal construction does not produce a result that is absurd and unjust and clearly inconsistent with the purposes and policies of the statute. The statute provides in clear terms that "[if,] after the making of a will, the testator ... marries ... such marriage shall operate as a revocation of the will," unless "provision is made in the will for such contingency." It is clear to us that "contingency" refers to a testator's marriage after having made a will. The will of the testator in the instant case does not contain any provision with respect to the marriage of the testator as the trial court so found in its order denying the motion.

Appellee argues that to revoke the will would produce a result that is absurd and unjust and clearly inconsistent with the purpose of the statute by reducing her share of testator's estate by two-thirds. Notwithstanding revocation of the will, however, the appellee, although no longer entitled to testator's entire estate, is protected by her dower rights under HRS Chapter 533....

Moreover, merely designating "Sandra Jean Cantwell" as the beneficiary of his entire estate did not provide in the will for the contingency of subsequent marriage, for in doing so, the testator did no more than he would have done in leaving any testamentary gift and the statute requires more than this....

The testator's will was revoked by operation of HRS §536-11 (1975 Supp.) for failure to comply with the statutory requirement. The orders entered by the court below are reversed.

RICHARDSON, C.J., OGATA and MENOR, JJ. concur.

Notes and Question

1. *Question.* Suppose that Robert had died on December 27, 1974. What result?

2. *Scrivener's Error?* Erickson v. Erickson, 716 A.2d 92 (Conn. 1998), involved a similar set of facts and a nearly identical statute. On September 1, 1988, Ronald K. Erickson executed a will. At that time, he was a widower and had three grown children from his previous marriage. Two days later, on September 3, 1988, he married Dorothy A. Mehring, a widow with four grown children from her previous marriage. Ronald died on February 22, 1996. His will devised the residue of his estate "to Dorothy A. Mehring" and also named her executor of his estate.

The decedent's daughters claimed that under Conn. Gen. Stat. §45a-257(a),[17] a statute nearly identical to the Hawaii statute in the *Spencer* case, their father's will was automatically revoked upon his marriage to Dorothy. The trial court held that Ronald's will was not revoked because it provided for the contingency of marriage. The trial court reasoned:

> [The decedent's] will bequeathed all of his estate to the woman he was licensed to marry and did marry two days later. In his will, he named her executrix and designated her the guardian of his daughters, whose mother had previously died. The nature of these provisions, coupled with the extreme closeness in time of the marriage constitutes clear and convincing evidence of provision for the contingency of marriage. It would be preposterous to assume that [the decedent] was instead executing a will to make provisions that were to be revoked two days later.

On appeal, the Connecticut Supreme Court held that "[o]n the basis of existing case law, the question of whether a will provides for the contingency of a subsequent marriage must be determined: (1) from the language of the will itself; and (2) without resort to extrinsic evidence of the testator's intent." Consequently, the court concluded that "the will, in and of itself, did not provide for the contingency of the subsequent marriage of the decedent and, therefore, under existing case law, properly would have been revoked by that marriage pursuant to §45a-257(a)."

---

17. This statute was repealed in 1996 and replaced with a statute based on the original version of UPC §2-301, which we study in Chapter 8.

The court held, however, "that under the circumstances of this case, the trial court improperly excluded evidence of a mistake by the scrivener that, if believed, would permit a finding that the will provided for the contingency of marriage." Dorothy had made an offer of proof that the decedent's attorney would, if permitted, testify as follows:

> During the course of the execution of the wills there was no conversation whatsoever about the fact that the Saturday marriage would revoke the will that had been drafted on Thursday.... [He] would testify that the reason that he did not place in the will any specific mention of the marriage ... was because in his view when a man executes a will two days before his marriage in which he leaves everything to the woman that he's about to marry, makes her guardian of his children, makes her administrator of the ... estate, and if she should predecease him, leaves half of his estate to her kids ...[, that c]learly makes provision in the will for not just a contingency, but the imminen[ce] ... of the marriage that's going to take place two days later.

The court concluded:

> [T]he extrinsic evidence offered, if believed, could prove clearly and convincingly that there was a scrivener's error that induced the decedent to execute a will that he intended to be valid despite his subsequent marriage. The offer of proof indicates that the evidence would be susceptible to an inference by the fact finder that there had been an implied assertion by the scrivener that the will would be valid despite the decedent's subsequent marriage.

On remand, the Connecticut Superior Court held that the decedent's widow failed to meet her burden of proof, which resulted in the decedent dying intestate. Erickson v. Estate of Erickson, 1999 WL 1063260 (Conn. Super. Ct. Nov. 4, 1999).

———

Revocation upon Divorce. Statutes in a large number of states once provided for revocation by operation of law in cases of "subsequent changes in the conditions or circumstances of the testator." Led by Lansing v. Haynes, 54 N.W. 699 (Mich. 1893), it was widely held that divorce accompanied by a property settlement constituted a subsequent change in the circumstance of the testator sufficient to revoke provisions in a pre-divorce will in favor of the decedent's former spouse. A few states still follow this principle despite the absence of a statute on the subject. See Rasco v. Estate of Rasco, 501 So.2d 421 (Miss. 1987) (holding no revocation occurred under this principle in situation where the divorced couple continued to live together after the divorce and the couple apparently never carried out the property settlement agreement).

In the vast majority of states, the generally worded statutes have disappeared,[18] having been replaced by more specific statutory provisions based on original UPC §2-508 or on current UPC §2-804, under which the statute specifically provides that divorce (or annulment) alone revokes any testamentary provision favoring the former spouse. The statutes typically go on to provide that revoked devises pass as if the former spouse failed to survive the decedent. See original UPC §2-508; cf. current UPC §2-804(d) (giving effect to revoked provisions as if the former spouse disclaimed).

Problem

A and B had no children by their marriage to each other, but each had adult children by a former marriage. During their marriage to each other, A executed a will devising all of his property to B if B survived A. If B failed to survive him, A devised one-half of his property to his children and one-half to B's children. (B also executed a will, which contained reciprocal provisions.)

A and B were subsequently divorced. A died soon after the divorce, survived by B, A's children, and B's children. A had never revoked his will. How is A's estate to be distributed? Assume that the case arose in a jurisdiction that has a provision similar or identical to the original version of UPC §2-508. See, e.g., Estate of Kerr, 520 N.W.2d 512 (Minn. Ct. App. 1994); Estate of Coffed, 387 N.E.2d 1209 (N.Y. 1979).

How would the outcome be changed if the case were governed by the current version of UPC §2-804? See also UPC §2-604. Cf. Hermon v. Urteago, 46 Cal. Rptr. 2d 577 (Ct. App. 1995) (holding that the decedent's former stepchildren were not eligible to take under a devise to "my spouse's children" and "my spouse's issue" subsequent to the divorce and urging the legislature to consider enacting a statute modeled after UPC §2-804); In re Walker, 849 S.W.2d 766 (Tenn. 1993) (holding, through a strained interpretation of trust provisions, that the children of the testator's former spouse did not take under a will that provided for them to take in the event "my wife [should] predecease me"). For further discussion of revocation by changes in circumstances, see Chapter 7 on will substitutes.

---

18. The District of Columbia seems to be the last remaining jurisdiction following this rule. See Luff v. Luff, 359 F.2d 235 (D.C. Cir. 1966) (holding that, under a statute providing that a will is revoked "by implication of law," D.C. Code Ann. §18-109, divorce accompanied by a property settlement revokes provisions in a pre-divorce will in favor of former spouse).

PART D. REVIVAL—REINSTATING A REVOKED WILL

Primary Statutory Reference: *UPC §2-509*

Restatement 3d of Property

§4.2 Revival of Revoked Wills

(a) A will that was revoked by a later will is revived if the testator: (i) reexecuted the previously revoked will; (ii) executed a codicil indicating an intent to revive the previously revoked will; (iii) revoked the revoking will by act intending to revive the previously revoked will; or (iv) revoked the revoking will by another, later will whose terms indicate an intent to revive the previously revoked will.

(b) A will that was revoked by act is revived if the testator: (i) reexecuted the will; (ii) executed a codicil indicating an intent to revive the previously revoked will; or (iii) performed an act on the will that clearly and convincingly demonstrates an intent to reverse the revocation.

(c) A testamentary provision that was revoked by dissolution of the testator's marriage is revived if: (i) the testator remarried the former spouse, reexecuted the will, or executed a codicil indicating an intent to revive the previously revoked provision; or (ii) the dissolution of the marriage is nullified.

———

Consider G, a testator who had previously executed two wills. Will #2 expressly revoked Will #1. Shortly before her death, G revoked Will #2 by drawing a large "X" across each of its pages. Has G died intestate, or is Will #1 her valid will? In jurisdictions that follow the view that the execution of Will #2 revoked Will #1—this is not the view universally followed, as we shall see—the question, framed in legal terminology, is whether Will #1 has been "revived" or "reinstated." A somewhat different way of thinking about the same question is: Did the revocation of the revoking document (Will #2) revoke the revocation (of Will #1)?

In England, prior to the Wills Act 1837, there was no statutory provision on revival. Although the Statute of Frauds 1677 provided for revocation by later instrument or by act to the document, that statute was silent on the matter of revival. Two approaches emerged in the English decisions: one came from the ecclesiastical courts, which had jurisdiction over succession to personal property; the other came from the common-law courts, which passed on questions of revocation (as well as of due execution) when an issue of title to land was raised.

The Ecclesiastical Rule. Under the ecclesiastical rule, whether G's Will #1 would be revived would depend on G's intent. In a lengthy opinion in Williams v. Miles, 94 N.W. 705 (Neb. 1903), then Commissioner Roscoe Pound (who later became Dean of the Harvard Law School) canvassed the state of English and American law on revival and described the ecclesiastical rule as follows:

[T]he ecclesiastical courts ... endeavor[ed] in each case to ascertain the testator's intention, ... making that intention the criterion. In a leading case the doctrine of those courts was stated thus:

> The legal presumption is neither adverse to, nor in favor of, the revival of a former uncanceled [will], upon the cancellation of a later revocatory will. Having furnished this principle, the law withdraws altogether, and leaves the question as one of intention purely, and open to a decision either way, solely according to facts and circumstances.

94 N.W. at 708, quoting Usticke v. Bawden, 2 Addams (Eng. Eccle.) 116, [162 Eng. Rep. 238] (1824). In practice, of course, the proponent of the revoked will presumably has the burden of establishing an intent to reinstate that will. A court would deny probate of the will unless the proponent could produce some evidence of such intent.

The Common-Law Rule. The common-law rule would treat Will #1 as G's valid will, regardless of her intention. The common-law rule is sometimes (erroneously) referred to as a rule of "automatic revival." This is how Commissioner Pound, in *Williams*, above, described it:

> Lord Mansfield announced a rule, which was followed by the common-law courts, when questions as to wills disposing of real property came before them, to the effect that if the first will is preserved, and a subsequent will, revoking it expressly or by implication, is destroyed or canceled, the revocation is repealed, and the original will revived and continued in force, by virtue of these circumstances.

Strictly speaking, Commissioner Pound did not get the common-law rule quite right. Lord Mansfield's actual view, enunciated in the leading case of Goodright v. Glazier, 4 Burr. 2512, 2514, 98 Eng. Rep. 317 (K.B. 1770), was that the first will had never been revoked:

> A will is ambulatory till the death of the testator. If the testator lets it stand till he dies, it is his will: if he does not suffer it to do so, it is not his will. Here, he had two. He has canceled the second: it had no effect, no operation; it is as no will at all, being canceled before his death. But the former, which was never canceled, stands as his will.

The second will in *Goodright* apparently contained no express revocation clause, but Lord Mansfield later made it clear that the position he had taken would apply even though it had. See Harwood v. Goodright, 1 Cowp. 87, 98 Eng. Rep. 981 (K.B. 1774).

American Rules on Revival in the Absence of a Statute. In the minority of states in which revival is not controlled by statute,[19] there appears to be a preference for the

---

19. Those states are Connecticut, Louisiana, Mississippi, New Hampshire, Texas, Vermont, and Wyoming. For Mississippi, see Bohanon v. Walcot, 2 Miss. 336 (Miss. Err. & App. 1836) (requiring "some express and direct act" to revive a prior will).

English ecclesiastical rule. See Hawes v. Nicholas, 10 S.W. 558 (Tex. 1889) (ruling that the destruction of a subsequent will was not itself sufficient to demonstrate intent to revive); Gould's Will, 47 A. 1082 (Vt. 1900) (placing burden of proof on proponent of a revoked will and further stating that careful preservation of the revoked will by testator can be counted as an indication of an intent to revive); May v. Estate of McCormick, 769 P.2d 395 (Wyo. 1989) (holding that, in the absence of evidence of an intention to revive, a revoked will is not revived by the destruction of a later will that expressly revoked all prior wills). The English common-law rule also has its adherents, however, as in Whitehill v. Halbing, 118 A. 454 (Conn. 1922); Succession of Dambly, 186 So. 7 (La. 1938).

Statutory Rules on Revival. In England, the common-law rule of "automatic revival" and the ecclesiastical rule giving effect to intention however proved were abrogated in 1837. The Wills Act 1837 replaced those rules by a so-called "antirevival" rule. Under the statutory "antirevival" rule, G's Will #1 would be revived only if G either reexecuted that will or executed a codicil showing an intention to revive that will.

In the United States, statutes in fourteen jurisdictions maintain the antirevival stance of the English Wills Act and require either a reexecution of the revoked will or the execution of a codicil showing an intention to revive. See Statutory Note to Restatement 3d of Property §4.2.

The statutes in the remaining states have liberalized the strict requirements of the English Wills Act and moved in the direction of the English ecclesiastical rule. Under early versions of these statutes, revival of Will #1 would occur if it "appears by the terms of" the revocation of Will #2 that it was G's intention to revive and give effect to Will #1 or if Will #1 was "republished." Today, this version exists in only five states (Indiana, Kansas, Nevada, Ohio, and Oklahoma).

The other states have replaced the early version permitting revival with more liberal versions modeled after either the original UPC or the current UPC. See Statutory Note, above. Estate of Boysen, below, applied the original UPC, which was then in effect in Minnesota.

Estate of Boysen
309 N.W.2d 45 (Minn. 1981)

PETERSON, J. Genevieve Thompson appeals from the order of a three-judge panel of the Dodge County District Court affirming the order of the county court, probate division, admitting to probate a will of decedent Chris Boysen. The issue raised by this appeal is whether decedent revived the will. Because we believe the relevant statute, Minn. Stat. §524.2-509(a) (1980), was misapplied below, we reverse and remand for a new trial.

Decedent was the father of appellant Genevieve Thompson and respondent Raymond Boysen, proponent of the will in question. Decedent's wife predeceased him by 30 years. [Genevieve] married and moved to Austin, Minnesota. After [Raymond] married, decedent made his home with [Raymond] and his wife in Hayfield, Minnesota. In 1964 [Raymond] was appointed guardian of decedent's person and estate. In 1973 decedent moved from [Raymond]'s home to a residence for the elderly located in Hayfield. He lived there until his death in 1977.

Decedent executed the will on March 12, 1964, when he was 75 years old. In the will he devised all his real property—in large part a 200-acre farm near Hayfield—to [Raymond] on the condition that [Raymond] pay [Genevieve] $7,000. Decedent bequeathed his personal property to [Raymond] and [Genevieve] in equal shares.

After its execution the will was filed with the Dodge County clerk of court. In 1972 the court removed the will from the courthouse vault in order to review it in connection with a proceeding for the dissolution of [Raymond]'s marriage. A few years later [Raymond] learned the will had never been returned to the clerk of court's custody. When attempts by decedent's attorney to locate the will proved unsuccessful, decedent discussed the preparation of a new will with a paralegal employed by the attorney. At the probate court hearing the paralegal described their conversation:

> When he came in, he said that his will had been lost so it was necessary for him to make another will, ... I had been present and witnessed the first will. He thought perhaps I remembered what was in it. I said too long a time had gone by. I didn't ... could not remember the details of the first will and we had no copy. He said at that time that it was necessary to make one because he wanted the farm to go to Raymond. He said at the first will he had given money to Genevieve, the farm to Raymond and a sum of money to Genevieve. He was indecisive as to this amount of money that he should put in to her because he didn't know what money he'd have, you know, what money there would be left to divide for her. He didn't know what ... valuations would be to ... things have changed. So he ... he did ask if this ... We discussed and we said, well, how did you determine the first amount of money? And he said, well, he had thought that 3/4 to 1/4 would be a ... set that sum of money. So we said, 'Well, you can use fractions; you don't have to use sums of money if you don't want to.' And that is why he made a fraction in place of a total sum of money.

Decedent executed the new will on May 13, 1975. It differs from its predecessor in one significant respect: it provides that in order to take decedent's real property [Raymond] must pay [Genevieve] a sum equal to one-fourth the property's appraised value. The farm is worth approximately $600,000.

Decedent filed the new will with the clerk of court. He gave [Raymond] an unsigned copy of the will. [Raymond] put the copy in a safe deposit box.

Efforts to determine the whereabouts of the old will continued. In June 1975 the clerk of court notified decedent's attorney that the old will had been found. In February 1976 the attorney, acting at decedent's direction, withdrew the new will from the court files.

Shortly thereafter, Raymond drove decedent to the attorney's office. The secretary gave decedent the new will and he signed a receipt for it. During the drive back to Hayfield decedent tore the new will in half. At the probate court hearing Raymond testified that decedent handed him the torn will and said:

> They maybe have lost it yet. This will give us ... some sort of an idea on my likes ... you take care of it.

Raymond placed the torn will in a locked box at his home. He removed the copy from the safe deposit box and returned it to decedent. Decedent tore the copy in half.

Decedent died in April of the following year. Raymond, as the executor of decedent's estate, filed a petition for probate of the 1964 will. Genevieve objected to the petition and sought an adjudication of intestacy. The probate court found that decedent revived the 1964 will and accordingly admitted the will to probate. A three-judge panel of the district court affirmed the probate court's order. We granted Genevieve leave to appeal to this court from the district court's determination.

Minn. Stat. §524.2-509(a) (1980) [original UPC §2-509(a)] governs the question whether decedent revived the 1964 will. That statute provides:

> If a second will which, had it remained effective at death, would have revoked the first will in whole or in part, is thereafter revoked by acts under section 524.2-507 [original UPC §2-507], the first will is revoked in whole or in part unless it is evident from the circumstances of the revocation of the second will or from testator's contemporary or subsequent declarations that he intended the first will to take effect as executed.

The 1975 will expressly revoked all prior wills and codicils of decedent. The 1975 will was revoked when decedent tore it in half. Under section 524.2-509(a) the 1964 will is not revived unless from "the circumstances of the revocation" of the 1975 will or from decedent's "contemporary or subsequent declarations" it is evident that he intended the 1964 will "to take effect as executed."

The probate court found that decedent did so intend. The district court panel held the probate court's finding not clearly erroneous. Our review of a factual finding of a court sitting without a jury is likewise limited to the question whether the finding is clearly erroneous.... Here, however, we are presented with a case involving the application of a statute we have not previously had occasion to interpret. On this appeal we must initially determine the correct interpretation of section 524.2-509(a) and then decide whether the district court's application of the statute to the facts of this case was consistent with that interpretation.

Where a later will which would have revoked an earlier will is itself revoked, section 524.2-509(a) establishes a presumption against revival of the earlier will. That presumption is rebutted if "the circumstances of the revocation" of the later will or the "testator's contemporary or subsequent declarations" make evident his intent that the earlier will "take effect as executed." In the present case decedent made no declarations indicating such an intent. Our concern, then, is with the meaning of the phrase "the circumstances of the revocation." No court in another jurisdiction that has enacted the [original] Uniform Probate Code appears to have interpreted this phrase.

The question under section 524.2-509(a) is whether a testator, at the time he revoked a will, intended to die intestate or to revive an earlier will. We believe that in allowing the trier of fact to consider "the circumstances of the revocation" when deciding this question the legislature meant to permit an examination of all matters relevant to the testator's intent. Accordingly, the trier of fact should consider the following:

> 1. Did the testator, at the time he revoked the later will, know whether the earlier will was in existence?
>
> 2. If the testator did know that the earlier will was in existence, did he know the nature and extent of his property and the disposition made of his property by the earlier will, particularly with respect to persons with a natural claim on his bounty?
>
> 3. Did the testator, by action or nonaction, disclose an intent to make the disposition which the earlier will directs?

Only if these questions are affirmatively answered should the earlier will be admitted to probate. Because these questions were not addressed below, the district court's order must be reversed and this case remanded for a new trial. By remanding the case we do not intimate an opinion regarding the ultimate result.

Reversed and remanded.

[The dissenting opinion of SCOTT, J. is omitted.]

Notes and Questions

1. *Subsequent History.* On remand, the trial court applied the supreme court's directives and determined that the 1964 will was not revived. The trial court also, however, applied the doctrine of dependent relative revocation, which we study in Part E, as a way of giving effect to the 1975 will. On appeal, the Minnesota Court of Appeals held that the procedural rules of the prior appeal rendered this determination improper. See Estate of Boysen, 351 N.W.2d 398 (Minn. Ct. App. 1984). In the end, Chris Boysen died intestate.

2. *Boysen's Discrete Subrequirements Approach.* Is *Boysen* an example of a hard case making bad law? The court was surely correct in saying that "the legislature meant to permit an examination of all matters relevant to the testator's intent" in determining whether one of the statutory requirements for revival were met. Do you agree, however, that it is appropriate to translate that general statutory prescription into discrete subrequirements, all of which must be met? Such an approach surely makes the proponent's case harder than the legislature intended it to be.

3. *Disapproval of the* Boysen *Approach.* UPC §2-509 continues to employ the same statutory language interpreted in *Boysen*. The comment to the section, however, explicitly rejects the *Boysen* discrete subrequirements approach, but does not disapprove of the result that the 1964 will was not revived.

4. *Mistake in the Inducement?* The Restatement 3d of Property §4.2 comment f provides that "[a]n intent to revive a former will is ineffective if it was the product of a mistake in inducement. The burden of proof is on the party claiming that it was the product of a mistake in inducement." Could Genevieve have carried that burden in *Boysen*?

5. *Revival of a Will That Was Revoked by Act.* Suppose that after G's death, an attested will, which earlier had been torn into a number of pieces, was found among G's important papers taped back together. Evidence shows that G was at all times in control of the document. What result under UPC §2-509? Should a court treat the will as having been revived? See Breathitt v. Whittaker's Executors, 47 Ky. 530 (1848). What standard of proof should be required to show revival in this type of case? See Restatement 3d of Property §4.2(b).

———

Revocation of a Codicil. In Estate of Hering, 166 Cal. Rptr. 298 (Ct. App. 1980), the decedent, Henry Hering, executed an eight-page typewritten will on October 21, 1976. Elaine Bockin was to receive a specific devise of the decedent's personal effects and rent-free use of certain premises. She was to be the income beneficiary of a testamentary trust, with the trustee also having power to invade the corpus of the trust for her benefit. At Elaine's death, any remaining corpus of the trust was to be distributed to the Braille Institute of America, Inc.

On January 13, 1977, Henry executed a typewritten three-page "First Codicil to Will of Henry Richard Hering." The codicil referred to the specific articles of the will containing Elaine's name and amended those articles by deleting her name and inserting the words "Evelyn Salib." The codicil also expressly confirmed and republished the will in all other respects.

On December 2, 1977, in the presence of his attorney and with intent to revoke the codicil, Henry made a large "X" through all of the writing on each page of the codicil and on each page wrote the words, "Revoked December 2, 1977 Henry R. Hering."[20] Henry's attorney testified that, shortly before Henry made these marks on the codicil, Henry stated that he thought that the X's would reinstate the provisions in the original will, devising the income interest to Elaine rather than Evelyn.

---

20. Bockin argued in the alternative that even if the antirevival provisions applied, the December 1977 writing was a valid holographic codicil that republished the original will. The court declined to address this issue once it found that the antirevival statute did not apply to a revoked codicil.

When the case was decided, the California statute on revival provided:[21]

If, after making a will, the testator makes a second will, the destruction or other revocation of the second will does not revive the first will, unless it appears by the terms of such revocation that it was the intention to revive and give effect to the first will, or unless, after such destruction or other revocation, the first will is duly republished.

The court gave effect to Henry's 1976 will as originally written but not on the theory that the revoked provisions of the 1976 will had been revived under the above revival statute. The above revival statute was, in fact, held inapplicable to cases of partial revocation by codicil. (Although UPC §1-201 defines the term "will" as including a "codicil," California then had no similar statutory provision.[22]) With the legislation held to be inapplicable, the court applied the common-law rule on revival, under which a subsequent revocation of the codicil "leaves the will in force and effect as written."[23]

How would the *Hering* case be decided under UPC §2-509? How would the *Hering* case have been decided under the court's approach and under the approach of the UPC if, just before he made the "X" marks on his 1977 codicil, Henry had said "Now neither Evelyn nor Elaine will get any of my property"?

PART E. DEPENDENT RELATIVE REVOCATION (INEFFECTIVE REVOCATION)

As we shall see, dependent relative revocation is a remarkable doctrine, ingeniously devised to give a testator results that come close to actual intention when actual intention, though established to a court's satisfaction, cannot be given effect. The Restatement 3d of Property seeks to rename the doctrine[24] and formulates it as follows.

---

21. The California provision has now been repealed and replaced by the original version of UPC §2-509. See Cal. Prob. Code §6123.

22. One was added in 1983. See Cal. Prob. Code §88.

23. But see Estate of Lagreca, 687 A.2d 783 (N.J. Super. Ct. App. Div. 1997) (holding under an antirevival statute that a revocation of a codicil by act does not revive the revoked will provisions and therefore the decedent died partially intestate).

24. In Goods of Brown, [1942] P. 136, the judge decried the term "dependent relative revocation," saying: "The name of this doctrine seems to me to be somewhat overloaded with unnecessary polysyllables. The resounding adjectives add very little, it seems to me, to any clear idea of what is meant."

Restatement 3d of Property

§4.3 Ineffective Revocation (Dependent Relative Revocation)

(a) A partial or complete revocation of a will is presumptively ineffective if the testator made the revocation:

(1) in connection with an attempt to achieve a dispositive objective that fails under applicable law, or

(2) because of a false assumption of law, or because of a false belief about an objective fact, that is either recited in the revoking instrument or established by clear and convincing evidence.

(b) The presumption established in subsection (a) is rebutted if allowing the revocation to remain in effect would be more consistent with the testator's probable intention.

———

Although the development of the doctrine of dependent relative revocation (ineffective revocation) is commendable, it is still the law of second best. Of prime concern as you study the following materials is whether the law can do better.

EXTERNAL REFERENCES. George E. Palmer, Dependent Relative Revocation and Its Relation to Relief for Mistake, 69 Mich. L. Rev. 989 (1971); Joseph Warren, Dependent Relative Revocation, 33 Harv. L. Rev. 337 (1920).

Callahan's Estate
29 N.W.2d 352 (Wis. 1947)

Eva Callahan died in June 1945 at the age of eighty-seven years as a result of an illness with which she was stricken on the preceding January 21st. Her husband, Dr. John L. Callahan, Sr., died on January 5, 1945 at the age of eighty-four. The Callahans were the parents of two children then living, John Jr. and Albert.

In July 1932 Eva Callahan and her husband executed wills almost identical in their provisions. In December 1936, September 1938, February 1940 and August 1944, further wills were drawn by each clearly evidencing common design and collaboration in their preparation. On the night of January 1, 1945 Quincy H. Hale, an attorney in the city of La Crosse who had drawn the various wills for the Callahans, visited them in the company of his wife. At the conclusion of the visit Dr. Callahan accompanied the Hales to the door and informed them that he and his wife had destroyed their 1944 wills for the purpose of reinstating their 1940 wills, and had done so because Albert had begun drinking heavily again and they desired to put him back in the position he occupied under their 1940 wills. Albert had been addicted to the excessive use of intoxicating liquor and had received less than equal treatment with John in the 1940 wills. In the 1944 wills his position was improved because he had at that time given up drinking. At the time of Dr. Callahan's statement Mrs. Callahan was in the room but said nothing.

The next day, January 2, Mr. Hale determined that the destruction of the 1944 wills did not reinstate the 1940 wills. He drew a new will for Dr. Callahan almost identical with his 1940 will and took it to him for execution. He then informed the doctor and Mrs. Callahan that their 1940 wills had not been revived by destruction of the later wills. He had not been requested to draw the new will by Dr. Callahan either on the preceding night or on the day following, but did so purely of his own volition. He stated that he acted in haste because he was convinced that the doctor would not live long. He did not prepare a similar will for Mrs. Callahan because she was in good health and he was not concerned about her. Dr. Callahan executed the will on January 2 and died three days later.

Mrs. Callahan was stricken on January 21. She was taken to the hospital immediately and died the following June. While she was at the hospital two additional wills were drawn.... Mr. Hale testified that Mrs. Callahan was incompetent [to execute a will] after she entered the hospital on January 21....

[Mrs. Callahan's] will of 1940 [and] will of 1944 ... were offered for probate in the alternative. The petition for probate was made by Mr. Hale who had retained a copy of the destroyed 1944 will. John and Albert objected to the probate. [A] decree was entered admitting the 1944 will to probate, from which John and Albert appeal....

RECTOR, J. The appeal of ... Albert and John from the judgment admitting the 1944 will to probate raises the question whether the trial court properly applied the doctrine of 'dependent relative revocation'.

That rule is ordinarily applied in cases where a testator having executed one will thereafter revokes it by the execution of a later will which, for some reason fails to become effectual. In such cases revocation of the earlier instrument 'is treated as relative and dependent upon the efficiency of the later disposition, which was intended to be substituted.' Will of Lundquist, 1933, 211 Wis. 541, 543, 248 N.W. 410, 411. The revocation of the earlier document is held to be dependent upon the validity of the later one and the later one being invalid, the earlier one stands. The rule has been criticized by some courts and some textwriters, but it is the law in this jurisdiction.

The situation presented here differs somewhat from the usual case in which the doctrine is applied. Here we have a revocation of a later will with an announced intention of reinstating a former one. But the rule was applied to such a situation in Powell v. Powell, 1866, L.R. 1 Prob. 209. The reasoning upon which it is based applies to the same extent that it does in the typical case. Adherence to the rule requires that we apply it here.

It is argued that there is a distinction between this case and other cases in which the rule has been applied. It is said that here the testatrix was advised the destruction of the 1944 will did not reinstate the 1940 will, that she had an adequate opportunity thereafter to prepare a new will if she had desired to do so, and that her failure to prepare a will indicated that her destruction of the 1944 will was not conditioned but was accompanied by an intention to revoke the document absolutely. There is considerable force in the argument. The doctrine of dependent relative revocation is based upon the testator's inferred intention. It is held that as a matter of law the destruction of the later document is intended to be conditional where it is accompanied by the expressed intent of reinstating a former will and where there is no explanatory evidence. Of course if there is evidence that the testator intended the destruction to be absolute, there is no room for the application of the doctrine of dependent revocation. Failure to prepare a new will may or may not be significant. The inferences to be derived from such a failure will vary according to the circumstances. If it were due to lack of opportunity, it would be difficult to attribute any great significance to it. The inferences, as in other factual questions, are to be drawn by the trier of fact.

Here the trial court evidently did not consider the delay in preparing a new will sufficient to establish that the 1944 will was destroyed with the intent to revoke it absolutely. It was justified in arriving at that conclusion.

Three days after Mr. Hale's advice to Mrs. Callahan, her husband died and she was stricken sixteen days after his death with an illness which rendered her incompetent thereafter. Both she and her husband were advanced in years. She was eighty-seven and he was eighty-four. They had lived together for many years. Her grief at his death, the necessity for arrangements that were then required and the loss that she must have felt, constitute adequate explanation of her failure to discuss the matter of a new will in the short time before she became ill.

There is a further argument to the effect that Mr. Hale's testimony as to the testatrix's intention in destroying her 1944 will is incompetent and of no probative force. [The court then held that Dr. Callahan's statement to Mr. Hale was in the course of a social visit and that Mr. Hale's testimony was not incompetent under a statute prohibiting disclosure by an attorney of communications of a client made to him "in the course of his professional employment."]

So far as the matter of probative force is concerned, it strikes us that the circumstances are persuasive as to the testatrix' intention. We must bear in mind that prior to the doctor's statement to Mr. Hale he and his wife had each executed five wills and these wills carried the clearest indication that they were the result of collaboration and execution of a common design. The fact that they acted in concert in preparing these wills carries an inference that they collaborated in destroying their 1944 wills. Dr. Callahan's statement to Mr. Hale in the presence of Mrs. Callahan that they had acted together must be considered as the statement of one who without doubt had consulted with her in the matter....

JUDGMENT AFFIRMED.

Notes and Questions

1. *Theory of Dependent Relative Revocation—Mistake or Conditional Revocation?* In the earliest English decision on the general problem, the court based relief partly upon the ground that the revocation "ought to be relieved against and the will set up again in equity, under the head of accident." Onions v. Tyrer, 2 Vern. 742, 23 Eng. Rep. 1085, 1 P. Wms. 343, 24 Eng. Rep. 418 (Ch. 1716). Recognition that the problem is essentially one of giving relief for mistake still appears in some of the cases, but the conventional analysis is the conditional-revocation theory. As the Restatement 3d of Property explains, neither theory is completely satisfactory.

> *§4.3, [Comment] a. Rationale and historical note....* This Restatement treats the doctrine of ineffective revocation as one of independent integrity, grounded neither in a conditional-revocation analysis nor exclusively in a mistake analysis.... The conditional-revocation theory is thoroughly unsatisfactory as a basis of the doctrine. The notion that the testator actually intended to make the revocation conditional is a fiction .... The mistake theory is unsatisfactory as an exclusive basis of the doctrine. Equity only grants relief for mistake if the actor was laboring under an erroneous belief *at the time of the act* .... This restriction makes the mistake theory too limiting, and the doctrine of ineffective revocation has properly been extended to cases in which the testator was not mistaken when he or she revoked ....

2. *Giving Effect to the Testator's Intention.* As noted in the introductory text to this Part, dependent relative revocation is the law of second best. Callahan's intention was to revive her 1940 will. She did not intend her destroyed 1944 will to stand unrevoked under the doctrine of dependent relative revocation. The 1940 will could not be given effect because the applicable Wisconsin legislation contained an antirevival provision similar to the one in the English Wills Act 1837, requiring reexecution of the revoked will.[25] Dependent relative revocation in cases like *Callahan* should all but disappear in states adopting a liberal revival rule like the one found in UPC §2-509.

———

Giving Effect to the Testator's Intention in Other Dependent Relative Revocation Cases. The factual pattern faced by the court in the *Callahan* case—revocation of a later will for the purpose of reviving a former one—is only one of several factual patterns that lend themselves to a dependent-relative-revocation analysis. Another typical situation in which courts have applied dependent relative revocation is one in which a testator revokes a will by revocatory act in connection with an ineffective attempt to execute a replacement will. We will study these revocation-to-make-a-replacement-will cases below. As you study them, consider the extent to which adoption of a harmless-error rule would give the law a mechanism by which to give effect to the testator's intention, the later will.

---

25. The current Wisconsin statute on revival tracks UPC §2-509. See Wis. Stat. §853.11(6).

The widespread enactment of UPC §2-503 or widespread judicial adoption of the harmless-error rule of Restatement 3d of Property §3.3 is probably years away. Therefore, it is important to consider how the courts should administer the law of second best. The Restatement 3d of Property provides the following guidance:

> *§4.3, [Comment] a. Rationale and historical note....* A revocation [that is made in connection with an attempt to achieve a dispositive objective that fails under applicable law] is only presumptively ineffective, not automatically ineffective. The revocation is still given effect when the court determines that the testator, if given the choice, would probably have preferred the revocation to remain in effect rather than to have it set aside. This is a question of fact, to be determined on the basis of relevant evidence. [A]n always relevant and often decisive factor on the question of probable intention is whether the outcome of treating the revocation as ineffective comes closer to the testator's failed dispositive objective than the outcome of allowing the revocation to remain in effect. If the outcome of allowing the revocation to remain in effect comes closer to the testator's failed dispositive objective, this tends to rebut the presumption. Consequently, if, from this comparison or from other relevant evidence, it is established that the testator's probable intention would have been for the revocation to stand, the presumption is rebutted and the revocation remains in effect. Otherwise, the presumption prevails and the revocation is nullified on the theory that, had the testator known that revoking the will would not facilitate intention, the testator would not have formed an intent to revoke. Under this doctrine, then, if the presumption is not rebutted, the will is valid and effective because it was never revoked.

See also George E. Palmer, Dependent Relative Revocation and Its Relation to Relief for Mistake, 69 Mich. L. Rev. 989 (1971).

Estate of Patten
587 P.2d 1307 (Mont. 1978)

[Ella D. Patten died in 1973, survived by her two sons, Donald and Robert. In 1970, about three years before her death, she had attempted to execute a will that devised the bulk of her $200,000 estate to Donald. This 1970 will was found in her safe-deposit box after her death, and Donald presented it for probate. Robert, however, successfully contested its validity on the ground of improper execution. See Patten v. Patten, 558 P.2d 659 (Mont. 1976).

The 1970 will consisted of two pages. Ella Patten's signature appeared at the bottom of the first page. The second page contained only an attestation clause, with the signatures of three members of her doctor's office staff. The ineffective attempt at proper execution occurred on July 6, 1970. Ella Patten took the will with her to a doctor's appointment. After being attended by her doctor, "a request was transmitted to the office staff to witness her will." Ella, who one witness described as habitually secretive about her personal affairs, folded the document over so that only the second page was visible to the witnesses. Contrary to the will formality requirements of the then-existing Montana statute, Ella neither signed in the presence of the witnesses nor acknowledged her signature to them.

After failing to get the 1970 will probated, Donald presented for probate a copy of a 1968 will. The original of the 1968 will had been given to Ella by her attorney after its proper execution, but could not be found after her death. The copy presented for probate was a copy retained by her attorney. The district court granted summary judgment to Robert, denying probate of the copy of his mother's 1968 will.]

HASWELL, C.J.... Both [the 1968 and 1970] wills left the bulk of decedent's estate, approximately $200,000, to Donald Patten. There are some differences between the wills. In the 1968 will, Robert Patten was named executor of the estate. In the 1970 will, this appointment was deleted. The 1970 will omits some specific bequests which were in the 1968 will. The remaining paragraphs in the wills are almost identical in language and in form....

The doctrine [of dependent relative revocation] is applied with caution. The mere fact that a testator made a new will, which failed of effect, will not of itself prevent the destruction of an earlier will from operating as a revocation. The doctrine can only apply where there is a clear intent of the testator that the revocation of the old is conditional upon the validity of the new will. For the doctrine to apply, the new will must also not have changed the testamentary purpose of the old will and essentially repeated the same dispositive plans such that it is clear that the first will is revoked only because the second duplicated its purpose. Thus, while the doctrine may be widely recognized, it is narrowly applied....

In deciding whether to apply the doctrine in a given case, the testator's "intent" is the controlling factor. The testator must intend that the destruction of the old will is dependent upon the validity of the new will. Thompson on Wills, supra. Evidence of this intent cannot be left to speculation, supposition, conjecture or possibility. The condition that revocation of a will is based upon the validity of the new will must be proved by substantial evidence of probative value. A showing of immediate intent to make a new will and of conditional destruction are required to re-establish a destroyed will under the theory of dependent relative revocation. [T]o prove this intent the proponents of the revoked will must show that the new will was executed concurrently with or shortly after the destruction of the old will and both wills must be similar in content. In the present case, Donald Patten, the proponent of the copy of the 1968 will, has not proven that decedent intended the destruction of the 1968 will to depend upon the validity of the 1970 will.... No one knows when the decedent destroyed her will or how she did it. The record does not show that the 1970 will was executed concurrently or shortly after the destruction of the 1968 will.

While the content of both wills is similar in some respects, the dissimilarities are such that they reveal decedent's revocation of the 1968 will was not conditioned on the validity of the 1970 will. In the 1968 will, decedent bequeathed $5,000 and $2,500 to her grandchildren, the son and daughter of Robert Patten. In the 1970 will, Donald Patten's name was written in by pen and ink as executor. In the 1968 will,

Robert Patten was the named executor. These differences in the wills show that decedent may not have intended the same dispositive plan.

Here, the evidence that decedent intended the revocation of the 1968 will to depend upon the validity of the 1970 will is merely conjecture and speculation. As that is the case, the District Court was correct in granting summary judgment to Robert L. Patten. The doctrine of dependent relative revocation can only be applied where the evidence of the testator's intent is clear and convincing. Such is not the case here.

.... Here, we have no evidence that the revocation of the 1968 will depended upon the validity of the 1970 will. The doctrine of dependent relative revocation has no application under these circumstances....

JUDGMENT AFFIRMED.

DALY, HARRISON, SHEA AND SHEEHY, JJ., concur.

Notes and Questions

1. *Question.* Did intestacy come closer to Ella's dispositive plan exemplified by her invalidly executed 1970 will than her validly executed but revoked 1968 will? Section 4.3 comment c of the Restatement 3d of Property provides:

> *§4.3, [Comment] c. Revocation intending to make a replacement will....* After death, the only evidence available may be the ineffectively executed replacement will, and sometimes but not necessarily the revoked first will. Consequently, the doctrine of ineffective revocation would be too restricted if it required evidence of the time of revocation and of a contemporaneous intent to make a replacement will. There need not be affirmative proof of the time of revocation or that, at the time of revocation, the testator intended to replace the first will with a replacement will.

2. *Subsequent Montana Legislation.* In 1974, Montana enacted the original UPC, including §2-502. In 1993, it enacted the current UPC, including §§2-502 and 2-503. See Mont. Code §§72-2-522, -523. What would have been the outcome of *Patten* if Ella Patten had died in 1975? In 1994?

———

Uncompleted Plan? In Dougan's Estate, 53 P.2d 511 (Or. 1936), Dougan made numerous pen and pencil marks on her will and then took the mutilated will to her lawyer, together with an outline of the provisions of a new will, which she requested him to prepare. The will was prepared, but she suffered a stroke and died before she could get to the attorney's office to execute it. Estate of Ausley, 818 P.2d 1226 (Okla. 1991), involved similar facts. Ausley marked up his will with "X's" and the words "void." He then hired an attorney to draft a new will for him. The attorney presented Ausley with a draft of a proposed new will on June 16, 1988. Some unspecified changes regarding some property in Oklahoma were required. Ausley died on June 20, 1988, before a new draft was presented to him. Both the *Dougan* and the *Ausley* courts held that the mutilated wills could not be given effect under dependent relative revocation. Why not? The Restatement 3d of Property states:

> *§4.3, [Comment] c. Revocation intending to make a replacement will....* If the testator never had a plan to make a replacement will, the doctrine of ineffective revocation is inapplicable. Similarly, if the testator intended to make a replacement will but never took steps to complete the plan, the doctrine cannot be applied. The testator's uncompleted plan to make a replacement will provides no benchmark against which to gauge whether the testator's probable intention would be to have the revocation stand or fall. The revocation stands....
>
> Between an ineffective attempt to make a replacement will ... and a wholly uncompleted plan to make a replacement will ... is an intermediate case ... in which the testator's actual intention, though not embodied in a defectively executed replacement will, is sufficiently provable to use as a benchmark against which to gauge whether or not the testator's probable intention would have been for the revocation to prevail.

In Trust Estate of Daoang, 953 P.2d 959 (Haw. 1998), the court held that the settlor of a revocable trust had "sufficiently manifested his intent to amend the trust" by "signing a letter sent by his attorney to confirm [the settlor's] plans to amend... the trust, even assuming the subsequent execution of a more formal document was contemplated."

Unattested Handwritten Alteration of Attested Will. Testators sometimes attempt to alter their wills by marking them up—by crossing out attested language and inserting unattested substitute language. The purpose is usually to alter one or more dispositions of property or designations of persons. In the absence of a harmless-error rule, the inserted unattested language cannot be given effect. The question then becomes whether the crossed-out attested language stands as a partial revocation or whether the revocation is ineffective under the doctrine of dependent relative revocation.

Schneider v. Harrington
71 N.E.2d 242 (Mass. 1947)

[Letitia Bliss's will provided that her entire estate was to be disposed of in the following manner:

> 1. To my niece Phyllis H. Schneider, of 2368 Washington Avenue Bronx, New York, one third (1/3).
>
> 2. One third (1/3) to my sister, Margaret J. Sugarman, of 177 West 95th Street New York City, New York.
>
> 3. One third (1/3) to my sister, Amy E. Harrington, of New York City, New York.

The will contained no residuary clause, but it did contain a provision stating: "I am intentionally omitting my other sisters and brothers for I feel that they are well taken care of." At some time after the execution of the will, Letitia used a pencil to cross out all of clause 3 and the figures "1/3" in clauses 1 and 2. She then inserted by pencil the figures ½ in clauses 1 and 2, leaving uncancelled in these clauses the words "one third."

Letitia left no husband or children. Her heirs were four sisters and twenty-two nieces and nephews.]

SPALDING, J.... The judge of probate entered a decree allowing the will with the exception of certain portions which had been crossed out by the testatrix. The case comes here on the appeal of Amy E. Harrington, a sister of the testatrix, who took one third of the estate under the will as executed, but nothing under the will as allowed....

The decree of the court below provided that the will was to be allowed except for clause 3 and the figures "1/3" in clauses 1 and 2; it also provided that the figures "1/2" which had been substituted for the figures "1/3" in clauses 1 and 2 were not part of the will.

By the law of this Commonwealth a will can be revoked "By burning, tearing, cancelling or obliterating it with the intention of revoking it, by the testator himself or by a person in his presence and by his direction." G.L.(Ter.Ed.) c. 191, §8. In the case before us there was clearly a "cancelling" of the third clause of the will which, if done with the requisite revocatory intent, would constitute a revocation pro tanto; a part of a will may be canceled, leaving the rest in full force. For reasons that will presently appear, it is not necessary to decide whether the canceling of the figures "1/3" in the first and second clauses, leaving the words "one third" intact, would, if coupled with the necessary intent, effect a revocation of the legacies therein provided.

The appellant argues that the cancellation of clause 3 was made conditional on the validity of the attempted substitutions in clauses 1 and 2, and that since these failed for want of proper authentication there was no revocation. The doctrine of conditional revocation (frequently, but less aptly, called dependent relative revocation) is recognized in this Commonwealth. In Sanderson v. Norcross, 242 Mass. 43, 45, 136 N.E. 170, 171, it was said, "The doctrine is widely established that a revocation of a valid will, which is so intimately connected with the making of another will as to show a clear intent that the revocation of the old is made conditional upon the validity of the new, fails to become operative if the new will is void as a testamentary disposition for want of proper execution. Revocation in its last analysis is a question of intent. A revocation grounded on supposed facts, which turn out not to exist, falls when the foundation falls." After recognizing the doctrine as part of our law, the court went on to say that "It is a principle to be applied with caution.... Courts have no power to reform wills.... Omissions cannot be supplied.... The only means for ascertaining the intent of the testator are the words written and the acts done by him." 242 Mass. at pages 45, 46, 136 N.E. at page 172. It has been held on the authority of Sanderson v. Norcross that where a testator cancels or obliterates portions of his will in order to substitute different provisions, and in such a way as to show a clear intent that the revocation is conditional on the validity of the substitution, and the substitution fails for want of proper authentication, the will stands as originally drawn. Thus in Walter v. Walter, 301 Mass. 289, 17 N.E.2d 199, the testatrix, after her will had been executed, obliterated the description of real estate in two devises, and then interlined different descriptions which were not properly authenticated. The decree of the Probate Court allowed the will, but disallowed the devises which had been obliterated. On appeal, this court reversed the decree, holding that the obliterations when considered with the interlineations disclosed an intent on the part of the testatrix to revoke only if the interlineations were valid as a substitute, and that parol evidence was admissible to prove the original wording of the obliterated clauses.

We think that the principle discussed above is applicable here. It is clear that the cancellations and the substitutions were inextricably linked together as parts of one transaction; and it is evident that the testatrix intended the cancellations to be effective only if the substitutions were valid. But the substitutions, inasmuch as they were not authenticated by a new attestation as required by statute, were invalid. Consequently the cancellations never became operative. Additional support for this conclusion, if any is needed, may be found in the fact that the will contained no residuary clause, and if the decree entered in the court below should stand there would be a partial intestacy—a result which we think the testatrix did not intend. It follows that the decree of the Probate Court is reversed, and a new decree is to be entered allowing the will as worded prior to the attempted changes....

So ordered.

Notes and Question

1. *Harmless-Error Rule?* Under the harmless-error rule of the Restatement 3d of Property or the UPC §2-503, could the words written on the will be given effect?[26]

2. *Handwritten Alteration of a Holographic Will.* In contrast to the position taken with respect to an attested will, the courts have held that a decedent *can* validly alter a holographic will by making handwritten changes thereon without signing the will again or signing or initialing the alteration. See, e.g., Estate of Archer, 239 Cal. Rptr. 137 (Ct. App. 1987); Randall v. Salvation Army, 686 P.2d 241 (Nev. 1984); Stanley v. Henderson, 162 S.W.2d 95 (Tex. Comm'n Appeals 1942); Moyers v. Gregory, 7 S.E.2d 881 (Va. 1940); Charleston Nat'l Bank v. Thru The Bible Radio Network, 507 S.E.2d 708 (W. Va. 1998).

---

26. Under conventional law, of course, the testator's actual intention could not be carried out because the alterations were unattested. Even under conventional law, however, the case would be open to proof that the will was in the altered form at the time of execution. See Cravens' Estate, 242 P.2d 135 (Okla. 1952); and cases collected in Annot., Interlineations and Changes Appearing on Face of Will, 34 A.L.R.2d 619.

3. *Attempted Reduction of the Devised Amount.* In Ruel v. Hardy, 6 A.2d 753 (N.H. 1939), a clause of Ethel Smith's will provided: "To Frank ..., and to Walter ... and ... Lilla ..., I give five hundred dollars to each one." After execution, in an unattested act, Ethel struck out "five" and inserted "one." The residuary devisee was her husband, Benjamin. The court found dependent relative revocation inapplicable and held that legacies to Frank, Walter, and Lilla were revoked.

> A reduction of eighty per cent of the legacy tends more to show a preference on her part that her legatees should have nothing rather than that they should have the full sum ....

Accord Estate of Lyles, 615 So. 2d 1186 (Miss. 1993).

Problems

Analyze the following problems under the Restatement 3d of Property §4.3 and the UPC.

1. As originally executed, G's attested will devised $10,000 to her brother, A, and $20,000 to her brother, B. After G's death, G's will was found with "$10,000" crossed out and the figure "$12,000" written in above it and with "$20,000" crossed out and the figure "$3,000" written in above it. All of the alterations were in G's handwriting. Assume that neither A nor B would be an heir of G. What result?

2. G's will devised the residue of her estate to her live-in companion A. Thereafter, G and A separated. Some years later, G began living with B, and G eventually adopted B's son X. At G's death, G and B were still living together. After G's death, her will was found, and "A" had been crossed out and "B" written in. What result?

3. G's will devised the residue of her estate to her live-in companion A. Then G and A separated. G began living with B, but then they separated and G went back to living with A. At G's death, G and A were living together. G's will showed that G had crossed out "A" and written in "B," then crossed out "B" and written in "A." A and B survived G. G's heirs are her brothers and sisters. What result?

———

Revocation Based on a Mistake of Fact. Although most dependent relative revocation cases involve an attempt to achieve a dispositive objective that fails under applicable law, the category is not restricted to such situations. See Restatement 3d of Property §4.3(a)(2). Consider how the doctrine of dependent relative revocation might apply to the following problems.

Problems

1. G, having been informed that her favorite nephew, N, a soldier, had been killed in combat, wrote across a $10,000 devise to him in her will the word "Canceled." Extrinsic evidence establishes that G revoked the devise because she thought N had

died in combat. Shortly after G's death, N, who had not died in combat but had been taken prisoner of war, was released. What result? Compare Campbell v. French, 30 Eng. Rep. 1033 (Ch. 1797); Gillespie v. Gillespie, 126 A. 744 (N.J. Eq. 1924), with Witt v. Rosen, 765 S.W.2d 956 (Ark. 1989); Salmonski's Estate, 238 P.2d 966 (Cal. 1951). See also Restatement 3d of Property §4.3 comment i; UPC §2-302(c).

2. G's will contains a $10,000 devise to his niece, N. G executed a codicil stating that he revoked the devise to N because G had made substantial gifts to N. N can establish that G did not give her substantial gifts. What result? See Restatement 3d of Property §4.3 comment i, illus. 24.

———

Express Revocation by Subsequent Instrument. Can dependent relative revocation be applied if a will was *expressly* revoked in connection with an attempt to achieve a dispositive objective that fails under applicable law? Most courts have held that it can be. See, e.g., Linkins v. Protestant Episcopal Cathedral Foundation, 187 F.2d 357 (D.C. Cir. 1950); Kaufman's Estate, 155 P.2d 831 (Cal. 1945); La Croix v. Senecal, 99 A.2d 115 (Conn. 1953); Charleston Library Society v. Citizens & Southern Nat'l Bank, 20 S.E.2d 623 (S.C. 1942).

Crosby v. Alton Ochsner Medical Foundation, 276 So. 2d 661 (Miss. 1973) (5-to-4 decision), is one of the few cases in which the court refused to apply the doctrine. Hollis Crosby died leaving a will that devised one-half of the residue of his estate to his widow and the other half to the Alton Ochsner Medical Foundation. The devise to the Medical Foundation, having been made in a will executed within ninety days of Hollis's death, was void under the now-repealed Mississippi mortmain statue.[27] The will contained a clause expressly revoking all former wills.

Hollis's former will, executed more than ninety days prior to death, contained a similar devise to the Medical Foundation. The Medical Foundation argued that the doctrine of dependent relative revocation should be applied so as to render ineffectual the revocation of the devise in its favor in the prior will.

The court rejected the Medical Foundation's argument, saying in part:

> [In Hairston v. Hairston, 30 Miss. 276 (1855)], this Court ... said: "[When] the will contains an express clause of revocation, ... there is nothing from which it could be inferred that the testator intended only to revoke conditionally .... [I]t would be incompetent to introduce evidence to prove that the declaration was not designed to operate as an absolute, but only as a conditional revocation ...." (30 Miss. at 301-303)....
>
> We do not think that it can be maintained that *Hairston* was wrongly decided or that its results are detrimental to the public. In fact, we are of the opinion that the law announced therein is sound. A person has a right to make a will and so long as it is in conformity with the law, he or she may leave his or her property as desired. By the same token such person

---

27. See Restatement 3d of Property §9.7.

has the right to revoke a will for any reason he or she may have. Due to the construction we have placed on our revocation statute, the only way that a person may be sure that the revocation of a will is unequivocal and certain is by a declaration in writing either in another will or in a separate writing duly attested revoking the former will. When so revoked such a person is assured that after death no one will be heard to say that he or she did not intend to revoke the former will. We think this is a valuable right and should not be disturbed.

Is the Mississippi court's conclusion and reasoning persuasive? If not, how would you answer the court's point that a revocation that is unambiguously and unconditionally declared in a validly executed will cannot be rendered conditional by extrinsic evidence?

Partial Application of Dependent Relative Revocation. The court in Arrowsmith v. Mercantile-Safe Deposit & Trust Co., 545 A.2d 674 (Md. 1988), was asked to apply dependent relative revocation to only one will provision and to treat the rest of the will as revoked. George H. C. Arrowsmith died in 1983, leaving a will dated July 29, 1982. George's 1982 will expressly revoked all prior wills and exercised a testamentary power of appointment over some $7 million in assets of an irrevocable inter vivos trust created by his mother in 1953.

George's 1982 will did not contain a perpetuity saving clause, a device routinely used by lawyers to avoid violating the Rule Against Perpetuities. See Chapter 17. In the absence of the perpetuity saving clause, George's exercise of the power of appointment violated the Rule.

George had executed two prior wills, one in 1976 and the other in 1966. His 1976 will expressly revoked all prior wills and exercised his testamentary power of appointment in terms similar to those contained in the 1982 will. The 1976 will also failed to contain a perpetuity saving clause.

George's 1966 will exercised his testamentary power of appointment, but in terms quite dissimilar to the 1982 or 1976 wills. The 1966 will, however, contained a perpetuity saving clause.

The court was asked to apply dependent relative revocation to conclude that the revocation of the perpetuity saving clause in the 1966 will was conditioned upon the validity of the exercise of the power of appointment in the 1976 will and, in turn, in the 1982 will. The court declined to apply dependent relative revocation in this manner, saying:

> Plucking the perpetuities saving clause from the 1966 will and inserting it in the 1982 will is inconsistent with the theoretical justification for the doctrine.... [T]he doctrine's underlying theory of conditional revocation limits the relief which a court can grant. If a later will which expressly revokes earlier wills itself fails in whole or in part, the doctrine requires a court to decide whether the decedent would have preferred the prior will to the result under the later will, which may be partial invalidity or intestacy.... The doctrine ... does not present a court with a menu. It is not the judicial function to select some provisions from column A and some provisions from column B in order to put together a valid will.

In contrast to *Arrowsmith*, the California Court of Appeal held in Estate of Anderson, 65 Cal. Rptr. 2d 307 (Ct. App.), rev. denied (1997), that dependent relative revocation applied with regard to a provision in the testator's first will that was otherwise wholly revoked by her second will. As a result of an attorney error, the testator's second will failed to include a specific reference to a power of appointment that she had received under her husband's will. A valid exercise of the power depended on her will containing a specific reference to it. See Chapter 14. Extrinsic evidence established the testator's intent to exercise her power in the second will just as she had in article eighth of her first will. The court held that:

> On these facts, we conclude that a "question [has] arise[n] as to the effectiveness of the second instrument,... so that upon its failure to be operative for want of proper execution *or other cause*, the testator will be presumed to have intended the original instrument to stand *to the extent that the later proves ineffective.*" (Estate of Salmonski, [38 Cal.2d 199, 212, 238 P.2d 966], italics added.) Because the second will did not effectively exercise the power of appointment, article eighth of the first will remained in effect under the doctrine of dependent relative revocation.

The result in *Anderson* is supported by Restatement 3d of Property §4.3 comment e and illustration 18.

INTERNAL REFERENCE. See the discussion in Chapter 17 of UPC §§2-901 to -906, which incorporates the Uniform Statutory Rule Against Perpetuities (USRAP) into the UPC. Generally speaking, the effect of USRAP is to insert a perpetuity saving clause into all trusts that contain a perpetuity violation. Had the *Arrowsmith* case been governed by USRAP, George's 1982 will would have been valid, and there would have been no reason to go into court to correct the mistaken omission of the perpetuity saving clause.

PART F. CONTRACTS NOT TO REVOKE A WILL

Primary Statutory Reference: *UPC §2-514*

Mutual and Joint Wills. Litigation over the existence of a contract not to revoke typically occurs in the context of mutual or joint wills executed by a married couple. Mutual wills are separate wills, executed by each of two persons; they contain similar or reciprocal provisions. Mutual wills are frequently executed by married couples as part of an overall estate plan for the disposition of their property. A *joint will* is a single instrument, executed by two persons, that they intend to operate as the will of each. Typically, joint wills are executed by a husband and wife. Because it acts twice, as the will for each party, a joint will must be probated twice, upon the death of each testator. Joint wills that contain reciprocal provisions, as they commonly do, are sometimes called *joint and mutual*. Because they tend to invite litigation over the existence of a will contract, joint wills are not favored by estate planners.

Where a couple has executed mutual wills or a joint will and the survivor subsequently changes his or her will, the existence of a common scheme expressed by mutual wills or a joint will may lead disappointed beneficiaries later to claim that the original will was executed pursuant to a will contract. The initial question is what evidence is required to prove that a contract not to revoke was made.

Junot v. Estate of Gilliam
759 S.W.2d 654 (Tenn. 1988)

HARBISON, C.J. Appellants brought this action to set aside the probate of a will executed on January 28, 1985, by decedent, Emma Jean Gilliam. The theory of the suit was that Mrs. Gilliam and her deceased husband, Thaddeaus Evans Gilliam, had executed mutual and reciprocal wills in 1974 and that upon the death of Mr. Gilliam in January, 1985, the 1974 will of Mrs. Gilliam had become irrevocable.

Appellants also filed a claim against the estate of Mrs. Gilliam for the portion of the estate which they claim under her 1974 will. Appellee filed a response, alleging that there was no contract between the parties and that the 1985 will of Mrs. Gilliam, already admitted to probate, should stand and be carried out according to its terms....

After a full trial, the judge held that appellants had not carried their burden of proof to establish a contract between Mr. and Mrs. Gilliam that would make her 1974 will irrevocable. The Court of Appeals affirmed. After careful consideration of all of the issues, we also affirm....

The 1974 Wills. Mr. and Mrs. Gilliam were married in 1967. This was the second marriage for each. Mr. Gilliam had three children by his former marriage, and Mrs. Gilliam had two. No children were born to this second marriage.

Prior to February 22, 1974, Mr. and Mrs. Gilliam had discussed making their wills. Mr. Gilliam is shown to have had a separate estate, the amount of which does not appear in the record. It is shown that he owned several pieces of real estate. Whether Mrs. Gilliam had a separate estate does not appear.

On or about February 1, 1974, Mr. and Mrs. Gilliam made an appointment with Mr. Thomas McKinney, Jr., an attorney who had practiced in Kingsport, Tennessee, for several years. He had never met either of the Gilliams previously. He testified that he discussed with them a number of possible dispositions which they might make of their property, including life estates with remainder. There was a general discussion of the subject of wills, the revocation thereof and contracts to make wills irrevocable. Inter vivos gifts were also discussed, but no conclusions were reached during the first meeting.

About three weeks later, on February 22, 1974, Mr. and Mrs. Gilliam returned to the attorney's office and instructed him to write the wills which are in question. They also instructed him to write a warranty deed from Mr. Gilliam to himself and his wife so as to create a tenancy by the entirety in the property on which their residence was situated. This warranty deed was duly executed and was recorded. It is in the record, and there is no issue between the parties concerning it.

The parties executed separate wills on February 22, 1974, which were mutual and reciprocal. In his will, Mr. Gilliam directed payment of debts and funeral expenses. He then left all of his property outright to his wife, Mrs. Gilliam, "except as otherwise directed in Item III hereof...."

In Item III the will provided that if Mrs. Gilliam did not survive the testator, or if she died within 90 days after his death as a result of a common disaster, then all of Mr. Gilliam's estate was to be divided equally among the five children of the parties; that is, Mr. Gilliam's three children and the two children of Mrs. Gilliam.

The will of Mrs. Gilliam was written in exactly the same language, leaving everything to Mr. Gilliam but to the five children of the parties in the event he did not survive her. The same persons witnessed both wills.

Mr. Gilliam died on January 21, 1985. Mrs. Gilliam did survive, and the parties were not involved in "a common accident." She survived for more than 90 days, although she did die a little less than 7 months later, on August 11, 1985.

In the meanwhile, shortly after the death of her husband, Mrs. Gilliam wrote another will, executed on January 28, 1985, leaving the entire estate to her children by her first marriage. They are the executors of her estate and are the appellees herein. There is no evidence of fraud, undue influence or lack of mental capacity, and no claim of such. Mr. McKinney, who also wrote the second will, did state that Mrs. Gilliam appeared to be very emotional and upset after the death of her husband. Her statements to him seem to indicate a feeling of insecurity as to whether Mr. Gilliam's children by his first marriage might be able to take the estate from her and leave her with very few assets. There is no testimony in the record, however, concerning any actual controversy between Mrs. Gilliam and the children of Mr. Gilliam's first marriage, who are the appellants here.

Under the terms of Mr. Gilliam's 1974 will, the entire estate vested in Mrs. Gilliam upon his death, unconditionally and without any kind of restraint or restriction. Unless a contract between the parties could be proved, so as to make her will of the same date irrevocable, she was free to dispose of the estate as she saw fit.

There was very little evidence concerning any such contract. Mr. Gilliam's brother and other witnesses testified that in the eleven years between the execution of the 1974 wills and the death of Mr. Gilliam in January, 1985, Mr. and Mrs. Gilliam made reference that they had "traded wills." Counsel for appellants insist that this is clear evidence that the wills were intended by Mr. and Mrs. Gilliam to be irrevocable after the death of the first of them and resulted from a contract between the parties to that effect.

We respectfully disagree. It is well settled that in order to establish a contract to make or not to revoke a will, where the contract is not otherwise documented, evidence of such a contract must be clear and convincing. The mere fact that parties have executed mutual and reciprocal wills on the same date is not, in and of itself, sufficient to establish the existence of such a contract. That fact, together with other evidence concerning the circumstances of the parties, may be sufficient to establish such a contract. The issue, however, in every case is one of fact, not law, to be determined in light of all of the surrounding circumstances....

In the present case, there is a concurrent finding of fact by the trial court and the Court of Appeals that no such agreement was established by the evidence. That conclusion ... is binding here if supported by material evidence.

The evidence to establish a contract not to revoke a will must be clear and convincing. The evidence offered by the appellants to show such a contract in the present case was not sufficiently clear or precise to establish a binding contract between Mr. and Mrs. Gilliam that the survivor would not revoke his or her 1974 will. The wills accomplished what each of the spouses apparently desired—that is, each left everything to the survivor provided they were not involved in a common accident with the survivor expiring within 90 days thereafter. Alternate dispositions in each will were identical, but it is clear that the children of the parties were no more than just that—alternate beneficiaries. Legally the entire estate vested in the survivor, and there is nothing in the text of the wills themselves nor in the brief and informal remarks of Mr. and Mrs. Gilliam shown in evidence to establish a firm and binding agreement that the survivor was restricted in any way in his or her subsequent disposition of the property covered by these wills. The residence of the parties, which was the subject of a simultaneous deed, of course, passed to the survivor under the tenancy by the entirety which was created, without restraint, condition or restriction.

Wholly apart from the testimony of the scrivener of the will, Mr. McKinney, the trier of fact was not compelled in this case to conclude that such a contract as contended for by appellants in fact existed. When the testimony of Mr. McKinney is considered, however, it clearly affords material evidence to support the conclusions of the trial court that no such contract was ever made.

Appellants contend that the testimony of Mr. McKinney as to the intention of Mr. and Mrs. Gilliam is inadmissible. In support of that proposition they cite *Fisher v. Malmo,* 650 S.W.2d 43, 45-46 (Tenn. App. 1983) and *Nichols v. Todd,* 20 Tenn. App. 564, 101 S.W.2d 486 (1936). Both of these cases hold that the draftsman of a will cannot express an opinion as to the intention of the testator with respect to the interpretation of legal terms such as "heirs."

Even if Mr. McKinney's testimony in the present case may have partly offended that rule, the bulk of it did not. Most of his testimony consisted of his general discussion of the law of wills and several possible dispositions with the parties on

February 1, 1974, and his testimony that they expressly disclaimed to him any contractual restrictions upon the survivor when they executed their wills on February 22 which contain no such restrictions.

The judgments of the courts below that the surviving spouse received the estate free of any contractual restrictions are affirmed.

The 1977-78 Statutes. The Court has been furnished excellent briefs by the parties in this case and has been greatly assisted by the able oral argument presented on both sides. The briefs of the parties refer to the numerous cases in Tennessee on the subject of joint wills and of mutual and reciprocal wills.

Probably because of the large body of case law in this state dealing with the subject, the General Assembly has enacted statutes rather rigidly prescribing the requirements of a contract to make a will, not to revoke a will or to die intestate. The first of the statutes was 1977 Tenn. Public Acts, chapter 88, which provided that contracts of this nature might be established in certain ways. This statute was replaced by 1978 Tenn. Public Acts, chapter 745, now codified as T.C.A. §32-3-107, providing that such contracts can be established only by:

(1) Provisions of a will stating material provisions of the contract;

(2) An express reference in a will to a contract and extrinsic evidence proving the terms of the contract; or

(3) A writing signed by the decedent evidencing the contract.

(b) The execution of a joint will or mutual wills does not create a presumption of a contract to make a will, or to refrain from revoking a will.

The latter statute ... is patterned after a model which has been enacted in a number of states. Unlike the provisions in most states, however, this statute contains no provision limiting its effect to wills executed on or after its effective date.

For this reason, counsel for appellees has insisted that the statute should be deemed retroactive and should apply to contracts to make wills entered into before its effective date. It is clear that the 1978 statute is more restrictive than that which was first enacted in 1977. If the 1978 provisions should be applicable to any alleged contract between Mr. and Mrs. Gilliam made in 1974, it is obvious that no contract meeting its requirements has been established.

While the omission from the Tennessee statutes of a provision contained in a model code could have some significance, in our opinion, the 1978 statute, which is the only one remaining in effect, should not be construed as applying retroactively. It prescribes exclusive methods by which a contract to make a will, to revoke a will or to die intestate may be established. There is some authority in other states that such statutes can be given retroactive effect without offending constitutional prohibitions against the impairment of contracts. Appellees particularly cite and rely upon the case of Floerchinger v. Williams, 260 Iowa 53, 148 N.W.2d 410 (1967).

The provisions of the Iowa statute are not the same as those of the Tennessee statute under consideration. Regardless of whether any constitutional limitations may be involved, it is our opinion that the General Assembly did not intend for the 1978 statute to be retroactive. The Legislature replaced a 1977 statute which was merely directory or permissive, prescribing certain ways in which such contracts "may be established." These provisions were replaced by the more stringent terms of the 1978 statute quoted above, to the effect that such contracts "can be established only" in certain prescribed ways.

The 1977 statute did not purport to be exclusive in its terms. The provisions of the 1978 statute were exclusive and mandatory. In our opinion, the rights of parties, contingent or otherwise, which might have come into existence prior to the adoption of the 1978 statute should not be deemed to be affected thereby, and we decline to give retroactive effect to that statute as requested by counsel for appellees.

The judgments of the courts below are affirmed at the cost of appellants. The cause will be remanded to the trial court for collection of costs accrued there and for any other proceedings which may be necessary.

FONES, COOPER, DROWOTA and O'BRIEN, JJ., concur.

Notes and Questions

1. *Proving a Contract Not to Revoke*. Exactly what did the court in *Junot* require the plaintiff to prove in order to establish that a mutual will is subject to a contract not to revoke? Compare the following statement from Wiemers v. Wiemers, 663 S.W.2d 25, 29-30 (Tex. Ct. App. 1983), rev'd, 683 S.W.2d 355 (Tex. 1984):

> In order to prevail the party asserting a binding contract must prove more than a mere agreement to make reciprocal wills.... The agreement must involve the assumption of an obligation to dispose of the property as therein provided, or not to revoke such will, which is to remain in force at the death of the testators.

The majority of decisions hold that contracts not to revoke must be proven by clear and convincing evidence and that the existence of mutual wills does not create a presumption of a contract.

Why are courts typically reluctant to find that mutual wills are subject to contracts not to revoke? Consider the following statement:

> The clear weight of authority, and certainly the sounder view, is that the mere presence of either joint or mutual wills does not raise any presumption that they were executed in pursuance of a contract. Nor is this rule altered by evidence that the parties had "agreed" to the making of such wills. Of course they had so agreed. The mere presence of such wills reveals that the parties must have talked the matter over and must have arrived at an understanding or agreement concerning their testamentary dispositions. Such discussions and such understandings between persons of close affinities, especially between husbands and wives, are not unusual and the fact that they have taken place is no indication that there has been any thought of a binding contract....

It is quite apparent that [the] cases which are contrary to the general rule stated above result from a confusion of evidence of an understanding or a common plan with evidence of a contract. This confusion has resulted in the finding of some contracts on extremely slender evidence and in the occasional suggestion that the presence of reciprocal provisions is sufficient without more to prove the contractual relationship.

Bertel M. Sparks, Contracts to Make Wills 27-28, 30 (1956).

2. *Presumptions*. Courts have disagreed on whether a *joint* will with reciprocal provisions is sufficient evidence of a contract. In a few decisions, joint and mutual wills have been *conclusively* presumed contractual. E.g., Estate of Knight v. Knight, 533 N.E.2d 949 (Ill. App. Ct. 1989) ("The provisions of a valid joint and mutual will become irrevocable upon the death of one of the testators ... and the survivor may not dispose of the property other than as contemplated in the will."); Rauch v. Rauch, 445 N.E.2d 77 (Ill. App. Ct. 1983) ("A joint and mutual will must be executed pursuant to a contract between the testators...."); Fiew v. Qualtrough, 624 S.W.2d 335 (Tex. Ct. App. 1981).

That a joint will with reciprocal provisions is *rebuttably* presumed contractual, at least in certain situations, is the rule adopted by some courts (see, e.g., Glass v. Battista, 374 N.E.2d 116 (N.Y. 1978)), while other courts reject that idea.

3. *Revocable Trusts*. Do the will-contract principles followed in a jurisdiction—particularly the presumptions, if any, arising from joint or mutual wills—apply to revocable trusts containing reciprocal provisions? Compare Reznik v. McKee, 534 P.2d 243 (Kan. 1975) (holding that they do), with Northern Trust Co. v. Tarre, 427 N.E.2d 1217 (Ill. 1981) (holding that they do not).

4. *Statutory Requirements*. The 1978 Tennessee statute held inapplicable in *Junot* is virtually identical to UPC §2-514.[28] Its purpose is to reduce the likelihood of litigation in circumstances like that in *Junot* by requiring that all will contracts be reduced to writing. Notice that §2-514 applies only to contracts executed after the statute's enactment. In Fryxell v. Clark, 856 S.W.2d 892 (Ky. 1993), the testator and her husband executed a joint will in 1951, devising their respective estates to the other and upon the death of the survivor, to be divided among their children from prior marriages. Apparently, there was no reference in the will to a contract not to revoke. After the husband's death, the wife executed a new will, revoking the joint will and devising her estate to her children only. The court held that the Kentucky statute, which was substantially the same as §2-514, could not be given retroactive effect and did not apply to the joint will. As a consequence, the court upheld the joint will, relying apparently on the common law presumption that execution of a joint will indicates intent to create a contract not to revoke.

---

28. Section 2-514 appeared without substantial amendment in the original UPC as §2-701.

See also Wis. Stat. §853.13(2), providing that "[t]he execution of a joint will or mutual wills does not create a presumption of a contract not to revoke the will or wills." Accord Colo. Rev. Stat. §15-11-514.

In the absence of a statute specifically directed at will contracts, most courts have held that the general provision of the Statute of Frauds requiring a writing for contracts for the sale of land applies to contracts to *devise* land. They have further held that the same statutory provision extends to contracts to devise both land and personal property on the theory that these contracts are indivisible. (The provision of the Statute of Frauds relating to contracts not to be performed within one year is held inapplicable to will contracts.)

When the Statute of Frauds does apply and is raised as a defense to the enforcement of an oral will contract, the defense is often unsuccessful *in cases involving joint or mutual wills.*[29] The familiar judicial techniques for avoiding the Statute of Frauds in other contexts may also be available in will-contract litigation. The most important of these theories for taking the case out of the Statute of Frauds are part performance and estoppel. See, e.g., Redke v. Silvertrust, 490 P.2d 805 (Cal. 1971); Notten v. Mensing, 45 P.2d 198, 200-01 (Cal. 1935).

Could a court justifiably adopt either theory to avoid UPC §2-514? In Juran v. Epstein, 28 Cal. Rptr. 2d 588 (Cal. Ct. App. 1994), the court held that Cal. Probate Code §150 [later replaced by Cal. Probate Code §21700], which was identical to UPC §2-514, did not abolish the doctrine of equitable estoppel as a basis for enforcing an oral will contract when the surviving promisor is still alive and able to testify.

Shimp v. Huff
556 A.2d 252 (Md. 1989)

MURPHY, C.J.... In the present case, the issue is whether Lester Shimp's second wife, upon his death, is entitled to receive an elective share and a family allowance under Maryland Code (1974, 1988 Cum.Supp.) §3-203 and §3-201 of the Estates and Trusts Article when Lester had previously contracted, by virtue of a joint will with his first wife, to will his entire estate to others.

Section 3-203 ... provides that "[i]nstead of property left to him by will, the surviving spouse may elect to take a one-third share of the net estate if there is also a surviving issue, or a one-half share of the net estate if there is no surviving issue." As to the family allowance, §3-201 provides in part, that a surviving spouse is entitled to "an allowance of $2000 for his personal use."

---

29. As we saw in Green v. Richmond, in Chapter 4, the Statute of Frauds is a more formidable obstacle in cases where a party attempts to enforce the decedent's promise to devise part or all of his or her property in exchange for services rendered to the decedent during life.

Lester Shimp married his first wife, Clara, in 1941. At the time of their marriage, neither Lester nor Clara possessed any property of consequence. Subsequently, in 1954, they acquired a farm which they sold in 1973; thereafter they bought a home. Lester and Clara took title to both the farm and the home as tenants by the entireties.

On May 8, 1974, in Washington County, the couple executed an instrument titled "Last Will and Testament of Clara V. Shimp and Lester Shimp." It stated in relevant part:

> WE, CLARA V. SHIMP AND LESTER SHIMP, of Washington County, Maryland, being of sound and disposing mind, memory and understanding, and capable of making a valid deed and contract, do make, publish and declare this to be our Last Will and Testament, hereby revoking all other Wills and Codicils by each of us made.
>
> After the payment of all just debts and funeral expenses, we dispose of our estate and property as follows:
>
> ITEM I. A. MUTUAL BEQUEST—We mutually give to whichever of us shall be the survivor the entire estate of which we may respectfully own at our death.
>
> B. SURVIVOR'S BEQUEST—The survivor of us gives the entire estate of his or her property which he or she may own at death as follows:
>
> 1) Unto James Shimp, if he is living at the death of the survivor of us, the sum of One Thousand ($1,000.00) Dollars.
>
> 2) Unto Emma Plotner, if living at the death of the survivor of us, the sum of One Thousand ($1,000.00) Dollars.
>
> 3) Unto Mary Virginia Huff and Betty Jane Moats all household goods and machinery to do with as they desire. This bequest is made unto them due to the care that they have given us.
>
> 4) All of the rest and residue of the estate of the survivor is hereby devised unto Mary Virginia Huff, Betty Jane Moats, Paul R. Mijanovich and Ruth C. Thomas to be divided equally among them. In the event of the death of any of said persons, their children shall inherit the share to which the parent would have been entitled, if living....
>
> ITEM III. We, the Testators, do hereby declare that it is our purpose to dispose of our property in accordance with a common plan. The reciprocal and other gifts made herein are in fulfillment of this purpose and in consideration of each of us waiving the right, during our joint lives, to alter, amend or revoke this Will in whole or in part, by Codicil or otherwise, without notice to the other, or under any circumstances after the death of the first of us to die. Unless mutually agreed upon, this Last Will and Testament is an irrevocable act and may not be changed.

Clara died in 1975 in Washington County. At the time of her death she did not own property solely in her name and possessed no probate estate. Lester did not offer the will for probate following his wife's death. He did, however, file a petition in the Circuit Court for Washington County seeking declaratory relief and requesting the right to execute a new last will and testament. The court found that the will was revocable, but that the contract under which the will was executed might be specifically enforced in equity or damages recovered upon it at law. Lester appealed to the Court of Special Appeals, and ultimately, by writ of certiorari, the case came before us.

In [Shimp v. Shimp, 412 A.2d 228 (Md. 1980)], we found that the Shimps had executed their joint will pursuant to and in accordance with a valid, binding contract. We held that Lester was "entitled to a declaratory decree stating that he may revoke his will but that an enforceable contract was entered into between him and his wife ... [and that] [a]t his death it may be specifically enforced in equity or damages may be recovered upon it at law." Thereafter, Lester did not execute another will or otherwise disturb the testamentary plan set forth in the joint will.

On April 4, 1985, in Washington County, Lester married Lisa Mae; they remained married until his death on January 11, 1986. Lester was not survived by any children.

Following Lester's death, Clara and Lester's joint will was admitted to probate in Washington County. Mary Virginia Huff and Wallace R. Huff were appointed Personal Representatives of the Estate on January 30, 1986. Lisa Mae and Lester had not entered into any marital agreement waiving Lisa Mae's marital rights, and she sought payment of a family allowance and filed an election for her statutory share of Lester's estate. On June 4, 1986, the Personal Representatives declined to pay Lisa Mae either her family allowance or her elective share. On July 10, 1986, Lisa Mae filed suit for a declaratory judgment in the Circuit Court for Washington County, requesting that the court pass an order that she was entitled to both a family allowance and an elective share of Lester's estate.

The court (Corderman, J.)... found that because Lester, before his marriage to Lisa Mae, had entered into a binding contract to devise all of his estate, he was not seized of an estate of inheritance at the time of his second marriage, but rather was merely a trustee of that estate. Because a widow is entitled to no part of her husband's estate except that of which he dies seized or possessed, the court concluded that since Lester was merely a trustee for the property, there was no estate from which Lisa Mae could take an elective share. Similarly, the court found that Lisa Mae could not claim a family allowance because there were no estate assets from which the allowance could be paid. Lisa Mae appealed to the Court of Special Appeals; we granted certiorari prior to a decision by that court to resolve the important issues raised in the case....

While we have not previously addressed the issue of a surviving spouse's right to take an elective share in conflict with claims under a contract to convey by will, courts in other jurisdictions have examined the issue under varying factual situations.

In a number of these cases one spouse, after entering into a divorce or separation agreement which requires that spouse to leave part or all of the estate to the first spouse, remarries and then dies. In other cases, the decedent has contracted to make a will leaving property to children or other relatives. Still other cases have arisen where the decedent had remarried after entering into an agreement to will property in exchange for services, or for forbearance from legal action, or to facilitate an adoption. In some cases, the decedent has executed a will conforming to the contract, while in others he has breached the contract by executing a nonconforming will or by dying intestate.

The majority of these cases arise from the decedent having breached a contract to devise property by executing a nonconforming will or by dying intestate. In these cases, the claimants under the contract generally proceed on a theory of specific performance. While the rights of beneficiaries of a contract vest after the contract is made, nevertheless, where suit is brought for specific performance of the contract, "the after-acquired rights of third parties are equitable considerations to be regarded in adjudicating the questions." Owens [v. McNally, 113 Cal. 444, 45 P. 710 (1896)]. In determining whether to award specific performance to contract beneficiaries, courts have considered several different factors, including whether the surviving spouse had notice of the contract prior to the marriage, the length of the marriage and the natural affection shared between the decedent and the surviving spouse, whether the surviving spouse would be deprived of the entire estate by enforcement of the contract, and the public policy concerning the marriage relationship and the rights of surviving spouses. In a great many cases consideration of these factors has led the court to determine that the superior equities were with the surviving spouse, while in other cases it has not.

In those cases where the decedent has executed a will conforming to the contract, the claimants cannot seek specific performance, and courts, therefore, do not use equitable powers in resolving these cases. Instead, courts have analyzed the conflicting claims by characterizing the competing claimants as either creditors or legatees and evaluating their claims under the applicable priority rules. In a number of cases involving divorce settlements, the courts have found that where the decedent executes a will, which conforms to the terms of a contract, the beneficiaries take as legatees under the will and not as contract creditors. Consequently, because the applicable statutes give a higher priority to a surviving spouse's elective share than to testamentary bequests, the courts upheld the surviving spouse's claim over the claims of the contract beneficiaries. As the court explained in In Re Hoyt's Estate[, 174 Misc. 512, 21 N.Y.S.2d 107 (Sur. Ct. 1940)]

... [we] hold that the claimants are not creditors under paragraph seventh of the separation agreement, but that the agreement merely created an enforceable obligation to make a testamentary provision for the benefit of the first wife of the testator and his children after her death. The testator performed that agreement. He undertook to do no more. The status of the claimants is therefore that of legatees or beneficiaries under the will. As such legatees or beneficiaries they take subject to the operation of the statutes relating to testamentary dispositions, including the right of the surviving widow to take her intestate share under Section 18 of the Decedent Estate Law. Their rights are also subordinate to all true creditors of the estate. The widow of the testator is therefore entitled to a one-third share of the net estate. The respective interests of the claimants as legatees or beneficiaries must be satisfied out of the balance. 21 N.Y.S.2d at 111.

At least one court, however, has suggested that analyzing the competing claims under the applicable priority statutes should be limited to cases involving divorce settlement agreements. In Rubenstein [v. Mueller, 225 N.E.2d 540 (N.Y. 1967)], which involved an ordinary contract to devise property rather than a separation agreement, the court distinguished those cases involving marital separation agreements, under which husbands covenanted to make a will, noting that different equitable considerations control in the two situations. The court explained:

> Separation agreements are usually attended by a present division of any jointly held property, and any provision for a future legacy is usually but an incident to the over-all settlement to be made with respect to the husband's individual property and his obligation of support. In the case of the joint will, however, this instrument typically represents the sole attempt by the signatories to effect a distribution of their collective property in a fashion agreeable to both. Most importantly, in those separation agreements there was no irrevocable obligation concerning the collective property. The husband did not ... become sole owner of jointly owned property by virtue of surviving the former wife. As the divorced husband's property after the agreement remains his own individual property, to which he holds beneficial as well as legal title, his widow's right of election may be asserted against such assets. 225 N.E.2d at 544, 278 N.Y.S.2d at 850.

Thus, the court suggests that in these cases whether the surviving spouse's claim is given priority does not depend upon whether the contract beneficiaries are characterized as contract creditors or legatees. Instead the court reasoned that this priority is based upon the decedent having held both the legal and beneficial title to the property completely independent of the first spouse as a result of the property division effectuated by the separation agreement—a division which does not occur when one spouse acquires rights in the property pursuant to a joint will.

Courts have cited other reasons for rejecting the practice of categorizing contract beneficiaries as legatees where the decedent has executed a conforming will. These courts acknowledge that technically the contract beneficiary becomes a creditor of the estate only after the decedent breaches the contract by dying intestate or executing a nonconforming will; and that where the decedent executes a conforming will the contract beneficiaries take as legatees under the will. Nevertheless, they note that this analysis leads to the anomalous result that the contract beneficiaries are in a better position where the decedent breaches the contract than where the decedent fully and properly performs in accordance with it. See In Re Erstein's Estate, supra, 129 N.Y.S.2d at 321 ("[i]t would be anomalous if the rights of the promisees would be substantially greater in the case of intestacy than they would be had the testator left a will which carried out his promise").

Other courts have suggested that the resolution of the conflict between the surviving spouse's rights and the rights of contract beneficiaries may be based upon public policy underlying wills statutes. Some courts have held that the right of election is personal to the surviving spouse and cannot be waived or otherwise defeated by the acts of the deceased spouse....

Other courts have upheld the surviving spouse's right to claim an elective share over the claims of contract beneficiaries by relying upon the general principle that the right to will property is not absolute, but instead is a privilege afforded the decedent by the State. Under these cases, the State may impose limitations on that privilege, including the condition that all bequests are subject to the surviving spouse's right to claim an elective share....

Other courts have relied upon the public policy surrounding the marriage relationship as the basis for upholding the surviving spouse's claim to an elective share over the claims of contract beneficiaries.... They characterize contracts which require a decedent to devise his entire estate to a third party as being contracts which might restrain or discourage marriage. Therefore, to prevent having these contracts declared void as against public policy, courts have construed the contract to imply that when entering into the agreement the parties contemplated that the testator might remarry....

This case does not present a claim for specific performance because Lester performed his obligation under the contract and died leaving a will which conformed to the contract. Thus, we need not consider whether the superior equities lie with the Personal Representatives or with Lisa Mae.

Because Lester died leaving a will which conformed to the contract, we might consider drawing an analogy between the present case and the divorce cases, wherein courts found that where the decedent died leaving a conforming will, the contract beneficiaries were more properly characterized as legatees rather than contract creditors. Under this approach, we would find the respondents to be legatees under Lester's will whose interest in the estate, like the interest of any other legatee under any will, is subject to the abatement procedure outlined in § 3-208 of the Estates and Trusts Article.[30] Under this procedure Lisa Mae's elective share would have priority over the respondents' claims and their share of the estate would be abated. Nevertheless, we acknowledge ... that this method of resolving the issue of priority leads to the anomalous result that the contract beneficiaries' rights would be greater where the contract is breached than where the testator performs in accordance with its terms. Consequently, we decline to adopt this theory as the controlling law in this case.

Instead, we find the question of priorities between a surviving spouse and beneficiaries under a contract to make a will should be resolved based upon the public policy which surrounds the marriage relationship and which underlies the elective share statute.... The Legislature on several occasions has limited [the right

---

30. Section 3-208(b) provides in relevant part that "[i]f there is an election to take an intestate share, contribution to the payment of it shall be prorated among all legatees."

to make a will] by enacting restrictions such as those contained in § 3-203, which grants a surviving spouse the right to receive an elective share of a decedent's estate, regardless of the provisions contained in the decedent's will. In addition, § 3-204 suggests that the right to receive the elective share is a personal right, which cannot be waived by the unilateral acts of others, including the actions of the deceased spouse. These statutes and principles of law suggest that there is a strong public policy in favor of protecting the surviving spouse's right to receive an elective share. This Court on other occasions has recognized the strong public policy interest in protecting the surviving spouse's elective share from the unilateral acts of a deceased spouse. For example, in a number of cases this Court has declared transfers in fraud of marital rights to be void. We have indicated that this doctrine also applies to transfers made prior to the marriage.

In addition to the public policy underlying these statutes, the public policy surrounding the marriage relationship also suggests that the surviving spouse's claim to an elective share should be afforded priority over the claims of beneficiaries of a contract to make a will. Like the majority of other courts, we have recognized the well settled principle that contracts which discourage or restrain the right to marry are void as against public policy. In executing a will, a testator is presumed to know that a spouse might renounce the will, thus extinguishing or reducing legacies contained in the will, and if the testator does not provide for this contingency then the beneficiaries under the will might lose the property left them. Thus, we find that the respondents' rights under the contract were limited by the possibility that the survivor might remarry and that the subsequent spouse might elect against the will. Consequently, we conclude that their claims under the contract are subordinate to Lisa Mae's superior right to receive her elective share.

Finally, we address the issue of whether Lisa Mae is entitled to a $2000 family allowance under §3-201....

The respondents' claim upon the estate of Lester Shimp must be characterized as being either that of a general creditor or of a legatee under the will. Under § 8-105, the family allowance receives priority over the claims of both contract creditors and legatees. Therefore, while the respondents' claim is more properly characterized as being that of a legatee, rather than that of a creditor, regardless of which characterization is used, Lisa Mae's claim for a family allowance takes precedence over the respondents' claim. Therefore, Lisa Mae is entitled to receive the family allowance provided for in § 3-201....

JUDGMENT VACATED; CASE REMANDED TO THE CIRCUIT COURT FOR WASHINGTON COUNTY FOR ENTRY OF A DECLARATORY JUDGMENT CONSISTENT WITH THIS OPINION. COSTS TO BE PAID BY THE APPELLEES.

Notes and Questions

1. *Uniform Probate Code.* How would *Shimp* be resolved if it were governed by the UPC? Had Lester's will not been contractual, what elective-share rights would

Lisa Mae have under §2-201? (We shall cover the elective share in detail in Chapter 8.) Would Lisa Mae have any rights to an intestate share under §2-301? Would Lester's will be found contractual under §2-514? If so, how would the contractual nature of the will affect Lisa Mae's rights under §§2-201 and 2-301?

2. *Theories Supporting the Contract Beneficiaries.* Quite a number of courts have held for the contract beneficiaries rather than for the surviving spouse in cases like *Shimp*. In Rubenstein v. Mueller, for example, cited in *Shimp*, the New York Court of Appeals held that the decedent's second spouse had no right to an elective share in the decedent's assets covered by a will contract entered into with his prior, deceased spouse. The reason given was that the will contract transformed the ownership interest in those assets into a life estate in the decedent and a remainder interest in the contract beneficiaries. Other courts have held for the contract beneficiaries on the similar theory that the surviving spouse's statutory rights attach only to assets equitably as well as legally owned by the decedent and that equitably owned assets do not include assets that the decedent received under a will executed pursuant to a will contract, since a court will impress those assets with a constructive trust for the contract beneficiaries. See, e.g., Estate of Stewart, 444 P.2d 337 (Cal. 1968); Bever v. Bever, 364 S.E.2d 34 (W. Va. 1987). Another theory is that breach of the will contract places the contract beneficiary in the position of a creditor and that creditors' rights are superior to the surviving spouse's elective-share right. See, e.g., Estate of Beeruk, 241 A.2d 755 (Pa. 1968).

3. *Enforcement of Contractual Wills and Remedies for Breach.* Apart from competing claims of a surviving spouse, most cases brought to enforce a will contract arise because the survivor has breached the contract by making a new will revoking the contractual will. Courts sometimes say that the contractual will became irrevocable. The logical implication of this is that the contractual will is entitled to probate despite the decedent's later attempt to revoke it. Occasionally this is what courts have done. See, e.g., Walker v. Yarbrough, 76 So. 390 (Ala. 1917); Helms v. Darmstatter, 215 N.E.2d 245 (Ill. 1966) (joint will). But this result conflicts with the long-accepted view that a will is always revocable. In most cases, then, the contract is enforced not by probating the contractual will, but rather through a subsequent proceeding for breach of contract. See, e.g., Estate of Chapman, 239 N.W.2d 869 (Iowa 1976).

This two-step process for enforcing will contracts, probate of the subsequent will followed by a proceeding on the contract, indicates the separate relationship between the contract and the will. The breach-of-contract proceeding may be one at law for damages or in equity for specific performance or a constructive trust. The usual remedy is a constructive trust upon the property passing in violation of the contract.

4. *Survivor's Rights to Consume or Make Gifts.* To what extent is the survivor free to consume or give away during his or her lifetime property that is subject to a will contract? To prevent the survivor from breaching an obligation under a will contract, courts have held that inter vivos gifts by the survivor of substantial portions of the

property can be set aside. See, e.g., Lawrence v. Ashba, 59 N.E.2d 568 (Ind. Ct. App. 1945); Schwartz v. Horn, 290 N.E.2d 816 (N.Y. 1972); Estate of Chayka, 176 N.W.2d 561 (Wis. 1970). Some courts have analyzed the question under a reasonableness requirement. Under this approach, the survivor is free to make "reasonable gifts"; the question is said to be "one of degree, and depends upon the proportion that the value of the gift bears to the amount of the donor's estate." Dickinson v. Lane, 85 N.E. 818 (N.Y. 1908). It has also been held that the survivor may set aside gifts made by the first to die that are in breach of the will contract. See, e.g., Conitz v. Walker, 541 P.2d 1028 (Mont. 1975). Is the survivor protected against testamentary gifts contrary to the contract? See Duhme v. Duhme, 260 N.W.2d 415 (Iowa 1977); Irving J. Kornfield, Note, 48 Calif. L. Rev. 858, 862-63 (1960).

An analogous problem arose in Blackmon v. Battcock, 587 N.E.2d 280 (N.Y. 1991). In that case, the testator, Elizabeth Battcock, had entered into a settlement contract with her late husband's estate, according to which in exchange for receiving a portion of his estate, she agreed to drop her elective share claim and further agreed not to revoke her existing will. The will devised the bulk of her estate to her two children. Several years later, after the death of one of her children, Battcock opened several savings account trusts, naming various charities as beneficiaries. Her surviving child brought an action seeking a declaration that the Totten trusts were in breach of the contract not to revoke. The Court of Appeals held, by a 4-3 vote, that a promise not to create Totten trusts could not be implied into the contract not to revoke a will. The court stated that the cases limiting freedom to make inter vivos gifts that would undermine the purpose of joint or mutual wills that are subject to a will contract were inapposite: "Inconsistent testamentary dispositions or inter vivos gifts would defeat the very purpose of particularized promises, expectations and mutuality of benefits involved with joint and mutual wills. That is not this case." Do you agree?

5. *What Property Is Covered by a Will Contract?* Questions frequently arise concerning whether a will contract covers property that the survivor acquired after the death of the first to die. Suppose that H died in 1950, survived by W. The value of H's estate, which passed to W pursuant to a contractual will, was $5,000. After H's death, W inherited real estate from a deceased friend, and acquired other property. W left a will devising $5,000 to the beneficiaries of the will contract, but left the remaining portion of her property to others. The terms of the will contract, however, bound the survivor as to "all the property... that the survivor may die seized and possessed of." Under these circumstances, courts have held that this language covered the after-acquired property. See, e.g., Wallace v. Turriff, 531 S.W.2d 692 (Tex. Civ. App. 1975); Estate of Jud, 710 P.2d 1241 (Kan. 1985).

A similar problem concerns post-death appreciation. Suppose, for example, that when H died in 1948, the value of the combined estates of H and W was approximately $60,000 and that at the time of W's death in 1969, it had grown to over $200,000. Courts have interpreted the contract as covering the entire estate as it existed at W's death. See, e.g., Matter of Wiggins, 360 N.Y.S.2d 129 (App. Div. 1974), aff'd per curiam, 350 N.E.2d 618 (N.Y. 1976).

Suppose that a will contract refers to the decedent's "property." Does this include non-probate assets? In Bergheger v. Boyle, 629 N.E.2d 1168 (Ill. App. Ct. 1994), the court held that a premarital contract to devise the "residue of the estate" referred only to the husband's probate estate and consequently did not include annuities.

6. *Lapse.* Suppose that a contract beneficiary predeceases the surviving contracting party. How should the survivor's estate be distributed? Most courts have held that the contract beneficiary's rights vest upon the death of the first of the contracting parties to die. The property covered by the will contract passes through the beneficiary's estate rather than under the otherwise applicable antilapse statute. (We shall cover antilapse statutes in detail in Chapter 6.) See, e.g., Rauch v. Rauch, 445 N.E.2d 77 (Ill. App. Ct. 1983); Estate of Maloney v. Carsten, 381 N.E.2d 1263 (Ind. Ct. App. 1978); Estate of Duncan, 638 P.2d 992 (Kan. Ct. App. 1982); Jones v. Jones, 692 S.W.2d 406 (Mo. Ct. App. 1985); Fiew v. Qualtrough, 624 S.W.2d 335 (Tex. Ct. App. 1981). Contra, e.g., Estate of Arends, 311 N.W.2d 686 (Iowa Ct. App. 1981). What theory or theories support the majority view? In this connection, consider the effect of the various approaches to the question of the surviving spouse's elective share. Professor Roberts argues that the majority view, that "a beneficiary need not survive when there is a contract not to revoke[, can be] intent-defeating." "[T]he lapse rule," she argues, "should still apply [, invoking the antilapse statute] if applicable. To the extent that [anti]lapse statutes effectuate intent, they would do so in this context as well." Patricia J. Roberts, Lapse Statutes: Recurring Construction Problems, 37 Emory L.J. 323, 384-93 (1988).

7. *Tax Consequences.* Married couples who have children by prior marriages may want special assurance that their property will be split between the two families when the survivor dies. The desirability of using contractual wills for this purpose may be greatly affected by tax consequences. The cost of using a contract not to revoke may be the loss of the estate-tax marital deduction.[31]

An alternative device, at least for assuring the decedent's control over the disposition of his or her property on the survivor's death, is to devise a life estate (or, more likely, an income interest for life in a trust) to the surviving spouse, coupled

---

31. E.g., Estate of Opal v. Commissioner, 450 F.2d 1085 (2d Cir. 1971); Estate of Krampf v. Commissioner, 56 T.C. 293 (1972); Estate of Siegel v. Commissioner, 67 T.C. 662 (1977). The disallowance of the marital deduction applies only to property passing under the decedent's will. Property passing outside of probate—for example, joint tenancy property and life insurance proceeds—can qualify for the estate tax marital deduction even though the surviving spouse is under a contractual obligation as to how this property is to be disposed of on the surviving spouse's death. Rev. Rul. 71-51, 1971-1 Cum. Bull. 274. The tax consequences are discussed in Joel C. Dobris, Do Contractual Will Arrangements Qualify for Qualified Terminable Interest Treatment Under ERTA?, 19 Real Prop. Prob. & Tr. J. 625 (1984); Amy M. Hess, The Federal Transfer Tax Consequences of Joint and Mutual Wills, 24 Real Prop. Prob. & Tr. J. 469 (1990).

with a remainder interest in favor of beneficiaries selected by the decedent. Until the early 1980s, this device suffered the same tax disadvantage—the loss of the estate tax marital deduction. The Economic Recovery Tax Act of 1981, however, amended the Internal Revenue Code so that the life estate/remainder combination, called a "QTIP," can qualify for the estate tax marital deduction, provided that certain technical requirements are satisfied. The allowance of a favorable tax consequence for the life estate/remainder combination has made it a more attractive device for controlling the disposition of the decedent's property on the surviving spouse's death than the contract not to revoke. This device, however, does not control after-acquired property.

8. *Planning and Drafting.* Couples who use joint or mutual wills should insert in their wills language clearly indicating whether or not they have contractually bound themselves not to revoke. If the parties *do* want to be contractually bound not to revoke, the contract should be reduced to writing and should spell out what property is covered and the survivor's powers with respect to making gifts.

In preparing this contract, can one lawyer ethically represent both parties, or must each party engage a lawyer? See Report, Developments Regarding the Professional Responsibility of the Estate Planning Lawyer: The Effect of the Model Rules of Professional Conduct, 22 Real Prop. Prob. & Tr. J. 1, 10-23 (1987). Cf. Whitney v. Seattle-First Nat'l Bank, 560 P.2d 360 (Wash. Ct. App. 1977); Bank of New York v. United States, 526 F.2d 1012 (3d Cir. 1975).

EXTERNAL REFERENCE. Annot., Surviving Spouse's Right to Marital Share as Affected by Valid Contract to Convey by Will, 85 A.L.R.4th 418.

Chapter 6

Post-Execution Events Affecting Wills

There will always be some interval between a will's execution and the testator's death. Sometimes the interval will be measured in decades. An older will, sometimes called a "stale" will, is just as valid as a "fresh" one but has the potential to do mischief because it is out of date.[1] In this Chapter, we study how the law is responding to changes in a testator's property and changes in the circumstances of a testator's devisees.

It is difficult to overemphasize the obvious point that many of these issues could—and should—be avoided by foresight and careful drafting. The doctrines studied in this Chapter operate as default rules. They apply because, and only to the extent that, the testator and the testator's attorney failed to address the issue in a will provision.

PART A. PROFESSIONAL RESPONSIBILITY

Formal Opinion 210 (March 15, 1941)[2]
Opinions on Professional Ethics 498-499 (ABA 1967)

An attorney may properly advise a client for whom he has drawn a will of the advisability of reexamining the will periodically and may from time to time send notices to the clients advising him of changes in law or fact which may defeat the client's testamentary purpose, unless the attorney has reason to believe that he has been supplanted by another attorney.

Canon Interpreted: Professional Ethics 27. A member calls attention to the effect on testamentary dispositions of subsequent changes in general economic conditions, of changes in the attitude or death of named fiduciaries in a will, of the removal of the testator to a different jurisdiction where different laws of descent may prevail, of changes in financial conditions, family relationship and kindred matters, and then inquires whether it is proper for the lawyer who drew the will to call attention of the testator from time to time to the importance of going over his will....

The inquiry presents the question as to whether such action on the part of the lawyer is solicitation of legal employment and so to be condemned. Many events transpire between the date of making the will and the death of the testator. The legal significance of such occurrences are [sic] often of serious consequence, of which the

---

1. For a discussion of the problem, see Adam J. Hirsch, Text and Time: A Theory of Testamentary Obsolescence, 86 Wash. U.L. Rev. 609 (2009).

2. The Canon referred to in this opinion is from the Canons of Professional Ethics, an antecedent of the Model Rules of Professional Conduct. Ed.

testator may not be aware, and so the importance of calling the attention of the testator thereto is manifest.

It is our opinion that where the lawyer has no reason to believe that he has been supplanted by another lawyer, it is not only his right, but it might even be his duty to advise his client of any changes of fact or law which might defeat the client's testamentary purpose as expressed in the will.

Periodic notices might be sent to the client for whom a lawyer has drawn a will, suggesting that it might be wise for the client to reexamine his will to determine whether or not there has been any change in his situation requiring a modification of his will.

Gerald P. Johnston, Legal Malpractice in Estate Planning: Perilous Times Ahead for the Practitioner
67 Iowa L. Rev. 629, 656-657 (1982)

The potential malpractice exposure that could result from the failure to notify present and former wills and trusts clients of the changes in estate and gift tax laws contained in the Economic Recovery Tax Act of 1981 is enormous. All lawyers would be well advised to write to each of the persons for whom they have drawn wills or revocable trusts to inform them of the potential impact of the newly enacted law on their estate plans....

The possibility of malpractice in such situations cannot simply be rejected on the ground that representation of the testator ended when the will was executed....

A determination of whether there was a continuing attorney-client relationship on which to posit liability for malpractice could substantially be affected by other recurring factors. For example, if the original will were kept in the attorney's office for "safekeeping," that might indicate a continuing relationship and a corresponding duty on the part of the attorney to keep the testator informed of changes in the law. Also, if the testator not only had the attorney prepare a will, but the company that employed the testator was also a client of the attorney or the attorney's firm, then a court could well find that there was a continuing relationship....

Questions
When *may* a lawyer notify clients of changes in the law requiring modifications of their wills? When *must* a lawyer do so?

PART B. CHANGES IN THE CLIENT'S ESTATE

"Remember that the residuary legatee gets everything which isn't specifically left to somebody else...."
– Lord Peter Wimsey to Miss Murchison[3]

Classification of Devises. Many of the doctrines studied in this Part traditionally involve a two-stage analysis. The first stage is classifying the devise as one of four types of devises—specific, general, demonstrative, or residuary. The Restatement 3d of Property §5.1 defines these classes as follows:

(1) A *specific devise* is a testamentary disposition of a specifically identified asset.

(2) A *general devise* is a testamentary disposition, usually of a specified amount of money or quantity of property, that is payable from the general assets of the estate.

(3) A *demonstrative devise* is a testamentary disposition, usually of a specified amount of money or quantity of property, that is primarily payable from a designated source, but is secondarily payable from the general assets of the estate to the extent that the primary source is insufficient.

(4) A *residuary devise* is a testamentary disposition of property of the testator's net probate estate not disposed by a specific, general, or demonstrative devise.

The second stage is to apply the doctrine based on the classification of the devise. In other words, the classification of the devise governs the legal outcome.

This two-stage analysis suggests that courts are involved in highly formalistic rule-making. Traditionally, this has been true, and to a great extent still is. The materials that follow, however, also show that courts and legislatures have now begun to erode that formalism by moving to a more generalized inquiry into intention.

1. Ademption of Specific Devises by Extinction

Primary Statutory Reference: *UPC §2-606*

Specific devises normally are used to transfer to particular relatives or friends property the testator holds especially dear. Often, these are items of tangible personal property—a particular piece of jewelry, a piano, a coin or stamp collection, a particular work of art. Also, a piece of real estate is sometimes specifically devised—the family farm, the family home, the vacation house, and so on. In addition, on occasion, testators devise specific financial assets, such as particular stocks or bonds or a savings account.

Although devises of specific financial assets sometimes prove troublesome,

---

3. Dorothy L. Sayers, Strong Poison 149 (Harper Perennial 1993) (originally published 1930).

specific devises of tangible personal property or land do not, for the most part, raise many issues. Occasionally, though, the testator might give the piano or the diamond ring to the devisee in advance of death, might sell a particular painting and purchase another one in its place, or might sell the family home and move to another one. Also, as the population ages, more and more elderly testators eventually become incapacitated to some degree. As a testator's financial affairs are taken over by a guardian or conservator, or by an agent acting under a durable power of attorney, specifically devised property becomes more likely to be sold so that the proceeds can be used to pay for nursing care and associated expenses. Occasionally, also, specifically devised property is stolen in a burglary or destroyed in a fire. Finally, it is quite possible that the testator becomes annoyed with the devisee and disposes of the specifically devised property as a method of revoking the devise—revocation by act to the property, so to speak, as opposed to revocation by subsequent instrument or by revocatory act to the will.

Under the doctrine of ademption by extinction, a specific devise is adeemed—i.e., rendered ineffective—if the testator no longer owns the specifically devised property at death. As Estate of Hume, below, shows, the generally accepted interpretation of the doctrine follows the so-called identity theory, which means that the court does not inquire into the reason why the specifically devised property is not found in the estate.

Estate of Hume
984 S.W.2d 602 (Tenn. 1999)

ANDERSON, Chief Justice. We granted this appeal to determine whether the probate rule of ademption by extinction applies to the specific bequest of a house, where the house is sold at foreclosure before the testator's death and sales proceeds representing the testator's interest are identifiable after his death.

The trial court, emphasizing the testator's intent as reflected by the will, concluded that the bequest had not been adeemed because there were proceeds remaining from the foreclosure sale. The foreclosure sale proceeds were ordered to be distributed to the beneficiary of the specific bequest. The Court of Appeals affirmed.

After our review of the record and applicable authority, we conclude that the foreclosure of the house prior to the testator's death resulted in an ademption by extinction of the specific bequest and that the foreclosure sale proceeds should have been distributed to the residuary beneficiary of the estate. Accordingly, we reverse the judgment of the Court of Appeals and remand the case to the trial court for further proceedings.

Background. Foster Hume, III, a licensed attorney, executed a valid holographic will dated August 1, 1990. In addition to other bequests, Hume specifically devised his house in Atlanta to his niece, Meredith Klank ("Klank"), stating in his will, "my Atl. House to ... Meredith. (Clank [sic] I believe)." Hume named the appellant, University of the South ("University"), residuary beneficiary.

Hume purchased the Atlanta house in 1986, subject to a mortgage in favor of NationsBanc. Hume faithfully made his mortgage payments to NationsBanc until the late summer of 1991. Because of Hume's delinquency, NationsBanc sold the house at foreclosure before Hume's death on November 12, 1991.

The surplus proceeds of $55,745.07, after satisfying the mortgage debt, were paid to the estate's Executrix, who took the position that the Atlanta house had been adeemed and that the proceeds should be paid to the University, the residuary beneficiary, and not to Klank, the beneficiary of the specific bequest. Klank, claiming the right to the surplus proceeds, filed an exception to the Executrix's final accounting in Davidson County Probate Court. The Executrix moved to have her final accounting approved.

The Davidson County Probate Court denied the Executrix's motion and ordered that the proceeds be paid to Klank. Relying on the lack of proof in the record to indicate Hume had actual knowledge of the foreclosure proceeding, the court reasoned that Hume had not voluntarily parted with his house and thus must have intended Klank to receive it, as indicated by the will.

The Court of Appeals affirmed the trial court, finding that an ademption by extinction had not occurred in this case for two main reasons. First, the court noted that "Testator's only contribution to the foreclosure was his inability or failure to pay the debt which cannot be presumed to be a voluntary act; and there is no evidence that it was deliberate or voluntary." Second, the Court of Appeals distinguished between cases in which the foreclosure sale was insufficient to satisfy the debt, where an ademption by extinction would occur, and cases in which the foreclosure sale resulted in surplus proceeds, where an ademption by extinction would not occur.

We granted the University's application for permission to appeal.

Analysis. The only issue presented for our review, whether the bequest of the Atlanta house has been adeemed by extinction, is purely a question of law; thus, our review is de novo with no presumption of correctness given the judgments of either the trial court or the Court of Appeals....

Ademption by extinction results because of "the doing of some act with regard to the subject-matter which interferes with the operation of the will." American Trust & Banking Co. v. Balfour, 198 S.W. 70, 71 (Tenn. 1917). In these cases:

> [t]he rule [of ademption by extinction] prevails without regard to the intention of the testator or the hardship of the case, and is predicated upon the principle that the subject of the gift is annihilated or its condition so altered that nothing remains to which the terms of the bequest can apply.

Wiggins v. Cheatham, 143 Tenn. 406, 225 S.W. 1040, 1041 (1920) (emphasis added) (citation omitted). In other words, it only matters that the subject of the specific bequest no longer exists because of "the doing of some act;" it is irrelevant who or what initiates "the doing." *Balfour*, 198 S.W. at 71....

This rule that the intent of the testator is irrelevant in ademption by extinction cases is in harmony with the modern holdings found in the majority of states. E.g., McGee v. McGee, 122 R.I. 837, 413 A.2d 72 (R.I. 1980). In *McGee*, the Rhode Island Supreme Court defines the rule and persuasively analyzes the policy supporting it. The *McGee* court stated with respect to the "in specie" test:

> This test focuses on two questions only: (1) whether the gift is a specific legacy and, if it is, (2) whether it is found in the estate at the time of the testator's death. The extinction of the property bequeathed works an ademption regardless of the testator's intent. ...
>
> Moreover, under the principles enunciated by Lord Thurlow ... only the fact of change or extinction, not the reason for the change or extinction, is truly relevant. The vast majority of jurisdictions adhere to this rule. This "in specie" theory of ademption, although it may occasionally result in a failure to effectuate the actual intent of a testator, has many advantages. Significant among these advantages is simplicity of application, as opposed to ad hoc determination of intent from extrinsic evidence in each particular case. This theory further has the advantages of stability, uniformity, and predictability. [Id. at 76-77 (citations omitted).]

The rule of ademption by extinction has been applied in several Tennessee cases similar to the case before us....

Applying the foregoing rule, we conclude that the specific bequest of the Atlanta property was adeemed in its entirety by the foreclosure sale regardless of Hume's presumed intentions.... It is of no significance that a third party and not Hume initiated the sale in the present case because, as previously stated, the rule of ademption by extinction applies without regard to the testator's intentions. Thus, the foreclosure sale constituted "the doing of some act with regard to the subject-matter which interferes with the operation of the will." *Balfour*, 198 S.W. at 71. Accordingly, in our view, the foreclosure sale prior to Hume's death adeemed the specific bequest of the house.

We further conclude that the proceeds cannot be substituted for the specific bequest of the house because "a specific legacy is adeemed when there has been a material alteration or change in the subject-matter, and ... the property into which it was converted in such change cannot be substituted as or for the specific bequest." *Balfour* 198 S.W. at 71....

Conclusion. We conclude that the testator's intent is irrelevant in deciding the question of whether a specific bequest has been adeemed by extinction. We further conclude that a foreclosure sale so alters the form of the specific bequest of a house that an ademption by extinction results regardless of whether identifiable proceeds remain from the foreclosure sale.

We therefore reverse the judgments of the trial court and the Court of Appeals and remand to the trial court for further proceedings. Costs of this appeal are taxed to the appellee.

DROWOTA, HOLDER, and BARKER, JJ., concur.

BIRCH, J., not participating.

Notes and Questions

1. *The Identity Theory vs. The Intent Theory. Hume* is a rather stark example of the "identity" theory of ademption, in contrast to the "intent" theory. According to the identity theory, ademption depends solely upon whether the subject matter of a specific devise exists as part of the testator's estate at death, and the testator's intent concerning the continued validity of the devise is irrelevant. According to the intent theory, ademption depends upon the testator's subjective intent, determined on a case-by-case basis. What reasons do you suppose have led courts, in an area of law seemingly dedicated to carrying out the testator's intent, to adopt a rule that disregards intent? See John C. Paulus, Ademption by Extinction: Smiting Lord Thurlow's Ghost, 2 Tex. Tech. L. Rev. 195 (1971); John C. Paulus, Special and General Legacies of Securities—Whither Testator's Intent, 43 Iowa L. Rev. 467 (1958).

2. *Adoptions of the Intent Theory.* Although the identity theory has been broadly accepted in this country, some courts have departed from that approach. See, e.g., Newbury v. McCammant, 182 N.W.2d 147 (Iowa 1970); Estate of Austin, 169 Cal. Rptr. 648 (Cal. Ct. App. 1980); Wachovia Bank & Trust Co. v. Ketchum, 333 S.E.2d 542 (N.C. Ct. App. 1985); Rodgers v. Rodgers, 406 S.W.3d 422 (Ark. 2012).

The Restatement 3d of Property adopts the intent theory, placing the burden of proof on the devisee to show that failure of the devise would be inconsistent with the testator's intent:

§5.2 Failure ("Ademption") of Specific Devises by Extinction

(a) If specifically devised property, in its original or in a changed form, is in the testator's estate at death, the devisee is entitled to the specifically devised property.

(b) If specifically devised property is not in the testator's estate at death, the devisee is entitled to any proceeds remaining unpaid at death of (i) any sale, (ii) any condemnation award, or (iii) any insurance on or other recovery for damage to or loss of the property.

(c) Subject to subsection (b), if specifically devised property is not in the testator's estate at death, the specific devise fails unless failure of the devise would be inconsistent with the testator's intent.

UPC §2-606(a)(6) also adopts the intent theory, placing on the devisee the burden of showing that "ademption would be inconsistent with the testator's manifested plan of distribution or that at the time the will was made, the date of disposition, or otherwise, the testator did not intend ademption of the devise." How would a court have decided *Hume* if subsection (a)(6) had applied? (Tennessee subsequently adopted a version of §2-606 but without (a)(6), see Tenn. Code §32-3-111.) At least one non-UPC statute expressly adopts an intent approach. See Ky. Rev. Stat. §394.360.

3. *Amendment to the UPC*. In 1997, the Uniform Law Commission substantially revised the 1990 version of UPC §2-606(a)(6). The 1990 version had provided:

> (a) A specific devisee has a right to the specifically devised property in the testator's estate at death and:...
>
> (6) unless the facts and circumstances indicate that ademption of the devise was intended by the testator or ademption of the devise is consistent with the testator's manifested plan of distribution, the value of the specifically devised property to the extent the specifically devised property is not in the testator's estate at death and its value or its replacement is not covered by paragraphs (1) through (5).

To understand why the amendment was made, try Problem #1 below.

4. *Dispositions by Guardians or Conservators*. One situation in which the courts have been reluctant to disregard the testator's intention arises where a guardian or conservator, acting on behalf of an incapacitated testator, sold or otherwise disposed of an item of specifically devised property.

In the leading case of Morse v. Converse, 113 A. 214 (N.H. 1921), the testator's guardian withdrew a savings bank deposit that had been specifically devised, and used part of the proceeds to buy a Liberty bond, which remained in the estate at the testator's death. The court awarded the Liberty bond to the devisee. As for the part of the withdrawal that had been spent by the guardian, the court held that the devisee had no claim, since "nothing has come to the executor's hands upon which the will can operate." The tendency of the guardianship cases has been in favor of the New Hampshire view,[4] and a few states have adopted that view by statute, so as to provide that the specific devisee "becomes entitled to receive any remaining money or other property."[5]

In Estate of Mason, 397 P.2d 1005 (Cal. 1965), the California Supreme Court refused to limit the devisee to the traceable proceeds of the sale. Several years after the testator had executed a will specifically devising her home to Fairbank, she became mentally incompetent and a guardian of her estate was appointed. The

---

4. See, e.g., Stake v. Cole 133 N.W.2d 714 (Iowa 1965); Estate of Graham 533 P.2d 1318 (Kan. 1975); Walsh v. Gillespie 154 N.E.2d 906 (Mass. 1959); Estate of Warren 344 S.E.2d 795 (N.C. Ct. App. 1986); Estate of Swoyer, 439 N.W.2d 823 (S.D. 1989). Cases are collected in Annots., Ademption or Revocation of Specific Devise or Bequest by Guardian, Committee, Conservator, or Trustee of Mentally or Physically Incompetent Testator, 84 A.L.R.4th 462; Annot., Ademption or Revocation of Specific Devise or Bequest by Guardian, Committee, Conservator, or Trustee of Mentally or Physically Incompetent Testator, 84 A.L.R.4th 462.

5. See, e.g., N.Y. Est. Powers & Trust Law §3-4.4 (this is an amended version of an earlier statute that reversed the position adopted by the Court of Appeals in Ireland's Estate, 177 N.E. 405 (N.Y. 1931), a case in opposition to Morse v. Converse).

guardian sold the home for $21,000, deposited the proceeds into a special account, and spent all but $556 for the support of the testator. The court held that the amount spent should be paid to Fairbank out of the residuary estate.[6] Any other result, Justice Traynor said, "would allow the guardian to destroy his ward's testamentary plan even though the guardian was acting to protect the ward's economic interests."

UPC §2-606(b) explicitly adopts a guardianship exception, adopting the Estate of Mason, rather than Morse v. Converse, view about the amount to which the devisee is entitled. UPC §5-418 directs the conservator to take into account the protected person's estate plan when making investment and expenditure decisions and authorizing the conservator to examine the will.

5. Dispositions by Attorneys-in-fact Acting Under Durable Powers of Attorney. In modern practice, durable powers of attorney—powers of attorney that are not automatically revoked when the principal becomes incompetent—have become popular substitutes for guardianships or conservatorships. See Chapter 18. Some courts have expressly extended the guardianship exception to dispositions made under authority of durable powers. See Estate of Graham, 533 P.2d 1318 (Kan. 1975); Estate of Anton, 731 N.W.2d 19 (Iowa 2007); Rodgers v. Rodgers, 406 S.W.3d 422 (Ark. 2012).[7]

UPC §2-606(b) likewise extends the guardianship exception to sales by an agent on behalf of an incapacitated testator under a durable power. To ease the administrative burden of a post-death inquiry into the mental state of the testator, §2-606(e) establishes a rebuttable presumption that a sale or other disposition by an agent is on behalf of a testator who is incapacitated.

Problems

1. G, an absent-minded classics professor, collected ancient Roman coins. G specifically devised the coins to his good friend, A. G spent his final years in a costly nursing home and, at his death, the coins were nowhere to be found. G might have sold them to pay for the nursing home, or the coins might have been stolen. No one knows. What are A's rights under the common-law identity theory? Under the 1990 version of UPC §2-606(a)(6)? Under the current UPC?

---

6. Accord, e.g., 20 Pa. Cons. Stat. Ann. §2514(16.1), construed in Estate of Fox, 431 A.2d 1008 (Pa. 1981).

7. See also Hobin v. O'Donnell 451 N.E.2d 30 (Ill. App. Ct. 1983) ("[A]demption requires some act of the testator indicative of an intention to revoke.... If someone other than the decedent sold the stock without permission or if the decedent was incapable of forming the requisite intent, then there was no ademption."); Estate of Warren, 344 S.E.2d 795 (N.C. Ct. App. 1986); Annot., Ademption or Revocation of Specific Devise or Bequest by Guardian, Committee, Conservator, or Trustee of Mentally or Physically Incompetent Testator, 84 A.L.R.4th 462. But see Estate of Hegel, 668 N.E.2d 474 (Ohio 1996).

2. G executed a will devising "my Ford car" to X and the residue of her estate to Y. In the following fact-patterns, to what, if anything, is X entitled under the UPC?

    a. G later sold the Ford and bought a Rolls-Royce.

    b. G later sold the Ford and bought a Honda and a Rolls-Royce.

    c. G later sold the Ford and bought a motorcycle.

    d. G later sold the Ford and bought office furniture.

––––––

EXTERNAL REFERENCES. Gregory S. Alexander, Ademption and the Domain of Formality in Wills Law, 55 Alb. L. Rev. 1067 (1992); Mary Kay Lundwall, The Case Against the Ademption by Extinction Rule: A Proposal for Reform, 29 Gonzaga L. Rev. 105 (1993/94).

2. Accessions and Accretions

Primary Statutory Reference: *UPC §2-605*

What rights does a devisee have to assets that were produced by a devised asset after execution of the will? This is a matter of "accessions" or "accretions." In most situations, the choice is between awarding the product to the devisee of the underlying asset or awarding it to the residuary devisee(s). Accession questions can involve many forms of wealth, including corporate stock, mortgages, promissory notes, oil and gas leases, and cultivated farm land.

In general, courts have held that specific devises transfer that specific asset together with accessions and accretions occurring *after the testator's death*. Thus, for example, rent becoming due after the testator's death goes to the devisee of the land. See Atkinson on Wills §135, at 750-51. Specific devises do not bear interest, strictly speaking. If the specifically devised asset has not actually produced any income or interest, the devisee is not entitled to any interest. By contrast, general devises do bear interest, beginning ordinarily one year after the testator's death.

Specific devises of debts or obligations usually carry with them interest accrued but unpaid *at* the testator's death. Thus specific devises of mortgages or debts pass any accrued but uncollected interest to the devisees. See id. Similarly, courts have held that a specific devise of a bond passes to the devisee an overdue interest coupon that was attached to the bond at the testator's death. See id.

Post-Execution, Pre-Death Accessions and Accretions. What if the accession or accretion occurs after execution of the will but before death? It is well settled that collected interest on a specifically devised bond does not pass to the specific devisee even if the interest remained part of the testator's estate. The law has had more difficulty in analyzing the effect of post-execution accessions upon devises of corporate stock. This is especially so where the accession results from a corporate restructuring. Corporate restructuring of stock by means of stock splits or stock dividends may affect devises of the stock in fundamental ways, because they potentially alter the economic interests that will be received by the devisee.

Stock Splits. A *stock split* occurs when a corporation amends its charter to increase the number of shares outstanding and issues these shares on a pro-rata basis to existing shareholders. For example, if a corporation has 1,000,000 shares of stock outstanding selling at $50 per share, a two-for-one stock split will increase the number of shares outstanding to 2,000,000. Existing shareholders will receive two shares for every share they own, but each share will be worth only $25.

The traditional approach to resolving questions of stock accessions resulting from stock splits has been to pin the result on whether the devise is classified as specific or general. If the devise is classified as specific, then the virtually uniform result has been to give to the devisee the increase in the number of shares resulting from a stock split. If the devise is classified as general, the devisee does not receive the benefit of the stock split.

Original UPC §2-607 adhered to the traditional view concerning stock splits—that whether the devisee is entitled to the additional number of shares resulting from stock splits depends upon the specific-general distinction.

Watson v. Santalucia, below, illustrates how some courts have abandoned the specific-general distinction to determine who receives the benefits of stock splits.

Watson v. Santalucia
427 S.E.2d 466 (W. Va. 1993)

NEELY, J. The question before us is what happens when a stock splits immediately before the death of a testator, and the testator has left a specific number of shares to his heirs. Traditionally, we viewed such a question as turning on whether the bequest was "specific" or "general" and then applied the result thought to follow automatically from the chosen label. However, the problems created by the use of the distinction between "general" and "specific" legacies in the stock split situation far outweigh any advantages to be gained by relying on those classifications. Instead we adopt today the rule that, in the absence of anything manifesting a contrary intent, a legatee of stock is entitled to any additional shares received by a testator as the result of a stock split occurring in the interval between the execution of a will and the testator's death. Accordingly, we reverse the decision of the Circuit Court of Lewis County.

The facts are not disputed. Frank Cirigliano (testator) died testate on 15 May 1990. The testator's will, dated 30 June 1988, as modified by two codicils executed in February 1990, was admitted to probate on 21 May 1990. The appellants are John T. Law, Marino Paletti and Teresa Calabrese, each the legatee of 100 shares of stock in Citizens Bancshares, Inc. The appellees, plaintiffs below, Geraldine C. Watson and Virginia Paletti, are the co-executrices of the estate and the beneficiaries under the residuary clause of the testator's will.

On 30 June 1988, (as well on 27 February 1990 when the most recent codicil to the will was executed) the testator owned 2,000 shares of the capital stock of Citizens Bancshares, Inc. The following provisions are relevant to this case:

FOURTH: I give and bequeath unto John T. Law 100 shares of the capital stock of Citizens Bancshares, Inc.

FIFTH: I give and bequeath unto Marino Paletti 100 shares of the capital stock of Citizens Bancshares, Inc.

SIXTH: I give and bequeath unto Teresa Calabrese 100 shares of the capital stock of Citizens Bancshares, Inc.... .

NINTH: I hereby authorize, empower and direct the personal representatives of this, my Will, as soon after my death as my said personal representatives may consider it advantageous, to sell, convey and otherwise transfer and convert to money all my property and estate, real, personal and mixed, wheresoever situate, which at my death may not already be in the form of cash, except for and subject always to the provisions of Items 'Second' through 'Eighth', above, and any and all sales by my personal representatives, pursuant to the authority vested in said personal representatives by this item, may be made by my said personal representatives at private or public sale, at such time or times, at such place, or places, at such price or prices, and upon such terms and conditions as to cash or credit as may be fixed by my said personal representatives....

TWENTY-SEVENTH: I give and bequeath all of the rest, residue and remainder of my estate unto the following persons in the following proportions:

Pasquale Cirigliano, my nephew, one-ninth (1/9th);

Maria Cirigliano Covelli, my niece, one-ninth (1/9th);

Angiolina Cirigliano, my niece, one-ninth (1/9th);

Antonio Santalucia, my nephew, one-ninth (1/9th);

Francesca Santalucia Petrocelli, my niece, one-ninth (1/9th);

Teresina Santalucia, my niece, one-ninth (1/9th);

Rosa Santalucia, my niece, one-ninth (1/9th);

Pasquale Santalucia, my nephew, one-ninth (1/9th); and

The children of Giuseppe Santalucia, my nephew, who are living at the time of my death, one-ninth (1/9th).

On 21 April 1990, the shareholders of Citizens Bancshares, Inc., at its regular annual meeting, caused a four-for-one split of the shares of the corporation. The par value of the stock was commensurately reduced from one dollar a share to twenty-five cents per share. This stock split became effective on 1 May 1990. On 15 May 1990, after a protracted illness that confined him to his home, Mr. Cirigliano died; at that time his 2,000 shares of stock in Citizens Bancshares, Inc., had become 8,000 shares as a result of the stock split.

On 11 December 1991, the Circuit Court of Lewis County entered its order that Mr. Law, Mr. Paletti and Ms. Calabrese are entitled only to the 100 shares mentioned in the will, as opposed to the same proportional interest in the bank, now represented by four hundred shares each, that they would have had if the testator had died fifteen days earlier. Mr. Law, Mr. Paletti and Ms. Calabrese appeal from that decision.

"The paramount principle in construing or giving effect to a will is that the intention of the testator prevails, unless it is contrary to some positive rule of law or principle of public policy." Syl. pt. 1, Farmers & Merchants Bank v. Farmers & Merchants Bank, 158 W.Va. 1012, 216 S.E.2d 769 (1975). However, in reaching his decision, the circuit court relied to a large extent on W.Va. Code 41-3-1 [1923], which states, in full:

A will shall be construed, with reference to the estate comprised in it, to speak and take effect as if it had been executed immediately before the death of the testator, *unless a contrary intention shall appear by the will*. [Emphasis added]

Code 41-3-1 [1923] is a codification of a common law rule. In construing similar statutes or the common law rule, most jurisdictions have concluded that this rule "relates to the effect and operation of the instrument, not to its construction." Egavian v. Egavian, 102 R.I. 740, 745, 232 A.2d 789, 792 (1967); Lee v. Foley, 224 Miss. 684, 689, 80 So.2d 765, 767 (1955). Indeed, a common sense reading of the "unless a contrary intention shall appear by will" exception to W.Va. Code 41-3-1 [1923] means that we need to determine the intent of the testator *before* this statute has any meaning. Weiss v. Soto, 142 W. Va. 783, 98 S.E.2d 727 (1957). Indeed, reference to W. Va. Code 41-3-1 [1923] in this situation merely serves to confuse the issue, not to clarify. Our mission is to follow our cardinal rule of will construction: We must determine the testator's intent.

Traditionally, most courts (including this Court) relied on the distinction between a "general" bequest and a "specific" bequest to determine to whom the shares of stock acquired in a split after the will was executed, but before the death of the testator, belonged: the named legatee or the residuary legatee. However, the general/specific distinction was not initially designed for use in this area, but only for purposes of ademption, abatement, or disposition of income earned on the principal of the bequest during administration of the estate.[8] Furthermore, most

---

8. An excellent summary of the appropriate use of the general/specific legacy distinction is found in Re Estate of Parker, 110 So.2d 498, 500-501 (Fla. App. 1959), cert. denied, 114 So.2d 3 (Fla. 1959):

> A specific legacy is a gift by will of property which is particularly designated and which is to be satisfied only by the receipt of the particular property described. Income received during administration on property specifically devised shall become property of the specific devisee. A general legacy or devise is one which does not direct the delivery of any particular property; is not limited to any particular asset; and may be satisfied out of the general assets belonging to the estate of the testator and not otherwise disposed of in the will. Income received on the property which is the subject of a general bequest passes to the residue of the estate.
>
> It was held at common law that if the particular property described in a specific bequest is disposed of by the testator during his life, or cannot be located, the bequest must fail or adeem. It was also the rule at common law that if the subject of a bequest was described in general terms, it was considered to be a general bequest and disposition by testator during his life of all or a part of the property so bequeathed did not create an ademption. In such case the personal representative was required to obtain and deliver to the legatee property satisfying the

courts have found that relying on such a standard does not comport with the notion of effecting the testator's intent[.]

The two principal difficulties with the general versus specific classification approach are that it fails to consider the testator's intent with specific reference to the additional shares created by a stock split and that it also fails to recognize the basic nature of a stock split. Bostwick v. Hurstel, 364 Mass. 282, 287, 304 N.E.2d 186 (1973). We agree with the reasoning of the Bostwick court and adopt the rule that the distinction between a "specific" bequest and a "general" bequest is not applicable to a stock split.[9] A stock split is merely a bookkeeping adjustment on the part of the corporation; "it does not alter the pre-existing proportionate interest of any stockholder or increase the intrinsic value of his holding or of the aggregate holdings of the other stockholders as they stood before. The new certificates simply increase the number of shares, with consequent dilution of the value of each share." Eisner v. Macomber, 252 U.S. 189, 211, 40 S.Ct. 189, 194 (1920). Furthermore, a stock split is an event over which a testator rarely has control or advance knowledge. Therefore, our question becomes: When the testator bequeathed 100 shares of stock in Citizens Bancshares, Inc., did he intend to give the control over the corporation that 100 shares provided at the time of execution, or did he intend to give exactly 100 shares, no matter what percentage of the corporation those shares represented at the time of his death?

In Cuppett v. Neilly, 143 W.Va. 845, 105 S.E.2d 548 (1958) (the only West Virginia case on point), this Court was presented with a situation where a woman left 100 shares of General Motors common stock to a legatee. General Motors then split its stock three-for-one two years after the testatrix executed her will, but two-and-a-half years before the testatrix died. After the split, the testatrix sold fifty of the shares and died owning 250 shares of General Motors common stock. The dispute was over whether the 150 shares of General Motors common stock that remained from the split would pass to the beneficiary of the stock bequest or to the residuary estate.

Although this Court could have relied on the intent of the testator to reach its decision, this Court instead relied on the general/specific bequest distinction. As we have seen above, however, reliance on this distinction is misplaced in the stock split situation. Therefore, to the extent that the Cuppett decision relied upon the general/specific bequest distinction to decide the distribution of the additional shares

---

general description of the bequest. If, however, the property designated in the will for payment of charges against the estate was insufficient for that purpose, general bequests would abate prior to specific bequests.

The technical distinction between general and specific bequests becomes important only when considering situations involving ademption, abatement or disposition of income earned on the subject of the bequest during administration.

9. We express no opinion today on the applicability of the "specific"/"general" distinction to other events that may occur between the execution of a will and the death of the testator, such as dividend reinvestments or stock dividends; the issue is not before us.

as a result of the stock split, it is overruled.

Without the general/specific fiction to rely on, we must now determine what this testator would have wanted done with the shares that accrued as a result of the stock split. A stock split is an occurrence that a testator has little reason to anticipate at the time he executes his will and one over which he has little or no control. Moreover, the intent of a testator in bequeathing stock rather than cash seems to imply that the testator intends to give a certain share of a corporation rather than a specific dollar value. The best way to effect the testator's intent, then, is to behave as if the stock split had never happened and to award to beneficiaries of specific stock bequests accretions as a result of stock splits between execution of the will and the death of the testator. Therefore, in the absence of anything manifesting a contrary intent, a legatee of stock is entitled to any additional shares received by a testator as the result of a stock split occurring in the interval between the execution of a will and the death of the testator. The result of this rule is that the interests are divided in the same manner as the testator intended; they are apportioned *as if the split had never occurred*.

In this case, we apply our presumption that the testator would intend that the same interests be given to the legatees of stock shares as if the split had never occurred. John T. Law, Marino Paletti and Teresa Calabrese, the legatees of 100 shares of stock in Citizens Bancshares, Inc. (each) in the will are to receive 400 shares each, with the balance of the stock passing, as per the will, to the residuary legatees.

Accordingly, the decision of the Circuit Court of Lewis County is reversed, and the case is remanded for further proceedings consistent with this opinion.

Reversed and remanded.

Notes and Problems

1. *Uniform Probate Code and Restatement 3d of Property.* UPC §2-605 basically adopts the approach used in *Watson*. That approach was codified in Massachusetts following the decision in Bostwick v. Hurstel, referred to in *Watson*. See Mass. Gen. Law c. 191, §1A(3). (Massachusetts subsequently repealed that statute when it adopted the Uniform Probate Code. See Mass. Gen. Law c. 190B, §2-605.) The Restatement 3d of Property also adopts the *Watson* approach:

> *§5.3 Effect of Stock Splits, Stock Dividends, and Other Distributions on Devises of a Specified Number of Securities.* A devise of a specified number of securities carries with it any additional securities acquired by the testator after executing the will to the extent that the post-execution acquisitions resulted from the testator's ownership of the described securities.

2. *Stock Dividends.* A stock dividend is a distribution to existing shareholders of stock in lieu of a cash dividend. Usually, stock dividends are distributed from a corporation's own authorized but unissued shares. Sometimes, however, stock dividends are distributed from shares in the stock of other firms that the corporation

owns. Courts have had difficulty determining who should receive shares obtained as a result of a stock dividend.

The majority of decisions appear to treat stock dividends the same as cash dividends, denying the benefit of the stock dividend accession to the stock devisee. See Note, 36 Alb. L. Rev. 182, 188-92 (1971); Annot., Change in Stock or Corporate Structure, or Split or Substitution of Stock of Corporation, as Affecting Bequest of Stock, 46 A.L.R.3d 7. Contra, Edmundson v. Morton, 420 S.E.2d 106 (N.C. 1992) (announcing a presumption that accretions of stock through splits or dividends pass to the devisee of the originally devised stock). The usual rationale for the majority view is that stock dividends are like cash dividends because they are both paid out of the firm's earned surplus (sometimes called "retained earnings").

3. *Problem on Stock Dividends*. For much of his life, G owned 1000 shares of stock in Acme Corporation. Shortly before G's death, the company paid out its annual dividend in stock rather than in cash. In G's case, the dividend amounted to an additional 100 shares. G's will provided: "I give my 1000 shares of stock in Acme Corp. to my son A and the residue of my estate to my daughter B." Under the majority view, how many shares of stock does A receive? Under the UPC? Why?

4. *Reverse Stock Split*. A reverse stock split occurs when a corporation reduces the number of its shares (perhaps to avoid being delisted from its stock exchange) and increases the share price proportionately. For example, if X originally owned 1000 shares and the corporation declares a 1-for-2 reverse split, X now owns 500 shares. The 500 new shares are as valuable as the 1000 old shares; each share has simply been doubled in value.

5. *Problem on Reverse Stock Splits*. Owning 500 shares of stock in ACME Corporation, G executed a will devising 100 shares to A, 100 shares to B, with the remaining 300 shares passing under the residuary clause to C. ACME later declared a 1-for-2 reverse split. Later, G died. You are G's executor. How many shares of stock do A, B, and C receive? Why?

3. Abatement

Primary Statutory Reference: *UPC §3-902*

Suppose a will leaves "my antique desk to A, $10,000 to B, $5,000 to C, and the residue of my estate to D." The testator dies owning the antique desk and net assets of $20,000, consisting of stocks and bonds. Because all the provisions of the will can be satisfied leaving a residue of $5,000 for D, there is no problem of funding the specific and general devises.

But if the net assets apart from the antique desk are worth only $10,000, a question arises about how to distribute the decedent's estate. The different systems of reducing the devises, referred to as "abatement" systems, are the subject of this Section. In the absence of a will provision providing for an order of abatement, the default rule of abatement statutes and judge-made law control. As with the doctrine of ademption, the common-law doctrine of abatement turns on classification of the gifts. Under the usual common-law rules, the residuary devisee will take nothing and there will be a pro rata reduction of the general devises to B and C. The devise of the antique desk is specific and abates last, so that A will get the desk unless its sale is necessary to pay debts or expenses of administration. If the will also contained a demonstrative devise, this would be treated as specific for purposes of abatement. See Atkinson on Wills §136.

Land. The estate included no land in the above example. Abatement may become more complicated when land is involved. At common law, title to personal property passed on the testator's death to the personal representative, but title to land passed directly to the devisee. Unless the will provided otherwise, land could not be reached to satisfy the decedent's debts unless the creditor had a claim secured by a lien on the land. The common-law rules concerning passage of title have persisted to this day, but land is now subject to the decedent's debts. In some states, however, all the personal property abates before any land. In some others, personal property devised in the residue abates before land devised in the residue and specifically devised personal property abates before specifically devised land. The UPC eliminates any distinction between real and personal property. See UPC §§1-201(10), (38), 3-902.

Devisees. Many states have statutes covering some or all of the problems of abatement, but they vary considerably in their treatment of the problem. Some, for example, give priority to specific devises to certain relatives over specific devises to others. See, e.g., 20 Pa. Cons. Stat. Ann. §3541.

Estate Taxes. Under the federal estate tax, the taxable estate may include nonprobate property. Examples include life insurance and property the decedent gratuitously transferred reserving a life estate. See Chapter 19. The position usually taken in the earlier cases followed the "burden on the residue" rule, under which the burden of the estate taxes on nonprobate property was borne by the probate assets.[10] In recent years, a significant number of courts have held that there should be an "equitable apportionment," placing a proportionate part of the estate tax burden on nonprobate assets. That is to say, assets not forming a part of the decedent's probate estate but nevertheless includable in his or her taxable estate abate proportionally to pay the federal estate tax liability owed by the estate.[11] Legislation providing for a

---

10. See, e.g., Ericson v. Childs, 198 A. 176, 115 A.L.R. 907 (Conn. 1938); Bemis v. Converse, 140 N.E. 686 (Mass. 1923); Austin Fleming, Apportionment of Federal Estate Taxes, 43 Ill. L. Rev. 153, 159 (1948); William P. Sutter, Apportionment of Federal Estate Tax in the Absence of Statute or an Expression of Intention, 51 Mich. L. Rev. 53 (1952).

11. See, e.g., Estate of Gowling, 411 N.E.2d 266 (Ill. 1980) (testate estate); Roe v. Farrell, 372 N.E.2d 662 (Ill. 1978) (intestate estate); Sebree v. Rosen, 349 S.W.2d 865, 884 (Mo. 1961); Beatty v. Cake, 387 P.2d 355 (Or. 1963), rehearing denied 390 P.2d 176 (Or. 1964); Industrial Trust Co. v. Budlong, 76 A.2d 600 (R.I. 1950). Other cases are cited in Douglas A. Kahn, The Federal Estate Tax

similar apportionment was enacted in 1930 in New York, and is now in force in about one-half of the states.

The typical provision in the apportionment statutes is similar to that contained in the Uniform Estate Tax Apportionment Act (UETAA), which is incorporated in UPC §§3-9A-101 to -115. UETAA apportions the burden among all recipients of property, whether probate or nonprobate, included in the taxable estate. UETAA provides for an apportionment among those who take probate assets, instead of placing the whole burden on the residuary estate where the decedent dies testate. This goes beyond the decisions favoring an equitable apportionment among nonprobate assets. Do you think treating probate and nonprobate assets alike for purposes of discharging the estate tax liability is likely to coincide with most testators' intent? Restatement 3d of Property §1.1 comment g takes the position that, unless the decedent's will provides otherwise, liability for estate taxes is "equitably apportioned" among nonprobate assets that are includible in the taxable estate, but within the probate estate, the full burden falls on the taxable portion of the residue.

Should nonprobate assets also be available to pay debts of the estate other than estate tax liability? Generally, the law requires the probate assets first to bear the burden of the estate's debts. Unsecured estate creditors are allowed to reach some types of nonprobate assets, but typically they can do so only if the probate assets are insufficient. Creditors' rights to nonprobate assets are considered in Chapter 7.

EXTERNAL REFERENCE. Ira Mark Bloom, Unifying the Rules for Wills and Revocable Trusts in the Federal Estate Tax Apportionment Arena: Suggestions for Reform, 62 U. Miami L. Rev. 767 (2008).

Problems

1. G's will provides: "I give my heirloom brooch to A, $10,000 to B, $5,000 to C, and the residue of my estate to D." G died owning the brooch as well as stocks and bonds worth $12,000. Under the UPC, who gets what?

2. Suppose instead that G died owning the brooch, stocks and bonds worth $5,000, and land worth $7,000. Under the UPC, who gets what?

Burden Borne by a Dissenting Widow, 64 Mich. L. Rev. 1499, 1506 n.36 (1966). See also John H. Minan, The Allocation of Estate Taxes by Judicial Rule: A Case for Reform, 38 Ohio St. L.J. 539 (1977); Joan M. Sherwin, Note, 1979 U. Ill. L. F. 703.

4. Ademption By Satisfaction

Primary Statutory Reference: *UPC §2-609*

Restatement 3d of Property

§5.4 Ademption by Satisfaction

An inter vivos gift made by a testator to a devisee or to a member of the devisee's family adeems the devise by satisfaction, in whole or in part, if the testator indicated in a contemporaneous writing, or if the devisee acknowledged in a writing, that the gift was so to operate.

————

If a testator makes a lifetime gift to a devisee, that gift might be treated as satisfying the devise, in whole or in part. The doctrine of satisfaction essentially provides for the situation in which the testator decides to change the timing of a gift to permit the beneficiary to enjoy the gift before the testator's death. It is analogous to the doctrine of advancements that applies to lifetime gifts made by decedents who die intestate. See Chapter 2.

When the doctrine of satisfaction is applied, the distribution of the property owned at death is not made in accordance with the literal terms of the will. However, if we consider the subject of the gift *as if* it were a part of the distributable estate, then the will can be said to be enforced as written. It is *as if* part of the decedent's estate had been distributed pursuant to the terms of the will in advance of the testator's death. The words "as if" need to be emphasized, because the property given is not treated as part of the estate for other purposes. For example, it is not subject to the claims of creditors of the estate.

Writing. In contrast to advancements, the satisfaction doctrine was not the subject of widespread statutory enactment. In the nineteenth century, a handful of states adopted a writing requirement to prove a satisfaction. Today, approximately half of the states impose a writing requirement. See Restatement 3d of Property §5.4 Statutory Note. A writing requirement avoids difficult factual inquiries about whether the testator intended a lifetime gift to be taken into account in distributing the estate. The writing requirement may be satisfied by a provision in the will expressly providing for lifetime advances. An attorney should raise this issue with the client and provide expressly whether lifetime gifts should or should not be taken into account for purposes of distributing the estate. Any other document written by the testator contemporaneously with the gift also qualifies. A satisfaction can also be proven by a writing in which the devisee acknowledges that the gift is in whole or in part satisfaction of a devise.

The UPC's provision concerning satisfaction allows the testator to make a gift in satisfaction of a devise to a person other than the devisee. The statutory change is a recognition that testators may want to reduce or eliminate a devise when they make gifts to family members of a devisee. See UPC §2-609 comment.

Specific Devise. A lifetime gift can satisfy a specific devise. If the testator makes a lifetime gift of the devised property, the doctrine of ademption applies and no writing is necessary. If the testator makes a lifetime gift of different property, the application of the satisfaction doctrine under the UPC depends upon whether the gift was accompanied by a writing. Other than the writing requirement, this is not a change from the common law. The common law recognized that the doctrine could apply even if the nature of the lifetime gift differed significantly from the nature of the devise. In some jurisdictions, however, a substantial difference between the subject matter of the lifetime gift and the devise raises a presumption that the testator did not intend to make a satisfaction. See, e.g., Dugan v. Hollins, 4 Md. Ch. 139 (1853); Scholze v. Scholze, 2 Tenn. App. 80 (1925).

Land. Although the UPC and non-UPC statutes eliminate any distinction under the satisfaction doctrine between devises of real and personal property, that was not the early rule. Historically, satisfaction has not been applied to devises of land. If the testator's will devised Greenacre to A and thereafter the testator conveyed the land to B, the courts treated the transfer as a revocation of the devise. They did this even though it could have been regarded as an ademption by extinction. If the testator retained Greenacre, but gave other property to A, intending this as a satisfaction of the devise, this transfer also was regarded as an attempted revocation. When the second situation came before the English courts after the passage of the Statute of Frauds of 1677, which prescribed the methods of revocation, the English courts held that this was not a permitted method and hence was ineffective. See Davys v. Boucher, 2 Y. & C. Ex. 397, 160 Eng. Rep. 757 (Ex. 1839). Older American cases took the same view: The question was decided, that is, by putting the transaction into the category of an attempted revocation of the devise, instead of an attempted satisfaction of the devise. See, e.g., Burnham v. Comfort, 15 N.E. 710, 2 Am. St. Rep. 462 (N.Y. 1888). Whether these older cases would still be followed today is uncertain.

Partial Satisfaction. At an early time, a gift of an amount less than the amount of a devise was presumed to have been intended to satisfy the whole devise. The theory was that the testator viewed the gift as a substitute for the devise. This rule is no longer followed. In the absence of evidence that the testator intended a satisfaction in whole, courts now hold that a gift of a part of a devise is a pro tanto satisfaction only.

UPC §2-609(b) explicitly addresses the question of partial satisfaction. It provides that for purposes of a partial satisfaction, the lifetime gift of property should be valued when the devisee obtains possession or when the testator dies, whichever occurs first.

Problems

1. G's daughter A was graduated five years ago from the Mayo Clinic Medical School at a four-year cost to G of $100,000. If G were to die now with a will leaving "$100,000 to A, residue to B," how much, if anything, would A receive under the will?

2. Suppose instead that G paid A's tuition by check. On the memo line of each check, G wrote: "This gift is in partial satisfaction of A's devise under my will." One year after her graduation, A died, survived by G, B, and A's daughter X. If G were to die now, under what circumstances would X receive A's devise? See UPC §2-603.

PART C. POST-EXECUTION DEATHS—LAPSE AND ANTILAPSE

Primary Statutory References: *UPC §§2-601, -603, -604, -702*

What happens to a devise if the devisee fails to survive the testator? The short answer is that the devise "lapses" (fails). This is because a will transfers property when the testator dies, not when the will was executed, and because property can only be transferred to a living person. All devises, then, are automatically and by law conditioned on surviving the testator.

120-Hour Requirement of Survival. Although at common law, survival by only an instant prevents lapse, UPC §2-702 extends—as a rule of construction—the 120-hour requirement of survival to all "governing instruments" (as defined in §1-201).

In Estate of Kerlee, 557 P.2d 599,(Idaho 1976), the court held that the applicable statute (original UPC §2-601) did not apply to a will that devised property to the testator's sister and provided that "if [she] does not survive me" the property was to go to the North Idaho Children's Home. The testator's sister survived him by 74 hours. The court held that the devise in favor of the testator's sister did not lapse because the statute states that its 120-hour requirement of survival is nullified by language in the will "requiring that the devisee survive the testator."[12] Because the law itself already requires devisees to survive the testator, the will need not do so. Nevertheless, will forms commonly attach boilerplate language requiring survival. How would *Kerlee* be decided under UPC §2-702?

Devolution of a Lapsed Devise. If a devise lapses, what happens to it? In the absence of an applicable antilapse statute and in the absence of an expressly designated alternative taker, lapsed devises devolve in accordance with the following rules.

---

12. See also Estate of Acord v. Commissioner, 946 F.2d 1473 (9th Cir. 1991) (the 120-hour rule was nullified by a provision dealing with simultaneous deaths, resulting in the devisee's estate incurring an additional $150,000 in estate taxes)

Lapse of a nonresiduary devise. If lapse occurs in a dispositive provision other than the residuary clause, the judicial rule is uniform that lapsed devises of personal property pass to the decedent's residuary devisees. Under early common law, this rule was not followed for land. The view that a will could not dispose of after-acquired land was thought to prevent the residuary clause from passing lapsed nonresiduary devises of land. Thus, they bypassed the residuary clause and passed to the decedent's heirs by intestacy. Many states have enacted legislation that usually causes real as well as personal property to pass under the residuary clause. A few statutes, however, preserve the common-law rule for land.

Lapse in the residue. When all the residuary devisees predecease the testator, the residue becomes intestate property. If the residuary clause is in favor of more than one person, and if that clause does not create a class gift, the conventional view is that the death of one or more, but not all, causes the share intended for the deceased devisee(s) to pass by intestacy.[13] This is known as the *no-residue-of-a-residue-rule.* As the judges follow the rule, they sometimes express dissatisfaction with it. For example, in In re Dunster, [1909] 1 Ch. 103, the court said: "I think the effect of [the no-residue-of-a-residue-rule] is to defeat the testator's intention in almost every case in which it is applied."

A number of decisions have rejected the no-residue-of-a-residue-rule and have held that the lapsed share passes to the other residuary devisees, if there are others who survive.[14] The UPC and the Restatement 3d of Property are aligned with this position. See UPC §2-604(b); Restatement 3d of Property §5.5 comment o.

Problems

1. G's will devised her watch to A, $10,000 to B, residue to C. A and B predeceased G. What result at common law?

2. G's will made specific devises to X and Y and then divided the residue as follows: one-half to B and one-half to C. B predeceased G. What result at common law? What result under the UPC?

Class Gifts. A class gift is a gift of property to a group of persons identified by a group label, such as "children," "grandchildren," "issue," "descendants," "brothers," "sisters," "nieces," "nephews," or "first cousins." According to the Restatement 3d of Property §13.1, a class gift "is a disposition to beneficiaries who take as members

---

13. See, e.g., Estate of Levy, 415 P.2d 1006 (Okla. 1966); Estate of McFarland, 167 S.W.3d 299 (Tenn. 2005); Swearingen v. Giles, 565 S.W.2d 574 (Tex. Civ. App. 1978); Estate of Mory, 139 N.W.2d 623 (Wis. 1966).

14. See, e.g., Estate of Jackson, 471 P.2d 278 (Ariz. 1970); Corbett v. Skaggs, 207 P. 819 (Kan. 1922); Niemann v. Zacharias, 176 N.W.2d 671 (Neb. 1970); Frolich Estate, 295 A.2d 448 (N.H. 1972); Commerce Nat'l Bank v. Browning, 107 N.E.2d 120 (Ohio 1952); Slack Trust, 220 A.2d 472 (Vt. 1966).

of a group." The Restatement explains that "[t]aking as a members of a group means that the membership of the group is subject to fluctuation by increase (i.e., by the addition of new members), by decrease (i.e., by the subtraction of existing members), or both... [and] that the ultimate share of each beneficiary is determined on a fractional basis." Restatement 3d of Property §13.1 comments h & i.

Not all gifts to multiple beneficiaries are class gifts, however. Generally speaking, the following rules of thumb determine whether a gift is or is not a class gift:

> *A gift is presumptively a class gift if the group members are identified only by a group label (such as "to my children").*
>
> *A gift is presumptively not a class gift, although the takers are identified by a group label, if the group members also are identified by name (such as "to my children, C1, C2, and C3") or by number ("to my three children") or by both name and number ("to my three children, C1, C2, and C3"). Gifts like these are gifts of a fixed fraction to each of the designated individuals—in this case, a gift of one-third to C1, one-third to C2, and one-third to C3.*

Although the law treats these rules as *presumptions* that can be rebutted by a contrary intent "found from additional language or circumstances," see Restatement 3d of Property §§13.1, 13.2, the case law shows that the presumptions are seldom rebutted. Because of the infrequency of actual rebuttal, the following examples assume that these presumptions are controlling.

The distinguishing feature typical of a class gift is the ability of the group to fluctuate in number. Fluctuations in number can come about through an *increase* in the number of takers (caused by births or adoptions), and/or through a *decrease* in the number of takers (caused by deaths).

Increase in class membership. The ability of the takers to increase in number is unique to class gifts.

> *Example 6.1:* G devised land "to my children." When the will was executed, G had two children (C1 and C2). Subsequently, G had a third child (C3). G was survived by C1, C2, and C3. No children were in gestation at G's death.
>
> Because G's will created a class gift, C1, C2, and C3 each take an undivided one-third interest in the devised land.
>
> If, on the other hand, G's will had created individual gifts (suppose, for example, that the dispositive language had been "to my two children, C1 and C2"), the result would have been different. The shares of C1 and C2 would have remained constant at one-half each. Not being a class gift, the devise would not have been subject to increase, and C3 would not have been entitled to share in the devised land.[15]

---

15. This analysis is based on the common law. In Chapter 8, we shall learn that omitted-child statutes might produce a different result.

Decrease in class membership. The rule of lapse—that devisees must survive the testator to take—applies to class gifts as well as individual gifts. In the absence of an applicable antilapse statute (see below), a class gift imports a built-in gift-over to the other takers. The traditional rule at common law is that there is no such gift-over in the case of individual gifts. The Restatement 3d of Property takes a slightly more nuanced view and provides that the question is one of construction: whether the result of implying a gift-over or not doing so is more consistent with the transferor's overall dispositive plan. Restatement 3d of Property §13.2 comment g.

> *Example 6.2:* G devised land "to my children." When the will was executed, G had three children (C1, C2, and C3). C1 predeceased G, but C2 and C3 survived G.
>
> Because G's will created a class gift, C2 and C3 each take an undivided one-half interest in the devised land, probably as tenants in common.
>
> If, on the other hand, G's will had created individual gifts of a one-third share to each of G's three children (suppose, for example, that the dispositive language had been "to my three children, C1, C2, and C3"), the traditional rule would say that C1's lost one-third share goes to G's residuary devisees or, in the unlikely event that there was no residuary clause, to G's heirs by intestate succession. Under the Restatement view, there could be an implied gift-over, but only if the court finds that such a construction is more consistent with the transferor's overall dispositive plan.

Problem

G's will devised $10,000 to A's children and the residue to B's children. If one of A's children predeceased G, what result at common law? If instead one of B's children predeceased G, what result at common law?

————

Antilapse Statutes. Almost all jurisdictions have antilapse statutes.[16] The "antilapse" label, however, is misdescriptive. Strictly speaking, antilapse statutes (other than in Maryland and perhaps Iowa) do not reverse the common-law rule of lapse. In other words, they do not eliminate the requirement of survival so that devised property passes to the estates of predeceasing devisees. Instead, antilapse statutes leave the requirement of survival intact, and provide a statutory substitute gift, usually to the devisee's descendants who survive the testator.[17]

Application to class gifts. Do antilapse statutes apply to class gifts? At one time, a few courts said no. Their reasoning was that the will makes a devise only to the members of the class who are living at the testator's death. The statute, therefore, would have no application to a potential class member who predeceased the testator.

---

16. For a state-by-state compilation, see Restatement 3d of Property, Statutory Note to §5.5.

17. Under the UPC, the substituted descendants must survive the testator by 120 hours. See above p. 319. Therefore, the UPC antilapse statutes apply even though the devisee survives the testator if the devisee fails to survive the testator by 120 hours.

In many decisions, however, the statutes have been construed to apply to class gifts, and the UPC and a growing number of non-UPC statutes explicitly apply to class gifts. The basis for applying antilapse statutes to class gifts is the idea that the remedial purpose of these statutes—to preserve equality of treatment among different lines of succession—would be frustrated if the testator happened to use class gift language. See Hoverstad v. First Nat'l Bank & Trust Co., 74 N.W.2d 48 (S.D. 1955).

The Restatement 3d of Property §5.5 comment j provides:

> *j. Application to class gifts.* Antilapse statutes apply to class gifts to single-generation classes, whether or not the language of the statute explicitly covers class gifts. Antilapse statutes do not, however, apply to class gifts to multiple-generation classes, such as gifts to "issue," "descendants," "heirs of the body," "heirs," "next of kin," "relatives," or "family," because these types of class gifts already pass the shares of deceased class members to their surviving descendants without statutory intervention.

Rule of construction. Antilapse statutes establish a rule of construction, not a mandatory rule. They apply in the absence of a contrary intention on the part of the testator. See UPC §2-601. The language that suffices to make an antilapse statute inapplicable has been the source of controversy, as we will see in Ruotolo v. Tietjen, below.

Antilapse statutes were enacted in the belief that the statutory substitute gift for which they make provision is one the testator probably would have made if he or she had thought about the matter. At the least, the substitute gift is thought to produce a result closer to the testator's probable intention than the disposition that would result under the common-law doctrine of lapse.

Protected categories. The antilapse statutes of most jurisdictions only apply to certain categories of predeceased devisees—relatives[18] or specified relatives of the testator. Very few statutes apply to any devisee who predeceases the testator leaving descendants who survive the testator. The UPC antilapse provision applies to devisees who are grandparents or descendants of grandparents of the testator. See UPC §2-603(b). The UPC also extends its antilapse protection to the testator's stepchildren.

The UPC, like most antilapse statutes, does not apply to devises to the testator's spouse. Antilapse statutes also typically exclude spouses of predeceased descendants as statutorily-substituted takers.

Questions of status. Antilapse statutes raise two questions of status. First, assuming that the statute includes "descendants" among the class of *protected relatives*, does the term "descendants" here carry the meaning it has under the intestacy laws or the meaning it has under rules of construction for donative

---

18. The term "relative" often is interpreted to mean blood relative. See, e.g., Estate of Bloomer, 620 S.W.2d 365 (Mo. 1981); Estate of Haese, 259 N.W.2d 54 (Wis. 1977).

documents?

Second, assuming that the statute describes the *substitute takers* as "descendants" of a protected relative, does the term "descendants" here carry the meaning it has under the intestacy laws or the meaning it has under rules of construction for donative documents?

Note that the UPC antilapse statute answers these questions of status in §2-603(a)(3), (4).

Problem

G's will provides: "I give $100,000 to my uncle A, if A survives me, and the residue of my estate to my alma mater, the University of Michigan." A predeceased G, leaving a daughter D, a graduate of arch-rival The Ohio State University, who survived G. What result? Consider the following materials.

Ruotolo v. Tietjen

890 A.2d 166 (Conn. App. Ct. 2006), aff'd per curiam, 916 A.2d 1 (Conn. 2007)

LAVERY, C.J. This appeal presents a question of statutory interpretation of General Statutes §45a-441, our testamentary antilapse statute. The appellant, Kathleen Smaldone,[19] appeals from the judgment of the Superior Court on appeal from the Probate Court, which found the statute inoperative in the present case. We disagree and, accordingly, reverse the judgment of the Superior Court.

The facts are undisputed. On March 1, 1990, John N. Swanson executed a will. The residuary clause contained therein bequeathed, inter alia, "one-half ... of [the residue] property to Hazel Brennan of Guilford, Connecticut, if she survives me ...." Brennan died on January 2, 2001, seventeen days prior to the testator's death. Brennan was the testator's stepdaughter, a relation encompassed by §45a-441. The appellant is the child of the deceased legatee, Brennan, and is a residuary legatee in the will, and, thus, was an object of affection of the testator....

The sole issue on appeal is whether the court properly concluded that the antilapse statute does not apply. Section 45a-441 has never been scrutinized by appellate eyes and, thus, presents a question of first impression. Accordingly, our review is plenary.

Pursuant to General Statutes §1-2z,[20] we consider first the text of §45a-441 to

---

19. Kathleen Smaldone is also known as Kathleen Ziegler. The plaintiffs in the appeal from probate were Fred Ruotolo and Charlene Ruotolo, while the defendants were Riefe Tietjen, executor of the estate of John N. Swanson, and Smaldone, Stella Szollosi, Yolanda Szollosi, Marion Fessenden, Geraldine Augeri and Michael Pesce. Only Smaldone has appealed to this court. For clarity, we refer in this opinion to Smaldone as the appellant and the other parties as appellees or by name.

20. General Statutes §1-2z provides: "The meaning of a statute shall, in the first instance, be ascertained from the text of the statute itself and its relationship to other statutes. If, after examining such text and considering such relationship, the meaning of such text is plain and unambiguous and does not yield absurd or unworkable results, extratextual evidence of the meaning of the statute shall

determine whether it is ambiguous. The statute provides: "When a devisee or legatee, being a child, stepchild, grandchild, brother or sister of the testator, dies before him, and no provision has been made in the will for such contingency, the issue of such devisee or legatee shall take the estate so devised or bequeathed." General Statutes §45a-441. The bequest in the present case specified "one-half ... of [the residue] property to Hazel Brennan of Guilford, Connecticut, if she survives me ...." Because the bequest contained the condition, "if she survives me," both the Probate Court and the Superior Court concluded that a provision had been made in the will for such contingency. The appellant disagrees, arguing that because the will contained no provision as to the fate of Brennan's share in the event that she predeceased the testator, a provision had not been made in the will for such contingency. Both readings present plausible interpretations of the salient statutory language. In light of that ambiguity, we turn our attention to extratextual evidence to determine its proper meaning.

According to our long-standing principles of statutory construction, our fundamental objective is to ascertain and give effect to the intent of the legislature.... In determining the intent of a statute, we look to the words of the statute itself, to the legislative history and circumstances surrounding its enactment, to the legislative policy it was designed to implement, and to its relationship to existing legislation and common law principles governing the same general subject matter....

I. History

At common law, when a named beneficiary under a will predeceased the testator, the share of the deceased beneficiary passed not to his descendants, but rather "lapsed." Thus, the rule of lapse automatically conditions all devises on the survival of the legatee....

As Judge O'Sullivan explained in [Ackerman v. Hughes, 11 Conn.Supp. 133, 135 (1942)], "[s]ome pretty oppressive results were occasioned by these principles which frequently blocked the way for carrying out the testator's expressed intention. These injustices were most significant in those instances where the will provided legacies for close relatives." Id. To prevent such a harsh and presumably unintended result, legislatures of the United States in the late eighteenth century began crafting statutes designed to protect certain devises from lapsing.

In 1783, the Massachusetts legislature enacted the first antilapse statute. It provided: "When a devise of real or personal estate is made to any child or other relation of the testator, and the devisee shall die before the testator, leaving issue who survive the testator, such issue shall take the estate so devised, in the same manner as the devisee would have done, if he had survived the testator; unless a different disposition thereof shall be made or required by the will." 1783 Mass. Acts, ch. 24, § 8 .... Today, antilapse statutes have been enacted in every state except

---

not be considered."

Louisiana....

II. Our Antilapse Statute

Connecticut's antilapse statute was enacted in 1821 as part of "An Act for the settlement of Estates, testate, intestate, and insolvent." It provided: "Whenever a devisee or legatee in any last will and testament, being a child or grand-child of the testator, shall die before the testator, and no provision shall be made for such contingency, the issue, if any there be, of such devisee or legatee, shall take the estate devised or bequeathed, as the devisee or legatee would have done, had he or she survived the testator; and if there be no such issue, at the time of the testator's death, the estate disposed of by such devise or legacy, shall be considered and treated as intestate estate." General Statutes (1821 Rev.) tit. 32, ch. 1, §4. The antilapse statute today provides that "[w]hen a devisee or legatee, being a child, stepchild, grandchild, brother or sister of the testator, dies before him, and no provision has been made in the will for such contingency, the issue of such devisee or legatee shall take the estate so devised or bequeathed." General Statutes §45a-441. Other than adding siblings and stepchildren to the class of applicable devisees and legatees; see Public Acts 1987, No. 87-355, §2; no substantive change has been made to our antilapse statute since 1821. Moreover, the pertinent language at issue in the present dispute, namely, "and no provision shall be made for such contingency," was part of the original 1821 statute and remains unaltered today....

Under Connecticut law, the antilapse statute applies unless a "provision has been made in the will for such contingency ...." General Statutes §45a-441. A review of the antilapse statutes presently in effect in forty-eight other jurisdictions reveals that this language is unique to our statute. It is not disputed that the "contingency" referenced in §45a-441 is the death of a devisee or legatee prior to that of the testator. What is contested is the proper construction of the "provision has been made in the will" language.

The appellees contend that inclusion of words of survivorship in a will constitutes a provision for such contingency, thereby rendering the antilapse statute inapplicable. Because the bequest in the present case contains the condition "if she survives me," they claim §45a-441 is inoperative. That simple and seemingly persuasive argument fails, however, on closer examination.

First, it is significant that the language at issue dates back to 1821, the inception of our antilapse statute. The first antilapse statute, enacted in Massachusetts in 1783, provided that it would apply "unless a different disposition thereof shall be made or required by the will." 1783 Mass. Acts, ch. 24, §8 .... The Maryland statute enacted in 1810 contained no such condition. Like every other antilapse statute that followed, ours was modeled on those statutes. Today, a majority of jurisdictions contain some variation of the "unless a different disposition thereof" condition.[21] ... Thus, although the precise wording of the condition in our antilapse statute is unique, its existence is not. Like other states, Connecticut enacted its statute to counteract the harsh results of the common-law rule of lapse. Like other states, Connecticut conditioned operation of the antilapse statute on the intent of the testator as expressed in the will. Accordingly, the critical inquiry is whether an intent contrary to §45a-441 is so manifested.

Our inquiry into whether words of survivorship evince a contrary intent sufficient to defeat the antilapse statute is guided by the following principles. Antilapse statutes "will apply unless testator's intention to exclude its operation is shown with reasonable certainty." (citation omitted). Section 5.5 of the Restatement (Third) of Property, Wills and Other Donative Transfers (1999), addresses antilapse statutes. Comment (f) to that section provides in relevant part: "Antilapse statutes establish a strong rule of construction, designed to carry out presumed intention. They are based on the constructional preference against disinheriting a line of descent .... Consequently, these statutes should be given the widest possible sphere of operation and should be defeated only when the trier of fact determines that the testator wanted to disinherit the line of descent headed by the deceased devisee." 1 Restatement (Third), Property, Wills and Other Donative Transfers §5.5, comment (f), p. 383 (1999). Hence, the burden is on those who seek to deny the statutory protection rather than on those who assert it.

Finally, we are mindful that our statute was enacted to prevent operation of the rule of lapse. Our statute is remedial in nature and must be liberally construed. Accordingly, we resolve any doubt in favor of the operation of §45a-441.

The bequest at issue states, "one-half ... of [the residue] property to Hazel Brennan of Guilford, Connecticut, *if she survives me* ...." (Emphasis added.) Our task is to determine the significance of those words of survivorship. While the present case is one of first impression in Connecticut, numerous other states have considered the question of whether words of survivorship, such as "if she survives me," demonstrate a contrary intent on the part of the testator sufficient to negate operation of the antilapse statute.

III. Other Authority

Whether words of survivorship alone constitute sufficient evidence of a contrary

---

21. The antilapse statutes of sixteen states operate unconditionally. See Ala. Code §43-8-224 (Michie 1991); Ga. Code §53-4-64(b) (Michie 1997) ("unless there appears a clear intent of the contrary" provision applicable only to class gifts); Idaho Code §15-2-605 (Michie 2001); Ind. Code §29-1-6-1(g) (Lexis 2000); Minn. Stat. §524.2-603 (West 2002); Miss. Code §91-5-7 (Lexis 2004); Mo. Rev. Stat. §474.460 (2000); Neb. Rev. Stat. §30-2343 (1995); N.H. Rev. Stat. §551:12 (Michie 1997); N.J. Stat. §3B:3-35 (West 1983); N.D. Cent. Code §30.1-09-05 (Michie 1996); Okla. Stat. tit. 84, §142 (West 1990); 20 Pa. Cons. Stat. §2514(9) (West 2005); S.C. Code §62-2-603 (Law. Co-op. 1987); S.D. Codified Laws §29A-2-603 (Michie 1997); Wyo. Stat. §2-6-106 (LexisNexis 2005).

intent on the part of the testator so as to prevent application of the antilapse statute is a question on which sibling authority is split. Some courts have concluded that words of survivorship demonstrate sufficient contrary intent. Illustrative of that line of cases is Bankers Trust Co. v. Allen, 257 Iowa 938, 135 N.W.2d 607 (1965). In that case, the Supreme Court of Iowa stated: "The bequest to Mary in Item III is conditioned on her surviving the testator. We have held many times ... that our antilapse statute ... does not apply to a bequest so conditioned. ... This is on the theory that a bequest to one 'if she survives me' manifests an intent that the bequest would lapse if the named beneficiary dies before the testator." (Citations omitted.)...

Underlying that view is the presumption that the testator knowingly and deliberately included the words of survivorship. As one New York court explained: "[T]hese words were used by the testator in a will drawn by an experienced attorney. Some meaning must be attributed to them-and the meaning is clear-that survivorship was a condition precedent to the receipt of the residuary estate. If words were held to be devoid of meaning, then this court would be rewriting the testator's will." In re Robinson's Will, 236 N.Y.S.2d 293 (1963). That presumption has pitfalls of its own, however.

Inclusion of words of survivorship provides neither objective evidence that a conversation about §45a-441 took place nor objective evidence that the testator considered seriously the possibility of nonsurvival or inquired about the meaning of expressions such as "lapsed bequest" and the protections of the antilapse statute. "Because such a survival provision is often boiler-plate form-book language, the testator may not understand that such language could disinherit the line of descent headed by the deceased devisee. When the testator is older than the devisee and hence does not expect the devisee to die first ... it seems especially unlikely that a provision requiring the devisee to survive the testator was intended to disinherit the devisee's descendants." 1 Restatement (Third), supra, §5.5, comment (h), p. 385.

At oral argument, counsel for the appellees alleged that inclusion of the words "if she survives me" indicates that the testator intended for the bequest to Brennan to lapse. While plausible, it remains conjecture nonetheless.... As this court recently observed, "[s]peculation and conjecture have no place in appellate review." Narumanchi v. DeStefano, 89 Conn.App. 807, 815, 875 A.2d 71 (2005). Put simply, the intent of the testator cannot definitely be discerned on the basis of words of survivorship alone.

If he intended the bequest to lapse, the testator could have explicitly so provided. The testator also could have made an alternative devise, which "indicates a contrary intent, and hence overrides an antilapse statute ...." 1 Restatement (Third), supra, §5.5, comment (g), p. 384. That the testator did neither in the present case informs our consideration of whether he intended disinheritance.

The argument is further weakened by the fact that, under the interpretation of §45a-441 provided by the Probate Court and the Superior Court, the result is not merely that Brennan's share lapses; her share passes to the intestate estate. Thus, at its crux, the contention of the appellees asks us to presume that, although not explicitly provided for, the testator intended intestacy as to Brennan's share. That argument confounds Connecticut law, which presumes that a testator designed by his will to dispose of his entire estate and to avoid intestacy as to any part of it. (Citations omitted.) ...

[Some] jurisdictions conclude[] that words of survivorship alone are insufficient to defeat an antilapse statute. As the Supreme Court of Appeals of West Virginia stated, "In order to prevent application of the [antilapse] statute ... a testator must clearly and unequivocally indicate his intent that the statute not apply." Kubiczky v. Wesbanco Bank Wheeling, 208 W.Va. 456, 460, 541 S.E.2d 334 (2000); see also In re Estate of Bulger, 224 Ill.App.3d 456, 166 Ill.Dec. 715, 586 N.E.2d 673 (1991); Galloupe v. Blake, 248 Mass. 196, 142 N.E. 818 (1924); In re Estate of Ulrikson, 290 N.W.2d 757, 759 (Minn.1980); Royston v. Watts, 842 S.W.2d 876, 880 (Mo.App.1992); Estate of Kehler, 488 Pa. 165, 411 A.2d 748 (1980); In re Estate of Allmond, 10 Wash.App. 869, 520 P.2d 1388, review denied, 84 Wash.2d 1004 (1974)....

In 1990, a revised Uniform Probate Code was promulgated, which contained a substantially altered antilapse statute. Notably, §2-603(b)(3) provides that "words of survivorship, such as in a devise to an individual 'if he survives me,' or in a devise to 'my surviving children,' are not, in the absence of additional evidence, a sufficient indication of an intent contrary to the application of this section." Unif. Prob. Code §2-603(b)(3). The comment to that section explains that this expansion of antilapse protection was necessary because "an antilapse statute is remedial in nature .... [T]he remedial character of the statute means that it should be given the widest possible latitude to operate" in considering whether in an individual case there is an indication of a contrary intent sufficiently convincing to defeat the statute. Id., comment. The Restatement Third of Property agrees; see 1 Restatement (Third), supra, §5.5, comment (f), p. 383; and that proposition is consonant with Connecticut law. In sum, we agree with those jurisdictions that have held that mere words of survivorship do not defeat antilapse statutes.

IV. Conclusion

Our antilapse statute was enacted to prevent operation of the rule of lapse and unintended disinheritance. The statute is remedial and receives a liberal construction. Any doubts are resolved in favor of its operation. We therefore conclude that words of survivorship, such as "if she survives me," alone do not constitute a "provision" in the will for the contingency of the death of a beneficiary, as the statute requires, and thus are insufficient to negate operation of §45a-441. Our conclusion today effectuates the intent of the General Assembly in enacting this remedial statute. Should a testator desire to avoid application of the antilapse statute, the testator must either unequivocally express that intent or simply provide for an alternate bequest. Because the testator in the present case did neither, the protections of the antilapse statute apply. Accordingly, the bequest to Brennan does not lapse, but rather descends to her issue.

The judgment is reversed and the case is remanded for further proceedings consistent with this opinion.

In this opinion the other judges concurred.

Notes and Questions

1. In affirming per curiam the Appellate Court decision in *Ruotolo*, the Connecticut Supreme Court stated: "Our examination of the record and briefs and our consideration of the arguments of the parties persuades us that the judgment of the Appellate Court should be affirmed on the certified issue. The Appellate Court properly resolved that issue in its concise and well reasoned opinion. Because that opinion fully addresses all arguments raised in this appeal, we adopt it as a proper statement of the issue and the applicable law concerning that issue. It would serve no useful purpose for us to repeat the discussion contained therein." 916 A.2d at 2.

2. *Survival Language—Restatement 2d of Property.* The Restatement 2d of Property stated in 1986:

> §18.6 *Operation of Antilapse Statutes....*
> a. *Rationale.* ... The result provided by the antilapse statute is applicable only if the disposition under the will ... does not manifest an intent that the antilapse statute not apply. Such manifestation of intent is present if the will specifically provides for an alternative taker if the originally designated taker does not survive the decedent whose will is involved. If the will provides that the named beneficiary is to take "if he [or she] survives the testator," this shows the decedent recognized the possibility the named beneficiary might not survive and did not choose to provide an alternative taker. The decision in this situation not to provide an alternative taker eliminates the applicability of the antilapse statute.

3. *Survival Language—Restatement 3d of Property.* The Restatement 3d of Property §5.5 comments h and i provide:

> h. *Contrary intent; survival language.* An often litigated question is whether language requiring the devisee to survive the testator, without more, constitutes a sufficient expression of a contrary intent to defeat the antilapse statute. The majority view is that such language signifies a contrary intent. Because such a survival provision is often boiler-plate form-book language, the testator may not understand that such language could disinherit the line of descent headed by the deceased devisee. When the testator is older than the devisee and hence does not expect the devisee to die first, or if the devisee was childless when the will was executed, it seems especially unlikely that a provision requiring the devisee to survive the testator was intended to disinherit the devisee's descendants....
>
> [T]he courts should be cautious in automatically concluding that survival language manifests a deliberate decision by the testator to disinherit the line of descent headed by a deceased devisee.
>
> i. *Contrary intent; clear, direct, unmistakable statement.* The clearest way of stating a

contrary intent is to do so directly, in language that is understandable to the testator, language that leaves no doubt that the testator considered the possibility of the devisee failing to survive the testator and decided against substituting the devisee's descendants. Language such as "and not to [the devisee's] descendants if [the devisee] fails to survive me" is an unmistakable expression of a contrary intent. If the language occurs in a will drafted by an attorney, the client has the opportunity to approve or disapprove of the result. A blanket provision stating that if any devisee fails to survive the testator, the devised property is "not to pass to the devisee's descendants" is equally clear.

Capable lawyers do not and should not want an antilapse statute to apply to wills they draft. The Restatement 3d suggests that clients would be better served if lawyers used words like "and not to [the devisee's] descendants if [the devisee] fails to survive me" to avoid the antilapse statute.

4. *Uniform Probate Code.* As noted in *Ruotolo*, the UPC addresses the survival-language question explicitly, by providing that survival language does not, in the absence of additional evidence, indicate a contrary intent. See UPC §2-603(b)(3).[22]

UPC §2-603 also establishes rules for determining when the statute's substitute gift takes effect. The statute looks more complex than it really is.

The design of UPC §2-603 is to follow the priorities established by the testator. *First priority* goes to the "primary" devisee. For example, suppose a devise of $10,000 "to son C1 if he survives me; if not, to daughter C2 if she survives me." If the primary devisee, C1, survives the testator (*i.e.*, survives by 120 hours or more), C1 takes. It makes no difference whether C2 survived the testator or not. It also makes no difference whether C1 or C2 had descendants who survived the testator.

Second priority goes to the secondary[23] devisee. If C1 fails to survive the testator (*i.e.*, by 120 hours) but C2 survives the testator, C2 takes. It makes no difference whether C1 or C2 had descendants who survived the testator.

Third priority goes to the descendants of either devisee if both fail to survive the testator but only one leaves descendants who survive the testator. If C1 and C2 fail to survive the testator, and only one of them leaves descendants who survive the testator, those descendants take by representation.

Fourth priority goes to the descendants of the primary devisee if both fail to survive the testator and both leave descendants who survive the testator, except that

---

22. For the opposite approach see Fla. Stat. §§732.603 (devises), 736.1106(3)(a) (future interests under the terms of a trust).

Will UPC §2-603 impose malpractice liability on a lawyer who uses survival language to avoid the antilapse statute? Compare Martin D. Begleiter, Article II of the Uniform Probate Code and the Malpractice Revolution, 59 Tenn. L. Rev. 101, 126-30 (1991), with Edward C. Halbach, Jr. & Lawrence W. Waggoner, The UPC's New Survivorship and Antilapse Provisions, 55 Alb. L. Rev. 1091, 1108 n.62 (1992).

23. The term "secondary" devisee is not used in the statute. The statute treats C1 and C2 as "alternative" devisees.

if the secondary devisee is a descendant of the primary devisee, the priority goes to the descendants of the secondary devisee. If C1 and C2 fail to survive the testator, and both leave descendants who survive the testator, C1's descendants take. (If C2 had been a descendant of C1, C2's descendants would have taken.)

Problems

With the design of UPC §2-603 in mind, consider how the following problems would be resolved under the current UPC. (The cases cited in the footnotes were decided under the original version of the UPC or a non-UPC antilapse statute. They are cited to demonstrate the split of authority that exists under conventional antilapse statutes with respect to most of the problems presented. These splits of authority led the UPC's framers to develop the current §2-603.)

1. Testator's will devised $50,000 "to my sister, Sally." Sally predeceased Testator, leaving a child, Nick, who survived Testator by 120 hours.

    (a) Testator's residuary clause devised "the residue of my estate to X Charity."

    (b) Testator's residuary clause devised "the residue of my estate, including all failed and lapsed devises, to X Charity." [24]

2. Testator had two children, Alex and Betty. Alex survived Testator by 120 hours. Betty predeceased Testator, leaving descendants who survived Testator by 120 hours.

    (a) Testator's will devised $100,000 "to my children."

    (b) Testator's will devised $100,000 "to my surviving children."[25]

    (c) Testator's will devised $100,000 "to my surviving children and not to the descendants of any child who fails to survive me."

3. Testator had two children, Alex and Betty. Alex and Betty predeceased Testator, both leaving descendants who survived Testator by 120 hours. Testator's

---

24. For a case holding that a conventional antilapse statute is counteracted (*i.e.*, X Charity takes the $50,000 devise; Nick takes nothing) by this type of provision, see Estate of Salisbury, 143 Cal. Rptr. 81 (Ct. App. 1978); contra, Blevins v. Moran, 12 S.W.3d 698 (Ky. Ct. App. 2000). Cf. Larson v. Anderson, 167 N.W.2d 640 (Iowa 1969) (antilapse statute counteracted by clause stating that "if any [devisee] die[s] prior to [my death], such gifts shall lapse and become a part of the residue of my estate."); Starkey v. District of Columbia, 377 A.2d 382 (D.C. 1977) (antilapse statute counteracted by clause stating that if "any of the [devisees] do not survive me, then, in that event, his or her devise and bequest shall lapse.").

25. For cases holding that a conventional antilapse statute is counteracted (*i.e.*, C2 takes $100,000; GC1 takes nothing), see Estate of Price, 454 P.2d 411 (Wash. 1969) (6-to-3 decision). Cf. Estate of Fitzpatrick, 406 N.W.2d 483 (Mich. Ct. App. 1987). For cases holding that a conventional antilapse statute is not counteracted (*i.e.*, GC1 takes $50,000; C2 takes $50,000) if A was living when Testator's will was executed, see Henderson v. Parker, 728 S.W.2d 768 (Tex. 1987) (court said: "[W]e read the phrase 'surviving children of this marriage' to mean children 'surviving' at the time the will was executed."). Accord Restatement 2d of Property §27.2 comment f illustration 5. Cf. id. §27.1 comment e illustration 6.

will made two nonresiduary devises:

(a) $50,000 "to my son, Alex, if he survives me; if not, to my daughter, Betty."

(b) $75,000 "to my daughter, Betty, if she survives me; if not, to my son Alex."

4. Testator had one child, Carl. Carl had two children, Mary and Ned. Mary was married and had three children. Ned was married and had two children. Carl and Ned predeceased Testator. All of the others survived Testator by 120 hours, i.e., Mary, Mary's husband, Mary's children, Ned's widow, and Ned's children.

(a) Testator's will devised $50,000 "to my son, Carl, if he survives me; if not, to Carl's children."

(b) Testator's will made the following two pecuniary devises:

(1) "$25,000 to my son Carl, if he survives me; if not, to Carl's daughter, Mary."

(2) "$25,000 to my son Carl, if he survives me; if not, to Carl's son, Ned."

(c) Testator's will devised $50,000 "to my son, Carl, if he survives me; if not, to Carl's children, Mary and Ned."

———

EXTERNAL REFERENCES. The scope and rationale of §2-603 are explained in Edward C. Halbach, Jr. & Lawrence W. Waggoner, The UPC's New Survivorship and Antilapse Provisions, 55 Alb. L. Rev. 1091 (1992). The section is debated in Mark L. Ascher, The 1990 Uniform Probate Code: Older and Better, or More Like the Internal Revenue Code?, 77 Minn. L. Rev. 639 (1993) (sharply critical); Mary L. Fellows, Traveling the Road to Probate Reform: Finding the Way to Your Will (A Response to Professor Ascher), 77 Minn. L. Rev. 659 (1993). See also Adam J. Hirsch, When Beneficiaries Predecease: An Empirical Analysis, 72 Emory L.J. 307 (2022).

Chapter 7

Revocable Trusts and Other Will Substitutes

As noted in Chapter 1, will substitutes are increasingly important in the deathtime transmission of wealth. A "pure" will substitute allows the donor to retain lifetime enjoyment of, and control over, the asset while designating another person to receive future possession. Life insurance, pension accounts, joint accounts, and revocable trusts fit this mold and are widely used. Joint tenancies also count as will substitutes, because they provide for a right of survivorship. They are not pure will substitutes, however. The right to sever does not operate as a power to revoke; it does not allow a joint tenant to regain his or her contribution toward the property's acquisition.[1] Instead, the right to sever merely allows a joint tenant to convert the joint tenancy into tenancy in common, destroying the right of survivorship.[2]

Will substitutes function to pass property at death without being subject to the statutory formalities required for wills. Also, although the affected property passes at death, it passes outside of probate. Will substitutes are sometimes referred to as probate-avoidance devices, or as nonprobate wills. They do not, of course, eliminate the desirability of having a will. Will substitutes tend to be asset-specific, so a will remains necessary for the decedent's other property. Also, a will is helpful as a back-stop even for property affected by a will substitute, in case the decedent outlives the designated beneficiary.

Because of their will-like characteristics, will substitutes have been exerting increasing pressure on the law of succession. If will substitutes are not wills for purposes of the statutory formalities, are they wills for other purposes, such as the law of lapse or the revocation of wills by changed circumstances such as divorce? There is no necessary reason why they cannot be treated as wills for some purposes but not for others. As we shall see, the law of succession is tending in the direction of a unification of its testamentary and nontestamentary branches. In particular, the UPC and the Restatement 3d of Property include rules that extend the subsidiary law of wills to various nonprobate arrangements.

---

1. But see, e.g., Blanchette v. Blanchette, 287 N.E.2d 459 (Mass. 1972) (joint tenancy unscrambled because husband, who bought AT&T stock in joint tenancy with his then wife under an employee stock-purchase plan, established that he had not created the joint tenancy with donative intent).

2. See Powell on Real Property §51.04; Cal. Civ. Code §683.2.

PART A. VALIDITY OF WILL SUBSTITUTES— FORM OVER SUBSTANCE

Primary Statutory References: *UPC §§6-101, 6-102*

Restatement 3d of Property

§7.1 Will Substitutes—Definition and Validity.

(a) A will substitute is an arrangement respecting property or contract rights that is established during the donor's life under which (1) the right to possession or enjoyment of the property or to a contractual payment shifts outside of probate to the donee at the donor's death; and (2) substantial lifetime rights of dominion, control, possession, or enjoyment are retained by the donor.

(b) To be valid, a will substitute need not be executed in compliance with the statutory formalities required for a will.

1. Revocable Trusts—The Present Transfer Test

Primary Statutory References: *UTC §§406, 601-604*

Property law recognizes the validity of a revocable inter vivos trust, even one in which the person creating the trust (called the "settlor") retains the right to income for life. It does so on the basis of the so-called "present transfer" test: *Upon creation of the trust*, the settlor transfers an equitable remainder interest in the trust property ("corpus") to the remainder beneficiary. The fact that the remainder interest is subject to divestment does not jeopardize the validity of the trust. A present transfer of a remainder interest—even one subject to divestment by the settlor's exercise of the power to revoke—satisfies the present transfer test and obviates the necessity of memorializing the trust in a document that is executed in accordance with the formalities for a valid will. The transfer is treated as inter vivos, not testamentary. See Restatement 3d of Property §7.1 comment b.

The present transfer test was critiqued in John H. Langbein, The Nonprobate Revolution and the Future of the Law of Succession, 97 Harv. L. Rev. 1108, 1128 (1984):

> The odor of legal fiction hangs heavily over the present-[transfer] test. We see courts straining to reach right results for wrong reasons and insisting that will-like transfers possess gift-like incidents. Courts have used such doctrinal ruses to validate not only the revocable inter vivos trust, but other will substitutes as well.... What is the difference between the revocable and ambulatory interest created by a will, and a vested but defeasible interest in life insurance or pension proceeds? None at all, except for the form of words.

Compare the following two cases, Mathias v. Fantine and Farkas v. Williams. Which was rightly decided, and why?

Mathias v. Fantine

1990 WL 21446 (Ohio App. 5 Dist.)

MILLIGAN, P[residing].J. The administrator of the estate of Lawrence H. Mathias, deceased, sought judgment from the Tuscarawas County Common Pleas Court, Probate Division, declaring (1) decedent's trust instrument titled "Declaration of Trust" void ab initio because the grantor, trustee, and beneficiary are one in the same person.... The court granted plaintiff's motion for summary judgment finding the "Trust instrument and its Addenda" void and ineffective....

The "Declaration Of Trust" [provided]:

I, Lawrence H. Mathias, aka L.H. Mathias of R.D. # 1 Dover, Ohio, (called Grantor), hereby transfer the property described in schedule "A" attached hereto to the Lawrence H. Mathias Trust of Dover, Ohio in trust to hold such securities, real estate, and all substitutions thereof and additions thereto for my benefit during my lifetime and thereafter for the benefit of others as follows:

Article I. Distribution During Grantor's Lifetime

1. During the life of the Grantor the Trustee (whether the Grantor or otherwise) shall distribute the net income from the Trust property to the Grantor, in at least quarterly installments or in such other installments as he may request, or make expenditures therefrom on behalf of Grantor.

2. In addition thereto the Trustee (whether Grantor or otherwise) is authorized from time to time to distribute to the Grantor, or make expenditures therefrom on his behalf, such portion of the principal of the Trust property as when added to his available income from this and all other sources, shall in the judgment of the Trustee be necessary or proper to provide for his maintenance, health, comfort, care and support.

3. Any unpaid income may be added to principal from time to time....

Article IV. Trustee

1. I hereby appoint myself, Lawrence H. Mathias as Trustee....

A trust is a fiduciary relationship in which one person holds a property interest subject to an equitable obligation to keep or use that interest for a benefit of another. In creating the trust, there must be a declaration of trust, accompanied with an intention to create a trust, followed by an actual conveyance or transfer of property.

Classification of an express trust traditionally hinges upon whether the beneficiary's interest in the trust vests during the lifetime of the settlor or after his death. There are two classifications: an inter vivos trust and a testamentary trust.

An inter vivos trust, also called a living trust, is created during the settlor's lifetime and exists at the time of the settlor's demise. A testamentary trust is created by a will and comes into existence after the settlor's death.....

The bedrock element of a valid express trust is the separate coexistence of the legal estate and the equitable estate. Where both the legal and equitable interests are in the same person, a merger is created rendering the attempted trust invalid and conferring a fee simple in the person holding both interests.

In the case sub judice, the trial court found that Article I did create a merger of interests in Lawrence H. Mathias making the "declaration of trust" void ab initio....

...[W]here the owner of property purports to create a trust inter vivos but no interest passes to the beneficiary before the death of the settlor, the intended trust is testamentary in character and is invalid unless there is compliance with the statute relating to wills.

Here, no interest passed during "Grantor's" lifetime. The merging of legal and equitable title in "Grantor" defeated the attempted trust and conferred a fee simple of the corpus in "Grantor." The testamentary provisions are invalid for failure to comply with the statute of wills....

SMART, and GWIN, JJ., concur.

Farkas v. Williams
125 N.E.2d 600 (Ill. 1955)

HERSHEY, J. This is an appeal from a decision of the Appellate Court, First District, which affirmed a decree of the circuit court of Cook County finding that certain declarations of trust executed by Albert B. Farkas and naming Richard J. Williams as beneficiary were invalid and that Regina Farkas and Victor Farkas, as coadministrators of the estate of said Albert B. Farkas, were the owners of the property referred to in said trust instruments, being certain shares of capital stock of Investors Mutual, Inc. ....

Albert B. Farkas died intestate at the age of sixty-seven years, a resident of Chicago, leaving as his only heirs-at-law brothers, sisters, a nephew and a niece. Although retired at the time of his death, he had for many years practiced veterinary medicine and operated a veterinarian establishment in Chicago. During a considerable portion of that time, he employed the defendant Williams, who was not related to him.

On four occasions (December 8, 1948; February 7, 1949; February 14, 1950; and March 1, 1950) Farkas purchased stock of Investors Mutual, Inc. At the time of each purchase he executed a written application to Investors Mutuals, Inc., instructing them to issue the stock in his name "as trustee for Richard J. Williams." Investors Mutual, Inc., by its agent, accepted each of these applications in writing by signature on the face of the application. Coincident with the execution of these applications, Farkas signed separate declarations of trust, all of which were identical except as to dates. The terms of said trust instruments are as follows:

> "Declaration of Trust-Revocable. I, the undersigned, having purchased or declared my intention to purchase certain shares of capital stock of Investors Mutual, Inc. (the Company), and having directed that the certificate for said stock be issued in my name as trustee for Richard J. Williams as beneficiary, whose address is 1704 W. North Ave. Chicago, Ill., under this Declaration of Trust Do Hereby Declare that the terms and conditions upon which I shall hold said stock in trust and any additional stock resulting

from reinvestments of cash dividends upon such original or additional shares are as follows:

"(1) During my lifetime all cash dividends are to be paid to me individually for my own personal account and use....

"(2) Upon my death the title to any stock subject hereto and the right to any subsequent payments or distributions shall be vested absolutely in the beneficiary....

"(3) During my lifetime I reserve the right, as trustee, to vote, sell, redeem, exchange or otherwise deal in or with the stock subject hereto, but upon any sale or redemption of said stock or any part thereof, the trust hereby declared shall terminate as to the stock sold or redeemed, and I shall be entitled to retain the proceeds of sale or redemption for my own personal account and use.

"(4) I reserve the right at any time to change the beneficiary or revoke this trust, but it is understood that no change of beneficiary and no revocation of this trust except by death of the beneficiary, shall be effective as to the Company for any purpose unless and until written notice thereof in such form as the Company shall prescribe is delivered to the Company at Minneapolis, Minnesota. The decease of the beneficiary before my death shall operate as a revocation of this trust.

"(5) In the event this trust shall be revoked or otherwise terminated, said stock and all rights and privileges thereunder shall belong to and be exercised by me in my individual capacity...."

It is conceded that the instruments were not executed in such a way as to satisfy the requirements of the statute on wills; hence, our inquiry is limited to whether said trust instruments created valid inter vivos trusts effective to give the purported beneficiary, Williams, title to the stock in question after the death of the settlor-trustee, Farkas....

If no interest passed to Williams before the death of Farkas, the intended trusts are testamentary and hence invalid for failure to comply with the statute on wills.

But considering the terms of these instruments we believe Farkas did intend to presently give Williams an interest in the property referred to. For it may be said, at the very least, that upon his executing one of these instruments, he showed an intention to presently part with some of the incidents of ownership in the stock. Immediately after the execution of each of these instruments, he could not deal with the stock therein referred to the same as if he owned the property absolutely, but only in accordance with the terms of the instrument.... Thus assuming to act as trustee, he is held to have intended to take on those obligations which are expressly set out in the instrument, as well as those fiduciary obligations implied by law. In addition, he manifested an intention to bind himself to having this property pass upon his death to Williams, unless he changed the beneficiary or revoked the trust, and then such change of beneficiary or revocation was not to be effective as to Investors Mutual, Inc., unless and until written notice thereof in such form as the company prescribed was delivered to them at Minneapolis, Minnesota. An absolute owner can dispose of his property, either in his lifetime or by will, in any way he sees fit without notifying or securing approval from anyone and without being held to the duties of a fiduciary in so doing.

It seems to follow that what incidents of ownership Farkas intended to relinquish, in a sense he intended Williams to acquire. That is, Williams was to be the beneficiary to whom Farkas was to be obligated, and unless Farkas revoked the instrument in the manner therein set out or the instrument was otherwise terminated in a manner therein provided for, upon Farkas's death Williams was to become absolute owner of the turst property. It is difficult to name this interest of Williams, nor is there any reason for so doing so long as it passed to him immediately upon the creation of the trust....

For the reasons stated, we conclude that these trust declarations executed by Farkas constituted valid inter vivos trusts and were not attempted testamentary dispositions. It must be conceded that they have, in the words of Mr. Justice Holmes in *Bromley v. Mitchell*, 155 Mass. 509, 30 N.E. 83, a "Testamentary look." Moreover, it must be admitted that the line should be drawn somewhere, but after a study of this case we do not believe that point has here been reached.

The judgment of the Appellate Court affirming the decree of the circuit court of Cook County is reversed, and the cause is remanded to the circuit court of Cook County, with directions to enter a decree in favor of the defendants.

Notes and Question

1. *Aftermath of Mathias v. Fantine.* After the decision in *Mathias*, the Ohio General Assembly enacted Ohio Rev. Code §1335.01(C) (now renumbered as §5804.02(E) with substantially similar wording):

> A trust is not invalid because a person, including but not limited to, the creator of the trust, is or may become the sole trustee and the sole holder of the present beneficial enjoyment of the corpus of the trust, provided that one or more other persons hold a vested, contingent, or expectant interest relative to the enjoyment of the corpus of the trust upon the cessation of the present beneficial enjoyment. A merger of the legal and equitable titles to the corpus of such a trust shall not be considered as occurring in its creator, and, notwithstanding any contrary provision of Chapter 2107 of the Revised Code, the trust shall not be considered to be a testamentary trust that must comply with that chapter in order for its corpus to be legally distributed to other beneficiaries in accordance with the provisions of the trust upon the cessation of the present beneficial enjoyment.

2. *Validity of Revocable, Self-Declared Trusts.* The trusts in *Mathias* and *Farkas* were self-declared. A self-declared trust is a trust in which the *settlor* acts as trustee. Typically, the settlor declares himself or herself trustee for the benefit of himself or herself for life, remainder at the settlor's death to the settlor's chosen beneficiaries. Because a self-declared trust involves no transfer of title to a third-party trustee, a self-declared trust might seem to present special difficulties under the present-transfer test. See *Mathias*. The clear weight of the authorities, however, is aligned

with *Farkas* and in favor of validity as an inter vivos transaction. The transfer that satisfies the present transfer test is the transfer of the equitable remainder interest to the beneficiary who is scheduled to take in possession or enjoyment at the settlor's death. See Restatement 2d of Trusts §57 comment h.

3. *Liability for Breach of Fiduciary Duties or Implied Amendment?* Suppose that Farkas breached his fiduciary duties in the administration of the trust. Would he or his estate be liable, or would the breach of fiduciary duties be regarded as an implied exercise of the settlor's power of amendment? See UTC §603(b). See also Moon v. Lesikar, 230 S.W.3d 800 (Tex. App. 2007), holding that a trust beneficiary has no standing to challenge the trustee's actions while the settlor has the power to revoke the trust.

4. *Mental Capacity Required for Creating a Trust.* The Restatement 3d of Trusts provides:

§11. Capacity of Settlor to Create a Trust.

(1) A person has capacity to create a trust by will to the same extent that the person has capacity to devise or bequeath the property free of trust.

(2) A person has capacity to create a revocable inter vivos trust by transfer to another or by declaration to the same extent that the person has capacity to create a trust by will.

(3) A person has capacity to create an irrevocable inter vivos trust by transfer to another or by declaration to the same extent that the person has capacity to transfer the property inter vivos free of trust in similar circumstances.

Accord, UTC §601; Restatement 3d of Property §8.1.

5. *Undue Influence, Duress, Fraud.* A trust is void to the extent that its creation was induced by undue influence, duress, or fraud. See Restatement 3d of Trusts §12; UTC §406; Restatement 3d of Property §8.3.

————

Rights of the Grantor's Surviving Spouse. In some jurisdictions, the grantor's surviving spouse may claim an elective share in the assets of a revocable trust. This subject is addressed in Chapter 8.

Rights of the Grantor's Creditors and Creditors of the Grantor's Estate. If a grantor transfers assets to a trust in fraud of his or her creditors, the grantor's creditors can set the transfer aside to the extent necessary to satisfy the indebtedness, whether the indebtedness arose before or after the transfer. Restatement 2d of Property §34.3; Unif. Fraudulent Transfer Act (1984); Unif. Voidable Transactions Act (2014). A transfer in fraud of creditors is one made with actual intent to hinder, delay, or defraud a creditor or one that leaves the grantor's remaining assets insufficient to satisfy current debts or debts the grantor intended to incur. A transfer to a trust that is in fraud of creditors can be set aside under the "fraudulent transfer" principle, whether the trust is revocable or irrevocable.

If the transfer to a *revocable* trust was *not* in fraud of creditors, can the grantor's creditors nevertheless satisfy an indebtedness out of the trust assets on the ground of the revocability of the trust? The traditional view was that the unexercised power to revoke is not property and therefore cannot be reached by the grantor's creditors. See Restatement 2d of Trusts §330 comment o.

The UTC, UPC, Restatement 3d of Trusts, and several decisions have broken away from the traditional position and allow the grantor's creditors to reach assets in a revocable trust, even though the transfer to the trust was not in fraud of creditors. See UTC §505 (applies to lifetime and estate creditors); UPC §6-102 (only applies to estate creditors); Restatement 3d of Trusts §25 comment e (applies to lifetime and estate creditors); State Street Bank & Trust Co. v. Reiser, 389 N.E.2d 768 (Mass. App. 1979); Estate of Kovalyshyn, 343 A.2d 852 (Hudson Co., N.J., 1975); Johnson v. Commercial Bank, 588 P.2d 1096 (Or. 1978); see also Restatement 3d of Property §7.2 comment b. The cases cited all involved creditors' claims to the grantor's estate, but the holdings would seem to apply also to creditors' suits brought during the grantor's lifetime. For a discussion of UPC §6-102 and how it might be improved, see Elaine H. Gagliardi, Remembering the Creditor at Death: Aligning Probate and Nonprobate Transfers, 41 Real Prop., Prob. & Tr. J. 819 (2007).

Several states have enacted statutes that allow the grantor's estate and lifetime creditors to reach assets of a revocable trust.[3] The federal Bankruptcy Code, adopted in 1978, is less clear than its predecessor on whether the grantor's bankruptcy trustee can reach a revocable trust. If the Bankruptcy Code addresses the question at all, it is by negative implication in the following provision:

> *Bankruptcy Code, 11 U.S.C. §541. Property of the Estate:*... (b) Property of the estate does not include... any power that the debtor may exercise solely for the benefit of an entity other than the debtor....

No provision explicitly declares that "property of the estate" *includes* property over which the debtor retains a power exercisable for the debtor's own benefit, such as a power of revocation.

Federal Taxation of Revocable Trusts: Substance Over Form. The federal system of income, estate, and gift taxation taxes revocable trusts according to their substance, not their form, as illustrated by the following example:

> *Example 8.1:* G transferred property to T, in trust, directing the trustee to pay the net income from the property to G for life and at G's death to deliver the trust corpus to X. G retained a power to revoke the trust.

---

3. See, e.g., Cal. Prob. Code §§18200-18201; Mich. Comp. Laws §556.128; Mo. Rev. Stat. §461.071 (see Committee Report, Rights of Creditors to Reach Assets of a Revocable Trust After the Death of the Grantor—The Missouri Approach, 20 Real Prop., Prob. & Tr. J. 1189 (1985)).

The tax consequences of G's transfer are as follows:

(1) Gift tax consequences: Because of his power to revoke, G's transfer of a remainder interest to X was not a taxable gift. See Treas. Reg. §25.2511-2(c).

(2) Income tax consequences: G will continue until his death to be taxed on both the ordinary income generated by the property and also on capital gains (or losses) realized by the trust. See IRC §§676, 677(a)(1); Treas. Reg. §1.671-3(b).

(3) Estate tax consequences: When G dies, the full value of the corpus of the trust will be included in G's gross estate under IRC §2036(a)(1) or §2038.

———

Marketing Revocable Trusts: Consumer Fraud and the Unauthorized Practice of Law. The self-declared revocable trust has become enormously popular. Part of the reason for its popularity is the way that it has been marketed. Beginning with the 1965 best-selling book by Norman Dacey, *How to Avoid Probate!*, non-attorneys have aggressively promoted the use of revocable trusts through a variety of media, including newspaper ads, telephone solicitations, and hotel "seminars." The promoters, sometimes called "trust mills," push standard-form inter vivos trust instruments (usually termed "living trusts") on targeted segments of the population, especially the elderly. These activities raise a number of potential legal problems, including consumer fraud and the unauthorized practice of law. See, e.g., Cleveland Bar Ass'n v. Sharp Estate Services, Inc., 837 N.E.2d 1183 (Ohio 2005) (trust mill permanently enjoined from marketing living trusts in Ohio and fined $1,027,260); Martha Neil, Court Fines 2 Cos. $6.4M for Unauthorized Law Practice, ABA J., Oct. 14, 2009 (reporting that the Ohio Supreme Court fined two "trust mill" companies $6,387,990 and banned them from doing business in the state).

A growing number of consumer fraud cases have been filed against trust mills. State attorneys general in at least ten states have charged promoters with deceptive sales practices, such as telling customers that revocable trusts are immune from creditor claims and income taxes. Another common practice is marketing standardized trust forms without informing customers that the terms may not meet their individual needs or interests. State legislatures are also cracking down on trust mills. For example, a Florida statute requires revocable inter vivos trusts to be executed in accordance with the formalities of a will, an Illinois statute prohibits the "assembly, drafting, execution, and funding" of an inter vivos trust by anyone other than a lawyer or an institutional trustee, and an Oregon statute prohibits, with very narrow exceptions, the preparation of a living trust by a non-lawyer.[4]

---

4. See Fla. Stat. §736.0403; Ill. Comp. Stat. ch. 815, §505/2BB; Or. Rev. Stat. §128.001. The Florida statute provides that "[t]he testamentary aspects of a revocable trust... are invalid unless the trust instrument is executed by the settlor with the formalities required for the execution of a will." The term "testamentary aspects" is defined as "those provisions of the trust instrument that dispose of the trust property on or after the death of the settlor other than to the settlor's estate."

External Reference. ACTEC Practice Committee, State and Local Action Against Trust Mills: The Unauthorized Practice of Law, 27 ACTEC J. 162 (2001).

2. Other Will Substitutes—The Present Transfer Test

Primary Statutory References: *UPC §§6-101, 6-203, 6-211 to 6-214*

The present transfer test is widely used to validate many will substitutes, not only revocable trusts. Though wills in substance, transfers that can be characterized as having presently passed to a donee any *interest in property*, whether present or future, vested or contingent, are treated as inter vivos, not testamentary, and their validity does not depend upon compliance with the execution formalities required of wills. Likewise, transfers that can be characterized as presently conferring a *contract right* on another are exempted from the statutory formalities for wills, even though the time of performance of the contract is geared to the time of the transferor's death. One such contract is a contract for life insurance.

Wilhoit v. Peoples Life Insurance Co.
218 F.2d 887 (7th Cir. 1955)

Major, Circuit Judge. The plaintiff, Robert Wilhoit, instituted this action against the defendants, Peoples Life Insurance Company (sometimes referred to as the company) and Thomas J. Owens, for the recovery of money held by the company. Roley Oscar Wilhoit was the insured and Sarah Louise Wilhoit, his wife, the beneficiary in a life insurance policy in the amount of $5,000, issued by Century Life Insurance Company and later reinsured in Peoples Life Insurance Company of Frankfort, Indiana. Mr. Wilhoit died prior to October 22, 1930 (the exact date not disclosed by the record), without having changed the beneficiary designated in the policy, and the proceeds thereof became due and payable to Mrs. Wilhoit. The amount due was paid to her and the policy surrendered....

On November 14, 1930, Mrs. Wilhoit (twenty-three days after she had acknowledged receipt of the amount due her under the policy) from her home in Indiana signed and addressed a letter to the company in the same State, which in material parts reads as follows:

> I hereby acknowledge receipt of settlement in full under Policy No. C172 terminated by the death of Roley O. Wilhoit, the Insured, and I direct that the proceeds of $4,749.00 be held in trust by the Peoples Life Insurance Company under the following conditions:
>
> (1) Said amount or any part thereof (not less than $100.00) to be subject to withdrawal on demand of the undersigned.
>
> (2) While on deposit, said amount or part thereof shall earn interest at the rate of 3½%, compounded annually, plus any excess interest authorized by the Board of Directors of the Company. Interest may be withdrawn at the end of each six months period or whenever the principal of the fund is withdrawn or may be allowed to accumulate compounded annually. Interest on this trust fund shall begin as of October 9th, 1930.

(3) In the event of my death, while any part of this trust fund is still in existence, the full amount, plus any accrued interest, shall be immediately payable to Robert G. Owens (Relationship) Brother.

The proposal contained in this letter was, on November 17, 1930, accepted by the company....

Robert G. Owens, a brother of Mrs. Wilhoit and the person mentioned in her November 14 letter to the company, died January 23, 1932, and Mrs. Wilhoit died April 12, 1951, each leaving a last will and testament. The will of the former by a general clause devised all his property to Thomas J. Owens, a defendant, and was admitted to probate in Marion County, Indiana. The will of Mrs. Wilhoit was admitted to probate in Edgar County, Illinois, and contained the following provision:

> I now have the sum of Four Thousand Seven Hundred Forty Nine Dollars ($4,749.00), or approximately that amount, which is the proceeds of an insurance policy on the life of my deceased husband, Oscar Wilhoit, on deposit with the insurance company, the Peoples Life Insurance Company of Frankfort, Indiana. This I give and bequeath to Robert Wilhoit, now of Seattle, Washington, who is another son of my said stepson, the same to be his property absolutely....

The fund in controversy, deposited with the company by Mrs. Wilhoit on November 17, 1930, remained with the company continuously until the date of her death, April 12, 1951. The company refused to recognize the claim to the fund made by the executor of her estate. Thereupon, the executor assigned his interest to Robert Wilhoit, the legatee named in the will of Mrs. Wilhoit and the plaintiff in the instant action....

...[P]laintiff argues, in support of the judgment [in the lower court], that the disposition of the fund is not controlled by the law of insurance because the agreement between Mrs. Wilhoit and the company was not an insurance contract or a supplement thereto but was nothing more than a contract of deposit, and that the provision in the agreement by which Robert G. Owens was to take the funds in the event of her death was an invalid testamentary disposition....

...[W]e have reached the conclusion that ... the arrangement between the parties was the result of a separate and independent agreement, unrelated to the terms of the policy....

...Mrs. Wilhoit deposited her money with the company, which obligated itself to pay interest and return the principal to her on demand. Only "in the event of her death" was the deposit, if it still remained, payable to Robert G. Owens. If Mrs. Wilhoit had deposited her money with a bank rather than with the insurance company under the same form of agreement, we think that it would have constituted an ineffectual disposition because of failure to comply with the Indiana statute of wills....

The judgment of the District Court is affirmed.

Notes

1. *Life Insurance as a Will Substitute.* Compliance with the statutory formalities for wills is not required of beneficiary designations of life insurance policies. Although life insurance contracts pay out at death, the beneficiary designation—when made—is treated as conferring a present contract right on the beneficiary. The will-like characteristics of life insurance can, therefore, be ignored, among which are the retained lifetime right of the owner of the policy (who typically is the person whose life is insured by the policy) to terminate the policy or to revoke the beneficiary designation and name a different beneficiary.

An additional will-like characteristic of life insurance is the requirement that the beneficiary must survive the insured in order to be entitled to the policy's proceeds. The requirement of survival is contained in the printed terms of all life insurance policies. Non-UPC antilapse statutes do not cover life insurance beneficiary designations. The current UPC broke new ground by adopting an antilapse statute for life insurance (UPC §2-706), but the life insurance industry, spearheaded by the American Council of Life Insurance (ACLI), the industry's trade association with paid lobbyists in every state, has mounted a well-funded lobbying effort to defeat the provision where it has been introduced.

In many states, due again to effective industry lobbying, the proceeds of life insurance policies are wholly or partly exempt from the claims of the insured's creditors. The statutes vary, and may only apply if the proceeds are payable to specified members of the insured's family.

2. *Life Insurance Trusts.* A popular estate planning technique is to establish a life insurance trust. Life insurance trusts take different forms. One type of life insurance trust is created by irrevocably transferring the full ownership of the policy to the trustee. Estate planners refer to irrevocable life insurance trusts as ILITs. ILITs are tax motivated—that is, the arrangement is designed to avoid the inclusion of the value of the proceeds of the policy in the insured's gross estate under IRC §2042. Trusts of this sort are sometimes "funded"—that is, other assets are irrevocably transferred to the trustee, in addition to the life insurance policy, with directions to the trustee to pay the life insurance premiums out of the income generated by the other assets. If the trust is not "funded," the grantor of the trust (the previous owner of the policy and the insured) usually continues to pay the premiums on the policy out of his or her own pocket.

A second type of life insurance trust is created by naming the trustee as the beneficiary of the life insurance policy, with directions to the trustee to collect the proceeds on the insured's death and carry out the terms of the trust. Trusts of this sort typically are revocable and hence are not tax motivated. Rather, the motive usually is the administrative convenience of having insurance proceeds added at death to an existing inter vivos trust. Not only is the trust itself revocable, but so is the designation of the trustee as the beneficiary of the policy. The insured, as owner of the policy, retains the right to renounce the beneficiary designation, to terminate the policy, to surrender the policy for its cash value, if any, and so on. Although the validity of this type of trust was at one time in doubt, it is now settled that this type of arrangement creates a valid trust. See Gordon v. Portland Trust Bank, 271 P.2d 653 (Or. 1954); Gurnett v. Mutual Life Insurance Co., 191 N.E. 250 (Ill. 1934).

3. *Does the Trustee Have an Insurable Interest in the Settlor's Life?* Insurance law requires that the purchaser of a life insurance policy have an insurable interest in the life of the insured. The insured always is regarded as having an insurable interest in his or her own life. The great majority (but not universal) rule is that a policy purchased by one who has an insurable interest can designate a beneficiary who has no insurable interest or can assign ownership of the policy to an assignee who has no insurable interest.

A problem that has surfaced is whether a *trustee* has an insurable interest in the settlor's life. Inter vivos trusts commonly authorize the trustee to purchase life insurance on the life of the settlor. Such a device has tax advantages if the insured dies within three years. To obtain the tax advantages, however, the trustee must purchase the life insurance policy; the tax advantages do not arise if the settlor purchases the life insurance policy and then assigns ownership of the policy to the trustee within three years of death. See Douglas A. Kahn & Lawrence W. Waggoner, Tax Consequences of Assigning Life Insurance—Time for Another Look, 4 Fla. Tax Rev. 381 (1999).

In Chawla, Trustee v. Occidental Life Ins. Co., 2005 WL 405405 (E.D. Va. 2005),[5] the court, applying Maryland law, held, among other things, that a trustee has no insurable interest in the settlor's life. That part of the district court's ruling was vacated as unnecessary by the Fourth Circuit in Chawla v. Transamerica Occidental Life Ins. Co., 440 F.3d 639 (2006). Still, the ruling inserted an uncertainty into the estate planning strategy, previously thought routine, of authorizing the trustee to purchase the policy. The Uniform Law Commission responded by approving curative legislation in the form of an amendment to the Uniform Trust Code, clarifying that a trustee has an insurable interest in the life of the settlor. See UTC §113.

———

We now consider other forms of will substitutes, focusing on the following: pension plan accounts; multiple party and pay on death (POD) accounts; joint tenancies and tenancies by the entirety; and the transfer on death (TOD) registration of securities and land.

---

5. The *Chawla* case is discussed in Mary Ann Mancini, The *Chawla* Case, Insurance Trusts and the Insurable Interest Rule: "Houston, We Have a Problem," 31 ACTEC J. 125 (2005).

Pension Plan Accounts. The first formal pension plan in the United States was established in 1875 by the American Express Company. But it was not until the second half of the twentieth century that the U.S. saw significant growth in the number of workers covered by pension plans, due in part to pressure from labor unions for such plans to be offered and in part by favorable federal tax treatment of pension and retirement savings. In the current era, pension plan participation is widespread, though far from universal. A recent study estimates that approximately 52.3 percent of U.S. workers are covered by a workplace retirement plan. See John Sabelhaus, The Current State of U.S. Workplace Retirement Plan Coverage, Wharton School Pension Research Council Working Paper (March 2022). Some employer-sponsored plans are so-called "defined benefit" plans, which entitle the participant to a benefit at retirement according to a predetermined formula, for example an annual income in retirement that is equal to the person's average salary while working multiplied by the number of years of employment with the company. Today, however, most employer-sponsored pension plans are not "defined benefit" plans. Instead, they are "defined contribution" plans, wherein the employer makes a specified contribution each pay period to the employee's pension account (in many instances, the employee also contributes), and then the funds available at retirement are determined by the investment performance of the account, with the investment choices under the employee's control. In a defined contribution plan, the risk of poor investment performance rests wholly on the employee. A common example of a defined contribution plan is the so-called "401(k) plan"—in which the employee can elect to make pre-tax contributions each pay period to the pension account. The 401(k) plan is named for the section of the Internal Revenue Code authorizing it.

In addition to employer-sponsored plans, there are also other vehicles for retirement savings, including individual plans (e.g., Keogh plans for self-employed individuals, farmers, and other professionals) and individual retirement accounts (IRAs). At the end of the first quarter of 2023, according to data from the Investment Company Institute (www.ici.org), IRAs held approximately $12.5 trillion, and private sector employer-sponsored plans held approximately $13.0 trillion. With such wealth in pensions and retirement accounts, understanding these vehicles for wealth transmission is crucial for the estate planner. Federal law authorizes the owner of each of these types of funds to designate beneficiaries to receive the (remaining) asset at the owner's death.

Multiple Party and Pay on Death (POD) Accounts. Bank and other financial intermediary accounts frequently are registered in the names of more than one person. These accounts generally take one of four forms: joint accounts, trust accounts (so-called "Totten" trusts), payable on death (POD) accounts, or agency accounts. These forms themselves are ambiguous concerning the depositor's substantive purpose. The depositor may intend to confer on the other party beneficial lifetime rights or survivorship rights or both. For example, if Alice deposits funds in a savings account registered jointly in the names of "Alice or Bill," Alice may have used the joint form for any one of three different purposes: (1) to give Alice and Bill lifetime rights to withdraw funds for their personal benefit, with the survivor receiving funds remaining in the account upon the death of the first to die (a true joint tenancy); (2) to give Bill the legal power to draw from the account for Alice's benefit but not Bill's and no survivorship right (an agency account, in which Bill acts as Alice's agent); or (3) to give Bill the right to any funds remaining in the account at Alice's death, but no lifetime rights or powers (the equivalent of a Totten trust or a payable on death account).

Totten trusts. The Totten trust is created when a person deposits his or her funds in a savings or bank account in his or her name "in trust for" another person. The depositor typically retains exclusive control of the account until death, when any remaining funds pass to the beneficiary. Totten trusts have been called the "poor person's will," but as Professor Friedman has observed, "It would be more accurate to call it a middle-class will." Lawrence M. Friedman, The Law of the Living, The Law of the Dead: Property, Succession, and Society, 1966 Wis. L. Rev. 340, 369 (1966). Totten trusts usually are created without legal advice, specifically for the purpose of bypassing probate. They are functionally equivalent to a will in every respect; only form distinguishes them from wills.

The Totten trust takes its name from the leading New York case validating the arrangement, Matter of Totten, 71 N.E. 748 (N.Y. 1904).

The Totten trust has been accepted in a substantial number of states besides New York. See, e.g., Brucks v. Home Federal Saving & Loan Association, 228 P.2d 545 (Cal. 1951); Seymour v. Seymour, 85 So.2d 726 (Fla. 1956); Estate of Petralia, 204 N.E.2d 1 (Ill. 1965); Estate of Morton, 769 P.2d 616 (Kan. 1987); Estate of McFetridge, 372 A.2d 823 (Pa. 1977); Reynolds v. Shambeau, 437 A.2d 1101 (Vt. 1981). Totten trusts have been validated by statute in several states. In some jurisdictions, however, the question is still open. The Restatement 3d of Trusts §26 and the Restatement 3d of Property §7.1 comment i recognize the validity of Totten trusts. One case upholds the trust but treats it as irrevocable. See Cazallis v. Ingraham, 110 A. 359 (Me. 1920).

Courts have held that creditors of the depositor can reach the deposit to satisfy their claims, both while the depositor is living, see Workmen's Compensation Board v. Furman, 106 N.Y.S.2d 404 (Sup. Ct. 1951), and after his or her death, see, e.g., Reich's Estate, 262 N.Y.S. 623 (Sur. Ct. 1933). Where the beneficiary dies before the depositor, it has been held that the trust "terminated ipso facto, and that the funds on deposit thereafter remained the sole property of the depositor, unimpressed by any trust...." See In re United States Trust Co., 102 N.Y.S. 271 (App. Div. 1907).

There seems no reason to doubt that a Totten trust can be made irrevocable, but there has been very little discussion of what evidence of intent is needed for this purpose. The question was presented in Estate of Sulovich v. Commissioner, 587

F.2d 845 (6th Cir. 1978); Ingels' Estate, 92 A.2d 881 (Pa. 1952); and In re Farrell, 81 N.E.2d 51 (N.Y. 1948).

Joint accounts; POD accounts. Like Totten trust accounts, joint bank and other financial organization accounts contain a survivorship feature. The balance on hand in the account at the death of a depositor shifts to the surviving co-account holder without going through probate.

Except in a very few states, however, the funds in a joint account are not owned in joint tenancy (or tenancy by the entirety, if between spouses). That is to say, a deposit into such an account does not transfer an undivided interest therein to the other co-account holder. The fact that each account holder can, in practice, withdraw the whole of the account masks the true ownership of the funds in the account. The true ownership is that each account holder continues to own his or her own contribution to the balance on hand.[6] If one co-account holder withdraws an amount in excess of his or her own contributions, the other co-account holder normally has a right to force that excess to be returned. This right is routinely waived by inaction, possibly triggering federal gift tax consequences when the statute of limitations expires. See Treas. Reg. §25.2511-1(h)(4); Estate of Lang v. Commissioner, 613 F.2d 770 (9th Cir. 1980). Consequently, as between the co-account holders, a deposit into a joint bank account is revocable; no federal gift tax consequences are triggered because the tax law treats the deposit as an "incomplete" gift.

As with a revocable inter vivos trust, the validity of the survivorship feature depends upon satisfaction of the present transfer test. Most courts have found the test to be satisfied on the same theory used to uphold life-insurance beneficiary designations, that is, upon deposit the non-depositing co-account holder acquires a present (though defeasible) contract right to the deposit, payable on the death of the depositor. Legislation in many states also validates or is treated as validating the survivorship feature of joint bank accounts. Finally, in seeming contradiction of the predominant view concerning the rights of each party during life, a group of cases validates the survivorship feature by utilizing a joint tenancy analysis, especially when the deposit agreement, in tracking the language of a widely enacted bank-protection statute, describes the co-depositors as "joint tenants."

Payable on death (POD) accounts are created when a depositor registers the account in his or her name "payable on death" to another person. Unlike joint accounts, the form of POD accounts discloses the intention to transfer benefits only at the depositor's death. This difference in form has led most courts to treat joint and POD accounts differently. In the absence of validating legislation, POD accounts are generally held by courts to be testamentary, invalidating the attempted transfer of

---

6. See, e.g., Enright v. Lehmann, 735 N.W.2d 326 (Minn. 2007), holding that, of the funds in a joint account, a creditor may only garnish the funds contributed by the debtor, unless the creditor proves by clear and convincing evidence that the depositor(s) of the other funds intended to confer them on the debtor.

ownership on the depositor's death. See generally William M. McGovern, Jr., The Payable on Death Account and Other Will Substitutes, 67 Nw. U.L. Rev. 7 (1972).

POD accounts have fared much better in the legislatures. Legislation in many states validates the survivorship feature of such accounts, without requiring compliance with the execution formalities required of wills. Restatement 3d of Property §7.1 comment g recognizes the validity of POD accounts.

Multiple-party accounts under the UPC. UPC Article VI deals with nonprobate transfers. The original version separately identified and defined lifetime and survivorship rights in three types of multiple-party accounts: joint accounts, POD accounts, and trust accounts. Another group of provisions defined various protections for financial intermediaries in making payments according to the terms of account contracts.

Under this original version, lifetime ownership of co-account holders in joint accounts was presumptively proportionate to each party's contribution to the balance on deposit. A POD account was owned solely by the depositor and a trust account was owned solely by the trustee.

Concerning survivorship rights, §6-104 of the original version presumptively created a survivorship feature in all accounts that were presently payable to two or more parties, regardless of whether the account form described them as joint tenants or referred in any way to a right of survivorship. The original version did recognize, however, that a multiple-party account need not contain a survivorship feature. Although a joint account was presumed to provide survivorship rights, this presumption was rebuttable by clear evidence of a contrary intent. Section 6-104 also established a presumptive death benefit for the named beneficiary of a trust account, but this presumption similarly was rebuttable by clear and convincing evidence. Finally, the section expressly provided a death benefit for the beneficiary of a POD account. Unlike the death benefits under joint or trust accounts, the death benefit for a POD account beneficiary was unqualified, rather than merely presumptive. Of course, evidence of incapacity, fraud, or undue influence affecting the creation of a POD account was admissible to defeat a beneficiary's claim.

For trust and POD accounts, the original version negated survivorship rights among multiple surviving beneficiaries. In contrast, survivorship continued for multiple joint account beneficiaries who survived the death of a third or other co-depositor. Moreover, §6-104(e) of the original version explicitly negated any effort by an owner-party to use a will to alter the death benefit arising from the form of a deposit or the statute, thereby reversing a considerable body of case law involving Totten trusts. Finally, §6-107 provided that, to the extent the decedent's probate estate proved insufficient, any right of a surviving party or account beneficiary was subject to claims of the decedent's creditors, the payment of estate administration expenses, and statutory allowances to the decedent's surviving family members.[7] This section also included procedures, subject to a two-year limitations period, for recovering sums necessary to satisfy the described charges from surviving account parties and beneficiaries.

The 1989 revision of Article VI's coverage of multiple-party accounts is basically consistent with the original version. The major changes include: (1) folding Totten trust accounts into the definition and coverage of POD accounts; (2) providing statutory forms for joint accounts with or without survivorship, transfer-on-death (TOD) accounts, and joint and single-name accounts designating an agent to act for the owner, (3) subjecting survivors' benefits in accounts covered by the legislation to an order (check) of any party who dies before the check is paid; and (4) providing that, when two persons named as parties to a survivorship joint account are married to each other and the account includes one or more additional parties, only the surviving spouse may receive additional ownership of account balances following the other spouse's death. In addition to these changes, the two-year statute of limitations is reduced to one year.

A major goal of the 1989 revision was to encourage financial institutions to use the statutory forms and abandon their practice of routinely offering joint accounts to customers who merely wish to add another person's name to an account for agency, death beneficiary, or multiple-owners-with-no-survivorship purposes. The statutory forms and depository protection provisions extend greater and more explicit protection to financial institutions in connection with payments they make, pursuant to an agent's instructions, after a principal's death and payments they make to a surviving co-depositor after a party to a "non-survivorship" account has died.

Problems

Under the current version of UPC Article VI, analyze the following bank accounts and the rights of the persons named. Assume initially that all of the persons are alive; then explore how the law responds if the persons die one by one, in the order in which their names appear.

1. A, B and C create an account payable on request to any one of them.

2. A and B create an account payable on request to either of them, and at death to C and D.

3. A and B create an account "in trust for" C and D.

4. A and B create an account so that B can act on A's behalf. What happens if, after establishing the account, A becomes incapacitated? What happens at A's death?

---

7. In Estate of Reed, 681 A.2d 460 (Me. 1996), the court held that IRA accounts were not "accounts" within the meaning of §6-107 and, therefore, were not available to satisfy the claims of estate creditors.

Joint Tenancies and Tenancies by the Entirety in Land. Joint tenancy, tenancy by the entirety, and tenancy in common are concurrent estates; each tenant holds an undivided interest in the property. Of these three estates, only joint tenancy and tenancy by the entirety function as will substitutes, for only they—and not tenancy in common—have a survivorship feature. (Recall the discussion in Chapter 1.) The validity of joint tenancy or tenancy by the entirety, however, does not depend on compliance with the formalities of execution required for wills. This point is beyond argument, for the present transfer test in these cases is well satisfied: Titling property in joint tenancy or in tenancy by the entirety irrevocably creates a present undivided interest in the entire property in each tenant.

This undivided interest of a joint tenant or tenant by the entirety includes the right of survivorship. At death, the interest of a joint tenant or a tenant by the entirety terminates—like a life estate. The property ownership shifts outside of probate to the surviving co-tenant(s). Tenancy by the entirety is restricted to spouses, and the surviving spouse's interest becomes a fee simple absolute. In the case of a joint tenancy, the interest of a surviving joint tenant also becomes a fee simple absolute, unless there is more than one surviving joint tenant, in which case the surviving joint tenants continue to hold the property in joint tenancy among themselves.

Unless a statute or case law makes joint tenancies indestructible, they are unilaterally severable by any joint tenant, thereby turning that tenant's interest into a tenancy in common. To accomplish a severance, the severing tenant can simply use a deed to transfer his or her interest. If the severing tenant wants to retain ownership (albeit as a tenant in common), the traditional method involves a "straw person": the severing tenant conveys the interest to a straw person who, in turn, conveys the interest back to the severing tenant. In some states, the procedure is modernized: the severing tenant can execute a so-called "severance deed" to himself or herself as a tenant in common. See, e.g., Riddle v. Harmon, 102 Cal.App.3d 524 (1980).

There is no requirement that a severing joint tenant notify the other joint tenant, although recordation of the severing instrument may be required to terminate the other joint tenant's right of survivorship. See, e.g., Cal. Civ. Code §683.2. Whatever method is used, it must be effected during the severing tenant's lifetime.

A tenancy by the entirety can be conveyed to a third party, but only if both spouses agree. Absent conveyance (or partition), a tenancy by the entirety will terminate only on the first spouse's death or on the couple's divorce. In the latter event, jurisdictions are divided on whether the former spouses—if they continue to hold concurrent estates—are tenants in common or joint tenants.

Since the interest of a joint tenant or a tenant by the entirety terminates upon a co-tenant's death, the creditors of the deceased co-tenant's estate have no claim against the property, unless a statute provides otherwise. Tenancy by the entirety additionally offers creditor protection while the spouses are alive. Some states enable this creditor protection to remain even if the spouses transfer the property into a revocable (or irrevocable) trust. See, e.g., 12 Del. Code §3334; Mo. Stat. §456.950; N.C. Gen. Stat. §41-65; Tenn. Code §35-15.510; Va. Code §55.1-136.

Transfer on Death (TOD) Registration of Securities. The amendments to Article VI of the Uniform Probate Code also added provisions authorizing a new form of ownership of investment securities, called Transfer on Death (TOD) registration. The "TOD" provisions, §§6-301 to 6-310, are discussed in Richard V. Wellman, Transfer-On-Death Securities Registration: A New Title Form, 21 Ga. L. Rev. 789 (1987).

Transfer on Death (TOD) Deeds. Transfer on death (TOD) beneficiary designations are not limited to investment securities. More than half the states—including Alaska, Arizona, Arkansas, California, Colorado, Hawaii, Illinois, Indiana, Kansas, Maine, Minnesota, Mississippi, Missouri, Montana, Nebraska, Nevada, New Mexico, North Dakota, Ohio, Oklahoma, Oregon, South Dakota, Texas, Utah, Virginia, Washington, West Virginia, Wisconsin, and Wyoming—and the District of Columbia authorize so-called TOD deeds of interests in real property. Pursuant to these statutes, a person who owns an interest in real property may designate one or more primary TOD beneficiaries and one or more contingent TOD beneficiaries. While the owner is alive, the beneficiaries have no interest in the property. At the owner's death, the property interest passes directly and outside of probate as specified in the TOD deed, usually to the primary beneficiary or beneficiaries who survive the owner or, if none survives, to the contingent beneficiary or beneficiaries who survive the owner. The transfer is not testamentary and, therefore, need not comply with the formalities for wills. If none of the beneficiaries survives the owner, the property interest passes through the owner's probate estate, unless the jurisdiction's antilapse statute applies to the TOD deed. See, for example, UPC §2-706. In 2007, the Uniform Law Commission (ULC) appointed a drafting committee to prepare a Uniform Real Property Transfer on Death Act. The chair of the drafting committee was Nathaniel Sterling, a commissioner from California, and the reporter was Thomas P. Gallanis, then of the University of Iowa. In July 2009, the final version of the Uniform Real Property Transfer on Death Act was approved by the ULC and has been incorporated into the Uniform Probate Code as Article VI, Part 4.

EXTERNAL REFERENCE. Susan N. Gary, Transfer-on-Death Deeds: The Nonprobate Revolution Continues, 41 Real Prop., Prob. & Tr. J. 529 (2006).

PART B. REVOKING OR AMENDING A WILL SUBSTITUTE

Primary Statutory References: *UTC §§602-604*

1. Revoking or Amending a Revocable Trust

Estate and Trust of Pilafas
836 P.2d 420 (Ariz. Ct. App. 1992)

McGregor, J. The remainder beneficiaries (appellants) under an inter vivos trust agreement appeal the trial court's determination that Steve J. Pilafas (decedent) revoked his inter vivos trust and will and died intestate. Appellants raise two issues on appeal. The first is whether appellees presented sufficient evidence that decedent revoked his will. We find the evidence sufficient and affirm that part of the trial court's judgment. The second issue is whether the trial court erred in determining that decedent effectively revoked his inter vivos trust. We hold that the court did err and reverse....

On August 30, 1982, decedent executed a trust agreement appointing himself trustee of certain described properties for the benefit of himself and other specified beneficiaries....

Article X of the trust agreement, entitled "Revocation," provided:

> The Settlor may at any time or times during the Settlor's lifetime by instrument in writing delivered to the Trustee amend or revoke this Agreement in whole or in part.... This power is personal to the Settlor and may not be exercised by the Settlor's Personal Representative or others.

In accord with the revocation provision, decedent twice amended the trust agreement by instrument in writing. On September 16, 1982, decedent executed a "First Amendment to Trust Agreement" that substituted a new article VIII regarding trustee succession and added a new article XI regarding the sale of trust property. On January 19, 1987, after his divorce, decedent executed a "Second Amendment to Trust Agreement" that revoked article XI and added an amended article III, thereby deleting his former wife as a trust beneficiary and increasing the share to be distributed to the eight nonprofit beneficiary organizations.

Decedent simultaneously executed a will and the second trust amendment. The will explicitly excluded decedent's former wife, disposed of certain personal property, and directed that other personal property be distributed in accordance with a separate written statement. The will gave the residue of decedent's estate to the trust.

After executing the second amendment to his trust agreement and his new will, decedent apparently improved his relationships with appellees Irene Pappas, James S. Pilafas and Nicholas Pilafas. In communications with his attorney and his family during the last month of his life, decedent indicated an intention to revise his estate plan to include all his children.

Decedent's attorney prepared the trust agreement, the two amendments, and the will, and assisted decedent in executing them. The attorney did not retain decedent's original documents and, to the best of his knowledge, gave decedent the signed originals of the trust agreement, the amendments and the will immediately after they were executed.

Decedent died on September 28, 1988. Subsequently, decedent's son, appellee James S. Pilafas, unsuccessfully searched decedent's house and belongings for the original will and trust documents. No information of record indicates their possible whereabouts.

According to appellees James S. Pilafas and Nicholas S. Pilafas, decedent fastidiously saved important records and was unlikely to have lost his original will and trust. At his death, decedent had a room filled with important documents, including photographs, old divorce papers, his selective service card from 1945, and letters from his children. Appellees also testified that decedent was a man of direct action who sometimes acted impulsively, and who had been known to tear or discard papers that offended him....

Appellees claim that decedent revoked his will because that document could not be found in a diligent search of his personal effects and papers after his death. This argument relies on the common law presumption that a testator destroyed his will with the intention of revoking it if the will is last seen in the testator's possession and cannot be found after his death....

...In our opinion, the trial court correctly determined that decedent revoked his will and died intestate....

Appellees ask us to extend to revocable inter vivos trusts the common law presumption that a will last seen in the testator's possession that cannot be found after his death has been revoked. Appellees' reliance on this common law presumption is misplaced, however, if decedent's trust agreement was not susceptible to revocation by physical destruction....

This court, when not bound by previous decisions or legislative enactments, follows the Restatement of the Law. Restatement (Second) of Trusts §330 (1959) provides:

> (1) The settlor has power to revoke the trust if and to the extent that by the terms of the trust he reserved such a power.
>
> (2) Except as stated in §§332 and 333, the settlor cannot revoke the trust if by the terms of the trust he did not reserve a power of revocation.

Restatement §330(2) makes it clear that, with two narrow exceptions, a trust is revocable only if the settlor expressly reserves a power to revoke, and the terms of the trust strictly define and limit the reserved power of revocation.

These general principles necessarily entail the more specific rule that when the settlor reserves a power to revoke his trust in a particular manner or under particular circumstances, he can revoke it only in that manner or under those circumstances....

Because appellees presented no evidence showing that decedent complied with the required method of revocation, the inter vivos trust was not revoked and remained valid....

For the foregoing reasons, we affirm the trial court's ruling that decedent revoked his will and died intestate, reverse the court's ruling that decedent revoked his trust agreement and the amendments thereto, and remand for proceedings consistent with this opinion.

GERBER, P.J., AND MELVYN T. SHELLEY, Retired Judge, concur.

Notes and Questions

1. *Revocability of Inter Vivos Trusts.* At common law, an inter vivos transfer in trust is treated like any other inter vivos transfer of property: it is *irrevocable* unless the settlor expressly retains a power to revoke.[8] This contrasts, of course, with wills, which are revocable without the necessity of an explicit reservation of a power to revoke or amend.

Statutes in a few states establish the opposite rule. They provide that transfers in trust are revocable unless expressly made irrevocable. See, e.g., Cal. Prob. Code §15400; Okla. Stat. tit. 60 §175.41; Tex. Prop. Code §112.051.

UTC §602(a) also reverses the common-law rule and provides: "Unless the terms of a trust expressly provide that the trust is irrevocable, the settlor may revoke or amend the trust." Section 602(a) provides that its rule "does not apply to a trust created under an instrument executed before [the effective date of this [Code]]."

The Restatement 3d of Trusts §63 provides that "[t]he settlor of an inter vivos trust has power to revoke and modify the trust to the extent the terms of the trust so provide." Comment b, however, provides that "[i]f the terms of the trust are otherwise expressed in writing but fail to provide whether or to what extent the settlor reserves the power to revoke or modify the trust, the writing is incomplete and its meaning is uncertain." Comment c amplifies this point further by providing:

> c. *Presumptions regarding revocability.* Where the settlor has failed expressly to provide whether a trust is subject to revocation or amendment, if the settlor has retained no interest in the trust..., it is rebuttably presumed that the settlor has no power to revoke or amend the trust. If, however, the settlor... has retained an interest in the trust..., the presumption is that the trust is revocable and amendable by the settlor.

2. *How to Revoke a Revocable Trust.* The Restatement 3d of Trusts §63 comments h and i provide:

> h. *Form of exercise when no method is specified.* If the settlor reserves the power to revoke or modify the trust but does not specify the manner or form in which the power is

---

8. This is also the position taken by statute in New York: "A lifetime trust shall be irrevocable unless it expressly provides that it is revocable." N.Y. Est. Powers & Trusts Law §7-1.16.

to be exercised, the power can be exercised in any way that provides clear and convincing evidence of the settlor's intention to do so. Thus, the power can be exercised by a will or codicil that is executed after the creation of the trust and remains unrevoked at the settlor's death, and that refers expressly to the trust or the power or that otherwise clearly manifests the settlor-testator's intent to exercise the power.

Similarly, a definitive manifestation by the settlor during life of his or her intention that the trust is thereby revoked is sufficient....

i. Where method of revocation specified. If the terms of the trust reserve to the settlor a power to revoke or amend the trust *exclusively* by a particular procedure, the settlor can exercise the power only by substantial compliance with the method prescribed....

Although the terms of the trust provide a method for the exercise of a power of revocation or amendment, if the terms do not make that method exclusive, this is not a "contrary provision" for purpose of Subsection (3). Thus, the settlor's power can be exercised either in the specified manner or by a method described in Comment *h*, above.

Section 602(c) of the UTC provides similar rules. See also Restatement 3d of Property §7.2 comments d, e, and h. These statutes and authorities liberalize the common law.

3. *Application to* Pilafas. How would *Pilafas* have been decided under UTC 602? Under the Restatement 3d of Trusts §63?

4. *Revoking or Amending a Joint Revocable Trust.* If a revocable trust is jointly created by two settlors, can the trust be amended or revoked by the sole survivor? For two cases answering in the negative, on the basis that the trusts did not explicitly so provide, see Mangels v. Cornell, 189 P.3d 573 (Kan. App. 2008); Scalfaro v. Rudloff, 934 A.2d 1254 (Pa. 2007).

2. Revoking or Amending Will Substitutes by a Later Will

Can the settlor of a revocable trust revoke the trust through an express provision in the settlor's later will? UTC §602(c), Restatement 3d of Trusts §63 comment h, and Restatement 3d of Property §7.2 comment e all say yes. So also does N.Y. Est. Powers & Trusts Law §7-1.16 ("[A] revocable lifetime trust can be revoked or amended by an express direction in the creator's will which specifically refers to such lifetime trust or a particular provision thereof"). But the cases are divided. See, e.g., Estate of Kovalyshyn, 343 A.2d 852 (Hudson Co., N.J., 1975), holding that a decedent could not exercise the power to revoke a revocable trust in a will.

If courts are divided about whether the settlor may revoke a revocable trust by will, may a transferor revoke other will substitutes by will?

Totten Trusts; Multiple-Party Accounts; POD Accounts. Some cases have held that a Totten trust may be revoked by appropriate provisions in the depositor's will. See Scanlon's Estate, 169 A. 106 (Pa. 1933); In Estate of Bol, 429 N.W.2d 467 (S.D. 1988). However, UPC §6-213(b) provides that a will may *not* alter the survivorship right in any multiple-party account or POD designation. See generally Scott and

Ascher on Trusts §8.3.4; Annot., Revocation of Tentative ("Totten") Trust of Savings Bank Account by Inter Vivos Declaration or Will, 46 A.L.R.3d 487.

Life Insurance. Most cases follow the view expressed in Stone v. Stephens, 99 N.E.2d 766 (Ohio 1951), that a will is not effective to change the beneficiary designation of a life insurance policy:

> To hold that a change in beneficiary may be made by testamentary disposition alone would open up a serious question as to payment of life insurance policies. It is in the public interest that an insurance company may pay a loss to the beneficiary designated in the policy as promptly after the death of insured as may reasonably be done. If there is uncertainty as to the beneficiary upon the death of insured, in all cases where the right to change the beneficiary had been reserved there would always be a question as to whom the proceeds of the insurance should be paid. If paid to the beneficiary, a will might later be probated designating a different disposition of the fund, and it would be a risk that few companies would be willing to take, unless some specified time had elapsed after the death of insured, or that there had been some court adjudication as to whom the proceeds should be paid. [quoting from Wannamaker v. Stroman, 166 S.E. 621, 623 (S.C. 1932).]
>
> It may also be observed that further delay in the payment of the proceeds of policies might be caused by a contest of such will or by a proceeding involving the construction of such will. The question of law involved herein is not affected by the interpleader of the insurers and their deposit of the disputed funds in court. There is substantial authority for the proposition that rights which become vested on the death of the insured and thus fixed by law can not thereafter be affected by such action of the insurer. 78 A.L.R. 981, and cases cited.

See, e.g., McCarthy v. Aetna Life Ins. Co., 704 N.E.2d 557 (N.Y. 1998); Cook v. Equitable Life As. Soc., 428 N.E.2d 110 (Ind. Ct. App. 1981). For a case reaching the same result as in *Stone* in the context of an ERISA-covered employee pension benefit plan on the basis of ERISA's preemption of state law, see MacLean v. Ford Motor Co., 831 F.2d 723 (7th Cir. 1987). (ERISA is the acronym for the Employee Retirement Income Security Act of 1974, the federal law that governs most tax-qualified pension plans; see discussion below.)

A few courts, however, have permitted testators to change a life insurance beneficiary by will. See, e.g., Liberty Life Assurance Co. of Boston v. Kennedy, 358 F.3d 1295 (11th Cir. 2004) (the company's instructions for changing beneficiaries provided that a change of beneficiary "can be" on forms approved by the company); Connecticut General Life Ins. Co. v. Peterson, 442 F. Supp. 533 (D.C. Mo. 1978); Burkett v. Mott, 733 P.2d 673 (Ariz. Ct. App. 1986).

Joint Tenancies. Because of the right of survivorship, joint tenants who predecease their co-tenants have no power to devise their interest in joint tenancy property.

Suppose G, who owns Blackacre as joint tenant with A, leaves a will devising "$20,000 to A, and all my interest in Blackacre to B." Can the devise to B be given effect? Not under the law of joint tenancy. But under the wills doctrine of *equitable election*, it can. Equitable election is a device of ancient origin by which testamentary power over owned property is extended to property owned by another.[9] In effect, the court would be treating the devise to A as if it were a conditional devise, that is, as if it said "$20,000 to A *if* A transfers Blackacre to B." See Restatement 3d of Property §6.1 comment f. Is this characterization of the devise to A justified? See Neville Crago, Mistakes in Wills and Election in Equity, 106 L.Q. Rev. 487 (1990) (arguing that G never actually intended the devise to be conditional; rather, G's devise to B was merely the product of a mistake on G's part as to his testamentary power to devise it). In Williamson v. Williamson, 657 N.E.2d 651 (Ill. App. Ct. 1995), appeal den., 664 N.E.2d 640 (Ill. 1996), the court refused to apply the doctrine in the context of a devise of jointly-owned property, stating that the doctrine should be restricted to circumstances where it prevents injustice or where the testator has expressly put the devisee to an election.

A Superwill? There has been discussion of permitting a so-called "superwill." The idea behind that term is that testamentary control should be expanded to allow testators to change the beneficiary designations of certain nonprobate transfers. In 1998, the superwill became a reality in the State of Washington, but only for certain will substitutes. Excluded are real property joint transfers and life insurance and retirement plan beneficiary designations:

> *Rev. Code Wash. §11.11.020. Disposition of Nonprobate Assets Under Will.* (1) Subject to community property rights, upon the death of an owner the owner's interest in any nonprobate asset[10] specifically referred to in the owner's will belongs to the testamentary

---

9. A modern use of the doctrine of equitable election is the spouse's-election device in community-property states. Under community-property regimes, property acquired during the marriage, other than by gift, inheritance, or devise, becomes community property. Unlike joint tenancy or tenancy by the entirety, community property is a form of co-ownership that operates like a tenancy in common, in that each spouse owns an undivided one-half interest with no rights of survivorship in the other. When one spouse dies, that spouse has testamentary power over his or her half of the couple's community property, but not over the survivor's half.

The spouse's-election device seeks to extend the deceased spouse's testamentary power to the *entire* community. In effect, the decedent's will might say to the survivor: I devise my half of the community into a trust, income to you for life, remainder to our descendants, if you agree to contribute your half of the community into the same trust. The survivor is thus put to an election as to whether to (i) keep his or her half of the community outright and forfeit the income interest in the decedent's half or (ii) transfer his or her half into the same trust, thereby enjoying the right to the income from the whole.

10. As defined in §§11.11.010(7)(a) and 11.02.005(10), the term "nonprobate assets" does not include: a payable-on-death provision of a life insurance policy, annuity, or other similar contract, or of an employee benefit plan; a right or interest if, before death, the person has irrevocably transferred the right or interest, the person has waived the power to transfer it or, in the case of contractual arrangement, the person has waived the unilateral right to rescind or modify the arrangement; a right or interest held by the person solely in a fiduciary capacity; a right or interest in real property passing under a joint tenancy with right of survivorship; a deed or conveyance for which possession has been postponed until the death of the owner; a right or interest passing under a community property agreement; and an individual retirement account or bond.

beneficiary named to receive the nonprobate asset, notwithstanding the rights of any beneficiary designated before the date of the will.

(2) A general residuary gift in an owner's will, or a will making general disposition of all of the owner's property, does not entitle the devisees or legatees to receive nonprobate assets of the owner.

(3) A disposition in a will of the owner's interest in "all nonprobate assets" or of all of a category of nonprobate asset under RCW 11.11.010(7), such as "all of my payable on death bank accounts" or similar language, is deemed to be a disposition of all the nonprobate assets the beneficiaries of which are designated before the date of the will.

(4) If the owner designates a beneficiary for a nonprobate asset after the date of the will, the specific provisions in the will that attempt to control the disposition of that asset do not govern the disposition of that nonprobate asset, even if the subsequent beneficiary designation is later revoked. If the owner revokes the later beneficiary designation, and there is no other provision controlling the disposition of the asset, the asset shall be treated as any other general asset of the owner's estate, subject to disposition under the other applicable provisions of the will. A beneficiary designation with respect to an asset that renews without the signature of the owner is deemed to have been made on the date on which the account was first opened.

What are the advantages and disadvantages of superwills? For discussion, see Roberta R. Kwall & Anthony J. Aiello, The Superwill Debate: Opening the Pandora's Box?, 62 Temple L. Rev. 277 (1989); Cynthia J. Artura, Comment, Superwill to the Rescue? How Washington's Statute Falls Short of Being a Hero in the Field of Trust and Probate Law, 74 Wash. L. Rev. 799 (1999).

3. Revoking or Amending Will Substitutes Governed by ERISA

The Employee Retirement Income Security Act of 1974 (ERISA) provides that ERISA "shall supersede any and all State laws insofar as they may now or hereafter relate to any employee benefit plan" covered by ERISA. 29 U.S.C. §1144(a).

Metropolitan Life Insurance Company v. Johnson
297 F.3d 558 (7th Cir. 2002)

MANION, Circuit Judge. Metropolitan Life Insurance Company ("MetLife") filed an interpleader action, requesting the district court to designate the proper beneficiary of Jimmie Johnson's life insurance policy. The district court ruled in favor of LaShanda Smith, Leonard Smith and Carolyn Hall, and the insured's former wife, Mildred Johnson, appeals. We affirm.

I. Jimmie Johnson was an employee of General Electric ("GE") from 1968 until his death on February 15, 1999. During his employment, he was a participant in the GE Life, Disability and Medical Plan (the "Plan"), an employee welfare benefit plan governed by the Employee Retirement Income Security Act of 1974 ("ERISA"). GE funded the Plan through an insurance policy issued by MetLife. Johnson had $104,902.00 in life insurance as of the date of his death. The Plan provides that the life insurance benefits will be paid to the beneficiary designated by the insured.

On October 8, 1968, Johnson designated his then-wife Mildred Johnson as sole beneficiary of the Plan. Several years later, Jimmie and Mildred divorced. On approximately December 27, 1996, Johnson completed a beneficiary designation form, naming LaShanda Smith, Leonard Smith and Carolyn Hall (jointly referred to as "SS & H") as co-beneficiaries.[11] The 1996 form contained a number of errors. First, Johnson checked the box for "GE S & SP Life Insurance Plan." However, he was never enrolled in that plan; rather, he should have checked the box for "GE Life or GE Leadership Life Insurance Plan." Also, Johnson listed his mother's address instead of his own. Finally, he indicated on the form that he was "separated" from his wife, Mildred, rather than divorced.

When Johnson died on February 15, 1999, GE informed Mildred that she was the beneficiary of his life insurance policy, and she filed a beneficiary claim. Subsequently, on March 1, 1999, LaShanda Smith sent GE a letter stating that she was aware that her father had made her "the only primary beneficiary to receive his life insurance benefits" and inquiring how to receive those proceeds. In her letter, she stated that, in late 1996, she and her brother had signed a change of beneficiary form, and that, in January 1997, her father had received confirmation of the change of beneficiary. MetLife claimed to have no record of the change of beneficiary designation and requested LaShanda to provide documentation of the change. She provided a copy of the 1996 form and a copy of a letter sent to Jimmie Johnson from the General Electric Enrollment Center dated January 1, 1997. In this letter, GE confirms receipt of Johnson's completed beneficiary designation form. However, the letter did not refer to a particular plan, nor did it indicate the identity of the newly designated beneficiaries.[12]

In response to the multiple claims to the proceeds of Johnson's life insurance policy, MetLife filed an interpleader action, requesting the court to determine who was properly entitled to the proceeds.[13] After Mildred Johnson and Carolyn Hall

---

11. According to the 1996 designation form, LaShanda Smith and Leonard Smith are Johnson's children, and Carolyn Hall is his friend. LaShanda and Leonard are not Mildred's children, but were born while Jimmie was still married to Mildred. She claimed that she did not know of their existence until notified of their claim on the life insurance proceeds. SS & H disputed this, but this dispute is immaterial for purposes of this appeal. The record reveals that Jimmie had at least one other child, Jimmie Johnson, Jr., his son by Mildred, born in 1965.

12. The confirmation letter provides, in its entirety: "This letter confirms receipt of your completed beneficiary designation form. The beneficiaries designated on this form will replace any beneficiaries you may have previously named. Please remember that if in the future you enroll in a plan requiring a beneficiary designation, or if you want to change your beneficiaries, you must submit another form at that time. If you have any questions please call the GE Enrollment Center at 1-800-252-5259."

13. On January 9, 2001, the district court granted MetLife leave to deposit $114,552.97 (the amount of the policy plus interest) with the Registry of the United States District Court for the Northern District of Illinois, granted MetLife's motion for entry of a final decree of interpleader and dismissed MetLife

filed answers, all parties moved for summary judgment, agreeing that the sole issue was whether Johnson had executed a valid change of beneficiary form in 1996. The court denied Mildred's motion and granted summary judgment to SS & H, concluding that the 1996 form evidenced Jimmie Johnson's intent to change his beneficiary from Mildred to SS & H and that he substantially complied with the requirements of the Plan in doing so. Mildred Johnson appeals.

II. A. Standard of Review. [We conduct *de novo* review of a district court's decision involving cross-motions for summary judgment, construing all inferences in favor of Mildred Johnson, the party against whom summary judgment was granted.]

B. Applicable Law. 1. Preemption. Consequently, the only issue before us is whether, as a matter of law, Johnson effectively changed his beneficiary designation by executing the 1996 form.... The terms of the Plan, in Part I(C) entitled, "Designation of Beneficiary," provide in relevant part:

> In the event of your death from any cause, the amount of your Life Insurance then in force will be payable to the beneficiary designated by you. You may change your beneficiary at any time. *Any designation of beneficiary or any change of beneficiary should be made in a form acceptable to the carrier and must be filed with the records maintained by your employee relations or personnel accounting office....* Upon receipt of written notice of change of beneficiary by such office, the change shall relate back and take effect as of the date you signed such written notice, whether or not you are living at the time of such receipt.... (Emphasis added.)

Here, Johnson attempted to designate SS & H as his beneficiaries by executing the 1996 form and, according to the 1997 letter from the GE Enrollment Center to Johnson, that form was filed and accepted by his employer. Nevertheless, it is undisputed that Johnson made several errors in executing the form. Thus, the question before us is whether the beneficiary change form was effective, notwithstanding those errors.

To address this issue, we must first determine the controlling law. As noted, the Plan is governed by ERISA. However, ERISA does not contain any provisions governing disputes between claimants to plan proceeds, or addressing whether an insured has effectively changed a beneficiary designation. *Phoenix Mut. Life Ins. Co. v. Adams,* 30 F.3d 554, 559 (4th Cir. 1994). Thus, Mildred advocates that we apply the Illinois doctrine of "substantial compliance,"[14] relying on the principle

---

from the action with prejudice.

14. The Illinois doctrine of substantial compliance requires that, for a change of beneficiary to be effective, "the party asserting that a change has occurred must establish: (1) the certainty of the insured's intent to change his beneficiary; and (2) that the insured did everything he could have reasonably done under the circumstances to carry out his intention to change the beneficiary." *Aetna Life Ins. Co. v. Wise,* 184 F.3d 660, 663 (7th Cir. 1999) (citing *Dooley v. James A. Dooley Assoc.*

enunciated in *John Hancock Mut. Life Ins. Co. v. Harris Trust & Sav. Bank,* 510 U.S. 86, 98 (1993), that ERISA "leaves room for complementary or dual federal and State regulation." SS & H, on the other hand, argue that ERISA preempts state law and, therefore, urge us to apply federal common law to resolve the dispute.

Generally, ERISA preempts all state laws "insofar as they may now or hereafter relate to any employee benefit plan" which is subject to ERISA. *See* 29 U.S.C. § 1144(a)....

We have not directly addressed the precise issue of whether ERISA preempts a state's substantial compliance doctrine because the doctrine "relates to" an ERISA plan. Other circuits have had occasion to do so, and their conclusions are split. For instance, the Ninth Circuit concluded that ERISA did not preempt the state doctrine of substantial compliance because it would not affect the administration of the plan, but would merely "aid in determining the identity of the proper recipient of the proceeds." *BankAmerica Pension Plan v. McMath,* 206 F.3d 821, 829 (9th Cir. 2000), *cert. denied, McMath v. Montgomery,* 531 U.S. 952....

In contrast, the Fourth Circuit, while agreeing that the doctrine of substantial compliance did not *modify* a plan, nevertheless concluded that the state law "relates to" such a plan because it involved the designation of the beneficiary of an ERISA plan. *Phoenix Mut. [Life Ins. Co v. Adams,* 30 F.3d 554 (4th Cir. 1994)]....

.... [W]e believe that a state law affecting the designation of a beneficiary is sufficiently "related to" an ERISA plan such that a state law doctrine of substantial compliance is preempted by ERISA. Thus, we find the Fourth Circuit's decision in *Phoenix Mutual* persuasive and believe this conclusion is consistent with our own precedent....

2. Federal common law. The question then is whether the 1996 change of beneficiary form is valid under ERISA. But, as we previously noted, ERISA is silent as to the resolution of disputes between putative beneficiaries of a life insurance policy. The Supreme Court has recognized, in situations where ERISA preempts state law but is silent on a topic, that courts would have to develop a body of federal common law, where appropriate, based on principles of state law....

On appeal, Mildred argues that, even if ERISA preempts state law, in formulating federal common law we should still look to Illinois' doctrine of substantial compliance. SS & H argue that we should instead adopt the Fourth Circuit's standard [of substantial compliance as federal common law] from *Phoenix Mutual.* Under the Fourth Circuit's test, we look at whether the insured "evidences his or her intent" and "attempts to effectuate the change by undertaking positive actions." .... The Illinois doctrine of substantial compliance and the test enunciated by the Fourth Circuit invoking federal common law are essentially the same, and in this particular case, it would make no practical difference which standard we applied. We

Employees Ret. Plan, 442 N.E.2d 222, 227 (Ill. 1982)).

recognize, however, the need to ensure uniformity in ERISA jurisprudence, and of the principle that "federal common law should be consistent across the circuits." *Phoenix Mutual,* 30 F.3d at 564.... Therefore, we will apply [*Phoenix Mutual*'s] formulation of the federal common law doctrine of substantial compliance.

C. Substantial Compliance. Applying this test, we now turn to the 1996 form to determine whether Johnson substantially complied with the instructions on the form by evidencing his intent to make a change of beneficiary, and by attempting to effectuate that change by undertaking positive action. The instructions attached to the change of beneficiary form told Johnson that he could "designate a beneficiary only for the plans in which you are currently participating or have an account balance. CHECK ONLY THOSE PLANS FOR WHICH YOU WANT THIS BENEFICIARY DESIGNATION TO APPLY." The completed form was to be sent to the GE Enrollment Center. As already noted, Johnson checked the box for the wrong life insurance policy. However, aside from that error, Johnson took positive action to effectuate a change in his life insurance policy. Specifically, the undisputed facts show that Johnson filled out GE's form indicating he wished to change the beneficiary designation on his life insurance policy (although he checked the wrong box), that he designated SS & H as the new beneficiaries of a life insurance plan and that the GE Enrollment Center (the place he was instructed to mail the form) sent him a confirmation letter indicating that he mailed the form as required. Moreover, the GE Enrollment Center's letter did not alert him that he had checked the box for an insurance policy different than the one covering him. Under these circumstances, we conclude that Johnson clearly evidenced an intent to change his beneficiary designation, that he took positive action to effectuate that intent, and that checking the wrong box does not serve to negate that intent. It is true that Johnson made some errors, but the doctrine of substantial compliance by its very nature contemplates something less than actual compliance....

III. For the reasons stated herein, we conclude that the evidence establishes that, under the federal common law doctrine of substantial compliance, Jimmie Johnson met the criteria for changing his beneficiary designation on his life insurance policy, and we therefore AFFIRM the district court's grant of summary judgment to LaShanda Smith, Leonard Smith and Carolyn Hall.

Notes

1. *The Fourth Circuit's* Phoenix *Test.* The Seventh Circuit in *Metropolitan Life* stated that it was applying the *Phoenix* substantial compliance test as federal common law. In Phoenix Mut. Life Ins. Co. v. Adams, 30 F.3d 554 (4th Cir. 1994), the court held that ERISA preempted South Carolina law regarding the validity of an attempted change of beneficiary of an ERISA-covered life insurance policy. Instead, the court recognized a federal common law of substantial compliance, which the court defined as follows:

[A]n insured substantially complies with the change of beneficiary provisions of an ERISA life insurance policy when the insured: (1) evidences his or her intent to make the change and (2) attempts to effectuate the change by undertaking positive action *which is for all practical purposes similar to the action required by the change of beneficiary provisions of the policy.* (Emphasis added.)

Did the court in *Metropolitan Life* alter this test while purporting to apply it? Suppose that Jimmie Johnson had telephoned the GE Enrollment Center, telling a plan coordinator that he wanted to change the beneficiary of his life insurance plan to LaShanda Smith, Leonard Smith, and Carolyn Hall. The coordinator took the information down in a handwritten note (or typed it into a computer database of incoming telephone inquiries), and told Jimmie that a change of beneficiary form would be mailed to him to fill out and return. Jimmie died before the postal service delivered the form. What result? Cf. Prudential Ins. Co. v. Schmid, 337 F.Supp.2d 325 (D. Mass. 2004).

2. *Split in the Circuits.* The Sixth Circuit has declined to endorse a doctrine of substantial compliance. See Guinn v. General Motors LLC, 766 Fed. Appx. 331 (6th Cir. 2019) (unpublished); Kmatz v. Metropolitan Life Ins. Co., 232 Fed. Appx. 451 (6th Cir. 2007) (unpublished); Swedish Match North America Inc. v. Tucker, 2010 WL 2721875 (W.D.Ky. 2010) (observing that "every other circuit that has addressed the question has found that the doctrine of substantial compliance is available to determine an ERISA beneficiary").

3. *Unsigned Change-of-Beneficiary Form.* The Seventh Circuit applied the substantial compliance doctrine as federal common law to an ERISA-covered life insurance change-of-beneficiary form in another decision, Davis v. Combes, 294 F.3d 931 (7th Cir. 2002). The execution defect that the court excused in *Davis* was that the insured-employee failed to sign the form. The court said:

We are aware that there will be situations in which a failure to sign and date a beneficiary designation may cast significant doubt on whether the policy holder actually decided to go through with the change. But it is equally true that there are other cases in which the evidence will unequivocally establish that the policy holder intended to make the new beneficiary designation and took positive action to effectuate that intent....

The evidence in the case before us leaves no doubt about Brenda's intent to make Linda the sole beneficiary of her NovaCare policy. Brenda attempted to make the change at the same time that she successfully named Linda the beneficiary of the Continental and the Life Investors policies. She requested the change of beneficiary form from her employer and filled it out in her own handwriting. She completed the form in its entirety (including a September 1, 1996 effective date) with the exception of the signature and date lines. She then turned the form in to the NovaCare benefits coordinator, who accepted and processed the application as though it were complete.

In BankAmerica Pension Plan v. McMath, 206 F.3d 821 (9th Cir. 2000), however, the court held that an unsigned change-of-beneficiary form was ineffective. The

Ninth Circuit applied the substantial compliance doctrine of California law, which required the insured to "do all that he [or she] could [do] to effectuate the change of beneficiary," as opposed to the *Phoenix* standard applied by the Seventh Circuit, which merely required the insured to "undertak[e] positive action" to effectuate the change.

4. *The Future of Federal Common Law.* In Rodriguez v. Federal Deposit Insurance Corporation, 140 S.Ct. 713 (2020), the U.S. Supreme Court stated that "[t]he cases in which federal courts may engage in common lawmaking are few and far between... [and] must be necessary to protect uniquely federal interests." Id. at 716-717 (internal quotation marks omitted).

EXTERNAL REFERENCE. Thomas P. Gallanis, ERISA and the Law of Succession, 65 Ohio St. L.J. 185 (2004).

PART C. WILL SUBSTITUTES AND THE SUBSIDIARY LAW OF WILLS

Primary Statutory Reference: *UTC §112*

The question whether will substitutes should be treated as testamentary for purposes of the statutory formalities of execution implicates rules that are mandatory. Apart from a harmless-error rule, such as set forth in UPC §2-503 or Restatement 3d of Property §3.3, wills statute requirements apply regardless of the testator's intent. Indeed, as we have seen, the harmless-error rule was promulgated to prevent those requirements from defeating the testator's intent.

Other rules of the law of wills, including antilapse statutes and statutes providing for revocation upon changed circumstances, are different in character. These rules yield to the contrary intentions of testators. The question that we study in this Part is whether these intent-effectuating rules should apply to wills and will substitutes alike. Put differently, should will substitutes be treated as testamentary for purposes of the subsidiary (or default) law of wills even if they are not so treated for purposes of the mandatory requirements of will execution?

The Restatement 3d of Property provides:

> *§7.2 Application of Will Doctrines to Will Substitutes*
> Although a will substitute need not be executed in compliance with the statutory formalities required for a will, such an arrangement is, to the extent appropriate, subject to substantive restrictions on testation and to rules of construction and other rules applicable to testamentary dispositions.

EXTERNAL REFERENCES. Grayson M.P. McCouch, Probate Law Reform and Nonprobate Transfers, 62 U. Miami L. Rev. 757 (2008); John H. Langbein, The Nonprobate Revolution and the Future of the Law of Succession, 97 Harv. L. Rev. 1108 (1984).

1. Revocation Upon Divorce

Primary Statutory References: *UPC §§2-508, 2-804*

Clymer v. Mayo
473 N.E.2d 1084 (Mass. 1985)

HENNESSEY, C.J. ...At the time of her death in November, 1981, the decedent, [Clara A. Mayo,] then fifty years of age, was employed by Boston University as a professor of psychology. She was married to James P. Mayo, Jr. (Mayo), from 1953 to 1978. The couple had no children. The decedent was an only child and her sole heirs at law are her parents, Joseph A. and Maria Weiss.

In 1963, the decedent executed a will designating Mayo as principal beneficiary. In 1964, she named Mayo as the beneficiary of her group annuity contract with John Hancock Mutual Life Insurance Company; and in 1965, made him the beneficiary of her Boston University retirement annuity contracts with Teachers Insurance and Annuity Association (TIAA) and College Retirement Equities Fund (CREF). As a consequence of a $300,000 gift to the couple from the Weisses in 1971, the decedent and Mayo executed new wills and indentures of trust on February 2, 1973, wherein each spouse was made the other's principal beneficiary. Under the terms of the decedent's will, Mayo was to receive her personal property. The residue of her estate was to "pour over" into the inter vivos trust she created that same day.

The decedent's trust instrument named herself and John P. Hill as trustees. As the donor, the decedent retained the right to amend or revoke the trust at any time by written instrument delivered to the trustees. In the event that Mayo survived the decedent, the trust estate was to be divided into two parts. Trust A, the marital deduction trust, was to be funded with an amount "equal to fifty (50%) per cent of the value of the Donor's 'adjusted gross estate,'... for the purpose of the United States Tax Law, less an amount equal to the value of all interest in property, if any, allowable as 'marital deductions' for the purposes of such law...." Mayo was the income beneficiary of Trust A and was entitled to reach the principal at his request or in the trustee's discretion. The trust instrument also gave Mayo a general power of appointment over the assets in Trust A.

The balance of the decedent's estate, excluding personal property passing to Mayo by will, or the entire estate if Mayo did not survive her, composed Trust B. Trust B provided for the payment of five initial specific bequests totaling $45,000. After those gifts were satisfied, the remaining trust assets were to be held for the benefit of Mayo for life. Upon Mayo's death, the assets in Trust B were to be held for "the benefit of the nephews and nieces of the Donor" living at the time of her death. The trustee was given discretion to spend so much of the income and principal as necessary for their comfort, support, and education. When all of these nephews and nieces reached the age of thirty, the trust was to terminate and its remaining assets were to be divided equally between Clark University and Boston University to assist in graduate education of women.

On the same day she established her trust, the decedent changed the beneficiary of her Boston University group life insurance policy from Mayo to the trustees. One month later, in March, 1973, she also executed a change in her retirement annuity contracts to designate the trustees as beneficiaries. At the time of its creation in 1973, the trust was not funded. Its future assets were to consist solely of the proceeds of these policies and the property which would pour over under the will's residuary clause. The judge found that the remaining trustee has never received any property or held any funds subsequent to the execution of the trust nor has he paid any trust taxes or filed any trust tax returns.

Mayo moved out of the marital home in 1975. In June, 1977, the decedent changed the designation of beneficiary on her Boston University life insurance policy for a second time, substituting Marianne LaFrance for the trustees. LaFrance had lived with the Mayos since 1972, and shared a close friendship with the decedent up until her death. Mayo filed for divorce on September 9, 1977, in New Hampshire. The divorce was decreed on January 3, 1978, and the court incorporated into the decree a permanent stipulation of the parties' property settlement. Under the terms of that settlement, Mayo waived any "right, title or interest" in the decedent's "securities, savings accounts, savings certificates, and retirement fund," as well as her "furniture, furnishings and art." Mayo remarried on August 28, 1978, and later executed a new will in favor of his new wife. The decedent died on November 21, 1981. Her will was allowed on November 18, 1982, and the court appointed John H. Clymer as administrator with the will annexed.

What is primarily at issue in these actions is the effect of the Mayos' divorce upon dispositions provided in the decedent's will and indenture of trust....

2. *Validity of "Pour-over" Trust*. The Weisses claim that the judge erred in ruling that the decedent's trust was validly created despite the fact that it was not funded until her death. They rely on the common law rule that a trust can be created only when a trust res exists. Arguing that the trust never came into existence, the Weisses claim they are entitled to the decedent's entire estate as her sole heirs at law.

In upholding the validity of the decedent's pour-over trust, the judge cited the relevant provisions of the Commonwealth's version of the Uniform Testamentary Additions to Trusts Act [original UPC §2-511]:

> "A devise or bequest, the validity of which is determinable by the laws of the commonwealth, may be made to the trustee or trustees of a trust established or to be established by the testator ... including a funded or unfunded life insurance trust, although the trustor has reserved any or all rights of ownership of the insurance contracts, if the trust is identified in the will and the terms of the trust are set forth in a written instrument executed before or concurrently with the execution of the testator's will ... *regardless of the existence, size or character of the corpus of the trust* (emphasis added)."

The decedent's trust instrument, which was executed in Massachusetts and states that it is to be governed by the laws of the Commonwealth, satisfies these statutory conditions....

4. *Termination of Trust A.* The judge terminated Trust A upon finding that its purpose—to qualify the trust for an estate tax marital deduction—became impossible to achieve after the Mayos' divorce. Mayo appeals this ruling. It is well established that the Probate Courts are empowered to terminate or reform a trust in whole or in part where its purposes have become impossible to achieve and the settlor did not contemplate continuation of the trust under the new circumstances....

5. *Mayo's Interest in Trust B.* The judge's decision to uphold Mayo's beneficial interest in Trust B was appealed by the Weisses, as well as by Boston University and Clark University. The judge reasoned that the decedent intended to create a life interest in Mayo when she established Trust B and failed either to revoke or to amend the trust after the couple's divorce. The appellants argue that we should extend the reach of G.L. c. 191, §9 [original UPC §2-508], to revoke all Mayo's interests under the trust. General Laws c. 191, §9, as amended through St.1977, c. 76, §2, provides in relevant part:

> "If, after executing a will, the testator shall be divorced or his marriage shall be annulled, the divorce or annulment shall revoke any disposition or appointment of property made by the will to the former spouse, any provision conferring a general or special power of appointment on the former spouse, and any nomination of the former spouse, as executor, trustee, conservator or guardian, unless the will shall expressly provide otherwise. Property prevented from passing to a former spouse because of revocation by divorce shall pass as if a former spouse had failed to survive the decedent, and other provisions conferring a power or office on the former spouse shall be interpreted as if the spouse had failed to survive the decedent."...

During her lifetime, the decedent retained power to amend or revoke the trust. Since the trust was unfunded, her co-trustee was subject to no duties or obligations until her death. Similarly, it was only as a result of the decedent's death that Mayo could claim any right to the trust assets. It is evident from the time and manner in which the trust was created and funded, that the decedent's will and trust were integrally related components of a single testamentary scheme. For all practical purposes the trust, like the will, "spoke" only at the decedent's death. For this reason Mayo's interest in the trust was revoked by operation of G.L. c. 191, §9, at the same time his interest under the decedent's will was revoked....

Treating the components of the decedent's estate plan separately, and not as parts of an interrelated whole, brings about inconsistent results....

Restricting our holding to the particular facts of this case—specifically the existence of a revocable pour-over trust funded entirely at the time of the decedent's death—we conclude that G.L. c. 191, §9, revokes Mayo's interest under Trust B.

6. *Nephews and Nieces of Donor.* According to the terms of G.L. c. 191, §9,

"[p]roperty prevented from passing to a former spouse because of revocation by divorce shall pass as if a former spouse had failed to survive the decedent..." In this case, the decedent's indenture of trust provides that if Mayo failed to survive her, "the balance of 'Trust B' shall be held . . . for the benefit of the nephews and nieces of the Donor living at the time of the death of the Donor." The trustee is directed to expend as much of the net income and principal as he deems "advisable for [their] reasonable comfort, support and education" until all living nephews and nieces have attained the age of thirty. At that time, the trust is to terminate and Boston University and Clark University are each to receive fifty per cent of the trust property to assist women students in their graduate programs.

The decedent had no siblings and therefore no nephews and nieces who were blood relations. However, when she executed her trust in 1973, her husband, James P. Mayo, Jr., had two nephews and one niece—John and Allan Chamberlain and Mira Hinman. Before her divorce, the decedent maintained friendly relations with these young people and, along with her former husband, contributed toward their educational expenses. The three have survived the decedent....

The judge concluded that the trust language created an ambiguity, and thus he considered extrinsic evidence of the decedent's meaning and intent. Based upon that evidence, he decided that the decedent intended to provide for her nieces and nephews by marriage when she created the trust. Because the decedent never revoked this gift, he found that the Chamberlains and Hinman are entitled to their beneficial interests under the trust. We agree....

... General Laws c. 191, § 9, does not provide the authority for revoking gifts to the blood relatives of a former spouse. The law implies an intent to revoke testamentary gifts between the divorcing parties because of the profound emotional and financial changes divorce normally engenders. There is no indication in the statutory language that the Legislature presumed to know how these changes affect a testator's relations with more distant family members. We therefore conclude that the Chamberlains and Hinman are entitled to take as the decedent's "nephews and nieces" under Trust B....

So ordered.

WILKINS, ABRAMS, and NOLAN, JJ., concur.

Notes

1. Pour-Over Devises. The Restatement 3d of Property §3.8 defines a pour-over devise as "a provision in a will that (i) adds property to an inter vivos trust or (ii) funds a trust that was not funded during the testator's lifetime but whose terms are in a trust instrument that was executed during the testator's lifetime." At common law, there was substantial uncertainty about the validity of an attempted pour-over into a revocable trust. Acting to facilitate pour-over devises, legislatures began to enact statutes that authorized testamentary additions to revocable or amendable trusts. The Uniform Testamentary Additions to Trusts Act was approved by the Uniform Law Commissioners in 1960, and was incorporated into the original version of the UPC as §2-511.

Section 2-511 of the current UPC makes it clear that the inter vivos trust receptacle need not have been funded during the testator's lifetime, but can be funded by the pour-over devise itself. The UPC also now allows the terms of the trust to be stated in a writing executed after as well as before or concurrently with the execution of the testator's will. It further allows the testator's will to provide that the pour-over devise is not to lapse even if the trust terminates or is revoked before the testator's death.

See also Uniform Trust Code §401(1) (stating that a trust may be created by a "transfer of property to another person as trustee during the settlor's lifetime or by will or other disposition taking effect upon the settlor's death").

2. *Will Substitutes and Conventional Revocation-upon-Divorce Statutes.* The revocation-on-divorce statute in *Clymer* is of a type widely enacted and is nearly identical to original UPC §2-508. These statutes expressly apply only to "wills."

Should the courts extend the application of these statutes beyond their express scope and apply them to "will substitutes," on the theory that will substitutes are substantively indistinguishable in function from wills?[15] Although the court in *Clymer* moved in this direction, some other courts—faced with will substitutes such as life-insurance and pension death-benefit beneficiary designations—have not been willing to do so. See, e.g., Pepper v. Peacher, 742 P.2d 21 (Okla. 1987) (retirement plan); Estate of Adams, 288 A.2d 514 (Pa. 1972) (retirement plan); Equitable Life Assurance Society v. Stitzel, 1 Fiduc.Rep.2d 316, 19 Pa. D. & C. 3d 55 (Ct. C.P. 1981) (life insurance). Notice, too, that even the court in *Clymer* was reluctant to extend the Massachusetts statute to *all* revocable inter-vivos trusts. The court took care to say that it was "restricting [its] holding to the particular facts of this case—specifically the existence of a revocable pour-over trust funded entirely at the time of the decedent's death."

3. *Current UPC §2-804.* The current UPC significantly changes the original version of §2-508. As revised and renumbered, §2-804 expressly calls for the revocation, upon divorce or annulment, of any revocable disposition or appointment of property made by either divorced individual to his or her former spouse, in a deed, will, trust, beneficiary designation, power of attorney, transfer-on-death account, or donative instrument of any other type executed by the divorced individual before the divorce or annulment of his or her marriage to the former spouse. UPC §2-804 not

---

15. In an influential article on statutory construction, Karl Llewellyn pointed out that "there are two opposing canons on almost every point." Among the opposing canons are the following: "A statute cannot go beyond its text." But "[t]o effect its purpose a statute may be implemented beyond its text." Karl N. Llewellyn, Remarks on the Theory of Appellate Decision and the Rules or Canons About How Statutes Are to be Construed, 3 Vand. L. Rev. 395, 401 (1950).

only revokes benefits to the former spouse, but also to the former spouse's relatives.

4. *Restatement 3d of Property*. The Restatement 3d of Property §4.1 comment p provides:

> *§4.1 [comment] p. Application to will substitutes.* The principles of Comment *o* [relating to revocation upon divorce] also apply to a donative transfer in the form of a will substitute, such as a revocable trust or a life-insurance-beneficiary-designation. On the application of these principles to a revocable trust, see Restatement Third, Trusts §25 comment *c* and Illustration 11. Any revocable provision in favor of the former spouse or relative of the former spouse in a will substitute is revoked upon dissolution of the marriage. The principles of Comment *o* also apply to a joint tenancy, effecting a severance of the joint tenancy and transforming the interests of the former spouses into an equal tenancy in common.

5. *Retroactive Application of the UPC*. Under UPC §8-101(b)(1), the provisions of the UPC apply to decedents dying after the effective date of the Code's enactment by a state legislature, irrespective of when the decedent's will or will substitute was executed. Thus §2-804, once enacted, operates to revoke on divorce beneficiary designations executed before the state's adoption of the UPC. In 1991, the Joint Editorial Board for Uniform Trust and Estate Acts issued a statement supporting the constitutionality of this approach under the Contracts Clause of the U.S. Constitution.[16] See Joint Editorial Board Statement Regarding the Constitutionality of Changes in Default Rules as Applied to Pre-Existing Documents, 17 ACTEC Notes 184 (1991). In 2018, the U.S. Supreme Court agreed. See Sveen v. Melin, 138 S.Ct. 1815 (2018).

———

ERISA-Covered Plans. The Employee Retirement Income Security Act of 1974 (ERISA) provides that ERISA "shall supersede any and all State laws insofar as they may now or hereafter relate to any employee benefit plan" covered by ERISA. 29 U.S.C. §1144(a). Are UPC §2-804 and similar statutes as applied to ERISA-covered plans preempted under this provision?

Egelhoff v. Egelhoff
532 U.S. 141 (2001)

JUSTICE THOMAS delivered the opinion of the Court. A Washington statute provides that the designation of a spouse as the beneficiary of a nonprobate asset is revoked automatically upon divorce. We are asked to decide whether the Employee Retirement Income Security Act of 1974 (ERISA) pre-empts that statute to the extent it applies to ERISA plans. We hold that it does.

---

16. The Contracts Clause provides that "[n]o state shall...pass any... law impairing the obligation of contracts." U.S. Const. art. I, §10 (capitalization omitted).

I. Petitioner Donna Rae Egelhoff was married to David A. Egelhoff. Mr. Egelhoff was employed by the Boeing Company, which provided him with a life insurance policy and a pension plan. Both plans were governed by ERISA, and Mr. Egelhoff designated his wife as the beneficiary under both. In April 1994, the Egelhoffs divorced. Just over two months later, Mr. Egelhoff died intestate following an automobile accident. At that time, Mrs. Egelhoff remained the listed beneficiary under both the life insurance policy and the pension plan. The life insurance proceeds, totaling $46,000, were paid to her.

Respondents Samantha and David Egelhoff, Mr. Egelhoff's children by a previous marriage, are his statutory heirs under state law. They sued petitioner in Washington state court to recover the life insurance proceeds. Respondents relied on a Washington statute that provides:

> "If a marriage is dissolved or invalidated, a provision made prior to that event that relates to the payment or transfer at death of the decedent's interest in a nonprobate asset in favor of or granting an interest or power to the decedent's former spouse is revoked. A provision affected by this section must be interpreted, and the nonprobate asset affected passes, as if the former spouse failed to survive the decedent, having died at the time of entry of the decree of dissolution or declaration of invalidity." Wash. Rev.Code §11.07.010(2)(a).

That statute applies to "all nonprobate assets, wherever situated, held at the time of entry by a superior court of this state of a decree of dissolution of marriage or a declaration of invalidity." §11.07.010(1). It defines "nonprobate asset" to include "a life insurance policy, employee benefit plan, annuity or similar contract, or individual retirement account." §11.07.010(5)(a).

Respondents argued that they were entitled to the life insurance proceeds because the Washington statute disqualified Mrs. Egelhoff as a beneficiary, and in the absence of a qualified named beneficiary, the proceeds would pass to them as Mr. Egelhoff's heirs. In a separate action, respondents also sued to recover the pension plan benefits.[17] Respondents again argued that the Washington statute disqualified Mrs. Egelhoff as a beneficiary and they were thus entitled to the benefits under the plan.

The trial courts, concluding that both the insurance policy and the pension plan "should be administered in accordance" with ERISA, granted summary judgment to petitioner in both cases. The Washington Court of Appeals consolidated the cases and reversed. It concluded that the Washington statute was not pre-empted by ERISA. Applying the statute, it held that respondents were entitled to the proceeds of both the insurance policy and the pension plan.

---

17. The pension benefits were then held by Boeing. In re Egelhoff, 989 P.2d 80, 83 (Wash. 1999) Ed.

The Supreme Court of Washington affirmed....

II. Petitioner argues that the Washington statute falls within the terms of ERISA's express pre-emption provision and that it is pre-empted by ERISA under traditional principles of conflict pre-emption. Because we conclude that the statute is expressly pre-empted by ERISA, we address only the first argument.

ERISA's pre-emption section, 29 U.S.C. §1144(a), states that ERISA "shall supersede any and all State laws insofar as they may now or hereafter relate to any employee benefit plan" covered by ERISA. We have observed repeatedly that this broadly worded provision is "clearly expansive." New York State Conference of Blue Cross & Blue Shield Plans v. Travelers Ins. Co., 514 U.S. 645, 655 (1995)....

We have held that a state law relates to an ERISA plan "if it has a connection with or reference to such a plan." Shaw v. Delta Air Lines, Inc., 463 U.S. 85, 97 (1983).... "[T]o determine whether a state law has the forbidden connection, we look both to 'the objectives of the ERISA statute as a guide to the scope of the state law that Congress understood would survive,' as well as to the nature of the effect of the state law on ERISA plans." California Div. of Labor Standards Enforcement v. Dillingham Constr., N. A., Inc., 519 U.S. 316 (1997).

Applying this framework, petitioner argues that the Washington statute has an impermissible connection with ERISA plans. We agree. The statute binds ERISA plan administrators to a particular choice of rules for determining beneficiary status. The administrators must pay benefits to the beneficiaries chosen by state law, rather than to those identified in the plan documents. The statute thus implicates an area of core ERISA concern. In particular, it runs counter to ERISA's commands that a plan shall "specify the basis on which payments are made to and from the plan," §1102(b)(4), and that the fiduciary shall administer the plan "in accordance with the documents and instruments governing the plan," §1104(a)(1)(D), making payments to a "beneficiary" who is "designated by a participant, or by the terms of [the] plan." §1002(8).[18]... [T]his statute governs the payment of benefits, a central matter of plan administration.

---

18. One can of course escape the conflict between the plan documents (which require making payments to the named beneficiary) and the statute (which requires making payments to someone else) by calling the statute an "invalidation" of the designation of the named beneficiary, and by observing that the plan documents are silent on whether "invalidation" is to occur upon divorce. The dissent employs just such an approach. Reading a clear statement as an ambiguous metastatement enables one to avoid all kinds of conflicts between seemingly contradictory texts. Suppose, for example, that the statute required that all pension benefits be paid to the Governor of Washington. That seems inconsistent with the plan documents (and with ERISA), but the inconsistency disappears if one calls the statute an "invalidation" of the principal and alternate beneficiary designations. After all, neither the plan nor ERISA actually says that beneficiaries cannot be invalidated in favor of the Governor. This approach exploits the logical inability of any text to contain a complete set of instructions for its own interpretation. It has the vice—or perhaps the virtue, depending upon one's point of view—of draining all language of its meaning.

The Washington statute also has a prohibited connection with ERISA plans because it interferes with nationally uniform plan administration. One of the principal goals of ERISA is to enable employers "to establish a uniform administrative scheme, which provides a set of standard procedures to guide processing of claims and disbursement of benefits." Fort Halifax Packing Co. v. Coyne, 482 U.S. 1, 9 (1987). Uniformity is impossible, however, if plans are subject to different legal obligations in different States.

The Washington statute at issue here poses precisely that threat. Plan administrators cannot make payments simply by identifying the beneficiary specified by the plan documents. Instead they must familiarize themselves with state statutes so that they can determine whether the named beneficiary's status has been "revoked" by operation of law. And in this context the burden is exacerbated by the choice-of-law problems that may confront an administrator when the employer is located in one State, the plan participant lives in another, and the participant's former spouse lives in a third. In such a situation, administrators might find that plan payments are subject to conflicting legal obligations.

To be sure, the Washington statute protects administrators from liability for making payments to the named beneficiary unless they have "actual knowledge of the dissolution or other invalidation of marriage," Wash. Rev.Code §11.07.010(3)(a), and it permits administrators to refuse to make payments until any dispute among putative beneficiaries is resolved, §11.07.010(3)(b). But if administrators do pay benefits, they will face the risk that a court might later find that they had "actual knowledge" of a divorce. If they instead decide to await the results of litigation before paying benefits, they will simply transfer to the beneficiaries the costs of delay and uncertainty.[19] Requiring ERISA administrators to master the relevant laws of 50 States and to contend with litigation would undermine the congressional goal of "minimiz[ing] the administrative and financial burden[s]" on plan administrators—burdens ultimately borne by the beneficiaries. Ingersoll-Rand Co. v. McClendon, 498 U.S. 133, 142 (1990).

.... We conclude that the Washington statute has a "connection with" ERISA plans and is therefore pre-empted.

III. Respondents suggest several reasons why ordinary ERISA pre-emption analysis should not apply here. First, they observe that the Washington statute allows employers to opt out....

Second, respondents emphasize that the Washington statute involves both family law and probate law, areas of traditional state regulation. There is indeed a

---

19. The dissent observes that the Washington statute permits a plan administrator to avoid resolving the dispute himself and to let courts or parties settle the matter. This observation only presents an example of how the costs of delay and uncertainty can be passed on to beneficiaries, thereby thwarting ERISA's objective of efficient plan administration. Cf. Fort Halifax Packing Co. v. Coyne, 482 U.S. 1, 9 (1987).

presumption against pre-emption in areas of traditional state regulation such as family law. But that presumption can be overcome where, as here, Congress has made clear its desire for pre-emption. Accordingly, we have not hesitated to find state family law pre-empted when it conflicts with ERISA or relates to ERISA plans.

Finally, respondents argue that if ERISA pre-empts this statute, then it also must pre-empt the various state statutes providing that a murdering heir is not entitled to receive property as a result of the killing. In the ERISA context, these "slayer" statutes could revoke the beneficiary status of someone who murdered a plan participant. Those statutes are not before us, so we do not decide the issue. We note, however, that the principle underlying the statutes—which have been adopted by nearly every State—is well established in the law and has a long historical pedigree predating ERISA. And because the statutes are more or less uniform nationwide, their interference with the aims of ERISA is at least debatable....

The judgment of the Supreme Court of Washington is reversed, and the case is remanded for further proceedings not inconsistent with this opinion.

JUSTICE SCALIA, with whom JUSTICE GINSBURG joins, concurring.

I join the opinion of the Court, since I believe that the "relate to" pre-emptive provision of the Employee Retirement Income Security Act of 1974 (ERISA) is assuredly triggered by a state law that contradicts ERISA.... I remain unsure (as I think the lower courts and everyone else will be) as to what else triggers the "relate to" provision, which—if it is interpreted to be anything other than a reference to our established jurisprudence concerning conflict and field pre-emption—has no discernible content that would not pick up every ripple in the pond, producing a result "that no sensible person could have intended." California Div. of Labor Standards Enforcement v. Dillingham Constr., N. A., Inc., 519 U.S. 316, 336 (1997) (SCALIA, J., concurring). I persist in the view that we can bring some coherence to this area, and can give the statute both a plausible and precise content, only by interpreting the "relate to" clause as a reference to our ordinary pre-emption jurisprudence.

JUSTICE BREYER, with whom JUSTICE STEVENS joins, dissenting.

Like JUSTICE SCALIA, I believe that we should apply normal conflict pre- emption and field pre-emption principles where, as here, a state statute covers ERISA and non-ERISA documents alike. Our more recent ERISA cases are consistent with this approach....

I do not agree with JUSTICE SCALIA or with the majority, however, that there is any plausible pre-emption principle that leads to a conclusion that ERISA pre-empts the statute at issue here. No one could claim that ERISA pre-empts the entire field of state law governing inheritance—though such matters "relate to" ERISA broadly speaking. Neither is there any direct conflict between the Washington statute and ERISA, for the one nowhere directly contradicts the other.

The Court correctly points out that ERISA requires a fiduciary to make payments to a beneficiary "in accordance with the documents and instruments governing the plan." 29 U.S.C. §1104(a)(1)(D). But nothing in the Washington statute requires the contrary. Rather, the state statute simply sets forth a default rule for interpreting documentary silence. The statute specifies that a nonprobate asset will pass at A's death "as if" A's "former spouse" had died first—unless the "instrument governing disposition of the nonprobate asset expressly provides otherwise." Wash. Rev.Code § 11.07.010(2)(b)(i). This state-law rule is a rule of interpretation, and it is designed to carry out, not to conflict with, the employee's likely intention as revealed in the plan documents.

There is no direct conflict or contradiction between the Washington statute and the terms of the plan documents here at issue. David Egelhoff's investment plan provides that when a "beneficiary designation" is "invalid," the "benefits will be paid" to a "surviving spouse," or "if there is no surviving spouse," to the "children in equal shares." The life insurance plan is silent about what occurs when a beneficiary designation is invalid. The Washington statute fills in these gaps, i.e., matters about which the documents themselves say nothing. Thus, the Washington statute specifies that a beneficiary designation—here "Donna R. Egelhoff wife" in the pension plan—is invalid where there is no longer any such person as Donna R. Egelhoff, wife. See Appendix, infra. And the statute adds that in such instance the funds would be paid to the children, who themselves are potential pension plan beneficiaries.

The Court's "direct conflict" conclusion rests upon its claim that "administrators must pay benefits to the beneficiaries chosen by state law, rather than to those identified in the plan documents." But the Court cannot mean "identified anywhere in the plan documents," for the Egelhoff children were "identified" as recipients in the pension plan documents should the initial designation to "Donna R. Egelhoff wife" become invalid. And whether that initial designation became invalid upon divorce is a matter about which the plan documents are silent.

To refer to state law to determine whether a given name makes a designation that is, or has become, invalid makes sense where background property or inheritance law is at issue, say, for example, where a written name is potentially ambiguous, where it is set forth near, but not in, the correct space, where it refers to a missing person perhaps presumed dead, where the name was written at a time the employee was incompetent, or where the name refers to an individual or entity disqualified by other law, say, the rule against perpetuities or rules prohibiting a murderer from benefiting from his crime. Why would Congress want the courts to create an ERISA-related federal property law to deal with such problems? Regardless, to refer to background state law in such circumstances does not directly conflict with any explicit ERISA provision, for no provision of ERISA forbids reading an instrument or document in light of state property law principles. In any event, in this case the plan documents explicitly foresee that a beneficiary designation may become "invalid," but they do not specify the invalidating circumstances. To refer to state property law to fill in that blank cannot possibly create any direct conflict with the plan documents.

The majority simply denies that there is any blank to fill in and suggests that the plan documents require the plan to pay the designated beneficiary under all circumstances. But there is nonetheless an open question, namely, whether a designation that (here explicitly) refers to a wife remains valid after divorce.... The plan documents themselves do not answer the question any more than they describe what is to occur in a host of other special circumstances (e.g., mental incompetence, intoxication, ambiguous names, etc.). To determine whether ERISA permits state law to answer such questions requires a careful examination of the particular state law in light of ERISA's basic policies. We should not short-circuit that necessary inquiry simply by announcing a "direct conflict" where none exists....

The more serious pre-emption question is whether this state statute "'stands as an obstacle to the accomplishment and execution of the full purposes and objectives of Congress.'"....

The Court claims that the Washington statute "interferes with nationally uniform plan administration" by requiring administrators to "familiarize themselves with state statutes." But administrators have to familiarize themselves with state law in any event when they answer such routine legal questions as whether amounts due are subject to garnishment, who is a "spouse," who qualifies as a "child," or when an employee is legally dead. And were that "familiarizing burden" somehow overwhelming, the plan could easily avoid it by resolving the divorce revocation issue in the plan documents themselves, stating expressly that state law does not apply. The "burden" thus reduces to a one-time requirement that would fall primarily upon the few who draft model ERISA documents, not upon the many who administer them. So meager a burden cannot justify pre-empting a state law that enjoys a presumption against pre-emption.

The Court also fears that administrators would have to make difficult choice-of-law determinations when parties live in different States. Whether this problem is or is not "major" in practice, the Washington statute resolves it by expressly setting forth procedures whereby the parties or the courts, not the plan administrator, are responsible for resolving it.

....[I]f one looks beyond administrative burden, one finds that Washington's statute poses no obstacle, but furthers ERISA's ultimate objective—developing a fair system for protecting employee benefits. The Washington statute transfers an employee's pension assets at death to those individuals whom the worker would likely have wanted to receive them. As many jurisdictions have concluded, divorced workers more often prefer that a child, rather than a divorced spouse, receive those assets. Of course, an employee can secure this result by changing a beneficiary form; but doing so requires awareness, understanding, and time. That is why Washington and many other jurisdictions have created a statutory assumption that divorce works a revocation of a designation in favor of an ex-spouse....

In forbidding Washington to apply that assumption here, the Court permits a divorced wife, who already acquired, during the divorce proceeding, her fair share of the couple's community property, to receive in addition the benefits that the divorce court awarded to her former husband.... As a result, Donna will now receive a windfall of approximately $80,000 at the expense of David's children. The State of Washington enacted a statute to prevent precisely this kind of unfair result. But the Court, relying on an inconsequential administrative burden, concludes that Congress required it.

Finally, the logic of the Court's decision does not stop at divorce revocation laws. The Washington statute is virtually indistinguishable from other traditional state-law rules, for example, rules using presumptions to transfer assets in the case of simultaneous deaths, and rules that prohibit a husband who kills a wife from receiving benefits as a result of the wrongful death. It is particularly difficult to believe that Congress wanted to pre-empt the latter kind of statute. But how do these statutes differ from the one before us? Slayer statutes—like this statute—"gover[n] the payment of benefits, a central matter of plan administration." And contrary to the Court's suggestion, slayer statutes vary from State to State in their details just like divorce revocation statutes. Indeed, the "slayer" conflict would seem more serious, not less serious, than the conflict before us, for few, if any, slayer statutes permit plans to opt out of the state property law rule....

...The state statute poses no significant obstacle to the accomplishment of any federal objective. Any effort to squeeze some additional pre-emptive force from ERISA's words (i.e., "relate to") is inconsistent with the Court's recent case law. And the state statute before us is one regarding family property—a "fiel[d] of traditional state regulation," where the interpretive presumption against pre-emption is particularly strong. Travelers, 514 U.S., at 655. For these reasons, I disagree with the Court's conclusion. And, consequently, I dissent.

APPENDIX TO OPINION OF BREYER, J.

Notes and Questions

1. *Federal Common Law?* In *Egelhoff*, the majority opinion and the concurring opinion said that the Washington revocation-on-divorce statute was preempted because it was in direct conflict with ERISA. The majority opinion stated:

> [The Washington statute revoking a beneficiary designation to the employee's former spouse] runs counter to ERISA's commands that a plan shall "specify the basis on which payments are made to and from the plan," §1102(b)(4), and that the fiduciary shall administer the plan "in accordance with the documents and instruments governing the plan," §1104(a)(1)(D), making payments to a "beneficiary" who is "designated by a participant, or by the terms of [the] plan." §1002(8).

Accord, Kennedy v. Plan Administrator for DuPont Savings and Investment Plan, 129 S.Ct. 865 (2009), holding that a plan administrator properly distributed benefits to a decedent's divorced spouse who was named on the beneficiary designation form, despite the terms of the divorce decree divesting her of the benefits.

Does this mean that *any* state law that could invalidate a beneficiary designation is preempted because it is in conflict with ERISA's command that the fiduciary "shall" make payments to the beneficiary who is designated by the participant? Suppose that the employee's signature on the beneficiary designation form is forged, or that the employee lacked mental capacity[20] or was subject to undue influence when signing the beneficiary designation?

In Tinsley v. General Motors Corp., 227 F.3d 700 (6th Cir. 2000), Edward B. Williams, who died on December 18, 1996, had initially designated his niece, Willie Lee Tinsley, as the beneficiary of the life insurance plan under the General Motors Life Insurance and Disability Program. Before his death, Williams executed a new "Designation of Beneficiary" form, naming his neighbor, Beulah Calloway, instead. Calloway had cared for Williams while he was ill and resided with him for a time. Tinsley brought suit in federal district court, claiming that the beneficiary designation form naming Calloway as beneficiary was the product of undue influence. Reversing the decision of the district court, the Sixth Circuit said:

> Although the district court, like the parties, looked to Michigan state law in its discussion of Tinsley's claims, we believe that federal law governs this case, because it involves an employee welfare benefit plan that is governed by the Employee Retirement Income Security Act ("ERISA"), 29 U.S.C. § 1001 *et seq.* ERISA preempts any state law

---

20. See Metropolitan Life Ins. Co. v. Hall, 9 F.Supp.2d 560 (D. Md. 1998), in which the court applied the following federal common law standard of mental capacity, which the court derived from Taylor v. United States, 113 F. Supp. 143 (W.D. Ark. 1953), aff'd, 211 F.2d 794 (8th Cir. 1954):

> To be capable of effecting a valid change of beneficiary a person should have clearness of mind and memory sufficient to know the nature of the property for which he is about to name a beneficiary, the nature of the act which he is about to perform, the names and identities of those who are the natural objects of his bounty; his relationship towards them, and the consequences of his act, uninfluenced by any material delusions.

that relates to—that is, that "has a connection with or reference to"—an ERISA-covered plan....

.... We therefore conclude that the question whether Tinsley is entitled to the proceeds from Williams's life insurance plan due to the ... alleged exercise of undue influence by Calloway is preempted by ERISA and governed by federal law.

The court went on to conclude that federal law is to be determined by "review[ing] the case law regarding undue influence in the various states that comprise this circuit" and "extract[ing] some shared general principles to guide our federal-common-law analysis of Tinsley's undue influence claim."

How is the administrative burden on plan administrators eased by forcing them to distill the possibly conflicting law of the various states in each circuit, as opposed to the law of one state? If federal common law is to be distilled from general state law, would the ALI Restatements of the Law be a more accessible source for determining such principles? An article by Thomas P. Gallanis, ERISA and the Law of Succession, 65 Ohio St. L.J. 185 (2004), answers this question in the affirmative. On undue influence specifically, the Restatement 3d of Property §8.3, reproduced in Chapter 4, sets forth principles of undue influence applicable to all donative transfers, including the various will substitutes. See Restatement 3d of Property §8.3 comment a.

2. *Revocation on Divorce as Federal Common Law?* If an ERISA beneficiary designation can be set aside on the ground of forgery, mental incapacity, or undue influence, and if these grounds are to be imported into federal common law on the basis of generally accepted state law (matters not yet decided by the Supreme Court), why is revocation by divorce not a matter of federal common law? The Restatement 3d of Property, as well as UPC §2-804, provides that a revocable beneficiary designation of the former spouse in a will substitute is set aside by divorce. Restatement 3d of Property §4.1 comment p. See David S. Lebolt, Making the Best of *Egelhoff*: Federal Common Law for ERISA-Preempted Beneficiary Designations, 28 J. Pension Plan. & Compliance 29 (Fall 2002).

3. *Effect on Slayer Statutes.* As discussed later in this chapter, most states have statutes providing that killers cannot succeed to their victim's property. Citing *Egelhoff*, an Ohio case held ERISA preempted the state's slayer statute, but recognized revocation by homicide as a doctrine of federal common law. See Ahmed v. Ahmed, 817 N.E.2d 424 (Ohio Ct. App. 2004). Accord Atwater v. Nortel Networks, Inc., 388 F.Supp.2d 610 (M.D. N.C. 2005); Connecticut General Life Ins. Co. v. Riner, 351 F.Supp.2d 492 (W.D. Va. 2005). For post-*Egelhoff* cases applying state slayer law to ERISA-governed benefits, see Laborers' Pension Fund v. Miscevic, 880 F.3d 927 (7th Cir. 2018)(pension plan); First Nat. Bank & Trust Co. of Mountain Home v. Stonebridge Life Ins. Co., 619 F.3d 951 (8th Cir. 2010) (life insurance). Oregon extended its slayer statute to deny "proceeds under any pension, profit-sharing, or other plan" to an "abuser," defined as "a person who is convicted

of a felony by reason of conduct that constitutes physical abuse ... or financial abuse ... [within five years of the decedent's death]." Or. Rev. Stat. §§112.455, 112.515. Would this statute be preempted by ERISA? See Herinckx v. Sanelle, 385 P.3d 1190 (Or. Ct. App. 2016), holding the statute preempted but allowing the plaintiffs to amend their complaint to assert a claim based in part on federal common law.

4. *Codified Constructive Trust.* UPC §2-804 provides that, in the event that federal courts decide that ERISA preempts §2-804, subsection (h)(2) imposes an offsetting personal liability on the recipient of the proceeds in the amount of any payment received as a result of preemption. Put differently, the statute creates a constructive trust to avoid unjust enrichment. There are corresponding provisions in four other sections of the UPC: §2-210 (elective share), §2-702 (survival by 120 hours), §2-706 (antilapse), and §2-803 (slayer rule). Does ERISA preempt these provisions?

Hillman v. Maretta
133 S.Ct. 1943 (2013)

JUSTICE SOTOMAYOR delivered the opinion of the Court. The Federal Employees' Group Life Insurance Act of 1954 (FEGLIA), 5 U.S.C. §8701 et seq., establishes a life insurance program for federal employees. FEGLIA provides that an employee may designate a beneficiary to receive the proceeds of his life insurance at the time of his death. Separately, a Virginia statute addresses the situation in which an employee's marital status has changed, but he did not update his beneficiary designation before his death. Section 20–111.1(D) of the Virginia Code renders a former spouse liable for insurance proceeds to whoever would have received them under applicable law, usually a widow or widower, but for the beneficiary designation. Va.Code Ann. §20–111.1(D). This case presents the question whether the remedy created by §20–111.1(D) is pre-empted by FEGLIA and its implementing regulations. We hold that it is.

I.A

... FEGLIA provides that, upon an employee's death, life insurance benefits are paid in accordance with a specified "order of precedence." 5 U.S.C. §8705(a). The proceeds accrue "[f]irst, to the beneficiary or beneficiaries designated by the employee in a signed and witnessed writing received before death.""...

FEGLIA also includes an express pre-emption provision. That provision states in relevant part that "[t]he provisions of any contract under [FEGLIA] which relate to the nature or extent of coverage or benefits (including payments with respect to benefits) shall supersede and preempt any law of any State..., which relates to group life insurance to the extent that the law or regulation is inconsistent with the contractual provisions." §8709(d)(1).

This case turns on the interaction between these provisions of FEGLIA and a Virginia statute. Section 20–111.1(A) (Section A) of the Virginia Code provides that a divorce or annulment "revoke[s]" a "beneficiary designation contained in a then existing written contract owned by one party that provides for the payment of any death benefit to the other party." A "death benefit" includes "payments under a life insurance contract." §20.111.1(B).

In the event that Section A is pre-empted by federal law, §20–111.1(D) (Section D) of the Virginia Code applies. Section D provides as follows:

> If [Va.Code Ann. §20–111.1] is preempted by federal law with respect to the payment of any death benefit, a former spouse who, not for value, receives the payment of any death benefit that the former spouse is not entitled to under [§20–111.1] is personally liable for the amount of the payment to the person who would have been entitled to it were [§20.111.1] not preempted.

In other words, where Section A is pre-empted, Section D creates a cause of action rendering a former spouse liable for the principal amount of the insurance proceeds to the person who would have received them had Section A continued in effect.

B

Warren Hillman (Warren) and respondent Judy Maretta were married. In 1996, Warren named Maretta as the beneficiary of his FEGLI policy. Warren and Maretta divorced in 1998 and, four years later, he married petitioner Jacqueline Hillman. Warren died unexpectedly in 2008. Because Warren had never changed the named beneficiary under his FEGLI policy, it continued to identify Maretta as the beneficiary at the time of his death despite his divorce and subsequent remarriage to Hillman.

Hillman filed a claim for the proceeds of Warren's life insurance, but the FEGLI administrator informed her that the proceeds would accrue to Maretta, because she had been named as the beneficiary. Maretta filed a claim for the benefits with OPM and collected the FEGLI proceeds in the amount of $124,558.03.

Hillman then filed a lawsuit in Virginia Circuit Court, arguing that Maretta was liable to her under Section D for the proceeds of her deceased husband's FEGLI policy. The parties agreed that Section A, which directly reallocates the benefits, is pre-empted by FEGLIA. Maretta contended that Section D is also pre-empted by federal law and that she should keep the insurance proceeds. The Circuit Court rejected Maretta's argument and granted summary judgment to Hillman, finding Maretta liable to Hillman under Section D for the proceeds of Warren's policy.

The Virginia Supreme Court reversed and entered judgment for Maretta....

We granted certiorari to resolve a conflict among the state and federal courts over whether FEGLIA pre-empts a rule of state law that automatically assigns an interest in the proceeds of a FEGLI policy to a person other than the named beneficiary or grants that person a right to recover such proceeds. We now affirm.

II

Under the Supremacy Clause, Congress has the power to pre-empt state law expressly. Although FEGLIA contains an express pre-emption provision, see §8709(d)(1), the court below considered only whether Section D is pre-empted under conflict pre-emption principles. We limit our analysis here to that holding.

A

To determine whether a state law conflicts with Congress' purposes and objectives, we must first ascertain the nature of the federal interest.

Hillman contends that Congress' purpose in enacting FEGLIA was to advance administrative convenience by establishing a clear rule to dictate where the Government should direct insurance proceeds. There is some force to Hillman's argument that a significant legislative interest in a large federal program like FEGLIA is to enable its efficient administration. If Hillman is correct that administrative convenience was Congress' only purpose, then there might be no conflict between Section D and FEGLIA: Section D's cause of action takes effect only after benefits have been paid, and so would not necessarily impact the Government's distribution of insurance proceeds.

For her part, Maretta insists that Congress had a more substantial purpose in enacting FEGLIA: to ensure that a duly named beneficiary will receive the insurance proceeds and be able to make use of them. If Maretta is correct, then Section D would directly conflict with that objective, because its cause of action would take the insurance proceeds away from the named beneficiary and reallocate them to someone else. We must therefore determine which understanding of FEGLIA's purpose is correct....

B

... Section D interferes with Congress' scheme, because it directs that the proceeds actually "belong" to someone other than the named beneficiary by creating a cause of action for their recovery by a third party. It makes no difference whether state law requires the transfer of the proceeds, as Section A does, or creates a cause of action, like Section D, that enables another person to receive the proceeds upon filing an action in state court. In either case, state law displaces the beneficiary selected by the insured in accordance with FEGLIA and places someone else in her stead....

One can imagine plausible reasons to favor a different policy. Many employees perhaps neglect to update their beneficiary designations after a change in marital status. As a result, a legislature could have thought that a default rule providing that insurance proceeds accrue to a widow or widower, and not a named beneficiary, would be more likely to align with most people's intentions. Or, similarly, a legislature might have reasonably believed that an employee's will is more reliable evidence of his intent than a beneficiary designation form executed years earlier.

But that is not the judgment Congress made. Rather than draw an inference about an employee's probable intent from a range of sources, Congress established a clear and predictable procedure for an employee to indicate who the intended beneficiary of his life insurance shall be....

In short, where a beneficiary has been duly named, the insurance proceeds she is owed under FEGLIA cannot be allocated to another person by operation of state law. Section D does exactly that. We therefore agree with the Virginia Supreme Court that it is pre-empted....

JUSTICE THOMAS, concurring in the judgment. ...Section D directly conflicts with [FEGLIA's] statutory scheme, because it nullifies the insured's statutory right to designate a beneficiary. The right to designate a beneficiary encompasses a corresponding right in the named beneficiary not only to receive the proceeds, but also to retain them. Indeed, the "right" to designate a beneficiary—as well as the term "beneficiary" itself—would be meaningless if the only effect of a designation were to saddle the nominal beneficiary with liability under state law for the full value of the proceeds. But Section D accomplishes exactly that: It transforms the designated beneficiary into a defendant in state court, a defendant who is now liable to the individual the State has designated as the true beneficiary. While Hillman does not insist that the insurer should have mailed the check to her (as opposed to Maretta, the designated beneficiary), Section D requires, in effect, this very result. If the right to designate a beneficiary means anything, we must conclude that Section D directly conflicts with FEGLIA's order of precedence.

The direct conflict between Section D and FEGLIA is also evident in the fact that Section D's only function is to accomplish what Section A would have achieved, had Section A not been pre-empted....

... Of course, Section D does not preclude the direct payment of benefits to the designated beneficiary; however, it accomplishes the same prohibited result by transforming the designated party into little more than a passthrough for the true beneficiary. This cannot be squared with FEGLIA. Consequently, Section D must yield.

For these reasons, I agree with the Court's conclusion that Section D is pre-empted and, therefore, concur in the judgment.

JUSTICE ALITO, concurring in the judgment. ...Because one of the purposes of the Federal Employees' Group Life Insurance Act of 1954 (FEGLIA) is to implement the expressed wishes of the insured, I would hold that a state law is pre-empted if it effectively overrides an insured's actual, articulated choice of beneficiary. The challenged provision of Virginia law has that effect....

...FEGLIA seems to me to have two primary purposes or objectives.

The first is administrative convenience. It is easier for an insurance administrator to pay insurance proceeds to the person whom the insured has designated on a specified form without having to consider claims made by others based on some other ground. But §20–111.1(D) does not affect the initial payment of proceeds. It operates *after* the funds are received by the designated beneficiary, and it thus causes no inconvenience for those who administer the payment of FEGLIA proceeds.

The second purpose or objective is the effectuation of the insured's *expressed* intent above all other considerations....

... To be sure, Virginia's provision may well reflect the *unexpressed* preferences of the majority of insureds whose situations are similar to that of the insured in this case—that is, individuals who, after divorce and remarriage, fail to change a prior designation of a former spouse as the beneficiary of the policy. But FEGLIA prioritizes the insured's *expressed* intent....

In affirming the decision below, the Court goes well beyond what is necessary and opines that the party designated as the beneficiary under a FEGLIA policy must be allowed to keep the insurance proceeds even if the insured's contrary and expressed intent is indisputable—for example, when the insured writes a postdivorce will specifically leaving the proceeds to someone else.... Needless to say, this circular reasoning does not explain *why* Congress might have wanted the designated beneficiary to keep the proceeds even when that is indisputably contrary to the insured's expressed wishes at the time of death. I am doubtful that any purpose or objective of FEGLIA would be honored by such a holding, but it is not necessary to resolve that question in this case.

For these reasons, I concur in the judgment.

Note

Response of the Uniform Law Commission. In 2014, the Uniform Law Commission amended the Official Comment to UPC §2-804 to explain, among other things, why the *Hillman* decision was wrong:

> The Court's decision in *Hillman* has many unfortunate consequences. First, the decision frustrates the dominant purpose of wealth transfer law, which is to implement the transferor's intention. The result in *Hillman*, that the decedent's ex-spouse remained entitled to the proceeds of the decedent's life insurance policy purchased through a program established by FEGLIA, frustrates the decedent's intention. Second, the *Hillman* decision ignores the decades-long trend of unifying the law governing probate and nonprobate transfers. The revocation-on-divorce rule has long been a part of probate law (see, e.g., pre-1990 Section 2-508). In 1990, this section extended the rule of revocation on divorce to nonprobate transfers. Third, the decision in *Hillman* fosters a division between state- and federally-regulated nonprobate mechanisms. If the decedent in Hillman had purchased a life insurance policy individually, rather than through the FEGLIA program, the policy would have been governed by the Virginia counterpart of this section.

EXTERNAL REFERENCES. For critiques of *Hillman*, see Thomas P. Gallanis, The U.S. Supreme Court and the Law of Trusts and Estates: A Law Reformer's Perspective, 42 ACTEC L.J. 11 (2016); John H. Langbein, Destructive Federal

Preemption of State Wealth Transfer Law in Beneficiary Designation Cases: *Hillman* Doubles Down on *Egelhoff*, 67 Vand. L. Rev. 1665 (2014); Lawrence W. Waggoner, The Creeping Federalization of Wealth-Transfer Law, 67 Vand. L. Rev. 1635 (2014).

2. Antilapse Statutes

Primary Statutory References: *UPC §§2-702, 2-706, 2-707*

Antilapse statutes apply by their terms only to "wills." This is true of the antilapse statute contained in the original UPC and of almost all the antilapse statutes in non-UPC states.

Suppose the beneficiary of a revocable inter vivos trust predeceases the settlor, or the beneficiary of a life insurance policy predeceases the insured, or the beneficiary of a death benefit under a retirement plan predeceases the participant. Should antilapse statutes be extended to these situations? Compare the following two cases.

First National Bank of Bar Harbor v. Anthony
557 A.2d 957 (Me. 1989)

ROBERTS, J. The children of John M. Anthony, Deborah Alley and Christopher Anthony Perasco, appeal from a summary judgment of the Superior Court, Hancock County (Smith, J.), that denied their claim to a remainder interest in an inter vivos trust created by their now deceased grandfather, J. Franklin Anthony. The court determined that the gift to John M. Anthony, a child of the settlor, of the remainder interest lapsed as a result of John M. Anthony's death prior to the death of the settlor. Because we hold that the remainder interest of John M. Anthony was a present, vested interest at the time of the creation of the inter vivos trust, we vacate the judgment.

Facts. On May 14, 1975, J. Franklin Anthony, of Bar Harbor, established a revocable inter vivos trust with the First National Bank of Bar Harbor. The income was payable to the settlor for life, then to his widow, Ethel L. Anthony, should she survive him. Upon the death of both J. Franklin and Ethel L. Anthony, the corpus would be divided "in equal shares to [the settlor's] children, John M. Anthony, Peter B. Anthony and Dencie S. Tripp [now Fenno] free and clear of any trust."

Ethel Anthony predeceased her husband on November 22, 1982. On September 9, 1983, John M. Anthony died unmarried, leaving three children: Deborah Alley, Christopher Anthony Perasco and Paul Anthony.

J. Franklin Anthony died on April 2, 1984. On April 10, 1984, his will was admitted to Probate by the Hancock County Probate Court. The will left two-thirds of his estate to Peter B. Anthony and one-third to Dencie S. Fenno; the heirs of John M. Anthony were expressly omitted from the will.

Procedure. The First National Bank of Bar Harbor, in its capacity as trustee, filed a complaint in the Superior Court requesting construction of the Anthony Trust. The children of John M. Anthony, grandchildren of the settlor, filed a motion for summary judgment. The grandchildren asserted that John M. Anthony's interest in the trust was vested, not contingent, at the time of its creation. John M.'s heirs, therefore, were entitled to his one-third interest in the trust.

The motion was opposed by Dencie S. Fenno and Peter B. Anthony, at that time arguing that the terms of the trust were ambiguous and that extrinsic evidence should be permitted to determine the intent of the settlor. Their memorandum was accompanied by two affidavits stating that affiant's understanding that the deceased settlor wished the children of John M. Anthony to receive nothing from the settlor's estate. In granting summary judgment against the movants, the court (1) declined to consider extrinsic evidence on the ground that the language of the trust was unambiguous, (2) determined that the gift of the remainder to named individuals "in equal shares" was a gift to the individuals and not to a class, (3) held that the gift to John M. Anthony lapsed because his interest did not vest until the death of the survivor of the settlor and his wife, and (4) declined to apply the Anti-Lapse Statute, 18-A M.R.S.A. §2-605, because the statute applies only to testamentary gifts. The court therefore directed the trustee to pay over the lapsed gift to John M. Anthony to the personal representative of the deceased settlor. This appeal followed.

Discussion. Before us all parties now agree that the terms of the trust are unambiguous and that a summary judgment is appropriate. Moreover, all parties agree that the gift of the remainder interest "in equal shares" to the named children of the settlor was a gift to the individuals and not to a class. As a result, we need address only the court's holding that the gift to John M. Anthony lapsed upon his death prior to the death of the settlor.

The parties rely almost exclusively on our prior cases dealing with testamentary dispositions. These cases are of little assistance on the issue before us. Because a will is not operative until the death of the testator, an interest in a testamentary trust cannot vest prior to that event. On the other hand, an inter vivos trust is operative from the date of its creation. We must determine the settlor's intent as expressed in the trust instrument by examining the settlor's overall plan of disposition.

We note the following: (1) the settlor explicitly retained the right to change his beneficiaries if he wanted to alter the trust's disposition; (2) the settlor imposed no restrictions on what his children could do with their respective shares; (3) aside from his power to revoke or amend the trust, the settlor specifically limited his own benefit to income during his lifetime and payment of certain expenses associated with his death; (4) the settlor made survival an explicit condition of any benefit to his wife, but did not include such language in the case of his children. The unexercised right to make a change in beneficiaries, the absence of any control over how the children might dispose of their shares, and the overall assignment of economic benefits lead us to conclude that this plan of disposition effectively eliminated any further interest of the settlor in the trust principal unless he affirmatively chose to intervene. His failure to change the plan coupled with the omission of a survival requirement in the case of the children's shares, suggests a disposition to a predeceased child's estate rather than a reversion to the settlor's estate. As a result of this construction of the instrument, it may be said that the children's interests were vested, subject to defeasance or divestment if the settlor chose to amend or revoke the trust or change his beneficiaries.

We next address the question whether the settlor's reservation of the power of amendment or revocation should alter our conclusion that the children's interests vested. Substantial case law from other jurisdictions persuades us that it should not. A leading case decided by the Ohio Supreme Court holds that an inter vivos trust reserving to the settlor the income for life plus the power to revoke, with a remainder over at the death of the settlor, creates a vested interest in the remainderman subject to defeasance by the exercise of the power of revocation. First National Bank v. Tenney, 165 Ohio St. 513, 138 N.E.2d 15 (1956)....

The trust instrument before us contains no requirement that the remainder beneficiaries survive the life tenants and we see no reason to imply a requirement of survival. Only the settlor's subsequent revocation or substitution would divest the remainder interest. Evidence presented by affidavit of the settlor's desire to revoke the contingent remainder and disinherit his son and son's heirs is simply not relevant. Although the settlor's intention is critical in interpreting the terms of a trust, that intention must be ascertained by analyzing the trust instrument. Mooney v. Northeast Bank & Trust Co., 377 A.2d 120, at 122 (Me. 1977). Only when the instrument is ambiguous can a court consider extrinsic evidence. Id. at 122.

Because John M. Anthony's interest vested at the time of the creation of the trust, we do not consider whether Maine's anti-lapse statute, 18-A M.R.S.A. §2-605, could apply to an inter vivos trust.

Judgment vacated.

Estate of Button

490 P.2d 731 (Wash. 1971)

ROSELLINI, J. This action was instituted by the Old National Bank of Washington, asking the Superior Court for Whitman County to determine its obligations under [a revocable] trust instrument[] and the applicable Washington law.

The evidence presented at the hearing of the matter showed that in 1940, Robert H. Button executed a revocable trust, covering certain real property located in Whitman County, retaining a life estate, and naming the Old National Bank of Washington as trustee.... The trust contained the following provision:

> Upon the death of the Trustor without having withdrawn the entire fund, the balance of investments and cash remaining in the trust fund shall be delivered to the Trustor's mother, Audrey A. Burg, and her receipt for the residue of said trust fund shall thereupon release the Trustee from any further responsibility therefor.

There was no provision for the disposition of the trust property in the event the trustor's mother should predecease him....

On November 15, 1966, Audrey A. Burg died intestate, and on November 28, 1966, the trustor, Button, died, leaving a will....

We are thus brought to the question of the proper disposition of the trust property, the only named beneficiary of the 1940 trust (other than the trustor himself) having died prior to the death of the trustor.

It was the rule at common law that a gift in trust lapsed upon the death of the beneficiary prior to the death of the trustor. Restatement (Second) of Trusts §112 comment f at 245 (1959); A. Scott, The Law of Trusts §112.3 (3d ed. 1967). And in this state, if the named legatee in a will is not a relative by consanguinity, the common law rule that the gift lapses is still in effect.

However, by the terms of RCW 11.12.110, when an estate is devised or bequeathed to any child, grandchild, or other relative of the testator, and the devisee or legatee dies before the testator, leaving lineal descendants, such descendants shall take the estate.

The act declares that under the provisions of that section a spouse is not a relative. It does not, however, exclude a parent from the definition of "relative."

Of course, the gift to Audrey A. Burg was not made by will, but by inter vivos trust. If it were made by testamentary trust, we do not think that it could be seriously suggested that this statute was not meant to affect it, and the only difference between such a gift and that involved here is that the inter vivos trust disposes of property upon the death of the settlor without the necessity of complying with the statute of wills. Similar statutes do indeed apply to trusts. Restatement (Second) of Trusts §112 comment f (1959); A. Scott, The Law of Trusts §112.3, n.3 (3d ed. 1967). Courts in other jurisdictions which have considered the question also have held that similar statutes apply to beneficiaries of testamentary trusts. See Annot., Statute to prevent lapse in event of death of devisee or legatee before testator as applicable to interest of beneficiary under trust who dies before testator, 118 A.L.R. 559 (1939).

A gift to be enjoyed only upon or after the death of the donor is in practical effect a legacy, whether it is created in an inter vivos instrument or in a will. RCW 11.12.110 declares the policy of the law of this state, and that policy is against the lapsing of gifts to relatives of the deceased. This does not mean that a testator or trustor cannot provide for a different disposition. If he does, of course, the statute has no application....

We conclude that the gift to Audrey A. Burg did not lapse, and that the trustee holds the residue for her [two other sons, Kerry and Fredric].

The judgment of the Court of Appeals is reversed... and the cause is remanded to the Superior Court for Whitman County with directions to enter an order in conformity with the views expressed herein.

Notes

1. *Current Washington Statute.* Washington's antilapse statute was amended in 1994 to apply not only to wills but also to "a trust of which the decedent is a grantor and which by its terms becomes irrevocable upon or before the grantor's death...." Wash. Rev. Code §11.12.110.

2. *State of the Authorities.* The *Button* case represents a minority but growing view. The weight of authority favors the view in *Anthony* that a future interest in a revocable trust is not conditioned on survival of the settlor unless the trust document expressly so provides.

The Restatement 3d of Property and the Restatement 3d of Trusts side with the *Button* case, the Restatement 3d of Property stating that antilapse statutes should "apply by analogy to revocable trusts and other will substitutes." Restatement 3d of Property §5.5 comment p; Restatement 3d of Trusts §25 comment e.

The Comment to §2-603, the antilapse provision contained in the UPC, states that §2-603 applies only to wills. However, §2-707, which we consider in more detail in Chapter 16, establishes a similar rule with respect to revocable and irrevocable trusts.

———

"Beneficiaries Who Don't Benefit." On January 23, 2000, financial columnist and author Jane Bryant Quinn published a column in the Washington Post, at page H2, titled "Beneficiaries Who Don't Benefit." She observed: "When you buy life insurance or a tax-deferred annuity, or start a retirement plan such as an IRA or 401(k), you're given standard forms to sign. The forms ask who you want as beneficiaries." The problem with these forms, she noted, is that they call for named beneficiaries, rather than for class gifts such as *to my descendants who survive me per stirpes*. This emphasis on named beneficiaries raises two concerns: (1) future-born relatives who would be included in a class gift are excluded by not being specifically named, and (2) one or more of the named beneficiaries might fail to survive. In the column, she quoted Professor Lawrence Waggoner of the University of Michigan, who commented that "insurers and retirement plans are to blame. If they wanted, they could give you some options on the beneficiary form. You could choose whether or not to include children born in the future, or whether your grandchildren could inherit your dead child's share." Why do most plans and insurers fail to do this? "'It's for their administrative convenience,' Waggoner says. 'They don't want to have to investigate who the grandchildren are.'"

Quinn advised her readers to change their beneficiary designations as often as needed and to keep records of each change. As she observed, "If the company loses the amendment, your family will need proof."

Notes

1. *Predeceasing Beneficiaries of Life Insurance, Retirement Plan Death Benefits, and POD Accounts.* The case for extending antilapse statutes to other types of will substitutes such as life-insurance beneficiary designations, retirement-plan death benefits, and POD accounts is much stronger than it is for revocable inter vivos trusts. The reason is that beneficiaries of these types of contractual arrangements *do* lose their interests by virtue of predeceasing the decedent because, like wills, the arrangements impose a survival requirement on the beneficiaries.

In direct response to this problem, the UPC contains a provision, §2-706, which applies language similar to that of §2-603 to "beneficiary designations" in favor of the decedent's grandparents, descendants of the decedent's grandparents, and the decedent's stepchildren. As defined in §1-201, the term "beneficiary designation" refers to "a governing instrument naming a beneficiary of an insurance or annuity policy, of an account with POD designation, of a security registered in beneficiary form (TOD), or of a pension, profitsharing, retirement, or similar benefit plan, or other nonprobate transfer at death."

Would this section be controlling in the case of an employee benefit plan covered by ERISA? See Egelhoff v. Egelhoff, discussed earlier in this chapter.

2. *Subsequent Response of the Pension-Account Industry.* Some mutual fund companies, such as Fidelity and Vanguard, have changed their pension-account beneficiary designation forms to accommodate the common desire to substitute the descendants of a deceased beneficiary and, in some cases, to allow the use of a class-gift designation in order to include after-born or after-adopted members of the class. However, these forms often specify the "per stirpes" method of representation as the one that must be used to distribute property among surviving descendants.

Still common, though, are forms such as the University of Michigan Group Life Insurance beneficiary form providing that "[i]f you name more than one beneficiary, payment will be made in equal shares to the named beneficiaries who survive you (or in full to the survivor if only one beneficiary survives you), unless you enter a specific percentage for each person."

3. *Simultaneous or Near Simultaneous Death*

Primary Statutory References: *UPC §2-702*

Section 5 of the 1953 version of the Uniform Simultaneous Death Act provides that, when the person whose life is insured and the beneficiary of the policy die under circumstances in which there is "no sufficient evidence" that they died otherwise than simultaneously, the policy proceeds are to be distributed as if the beneficiary predeceased the insured.

Janus v. Tarasewicz
482 N.E.2d 418 (Ill. App. Ct. 1985)

[Stanley and Theresa Janus, having just returned from their honeymoon, gathered on September 29, 1982, with other family members to mourn the death of Stanley's brother, who had died earlier that day from ingesting what turned out to be cyanide-laced Tylenol capsules.[21] In the stress of the moment, Stanley and Theresa took some of the Tylenol capsules, not knowing these were poisoned. Within a short while, Stanley fell to the floor. While a neighbor, who was a registered nurse, applied emergency CPR on Stanley, Theresa began having seizures and within a few minutes she fell unconscious. Paramedics testified that Stanley's vital signs disappeared while he and Theresa were in the ambulance en route to the hospital. He was pronounced dead an hour and a half after arriving at the emergency room. Theresa required an artificial respirator in order to breathe by the time she was in the ambulance, but when she arrived at the hospital she did have a palpable pulse and blood pressure. She maintained a "measurable, though unsatisfactory" blood pressure later while she was in the emergency room. The next day, after receiving several tests to assess her brain function, Theresa was diagnosed as having sustained total brain death. Her life support systems were terminated, and she was pronounced dead on October 1, 1982. The death certificates listed Stanley's date of death as September 29, and Theresa's as October 1.

Theresa was the primary beneficiary of Stanley's life-insurance policy. The Metropolitan Life Insurance Company paid the proceeds to the administrator of Theresa's estate. Stanley's mother, Alojza Janus, as the contingent beneficiary of Stanley's policy, brought an action to recover the proceeds, claiming that there was insufficient evidence that Theresa survived Stanley. The trial court found that sufficient evidence that Theresa survived Stanley did exist. On appeal, Alojza's main argument was that there was insufficient evidence to prove that both victims did not suffer brain death before arriving at the hospital on September 29.]

O'CONNOR, J.... Dual standards for determining when legal death occurs in Illinois were set forth in the case of In Re Haymer (1983), 115 Ill.App.3d 349, 71 Ill.Dec. 252, 450 N.E.2d 940. There, the court determined that a comatose child attached to a mechanical life support system was legally dead on the date he was medically determined to have sustained total brain death, rather than on the date that his heart stopped functioning. The court stated that in most instances death could be determined in accordance with the common law standard which is based upon the irreversible cessation of circulatory and respiratory functions. If these functions are

---

21. Stanley and Theresa Janus and Stanley's brother were among seven people in the Chicago area murdered in 1982 by ingesting cyanide-laced Tylenol capsules. More than ten years later, these murders were still not solved. The killings led to new federal regulations requiring protective seals to be placed on nonprescription drugs. See Tylenol Deaths Leave Legacy of Fear, Detroit Free Press, Sept. 30, 1992, p. 2A.

artificially maintained, a brain death standard of death could be used if a person has sustained irreversible cessation of total brain function....

Even though *Haymer* was decided after the deaths of Stanley and Theresa, we find that the trial court properly applied the *Haymer* standards under the general rule that a civil case is governed by the law as it exists when judgment is rendered, not when the facts underlying the case occur....

Regardless of which standard of death is applied, survivorship is a fact which must be proven by a preponderance of the evidence by the party whose claim depends on survivorship. The operative provisions of the Illinois version of the Uniform Simultaneous Death Act provides in pertinent part:

> If the title to property or its devolution depends upon the priority of death and there is no sufficient evidence that the persons have died otherwise than simultaneously and there is no other provision in the will, trust agreement, deed, contract of insurance or other governing instrument for distribution of the property different from the provisions of this Section:
> (a) The property of each person shall be disposed of as if he had survived....
> (d) If the insured and the beneficiary of a policy of life or accident insurance have so died, the proceeds of the policy shall be distributed as if the insured had survived the beneficiary.

Ill.Rev.Stat.1981, ch. 110½, par. 3-1.

In cases where the question of survivorship is determined by the testimony of lay witnesses, the burden of sufficient evidence may be met by evidence of a positive sign of life in one body and the absence of any such sign in the other. In cases such as the instant case where the death process is monitored by medical professionals, their testimony as to "the usual and customary standards of medical practice" will be highly relevant when considering what constitutes a positive sign of life and what constitutes a criteria for determining death. Although the use of sophisticated medical technology can also make it difficult to determine when death occurs, the context of this case does not require a determination as to the exact moment at which the decedents died. Rather, the trial court's task was to determine whether or not there was sufficient evidence that Theresa Janus survived her husband. Our task on review of this factually disputed case is to determine whether the trial court's finding was against the manifest weight of the evidence.... We hold that it was not.

In the case at bar, both victims arrived at the hospital with artificial respirators and no obvious vital signs. There is no dispute among the treating physicians and expert witnesses that Stanley Janus died in both a cardiopulmonary sense and a brain death sense when his vital signs disappeared en route to the hospital and were never reestablished. He was pronounced dead at 8:15 p.m. on September 29, 1982, only after intensive procedures such as electro-shock, medication, and the insertion of a pacemaker failed to resuscitate him.

In contrast, these intensive procedures were not necessary with Theresa Janus because hospital personnel were able to reestablish a spontaneous blood pressure and pulse which did not have to be artificially maintained by a pacemaker or medication. Once spontaneous circulation was restored in the emergency room, Theresa was put on a mechanical respirator and transferred to the intensive care unit. Clearly, efforts to preserve Theresa Janus' life continued after more intensive efforts on Stanley's behalf had failed.

It is argued that the significance of Theresa Janus' cardiopulmonary functions, as a sign of life, was rendered ambiguous by the use of artificial respiration. In particular, reliance is placed upon expert testimony that a person can be brain dead and still have a spontaneous pulse and blood pressure which is indirectly maintained by artificial respiration. The fact remains, however, that Dr. Kim, an intensive care specialist who treated Theresa, testified that her condition in the emergency room did not warrant a diagnosis of brain death. In his opinion, Theresa Janus did not suffer irreversible brain death until much later, when extensive treatment failed to preserve her brain function and vital signs. This diagnosis was confirmed by a consulting neurologist after a battery of tests were performed to assess her brain function. Dr. Kim denied that these examinations were made merely to see if brain death had already occurred. At trial, only Dr. Vatz disagreed with their finding, but even he admitted that the diagnosis and tests performed on Theresa Janus were in keeping with the usual and customary standards of medical practice.

There was also other evidence presented at trial which indicated that Theresa Janus was not brain dead on September 29, 1982. Theresa's EEG, taken on September 30, 1982, was not flat but rather it showed some delta waves of extremely low amplitude. Dr. Hanley concluded that Theresa's EEG taken on September 30 exhibited brain activity. Dr. Vatz disagreed. Since the trier of fact determines the credibility of expert witnesses and the weight to be given to their testimony..., the trial court in this case could have reasonably given greater weight to Dr. Hanley's opinion than to Dr. Vatz'. In addition, there is evidence that Theresa's pupil reacted to light on one occasion. It is argued that this evidence merely represents the subjective impression of a hospital staff member which is not corroborated by any other instance where Theresa's pupils reacted to light. However, this argument goes to the weight of this evidence and not to its admissibility. While these additional pieces of neurological data were by no means conclusive, they were competent evidence which tended to support the trial court's finding, and which also tended to disprove the contention that these tests merely verified that brain death had already taken place.

In support of the contention that Theresa Janus did not survive Stanley Janus, evidence was presented which showed that only Theresa Janus suffered seizures and exhibited a decerebrate posture shortly after ingesting the poisoned Tylenol. However, evidence that persons with these symptoms tend to die very quickly does not prove that Theresa Janus did not in fact survive Stanley Janus. Moreover, the evidence introduced is similar in nature to medical presumptions of survivorship based on decedents' health or physical condition which are considered too speculative to prove or disprove survivorship. Similarly, we find no support for the allegation that the hospital kept Theresa Janus on a mechanical respirator because her family requested that termination of her life support systems be delayed until the arrival of her brother, particularly since members of Theresa's family denied making such a request.

In conclusion, we believe that the record clearly established that the treating physicians' diagnoses of death with respect to Stanley and Theresa Janus were made in accordance with "the usual and customary standards of medical practice." [The physicians'] conclusion that Theresa Janus did not die until October 1, 1982, was based on various factors including the restoration of certain of her vital signs as well as other neurological evidence. The trial court found that these facts and circumstances constituted sufficient evidence that Theresa Janus survived her husband. It was not necessary to determine the exact moment at which Theresa died or by how long she survived him, and the trial court properly declined to do so. Viewing the record in its entirety, we cannot say that the trial court's finding of sufficient evidence of Theresa's survivorship was against the manifest weight of the evidence.

Because of our disposition of this case, we need not and do not consider whether the date of death listed on the victims' death certificates should be considered "facts" which constitute prima facie evidence of the date of their deaths. See Ill.Rev.Stat.1981, ch. 111½, par. 73-25; People v. Fiddler (1970), 45 Ill.2d 181, 184-86, 258 N.E.2d 359.

Accordingly, there being sufficient evidence that Theresa Janus survived Stanley Janus, the judgment of the circuit court of Cook County is affirmed.

AFFIRMED.

Notes and Questions

1. *Definition of Death; Uniform Determination of Death Act.* The definition of death used by the Illinois court in *Janus* is similar to that employed in the Uniform Determination of Death Act (1980). The Uniform Determination of Death Act was incorporated into §1-107 of the UPC in 1991.

2. *Questions.* If *Janus* had been governed by the current UPC, what result? Would the case even have been litigated?

3. *Joint Tenancies and Multiple-Party Accounts Under the UPC.* Section 2-702 of the UPC extends the 120-hour requirement of survival to joint tenancies, tenancies by the entirety, and multiple-party accounts.

4. *Revised Uniform Simultaneous Death Act.* In 1991, a revised version of the USDA adopting the provisions of UPC §2-702 was approved by the Uniform Law Commission.

EXTERNAL REFERENCES. Thomas P. Gallanis, Death by Disaster: Anglo-American Presumptions 1766-2006, in R.H. Helmholz & W. David H. Sellar, The Law of Presumptions: Essays in Comparative Legal History (2009).

4. Ademption by Extinction

Wasserman v. Cohen
606 N.E.2d 901 (Mass. 1993)

LYNCH, J. This appeal raises the question whether the doctrine of ademption by extinction applies to a specific gift of real estate contained in a revocable inter vivos trust. The plaintiff, Elaine Wasserman, brought an action for declaratory judgment in the Middlesex Division of the Probate and Family Court against the defendant, David E. Cohen (trustee), as he is the surviving trustee of a trust established by Frieda M. Drapkin (Drapkin). In her complaint the plaintiff requested that the trustee be ordered to pay her the proceeds of the sale of an apartment building which, under the trust, would have been conveyed to the plaintiff had it not been sold by Drapkin prior to her death. Pursuant to the trustee's motion to dismiss under Mass. R. Civ. P. 12 (b) (6), 365 Mass. 754 (1974), the probate judge dismissed the action. The plaintiff appealed. We granted the plaintiff's application for direct appellate review and now affirm.

1. We summarize the relevant facts. Frieda Drapkin created the Joseph and Frieda Drapkin Memorial Trust (trust) in December, 1982, naming herself both settlor and trustee. She funded the trust with "certain property" delivered on the date of execution, and retained the right to add property by inter vivos transfer and by will. Drapkin also reserved the right to receive and to direct the payment of income or principal during her lifetime, to amend or to revoke the trust, and to withdraw property from the trust. On her death, the trustee was directed to distribute the property as set out in the trust. The trustee was ordered to convey to the plaintiff "12-14 Newton Street, Waltham, Massachusetts, Apartment Building, (consisting of approximately 11,296 square feet)."

When she executed the trust, Drapkin held record title to the property at 12-14 Newton Street in Waltham, as trustee of Z.P.Q. Realty Trust. However, she sold the property on September 29, 1988, for $575,000, and had never conveyed her interest in the property to the trust.[22]

Drapkin died on March 28, 1989. Her will, dated December 26, 1982, devised all property in her residuary estate to the trust to be disposed of in accordance with the trust's provisions.

2. The plaintiff first contends that the probate judge erred in failing to consider

---

22. Drapkin amended the trust by instruments dated December 16, 1982, and February 8, 1989. The amendments did not reference the gift to the plaintiff.

Drapkin's intent in regard to the gift when she sold the property. We disagree.

We have long adhered to the rule that, when a testator disposes, during his lifetime, of the subject of a specific legacy or devise in his will, that legacy or devise is held to be adeemed, "whatever may have been the intent or motive of the testator in doing so." Walsh v. Gillespie, 338 Mass. 278, 280 (1959), quoting Richards v. Humphreys, 15 Pick. 133, 135 (1833). The focus is on the actual existence or nonexistence of the bequeathed property, and not on the intent of the testator with respect to it. To be effective, a specific legacy or devise must be in existence and owned by the testator at the time of his death.

The plaintiff asks us to abandon the doctrine of ademption. She contends that, because the doctrine ignores the testator's intent, it produces harsh and inequitable results and thus fosters litigation that the rule was intended to preclude. See Note, Ademption and the Testator's Intent, 74 Harv. L. Rev. 741 (1961). This rule has been followed in this Commonwealth for nearly 160 years. See Richards v. Humphreys, supra. Whatever else may be said about it, it is easily understood and applied by draftsmen, testators, and fiduciaries. The doctrine seeks to give effect to a testator's probable intent by presuming he intended to extinguish a specific gift of property when he disposed of that property prior to his death. As with any rule, exceptions have emerged.[23] These limited exceptions do not lead us to the abandonment of the rule. Its so-called harsh results can be easily avoided by careful draftsmanship and its existence must be recognized by any competent practitioner. When we consider the myriad of instruments drafted in reliance on its application, we conclude that stability in the field of trusts and estates requires that we continue the doctrine....

4. We have held that a trust, particularly when executed as part of a comprehensive estate plan, should be construed according to the same rules traditionally applied to wills. See Second Bank-State St. Trust Co. v. Pinion, 341 Mass. 366, 371 (1960) (doctrine of independent legal significance applied to pour-over trusts); Clymer v. Mayo, 393 Mass. 754 (1985) (G. L. c. 191, §9, which revokes dispositions made in will to former spouses on divorce or annulment, applied to trust executed along with will as part of comprehensive estate plan). In Clymer v. Mayo, supra at 766, we reasoned that "[t]reating the components of the decedent's estate plan separately, and not as parts of an interrelated whole, brings

---

23. This court has created two exceptions to the "identity" theory. In Walsh v. Gillespie, 338 Mass. 278 (1959), a conservator appointed for the testatrix five years after her will was executed sold shares of stock that were the subject of a specific legacy. The court held that the sale did not operate as an ademption as to the unexpended balance remaining in the hands of the conservator at the death of the testatrix. Id. at 284. In Bostwick v. Hurstel, 364 Mass. 282 (1973), a conservator had sold, then repurchased, stock that was the subject of a specific legacy and that had been split twice, before the death of the testatrix. The court held that the bequest of stock was not adeemed but emphasized, "we do not violate our rule that 'identity' and not 'intent' governs ademption cases." Id. at 296. See BayBank Harvard Trust Co. v. Grant, 23 Mass. App. Ct. 653, 655 (1987).

about inconsistent results." We also quoted one commentator who wrote, "The subsidiary rules [of wills] are the product of centuries of legal experience in attempting to discern transferors' wishes and suppress litigation. These rules should be treated presumptively correct for will substitutes as well as for wills." Id. at 768, quoting Langbein, The Nonprobate Revolution and the Future of the Law of Succession, 97 Harv. L. Rev. 1108, 1136-1137 (1984). We agree with this reasoning. As discussed above, the doctrine of ademption has a "long established recognition" in Massachusetts. Furthermore, Drapkin created the trust along with her will as part of a comprehensive estate plan. Under the residuary clause of her will, Drapkin gave the majority of her estate to the trustee, who was then to dispose of the property on her death according to the terms of the trust. We see no reason to apply a different rule because she conveyed the property under the terms of the trust, rather than her will. Thus, we conclude that the doctrine of ademption, as traditionally applied to wills, should also apply to the trust in the instant case.

5. Conclusion. Since the plaintiff does not contest that the devise of 12-14 Newton Street was a specific devise,[24] it follows that the devise was adeemed by the act of Drapkin.

So ordered.

Notes and Questions

1. *Questions*. Assuming that you share Professor Langbein's view that what he calls the "subsidiary rules of wills" are presumptively as correct for will substitutes as they are for wills, was the court correct in extending the identity theory of ademption, studied in Chapter 6, to the situation in *Wasserman*?

Suppose that the revocable trust that Frieda Drapkin created had not been part of a pour-over arrangement but was freestanding. Would the court have applied the identity theory in that situation? Should it?

2. *Restatement 3d of Property*. The Restatement 3d of Property §5.2 comment i provides that its principle of ademption by extinction, which adopts the intent theory and rejects the identity theory, applies to a will substitute, such as a revocable trust, that contains the equivalent of a specific devise.

3. *UTC*. UTC §112 provides that the rules of construction for wills apply also "to the interpretation of the terms of a trust and the disposition of the trust property." Does this section extend the rule of ademption by extinction to trusts? For a case answering in the affirmative, see Connary v. Shea, 259 A.3d 118 (Me. 2021).

---

24. "A specific legacy is one which separates and distinguishes the property bequeathed from the other property of the testator, so that it can be identified. It can only be satisfied by the thing bequeathed; if that has no existence, when the bequest would otherwise become operative, the legacy has no effect." Moffatt v. Heon, 242 Mass. 201, 203 (1922), quoting Tomlinson v. Bury, 145 Mass. 346, 347 (1887).

5. Homicide: The Slayer Rule

"Winston, if I were your wife, I would flavor your coffee with poison."
"Madam, if I were your husband, I would drink it."
 – Exchange between Lady Nancy Astor and Sir Winston Churchill

Primary Statutory Reference: *UPC §2-803*

Can a killer succeed to his or her victim's property? In cases of homicide, how does the state protect the right of the victim, now dead, to decide that his or her killer is no longer a preferred beneficiary? As indicated in Chapter 3, some state statutes provide that spouses and parents forfeit their intestate succession shares if they commit certain statutorily proscribed acts, such as abandonment, nonsupport, or bigamy. In some respects, homicide is just another in the list of reprehensible acts that result in forfeiture because denying an heir the right to take accords with the community's sense of justice and likely reflects the decedent's dispositive preference.

Homicide is different from other wrongful conduct, however, because of the nexus between the killing and the transfer of the victim's property by operation of an intestacy statute, will, or property or contractual arrangement. After all, succession rights are determined by the order of the victim's and killer's deaths. The nexus between the act and property transfers, along with the moral imperative of preventing a killer from succeeding to the victim's property, has led many courts, in the absence of a statutory directive, to deny killers succession rights to their victims' property, and has led many legislatures to enact statutes denying killers succession rights.

The Restatement 3d of Property formulates the slayer rule as follows:

§8.4 Slayer Rule

(a) A slayer is denied any right to benefit from the wrong. For purposes of this section, a slayer is a person who, without legal excuse or justification, is responsible for the felonious and intentional killing of another.

(b) Whether or not a person is a slayer is determined in a civil proceeding under the preponderance of the evidence standard rather than beyond a reasonable doubt. For purposes of the civil proceeding, however, a final judgment of conviction for the felonious and intentional killing of the decedent in a criminal proceeding conclusively establishes the convicted person as the decedent's slayer.

Neiman v. Hurff
93 A.2d 345 (N.J. 1952)

VANDERBILT, C.J. On July 31, 1950 the defendant killed his wife and thereafter pleaded *non vult* to an indictment for second degree murder for which he is now confined in prison. During her lifetime the decedent and the defendant owned a residence in Collingswood, New Jersey, as tenants by the entirety, and certain shares of corporate stock as joint tenants. In her will the decedent named as her sole beneficiary the Damon Runyon Memorial Fund for Cancer Research, Inc.

The plaintiff Alberta A. Neiman as executrix of the decedent sought, first, the direction of the court in regard to the rights of the Cancer Fund and of the defendant respectively in the corporate stock owned jointly by the decedent and the defendant during her lifetime .... The Cancer Fund sought an adjudication that the real property held by the entirety and the jointly owned corporate stock be held in trust for it by the defendant and that he be ordered to convey them to it.

The defendant contended that the title to both the realty and the corporate stock vested in him on his wife's death....

The trial court ruled that the decedent having met her death at the hands of the defendant, the title to the realty was vested in him as trustee for himself individually and for the Cancer Fund; that its value at the time of her death was $14,000; that the value of the Cancer Fund's interest was $11,597.98 (this sum representing the difference between $14,000 and "the commuted value as of the date of decedent's death of the net income of one-half of said property for the number of years of defendant's expectancy of life as determined according to the mortality tables used by this Court"); that $11,597.98 was imposed as a lien on the real property in favor of the Cancer Fund; that the defendant pay the Cancer Fund $11,597.98 within 45 days of service of the judgment or that the Cancer Fund have execution issue. The trial court further ruled that the title to the shares of stock likewise be held by the defendant as trustee for himself and the Cancer Fund; that the value of the stock at the time of the wife's death was $2,495.63; that the value of the interest of the Cancer Fund as the sole beneficiary under the decedent's will was $2,062.61 (representing the difference between $2,495.63 and "the commuted value as of the date of the decedent's death of the net income of one-half of the said shares of stock for the number of years of defendant's expectancy of life as determined according to the mortality tables used by this Court"); that $2,062.61 was imposed as a lien in favor of the Cancer Fund and that the defendant pay said sum within 45 days after service of the judgment or that execution issue....

From this judgment the defendant appealed.... The question here presented is whether or not a murderer can acquire by right of survivorship and keep property the title to which he had held jointly with his victim. This question has never been before a court of last resort in this State.... Some states have held that the legal title passes to the murderer despite his crime and that he may retain it .... Some other states have held that the legal title will not pass to the murderer at all .... A third group of states has held that legal title passes to the murderer but that equity will treat him as a constructive trustee because of his unconscionable acquisition of the property and compel him to convey it to those to whom it has been devised or bequeathed by the will of his victim, or in the absence of a will to the heirs or next of kin of the decedent exclusive of the murderer....

To permit the murderer to retain title to the property acquired by his crime as permitted in some states is abhorrent to even the most rudimentary sense of justice. It violates the policy of the common law that no one shall be allowed to profit by his own wrong.... On the other hand, to divest the surviving murderer of all legal title violates or does violence to the doctrine of vested rights and would conflict with N.J.S. 2A:152-2, N.J.S.A.: "No conviction or judgment for any offense against this state, shall make or work corruption of blood, disinherison of heirs, loss of dower, or forfeiture of estate." But to follow the principle enunciated in the [third group of states discussed above] does not interfere with vested legal rights, yet by applying the equitable doctrine of a constructive trust force is given to the sound principle of equity that a murderer or other wrongdoer shall not enrich himself by his inequity at the expense of an innocent person....

This doctrine is so consistent with the equitable principles that have obtained here for centuries that we have no hesitancy in applying it, and we find no merit at all in the defendant's argument that the decision below works a corruption of blood or a forfeiture of estate. It would be a strange system of jurisprudence that would be able to grant relief against many kinds of accidents, mistake and fraud, by compelling a defendant to act as a constructive trustee with respect to property vouchsafed him by the common law, and yet be unable similarly to touch the legal rights of a defendant who sought to profit by a heinous crime.

A more difficult question is involved in determining how much, if any, of the realty and of the shares of stock shall be held in constructive trust by the defendant for the benefit of the Cancer Fund. In the ordinary course of events the estate by the entirety in the real property would vest in the survivor absolutely and so would the ownership of the corporate stock, but it is now impossible here to determine whether husband or wife would have survived in the ordinary course of events and thus which would have become the sole owner of the property in question. Inasmuch as the husband by his wrongful act has prevented the determination in the natural course of events of whether he or his wife would survive, it is not inequitable to presume that the decedent would have survived the wrongdoer. In this situation there is no justification for determining survivorship according to the mathematical life expectancies of the decedent and her murderer. The wrongdoer, having prevented the natural ascertainment of the answer to the question of survivorship, should not be permitted to avail himself of mortality tables which may have no applicability as between him and the decedent in respect to their respective individual possibilities of survivorship. Equity therefore conclusively presumes for the purpose of working out justice that the decedent would have survived the wrongdoer. In no other way can complete justice be done and the criminal prevented from profiting through his crime.

This view inevitably leads us to the conclusion that both as to the realty and the corporate stock the Cancer Fund is entitled in equity to an absolute one-half interest and a remainder interest in the other half, subject only to the value of the life estate of the defendant in such half. Thus the defendant will hold the realty in trust for the Cancer Fund subject to a lien thereon for the commuted value at the time of the decedent's death of the net income of one-half of the real property for the number of years of his expectancy of life as determined according to the mortality tables used in our courts, i.e., $2,402.02. Likewise the defendant will hold the shares of stock in trust for the Cancer Fund subject to the commuted value at the date of the decedent's death of the net income of one-half of the shares of stock for the number of years of defendant's expectancy of life as determined according to the mortality tables, or $433.02....

The judgment below is modified in accordance with this opinion but without costs to either party and the cause is remanded for such further proceedings as may be necessary.

Note

Severance of Joint Tenancies and Tenancies by the Entirety. State laws conflict over the treatment of joint tenancies with the right of survivorship.[25] Some states adopt the *Neiman* rule that the killer should retain only a one-half share in the property for life.

The majority of state statutes and UPC §2-803, adopt the rule that the killer should retain a one-half share in fee. There is a general theory in property law that "[t]he power to become the owner at will is in essence ownership." Restatement of Property, Introductory Note to Chapter 25. The right of severance of a joint tenancy gives each joint tenant a power to become the owner at will of his or her fractional interest.

Felonious and Intentional Killing. States generally provide for forfeiture only if the killing is felonious and intentional. The Restatement 3d of Property §8.4 comment f provides that "[t]he term 'felonious' refers to criminal offenses that are felonies"[26] and that "[t]he term 'intentional' is not confined to consequences that the actor has the purpose of producing, but includes consequences that the actor knows to a substantial certainty will ensue from the actor's conduct."

---

25. A few states go so far as to deny the killer all rights to the jointly-held property. See, e.g., Estate of Castiglioni, 47 Cal.Rptr.2d 288 (Ct. App. 1995), petition for review denied (Feb. 15, 1996); Ohio Rev. Code § 2105.19(A); Oleff v. Hodapp, 195 N.E. 838 (Ohio 1935); Estate of Fiore, 476 N.E.2d 1093 (Ohio Ct. App. 1984). The *Castiglioni* decision, which was rendered under a statute patterned after the original UPC provision, is criticized in Charlotte K. Goldberg, Estate of Castiglioni: Spousal Murder and the Clash of Joint Tenancy and Equity in California Community Property Law, 33 Idaho L. Rev. 513 (1997).

26. The Model Penal Code §1.04(2) provides that "[a] crime is a felony if it is so designated in this Code or if persons convicted thereof may be sentenced [to death or] to imprisonment for a term that, apart from an extended term, is in excess of one year."

The fact that the killing was not motivated by greed is appropriately treated as irrelevant to whether the state requires a forfeiture of succession rights, because, regardless of the reason for the intentional killing, the victim lost enjoyment of the property, the opportunity to change the distribution, and the possibility of surviving the killer.

A person who acts in self-defense is not treated as a felonious and intentional killer. See, e.g., State Farm Life Insurance Co. v. Smith, 363 N.E.2d 785 (Ill. 1977); Restatement 3d of Property §8.4 comment h. The majority of states do not deny succession rights to a killer who was insane at the time of the killing. See, e.g., Ford v. Ford, 512 A.2d 389 (Md. 1986); Restatement 3d of Property §8.4 comment h. But see, e.g., Conn. Gen. Stat. §45a-447; Ind. Code §29-1-2-12.1.

A minority of states require the killing to constitute murder before denying the killer the right to succeed to the victim's property. Other states require a person to be convicted of murder or an intentional homicide. Whether a state requires the killing to constitute murder, or whether it requires the killer to be convicted of an intentional homicide, can vary depending on the type of property transfer involved.[27]

In a jurisdiction that does not require a criminal conviction, a civil proceeding is necessary to determine whether a person claiming the decedent's property feloniously and intentionally killed the victim. Most jurisdictions require that the issue of whether a person feloniously and intentionally killed the decedent be decided by a preponderance of the evidence standard. The UPC and the Restatement 3d of Property take this position. At least one state imposes a clear and convincing standard of proof. See Estate of Safran, 306 N.W.2d 27 (Wis. 1981). Most of the statutes provide that a conviction for a felonious and intentional killing conclusively denies the killer succession rights.[28] No jurisdiction, however, treats an acquittal as conclusive evidence of the innocence of the accused or the lawfulness of the killing. This is because of the higher standard of proof necessary to obtain a conviction in a criminal trial. See Restatement 2d of Judgments §85(2)(a).

---

27. For example, in Seipel v. State Employees' Retirement System, 289 N.E.2d 288 (Ill. App. Ct. 1972), a widow convicted of voluntary manslaughter of her husband was barred from receiving death benefits under her husband's state pension by the common-law principle that one may not profit by his own wrong; the pension benefits were ordered paid to the husband's estate. But, in Estate of Seipel, 329 N.E.2d 419 (Ill. App. Ct. 1975), the same widow was not barred from succeeding to her husband's estate as his sole heir because, as to the right of inheritance, the state statute barring inheritance in cases of "murder" superseded the common law. But see Life Insurance Co. of North America v. Wollett, 766 P.2d 893 (Nev. 1988) (statutory provision requiring conviction for murder to deny a killer an inheritance preempted the common law and, therefore, killer who entered a plea of voluntary manslaughter received insurance proceeds as beneficiary of a policy on the victim's life).

28. But see Estates of Swanson, 187 P.3d 631 (Mont. 2008), holding that a guilty plea is within the definition of a "conviction" but does not conclusively establish that the killing was felonious and intentional within the meaning of the slayer statute.

Suppose that X, who is the sole devisee under D's will, intentionally murders D but is able to prove by clear and convincing evidence that he did so for the purpose of relieving D's suffering from pain associated with a terminal illness. Should X be entitled to inherit under D's will? For an argument that he should, see Jeffrey G. Sherman, Mercy Killing and the Right to Inherit, 61 U. Cin. L. Rev. 803 (1993).

Property Owned by the Victim. All but a handful of states have statutes that deny the killer the right to receive property from the victim's estate by will or by intestacy and provide that the estate or the failed interest should be distributed in accordance with the fiction that the killer predeceased the victim. In the states without statutes expressly providing for forfeiture, the courts have reached the same result. See, e.g., Wright v. Wright, 449 S.W.2d 952 (Ark. 1970) (intestacy); Welch v. Welch, 252 A.2d 131 (Del. Ch. 1969) (will). Under UPC §2-803(b), if the decedent died intestate, the estate passes as if the killer disclaimed his or her intestate interest. Under the UPC's disclaimer provision, §2-1106, this means that the killer is treated as having predeceased the decedent for purposes of allowing the killer's interest to pass to his or her surviving descendants, if any, but not for purposes of changing the shares.

Will Substitutes. Section 2-803 of the current UPC, while retaining the major thrust of the original version, is more comprehensive. Subsection (c) covers property arrangements that were not expressly treated by the original UPC. For example, subsection (c)(1) provides that the felonious and intentional killing of the decedent revokes any revocable disposition made by the decedent to the killer. This includes life insurance beneficiary designations and interests in revocable trusts.

General Principle. For situations not expressly covered, §2-803(f) provides that they are controlled by the principle that a killer cannot profit from his or her wrong.

Problems

1. G makes an irrevocable transfer in trust directing the trustee to pay income to A for life, and at A's death, to distribute the corpus of the trust to B. B kills A. Should A's estate be able to obtain an amount equal to the present value of the income interest based on A's life expectancy? See Restatement 3d of Property §8.4 comment m illus. 6.

2. Same facts as in Problem 1, except the trust directs that if B fails to survive A, the corpus should be distributed to C. Should A's estate be able to obtain an amount equal to the present value of the income interest based on A's life expectancy or should C receive the entire corpus? See Restatement 3d of Property §8.4 comment m illus. 7.

3. Same facts as in Problem 2, except that A kills B. Should A be able to retain her income interest? Should B or C receive the remainder interest? See Restatement 3d of Property §8.4 comment o illus. 10.

4. G purchases a single-premium insurance policy on her own life and irrevocably assigns ownership of the policy to X. X feloniously and intentionally kills G. Should X be able to enjoy the proceeds? Should the result be different if the policy does not require X to survive G? Cf. Restatement 3d of Property §8.4 comment k illus. 3.

5. W's pension plan, which is an employee benefit plan covered by the Employee Retirement Income Security Act of 1974 (ERISA), provides that a surviving spouse shall be entitled to an annuity. H kills W. Should H receive the annuity payments? Should the answer depend on state or federal law? See Egelhoff v. Egelhoff, above p. 373; Mendez-Bellido v. Board of Trustees, 709 F. Supp. 329 (E.D.N.Y. 1989); cf. Restatement 3d of Property §8.4 comment k illus. 4.

———

Property Owned by the Killer. The general, and seemingly appropriate, rule is that the killer should not forfeit any property he or she owns. See, e.g., Luecke v. Mercantile Bank of Jonesboro, 691 S.W.2d 843 (Ark. 1985); Meyer's Estate, 94 N.Y.S.2d 620 (App. Div. 1950); Restatement 3d of Property §8.4 comment o. But see *Neiman*, above. Nevertheless, issues can arise that suggest that some exceptions to that rule are warranted. For example, if H feloniously and intentionally killed W and then committed suicide, should W's estate be able to claim an elective share against H's estate? See, e.g., Luecke v. Mercantile Bank of Jonesboro, 691 S.W.2d 843 (Ark. 1985); National City Bank of Evansville v. Bledsoe, 144 N.E.2d 710, 716 (Ind. 1957) (disapproving Debus v. Cook, 154 N.E. 484 (Ind. 1926)); Parker v. Potter, 157 S.E. 68 (N.C. 1931). Could W's executor sue H's estate for wrongful death? See Fowler V. Harper et al., Law of Torts §§8.10, 24.5 (2d ed. 1986).

Another troubling case concerns life insurance policies on the life of the victim where the killer is the owner and primary beneficiary. Should the killer be able to receive the life insurance proceeds? See, e.g., New York Mutual Ins. Co. v. Armstrong, 117 U.S. 591 (1886). Should the killer be able to obtain the cash surrender value, if any, on the policy? See, e.g., Manufacturers Life Ins. Co. v. Moore, 116 F. Supp. 171 (D.C.Cal. 1953); Restatement 3d of Property §8.4 comment o illus. 11. If the killer named Y to take in the event the killer failed to survive the insured, should Y be able to take? Compare, e.g., First Kentucky Trust Co. v. United States, 737 F.2d 557 (6th Cir. 1984) with, e.g., Manufacturers Life Ins. Co. v. Moore, supra. See also Seidlitz v. Eames, 753 P.2d 775 (Colo. App. 1987) (children of the killer received proceeds as named successor-owners and contingent beneficiaries of a policy owned by the killer). Should the insured's estate be able to take? See, e.g., First Kentucky Trust Co. v. United States, supra. Should the insurance company be relieved of all liability? See, e.g., Travelers Ins. Co. v. Thompson, 163 N.W.2d 289 (Minn. 1968), appeal dismissed, 395 U.S. 161 (1969).

Extension of Slayer Rule Beyond Homicide? Should the slayer rule be extended to fact-patterns other than homicide? In 2009, the State of Washington expanded its slayer rule to apply to someone who participates, either as a principal or an accessory before the fact, in the willful and unlawful financial exploitation of a vulnerable adult. See Rev. Code Wash. §§11.84.010(1), 11.84.020 et seq. Some other states also have enacted legislation expanding the application of the slayer rule. See, e.g., Conn. Gen. Stat. §45a-447; Fla. Stat. §732.8031; Ky. Rev. Stat. §381.280; Mich. Comp. Laws §700.2803, -.2804, -2805; Md. Code Est. & Tr. §§11-111, -112; Mont. Code §72-2-813; Or. Rev. Code §112.455 et seq.; W.Va. Stat. §42-4-2.

EXTERNAL REFERENCES. Fredrick E. Vars, The Slayer Rule: An Empirical Examination, 48 ACTEC L.J. 201 (2023); Michelle Antao, The Standards of Slayer Statutes: Should a Criminal Conviction Be Required to Disqualify an Alleged Slayer from Benefitting Under a Decedent's Will, 35 Quin. Prob. L.J. 207 (2022); Carla Spivack, Killers Shouldn't Inherit from Their Victims—Or Should They?, 48 Ga. L. Rev. 145 (2013); Nili Cohen, The Slayer Rule, 92 B. U. L. Rev. 793 (2012); Karen J. Sneddon, Should Cain's Children Inherit Abel's Property?: Wading into the Extended Slayer Rule Quagmire, 76 UMKC L. Rev. 101 (2007); Mary Louise Fellows, The Slayer Rule: Not Solely a Matter of Equity, 71 Iowa L. Rev. 489 (1986); Linda J. Maki & Alan M. Kaplan, Elmer's Case Revisited: The Problem of the Murdering Heir, 41 Ohio St. L.J. 905 (1980); William M. McGovern, Jr., Homicide and Succession to Property, 68 Mich. L. Rev. 65 (1969).

Chapter 8

Protection of the Family: Limitations on the Freedom of Disposition

Freedom of disposition is a hallmark of the American law of succession. In the United States, testamentary freedom is abridged only in limited circumstances and only in a limited way. In contrast, in Continental Europe, a decedent cannot totally disinherit his or her children and sometimes cannot totally disinherit other blood relatives. In England and the principal commonwealth jurisdictions (the Australian states, most of the Canadian provinces, New Zealand), family provision legislation empowers the judge to revise the dispositive provisions of a testator's will (including intestate shares, in an intestate estate) to provide support for the decedent's relatives and other dependents.[1]

In American law, the decedent's spouse is the only relative favored by a protection against intentional disinheritance. The decedent's children and possibly more remote descendants are granted protection only against unintentional disinheritance.

PART A. THE SPOUSE'S ELECTIVE SHARE

1. The Partnership Theory of Marriage

Primary Statutory References: *UPC §§2-202, 2-203, 2-204, 2-207, 2-209*
Model Marital Property Act

Disinheritance of a surviving spouse brings into question the fundamental nature of the economic rights of parties to a marital relationship, and how the institution of marriage is viewed in society. The contemporary view of marriage is that it is an economic partnership.[2] The partnership theory of marriage, sometimes also called

---

1. See, e.g., Inheritance (Provision for Family and Dependants) Act 1975, c. 63 (U.K.). Some commentators have argued that the family provision approach, because of its discretionary character, should not be adopted in the United States. See Mary Ann Glendon, Fixed Rules and Discretion in Contemporary Family Law and Succession Law, 60 Tul. L. Rev. 1165, 1186-91 (1986); John H. Langbein & Lawrence W. Waggoner, Redesigning the Spouse's Forced Share, 22 Real Prop. Prob. & Tr. J. 303, 314 (1987). See generally Kenneth G.C. Reid, Marius J. De Waal & Reinhard Zimmermann, Mandatory Family Provision: Comparative Succession Law, Volume III (2020).

2. One of the earliest American expressions of the partnership theory of marriage appears in the 1963 Report of the Committee on Civil and Political Rights to the President's Commission on the Status of Women. As quoted in the Prefatory Note to the Uniform Marital Property Act, the Report states:

the marital-sharing theory, is that each spouse is entitled to an equal share of the "marital property"—property acquired by the couple during the marriage other than by gift, devise, or inheritance. The theory of equal sharing is explained in the American Law Institute's Principles of the Law of Family Dissolution §4.09 comment c (2002) as follows:

> It makes far more sense to ground an equal-division presumption on the spouses' contribution to the entire marital relationship, not just to the accumulation of financial assets. The spousal contribution of domestic labor may not confer an equal financial benefit, but may have made it possible for the couple to raise children as well as accumulate property. One spouse may have contributed more than the other in emotional stability, optimism, or social skills, and thereby enriched the marital life. Property may be the only thing left at dissolution for the court to divide, but it is not usually the only thing produced during the marriage. An equal allocation of the property at divorce might thus be grounded on a presumption that both spouses contributed significantly to the entire relationship whether or not they contributed equally to accumulation of property during it.
>
> It is certainly common for persons to believe they derive great benefit from their marriage even when their financial contribution to it is more than their spouse's. But the incommensurability of the spouses' nonfinancial contributions frustrates any effort to attach monetary value to them. Faced with this measurement difficulty, it may be sensible for the law to presume irrebuttably that the spouses contributed equally to their entire relationship. Even though the presumption will sometimes be incorrect, case-by-case measurement offers no promise of greater accuracy. Moreover, the measurement attempt itself would require a retrospective examination of the parties' marital life that would often be burdensome and intrusive, as well as futile in its purpose.

Other relevant areas of the law of marriage are based on and coordinated with the partnership theory. In the community property states,[3] property law implements the

---

Marriage is a partnership to which each spouse makes a different but equally important contribution. This fact has become increasingly recognized in the realities of American family living. While the laws of other countries have reflected this trend, family laws in the United States have lagged behind.

3. By way of background, for students who have not taken a course in family law: There are two marital-property systems prevailing in the U.S.—common law (or separate property) and community property. The separate property (title-based) system derives from English common law, while community property developed in continental Europe and was transplanted to the new world by French and Spanish settlers. The basic distinction between the two systems is this: Under the common law's system of separate property, the spouses are separate owners of the assets that each acquires during the marriage, except for items they agree to hold jointly. Under the community property system, the spouses own all assets acquired by either of them during the marriage—except by gift, inheritance, or devise—in equal undivided shares.

Nine states can be called community property states: Arizona, California, Idaho, Louisiana, Nevada, New Mexico, Texas, Washington, and Wisconsin. Wisconsin's enactment of the Uniform Marital Property Act (now the Model Marital Property Act, or MMPA) made it a community property state, though the Wisconsin legislature modified the MMPA in several respects. See Howard S. Erlanger & June M. Weisberger, From Common Law Property to Community Property: Wisconsin's Marital Property Act Four Years Later, 1990 Wis. L. Rev. 769 (1990). Some additional states—such as Alaska,

partnership theory *during the marriage*. Under the community property system, each spouse owns an undivided half interest in marital/community property, defined as property acquired during the marriage other than by gift, devise, or inheritance. Property acquired before the marriage and property acquired during the marriage by gift, devise, or inheritance are not counted in the community (or marital estate), and remain separate property. The community property states do not have or need elective share statutes because the marital assets have already been equalized through the ownership rights that attached during the marriage.

Family law implements the partnership theory *upon divorce* through regimes of equitable distribution. The specifics of the equitable distribution regimes vary from state to state regarding the property that is subject to equitable distribution, the factors to be considered, and the amount of discretion granted to the courts in dividing up that property. Despite the differences, equitable distribution echoes community property at divorce by implementing the partnership theory. See ALI Principles of the Law of Family Dissolution §4.09 comment b (2002).

Conventional elective share law is the odd one out.

a. Conventional Elective Share Law

All but one of the separate property states[4] have decided that disinheritance of the surviving spouse at death is one of the few instances in which the decedent's testamentary freedom must be curtailed. No matter what the decedent's intent, the separate property states recognize that the surviving spouse has a claim to a portion of the decedent's estate. These statutes, which in all but a few states have replaced the common-law estates of dower and curtesy,[5] provide the spouse a so-called "forced" share. Because the forced share is expressed as an option that the survivor can elect or let lapse during the administration of the decedent's estate, the UPC uses the more descriptive term, "elective" share.

Florida, Kentucky, South Dakota, and Tennessee—are optional community property states. Married persons resident in one of these states may, if they choose, classify some or all of their assets as community property. Often this is accomplished by creating a community property trust.

4. Georgia is the only separate property state lacking an elective share statute. For a discussion of the reasons for Georgia's position, including its unusual "year's support" practice, and an argument that elective share statutes are generally unnecessary, see Verner F. Chaffin, A Reappraisal of the Wealth Transmission Process: The Surviving Spouse, Year's Support and Intestate Succession, 10 Ga. L. Rev. 447 (1976). For an opposing view, see Note, Preventing Spousal Disinheritance in Georgia, 19 Ga. L. Rev. 427 (1985).

5. The Restatement 2d of Property, Statutory Note to §34.1, lists five jurisdictions as providing the surviving spouse a dower or dower-like interest in the decedent's real property: Arkansas, the District of Columbia, Kentucky, Ohio, and West Virginia. The District of Columbia and West Virginia should be dropped from this list; dower and curtesy were abolished there. See D.C. Code §19-102; W. Va. Code §43-1-1. North Carolina, which statutorily provides a dower right for both spouses, should be added to the list. See N.C. Gen. Stat. §29-30.

Elective share law in the separate property states has not caught up to the partnership theory of marriage. Under traditional American elective share statutes, including the elective share provided by the original version of the UPC promulgated in 1969, a surviving spouse is granted a personal non-transferable right to claim a one-third share of the decedent's estate. (Note that this is a far cry from the transmissible right to claim the fifty percent share of the couple's combined assets that the partnership theory would imply.) Indeed, in a few states the elective share is not even a right to a fee interest but, like common-law dower, only a life interest in one-third or one-half.[6]

Although there are an infinite variety of marriages, three dominant patterns recur. The three are first marriages, remarriages after divorce, and remarriages after widowhood or widowerhood.

Consider a first marriage lasting until death, in which the couple's combined assets were accumulated mostly during the marriage. The elective share fraction of one-third of the decedent's estate plainly does not implement a partnership principle. The actual result is governed by which spouse happens to die first and how the property accumulated during the marriage was titled.

To illustrate this sort of marriage, consider Harry and Wilma. Assume that Harry and Wilma were married in their mid-to-late twenties. They never divorced, and Harry died at age 73, survived by Wilma. For whatever reason, Harry left a will entirely disinheriting Wilma. Throughout their long life together, the couple managed to accumulate assets worth $600,000, marking them as a somewhat affluent but hardly wealthy couple.

Under conventional elective share law, Wilma's ultimate entitlement is governed by the manner in which the $600,000 in assets were titled. Wilma could end up much poorer or much richer than a 50/50 principle would suggest. The reason is that under conventional elective share law, Wilma has a claim to one-third of Harry's *"estate."*

When the marital assets have been disproportionately titled in the decedent's name, conventional elective share law often entitles the survivor to less than an equal share. Thus, if all $600,000 of the marital assets were titled in Harry's name, Wilma's claim against Harry's estate would be for $200,000—well below Wilma's $300,000 ideal entitlement under a partnership/marital-sharing principle.

---

6. See, e.g., Conn. Gen. Stat. §45a-436.

Before 1992, the New York statute allowed the decedent to satisfy the elective share by giving the surviving spouse $10,000 plus a life income interest in a trust. Criticized for leaving surviving spouses—particularly women, who are more likely to be the survivor—with a lack of control, the statute was amended. As of 1992, the survivor is entitled to an outright one-third share or $50,000, whichever is greater. N.Y. EPTL §5-1.1-A(a)(4)-(5). The current South Carolina statute allows the decedent to satisfy the elective share by transferring one-third of the estate into a trust that qualifies for the federal estate tax marital deduction. S.C. Code §§62-2-201, 62-2-207.

When, on the other hand, the marital assets already have been more or less equally divided, conventional elective share law grants the survivor a right to take even more. If $300,000 were titled in Wilma's name, Wilma still is granted a claim against Harry's estate for an additional $100,000 (one-third of the $300,000 titled in Harry's name).

Finally, when the marital assets have been disproportionately titled in the survivor's name, conventional elective share law entitles the survivor to magnify the disproportion. If only $150,000 were titled in Harry's name, Wilma still would have a claim against Harry's estate for $50,000 (one-third of $150,000), even though Wilma was *already* overcompensated as measured by the partnership/marital-sharing theory.

Let us now turn our attention to a very different sort of marriage—the post-widow(er)hood remarriage—a marriage following the death of the prior spouses. In such a marriage, the one-third fraction of the decedent's estate often far exceeds a fifty/fifty division of assets acquired during the marriage. The reason is that such spouses are likely to come into the marriage with substantial individual property, typically carried over from their prior marriages.

To illustrate this sort of marriage, consider Wilma and Sam. Suppose that a few years after Harry's death, Wilma married Sam, whose prior spouse also had died. Then suppose that, after some years of marriage, Wilma died survived by Sam. Assume further that both Wilma and Sam have adult children by their prior marriages, and that each would prefer to leave most or all of his or her property to his or her children.

The value of the couple's combined assets is $600,000, $300,000 of which is titled in Wilma's name (the decedent) and $300,000 of which is titled in Sam's name (the survivor).

Under conventional elective share law, Sam would have a claim to one-third of Wilma's estate, or $100,000. Keep in mind that when this marriage ended by Wilma's death, Wilma's assets were $300,000 and Sam's assets were $300,000. For reasons that are not immediately apparent, conventional elective share law gives the survivor, Sam, a right to shrink Wilma's estate (and hence the share passing to Wilma's children from her prior marriage to Harry) by $100,000 (reducing it to $200,000) while supplementing Sam's assets (which likely will go to Sam's children from his prior marriage) by $100,000 (increasing their value to $400,000).

Conventional elective share law, in other words, basically rewards the children of the remarried spouse who manages to outlive the other, arranging for those children a windfall share of one-third of the "loser's" estate. The "winning" spouse—the one who chanced to survive—gains a windfall, for this "winner" is unlikely to have made a contribution, monetary or otherwise, to the "loser's" wealth remotely worth one-third.

That these results are seen as unjust by the children of the decedent's former marriage is both unsurprising and well documented in the elective share case law. In a case like that of Wilma and Sam, a decedent who disinherits or largely disinherits the surviving spouse often is not acting from malice toward the surviving spouse but from love for the children of the prior marriage.

There is also another concern: caregivers marrying their patients for an elective share. If the surviving spouse is entitled to a one-third elective share no matter how brief the marriage, there is an incentive for an unscrupulous caregiver to arrange a wedding. Consider the case of Irving Berk, a 91-year-old businessman diagnosed with dementia who was nevertheless married to his abusive caregiver. When he died the following year, the Surrogate's Court of New York held that the caregiver was entitled to an elective share. See John T. Brooks & Samantha E. Weissbluth, Marrying for the Money: A New Twist?, Tr. & Est. Online, April 20, 2010, discussing In re Berk, 897 N.Y.S.2d 475 (N.Y. App. Div. 2010).

b. The Uniform Probate Code's Elective Share

The current UPC, as refined in 2008, brings elective share law broadly into line with the partnership theory. The purpose is to grant the surviving spouse a right of election that implements the partnership theory for the division of marital property at death.

Partnership by Approximation. The UPC elective share system adopts a mechanical system that attempts to implement the partnership theory by approximation. It has three essential features. The first, implemented by §2-202(a), provides that the elective share percentage is fifty percent of the "marital-property portion" of the augmented estate. The augmented estate, as defined in §2-203(a) and then more specifically in §§2-204 through 2-208, consists of the sum of the values of four components: (1) the decedent's net probate estate, (2) the decedent's nonprobate transfers to others,[7] (3) the decedent's nonprobate transfers to the surviving spouse,[8] and (4) property owned by the surviving spouse and amounts that would have been included in the surviving spouse's nonprobate transfers to others had the spouse been the decedent. The purpose of combining the couple's assets is to implement the marital-sharing theory by denying significance to how the spouses happen to have taken title to particular assets.

---

7. The content of the decedent's nonprobate-transfers-to-others component and its role in preventing "fraud on the spouse's share" are discussed below at p. 427.

8. This component covers items such as the decedent's fractional interest in property held by the decedent and surviving spouse in joint tenancy and life insurance on the decedent's life payable to the surviving spouse.

The second feature, implemented by §2-203(b), establishes a schedule under which the marital-property portion of the augmented estate adjusts to the length of the marriage. The longer the marriage, the larger the marital-property portion. After 15 years of marriage, all of the couple's assets are deemed to be marital.

The third feature, implemented by §2-209, is that the surviving spouse's own assets are counted first (or a portion of them in marriages under 15 years) in making up the spouse's ultimate entitlement, so that the decedent's assets are liable only if there is a deficiency.

The UPC elective share system differs from the community property regime in two ways. First, the rights accorded a spouse under the UPC are conditioned on surviving the decedent. In contrast, under a community property regime each spouse has a right to control one-half of the marital estate regardless of the order of deaths. The second difference is that the UPC adds together and then splits all of the couple's assets, including assets acquired before marriage to each other and assets acquired by gift or inheritance, rather than only acquisitions from earnings during marriage to each other. The reason for this more inclusive approach is to make the system more administratively convenient by avoiding the tracing problems that arise under the community property system. In practice, the gap between the two systems is unlikely to be great. It is unusual for either spouse to bring substantial separate property to a long-duration first marriage. In cases of short-duration marriages, the accrual mechanism abates some of the consequences of an expanded forced share by reducing the vested portion of the survivor's entitlement. Finally, where there is substantial disparity in the wealth of the parties, they can contract out of the elective share through a premarital or marital agreement or waiver under §2-213.

Implementation of a Support Theory; Supplemental Share Amount. The partnership/marital-sharing theory is not the only driving force behind elective share law. Another theoretical basis for elective share law is that the spouses' mutual duties of support during their joint lifetimes should be continued in some form after death in favor of the survivor, as a claim on the decedent's estate. Conventional elective share law implements this theory poorly. The fixed fraction, whether it is the typical one-third or some other fraction, disregards the survivor's actual needs. A one-third share may be inadequate to the surviving spouse's needs, especially in a modest estate. On the other hand, in a very large estate, a one-third share may go far beyond the survivor's needs. In either a modest or a large estate, the survivor may or may not have ample independent means, and this factor, too, is disregarded in conventional elective share law.

The UPC elective share system seeks to implement the support theory by granting the survivor a supplemental share related to the survivor's actual needs. In implementing a support rationale, the length of the marriage is irrelevant. Because the duty of support is founded upon status, it arises upon the marriage.

Section 2-202(b) of the UPC implements the support theory by providing a supplemental share of $75,000. Counted first in satisfying this $75,000 are the surviving spouse's own ownership interests, including amounts shifting to the survivor at the decedent's death, and amounts owing to the survivor from the decedent's estate under the elective share discussed above, but excluding amounts going to the survivor under the UPC's probate exemptions and allowances and the survivor's Social Security and other governmental benefits.

Gender Inequality and the Elective Share. Some commentators have criticized the partnership theory generally and the UPC elective share specifically on the ground that they fail adequately to take account of the disparity in the economic circumstances of married men and women. The critics argue that the partnership theory is fundamentally flawed because wives are much less likely to be self-sufficient than husbands. In general, men earn more than women do, and men have more assets titled in their names than do women. These circumstances have led to criticism of the partnership theory as applied to divorce law on the ground that it sometimes leaves divorced women without an adequate means of support. This is especially so with respect to divorced women who have children and invested more time in raising their children than they did in their jobs. See, e.g., Lenore J. Weitzman, The Divorce Revolution: The Unexpected Social and Economic Consequences for Women and Children in America Ch. 7 (1985); Deborah L. Rhode & Martha Minow, Reforming the Questions, Questioning the Reforms, in Divorce Reform at the Crossroads 191, 201-04 (Stephen D. Sugarman & Herma Hill Kay eds. 1990); Bea A. Smith, The Partnership Theory of Marriage: A Borrowed Solution Fails, 68 Tex. L. Rev. 689 (1990). For criticism of the Weitzman study, see Stephen D. Sugarman, Dividing Financial Interests on Divorce, in Divorce Reform at the Crossroads 130 (Stephen D. Sugarman & Herma Hill Kay eds. 1990).

The same criticism has been extended to elective share law. Because women's average life expectancy is longer than men's, the surviving spouse is more likely to be a woman. The economic disparity between men and women increases as they age. Among men and women age 65 and older, for example, women are approximately 1.3 times as likely as men to be poor. See Administration for Community Living, Profile of Older Americans: 2021, available at www.acl.gov. Thus, some have argued that the UPC's supplemental elective share amount is too small adequately to protect substantial numbers of women, especially those who gave up a career to be homemakers and whose husbands die within ten years of marriage. See Margaret V. Turano, UPC Section [2-202]: Equal Treatment of Spouses?, 55 Alb. L. Rev. 983 (1992).

On the other hand, a special subcommittee of the Massachusetts, Boston, and Women's Bar Associations issued a report in 2007 stating that, after two years of review, all members of the committee agree that the "UPC model produces results that are the most fair."

Criticizing the UPC elective share from another direction, it has been argued that while the statute makes a nod to the contribution theory, its actual rationale is support or need. See Mary Moers Wenig, The Marital Property Law of Connecticut: Past, Present and Future, 1990 Wis. L. Rev. 807. See also Charles H. Whitebread, The Uniform Probate Code's Nod to the Partnership Theory of Marriage, 11 Prob. L.J. 125 (1992).

The Partnership Theory and the Problem of Nonmarital Property. Yet another criticism concerns the UPC's use of a 15-year phase-in period to deal with the problem of nonmarital property. It has been argued that this approach is arbitrary and may often result in the elective share amount not being consistent with the objective of one-half the marital, and only the marital, property. For example, it is possible even after a 15-year marriage that most of the assets of both spouses are separate property, if the marriage occurred late in life. Conversely, property owned by both spouses after a five-year marriage in some cases may be entirely marital property. To deal with this problem of over- and under-inclusiveness, it has been suggested that the accrual approach be replaced with a flat elective share percentage of 50% coupled with an exception for separate property to the extent that either the decedent's estate or the surviving spouse can prove it. To ameliorate proof problems, there would be a strong rebuttable presumption that all property is marital property. See Susan N. Gary, Marital Partnership Theory and the Elective Share: Federal Estate Tax Law Provides a Solution, 49 U. Miami L. Rev. 567 (1995); Alan Newman, Incorporating the Partnership Theory of Marriage into Elective-Share Law: The Approximation System of the Uniform Probate Code and the Deferred-Community-Property Alternative, 49 Emory L.J. 487 (2000).

The 2008 revisions added an alternative deferred marital property approach for states that prefer that method. See §2-203 Alternative Subsection (b).

Problems

In the following scenarios, to how much is the surviving spouse (S) entitled? Analyze the scenarios under three legal regimes:

(i) the original UPC's elective share;[9]

---

9. The relevant provisions of the original UPC are:

2-201(a). If a married person domiciled in this state dies, the surviving spouse has a right of election to take an elective share of one-third of the augmented estate under the limitations and conditions hereinafter stated.

2-202. The augmented estate means the estate reduced by funeral and administration expenses, homestead allowance, family allowances and exemptions, and enforceable claims, to which is added the sum of the following amounts:

(1) The value of property transferred to anyone other than a bona fide purchaser by the decedent at any time during the marriage, to or for the benefit of any person other than the surviving spouse, to the extent that the decedent did not receive adequate and full consideration in money or money's worth for the transfer, if the transfer is of any of the following types:....

(ii) the current UPC's elective share;

(iii) a community property regime as implemented by the Model Marital Property Act (MMPA).

Assume that D died with a will completely disinheriting S and that D made no nonprobate transfers. In these problems, the term "D's net probate estate" refers to the amount that would be included in the augmented/marital estate under §§2-203 and 2-204. The term "S's net assets" refers to the amount that would be included in the augmented/marital estate under §§2-203 and 2-207.

With respect to the original UPC, assume that S's assets are not derived from D. With respect to the MMPA, make all-or-nothing assumptions about whether the property is marital or individual.

1. Married in their twenties, D and S lived a long life together. D died at age 75, survived by S.

    (a) D's net probate estate is valued at $500,000; S's net assets at D's death are valued at $100,000.

    (b) D's net probate estate is valued at $100,000; S's net assets at D's death are valued at $500,000.

2. D and S got married late in life, after having previously been married; each had children by the prior marriage. Five years after their marriage to each other, D died, survived by S.

    (a) D's net probate estate is valued at $600,000 and S's net assets at D's death are valued at $400,000.

    (b) D's net probate estate is valued at $400,000; S's net assets at D's death are valued at $600,000.

    (c) D's net probate estate is valued at $90,000; S's net assets at D's death are valued at $10,000.

What do these results tell you about the way the various legal regimes view marriage? In each regime that has an elective share, what is the elective share designed to do?

———

EXTERNAL REFERENCES. Ronald Z. Domsky, 'Til Death Do Us Part ... After That, My Dear, You're on Your Own: A Practitioner's Guide to Disinheriting a Spouse

---

(2) The value of property owned by the surviving spouse at the decedent's death, plus the value of property transferred by the spouse at any time during the marriage to any person other than the decedent which would have been includible in the spouse's augmented estate if the surviving spouse had predeceased the decedent to the extent the owned or transferred property is derived from the decedent by any means other than testate or intestate succession without a full consideration in money or money's worth....

in Illinois, 29 S. Ill. U. L.J. 207 (2005); John W. Fisher II & Scott A. Curnutte, Reforming the Law of Intestate Succession and Elective Shares: New Solutions to Age-Old Problems, 93 W. Va. L. Rev. 61 (1990); Lawrence W. Waggoner, Spousal Rights in our Multiple-Marriage Society: The Revised Uniform Probate Code, 26 Real Prop. Prob. & Tr. J. 683 (1992); Lawrence W. Waggoner, The Uniform Probate Code's Elective Share: Time for a Reassessment, 37 U. Mich. J. L. Reform 1 (2003).

2. Protection Against Will Substitutes

Primary Statutory References: *UPC §§2-205, 2-206*

One of the most troublesome issues regarding elective share law is the extent to which the surviving spouse's rights sometimes fail to extend to will substitutes. An elective share is of little value to a surviving spouse if it applies only to the decedent's probate estate. The decedent could use one or more will substitutes to implement a dispositive plan that effectively disinherits his or her spouse. Many courts, using different approaches, have worked to preserve the effectiveness of the statutory elective share. These judicial doctrines remain important in those states that have not amended their elective share statutes to extend to will substitutes. We shall first examine these judicial approaches and then address the statutory extension of elective share law to will substitutes under the UPC.

a. Common-Law Theories

Seifert v. Southern National Bank of South Carolina
409 S.E.2d 337 (S.C. 1991)

TOAL, J.

Widow (Agnes T. Seifert, appellant) instituted this declaratory judgment action alleging that a revocable inter-vivos trust, established by Husband (Harry E. Seifert) in favor of respondents Barbara S. Meyers and Charlotte S. Knaub, should be included in Husband's estate. We agree and reverse the Master's finding to the contrary.

Facts. Widow and Husband were married approximately ten (10) years. On August 5, 1987, Husband created a revocable inter-vivos trust in favor of respondents, Husband's daughters from a former marriage, to which he transferred the better part of his estate. At his death, the value of the trust was approximately $800,000.

Under the terms of the trust, upon Husband's death, a separate trust containing $150,000, known as the Agnes T. Seifert Trust, was carved from respondents' trust. Widow received a life interest in the income of the Agnes T. Seifert Trust and could invade the principal for medical purposes only. Under Husband's will, Widow received a one-half life interest in the marital home, half of which she already owned. The will also provided that the residue of the estate be transferred to respondents' trust.

Widow made a timely request for her elective share pursuant to S.C. Code Ann. §62-2-201 (1990 Supp.); however, Husband's will was designed so that there were no other assets in the estate, other than the life interest in the house, his personal property, and what was contained in the residue.

Widow challenged Husband's dispositions by filing a complaint in Anderson County probate court. The matter was removed to circuit court. From there it was transferred to the Master-in-Equity with direct appeal to this Court.

The Master found that the revocable, inter-vivos trust should not be included in the probate estate. Widow then instituted this appeal.

Law/Analysis. Widow contends that Husband's revocable inter-vivos trust is void because it is illusory, since he used it to reduce her elective share, and that the trust assets should be included in Husband's estate for purposes of valuing her elective share. This is a question of first impression in this Court. Other jurisdictions have held that a trust was invalid where the settlor retained powers over the trust assets so extensive that he had until his death the same rights in the assets of the trust after creating it that he had before its creation. See, e.g., Moore v. Jones, 44 N.C. App. 578, 261 S.E.2d 289 (1980); Newman v. Dore, 275 N.Y. 371, 9 N.E.2d 966 (1937).

Husband's trust was completely revocable. The role of the trustee was described in the trust agreement and in a subsequent amendment as "custodial." Article XIV of the trust agreement granted settlor extensive powers. Furthermore, the trustee was expressly forbidden from exercising any powers of sale, investment or reinvestment during Husband's lifetime unless by (1) written notice of Husband or (2) certification of Husband's incompetence. In light of the evidence of Husband's extensive control over the trust, we find that the trust is illusory and, thus, invalid.

Respondents point to S.C. Code Ann. §§62-2-201 and 202 (1990 Supp.) as specifically barring inclusion of the trust in the estate. Section 62-2-201 (1986) originally provided in pertinent part: "(a) If a married person domiciled in this state dies, the surviving spouse has a right of election to take an elective share of one-third of the decedent's estate, as computed under §62-2-202." In 1987, §62-2-201 was amended by the legislature to insert the adjective "probate" between the words "decedent's" and "estate."

Section 62-2-201 originally defined "estate" as the "estate reduced by funeral and administration expenses and enforceable claims." In 1987, §62-2-201 was revised. It now provides: "For purposes of this Part, probate estate means the decedent's property passing under the decedent's will plus the decedent's property passing by intestacy, reduced by funeral and administration expenses and enforceable claims."

Respondents argue that the legislature's addition of the word "probate" in the 1987 amendment to §62-2-201 and the revision of §62-2-202 indicate the legislature's intention to keep trusts like the one at issue out of the estate because the "decedent's probate estate" only includes property passing under the will and by intestacy and does not include property in trusts.

We disagree with respondents' interpretation of the §§62-2-201 and -202 because those sections do not specifically preclude the proceeds of the trust from being included in decedent's estate. We see very little difference between this situation and one in which an otherwise valid trust fails. The proceeds of the failed trust would revert back to the settlor's estate and become part of the residue. The trust property would then be part of the estate for elective share purposes. Similarly, nothing in the Probate Code prohibits a trust, declared invalid as illusory, from reverting to the probate estate and being included in it for elective share purposes.

Respondents also point to the legislature's purported rejection of the Uniform Probate Code's "augmented estate," as evidenced by the reporter's comment to §62-2-202. The augmented estate, however, is an elaborate system of incorporating various non-probate assets into the estate. See [original] Uniform Probate Code, §2-202, 8 U.L.A. 75 (1983). Rejection of it does not prohibit invalidation of husband's inter-vivos trust in this situation.

Furthermore, contrary to respondents' contentions, we note that S.C. Code Ann. §62-2-204 (1986) protects the spouse's elective share by requiring that any waiver be made in writing. Thus, the legislature has indicated that the right to receive the elective share is a substantial one. Surely, then, it was not the legislature's intent to allow this substantial right to be circumvented as respondents urge. Thus, we hold that, where a spouse seeks to avoid payment of the elective share by creating a trust over which he or she exercises substantial control, the trust may be declared invalid as illusory, and the trust assets will be included in the decedent's estate for calculation of the elective share.

Since nothing in §§62-2-201 and 62-2-202 prohibits the proceeds of a trust, once declared invalid or illusory from being included in the probate estate, we hold that the proceeds of the trust should be included in Husband's estate for the purpose of calculating Widow's elective share. Due to our disposition of this issue, we need not reach Widow's remaining exception. We remand the matter for determination of Widow's elective share.

REVERSED AND REMANDED.

Notes

1. *Newman v. Dore and its Progeny.* Courts unwilling to permit a decedent to use will substitutes to deprive the surviving spouse of an elective share have historically adopted either of two judicial approaches: the *illusory-transfer* test or the *fraudulent-transfer* test. The first of these—the illusory-transfer test, illustrated in *Seifert*, above—is the predominant view. The leading case adopting the illusory-transfer test was Newman v. Dore, 9 N.E.2d 966 (N.Y. 1937). In that case, Ferdinand Straus, an 80-year-old testator, executed trust agreements by which he transferred all his real and personal property to his trustees. The trust agreements were executed

three days before his death and when cross-actions for dissolution of his marriage were pending. The terms of the trusts reserved to Straus the right to the income for life, the power to revoke the trusts, and the power to control the trustees in all aspects of the trusts' administration; needless to say, Straus's wife of four years, a woman in her thirties, received no beneficial interest in these trusts. She challenged the validity of the transfers to the trustees. The trial court found that Straus's motive in creating the trusts was to evade New York's elective share statute, and held that the transfers were not valid. In holding that the trusts were illusory, and therefore part of Straus's estate for purposes of his widow's rights, the New York Court of Appeals held:

> In this case the decedent... retained not only the income for life and power to revoke the trust, but also the right to control the trustees. We need not now determine whether such a trust is, for any purpose, a valid present trust....
>
> Judged by the substance, not by the form, the testator's conveyance is illusory, intended only as a mask for the effective retention by the settlor of the property which in form he had conveyed.

Although promising in theory, the illusory-transfer doctrine of Newman v. Dore, as applied by subsequent courts, gave the surviving spouse very limited protection against will substitutes. The reason is that, among the courts accepting the doctrine, one of the most common will substitutes—the revocable trust with a retained life estate—was typically held *not* to be illusory.[10]

2. *Aftermath of Seifert.* In South Carolina, *Seifert* has been superseded by statute. S.C. Code §62-2-202(b) states: "Except as provided in Section 62-7-401(c) with respect to a revocable trust found to be illusory, the elective share shall apply only to the decedent's probate estate." S.C. Code §62-7-401(c) provides in pertinent part: "A revocable inter vivos trust... is not rendered invalid because the settlor retains substantial control over the trust.... This subsection does not prevent a finding that a revocable inter vivos trust, enforceable for other purposes, is illusory for purposes of determining a spouse's elective share rights...."

3. *Recent Judicial Approaches.* In recent years, there has been a growing willingness to apply the elective share to revocable trusts. A leading case here is Sullivan v. Burkin, 460 N.E.2d 572 (Mass. 1984). Ernest Sullivan created a revocable trust while he was married to, but separated from, his wife Mary. Upon Ernest's death, Mary claimed an elective share right against the assets in the trust, relying upon the following statutory language: "The surviving husband or wife of a deceased person... [may claim a] portion of the estate of the deceased." Mass. Gen.

---

10. See, e.g., Johnson v. LaGrange State Bank, 383 N.E.2d 185 (Ill. 1978) (see also 755 Ill. Rev. Stat. §5/2-8); Kerwin v. Donaghy, 59 N.E.2d 299 (Mass. 1945) (prospectively overruled in Sullivan v. Burkin, 460 N.E.2d 572 (Mass. 1984)); Beirne v. Continental-Equitable Trust Co., 161 A. 721 (Pa. 1932); see Johnson v. Farmers & Merchants Bank, 379 S.E.2d 752 (W. Va. 1989) (West Virginia subsequently enacted the UPC augmented-estate system); Restatement 2d of Trusts §57 comment c.

Laws ch. 191, §15. The Supreme Judicial Court of Massachusetts held that the revocable trust was valid and thus, under the earlier Massachusetts case of Kerwin v. Donaghy, not part of Ernest's "estate" and not subject to the elective share. However, the court declared that it would apply a different rule in the future:

> We announce for the future that, as to any inter vivos trust created or amended after the date of this opinion, we shall no longer follow the rule announced in Kerwin v. Donaghy. There have been significant changes since 1945 in public policy considerations bearing on the right of one spouse to treat his or her property as he or she wishes during marriage. The interests of one spouse in the property of the other have been substantially increased upon the dissolution of a marriage by divorce. We believe that, when a marriage is terminated by the death of one spouse, the rights of the surviving spouse should not be so restricted as they are by the rule in Kerwin v. Donaghy. It is neither equitable nor logical to extend to a divorced spouse greater rights in the assets of an inter vivos trust created and controlled by the other spouse than are extended to a spouse who remains married until the death of his or her spouse.
>
> The rule we now favor would treat as part of "the estate of the deceased" for the purposes of G.L. c. 191, §15, assets of an inter vivos trust created during the marriage by the deceased spouse[11] over which he or she alone had a general power of appointment, exercisable by deed or by will. This objective test would involve no consideration of the motive or intention of the spouse in creating the trust. We would not need to engage in a determination of "whether the [spouse] has in good faith divested himself [or herself] of ownership of his [or her] property or has made an illusory transfer" (Newman v. Dore, [9 N.E.2d 966 (N.Y.1937)]) or with the factual question whether the spouse "intended to surrender complete dominion over the property" (Staples v. King, 433 A.2d 407, 411 [Me. 1981]). Nor would we have to participate in the rather unsatisfactory process of determining whether the inter vivos trust was, on some standard, "colorable," "fraudulent," or "illusory."
>
> What we have announced as a rule for the future hardly resolves all the problems that may arise. There may be a different rule if some or all of the trust assets were conveyed to such a trust by a third person. Cf. Theodore v. Theodore, [249 N.E.2d 3 (Mass. 1969)]. We have not, of course, dealt with a case in which the power of appointment is held jointly with another person. If the surviving spouse assented to the creation of the inter vivos trust, perhaps the rule we announce would not apply. We have not discussed which assets should be used to satisfy a surviving spouse's claim. We have not discussed the question whether a surviving spouse's interest in the intestate estate of a deceased spouse should reflect the value of assets held in an inter vivos trust created by the intestate spouse over which he or she had a general power of appointment. That situation and the one before us, however, do not seem readily distinguishable. A general power of appointment over assets in a trust created by a third person is said to present a different situation. Restatement (Second) of Property: Donative Transfers, Supplement to Tent. Draft No. 5, reporter's note to § 13.7 at 29 (1982). Nor have we dealt with other assets not passing by will, such as a trust created

---

11. The Supreme Judicial Court emphasized the importance of this requirement in Bongaards v. Millen, 793 N.E.2d 335 (Mass. 2003) (holding that the *Sullivan* rule applies only to trusts created by the deceased spouse, not trusts created by third parties). Ed.

before the marriage or insurance policies over which a deceased spouse had control.[12]

The question of the rights of a surviving spouse in the estate of a deceased spouse, using the word "estate" in its broad sense, is one that can best be handled by legislation. See [Original] Uniform Probate Code, §§2-201, 2-202.... See also Uniform Marital Property Act, §18 (Nat'l Conference of Comm'rs on Uniform State Laws, July, 1983), which adopts the concept of community property as to "marital property." But, until it is, the answers to these problems will "be determined in the usual way through the decisional process." Tucker v. Badoian, [384 N.E.2d 1195 (Mass. 1978)] (Kaplan, J., concurring).

See also Knell v. Price, 569 A.2d 636 (Md. 1990) (holding that any transfer in which the decedent retained "dominion and control" over the property during life is subject to the spouse's elective share); Dreher v. Dreher, 634 S.E.2d 646 (S.C. 2006) (holding that the decedent retained sufficient control over the revocable trust to render it illusory for purpose of the surviving spouse's elective share but valid for other purposes); Karsenty v. Schoukroun, 959 A.2d 1147 (Md. 2008) (explicating the factors to be considered in determining whether a revocable trust should be subject to the elective share).

4. *Restatement 3d of Property.* The Restatement 3d of Property supports the judicial application of the elective share to will substitutes. See Restatement 3d of Property §9.1(c) and the accompanying comment.

———

Computation; Contribution. For purposes of computing the amount of the elective share, the value of a will substitute that is subject to the elective share is added to the value of the decedent's probate estate. In satisfying the elective share amount, however, is the probate estate used first, so that the beneficiaries of the will substitutes are liable for contribution only to the extent the probate estate is insufficient to satisfy the elective share amount? Or are the beneficiaries of will substitutes liable to contribution of a proportional part of their gifts in making up the spouse's elective share? UPC §2-209 establishes the latter rule. The Restatement 3d of Property §9.1 comment *l* suggests that the court should try to retain the decedent's dispositive plan to the extent possible.

Will Substitutes and Intestate Estates. Note that the elective share provisions of the UPC apply to intestate as well as testate estates. Why?

———

Protection of Spousal Rights in Pension Benefits Under ERISA. The rights of a spouse in an employee spouse's ERISA-covered pension are protected under the Retirement Equity Act of 1984 (REAct). With respect to marriages ending at death, REAct creates new spousal interests in the form of survivorship rights. These rights

———

12. See Bongaards v. Millen, above (applying *Sullivan* to a bank account held by the deceased spouse "as trustee for" a third party). Ed.

exist only if the nonemployee spouse survives the employee spouse. If the employee spouse survives to retirement age, the pension must be paid as a "qualified joint and survivor annuity" (QJSA), unless the nonemployee spouse consents to some other form of payment. If the employee spouse dies before retirement age and the pension is vested, the surviving spouse is entitled to a "qualified preretirement survivor annuity" (QPSA). The Pension Protection Act of 2006 mandates a third survivor annuity option, called a "qualified optional survivor annuity" (QOSA) for spouses who decline a QJSA. These annuities are discussed in John H. Langbein et al., Pension and Employee Benefit Law (6th ed. 2015).

For marriages ending on divorce, REAct basically authorizes deference to state law. It prescribes certain conditions for enforcing state-court decrees that divide or transfer pension property, referred to as "qualified domestic-relations orders" (QDROs). In effect, this represents an exception to both ERISA's anti-alienation[13] and preemption rules, which would otherwise have immunized pension wealth from domestic relations judgments.

In Boggs v. Boggs, 520 U.S. 833 (1997), the Supreme Court held that ERISA preempts state property law. The employee's first wife of 30 years predeceased him. Her will devised part of her community share of his then-undistributed pension plan benefits to their three children. He remarried within a year after her death, retired five years later, and died four years after retirement, survived by his second wife. Upon retirement, the employee received certain shares of stock, a cash payment, and an annuity for his life and afterwards for his surviving second wife.

After the employee's death, his second wife began collecting the annuity payments. His children filed a suit in state court against their stepmother and their father's estate, seeking an accounting for the portion of his pension benefits devised to them under their predeceased mother's will. The employee's surviving second wife then filed a complaint in federal district court, seeking a declaratory judgment that ERISA preempts the application of the state's community property and succession laws to the extent they recognize the children's claim to an interest in the disputed pension benefits. The district court held for the children. The Fifth Circuit affirmed, holding that the first wife's ownership interest and devise were valid and not preempted by ERISA. The Supreme Court reversed, holding that ERISA preempts state community property law to the extent it allowed the employee's first wife to devise her community share of his pension benefits. Writing for the majority, JUSTICE KENNEDY stated:

---

13. For a decision that ERISA's anti-alienation rule ceases to apply once the pension benefits are received by the beneficiary, see Guidry v. Sheet Metal Workers National Pension Fund, 39 F.3d 1078 (10th Cir. 1994) (en banc).

The principal object of [ERISA] is to protect plan participants and beneficiaries. ...

.... ERISA's silence with respect to the right of a nonparticipant spouse to control pension plan benefits by testamentary transfer provides powerful support for the conclusion that the right does not exist....

We conclude the [children] have no claim under ERISA to a share of the retirement benefits. To begin with, the [children] are neither participants nor beneficiaries....

.... Reading ERISA to permit nonbeneficiary interests, even if not enforced against the plan, would result in troubling anomalies....

.... [R]etirees could find their retirement benefits reduced by substantial sums because they have been diverted to testamentary recipients. Retirement benefits and the income stream provided for by ERISA-regulated plans would be disrupted in the name of protecting a nonparticipant spouse's successors over plan participants and beneficiaries....

.... If state law is not pre-empted, the diversion of retirement benefits will occur regardless of whether the interest in the pension plan is enforced against the plan or the recipient of the pension benefit....

.... It does not matter that [the children] have sought to enforce their rights only after the retirement benefits have been distributed since their asserted rights are based on the theory that they had an interest in the undistributed pension plan benefits. Their state-law claims are pre-empted.

JUSTICE BREYER filed a dissenting opinion, in which JUSTICE O'CONNOR joined, and in which CHIEF JUSTICE REHNQUIST and JUSTICE GINSBERG joined in part, saying in part:

I can find no basis for pre-emption....

The state law in question concerns the ownership of benefits.... I cannot say that the state law at issue here concerns a subject that Congress wished to place outside the State's legal reach.

My reason in part lies in the fact that the state law in question involves family, property, and probate—all areas of traditional, and important, state concern....

....This case does not involve a lawsuit against a [pension] fund.... ERISA would likely pre-empt state law that permitted such a suit....

The lawsuit before us concerns benefits that the [pension] fund has already distributed; it asks not the fund, but others, for a subsequent accounting. [T]his lawsuit will not interfere with the payment of a survivor annuity to [the surviving spouse]. Under these circumstances, I do not see how allowing the respondents' suit to go forward could interfere with the administration of the [company] pension plan according to ERISA's requirements. Whether or not the children are allowed to seek an accounting, the plan fiduciaries will continue to owe a duty only to plan participants and beneficiaries.... Moreover, the children here are seeking an accounting only after the plan participant has died. But even were that not so, any threat the children's lawsuit could pose to plan administration is far less than that posed by the division of plan assets upon separation or divorce, which is allowed under §1056(d).

b. The Uniform Probate Code

Primary Statutory References: *UPC §§2-205, 2-207*

We saw earlier that, under the UPC, the surviving spouse's elective share percentage is applied to the augmented estate. The augmented estate serves two basic functions. By *combining* the couple's assets, it plays a crucial part in implementing the UPC's marital-sharing theory. The other function is to provide a means of dealing with "fraud on the spouse's share." To these ends, the augmented estate consists of the sum of the values of four components: (1) the decedent's net probate estate; (2) the decedent's nonprobate transfers to others; (3) the decedent's nonprobate transfers to the surviving spouse; and (4) property owned by the surviving spouse and amounts that would have been included in the surviving spouse's nonprobate transfers to others had the spouse been the decedent.

We are concerned here with the second of the two functions—preventing "fraud on the spouse's share." This function is performed by the decedent's nonprobate-transfers-to-others component of the augmented estate. Section 2-205 gives a detailed list of will substitutes that are included in this component. Examine §2-205 for a complete rundown of the specific types of will substitutes included. The listed items are, in general, quite similar to the will substitutes included in a decedent's gross estate for federal estate tax purposes.

The concept of providing in the statute itself a list of will substitutes to be subjected to the surviving spouse's elective share was pioneered by legislation in New York and Pennsylvania and adopted by the original version of the UPC. This approach resolves the problem that arises under conventional elective share statutes, illustrated by Newman v. Dore, of shifting to the courts the burden of deciding whether and under what circumstances will substitutes are subject to the elective share.

The 1990 revisions to the UPC sought to strengthen the decedent's nonprobate-transfers-to-others component. The original version contained several loopholes. The most important of these was life insurance that the decedent purchased, naming someone other than his or her spouse as the beneficiary. Under the current version, proceeds of these policies are included.[14]

The other important feature of the current version is that the decedent's nonprobate transfers to others now include property that is subject to a presently exercisable general power of appointment (including a power to revoke) held solely by the decedent. Such powers are viewed as substantively indistinguishable from

---

14. The American Council of Life Insurers (ACLI) has opposed the inclusion of life insurance in the augmented estate, claiming that the decedent "is best suited to evaluate" whom the policy should benefit. Letter from Carroll A. Campbell Jr., President and CEO, ACLI, to Lawrence W. Waggoner, Director of Research, JEB-UTEA, February 26, 1996. Do you agree?

outright ownership. It is immaterial whether the power was created by the decedent or another and whether the power was created during the marriage. The decedent need only have held the power immediately before his or her death or have exercised or released the power in favor of someone other than the decedent, the decedent's estate, or the decedent's spouse while married to the spouse and during the two-year period immediately preceding the decedent's death.

Problem

Hector died on May 7, 2005, survived by his wife, Wanda. He was also survived (i) by his father, Fred; and (ii) by his three children from his prior marriage to Martha that ended in divorce, Alice, Betty, and Carl.

Hector and Wanda were married to each other on June 14, 1994. Hector's will, executed on April 20, 2003, devised $100,000 to Wanda and the residue of his estate to his children in equal shares.

Hector's net probate estate, after payment of expenses and enforceable claims (excluding estate and inheritance taxes) and after payment of probate exemptions and allowances, was worth $2.5 million.

On December 23, 1985, Hector signed a written declaration of trust of certain financial assets; the trust was to pay the income to Hector's father for life, remainder in corpus to his children in equal shares; Hector retained no property interest in the trust, but did retain the power of revocation until his death. At the time of Hector's death, the value of the trust corpus was $200,000.

On September 1, 1994, Hector transferred his summer house and lot, title to which had been solely in his name, to Alice, retaining the right to use and possess the property until his death. At the time of Hector's death, the value of the summer house and lot was $110,000.

On July 21, 1995, Hector deposited $60,000 in a savings account registered in the names of "Hector, in trust for Betty." At Hector's death, the account had a balance of $100,000.

On October 5, 1996, Hector purchased a $90,000 life-insurance policy naming Carl as the beneficiary.

On May 20, 1997, Hector purchased a $200,000 life-insurance policy naming Wanda as the beneficiary.

When Hector died, Wanda's property was valued at $800,000, not counting the $200,000 in life-insurance proceeds she collected by reason of Hector's death or the $100,000 devised to her by Hector's will.

Wanda believes that Hector shortchanged her, and has decided to explore the possibility of obtaining a larger share of Hector's assets.

Under (1) a statute granting the surviving spouse an elective share of one-third of the decedent's net probate estate (assume that there are no illusory or fraudulent transfers) and (2) the UPC, what are Wanda's rights and what impact on the distribution of Hector's estate would occur if Wanda chooses to exercise those rights?

Matter of Scheiner

535 N.Y.S.2d 920 (Sur. Ct. 1988)

BLOOM, S. All objections filed by the surviving spouse in this contested accounting proceeding, except those relating to her right to elect against certain United States Treasury bills, were withdrawn after conference with the court.

All issues pertaining to the validity of the spouse's right to elect against the Treasury bills, purchased by the decedent in the joint names of himself and his sister prior to his marriage to the electing spouse, were submitted to the court for determination.

Based upon the facts and the circumstances herein, the court determines that these United States Treasury bills cannot be considered testamentary substitutes against which a surviving spouse can elect for the following reasons:

(1) All inter vivos transactions against which a spouse can elect as testamentary substitutes pursuant to EPTL 5-1.1(b)[15] are exempt from that right where the transaction occurred prior to the marriage (EPTL 5-1.1[b][1]). Even if these Treasury bills were usually considered as testamentary substitutes pursuant to the EPTL, which they are not for the reasons set forth later in the decision, the spouse's right to elect against them would be nullified by the fact that they were purchased prior to the marriage even though they rolled over during the course of the marriage.

(2) Certain money transactions, under EPTL 5-1.1(b)(2), are never deemed to be testamentary substitutes against which a spouse can elect. Included in this exempt category are "any United States savings bonds payable to a designated person" (EPTL 5-1.1[b][2][C]). The Practice Commentary to EPTL 5-1.1 (Rohan,

---

15. EPTL §5-1.1(b) provides in relevant part as follows:

(b) Inter vivos dispositions treated as testamentary substitutes for the purpose of election by surviving spouse.

(1) Where a person dies after August thirty-first, nineteen hundred sixty-six and is survived by a spouse who exercises a right of election under paragraph (c), the following transactions effected by such decedent at any time after the date of the marriage and after August thirty-first, nineteen hundred sixty-six, whether benefitting the surviving spouse or any other person, shall be treated as testamentary substitutes and the capital value thereof, as of the decedent's death, included in the net estate subject to the surviving spouse's elective right: ....

(D) Any disposition of property made by the decedent after August thirty-first, nineteen hundred sixty-six whereby property is held, at the date of his death, by the decedent and another person as joint tenants with a right of survivorship or as tenants by the entirety....

(2) Nothing in this paragraph shall affect, impair or defeat the right of any person entitled to receive ... (C) payment of any United States savings bond payable to a designated person, and such transactions are not testamentary substitutes within the meaning of this paragraph.

McKinney's Cons Laws of NY, Book 17B, at 18) gives a reason for their omission as testamentary substitutes the fact that their inclusion would conflict with existing Federal regulations and present serious constitutional questions.

The United States Department of the Treasury adopted regulations on July 1, 1986 that are found in 31 CFR part 357 and are known as Treasury Direct. One of the purposes for the enactment of Treasury Direct was to override any inconsistent State law concerning Treasury bills so that they would be treated in the exact manner as United States savings bonds. Evidence of the Government's intent to treat both United States savings bonds and Treasury bills in the same manner thereby enabling them to pass as registered free of the spouse's right of election is clearly set forth in Appendix A (Discussion of Final Rule) to the Federal regulations (31 CFR part 357). It states:

> *Forms of Registration.* The proposed rule provides the investor with a variety of registration options. They are essentially similar to those provided for registered, definitive marketable treasury securities. Investors should be particularly aware that, where the security is held in the names of two individuals, the registration chosen may establish rights of survivorship.
>
> The reason for establishing the rights of ownership for securities held in Treasury Direct is that it will give investors the assurance that the forms of registration they select will establish conclusively the rights to their book-entry securities. It will also serve to eliminate some of the uncertainties, as well as possible conflicts, between the varying laws of the several States.
>
> A Federal rule of ownership is being adopted by the Treasury for Treasury Direct securities. This regulatory approach is consistent with the one previously taken in the case of United States Savings Bonds. It will have the effect of overriding inconsistent State laws. See, Free v. Bland, 369 U.S. 663 (1962).

Accordingly, the Treasury bills in dispute are not testamentary substitutes against which a spouse can elect. The Federal regulations known as Treasury Direct preempted any existing inconsistent State law by mandating that these securities should pass as registered. In order to be consistent with the regulations in Treasury Direct, EPTL 5-1.1(b)(2)(C) must be construed to include United States Treasury bills within the term United States savings bonds.

All remaining objections are dismissed.

Note

Federal Preemption of State Elective Share Law. The decision in *Scheiner* interpreting the Treasury Direct Book-Entry regulations as preempting state law creates an opportunity for individuals to evade the surviving spouse's elective share through United States Treasury bills purchased through the book-entry account system of the Federal Reserve Banks. In reaching its decision, the court relied on Free v. Bland, 369 U.S. 663 (1962). In *Free*, the husband, who was the manager of the couple's community property under Texas law, purchased United States savings bonds in the names of "Mr. or Mrs." Free. The Treasury Department's savings bonds regulations provide that the bond's surviving coowner or beneficiary "will be recognized as [the bond's] sole and absolute owner" and that the Department "will not recognize ... a judicial determination that impairs the rights of survivorship conferred by these regulations upon a coowner or beneficiary." 31 C.F.R. §§315.20(a), 315.70(b)(1).

The wife died first, and her son, Bland, as the devisee under her will, claimed that one-half of the savings bonds were part of her estate as community property. The Texas court held that, although Free had full title by virtue of the federal regulations, Bland was entitled to be reimbursed for his mother's one-half interest. The Supreme Court reversed, holding that under the Supremacy Clause of the Constitution the savings bonds registration allowed by federal regulations must prevail over Texas's community property law. The Court, however, found that there was an implicit exception in the savings bond regulations in cases of fraud. The Court stated: "The regulations are not intended to be a shield for fraud, and relief would be available in a case where the circumstances manifest fraud or a breach of trust tantamount thereto on the part of a husband while acting in his capacity as manager of the general community property." 369 U.S. at 670. Although *Free* involved savings bond regulations rather than Treasury Direct regulations governing treasury bills, the latter regulations are a clone of the savings bond regulation insofar as they provide that "[r]egistration of a security conclusively establishes ownership...." 31 C.F.R. §357.21(a)(1).

The opinion in *Scheiner* does not mention another federal preemption case decided two years after *Free*. In Yiatchos v. Yiatchos, 376 U.S. 306 (1964), the Supreme Court developed the "fraud or breach of trust" exception that it had recognized in dictum in *Free*. In *Yiatchos*, the decedent husband, manager of the community property under Washington law, used community funds to purchase United States savings bonds in his name, payable on his death to his brother. The Court held that, unless the wife had consented to the POD registration or would receive her full half of the community property without the bonds, she was entitled to her one-half community property interest in the bonds. Applying the "fraud or breach of trust" exception, the Court stated: "[W]e shall be guided by state law insofar as the property interests of the widow created by state law are concerned. It would seem obvious that the bonds may not be used as a device to deprive the widow of property rights which she enjoys under [state] law and which would not be transferable by her husband but for the survivorship provisions of the federal bonds." 376 U.S. at 309.

Was *Yiatchos* relevant to the problem in *Scheiner*? Unlike a spouse's community property interest, the elective share is technically not a property interest. Should this fact preclude application of the "fraud or breach of trust" exception to the preemption doctrine? See Charles F. Gibbs & Marilyn G. Ordover, Right of Election by Surviving Spouse, N.Y. L.J., Sept. 13, 1989.

Note that §2-210(b) of the UPC attempts to handle the preemption problem by imposing a personal liability on the recipient. But recall the U.S. Supreme Court's decision in Hillman v. Maretta, discussed in Chapter 7.

3. *The Incapacitated Surviving Spouse*

As longevity increases, so does the incidence of mental deficiency, often due to Alzheimer's disease.[16] Should the elective share be available to a mentally incapacitated surviving spouse? If so, who should have the power to make the election and by what standard should that power be exercised? Clarkson v. First National Bank raises these issues.

Clarkson v. First National Bank
226 N.W.2d 334 (Neb. 1975)

SPENCER, J. This is an action under section 30-108(2), R.R.S.1943. It involves an election on behalf of an incompetent surviving spouse to either take under or against her husband's will. The District Court vacated an order of the county court electing on behalf of the widow to take the provision made for her in her husband's will. The executor prosecutes this appeal. We affirm.

Joseph D. Clarkson, deceased, married Evelyn Bell Clarkson April 16, 1953. Mr. Clarkson had two daughters from a prior marriage. Mrs. Clarkson had a son and a daughter by a prior marriage. No children were born of the second marriage. Mrs. Clarkson, who is 80 years of age, has been mentally incompetent since June 1965. The record indicates that her chances of recovery were and are nil. The will in question was executed November 18, 1969. The inventory filed in the estate indicates the value of the estate to be $1,229,263.56. The report of the guardian ad litem indicates the net value of the estate is $1,372,224. Only $62,000 is real estate, a Missouri farm valued at $40,000 and the residence property valued at $22,000.

The will makes the following provision for the incompetent:

> If my wife, Evelyn Bell Clarkson, survives me, I give, devise and bequeath to the FIRST NATIONAL BANK OF OMAHA, as TRUSTEE for my said wife, an amount equal to one-fourth (1/4) of the value of my net estate as finally determined for Federal Estate Tax purposes, unreduced by any taxes.

The will directs the trustee to pay all income therefrom to Mrs. Clarkson and in addition provides for such amounts of principal to be paid to her from time to time as the trustee deems necessary or desirable to provide for her proper support and maintenance. The will further provides that upon Mrs. Clarkson's death the trust

---

16. Alzheimer's disease, a form of dementia that progressively impairs intellectual abilities, has become a major problem among the over-65 portion of the American population. As American society ages, it is likely that the percentage of the population afflicted with the disease, the incidence of which increases sharply with age, will grow yet higher.

estate shall terminate and the assets remaining in the trust shall then be distributed and disposed of to such persons in such manner as Mrs. Clarkson by her last will and testament shall direct and appoint. If Mrs. Clarkson fails to exercise the general testamentary power of appointment upon her death, the will provides that the remaining assets shall be distributed as follows:

> Twenty-five Thousand Dollars ($25,000) thereof shall be paid to each of my wife's children, JERRY W. MENCK and PEGGY LOU McVEA, with the children of either of them who may be then deceased to take equally the share which the parent would have taken if then living; and the balance of said assets remaining shall be distributed to my daughters, HELEN E. CLARKSON and RUTH C. BOLLINGER, share and share alike.

The will was made at a time when Mrs. Clarkson was incompetent. There is no possibility of her exercising the power of appointment granted in the will because her condition cannot improve....

The incompetent, as the second wife of deceased, would receive one-fourth of the estate if she takes under the statute rather than the will. The parties are in agreement that there is no dollar difference between what Mr. Clarkson left his wife in trust and what she would take by an election. The difference comes about in that a fee title is of much greater value than a beneficial interest in the trust.

While this is a case of first impression in Nebraska, the question has arisen in many other jurisdictions.... [T]here is an irreconcilable conflict in the decisions. This conflict arises because of various theories used by the courts in interpreting and defining the meaning of the words "best interests" or similar words which are found in the several statutes under consideration....

In the so-called minority view, all the decisions in one way or another indicate that the best interests of the incompetent will be served by electing the method which is the most valuable to the surviving spouse. This usually means the one having the greater pecuniary value is the one selected.

The language of the various statutes may differ but essentially most of them will provide that the election should be made which is to the best interests, advantage, welfare, or the like of the incompetent person. Our statute provides that the court should make such election as it deems *the* best interests of the surviving wife or husband shall require. This seems to narrow the range of consideration.[17]

The majority view, as stated in Kinnett v. Hood (1962), 25 Ill.2d 600, 185 N.E.2d 888, 3 A.L.R.3d 1, is that all the surrounding facts and circumstances should be

---

17. Nebraska repealed this statute, incident to enactment of the original version of the UPC in 1974. However, Neb. Rev. Stat. §30-2315, the Nebraska counterpart of original UPC §2-203, substitutes "in the best interests of" for the UPC's "necessary to provide adequate support for." In 2017, the Nebraska Supreme Court held that "to the extent *Clarkson* adopted the minority 'pecuniary approach,' that holding has been superseded by statute, specifically §30-2315." In re Kaiser, 891 N.W.2d 84, 91 (Neb. 2017). Ed.

taken into consideration by the court in order to make the election to take under the will or against it....

The majority rule emphasizes other considerations than monetary. It characterizes the minority cases as placing the election purely on monetary standards or what would result in the larger pecuniary value, to the detriment of other considerations. We concede that in some instances there may be other considerations than monetary which may promote the best interests of the incompetent. What, however, are those other considerations? It is impractical to delineate factors which could apply in every case or to specify the relative weight which should be given to such other possible considerations. If we follow our statutes, the best interests of an incompetent in most instances will require the election which will result in the larger pecuniary value. We cannot agree that the preservation of the decedent's estate plan is a major consideration ... as it appears to be in many cases espousing the majority view. Under our law the testator's testamentary desires have little or no importance in relation to the best interests of the surviving spouse....

Many of the majority view cases criticize the minority cases, suggesting that they tend to sanction: (1) The interests of the heirs of the incompetent as a consideration; and (2) give too much weight to what the surviving spouse would have done had she made her own election as a consideration. We are in full accord with the view that the interests of possible heirs of the incompetent should play no part in the decision. We would not, however, entirely ignore what the surviving spouse might have done had she made her own election....

It seems a little inconsistent under our law to say, as do some of the majority cases, that the election by the court to renounce the will should be made only if necessary to provide for the widow's needs. This would write a restriction into our statute. The statute requires the court to make the election which it deems is in the best interests of the incompetent spouse. This must be made without reference to whether she may be provided for otherwise. We observe that neither section 30-107 nor section 30-108, which create the right of election and provide the necessary procedural steps, make any mention of or suggest any restrictions under which an election might be made. While a competent surviving spouse may elect to take against the will, even if it would seem obviously against her best interests to do so, a court in making the choice for an incompetent does not have that privilege. It must consider only the best interests of the incompetent.

On the record we find no considerations other than the monetary value of the estate. We find that an estate in fee is of much greater value than a beneficial interest in a trust....

The judgment is affirmed.

[The dissenting opinion of MCCOWN, J., in which NEWTON and CLINTON, JJ., joined, is omitted.]

Notes

1. *"Best Interests."* Whose "best interests" were served by the decision in *Clarkson*?

2. *Current Cost of Long Term Care.* The cost of long term care for an incapacitated person varies considerably from state to state. Current costs in particular cities can be estimated by clicking on the map at the John Hancock Group Long-Term Care Insurance website, caregiveradvocate.com/johnhancock-cost-of-care/wellness/cost-care-public. According to the site, care in a private room in a nursing home in Lincoln, Nebraska, averages $335 per day. The average daily cost in Manhattan is $534; in San Francisco it is $453; and in Chicago it is $411.

3. *Uniform Probate Code.* UPC §2-212 includes several innovations. The most important of these is that, under subsection (b), an election made on behalf of a surviving spouse who is incapacitated requires that the portion of the elective share and supplemental elective share amounts that are payable from the decedent's probate estate and nonprobate transfers to others under §2-209(c) and (d) goes into a custodial trust created under the Uniform Custodial Trust Act. The purpose of this provision is to assure that the portion of the elective share amount that represents involuntary transfers from the decedent is used to benefit the surviving spouse personally rather than the spouse's heirs or devisees. Upon the surviving spouse's death, the remaining custodial trust property passes to the predeceased spouse's residuary devisees or heirs.

4. *Timing of the Election.* The statutory right of election is personal and does not survive the surviving spouse's death. See, e.g., Estate of Anderson, 394 So.2d 1146 (Fla. Dist. Ct. App. 1981), where the court explained that the elective share "is a substitute for dower and curtesy, which were abolished [by statute]. The purpose of dower and curtesy was to insure provision for the surviving spouse's needs [and not for the spouse's heirs or devisees]. When the surviving spouse dies, no like purpose remains."[18]

5. *Incapacitated Spouse's Elective Share and Medicaid Eligibility.* In Estate of Cross, 664 N.E.2d 905 (Ohio 1996), the surviving spouse, who had been declared incompetent, was dependent on Medicaid benefits to pay her nursing home expenses. Her husband had devised his entire estate to his child from an earlier marriage. The court held that the probate court, acting on behalf of the incompetent spouse, had properly decided to elect her statutory share. Under Ohio law, the spouse's statutory share is a "potential resource" for purposes of Medicaid

---

18. In Will of Sayre, 415 S.E.2d 263 (W.Va. 1992), the testator's wife was unable to make the election because she had previously suffered a mentally debilitating stroke. She was not declared incompetent until shortly after her husband's death. Three weeks after the declaration of incompetency, her committee filed her elective share claim. She died while the claim was being processed but before it was finally allowed. The court held that because the spouse's committee had timely commenced the election, the elective share right survived her death.

eligibility, and the nonutilization of it would disqualify her for Medicaid. In order to maintain her eligibility, the probate judge was required to elect to take against the will. Accord Miller v. State Dep't of Soc. & Reb. Services, 64 P.3d 395 (Kan. 2003).

4. Premarital and Marital Agreements

Primary Statutory References: *UPC §2-213*
Uniform Premarital and Marital Agreements Act

The right to an elective share (and other death benefits, such as homestead and family allowances) may be waived by premarital or marital agreement.[19] In the absence of statute, the validity of these agreements depends upon general principles of contract law. However, because of the confidential relationship between the parties, the law has moved largely to the view that these agreements will be closely scrutinized for any overreaching by either party.

This was not always the standard. In an early Massachusetts decision, the court in Wellington v. Rugg, 136 N.E. 831 (Mass. 1922), held that mere failure to disclose a party's true financial situation was not a sufficient ground for setting aside a premarital agreement; it took a showing of actual fraud to avoid enforcement. The rule of the *Wellington* case was prospectively overruled, however, in Rosenberg v. Lipnick, 389 N.E.2d 385 (Mass. 1979). In place of the *Wellington* rule, the *Rosenberg* decision announced the following position, believed to reflect the prevailing position today, in the absence of statute:

> [I]n future cases... we shall feel free to hold that the parties by definition occupy a confidential relationship and that the burden of disclosure rests upon both of them.
>
> In judging the validity of such an antenuptial agreement, other relevant factors which we may consider are whether (1) it contains a fair and reasonable provision as measured at the time of its execution for the party contesting the agreement; (2) the contesting party was fully informed of the other party's worth prior to the agreement's execution, or had, or should have had, independent knowledge of the other party's worth; and (3) a waiver by the contesting party is set forth. It is clear that the reasonableness of any monetary provision in an antenuptial contract cannot ultimately be judged in isolation. Rather, reference may appropriately be made to such factors as the parties' respective worth, the parties' respective ages, the parties' respective intelligence, literacy, and business acumen, and prior family ties or commitments....
>
> The right to make antenuptial agreements settling property rights in advance of marriage is a valuable personal right which courts should not regulate destructively. Neither should the exercise of that right be looked upon with disfavor. Thus, we recognize that antenuptial

---

19. At one time, agreements governing property rights on *divorce* were held to encourage divorce, and hence unenforceable as against public policy. Today, the prevailing view is that such agreements are enforceable if fair and reasonable. Posner v. Posner, 233 So.2d 381 (Fla. 1970), was the leading decision breaking new ground on the question.

agreements must be so construed as to give full effect to the parties' intentions, but we are concerned that such agreements be executed fairly and understandingly and be free from fraud, imposition, deception, or over-reaching.[20]

For other decisions adopting a similar set of standards, see Martin v. Farber, 510 A.2d 608 (Md. Ct. Spec. App.1986); Estate of Benker, 331 N.W.2d 193 (Mich. 1982); Juhasz v. Juhasz, 16 N.E.2d 328 (Ohio 1938); Estate of Crawford, 730 P.2d 675 (Wash. 1986). A decision of the Supreme Court of Pennsylvania, Estate of Geyer, 533 A.2d 423 (Pa. 1987), also adopted a similar set of standards, but that decision was reexamined in the *Simeone* decision, below.

Simeone v. Simeone
581 A.2d 162 (Pa. 1990)

FLAHERTY J. At issue in this appeal is the validity of a prenuptial agreement executed between the appellant, Catherine E. Walsh Simeone, and the appellee, Frederick A. Simeone. At the time of their marriage, in 1975, appellant was a twenty-three year old nurse and appellee was a thirty-nine year old neurosurgeon. Appellee had an income of approximately $90,000 per year, and appellant was unemployed. Appellee also had assets worth approximately $300,000. On the eve of the parties' wedding, appellee's attorney presented appellant with a prenuptial agreement to be signed. Appellant, without the benefit of counsel, signed the agreement. Appellee's attorney had not advised appellant regarding any legal rights that the agreement surrendered. The parties are in disagreement as to whether appellant knew in advance of that date that such an agreement would be presented for signature. Appellant denies having had such knowledge and claims to have signed under adverse circumstances, which, she contends, provide a basis for declaring it void.

The agreement limited appellant to support payments of $200 per week in the event of separation or divorce, subject to a maximum total payment of $25,000. The parties separated in 1982, and, in 1984, divorce proceedings were commenced. Between 1982 and 1984 appellee made payments which satisfied the $25,000 limit. In 1985, appellant filed a claim for alimony pendente lite. A master's report upheld the validity of the prenuptial agreement and denied this claim. Exceptions to the master's report were dismissed by the Court of Common Pleas of Philadelphia County. The Superior Court affirmed....

[T]here is need for a reexamination of the foundations upon which ... and a need for clarification of the standards by which the validity of prenuptial agreements will be judged. There is no longer validity in the implicit presumption that ... spouses are of unequal status and that women are not knowledgeable enough to understand the

---

20. The Massachusetts court subsequently extended the *Rosenberg* rules to the validity of a premarital contract relating to divorce as well as death. See Osborne v. Osborne, 428 N.E.2d 810 (Mass. 1981).

nature of contracts that they enter. Society has advanced ... to the point where women are no longer regarded as the "weaker" party in marriage, or in society generally. Indeed, the stereotype that women serve as homemakers while men work as breadwinners is no longer viable. Quite often today both spouses are income earners. Nor is there viability in the presumption that women are uninformed, uneducated, and readily subjected to unfair advantage in marital agreements. Indeed, women nowadays quite often have substantial education, financial awareness, income, and assets.

Accordingly, the law has advanced to recognize the equal status of men and women in our society.... Paternalistic presumptions and protections that arose to shelter women from the inferiorities and incapacities which they were perceived as having in earlier times have, appropriately, been discarded....

Further, [prior law] embodied substantial departures from traditional rules of contract law, to the extent that they allowed consideration of the knowledge of the contracting parties and reasonableness of their bargain as factors governing whether to uphold an agreement. Traditional principles of contract law provide perfectly adequate remedies where contracts are procured through fraud, misrepresentation, or duress. Consideration of other factors, such as the knowledge of the parties and the reasonableness of their bargain, is inappropriate. Prenuptial agreements are contracts, and, as such, should be evaluated under the same criteria as are applicable to other types of contracts. Absent fraud, misrepresentation, or duress, spouses should be bound by the terms of their agreements.

Contracting parties are normally bound by their agreements, without regard to whether the terms thereof were read and fully understood and irrespective of whether the agreements embodied reasonable or good bargains....

Accordingly, we find no merit in a contention raised by appellant that the agreement should be declared void on the ground that she did not consult with independent legal counsel. To impose a per se requirement that parties entering a prenuptial agreement must obtain independent legal counsel would be contrary to traditional principles of contract law, and would constitute a paternalistic and unwarranted interference with the parties' freedom to enter contracts.

Further, the reasonableness of a prenuptial bargain is not a proper subject for judicial review.... [E]arlier decisions required that, at least where there had been an inadequate disclosure made by the parties, the bargain must have been reasonable at its inception. Some have even suggested that prenuptial agreements should be examined with regard to whether their terms remain reasonable at the time of dissolution of the parties' marriage.

By invoking inquiries into reasonableness, however, the functioning and reliability of prenuptial agreements is severely undermined. Parties would not have entered such agreements, and, indeed, might not have entered their marriages, if they did not expect their agreements to be strictly enforced. If parties viewed an agreement as reasonable at the time of its inception, as evidenced by their having signed the agreement, they should be foreclosed from later trying to evade its terms by asserting that it was not in fact reasonable. Pertinently, the present agreement contained a clause reciting that "each of the parties considers this agreement fair, just and reasonable...."

Further, everyone who enters a long-term agreement knows that circumstances can change during its term, so that what initially appeared desirable might prove to be an unfavorable bargain. Such are the risks that contracting parties routinely assume. Certainly, the possibilities of illness, birth of children, reliance upon a spouse, career change, financial gain or loss, and numerous other events that can occur in the course of a marriage cannot be regarded as unforeseeable. If parties choose not to address such matters in their prenuptial agreements, they must be regarded as having contracted to bear the risk of events that alter the value of their bargains.

We are reluctant to interfere with the power of persons contemplating marriage to agree upon, and to act in reliance upon, what they regard as an acceptable distribution scheme for their property. A court should not ignore the parties' expressed intent by proceeding to determine whether a prenuptial agreement was, in the court's view, reasonable at the time of its inception or the time of divorce. These are exactly the sorts of judicial determinations that such agreements are designed to avoid. Rare indeed is the agreement that is beyond possible challenge when reasonableness is placed at issue. Parties can routinely assert some lack of fairness relating to the inception of the agreement, thereby placing the validity of the agreement at risk. And if reasonableness at the time of divorce were to be taken into account an additional problem would arise. Virtually nonexistent is the marriage in which there has been absolutely no change in the circumstances of either spouse during the course of the marriage. Every change in circumstance, foreseeable or not, and substantial or not, might be asserted as a basis for finding that an agreement is no longer reasonable.

In discarding the [prior] approach... that permitted examination of the reasonableness of prenuptial agreements and allowed inquiries into whether parties had attained informed understandings of the rights they were surrendering, we do not depart from the longstanding principle that a full and fair disclosure of the financial positions of the parties is required. Absent this disclosure, a material misrepresentation in the inducement for entering a prenuptial agreement may be asserted. Parties to these agreements do not quite deal at arm's length, but rather at the time the contract is entered into stand in a relation of mutual confidence and trust that calls for disclosure of their financial resources. It is well settled that this disclosure need not be exact, so long as it is "full and fair." Kaufmann Estate, 404 Pa. 131, 136 n. 8, 171 A.2d 48, 51 n. 8 (1961). In essence therefore, the duty of disclosure under these circumstances is consistent with traditional principles of contract law.

If an agreement provides that full disclosure has been made, a presumption of full disclosure arises. If a spouse attempts to rebut this presumption through an assertion of fraud or misrepresentation then this presumption can be rebutted if it is proven by clear and convincing evidence.

The present agreement recited that full disclosure had been made, and included a list of appellee's assets totaling approximately $300,000....

Appellant's final contention is that the agreement was executed under conditions of duress in that it was presented to her at 5 p.m. on the eve of her wedding, a time when she could not seek counsel without the trauma, expense, and embarrassment of postponing the wedding. The master found this claim not credible. The courts below affirmed that finding, upon an ample evidentiary basis.

Although appellant testified that she did not discover until the eve of her wedding that there was going to be a prenuptial agreement, testimony from a number of other witnesses was to the contrary. Appellee testified that, although the final version of the agreement was indeed presented to appellant on the eve of the wedding, he had engaged in several discussions with appellant regarding the contents of the agreement during the six month period preceding that date. Another witness testified that appellant mentioned, approximately two or three weeks before the wedding, that she was going to enter a prenuptial agreement. Yet another witness confirmed that, during the months preceding the wedding, appellant participated in several discussions of prenuptial agreements. And the legal counsel who prepared the agreement for appellee testified that, prior to the eve of the wedding, changes were made in the agreement to increase the sums payable to appellant in the event of separation or divorce. He also stated that he was present when the agreement was signed and that appellant expressed absolutely no reluctance about signing. It should be noted, too, that during the months when the agreement was being discussed appellant had more than sufficient time to consult with independent legal counsel if she had so desired. Under these circumstances, there was plainly no error in finding that appellant failed to prove duress.

Hence, the courts below properly held that the present agreement is valid and enforceable. Appellant is barred, therefore, from receiving alimony pendente lite.

Order affirmed.

PAPADAKOS, J., Concurring. Although I continue to adhere to the [prior] principles... I concur in the result because the facts fully support the existence of a valid and enforceable agreement between the parties and any suggestion of duress is totally negated by the facts. The full and fair disclosure, as well as the lack of unfairness and inequity,... are supported by the facts in this case so that I can concur in the result.

However, I cannot join the opinion authored by Mr. Justice Flaherty, because, it must be clear to all readers, it contains a number of unnecessary and unwarranted declarations regarding the "equality" of women. Mr. Justice Flaherty believes that, with the hard-fought victory of the Equal Rights Amendment in Pennsylvania, all vestiges of inequality between the sexes have been erased and women are now treated equally under the law. I fear my colleague does not live in the real world. If I did not know him better I would think that his statements smack of male chauvinism, an attitude that "you women asked for it, now live with it." If you want to know about equality of women, just ask them about comparable wages for comparable work. Just ask them about sexual harassment in the workplace. Just ask them about the sexual discrimination in the Executive Suites of big business. And the list of discrimination based on sex goes on and on.

I view prenuptial agreements as being in the nature of contracts of adhesion with one party generally having greater authority than the other who deals in a subservient role. I believe the law protects the subservient party, regardless of that party's sex, to insure equal protection and treatment under the law.

The present case does not involve the broader issues to which the gratuitous declarations in question are addressed, and it is injudicious to offer declarations in a case which does not involve those issues. Especially when those declarations are inconsistent with reality.

[The dissenting opinion of MCDERMOTT, J.,in which LARSEN, J., joined, is omitted.]

Notes and Questions

1. *Equal Bargaining Power?* Do you think an unemployed twenty-three year old nurse and a thirty-nine year old practicing neurosurgeon have equal bargaining power regarding a premarital agreement drafted by the neurosurgeon's attorney?

Consider how the following conclusions bear on the bargaining power of a woman with respect to a premarital agreement presented to her by the man's attorney on the eve of the wedding:

> Despite more than twenty-five years of experience with federal and state laws prohibiting discrimination in employment based on sex,... in most cases, marriage is still the most promising opportunity open to women who want to raise their standard of living. If the marriage terminates in divorce,... remarriage is the most efficient path to an immediate return to a higher standard of living. Marriage, it seems, is both a long-term cause and a short-term cure of female poverty.

Herma Hill Kay, Beyond No-Fault, in Divorce Reform at the Crossroads 6, 30 (Stephen D. Sugarman & Herma Hill Kay eds. 1990).

2. *Is Separate Counsel Required?* The court in *Simeone* rejected the argument that agreements should be declared void if one party did not have independent counsel. This is the prevailing view. See, e.g., In re Matson, 730 P.2d 668 (Wash. 1986) (rejecting a requirement of separate counsel but nonetheless stating: "We still strongly urge both parties to seek advice from independent counsel before signing

a premarital agreement. This would provide the best opportunity for both sides to receive objective and independent information regarding the legal consequences of the agreement.")

Restatement 3d of Property

§9.4 Premarital or Marital Agreement

(a) The elective share and other statutory rights accruing to a surviving spouse may be waived, wholly or partially, or otherwise altered, before or during marriage, by a written agreement that was signed by both parties. An agreement that was entered into before marriage is a premarital agreement. An agreement that was entered into during marriage is a marital agreement. Consideration is not necessary to the enforcement of a premarital or a marital agreement.

(b) For a premarital or a marital agreement to be enforceable against the surviving spouse, the enforcing party must show that the surviving spouse's consent was informed and was not obtained by undue influence or duress.

(c) A rebuttable presumption arises that the requirements of subsection (b) are satisfied, shifting the burden of proof to the surviving spouse to show that his or her consent was not informed or was obtained by undue influence or duress, if the enforcing party shows that:

(1) before the agreement's execution, (i) the surviving spouse knew, at least approximately, the decedent's assets and asset values, income, and liabilities; or (ii) the decedent or his or her representative provided in timely fashion to the surviving spouse a written statement accurately disclosing the decedent's significant assets and asset values, income, and liabilities; and either

(2) the surviving spouse was represented by independent legal counsel; or

(3) if the surviving spouse was not represented by independent legal counsel, (i) the decedent or the decedent's representative advised the surviving spouse, in timely fashion, to obtain independent legal counsel, and if the surviving spouse was needy, offered to pay for the costs of the surviving spouse's representation; and (ii) the agreement stated, in language easily understandable by an adult of ordinary intelligence with no legal training, the nature of any rights or claims otherwise arising at death that were altered by the agreement, and the nature of that alteration.

Notes

1. *Scope of the Restatement.* The Restatement (above) applies to premarital and marital agreements dealing with the elective share and other spousal statutory rights arising on death. The American Law Institute's position on the enforceability of premarital and marital agreements dealing with dissolution of marriage during life is set forth in similar terms in Chapter 7 of The Principles of the Law of Family Dissolution. For a dissenting view regarding Chapter 7 of the Principles, see David

Westfall, Forcing Incidents of Marriage on Unmarried Cohabitants: The American Law Institute's *Principles of Family Dissolution*, 76 Notre Dame L. Rev. 1467, 1478-90 (2001).

2. *1983 Uniform Premarital Agreement Act.* Under the Uniform Premarital Agreement Act (1983) (UPAA),[21] agreements pertaining to property rights on divorce or death are enforceable unless the party against whom enforcement is sought proves (a) that he or she did not execute the agreement voluntarily; or (b) that the agreement was unconscionable[22] when made *and* that, before execution of the agreements, he or she (1) was *not* provided a fair and reasonable disclosure of the property or financial obligations of the other party, (2) did *not* voluntarily and expressly waive, in writing, any right to disclosure of the property or financial obligations of the other party beyond the disclosure provided, *and* (3) did *not* have, or reasonably could not have had, an adequate knowledge of the property and financial obligations of the other party.

3. *2012 Uniform Premarital and Marital Agreements Act.* In 2012, the Uniform Law Commission approved the Uniform Premarital and Marital Agreements Act (UPMAA), designed to replace the 1983 UPAA. Under §9(a) of the UPMAA, a premarital or marital agreement is unenforceable if the party against whom enforcement is sought proves that (1) the party's consent was involuntary or the result of duress, or (2) the party did *not* have access to independent legal representation as defined in §9(b), or (3) unless the party had access to independent legal representation, the agreement did *not* provide a notice of waiver of rights as defined in §9(c), or (4) before signing the agreement, the party did *not* receive adequate financial disclosure as defined in §9(d).

4. *Conforming Amendments to UPC §2-213.* In 2016, the Uniform Law Commission approved amendments to UPC §2-213 to conform it to §9 of the UPMAA.

5. *Premarital Waiver of Spousal Rights Under ERISA.* As noted earlier, ERISA was amended in 1984 by the Retirement Equity Act (REAct) to require each employee benefit plan subject to its provisions to provide the surviving spouse with the right to an annuity. The spouse may, however, elect to waive that right, but the waiver is invalid unless:

---

21. The UPAA was enacted in 26 states (Arizona, Arkansas, California, Connecticut, Delaware, Florida, Hawaii, Idaho, Illinois, Indiana, Iowa, Kansas, Maine, Montana, Nebraska, Nevada, New Mexico, North Carolina, North Dakota, Oregon, Rhode Island, South Dakota, Texas, Utah, Virginia, and Wisconsin) and the District of Columbia. North Dakota later enacted the 2012 Uniform Premarital and Marital Agreements Act (UPMAA), as has Colorado.

22. The term "unconscionable," derived from §306 of the Model Marriage and Divorce Act, is explained in a Commissioner's Note to §306 as encompassing overreaching, concealment of assets, or sharp dealings inconsistent with the obligations of marital partners to deal fairly with each other.

(i) the spouse of the participant consents in writing to such election, (ii) such election designates a beneficiary (or a form of benefits) which may not be changed without spousal consent (or the consent of the spouse expressly permits designations by the participant without any requirement of further consent by the spouse), and (iii) the spouse's consent acknowledges the effect of such election and is witnessed by a plan representative or a notary public.

See 29 U.S.C. §1055(c)(2)(A); IRC §417(a)(2)(A).

In Hurwitz v. Sher, 982 F.2d 778 (2d Cir. 1992), the court held that a premarital agreement was not an effective waiver of a wife's rights under an ERISA-covered profit sharing plan in which the deceased husband was the sole participant. The premarital agreement provided, in part, that "each party hereby waives and releases to the other party and to the other party's heirs, executors, administrators and assigns any and all rights and causes of action which may arise by reason of the marriage between the parties... with respect to any property, real or personal, tangible or intangible... now owned or hereafter acquired by the other party, as fully as though the parties had never married...." The court held that the premarital agreement was not an effective waiver because it "did not designate a beneficiary and did not acknowledge the effect of the waiver as required by ERISA." Although the district court had held that the premarital agreement was also ineffective because the wife was not married to the participant when she signed the agreement, the Second Circuit "reserve[d] judgment on whether the [premarital] agreement might have operated as an effective waiver if its only deficiency were that it had been entered into before marriage." The court did, however, quote Treas. Reg. § 1.401(a)-20, which specifically states that "an agreement entered into prior to marriage does not satisfy the applicable consent requirements...." But see Estate of Hopkins, 574 N.E.2d 230 (Ill. App. 1991) (holding that premarital agreement was valid waiver under 29 U.S.C. §1055 even though parties were not yet married). See Lynn Wintriss, Waiver of REA Rights in Premarital Agreements, Probate & Property 16 (May/June 1993); Michael D. Rose, Pension Plans: Why Antenuptial Agreements Cannot Relinquish Survivor Benefits, 43 Fla. L. Rev. 723 (1991).

EXTERNAL REFERENCES. Wendy S. Goffe, Peter M. Walzer & Kimberly R. Willoughby, When Estate Planning and Marital Agreements Collide, 68 Prac. Law 26 (Oct. 2022) (Part I), 68 Prac. Law 20 (Dec. 2022) (Part II); Elizabeth R. Carter, Are Premarital Agreements Really Unfair?: An Empirical Study, 48 Hofstra L. Rev. 387 (2019); Linda J. Ravdin, Postmarital Agreements: Validity and Enforceability, 52 Fam. L.Q. 245 (2018); Arlene G. Dubin & Carole M. Bass, Ten Tips for Estate Planners Who Draft Prenuptial Agreements, 42 Est. Plan. 3 (June 2015); Annot., Failure to Disclose Extent or Value of Property Owned as Ground for Avoiding Premarital Contract, 3 A.L.R.5th 394.

5. Tax Implications of an Election

In an age in which married partners often have children from prior marriages, an aspect of elective share law that makes election attractive is that, by electing, the spouse receives absolute ownership of all (or part of[23]) his or her entitlement. Absolute ownership means that the spouse has power to give the property to his or her children during life or at death.

To the extent that an elective share confers an absolute-ownership interest on the surviving spouse, it qualifies for the federal estate tax marital deduction. Under the UPC scheme, that part of the elective share made up of augmented-estate property that passes or has passed to the surviving spouse might also qualify for the federal estate tax marital deduction, depending on the terms of the disposition.

The Economic Recovery Tax Act of 1981 amended the federal estate tax by allowing a marital deduction for qualified terminable interest property—"QTIPs" in estate-planning parlance. See IRC §2056(b)(7). The great attraction of QTIPs is that they allow the decedent spouse to create a deductible trust in which the surviving spouse receives only a lifetime income interest in the property. QTIPs are now in widespread use. In a QTIP, of course, the surviving spouse does not have testamentary control over the devolution of the trust property after his or her death.[24]

Consider a surviving spouse who has not been disinherited in any strict sense, but rather has been provided for by means of a QTIP trust. The elective-share provisions, as they are currently constituted in non-UPC states, where the forced share entitles the survivor to an absolute-ownership interest, provide this surviving spouse with an incentive to elect the statutory share if he or she has children by a former marriage. To the extent that the electing spouse can take an absolute-ownership interest, as opposed to an interest that expires on his or her death (such as a life estate), the elective share is attractive because it gives the survivor the power to benefit those children upon his or her death.

In an estate large enough to incur federal estate tax, a more subtle problem pertains to the calculation of the elective share. (The same problem exists, incidentally, in the calculation of the spouse's intestate share in an intestate estate.) The problem is whether the elective-share fraction (or intestate-share fraction) is applied to the estate before or after the federal estate tax has been subtracted. The elective or intestate share will be greater, perhaps substantially greater, under the before-tax approach

---

23. To repeat a point made earlier: UPC §2-209(a)(1) provides that the elective share is funded first with property interests passing to the surviving spouse that may or may not be absolute ownership interests.

24. Prior to the 1981 tax law changes, the only methods available for qualifying for the marital deduction required the surviving spouse to be given testamentary control over the property, either through outright ownership of that property or under a general power of appointment. See IRC §2056(b)(5).

than under the after-tax approach; also, under the before-tax approach, the federal estate tax itself will be lower, to the extent that the amount of the elective or intestate share qualifies for the marital deduction and reduces the amount subject to estate taxation.

The UPC incorporates as §§3-9A-101 to 3-9A-115 the Uniform Estate Tax Apportionment Act. The Act apportions the estate tax among the "[a]pportionable estate," defined in §3-9A-102 as including "the value of the gross estate as finally determined for purposes of the estate tax... reduced by... the value of any interest in property that, for purposes of the tax, qualifies for a marital or charitable deduction or otherwise is deductible or is exempt...." Consequently, under the Uniform Act or similar tax-apportionment legislation, the amount of the spouse's elective share (and the amount of the spouse's intestate share in an intestate estate) is calculated on the basis of the estate *before* estate taxes have been subtracted.[25]

Unfortunately, some non-UPC states do not have tax-apportionment legislation. In the absence of such legislation, the decisions on the question are divided. Spurrier v. First Nat'l Bank, 485 P.2d 209 (Kan. 1971), a leading decision for the view that the spouse's elective or intestate share is calculated on a before-tax basis, reasoned:

> When K.S.A. 59-502 [providing that all interests by intestate succession are subject to "homestead rights, the allowances ..., and the payment of reasonable funeral expenses, expenses of last sickness and costs of administration, taxes and debts"] was enacted in 1939, the tax advantage of the marital deduction did not exist.... We cannot attribute legislative inaction in this instance as an indication that taxpayers of this state were intended to be deprived of the benefits of the marital deduction.

This is the position adopted in the Restatement 3d of Property §9.3.

A pair of leading decisions for the contrary view, that the spouse's elective share and intestate share are calculated on an after-tax basis,[26] are Del Mar v. United States, 390 F.2d 466 (D.C. Cir. 1968) (elective share); Herson v. Mills, 221 F. Supp. 714 (D.D.C. 1963) (intestate share). In *Del Mar*, the court said:

> Other jurisdictions have permitted the result for which appellants contend, either by specific statute or judicial adoption of general equitable apportionment of estate taxes. However, we are not inclined to modify our settled course of decisions—either to upset the general law of decedents' estates in the District of Columbia merely to allow a dissenting

---

25. With respect to the elective share, the original and current versions of the UPC do not rely solely on §3-916(e)(2). Section 2-204 of the current UPC provides that the fraction (or percentage) applies to an amount "reduced by funeral and administration expenses, homestead allowance, family allowances, exempt property, and enforceable claims." The definition of the word "claims" in §1-201 carefully states that the "term does not include estate or inheritance taxes...." See original UPC §1-202(4); current UPC §1-201(6).

26. This approach makes the amount of the forced or intestate share dependent on the amount of the estate tax, which in turn is dependent on the amount of the forced or intestate share! The calculations must be done algebraically.

widow a larger portion of the estate at the expense of the remaining legatees and the Government, or to carve out a narrow exception for the widow's intestate share, a course which other states have taken only through actions of their legislatures.

If the marital deduction provision of the tax law reflects a policy that Congress considers applicable to govern local law in the District of Columbia, Congress can easily provide a remedy. If Congress has been sluggish as a local legislature in making available to the District of Columbia benefits it has enabled the various legislatures to provide to the citizens of the states and commonwealths, petitions for relief from this anomaly are properly addressed to Congress.

Subsequently, in 1987, the District of Columbia enacted an apportionment statute reversing the rule of *Del Mar* and *Herson*. See D.C. Code §47-3714.

PART B. PROBATE EXEMPTIONS AND ALLOWANCES

Primary Statutory References: *UPC §§2-401 to -405*

The elective share in the common-law states and the community interest in the community-property states are not the only protections against disinheritance afforded the surviving spouse. Additional layers of protection routinely run in favor of the decedent's surviving spouse (and often also in favor of the decedent's children, sometimes limited to minor or dependent children). These are the right of homestead, the exempt property allowance, and the family allowance.

Although the statutes vary in considerable detail, the UPC provisions are fairly representative of the type of legislation likely to be found even in non-UPC states, but with one exception: The UPC's homestead allowance is unique, in that it provides for a lump-sum amount rather than a right to occupy the spouses' dwelling house as long as the surviving spouse or minor children wish to do so.

Effect of the Probate Exemptions and Allowances In Small Estates. Under the UPC, the probate exemptions and allowances—homestead, exempt property, and family allowance (up to the maximum that can be made without special court order)—can be distributed to the surviving spouse without delay, other than as may be necessary for the personal representative to locate, liquidate, and distribute the necessary estate funds or assets in kind. Estates worth less than this amount can be closed by distribution of these probate exemptions and allowances, once a personal representative has been appointed. The decedent's will is rendered irrelevant in such cases.

Probate Exemptions and Allowances and Nonprobate Transfers. On the relationship between the probate exemptions and allowances and nonprobate transfers, see UPC §6-102(b).[27]

---

27. UPC §6-102(b) provides:

(b) Except as otherwise provided by statute, a transferee of a nonprobate transfer is subject to liability to any

Probate Exemptions and Allowances Are Neither Charged Against the Elective Share Nor Against Devises Unless the Decedent's Will So Directs. The UPC clarifies a matter on which many non-UPC statutes are silent, which is whether the exemptions and allowances are in addition to or are charged against devises to the persons entitled to the exemptions and allowances. The UPC does not charge the exemptions and allowances against devises unless the decedent's will directs otherwise. Nor are they charged against the elective share.

Homestead. The homestead allowance provided for by UPC §2-402 is derived, in name at least, from a uniquely American contribution to laws giving a decedent's dependent survivors limited protection in the family home.[28] English law is the source of a different idea. Under the Magna Carta, the widow had a right, called the widow's quarantine, to "tarry in the chief house of her husband for forty days,"[29] and there are early American decisions recognizing this as a part of the common law. Some American legislation has extended this right for a year, as in Ohio.[30] By contrast, more prevalent American homestead legislation, though framed primarily in terms of exempting the homestead from the claims of the owner's creditors during his or her lifetime, commonly grants a decedent's spouse or minor children a right of occupancy in certain real estate of the decedent that may continue for much longer periods. (A title in fee simple passes to homestead beneficiaries in Wyoming.) These homestead statutes vary markedly in the amount and scope of protection given to family survivors.

The UPC homestead allowance shifts the exemption from a right of occupancy of realty to a money substitute. In doing so, the UPC protects all surviving spouses and minor children, including those of renters, owners of mobile homes not classified as

---

probate estate of the decedent for allowed claims against decedent's probate estate and statutory allowances to the decedent's spouse and children to the extent the estate is insufficient to satisfy those claims and allowances. The liability of a nonprobate transferee may not exceed the value of nonprobate transfers received or controlled by that transferee.

Note that §6-212(a) gives a further right to a surviving spouse in multiple-party accounts by providing:

(a) Except as otherwise provided in this part, on death of a party sums on deposit in a multiple-party account belong to the surviving party or parties. If two or more parties survive and one is the surviving spouse of the decedent, the amount to which the decedent, immediately before death, was beneficially entitled under Section 6-211 belongs to the surviving spouse. If two or more parties survive and none is the surviving spouse of the decedent, the amount to which the decedent, immediately before death, was beneficially entitled under Section 6-211 belongs to the surviving parties in equal shares, and augments the proportion to which each survivor, immediately before the decedent's death, was beneficially entitled under Section 6-211, and the right of survivorship continues between the surviving parties.

28. The laws are said to have originated in 1839 in the Republic of Texas.

29. The quotation is from 4 James Kent, Commentaries 59 (1st ed. 1830). See generally, Annot., \Widow's Right of Quarantine, 126 A.L.R. 796.

30. Ohio Rev. Code §2106.15: "A surviving spouse may remain in the mansion house free of charge for one year...."

real estate, and decedents who owned no interest in a residence of any sort. The fact that the UPC's homestead allowance does not grant a right of occupancy does not mean that a surviving spouse has no prospect of remaining in possession of realty in the name of the deceased spouse. With the cooperation of the personal representative, a spouse's right to money from an estate can readily be converted into a title to real estate—as a distribution in kind to the spouse, as a sale of land to the spouse, or as some combination of the two. In this connection, it may be noted that under the UPC, the surviving spouse has priority either to serve as the personal representative or to choose who serves, unless a probated will nominates someone else who qualifies and accepts the appointment.

EXTERNAL REFERENCE. On homestead legislation generally, see Restatement 3d of Property §1.1 comment j and Statutory Note.

PART C. PROTECTION AGAINST UNINTENTIONAL DISINHERITANCE

In this Part, we consider two measures that protect the family against unintentional disinheritance: omitted children (pretermitted heir) statutes and omitted spouse statutes. The former protect children; the latter protect surviving spouses.

1. Omitted Child (Pretermitted Heir) Statutes

Primary Statutory Reference: *UPC §2-302*

Putting aside the probate exemptions and allowances considered in Part B, children may be *intentionally* disinherited in every American state except Louisiana.[31] The power to disinherit one's children is a major difference between American succession law and the system that exists in all civil-law nations. The civil law recognizes the *legitime*, a device that guarantees that close family members will inherit a fixed share of a decedent owner's estate.[32] Although the legitime is

---

31. The Louisiana constitution was amended in 1995 to limit forced heirship to children who are 23 years of age or younger or are incapable of taking care of their persons or administering their estates because of mental incapacity or physical infirmity. See La. Const. of 1974 art. XII, § 5, as amended in 1995. If the testator leaves one forced heir, the forced heir is entitled to one-fourth of the testator's estate. If the testator leaves more than one forced heir, the forced heirs are entitled to one-half of the testator's estate. See La. Civ. Code art. 1495. For discussion, see Max Nathan, Jr., Forced Heirship: The Unheralded "New" Disinherison Rules, 74 Tul. L. Rev. 1027 (2000).

32. Early English law also recognized restrictions on an owner's power to disinherit his heirs. The treatise that we know as Glanvill states that an owner could give away to the exclusion of his heirs only a "reasonable" part of his land. See 2 Frederick Pollock & Frederic W. Maitland, The History of English Law 308 (2d ed. 1898, reprinted 1968). Reference to these restraints disappeared around 1200, probably because they could not be well-enforced in the king's courts. See S. F. C. Milsom, The Legal Framework of English Feudalism 122 (1976).

frequently said to have originated in Roman law, Professor Dawson determined that it owes to classical Roman law not much more than the name. The origins of forced heirship lie elsewhere, he wrote:

> The antecedents of these ideas [guaranteed share for the forced heir] lie far back in the forms of social organization among the races of Germanic origin that came to occupy Europe, including Gaul, as Roman power declined. They had notions of family solidarity and of the subordination of individuals to the decisions of family groups that were no part of the heritage from Rome.

John P. Dawson, Gifts and Promises 29 (1980).

What advantages might be attributed to this system in modern society? Professor James Buchanan, a Nobel laureate in economics, has suggested that fixed shares would reduce waste of economic resources on the part of hopeful beneficiaries attempting to induce gifts and devises to them.[33] Other commentators have argued that the increasing incidence of multiple marriages increases the need to protect dependent children from intentional disinheritance by noncustodial parents. See Deborah A. Batts, I Didn't Ask to Be Born: The American Law of Disinheritance and a Proposal for Change to a System of Protected Inheritance, 41 Hastings L.J. 1197 (1990). One counterargument is that testators should have the freedom to favor the children (or grandchildren) who bear the burden of caring for the testator during lifetime. See Joshua C. Tate, Caregiving and the Case for Testamentary Freedom, 42 U.C. Davis L. Rev. 129 (2008).

Unintentional disinheritance is another matter: Nearly all states have statutes, called "pretermitted heir" statutes, that grant children a measure of protection from being unintentionally disinherited. Some statutes are expressly framed as default rules that do not apply if it appears from the will that the omission of the child was intentional. Other statutes make no mention of the testator's intention and provide simply that a child (occasionally, any "issue") not named or provided for in the testator's will takes an intestate share.[34] Most statutes, like the UPC, protect only a child who became a child of the testator *after* the execution of the will;[35] a few protect any omitted child. The UPC appears to have broken new ground by providing

---

33. James M. Buchanan, Rent-Seeking, Noncompensated Transfers, and Laws of Succession, 26 J.L. & Econ. 71 (1983). Similarly, in criticizing a previous amendment to Louisiana's forced heirship law, Professor Cynthia Samuel has stated: "Greed, prejudice, jealousy, meanness and fear will henceforth have a much freer hand in influencing a parent's testamentary plans." Moreover, she contends that the traditional legitime device serves the modern function of "guaranteeing that kids don't get divorced from their inheritance when their parents get divorced from each other." Francis Frank Marcus, N.Y. Times, Dec. 1, 1989, at B7.

34. The constitutionality of this type of a statute was upheld in Holland v. Willis, 739 S.W.2d 529 (Ark. 1987).

35. See, e.g., Lanier v. Rains, 229 S.W.3d 656 (Tenn. 2007).

that nonprobate transfers to a child can defeat that child's statutory protection.[36]

The current UPC substantially amends the original version of §2-302. Two basic changes were made. First, if the testator had no child alive when the will was executed, an omitted child takes no portion of the estate if the testator devised all or substantially all of the estate to another parent of the omitted child and that parent survives the testator and is entitled to take the property. This extends the rule of the original version of §2-302, namely that an omitted child does not receive an intestate share if at the time of execution the testator had one or more children and the testator devised substantially all of the estate to the other parent of the omitted child. Whether or not a testator has children at the time of execution, a devise of the bulk of the estate to another parent of the omitted child usually indicates that the testator trusts that surviving parent to use the property to benefit the child.

The other major change concerns situations in which the testator had one or more children alive when the will was executed and devised property to at least one of the then-living children. An omitted child does not take a full intestate share in this situation but only a pro rata share of the property devised to the then-living children.

On pretermitted heir statutes generally, see Restatement 3d of Property §9.6.

Problems, Note and Question

1. H and W were married. W then prepared her will, providing as follows: $10,000 to X Charity, residue to H. Later, H and W had a son, S. W died without revising her will, with a net probate estate valued at $500,000. To what extent can S claim a share of her estate under the original UPC? Under the current UPC?

2. Dawson, a freshman at the University of Southern California, recently returned home to the town of Capeside. During Dawson's visit, his father was killed in a car accident. The father's will established a trust for his wife (Dawson's mother) and Dawson. The document contained no mention of Dawson's recently born baby sister, Lily. (Lily is the child of Dawson's parents.) Dawson and his mother searched through the house to see whether Dawson's father executed a codicil including Lily in the trust. They found the codicil, prepared by the family's lawyer, but Dawson's father had not yet signed it. Dawson and his mother, both of whom want to remedy this exclusion of Lily, have come to you for legal advice. What result under the current UPC?

3. *Application to Will Substitutes?* Pretermitted heir statutes apply to the decedent's probate estate. See, e.g., Estate of Jackson, 194 P.3d 1269 (Okla. 2008); Kidwell v. Rhew, 268 S.W.3d 309 (Ark. 2007). Should the statutes be extended to will substitutes? See Restatement 2d of Property §34.2 (affirmative); Restatement 3d of Property §9.6 (silent).

---

36. For a collection of cases dealing with what constitutes a sufficient indication of a contrary intent, see Annot., Pretermitted Heir Statutes: What Constitutes Sufficient Testamentary Reference to, or Evidence of Contemplation of, Heir to Render Statute Inapplicable, 83 A.L.R.4th 779.

_____

Azcunce v. Estate of Azcunce
586 So. 2d 1216 (Fla. Ct. App. 1991)

HUBBART, J. The central issue presented by this appeal is whether a child who is born after the execution of her father's will but before the execution of a codicil to the said will is entitled to take a statutory share of her father's estate under Florida's pretermitted child statute—when the will and codicils fail to provide for such child and all the other statutory requirements for pretermitted-child status are otherwise satisfied. We hold that where inter alia the subject codicil expressly republishes the original will, as here, the testator's child who is living at the time the codicil is executed is not a pretermitted child within the meaning of the statute. We, accordingly, affirm the final order under review which denies the child herein a statutory share of her father's estate as a pretermitted child.

I. The facts of this case are entirely undisputed. On May 4, 1983, the testator Rene R. Azcunce executed a will which established a trust for the benefit of his surviving spouse and his then-born children: Lisette, Natalie, and Gabriel; the will contained no provision for after-born children.[37] On August 8, 1983, and June 25, 1986, the testator executed two codicils which did not alter in any way this testamentary disposition and also made no provision for after-born children.

On March 14, 1984, the testator's daughter Patricia Azcunce was born—after the first codicil was executed, but before the second codicil was executed. The first codicil expressly republished all the terms of the original will; the second codicil expressly republished all the terms of the original will and first codicil.

On December 30, 1986, the testator, who was thirty-eight (38) years old, unexpectedly died of a heart attack—four months after executing the second codicil. After the will and codicils were admitted to probate, Patricia filed a petition seeking a statutory share of her father's estate as a pretermitted child; the trial court denied this petition. Patricia appeals.

II. The statute on which Patricia relies for a share of her father's estate provides:

When a testator omits to provide in his will for any of his children *born or adopted after making the will* and the child has not received a part of the testator's property equivalent to a child's part by way of advancement, the child shall receive a share of the estate equal in value to that he would have received if the testator had died intestate, unless:

(1) It appears from the will that the omission was intentional; or

(2) The testator had one or more children when the will was executed and devised substantially all his estate to the other parent of the pretermitted child.

---

37. Because the trust was designed to qualify for the federal estate tax marital deduction, the precise terms of the trust were undoubtedly to pay the income to the decedent's surviving spouse for life, remainder in corpus to Lisette, Natalie, and Gabriel. Ed.

Section 732.302, Florida Statutes (1985) (emphasis added). Without dispute, Patricia was a pretermitted child both at the time the testator's will and the first codicil thereto were executed, as, in each instance, the testator "omitted to provide in his will [or codicil] for [Patricia who was] born ... after ... the will [or codicil was executed]"; moreover, Patricia at no time received a part of the testator's property by way of advancement, the will and first codicil do not expressly disinherit Patricia, and the testator did not substantially devise all of his estate to Patricia's mother. The question in this case is whether the testator's execution of the *second* codicil to the will *after* Patricia had been born destroyed her prior statutory status as a pretermitted child.

It is well settled in Florida that, as a general rule, the execution of a codicil to a will has the effect of republishing the prior will as of the date of the codicil. Although this is not an inflexible rule and must at times give way to a contrary intent of the testator, it always applies where, as here, the codicil expressly adopts the terms of the prior will; this is so for the obvious reason that such a result comports with the express intent of the testator.

III. Turning to the instant case, it is clear that the testator's second codicil republished the original will and first codicil because the second codicil expressly so states. This being so, Patricia's prior status as a pretermitted child was destroyed inasmuch as Patricia was alive when the second codicil was executed and was not, as required by Florida's pretermitted child statute, born after such codicil was made. Presumably, if the testator had wished to provide for Patricia, he would have done so in the second codicil as she had been born by that time; because he did not, Patricia was, in effect, disinherited which the testator clearly had the power to do. Indeed, the result we reach herein is in full accord with the results reached by courts throughout the country based on identical circumstances.

To avoid this inevitable result, Patricia argues that the will and two codicils are somehow ambiguous and that, accordingly, the court should have accepted the parol evidence adduced below that the testator intended to provide for Patricia; Patricia also urges that the will should have been voided because the draftsman made a "mistake" in failing to provide for Patricia in the second codicil. These arguments are unavailing. First, there is utterly no ambiguity in the subject will and codicils which would authorize the taking of parol evidence herein, and the trial court was entirely correct in rejecting same. Second, the mistake of which Patricia complains amounts, at best, to the draftsman's alleged professional negligence in failing to apprise the testator of the need to expressly provide for Patricia in the second codicil; this is not the type of mistake which voids a will under Section 732.5165, Florida Statutes (1987).

For the above-stated reasons, the final order under review is, in all respects,

Affirmed.

LEVY, J. (specially concurring). I write separately only to express my frustration with the apparent inability of the justice system of this State to be in a position to provide relief to someone who is clearly entitled to it, to-wit: Patricia Azcunce, the appellant herein who was the daughter of Rene R. Azcunce....

On June 25, 1986, decedent executed a second codicil which removed a certain person as a Trustee in order to qualify for a marital deduction under the federal and state tax laws. Testimony from the attorney who prepared the second codicil revealed that the decedent had contacted him and mentioned that he (the decedent) and his wife had another child. At the request of the decedent, the attorney prepared a new will which included that child, Patricia, as a beneficiary. A copy of the new will was mailed to the decedent on April 4, 1986, for the decedent to review. The new will, however, was not executed due to a disagreement that the attorney had with the decedent over the worth of decedent's assets. The disagreement between the decedent and the attorney, which caused the decedent not to sign the new will, was totally unrelated to the provision in the new will relating to Patricia. Based upon decedent's concern that a change in the marital trust, contained in the original will, had to be effected expeditiously, the second codicil was prepared by the attorney, and signed by decedent, so that the marital trust change could be effectuated immediately, rather than waiting for the preparation of another draft of a new will. The second codicil contained language that specifically republished the terms of the original will and the first codicil. Not long thereafter, decedent died.

The lower court held there was no ambiguity between the will and the first and second codicils as to the definition of issue or children and, thus, there was no ambiguity as to the testator's intent. Because the second codicil made no reference to Patricia, but did specifically republish the original will, her status as a pretermitted child was destroyed, pursuant to Section 732.02, Florida Statutes (1985), and she was no longer able to share in her father's estate.

What makes this case so troubling is that, beyond the fact that she is being denied the opportunity to share in her deceased father's assets, the record in this case ... clearly reflects that it is virtually uncontroverted that Rene R. Azcunce intended that his daughter, the appellant herein, share in his assets after his death. Based upon the evidence presented before the trial court, it is clear that her apparent inability to receive that which her father clearly wanted her to have is the result of the current state of the case law in the State of Florida.

Lest there be any misunderstanding, I hasten to add that I understand that the majority opinion has correctly interpreted and applied the current law of this State that relates to the facts of this case. The majority opinion reflects that the current posture of the law in this area is designed to give effect to the testator's wishes and to deny any relief to false or fraudulent claimants. However, the fear of false or fraudulent claims should never be allowed to be used as the reason to bar claimants from filing their claims with the courts of this State. Rather, the courthouse doors must always remain open in the hope that the justice system will do what it is supposed to do—render justice. In furtherance of that end, hopefully, valid claims will prevail and false claims will fail. If, however, courthouse doors are barred to any type of claimant, then we all, as members of a supposedly free and just society, suffer from such a denial of access to the courts.

As I indicated above, the unrefuted evidence in this case reflects that Patricia's father, the decedent herein, intended Patricia to receive her fair share. It is only through an unfortunate series of circumstances, and the legal implications springing therefrom, that Patricia is being denied what her father wanted her to receive.

The next to last paragraph of the majority opinion seems to suggest the possibility that Patricia might find relief in a professional malpractice action against the professional draftsman who prepared the second codicil knowing, according to the undisputed evidence, that Patricia's father wanted Patricia to receive her fair share of his estate, but still allowed Patricia's father to sign it (thereby extinguishing Patricia's right to receive her share as a "preoterimitted child") without either advising her father of the legal consequences of signing the second codicil (to-wit: that Patricia would lose her status as a pretermitted child) or providing for her in the second codicil, or some other such document, so as to give life and vitality to her father's (the testator's) wishes. However, this flicker of light of possible relief, that might appear to offer hope to Patricia, is soon doused as one reads the majority opinion of this Court in *Espinosa v. Sparber Shevin, et al.*, which is the appeal growing out of the trial court's dismissal of the professional malpractice case filed, on behalf of Patricia, against the draftsman of the codicil. For the reasons stated in my concurring opinion in the case of *Espinosa v. Sparber Shevin, et. al.*, and the cases that I refer to therein, it would appear that the case law of this State has "missed the boat" in its efforts to make sure that there is "a remedy for every wrong."

Notes and Question

1. *Aftermath: The Malpractice Action.* As Judge Levy's opinion indicates, Patricia Azcunce received no relief in the malpractice action brought against the law firm that drafted Rene Azcunce's will and codicils. In Espinosa v. Sparber, Shevin, Shapo, Rosen & Heilbronner, 612 So.2d 1378 (Fla. 1993), the Florida Supreme Court held that the action could not be brought on behalf of Patricia because she was not in privity of estate with the attorney. An action by the estate, however, could be brought.

2. *Restatement 3d of Property.* The Restatement 3d of Property §3.4 comment b states:

> *b. Intent-effecting doctrine.* The doctrine of republication by codicil is to be applied unless the effect would be inconsistent with the testator's intent. That a codicil contains a provision expressly republishing the prior will does not require the doctrine to be applied. The doctrine is still inapplicable if the effect of applying it would be inconsistent with the testator's intent.

See also Restatement 3d of Property §9.6 comment e.

2. *Omitted Spouse Statutes*

Primary Statutory Reference: *UPC §2-301*

Although pretermitted heir statutes are common, protection for the decedent's surviving spouse in that form is rare—apart from the UPC states. The earlier approach to the problem took the form of the common-law doctrines revoking a person's will if he or she later married. As elective share statutes came to replace dower and curtesy, the elective share was thought to provide sufficient protection in the situation of a premarital will. The UPC embarks on a different course by providing, in §2-301, an omitted spouse provision in addition to the apparatus of the elective share. The purpose is not only to reduce the frequency of elections under the elective share but also to provide a share for the surviving spouse more related to the amount the decedent probably would have wanted to give, had he or she gotten around to revising the premarital will. As revealed by the following problems, however, there is a marked difference in detail between the original and current versions of UPC §2-301.

Problems

H and W enjoyed a long marriage to each other, which produced two children, C1 and C2, and three grandchildren (C1's children, GC1 and GC2; and C2's child, GC3). W died at age 70, survived by H, age 68. W's will devised her entire estate to H if he survived her; if not, to C1 and C2 in equal shares. H's will, executed at the same time, devised his entire estate to W if she survived him; if not, to C1 and C2 in equal shares.

Some few years after W's death, H remarried. A few months after the remarriage, his son C2, age 48, was killed in an airplane crash. C2 was survived by his wife and by his 19-year-old child GC3. Upon learning of C2's tragic death, H suffered a heart attack and died. H was survived (by 120 hours) by his second wife, W2, and by C1, GC1, GC2, and GC3.

H's net estate was valued at $500,000.

1. How would H's estate be distributed under the original version of UPC §2-301?

2. How would H's estate be distributed under the current version of UPC §2-301? (Assume that W2's assets at H's death are valued at $600,000.)

EXTERNAL REFERENCES. Restatement 3d of Property §9.5; Lawrence W. Waggoner, Spousal Rights in Our Multiple-Marriage Society: The Revised Uniform Probate Code, 26 Real Prop., Prob. & Tr. J. 683 (1992).

Chapter 9

Trusts: Formation and Formality

PART A. INTRODUCTION

Maitland, the leading historian of English law, called the trust "the greatest and most distinctive achievement performed by Englishmen in the field of jurisprudence."[1] The trust is a remarkably flexible tool used for a variety of purposes, both commercial and non-commercial. As an instrument for gratuitous transfers of wealth, the trust sits at the core of modern estate planning practice. The following excerpt explains how the character and basic function of the trust have changed over the past century.

John H. Langbein, Rise of the Management Trust
143 Tr. & Est. 52, 53, 57 (Oct. 2004)

Although the trust comes with a long historical pedigree, it has undergone a radical transformation in the past century. The core function of the trust has changed, giving rise both to the modern trust industry and to a profoundly altered legal regime that was necessary to support and govern the industry.... The trust first developed from an age in which real estate was the principal form of wealth.

Today's trust has ceased to be a conveyancing device for land and has become, instead, a management device for holding a portfolio of financial assets.... Most modern wealth takes the form of financial assets: equities, bonds, mutual fund shares, insurance contracts, pension and annuity interests, and bank accounts.... Such a portfolio requires skilled and active management. Investment decisions must be made and monitored, the portfolio rebalanced and proxies voted.... By contrast,

---

1. Frederic W. Maitland, The Unincorporate Body, in 3 Frederic W. Maitland, Collected Papers 271, 272 (1911). This is not to suggest, however, that concepts similar to the trust have not been developed by other legal systems. A statutory adoption of the trust is in place in Louisiana. See La. Rev. Stat. §§9:1721-9:2252. And several civil-law countries have adopted concepts serving similar purposes, such as the German *Treuhand*. See Itinera Fiduciae: Trust and Treuhand in Historical Perspective (Richard Helmholz & Reinhard Zimmermann eds. 1998). Also, the Islamic legal system developed a concept similar to a charitable trust, called a *waqf*. One type of *waqf*—the family *waqf*, also known as the *waqf ahli* or the *waqf dhurri*—has some features similar to the private express trust. See David Powers, The Islamic Family Endowment (*Waqf*), 32 Vand. J. Transnat'l L. 1167 (1999); Jeffrey A. Schoenblum, The Role of Legal Doctrine in the Decline of the Islamic *Waqf*: A Comparison with the Trust, id. at 1191. Trust law, or something like it, has developed in other civil-law countries. See Alexandra Braun, The State of the Art of Comparative Research in the Area of Trusts, in Comparative Property Law: Global Perspectives (Michele Graziadei & Lionel Smith eds. 2017), and the sources cited therein. China also has begun to develop trust law. See Lusina Ho, Trust Law in China (2003); Lusina Ho, Rebecca Lee & Jin Jinping, Trust Law in China: A Critical Evaluation of Its Conceptual Foundation, in Trust Law in Asian Civil Law Jurisdictions: A Comparative Analysis (Lusina Ho & Rebecca Lee eds. 2013).

under the old conveyancing trust that held ancestral land, the beneficiaries commonly lived on the land and managed it. The trustees were... in effect, nominees, with no serious powers or duties....

1. Historical Development of Trusts

The modern trust grew out of the *feoffment to uses*. In the thirteenth century, shortly after the Norman Conquest, people (nearly always men) from time to time enfeoffed land to another "to the use" of a third.[2] There was "a darker side to the picture," as Professor Scott put it.[3] Uses provided a means of defrauding creditors and purchasers. To the annoyance of the overlords and the Crown, they also provided a means of escaping the consequences of many rules of law that landowners had come to regard as burdensome. Through the device of a use, an individual could in effect dispose of land at death at a time when wills of land were not recognized. This was done by conveying land to another to hold to the use of the feoffor and then to the use of such persons as the feoffor should designate in his will. In this way, land could be passed to younger sons or daughters, or even strangers, to the exclusion of the eldest son and heir. Furthermore, the burden of feudal obligations could be escaped or lessened by depriving the lord of feudal rights that arose when his tenant died and the land passed to the tenant's heir. In the eyes of the law, legal title to the land was in the feoffee; thus nothing passed on the death of the grantor ("feoffor") or beneficiary ("cestui que use"). Of course, the feudal rights attached on inheritance from the feoffee, but inheritance here could be avoided for a long period by placing the title in a large group as joint tenants.[4]

The Crown finally got fed up. Henry VIII, in need of more revenue, insisted that something be done about the situation.[5] In 1536, Parliament enacted the Statute of Uses to eliminate "subtile practiced feoffementes,... abuses and errours... to the subversion of the good and anncyent laws of the [realm]." The statute itself provided:

> *Statute of Uses, 27 Henry 8, ch. 10.* That where any person or persons stand or be seized... of... lands... to the use, confidence or trust of any other person or persons, or of any body politick,... in every such case, all and every such person and persons..., shall henceforth stand and be seized... of... the same... lands... in such like estates as they had or shall have in use, trust or confidence.

---

2. In these early times, the use arrangement was often made for the benefit of the Franciscan friars, whose poverty vows made it impossible for them to own property but who still had to have shelter and land to cultivate.

3. Scott on Trusts §1.

4. Frederic W. Maitland, Equity 26-27 (2d ed. 1936).

5. The story is told in Sir John Baker, An Introduction to English Legal History 271-278 (5th ed. 2019).

Although the statute sought to abolish existing uses, the mechanism used to achieve that objective was not to deprive the cestui que use of his beneficial interest; rather, the statute converted that beneficial interest into a legal interest. In the words of the statute, the cestui shall "henceforth stand and be seized" of the land "in such like estates as they had... in use." Converting the beneficial interest into a legal one brought it under the jurisdiction of the courts of common law rather than the Court of Chancery. For our purposes, conversion rather than abolition was a crucial development, for it meant that, in one form or another, the use was allowed to persist.

The modern trust arises out of those situations in which the statute did *not* apply. The statute did not apply to a use on a use. If G conveyed to X to the use of T to the use of B, the statute executed the first use, so that T got legal title; the second use was void at law. But what was void at law was soon enforced in equity. As explained by Professor Sir John Baker,

> ...what began as a mere trickle of special cases grew within a century into common form, so that from the seventeenth century until the repeal of the Statute of Uses in 1926 the most usual way of creating trusts was by a conveyance "to X and his heirs unto and to the use of Y and his heirs, in trust nevertheless for Z." This vested the legal estate in Y as trustee for Z.... Not for the first time, the courts had allowed policy to triumph over unintended legislative hindrances. It could be said in 1738 that "a statute made upon great consideration, introduced in a solemn and pompous manner ... had no other effect than to add at most three words to a conveyance."[6]

2. Parties to a Trust

The trust has three basic legal parties: the *settlor*, who creates the trust;[7] the *trustee*, who holds legal title to the trust property; and the *beneficiary*, for whose benefit the trustee holds title to the trust property.[8] The settlor can create a trust during his or her lifetime (an inter vivos or "living" trust) or by will (a "testamentary" trust). An inter vivos trust can be either irrevocable or, as we know from Chapter 7, revocable. The settlor of an inter vivos trust can name himself or herself as trustee (a self-declared trust) or name a third party as trustee. The settlor can also reserve for himself or herself a beneficial interest in the trust; chapter 7

---

6. Baker, Introduction to English Legal History at 310-311, quoting Hopkins v. Hopkins, 1 Atk. 581, 591 (1738), per Lord Hardwicke. Professor Baker wryly observes, however: "His lordship's historical sense on this occasion was no better than his arithmetic." Id. at 311 n. 73.

7. Can an agent under a power of attorney create a trust on the settlor's behalf? Under Uniform Power of Attorney Act §201, the answer is "yes" but only if the power of attorney expressly grants the agent the authority to do so. See also Barbetti v. Stempniewicz, 189 N.E.3d 264 (Mass. 2022).

8. There are three legal parties to a trust but not necessarily three different persons. As we explain later, the same person can occupy two or even all three roles, settlor, trustee, and beneficiary (though the sole trustee cannot be the sole beneficiary).

taught us that this often happens in the case of a revocable inter vivos trust, where the arrangement is essentially a probate-avoidance device, with the settlor commonly being the beneficiary of the income interest.

Normally, there is more than one beneficiary, such as when G transfers property to T, in trust, with a direction to pay income to A for life, then at A's death to transfer the corpus to B. Such a trust gives A an "equitable life estate" and B an "equitable remainder." T's interest usually is a "legal" estate, typically a fee simple.[9]

Nature of the Beneficiary's Interest. It was once thought that the beneficiary's interest was nothing more than a right in personam, enforceable in equity against the trustee.[10] But today a trust is seen as a property arrangement under which ownership of the property is divided. The trust property's *legal* title goes to the trustee and the *equitable* (or beneficial) title goes to the beneficiary or, more usually, is divided along temporal lines between income beneficiaries and beneficiaries of future interests in corpus.

Historically, to say that the trustee held "legal" title signified that the courts of common law recognized the feoffee (the trustee) as the owner of the trust property, with the chancery or equity courts recognizing and enforcing the rights of the cestuis que use (the beneficiaries). Despite the subsequent merging of law and equity, we still speak of "legal" and "equitable" obligations, though in most states today they are enforced by the same court. This division-of-ownership idea embraces within it an allocation of rights and duties. Holding legal but not beneficial title carries fiduciary duties with respect to the property; holding equitable title confers rights in personam to enforce those duties. But it is now generally agreed that the beneficiary also has rights in rem, an equitable property interest in the assets held in trust. See Restatement 3d of Trusts Introductory Note to Part 4; Restatement 2d of Trusts §130. Of decisive influence in this regard is the application of the Rule Against Perpetuities to beneficial interests in trust. The Rule Against Perpetuities is strictly a rule of property law, yet it applies to interests in trust. Indeed, most modern perpetuity cases are concerned with the validity of a beneficial interest in trust.

Enforcement. In the beginning stages, the feoffor could do little more than trust to the honor of the feoffee. When that trust was misplaced, the law courts gave no remedy.[11] In such circumstances, it was to be expected that appeals would be made

---

9. This statement requires some qualification. As the Restatement 3d of Trusts points out, while the trust beneficiaries' interest is always equitable in nature, the trustee's interest may be legal or equitable: "Although it is usually true (and is, unfortunately, often stated without qualification in cases and texts) that the trustee has legal title, in some instances the trustee will hold only an equitable title." Restatement 3d of Trusts §2 comment d.

10. Frederic W. Maitland, Equity 29, 107 (2d ed. 1936); James B. Ames, Lectures on Legal History 76, 262 (1913); Harlan F. Stone, The Nature of the Rights of the Cestui Que Trust, 17 Colum. L. Rev. 467 (1917).

11. Pollock and Maitland suggested that some of the earlier uses "may have been enforced by the

to the Chancellor for relief, and in the first half of the fifteenth century, at the suit of the cestui que use (beneficiary), the Chancellor began to force the feoffee (trustee) to perform his undertakings.[12]   Today, the action against a trustee for breach of duties is not in contract or at law. Except in very limited circumstances, the jurisdiction of equity has remained exclusive.[13] Moreover, the remedy against the trustee remains in the beneficiary. Traditionally, only the beneficiaries have had standing to enforce the trust.[14]

While the law traditionally has not treated trusts as contracts, legal scholars have long acknowledged that there is a contractual aspect to trusts.[15] The Restatement 3d of Trusts points out, however, that "[t]his 'contractual approach'... was certainly a limited one...."[16] Professor Langbein, however, has extended the contractual approach, arguing that "[t]rusts *are* contracts." See John H. Langbein, The Contractarian Basis of Trusts, 105 Yale L.J. 625, 627 (1995) (emphasis added). Professors Hansmann and Mattei take a somewhat different view:

> [I]t is precisely the property-like aspects of the trust that are the principal contributions of trust law.... In effect, trust law provides for the creation of an entity—the trust—that is separate from the three principal parties.... [T]he essential purpose served by trust law ... is to facilitate an accompanying reorganization of rights and responsibilities between the three principal parties and third parties, such as creditors, with whom the principal parties deal. That reorganization of the rights of third parties—which is the property-like aspect of the trust relationship—is difficult to accomplish without the law of trusts.

Hansmann & Ugo Mattei, The Functions of Trust Law: A Comparative Legal and Economic Analysis, 73 N.Y.U. L. Rev. 434, 469-72 (1998). For a third point of view, applicable not only to trusts but to all fiduciary arrangements, see James Edelman, When Do Fiduciary Duties Arise?, 126 Law Q. Rev. 302 (2010) (arguing that "fiduciary duties arise as a result of express or implied manifestations of consent

---

ecclesiastical courts." 2 Frederick Pollock & Frederic W. Maitland, History of English Law 232 (2d ed. 1911). Historical evidence has since been uncovered suggesting that Pollock and Maitland were right about this. Professor Helmholz has established that, from the last quarter of the 14th century through the middle of the 15th century, some ecclesiastical courts regularly enforced feoffments to uses. Richard H. Helmholz, The Early Enforcement of Uses, 79 Colum. L. Rev. 1503 (1979).

12. James B. Ames, Lectures on Legal History 237 (1913).

13. A legal remedy is available to the beneficiary where the trustee is under an immediate and unconditioned obligation to pay money or transfer property to the beneficiary. Scott and Ascher on Trusts §24.2.

14. Restatement 2d of Trusts §200 and comment b. The UTC has changed the traditional law somewhat by granting standing to settlors to enforce charitable trusts. UTC §405(c). It also allows the settlor of an irrevocable trust to petition for removal of a trustee. Id. §706(a).

15. See, e.g., Maitland, Equity, at 28, 29.

16. Restatement 3d of Trusts, Reporter's Notes on §2, at 38.

in voluntary undertakings" that the law "does not confine ... to contract").

Trust Property (or Res). During the medieval period, the nearly invariable subject of a use was land. Today, the subject of a trust can still be land, but more commonly, as the excerpt from the Langbein article above suggests, it is personal property in the form of investment securities. Whether real or personal property, the subject of the trust is also called the corpus, the principal, or the *res*.

3. The Uses of Trusts

Estate Planning. We began this chapter by noting that express trusts are at the core of modern estate planning practice. This is so because trusts are responsive to so many financial and estate planning needs. The variety of reasons why settlors create trusts, or are led by their lawyers to create trusts, include probate avoidance, property management, tax minimization, and control through successive generations. Ultimately, trusts serve donative purposes, but different types of trusts satisfy one or more additional purposes.

As we saw in Chapter 7, revocable inter vivos trusts carry no tax advantages, but do avoid probate. They also may provide independent property management, but not if self-declared. A self-declared, revocable inter vivos trust allows the settlor to retain lifetime management control of his or her own property. A standby trust with an independent trustee, to be more fully funded through the exercise of a durable power of attorney in case of the settlor's incapacity, is a superior alternative to a guardianship or conservatorship.

Whether self-declared or not, a revocable inter vivos trust acts as a will substitute. On the settlor's death, such a trust may provide for outright distributions, in the manner of outright specific, general, or residuary devises; or, it may provide for the property or a portion of it to continue in trust, in which case it serves the same purposes as a testamentary trust. The trust may receive additional property from the settlor's estate as the result of a pour-over devise.

Irrevocable inter vivos trusts satisfy entirely different purposes. They can be structured to offer significant tax advantages, by freezing the value of assets at the date of conveyance and by providing for the receipt of supplemental fundings that qualify for the annual gift tax exclusion. Pour-over devises from the settlor's estate can also provide additional funding of irrevocable inter vivos trusts.

In the case of a married testator, testamentary trusts are typically structured to qualify for the estate tax marital deduction; the continuation after the settlor's death of a revocable inter vivos trust also can serve this purpose. See the sample trust instrument, set forth below. After the surviving spouse's death, marital deduction trusts can continue for a further time, for the benefit of successive generations of descendants or down collateral lines. Bypass trusts also can continue for successive generations. The Rule Against Perpetuities places an outer limit on the duration of such trusts. Successive-generation trusts can provide considerable transfer tax savings, to the extent they come within the protection of the exemption from the federal generation-skipping transfer tax. Where the corpus of a trust consists of intangible personal property, such as corporate securities, a trust preserves the integrity of the fund in a manner not possible in the case of a succession of legal interests not in trust.

Trusts Compared to Other Types of Management Arrangements. There are other kinds of arrangements under which property is managed for persons other than the owners. There are also property arrangements that in the circumstances may leave the nature of the transaction in some doubt.

Section 5 of the Restatement 3d of Trusts distinguishes trusts from a series of arrangements, some of which also create fiduciary relationships. The distinction between a trustee and the *personal representative* (executor or administrator) of a decedent's estate is more practical than theoretical. Some but not all of the duties of a trustee are imposed upon a personal representative. The latter must be appointed by a court, and his or her duties are limited to winding up the estate of a decedent and so are implicitly temporary in duration. For different reasons, an *officer* or *director* of a corporation is a fiduciary, but not a trustee. So also with a guardian or with a receiver of the property of an insolvent person or corporation. In several of these instances, the fiduciary does not take title to the property involved, whereas a trustee is regarded as taking the legal title to the trust property.

A *bailee* of personal property owes certain duties to the bailor, but takes only possession of the property, not legal title, and is not a trustee. Similarly, an *agent* is not a trustee; but the distinction between an agent who is authorized to transfer title to property and a trustee is sometimes not easy to draw.

A conveyance of property upon a *condition subsequent* or subject to a *lien* or an *equitable charge* does not create a trust. The most difficult problem to resolve in a variety of circumstances involves the distinction between trust law and certain aspects of the law of contract, specifically the distinction between a trust and a *debt* (see, e.g., Estate of Stephano, 981 A.2d 138 (Pa. 2009)) or between a trust and a *third-party-beneficiary* contract.

EXTERNAL REFERENCE. A. Joseph Warburton, Trusts Versus Corporations: An Empirical Analysis of Competing Organizational Form, 36 J. Corp. L. 183 (2010).

Sample Revocable Inter Vivos Trust

The following trust instrument is reproduced here to give you some idea of what a modern trust instrument looks like. The instrument suggests especially (1) how a trust can be used to make provision for successive generations, (2) the possibility of giving some flexibility to the dispositions through the use of powers, and (3) the amount of detail commonly found in the administrative provisions of a trust instrument.

This trust agreement is made this _____ day of ____, 20_, between JOHN DOE, the Grantor, and OLD FAITHFUL TRUST COMPANY OF ___, as Trustee.

The Grantor hereby transfers to the trustee the property described in the attached schedule. Such property, and any other property that may be received by the trustee, shall be held and disposed of upon the following trusts:

ARTICLE I

The Grantor may by signed instruments delivered to the trustee revoke the trusts hereunder in whole or in part or amend this agreement from time to time in any manner. No amendment changing the powers or duties of the trustee shall be effective unless approved in writing by the trustee.

ARTICLE II

The trustee shall pay all the net income of the trust estate, and such portions of the principal as the Grantor from time to time directs in writing, to the Grantor, or otherwise as he directs in writing, during his life. In addition, the trustee may in its discretion pay to the Grantor, or use for his benefit, such portions or all of the principal of the trust estate as the trustee determines to be required for the Grantor's support and comfort, or for any other purpose which the trustee determines to be to his best interests.

ARTICLE III

After the Grantor's death the trustee shall hold and dispose of the trust estate as follows:

1. (a) The trustee shall pay all the net income of the trust estate to MARY DOE, wife of the Grantor, during her life, beginning as of the date of the Grantor's death and payable at least as often as quarter-annually. Unproductive property shall not be held as an asset of the trust estate for more than a reasonable time during the life of the Grantor's said wife without her consent.

(b) Whenever the trustee determines that the income of the Grantor's said wife from all sources known to the trustee is not sufficient for her reasonable support and comfort, the trustee shall pay to her, or use for her benefit, so much of the principal of the trust estate as the trustee determines to be required for those purposes.

2. Upon the death of the Grantor's said wife the trustee shall distribute the trust estate to such person or persons, or the estate of the Grantor's said wife, upon such conditions and estates, in trust or otherwise, in such manner and at such time or times as she appoints and directs by will specifically referring to this power of appointment.

3. In default of appointment by the Grantor's wife as aforesaid the trustee shall upon her death, or if she does not survive the Grantor the trustee shall upon the Grantor's death, divide the trust estate into equal funds, one for each child of the Grantor then living and one for the then-living descendants of each child of the

Grantor then deceased. Each such fund shall be held and administered as a separate trust and shall be held and disposed of as follows:

(a) While any child of the Grantor is under the age of twenty-one years, the trustee shall use so much of the income of his or her fund for his or her reasonable support, comfort and education as the trustee determines to be required for those purposes. After he or she attains that age, the trustee shall pay all the current net income of his or her fund to him or her.

(b) Whenever the trustee determines that the income of any child of the Grantor from all sources known to the trustee is not sufficient for his or her reasonable support, comfort and education, the trustee shall pay to him or her, or use for his or her benefit, so much of the principal of his or her fund as the trustee determines to be required for those purposes.

(c) When any child of the Grantor shall have attained the age of twenty-five years, the trustee shall distribute to him or her one-third of the principal of his or her fund as constituted at the time of distribution. When he or she shall have attained the age of thirty years, the trustee shall further distribute to him or her one-half of the remaining principal of his or her fund as constituted at the time of distribution. When he or she shall have attained the age of thirty-five years, the trustee shall further distribute to him or her the balance of his or her fund.

(d) Upon the death of any child of the Grantor before he or she becomes entitled to receive the entire principal of his or her fund, the trustee shall distribute his or her fund, or any remaining portion of it, to, or in trust for the benefit of, such person or persons among the Grantor's descendants and their spouses, including such child's own spouse, upon such conditions and estates, in such manner and at such time or times as he or she appoints and directs by will specifically referring to this power of appointment, and in default of such appointment, to his or her descendants then living, by representation, or if there is no descendant of his or her then living, to the Grantor's descendants then living, by representation; provided that if the trustee is then holding another fund or portion hereunder for the primary benefit of any such descendant, his or her share shall be added to and commingled with such other fund or portion and held, or partly held and partly distributed, as if it had been an original part thereof.

(e) The trustee shall distribute each fund set aside for the descendants of a deceased child of the Grantor to such descendants, by representation.

4. Notwithstanding anything in this instrument to the contrary, if any descendant of a deceased child of the Grantor is under the age of twenty-one years when the trustee is directed in the foregoing provisions of this instrument to distribute to him or her any portion of the principal of the trust property, his or her portion shall immediately vest in interest in him or her indefeasibly, but the trustee may in its discretion withhold possession of it and hold it in trust for his or her benefit until he or she attains that age. In the meantime, the trustee shall use so much of the income

and principal for his or her reasonable support, comfort, and education as the trustee determines to be required for those purposes.

1. If at any time any person to whom the trustee is directed in this instrument to pay any income is under legal disability or is in the opinion of the trustee incapable of properly managing his or her affairs, the trustee may use so much of such income for his or her support and comfort as the trustee determines to be required for the purposes.

2. The trustee either may expend directly any income or principal that it is authorized in this instrument to use for the benefit of any person, or may pay it over to him or her or for his or her use to his or her parent or guardian, or to any person with whom he or she is residing, without responsibility for its expenditure. The trustee shall withhold any such income not so used, and at its discretion add it to principal; provided that during the life of the Grantor's wife the trustee shall in any event pay all the net income of the trust estate to her or use it for her benefit.

3. No interest of any beneficiary in the income or principal of this trust shall be assignable in anticipation of payment or be liable in any way for the beneficiary's debts or obligations and shall not be subject to attachment.

4. Upon the death of my wife, any income accrued or undistributed shall be paid to her estate; upon the death of any other beneficiary, any income accrued or undistributed shall be held and accounted for, or distributed, in the same manner as if it had been income accrued and received after such beneficiary's death.

5. Notwithstanding anything herein to the contrary, the trusts hereunder shall terminate not later than twenty-one years after the death of the last survivor of the Grantor's wife and his descendants living at the Grantor's death, at the end of which period the trustee shall distribute each remaining portion of the trust property to the beneficiaries, at that time, of the income thereof, and in the proportions in which they are beneficiaries of such income.

ARTICLE V

1. The trustee shall have the following powers with respect to each trust hereunder, to be exercised as the trustee in its discretion determines to be to the best interests of the beneficiaries:

(a) Subject to Article III, paragraph 1(a), to retain any property transferred, devised, or bequeathed to the trustee, or any undivided interest therein, regardless of any lack of diversification, risk, or non-productivity;

(b) To invest and reinvest the trust estate in any property or undivided interests therein, wherever located, including bonds, notes (secured or unsecured), stocks of corporations, real estate, or any interest therein, and interests in trusts including common trust funds, without being limited by any statute or rule of law concerning investments by trustees;

(c) To sell any trust property, for cash or on credit, at public or private sale; to exchange any trust property for other property; to grant options to purchase or acquire any trust property; and to determine the prices and terms of sales, exchanges, and options;

(d) To execute leases and sub-leases for terms as long as two hundred years, even though such terms may extend beyond the termination of the trust; to subdivide or improve real estate and tear down or alter improvements; to grant easements, give consents, and make contracts relating to real estate or its use; and to release or dedicate any interest in real estate;

(e) To borrow money and to mortgage or pledge any trust property;

(f) To take any action with respect to conserving or realizing upon the value of any trust property, and with respect to foreclosures, reorganizations, or other changes affecting the trust property; to collect, pay, contest, compromise, or abandon demands of or against the trust estate, wherever situated; and to execute contracts, notes, conveyances, and other instruments containing covenants and warranties binding upon and creating a charge against the trust estate, and containing provisions excluding personal liability;

(g) To keep any property in the name of a nominee with or without disclosure of any fiduciary relationship;

(h) To employ agents, attorneys, auditors, depositories, and proxies, with or without discretionary powers;

(i) To determine the manner of ascertainment of income and principal, and the apportionment between income and principal of all receipts and disbursements, and to select an annual accounting period;

(j) To receive additional property from any source and add it to and commingle it with the trust estate;

(k) To enter into any transaction authorized by this Article with trustees or legal representatives of any other trust or estate in which any beneficiary hereunder has any beneficial interest, even though any such trustee or legal representative is also trustee hereunder;

(l) To make any distribution or division of the trust property in cash or in kind or both, and to allot different kinds or disproportionate shares of property or undivided interests in property among the beneficiaries or portions, and to determine the value of any such property; and to continue to exercise any powers and discretion herein given for a reasonable period after the termination of the trust, but only for so long as no rule of law relating to perpetuities would be violated.

2. To the extent that any such requirements can legally be waived, no trustee shall ever be required to give any bond as trustee or qualify before, be appointed by, or in the absence of breach of trust account to any court, or obtain the order or approval

of any court in the exercise of any power or discretion herein given. No person paying money or delivering any property to any trustee shall be required to see to its application.

3. Any trustee shall be entitled to reasonable compensation for services in administering and distributing the trust property, and to reimbursement for expenses.

ARTICLE VI

1. Any trustee may resign at any time by giving written notice, specifying the effective date of such resignation, to the beneficiaries, at the time of giving notice, of the current income of the trust property.

2. If any trustee at any time resigns or is unable to act, another corporation authorized under the law of any State or of the United States to administer trusts may be appointed as successor trustee, by an instrument delivered to such successor and signed by the beneficiaries, at the time of such appointment, of at least two-thirds of the current income of the trust property, and such beneficiaries may direct the successor trustee to accept the accounts of any former trustee, in which event the successor trustee shall have no responsibility thereof.

3. Every successor trustee shall have all the title, powers, and discretion herein given the trustee, without any act of conveyance or transfer.

4. The guardian or conservator of the estate of a beneficiary under legal disability, or the parents or surviving parent of a minor beneficiary for whose estate no guardian has been appointed, may act for such beneficiary in making any appointment and giving any direction under this Article.

5. If another corporation succeeds to the trust business of any corporate trustee hereunder, such successor shall become trustee hereunder.

ARTICLE VII

After the Grantor's death, the trustee may in its discretion make loans, with or without security, to the executor or administrator of the Grantor's estate, purchase from such executor or administrator, at such value as may be determined by the trustee, any property constituting part or all of the Grantor's estate, and, subject to Article III, paragraph 1(a), retain all or any part of such property regardless of risk, unproductivity, or lack of diversification.

IN WITNESS WHEREOF, the parties hereto have signed and sealed this instrument on the date first above written.

_____(Seal)
Grantor

OLD FAITHFUL TRUST
COMPANY OF _____

By _____
                                            President
                                    Attest_____
                                            Trust Officer

———

Trusts for Commercial Purposes. While we are primarily concerned in this book with trusts as a mechanism for transmitting and managing family wealth, we note that the trust is also widely used for commercial purposes. As Professor Langbein has noted, "[M]ost of the wealth that is held in trust in the United States is placed there incident to business deals, and not in connection with gratuitous transfers." John H. Langbein, The Secret Life of the Trust: The Trust as an Instrument of Commerce, 107 Yale L.J. 165, 166 (1997). These commercial purposes include pension plans and mutual funds. For further discussion of trusts for commercial purposes, see Steven L. Schwarcz, Commercial Trusts as Business Organizations: Unraveling the Mystery, 58 Bus. Law. 559 (2003); Robert H. Sitkoff, Trust as "Uncorporation": A Research Agenda, 2005 U. Ill. L. Rev. 31.

Blind Trusts. Yet another purpose of trusts is to avoid impermissible conflicts of interest. Political figures and corporate officers commonly are placed in positions in which a conflict of interest would arise if they owned certain assets outright. To avoid these conflicts (or potential conflicts), these individuals place their assets in a so-called "blind trust." The trustee of such a trust is an independent third party, and the settlor retains no control over management of the assets and no authority to inquire about the exact nature of investments of the assets while the settlor is in office. The federal government's blind trust forms can be found at http://www.oge.gov.

EXTERNAL REFERENCE. Wendy S. Goffe, Oddball Trusts and the Lawyers Who Love Them, or Trusts for Politicians and Other Animals, 46 Real Prop., Tr. & Est. J. 543 (2012).

4. Types of Trusts

Express Trusts. When we speak of the estate planning uses of trusts, we are referring to *express* trusts. Express trusts are intentionally created for the ongoing management of the trust property, whether for private or charitable beneficiaries or for a combination of the two. Express trusts persist over some period of time.

We have already briefly mentioned two other trust categories—the *constructive* trust and the *resulting* trust. Neither type is truly a "trust" in the sense of requiring ongoing management of trust property. Their functions are quite different.

Constructive Trusts. The constructive trust is not a trust at all, but a remedy. It is closely associated with quasi-contract, which likewise is not a contract but a remedy.

In fact, one can say that if quasi-contract is the law's principal answer to unjust enrichment, then constructive trust is equity's principal answer. Recall the discussion of constructive trusts in Chapter 4.

Resulting Trusts. At several points in the succeeding materials, we will also encounter one kind of resulting trust, that is, the kind of "trust" that arises when an express trust fails or does not completely dispose of the trust property. Like the constructive trust, the resulting trust is no trust at all in the sense of prescribing ongoing management of the property. It is, rather, a property interest analogous to the reversion retained by a grantor who conveys one or more legal interests in property for life or for years without creating a remainder thereafter. In other words, a reversion is a legal interest, whereas the beneficial interest under a resulting trust is equitable, since a resulting trust arises from a conveyance of the legal title in fee simple, but without disposing of the complete beneficial interest.

Another kind of resulting trust is the so-called "purchase-money" resulting trust. The "purchase-money" resulting trust further demonstrates the versatility of the "trust" idea or label, but it is not part of this course. The basic principle is that where property is transferred to one person and the purchase price is paid by another person, a resulting trust presumptively arises in favor of the person who pays the purchase price. For further elaboration of the purchase-money resulting trust, see Restatement 3d of Trusts §9.

EXTERNAL REFERENCES. Gregory S. Alexander, The Transformation of Trusts as a Legal Category, 1800-1914, 5 Law & Hist. Rev. 303 (1987); A.I. Ogus, The Trust as a Governance Structure, 36 U. Toronto L.J. 186 (1986).

PART B. SUBSTANTIVE REQUIREMENTS: THE THREE CERTAINTIES

Primary Statutory References: *UTC §§401-404*

Trusts, other than charitable trusts, have three substantive requirements, known as the "three certainties." These are: (1) certainty of subject (specific trust property, or *res*), (2) certainty of object (identifiable beneficiaries), and (3) certainty of intent (specific intent to create a trust). We examine each of these in turn.

1. Certainty of Subject

Trust law requires that there be an identifiable trust property, often called the trust *res*. See Restatement 3d of Trusts §2 comment f, §§3, 10, 40. The requirement of trust property is sometimes codified, as in the Uniform Trust Code and in the California and Texas codifications of trust law. See UTC §401; Cal. Prob. Code §15202; Tex. Prop. Code §112.005. Any legally recognized property interest that is transferable can be the subject of a trust. See Restatement 3d of Trusts §40. In most trusts, the requirement of a trust *res* presents no difficulties, but occasionally it does, as the *Brainard* case, below, illustrates. Relevant to *Brainard* is §41 of the Restatement 3d of Trusts, which provides:

> §41. *Expectancies; Nonexistent Property Interests.* An expectation or hope of receiving property in the future, or an interest that has not come into existence or has ceased to exist, cannot be held in trust.

Brainard v. Commissioner
91 F.2d 880 (7th Cir. 1937)

SPARKS, J. This petition for review involves income taxes for the year 1928. The question presented is whether under the circumstances set forth in the findings of the Board of Tax Appeals, the taxpayer created a valid trust, the income of which was taxable to the beneficiaries under section 162 of the Revenue Act of 1928.

The facts as found by the Board of Tax Appeals are substantially as follows: In December, 1927, the taxpayer, having decided that conditions were favorable, contemplated trading in the stock market during 1928. He consulted a lawyer and was advised that it was possible for him to trade in trust for his children and other members of his family. Taxpayer thereupon discussed the matter with his wife and mother, and stated to them that he declared a trust of his stock trading during 1928 for the benefit of his family upon certain terms and conditions. Taxpayer agreed to assume personally any losses resulting from the venture, and to distribute the profits, if any, in equal shares to his wife, mother, and two minor children after deducting a reasonable compensation for his services. During 1928 taxpayer carried on the trading operations contemplated and at the end of the year determined his compensation at slightly less than $10,000, which he reported in his income tax return for that year. The profits remaining were then divided in approximately equal shares among the members of his family, and the amounts were reported in their respective tax returns for 1928. The amounts allocated to the beneficiaries were credited to them on taxpayer's books, but they did not receive the cash, except taxpayer's mother, to a small extent.

In addition to these findings the record discloses that taxpayer's two children were one and three years of age. Upon these facts the Board held that the income in controversy was taxable to the petitioner as a part of his gross income for 1928, and decided that there was a deficiency. It is here sought to review that decision.

In the determination of the questions here raised it is necessary to consider the nature of the trust, if any, that is said to have been created by the circumstances hereinbefore recited. It is clear that the taxpayer, at the time of his declaration, had no property interest in "profits in stock trading in 1928, if any," because there were none in existence at that time. Indeed it is not disclosed that the declarer at that time owned any stock. It is obvious, therefore, that the taxpayer based his declaration of trust upon an interest which at that time had not come into existence and in which no one had a present interest. In the Restatement of the Law of Trusts, vol. 1, §75, it is said that an interest which has not come into existence or which has ceased to exist can not be held in trust. It is there further said:

> A person can, it is true, make a contract binding himself to create a trust of an interest if he should thereafter acquire it; but such an agreement is not binding as a contract unless the requirements of the law of Contracts are complied with ...
>
> Thus, if a person gratuitously declares himself trustee of such shares as he may thereafter acquire in a corporation not yet organized, no trust is created. The result is the same where instead of declaring himself trustee, he purports to transfer to another as trustee such shares as he may thereafter acquire in a corporation not yet organized. In such a case there is at most a gratuitous undertaking to create a trust in the future, and such an undertaking is not binding as a contract for lack of consideration ....
>
> If a person purports to declare himself trustee of an interest not in existence, or if he purports to transfer such an interest to another in trust, he is liable as upon a contract to create a trust if, but only if, the requirements of the law of Contracts are complied with.

See, also, Restatement, §30b; Bogert, Trusts and Trustees, vol. 1, §112. In 42 Harvard Law Review 561, it is said:

> With logical consistency, the courts have uniformly held that an expectancy cannot be the subject matter of a trust and that an attempted creation, being merely a promise to transfer property in the future, is invalid unless supported by consideration.

Citing Lehigh Valley R. R. Co. v. Woodring, 116 Pa. 513, 9 A. 58. Hence, it is obvious under the facts here presented that taxpayer's declaration amounted to nothing more than a promise to create a trust in the future....

The questions with which we are concerned are at what times did the respective earnings which constitute the trust fund come into existence, and at what times did the trust attach to them. It is obvious that the respective profits came into existence when and if such stocks were sold at a profit in 1928. Did they come into existence impressed with the trust, or was there any period of time intervening between the time they came into existence and the time the trust attached? If there were such intervening time, then during that time the taxpayer must be considered as the sole owner of the profits and they were properly taxed to him as a part of his income.

It is said in the Restatement of the Law of Trusts, §75c:

> If a person purports to declare himself trustee of an interest not in existence or if he purports to transfer such an interest to another in trust, no trust arises even when the interest comes into existence in the absence of a manifestation of intention at that time.

This we think is especially applicable where, as here, there was no consideration for the declaration. It is further stated, however, in the Restatement, §26k:

> If a person manifests an intention to become trustee at a subsequent time, his conduct at that subsequent time considered in connection with his original manifestation may be a sufficient manifestation of intention at that subsequent time to create a trust ... the act of

acquiring the property coupled with the earlier declaration of trust *may be* a sufficient manifestation of an intention to create a trust at the time of the acquisition of the property. (Our italics, here and hereafter.)

In subsection 1 it is said "...Mere silence, however, ordinarily will not be such a manifestation....." ...

From what has been said we are convinced that appellant's profits in question were not impressed with a trust when they first came into existence. The Board was obviously of the impression that the trust first attached when appellant credited them to the beneficiaries on his books of account. This act, it seems to us, constituted his first subsequent expression of intention to become a trustee of the fund referred to in his original and gratuitous declaration. Prior to that time we think it is clear that the declaration could not have been enforced against him, and that his mere silence with respect thereto should not be considered as an expression of his intention to establish a trust at a time earlier than the credits....

The order of the Board is affirmed.

Notes and Questions

1. *Market Performance 1928.* The year 1928 was a good year in the stock market. At the close of 1927, the Dow Jones Industrial Average stood at 202, and closed the year 1928 at 300, for nearly a 50 percent gain.

2. *Expectancies.* That mere expectancies cannot be the subject of a trusts is well-settled. See Restatement 3d of Trusts §41. The question is, what *is* an "expectancy"?

The interests of presumptive heirs or devisees of a living person traditionally have been characterized as "expectancies" and not as property. See Simes & Smith on Future Interests §391. Nevertheless, historically, equity courts enforced expectancy assignments but only if "value" was given, by which the courts meant that they retained the power to review the fairness of the exchange. Recall the discussion in Chapter 2.

3. *Pour-Over Devises and Testamentary Appointments.* On the validity of pour-over devises, recall the discussion of UPC §2-511 and UTC §401(1) in Chapter 7. What about a testamentary exercise of a power of appointment in favor of a trust not funded before the testator's death? See Benjamin v. Carasaniti, 267 A.3d 108 (Conn. 2021) (upholding the trust).

4. *Debts as Trust Property.* Any legally recognized property interest or contract right that is transferrable can be the subject of a trust. If A has a legally enforceable claim against B, A can create a trust of that debt, either by declaration of a trust or by transfer. However, if B declares that he or she holds the debt he or she owes to A in trust for A, no trust is created. B is a debtor, and a debtor cannot be a trustee of his or her own debt. Why might it matter whether B is treated as a debtor or a trustee?

5. *Uncashed Checks as Trust Property.* Suppose that prior to her death, Susan

delivered to her daughter, Emily, a check for $20,000, designating on the check that it was to be held in trust for Emily's minor child. Before Emily was able to cash the check, Susan died. Was a trust created? Is there a legally recognized property interest that can serve as the subject matter of the trust? Compare Estate of Bolton, 444 N.W.2d 482 (Iowa 1989) (an uncashed check is not a completed gift) with Sinclair v. Fleischman, 773 P.2d 101 (Wash. Ct. App. 1989) (an uncashed check constituted a completed gift because it was legally delivered by the donor and accepted by the donee prior to the donor's death).

Where the check was to a charity, the Tax Court has held that the gift became complete upon the delivery of the check. See Estate of Belcher v. Commissioner, 83 T.C. 227 (1984). Under state law, charitable pledges if relied upon by the charity are enforceable even though not supported by consideration. See, e.g., King v. Trustees of Boston University, 647 N.E.2d 1196 (Mass. 1995).

————

When Is an Inter Vivos Trust Created? The Restatement 3d of Trusts provides that "[an inter vivos] trust may be created by an owner's inter vivos *transfer* of property to another person as trustee...." Restatement 3d of Trusts §10 comment d (emphasis added).

What if the trust is a self-declared trust? Does the declaration constitute the transfer or does the transfer occur when the property is retitled in the settlor's name as trustee? The Restatement 3d of Trusts §10 comment e provides that "[i]f the owner of property declares himself or herself trustee..., a trust is created, even though there is no transfer of the title to the trust property to another...." Comment e then provides:

> e. *Declaration of trust....* In this Restatement, the declaration of trust is generally considered to be an additional means of creating a trust inter vivos, and is thus an exception to or substitute for the usual requirement that there be a transfer of the trust property to the trustee. Conceptually, however, it is not inappropriate for the declaration of trust to be viewed as a form of "transfer" from the property owner individually to the property owner in a representative capacity. Accordingly, regardless of which of these views may be preferred in a particular jurisdiction, an owner of property may create a trust by executing an instrument worded as a transfer of the property to himself or herself as trustee....
>
> In addition, except as precluded by statute, a trust may be established by the settlor's signing of an instrument that begins, essentially, "I hereby declare myself trustee of the property listed in Schedule A attached hereto" or "O, as settlor, hereby transfers to O, as trustee, the property listed in the attached Schedule A," even though in either case the document is not supported at the time of execution, or by the time of the settlor's death or incompetency, by other acts or other documents of transfer or title.

See also UTC §401; Estate of Heggstad, 20 Cal. Rptr. 2d 433 (Cal. Ct. App. 1993). But see N.Y. Est. Powers & Trust Law §7-1.18(b) (requiring further steps).

2. Certainty of Object

Primary Statutory Reference: *UTC §402*

Restatement 3d of Trusts

§44. Definite Beneficiary Requirement. A trust is not created, or if created will not continue, unless the terms of the trust provide a beneficiary who is ascertainable at the time or who may later become ascertainable within the period and terms of the rule against perpetuities.

§48. Beneficiaries Defined; Incidental Benefits. A person is a beneficiary of a trust if the settlor manifests an intention to give the person a beneficial interest; a person who merely benefits incidentally from the performance of the trust is not a beneficiary.

There is no doubt that a trust can be created that includes unborn and unascertained persons among its beneficiaries. Suppose, for example, a parent transfers property to a trustee, directing that the income from the property be paid to the parent for life, corpus at the parent's death to be equally divided among his or her then-living children. The trust would be valid without question. See Restatement 3d of Trusts §44 comment c.

Can a trust be validly created if *all* of its beneficiaries are unborn, unascertained, or both?

Morsman v. Commissioner
90 F.2d 18 (8th Cir. 1937)

[On January 28, 1929, Robert P. Morsman, president of the United States Trust Company, signed a document declaring himself trustee of certain publicly traded securities; the United States Trust Company was named successor trustee. The securities had substantially appreciated in value during Morsman's ownership. Morsman, being in a high income-tax bracket, hoped that putting the securities into the self-declared trust would cause the ordinary income and any capital gain realized on sale to be taxed to the lower-bracket trust.

The trust document provided that the trust income was to be accumulated and added to principal until January 1, 1934. Thereafter, income was to be paid to Morsman himself for life. On termination of the trust, the principal was to go to his issue, or to his widow if there were no issue, or to his legal heirs if he had neither issue nor a widow then living.

Throughout the period in question, Mr. Morsman was unmarried and had no issue. Apparently his closest blood relative was a brother, who was Morsman's heir apparent.

Shortly after signing the trust document, Morsman sold the securities at a profit. Then, on May 3, 1929, he turned the trust property over to the United States Trust

Company as successor trustee. The gains realized on these sales were reported as income of the trust. The Commissioner of Internal Revenue determined that the gains should have been reported as income on Morsman's personal return.]

THOMAS, J.... The question for consideration is whether or not the arrangement so devised resulted in the creation of an express trust covering the period and the transactions between January 28 and May 3, 1929. No claim is made that a charitable trust is involved. [Morsman] contends that a private express trust did exist during the period in question and that the profits realized from the sale of the securities should be taxed as income to the trust and not as income to himself individually....

First. With respect to the position of Morsman, it is settled that a trust cannot exist where the same person possesses both the legal and equitable titles to the trust fund at the same time. In such a case the two titles are said to merge.... This principle is not denied. The result, of course, is different where one person conveys property to another who agrees to hold in trust for the grantor, as in the case of Doctor v. Hughes, 225 N.Y. 305, 122 N.E. 221. In such a case there is an immediate severance of the legal and equitable titles, and a trust arises at once. In the instant case that provision of the agreement by which [Morsman] undertook to hold for himself, standing alone, therefore, contributes nothing toward the creation of a trust....

Second. With respect to the possibility of issue, it... is true that... it has been held in several cases that a present trust may be created where the beneficiary of an express trust is an unborn child. [E.g.,] Folk v. Hughes, 100 S.C. 220, 84 S.E. 713. The rationale of these cases, however, is not believed to rest on the theory that an unborn child can be the express cestui of an immediate trust. To so hold would violate fundamental principles of trusts which require a present conveyance of the beneficial interest and the existence of present enforceable duties and it would permit the suspension of the beneficial ownership, a notion repugnant to the requirements of a trust. The rationale of such a case is that the instrument has the effect of creating an immediate resulting trust for the settlor (which will cease if the expected child is born) "with an express trust for the child springing up when and if such child ever materializes." Bogert, Trusts and Trustees, §163.... So if A, a bachelor, transfers property to B in trust to accumulate the rents and profits and to convey the same to A's eldest son on reaching its majority (Trusts, Restatement, §112, Illustration 6), a trust will arise at once—B now holding as a resulting trustee for A with the express trust arising if and when the eldest son comes into existence—the resulting trust then to cease. But in that view if A, a bachelor, or any person without issue, declares himself trustee of property for his own eldest son on identical or similar terms, no trust will presently arise. The express trust for the child cannot arise until the child comes into existence, and A cannot hold as a resulting trustee for himself during his lifetime because of the necessary merger in such a case of the legal and equitable interests in the same person. If A should die without issue under these circumstances, the property constituting the so-called trust fund is as much a part of his estate as if he had never made the purported declaration. The distinction thus noted between the case where A declares himself trustee for his unborn issue and where he conveys to B to hold in trust for such issue is vital; and this is the point at which Morsman failed in his attempt to create a present trust....

To hold that a *present* trust arises where the owner of property declares that he holds it in trust for himself and other persons who are as yet nonexistent not only lacks a logical explanation but is incapable of practical application. To a creditor seeking to subject the property to the satisfaction of a debt [Morsman] would say that it was no longer his, but belonged, in equity, to others who were not yet in existence. But if he sought to dissipate the property, there is no person in being who has such an interest that he may go into a court of equity and prevent the dissipation. To say that [Morsman] in this case has an interest in enforcing such an obligation against himself or that the community at large is interested in preserving the rights of issue as yet not conceived is, to say the least, an unwarranted assumption. For the court to regard possible unborn issue as present beneficiaries is to permit the substance and realities of the transaction to be obscured by words and phrases....

Third. With respect to the "heirs" as present beneficiaries and to the possible suggestion that [Morsman's] brother now living may take a present equitable interest under paragraph (8) of the trust agreement, it is observed that one of the elementary rules of law is that "A living person has no heirs".... Only on death do heirs come into existence, "for the ancestor during his life beareth in his body (in judgment of law) all his heirs, and therefore, it is truly said that haeres est pars antecessoris." Co. Litt. 22b. Quoted in Doctor v. Hughes, 225 N.Y. 305, 122 N.E. 221, 222.[17] What has been said with reference to the rights of unborn children applies with equal force to the rights of heirs, two classes equally nonexistent. "Heirs," therefore, have no present beneficial interest, and cannot be considered beneficiaries....

Finally, with respect to the status of a widow as a beneficiary, what has been said in reference to the nonexistence of issue and heirs is applicable here. The record, as pointed out above, does not show the existence of a wife. A widow is, therefore, a mere potentiality without existence and with no one to represent her. As a fiction, she belongs to no class. In case of an hypothetical breach of duty of the trustee, no woman in all the world, upon the record here, has a present right to come forward and enforce any rights under the trust agreement, and no existing person is authorized to enforce her imaginary rights.

---

17. This case concerned the Doctrine of Worthier Title, which states that a remainder in the grantor's heirs is transformed into a reversion in the grantor. Thus, a remainder in Morsman's heirs would be transformed into a reversion in Morsman. Many states have abolished the Doctrine of Worthier Title as a rule of law, and the UPC abolishes it as a rule of law and as a rule of construction. See UPC §2-710. If we put aside the Doctrine of Worthier Title, should the court in *Morsman* have reached a different result? Ed.

The trust agreement, therefore, failed to effect the creation of a trust on January 28, 1929. This results from the fact that no existing beneficiaries were named therein and, consequently, there was no present severance of the legal and equitable titles to the property. The question here determined is whether there was a valid declaration of trust operating in praesenti between January 28 and May 3, 1929. That question must necessarily be answered in the negative since there was at that time no person in being who could claim any beneficial interest in the property other than the holder of the legal title. It is true, of course, that in equity a trust may not fail for want of a trustee, nevertheless the courts cannot supply a private express beneficiary....

AFFIRMED.

GARDNER, J. dissenting.... Authority is not wanting to the effect that a trust may be created even though the cestui que trust at the time of its creation is not in existence. For instance, the case of Folk v. Hughes, 100 S.C. 220, 84 S.E. 713, 714, cited in the majority opinion, specifically so holds.... But if it be assumed that there must have been in existence at the time of the creation of the trust a cestui que capable of taking, yet a prospective or potential heir, who under the terms of the trust may, under certain contingencies, be a beneficiary, fulfills this requirement.

Note and Questions

1. *Trusts With Unborn Beneficiaries.* Compare with *Morsman*, Folk v. Hughes, 84 S.E. 713 (S.C. 1915), cited in both the majority and dissenting opinions in *Morsman*. In *Folk*, a father transferred real property to his son under a deed that provided:

> To have and to hold the said described tract of land with all privileges and appurtenances thereof to [my son] for his uses and benefits, and for the maintenance and support of [my son's] children during the term of [my son's] natural life. And I... for and in consideration of the love and affection I have for the lawful children of [my son], do hereby grant, release and convey unto the lawful children of [my son] all the above described tract of land. To have and to hold the same immediately after the death of [my son]. Together with all the rights and appurtenances thereto belonging. To have and to hold all and singular the said premises unto the children of [my son], their heirs and assigns forever.

At the time of the transfer, the son was married but childless. A child was born to the son later, however, and the court held that a valid trust had been created for that child at the time of the original transfer. As a consequence, the son was unable by reconveying the property to his father to destroy the contingent remainder in his unborn children. The court said, in part:

> It is not necessary to the creation of a trust estate that the cestui que trust should be in existence at the time of its creation. In [Ashurst v. Given, 5 Watts & S. (Pa.) 329], a devise to a father in trust for his children at the time of his death was held to be good, although the father had no children at the time of the vesting of the estate in him as trustee.

A trustee will not be allowed by his own act to defeat or destroy his trust, and those who deal with him in respect of the trust estate, with knowledge of the trust, are bound by the terms of the trust, and if they purchase the trust estate, they take it incumbered with the trust.

Are *Folk* and *Morsman* distinguishable, as the *Morsman* majority thought, or was the dissenting judge right that they are inconsistent? Should it matter that in *Folk* the trust was created by transfer of legal title, while the *Morsman* trust was self-declared?[18]

2. *Uniform Trust Code.* Would *Morsman* have been decided differently under UTC §402(a)(5) and (b)? What if the trust had been revocable (see UTC §603(b))?

———

Merger: Beneficiary as Trustee. The court in *Morsman* spoke of the merger of legal and equitable title in one person. This raises a question: can the beneficiary also be the trustee?

One Person as Sole Trustee and Sole Beneficiary. The Restatement 3d of Trusts provides that "[t]he settlor or the trustee, or both, may be beneficiaries [of a trust]; but a sole trustee may not be the sole beneficiary." Restatement 3d of Trusts §3 comment d; see also id. §10. Accord, UTC §402(a)(5). A transfer of legal title to a person to hold in trust for himself or herself, as sole beneficiary, does not create a trust. This is commonly explained, as it was in the *Morsman* opinion, by saying that there is a merger of the legal and equitable titles. But in truth, no separation of legal and equitable title ever occurred so as to bring about a merger—in short, the transfer did not create a trust.

The problem of merger may arise, however, either *after* the inception of an admittedly valid trust or *at* the inception of an intended trust. If title is transferred to A to hold on active trust for B, there is of course a trust at the inception of the arrangement. Should A thereafter die intestate, leaving B as his or her sole heir, in a jurisdiction in which title to trust property passes to an intestate trustee's heirs, legal and equitable title will have become vested in one person, hence there will typically be a merger, which will normally put an end to the trust. See the Restatement 3d of Trusts §69, which provides that "[i]f the legal title to the trust property and the entire beneficial interest become united in one person, the trust terminates." Some statutes specifically recognize certain limited exceptions to the doctrine of merger. See, e.g., Tex. Prop. Code §112.034; Cal. Prob. Code §15209.

———

18. The Restatement 3d of Trusts §44 gives an illustration based on facts like those in *Folk* (declaring such a trust valid) but does not give an illustration based on facts like those in *Morsman*. The Reporter's Notes to §44 comment c, however, state the Reporter's view that "the dissent [in *Morsman*] seems correct, and the majority's generally criticized view seems strained in order to block a tax-avoidance plan." Reporter's Notes state the Reporter's view; they are not an official part of the Restatement.

Multiple Parties, Overlapping Interests as Trustee and Beneficiary. The problems are more complicated once we get beyond the situation of one person as sole trustee and sole beneficiary. Three situations are most troublesome:

Category (1): G transfers to A and B in trust for A and B, where the beneficial interests are concurrent.

Category (2): G transfers to A in trust for A and B, where the beneficial interests are concurrent—for example, the beneficiaries are given equal shares in income and principal.

Category (3): G transfers to A in trust for A and B, where the beneficial interests are successive—for example, income is to be paid to A for life, with principal then to be transferred to B.

A valid trust would be created in all these situations according to the Restatement 3d of Trusts §69 comment c. In Category (1), a technical argument favoring validity is that the trustees hold the legal title as joint tenants, while the beneficiaries hold as tenants in common. A purposeful argument is that applying the merger doctrine would defeat the expressed intent of the settlor, which public policy does not require inasmuch as a beneficiary exists who can enforce the trust against a trustee other than himself or herself. Most of the cases that have dealt with the above categories have avoided the merger of interests, and this is certainly the trend. A case in Alabama dealing with Category (1) sustained the trust and overruled a prior case to the contrary. See First Alabama Bank v. Webb, 373 So.2d 631 (Ala. 1979). The court said that merger should operate only where one person is both trustee and beneficiary.

A point applicable only to Category (3) is that, at the very least, it should be clear that A holds the remainder interest in trust for B. The only real question should be whether A's equitable life estate, which A holds as beneficiary, merges with the legal life estate, which A holds as trustee, so that A holds the life estate free of trust. The better authority holds that A does not hold the life estate free of trust. The ground, again, is that merger defeats the intention of the settlor for no good reason. Thus the trustee holds the entire legal title in trust, as intended by the settlor; a court should not reduce that legal title to separate undivided interests.

The Problem of Indefinite Beneficiaries. What happens if the settlor creates a trust in favor of a class of persons, but the class is described in such vague terms that it is difficult to say who is in the class and who is not?

Restatement 3d of Trusts

§46. Members of an Indefinite Class as Beneficiaries

(1) Except as stated in (2), where the owner of property transfers it upon intended trust for the members of an indefinite class of persons, no trust is created.

(2) If the transferee is directed to distribute the property to such members of the indefinite class as the transferee shall select, the transferee holds the property in trust with power but no duty to distribute the property to such class members as the transferee may select; to whatever extent the power (presumptively personal) is not exercised, the transferee will then hold for reversionary beneficiaries implied by law.

In connection with the above provision of the Restatement and UTC §402(c), read the following materials, including Clark v. Campbell, and consider whether a trust is created where G's will purports to create a trust on the following alternative terms:

1. "Income to A for life, remainder in corpus to my (G's) friends"; or

2. "Income to A for life, remainder in corpus to such of my (G's) friends as the trustee shall select"; or

3. "Income to A for life, remainder in corpus to such of my (G's) friends as A shall select."

Because the word "friends" is treated as an indefinite class, the remainder interest given to G's "friends" in Problem 1 is generally considered to be invalid.

The power given to A in Problem 3 is called a *discretionary* power of appointment, because the holder of the power—A—is not a fiduciary and thus is not under any fiduciary obligation to exercise the power.[19] Discretionary powers are almost always valid because the test for their validity is so easily satisfied. Discretionary powers are valid unless the group of permissible appointees (G's "friends" in Problem 3) is so indefinite that "it is impossible to identify any person the donor intended should be [permissible appointees] of the power." Restatement 2d of Property §12.1 comment h & illustration 18. Accord Restatement 1st of Property §323 comment h.

The power given to the trustee—to a fiduciary—in Problem 2 is called a *mandatory* power of appointment. Despite §46(2) of the Restatement 3d of Trusts and UTC §402(c), which treat mandatory and discretionary powers alike, Clark v. Campbell shows that the traditional test for validity of a mandatory power is much more stringent than for a discretionary power.

---

19. This chapter does not deal comprehensively with discretionary powers. Discretionary powers are considered in Chapter 14.

Clark v. Campbell
133 A. 166 (N.H. 1926)

Petition for instructions, by the trustees under the will of Charles H. Cummings. Questions, which appear in the opinion, were reserved without ruling by Sawyer, J. SNOW, J. The ninth clause of the will of deceased reads:

> My estate will comprise so many and such a variety of articles of personal property such as books, photographic albums, pictures, statuary, bronzes, bric-a-brac, hunting and fishing equipment, antiques, rugs, scrap books, canes and masonic jewels, that probably I shall not distribute all, and perhaps no great part thereof during my life by gift among my friends. Each of my trustees is competent by reason of familiarity with the property, my wishes and friendships, to wisely distribute some portion at least of said property. I therefore give and bequeath to my trustees all my property embraced within the classification aforesaid in trust to make disposal by the way of a memento from myself, of such articles to such of my friends as they, my trustees, shall select. All of said property, not so disposed of by them, my trustees are directed to sell and the proceeds of such sale or sales to become and be disposed of as a part of the residue of my estate.

....By the common law there cannot be a valid bequest to an indefinite person. There must be a beneficiary or a class of beneficiaries indicated in the will capable of coming into court and claiming the benefit of the bequest. This principle applies to private but not to public trusts and charities. Morice v. Bishop of Durham, 9 Vest. 399, 10 Ves. 521.

The basis assigned for this distinction is the difference in the enforceability of the two classes of trusts. In the former, there being no definite *cestui que trust* to assert his right, there is no one who can compel performance, with the consequent unjust enrichment of the trustee; while, in the case of the latter, performance is considered to be sufficiently secured by the authority of the Attorney General to invoke the power of the courts. The soundness of this distinction and the grounds upon which it rests, as applied to cases where the trustee is willing to act, has been questioned by distinguished authorities (5 Harvard Law Review, 390, 394, 395; 65 University of Pennsylvania Law Review, 538, 540; 37 Harvard Law Review, 687, 688) and has been supported by other authorities of equal note (15 Harvard Law Review, 510, 513-515, 530).[20] It is, however, conceded by the former that, since the doctrine was first stated in Morice v. Bishop of Durham, supra, more than a century ago, it has remained unchallenged, and has been followed by the courts in a practically unbroken line of decisions. Although it be conceded that the doctrine is not a legal necessity, the fact that it has never been impeached affords strong evidence that in its practical application it has been generally found just and reasonable. This is a

---

20. The distinguished authorities referred to are James B. Ames, The Failure of the "Tilden Trust," 5 Harv. L. Rev. 389 (1892); John C. Gray, Gifts for a Non-Charitable Purpose, 15 Harv. L. Rev. 509 (1902); and Austin W. Scott, Control of Property by the Dead, 65 U. Pa. L. Rev. 527 (1917), and Conveyances Upon Trusts Not Property Declared, 37 Harv. L. Rev. 653 (1924). Ed.

sufficient ground for continued adherence to the rule....

"A gift to trustees to dispose of the same as they think fit is too uncertain to be carried out by the court." Theobald on Wills, 7th ed., 495....

That the foregoing is the established doctrine seems to be conceded, but it is contended in argument that it was not the intention of the testator by the ninth clause to create a trust, at least as respects the selected articles, but to make an absolute gift thereof to the trustees individually. It is suggested that the recital of the qualifications of the trustees may be considered as investing them with personal and nonofficial character, and that the word "trustees" is merely descriptive of the persons who had been earlier named as trustees, and was not intended to limit the capacity in which they were to act here.... It is a sufficient answer to this contention that the language of the ninth clause does not warrant the assumed construction. The assertion of the competency of the trustees to wisely distribute the articles in question by reason of their familiarity with the testator's property, wishes and friendships seem quite as consistent with a design to clothe them with a trusteeship as with an intention to impose upon them a moral obligation only. Blunt v. Taylor, 230 Mass. 303, 305, 119 N.E. 954. If, however, the recited qualifications had the significance ascribed to them the language of the bequest is too plain to admit of the assumed construction. When the clause is ended of unnecessary verbiage the testator is made to say: "I give to my trustee my property (of the described class) in trust to make disposal of to such of my friends as they shall select." It is difficult to conceive of language more clearly disclosing an intention to create a trust. However, if the trust idea introduced by the words "trustees" and in "trust" were not controlling, all the evidence within the will confirms such idea. In the first clause of the will the testator nominates three trustees, and an alternate in case of vacancy. Throughout the will these nominees are repeatedly and invariably referred as "my trustees," whenever the testator is dealing with their trust duties. Whenever rights are conferred upon them individually, as happens in the fifth, sixth, and eighth clauses, they are as invariably severally referred to solely by their individual names. The clause under consideration (ninth) expressly provides for the disposal of only a portion of the classified articles, and imposes upon the trustees the duty of selling the balance thereof and adding the proceeds to the residue which they are to continue to hold, and administer in their capacity as trustees. The proceeds thus accruing under this clause are expressly referred to in the eleventh clause in enumeration of the ultimate funds to be distributed by them as trustees "in and among such charitable... institutions" as they shall select and designate. The conclusion is inescapable that there was no intention to bestow any part of the property enumerated is the ninth clause upon the trustees for their own benefit. This necessarily follows, since the direction to make disposal is clearly as broad as the gift.

It is further sought to sustain the bequest as a power. The distinction apparently relied upon is that a power, unlike a trust, is not imperative and leaves the act to be done at the will of the donee of the power. But the ninth clause by its terms imposes upon the trustees the imperative duty to dispose of the selected articles among the testator's friends. If, therefore, the authority bestowed by the testator by the use of a loose terminology may be called a power, it is not an optional power, but a power coupled with a trust, to which the principles incident to a trust so far as here involved, clearly apply.

We must therefore conclude that this clause presents the case of an attempt to create a private trust, and clearly falls within the principle of well-considered authorities. Nichols v. Allen, 130 Mass. 211, 212, 39 Am.Rep. 445; Blunt v. Taylor, 230 Mass. 303, 305, 119 N.E. 954. In so far as the cases cited by the petitioners upon this phase of the case are not readily distinguishable from the case at bar, they are in conflict with the great weight of authority.

The question presented, therefore, is whether or not the ninth clause provides for definite and ascertainable beneficiaries, so that the bequest therein can be sustained as a private trust. In this state the identity of a beneficiary is a question of fact to be found from the language of the will, construed in the light of all the competent evidence rather than by the application of arbitrary rules of law. It is believed that in no other jurisdiction is there greater liberality shown in seeking the intention of the testator in this, as in other particulars. We find, however, no case in which our courts have sustained a gift where the testator has attempted to delegate to a trustee the arbitrary selection of the beneficiaries of his bounty through means of a private trust.

Like the direct legatees in a will, the beneficiaries under a trust may be designated by class. But in such case the class must be capable of delimitation, as "brothers and sisters," "children," "issue," "nephews and nieces." A bequest giving the executor authority to distribute his property "among his relatives and for benevolent objects is such sums as in their judgment shall be for the best" was sustained upon evidence within the will that by "relatives" the testator intended such of his relatives within the statute of distributions as were needy, and thus brought the bequest within the line of charitable gifts, and excluded all other as individuals. Goodale v. Mooney, 60 N.H. 528, 526, 49 Am. Rep. 334. Where a testator bequeathed his stocks to be apportioned to his "relations" according to the discretion of the trustee, to be enjoyed by them after his decease, it was held to be a power to appoint amongst his relations who were next of kin under the statute of distribution. Varrell v. Wendell, 20 N.H. 431, 436. Likewise where a devise over after a particular estate was to the testator's "next of kin" simpliciter. Pinkham v. Blair, 57 N.H. 226, 243. Unless the will discloses a plain purpose to the contrary, the words "relatives" or "relations," to prevent gifts from being void for uncertainty, are commonly construed to mean those who would take under statutes of distribution or descent.

In the case now under consideration the cestuis que trust are designated as the "friends" of the testator. The word "friends," unlike "relations," has no accepted statutory or other controlling limitations, and in fact has no precise sense at all.

Friendship is a word of broad and varied application. It is commonly used to describe the undefinable relationships which exist, not only between those connected by ties of kinship or marriage, but as well between strangers in blood, and which vary in degree from the greatest intimacy to an acquaintance more or less casual. "Friend" is sometimes used in contradistinction to "enemy." "A friendless man is an outlaw." Cowell, Bouvier. Although the word was formerly sometimes used a synonymous with relatives, there is no evidence that it was so used here. The inference is to the contrary. The testator in the will refers to eight different persons, some of them already deceased, by the title of "friends." He never uses the appellation concurrently with "nephew" or "niece," which words occur several times in describing legatees. Nor is there anything to indicate that the word "friends" in the ninth clause was intended to apply only to those who had been thus referred to in the will. There is no express evidence that the word is used in any restricted sense....

It was the evident purpose of the testator to invest his trustees with the power after his death to make disposition of the enumerated articles among an undefined class with practically the same freedom and irresponsibility that he himself would have exercised if living; that is, to substitute for the will of the testator the will and discretion of the trustees. Such a purpose is in contravention of the policy of the statute which provides that

> No will shall be effectual to pass any real or personal estate... unless made by a person... in writing, signed by the testator or by some one in his presence and by his direction, and attested and subscribed in his presence by three or more credible witnesses.

Where a gift is impressed with a trust, ineffectively declared, and incapable of taking effect because of the indefiniteness of the cestui que trust, the donee will hold the property in trust for the next taker under the will or for the next of kin by way of a resulting trust.... The trustees therefore hold title to the property enumerated in the paragraph under consideration to be disposed of as a part of the residue, and the trustees are so advised. This conclusion makes it unnecessary to answer the question reserved, and it has not been considered....

Case discharged.

Notes and Questions

1. *Requirement of a Definite Class.* What reasoning explains the rule, applied in *Clark*, that where a fiduciary is under a duty to select the beneficiaries of a trust from amongst a class, the entire membership of the class must be definite and ascertainable? The court in *Clark* pointed to the policy of the statute of wills as a basis for the rule. But a moment's reflection should tell you that this cannot be so.

In Nichols v. Allen, 130 Mass. 211, 221 (1881), the leading American case on the problem, the court said:

The conclusion of the whole matter is, that, the testatrix having given the residue of her property to her executors in trust and not having defined the trust sufficiently to enable the court to execute it, the plaintiff, being her next of kin, is entitled to the residue by way of resulting trust.

Compare this statement with the explanation for the rule put forward by the court in *Clark*.

The first and leading case on the problem was Morice v. The Bishop of Durham, 10 Ves. 522, 32 Eng. Rep. 947 (Ch. 1805), in which property was given by will to the Bishop of Durham upon trust, after the payment of the testator's debts and legacies, "to dispose of the ultimate residue to such objects of benevolence and liberality as the Bishop of Durham in his own discretion shall most approve of." The Chancellor, Lord Eldon,[21] held that there was no intent that the Bishop take beneficially, and that the Bishop's discretion was not limited to purposes that were charitable, and that, therefore, the trust must fail because it was "for purposes not sufficiently defined to be controlled and managed by this Court." A decree in favor of the next of kin of the testatrix was affirmed.

Prior to this case, English equity judges had been more willing to exercise control over trustees' powers to select beneficiaries. The *Bishop of Durham's* case sharpened the distinction between trust powers and "bare" powers. As a result, the Court of Chancery embarked on a course that violated donors' intentions in a much wider range of cases.

2. *Discretionary Versus Mandatory Powers of Appointment.* Because the traditional tests for validity of discretionary and mandatory powers are so different, the process of identifying which type of power is created in a particular case can be crucial to the outcome. The distinction between mandatory and discretionary powers, however, is not always easy to draw. In Gibbs v. Rumsey, 2 Ves. & B. 294, 35 Eng. Rep. 331 (Ch. 1813), for example, a will devised the testator's estate to "my said trustees and executors [naming them] to be disposed of unto such person and persons and in such manner and form and in such sum and sums of money as they in their discretion shall think proper and expedient." In upholding the devise, the Master of the Rolls concluded that the will authorized appointment to anyone,

---

21. The Chancellorship of Lord Eldon (born John Scott), which lasted from 1801 to 1838, is widely considered to have exemplified the interventionist approach to trusts that prevailed in England before notions of economic liberalism began to influence equity doctrine.

Eldon's notorious dilatoriness is thought by some to have contributed to the backlog in Chancery practice that Dickens immortalized in the opening scene of his novel Bleak House: "Never can there come fog too thick, never can there come mind and mire too deep, to assort with the groping and floundering condition which this High Court of Chancery, most pestilent of hoary sinners, holds, this day, in the sight of heaven and earth." Charles Dickens, Bleak House 1 (Riverside ed. 1956; 1st pub. 1852-53). For a suggestion that Eldon's "legendary lack of expedition on the bench" owed more to "excessive zeal to get things right than to simple tardiness," see Simon Gardner, An Introduction to the Law of Trusts 194 n. 44 (1990).

including the fiduciaries, and so created "a purely arbitrary power of disposition." In District of Columbia v. Adams, 57 F. Supp. 946 (D.D.C. 1944), however, the court concluded that the following language created a mandatory power rather than a discretionary power in the executor: "I order that my executor shall collect all monies and property of any description due and belonging to me from any bank or insurance company, or from any other source, and dispose of all of the same according to his best judgment." The court held that the trust failed because no general power was intended and "those to whom the property is to be distributed are uncertain." In Leach v. Hyatt, 423 S.E.2d 165 (Va. 1992), the court treated a power in "executors" as a discretionary power, and seemed to be ignorant of the law on indefinite beneficiaries of a mandatory power.

3. *Reforming the Traditional Rules.* The Restatement 3d of Trusts §46(2), above, and UTC §402(c) attempt to change the traditional trust rules concerning indefinite beneficiaries. Both treat a power in a trustee to select a beneficiary from an indefinite class as a discretionary power, i.e., as a power that can but need not be exercised.

4. *"Friends" As an Indefinite Class.* Why does the word "friends" create a class too indefinite to sustain a trust? Recall what the court in Clark v. Campbell said about the point:

> The word "friends," unlike "relations," has no accepted statutory or other controlling limitations, and in fact has no precise sense at all. Friendship is a word of broad and varied application. It is commonly used to describe the undefinable relationships which exist, not only between those connected by ties of kinship or marriage, but as well between strangers in blood, and which vary in degree from the greatest intimacy to an acquaintance more or less casual.

The Restatement 3d of Trusts gives a somewhat different rationale for the indefiniteness of the word "friends":

> *§46 comment a.* A class of persons is indefinite... if the identity of all individuals comprising its membership cannot be ascertained. Although it is possible to determine that certain persons fall within a class and that others do not, it may be impossible to determine *all* of the persons who fall within it.... This is the case, for example, of a class consisting of all of the "friends" of the settlor or of another person.

5. *Meaning of "Relatives."* In Binns v. Vick, 538 S.W.2d 283 (Ark. 1976), a testator's residuary clause provided:

> All the rest and residue of my estate... I give, devise and bequeath [to] Kenneth Binns [a nephew of the testator and also the testator's executor] to distribute among my relatives as he sees fit.

The trial court held that a trust was intended, but failed for want of definite beneficiaries. The decision was affirmed. The court said that if "relatives" meant legal heirs, the appellant Binns' claim to the property beneficially must be denied because the testator's sole heir was a sister; and that if "relatives" meant all persons related to the testator, the bequest failed for uncertainty.

Compare the Restatement 3d of Trusts, which provides:

> *§45 comment d*. A trust for the benefit of "relatives" of the settlor or other designated person does not fail if the trustee has power to select who among the relatives shall take and in what portions.

See also UPC §2-711 (donative disposition of a present or a future interest to an individual's "relatives" or "family" is presumptively a disposition to the individual's heirs); Accord Cal. Prob. Code §21114.

EXTERNAL REFERENCES. George E. Palmer, Private Trusts for Indefinite Beneficiaries, 71 Mich. L. Rev. 359, 366-67 (1972); John Hopkins, Certain Uncertainties of Trusts and Powers, 29 Camb. L.J. 68 (1971).

———

Trusts for Pets. Can an animal be the beneficiary of a trust?

Estate of Searight
95 N.E.2d 779 (Ohio Ct. App. 1950)

HUNSICKER, J. George P. Searight, a resident of Wayne county, Ohio, died testate on November 27, 1948. Item "third" of his will provided:

> I give and bequeath my dog, Trixie, to Florence Hand of Wooster, Ohio, and I direct my executor to deposit in the Peoples Federal Savings and Loan Association, Wooster, Ohio, the sum of $1000.00 to be used by him to pay Florence Hand at the rate of 75 cents per day for the keep and care of my dog as long as it shall live. If my dog shall die before the said $1000.00 and the interest accruing therefrom shall have been used up, I give and bequeath whatever remains of said $1000.00 to be divided equally among those of the following persons who are living at that time, to wit: Bessie Immler, Florence Hand, Reed Searight, Fern Olson and Willis Horn.

At the time of his death, all of the persons, and his dog, Trixie, named in such item third, were living.

Florence Hand accepted the bequest of Trixie, and the executor paid to her from the $1000 fund, 75 cents a day for the keep and care of the dog. The value of Trixie was agreed to be $5....

We do not have, in the instant case, the question of a trust established for the care of dogs in general or of an indefinite number of dogs, but we are here considering the validity of a testamentary bequest for the benefit of a specific dog. This is not a charitable trust, nor is it a gift of money to the Ohio Humane Society or a county humane society, which societies are vested with broad statutory authority, Section 10062, General Code, for the care of animals.

Text writers on the subject of trusts and many law professors designate a bequest for the care of a specific animal as an "honorary trust"; that is, one binding the conscience of the trustee, since there is no beneficiary capable of enforcing the trust.

The rule in Ohio, that the absence of a beneficiary having a legal standing in court and capable of demanding an accounting of the trustee is fatal and the trust fails, was first announced in Mannix, Assignee, v. Purcell, 46 Ohio St. 102, 19 N.E. 572, 2 L.R.A. 753....

In 1 Scott on the Law of Trusts, Section 124, the author says:

> There are certain classes of cases similar to those discussed in the preceding section in that there is no one who as beneficiary can enforce the purpose of the testator, but different in one respect, namely, that the purpose is definite. Such, for example, are bequests for the erection or maintenance of tombstones or monuments or for the care of graves, and bequests for the support of specific animals. It has been held in a number of cases that such bequests as these do not necessarily fail. It is true that the legatee cannot be compelled to carry out the intended purpose, since there is no one to whom he owes a duty to carry out the purpose.
>
> Even though the legatee cannot be compelled to apply the property to the designated purpose, the courts have very generally held that he can properly do so, and that no resulting trust arises so long as he is ready and willing to carry it out. The legatee will not, however, be permitted to retain the property for his own benefit; and if he refuses or neglects to carry out the purpose, a resulting trust will arise in favor of the testator's residuary legatee or next of kin.

....To call this bequest for the care of the dog, Trixie, a trust in the accepted sense in which that term is defined is, we know, an unjustified conclusion. The modern authorities, as shown by the cases cited earlier in this discussion, however, uphold the validity of a gift for the purpose designated in the instant case, where the person to whom the power is given is willing to carry out the testator's wishes. Whether called an "honorary trust" or whatever terminology is used, we conclude that the bequest for the care of the dog, Trixie, is not in and of itself unlawful....

[As to the common-law Rule Against Perpetuities,] it is to be noted, in every situation where the so-called "honorary trust" is established for specific animals, that, unless the instrument creating such trust limits the duration of the trust—that is, the time during which the power is to be exercised—to human lives, we will have "honorary trusts" established for animals of great longevity, such as crocodiles, elephants and sea turtles....

If we then examine item third of testator's will, we discover that, although the bequest for his dog is for "as long as it shall live," the money given for this purpose is $1000 payable at the rate of 75¢ a day. By simple mathematical computation, this sum of money, expended at the rate determined by the testator, will be fully exhausted in three years and 238-1/3 days. If we assume that this $1000 is deposited in a bank so that interest at the high rate of 6% per annum were earned thereon, the time needed to consume both principal and interest thereon (based on semi-annual computation of such interest on the average unused balance during such six month period) would be four years, 57 ½ days.

It is thus very apparent that the testator provided a time limit for the exercise of the power given his executor, and that such time limit is much less than the maximum period allowed under the rule against perpetuities....

We therefore conclude that the bequest in the instant case for the care of the dog, Trixie, does not, by the terms of the creating instrument, violate the rule against perpetuities....

The judgment of the Probate Court is affirmed.

Notes

1. *The Tax Question in Searight.* Believe it or not, *Searight* was a state inheritance tax case. The Ohio Department of Taxation claimed that an inheritance tax was due on the amount devised to Trixie for Trixie's care and on the value of the devise of Trixie to Florence Hand. The Ohio statute imposed an inheritance tax on property passing "to or for the use of a person, institution or corporation." The court held that Trixie herself, a fox-terrier, was not any of these and no inheritance tax was due on the amount devised to Trixie for Trixie's care. An inheritance tax was, however, imposed on the devise of Trixie to Florence Hand. Trixie's value? $5.00.

2. *Trusts for Animals.* The UPC (in §2-907(b) and (c)) authorizes trusts for the care of a designated domestic or pet animal, authorizes the court to reduce extravagant amounts devised to such trusts, provides a mechanism for their enforcement, and limits the duration to the life of the animal. Similarly, UTC §408 provides that "[a] trust may be created to provide for the care of an animal alive during the settlor's lifetime" and directs that the trust terminate upon the animal's death. Under the UTC, you can create a trust for your favorite aunt or for your favorite ant!

3. *Honorary Trusts (Noncharitable Purpose Trusts).* Trusts have been upheld that provided for the saying of masses, for the erection of a tombstone, and the upkeep of a burial plot. Scott on Trusts §124.

Under the common-law Rule Against Perpetuities, a contingent future interest is invalid unless it is certain to vest, if at all, within a life in being plus 21 years from the creation of the interest. See Chapter 17. At common law, this period applies to honorary trusts; the trust is invalid if it may last longer than the perpetuities period. See Foshee v. Republic Nat'l Bank, 617 S.W.2d 675 (Tex. 1981) (perpetual trust to maintain family burial space in mausoleum). Neither courts nor writers have been in complete agreement on whether such a trust violates the rule against remoteness of vesting itself or only some associated rule. In Bryant Smith, Honorary Trusts and the Rule Against Perpetuities, 30 Colum. L. Rev. 60 (1930), the author suggested that the Rule Against Perpetuities was violated, on the theory that the trustee of the honorary trust has a nongeneral power of appointment, and that under perpetuities doctrine such a power is void if it is exercisable beyond a life in being plus 21 years. This position is embraced by other writers on perpetuities. See, e.g., John C. Gray, The Rule Against Perpetuities § 909.1 (4th ed. 1942); Scott on Trusts §124.1.

The UPC (in §2-907(a) and (c)) authorizes trusts for a specific lawful noncharitable purpose, authorizes the court to reduce extravagant amounts devised to such trusts, provides a mechanism for their enforcement, and limits the duration to 21 years. Similarly, UTC §409 provides that "[a] trust may be created for a noncharitable purpose without a definite or definitely ascertainable beneficiary or for a noncharitable but otherwise valid purpose to be selected by the trustee." The duration of such trusts is limited to 21 years.

The Restatement 3d of Trusts takes a somewhat different approach to the problem of noncharitable purpose trusts. Applying its "adapted trust" technique, it provides that a transferee of property for indefinite or general purposes, not limited to charitable purposes, holds the property "as trustee with the power but not the duty to distribute or apply the property...." Id. §47(1). Similarly, §47(2) provides:

> *§47(2). Trusts for Noncharitable Purposes.* If the owner of property transfers it in trust for a specific noncharitable purpose and no definite or ascertainable beneficiary is designated, unless the purpose is capricious, the transferee holds the property as trustee with power, exercisable for a specified or reasonable period of time normally not to exceed 21 years, to apply the property to the designated purpose; to whatever extent the power is not exercised (although this power is *not* presumptively personal), or the property exceeds what reasonably may be needed for the purpose, the trustee holds the property, or the excess, for distribution to reversionary beneficiaries implied by law.

Comment d goes on to explain that the 21-year period "is neither sacred nor necessarily suitable to all cases of adapted trust powers." Thus, for example, a trust power to maintain a grave "should be allowed for the lifetime of the decedent's spouse and children, or of other concerned individuals designated in the will...."

Some states, by statute, authorize perpetual noncharitable purpose trusts. Among these states are Oregon, see Or. Rev. Stat. §130.193 (authorizing a perpetual stewardship trust for a business purpose; other Oregon noncharitable purpose trusts are subject to the state's Rule Against Perpetuities), and Delaware, see 12 Del. Code §3556 (authorizing a perpetual noncharitable purpose trust for any "declared purpose that is not impossible of attainment"). Purposes might include stewardship of a business, preserving family vacation property, maintaining an art collection or a gravesite, publishing manuscripts that were unpublished at the author's death, promoting causes that do not meet the definition of "charitable" (see Chapter 12), or owning a family office (see Chapter 20).

EXTERNAL REFERENCES. Susan N. Gary, The Oregon Stewardship Trust, 88 U. Cin. L. Rev. 707 (2020); Richard C. Ausness, Non-Charitable Purpose Trusts: Past, Present, and Future, 51 Real Prop. Tr. & Est. L.J. 321 (2016).

3. Certainty of Intent

Primary Statutory References: *UTC §§401, 402*

Restatement 3d of Trusts

§13. Intention to Create Trust. A trust is created only if the settlor properly manifests an intention to create a trust relationship.

§14. Notice and Acceptance Not Required to Create Trust. A trust can be created without notice to or acceptance by any beneficiary or trustee.[22]

A trust is a property arrangement, requiring a *res* as its subject. Normally, the property forming the trust res is owned outright by the settlor. The trust is created when the ownership of that property is divided into its legal and equitable portions, with the legal title transferred to the trustee (or, in the case of a self-declared trust, retained by the settlor as trustee) and the equitable title portion transferred to (and further subdivided among) the beneficiaries.

The transfer of the equitable title to the beneficiaries via a self-declared trust does not require the same formalities as would be required for making an outright gift, such as physical, constructive, or symbolic delivery of the subject matter[23] or delivery of a document of transfer or some manifestation that the document is to be presently effective.[24] See UTC §§401(2), 402(a)(2). As the court said in Matter of Brown, 169 N.E. 612 (N.Y. 1930):

> [D]elivery is not necessary to constitute a valid trust. While a transfer of the property to a trustee for the purposes of the settlement may be the surest way to create a trust, yet the same result will be accomplished if the owner declares that he himself holds the property in trust for the person designated, and this trust may be created either in writing or, if relating to personal property, by parol. The declaration need not be made to the beneficiary, nor the writing given to him; in fact, his ignorance of the trust is immaterial. There must be proof of a declaration of trust in writing to pass real property, but the declaration varies with the circumstances of each case; it may be contained in a letter, or as here by formal witnessed statement. A declaration implies an announcement of an act

---

22. UTC §813(b), however, provides that a trustee "within 60 days after accepting a trusteeship, shall notify the qualified beneficiaries of the acceptance and of the trustee's name, address, and telephone number" and "within 60 days after the date the trustee acquires knowledge of the creation of an irrevocable trust, or the date the trustee acquires knowledge that a formerly revocable trust has become irrevocable, whether by the death of the settlor or otherwise, shall notify the qualified beneficiaries of the trust's existence, of the identity of the settlor or settlors, of the right to request a copy of the trust instrument, and of the right to a trustee's report...." Ed.

23. See Restatement 3d of Property §6.2.

24. See Restatement 3d of Property §6.2 comment yy, stating that "this Restatement adopts the position that a gift of personal property can be perfected on the basis of donative intent alone if the donor's intent to make a gift is established by clear and convincing evidence."

performed, not a mere intention, and in most instances to another party. However, a writing formally creating a trust, kept by the donor without delivery to any one, under such circumstances and conditions as to show that a trust was declared, created and intended, will be given effect....

The near absence of formality required to confer upon (transfer to) others the equitable interest in property, making them trust beneficiaries, has led to pressure to treat transactions that would otherwise fail, such as imperfect gifts, as self-declared trusts. This was the argument made, but not accepted, in the next case, Farmers' Loan & Trust Co. v. Winthrop. As background to understanding the *Winthrop* case, know that, unless modified by statute,[25] an agent's authority under a power of attorney is terminated by the death of the principal. For discussion of powers of attorney, see Chapter 18. Also note that an equitable interest, including the interest of a beneficiary of a trust, can itself be made the subject of a trust. Kekewich v. Manning, 1 DeG. M. & G. 176, 42 Eng. Rep. 519 (Ch. 1851); Merchants' Loan & Trust Co. v. Patterson, 139 N.E. 912 (Ill. 1923).

Farmers' Loan & Trust Co. v. Winthrop
144 N.E. 686 (N.Y. 1924)

CARDOZO, J. On February 3, 1920, Helen C. Bostwick executed her deed of trust to the Farmers' Loan & Trust Company as trustee. It is described as the 1920 deed, to distinguish it from an earlier one made in 1918, which is the subject of another action. By the later of the two deeds she gave to her trustee $5,000, "the said sum, and all other property hereafter delivered to said trustee as hereinafter provided," to be held upon the trusts and limitations therein set forth. The income was to be paid to her own use during life, and the principal on her death was to be divided into two parts—one for the benefit of the children of a deceased son, Albert; the other for the benefit of a daughter, Fannie, and the children of said daughter. The donor reserved "the right, at any time and from time to time during the continuance of the trusts, ... to deliver to said trustee additional property to be held by it" thereunder. She reserved also a power of revocation.

At the date of the execution of this deed, a proceeding was pending in the Surrogate's Court for the settlement of the accounts of the United States Trust Company as trustee of a trust under the will of [Helen's late husband,] Jabez A. Bostwick. The effect of the decree, when entered, would be to transfer to Mrs. Bostwick money, shares of stock, and other property of the value of upwards of $2,300,000. The plan was that this property, when ready to be transferred, should be delivered to the trustee, and held subject to the trust. On February 3, 1920,

---

25. The Uniform Power of Attorney Act §110(d) provides: "Termination of an agent's authority or of a power of attorney is not effective as to the agent or another person that, without actual knowledge of the termination, acts in good faith under the power of attorney. An act so performed, unless otherwise invalid or unenforceable, binds the principal and the principal's successors in interest."

simultaneously with the execution of the trust deed, three other documents, intended to effectuate this plan, were signed by the donor. One is a power of attorney whereby she authorized the Farmers' Loan & Trust Company as her attorney "to collect and receive any and all cash, shares of stock and other property" to which she might "be entitled under any decree or order made or entered" in the proceeding above mentioned. A second is a power of attorney authorizing the Farmers' Loan & Trust Company to sell and transfer any and all shares of stock then or thereafter standing in her name. A third is a letter, addressed to the Farmers' Loan & Trust Company, in which she states that she hands to the company the powers of attorney just described, and in which she gives instructions in respect of the action to be taken thereunder:

> My desire is and I hereby authorize you to receive from the United States Trust Company of New York all securities and property coming to me under the decree or order on the settlement of its account and to transfer such securities and property to yourself as trustee under agreement of trust bearing even date herewith executed by me to you.

The decree in the accounting proceeding was entered March 16, 1920. It established the right of Helen C. Bostwick to the payment or transfer of shares of stock and other property of the market value (then or shortly thereafter) of $2,327,353.70. On April 27, 1920, a representative of the Farmers' Loan & Trust Company presented the power of attorney to the United States Trust Company and stated that he was authorized to receive such securities as were ready for delivery. Shares of stock having a market value of $856,880 were handed to him then and there. No question is made that these became subject to the provisions of the deed of trust. The controversy arises in respect of the rest of the securities, $1,470,473.70 in value, which were retained in the custody of the United States Trust Company, apparently for the reason that they were not yet ready for delivery. During the night of April 27, 1920, Helen C. Bostwick died. She left a will, appointing the Farmers' Loan & Trust Company executor, and disposing of an estate of the value of over $20,000,000. The securities retained, as we have seen, in the custody of the United States Trust Company, were delivered on or about July 13, 1920, to the executor under the will. Conflicting claims of ownership are made by the legatees under the will and the remaindermen under the deed.

We think, with the majority of the Appellate Division, that the gift remained inchoate at the death of the donor. There is no occasion to deny that in the setting of other circumstances a power of attorney, authorizing a donee to reduce to possession the subject of a gift, may be significant as evidence of a symbolical delivery. We assume, without deciding, that such effect will be allowed if, apart from the power, there is established an intention that the title of the donor shall be presently divested and presently transferred.... [T]here is here no expression of a purpose to effectuate a present gift. The power of attorney, standing by itself, results, as all concede, in the creation of a revocable agency.

If something more was intended, if what was meant was a gift that was to be operative at once, the expression of the meaning will have to be found elsewhere, in the deed of trust or in the letter. Neither in the one, however, nor in the other, can such a purpose be discerned. Deed and letter alike are framed on the assumption that the gift is executory and future, and this though the addition of a few words would have established it beyond cavil as executed and present. In the deed there is a present transfer of $5,000 and no more. This wrought, there is merely the reservation of a privilege to augment the subject-matter of the trust by deliveries thereafter. The absence of words of present assignment is emphasized when we consider with what simplicity an assignment could have been stated. All that was needed was to expand the description by a phrase:

> The right, title, and interest of the grantor in the securities and other property due or to become due from the United States Trust Company as trustee under the will.

The deed and the other documents, we must remember, were not separated in time. They were parts of a single plan, and were executed together. In these circumstances, a present transfer, if intended, would naturally have found its place in the description of the deed itself. If omitted for some reason there, the least we should expect would be to find it in the letter. Again words of present transfer are conspicuously absent. What we have instead is a request, or at best a mandate, incompetent without more to divest title, or transfer it, serving no other purpose than a memorandum of instructions from principal to agent as a guide to future action. Deed and documents were prepared by counsel learned in the law. With industrious iteration, they rejected the familiar formulas that would have given unmistakable expression to the transfer of a present title. With like iteration, they chose the words and methods appropriate to a gift that was conceived of as executory and future. We must take the transaction as they made it. The very facility with which they could have made it something else is a warning that we are not at liberty, under the guise of construction, to make it other than it is. They were willing to leave open what they might readily have closed. Death overtook the signer before the gap was filled.

Viewed thus as a gift, the transaction was inchoate. An intention may be assumed, and indeed is not disputed, that what was incomplete at the moment should be completed in the future. The difficulty is that the intention was never carried out. Mrs. Bostwick remained free (apart from any power of revocation reserved in the deed of trust) to revoke the executory mandate, and keep the property as her own. Very likely different forms and instrumentalities would have been utilized, if he or she counsel had supposed that death was to come so swiftly. We might say as much if she had left in her desk a letter or memorandum expressing her resolutions for the morrow. With appropriate forms and instrumentalities available, she chose what the course of events has proved to be the wrong one. The court is without power to substitute another.

The transaction, failing as a gift, because inchoate or incomplete, is not to be sustained as the declaration of a trust. The donor had no intention of becoming a trustee herself. The donee never got title, and so could not hold it for another.

There was no equitable assignment. Equity does not enforce a voluntary promise to make a gift thereafter....

One other question is in the case. It concerns the right of the executor to charge a proportionate part of the estate and inheritance taxes upon the interest of the remaindermen under the 1920 deed of trust. For the reasons stated in another action between the same parties involving the 1918 deed, the federal taxes are to be borne by the residuary estate.

The judgment of the Appellate Division should be modified, so as to affirm the judgment entered on the report of the referee in respect of the payment of the federal estate taxes, and, as so modified, affirmed, with a separate bill of costs to each party or set of parties appearing by separate attorney and to the several guardians ad litem, all payable out of the estate.

Notes

1. *A Constructive Trust Approach.* The Restatement 3d of Trusts §16 adopts a different approach that would have changed the outcome in *Winthrop*. It provides that the trust intent of someone who dies or becomes incompetent before the transfer is completed "may be given effect by a constructive trust in order to prevent unjust enrichment of the property owner's successor's in interest." See id. comment c, illustration 8. See also Restatement 3d of Property §6.1 comment o; Restatement 3d of Restitution and Unjust Enrichment §11.

2. *Origins of the* Winthrop *Principle.* That an imperfect gift should not be salvaged by attributing to the would-be donor a fictitious intent to create a self-declared trust has pretty well been settled since Richards v. Delbridge, L.R. 18 Eq. 11 (1874). The principle is adopted in the Restatement 3d of Trusts §16(2) and is codified by statute in some states. See, e.g., Cal. Prob. Code §§15200, 15201; Tex. Prop. Code §§112.001, 112.002.

3. *Consideration Not Required.* The law is well settled that no consideration is required to support a self-declared trust. See Restatement 3d of Trusts §15. The point is stated explicitly in the California and Texas codifications of the law of trusts. Cal. Prob. Code §15208; Tex. Prop. Code §112.003. The California statute states:

> *§15208. Consideration.* Consideration is not required to create a trust, but a promise to create a trust in the future is enforceable only if the requirements for an enforceable contract are satisfied.

———

Precatory Language. The next case, Colton v. Colton, explores another aspect of an intent to create a trust—whether, in a given case, "precatory" language in a will or other governing instrument is properly interpreted as creating a trust. The Restatement 3d of Trusts §13 comment d provides:

> *d. Precatory language.* Unless a testator or other transferor manifests an intention to impose enforceable duties on the transferee, the intention to create a trust is lacking and no trust is created....

The distinction, therefore, is between imposing legally enforceable duties on the devisee and merely seeking to impose a moral obligation on the devisee. In determining whether the transferor intended to impose enforceable legal duties rather than a moral obligation, the Restatement 3d of Trusts §13 comment d lists the following factors to be considered:

> (1) the specific terms and overall tenor of the words used; (2) the definiteness or indefiniteness of the property involved; (3) the ease or difficulty of ascertaining possible trust purposes and terms, and the specificity or vagueness of the possible beneficiaries and their interests; (4) the interests or motives and the nature and degree of concerns that may reasonably be supposed to have influenced the transferor; (5) the financial situation, dependencies, and expectations of the parties; (6) the transferor's prior conduct, statements, and relationships with respect to possible trust beneficiaries; (7) the personal and any fiduciary relationships between the transferor and the transferee; (8) other dispositions the transferor is making or has made of his or her wealth; and (9) whether the result of construing the disposition as involving a trust or not would be such as a person in the situation of the transferor would be likely to desire.

In the *Colton* case below, what result would these factors have produced?

Colton v. Colton
127 U.S. 300 (1888)

These are two bills in equity, one filed by Martha Colton and the other by Abigail R. Colton, each of whom is a citizen of the state of New York, against Ellen M. Colton, a citizen of California.

Martha Colton alleges in her bill that she was a sister of David D. Colton, who died in San Francisco, Cal., on October 9, 1878, and that the defendant, Ellen M. Colton, is his widow; that on October 8, 1878, the said David D. Colton made and executed in due form his last will and testament, a copy of which is made a part of the bill, and is set out as follows:

> I, David D. Colton, of San Francisco, make this my last will and testament. I declare that all of the estate of which I shall die possessed is community property, and was acquired since my marriage with my wife. I give and bequeath to my said wife, Ellen M. Colton, all of the estate, real and personal, of which I shall die seized or possessed or entitled to. I recommend to her the care and protection of my mother and sister, and request her to make such gift and provision for them as in her judgment will be best....

The bill then alleges that the estate of David D. Colton thus distributed to the defendant was of the value of about $1,000,000, and that the defendant, though often demanded, has failed, neglected, and refused to make to the plaintiff any gift or provision whatever from the estate of said David D. Colton....

[The bill filed by Abigail, mother of the testator, was much the same as Martha Colton's bill, except that it also alleged that the petitioner was 75 years old and in poor health, that her only income was the interest on a sum of $15,000, and that she was in "very straitened circumstances." A demurrer was sustained to each bill. The trial judge concluded that the "precatory words" of the will did not create a trust. 21 F. 594 (1884).]

MATTHEWS J. These appeals bring before us the will of David D. Colton for construction. The question is whether his widow, Ellen M. Colton, by its provisions, takes the whole estate of which he died seized and possessed absolutely in her own right, or whether she takes it charged with a trust enforceable in equity in favor of the complainants, and, if so, to what extent.... No technical language... is necessary to the creation of a trust, either by deed or by will. It is not necessary to use the words "upon trust" or "trustee," if the creation of a trust is otherwise sufficiently evident. If it appear to be the intention of the parties from the whole instrument creating it that the property conveyed is to be held or dealt with for the benefit of another, a court of equity will affix to it the character of a trust, and impose corresponding duties upon the party receiving the title, if it be capable of lawful enforcement....

The situation of the testator at the time he framed these provisions is to be considered. He made his will October 8, 1878; he died the next day. It may be assumed that it was made in view of impending dissolution, in the very shadow of approaching death. There is room enough for the supposition that by this necessity the contents of his will were required to be brief; the conception of the general idea to give everything to his wife was simple and easily expressed, and capable of covering all other intended dispositions. The time and the circumstances perhaps disabled him from specifying satisfactory details concerning a provision for his mother and his sister, but he did not forget that he owed them care and protection. That care and protection, therefore, he recommended to his wife as his legatee; but he was not satisfied with that; he wished that care and protection to be embodied in a gift and provision for them out of the estate which he was to leave to her. He therefore requested her to make it, and that request he addressed to his legatee and principal beneficiary as expressive of his will that a gift and provision for his mother and sister should come out of it....

It is an error to suppose that the word "request" necessarily imports an option to refuse, and excludes the idea of obedience as corresponding duty. If a testator requests his executor to pay a given sum to a particular person, the legacy would be complete and recoverable. According to its context and manifest use, an expression of desire or wish will often be equivalent to a positive direction, where that is the evident purpose and meaning of the testator; as where a testator desired that all of his just debts, and those of a firm for which he was not liable, should be paid as soon as convenient after his decease, it was construed to operate as a legacy in favor of the creditors of the latter. Burt v. Herron, 66 Pa. St. 400. And in such a case as the present, it would be but natural for the testator to suppose that a request, which, in its terms, implied no alternative, addressed to his widow and principal legatee, would be understood and obeyed as strictly as though it were couched in the language of direction and command....

On the whole, therefore, our conclusion is that each of the complainants in these bills is entitled to take a beneficial interest under the will of David D. Colton, to the extent, out of the estate given by him to his wife, of a permanent provision for them during their respective lives, suitable and sufficient for their care and protection, having regard to their condition and necessities, and the amount and value of the fund from which it must come. It will be the duty of the court to ascertain after proper inquiry, and thereupon to determine and declare, what provision will be suitable and best under the circumstances, and all particulars and details for securing and paying it. The decrees of the circuit court are accordingly reversed, and the causes remanded, with directions to overrule the demurrers to the several bills, and to take with this opinion; and it is so ordered.

EXTERNAL REFERENCE. Frank L. Schiavo, Does the Use of "Request," "Wish," or "Desire" Create a Precatory Trust or Not?, 40 Real Prop., Prob. & Tr. J. 647 (2006).

4. Certainty of Trustee?

Primary Statutory References: *UTC §§701, 703-705*

Restatement 3d of Trusts

§31. Trust Does Not Fail for Lack of Trustee. A trust does not fail because no trustee is designated or because the designated trustee declines, is unable, or ceases to act, unless the trust's creation or continuation depends on a specific person serving as trustee; a proper court will appoint a trustee as necessary and appropriate (see §34).

Adams v. Adams
88 U.S. (21 Wall.) 185 (1874)

Appeal from the Supreme Court of the District of Columbia. The case was thus: Adams, a government clerk, in Washington, owning a house and lot there, on the 13th of August, 1861, executed, with his wife, a deed of the premises to one Appleton, in fee, as trustee for the wife. The deed by appropriate words *in praesenti* conveyed, so far as its terms were concerned, the property for the sole and separate use of the wife for life, with power to lease and to take the rents for her own use, as if she was a *feme sole*; the trustee having power, on request of the wife, to sell and convey the premises in fee and pay the proceeds to her or as she might direct; and after her death (no sale having been made), the trust being that the trustee should hold the property for the children of the marriage as tenants in common, and in default of issue living at the death of the wife, then for Adams, the husband, his heirs and assigns.

The deed was signed by the grantors, and the husband acknowledged it before two justices "to be his act and deed." The wife did the same; being separately examined. The instrument purported to be "signed, sealed, and delivered" in the presence of the same justices, and they signed it as attesting witnesses. The husband put it himself on record in the registry of deeds for the county of Washington, D.C., which was the appropriate place of record for it.

Subsequent to this, that is to say in September, 1870, the husband and wife were divorced by judicial decree.

And subsequently to this again, that is to say, in December, 1871—the husband being in possession of the deed, and denying that any trust was ever created and executed, and Appleton, [declining] the wife's request... to assert the trust, or to act as trustee, Mrs. Adams filed a bill in the court below against them both, to establish the deed as a settlement made upon her by her husband, to compel a delivery of it to her; to remove Appleton, the trustee named in it, and to have some suitable person appointed trustee in his place....

The bill further alleged the dissolution of the marriage by law, and that the complainant, relying upon the provisions of the deed referred to, neither sought nor obtained alimony in that suit; and further, that she has accepted, and still accepted the benefits of the trust; that Appleton declined to act as trustee, to allow the use of his name, or in any way to aid her in the matter; that her husband, the defendant, was in possession receiving the rents and profits, and declined to acknowledge her rights in the premises....

Appleton also answered, alleging that if any such deed as described was executed, it was executed without his knowledge or consent; that no such deed was ever delivered to him, and that he never accepted any trust imposed by it; that he was never informed of the existence of the deed till 1870, when he was informed of it by the complainant, and that he then declined to act as trustee....

The court below declared the trust valid and effective in equity as between the parties; appointed a new trustee; required the husband to deliver up the deed to the wife or to the new trustee; and to deliver also to him possession of the premises described in the deed of trust, and to account before the master for the rents and profits of it which had accrued since the filing of the bill, receiving credit for any payment made to the complainant in the meantime, and to pay the complainant's costs of the suit.

From a decree accordingly, the husband appealed.

HUNT J.... Upon the evidence before us we have no doubt that the deed was executed, acknowledged, and recorded by the defendant with the intent to make provision for his wife and children; that he took the deed into his own possession with the understanding, and upon the belief on his part, that he had accomplished that purpose by acknowledging and procuring the record of the deed, by showing the same to his wife, informing her of its contents, and placing the same in the house therein conveyed in a place equally accessible to her and to himself.

The defendant now seeks to repudiate what he then intended, and to overthrow what he then asserted and believed he had then accomplished.

It may be conceded, as a general rule, that delivery is essential, both in law and in equity, to the validity of a gift, whether of real or personal estate. What constitutes a delivery is a subject of great difference of opinion, some cases holding that a parting with a deed, even for the purpose of recording, is in itself a delivery.

It may be conceded also to have been held many times that courts of equity will not enforce a merely gratuitous gift of mere moral obligation.

These concessions do not, however, dispose of the present case....

We are of opinion that the refusal of Appleton, in 1870, to accept the deed, or to act as trustee, is not a controlling circumstance.

Although a trustee may never have heard of the deed, the title vests in him, subject to a disclaimer on his part. Such disclaimer will not, however, defeat the conveyance as a transfer of the equitable interest to a third person. A trust cannot fail for want of a trustee, or by the refusal of all the trustees to accept the trust. The court of chancery will appoint new trustees....

The defense rests upon the alleged non-delivery by Mr. Adams of the deed of August 13th, 1861, to Mrs. Adams, or for her benefit. We have referred at length to the authorities which show that as matter of law the deed was sufficiently delivered, and that it is the duty of the court to establish the trust.

We think that the decree of the court below was well made, and that it should be AFFIRMED.

Notes

1. *Resignation Distinguished from Disclaimer.* In *Adams*, the trustee, Appleton, disclaimed the trust. A trustee can always disclaim (refuse to accept) a trust (see UTC §701), but once accepted, the trustee can resign only with the permission of the appropriate court, or in accordance with the terms of the trust, or with the consent of the beneficiaries if they are competent to give such consent. See the differing provisions of UTC §705 and Restatement 3d of Trusts §36. See also Tex. Prop. Code §113.081; Cal. Prob. Code §15640. Trust instruments often provide that the trustee may resign, as in Article VI of the Sample Inter Vivos Trust reproduced above at p. 466.

2. *Devolution of a Trustee's Title Upon Death.* At common law, a sole trustee's title to the trust property passed to his or her heirs on the trustee's death intestate and

could also be disposed of by will. Restatement 2d of Trusts §§104, 105. In some states, this has been changed by statute; New York, for example, provides that title "vests in the supreme court or the surrogate's court, as the case may be, and the trust shall be executed by a person appointed by the court...." N.Y. Est. Powers & Trust Law §7-2.3. Trust documents commonly take control of this question by expressly designating a successor trustee.

Co-trustees hold title as joint tenants so that, on the death of one, legal title to the trust property is in the survivor. Reichert v. Missouri & Illinois Coal Co., 83 N.E. 166 (Ill. 1907); UTC §704(b); Restatement 3d of Trusts §34 comment d.

3. *Multiple Trustees; Exercise of Powers.* Traditionally, co-trustees of a private trust must all join in the exercise of their powers as trustees, unless the terms of the trust or of a statute provide otherwise. This rule did not apply, however, to charitable trusts, where action could be taken by a majority of the trustees if there are three or more. Restatement 3d of Trusts §39 and the UTC §703, however, break new ground by extending the majority-rule principle to private trusts having three or more trustees. Some states have statutes reaffirming the traditional rule. See, e.g., Cal. Prob. Code §15620 (two or more co-trustees). In other states statutes apply the majority-vote rule of charitable trusts to private non-charitable trusts. See, e.g., N.Y. EPTL §10-10.7 (three or more co-trustees).

4. *Lack of a Trustee.* Suppose that G dies leaving a will that devises his or her entire estate in trust to named beneficiaries. Or, suppose that the will names a trustee but the designated trustee dies prior to G's death. Is there a valid trust? In these circumstances, courts will appoint a trustee to carry out the term of the will, relying on the time-honored principle that a trust will not fail for lack of a trustee. See, e.g., Restatement 3d of Trusts §14 comment b; § 31; UTC §704; Estate of McCray, 268 P. 647 (Cal. 1928); Woodruff v. Woodruff, 16 A. 4 (N.J. Ch. 1888).

PART C. FORMALITIES IN THE CREATION OF A TRUST

Primary Statutory Reference: *UTC §407*

Apart from the substantive requirements just discussed—the three certainties—trust law imposes no formal requirements for creating a trust. A declaration of trust of personal property may be entirely oral.[26] See Restatement 3d of Trusts §20; UTC §407 (requiring proof of an oral trust by clear and convincing evidence). However, as the old maxim states, "equity follows the law." There are two situations in which certain statutory formalities apply. One situation is where the subject matter of an inter vivos trust is land. Here, the Statute of Frauds imposes

---

26. Only a few states have statutes that impose a writing requirement for inter vivos trusts of personalty. See, e.g., Ga. Code §53-12-20(a) (applying to all express trusts); Ind. Code §30-4-2-1(a). The UTC and California require clear and convincing evidence. UTC §407; Cal. Prob. Code §15207.

the requirement of a signed writing. The other situation involves trusts created at the settlor's death by will. Testamentary trusts are subject to the requirements of the Statute of Wills.

Both the Statute of Frauds and Statute of Wills impose formalities for evidentiary reasons. In some situations, however, the question arises whether other policy objectives should override these evidentiary concerns.

1. Inter Vivos Trusts of Land: Statute of Frauds

Most states have statutes that require trusts of real property to be evidenced by a signed writing. See Restatement 3d of Trusts §§22-24. The statutes vary in their language. Some explicitly provide that trusts of land must be "created or declared" by a writing,[27] while others require that trusts of real property be proved by a writing of the transferor or transferee.[28] Statutes of the latter type are based on §7 of the English Statute of Frauds 1677. The conceptual distinction between a writing requirement necessary to *effect* a transfer and one required only to *prove* the transfer, however, appears to have had little, if any, influence on the substantive development of the law. It is generally thought that the writing requirement affects the trust's enforcement and not its existence.

Typically, the writing requirement is met by a formal written instrument that is signed by both the settlor and the trustee or, in the case of a self-declared trust, by the settlor alone. In a few states, there is no statutory requirement that a trust of land be evidenced by a writing. See, e.g., Ellis v. Vespoint, 403 S.E.2d 542 (N.C. Ct. App. 1991); Burns v. Equitable Assoc., 265 S.E.2d 737 (Va. 1980). In these states, the problem becomes one under the parol-evidence rule: May extrinsic evidence be admitted to show that, despite a deed absolute in form, the grantee was merely to hold the land in trust? Usually, the extrinsic evidence is received. See, e.g., Boggs v. Yates, 132 S.E. 876 (W. Va. 1926); however, a few states do not permit proof of the oral trust where the grantor himself or herself was the intended beneficiary. The Restatement 3d of Trusts §21 provides that where a writing purporting to transfer the property does exist but does not affirmatively declare "that the transferee is to take the property for the transferee's own benefit or that the transferee is to hold it upon a particular trust...," extrinsic evidence is admissible to show that the transferor intended that the transferee hold the property in trust, either for the transferor or a third person. UTC §407 provides that "[e]xcept as required by a statute other than this [Code], a trust need not be evidenced by a trust instrument, but the creation of an oral trust and its terms may be established only by clear and convincing evidence."

Finally, as indicated earlier, even if the statute states that an oral trust of land is

---

27. See, e.g., Ga. Code §53-12-20(a); Mass. Gen. Laws ch. 203, §1; Me. Rev. Stat. tit. 33, §851.

28. E.g., Fla. Stat. §689.05; Mo. Stat. §456.4-407; Pa. Stat. tit. 33, §2.

void, courts have treated such trusts as voidable only. If the trustee does not raise the bar of the Statute of Frauds, the trust is enforceable. In consequence, creditors of an oral trustee cannot defeat the trust if the trustee chooses to recognize it.

Hays v. Regar
1 N.E. 386 (Ind. 1885)

MITCHELL, C. J. On the fifteenth day of August, 1872, William Regar was the owner of a lot in Davidson's Heirs' addition to the city of Indianapolis. On that day, his wife joining, he conveyed it to John Stumph by an absolute deed. This conveyance was made without any consideration, and upon a parol trust that the title should be held for the benefit of Regar, who remained in possession and paid the taxes. On the ninth day of February, 1878, by the direction of Regar, Stumph and wife conveyed the lot to the appellee, Regar's wife. While the title was in Stumph in the manner stated, Hays & Wiles recovered a judgment against him in the Marion superior court. After the lot was conveyed to Mrs. Regar, the city of Indianapolis, by due proceedings, condemned it for street purposes, assessing damages to Mrs. Regar at $412.50. This sum was paid into the city treasury. Hays & Wiles claimed the money, or part of it, from the city treasurer, on account of the alleged lien of their judgment, which was acquired while the legal title was in Stumph. This suit was brought by Mrs. Regar against the city and its treasurer, and Hays & Wiles, for the purpose of establishing her right to the money.

The determination of a single question which is raised on the record in various ways settles all there is in the case. Appellants claim that, because the deed from Regar and wife to Stumph was absolute, and the alleged trust in favor of Regar rested in parol, the lot was bound by the lien of the Hays & Wiles judgment, and that it was, therefore, not competent to aver and prove the parol trust. There is no claim of any fraud in the transaction. It is averred in an answer, to which a demurrer was sustained, that the judgment of Hays & Wiles was rendered upon a note executed by Stumph to them, and that the consideration of the note was goods and merchandise sold by them to him on the faith that he was the owner of the lot. The question is, not whether the parol trust may be enforced, but, the parties having voluntarily executed it, is it competent to aver and prove that it existed, in order to defeat the apparent lien of Hays & Wiles' judgment?

The case cannot be distinguished in principle from Moore v. Cottingham, 90 Ind. 239, in which it was decided, in a well-considered opinion by Best, C. J., that, although the trust rested in parol since it had been executed, proof of the facts will be allowed as against the claim of a judgment creditor. It is insisted that Moore v. Cottingham, supra, effects a virtual abrogation of section 2969, Rev. St. 1881, which inhibits the creation of trusts concerning lands, unless such trusts arise by implication of law, or are created by writing, signed by the party creating the same. We think no such consequences follow from the decision referred to. This statute, as also the statute of frauds, was enacted, not that parties might avoid trusts which were executed, but rather to enable them, in case of an attempt to enforce such trusts while they remained executory, to insist on certain modes of proof in order to establish them. The trust having been executed, we need not determine whether it was one arising by implication of law, or whether it was an express trust. Whether it was one or the other, the parties having voluntarily executed it, the authorities are that it may be proved by parol for the purpose of showing that the apparent owner had no interest which was subject to the lien of a judgment against him....

The interest which the lien of a judgment affects is the actual interest which the debtor has in property, and a court of equity will always permit the real owner to show, there being no intervening fraud, that the apparent ownership of another is or was not real, and when the judgment debtor has no other interest except the naked legal title, the lien of a judgment does not attach....

As Stumph had nothing but the naked legal title to the lot, Regar remaining in possession, and as it does not appear that there was any fraud or concealment, or that Stumph's deed was of record, even, or that Regar had any knowledge of the credit extended to him, the fact that goods were sold to him on the faith of his title cannot estop the appellee to show her right.

We find no error in the record. Judgment affirmed, with costs.

Note and Questions

1. *Questions.* Do you agree with *Hays*? Why did the court recognize the trust despite the settlor's failure to comply with the Statute of Frauds?

2. *Statutes.* The result in *Hays* is codified in some states. See, e.g., Tex. Prop. Code §101.002.

2. Testamentary Trusts: Statute of Wills

Suppose a testator's will devises property to a devisee outright. After the testator's death, a plaintiff alleges that the devisee had promised the testator that the devisee would hold the property in trust for the benefit of the plaintiff. Or, suppose a testator's will expressly indicates that a devisee is to hold the devised property in trust, but neglects to state the substantive terms of the trust, including the intended beneficiary. The two situations involve so-called "secret" and "partially secret" trusts, respectively. Both situations involve issues concerning compliance with the Statute of Wills.

Oral ("Secret") Testamentary Trusts. If the plaintiff, who claims to be the intended beneficiary of an oral testamentary trust, proves that the devisee promised to hold the property in trust for the plaintiff, whether the promise was made before or after the will was executed, most jurisdictions impose a constructive trust on the devisee in favor of the plaintiff. See Restatement 3d of Trusts §18.

In the leading case of Trustees of Amherst College v. Ritch, 45 N.E. 876 (N.Y. 1897), the court gave this explanation for the result:

[I]f the testator is induced either to make a will or not to change one after it is made, by a promise, express or implied, on the part of a legatee that he will devote his legacy to a certain lawful purpose, a secret trust is created, and equity will compel him to apply property thus obtained in accordance with his promise.... The trust springs from the intention of the testator and the promise of the legatee. The same rule applies to heirs and next of kin who induce their ancestor or relative not to make a will by promising, in case his property falls to them through intestacy, to dispose of it, or a part of it, in the manner indicated by him.... The rule is founded on the principle that the legacy would not have been given, or intestacy allowed to ensue, unless the promise had been made; and hence the person promising is bound, in equity, to keep it, as to violate it would be fraud. While a promise is essential, it need not be expressly made, for active co-operation or silent acquiescence may have the same effect as an express promise. If a legatee knows what the testator expects of him, and having an opportunity to speak, says nothing, it may be equivalent to a promise, provided the testator acts upon it. Whenever it appears that the testator was prevented from action by the action or silence of a legatee, who knew the facts in time to act or speak, he will not be permitted to apply the legacy to his own use when that would defeat the expectations of the testator....

The trust does not act directly upon the will by modifying the gift, for the law requires wills to be wholly in writing, but it acts upon the gift itself as it reaches the possession of the legatee, or as soon as he is entitled to receive it. The theory is that the will has full effect, by passing an absolute legacy to the legatee, and that then equity, in order to defeat fraud, raises a trust in favor of those intended to be benefited by the testator, and compels the legatee, as a trustee ex maleficio, to turn over the gift to them. The law, not the will, fastens the trust upon the fund, by requiring the legatee to act in accordance with the instructions of the testator and his own promise. Neither the statute of frauds nor the statute of wills applies, because the will takes effect as written and proved; but, to promote justice and prevent wrong, the courts compel the legatee to dispose of his gift in accordance with equity and good conscience.

The Restatement 3d of Trusts §18 comment h states that "the existence of the agreement to hold the property in trust must be shown by clear and convincing evidence." The rationale is that the proof must overcome "what appears on the face of the will to be an outright bequest or devise...." Accord, Restatement 3d of Property §12.1 comment b.

Although there is little dissent in the cases from the proposition of the *Ritch* case,[29] the result has been criticized. Professor Scott argued that the decisions giving relief in favor of the intended beneficiary are in conflict with the Statute of Wills.[30] In his view, the unjust enrichment should be remedied by imposing a constructive trust in favor of those who would be entitled to the property had the devise not been made. See, however, the following for discussions approving the results of the cases:

---

29. Cases are collected in Annots., 66 A.L.R. 156; 155 A.L.R. 106.

30. Scott on Trusts §55.1 (3d ed. 1967).

Restatement 3d of Trusts §18; John H. Langbein & Lawrence W. Waggoner, Reformation of Wills on the Ground of Mistake: Change of Direction in American Law?, 130 U. Pa. L. Rev. 521, 574-76 (1982).

———

Partially Oral ("Partially Secret") Testamentary Trusts. A partially secret trust typically arises where the transfer in trust is in writing but the terms of the trust are not. Should the trust be upheld? Consider the following case.

Olliffe v. Wells
130 Mass. 221 (1881)

[Ellen Donovan died in 1877. Her will devised the residue of her estate "to the Rev. Eleazer M.P. Wells... to distribute the same in such manner as in his discretion shall appear best calculated to carry out wishes which I have expressed to him or may express to him." Her will also nominated the Reverend Wells to be the executor. Donovan's heirs sued, claiming that the residue should be distributed to them. The Reverend Wells claimed the right to carry out Donovan's wishes, which she had expressed to him orally, and to which he had assented before she executed her will. According to Rev. Wells, her intention was that the residue be used to provide for persons who were under the care of the St. Stephen's Mission of Boston.[31] The heirs treated Rev. Wells' allegation as true.]

GRAY, C.J. Upon the face of this will the residuary bequest to the defendant gives him no beneficial interest. It expressly requires him to distribute all the property bequeathed to him, giving him no discretion upon the question whether he shall or shall not distribute it, or shall or shall not carry out the intentions of the testatrix, but allowing him a discretionary authority as to the manner only in which the property shall be distributed according to her intentions. The will declares a trust too indefinite to be carried out, and the next of kin of the testatrix must take by way of a resulting trust, unless the facts agreed show such a trust for the benefit of others as the court can execute. Nichols v. Allen, [130 Mass.] 211. No other written instrument was signed by the testatrix, and made part of the will by reference....

...[I]t has been held in England that, if a testator devises or bequeaths property to his executors upon trusts not defined in the will, but which, as he states in the will, he has communicated to them before its execution, such trusts, if for lawful purposes, may be proved by the admission of the executors, or by oral evidence, and enforced against them.... And in two or three comparatively recent cases it has been held that such trusts may be enforced against the heirs or next of kin of the testator,

---

31. The St. Stephen's Mission was destroyed in the great Boston fire of 1872. Rev. Wells worked to restore the mission, but to no avail. Rev. Wells died in 1878 at age 95. In reading the court's opinion, consider whether these facts might have influenced the result. (We owe information about the St. Stephen's Mission to Jesse Dukeminier & Stanley M. Johanson, Wills, Trusts, and Estates 485-86 n.32 (4th ed. 1990)). Ed.

as well as against the devisee.... But these cases appear to us to have overlooked or disregarded a fundamental distinction.

Where a trust not declared in the will is established by a court of chancery against the devisee, it is by reason of the obligation resting upon the conscience of the devisee, and not as a valid testamentary disposition by the deceased.... Where the bequest is outright upon its face, the setting up of a trust, while it diminishes the right of the devisee, does not impair any right of the heirs or next of kin, in any aspect of the case; for if the trust were not set up, the whole property would go to the devisee by force of the devise; if the trust set up is a lawful one, it enures to the benefit of the *cestuis que trust*; and if the trust set up is unlawful, the heirs or next of kin take by way of resulting trust....

[In the present case, w]here the bequest is declared upon its face to be upon such trusts as the testator has otherwise signified to the devisee, it is equally clear that the devisee takes no beneficial interest; and, as between him and the beneficiaries intended, there is as much ground for establishing the trust as if the bequest to him were absolute on its face. But as between the devisee and the heirs or next of kin, the case stands differently. They are not excluded by the will itself. The will upon its face showing that the devisee takes the legal title only and not the beneficial interest, and the trust not being sufficiently defined by the will to take effect, the equitable interest goes, by way of resulting trust, to the heirs or next of kin, as property of the deceased, not disposed of by his will. Sears v. Hardy, 120 Mass. 524, 541, 542. They cannot be deprived of that equitable interest, which accrues to them directly from the deceased, by any conduct of the devisee; nor by any intention of the deceased, unless signified in those forms which the law makes essential to every testamentary disposition. A trust not sufficiently declared on the face of the will cannot therefore be set up by extrinsic evidence to defeat the rights of the heirs at law or next of kin....

Decree for the plaintiffs.

Notes and Questions

1. *Contrary Authority.* As the court's opinion in *Olliffe* indicated, the English courts do not differentiate between partially oral and completely oral testamentary trusts; they uphold both types. The principal decision is Blackwell v. Blackwell, [1929] App. Cas. 318 (H.L.). In that case, Blackwell's will devised £12,000 to five named persons "upon trust... for the purposes indicated by me to them." Blackwell communicated to some of the trustees his intention that the fund be used to care for a "woman... who was not his wife" and their sixteen-year-old son,[32] and these

---

32. Historically, completely oral and partially oral trusts were sometimes created by wealthy men who wished to provide for their mistresses and/or nonmarital children. See Simon Gardner, An Introduction to the Law of Trusts 85-87 (1990). Disclosing the terms of the trust in the will was undesirable because a probated will is a public document. Nowadays, of course, there are other, more

trustees accepted the trust. The court held that a trust was created.

The Restatement 1st of Trusts adopted the English view in 1935 and has adhered to it in the most recent revision. See Restatement 3d of Trusts §18(1) comment c. However, the Reporter's Notes to comment c acknowledge that section 18(1) "probably does not reflect the current weight of authority," which continues to follow Olliffe v. Wells. Nevertheless, some American decisions accord with the Restatement, rejecting *Olliffe*. See, e.g., Curdy v. Berton, 21 P. 858 (Cal. 1889); Linney v. Cleveland Trust Co., 165 N.E. 101 (Ohio Ct. App. 1928); Hartman's Estate (No. 2), 182 A. 232 (Pa. 1936).

2. *Statute of Frauds Compared.* Very few cases have arisen concerning partially secret oral trusts with respect to deeds of land. One such case is Muhm v. Davis, 580 S.W.2d 98 (Tex. Civ. App. 1979). Perry McNeill conveyed by deed his undivided one-half interest in 300 acres of land to "Cleveland Davis, Trustee." The conveyance was made pursuant to a prior oral agreement under which Davis, McNeill's attorney, agreed to hold the land in trust until McNeill's youngest grandchild reached the age of eighteen, at which time Davis was to convey the land in equal shares to McNeill's two children and three grandchildren. Subsequently, McNeill's youngest grandchild reached eighteen, and Davis carried out his promise.

After McNeill's death, his principal devisee, one of his children, brought an action to set aside the conveyance from McNeill to Davis and the conveyance from Davis to McNeill's children and grandchildren. The trial court granted a motion for summary judgment in favor of the defendants. Affirming, the Texas Court of Civil Appeals said:

> The rule is thoroughly settled "that a trust in land declared by parol only, although wholly unenforceable against the trustee, has yet enough of vitality, so that, if voluntarily executed by the trustee at any time, it will become validated as of the date of the original oral agreement...." Blaha v. Borgman, 142 Wis. 43, 46, 124 N.W. 1047, 1048 (1910).
>
> The seventh section of the English Statute of Frauds which was enacted in many American states commonly provides that trusts of land shall be "void and of no effect", unless manifested or proved by a writing. In these states the word "void" has been held to mean "unenforceable against the objection of the trustee." In Bogert, Trusts and Trustees 2d ed., §69, the author says that the trustee in an oral trust is not forbidden to carry out his trust. He has a moral obligation to carry out his trust duties, and the performance of the oral trust is a legal and commendable act.
>
> This approach to the problem has been adopted in the Restatement of the Law of Trusts, where the Rule is stated in these words:

---

effective ways to keep confidential the terms of one's dispositions (including a pour-over will, as we saw in Chapter 7, or a multiple-party bank account), but these techniques were not available until modern times.

Where an oral trust of an interest in land is created inter vivos, the trustee can properly perform the trust if he has not transferred the interest, although he cannot be compelled to do so.

Restatement (Second) of Trusts, §43 at 112.

The summary judgment evidence presents no issues of material fact and establishes as a matter of law an executed parol express trust. The trial court did not err in granting summary judgment.

See also the Restatement 3d of Trusts §24 comments b and i.

EXTERNAL REFERENCE. Robi Blumenstein, Secret Trusts, 36 U. Toronto Fac. L. Rev. 108 (1978).

———

Testamentary Aspects of a Revocable Trust. Florida law requires the "testamentary aspects of a revocable trust" created by a settlor domiciled in Florida to be executed "with the formalities required for the execution of a will in this state." Fla. Stat. §736.0403(b). The term "testamentary aspects" is defined as "those provisions of the trust instrument that dispose of the trust property on or after the death of the settlor other than to the settlor's estate." Id.

EXTERNAL REFERENCE. Donna Litman, Revocable Trusts Under the Florida Trust Code, 34 Nova L. Rev. 1 (2009).

Chapter 10

Trust Administration

In this Chapter, we discuss selected aspects of trust administration. We concentrate on the fiduciary relationship created when a person becomes a trustee. While other relationships, such as attorney and client, principal and agent, corporate officer and stockholder, partner and joint venturer, are also conventionally labeled "fiduciary,"[1] the responsibilities imposed on trustees tend to be more specific and more onerous. Another difference between the fiduciary duties examined here and others is that non-corporate trustees are more likely to be unaware of the legal implications of the positions they have accepted. Friends and relatives often agree to act as trustee simply to be helpful.[2]

PART A. INTRODUCTION

Primary Statutory References: *UTC §§105, 201*

By way of background to the substantive rules regulating trustees, we first explore the conceptual distinction between mandatory and default rules in trust law. The distinction is important because only the default rules, not the mandatory rules, can be modified in the terms of the trust.[3]

We also use this introductory part to speak briefly about the role of the court in supervising the trustee's performance.

---

1. For general discussions of fiduciary law and obligations, see Oxford Handbook of Fiduciary Law (Evan J. Criddle et al. eds. 2019); Research Handbook on Fiduciary Law (D. Gordon Smith & Andrew Gold eds. 2018); Tamar Frankel, Fiduciary Law (2011).

2. For a fascinating historical account of the private trustee in the nineteenth century, see Chantal Stebbings, The Private Trustee in Victorian England (2002). Should individuals be allowed to serve as trustees, or should the role be available only to banks and similar financial service institutions? See Iris J. Goodwin, Why Civil Law Countries Might Forego the Individual Trustee: Provocative Insights from the New-to-the-Fold, in The Worlds of the Trust (Lionel Smith ed. 2013).

3. As defined in Uniform Trust Code §103(18), "terms of a trust" means:
   (A) except as otherwise provided in subparagraph (B), the manifestation of the settlor's intent regarding a trust's provisions as:
       (i) expressed in the trust instrument; or
       (ii) established by other evidence that would be admissible in a judicial proceeding; or
   (B) the trust's provisions as established, determined, or amended by:
       (i) a trustee or other person in accordance with applicable law; [or]
       (ii) court order[[; or]
       (iii) a nonjudicial settlement agreement under [Section 111]].

Mandatory and Default Rules in Trust Law. The substantive rules of trust law are, in the main, default rules—rules that are designed to implement the likely wishes of most settlors and that yield to expressions of contrary intention. Some rules of trust law, however, are mandatory. The Uniform Trust Code clarifies which are which, by explaining which fiduciary duties cannot be overridden in the terms of the trust. See UTC §105. These mandatory rules include the trustee's duties "to act in good faith and in accordance with the terms and purposes of the trust and the interests of the beneficiaries." UTC §105(b)(2). As the UTC explains in §105(b)(3), there is a mandatory "requirement that a trust and its terms be for the benefit of its beneficiaries...."

Much of trust law consists of default rules. The duties of loyalty and prudence, for instance, are default rather than mandatory rules. The Comment to UTC §802, which deals with the duty of loyalty, states that "Section 105 authorizes a settlor to override an otherwise applicable duty of loyalty in the terms of the trust." Similarly, the Uniform Prudent Investor Act states, "The prudent investor rule, a default rule, may be expanded, restricted, eliminated, or otherwise altered by the provisions of a trust." Unif. Prudent Investor Act §1(b). Of course, the settlor cannot be allowed to waive all of the trustee's fiduciary duties. There is always, as stated earlier, a core duty "to act in good faith and in accordance with the terms and purposes of the trust and the interests of the beneficiaries." UTC §105(b)(2). Indeed, if a trustee owed no duties, then the beneficiaries would have no rights, and the trust would be illusory. See the Comment to UTC §105(b)(1).

EXTERNAL REFERENCES. Daniel Clarry, The Irreducible Core of the Trust (2018); David M. Fox, Non-Excludable Trustee Duties, 17 Tr. & Trustees 17 (2011); Thomas P. Gallanis, The Trustee's Duty to Inform, 85 N.C. L. Rev. 1595 (2007); Melanie B. Leslie, Trusting Trustees: Fiduciary Duties and the Limits of Default Rules, 94 Geo. L.J. 67 (2005); John H. Langbein, Mandatory Rules in the Law of Trusts, 98 Nw. U. L. Rev. 1105 (2004); Donovan Waters, Settlor Control: What Kind of a Problem Is It?, 15 Tr. & Trustees 12 (2009).

Court Supervision? Inter vivos trusts typically are not subject to judicial involvement unless there is litigation between the trustee and the beneficiaries. See UTC §201. However, legislation in a few states permits any person interested in a trust to require that the trust be administered under the continuing supervision of a court.

More commonly, legislation requires *testamentary* trustees to qualify with the court having control of the testator's probate estate before undertaking the office. Qualification may or may not involve submission of the trust administration to continuing court supervision. To qualify, the trustee may be required to post bond unless the trust instrument excuses the requirement. Some statutes provide that nonresidents of the state of probate and foreign corporations not qualified to engage in local trust business cannot qualify for appointment as trustee.

Once qualified, a supervised testamentary trustee may be required to submit periodic accountings to the court. Judicial orders settling the accounts may or may not be binding on all beneficiaries. The scope of the review may indicate a different effect for a regular, periodic accounting to a supervising court as well as for a final accounting seeking the trustee's discharge. In both cases, an accounting purporting to bind is ineffective against the interest of a beneficiary to whom inadequate notice has been accorded. In the case of minor or unascertainable beneficiaries, the propriety of any claimed representation other than by a duly appointed guardian ad litem is likely to be governed by legislation, or by equitable principles in the absence of statute. Judicial orders favoring trustees over beneficiaries may be avoided or modified by collateral attack for extrinsic fraud if the trustee was guilty of actual or constructive fraud for failure to inform beneficiaries adequately of matters affecting their rights.

UPC Article VII (deleted from the UPC in 2010, on account of the promulgation of the Uniform Trust Code, but still in effect in some states) eliminated many of the problems involving court qualification and supervision of testamentary trustees. Article VII identified a passive, jurisdictional relationship between every trust and a court of the state of principal administration of the trust. It permitted mailed notice and provides for representation of unborn or unascertained interests. Furthermore, Article VII neither required court qualification of trustees nor the posting of bond, filing of inventories, or judicial approval of accounts periodically or at any other time.

Article VII required trustees to register trusts in the court of the principal place of administration. The purpose of trust registration was to assure that a particular court would be available to the parties on a permissive basis, rather than to subject the trust to compulsory continuing court supervision. A trustee registers a trust by filing a short statement acknowledging acceptance of a trust. The statement must identify the trust by the name of the settlor, date of the trust instrument, and the place of probate of the will if the trust is testamentary. Except for trusts created without a writing, the names of the beneficiaries, the nature and value of the assets, and the terms of the trust need not be disclosed. No sanctions for non-registration are provided, except that a trustee who refuses to register a trust within thirty days after receipt of a written demand for its registration by a settlor or beneficiary is subject to removal if an interested person petitions for removal. Trust registration was a controversial innovation. Several states adopting Article VII of the UPC omitted the trust registration provisions.

PART B. FIDUCIARY DUTIES OF TRUSTEES

Thomas P. Gallanis, The Trustee's Duty to Inform
85 N.C. L. Rev. 1595, 1615 (2007)

The essential structure of the trust, dividing ownership between one or more trustees holding legal title and one or more beneficiaries holding equitable title, presents a classic problem. The powers of trust administration are held by the trustees, who have no personal stake in the effect of their decisions on the trust corpus; conversely, the beneficiaries who do bear the risk of asset loss have no control over the trust's administration.

———

The purpose of trust fiduciary law is to guard against the danger that the trustee will breach a duty to the beneficiaries—either by negligence or, worse, by deliberate mismanagement. Accordingly, the law imposes fiduciary obligations on the trustee. In this part, we examine the central fiduciary duties of trust law: (1) the duties to inform and to account, (2) the duty of loyalty, (3) the duty of prudence, and (4) the duty of impartiality.

1. The Duties to Inform and to Account

Primary Statutory References: *UTC §§810, 813, 1001(b)(4), 1005*

Duty to Inform Beneficiaries. Trustees are under a duty to keep the beneficiaries reasonably informed about the administration of the trust. This duty is, as the Uniform Trust Code states, "a fundamental duty of the trustee." UTC §813 comment. Trust beneficiaries cannot enforce other duties that the trustee owes to them unless they know of their interests and the trustee's administration of the trust.

Although the existence of duty to inform is well settled, the scope of that duty is controversial. As Professor Edward Halbach, the Reporter for the Restatement 3d of Trusts, has observed, "[P]ractice, experience, and litigation... clearly demonstrate that there is considerable reluctance, and at least a fair amount of uncertainty, among fiduciaries concerning the applicability and performance of this general duty." Edward C. Halbach, Jr., Uniform Acts, Restatements, and Trends in American Trust Law at Century's End, 88 Calif. L. Rev. 1877, 1914 (2000). The Uniform Trust Code tries to strike a compromise between the settlor's views on how much information is provided to the beneficiaries and the need for beneficiaries to have sufficient information to protect their interests. See David M. English, The Uniform Trust Code (2000): Significant Provisions and Policy Issues, 67 Mo. L. Rev. 143,

203 (2002).[4] The UTC's provisions concerning the duty to inform have been controversial, and several states that have adopted other parts of the UTC have modified these provisions.

The UTC's disclosure provisions are more expansive in some ways and narrower in others than those provided in (the now superseded) Article VII of the Uniform Probate Code. For example, UTC §813(b)(1) requires disclosure of the entire trust instrument to a beneficiary upon demand, unlike UPC §7-303(b) which required disclosure only of those trust provisions that describe or affect the beneficiary's interest. On the other hand, unlike UPC §7-303, UTC §813(a) only requires the trustee to keep the "qualified beneficiar[ies]" informed; this term is defined in UTC §103(13).

One of the most controversial questions regarding the duty to inform is whether the settlor should be able to waive the beneficiaries' information rights. The UTC provides that most aspects of its duty to inform are waivable. As originally written, only two aspects of the duty to inform were mandatory: the duty under §813(a) to respond to a beneficiary's request for information reasonably related to the beneficiary's interest, and the duty under §813(b)(2)-(3) to notify the beneficiaries of an irrevocable trust "of the existence of the trust, of the identity of the trustee, and of their right to request trustee's reports." UTC §105(b)(8). But these subsections of §105 were later bracketed, indicating that they are optional. See Thomas P. Gallanis, The Trustee's Duty to Inform, 85 N.C. L. Rev. 1595, 1604-05 (2007).

The Restatement provides that "[t]he terms of a trust may alter the amount of information a trustee must give to the beneficiaries... and also the circumstances and frequency with which, and persons to whom, it must be given." Restatement 3d of Trusts §82 comment a(2). It goes on to state that "the duty to provide information to certain beneficiaries... may not be dispensed with entirely or to a degree or for a time that would unduly interfere with the underlying purposes or effectiveness of the information requirements," and that beneficiaries are "always entitled... to request such information... as is reasonably necessary to enable the beneficiary to prevent or redress a breach of trust and otherwise enforce his or her rights under the trust." Id. The duty to inform does not apply to beneficiaries of revocable trusts while the settlor is alive and competent. Id. comment a; see also UTC §603(b).

---

4. Section 813, for example, limits the trustee's duty to inform to the trust's "qualified beneficiaries," defined in §103(13) as "a distributee or permissible distributee of trust income or principal" as of specified dates. Remote remainder beneficiaries are not entitled to information about the trust's administration unless they have filed a specific request with the trustee. The Restatement similarly limits the range of beneficiaries to whom the duty to inform extends. It uses the term "fairly representative" beneficiaries rather than the UTC's term "qualified" beneficiaries. See Restatement 3d of Trusts §82.

Jacob v. Davis

738 A.2d 904 (Md. App. 1999)

ADKINS, J. Appellant William H. Jacob (Bill) is the sole remainderman of two trusts established under the last will and testament of his father, John B. Jacob (John). Appellant sued Michael W. Davis, the surviving trustee of those trusts, and Davis's law firm..., alleging numerous violations of appellees' fiduciary duties as trustees, and seeking an accounting, other equitable relief, and damages....

Facts

John died on January 22, 1994, leaving... a will that created two trusts known as the Marital Trust, and the Family Trust, respectively (collectively, "the Trusts"). John's surviving wife, Harriett Bell Jacob (Harriett) was the income beneficiary of the Trusts, and appellant was the remainder beneficiary....

Another subject of [Bill's] complaint is the refusal of Davis to provide... an accounting for the Trusts. [Bill] first requested an accounting in May of 1996, by letter to a paralegal at Ahlstrom & Davis, P.A., who assisted Davis in estate and trust matters. Responding in a May 28, 1996 letter (May 28 letter), Davis told appellant:

> Your letter raised an interesting point regarding my duties to you under the Trust Agreement for the aforesaid Trust. As you know, I am a co-Trustee with your stepmother, Harriett Bell Jacob, of this Trust. Pursuant to the provisions of the Trust, the Trustee is to render an annual account to the "current income beneficiaries" of the Trust. At present, your stepmother is the only income beneficiary. Thus, I as Trustee, have no obligation to provide to you an accounting for the Trust.
>
> If you wish, I will forward a copy of your letter to [the paralegal] to your stepmother for the purpose of obtaining her approval to give you an accounting for the Trust. Since she and I are co-Trustees, and since she is the sole income beneficiary, if I were to provide such an accounting to you without obtaining her consent first, I would be breaching my fiduciary obligations to her. Please let me know if you wish for me to do this.... Your stepmother is very active in the administration of this Trust, and, in fact, makes all decisions regarding any distributions from the Trust. My only role at this point is to facilitate her administration and to provide to her any counsel that she may wish regarding the Trust.

After receiving this letter, appellant called Harriett to request her permission for an accounting, but she declined. Harriett died in January 1997, leaving an estate valued at approximately $1,500,000.

On April 17, 1997, almost a year after his first request, appellant again requested by letter an accounting of the Trusts, this time through his attorneys, Christopher Wheeler and Gene C. Lange (collectively, "Wheeler"). In the letter Wheeler asked that the accountings "cover all assets, property, receipts, expenditures, distributions, trustee and other commissions, attorneys' and other professional fees, and any and all payments or transfers to and from the two trusts and [Harriett's] Estate." The letter also requested all "books, records, tax returns, court filings or other information" concerning these items. Wheeler requested that the information be furnished by April 25, 1997. In response to this letter, Davis wrote to Wheeler on April 18, 1997, and said, *inter alia:*

> [P]lease be advised that the John B. Jacob Marital Trust was never established since the total assets that were available from the Estate of John B. Jacob to be distributed to his Testamentary Trust did not exceed $600,000.

Davis enclosed in his letter copies of the following documents: 1) inventory and distribution account for John's estate; 2) statements from the brokerage firm of Ferris, Baker Watts for the Family Trust; 3) the check register for the Family Trust checking account; 4) 1995 and 1996 balance sheets, prepared by the accountant for the Family Trust; 5) 1995 and 1996 "general ledgers," prepared by the accountant, showing income and other deposits received, disbursements, plus sales of stocks; 6) income tax returns for 1995 and 1996 filed by the Family Trust; 7) a summary of profits and losses for 1995 and 1996 showing $143,543 in total distributions to Harriett over the two-year period; and 8) John's will and First and Final Accounting for John's Estate. Davis also provided a two-page document, unsigned, titled "John Jacob Family Trust, Recap of Transactions." ...

The recap summarizes distributions to Harriett, but often does not designate whether they were principal or income....

With respect to the other information requested by Wheeler, Davis said:

> With such short notice, the above is the best that we can do to comply with your request that we provide you information by April 25, 1997. From these documents, you should be able to understand the relationship between the Estate of John B. Jacob, the John B. Jacob Family Trust, and Harriett Bell Jacob. I think you will find that there were no distributions from the Trust that did not comply with both the intent and the provisions of the Last Will and Testament of John B. Jacob.

Davis did not provide any... information as to how the expenses of the trust, such as trustees' commissions and accountant fees, were allocated between the income beneficiary and the remainderman. Further, no information was provided to show how in kind distributions of stock to Harriett were valued, e.g., at inventory value or fair market value.

Davis did offer to meet with appellant and counsel and the accountant for the estate to discuss their concerns. On May 5, 1997, Wheeler replied that "a meeting would probably be beneficial, but [we] would prefer that we have a little longer to digest the information you provided." In that letter Wheeler also said: "We have noted an omission in the documents you provided. As a result we hereby request a complete accounting of (including all documents related to) the transfer of assets owned by John B. Jacob at his death, to the Family Trust, for the period October, 1994, through January, 1995." Wheeler also requested the federal estate tax return for John's estate.

Davis responded to Wheeler's letter on May 7, and enclosed the Ferris, Baker Watts statements for the period requested and the federal estate tax return. With respect to the statements, appellee Davis commented: "[p]lease note that there may be discrepancies between these statements and the accounting that was filed in the Orphan's Court.... The Accounting does not provide a means to show changes in the prices of the equities during the time from when the estate is opened until the time the estate is closed."...

On May 23, 1997, Wheeler again wrote to Davis, and requested that he "explain the justification for the removal of" five stocks and seven bonds from the trust, as well as other specific items, suggesting that these items "could only be removed from the Family Trust pursuant to the terms and intent of the Family Trust established by Mr. Jacob." The record does not reflect Davis's response to this letter. Bill testified that he never received any explanation or accounting from Davis regarding the trust principal that was distributed to Harriett. Appellees took the position at trial and on appeal that they had no obligation to account to Bill.

Although the letters refer to several telephone conversations between counsel, there is no indication that the parties ever had a meeting. Appellant filed suit on July 3, 1997....

Discussion

...Appellant complains that appellees never provided a full accounting of the Trusts created under John's will. Appellees contend that they had no obligation to provide an accounting to appellant either during the lifetime of Harriett or after her death. Alternatively, they claim that the documents they provided to appellant in April 1997, after her death, were a sufficient accounting of the Trusts.

Appellees rely on section 10.02 of John's will, which provides:

> My Trustee shall be excused from filing any account with any court; however, my Trustee shall render an annual (or more frequent) account and may, at any other time, including at the time of the death, resignation, or removal of any Trustee, render an intermediate account of my Trustee's administration to such of the then current income beneficiaries who are of sound mind and not minors at the time of such accounting. The written approval of such accounting by all of such income beneficiaries shall bind all persons then having or thereafter acquiring or claiming any interest in any trust, and shall be a complete discharge to my Trustee with respect to all matters set forth in the account as fully and to the same extent as though the account had been judicially settled in an action or proceeding in which all persons having, acquiring, or claiming any interest were duly made parties and were duly represented.

The trial court held that under the terms of the Trusts and applicable law, the trustees had no obligation to account to a remainderman such as appellant during the lifetime of the income beneficiary. The trial court seemingly agreed with appellant that an accounting was due after death, but found that the documents provided by appellees after Harriett's death sufficed....

We do not agree with appellees' view that appellant is not entitled to request and obtain an accounting of the Trusts. The leading authorities on trusts are unequivocal in their articulation of the right of the remainder beneficiary to an accounting during the lifetime of the income beneficiary and after his or her death. Austin W. Scott and William F. Fratcher, The Law of Trusts, (Vol. IIA 4 th ed.1987) §172 explains:

> A trustee is under a duty to the beneficiaries of the trust to keep clear and accurate accounts. His accounts should show what he has received and what he has expended. They should show what gains have accrued and what losses have been incurred on changes of investments. *If the trust is created for beneficiaries in succession, the accounts should show what receipts and what expenditures are allocated to principal and what are allocated to income ...*

Restatement (Second) of Trusts §172, comment (b) [sic: (c) Ed.] states the rule in like terms:

> The beneficiary may by a proper proceeding compel the trustee to render to the proper court an account of the administration of the trust.... The trustee may be compelled [to] account not only by a beneficiary presently entitled to the payment of income or principal, but also by a beneficiary who will be or may be entitled to receive income or principal in the future.

...Appellees argue that section 10.2 of the will relieves them from any obligation to account to a remainder beneficiary. This section allows the trustee to provide an accounting at any time, and provides that if such accounting is approved in writing by the then income beneficiaries, then the trustee is discharged with respect to the matters covered by the account. Appellees would have us apply this section to modify the common law obligation of a trustee to account.

To our knowledge, no Maryland appellate decision has addressed the extent to which a decedent or testator may limit the common law duty of a trustee to account in a court of equity. Nor do we find any statute or rule, addressing this point.... In the present case we need not decide this interesting issue because we do not interpret section 10.02 in light of the will as a whole, to limit the trustees' obligation to account under the present circumstances....

When section 10.02 is considered in light of section 10.08, the former cannot reasonably be construed to deny appellant an accounting based on Harriett's consent to some prior accounting. Section 10.08 provides:

> Notwithstanding any other provision hereunder, no Trustee hereunder shall have a vote or otherwise participate in any decision regarding whether, and to what extent, any discretionary payment of principal or interest shall be made or allocated to or for such Trustee's personal benefit or to or for the benefit of any person for whose support such Trustee may be legally obligated. Any such decision shall be made by the co-Trustee then serving, or if there is no such co-Trustee, then the Trustee shall appoint a co-Trustee to make such decision.

Clearly, if Harriett cannot participate in a decision to distribute principal to her, then her consent to such distribution cannot be considered binding upon a remainderman whose interest is adversely affected.... Since appellant's claim for accounting is based upon his contention that principal amounts were improperly distributed to Harriett, section 10.02 of the will does not bar his suit....

In sum, we hold that appellant was entitled to an accounting during the life of Harriett and at her death, notwithstanding the language in... John's will.

Note and Questions

1. How would *Jacob* have been decided under the UTC?

2. Section 603(b) of the UTC provides: "To the extent a trust is revocable [and the settlor has capacity to revoke the trust], rights of the beneficiaries are subject to the control of, and the duties of the trustee are owed exclusively to, the settlor." After the settlor of a revocable trust dies, do the beneficiaries have a right to information about the trust only as of the date the trust became irrevocable, or does their right to information reach back to earlier periods? Compare Matter of Trimble, 826 N.W.2d 474 (Iowa 2013) (only as of the date the trust became irrevocable), with Estate of Giraldin, 290 P.3d 199, 219 (Cal. 2012) (beneficiaries of a formerly revocable trust have standing, after the settlor's death, to assert a breach of fiduciary duty owed to the settlor "to the extent the breach harmed the beneficiaries").

EXTERNAL REFERENCES. Dana G. Fitzsimons Jr., Navigating the Trustee's Duty to Disclose, 23 Prob. & Prop. 40 (Jan./Feb. 2009); Thomas P. Gallanis, The Trustee's Duty to Inform, 85 N.C. L. Rev. 1595 (2007).

———

Duty to Account. Property fiduciaries, such as executors, administrators, and trustees, are required to file an accounting with the court prior to their discharge from office. For trustees, this normally occurs upon termination of the trust. For estate representatives, the accounting occurs at the end of administration. In addition, estate representatives must make earlier periodic accountings, beginning upon their appointment. Many statutes also require trustees of testamentary trusts to make intermediate accountings. Even where not required to do so, trustees often find it advantageous to file periodic accountings with the supervising court as a means of gaining judicial approval of their actions with respect to the trust property.

Traditionally, the accounting takes the form of a detailed description of the fiduciary's actions during the period covered by the accounting. The accounting must describe property received, income earned, disbursements made, taxes paid, and all distributions of income and/or principal made during the covered period. Under the traditional rules, the fiduciary must provide notice of an accounting to all persons having an interest in the estate or trust.

Upon settlement of the final accounting, the fiduciary makes final distribution and is then discharged by the court. Normally, if beneficiaries have received proper notice of an accounting and failed to object, the fiduciary is protected against subsequent objections, absent fraud, of course. The case that follows illustrates the potential breadth of the term "fraud."

National Academy of Sciences v. Cambridge Trust Company
346 N.E.2d 879 (Mass. 1976)

REARDON, J. This matter is before us for further appellate review, the Appeals Court having promulgated an opinion.

The facts which give rise to the case are essentially as follows. Leonard T. Troland died a resident of Cambridge in 1932 survived by his widow, Florence R. Troland. By his will executed in April, 1931, he left all of his real and personal property to be held in trust by the Cambridge Trust Company (bank) with the net income of the trust, after expenses, 'to be paid to, or deposited to the account of (his wife) Florence R. Troland' during her lifetime so long as she remained unmarried. He further provided that '(k)nowing my wife, Florence's, generosity and unselfishness as I do, I wish to record it as my intention that she should not devote any major portion of her income under the provisions of this will, to the support or for the benefit of people other than herself. It is particularly contrary to my will that any part of the principal or income of my estate should revert to members of my wife's family, other than herself, and I instruct the trustees to bear this point definitely in mind in making decisions under any of the options of this will.' The testator went on to provide in part that on his wife's death or second marriage the bank would transfer the trusteeship to The National Research Council of Washington, D.C., which the petition alleged to be an agency of the National Academy of Sciences (academy), to constitute a trust to be known as the Troland Foundation for Research in Psychophysics. He directed that income be accumulated and added to principal until sufficient to produce an annual income of $50,000 or the 1931 purchasing power equivalent of that amount of money, at which time the income was to be applied by the academy within certain specific guidelines set out in the will. The testator further provided instructions to the academy as successor trustee concerning his wife's support should she be widowed again after a second marriage or should her second husband fail to support her.

The will was allowed, the trust was established as provided by the testator, and the bank paid the income thereof to the widow until her death in 1967. During the period from 1932 to 1945 the widow provided eighteen different mailing addresses for income checks to be transmitted to her by the bank. On February 13, 1945, she married Edward D. Flynn in West Palm Beach, Florida, and failed to advise the bank of her remarriage. Following her remarriage she lived in Perth Amboy, New Jersey. Commencing on April 14, 1944, she directed the bank to forward all her monthly checks to her in care of Kenneth D. Custance, her brother-in-law through marriage to her sister. Over the years these checks were forwarded to two Boston addresses and were made payable to 'Florence R. Troland.' Custance in turn forwarded the checks to Florence R. Flynn who indorsed them in blank 'Florence R. Troland' and returned them to Custance who also indorsed them prior to depositing them in bank accounts in his name maintained at the State Street Bank and Trust Company in Boston and the National Bank of Wareham, Massachusetts. After Florence R. Flynn's death on December 25, 1967, the bank for the first time learned of her remarriage. Throughout her second marriage Florence R. Flynn lived with her husband who was able to provide support for her and who, although aware that she was receiving payments from the trust, was ignorant of the limitation on her rights to receive such payments. In March, 1968, the bank brought a suit in equity in the Superior Court, Suffolk County, against Custance, the National Bank of Wareham, the State Street Bank and Trust Company, and Edward D. Flynn for recovery of amounts 'represented by checks made payable to Florence R. Troland and collected by Florence R. Flynn subsequent to the date of her marriage.' In this litigation the bank recovered $41,416.64 from which it paid legal fees and disbursements of $14,475.49. The total of all checks collected by Florence R. Flynn following her marriage in 1945 up to the date of her death is $106,013.41. The twelfth through thirty-third accounts of the bank covering that period between her remarriage and October 8, 1966, were presented to the Probate Court for Middlesex County in separate proceedings and allowed. The academy had formal notice prior to the presentation of the twelfth through fourteenth accounts and the eighteenth through thirty-third accounts, and with respect to the fifteenth through seventeenth accounts assented in writing to their allowance. The academy, unaware of the widow's remarriage, did not challenge any of the accounts and they were duly allowed.

The petition brought in the Probate Court by the academy seeks revocation of the seven decrees allowing the twelfth through thirty-third accounts of the bank, the excision from those accounts of 'all entries purporting to evidence distributions to or for the benefit of 'Florence R. Troland'... subsequent to February 13, 1945,' the restoration by the bank to the trust of the amounts of those distributions with interest at the rate of six per cent, a final account reflecting the repayments and adjustments, appointment of the academy as trustee, and payment by the bank of the costs and expenses of the academy's counsel.

Following hearing a judge of the Probate Court revoked the seven decrees allowing the twelfth through thirty-third accounts, ordered restoration to the trust of $114,314.18, representing amounts erroneously distributed to Florence R. Flynn plus Massachusetts income taxes paid on those amounts from trust funds, together with interest thereon in the sum of $104,847.17 through March 31, 1973, and interest thereafter at the rate of six per cent per annum to the date of restoration in full....

The issues before us have to do with the power of the Probate Court judge to order the revocation of the decrees allowing the twelfth through thirty-third accounts, and the propriety of charging the bank for the amounts erroneously disbursed, as well as the disposition of the several claims for counsel fees, interest and disbursements.

The bank recited in the heading of each of the challenged accounts that the trust was 'for the benefit of Florence R. Troland,' and stated in schedule E of each account (in the first four accounts specifically as 'Distributions to Beneficiary') that monthly payments of $225 or more were made to 'Florence R. Troland.' The Appeals Court held that these recitals and statements 'constituted a continuing representation by the bank to the academy and to the court that the widow remained 'Florence R. Troland' despite her (then unknown) remarriage to Flynn, and that she remained the sole income beneficiary of the trust.'... The court further held that those representations were technically fraudulent in that '(t)hey were made as of the bank's own knowledge when the bank had no such knowledge and had made absolutely no effort to obtain it.'...

The doctrine of constructive or technical fraud in this Commonwealth is of venerable origin. As we pointed out in Powell v. Rasmussen, 355 Mass. 117, 118-119, 243 N.E.2d 167 (1969), the doctrine here was developed in two opinions by Chief Justice Shaw. In Hazard v. Irwin, 18 Pick. 95, 109 (1836), it was defined in the following terms: '(W)here the subject matter is one of fact, in respect to which a person can have precise and accurate knowledge, and ... he speaks as of his own knowledge, and has no such knowledge, his affirmation is essentially false.' This rule was reiterated by Chief Justice Shaw in Page v. Bent, 2 Met. 371, 374 (1841): 'The principle is well settled, that if a person make a representation of a fact, as of his own knowledge, in relation to a subject matter susceptible of knowledge, and such representation is not true; if the party to whom it is made relies and acts upon it, as true, and sustains damage by it, it is fraud and deceit, for which the party making it is responsible.' In this case the marital status of Mrs. Troland/Flynn was a fact susceptible of precise knowledge, the bank made representations concerning this fact of its own knowledge when it had no such knowledge, and the academy to whom the representations were made relied on them to its detriment. While this standard of fraud in law has been developed primarily in the context of actions seeking rescission of contracts and of tort actions for deceit, we have indicated in past decisions that an analogous standard might be applicable to misrepresentations in the accounts of fiduciaries. We hold today that 'fraud' as used in G.L. c. 206, §24, contemplates this standard of constructive fraud at least to the extent that the fiduciary has made no reasonable efforts to ascertain the true state of the facts it has misrepresented in the accounts. This rule is not a strict liability standard, nor does it make a trustee an insurer against the active fraud of all parties dealing with the trust. Entries in the accounts honestly made, after reasonable efforts to determine the truth or falsity of the representations therein have failed through no fault of the trustee, will not be deemed fraudulent or provide grounds for reopening otherwise properly allowed accounts. However, in the instant case the probate judge found that the bank, through the twenty-two years covered by the disputed accounts, exerted 'no effort at all... to ascertain if Florence R. Troland had remarried even to the extent of annually requesting a statement or certificate from her to that effect' and that 'in administering the trust acted primarily in a ministerial manner and in disregard of its duties as a trustee to protect the terms of the trust.' In these circumstances we have little trouble in concluding that the bank's representations as to the marital status of the testator's widow fully justified the reopening of the accounts.

Cases relied on by the bank in which this court refused to allow previously allowed accounts to be reopened are distinguishable in that either they did not involve representations of fact susceptible of precise knowledge but rather questions of judgment and discretion as to matters fully and frankly disclosed in the accounts, or that the alleged wrongful acts or mistakes of the trustee were discernible from an examination of the accounts, the trust documents and the law. We adhere to our decisions that it is the duty of beneficiaries 'to study the account presented to the Probate Court by the trustee, and to make their objections at the hearing.' Greene v. Springfield Safe Deposit & Trust Co., supra, 295 Mass. at 154, 3 N.E.2d at 257. However, in this case the fact of the widow's remarriage was not discernible from the most scrupulous examination of the accounts, the trust documents and the relevant law, and the bank cannot avoid responsibility here for its misrepresentations by alleging a breach of duty on the part of the academy.

As to the propriety of surcharging the bank for the amounts erroneously disbursed, when a trustee makes payment to a person other than the beneficiary entitled to receive the money, he is liable to the proper beneficiary to make restitution unless the payment was authorized by a proper court. Since, as we have held, the decrees allowing the twelfth through thirty-third accounts were revoked properly, the bank thus became liable to the academy to restore to the trust corpus the payments it made to Mrs. Troland/Flynn when she was not entitled to receive them. In addition to the amounts erroneously disbursed, the bank was also properly charged by the Probate Court judge with simple interest on those payments at the legal rate of six per cent per annum....

[T]he decree is affirmed.

[The dissenting opinion of WILKINS, J. is omitted.]

Notes

1. *"No Judicial Accounting" Provisions.* Settlors who wish to relieve their trustees of the burden of making repeated accountings often insert in the trust instrument a so-called "no judicial accounting" provision. Such a provision requires only that the trustee make periodic accountings to the adult beneficiaries and not to the court. Some jurisdictions have been unwilling to enforce such clauses in the case of testamentary trusts and, in a few instances, inter vivos trusts as well.

2. Section 813(c) of the Uniform Trust Code requires trustees to provide annual "reports" (the term used by the UTC for "accounting"). However, this provision is not on §105's list of mandatory rules, meaning that the settlor may waive this requirement.

2. The Duty of Loyalty

Primary Statutory References: *UTC §§603, 703, 802, 810, 1002, 1008, 1009*

It is commonly said that the "most fundamental" rule of trust fiduciary law is the duty of loyalty. See Scott and Ascher on Trusts §17.2, at 1200 (6th ed. 2021). A trustee must act "solely in the interest of the beneficiary." Restatement 2d of Trusts §170(1). Accord Restatement 3d of Trusts §78(1). Professor John Langbein explains the core policy behind the duty of loyalty this way:

> Any conflict of interest in trust administration, that is, any opportunity for the trustee to benefit personally from the trust, is potentially harmful to the beneficiary. The danger... is that a trustee "placed under temptation" will allow "selfishness" to prevail over the duty to benefit the beneficiaries. [John H. Langbein, Questioning the Trust Law Duty of Loyalty: Sole Interest or Best Interest?, 114 Yale L.J. 929, 934 (2005) (quoting George G. Bogert & George T. Bogert, The Law of Trusts and Trustees §543, at 227 (rev. 2d ed. 1993)).]

Matter of Green Charitable Trust
431 N.W.2d 492 (Mich. Ct. App. 1988)

HOOD, J. Respondents, Comerica Bank and Miles Jaffe, appeal as of right from an order of visiting Oakland County Probate Judge George E. Benko which removed respondents as trustees of the Leslie H. Green and Edith C. Green Charitable Trust, removed Comerica as personal representative of the estate of Edith C. Green, deceased, and surcharged respondents in the amount of $1,900,000. The petitioners are the Michigan Attorney General, St. Peter's Home for Boys, Bishop of the Episcopal Church—Diocese of Michigan, Dean of the Cathedral Church of St. Paul, and the Cathedral Church of St. Paul. This case is based on the petitioners' objections to respondents' sale of real property owned by the estate and charitable trust to Maurice Cohen, a client of respondent Jaffe.

Leslie and Edith Green owned and maintained a residence on 315 acres in Bloomfield Township, Oakland County, known as Turtle Lake Farms.

In 1969, Leslie and Edith Green created a charitable trust funded in part by a grant of an interest in Turtle Lake Farms. As finally amended, the beneficiaries of this trust are St. Peter's Home for Boys, the Cathedral Church of St. Paul and the Cathedral of the Episcopal Church, Diocese of Michigan. The named trustees were the Greens, Comerica and Miles Jaffe.

Mr. Green died in 1973. His will gave Mrs. Green a life estate in the portion of Turtle Lake Farms including their residence and created a marital trust for the benefit of his wife during her lifetime. The charitable trust was made the residuary beneficiary of the marital trust and would receive the marital trust's interest in Turtle Lake Farms upon Mrs. Green's death. Comerica was named sole trustee of the marital trust.

Mrs. Green died in March, 1983. Her will made specific bequests totaling $320,000 and directed the establishment of a million dollar trust fund for her granddaughter. The residue of her estate was left to the charitable trust. Mrs. Green's estate consisted of cash and securities valued at $1,340,000, plus her interest in Turtle Lake Farms. Comerica was designated personal representative of the estate.

Upon Mrs. Green's death, Bishop McGehee and Dean Herlong of the Episcopal Church became co-trustees of the charitable trust as provided for under the trust. Under the trust, only Comerica and Jaffe were empowered to make decisions regarding the disposition of the real property.

According to respondents, soon after Mrs. Green's death they determined that the liquid assets of the estate were insufficient to satisfy the cash bequests, the funding of the $1,000,000 trust fund for the granddaughter, the estate taxes and the administrative expenses. After reviewing the options, Comerica and Jaffe concluded that the interests of the estate and its beneficiaries would best be served by the sale of the Turtle Lake property.

At Mrs. Green's death, three entities owned undivided interests in Turtle Lake: the Edith Green estate, the marital trust, and the charitable trust. For the sale, Comerica acted in three capacities: as executor of the estate, as sole trustee of the marital trust, and as one of the trustees of the charitable trust. Jaffe also acted in several capacities. He was a trustee of the charitable trust. Also, Jaffe and his firm, Honigman, Miller, Schwartz & Cohn, were attorneys for the estate, for Comerica as executor, for Comerica as trustee of the marital trust, and for Comerica as trustee of the charitable trust. The record also contains testimony of Dean Herlong to the effect that Jaffe, at least on one occasion, provided legal advice to him in his role as trustee. Jaffe had been a personal friend of the Greens, as well as their attorney. He drafted their wills and the trust instruments.

During the time between Leslie Green's death and the death of his wife, Comerica's trust department received inquiries from individuals interested in purchasing Turtle Lake Farms. Since the intent was for Mrs. Green to live out her life on the property, Comerica informed inquiring developers that the property was not on the market and that they would be notified when it became available. The parties' briefs describe in detail the events following Mrs. Green's death and leading up to the sale of the Homestead, the real property concerned in this action. The Homestead is the western portion of the Turtle Lake property, consisting of 211 acres and including the Green's mansion and other buildings, Turtle Lake, and lakefront property on Upper Long Lake.

On September 15, 1983, Comerica accepted an offer from Maurice Cohen for the Homestead. The sale was closed on November 1, 1983, by execution of a land contract for $3,250,000, with $1,500,000 down payment and the balance over two years at twelve percent interest. Maurice Cohen is a successful real estate developer and was represented by the Honigman firm.

This case concerns the objections by the charitable trust beneficiaries to Jaffe's and his law firm's conflicts of interest in representing both buyer and seller, to Comerica's management of the sale of the property, and to the adequacy of the price received for the Homestead....

Testifying for Comerica were Gari Kersten and Cleveland Thurber. Kersten was vice president of Comerica's trust real estate department which supervised the management of trust real estate and the Comerica representative who apparently worked most closely with Jaffe on the sale of property. Thurber was in charge of Comerica's trust department, which generally oversaw the trust, and one of the trust officers who participated in decisions to sell the property to and accept the Cohen offer. Another Comerica employee, the sales manager, Mr. Keating, apparently supplied information to Kersten on the value of the property. David Wind was another trust officer involved in various decisions. Neither of these two men testified.

Leo Majzels, who had done an appraisal of the property in 1973, was retained by Comerica following Mrs. Green's death as part of the efforts to prepare a marketing plan and as a consultant to assist in evaluating the value of the property. Calvin Hall was retained to submit a development plan on the possible uses of the land. Donald Tilton was retained to study possible environmental problems caused by the wetlands on the property.

Also testifying was Paul C. Robertson, a local land developer and builder, who had expressed interest in developing the property prior to Mrs. Green's death and who contacted Comerica regarding the property again in May, 1983.

The Attorney General is a petitioner as a necessary party in interest to estate proceedings involving charitable trusts....

Maurice Cohen visited the Homestead in April, 1983, and expressed an interest in purchasing the Green residence and a few surrounding acres. Kersten told Cohen that the sale of such a small parcel was not desirable because it would reduce the marketability of the balance of the property. Jaffe put Cohen in touch with Calvin Hall and showed Cohen Hall's development plan to encourage Cohen's interest in a larger parcel. Throughout the summer, Jaffe continued to meet with Cohen to encourage him to make a suitable offer for the entire parcel.

According to Jaffe, when he realized in August that Cohen was interested in making "a hard offer" on the entire Homestead, he informed Thurber that there was a potential conflict of interest because his law firm represented Cohen. In a letter of August 12 to Thurber, Jaffe requested the consent of Comerica, Bishop McGehee and Dean Herlong, as trustees, to the Honigman firm's dual representation and indicated that, in any event, Jaffe would not act as co-trustee with respect to any offer by Cohen. It does not appear that Jaffe sent copies of the letter directly to Bishop McGehee or Dean Heriong.

On August 18, at a meeting of Comerica representatives and Honigman attorneys, Majzels expressed his opinion that the Homestead should sell for between $3 and $3.5 million.

On August 22, all of the trustees of the charitable trust met to discuss the possible sale of the land and the question of dual representation. Dean Herlong testified that Thurber informed them of the estate's cash needs and Jaffe discussed the various problems with development of the property. Jaffe, Thurber and Kersten also informed Bishop McGehee and Dean Herlong that they expected Cohen to make an offer for the western portion of the property. Jaffe explained the conflict of interest.

Former Chief Justice G. Mennen Williams was also present at this meeting in his capacity as Senior Warden of the Vestry of the Cathedral Church of St. Paul but he did not testify at trial. Dean Herlong testified that the Chief Justice was present at the Dean's request. The Senior Warden is the representative of the cathedral to whom Dean Herlong is ultimately responsible, and Dean Herlong felt it was in the best interest of the cathedral for the Chief Justice to be present. The Chief Justice... was precluded from practicing law, and we find no indication in the record that he was present as or in any way acted as a legal advisor....

On August 23, Cohen made an offer for the Homestead of $3 million. Neither the price nor the conditions were acceptable to Jaffe or Comerica, and Kersten directed Jaffe to go back to Cohen and see what could be done to better the offer.

On August 26, a one-page circular describing generally the land and its availability was sent to people who had expressed an interest in the property and to local real estate people. Kersten authorized the mailing against the advice of Jaffe.

On August 31, 1983, Bishop McGehee and Dean Herlong sent a letter to Jaffe consenting to the dual representation "subject to the satisfactory demonstration by the Comerica Bank after reasonable investigation that the offer is indeed suitable, appropriate, and in keeping with the present market situation."

On September 6, Kersten met with Robertson. Kersten apparently attempted to secure an offer on the entire parcel from Robertson, indicating that the asking price was $10 million, with $4 million down. Kersten met with Cohen on September 12, apparently in an attempt to secure a better offer and to obtain an extension of Cohen's offer, both of which Cohen refused. A revised offer at $3.25 million was prepared by the Honigman attorneys and accepted on September 15....

On September 19, Dean Herlong was informed of the sale. On September 26, Wind, Kersten, and Jaffe met with Dean Herlong, Bishop McGehee and Chief Justice Williams. Dean Herlong testified that he expressed at this meeting his concerns regarding the sale and Comerica's marketing of the property. The Cohen deal was closed on November 1, 1983. Bishop McGehee and Dean Herlong signed the land contract as trustees of the charitable trust. Dean Herlong testified that Jaffe told them that the sale was a "fait accompli" and that their signatures were a legal formality.

On December 29, Jaffe wrote to Bishop McGehee and Dean Herlong advising them that another Honigman client was interested in another part of the property and requesting their consent to the multiple representation. In a letter dated March 5, 1984, Dean Herlong consented to the multiple representation, but asked for a written appraisal of the property before sale. According to Jaffe, Dean Herlong indicated for the first time that he was dissatisfied with the way in which the Cohen sale had been handled. Dean Herlong testified that he had orally conveyed his dissatisfaction earlier.

After the present controversy arose, appraisals of the market value of the Homestead as of September 15, 1983, were prepared by Majzels, who was selected by Jaffe, and by Proctor, who was selected by Dean Herlong from a list of appraisers submitted by Jaffe. Over Dean Herlong's objection, the instructions to the appraisers included information on the Cohen sale. The appraisals were completed in 1985, with Majzels indicating a value of $3.35 million and Proctor arriving at a value of $5.15 million for the Homestead.

On September 9, 1984, Comerica filed its first account on the estate of Edith Green. On October 29, 1985, St. Peter's Home for Boys filed a petition and objection to the account. On December 2, 1985, the Attorney General filed a similar petition. On November 12, 1986, Bishop McGehee and Dean Herlong filed petitions in the probate court pursuant to M.C.L. § 700.805, to surcharge Comerica and Jaffe as trustees of the charitable trust, and the Attorney General filed a petition to surcharge and remove Comerica as executor of the Edith Green estate, as trustee of the marital trust, and as trustee of the charitable trust.

On November 13, 1986, Judge Benko began hearings on all of these petitions, excluding issues related to the marital trust because Comerica had been discharged as trustee when the Leslie Green estate had been closed in 1984. Following several days of testimony, the probate court issued its thirty-four page opinion, finding that Jaffe and Comerica violated their obligations as trustees to the settlors and beneficiaries of the charitable trust and that Comerica violated its obligation as personal representative to the Edith Green estate. As to Comerica, the court found that it had negligently handled the sale of the property, as evidenced by its inadequate efforts to determine the property's value and its failure to adequately market the property. Furthermore, the court found that Comerica was negligent in its response to Jaffe's acknowledged conflict of interest and in allowing Jaffe and his firm to control the negotiations. As to Jaffe, the court found that his conflict of interest, although acknowledged, tainted the sale because there was not full disclosure of the extent of his prior representation of Cohen on personal tax matters, because Jaffe actively participated in the negotiations and because his course of conduct insured that his client, Cohen, obtained the property at an inadequate price. The court found that both parties had failed in their duty to keep the beneficiaries reasonably informed and to fulfill a self-imposed duty to keep their co-trustees fully advised of developments....

We now turn to the substantive issue of whether Jaffe and Comerica violated their duties to the trust. As a preliminary matter, we note that, while Jaffe maintains that he declined to act as a trustee with respect to any offer by Cohen, he did not resign his position as trustee. Therefore, his duties to the beneficiaries and the trust as to matters related to the valuation and marketing of the property did not end when he chose to decline to act on the offer....

Paragraph VII of the trust gives the trustees broad powers "to do everything they in good faith deem advisable even though it would not be authorized or appropriate for fiduciaries (but for this power) under any statutory or other rule of law...." Paragraph V empowers Comerica and Jaffe "in their sole discretion" to determine the timing of any sale of the real property so as to realize its "full value."

Giving trustees discretionary or broad powers does not mean that there are no limits to those powers. Trustees' actions will be reviewed for abuse of that discretion. The trustee is bound to exercise his discretion honestly and in good faith....

As noted by the parties, the liability of the trustee may be limited by the terms of the trust instrument. Comerica's and Jaffe's liability for error, negligence, mistake of judgment, act or omission as trustees of the charitable trust was limited to actions done in bad faith. This provision is consistent with the common law principle that trustees may not be liable for mere mistakes or errors of judgment where they have acted in good faith and within the limits of the law and of the trust.

The exculpatory clause does not preclude judicial review or application of the required standard of care....

An exculpatory clause generally is not considered to reduce or enlarge the standard of care required of the trustee in administering the trust, but acts to relieve the trustee of personal liability under the stated circumstances. It will not generally be construed to mean that the trustee is not accountable to anyone for his actions. A trust implies an equitable duty to act for the benefit of the beneficiary and an all-inclusive exculpatory clause would connote either that there was no enforceable duty owed the beneficiary or that there was no remedy for a breach of duty even if the breach was found to be unconscionable.

The "bad faith" standard used in the Green trust has not been defined in the trust context in Michigan. However, the principle has been applied in trust situations in evaluating a trustee's diligence, honesty, and good faith. In the insurance context, bad faith has been defined as "arbitrary, reckless, indifferent, or intentional disregard of the interests of the person owed a duty." Commercial Union Ins. Co. v. Liberty Mutual Ins. Co., 426 Mich. 127, 136, 393 N.W.2d 161 (1986).

Bad faith is not a specific act in itself, but defines the character or quality of a party's actions. Its presence, as with a determination that a trustee has violated his duty to the trust, depends on the facts of the individual case....

Specific duties of trustees include keeping the beneficiaries "reasonably informed of the trust and its administration." M.C.L. §700.814. In the context of the sale of real property, there is an obligation to seek the highest price obtainable. The entire circumstances of the case will be considered in reviewing a contested sale. That the price realized at the sale was at or above the appraised value does not necessarily indicate that the best price was obtained.

The duty to obtain the best price has been expanded upon in other jurisdictions to specifically include consideration of those factors noted by the probate court: the determination of fair market value, the proper marketing of the property, and the adequacy of the price obtained. The parties have referred us to a number of cases from other courts, one of which, Allard v. Pacific National Bank, 99 Wash.2d 394, 663 P.2d 104 (1983), is strikingly similar to our situation. In *Allard*, the Supreme Court of Washington affirmed a finding that the trustee had breached its fiduciary duties in its management of the sale of real property located in downtown Seattle, the sole asset of the trust. The beneficiaries argued a breach of duty based on the trustee's failure to inform them of the sale and failure to either obtain an independent appraisal or place the property on the open market prior to the sale.

The Washington court found that the trustee "must inform beneficiaries... of all material facts in connection with a nonroutine transaction which significantly affects the trust estate and the interest of the beneficiaries prior to the transaction taking place." *Allard*, supra, 99 Wash.2d at 404-405, 663 P.2d 104. This duty is based on the generally recognized principle that the beneficiaries must know how the estate is being managed in order that they may hold the trustee to proper standards of care and honesty arid obtain the benefits to which they are entitled. Id.... In *Allard*, there was one offer made for the property by a leaseholder who had a right of first refusal. The court found that, at a minimum, the beneficiaries had a right to know of the offer prior to the sale to give them the opportunity to outbid the leaseholder.

We agree with the *Allard* court that this duty, especially in the instant case where the single most valuable asset was the real property, imposed on Jaffe and Comerica the responsibility of informing all the beneficiaries of the impending sale. It is not clear in what capacity, as co-trustees or as representatives of the beneficiaries, Dean Herlong and Bishop McGehee were first contacted. However, it is clear that Jaffe and Comerica had made a specific commitment to keep Dean Herlong and Bishop McGehee informed, and that commitment should also have been kept. The probate court did not err in finding that Jaffe and Comerica breached this duty.

We now turn to whether the trustees fulfilled their duties in the sale of the property. *Allard's* second issue requiring an appraisal or testing the market has been considered in other jurisdictions as part of the trustee's duty to establish the value of the property offered for sale. Knowledge of value is the basic assurance that any sale price is fair and just.

Factors which have been considered in determining whether adequate efforts were taken to determine value include the existence of a "sound" appraisal and consultation with competent local real estate people to obtain their expert advice. In general, the question is whether the trustee has done its homework.

In the absence of a thorough appraisal, the trustee may establish value by "testing the market." "Testing the market" is not limited to consideration of offers volunteered by actual potential buyers. It includes whatever actions may be available to encourage fair, legitimate and seasonable competition.

In *Allard*, the leaseholder made an initial offer of $139,000. The trustees demanded at least $200,000, and the leaseholder eventually met that price. The trustees' price was apparently based on an internal appraisal by the trustee bank's trust department. However, the court found that, by failing to obtain an independent outside appraisal or testing the market to determine what a willing buyer would pay, the trustees had breached their fiduciary duty.

In our case, respondents argue that they had two appraisals to guide them, Majzels' and Kersten's. But Jaffe, Kersten and Majzels testified that Majzels was not engaged as an appraiser, but as a consultant supplying his input on an appropriate asking price. Jaffe specifically testified that they did not want an appraisal "early on" for fear that it would establish a ceiling on the price that could deleteriously affect the manner of selling the property. That Kersten and Comerica's real estate department had an opinion regarding the value is relevant but not determinative. No evidence was presented by Keating as to the basis for his input, nor is there any indication that Kersten's opinion is equal to a sound and thorough independent appraisal. The last full appraisal on the property was done in 1973. The passage of time, as well as the duty of the trustees, indicated that obtaining a sound and thorough appraisal would have been prudent.

Nor do the facts indicate that the trustees, in the alternative, had "tested the market." Jaffe's reference to not wanting the appraisal "early on" highlights the weakness in crediting the contacts with local developers in early 1983 as part of "testing the market." Jaffe testified that these contacts were not for the purpose of soliciting offers, which might have helped establish value. There is no indication that these contacts were part of an organized effort to "test the market" in a manner which would reasonably take the place of a sound and thorough appraisal. The record does not indicate that the trial court clearly erred in finding that the trustees did not fulfill their duty of establishing the value of the property.

The probate court's next concern was the inadequate marketing of the property. Marketing means taking action to bring the property's "availability to the attention of a wide spectrum of potential purchasers." Lockwood v. OFB Corp., 305 A.2d 636, 639 (Del Ch, 1973). There is no one set method of marketing, rather the cases indicate that all the circumstances surrounding the sale are considered to determine adequacy. We agree with the Chancery Court of Delaware, that what we are looking for is "a reasonably aggressive program which men of prudence and intelligence would have followed." Id. Factors which have been considered include advertisement in appropriate publications, contact with local developers, listing with a local broker, use of "For Sale" signs, showing the property to prospective customers, consultation with local sources on whether the offer price was the best offer obtainable, canvassing for possible purchasers, wide circulation of brochures and taking advantage of events—such as free publicity—to give notice of the sale. In short, we are looking to see if the trustees adopted and followed "a comprehensive and thorough plan to assure that the reasonable and intelligent steps necessary to secure the best possible market price were taken." Lockwood, supra, 305 A.2d 640.

[T]he record indicates that, whatever early contacts with local developers occurred, they were not for the purpose of marketing the property. The indications from Jaffe and Kersten are that these early contacts, along with the information received from Hall and Tilton, were an attempt to formulate a plan for the orderly marketing of the property. According to Jaffe and Kersten, it was not until August that the trustees decided on the standard to be applied in selling the property. The distribution of the circular was their only marketing effort.

Even assuming that sending out a circular could be sufficient, this method of marketing is suspect in these circumstances. While the trustees were actively considering an offer on less than all of the property and for an initial cash payment of $1.5 million, the property was being marketed to the rest of the world in its entirety. At least one potential buyer was told that he needed an initial cash outlay of $4 million. Furthermore, the entire extent of the marketing effort encompassed approximately twenty days—the time between the mailing and the acceptance of the Cohen offer.

The testimony of Dean Herlong is that he was informed on August 22 that interested parties would be given thirty days to respond. However, the circular did not indicate a time limit or that time was of the essence. The record indicates that potential purchasers such as Robertson, who had previously expressed an interest, were originally told it would be nine months to a year before offers would be accepted. Other purchasers could easily have accepted the circular as the first step in the long-awaited offering. The general impression we are left with is that the trustees were basically dormant, waiting for offers to be brought to them. Such lack of activity does not indicate that they fulfilled their duty to the trust.

The third area considered was the adequacy of the price obtained. While an accurate determination of value gives the trustees a good idea of where the bidding should begin, it does not mean that a higher price may not be available. The entire range of activities and surrounding circumstances are examined to see if the trustees took steps to understand the value and qualities of the property, as well as the nature of the market, and then took appropriate steps to secure the maximum price available....

A review of the record indicates that the trustees took a number of actions similar to those mentioned in the cases above. Prior to the Cohen offer, there were phone calls to local developers, there was consultation with an appraiser regarding value, other experts—Hall and Tilton—were consulted as to the use and potential problems, and at least two prospective purchasers—Robertson and Johnson—were contacted. Following the offer, a flyer was widely circulated among those local entities apparently most likely to be interested. If this were a simple matter of checking off an appropriate number of boxes, it could be argued that the trustees fulfilled their duty. However, in viewing these actions as a whole, we cannot say that these actions amounted to any actual concerted effort to determine or obtain the highest price available. This is not to say that a written or established plan is required, but rather it is to say that individual actions which do not indicate a concerted effort towards understanding and achieving the maximum price are not enough.

In the absence of some contemporaneous evidence on the value of the property, the court was forced to consider the appraisals made in 1985 in determining what an adequate price might have been. Both Majzels and Proctor testified; both appraisals were available. Both respondents and petitioners were diligent in pointing out to the court the respective strengths and weaknesses of the appraisals.

We find that, as with any other means for the assessment of damages, an appraisal must establish with a reasonable degree of certainty what an adequate price would have been; however, the law does not require a higher degree of certainty than the nature of the case permits. Given the facts of this case regarding the inadequacies of the trustees' actions with regard to the sale, it is not logical to require proof of a known purchaser or the existence of another offer to establish a price. The inadequate marketing in this case virtually precludes such a finding.

The court's finding that Proctor's appraisal, which included consideration of the development potential of the property, was more compelling as an indicator of price than Majzels' appraisal is not clearly erroneous. That the probate court found the development potential relevant to the worth of the property is not the same as Comerica's argument that the court was requiring the fiduciaries to speculate in risky land ventures.

The remaining issue concerning the trustees involves the court's finding that Jaffe was involved in a conflict of interest situation which tainted the sale and established his bad faith and self-dealing. We agree... that this is not a case of self-dealing because there was no evidence that Jaffe was actually a party or that he directly profited from the sale. We have been given no authority for the proposition that whatever indirect interest Jaffe may have had in his firm's fees amounts to self-dealing. However... there is evidence of a potential conflict of interest or conflicting loyalties which must be considered....

As a trustee, Jaffe was bound to consider the interests of the trust as paramount to all others. If other interests would prevent him from making a sound decision from the point of view of the trust, a potential conflict of interest exists. It is a fundamental principle that the trustee must display complete loyalty to the interests of the beneficiary, to the exclusion of all selfish interests or consideration of the interests of third parties. This principle is based on the understanding that a person acting in two capacities or in behalf of two interests may consciously or unconsciously favor one side over the other. It is not necessary that the trustee gain from the transaction to find disloyalty. Bogert, [Trusts and Trustees] §543, p 204. "In its desire to guard the highly valuable fiduciary relationship against improper administration, equity deems it better to forbid disloyalty and strike down all disloyal acts, rather than to attempt to separate the harmless and the harmful by permitting the trustee to justify his representation of two interests." Id., p 207.

As an attorney, Jaffe also had an obligation to use his skills and judgment in representing his client, thereby assuming a position of the highest trust and confidence. "A lawyer who is also a fiduciary bears a doubly high degree of responsibility and accountability." State Bar Grievance Administrator v. Estes, 392 Mich. 645, 653, 221 N.W.2d 322 (1974). While the Code of Professional Responsibility is not directly in issue in this case, it is relevant as expressing a standard of professional conduct expected of lawyers by which Jaffe may be measured. At the very least, the Code puts the attorney on notice that he is to be sensitive to the potential problems accompanying the representation of multiple clients, Canon 5, and that it is his duty to avoid even the appearance of impropriety.

The cases cited by Jaffe for his proposition that multiple representation may be valid are not determinative, since in those cases the parties were fully informed of the nature of the conflict. As noted by the probate court, Dean Herlong and Bishop McGehee, as co-trustees, were not fully informed of the extent of Jaffe's past representations of Cohen. Nor is it clear that they were kept apprised of the extent of his involvement in the Cohen negotiations and eventual sale. Similarly, the beneficiaries were not fully informed.

The fact is that Jaffe, as a named trustee, as the agent of Comerica and as an attorney with the law firm representing both the buyer and the seller, had a responsibility to avoid even the appearance of a conflict. The record indicates that the multiplicity of his roles created a situation fraught with conflict that could not be avoided by simply withdrawing as trustee for purposes of approving the Cohen offer. Jaffe's own testimony indicates the difficulty of the position in which he found himself "It's very difficult in these kinds of situations, ... to differentiate the head that you're using as trustee from the head that you're using as counsel. After all, you only have one. You have a lot of hats but you only have one head." The record indicates that, even after he committed not to act as a trustee, he was actively involved in the negotiations, and yet he testified that he had declined to act as both attorney for the estate and trustee for the charitable trust. The only party left to represent was Cohen, but Jaffe maintains that his firm's representation of the buyer was kept separate from him.

We know that Jaffe was involved in meetings regarding the adequacy of the offer and that he indicated approval of it to Comerica. As noted by the trial court:

> Even had the one page circular been designed to expose the property in its most favorable light to the market, there obviously was no time for any developer to investigate the property, perform soil borings, conduct environmental studies, prepare site plans, have the property appraised and study development costs, let alone prepare a bid. Cohen, on the other hand, had the benefit of the Calvin Hall site plans and Tilton materials and had spent five months studying the property before he had Honigman lawyers submit his bid.

At the very least, the short time span between the mailing of the circular and the acceptance of the Cohen offer gives the appearance that matters had been manipulated to assure that no other offers would be submitted or considered. Given our earlier finding on the inadequacy of the sale efforts, we cannot say that Jaffe's actions were the fair and adequate dealings of the loyal fiduciary. The court did not clearly err in finding a conflict or in finding that the conflict resulted in a breach of Jaffe's fiduciary duties.

However, while it was appropriate for the probate court to consider the Code of Professional Responsibility as indicative of the standard to which Jaffe should be held, we find that its holding that he violated the Disciplinary Rules must be vacated. The appropriate context for consideration of this type of attorney misconduct appears to be proceedings by the attorney discipline board or an action brought by an aggrieved client. The probate court's holding on this issue was not a necessary part of this adjudication and, to the extent it may be considered a holding of the court, we vacate it.

We further agree, given the facts of this case, that it is clear that Comerica had a responsibility to monitor or in some way react to Jaffe's conflict. Comerica's duty of loyalty applied to Jaffe and his firm as Comerica's employees or agents. Where a trustee allows its agents to pursue their own interests while carrying on trust work, the trustee may be liable to the same extent as the agent.

On the basis of all of the above, we affirm the trial court's holding that Jaffe and Comerica failed in their duties as trustees. Their actions and inactions were not mere negligence or errors in judgment. Their actions, clearly in violation of their duties and done with reckless or indifferent disregard of the beneficiaries' interests, indicate they acted in bad faith and preclude any insulation from liability under the trust's exculpatory clause.

As to Comerica's liability as personal representative, by statute the personal representative stands in a position of confidence and trust with respect to the beneficiaries. Edith Green's will gave Comerica, as personal representative, the same broad powers it enjoyed as a trustee. But the similar limitation of liability, excluding negligence and mistake of judgment, was specifically made not applicable to a corporate fiduciary such as Comerica. As a fiduciary, Comerica is liable for loss resulting from its negligence in handling the estate and for any misfeasance, malfeasance, or other breach of duty.

As a fiduciary, Comerica is held to the same standards regarding the sale of the property as were discussed above. Furthermore, the loyalty rule considered above with regard to Jaffe applies to all fiduciaries and their agents, not just trustees. The reasons discussed above also support the court's finding that Comerica is liable for its failure to fulfill its duties as the personal representative....

As to whether Dean Herlong and Bishop McGehee were estopped to complain..., the general rule is that ratification occurs only where the beneficiary acted with full knowledge of all the facts and not under the influence of misrepresentation, concealment or other wrongful conduct of the trustee. The record supports the probate court's finding that there is no estoppel because their qualified consent was not based on a full disclosure of the facts or the extent of the Jaffe-Cohen dealings. Nor were they fully informed when they signed the Cohen land contract.

On the issue of damages..., [t]he probate court found Comerica, as personal representative and trustee, and Jaffe, as trustee, jointly and severally liable for their activities in the amount of $1,900,000. There was no finding concerning the marital trust, nor did there need to be. Comerica's liability was based on an evaluation of its activities. That Comerica was not found liable for its role as trustee of the marital trust does not make its liability in its other roles any the less. The same is true for Jaffe. That Jaffe was not a trustee or personal representative of the estate is irrelevant to the liability imposed because of his own breach of duty as a trustee of the charitable trust. To carve out identities and liabilities at this stage of the proceedings smacks of the artificial and appears to be an effort to avoid liability rather than define the limits of liability....

Finally, both Jaffe and Comerica ask that they be reinstated as co-trustees and personal representative. Removing a fiduciary is a question entrusted to the discretion of the probate court, and that court's decision will not be reversed absent an abuse of discretion. Given the facts of this case, we find no abuse of discretion.

With the exception of the finding regarding Jaffe's violation of the Code of Professional Responsibility, which is vacated, the probate court's order is affirmed.

Notes and Questions

1. *Aftermath.* The facts of *Green* make it an especially interesting case. Miles Jaffe, whom the court found had violated his duty of loyalty, was a highly respected Detroit lawyer specializing in estate planning. Following the court's decision, he lost his law practice and eventually died a broken man. How could a sophisticated lawyer like Jaffe allow himself to be placed in a situation in which the conflict of interest is so apparent? Are there any particular factors that might explain why he let his guard down as trustee of the Green trust?

2. *Exculpatory Clauses.* One factor that may have entered into Jaffe's thinking was the existence of an exculpatory (sometimes called exoneration) clause in the trust instrument. Why did the clause not relieve Jaffe of all liability? Should these

clauses be enforceable as written?

Generally, exculpatory clauses are not permitted to immunize trustees from bad faith, reckless indifference, or intentional or willful neglect. UTC §1008(a) provides that an exculpatory clause is unenforceable "to the extent that it (1) relieves the trustee of liability for breach of trust committed in bad faith or with reckless indifference to the purposes of the trust or the interest of the beneficiaries; or (2) was inserted as a result of an abuse by the trustee of a fiduciary or confidential relationship to the settlor." (This restriction on the validity of an exculpatory clause is a mandatory rule according to UTC §105(b)(10).) How would Miles Jaffe have fared under this standard? Was he guilty of acting in bad faith?

3. *Self-Dealing and the "No-Further-Inquiry" Rule.* The court in *Green* concluded that Jaffe's actions, while tainted by a conflict of interest, did not constitute self-dealing. Self-dealing exists when the trustee sells trust property to itself individually or sells individual property to the trust. In these circumstances, courts have applied a prophylactic rule known as the "no-further-inquiry" rule—a rule that makes all self-dealing transactions per se voidable by the beneficiaries, requiring no proof that such transactions were unreasonable or harmful. The beneficiaries may set the transaction aside even though it was made in good faith and for a reasonable price. See UTC §802(b). Moreover, the trustee is chargeable with any profit the trustee realized through the breach of trust. See UTC §1002(a)(2). If it has made no profit, the trustee is chargeable with any loss to the trust estate resulting from the breach of trust or any profit that would have accrued to the trust estate if there had been no breach of trust. See UTC §1002(a)(1).

Professor John Langbein has argued that the no-further-inquiry rule should be relaxed. He argues that "[a] transaction in which there has been a conflict or overlap of interest should be sustained if the trustee can prove that the transaction was prudently undertaken in the best interests of the beneficiaries." In such cases, he contends, "inquiry into the merits is better than 'no further inquiry.'" John H. Langbein, Questioning the Trust Law Duty of Loyalty: Sole Interest or Best Interest?, 114 Yale L.J. 929, 932 (2005). For the contrary view, see Melanie B. Leslie, In Defense of the No Further Inquiry Rule: A Response to Professor John Langbein, 47 Wm. & Mary L. Rev. 541 (2005).

4. *Indirect Self-Dealing.* In the past, courts have treated certain transactions that are not, strictly speaking, self-dealing as indirect forms of self-dealing and subjected them to the no-further-inquiry rule. Transactions between the trustee and the trustee's spouse or close relative, for example, have been held subject to the no-further-inquiry rule. See, e.g., Restatement 3d of Trusts §78 comment e; Hartman v. Hartle, 122 A. 615 (N.J. Ch. 1923). The same result has been reached when the sale is to the trustee's attorney, agent, or any entity in which the trustee has an interest. See, e.g., In re Clarke's Estate, 188 N.E.2d 128 (N.Y. 1962). The Uniform Trust Code, however, relaxes the treatment of such transactions. It provides that as to such transactions the rule "is less severe." These transactions are voidable, not void. See

UTC §802(c)(4) and comment. The trustee may avoid liability by showing that such a transaction was not affected by a conflict between fiduciary and personal interests.

5. *Corporate Trustee Purchase or Retention of Its Own Stock.* There is no self-dealing if a corporate trustee retains for the trust or purchases from others its own shares as trust property.[5] Nevertheless, the practice has been condemned on the basis of the possibility of conflict of interest. See Restatement 3d of Trusts §78 comment e(2); Restatement 2d of Trusts §170 comment n. The Restatement 3d relaxes the stricture somewhat by providing that "it would normally be permissible for a relatively modest portion of the trustee's stock to be held indirectly through an appropriate holding of shares in a mutual fund or other pooled-investment vehicle." Restatement 3d of Trusts §78 comment e(2). See also UTC §802(f).

6. *Liability of Co-Trustees.* The traditional rule is that where there is more than one trustee, co-trustee A is liable for the wrongful acts of co-trustee B to which A consented or which, through negligent inaction or improper delegation, A enabled. See Restatement 3d of Trusts §81(2) and comment e.[6]

7. *Consent to or Ratification of Breaches of Fiduciary Duty.* Trustee actions that would otherwise constitute a breach of the duty of loyalty may be consented to ex ante or ratified ex post, thereby relieving the trustee of liability. If the settlor holds the power to revoke the trust, the settlor may consent to or ratify the breach without the beneficiaries' consent. See UTC §603. Lacking such a power, the settlor's consent or ratification will not be binding on the beneficiaries. The beneficiaries, however, may consent to or ratify a breach. Uniform Trust Code §1009 provides that a trustee is not liable to a beneficiary for a breach of trust "if the beneficiary consented to the conduct constituting the breach, released the trustee from liability, or ratified the transaction constituting the breach, unless: (1) the consent, release, or ratification of the beneficiary was induced by improper conduct of the trustee; or (2) at the time of the consent, release, or ratification, the beneficiary did not know of the beneficiary's rights or of the material facts relating to the breach."

8. *Authorization or Approval of Actions Otherwise Constituting Breaches of Trust.* To be distinguished from consent or ratification is authorization by the terms of the trust, or approval by a court, of trustee actions that would otherwise constitute a

---

5. Self-dealing would exist, however, if a corporate trustee purchased for inclusion in the trust other assets, including securities, that the trustee owned.

6. UTC §703 provides in relevant part:

(f) Except as otherwise provided in subsection (g), a trustee who does not join in an action of another trustee is not liable for the action.

(g) Each trustee shall exercise reasonable care to:

    (1) prevent a cotrustee from committing a serious breach of trust; and

    (2) compel a cotrustee to redress a serious breach of trust.

The Comment states: "Trustees who dissent from the acts of a cotrustee are in general protected from liability. Subsection (f) protects trustees who refused to join in an action.... However, the protection[] provided in subsection[] (f) ... no longer appl[ies] if the action constitutes a serious breach of trust."

breach of trust. Uniform Trust Code §802(b) permits the terms of the trust to authorize or a court to approve transactions that would otherwise violate the trustee's duty of loyalty.

———

Duty to Earmark. Suppose a trustee causes trust assets to be registered in its name without any indication that the asset is subject to the trust. If the asset falls in value due to unforeseeable market developments beyond the control of the trustee, should the trustee be able to avoid liability for the loss by explaining away any inference of intentional wrongdoing? Although the failure to earmark is arguably prohibited by the rule against self-dealing, a distinct duty to earmark a trust investment so as to distinguish it from individual assets of the trustee is well recognized. See UTC §810(c); Restatement 3d of Trusts §84, comment d.

3. The Duty of Prudence

Primary Statutory References: *UTC §§804, 807, 809*
                                                      Uniform Prudent Investor Act

We now turn to the trustee's duty of prudence, expressed in what is today called the "Prudent Investor Rule." The duty of prudence has undergone profound changes within the past few decades. The following excerpts provide the historical background for the rethinking of trust law's duty of prudence in trust investment.

Restatement 3d of Trusts: Prudent Investor Rule
Topic 5. Investment of Trust Funds: Introduction (1992)

The foundation of trust investment law in the first and second Restatements has been the so-called "prudent man rule" of Harvard College v. Amory, 9 Pick. (26 Mass.) 446, 461 (1830). The opinion admonishes trustees "to observe how men of prudence, discretion and intelligence manage their own affairs, not in regard to speculation, but in regard to the permanent disposition of their funds, considering the probable income, as well as the probable safety of the capital to be invested." Thus, the rule of the Restatement, Second, of Trusts §227 (1959) directs trustees "to make such investments and only such investments as a prudent man would make of his own property having in view the preservation of the estate and the amount and regularity of the income to be derived." In generally similar language, influenced by the original Restatement, the prudent man rule has been adopted by decision or legislation in most American jurisdictions, often displacing the more restrictive, so-called "legal list" statutes.[7]

---

7. Legal lists were statutory lists of the supposedly safest investments. The lists, patterned after an English statutory list initially adopted by Parliament following the bursting of the South Sea "Bubble" in the early 18th century, were mostly limited to fixed income investments, such as government bonds,

Unfortunately, much of the apparent and initially intended generality and adaptability of the prudent man rule was lost as it was further elaborated in the courts and applied case by case. Decisions dealing with essentially factual issues were accompanied by generalizations understandably intended to offer guidance to other courts and trustees in like situations. These cases were subsequently treated as precedents establishing general rules governing trust instruments. Specific case results and flexible principles often thereby became crystallized into specific subrules prescribing the types and characteristics of permissible investments for trustees.

Based on some degree of risk that was abstractly perceived as excessive, broad categories of investments and techniques often came to be classified as "speculative" and thus as imprudent per se. Accordingly, the exercise of care, skill, and caution would be no defense if the property acquired or retained by a trustee, or the strategy pursued for a trust, was characterized as impermissible.

Knowledge, practices, and experiences in the modern investment world have demonstrated that arbitrary restrictions on trust investments are unwarranted and often counterproductive. For example, understandable concern has existed that widely accepted theories and practices of investment management cannot properly be pursued by trustees under present judicial and treatise statements of the law. Prohibitions that developed under the traditional prudent man rule have been potential sources of unjustified liability for trustees generally and, more particularly, of inhibitions limiting the exercise of sound judgment by skilled trustees. This is particularly so for trustees whose fiduciary circumstances call for, or at least permit, investment programs that would include some high-risk-and-return investment strategies (such as a venture capital program) or for the use of abstractly high-risk investments or techniques (such as futures or options trading) for the purpose of reducing the risk level of the portfolio as a whole.

These criticisms of the prudent man rule are supported by a large and growing body of literature that is in turn supported by empirical research, well documented and essentially compelling. Much... of this criticism is found in writings that have collectively and loosely come to be called modern portfolio theory.

Christopher P. Cline, The Uniform Prudent Investor and Principal and Income Acts: Changing the Trust Landscape
42 Real Prop., Prob. & Tr. J. 611, 613 (2008)

To understand the impetus behind the Prudent Investor Act..., the estate planning lawyer must be familiar with modern portfolio theory....

(first) mortgages, and fixed-income securities of large established companies. Most states had such statutes into the 1940s. [Ed.]

[Market portfolio theory conceptualizes] the existence of two distinct types of risk: (1) market risk, which deals with market volatility (for example, the stock market), and (2) firm-specific (or nonmarket) risk, which deals with the volatility of a particular asset (for example, a company that may go bankrupt). An investor should obtain higher returns by accepting greater market risk (for example, investments in stocks are riskier than investments in bonds, so as market risk increases so should the return on investment). On the other hand, firm-specific (or nonmarket) risk generates no additional return because an investor can avoid the risk through diversification. An investor should take at least two steps to deal with these risks. First, an investor should determine the level of volatility it is willing to accept for the return it hopes to achieve. This will determine the level of market risk it assumes. Second, to avoid nonmarket risk, an investor should diversify its portfolio in accordance with the chosen level of market risk.

Uniform Prudent Investor Act
Prefatory Note (1994) (citations omitted)

Over the quarter century from the late 1960s the investment practices of fiduciaries experienced significant change. The Uniform Prudent Investor Act (UPIA) undertakes to update trust investment law in recognition of the alterations that have occurred in investment practice....

This Act draws upon the revised standards for prudent trust investment promulgated by the American Law Institute in its Restatement (Third) of Trusts: Prudent Investor Rule (1992)....

UPIA makes five fundamental alterations in the former criteria for prudent investing. All are to be found in the Restatement....

(1) The standard of prudence is applied to any investment as part of the total portfolio, rather than to individual investments. In the trust setting, the term "portfolio" embraces all the trust's assets.

(2) The tradeoff in all investing between risk and return is identified as the fiduciary's central consideration.

(3) All categoric restrictions on the types of investments have been abrogated; the trustee can invest in anything that plays an appropriate role in achieving the risk/return objectives of the trust and that meets the other requirements of prudent investing.

(4) The long familiar requirement that fiduciaries diversify their investments has been integrated into the definition of prudent investing.

(5) The much criticized former rule of trust law forbidding the trustee to delegate investment and management functions has been reversed. Delegation is now permitted, subject to safeguards.

Estate of Janes

681 N.E.2d 332 (N.Y. 1997)

LEVINE, J. Former State Senator and businessman Rodney B. Janes (testator) died on May 26, 1973, survived solely by his wife, Cynthia W. Janes, who was then 72 years of age. Testator's $3,500,000 estate consisted of a $2,500,000 stock portfolio, approximately 71% of which consisted of 13,232 shares of common stock of the Eastman Kodak Company. The Kodak stock had a date-of- death value of $1,786,733, or approximately $135 per share.

Testator's 1963 will and a 1969 codicil bequeathed most of his estate to three trusts. First, the testator created a marital deduction trust consisting of approximately 50% of the estate's assets, the income of which was to be paid to Mrs. Janes for her life. In addition, it contained a generous provision for invasion of the principal for Mrs. Janes's benefit and gave her testamentary power of appointment over the remaining principal. The testator also established a charitable trust of approximately 25% of the estate's assets which directed annual distributions to selected charities. A third trust comprised the balance of the estate's assets and directed that the income therefrom be paid to Mrs. Janes for her life, with the remainder pouring over into the charitable trust upon her death.

On June 6, 1973, the testator's will and codicil were admitted to probate. Letters testamentary issued to petitioner's predecessor, Lincoln Rochester Trust Company, and Mrs. Janes, as coexecutors, on July 3, 1973. Letters of trusteeship issued to petitioner alone. By early August 1973, petitioner's trust and estate officers, Ellison Patterson and Richard Young had ascertained the estate's assets and the amount of cash needed for taxes, commissions, attorneys' fees, and specific bequests.

In an August 9, 1973 memorandum, Patterson recommended raising the necessary cash for the foregoing administrative expenses by selling certain assets, including 800 shares of Kodak stock, and holding "the remaining issues... until the [t]rusts [were] funded." The memorandum did not otherwise address investment strategy in light of the evident primary objective of the testator to provide for his widow during her lifetime. In a September 5, 1973 meeting with Patterson and Young, Mrs. Janes, who had a high school education, no business training or experience, and who had never been employed, consented to the sale of some 1,200 additional shares of Kodak stock. Although Mrs. Janes was informed at the meeting that petitioner intended to retain the balance of the Kodak shares, none of the factors that would lead to an informed investment decision was discussed. At that time, the Kodak stock traded for about $139 per share; thus, the estate's 13,232 shares of the stock were worth almost $1,840,000. The September 5 meeting was the only occasion where retention of the Kodak stock or any other investment issues were taken up with Mrs. Janes.

By the end of 1973, the price of Kodak stock had fallen to about $109 per share. One year later, it had fallen to about $63 per share and, by the end of 1977, to about $51 per share. In March 1978, the price had dropped even further, to about $40 per share. When petitioner filed its initial accounting in February 1980, the remaining 11,320 shares were worth approximately $530,000, or about $47 per share. Most of the shares were used to fund the trusts in 1986 and 1987.

In addition to its initial accounting in 1980, petitioner filed a series of supplemental accountings that together covered the period from July 1973 through June 1994. In August 1981, petitioner sought judicial settlement of its account. Objections to the accounts were originally filed by Mrs. Janes in 1982, and subsequently by the Attorney-General on behalf of the charitable beneficiaries (collectively, "objectants"). In seeking to surcharge petitioner for losses incurred by the estate due to petitioner's imprudent retention of a high concentration of Kodak stock in the estate from July 1973 to February 1980, during which time the value of the stock had dropped to about one third of its date-of-death value, objectants asserted that petitioner's conduct violated EPTL 11-2.2(a)(1), the so-called "prudent person rule" of investment. When Mrs. Janes died in 1986, the personal representative of her estate was substituted as an objectant.

Following a trial on the objections, the Surrogate found that petitioner, under the circumstances, had acted imprudently and should have divested the estate of the high concentration of Kodak stock by August 9, 1973. The court imposed a $6,080,269 surcharge against petitioner and ordered petitioner to forfeit its commissions and attorneys' fees. In calculating the amount of the surcharge, the court adopted a "lost profits" or "market index" measure of damages espoused by objectants' expert—what the proceeds of the Kodak stock would have yielded, up to the time of trial, had they been invested in petitioner's own diversified equity fund on August 9, 1973.

The Appellate Division modified solely as to damages, holding that "the Surrogate properly found [petitioner] liable for its negligent failure to diversify and for its inattentiveness, inaction, and lack of disclosure, but that the Surrogate adopted an improper measure of damages" (Matter of Janes, 223 A.D.2d 20, 22, 643 N.Y.S.2d 972). [T]he Court held that the Surrogate's finding of imprudence, as well as its selection of August 9, 1973 as the date by which petitioner should have divested the estate of its concentration of Kodak stock, were "well supported" by the record. The Court rejected the Surrogate's "lost profits" or "market index" measure of damages, however, holding that the proper measure of damages was "the value of the capital that was lost"—the difference between the value of the stock at the time it should have been sold and its value when ultimately sold. Applying this measure, the Court reduced the surcharge to $4,065,029. We granted petitioner and objectants leave to appeal, and now affirm.

I. Petitioner's Liability. Petitioner argues that New York law does not permit a fiduciary to be surcharged for imprudent management of a trust for failure to diversify in the absence of additional elements of hazard, and that it relied upon, and complied with, this rule in administering the estate. [P]etitioner claims that elements of hazard can be capsulized into deficiencies in the following investment quality factors: "(i) the capital structure of the company; (ii) the competency of its management; (iii) whether the company is a seasoned issuer of stock with a history of profitability; (iv) whether the company has a history of paying dividends; (v) whether the company is an industry leader; (vi) the expected future direction of the company's business; and (vii) the opinion of investment bankers and analysts who follow the company's stock." Evaluated under these criteria, petitioner asserts, the concentration of Kodak stock at issue in this case, that is, of an acknowledged "blue chip" security popular with investment advisors and many mutual funds, cannot be found an imprudent investment on August 9, 1973 as a matter of law. In our view, a fiduciary's duty of investment prudence in holding a concentration of one security may not be so rigidly limited.

New York followed the prudent person rule of investment during the period of petitioner's administration of the instant estate. This rule provides that "[a] fiduciary holding funds for investment may invest the same in such securities as would be acquired by prudent [persons] of discretion and intelligence in such matters who are seeking a reasonable income and the preservation of their capital" (EPTL 11-2.2[a][1]).[8] Codified in 1970, the prudent person rule's New York common-law antecedents can be traced to King v. Talbot, 40 N.Y. 76, wherein this Court stated:

> [T]he trustee is bound to employ such diligence and such prudence in the care and management [of the trust], as in general, prudent men of discretion and intelligence in such matters, employ in their own like affairs.
>
> This necessarily excludes all speculation, all investments for an uncertain and doubtful rise in the market, and, of course, everything that does not take into view the nature and object of the trust, and the consequences of a mistake in the selection of the investment to be made....
>
> *[T]he preservation of the fund, and the procurement of a just income therefrom, are primary objects* of the creation of the trust itself, and are to be primarily regarded" (id., at 85-86 [emphasis supplied]).

No precise formula exists for determining whether the prudent person standard has been violated in a particular situation; rather, the determination depends on an examination of the facts and circumstances of each case. In undertaking this inquiry, the court should engage in "'a balanced and perceptive analysis of [the fiduciary's] consideration and action in light of the history of each individual investment, viewed at the time of its action or its omission to act'" (Matter of Donner, 82 N.Y.2d 574, 585, 606 N.Y.S.2d 137, 626 N.E.2d 922 [quoting Matter of Bank of N.Y., 35 N.Y.2d 512, 519, 364 N.Y.S.2d 164, 323 N.E.2d 700]). And, while a court should not view

---

8. The recently enacted Prudent Investor Act requires a trustee "to diversify assets unless the trustee reasonably determines that it is in the interests of the beneficiaries not to diversify, taking into account the purposes and terms and provisions of the governing instrument" (EPTL 112.3[b][3][C]). The act applies to investments "made or held" by a trustee on or after January 1, 1995 and, thus, does not apply to the matter before us (EPTL 11-2.3 [a]).

each act or omission aided or enlightened by hindsight, a court may, nevertheless, examine the fiduciary's conduct over the entire course of the investment in determining whether it has acted prudently. Generally, whether a fiduciary has acted prudently is a factual determination to be made by the trial court.

As the foregoing demonstrates, the very nature of the prudent person standard dictates against any absolute rule that a fiduciary's failure to diversify, in and of itself, constitutes imprudence, as well as against a rule invariably immunizing a fiduciary from its failure to diversify in the absence of some selective list of elements of hazard, such as those identified by petitioner. Indeed, in various cases, courts have determined that a fiduciary's retention of a high concentration of one asset in a trust or estate was imprudent without reference to those elements of hazard. The inquiry is simply whether, under all the facts and circumstances of the particular case, the fiduciary violated the prudent person standard in maintaining a concentration of a particular stock in the estate's portfolio of investments.

Moreover, no court has stated that the limited elements of hazard outlined by petitioner are the only factors that may be considered in determining whether a fiduciary has acted prudently in maintaining a concentrated portfolio. Again, as commentators have noted, one of the primary virtues of the prudent person rule "lies in its lack of specificity, as this permits the propriety of the trustee's investment decisions to be measured in light of the business and economic circumstances existing at the time they were made" (Laurino, Investment Responsibility of Professional Trustees, 51 St John's L Rev 717, 723 [1977] [emphasis supplied]).

Petitioner's restrictive list of hazards omits such additional factors to be considered under the prudent person rule by a trustee in weighing the propriety of any investment decision, as: "the amount of the trust estate, the situation of the beneficiaries, the trend of prices and of the cost of living, the prospect of inflation and of deflation" (Restatement [Second] of Trusts §227 comment e). Other pertinent factors are the marketability of the investment and possible tax consequences (id. comment o). The trustee must weigh all of these investment factors as they affect the principal objects of the testator's or settlor's bounty, as between income beneficiaries and remainder persons, including decisions regarding "whether to apportion the investments between high-yield or high-growth securities" (Turano and Radigan, New York Estate Administration ch. 14, §P, at 409 [1986]).

Moreover, and especially relevant to the instant case, the various factors affecting the prudence of any particular investment must be considered in the light of the "circumstances of the trust itself rather than [merely] the integrity of the particular investment" (9C Rohan, N.Y. Civ. Prac-EPTL I 11- 2.2[5], at 11-513, n.106 [1996]). As stated in a leading treatise:

> [t]he trustee should take into consideration the circumstances of the particular trust that he is administering, both as to the size of the trust estate and the requirements of the beneficiaries. He should consider each investment not as an isolated transaction but in its

relation to the whole of the trust estate (3 Scott, Trusts §227.12, at 477 [4th ed]).

Our case law is entirely consistent with the foregoing authorities. Thus, in Matter of Bank of N.Y, although we held that a trustee remains responsible for imprudence as to each individual investment in a trust portfolio, we stated:

> *The record of any individual investment is not to be viewed exclusively, of course, as though it were in its own water-tight compartment*, since to some extent individual investment decisions may properly be affected by considerations of the performance of the fund as an entity, as in the instance, for example, of individual security decisions based in part on considerations of diversification of the fund or of capital transactions to achieve sound tax planning for the fund as a whole. The focus of inquiry, however, is nonetheless on the individual security as such and factors relating to the entire portfolio are to be weighed only along with others in reviewing the prudence of the particular investment decisions" (35 N.Y.2d, at 517, 364, N.Y.S.2d 164, 323 N.E.2d 700, supra [emphasis supplied]).

Thus, the elements of hazard petitioner relies upon as demonstrating that, as a matter of law, it had no duty to diversify, suffer from two major deficiencies under the prudent person rule. First, petitioner's risk elements too narrowly and strictly define the scope of a fiduciary's responsibility in making any individual investment decision, and the factors a fiduciary must consider in determining the propriety of a given investment.

A second deficiency in petitioner's elements of hazard list is that all of the factors relied upon by petitioner go to the propriety of an individual investment "exclusively... as though it were in its own water-tight compartment" (Matter of Bank of N.Y., supra, at 517, 364 N.Y.S.2d 164, 323 N.E.2d 700), which would encourage a fiduciary to treat each investment as an isolated transaction rather than "in its relation to the whole of the trust estate" (3 Scott, op. cit., at 477). Thus, petitioner's criteria for elements of hazard would apply irrespective of the concentration of the investment security under consideration in the portfolio. That is, the existence of any of the elements of risk specified by petitioner in a given corporate security would militate against the investment even in a diversified portfolio, obviating any need to consider concentration as a reason to divest or refrain from investing. This ignores the market reality that, with respect to some investment vehicles, concentration itself may create or add to risk, and essentially takes lack of diversification out of the prudent person equation altogether.

Likewise, contrary to petitioner's alternative attack on the decisions below, neither the Surrogate nor the Appellate Division based their respective rulings holding petitioner liable on any absolute duty of a fiduciary to diversify. Rather, those courts determined that a surcharge was appropriate because maintaining a concentration in Kodak stock, under the circumstances presented, violated certain critical obligations of a fiduciary in making investment decisions under the prudent person rule. First, petitioner failed to consider the investment in Kodak stock in relation to the entire portfolio of the estate, i.e., whether the Kodak concentration itself created or added to investment risk. The objectants' experts testified that even high quality growth stocks, such as Kodak, possess some degree of volatility because their market value is tied so closely to earnings projections. They further opined that the investment risk arising from that volatility is significantly exacerbated when a portfolio is heavily concentrated in one such growth stock.

Second, the evidence revealed that, in maintaining an investment portfolio in which Kodak represented 71 % of the estate's stock holdings, and the balance was largely in other growth stocks, petitioner paid insufficient attention to the needs and interests of the testator's 72-year-old widow, the life beneficiary of three quarters of his estate, for whose comfort, support and anticipated increased medical expenses the testamentary trusts were evidently created. Testimony by petitioner's investment manager, and by the objectants' experts, disclosed that the annual yield on Kodak stock in 1973 was approximately 1.06%, and that the aggregate annual income from all estate stockholdings was $43,961, a scant 1.7% of the $2.5 million estate securities portfolio. Thus, retention of a high concentration of Kodak jeopardized the interests of the primary income beneficiary of the estate and led to the eventual need to substantially invade the principal of the marital testamentary trust.

Lastly, there was evidence in the record to support the findings below that, in managing the estate's investments, petitioner failed to exercise due care and the skill it held itself out as possessing as a corporate fiduciary. Notably, there was proof that petitioner (1) failed initially to undertake a formal analysis of the estate and establish an investment plan consistent with the testator's primary objectives; (2) failed to follow petitioner's own internal trustee review protocol during the administration of the estate, which advised special caution and attention in cases of portfolio concentration of as little as 20%; and (3) failed to conduct more than routine reviews of the Kodak holdings in this estate, without considering alternative investment choices, over a seven-year period of steady decline in the value of the stock.

Since, thus, there was evidence in the record to support the foregoing affirmed findings of imprudence on the part of petitioner, the determination of liability must be affirmed.

II. Date of Divestiture. As we have noted, in determining whether a fiduciary has acted prudently, a court may examine a fiduciary's conduct throughout the entire period during which the investment at issue was held. The court may then determine, within that period, the "reasonable time" within which divestiture of the imprudently held investment should have occurred. What constitutes a reasonable time will vary from case to case and is not fixed or arbitrary. The test remains "the diligence and prudence of prudent and intelligent [persons] in the management of their own affairs."...

Again, there is evidentiary support in the record for the trial court's finding, affirmed by the Appellate Division, that a prudent fiduciary would have divested the estate's stock portfolio of its high concentration of Kodak stock by August 9, 1973, thereby exhausting our review powers on this issue. Petitioner's own internal documents and correspondence, as well as the testimony of Patterson, Young, and objectants' experts, establish that by that date, petitioner had all the information a prudent investor would have needed to conclude that the percentage of Kodak stock in the estate's stock portfolio was excessive and should have been reduced significantly, particularly in light of the estate's over-all investment portfolio and the financial requirements of Mrs. Janes and the charitable beneficiaries.

III. Damages. Finally, as to the calculation of the surcharge, we conclude that the Appellate Division correctly rejected the Surrogate's "lost profits" or "market index" measure of damages. Where, as here, a fiduciary's imprudence consists solely of negligent retention of assets it should have sold, the measure of damages is the value of the lost capital ....

In imposing liability upon a fiduciary on the basis of the capital lost, the court should determine the value of the stock on the date it should have been sold, and subtract from that figure the proceeds from the sale of the stock or, if the stock is still retained by the estate, the value of the stock at the time of the accounting. Whether interest is awarded, and at what rate, is a matter within the discretion of the trial court. Dividends and other income attributable to the retained assets should offset any interest awarded.

Here, uncontradicted expert testimony established that application of this measure of damages resulted in a figure of $4,065,029, which includes prejudgment interest at the legal rate, compounded from August 9, 1973 to October 1, 1994. The Appellate Division did not abuse its discretion in adding to that figure prejudgment interest from October 1, 1994 through August 17, 1995, $326,302.66 previously received by petitioner for commissions and attorneys' fees, plus postjudgment interest, costs, and disbursements.

Accordingly, the order of the Appellate Division should be affirmed, without costs.

Notes and Questions

1. *Settlor Authorization or Direction.* Given that over 70% of Rodney Janes' pre-death stock portfolio was comprised of Kodak stock, did Janes implicitly authorize the trustee to retain the stock? If yes, is the trustee relieved of the duty to diversify? For discussion, see John H. Langbein, Burn the Rembrandt?: Trust Law's Limits on the Settlor's Power to Direct Investments, 90 B.U. L. Rev. 375 (2010).

2. *Enactment of the Uniform Prudent Investor Act.* More than forty states and the District of Columbia have enacted the Uniform Prudent Investor Act. However, very few states have enacted the Act verbatim. For an analysis of some of the variations, see Trent S. Kiziah, Remaining Heterogeneity in Trust Investment Law After Twenty-Five Years of Reform, 37 ACTEC J. 317 (2011).

3. *Criticism of the Prudent Investor Rule.* Professor Stewart Sterk has argued that the Prudent Investor Rule has had the unfortunate effect of encouraging trustees to invest too heavily in equities. He argues, instead, for a regime of "safe harbors" to protect beneficiaries from excess market risk. See Stewart E. Sterk, Rethinking Trust Law Reform: How Prudent is Modern Prudent Investor Doctrine?, 95 Cornell L. Rev. 851 (2010).

4. *ESG Investing.* Can trustees, consistent with their fiduciary duties, take environmental, social, and governance ("ESG") factors into account in making investment decisions? Compare the views of Scott and Fratcher, The Law of Trusts §227.17 (4th ed. 1988),

> The directors of a business corporation owe fiduciary duties to the shareholders to conduct the business of the corporation so as to attempt to secure a profit. But it is well-settled that they should recognize that they and the corporation are part of the community. They may, within proper limits, make gifts of the money of the corporation for charitable purposes, although this may, for the immediate present at least, slightly diminish the profits of the corporation....
>
> Trustees in deciding whether to invest in, or to retain, the securities of a corporation may properly consider the social performance of the corporation....
>
> ...Of course they may well believe that a corporation that has a proper sense of social obligation is more likely to be successful in the long run than those that are bent upon obtaining the maximum amount of profits. But even if this were not so, the investor, though a trustee of funds for others, is entitled to consider the welfare of the community, and refrain from allowing the use of the funds in a manner detrimental to society.

with John H. Langbein & Richard A. Posner, Social Investing and the Law of Trusts, 79 Mich. L. Rev. 72, 85-86, 88 (1980),

> A portfolio constructed in accordance with social principles will be less diversified than a portfolio constructed in accordance with [modern portfolio theory]. This is because stocks are added to and subtracted from the portfolio by the social investor without regard to the effect on diversification. To be sure, if social responsibility were a random characteristic of firms... the effect on diversification of excluding the socially irresponsible firms from the investment portfolio would be limited to what is called sampling error....
>
> If socially irresponsible firms are not a random draw from the underlying universe of firms, then the use of social-investing criteria to design the portfolio will result not only in sampling error, but also in sampling bias....
>
> In sum, we are skeptical that a portfolio constructed in accordance with consistent, and consistently-applied, social principles could avoid serious underdiversification.

The Restatement 3d of Trusts §90 comment c takes the following position:

> [T]he trustee's [investment] decisions ordinarily must not be motivated by a purpose of advancing or expressing the trustee's personal views concerning social or political issues or causes. Such considerations, however, may properly influence the investment decisions of a trustee to the extent permitted by the terms of the trust or by the consent of the

beneficiaries.... In addition, social considerations may be taken into account in investing the funds of charitable trusts to the extent the charitable purposes would justify an expenditure of trust funds for the social issue or cause in question or to the extent the investment decision can be justified on grounds of advancing, financially or operationally, a charitable activity conducted by the trust.

───────

Delegation of Fiduciary Duties. A traditional rule of trust fiduciary law is that trustees may not delegate to others those responsibilities that they can reasonably be required to perform themselves. The line between delegable and non-delegable duties is not always clear. The courts usually articulate the line in terms of an equally uncertain distinction between discretionary and ministerial acts. It is clear, though, that while a trustee may employ investment advisors, delegating the power to select trust investments to an agent is a breach of the traditional duty not to delegate. Restatement 2d of Trusts §171 comment h. Commentators have criticized this rule on the ground that it inhibits trustees from taking advantage of specialized expertise in an industry that increasingly has become specialized. The question, they argue, should not be whether to delegate but how to delegate in the way most effective for the trust. See John H. Langbein, Reversing the Nondelegation Rule of Trust-Investment Law, 59 Mo. L. Rev. 105 (1994).

The Restatement 3d of Trusts, responding to these criticisms, abandons the traditional non-delegation rule. Section 80 provides that "[a] trustee has a duty to perform the responsibilities of the trusteeship personally, except as a prudent person of comparable skill might delegate those responsibilities to others." Restatement 3d of Trusts §90 comment j sheds further light on the subject, stating that "the trustee has power, and may sometimes have a duty, to delegate [investment] functions...." It requires that the power to delegate be exercised reasonably and with due care, eschewing any simple objective test for determining whether the delegation power has been properly exercised. Similarly, both the Uniform Prudent Investor Act §9 and Uniform Trust Code §807 abrogate the non-delegation rule.

Related to the question about the duty not to delegate is the widespread practice of trust investment in mutual funds. In a mutual fund, such as those marketed by Vanguard or Fidelity or other well-known companies, the selection of assets comprising the particular fund is made by the fund's manager. Thus, the decision to invest in one mutual fund versus another (or not in any mutual funds at all) is a decision of the trustee, but investments *within* a given mutual fund cannot be determined by the trustee but only by the fund manager. Hence the problem of delegation. Restatement 3d of Trusts §90 [Prudent Investor Rule §227] comment m approves of a strategy of achieving diversification through investing trust assets in mutual funds. Index funds are mutual or other investment funds comprised of a securities portfolio designed to approximate a market index such as the Standard & Poor's (S&P) 500 or the Russell 3000.

Surcharge for Breach of Fiduciary Duty. The Restatement 3d of Trusts provides: "A trustee who commits a breach of trust is chargeable with... the amount required to restore the values of the trust estate and trust distributions to what they would have been if the portion of the trust affected by the breach had been properly administered...." Restatement 3d of Trusts §100(a). How does this measure of loss compare with the measures of loss used by the trial and appellate courts in *Janes*?

Determining the Amount of Loss. How should a court determine "the amount required to restore the trust estate and trust distributions to what they would have been if the portion of the trust affected by the breach had been properly administered"? Consider the following advice from the Restatement 3d of Trusts §100 comment b(1):

> *b(1). Determining amount of loss.* If a breach of trust causes a loss, including any failure to realize income, capital gain, or appreciation that would have resulted from proper administration of the trust, the trustee is liable for the amount necessary to compensate fully for the breach.
>
> Occasionally a situation arises that offers an essentially objective means of ascertaining the loss for which a trustee is liable.... For example, if the trustee failed to retain (or to acquire) certain property as specifically required by the terms of the trust, whether and in what amount the trust suffered a loss can be determined by ascertaining the specified property's value and earnings as of the time of surcharge and comparing that with the results of the trustee's investment of the sale proceeds (or of the funds that would have been needed to purchase the property as directed)....
>
> If the breach of trust involved accepting too low a price in an otherwise proper sale of trust property, the trustee's liability would be the amount by which the sale price was inadequate, plus (or minus) a projected total return on that amount to the time of surcharge. In this situation, the return projection probably... can be based simply on the return received on the trustee's investment of the actual proceeds of the sale. (If the only breach was in selling the property for too little, the trustee is not chargeable with the amount of any subsequent increase in that property's value.)
>
> Illustrative of more difficult "loss" determinations is the determination of the recovery from a trustee for imprudent or otherwise improper investments. The recovery in such a case ordinarily would be the difference between (1) the value of those investments and their income and other product at the time of surcharge and (2) the amount of funds expended in making the improper investments, increased (or decreased) by a projected amount of total return (or negative total return) that would have accrued to the trust and its beneficiaries if the funds had been properly invested. (A return projection for "properly invested" funds should reflect the standards of prudent investment..., and should not rely on hindsight....
>
> Depending on the type of trustee and the nature of the breach involved, the availability of relevant data, and other facts and circumstances of the case, the projected returns on indefinite hypothetical investments during the surcharge period may appropriately be based,

inter alia, on: the return experience (positive or negative) for other investments, or suitable portions of other investments, of the trust in question; average return rates of portfolios, or suitable parts of portfolios, of a representative selection of other trusts having comparable objectives and circumstances; or return rates of one or more suitable common trust funds, or suitable index mutual funds or market indexes (with such adjustments as may be appropriate)....

On the danger of using hindsight in determining (1) whether the trustee breached a fiduciary duty and, if so, (2) the amount of the loss, see Randall W. Roth, Hindsight Bias and the Curse of Knowledge: Forewarned is Forearmed, ABA Tr. & Investments 30-34 (Jan./Feb. 2011).

Punitive Awards? Should trustees who commit a breach of trust be potentially subject to a punitive surcharge? Professor Wellman has identified some disadvantages of punitive awards:

[H]onest and able fiduciaries... may well be willing to administer the estate without extraordinary legal advice or court instructions if they know that the estate's fair market value at the time of its disposition will provide a ceiling on their liability. [But] [h]onest fiduciaries will be overly cautious...[or even decline to serve as fiduciaries] when threatened with surcharges they can neither estimate nor control....

Richard V. Wellman, Punitive Surcharges Against Disloyal Fiduciaries—Is Rothko Right?, 77 Mich. L. Rev. 95, 116 (1978).

A contrary argument is made by Robert Cooter & Bradley J. Freedman, The Fiduciary Relationship: Its Economic Character and Legal Consequences, 66 N.Y.U. L. Rev. 1045, 1070 (1991), wherein the authors argue that a punitive award for breaches of fiduciary duties *should* be more common in order effectively to deter wrongdoing. "[T]he strongest case for punitive damages," they contend, "can be made when the enforcement error is large—where there is a significant failure to sanction wrongdoing." See also John Pankauski et al., Punitive Damages Against Fiduciaries, Probate Cases, and Equitable Relief, Prob. & Prop. 43 (May/June 2011).

For a collection and discussion of cases and statutes allowing punitive awards, see Walter L. Nossaman & Joseph L. Wyatt, Jr., Trust Administration and Taxation §34.12A (2010).

———

Primary Statutory References: *Uniform Directed Trust Act*

"Directed" Trusts. Can the settlor relieve a trustee of liability by directing the trustee to follow the instructions of another—a co-trustee, an advisor, a committee? As stated in the Restatement 3d of Trusts §75 comment a, "The terms of a trust may reserve to the settlor or grant a designated person the authority to control the trustee in certain matters, by direction or by withholding a required consent. The person who holds a directory or veto power may be designated by name, by class or other description, or by inclusion in the trust provision of a list of persons to serve in the role concurrently or in sequence."

Aa originally enacted, UTC §808(b) and (d) provided in pertinent part:

(b) If the terms of the trust confer upon a person... power to direct certain actions of the trustee, the trustee shall act in accordance with an exercise of the power unless the attempted exercise is manifestly contrary to the terms of the trust or the trustee knows the attempted exercise would constitute a serious breach of a fiduciary duty that the person holding the power owes to the beneficiaries of the trust.

...

(d) A person, other than a beneficiary, who holds a power to direct is presumptively a fiduciary who, as such, is required to act in good faith with regard to the purposes of the trust and the interests of the beneficiaries. The holder of a power to direct is liable for any loss that results from breach of a fiduciary duty.

This provided some protection for the trustee, but still some fiduciary duty.

Some states, however, have gone further in insulating a directed trustee from any liability. For example, Nevada's directed trust statute provides that a trustee subject to a power to direct "is not liable, individually or as a fiduciary for any loss which results from... [c]omplying with a direction of a directing trust adviser, whether the direction is to act or to not act." Nev. Rev. Stat. §163.5549(1)(a). And what about the responsibility of the "trust adviser"? The statute grants the settlor the power to declare that the trust adviser owes no fiduciary duty whatsoever to the beneficiaries: "trust advisers shall be considered fiduciaries when exercising... [certain types of] authority unless the instrument provides otherwise." Nev. Rev. Stat. §163.5551. See also Nev. Rev. Stat. §163.5553(3).

In what sense is there a "trust" if there is no fiduciary duty?

Today, most of the states have statutes authorizing a trust director. Some of these statutes are enactments of UTC §808.

The first legislation on directed trusts was enacted in Delaware in 1986.[9] Since then, statutes on directed trusts other than UTC §808 have been enacted in more than half the states.

The Uniform Law Commission approved a Uniform Directed Trust Act in 2017 and, as a consequence, deleted UTC §808. The Uniform Directed Trust Act is well summarized in the act's prefatory note:

The Uniform Directed Trust Act addresses an increasingly common arrangement in contemporary estate planning and asset management known as a "directed trust." In a directed trust, the terms of the trust grant a person other than a trustee a power over some aspect of the trust's administration. There is no consistent vocabulary to describe the person other than a trustee that holds a power in a directed trust. Several terms are common in

---

9. See Del. Laws 1986, ch. 422 §5. For the current version, see 12 Del. Code §3313.

practice, including "trust protector," "trust adviser," and "trust director." There is much uncertainty in existing law about the fiduciary status of a nontrustee that has a power over a trust and about the fiduciary duty of a trustee, sometimes called an "administrative trustee" or "directed trustee," with regard to actions taken or directed by the nontrustee....

Under the Uniform Directed Trust Act, a trust director has the same default and mandatory fiduciary duties as a trustee in a like position and under similar circumstances. In complying with a trust director's exercise of a power of direction, a directed trustee is liable only for the trustee's own "willful misconduct." The logic behind these rules is that in a directed trust the trust director functions much like a trustee in an undirected trust. Accordingly, the trust director should have the same duties as a trustee in the exercise or nonexercise of the director's power of direction, and the fiduciary duty of the directed trustee is reduced with respect to the director's power of direction....

Compared with a non-directed trust in which a trustee holds all power over the trust, a directed trust subject to this act provides for more aggregate fiduciary duties owed to a beneficiary. All of the usual duties of trusteeship are preserved in the trust director, and in addition the directed trustee has a duty to avoid willful misconduct.

Wilmington Trust Company, based in Delaware, advertises directed trusts with the following slogan: "When you need a trust, but want to or must maintain control."

Directed Trusts and the Conflict of Laws. Should a settlor domiciled in one jurisdiction be able to establish and use a directed trust in another jurisdiction? For discussion, see Jeffrey A. Schoenblum, Directed Trusts and the Conflict of Laws, 97 Tul. L. Rev. 957 (2023); Thomas P. Gallanis, Trusts and the Choice of Law: What Role for the Settlor's Choice and the Place of Administration?, 97 Tul. L. Rev. 805 (2023).

———

EXTERNAL REFERENCES. Edward C. Halbach, Jr., Trust Investment Law in the Third Restatement, 77 Iowa L. Rev. 1151 (1992); John H. Langbein, The Uniform Prudent Investor Act and the Future of Trust Investing, 81 Iowa L. Rev. 641 (1996); Max M. Schanzenbach & Robert H. Sitkoff, The Prudent Investor Rule and Market Risk: An Empirical Analysis, 14 J. Empir. Legal Stud. 129 (2017).

4. The Duty of Impartiality

Primary Statutory References: *UTC §803*
Uniform Fiduciary Income and Principal Act §§203, 303, 506, 507

Trusts typically have multiple beneficiaries who have differing interests in income and principal. This situation creates the potential for conflicting preferences among beneficiaries. For example, beneficiaries who have a remainder interest in principal usually prefer that the trustee emphasize capital appreciation in making investment decisions, while life income beneficiaries prefer an investment strategy that emphasizes income production. Conflicts also frequently exist among concurrent beneficiaries. Concurrent life beneficiaries, for example, may have different tax positions or different preferences between income and growth. Responding to these problems, trust law has long recognized a duty on the trustee to act impartially. The duty of impartiality is involved in decisions concerning trust investments. The duty also applies in the context of decisions about how to allocate receipts and expenditures between income and principal.

The case that follows illustrates the first category, concerning the relationship between the trustee's duties of investment and the duty of impartiality.

Dennis v. Rhode Island Hospital Trust National Bank
744 F.2d 893 (1st Cir. 1984)

BREYER, C.J. The plaintiffs are the great-grandchildren of Alice M. Sullivan and beneficiaries of a trust created under her will. They claimed in the district court that the Bank trustee had breached various fiduciary obligations owed them as beneficiaries of that trust. The trust came into existence in 1920. It will cease to exist in 1991 (twenty-one years after the 1970 death of Alice Sullivan's last surviving child). The trust distributes all its income for the benefit of Alice Sullivan's living issue; the principal is to go to her issue surviving in 1991. Evidently, since the death of their mother, the two plaintiffs are the sole surviving issue, entitled to the trust's income until 1991, and then, as remaindermen, entitled to the principal.

The controversy arises out of the trustee's handling of the most important trust assets, undivided interests in three multi-story commercial buildings in downtown Providence. The buildings (the Jones, Wheaton-Anthony, and Alice Buildings) were all constructed before the beginning of the century, in an area where the value of the property has declined markedly over the last thirty years. During the period that the trust held these interests the buildings were leased to a number of different tenants, including corporations which subsequently subleased the premises. Income distribution from the trust to the life tenants has averaged over $34,000 annually.

At the time of the creation of the trust in 1920, its interests in the three buildings were worth more than $300,000. The trustee was authorized by the will to sell real estate. When the trustee finally sold the buildings in 1945, 1970, and 1979, respectively, it did so at or near the lowest point of their value; the trust received a total of only $185,000 for its interests in them. These losses, in plaintiffs' view, reflect a serious mishandling of assets over the years.

The district court... while rejecting many of plaintiffs' arguments, nonetheless found that the trustee had failed to act impartially, as between the trust's income beneficiaries and the remaindermen; it had favored the former over the latter, and, in doing so, it had reduced the value of the trust assets. To avoid improper favoritism, the trustee should have sold the real estate interests, at least by 1950, and reinvested the proceeds elsewhere. By 1950 the trustee must have, or should have, known that the buildings' value to the remaindermen would be small; the character of downtown commercial Providence was beginning to change; retention of the buildings would work to the disadvantage of the remaindermen. The court ordered a surcharge of $365,000, apparently designed to restore the real value of the trust's principal to its 1950 level.

On appeal, plaintiffs and defendants attack different aspects of the district court's judgment. [The court then announced that it affirmed the district court's judgment.]

I. a. The trustee first argues that the district court's conclusions rest on "hindsight." It points out that Rhode Island law requires a trustee to be "prudent and vigilant and exercise sound judgment," Rhode Island Trust Co. v. Copeland, 39 R.I. 193, 98 A. 273, 279 (1916), but "[n]either prophecy nor prescience is expected." Stark v. United States Trust Co. of New York, 445 F.Supp. 670, 678 (S.D.N.Y.1978). It adds that a trustee can indulge a preference for keeping the trust's "inception assets," those placed in trust by the settlor and commended to the trustee for retention. How then, the trustee asks, can the court have found that it should have sold these property interests in 1950?

The trustee's claim might be persuasive had the district court found that it had acted *imprudently* in 1950, in retaining the buildings. If that were the case, one might note that every 1950 sale involved both a pessimistic seller and an optimistic buyer; and one might ask how the court could expect the trustee to have known then (in 1950) whose prediction would turn out to be correct. The trustee's argument is less plausible, however, where, as here, the district court basically found that in 1950 the trustee had acted not imprudently, but *unfairly*, between income beneficiaries and remaindermen.

Suppose, for example, that a trustee of farmland over a number of years overplants the land, thereby increasing short run income, but ruining the soil and making the farm worthless in the long run. The trustee's duty to take corrective action would arise from the fact that he knows (or plainly ought to know) that his present course of action will injure the remaindermen; settled law requires him to act impartially, "with due regard" for the "respective interests" of both the life tenant and the remainderman. Restatement (Second) of Trusts § 232 (1959). See also A. Scott, The Law of Trusts § 183 (1967); G.G. Bogert & G.T. Bogert, The Law of Trusts and Trustees § 612 (1980). The district court here found that a sale in 1950 would have represented one way (perhaps the only practical way) to correct this type of favoritism. It held that instead of correcting the problem, the trustee continued to favor the life tenant to the "very real disadvantage" of the remainder interests, in violation of Rhode Island law.

To be more specific, in the court's view the problem arose out of the trustee's failure to keep up the buildings, to renovate them, to modernize them, or to take other reasonably obvious steps that might have given the remaindermen property roughly capable of continuing to produce a reasonable income. This failure allowed the trustee to make larger income payments during the life of the trust; but the size of those payments reflected the trustee's acquiescence in the gradual deterioration of the property. In a sense, the payments ate away the trust's capital.

The trustee correctly points out that it did take certain steps to keep up the buildings; and events beyond its control made it difficult to do more. In the 1920s, the trustee, with court approval, entered into very longterm leases on the Alice and Wheaton-Anthony buildings. The lessees and the subtenants were supposed to keep the buildings in good repair; some improvements were made. Moreover, the depression made it difficult during the 1930s to find tenants who would pay a high rent and keep up the buildings. After World War II the neighborhood enjoyed a brief renaissance; but, then, with the 1950s flight to the suburbs, it simply deteriorated.

Even if we accept these trustee claims, however, the record provides adequate support for the district court's conclusions. There is considerable evidence indicating that, at least by 1950, the trustee should have been aware of the way in which the buildings' high rents, the upkeep problem, the changing neighborhood, the buildings' age, the failure to modernize, all together were consuming the buildings' value. There is evidence that the trustee did not come to grips with the problem. Indeed, the trustee did not appraise the properties periodically, and it did not keep proper records. It made no formal or informal accounting in 55 years. There is no indication in the record that the trust's officers focused upon the problem or consulted real estate experts about it or made any further rehabilitation efforts. Rather, there is evidence that the trustee did little more than routinely agree to the requests of the trust's income beneficiaries that it manage the trust corpus to produce the largest possible income. The New Jersey courts have pointed out that an impartial trustee must

> view the overall picture as it is presented from all the facts, and not close its eyes to any relevant facts which might result in excessive burden to the one class in preference to the other.

Pennsylvania Co. v. Gillmore, 137 N.J.Eq. 51, 43 A.2d 667, 672 (1945). The record supports a conclusion of failure to satisfy that duty.

The district court also found that the trustee had at least one practical solution available. It might have sold the property in 1950 and reinvested the proceeds in other assets of roughly equivalent total value that did not create a "partiality" problem. The Restatement of Trusts foresees such a solution, for it says that

> the trustee is under a duty to the beneficiary who is ultimately entitled to the principal not to... retain property which is certain or likely to depreciate in value, although the property yields a large income, unless he makes adequate provision for amortizing the depreciation.

Restatement (Second) of Trusts § 232 comment b. Rhode Island case law also allows the court considerable discretion, in cases of fiduciary breach, to fashion a remedy, including a remedy based on a hypothetical, earlier sale. In, for example, Industrial Trust Co. v. Parks, 190 A. at 42, the court apportioned payments between income and principal "in the same way as they would have been apportioned if (certain) rights had been sold by the trustees immediately after the death of the testator" for a specified hypothetical value, to which the court added hypothetical interest. In the absence of a showing that such a sale and reinvestment would have been impractical or that some equivalent or better curative steps might have been taken, the district court's use of a 1950 sale as a remedial measure of what the trustee ought to have done is within the scope of its lawful powers.

In reaching this conclusion, we have taken account of the trustee's argument that the buildings' values were especially high in 1950 (though not as high as in the late 1920s). As the trustee argues, this fact would make 1950 an unreasonable remedial choice, other things being equal. But the record indicates that other things were not equal. For one thing, the district court chose 1950, not because of then-existing property values, but because that date marks a reasonable outer bound of the time the trustee could plead ignorance of the serious fairness problem. And, this conclusion, as we have noted, has adequate record support. For another thing, the district court could properly understand plaintiffs' expert witness as stating that the suburban flight that led to mid-1950s downtown decline began before 1950; its causes (increased household income; more cars; more mobility) were apparent before 1950. Thus, the court might reasonably have felt that a brief (1948-52) downtown "renaissance" should not have appeared (to the expert eye) to have been permanent or longlasting; it did not relieve the trustee of its obligation to do something about the fairness problem, nor did it make simple "building retention" a plausible cure. Finally, another expert testified that the trustee should have asked for power to sell the property "sometime between 1947 and 1952" when institutional investors generally began to diversify portfolios. For these reasons, reading the record, as we must, simply to see if it contains adequate support for the district court's conclusion as to remedy (as to which its powers are broad), we find that its choice of 1950 as a remedial base year is lawful.

Contrary to the trustee's contention, the case law it cites does not give it an absolute right under Rhode Island law to keep the trust's "inception assets" in disregard of the likely effect of retention on classes of trust beneficiaries. The district court's conclusion that the trustee should have sold the assets if necessary to prevent the trust corpus from being consumed by the income beneficiaries is reasonable and therefore lawful....

c. The trustee challenges the district court's calculation of the surcharge. The court assumed, for purposes of making the trust principal whole, that the trustee had hypothetically sold the trust's interests in the Wheaton-Anthony and the Alice buildings in 1950, at their 1950 values (about $70,000 and $220,000, respectively). It subtracted, from that sum of about $290,000, the $130,000 the trust actually received when the buildings were in fact sold (about $40,000 for the Wheaton-Anthony interest in 1970 and about $90,000 for the Alice interest in 1979). The court considered the difference of $160,000 to be a loss in the value of the principal, suffered as a result of the trustee's failure to prevent the principal from eroding. The court then assumed that, had the trustee sold the buildings in 1950 and reinvested the proceeds, the trustee would have been able to preserve the real value of the principal. It therefore multiplied the $160,000 by 3.6 percent, the average annual increase in the consumer price index from 1950 to 1982, and multiplied again by 32, the number of full years since 1950. Finally, the court multiplied again by an annual 0.4 percent, designed to reflect an "allowance for appreciation." It added the result ($160,000 X 4 percent X 32), about $205,000, to the $160,000 loss and surcharged the trustee $365,000. We are aware of a number of mathematical problems with this calculation. (Why, for example, was no account taken of inflation when subtracting sale receipts from 1950 values?) But, in the context of this specific litigation, fairness as between the parties requires us to restrict our examination to the two particular challenges that the trustee raises.

First, the trustee claims that the court improperly ascertained the 1950 values of the trust's interests because it simply took a proportionate share of the buildings' values. That is to say, it divided the total value of the Alice Building by four to reflect the fact that the trust owned a 1/4 undivided interest. The trustee argues that the building's values should have been discounted further to reflect the facts that the trust owned a fractional interest in the buildings and that fractional interests (with their consequent problems of divided control) typically sell at a discount.

This particular matter in this case, however, was the subject of conflicting evidence. On the one hand, the trustee showed that the marketplace ordinarily discounted the value of fractional interests. On the other hand, the plaintiffs introduced an expert study giving the 1950 values of the trust's interests at precisely the figure shown by the district court. When the trustee finally sold the trust's interests (in 1970 and 1979), their value *was* not significantly discounted. And, since the trustee also controlled (as a trustee) other fractional interests in the same building, the trustee arguably could have arranged to sell the entire building in 1950 as it did in 1970 and 1979. Evaluating this evidence and the merits of these arguments is a matter for the district court. We see no abuse of the district court's powers to make reasonable judgments as to hypothetical values in its efforts to devise an appropriate remedy for the trustee's breach of duty.

Second, the trustee argues that the district court should not have applied to the 1950 hypothetical sales value a 4 percent interest factor—a factor designed to compensate for 3.6 percent average annual inflation and for 0.4 percent "appreciation." We do not agree with the trustee in respect to the 3.6 percent.

Rhode Island law simply requires that the court's approach be reasonable and its calculations grounded in the record's facts. See generally Industrial Trust Co. v. Parks, supra. The trustee does not claim that it requires the court to follow any one particular calculation method, such as that, for example, contained in Restatement (Second) of Trusts § 241. And, we believe the inflation adjustment meets Rhode Island's broader requirements.

For one thing, it seems reasonable for the court—in devising a remedy for the trustee's violation of its duty of impartiality—to assume that a fair trustee would have maintained the property's real value from 1950 through 1982. Such an assumption is consistent with basic trust law policies of providing income to income beneficiaries while preserving principal for the remaindermen, and, consequently, of avoiding investment in wasting assets. Moreover, it is consistent with readily ascertainable general economic facts that wages and many asset values as well as prices have on average kept pace with inflation. See generally K. Hirsch, Inflation and the Law of Trusts, 18 Real Prop., Prob. & Tr. J. 601 (Win.1983); Comment, Investment and Management of Trust Funds in an Inflationary Economy, 126 U. of Pa.L.R. 1171, 1197 (1978). While the value of long term bonds has fallen, the value of common stocks and much property has risen. See generally R. Ibbotson & R. Sinquefield, Stocks, Bonds, Bills and Inflation: The Past and the Future (1982); J. Wiedemer, Real Estate Investment (1979). Where a court is trying to create, not a measure of the trustee's duty, but simply a plausible reconstruction of what would have occurred to a hypothetical 1950 reinvestment, we see nothing unreasonable in assuming that the value of the corpus would have kept pace with inflation.

We reach a different conclusion, however, in respect to the additional 0.4 percent, designed to reflect "appreciation." Neither the court nor the parties have provided us with any reason to believe that the trustee would have outperformed inflation. There is no evidence in the record suggesting that a hypothetical reinvestment of hypothetical proceeds from a hypothetical 1950 property sale would have yielded real appreciation over and above inflation's nominal increase. We have found no information about the performance of an average, or typical, trust. And the general publicly available sources offer insufficient support for a claim of likely real increase. See R. Ibbotson & R. Sinquefield, supra. Moreover, one can imagine reasonable disagreement about whether any such hypothetical real appreciation would belong to the life tenant or to the remainderman. These factors lead us to conclude that, in adding 0.4 percent interest for real appreciation, the district court exceeded its broad remedial powers. Our recalculation, omitting the 0.4 percent, reduces the surcharge from \$365,781.67 to \$345,246.56.

d. The trustee objects to the court's having removed it as trustee. The removal of a trustee, however, is primarily a matter for the district court. A trustee can be removed even if "the charges of his misconduct" are "not made out." Petition of Slatter, 108 R.I. 326, 275 A.2d 272, 276 (1971). The issue here is whether "ill feeling" might interfere with the administration of the trust. The district court concluded that the course of the litigation in this case itself demonstrated such ill feeling. Nothing in the record shows that the court abused its powers in reaching that conclusion. [The balance of the opinion, rejecting the plaintiff's contentions that (1) pre-judgment interest should have been awarded, and (2) that defendant should have been charged personally with plaintiff's attorneys fees, is omitted.]

The judgment of the district court is modified and as modified affirmed.

_____

Accounting for Principal and Income. The trustee's duty of impartiality extends beyond making investment decisions. The trustee must also be impartial when allocating receipts and expenditures between what is labeled "principal" (and thus available to the beneficiaries of principal) and what is labeled "income" (and thus available to the beneficiaries of income).

Estate of Bixby
295 P.2d 68 (Cal. App. 1956)

Fox, J. ....The decedent, Fred H. Bixby, died testate May 17, 1952, a resident of Long Beach, California....

The decedent was survived by his spouse, Florence G. Bixby (hereinafter called 'Mrs. Bixby'), by four children, Katharine Bixby Hotchkis, Florence Elizabeth Bixby Janeway, Deborah Bixby Green, and Fred H. Bixby, Jr., and by eight grandchildren....

By the terms of his will, the decedent gave his automobile and 19,000 shares of... stock to Mrs. Bixby and the residue of his estate in equal shares to four trusts.... each of the four trusts is to continue until the death of the survivor of the decedent's four children and thereupon the trust estate is to be distributed to the decedent's then living grandchildren [or their descendants].... During the continuation of each trust, the net income is to be paid to a designated child of the decedent for life [etc.]....

In his will, the decedent directed that all succession taxes be paid from the residue of his estate....

The 19,000 shares of stock bequeathed to Mrs. Bixby were distributed to her pursuant to an order for partial distribution rendered by the trial court September 3, 1953. The only dividends on said shares paid to the executor were the aforementioned dividends aggregating $76,000 received by the executor during the fiscal year ending April 30, 1953....

Mrs. Bixby has no interest in the estate's income except to the extent of the $76,000 in dividends, the residuary beneficiaries being entitled to the benefit of the balance ($84,602.92) of the gross income for the fiscal year in question. The utilization by the executor of administration expenses aggregating $120,270.28 as income tax deductions reduced ratably the portion of the income taxes allocable to the $76,000 in dividends and the portion of the income taxes allocable to the remaining income of $84,602.92....

[The guardian for Mrs. Bixby argues as follows:] Income taxes assessed against the income of the estate received by the executor during administration are expenses of administration chargeable against the residue of the estate. Mrs. Bixby, therefore, was entitled to receive the whole of the $76,000 in dividends undiminished by any amount on account of income taxes paid or payable by the executor. In any case, the dividends should not be diminished by more than the portion ($8,713.40) of the income taxes actually paid by the executor allocable against the dividends....

[The trustees for the remainder beneficiaries argue as follows:] Income taxes assessed against the income of the estate received by the executor during administration are not expenses of administration payable from the residue of the estate, but are charges against and payable from the income....

...[W]e are concerned with the dividends amounting to $76,000 which the executor received upon the 19,000 shares of stock of which Mrs. Bixby was the outright legatee. As legatee of this stock, title thereto vested in her... as of the date of the testator's death, at which time there also originated her right to receive the income (dividends) produced by this stock subsequent to the testator's death. Had the legatee received this income when her right thereto accrued, it is undisputed that the payment of an income tax on these funds would have been the legatee's obligation. However, distribution not having as yet been made and the estate being a taxable entity, the executor was required to pay an income tax on this and the other income received by him during the course of administration. Since such taxes are the subject of and measured by the income, it seems only fair that they should be paid therefore and not from the principal of the residue of the estate. Although the precise point has not been directly adjudicated in this state, such a rule is in harmony with the equitable principle that the burden of the tax accompanies companies the income and should be borne by the account into which the taxed item goes....

...To charge the estate's income taxes against the principal of the residue gives the persons entitled to the income substantial benefits over and above what they possibly could have realized if the income had been distributed to them as received, thus giving the person entitled to the income a windfall which he would not realize were it possible to effect distribution as of the date of the decedent's death. The windfall, moreover, comes from the pockets of the residuary legatees. Any such rule would be patently inequitable; its application would not mean that the income escapes taxation but that the onerous burden of the income taxes would be shifted from the recipients of the income to the persons entitled to the residue.

On the basis of logic and as a matter of equity, the conclusion is inescapable that income taxes assessed against the estate's income during the period required for administration should be charged against that income and not against the principal of the residue.

We pass now to the problem presented by the trustees' appeal, viz.: What is the effect on the rights of the beneficiaries of the executor's utilization of expenses of administration as federal income rather than federal estate tax deductions ...

In the case at bar, the executor discharged his responsibility wisely under the circumstances by electing to utilize the administration expenses as an income tax deduction, although such expenses were borne by the principal of the residuary estate. In so doing, having reported an income of some $160,000, he paid a tax of

$18,728.16. Had he not utilized this deduction on the estate income tax return, the tax would have been $120,378.11. He thus effected a tax saving of $101,649.95, resulting in a very substantial benefit to the legatees and beneficiaries entitled to the income. While this is a most obviously desirable result, its correlative effect on those entitled to corpus is unfortunate. For had the administrative expenses been used as a deduction in the federal estate tax return, the succession taxes payable from decedent's estate would have been reduced by $58,932.44. To that extent the remainder beneficiaries of the residuary trusts have been penalized to effect the income tax saving previously described.

It is at once manifest that the election to effect a tax saving afforded the executor under the Revenue Code does not justify the severe disruption and disarrangement of what would otherwise constitute the beneficial interests of the legatees and remaindermen under the will... In such a situation, the equitable solution is to reallocate enough of the tax saving to the principal account to make whole the detriment suffered by corpus....

Notes

1. *The Traditional Rules of Income and Principal.* Before 1997, nearly all states had enacted one of two versions of the Uniform Principal and Income Act (UPAIA): the original 1931 act or the 1962 act. These acts operated as default rules. They yielded to a contrary provision in the trust instrument.

Both acts set out detailed rules regarding the allocation of receipts and expenditures between income and principal. Both sets of rules tended to rely on form over substance. For example, with respect to corporate distributions, it was well settled that *income* beneficiaries receive ordinary cash dividends, and that *principal* beneficiaries receive any capital gains if the stock is sold. The states differed over allocation of stock dividends, but the two competing rules (the so-called "Pennsylvania" and "Massachusetts" rules) both emphasized form over substance.

The emphasis on form also appeared in rules concerning other sorts of receipts. The 1962 UPAIA, for example, allocated to *income* receipts like rent and interest on bonds and loans, while allocating to *principal* the proceeds of asset sales and the payment of bond principal.

2. *The Equitable Power to Adjust.* Recognizing the tension between the allocation of tax burdens and the duty of impartiality, some courts have held, without statutory authority, that trustees have an equitable power to adjust between income and principal. See *Bixby* above. The leading case is Estate of Warms, 140 N.Y.S.2d 169 (N.Y. Surr. 1955). For discussion, see Joel C. Dobris, Equitable Adjustments in Postmortem Tax Planning: An Unremitting Diet of *Warms*, 65 Iowa L. Rev. 103 (1979).

3. *Modern Portfolio Theory and the 1997 Uniform Principal and Income Act.* Modern portfolio theory (MPT), which is the foundation for the Uniform Prudent

Investor Act, teaches that trustees should invest in ways designed to maximize overall return and not be controlled by the form of a particular investment. However, trust law's duty of impartiality seems to require that a trustee pay attention to the form of investments to the extent that investments do not benefit all of the beneficiaries evenly. Suppose, for example, that from the perspective of overall return and diversification, prudence favors investing in the stock of a company that pays no dividends because the firm plows all of its earnings back into the company. How can the trustee invest in such a company without breaching its duty of impartiality by disfavoring the income beneficiary? Under the traditional rules regarding allocations between income and principal, trustees frequently faced such dilemmas.

In recent years, MPT has changed not only trust law's thinking about prudence but also its approach to income and principal. The Uniform Law Commission promulgated in 1997 and further revised in 2000 an updated Uniform Principal and Income Act expressly predicated on the principles of MPT. This UPAIA, which has been widely adopted, continued many of the 1962 Act's rules. However, to enable trustees to invest from a portfolio-maximizing perspective, §104 of the 1997 Act provided statutory authorization for the trustee to make adjustments between income and principal. Specifically, §104(a) stated:

> A trustee may adjust between principal and income to the extent the trustee considers necessary if the trustee invests and manages trust assets as a prudent investor, the terms of the trust describe the amount that may or must be distributed to a beneficiary by referring to the trust's income, and the trustee determines... that the trustee is [otherwise] unable to [administer the trust impartially].

For a discussion of this provision and the 1997 UPAIA generally, see Joel C. Dobris, Why Trustee Investors Often Prefer Dividends to Capital Gain and Debt Investments to Equity—A Daunting Principal and Income Problem, 32 Real Prop., Prob. & Tr. J. 255 (1997).

4. *Unproductive Assets.* Unproductive (and underproductive) assets present the opposite problem from that involved in *Dennis*. The income generated by unproductive assets is less rather than more than a return provided by normal trust investments. The trustee's duty of impartiality means that the portfolio must be diversified to compensate for the underproductive asset or, if not feasible to do so, the asset must be sold. See Restatement 3d of Trusts: Prudent Investor Rule §240. If the asset is sold, the proceeds must be allocated between income and principal.

5. *Allocation Rules for Not-for-Profit Institutions.* Most charitable institutions have long been permitted to implement an approach known as "total return"—taking income and appreciation into account together. The Uniform Management of Institutional Funds Act (1972) (UMIFA) allowed charitable trustees and directors of nonprofit institutions to count appreciation, realized and unrealized, in the value of a fund for purposes of establishing an income stream that balances corpus and

operating needs. See Joel C. Dobris, Real Return, Modern Portfolio Theory, and College, University, and Foundation Decisions on Annual Spending From Endowments: A Visit to the World of Spending Rules, 28 Real Prop., Prob & Tr. J. 49 (1993).

In 2006, the Uniform Law Commission promulgated a revised version of UMIFA, called the Uniform Prudent Management of Institutional Funds Act (UPMIFA). UPMIFA continues the total return approach and also incorporates other insights from modern prudent investing. UPMIFA has been enacted in the District of Columbia and every U.S. state except Pennsylvania.

6. *Total Return Unitrusts*. States are moving to enact statutes permitting trustees of private trusts to apply the total return approach to a conventional income-and-remainder trust. Under these statutes, a trustee may convert an income-and-remainder trust to a total return unitrust (TRU), or vice versa, after giving notice to current and remainder beneficiaries. (The payout of a unitrust is a percentage of the trust's fair market value.) The statutes vary regarding the extent of the trustee's discretion over important issues like rate of return. New York's statute, for example, adopts a fixed rate of return of 4%, with a smoothing rule after the first three years, while Delaware's statute gives the trustee a choice to set the rate between 3 and 5%, taking into account the settlor's expressed intentions, general economic conditions, projected earnings and capital appreciation, and projected inflation.

Another difference among states concerns the relationship between the TRU approach and the adjustment approach of the 1997 UPAIA. Some states do not provide adjustment powers, while others include both the power to adjust and a separate TRU provision. For the latter approach, see, e.g., N.Y. Est. Powers & Trusts Law §§11-2.3(5), -2.4.

The 1997 UPAIA did not include a unitrust conversion option because, at the time, the U.S. Treasury Department had not issued guidance on the tax treatment of unitrusts. The Treasury Department issued proposed regulations on unitrusts in 2001, and the regulations were finalized in late 2003, with an effective date of January 2, 2004. The regulations provide that "a unitrust amount [paid to the income beneficiary] of no less than 3% and no more than 5% of the fair market value of the trust assets... is a reasonable apportionment of the total return of the trust." Treas. Reg. §1-643(b)-1. The regulations also provide that "a state statute that permits the trustee to make adjustments between income and principal to fulfill the trustee's duty of impartiality between the income and remainder beneficiaries is generally a reasonable apportionment of the total return of the trust." Id.

7. *The 2018 Uniform Fiduciary Income and Principal Act*. In 2018, the Uniform Law Commission approved a revision of the 1997 UPAIA, this time called the Uniform Fiduciary Income and Principal Act (UFIPA). The goals of UFIPA are well stated in the following excerpts from the Act's prefatory note.

Uniform Fiduciary Income and Principal Act
Prefatory Note (2018)

The 2018 Uniform Fiduciary Income and Principal Act, like previous revisions of the Uniform Principal and Income Act, is intended to reflect and address changes in the design and use of modern trusts. Very long-term trusts are more common, as are totally discretionary trusts—that is, trusts in which income, as well as principal, is distributable to beneficiaries during the term of the trust not as a matter of right but solely in the discretion of the trustee. Even where income distributions are mandatory, including occasions where income distributions are mandated by requirements of tax law (such as the estate tax marital deduction), discretion in the trustee to supplement income distributions by invasions of principal is common.

One result of these developments in the design, use, and role of trusts is to make historical distinctions between income and principal less important as a technical matter in some cases. Discretionary accumulation of income has the effect of treating income as principal to the extent of the accumulation. And discretionary invasion of principal has the effect of treating principal as income to the extent of the invasion. Even so, the difference between income and principal is important to impartial trustees and beneficiaries alike. The 2018 Act retains the historical distinctions, including the historical technical rules that have evolved through changing legal and practical environments, while still allowing skilled and dedicated trustees to respond to legal and practical environments that inevitably will continue to change.

The basic premise of the current revision is that a trustee that is aware of the current practical environment of trust administration and sensitive to the evolving demands of impartiality should be able to determine standards for adjusting between income and principal that are reasonable in the circumstances, and to update those standards from time to time. Authority to make adjustments between income and principal from year to year, introduced as Section 104 in the 1997 Act, is retained, and indeed significantly expanded, as Section 203 in the 2018 Act. The most important way in which the authority to adjust is expanded is by eliminating the precondition that trust distributions are constricted by the concept of "income" in a way that economic results from year to year could arbitrarily affect. In other words, while the trustee of a more modern trust with greater, if not total, flexibility to make distributions from income and/or principal would actually have been *denied* the flexibility intended by former Section 104, new Section 203 ensures that designing a trust for greater flexibility will not ironically sacrifice the flexibility of adjustments....

The 2018 Act respects, and permits a trustee to respect, the simple notion of "income." Under Section 203, a trustee of a discretionary trust can make adjustments, taking into account a nonexclusive list of factors provided in Section 201(e), and still achieve the comfortable outcome of "distributing income." And if the interests of beneficiaries under the terms of the trust are still not appropriately served within the framework of "distributing income"—that is, when no reasonable adjustment would serve those interests, or when non-pro rata distributions are justified—then invasions of principal are still appropriate to the extent consistent with the terms of the trust.

The more traditional rules for allocating income and principal are retained, with updates, in Articles 4 through 7. The general substantive rules are in Articles 4 and 5, and the special temporal rules relating to the beginning and end of interests are moved from Articles 2 and 3 in the 1997 Act to Articles 6 and 7 in the 2018 Act, thus placing the substantive rules that are applicable on an ongoing basis ahead of the temporal rules that are applicable only at certain times. One useful result of these changes is that the former rules of Sections 401 through 415 and 501 through 503, with which many fiduciaries no doubt have considerable experience, are retained in the 2018 Act with the same section numbers.

Article 3 adds the authority for a trustee to convert to or from or change a unitrust. But the tax-sensitive limitations typically included in unitrust statutes, such as the limitation of the unitrust rate to a rate from 3 to 5 percent, are now provided only for trusts that are intended to qualify for tax benefits for the protection of which those limitations are needed. The new unitrust rules are discussed further in the Comments in Article 3....

EXTERNAL REFERENCE. Benjamin Orzeske, UFIPA: Trust Accounting for the 21st Century, Prob. & Prop. 6 (Nov./Dec. 2018).

PART C. POWERS, SELECTION, RESIGNATION, REMOVAL, AND COMPENSATION OF TRUSTEES

Primary Statutory References: *UTC §§705, 706, 708, 815, 816*

Trustee Powers. A brief word is in order about the trustee's powers. Typically these are enumerated in the trust instrument. By way of example, see Article V of the Sample Inter Vivos Revocable Trust, above on pp. 468-470.

The Uniform Trust Code offers default rules on the powers of the trustee in §815 (general powers) and §816 (specific powers).

Even in the absence of provisions in the trust instrument or applicable statutes, the trustee has the powers needed to administer the trust. The Restatement 3d of Trusts §70(a) provides: "In administering a trust, a trustee:... (a) has, except as limited by statute or the terms of the trust, the comprehensive powers described in §85 to manage the trust property and to carry out the terms and purposes of the trust." Section 85(1) of the Restatement provides in pertinent part: "In administering a trust, the trustee has, except as limited by statute or the terms of the trust,... all of the powers over trust property that a legally competent, unmarried individual has with respect to individually owned property...."

Selecting Trustees. Selecting trustees and other fiduciaries can be a tricky business. Often the persons whom the client wants to serve are not prepared to carry out the responsibilities of the job. Most settlors want their trustees to be people whom they know well and trust. These are, obviously, important criteria, but they should not be the only factors that the client takes into account. A trustee must be knowledgeable about investments, including their tax implications.

Clients often wish, initially at least, to select a family member to serve as trustee. While there is nothing inherently wrong with this, the client should be made aware of several potential issues. First, family members often do not possess the degree of financial sophistication that trustees usually need. Second, the family member whom the client wishes to act as fiduciary may also be a beneficiary. The problem here is not necessarily of merger but of potential conflicts of interests or at least the potential for disputes between the fiduciary-beneficiary and other beneficiaries. Finally, fiduciaries, even those who are family members, are liable for breach of fiduciary duties, and family members, once made aware of the issue, may not be able or willing to bear that risk. Corporate fiduciaries are usually much better able to bear the risk through a variety of risk-spreading techniques.

The mention of corporate fiduciaries raises another issue that is likely to occur to the client, namely, whether there should be two (or more) co-trustees, with at least one being a corporate entity. Here again, multiple considerations compete. On the one hand, there is the matter of cost. Family members may, and often do, waive the fiduciary's right to receive a fee; corporate fiduciaries, obviously, will not do so. On the other hand, corporate fiduciaries are more likely than family members or friends of the client to possess the desirable degree of financial sophistication. It is possible, however, for a personal fiduciary to obtain the benefits of such sophistication if the fiduciary is given the authority to retain accountants, investment advisors, and others who are in a position to provide the personal fiduciary with specialized assistance.

Where there are multiple fiduciaries, problems may arise in their relationship with each other. Not infrequently, disputes arise over such questions as the division of responsibilities among them, custody of assets, and fees. Corporate fiduciaries usually want to have custody over all assets and receive the full fee to which they are entitled. (We discuss below the amount to which a fiduciary is entitled to receive as a commission.)

A final, and very important, matter concerning the selection of fiduciaries involves appointment of the drafting attorney as the trustee. We raised this topic in Chapter 4 when we discussed the interrelationship between undue influence and the professional responsibilities of drafting attorneys. Briefly to summarize what we said there, while no per se rule bans lawyers from preparing documents that name the lawyer as a fiduciary, special disclosure and counseling is strongly advisable.

Family Offices. The tremendous growth in family wealth during in recent decades has led to growing popularity of a new institution for managing family wealth, the "family office." The central purpose of the family office is to provide coordinated management of family fortunes over several generations. It often originates in a family-owned business, handling shareholder record-keeping and legal compliance requirements for family members. As the business becomes more complex, these responsibilities are shifted to an entity that operates outside of, but complementary to, the family business.

Family offices typically serve multiple functions. Primary among these are asset-preservation and enhancement, financial education for younger generation family members, and fulfilling family philanthropic goals. The functions and organization of any family office change over time as the family grows larger and its needs become more diverse. We discuss family offices further in Chapter 20.

The executives of family offices may be trustees of family trusts or occupy other positions within the family firm. Even if they are not trustees, family office executives are fiduciaries, subject to all the usual duties of property fiduciaries. As such, they are subject to the risk of liability for failure to comply with duties of care, loyalty, prudence, and other customary fiduciary responsibilities. Not surprisingly, family office executives frequently require that exculpation and indemnification provisions be included in their employment contracts. They may also request liability insurance policies to provide more protection in the event of litigation brought against them.

Removal/Resignation of Fiduciaries. Over the coming decades, trillions of dollars may pass from one generation to the next. Much of this wealth will be transferred into private trusts and managed by professional trustees. The transfer and management of such vast sums of wealth by fiduciaries has already begun to generate closer scrutiny of fiduciaries by entitled recipients. Beneficiaries are increasingly objecting to fiduciary practices ranging from investment decisions to commissions. Indeed, organizations such as Heirs Inc. and Fiduciary Solutions have been formed for the purpose of providing advice to estate and trust beneficiaries who believe that estate representatives or trustees are mishandling fiduciary assets or charging excessive fees.[10]

One option, of course, is to get the fiduciary to resign. On the resignation of a trustee, see UTC §705.

Another option available to disgruntled beneficiaries is removal of the fiduciary. As the old saying goes, however, "Easier said than done." Courts view removal as a drastic action, one to be taken only under exceptional circumstances. UTC §706 provides that a court may remove a trustee, either at the request of a beneficiary, co-trustee or the settlor or on its own motion, only under four limited circumstances: (1) the trustee has committed a "serious breach of trust"; (2) lack of cooperation among the trustees "substantially impairs" trust administration; (3) removal would serve the

---

10. Brigid McMenamin, Don't Count Your Chickens, Forbes, March 6, 2000, at 104.

best interests of the beneficiaries because the trustee is unable or unwilling to administer the trust effectively; or (4) because of a "substantial change of circumstances" or upon the request of all the beneficiaries, the court finds that removal "best serves the interests of all the beneficiaries and is not inconsistent with a material purpose of the trust." For a discussion of trustee removal, see Ronald Chester & Sarah Reid Ziomek, Removal of Corporate Trustees Under the Uniform Trust Code and Other Current Law, 67 Mo. L. Rev. 241 (2002).

Fiduciary Compensation Practices. It goes without saying that clients are keenly interested in the fees charged by fiduciaries. The trustee's fee is usually established by agreement. In the absence of any explicit agreement, a standard of reasonable compensation is applied. See G. Bogert, The Law of Trusts and Trustees §975. UTC §708 adopts the reasonable compensation standard as the default rule and goes on to provide that if the trust instrument specifies the compensation level, the court may allow more or less in either of two circumstances: (1) the trustee's duties were "substantially different" from those initially contemplated; or (2) the specified compensation is "unreasonably low or high."

Clients are especially likely to be concerned about fees if the fiduciary is a corporate fiduciary (i.e., a bank or trust company). Corporate fiduciaries typically recommend including in wills or trust instruments compensation provisions that permit them to be paid without prior court approval. In addition, the suggested compensation provisions might state that the testator or grantor "recognizes that such compensation may exceed the compensation for [fiduciary] services in effect from time to time under applicable law."

PART D. LIABILITY TO THIRD PARTIES

Primary Statutory References: *UTC §1010*

Creditors' Claims. The rule at common law is that a trustee is personally liable on any contract that the trustee makes regardless of whether the trustee had the power to enter into the contract. One with whom the trustee contracts cannot obtain a legal judgment against the trustee as trustee so as to collect the judgment against trust assets. The trustee does not avoid personal liability merely by signing in its fiduciary role. See, e.g., Dolben v. Gleason, 198 N.E. 762 (Mass. 1935). The trustee is entitled to be indemnified out of trust assets, but if the contract is beyond the trustee's powers there is no right to indemnity.

The contract may expressly relieve the trustee of personal liability if the trustee had authority to enter into the contract. Under these circumstances, the creditor does have recourse against trust assets on the theory that the creditor is enforcing the trustee's right to indemnity (but only to the extent of the trustee's right of indemnification). The other theory upon which creditors may recover against trust assets is unjust enrichment. If the creditor has conferred a benefit upon the trust estate, the trustee is entitled to recover directly from the trust estate to that extent.

The trustee's tort liability follows the same general approach. The trustee is personally liable for torts committed by the trustee or the trustee's employee in the course of trust administration. The trustee, if not personally at fault, is entitled to indemnification from trust assets. See, e.g., Matter of Lathers, 137 Misc. 226, 243 N.Y.S. 366 (1930). It is likely that a court permitting a contract creditor to reach trust assets through substitution of the creditor for the trustee's right to indemnity will reach the same result when a tort claimant tries to reach trust assets, but courts have been somewhat cautious in committing themselves to this position. See, e.g., Johnston v. Long, 181 P.2d 645 (Cal. 1947).

Commentators have criticized the traditional rules as unfair to both creditors and the trustee where the trustee is not personally at fault and trust assets are insufficient to indemnify the trustee. See John D. Johnston, Jr., Developments in Contract Liability of Trusts and Trustees, 41 N.Y.U. L. Rev. 483 (1966). Reacting to these criticisms, statutes in many states have reversed the traditional rules. Uniform Trust Code §1010 is an example. For contract creditors, §1010 provides a default rule of no personal liability if the trustee properly entered into the contract and if the contract disclosed the fiduciary status. For tort creditors, it provides that the trustee is personally liable only if the trustee was personally at fault.

This modern approach—of representative liability, not personal liability, unless the trustee is personally at fault—is the approach adopted by the Restatement 3d of Trusts. See Restatement 3d of Trusts §§105, 106.

Fiduciary Liability Under CERCLA. One controversial basis of fiduciary liability in recent years has been the federal "superfund" act, the Comprehensive Environmental Response, Compensation, and Liability Act, 42 U.S.C. §9601-75, usually called "CERCLA." CERCLA imposes liability for the costs of cleaning up toxic waste sites on any "owner" of land on which hazardous substances are found. It is clear that a trustee can be an "owner" under CERCLA, but the statute does not say whether a trustee is personally liable or liable only in its fiduciary capacity, that is, only to the extent of the trust's assets. Obviously, personal liability has much greater financial ramifications for trustees than fiduciary liability.

The widely discussed decision in City of Phoenix v. Garbage Service Co., 827 F. Supp. 600 (D. Ariz. 1993), raised for fiduciaries great fear that they would be held personally liable under CERCLA any time land that they owned in trust was found to be contaminated with a hazardous substance. In that case, Valley National Bank (VNB) acquired in 1965, as an original trust asset of a testamentary trust, an option to repurchase a landfill site in Phoenix, Arizona, that the settlor had previously owned. VNB exercised the option. At the time it did so, Garbage Services, Inc., which the decedent settlor had completely owned and which VNB now owned, was managing the site. After exercising the option, VNB leased the land to Garbage Services, which managed the site until it was closed in 1972.

In 1980, the city of Phoenix acquired title to the site by condemnation. Later, in 1989, it sued VNB to recover the cleanup costs under CERCLA. VNB argued that because it owned the landfill as trustee, it was not personally liable and that its liability was limited to the amount of the assets held in the trust. The court held that VNB was personally liable.

In response to fiduciaries' fears of broad personal liability under CERCLA after *City of Phoenix*, Congress in 1996 enacted a statute limiting trustees' liability. The Asset Conservation, Lender Liability, and Deposit Insurance Protection Act of 1996 amended CERCLA to provide that the liability of a fiduciary is limited to the assets held in a fiduciary capacity. The Act made two major changes. First, it confined fiduciary personal liability to circumstances in which the fiduciary is liable "independently of [its] ownership as a fiduciary or actions taken in a fiduciary capacity." 42 U.S.C. §9607(n)(2). Second, it created certain safe harbors for fiduciaries to avoid personal liability. These include undertaking or directing others to undertake a clean-up or "any other lawful means of addressing hazardous substances" on the site, including in the trust instrument a term or condition that "relates to compliance with an environmental law," monitoring or enforcing such a term, providing "financial or other advice... to other parties to the fiduciary relationship, including the settlor or beneficiary," and administering, as a fiduciary, a facility that was contaminated before the fiduciary relationship began. 42 U.S.C. §9607(n)(4).

The 1996 statute mollifies many of the concerns that grew out of the *City of Phoenix* decision. It does not, however, apply to possible fiduciary liability under federal environmental legislation other than CERCLA.

Chapter 11

Support, Discretionary, and Spendthrift Trusts

Now that we have introduced the basic requirements to form a trust (in Chapter 9) and the law governing the duties of the trustee (in Chapter 10), we turn to a fundamental question of policy. Whose trust is it: the settlor's or the beneficiaries'? Once a trust has been properly formed, should the law ensure that it will continue? Or should the law enable the beneficiaries to terminate the trust against the wishes of the settlor? The question is one of distributing power between successive property owners, past and present. Where the preferences of beneficiaries conflict with those expressed by the settlor, the law cannot simultaneously respect the autonomy of both; instead, the law must choose between them.

Conflicts between the settlor's wishes and the preferences of trust beneficiaries arise primarily in the context of three types of trusts: support, discretionary, and spendthrift trusts. Most trusts created today fall into one or more of these categories. The principal features of each are briefly summarized as follows:

> *Support Trusts.* A support trust is a trust that contains a provision directing the trustee to pay to or apply for the benefit of the beneficiary so much of the income and principal or either as is necessary for the beneficiary's education and support.

> *Discretionary Trusts.* A discretionary trust is a trust that contains a provision giving the trustee discretion to pay to or apply for the benefit of the beneficiary so much of the income and principal or either as the trustee sees fit.

> *Spendthrift Trusts.* A spendthrift trust is a trust that contains a provision imposing a disabling restraint on the alienation of the beneficiaries' equitable interests. A disabling restraint on alienation is one that purports to nullify any attempted assignment by a beneficiary of his or her equitable interest and any attempted attachment of a beneficiary's interest by the beneficiary's creditors.

See Restatement 3d of Trusts §§58, 60.

To illustrate these trusts and the general problem they pose, consider Example 11.1.

Example 11.1: G has just died at age 75, survived by her 55-year-old daughter, A, and A's 21-year-old son, X. During the last few years of her life, G had been thinking about how to divide her $1 million estate between A and X. G decided to make a will giving most of the estate, say 80 percent of it, to A. In exploring how to formulate her will with A and X, a choice discussed was simply to devise $800,000 outright to A and $200,000 outright to X. A and X respectfully expressed preference for that form, although A was not so sure that X should be devised such an amount in a lump sum.

Although G did not mention her feelings to A or X, G secretly had reservations about devising lump-sum amounts to either one. G's concern was not about A's lack of maturity or ability to handle money, but she was worried that A's husband, H, whom she often described as that "no-good bum," might somehow get his hands on the money and squander it on some risky business venture. So, after consulting her lawyer (one of your former classmates), G decided to follow a different path. To the chagrin of A, H, and X, G's will devised the full $1 million into a trust, the terms of which are that A is to receive the income for life, with the corpus going to X at A's death.

Suppose that, using the actuarial tables currently in use for tax purposes (see IRC §7520), the present value of A's right to the income from $1 million for life is $800,000 and the present value of X's right to $1 million at A's death is $200,000.

With all due respect for G and her wishes, A and X still prefer the cash. Accompanied by H, they consult you as their lawyer and ask a straightforward question: Can they somehow exchange their trust interests for cash? Well, you tell them, there are two potential sources—the trust and outsiders. A and X could try to find a buyer for their interests (or find a lender who would loan them the cash, accepting the beneficial interests as security). Or A and X could try to terminate the trust and have the $1 million corpus distributed to them on an 80/20 basis.

Putting aside the impracticability of the first option,[1] your examination of G's will reveals that the trust is a spendthrift trust, i.e., it contains a disabling restraint on alienation. Under prevailing American law, disabling restraints on alienation of equitable interests in trust are valid. Moreover, a spendthrift trust is indestructible, meaning that the beneficiaries cannot compel the trustee to terminate such a trust prematurely. See Restatement 2d of Trusts §§152, 153, 330 & comment *l*.

These rules of American trust law represent a shift away from the English law of trusts. Under English law, disabling restraints on the alienation of equitable interests in trust are invalid. This was established by the Chancellor, Lord Eldon, in Brandon v. Robinson, 18 Ves. 429, 34 Eng. Rep. 379 (Ch. 1811). English law allows the beneficiaries to terminate the trust early, irrespective of the settlor's wishes, by demanding the trust property outright. This rule was adopted in Saunders v. Vautier, 4 Beav. 115, 49 Eng. Rep. 282 (Ch. 1841), aff'd, Cr. & Ph. 240, 41 Eng. Rep. 482 (Ch. 1841), and solidified in Wharton v. Masterman, [1895] App. Cas. 186 (H.L.). English law, then, empowers trust beneficiaries to control their interests and thereby limits the donor's control. American trust doctrine reverses this allocation of control.

The American shift away from the English rules occurred in the latter part of the nineteenth century. A pair of 1880s decisions of the Supreme Judicial Court of

---

1. A and X would have difficulty finding buyers for their interests, let alone buyers who would pay full actuarial value. A different situation exists in England, where it has been reported that organized auctions are held for the sale of future interests in property, either vested or contingent. See Speculation: Betting on Death, Newsweek, Jan. 25, 1971, at 66; Some Britishers Sell Birthrights for More Than Mess of Pottage, Wall St. J., May 10, 1971. In America, no such auction market exists.

Massachusetts are mainly credited with having engineered these departures from prior law: Broadway National Bank v. Adams (1882) and Claflin v. Claflin (1889). We shall study both of these cases in this Chapter.

EXTERNAL REFERENCES. Thomas P. Gallanis, The New Direction of American Trust Law, 97 Iowa L. Rev. 215 (2011); Gregory S. Alexander, The Dead Hand and the Law of Trusts in the Nineteenth Century, 37 Stan. L. Rev. 1189 (1985).

PART A. RESTRAINING ALIENABILITY OF BENEFICIAL INTERESTS/SHIELDING BENEFICIAL INTERESTS FROM CREDITORS

1. Support, Discretionary, and Discretionary-Support Trusts

Primary Statutory References: *UTC §§503, 504, 814*

Traditional Trust Law Classification. Traditional doctrine draws a distinction between support and discretionary trusts, defining them as follows.

A *support trust* is defined as one in which "by the terms of the trust the amount to be paid or applied for the beneficiary is limited to so much of the income or principal as is in fact necessary for his education or support." See Restatement 2d of Trusts §154 comment d.

A *discretionary trust* is defined as one in which the terms of the trust provide that "the trustee may in his absolute discretion refuse to make any payment to the beneficiary or to apply any of the trust property for his benefit." See Restatement 2d of Trusts §155 comment c.

These definitions led the Restatement 2d and many courts to resolve important disputes by classifying the trust. If the trust was classified as a *discretionary trust*, the beneficiary's interest was considered to be inalienable. As one court stated: "Because discretionary trusts give the trustee complete discretion to distribute all, some, or none of the trust assets, the beneficiary has a 'mere expectancy' in the non-distributed income and principal until the trustee elects to make a payment." United States v. O'Shaughnessy, 517 N.W.2d 574, 577 (Minn. 1994) (holding that the IRS could not enforce a tax levy against a discretionary trust beneficiary's interest). The same reasoning led courts to hold that *creditors* of the beneficiary of a discretionary trust cannot reach the beneficiary's interest. Restatement 2d of Trusts §155.

On the other hand, if the trust was not a discretionary trust, then the beneficiary's ability to alienate (and a creditor's ability to reach) the interest depended on whether the interest was limited to what was necessary for the beneficiary's support and education. If it was so limited, then the trust was called a *support trust*, and the beneficiary's interest was not transferable by the beneficiary and not reachable by the creditor. Otherwise, it was. See Restatement 2d of Trusts §154.

The effect of these rules has been substantial confusion in the case law. Different outcomes have turned on the slightest differences in the language used in the trust instruments. This was not how the authors of the Second Restatement envisioned the law would develop. See Restatement 2d of Trusts §154 comment d (stating that the "application of this section" on support trusts "is not dependent on the use of any particular form of words in the terms of the trust").

Question

Read Article III, paragraph 3, subparagraph (b) of the Sample Inter Vivos Trust, found on p. 467. Focusing only on this provision, answer the following question: Is the trust a support trust or a discretionary trust?

A New Approach. Recognizing the difficulty of classifying trusts into the separate categories of "support" and "discretionary," both the Restatement 3d of Trusts and the Uniform Trust Code have abandoned the traditional distinction between discretionary trusts and support trusts in favor of a single standard. As the Restatement Reporter's Notes on §60 explain, §§50 and 60

> depart[] significantly from prior Restatements, and from some lines of cases that were largely influenced by the prior Restatement positions... in that this Restatement Third does not attempt to draw a bright line between "discretionary" interests... and "support" interests.... The so-called "support trust" ... is viewed here as a discretionary trust with a support standard. This in turn requires asking and examining all of the questions that follow from that view, such as how a particular standard, in context, is to be interpreted and whether a beneficiary's other resources are to be taken into account in making a fiduciary judgment about appropriate distributions to the beneficiary.... The fact of the matter is that there is a continuum of discretionary trusts, with the terms of distributive powers ranging from the most objective... of standards (pure "support") to the most open ended (e.g., "happiness") or vague ("benefit") of standards, or even with no standards manifested at all (for which a court will probably apply "a general standard of reasonableness"). And these trusts use an unlimited variety of combinations of such terms or standards, with any standard or combination about as likely as another to be accompanied by language of extended discretion (such as "absolute" or "sole and uncontrolled").

UTC §504 similarly provides a single rule for all discretionary trusts. The materials that follow discuss some of the implications of this new approach.

a. Range of the Trustee's Discretion

By conferring discretion, a settlor manifests an intention to trust the trustee's judgment. Restatement 3d of Trusts §50 provides that a discretionary power of a trustee to determine the benefits to be paid to a beneficiary is subject to judicial control only to prevent misinterpretation or abuse of discretion. This raises the question: What constitutes an abuse of discretion? Consider the following excerpts from the Restatement 3d of Trusts.

Restatement 3d of Trusts

§50(2). [W]hat may constitute an abuse of discretion by the trustee... depend[s] on the terms of the discretion, including the proper construction of any accompanying standards, and on the settlor's purposes in granting the discretionary power and in creating the trust....

[Comment] b. Judicial review and control of trustee's discretion.... Court intervention may be obtained to rectify abuses resulting from bad faith or improper motive, and to correct errors resulting from mistakes of interpretation. Absent language of extended (e.g., "absolute" or "uncontrolled") discretion (Comment c), a court will also intervene if it finds that the payments made, or not made, to be unreasonable as a means of carrying out the trust provisions. For example, a beneficiary may be entitled to amounts sufficient to provide support, or to meet some other standard, and the amounts being paid by the trustee may be clearly excessive or inadequate for the purpose. It is not necessary, however, that the terms of the trust provide specific standards in order for a trustee's good faith decision to be found unreasonable and thus to constitute an abuse of discretion....

[Comment] c. Effect of extended discretion. Although the discretionary character of a power of distribution does not ordinarily authorize the trustee to act beyond the bounds of reasonable judgment (Comment b), a settlor may manifest an intention to grant the trustee greater than ordinary latitude in exercising discretionary judgment. How does such an intention affect the duty of the trustee and the role of the court?

It is contrary to sound policy, and a contradiction in terms, to permit the settlor to relieve a "trustee" of all accountability.... Once it is determined that the authority over trust distributions is held in the role of trustee..., words such as "absolute" or "unlimited" or "sole and uncontrolled" are not interpreted literally. Even under the broadest grant of fiduciary discretion, a trustee must act honestly and in a state of mind contemplated by the settlor. Thus, the court will not permit the trustee to act in bad faith or for some purpose or motive other than to accomplish the purposes of the discretionary power.[2] Except as the power is for the trustee's personal benefit, the court will also prevent the trustee from *failing* to act, either arbitrarily or from a misunderstanding of the trustee's duty or authority.

Within these limits, it is a matter of interpretation to ascertain the *degree* to which the settlor's language of extended (e.g., "absolute") discretion manifests an intention to relieve the trustee of normal judicial supervision and control in the exercise of a discretionary power over trust distributions....

---

2. See UTC §814(a), which provides that even where the trust instrument grants the trustee extended discretion through such terms as "absolute" or "uncontrolled," the trustee "shall exercise a discretionary power in good faith and in accordance with the terms and purposes of the trusts and the interests of the beneficiaries." For an argument that this provision does not change the common law, see Alan Newman, Spendthrift and Discretionary Trusts: Alive and Well under the Uniform Trust Code, 40 Real Prop., Prob. & Tr. J. 567, 601-614 (2005).

[Comment] e. Significance of beneficiary's other resources. It is important to ascertain whether a trustee, in determining the distributions to be made to a beneficiary under an objective standard (such as a support standard), (i) is *required* to take account of the beneficiary's other resources, (ii) is *prohibited* from doing so, or (iii) is to consider the other resources but *has some discretion* in the matter. If the trust provisions do not address the question, the general rule of construction presumes the last of these....

One qualification is that, if the discretionary power is one to invade principal for (or to distribute additional income to) a beneficiary who is entitled to all or a specific part of the trust income ..., the trustee must take the mandatory distributions into account before making additional payments under the discretionary power. Where the beneficiary is entitled to payments from another trust created by the same settlor... or as part of coordinated estate planning with another (such as the settlor's spouse), required distributions from the other trust—and the purposes of both trusts—are to be taken into account by the trustee in deciding whether, in what amounts, and from which trust(s) discretionary payments are to be made.

Another qualification is that, to the extent and for as long as the discretionary interest is intended to provide for the support, education, or health care of a beneficiary... for periods during which a beneficiary was probably not expected to be self-supporting, the usual inference is that the trustee is *not* to deny or reduce payments for these purposes because of a beneficiary's personal resources. (But contrast the effect of *another's* duty to support the beneficiary....)

EXTERNAL REFERENCES. Richard C. Ausness, Discretionary Trusts: An Update, 43 ACTEC L. J. 231 (2018); Ivan Taback & David Pratt, Where the Rubber Meets the Road: A Discussion Regarding a Trustee's Exercise of Discretion, 49 Real Prop., Prob. & Tr. J. 491 (2015).

Problems

Wilma Brown is a 50-year-old state supreme court justice. Wilma's spouse, Harry, age 47, is a self-employed cello teacher. Wilma and Harry have two children, Donny and Marie, both of whom are over 18 and are undergraduates at Snootymore University. All members of the family are in good health.

Major assets, liabilities, and annual income and expenses of the family are as follows:

MAJOR ASSETS		MAJOR LIABILITY	
House and Furnishings	$800,000	Mortgage	$400,000
Automobiles	$75,000		
Investments	$500,000		
Total	$1,375,000	*Net Worth*	$975,000
ANNUAL INCOME		ANNUAL EXPENSES	
Wilma's Salary	$200,000[3]	Automobile Loan Payments	$15,000
Harry's Income	$50,000	Mortgage Payments	$36,000
Interest	$55,000	College Expenses for Donny and Marie	$170,000
		Taxes (Income and Real Estate)	$45,000
		Other expenses (Food, clothing, donations, travel, medical, entertainment, etc.)	$60,000
Total Income	$305,000	Total Expenses	$326,000

1. Justice Brown's mother, Gertrude, died last year. Her will, executed five years earlier, devised $4.2 million in trust. You, as trustee, are directed to pay so much of the income, principal, or both as you, in your absolute and uncontrolled discretion, determine is necessary for Wilma's support and maintenance; unexpended income is to be accumulated and added to principal; upon Wilma's death, the principal (including accumulated income) is to go to Donny and Marie.

---

3. Wilma's salary is in the upper range of associate justices of highest state courts. See www.ncsc.org/salarytracker.

You have invested the $4.2 million in such a way that it produces income at the rate of about $165,000 per year. In light of the Restatement 3d's approach, what amount would you decide to distribute to Wilma this year? Why?

2. Same facts as Problem 1, except that Gertrude is Harry's mother, not Wilma's mother, and the beneficiary of the trust is Harry, not Wilma.

3. Same facts as Problem 1, except that the amount Gertrude devised in trust was $1,200,000, producing income at the rate of about $44,000 per year. See Tidrow v. Director, Missouri State Division of Family Services, 688 S.W.2d 9, 12 (Mo. Ct. App. 1985) (suggesting that the amount of the principal is a factor in deciding whether the beneficiary's other assets or sources of income can or must be taken into account by the trustee).

4. Same facts as Problem 1, except for the additional information that Wilma had been appointed by the governor to fill a vacancy on the state supreme court only two years ago. Prior to that time, Wilma had been a partner in and head of the trusts, estates, and personal financial counseling department of a medium-sized law firm, earning about $625,000 per year. The cut in pay Wilma took to become a judge considerably curtailed the style of living to which the family had previously been accustomed.

5. From your perspective as trustee, how could the drafting of Gertrude's trust have been improved?

6. Would the grant of discretion to pay income and principal to Wilma for her "support" permit you, as trustee, to distribute income and principal to pay for college tuition for Donny and Marie? See Estate of Stevens v. Lutch, 617 S.E.2d 736 (S.C. Ct. App. 2005).

"Incentive" and "Principle" Trusts. A growing phenomenon in recent years is the so-called "incentive" trust, a trust that conditions the payment of income or corpus on such things as the beneficiary obtaining a college, graduate, or professional education, getting or staying married (sometimes to a spouse of specified faith), being employed, or refraining from drug or alcohol use. See, e.g., Catherine M. Allchin, In Some Trusts, the Heirs Must Work for the Money, N.Y. Times, Jan. 29, 2006. The criteria the beneficiary must satisfy in order to receive, or continue receiving, trust funds are specified in significant detail. Some practitioners worry that the level of detail in an incentive trust can have unforeseen negative consequences, preferring instead the so-called "principle" trust, wherein the settlor articulates standards to guide, rather than rules to bind, the trustee. See David A. Handler & Alison E. Lothes, The Case for Principle Trusts and Against Incentive Trusts, 147 Tr. & Est. 30 (October 2008). For a discussion of whether incentive trusts can be modified on the petition of the beneficiaries, see Joshua C. Tate, Conditional Love: Incentive Trusts and the Inflexibility Problem, 41 Real Prop. Prob. & Tr. J. 445 (2006).

b. Creditors' Rights

Traditional Approach. According to the traditional approach, the position of a creditor of the beneficiary depended on the classification of the trust. If the trust was neither a support trust nor a discretionary trust, the creditor could reach the beneficiary's interest. If the trust was a support trust, meaning that the beneficiary's interest was limited to what was necessary for the beneficiary's support and education, the creditor could not reach the beneficiary's interest. See Restatement 2d of Trusts §154. If the trust was a discretionary trust, the beneficiary was viewed as having a mere expectancy, not a property interest. The creditor of the beneficiary therefore could not reach the beneficiary's interest. See Restatement 2d of Trusts §155.

The UTC Approach. As we have already pointed out, the UTC collapses the distinction between discretionary and support trusts. With respect to creditors' rights, UTC §504(b) provides that a creditor "may not compel a distribution that is subject to the trustee's discretion, even if (1) the discretion is expressed in the form of a standard of distribution; or (2) the trustee has abused the discretion." The Comment to this section states that "the power to force a distribution due to an abuse of discretion or failure to comply with a standard belongs solely to the beneficiary [under §814(a)]." This means that a beneficiary's creditor cannot successfully assert an abuse-of-discretion claim for non-payment by the trustee even if the beneficiary could have done so on the basis of an abuse of discretion or failure to comply with a standard of distribution. See Alan Newman, The Rights of Creditors of Beneficiaries Under the Uniform Trust Code: An Examination of the Compromise, 69 Tenn. L. Rev. 771, 803-816 (2002).

The Restatement 3d Approach. The Restatement 3d of Trusts takes a different approach. Section 60 provides:

> Subject to the rules [on spendthrift trusts], if the terms of a trust provide for a beneficiary to receive distributions in the trustee's discretion, a transferee or creditor of the beneficiary is entitled to receive or attach any distributions the trustee makes or is required to make in the exercise of that discretion after the trustee has knowledge of the transfer or attachment. The amounts a creditor can reach may be limited to provide for the beneficiary's needs..., or the amounts may be increased as where the beneficiary either is the settlor... or holds the discretionary power to determine his or her own distributions....

The Restatement permits creditors to compel the trustee to make discretionary distributions if the beneficiary could have compelled distributions. Comment e points out that "[t]he exercise or nonexercise of fiduciary discretion is always subject to judicial review to prevent abuse." At the same time, however, comment e states:

> On the other hand, a trustee's refusal to make distributions might not constitute an abuse as against an assignee or creditor even when, under the standards applicable to the [discretionary] power, a decision to refuse distributions to the beneficiary might have

constituted an abuse in the absence of an assignment or attachment. This is because the extent to which the designated beneficiary might actually benefit from a distribution is relevant to the justification and reasonableness of the trustee's decision in relation to the settlor's purposes and the effects on other beneficiaries. Thus, the balancing process typical of discretionary issues becomes, in this context, significantly weighted against creditors, and sometimes against a beneficiary's voluntary assignees.

Trustee Liability. What happens if the trustee pays money to the beneficiary-debtor? Because creditors cannot compel a trustee of a discretionary trust to pay them rather than the beneficiary, one might suppose that the trustee may pay the beneficiary without incurring liability to the creditor. According to Restatement 3d of Trusts §60 comment c, however, if there is no spendthrift restraint and if the trustee has knowledge that the beneficiary of a discretionary trust has assigned his or her interest or if the beneficiary's creditors have served the trustee with process in a proceeding to reach that interest, the trustee is liable to the assignee or the creditor if the trustee first pays the beneficiary.[4]

This principle was established in New York by Hamilton v. Drogo, 150 N.E. 496 (N.Y. 1926). In that case, the dowager Duchess of Manchester devised a large sum in trust, giving the trustees "sole and uncontrolled discretion" to pay the income for the benefit of all or any among her son (the ninth Duke of Manchester, who, incidentally, was a genuine spendthrift extraordinaire[5]), his wife, or his descendants. A judgment creditor of the Duke, after an execution was issued and returned unsatisfied, applied for an order that an execution issue against the trust income in the amount of ten percent thereof pursuant to N.Y. Civil Practice Law §684.[6] The court ordered that the execution be granted, relying on this reasoning:

> In the present case no income may ever become due to the judgment debtor. We may not interfere with the discretion which the testatrix has vested in the trustee.... But at least annually this judgment must be exercised. And if it is exercised in favor of the duke, then

---

4. Contrast this rule with the traditional rule of trustee liability with respect to a *support* trust that has no spendthrift restraint: "the trustee is not liable to the transferee or creditor though the trustee pays to or applies for the beneficiary so much of the property as is necessary for his education or support, even though the trustee has knowledge of the conveyance or has been served with process in proceedings instituted by the creditor to reach the interest of the beneficiary." Restatement 2d of Trusts §154 comment c.

5. See Time, June 17, 1935, at 19. According to Time, the Duke (born William Angus Drogo Montagu) once owed $5,000 for tennis balls.

6. N.Y. Civ. Prac. Law §684 then provided that "where any... income from trust funds... are due and owing to the judgment debtor or shall thereafter become due and owing to him," upon application of the creditor the justice must grant "an order directing that an execution issue against the... income from trust funds of said judgment debtor, and on presentation of such execution... to the person ... from whom such... income from trust funds... are due and owing or may thereafter become due and owing to the judgment debtor, said execution shall become a lien and a continuing levy upon the... income from trust funds... due or to become due to said judgment debtor" for "ten per centum thereof."

there is due him the whole or such part of the income as the trustee may allot to him. After such allotment, he may compel its payment. At least for some appreciable time, however brief, the award must precede the delivery of the income he is to receive, and during that time the lien of the execution attaches.[7]

California courts later adopted the rule of Hamilton v. Drogo. See, e.g., Canfield v. Security-First Nat'l Bank, 87 P.2d 830 (Cal. 1939). The rule is now codified and its scope expanded in the California Probate Code §15303, which provides that the trustee is liable to the beneficiary's transferee or creditor "to the extent that the payment to or for the benefit of the beneficiary impairs the right of the transferee or creditor." The statute further provides that it applies even if the trust was not a "pure" discretionary trust, i.e., the trust instrument provides a standard for the exercise of the trustee's discretion.[8]

Protective Trusts. A variation on discretionary trusts, the "protective trust," was developed by English lawyers.[9] At creation, a protective trust typically gives the beneficiary a *right* to the income, but provides that, upon an attempted alienation, voluntary or involuntary, the beneficiary's right is forfeited and the trust becomes a discretionary trust. The protective-trust device takes advantage of the English rule that forfeiture restraints on equitable life estates are valid.

Ronald Kessler, The Season: Inside Palm Beach and America's Richest Society 49-51 (1999)

Controlling much of the money [for many members of Palm Beach society] are trust-department officers....

Trust-fund babies try to outsmart trust officers.... That's their job, living off inherited wealth. They wake up late, go to their clubs, have a few drinks, and urge [their trust officers] to give them money.

One heir to an industrial fortune has homes in Palm Beach, New York, France, and Italy. He has a yellow Rolls-Royce Corniche convertible but wanted a red Ferrari as well. The trust department of his bank kept turning him down, considering the purchase frivolous. Finally, he bought the Ferrari using his American Express platinum card. The trust department automatically paid the charge....

---

7. This reasoning had been used in an earlier English case involving an assignment by the beneficiary of his interest under a discretionary trust. In re Neil, 62 L.T.R. 649 (1890).

8. An Oklahoma statute also embraces the substance of the Restatement's position, but the statute itself is based upon §5 of a proposed statute found in Erwin N. Griswold, Spendthrift Trusts, app. A (2d ed. 1947). See Okla. Stat. tit. 60 §175.25(F); First Nat'l Bank v. Clark, 402 P.2d 248 (Okla. 1965).

9. In re Bullock, 60 L.J. Ch. 341 (1891). In 1925, England enacted legislation under which a settlor may create a protective trust of income merely by providing that the income is to be held on a "protective trust" for a person for "his life or for any less period." Trustee Act, 1925, 15 Geo. 5, ch. 19, § 33(1).

In Palm Beach, I learned, people are judged not by their accomplishments—most do nothing but cash checks from trust departments—but by the quality of their balloon decorations [at the parties they give]....

2. Spendthrift Trusts

Primary Statutory References: *UTC §§501-502*

We begin our study of spendthrift trusts with Broadway National Bank v. Adams. Although *Broadway Bank* was not the first American decision to uphold the validity of a spendthrift trust, the decision—along with Justice Miller's dictum in Nichols v. Eaton, 91 U.S. 716 (1875), expressing approval of such trusts—is usually credited with having turned the tide of American law.

To put *Broadway Bank* into perspective, the subject of restraints on alienation of *legal* interests must be briefly examined. (When you read the *Broadway Bank* opinion, note that this is what the court is referring to when it mentions "the rule of the common law.") For our purposes, two types of restraints on alienation are relevant—disabling restraints and forfeiture restraints. On their definition and validity, consider the Restatement 2d of Property:

§3.1 *Disabling Restraint.* Terms of a donative transfer of an interest in property which seek to invalidate a later transfer of that interest, in whole or in part, constitute a disabling restraint on alienation (hereinafter referred to as a disabling restraint).

§4.1 *Validity of Disabling Restraint.* (1) A disabling restraint imposed in a donative transfer on an interest in property is invalid if the restraint, if effective, would make it impossible for any period of time from the date of the donative transfer to transfer such interest....

§3.2 *Forfeiture Restraint.* Terms of a donative transfer of an interest in property which seek to terminate, or to subject to termination, that interest, in whole or in part, in the event of a later transfer constitute a forfeiture restraint on alienation (hereinafter referred to as a forfeiture restraint). A forfeiture restraint may apply to any attempted later transfer or only to some types of such transfers and may be limited or unlimited in duration. But the person that is to take in the event of a forfeiture must have a valid interest under the rule against perpetuities.

§4.2 *Validity of Forfeiture Restraint.* (1) A forfeiture restraint imposed in a donative transfer on a life interest in property, or on an interest for a term of years that will terminate at the end of a life (or reasonable number of lives) in being at the time of the transfer, is valid....

In *Broadway National Bank,* the beneficiary, Charles Adams, was given an *equitable* life estate, with the statement that it was not to be subject (a) to voluntary alienation by him or (b) to the claims of his creditors. The second provision is often described as a restraint on involuntary alienation because if a creditor *is* permitted to reach an asset of the debtor the consequence sometimes will be a forced sale of the debtor's interest. The typical spendthrift trust restrains both voluntary and involuntary alienation.[10] See, for example, the clause in Article IV, paragraph 3, of the Sample Inter Vivos Trust, found on p. 468.

Had Charles Adams been given a *legal* life estate, the restraint would have been invalid. As the above provisions of the Restatement 2d demonstrate, the general position of the common law is that such "disabling" restraints on legal interests in property are invalid.

One of Lord Eldon's goals as Chancellor was to move the English rules of equity into greater alignment with those of the common law. This may account for his holding in Brandon v. Robinson (discussed in *Broadway National Bank*) voiding disabling restraints on equitable life estates. It may also explain his statement that the equitable interest of the beneficiary could validly have been subjected to a forfeiture restraint, which he expressed in terms of approval of a grant of an equitable interest to a beneficiary "until he shall become bankrupt."

Broadway National Bank v. Adams
133 Mass. 170 (1882)

MORTON, C.J. The object of this bill in equity is to reach and apply in payment of the plaintiff's debt due from the defendant Adams the income of a trust fund created for his benefit by the will of his brother. The eleventh article of the will is as follows:

> I give the sum of seventy-five thousand dollars to my said executors and the survivors or survivor of them, in trust to invest the same in such manner as to them may seem prudent, and to pay the net income thereof, semiannually, to my said brother Charles W. Adams, during his natural life, such payments to be made to him personally when convenient, otherwise, upon his order or receipt in writing; in either case free from the interference or control of his creditors, my intention being that the use of said income shall not be anticipated by assignment....

There is no room for doubt as to the intention of the testator. It is clear if the trustee was to pay the income to the plaintiff under an order of the court, it would be in direct violation of the intention of the testator and of the provisions of his will. The court will not compel the trustee thus to do what the will forbids him to do, unless the provisions and intention of the testator are unlawful....

It is true that the rule of the common law is, that a man cannot attach to a grant or transfer of property, otherwise absolute, the condition that it shall not be alienated;

---

10. The Restatement 3d of Trusts §58 comment b states that for policy reasons a spendthrift clause that restrains involuntary alienation but permits voluntary alienation is invalid. Accord, UTC §502(a). Massachusetts takes the contrary view. See Bank of New England v. Strandlund, 529 N.E.2d 394 (Mass. 1988).

such condition being repugnant to the nature of the estate granted. Co.Lit. 223a; Blackstone Bank v. Davis, 21 Pick. 42.

Lord Coke gives as the reason of the rule, that "it is absurd and repugnant to reason that he, that hath no possibility to have the land revert to him, should restrain his feoffee in fee simple of all his power to alien," and that this is "against the height and puritie of a fee simple." By such a condition, the grantor undertakes to deprive the property in the hands of the grantee of one of its legal incidents and attributes, namely its alienability, which is deemed to be against public policy. But the reasons for the rule do not apply in the case of a transfer of property in trust. By the creation of a trust like the one before us, the trust property passes to the trustee with all its incidents and attributes unimpaired. He takes the whole legal title to the property, with the power of alienation; the *cestui que trust* takes the whole legal title to the accrued income at the moment it is paid over to him. Neither the principal nor the income is at any time inalienable.

The question whether the rule of the common law should be applied to equitable life estates created by will or deed, has been the subject of conflicting adjudications by different courts.... [F]rom the time of Lord Eldon the rule has prevailed in the English Court of Chancery, to the extent of holding that when the income of a trust estate is given to any person (other than a married woman) for life, the equitable estate for life is alienable by, and liable in equity to the debts of, the *cestui que trust*, and that this quality is so inseparable from the estate that no provision, however express, which does not operate as a cesser or limitation of the estate itself, can protect it from his debts. Brandon v. Robinson, 18 Ves. 429. The English rule has been adopted in several of the courts of this country. Other courts have rejected it....

The founder of this trust was the absolute owner of his property. He had the entire right to dispose of it, either by any absolute gift to his brother, or by a gift with such restrictions or limitations, not repugnant to law, as he saw fit to impose. His clear intention, as shown in his will, was not to give his brother an absolute right to the income which might hereafter accrue upon the trust fund, with the power of alienating it in advance, but only the right to receive semiannually the income of the fund, which upon its payment to him, and not before, was to become his absolute property. His intentions ought to be carried out, unless they are against public policy. There is nothing in the nature or tenure of the estate given to the *cestui que trust* which should prevent this. The power of alienating in advance is not a necessary attribute or incident of such an estate or interest, so that the restraint of such alienation would introduce repugnant or inconsistent elements.

We are not able to see that it would violate any principles of sound public policy to permit a testator to give to the object of his bounty such a qualified interest in the income of a trust fund, and thus provide against the improvidence or misfortune of the beneficiary. The only ground upon which it can be held to be against public policy is, that it defrauds the creditors of the beneficiary.

It is argued that investing a man with apparent value tends to mislead creditors, and to induce them to give him credit. The answer is, that creditors have no right to rely upon property thus held, and to give him credit upon the basis of an estate which, by the instrument creating it, is declared to be inalienable by him, and not liable for his debts. By the exercise of proper diligence they can ascertain the nature and extent of his estate, especially in this Commonwealth, where all wills and most deeds are spread upon the public record. There is the same danger of their being misled by false appearances, and induced to give credit to the equitable life tenant when the will or deed of trust provides for a cesser or limitation over, in case of an attempted alienation, or of bankruptcy or attachment, and the argument would lead to the conclusion that the English rule is equally in violation of public policy....

The rule of public policy which subjects a debtor's property to the payment of his debts, does not subject the property of a donor to the debts of his beneficiary, and does not give the creditor a right to complain that, in the exercise of his absolute right of disposition, the donor has not seen fit to give the property to the creditor, but has left it out of his reach....

It follows that, under the provisions of the will which we are considering, the income of the trust fund created for the benefit of the defendant Adams cannot be reached by attachment, either at law or in equity, before it is paid to him.

Bill dismissed.

———

Application to Interests in Principal. The spendthrift clause held valid in *Broadway National Bank* applied to Charles' income interest. Were spendthrift clauses valid for interests in the principal (corpus) of the trust? The first Restatement of Trusts in 1935 answered this question in the negative: a spendthrift restraint on an interest in principal was invalid. See Restatement of Trusts §151. By 1959, the position of the American Law Institute had changed. The Restatement 2d of Trusts declared that spendthrift restraints on principal were valid. See Restatement 2d of Trusts §153. An important case on the subject was Estate of Vought, below.

Estate of Vought
250 N.E.2d 343 (N.Y. 1969)

[Clarence M. Vought, Sr., died in 1930, survived by his wife, Edna, and his two sons, Peter Vought and Chance M. Vought, Jr. The will of Chance, Sr., created a trust, the income to be paid to Edna for life, remainder in corpus in equal shares to the two sons. Edna died at age 67 in 1965, survived by Peter. Although Chance, Jr., predeceased his mother by about a year and a half, his remainder interest in half of the corpus (valued at about $1 million) was not conditioned on survivorship to the time of possession or enjoyment and so passed through his estate to his successors in interest, presumably his widow and surviving children.

The trust expressly prohibited alienation of the sons' remainder interests in principal. Nevertheless, Chance, Jr., during his lifetime, purported to assign his remainder interest in the corpus in a series of transactions as follows: (a) on October 27, 1959, he sold to Inheritance Estates Ltd. a right to $450,000, for which he allegedly received $78,750; (b) on October 27, 1959, he sold to the Allied Investment & Discount Corporation a right to $150,000, subject to the prior assignment, for which he allegedly received $15,000; (c) on January 8, 1960, he sold to Lex Company Inc. a right to $500,000, subject to the two prior assignments; and (d) on August 11, 1960, he sold to Leonard P. Levy, all his interest in the principal, subject to the three prior assignments. Chance, Jr., allegedly received $12,000 for these last two assignments. There was evidence that these amounts allegedly received by Chance, Jr. were substantially below the actuarial values of the interests purportedly assigned by him. There was also evidence that Chance, Jr., was, at the time of these transactions "an alcoholic suffering from chronic relapsing pancreatitis and diabetes and was addicted to the use of drugs as a result of the suffering caused by this condition [and] in the words of one witness [he was also] in 'desperate financial straights'...." The Surrogate's Court held that the clause restraining alienation of Chance, Jr.'s remainder interest in the trust principal was valid and, therefore, that his assignments were void. The Appellate Division affirmed, and the assignees appealed to the Court of Appeals.]

BREITEL, J. ...The precise question of whether a settlor has the power to make inalienable a principal remainder limited on an entrusted life estate is one of first impression. In this State, although there are many precedents which offer close analogies, they yield no conclusive or authoritative holding or doctrine. It is evident, however, that the prevailing weight of decisional authority in the Nation, based more or less on common-law principles, would sustain the restraint of alienation of a remainder limited on an equitable life interest, if so provided by the creator of the trust. Moreover, in policy, there are no persuasive modern reasons, and aside from conceptual and historical grounds, for nullifying attempts at restraining alienation on transfers in fee absolute, no compelling legal ground why the creator's wishes must be ignored during the measured period involved. Consequently, it is concluded that the determinations of the Surrogate and the Appellate Division should be affirmed....

In the instant case, the issue is whether generally a creator may postpone for a limited period the beneficiary's control of material wealth until a time when the beneficiary is believed to be more able to manage it more wisely. Such a desire is not unnatural in a creator of trusts, nor does it work an undue hardship on those who extend aid to the beneficiary, provided they extend aid with the knowledge that they will not be reimbursed out of the principal against the creator's wishes.

The weight of authority, where not controlled by statute, supports the power to impose inalienability of principal as well as of life interests (see 2 Scott, Law of Trusts [3d ed.], §153, p. 1170; see, also, 2 Bogert, Law of Trusts and Trustees [2d ed.], §222, p. 639, at n. 2). Scott has noted: "The courts seem to feel that the protection of the beneficiary of a trust should extend not merely to his right to receive income but to his right to receive principal in the future, whether in the meantime he or another person is entitled to receive the income" (op. cit., at pp. 1170-1171). As a reflection of a trend in favor of allowing principal inalienability, the Restatement, 2d Trusts, reversing the position of the first Restatement, now allows for inalienability of the principal (compare Restatement, 2d Trusts, §153, with Restatement, Trusts, §153)....

Given the history of the rules and the statutes expressing the rules, giving only limited value to the ideal of consistency of patterns in the law, and according substantial weight to modern policy considerations and the purpose of permitting owners enlarged freedom to dispose of their property as they will unless there is injury to the public, the law of this State should conform to the prevailing weight of authority. In this way, the intended beneficiaries of the remainders of principal will be protected as the settlors intend, and the assignees suffer no loss greater than that for which they bargained on the face of the instruments with which they were dealing. Interests in property are not restrained of alienation or transfer for any greater time than the permissible life interests and the legal title of the particular assets ...is always capable of being transferred [under the trustee's power of sale.]

In the absence of any strong statutory direction or any developed body of precedent restricting provisions making principal inalienable, the will of the testator should be given effect, and the interest of the assignor be deemed unassignable during the life of the trust.

The assignees argue, however, that even if the interest in principal be deemed unassignable, the assignees should be entitled to that interest now that the trust has ended and the principal is now to be paid out. They argue it would be inequitable to have allowed the assignor to renounce the assignment, and urge that his estate be charged with his obligation to facilitate a transfer.

Such a result, however, would render meaningless any provision providing for inalienability of the principal for, indeed, the beneficial owner has no present interest to be protected but the right to receive the principal at a later date. If by an assignment during the life of the trust he is deemed to have transferred this sole right of later possession he has transferred virtually all his interest. Moreover, the creator's wishes would be completely frustrated, the beneficiary not only getting the funds the creator had intended be delayed, but the beneficiary receiving a fraction, after discount, of what was eventually intended.

Thus the courts below correctly determined that the assignees were not entitled to the principal of the trust.

Accordingly, the order of the Appellate Division should be affirmed, with costs to all parties filing briefs payable out of the estate.

FULD, C.J., dissenting. I would reverse on the ground that the estate created in the will for the testator's son constituted both a legal and equitable vested remainder in fee, the alienability of which, under long-established principles, may not be proscribed. (EPTL, 7-1.5 [replacing former Personal Property Law, §15].) Moreover, the policy considerations in favor of permitting a restraint upon the alienability of property until such time as the beneficiary is believed to be equipped to manage it wisely do not operate where a remainderman is given an absolute and unqualified right to dispose of the property as he chooses, subject only to the prior life estate of another.

———

Policy Arguments For and Against Spendthrift Trusts. Spendthrift trusts raise what Professor Alexander has called the "dead hand dilemma,"[11] which is that the general idea of freedom of disposition can be invoked on either side—for or against the validity of spendthrift trusts. Several writers have opposed the validity of spendthrift trusts, focusing on the infringement of the beneficiary's freedom. One outspoken critic was John Chipman Gray, who was prompted by Nichols v. Eaton to write a book titled Restraints on the Alienation of Property (1883), arguing:

> The fallacy [of validating spendthrift trusts is in the notion] that the only objection to such inalienable life estates is that they defraud the creditors of the life tenant; and the courts labor, with more or less success, to show that these creditors are not defrauded.... But, with submission, this is not the ground why equitable life estates cannot be made inalienable and free from debts. The true ground is the same on which the whole law of property, legal and equitable, is based;—that inalienable rights of property are opposed to the fundamental principles of the common law; that it is against public policy that a man "should have an estate to live on, but not an estate to pay his debts with"; Tillinghast v. Bradford, 5 R.I. 205, 212; that a man should have the benefits of wealth without the responsibilities. The common law has recognized certain classes of persons who may be kept in pupilage, viz. infants, lunatics, married women; but it has held that sane grown men must look out for themselves,—that it is not the function of the law to join in the futile effort to save the foolish and the vicious from the consequences of their own vice and folly. It is wholesome doctrine, fit to produce a manly race, based on sound morality and wise philosophy....
>
> That grown men should be kept all their lives in pupilage, that men not paying their debts should live in luxury on inherited wealth, are doctrines as undemocratic as can well be conceived.... The general introduction of spendthrift trusts would be to form a privileged class, who could indulge in every speculation, could practice every fraud, and, provided they kept on the safe side of the criminal law, could yet roll in wealth. They would be an aristocracy, though certainly the most contemptible aristocracy with which a country was ever cursed.

---

11. Gregory S. Alexander, The Dead Hand and the Law of Trusts in the Nineteenth Century, 37 Stan. L. Rev. 1189, 1193 (1985).

Id. at 169-70, 174. Gray's opposition to spendthrift trusts was to little avail. In the preface to the second edition of his book, published in 1895, Gray lamented:

> State after State has given in its adhesion to the new doctrine.... Were it not for an occasional dissenting opinion... I should be *vox clamantis in deserto*.
>
> And yet I cannot recant. Doubtless I may exaggerate the importance of the matter; but, so far as it goes, I still believe, as I said in the first edition, that the old doctrine was a wholesome one, fit to produce a manly race, based on sound morality and wise philosophy; and that the new doctrine is contrary thereto.[12]

To the judges (and legislators) of the time (and since), the donor's freedom of disposition has seemed more worthy of protection. This is vividly expressed in the *Broadway National Bank* case, where the court said:

> The founder of this trust was the absolute owner of his property.... His clear intention... was not to give his brother an absolute right to the income... with power of alienating it in advance, but only the right to receive semiannually the income.... His intentions ought to be carried out, unless they are against public policy.... We are not able to see that it would violate any principles of sound public policy to permit a testator to give to the object of his bounty such a qualified interest in the income ... and thus provide against the improvidence or misfortune of the beneficiary.

See also Steib v. Whitehead, 111 Ill. 247, 250-52 (1884).

The term spendthrift trust is somewhat of a misnomer, since judicial recognition has not limited such trusts to spendthrifts or to persons who may be in need of special protection. Apart from statute, any person can be the beneficiary of a spendthrift trust in a state recognizing such trusts, without regard to the beneficiary's ability to look after himself or herself and his or her business affairs. Nor has the case law placed any limitation on the amount of income that can be validly protected from the claims of the beneficiary's creditors. In an Illinois case, Congress Hotel Co. v. Martin, 143 N.E. 838 (Ill. 1924), the beneficiary was entitled to income of over $171,000 for the year 1921. In that year, she ran up a hotel bill of some $6,700 and the hotel sought to reach income in the hands of the trustee by garnishment. The court denied relief because the will creating the trust included a spendthrift provision.

Today, no jurisdiction in the United States refuses recognition of spendthrift trusts. In the words of Professors Scott and Ascher, "In a few states the courts at first held that spendthrift trusts were against public policy, but even in these states the law is now otherwise, either as a result of legislation or a due to a judicial change of heart." Scott and Ascher on Trusts §15.2.1 (6th ed. 2021). One of the last holdouts was New Hampshire. See N.H. Rev. Stat. §564-B:5-502 (enacted 2004).

---

12. John C. Gray, Restraints on the Alienation of Property iv-v (2d ed. 1895).

For policy discussions of the spendthrift trust doctrine, see Mary Louise Fellows, Spendthrift Trusts: Roots and Relevance for Twenty-First Century Planning, 50 Rec. Assn. B. City N.Y. 140 (1995); Adam J. Hirsch, Spendthrift Trusts and Public Policy: Economic and Cognitive Perspectives, 73 Wash. U. L.Q. 1 (1995).

––––––

What Do Spendthrift Clauses Do? Let us be explicit about how spendthrift clauses work.

Effect Before Income/Principal Due. If the beneficiary of a spendthrift trust attempts to assign his or her interest in the trust to a creditor, in anticipation of future payments by the trustee, the spendthrift clause makes the assignment revocable by the beneficiary (though the beneficiary will still owe the debt) and not binding on the trustee. See Restatement 3d of Trusts §58 comment d; UTC §502.

Effect When Income/Principal Due But Not Yet Distributed. If a spendthrift provision is valid, does it continue to be effective once the time has arrived for, but prior to, actual distribution? Although the decisions are divided on the question (Scott and Ascher on Trusts §15.2.7 (6th ed. 2021)), the Restatement 3d of Trusts §58 comment d states that "property that has become distributable to the beneficiary but is retained by the trustee beyond a time reasonably necessary to make distribution to a beneficiary, and thus to which the beneficiary has a right to demand immediate distribution, is then subject to attachment by creditors of the beneficiary." This rule is codified in some states. See, e.g., Cal. Prob. Code §15301. UTC §506 similarly provides that "[w]hether or not a trust contains a spendthrift provision, a creditor or assignee of a beneficiary may reach a mandatory distribution of income or principal, including a distribution upon termination of the trust, if the trustee has not made the distribution to the beneficiary within a reasonable time after the designated distribution date."

Effect After Income/Principal Transferred to Beneficiary. All authorities agree that both income and principal are transferable and attachable once received by the beneficiary.

––––––

Spendthrift Trust Legislation. Spendthrift trusts are recognized by statute in many states, but the statutes take a variety of forms. No attempt at exhaustive classification is made here; for a state-by-state compilation, see Bogert on Trusts and Trustees §222 (3d ed. 2007 & 2023 Supp.).

As is true of the common-law decisions, most statutes place no limit on the amount that can be protected by or on who can be the beneficiary of a spendthrift trust, by reference to need, competency, or relationship to the settlor. In Nevada (see

Nev. Rev. Stat. §166.010 et seq.)[13] and Texas (see Tex. Prop. Code §112.035), for example, the statute authorizes the creation of spendthrift trusts in terms about as broad as could be devised. Both income and principal may be placed beyond the reach of creditors without regard to the amount of wealth involved. The Nevada statute is explicit that the validity of such a trust "does not depend on the character, capacity, incapacity, competency or incompetency of the beneficiary." Nev. Rev. Stat. §166.090.

The New York statute deserves mention because it has been copied in a number of states, in whole or in part. By legislation that had its beginnings in 1828, well before the *Broadway National Bank* case was decided, virtually all trusts are automatically made spendthrift trusts by statute, without the need of any provision to that effect in the trust instrument. The central provision in the present New York statute reads:

> *N.Y. Est. Powers & Trusts Law §7-1.5. When trust interest inalienable; exception.* (a)...
> (1) The right of a beneficiary of an express trust to receive the income from property and apply it to the use of or pay it to any person may not be transferred by assignment or otherwise unless a power to transfer such right, or any part thereof, is conferred upon such beneficiary by the instrument creating or declaring the trust....

Unlike the spendthrift trust at common law, the New York statute allows voluntary transfer of any amount of income in excess of $10,000 per year, provided the transfer is made to specified relatives, is gratuitous, and is not expressly prohibited by the trust instrument. N.Y. Est. Powers & Trusts Law §7-1.5(b).

The New York statute also places a limit on the amount of income that can be shielded from the claims of creditors. Creditors can reach income "in excess of the sum necessary for the education and support of the beneficiary." N.Y. Est. Powers & Trusts Law §7-3.4. This limitation has been substantially vitiated, however, by construing needs to relate to the beneficiary's "station in life."[14] In Kilroy v. Wood, 42 Hun. 636 (N.Y. 1886), for example, creditors were unsuccessful in trying to reach surplus income of a spendthrift trust because they failed to show that the income was more than sufficient for the beneficiary's support. The court said:

> [The beneficiary is] a gentleman of high social standing, whose associations are chiefly with men of leisure, and is connected with a number of clubs, with the usages and customs of which he seems to be in harmony both in practice and expenditure, and it is insisted on his behalf that his income is not more than sufficient to maintain his position according to his education, habits and associations.

---

13. But see Ambrose v. First Nat'l Bank, 482 P.2d 828 (Nev. 1971), which construed the statute as limiting spendthrift trusts to trusts for support.

14. Provisions of the N.Y. Civil Practice Law and Rules have removed some of the protection previously afforded by this station-in-life test. See Gregory S. Alexander, Spendthrift Trusts and Their Functional Substitutes, in Debtor-Creditor Law §39.03[1](a) (Theodore Eisenberg ed. 2008).

Id. at 638. See also Erwin N. Griswold, Spendthrift Trusts §379 (2d ed. 1947); Richard R. Powell, The Rule Against Perpetuities and Spendthrift Trusts in New York: Comments and Suggestions, 71 Colum. L. Rev. 688, 699 (1971) [hereinafter Powell, Spendthrift Trusts].

The California statute is a variation of the New York scheme. Unlike the New York statute, the restraint on alienation is imposed only if the settlor so provides. Cal. Prob. Code §15300. But once this has occurred, judgment creditors (as under the New York scheme) can reach any amount "in excess of the amount that is or will be necessary for education and support of the beneficiary"; unlike New York, however, there is apparently an additional cap preventing judgment creditors from reaching more than 25 percent of the amounts otherwise payable. Cal. Prob. Code §§15306.5, 15307.

In interpreting the education-and-support limit, the California courts also apply a station-in-life test. But the extremes of the New York cases have arguably been avoided, as the following passage from Canfield v. Security-First Nat'l Bank, 87 P.2d 830, 840-41 (Cal. 1939), suggests:

No set sum can be fixed to apply to all cases. The amount varies according to the station in life of the beneficiary. This does not mean, however, that the needs of the beneficiary are to be measured by his extravagance or his ability to spend. It does not mean that an allowance is to be made for extravagant entertaining, and for unbridled luxuries. The manner of living of the beneficiary in the past, if such living was unreasonably extravagant and profuse, is no criterion of the reasonable amount necessary for support and maintenance. Evidence as to cost of living, wages of servants, medical expense and reasonable entertainment, and other reasonably necessary expenses, fixes the amount....

The cost of living, cost of housing, medical cost, the manner in which the beneficiary has been reared, the number and health of his dependents, his own health, his entire background—all these and perhaps others should be considered. But cost of lavish entertaining, cost of betting on race horses and cost of obvious luxuries, etc.—these are all false factors.

The station-in-life test, even as administered by the California courts, shields from creditors' claims income sufficient to support a fairly luxurious style of living, if this is the style of living to which the beneficiary is accustomed. Dean Griswold and Professor Powell bridled at the station-in-life test and argued for a different approach. In Powell, Spendthrift Trusts, above, at 704-05, the author argued:

It would not be wise to prohibit *all* spendthrift trusts. There are occasions when a possessor of substantial wealth has, close to his heart, a relative who lacks the business experience to protect himself from the ever-present vultures. A modest sum, so set up as to protect such a person from dissipating his substance and unreachable by creditors generally, constitutes no threat to social welfare. The trouble arises when the amount entrusted becomes large and the immunities of the beneficiary cease to be reasonable.

Earlier, Dean Griswold had drafted a model spendthrift trust statute, which provided that all income "in excess of $5000 per annum shall be subject to attachment by a creditor of the beneficiary [of a spendthrift trust] and shall be freely alienable by the beneficiary." Griswold, above, at 648. Griswold wrote this in 1947; in today's dollars, the $5000 figure would translate roughly to $54,000 per year.

Griswold's model statute was enacted in Louisiana and Oklahoma. In Louisiana, the $5,000 figure was raised to $10,000 in 1964, then to $20,000 in 1985; in 1987, the limit was repealed altogether. See La. Rev. Stat. §9:2004. Oklahoma has also repealed the limit. See 60 Okla. Stat. §175.85.

Federal Bankruptcy. To the extent that a spendthrift restraint is valid under or automatically imposed by state law or federal law, it is also effective in bankruptcy. A provision of the federal Bankruptcy Code, 11 U.S.C. § 541(c)(2), provides that "[a] restriction on the transfer of a beneficial interest of the debtor in a trust that is enforceable under applicable nonbankruptcy law is enforceable in a case under this title." Courts have consistently construed this provision to exclude from a bankrupt debtor's estate any beneficial trust interest that is subject to a valid spendthrift restraint. E.g., Bass v. Denney (*in re* Bass), 171 F.3d 1016 (5th Cir. 1999).

One of the major changes made by the Bankruptcy Abuse Prevention and Consumer Protection Act of 2005 (BAPCPA) was the introduction of means testing in Chapter 7 bankruptcy, making it much harder for individuals to have their debts completely discharged in bankruptcy. Section 707 allows the court to dismiss the case of a debtor whose debts are primarily consumer debts if the court finds that granting relief would be an abuse of Chapter 7. Section 707(b)(2) provides that the court shall presume such an abuse exists if the "debtor's current monthly income," defined in section 101(10A) as "average monthly income from all sources that the debtor receives," is excessive, as determined according to a specified calculation. Although the meaning of this provision is not entirely clear, it is possible that under it the income from a spendthrift trust must be counted. Under that reading the beneficiary of a spendthrift trust generating a significant amount of monthly income may not qualify for bankruptcy discharge under Chapter 7 but be relegated to Chapter 13 bankruptcy, in which the debtor is required to pay off debts according to a court-approved plan.

———

Boilerplate Use of Spendthrift Clauses. In practice, most private trusts drafted by lawyers contain a spendthrift clause. A spendthrift clause is routinely included in law-office and published form-book trust forms. Here is the clause contained in the Sample Revocable Inter Vivos Trust from Chapter 9:

> No interest of any beneficiary in the income or principal of this trust shall be assignable in anticipation of payment or be liable in any way for the beneficiary's debts or obligations and shall not be subject to attachment.

The location of the spendthrift clause may also be significant. It is not unusual for a modern trust instrument to be lengthy, consisting of thirty or more typewritten pages. Unlike the testator's will in the *Broadway National Bank* case, where the spendthrift restraint was part of the same sentence granting Charles Adams the right to the income, modern trust forms bury the spendthrift clause in a separate Article toward the end of the document, near the perpetuity saving clause (see Chapter 17 on the Rule Against Perpetuities). We doubt that many clients are told the significance of the clause, except where the client expresses concern about one or more of the beneficiaries, such as G did in Example 11.1, above. Nor do we think that many clients notice the clause on their own and inquire about its significance; and, of those that do, we doubt they get much of an explanation of its significance beyond the standard "Oh, that's a technical-legal clause that we put in all the trusts we draft." To the extent that this is an accurate picture of current legal practice, what risk does this practice create for settlors, beneficiaries, or society in general?

3. Exception Creditors

Primary Statutory Reference: *UTC §503*

Hurley v. Hurley
309 N.W.2d 225 (Mich. Ct. App. 1981)

ALLEN, J. On March 31, 1980, Ingham County Circuit Court ordered garnishee-defendant, Michigan National Bank, to pay accrued and future income of a spendthrift trust to the court in satisfaction of an outstanding judgment for past due child support taken against defendant, James Hurley, former husband of plaintiff, Phyllis Hurley. Garnishee-defendant's motion for rehearing was denied on April 14, 1980. Garnishee-defendant appeals as of right.

The facts before this Court are undisputed. On September 26, 1966, Maybelle Hurley, defendant's mother and a resident of Missouri, executed a will in Missouri. The will devised [approximately one-half of her estate] in a spendthrift trust for James. He was to receive all income from the trust during his lifetime with the principal passing upon James' death into [trusts] for James' two daughters, Linda Kay and Cherri Ann, the decedent's granddaughters....

Plaintiff and defendant were divorced in Missouri approximately six years before the decedent executed her will in September 1966. The decedent did not provide for plaintiff in her will. In 1970, decedent moved from Missouri to Michigan where she remained until her death in 1978. Defendant, James Hurley, moved from Missouri and presently resides in California. He failed to maintain his child support payments. In 1977, plaintiff filed suit in Missouri for past due child support, and in 1979 obtained a Missouri judgment of $19,630 principal plus $5,728 interest. In 1978, Maybelle Hurley died in Michigan, and her will was admitted into probate in Ingham County, Michigan. Garnishee-defendant, Michigan National Bank, was appointed trustee under the will.

In 1979, plaintiff filed a complaint in the Ingham County Circuit Court against defendant and garnishee-defendant, seeking full faith and credit of the Missouri child support judgment. Plaintiff then moved to require the garnishee-defendant, as trustee, to pay plaintiff the past due and future income from defendant's trust to satisfy the outstanding Missouri child support judgment. Garnishee-defendant answered, claiming that the income from the spendthrift trust was not subject to process by the court. On March 31, 1980, the trial court granted plaintiff's motion and ordered garnishee-defendant to pay due and future income into the court to satisfy plaintiff's outstanding judgment. Only garnishee-defendant appeals as of right.

The sole issue before the Court is whether plaintiff, as defendant's former wife, can reach by judicial process the income from a spendthrift trust created in favor of defendant, her former husband, to obtain satisfaction of plaintiff's judgment against defendant for past due child support. The trust established under the terms of Maybelle Hurley's will meets the definition of a spendthrift trust....

Although the issue is one of first impression in Michigan,[15] it has been ruled upon in several other jurisdictions. The majority rule is that, in the absence of a specific state statute, the income of a spendthrift trust of which a former husband is the current income beneficiary may be reached to satisfy his former wife's claim for alimony, separate maintenance, or child support. Restatement, Trusts 2d, §157, p. 328 provides:

> Although a trust is a spendthrift trust or a trust for support, the interest of the beneficiary can be reached in satisfaction of an enforceable claim against the beneficiary,
>
> (a) by the wife or child of the beneficiary for support, or by the wife for alimony;[16]
>
> [(b) for necessary services rendered to the beneficiary or necessary supplies furnished to him;
>
> (c) for services rendered and materials furnished which preserve or benefit the interest of the beneficiary;
>
> (d) by the United States or a State to satisfy a claim against the beneficiary.]

See also II Scott on Trusts, 3d ed., §157.1, pp. 1206-1216.

---

15. Gilkey v. Gilkey, 162 Mich. 664, 127 N.W. 715 (1910), cited by garnishee-defendant, is not applicable to the present facts. Gilkey involved a discretionary trust, not a spendthrift trust....

16. The Comment on §157(a) of the Restatement, Trusts 2d, is as follows:

Although a trust is a spendthrift trust or a trust for support, the interest of the beneficiary can be reached in satisfaction of an enforceable claim against him for support by his wife or children. In some cases a spendthrift clause is construed as not intended to exclude the beneficiary's dependents. Even if the clause is construed as applicable to claims of his dependents for support, it is against public policy to give full effect to the provision. The beneficiary should not be permitted to have the enjoyment of his interest under the trust while neglecting to support his dependents.

Several reasons have been advanced in support of the rule. Some courts adhere to the rationale by finding an intention on behalf of the settlor of the trust to allow a wife to enforce a claim for alimony, maintenance, or child support. In Keller v. Keller, 284 Ill. App. 198, 1 N.E.2d 773 (1936), it was held that such an intention will be found unless the trust instrument discloses an intention that such a claim may not be enforced. Other courts have held that child support is not a "debt" contemplated by the spendthrift provision of a trust.... Still other courts have held that it would be against public policy to hold that a wife may not enforce child support claims against a recalcitrant husband.... In accord with holding a spendthrift provision contrary to public policy is Shelley v. Shelley, 354 P.2d 282 (Or. 1960), which opines that if the beneficiary's interest cannot be reached to satisfy claims for alimony or child support, the state may be called upon to support the wife and children. Further, O'Connor v. O'Connor, 3 Ohio Op.2d 186, 141 N.E.2d 691, 75 Ohio Law Abst. 420 (Oh.Com.Pl., 1957), holds that the husband has a legal duty to support his wife, that a father has a legal duty to support his minor children, and that these elements of public policy outweigh the public policy that an owner of property, such as the settlor of a trust, may dispose of it as he pleases and may impose spendthrift restraints on the disposition of income.

We find all of the above reasons persuasive and affirm, particularly in light of the existing law in Missouri at the time of the execution of the decedent's will and the creation of the present trusts. Missouri law provides, Mo.Rev.Stat. §456.080:

> All restraints... in the form of a spendthrift trust, or otherwise [are] of no effect, as against the claims of any wife, child or children, of [the beneficiary] for support and maintenance, or, as against the claim of any said wife for alimony.

This law was in effect at the time of the creation of the present trusts. Therefore, the trusts as created, even though of a spendthrift nature, could not bar the recovery of the income from the trust for child support. We do not find that the settlor of these trusts intended to exclude such claims but rather intended the trusts to be administered in accordance with the laws of the state in which the trusts were created thereby allowing such claims.

The lower court order... was proper and is sustained.

AFFIRMED.[17]

Notes and Questions

1. *Alimony and Child Support Claims to Spendthrift Trusts.* The view taken in *Hurley*—that a spendthrift clause does not protect a trust beneficiary's interest from claims for child support—represents the prevailing view. Though alimony awards

---

17. In Miller v. Department of Mental Health, 442 N.W.2d 617, 619 (Mich. 1989), the Michigan Supreme Court noted in dictum that "the interest of a beneficiary of [a spendthrift or a support trust] can be reached to enforce claims by the beneficiary's wife or child for alimony or support...." Ed.

are less common today than they once were, the same view prevails regarding the right of a recipient of an alimony award to reach the obligor's interest in a trust despite a spendthrift restraint on that interest. See Restatement 3d of Trusts §59(a). Several courts, however, have refused to permit a former spouse or children to reach a spendthrift trust to satisfy alimony or child support judgments. An example is Erickson v. Erickson, 266 N.W. 161, reh'g denied, 267 N.W. 426 (Minn. 1936). In that case, the court rejected the theory, mentioned in *Hurley*, that the exceptions in favor of alimony and child support claimants are justified, in part, on the basis of the settlor's imputed intent. The court stated: "If alimony or support money is to be an exception to the protection offered by spendthrift provisions it must be by some justifiable interpretation of the donor's language by which such implied exception may be fairly construed into the instrument of the trust."

From the perspective of the settlor's probable intent, should courts distinguish between the claims of the beneficiary's former spouse and those of the beneficiary's children?[18] As the opinion in *Hurley* indicates, of course, the settlor's imputed intention is not the only rationale for the exceptions in favor of alimony or support claimants.

2. *Claimants Who Provided Necessities/Government Claimants.* The Restatement 3d of Trusts §59 does, but UTC §503 does not, list as exception creditors claimants who provided the beneficiary with necessary services or supplies, such as medical personnel.

Both UTC §503 and Restatement 3d §59 comment a list government claimants as exception creditors.[19]

---

18. An article advocating the routine use of spendthrift trusts recommends a clause that specifically states that the interest of any beneficiary "shall be free from the control or interference... of any spouse of a married beneficiary," but does not mention claims of children for child support. See Nancy S. Roush & Robert K. Kirkland, Spendthrift Trusts Not Limited to Protection of Immature Dependents, 18 Est. Plan. 16, 18 (Jan.-Feb. 1991).

19. In United States v. Riggs Nat'l Bank, 636 F. Supp. 172 (D.D.C. 1986), a testamentary protective trust created by the will of Isabel G. Zantzinger provided for payment of a third of the income to her son, William, subject to a spendthrift restraint and a forfeiture provision providing that if William attempts to assign his interest or if his creditors attempt to subject his interest to a levy of execution, writ of attachment, or garnishment, the trustee should have discretion to apply income for the support of William or accumulate it and add it to corpus. A federal district court held that the protective-trust device was ineffective as against the federal tax lien. The court stated:

[W]hile [protective] trust clauses create a legitimate property right under state law which can shield the beneficiary from ordinary creditors, such trusts cannot be effective against a federal tax lien, as a matter of federal law.... It would be offensive and disruptive to federal tax law for a beneficiary to receive an income stream for years without paying taxes on it, only to have the income stream disappear once the IRS discovers the misfeasance and moves against it.

The trust's beneficiary, William Devereaux Zantzinger (d. 2009), was the subject of an early song by Bob Dylan, "The Lonesome Death of Hattie Carroll." According to the song's lyrics, "William

3. *Tort Claimants?* Are tort claimants exception creditors? Should they be? See the *Sligh* decision below and the Notes following.

Sligh v. First National Bank, Trustee
704 So.2d 1020 (Miss. 1997)

MILLS, J., for the Court: This case comes on appeal from the Chancery Court of Holmes County, where Will and Lucy Sligh sought to garnish Gene Lorance's beneficial interest in two spendthrift trusts in order to partially satisfy a tort judgment for damages resulting from injuries sustained by Will Sligh in an automobile accident with Gene Lorance. On December 15, 1995, the chancellor dismissed the Slighs' complaint, ruling that the assets of spendthrift trusts may not be garnished to satisfy the claims of tort judgment creditors. Aggrieved, the Slighs appeal to this Court....

Facts. On January 30, 1993, William B. Sligh was involved in an automobile accident with Gene A. Lorance, an uninsured motorist who was operating a vehicle while intoxicated. As a result, Will Sligh suffered a broken spine and resulting paralysis, including loss of the use of both legs, loss of all sexual functions and loss of the ability to control bowel and urinary functions. Lorance was convicted of the felony of driving under the influence and causing bodily injury to another, for which he was sentenced to serve ten years, with six years suspended, in the custody of the Mississippi Department of Corrections.

On April 2, 1993, Will and his wife, Lucy M. Sligh, filed in the Circuit Court of Holmes County an action against Lorance alleging gross negligence resulting in personal injury, property damage and loss of consortium, for which they sought compensatory and punitive damages. Lorance failed to respond, and after entry of default and a hearing on the Slighs' Motion for Writ of Inquiry on January 25, 1994, the circuit court entered default judgment against Lorance for $5,000,000 in compensatory and punitive damages.

Lorance has no assets other than his interest as beneficiary of two spendthrift trusts established by his mother in 1984 and 1988, respectively, before she died in 1993. Both trusts, whose trustee is First National Bank of Holmes County ("First National Bank"), provide as follows:

> 1. My said Trustee shall have full and complete authority to expend all or any part of the income or corpus of said trust property for the benefit of myself and my said son, Gene Lorance, and shall have the right to make payments directly to me and to my said son or to anyone for myself or my said son.

Zantzinger killed poor Hattie Carroll/With a cane that he twirled around his diamond ring finger/At a Baltimore hotel society gath'rin'." See Bob Dylan, *The Times They Are A-Changin'* (1964). (Many thanks to Kevin FitzPatrick, Esq., of Detroit, Michigan, for providing this information. Ed.) For a detailed obituary, see Douglas Martin, W.D. Zantzinger, Subject of Dylan Song, Dies at 69, N.Y. Times, Jan. 9, 2009.

2. The Trustee shall have the right to invest, re-invest, manage and care for said property in the same manner as though said property was the individual property of said Trustee, and my said Trustee shall not be required to give bond, or account to Court, and shall have all the powers conferred by the Uniform Trustees' Powers Act as the same is now in force in the State of Mississippi and the power to sell, lease or encumber real property. My said Trustee shall exercise the powers herein granted for what may be, in the discretion of my said Trustee, in the best interest of myself and said Gene Lorance, and shall pay to me or the said Gene Lorance such sums and at such times as my said Trustee thinks in my or his best interest. *No part of this trust, either principal or income, shall be liable for the debts of the said Gene Lorance, nor shall the same be subject to seizure by any creditor of his* and he shall not have the right to sell, assign, transfer, encumber or in any manner anticipate or dispose of his interest in said property, or any part of same, or the income produced from said trust or any part thereof.

(emphasis added). Lorance is the lifetime beneficiary of the two trusts, which each have two remaindermen, Virginia Tate and William C. Bardin.

On June 29, 1994, Will and Lucy Sligh filed in the Circuit Court of Holmes County a Suggestion for Writ of Garnishment as to First National Bank, either in its corporate capacity or in its capacity as trustee of the two trusts. A Writ of Garnishment was issued and served upon First National Bank, who, in its answer filed on June 30, 1994, admitted that it was indebted to Lorance in the amount of $313,677.48, but asserted that such sum was held in trust for Lorance and was not subject to seizure. After the Slighs filed a motion for judgment on the answer and First National Bank filed its response, First National Bank moved for a dismissal or, in the alternative, for a transferal of the garnishment proceeding to chancery court. On October 5, 1994, the circuit court transferred the proceeding to the Chancery Court of Holmes County.

On October 25, 1994, the Slighs filed in that court their complaint naming as defendants First National Bank, Gene Lorance, Virginia Tate and William Bardin. The Slighs alleged, in addition to the aforementioned facts, that Lorance's mother, Edith Lorance, had actual knowledge of the following facts: her son was an habitual drunkard who had been unsuccessfully treated for alcoholism; he was mentally deficient and had been previously committed to mental institutions; he had impaired facilities due to his alcoholism and mental disorders; he regularly operated motor vehicles while intoxicated; he was a reckless driver who had been involved in numerous automobile accidents; and he had been arrested and convicted on numerous occasions for driving under the influence. The complaint alleged that despite her actual knowledge of these facts, Mrs. Lorance established the two trusts as part of her intentional plan and design to enable her son to continue to lead his intemperate, debauched, wanton and depraved lifestyle while at the same time shielding his beneficial interest in the trusts from the claims of his involuntary tort creditors. The Slighs alleged that it was a violation of public policy to enforce and give priority to spendthrift trust provisions over involuntary tort judgments against the beneficiary, and they urged the court to recognize and enforce a public policy exception to the spendthrift trust doctrine in favor of involuntary tort creditors by subjecting Lorance's beneficial interests to the payment of their tort judgment in one or more of several equitable ways suggested in their complaint.

After the defendants filed their respective answers, First National Bank filed a Motion for Dismissal on October 27, 1995. On December 15, 1995, the chancellor granted the motion, ruling that the Slighs failed to state a claim upon which relief can be granted. The chancellor ruled that "a tort judgment creditor may not garnish the trustee of a spendthrift trust in which the tort judgment defendant is a mere lifetime discretionary income beneficiary, nor are the assets of such trust subject to the claims of the tort judgment creditor."

Discussion.... The spendthrift trust doctrine is codified by statute in some states and is a judicially created doctrine in others....

Legal scholars for years have called for the recognition of a public policy exception to the spendthrift trust doctrine in favor of tort judgment creditors.[20] However, there is little case law on the matter. In Thackara v. Mintzer, 100 Pa. 151, 154-55 (1882), the Pennsylvania Supreme Court, in upholding the validity of a spendthrift trust, declared in dicta that "whether the judgment be for a breach of contract or for a tort, matters not." In Kirk v. Kirk, 254 Ore. 44, 456 P.2d 1009 (1969), the Oregon Supreme Court held that the interest of a spendthrift trust created by the United States for the Klamath Tribe of American Indians was unreachable by the Indian beneficiary's tort judgment creditor. However, at least one state, Louisiana, has recognized an exception to the spendthrift trust doctrine in favor of tort judgment creditors, which doctrine and exception were codified by the Louisiana Legislature[21]....

[O]ne can identify three public policy considerations ... when enforcing spendthrift trust provisions: (1) the right of donors to dispose of their property as they wish; (2) the public interest in protecting spendthrift individuals from personal pauperism, so that they do not become public burdens; and (3) the responsibility of creditors to make themselves aware of their debtors' spendthrift trust protections. Upon consideration of these public policy concerns in the present context, we find

---

20. See Laurene M. Brooks, Comment, A Tort-Creditor Exception to the Spendthrift Trust Doctrine: A Call to the Wisconsin Legislature, 73 Marq. L. Rev. 109 (1989); Frank A. Gregory, Note, Trusts: Tort Claims as an Exception to the Spendthrift Trust Doctrine, 17 Okla. L. Rev. 235 (1964); Antonis, Spendthrift Trusts, Attachability of a Beneficiary's Interests in Satisfaction of a Tort Claim, 28 Notre Dame L. Rev. 509 (1953); Costigan, Those Protective Trusts Which Are Miscalled "Spendthrift Trusts" Reexamined, 22 Cal. L. Rev. 471 (1934); Griswold, Reaching the Interest of a [Beneficiary of a] Spendthrift Trust, 43 Harv. L. Rev. 63 (1929).

21. The Louisiana Trust Code provides that the beneficiary's interest in a spendthrift trust may be seized to satisfy a judgment for "an offense or quasi-offense committed by the beneficiary or by a person for whose acts the beneficiary is individually responsible." La. Rev. Stat. §9:2005. [This provision was repealed in 2004. Ed.]

that they do not weigh in favor of enforcing spendthrift trust provisions as against the claims of tort creditors or those found liable for gross negligence.

Regarding the responsibility of creditors when entering into transactions with spendthrift trust beneficiaries, Austin W. Scott stated in The Law of Trusts:

> In many of the cases in which it has been held that by the terms of the trust the interest of a beneficiary may be put beyond the reach of his creditors, the courts have laid some stress on the fact that the creditors had only themselves to blame for extending credit to a person whose interest under the trust had been put beyond their reach. The courts have said that before extending credit they could have ascertained the extent and character of the debtor's resources. Certainly, the situation of a tort creditor is quite different from that of a contract creditor. A man who is about to be knocked down by an automobile has no opportunity to investigate the credit of the driver of the automobile and has no opportunity to avoid being injured no matter what the resources of the driver may be.

Scott [§157.5 (4th ed. 1987)], supra. Likewise, George T. Bogert reasoned in Trusts and Trustees:

> It is true that a tort creditor has had no chance to choose his debtor and cannot be said to have assumed the risk of the collectibility of his claim. The argument for the validity of spendthrift trusts based on notice to the business world of the limited interest of the beneficiary does not apply. It may be argued that the beneficiary should not be permitted to circumvent the case and statute law as to liability for wrongs by taking advantage of the spendthrift clause.

Bogert on Trusts and Trustees §224 (rev. 2d ed. 1992). As these scholars point out, it is plain to see that one of the main reasons for enforcing spendthrift trust provisions—the responsibility of creditors to be aware of the law and of the substance of such provisions—simply does not apply in the case of tort judgment creditors.

As for the public interest in protecting spendthrift individuals from personal pauperism, we believe that this interest is not as strong in the case of tort judgment creditors, where the inability to collect on their claims may well result in their own personal pauperism. While it is true that most contract creditors do not risk becoming insolvent if they do not collect on a particular claim, such is often not the case with tort judgment creditors, particularly those who have suffered such devastating and expensive injuries as did the Slighs. The public interest against individuals becoming public burdens would not be served by protecting a spendthrift tortfeasor from personal pauperism where such protection would result merely in the pauperism of his victim. If one must choose whom to reduce to personal pauperism in such a case, the spendthrift tortfeasor or the innocent tort judgment creditor, we are inclined to choose the party at fault, especially where that fault rises to the level of gross negligence or intentional conduct.

This limitation on the public interest in protecting individuals from personal pauperism is reflected in our federal bankruptcy laws, whose very purpose is to protect debtors from pauperism. Under the Federal Bankruptcy Act, debtors may not discharge their debts to tort victim creditors whose claims are based on "willful and malicious" injuries. 11 U.S.C.A. §523(a)(6). Thus, it has been recognized that the rights of intentional tort creditors are greater than the public interest in protecting debtors from personal pauperism.

Perhaps the most important policy consideration in favor of enforcing spendthrift trust provisions is the right of donors to dispose of their property as they wish. On this subject, Austin W. Scott stated in The Law of Trusts:

> It may be argued that the settlor can properly impose such restrictions as he chooses on the property that he gives. But surely he cannot impose restrictions that are against public policy. It is true that the tortfeasor may have no other property than that which is given him under the trust, and that the victim of the tort is no worse off where the tortfeasor has property that cannot be reached than he would if the tortfeasor had no property at all. Nevertheless, there seems to be something rather shocking in the notion that a man should be allowed to continue in the enjoyment of property without satisfying the claims of persons whom he has injured. It may well be held that it is against public policy to permit the beneficiary of a spendthrift trust to enjoy an income under the trust without discharging his tort liabilities to others.

Scott, supra.

Clearly, the right of donors to place restrictions on the disposition of their property is not absolute, for... there are several generally recognized exceptions to the spendthrift trust doctrine. Rather, a donor may dispose of his property as he sees fit so long as such disposition does not violate the law or public policy. We find that it is indeed against public policy to dispose of property in such a way that the beneficiary may enjoy the income from such property without fear that his interest may be attached to satisfy the claims of his gross negligence or intentional torts.

Our tort doctrine has evolved into two types of torts, ordinary torts and intentional torts. Public policy deems it so important to deter the commission of intentional torts or acts of gross negligence, that we allow victims of gross negligence or intentional torts to recover damages above and beyond what is necessary to compensate them for their injuries, i.e., punitive damages. However, the intended deterrent effect would be completely lost upon individuals whose interests are immune from the satisfaction of such claims.

The Slighs have alleged facts to the effect that Lorance's mother intended that her son should be able to commit acts of gross negligence or intentional torts without fear that his beneficial interests would be attached as a result thereof. However, in cases such as this where the donor has died, such facts may often be difficult, if not impossible, to prove. We hold that plaintiffs need not prove such facts but that such intent shall be presumed where a party has obtained a judgment based upon facts evidencing gross negligence or an intentional tort against the beneficiary of a spendthrift trust. Furthermore, we state the natural corollary that when assessing punitive damages against a tortfeasor found to have committed gross negligence or an intentional tort who is a spendthrift trust beneficiary, the beneficiary's interest should be taken into account as a factor in determining his monetary worth. However, in order to uphold spendthrift trust provisions so much as is reasonably possible, we hold that the beneficiary's interest in a spendthrift trust should not be attached in satisfaction of a claim until all of his other available assets have first been exhausted....

The parties agree that the trusts' two remaindermen, Virginia Tate and William Bardin, have vested remainders. The trusts provide that First National Bank "shall have full and complete authority to expend *all or any part* of the income or corpus of said trust property for the benefit of myself and my said son." (emphasis added). Therefore, the interests of Ms. Tate and Mr. Bardin are vested remainders subject to complete defeasance in the event that all of the trust assets are expended to satisfy the interest of Lorance. Put another way, Lorance has a beneficial interest in all of the trust assets. Accordingly, we hold that all of the trust assets should be subject to the Slighs' claim, thereby defeating the interests of the two remaindermen.

In Deposit Guaranty Nat'l Bank v. Walter E. Heller & Co., 204 So. 2d 856 (Miss. 1967), the settlor of the trust created a lifetime beneficial interest in himself with a single remainderman. As a matter of public policy, we held the trust's spendthrift provisions invalid as against the claim of the donor/beneficiary's creditor, ruling that the remainderman would take subject to the claim of the creditor. Deposit Guaranty Nat'l Bank, 204 So. 2d at 862-63. Likewise, the Slighs' claim shall take priority over the interests of the two remaindermen.

Conclusion. We find, as a matter of public policy, that a beneficiary's interest in spendthrift trust assets is not immune from attachment to satisfy the claims of the beneficiary's intentional or gross negligence tort creditors, and that such claims take priority over any remainder interests in such assets. Accordingly, we reverse and render.

REVERSED AND RENDERED.

DAN LEE, C.J., SULLIVAN, P.J., and PITTMAN, BANKS, MCRAE AND JAMES L. ROBERTS, JR., JJ., concur.

PRATHER, P.J., dissents with separate written opinion joined by SMITH, J.

PRATHER, Presiding Justice, dissenting: I must respectfully dissent to the limitations placed by the majority on the exempt status of spendthrift trust benefits. The majority acknowledges that Louisiana is the only other State to place such limitations on spendthrift trust benefits for tort creditors, and said limitations were implemented by the Louisiana legislature rather than the courts of said state. This Court is thus, apparently, the first to so limit the exempt status of spendthrift trust benefits. I am aware of the public policy considerations which motivated the majority's decision, but, in my view, the general rule favoring the exempt status of spendthrift trusts benefits is a sound one which is in no need of revision.

Spendthrift trusts provide a means for a parent or other concerned party to provide for the basic needs of a beneficiary, and the largely exempt status of the trust benefits has given comfort and support to countless settlors and beneficiaries. The facts of the present case are tragic, but this Court should, in my view, avoid changing longstanding precedent based on the fact pattern of a particular case. Creditors in this state have at their disposal a number of means of collecting judgments, and I fear that the majority opinion signals the start of a gradual decline of the spendthrift trust in this state. I would affirm the ruling of the trial court, and I must accordingly dissent.

SMITH, J., joins this opinion.

Notes and Questions

1. *Questions.* Was the trust in *Sligh* a spendthrift trust or was it a discretionary trust with a spendthrift provision? If it was a discretionary trust with a spendthrift provision,[22] should exception-creditor status have applied?

2. *Aftermath in Mississippi.* After *Sligh* was decided, the Mississippi legislature enacted legislation stating that a beneficiary's interest protected by a spendthrift clause "may not be transferred and is not subject to the enforcement of a money judgment until paid to the beneficiary." Miss. Code §91-9-503, now codified at Miss. Code §91-8-502(a). This legislation was supported and drafted by the estate planning bar. Does this legislation also eliminate preferred-creditor status for spouses for alimony and children for child support?

3. *Contrasting Views of the* Sligh *Decision.* Citing Charles D. Fox IV & Rosalie Murphy, Are Spendthrift Trusts Vulnerable to a Beneficiary's Tort Creditors?, 136 Tr. & Est. 57 (Feb. 1998), a prominent Michigan estate planning practitioner wrote: "The Mississippi Supreme Court abused basic trust, property and contract law by creating a common law exception to the spendthrift doctrine for a beneficiary who engages in gross negligence and intentional torts." Allan J. Claypool, Asset Protection Overview (Techniques in the United States and Offshore), 24 ACTEC Notes 302, 312 (1999). Professor Edward Halbach, the reporter for the Restatement 3d of Trusts, however, described the *Sligh* decision as "widely acclaimed." Edward C. Halbach, Jr., The 1999 Joseph Trachtman Lecture—Uniform Acts, Restatements and Other Trends in American Trust Law at Century's End, 25 ACTEC Notes 101, 108 (1999).

4. *Uniform Trust Code.* The drafting committee for the Uniform Trust Code debated whether to include tort creditors in the category of exception creditors, and ultimately decided not to do so. See UTC §503.

5. *Restatement 3d.* The Restatement 3d of Trusts §59 comment a states: "The nature or a pattern of tortious conduct by a beneficiary... may on policy grounds

22. Most discretionary trusts have a spendthrift provision.

justify a court's refusal to allow spendthrift immunity to protect the trust interest and the lifestyle of the beneficiary, especially one whose willful or fraudulent conduct or persistently reckless behavior causes serious harm to others."

EXTERNAL REFERENCE. Kevin D. Millard, Rights of a Trust Beneficiary's Creditors Under the Uniform Trust Code, 34 ACTEC J. 58 (2008).

4. Asset Protection Trusts

Primary Statutory Reference: *UTC §505*

Background: Common-Law Prohibition of Self-Settled Spendthrift and Discretionary Trusts. The traditional rule has long been that a settlor may not create an effective spendthrift or discretionary trust for his or her own benefit. Such a "self-settled" trust is not void, but the settlor's interest in a spendthrift trust is alienable and can be reached by creditors, and in a discretionary trust the maximum amount that the trustee can pay the settlor or apply for his or her benefit is alienable and can be reached by creditors.[23] See Restatement 3d of Trusts §58(2), §60 comment f.

Offshore Asset Protection Trusts. The traditional rule has been reversed in some jurisdictions, beginning overseas. These jurisdictions permit self-settled spendthrift trusts, which have come to be known as asset protection trusts (APTs). APTs first appeared in the 1980s as several countries in the British Commonwealth, including the Bahamas, the Cayman Islands, Bermuda, and the Cook Islands, as well as other small countries in the Caribbean and other exotic locations, amended their trust legislation to permit the creation of self-settled trusts for purposes of protecting assets from creditors. The Cook Islands International Trusts Act of 1984 is typical of this legislation. The Act drastically narrows the range of transfers to international trusts[24] that creditors may attack as fraudulent. It also provides that the Cook Island courts shall not enforce or recognize a foreign judgment against an international trust

---

23. Congress has enacted a complicated set of rules designed to prevent a settlor from using a self-settled inter vivos trust to qualify himself or herself or his or her spouse for Medicaid.

24. *International Trusts and the Hague Convention on Trusts.* Offshore asset protection trusts are only one example of the expanding market of international trusts. The growth of international trusts results from the general globalization of wealth management. This development has heightened the need for legislation that clarifies the status of trusts in other countries, especially in civil-law jurisdictions, whose legal systems do not recognize the trust. The most serious effort to date at responding to this need is the Hague Convention on the Law Applicable to Trusts, first signed in 1985. Unfortunately, the Hague Convention has had only limited success in answering questions about the effect of trusts in civil-law countries. It has been signed only by a handful of nations and has gone into force in only one major civil-law country, Italy. Lawyers who work in the field of offshore trusts have criticized many of its provisions on important topics. For a perceptive critique, see Jeffrey A. Schoenblum, The Hague Convention on Trusts: Much Ado About Very Little, 3 J. Int'l Trust & Corp. Planning 5 (1994).

if the judgment is based on a law inconsistent with the Cook Islands statute.[25]

Offshore APTs commonly include several features designed to immunize them from creditors. Professor Danforth usefully summarizes these features:

> First, if the APT is properly established in a foreign country, in most cases a court of the United States will lack personal jurisdiction over the trustee. Consequently, regardless of whether the United States court is inclined to respect the asset protection features of the APT, the court will be unable to exert any powers over the foreign trustee. Second, many offshore jurisdictions recognize the role of a trust "protector," a person granted special non-fiduciary powers to control the administration of the trust, with respect to such matters as removal and replacement of trustees, control over discretionary action of the trustees, etc. By use of the trust protector mechanism, the settlor is able to vest in some trusted person substantial control over trust administration, while at the same time being able to resist the claim that the settlor himself or herself (whose actions will be subject to the authority of a United States court) retains such control. If the trust protector is United States person (and thus subject to the authority of a United States court), the trust instrument will typically give the protector no affirmative powers, but only veto powers, with the consequence that a United States court will be unable to compel the protector to force administration of the trust in a certain manner. Third, many offshore APTs include a so-called duress clause, under which the trustee is directed to ignore any directions received from a settlor or trust protector who is under duress. Thus, for example under a duress clause, the trustee of an APT would be required to disregard a direction from the settlor or protector to repatriate trust assets, if the settlor's order was compelled by a United States court's order. Finally, most offshore APTs also include a "flight" clause, under which the trustee is authorized to change the situs of the trust, if a claim against the trust threatens to be successful. Flight provisions virtually guarantee that an offshore APT will never be subjected to a creditor's claim.[26]

Offshore APTs have become especially popular with American professionals, such as physicians and lawyers, who wish to shield assets from potential malpractice liability judgments.

FTC v. Affordable Media; In re Lawrence. In widely noted cases, FTC v. Affordable Media, LLC, 179 F.3d 1228 (9th Cir. 1999), and In re Lawrence, 279 F.3d 1294 (11th Cir. 2002), the settlors of offshore APTs were jailed for failure to repatriate the trust assets.

In *Affordable Media*, Denyse and Michael Anderson, a married couple, were

---

25. The Cayman Islands statute takes the asset-protection idea one step further by allowing an individual to shield his or her assets in a trust *after* a suit is filed against him or her. See Gene Epstein, Pocket Protector, Barron's, Aug. 7, 1995, at 37.

26. Robert T. Danforth, Rethinking the Law of Creditors' Rights in Trusts, 53 Hastings L.J. 287, 309-310 (2002) (footnotes omitted).

engaged in what amounted to a Ponzi scheme.[27] The Federal Trade Commission brought a civil action against the Andersons, seeking to recover as much money as possible for the defrauded investors. The Andersons, however, had previously moved their millions of dollars in profits to a Cook Islands trust. The Andersons, claiming that they were unable to repatriate those assets, refused to comply with the district court's preliminary injunction. The district court then found them in civil contempt of court and sent them to jail.

In *Lawrence*, Stephan Jay Lawrence, a high-flying options trader on Wall Street, created a $7 million APT in Mauritius. Two months after creating the trust, he lost an arbitration proceeding that resulted in a $20 million judgment against him. Lawrence filed for bankruptcy, and the bankruptcy court ordered him to turn over to the bankruptcy trustee the assets in the APT. Lawrence refused, claiming that he had no control over the assets, and therefore that compliance with the order was impossible. The bankruptcy court held Lawrence in contempt and sent him to jail until he complied with the turnover order. On appeal, the Eleventh Circuit affirmed the contempt order.

In both *Affordable Media* and *Lawrence*, the settlors relied on a so-called duress clause that had been inserted in the APTs. Under the Andersons' trust agreement, an event of duress purported to terminate the Andersons as co-trustees, so that control over the trust assets would appear to be exclusively in the hands of the foreign trustee, beyond the jurisdiction of a United States court. An event of duress includes "[t]he issuance of any order, decree or judgment of any court or tribunal in any part of the world which in the opinion of the protector will or may directly or indirectly, expropriate, sequester, levy, lien or in any way control, restrict or prevent the free disposal by a trustee of any monies, investments or property which may from time to time be included in or form part of this trust and any distributions therefrom." In *Lawrence*, the duress clause purported to remove Lawrence as a beneficiary of the trust, thereby extinguishing his interest in the trust.

The duress-clause argument failed in both cases because of a flaw in drafting. In *Affordable Media*, the Andersons were not only beneficiaries but also trust directors—i.e., persons with control over the trustees. Indeed, the Andersons had the

---

27. As defined on the website of the Securities and Exchange Commission, Ponzi schemes are a type of illegal pyramid scheme named for Charles Ponzi, who duped thousands of New England residents into investing in a postage stamp speculation scheme back in the 1920s. Ponzi thought he could take advantage of differences between U.S. and foreign currencies used to buy and sell international mail coupons. Ponzi told investors that he could provide a 40% return in just 90 days compared with 5% for bank savings accounts. Ponzi was deluged with funds from investors, taking in $1 million during one three-hour period—and this was 1921! Though a few early investors were paid off to make the scheme look legitimate, an investigation found that Ponzi had only purchased about $30 worth of the international mail coupons. Decades later, the Ponzi scheme continues to work on the "rob-Peter-to-pay-Paul" principle, as money from new investors is used to pay off earlier investors until the whole scheme collapses. See www.investor.gov/introduction-investing/investing-basics/glossary/ponzi-schemes.

power to appoint new trustees. That power, the court held, "makes the anti-duress provisions subject to the protectors' powers, [and] therefore, they can force the foreign trustee to repatriate the trust assets to the United States." In *Lawrence*, the court pointed to the fact that the trust instrument gave Lawrence the power to appoint trustees. These new trustees, the court said, would have discretion to reinstate Lawrence as a beneficiary. The court brushed aside the duress provision, saying, "The sole purpose of this provision appears to be an aid to the settlor to evade contempt while merely feigning compliance with the court's order.... [W]here the person charged with contempt is responsible for the inability to comply, impossibility is not a defense to the contempt proceedings."

Trust Directors. Nearly all offshore APTs today include trust directors, also known as trust protectors. The purpose of trust directors in APTs is to allow the settlor, through the settlor's agent—the trust director—to exercise control over the local trustees while still shielding trust assets from creditors. The trust instrument may name a third party or the settlor as the trust director, although many lawyers engaged in the business of setting up offshore APTs now point out that the settlor should not be the trust director, as the Andersons were in *Affordable Media.* They further counsel against granting broad powers to a trust director who is United States person or institution subject to the jurisdiction of United States courts. The court may treat the director as the settlor's agent and order the director to act, subjecting the director to contempt if the director refuses to comply. See Alexander A. Bove, Jr., Drafting Offshore Trusts, 143 Tr. & Est. 44, 45-46 (2004); Gideon Rothschild, Establishing and Drafting Offshore Asset Protection Trusts, 23 Est. Plan. 65 (1996).

———

Offshore APTs are subject to numerous federal tax compliance and reporting requirements. Severe civil and criminal penalties may be imposed on American lawyers for failure to file the required tax returns. See J. Richard Duke, Offshore Trusts: Crossing the "T"s, 144 Tr. & Est. 49 (2005).

———

Domestic Asset Protection Trusts—The New Frontier. Prompted by competition for trust business and trust funds, several American states have enacted statutes that authorize a domestic version of asset protection trusts. Alaska was the first state to take this step. The 1997 Alaska Trust Act, Alaska Stat. §34.40.110, is carefully crafted to allow a client to protect owned assets from creditors and claims of all types (including his or her child-support obligations and, perhaps, his or her spouse in a divorce proceeding) by transferring those assets into an irrevocable discretionary trust (with a friendly trustee?). Another provision of the Act seeks to exempt discretionary trusts from the Rule Against Perpetuities (see Chapter 17), making it possible to create perpetual asset protection trusts. The Alaska Trust Act was developed and principally authored by Jonathan Blattmachr, a New York lawyer, in partnership with Donald Blattmachr, his brother and the CEO of an Anchorage Trust Company, and Robert Manley, an Anchorage attorney. See Robert H. Sitkoff and Max M. Schanzenbach, Jurisdictional Competition for Trust Funds: An Empirical Analysis of Perpetuities and Taxes, 115 Yale L.J. 356, 381 (2005).

Twenty states now have statutes authorizing domestic asset protection trusts (DAPTs): Alabama, Alaska, Connecticut, Delaware, Hawaii, Indiana, Michigan, Mississippi, Missouri, Nevada, New Hampshire, Ohio, Oklahoma, Rhode Island, South Dakota, Tennessee, Utah, Virginia, West Virginia, and Wyoming. In addition, Florida now provides by statute that

> the assets of an irrevocable trust may not be subject to the claims of an existing or subsequent creditor or assignee of the settlor, in whole or in part, solely because of the existence of a discretionary power granted to the trustee by the terms of the trust, or any other provision of law, to pay directly to the taxing authorities or to reimburse the settlor for any tax on trust income or principal which is payable by the settlor under the law imposing such tax.

Fla. Stat. §736.0505(1)(c).

The following article, written by two attorneys who are advocates of asset protection planning, gives a practitioner's perspective on the growing desire for asset protection trusts.

Duncan E. Osborne & Elizabeth M. Schurig, What ACTEC Fellows Should Know About Asset Protection
25 ACTEC Notes 367 (2000)

ACTEC[28] lawyers probably have a duty to engage in asset protection planning for their clients, but if they do not, then to protect themselves from potential malpractice liability, they should clearly communicate to their clients that their representation does not involve any advice regarding asset protection....

There are certainly ACTEC Fellows who resist the notion that asset protection planning is a part of the service owed to clients. Some argue that the potential for unwittingly assisting a client in defrauding his creditors is enough of a risk that this representation should not be undertaken. Indeed, some argue that this risk may itself serve as the basis for a defense to a malpractice claim founded on a duty to provide asset protection advice. Some would go further and say that under the fraudulent conveyance and fraudulent transfer laws, all potential creditors are protected, no matter how removed in time and events from a transfer, so it is wrong under all circumstances to engage in asset protection planning. In support of such a position, those Fellows might refer to the language of the fraudulent transfer laws dealing with the rights of present and future creditors. They might also cite the recent cases

---

28. ACTEC is an acronym for the American College of Trust and Estate Counsel. Ed.

which have held against the debtor and have struck down foreign asset protection trusts and that have, in some cases, subjected the settlors to imprisonment in civil contempt proceedings. Finally, they might argue the long-standing policies of Anglo-Saxon jurisprudence which generally tend to support creditors' rights to access self-settled spendthrift trusts.

The problem with these arguments is that they are superficial and they do not withstand serious analysis of the statutes and of the case law. Fraudulent transfer law is extraordinarily complex. While it is absolutely true that the fraudulent transfer law of any given state may, on its face, appear to be susceptible to the interpretation that future creditors, remote in time and circumstances from the "transfer" are protected, that is not, and never has been, the way in which the courts have interpreted those laws. Courts have always fixed on the relative proximity of the various creditors to the events that led to the insolvency or to the financial injury to the creditors. Indeed, for those who take the time to study the bankruptcy cases, the creditors' rights cases, and the articles written by the creditors' rights bar, it is almost alarming what the courts do permit in relation to the federal fraudulent transfer law applied in a bankruptcy context. There is even an area of the law called pre-bankruptcy planning which allows asset transfers far beyond what these authors have ever advocated. In short, a serious legal analysis of what can and cannot be done to protect assets from creditors under both state and federal law reveals wide latitude for asset protection planning.

One reason that there is such wide latitude for protecting assets is that the law (either common law or federal or state statutory law) has never required an individual to preserve his or her assets for the benefit of future creditors. Fraudulent transfer statutes focus on "intent" and one cannot "intend" to defraud a creditor who does not exist. If the law did require individuals to preserve assets for the benefit of future creditors, then gratuitous transfers of all kinds (to family members, to charities, etc.) would be prohibited and the ability to use limited liability entities, e.g., corporations, limited liability partnerships, and limited liability corporations, would not be allowed. However, from the earliest times in our history, persons have had the ability to limit their liability, and creditors have had fraudulent transfer laws and bankruptcy laws to protect them.

What has changed, and what has consequently fueled the debate about asset protection planning, is the legislative evolution in jurisdictions in which individuals may legally protect assets from their creditors by establishing and funding trusts for their own benefit, the assets of which are statutorily protected from the settlor's creditors....

In addition to the fact that there is planning flexibility under creditors' rights law, there are some powerful forces working in favor of asset protection. First and foremost is client demand; the interest in protecting assets is not universal, but it is both widespread and incessant, and it is driven in large measure by a serious lack of faith in our legal system to render fair results. Many persons of wealth perceive themselves to be at risk no matter what sort of professional, business, or personal activities they undertake. They genuinely believe that the plaintiff's bar can make a case and generate liability under the most absurd and unlikely set of facts. This concern reaches across the spectrum of those who have wealth: doctors, lawyers, accountants, architects, entrepreneurs, entertainers, professional athletes, heirs to fortunes, etc. Whether the perceptions are well-grounded or not, they are real, and they drive the decisions of these individuals. As a result, most wealthy clients are interested in asset protection advice....

If the ACTEC Fellow does decide to engage in asset protection planning, he or she must be educated about the fraudulent transfer laws applicable in the jurisdictions in which that person practices. At a minimum, the lawyer should have a working knowledge of the statutes and the cases decided under them. Knowledge of the federal bankruptcy statutes that protect creditors is also necessary, although as a practical matter, state statutes are usually more protective of creditors' rights than the bankruptcy laws. If a lawyer plans under the guidance of the state laws, the resulting plan is generally more conservative than would be the case under the federal laws. Finally, a lawyer must know the so-called shield laws of his or her state, i.e., those laws that exempt certain assets from the claims of creditors....

In summary, what should an ACTEC Fellow know about asset protection planning?

• You may well have a duty to deal with it either by undertaking it or expressly confirming that you are not undertaking it.

• Clients want it. More and more clients are interested in asset protection counsel. There is a demand, and it is being encouraged by marketers of asset protection plans. Do not be surprised by clients asking for it.

• If you undertake asset protection planning on behalf of a client, educate yourself on the applicable state and federal laws that protect creditors and identify and establish a relationship with a leading creditors' rights attorney in your locale.

• Undertake an in depth solvency analysis of the client's assets, liabilities, and creditor protected assets. Make sure you know the extent of your client's real and likely risks.

• Educate yourself about the asset protection options in your state. Domestic solutions frequently work in debtor friendly states like Texas and Florida, but even in creditor friendly states, you may be able to achieve all that is necessary, for example, with a life insurance plan, a retirement plan, and a family limited partnership. Offshore trusts and out-of-state trusts can be complex and expensive and may not really be necessary.

• Always be aware that you may be at risk for potentially engaging in a conspiracy to commit a fraudulent transfer and plan conservatively.

• Remember, in the context of asset protection planning, you are damned if you do (under a potential conspiracy theory) and damned if you don't (under a theory that you have a duty to your client to render asset protection advice). No one ever said the practice of law was not challenging!

———

Domestic Asset Protection Trusts and Federal Bankruptcy Law. Domestic APTs have been heavily marketed in recent years. However, the attractiveness of domestic APTs was clouded by the 2005 amendments to the federal bankruptcy code. The Bankruptcy Abuse Prevention and Consumer Protection Act of 2005 added provisions directly dealing with domestic APTs. Section 548(e)(1) provides that a bankruptcy trustee may avoid any transfer by the debtor to a self-settled spendthrift trust "or similar device" made within 10 years before the filing of the bankruptcy petition where the transfer was made "with actual intent to hinder, delay, or defraud any entity to which the debtor was or became, on or after the date that such transfer was made, indebted." This provision was added to the bill after press reports about DAPTs suggested that these trusts permitted the rich to protect vast amounts of wealth even as Congress stripped bankruptcy protections for the poor.

Domestic Asset Protection Trusts and the Conflict of Laws. On May 17, 2013, the U.S. Bankruptcy Court for the Western District of Washington decided In re Huber, 493 B.R. 798 (W.D.Wash. 2013), the first case to address the application of conflict-of-laws analysis to a DAPT. *Huber* involved the creation of an Alaska DAPT by a property developer from the State of Washington. In addition to determining that the funding of the trust was a fraudulent transfer avoidable under §§544(b)(1) and 548 (e) of the Bankruptcy Code, the court held that the trust was invalid under the conflict of laws. The court relied on Section 270 of the Restatement (Second) of Conflict of Laws (1971), which provides that an

> inter vivos trust of movables is valid if valid... under the local law of the state designated by the settlor to govern the validity of the trust, provided that this state has a substantial relation to the trust and that the application of its law does not violate a strong public policy of the state with which, as to the matter at issue, the trust has its most significant relationship...

The court found that "Alaska had only a minimal relation to the [t]rust"; that "Washington had a substantial relation to the [t]rust"; and that "Washington State has a strong public policy against self-settled asset protection trusts." Id. at 809. Accordingly, the court disregarded the settlor's choice of Alaska law as the governing law and instead applied the law of Washington.

The Alaska Trust Act, at §34.40.110(k), also had a provision stating in pertinent part: "A court of this state has exclusive jurisdiction over an action brought under a cause of action or claim for relief that is based on a transfer of property to a trust that is the subject of this section." The constitutionality of this provision was litigated in Toni 1 Trust v. Wacker, 413 P.3d 1199 (Alaska 2018). The facts of the case are well summarized in the opinion of the Alaska Supreme Court:

> In 2007 Donald Tangwall sued William and Barbara Wacker in Montana state court. The Wackers counterclaimed against Tangwall; his wife, Barbara Tangwall; his mother-in-law, Margaret "Toni" Bertran; and several trusts and businesses owned or run by the family. In the ensuing years, several default judgments were entered against Tangwall and his family.
>
> In 2010, before the last of these judgments was issues, Bertran and Barbara Tangwall transferred parcels of real property to an Alaska trust called the "Toni 1 Trust". The Wackers filed a fraudulent transfer action under Montana law in Montana state court, alleging that the transfers were made to avoid the judgments. Default judgments in the fraudulent transfer action were entered against Barbara Tangwall, the Toni 1 Trust, and Bertran....
>
> Tangwall... sought relief in Alaska state court, where he filed the complaint that led to this appeal. The crux of his argument was that [Alaska Stat. §]34.40.110 grants Alaska courts exclusive jurisdiction over any fraudulent transfer actions against the Trust....

The Alaska Supreme Court held that the provision in §34.40.110(k) was an unconstitutional violation of the U.S. Constitution's Full Faith and Credit Clause and its Supremacy Clause. The court held that the Alaska legislation cannot limit the scope of other states' jurisdiction, nor can it limit the scope of a federal court's jurisdiction. (One of the judgments against Tangwall had been issued in federal bankruptcy court.)

As this edition of the casebook goes to press, the Uniform Law Commission is working on a uniform act on the conflict of laws in trusts and estates.

Domestic Asset Protection Trusts and the Law of Fraudulent or Voidable Transfers. Section 4(a)(1) of the Uniform Fraudulent Transfer Act (1984) provides that a transfer is "fraudulent" if a debtor "made the transfer... with actual intent to hinder, delay, or defraud any creditor of the debtor." The same language, except with the substitution of "voidable" for "fraudulent," is carried forward in the revised version of the Act, now re-named the Uniform Voidable Transactions Act (2014) (UVTA). As the Comment to Section 4 of the UVTA explains:

> The phrase "hinder, delay, or defraud" in §4(a)(1), carried forward from the primordial Statute of 13 Elizabeth, is potentially applicable to any transaction that unacceptably contravenes norms of creditors' rights.... Fraud is not a necessary element of a claim for relief.... By its terms §4(a)(1) applies to a transaction that "hinders" or "delays" a creditor, even if it does not "defraud" the creditor."...
>
> Because the laws of different jurisdictions differ in their tolerance of particular creditor-thwarting devices, choice of law considerations may be important in interpreting §4(a)(1) as in force in a given jurisdiction.... Suppose that jurisdiction X, in which this Act is in force, also has in force a statute permitting an individual to establish a self-settled spendthrift trust and transfer assets thereto, subject to stated conditions. If an individual Debtor whose principal residence is in X establishes such a trust and transfers assets

thereto, then under §10 of this Act, the voidable transfer law of X applies to that transfer. The transfer cannot be considered voidable in itself because the legislature of X, having authorized the establishment of such trusts, must have expected them to be used.... By contrast, if Debtor's principal residence is in jurisdiction Y, which also has enacted this Act but has no legislation validating such trusts, and if Debtor establishes such a trust under the law of X and transfers assets to it, then the result would be different. Under §10 of this Act, the voidable transfer law of Y would apply to the transfer.

Domestic Asset Protection Trusts and Divorce. Suppose a married individual domiciled in a state (Utah) allowing DAPTs establishes a DAPT in a different state allowing them (Nevada). Then suppose the individual divorces his spouse and attempts to use the DAPT to shield assets? In Dahl v. Dahl, 345 P.3d 566 (Utah 2015), the Utah Supreme Court declined to follow a choice-of-law provision in a DAPT providing that the "validity, construction, and effect of the provisions" of the trust shall be governed by Nevada law. Instead, the court held that the forum's law (Utah law) should govern because Utah has "a strong policy of equitable distribution of marital assets" at divorce.

EXTERNAL REFERENCES. Thomas P. Gallanis, Trusts and the Choice of Law: What Role for the Settlor's Choice and the Place of Administration?, 97 Tul. L. Rev. 805 (2023); Alexander A. Bove Jr. ed., Asset Protection Strategies: Planning with Domestic and Offshore Entities (2019); Thomas P. Gallanis, The Use and Abuse of Governing-Law Clauses in Trusts: What Should the New Restatement Say?, 103 Iowa L. Rev. 1711 (2018); Duncan E. Osborne & Elizabeth Morgan Schurig, Asset Protection: Domestic and International Law and Tactics, 4 vols. (updated quarterly); Stewart E. Sterk, Asset Protection Trusts: Trust Law's Race to the Bottom? 85 Cornell L. Rev. 1035 (2000).

PART B. TERMINATION (OR MODIFICATION) BY THE BENEFICIARIES

Primary Statutory References: *UTC §§301-305, 410-411, 414*

As we stated at the beginning of this Chapter, a fundamental policy question that courts frequently face when the preferences of the settlor and the trust beneficiaries conflict is which side the law should empower. In this part, we consider another aspect of this question: Once a trust has been properly formed, should the law ensure that it will continue? Or should the law enable the beneficiaries to terminate or modify the trust against the stated or implied wishes of the settlor?

Consider, again, Example 11.1, where A and X—both of whom are competent adults—prefer cash to their income and remainder interests in the spendthrift trust created by A's mother, G. Recall that under English law, A and X could fulfill their wish by either finding a buyer for their interests (disabling restraints on alienation being invalid in England) or terminating the trust.

In the United States, however, spendthrift restraints, as we have seen, are valid in all states. A and X can neither sell their interests nor borrow against them. In their quest for funds, of course, the inalienability of their interests would not be of much concern if they could terminate the trust. Practically speaking, third-party purchasers are hard to find. The trust itself is a far more promising source of funds.

Under English law, as noted, A and X could compel the termination of the trust. In Saunders v. Vautier, 49 Eng. Rep. 282 (Ch. 1841), the testator, Richard Wright, died in 1832, devising all his East India stock (worth £2,000) to trustees, in trust, directing them to accumulate the interest and dividends accruing thereon until his great-nephew, Daniel Wright Vautier, became 25; when Daniel became 25, the trustees were to transfer the East India stock, together with the accumulated interest and dividends, to Daniel, absolutely.

Daniel had grander ideas. Promptly upon becoming 21, Daniel petitioned the court for the fund's immediate transfer to him. The Master of the Rolls upheld Daniel's claim, saying:

> I think that principle has been repeatedly acted upon; and where a legacy is directed to accumulate for a certain period, or where the payment is postponed, the legatee, if he has an absolute indefeasible interest in the legacy, is not bound to wait until the expiration of that period, but may require payment the moment he is competent to give a valid discharge.

On appeal, Lord Langdale's decision was affirmed by the Chancellor, Lord Cottenham. Saunders v. Vautier, 41 Eng. Rep. 482 (Ch. 1841).

In his article, The Dead Hand and the Law of Trusts in the Nineteenth Century, 37 Stan. L. Rev. 1189, 1201 (1985), Professor Alexander gives this account of the developments following *Saunders*:

> Although the doctrine of *Saunders* was not accepted by the House of Lords until some fifty years later,[29] it was quickly and widely followed in equity practice. In Curtis v. Luken, decided in 1842,[30] the Master of the Rolls explained the *Saunders* doctrine:
>
> > [The beneficiary] has the legal power of disposing of it, he may sell, charge, or assign it, for he has an absolute, indefeasible interest in a thing defined and certain; the Court, therefore, has thought fit ... to say, that since the legatee has such the legal right and power over the property, and can deal with it as he pleases, it will not subject him to the

---

29. Wharton v. Masterman, 1895 App. Cas. 186 (H.L.).

30. 5 Beav. 147, 49 Eng. Rep. 533 (Ch. 1842).

disadvantage of raising money by selling or charging his interest, when the thing is his own, at this very moment.[31]

The court here explicitly connected the question of a beneficiary's power to compel termination in anticipation of the time prescribed by the trustor with the question of the beneficiary's power to alienate his equitable interest. Since no valid restraint could be imposed upon an equitable fee, a provision postponing possession of the trust estate could not be given effect, since it would be inconsistent with the property interest given to him. The *Saunders* doctrine thereafter was understood to require premature termination when all parties having an equitable interest in the trust and having legal capacity to consent petitioned for termination and distribution of the trust estate.

The English doctrine was generally followed by American courts prior to 1889.[32] Since American courts had followed the English position on the validity of restraints on alienation of equitable interests, including equitable fees and more limited interests such as life estates in income, it was to be expected that they would not enforce provisions postponing possession of trust property by legally competent beneficiaries who, individually or collectively, held the entire equitable interest.

Claflin v. Claflin
20 N.E. 454 (Mass. 1889)

FIELD, J. By the eleventh article of his will, as modified by a codicil, Wilbur F. Claflin gave all the residue of his personal estate to trustees,

> to sell and dispose of the same, and to pay to my wife, Mary A. Claflin, one-third part of the proceeds thereof, and to pay to my son Clarence A. Claflin, one-third part of the proceeds thereof, and to pay the remaining one-third thereof to my son Adelbert E. Claflin, in the manner following, viz.: Ten thousand dollars when he is of the age of twenty-one years, ten thousand dollars when he is of the age of twenty-five years, and the balance when he is of the age of thirty years.

Apparently, Adelbert E. Claflin was not quite 21 years old when his father died, but he some time ago reached that age, and received $10,000 from the trust. He has not yet reached the age of 25 years, and he brings this bill to compel the trustees to pay to him the remainder of the trust fund. His contention is, in effect, that the provisions of the will postponing the payment of the money beyond the time when he is 21 years are void. There is no doubt that his interest in the trust fund is vested and absolute, and that no other person has any interest in it; and the authority is undisputed that the provisions postponing payment to him until some time after he reaches the age of 21 years would be treated as void by those courts which hold that restrictions against the alienation of absolute interests in the income of trust property

---

31. Id. at 156, 49 Eng. Rep. at 536.

32. E.g., Sanford v. Lackland, 21 Fed. Cas. 358 (C.C.D. Mo. 1871) (No. 12,312); Gray v. Obear, 54 Ga. 231 (1875); Thompson v. Ballard, 70 Md. 10, 16 A. 378 (1889); Philadelphia v. Girard, 45 Pa. 9, 27 (1863).

are void. There has indeed, been no decision of this question in England by the House of Lords, and but one by a Chancellor, but there are several decisions to this effect by Masters of the Rolls, and by Vice-Chancellors....

These decisions do not proceed on the ground that it was the intention of the testator that the property should be conveyed to the beneficiary on his reaching the age of 21 years, because in each case it was clear that such was not his intention, but on the ground that the direction to withhold the possession of the property from the beneficiary after he reached his majority was inconsistent with the absolute rights of property given him by the will.

This court has ordered trust property conveyed by the trustee to the beneficiary when there was a dry trust, or when the purposes of the trust had been accomplished, or when no good reason was shown why the trust should continue, and all the persons interested in it were *sui juris*, and desired that it be terminated; but we have found no expression of any opinion in our reports that provisions requiring a trustee to hold and manage the trust property until the beneficiary reached an age beyond that of 21 years are void if the interest of the beneficiary is vested and absolute. This is not a dry trust, nor have the purposes of the trust been accomplished, if the intention of the testator is to be carried out....

In the case at bar nothing has happened which the testator did not anticipate, and for which he has not made provision. It is plainly his will that neither the income nor any part of the principal should now be paid to the plaintiff. It is true that the plaintiff's interest is alienable by him, and can be taken by his creditors to pay his debts, but it does not follow because the testator has not imposed all possible restrictions that the restrictions which he has imposed should not be carried into effect.

The decision in Broadway National Bank v. Adams, 133 Mass. 170, rests upon the doctrine that a testator has a right to dispose of his own property with such restrictions and limitations, not repugnant to law, as he sees fit, and that his intentions ought to be carried out, unless they contravene some positive rule of law, or are against public policy. The rule contended for by the plaintiff in that case was founded upon the same considerations as that contended for by the plaintiff in this, and the grounds on which this court declined to follow the English rule in that case are applicable to this; and for the reasons there given we are unable to see that the directions of the testator to the trustees to pay the money to the plaintiff when he reaches the ages of 25 and 30 years are against public policy, or are so far inconsistent with the rights of property given to the plaintiff that they should not be carried into effect. It cannot be said that these restrictions upon the plaintiff's possession and control of the property are altogether useless, for there is not the same danger that he will spend the property while it is in the hands of the trustees as there would be if it were in his own....

Decree affirmed.

Notes

1. *State of the Authorities.* The *Claflin* doctrine is widely followed in this country. See Scott and Ascher on Trusts §34.1 (6th ed. 2023). The American rule, as expressed in Restatement 2d of Trusts §337, is that the beneficiaries of a trust cannot compel the trust's premature termination (or modification) unless: (1) all beneficiaries consent (and are competent to do so) and (2) premature termination (or modification) will not defeat a "material purpose" of the trust. The Uniform Trust Code codifies the *Claflin* doctrine regarding irrevocable trusts. See UTC §411(b). (As to revocable trusts, see UTC §§602, 603.)

The state of Washington has effectively abolished the material purpose aspect of the *Claflin* doctrine. Rev. Code Wash. §11.96A.210-240 provides a binding nonjudicial procedure through which all parties interested in a trust may agree in writing to resolve "any matter." The term "any matter" is broadly defined to include "any issue, question, or dispute" involving trusts and estates. Rev. Code Wash. §11.96A.030. The comment to this provision states that "Washington formally... adopts a rule that allows all interested parties to agree to the... modification of an applicable document." There is no requirement that the requested action be consistent with the settlor's purposes.

2. *Consent of the Settlor.* Although a trust contains a "material purpose," it is widely (though not universally) held that the beneficiaries can compel its termination (or modification) if they obtain the settlor's consent. See UTC §411(a); Restatement 3d of Trusts §65; Restatement 2d of Trusts §338.

3. *Premature Termination of Uneconomical Trusts.* Both the Uniform Trust Code and an Alaska statute permit the trustee, upon notice to beneficiaries, to terminate a trust whose value is less than $50,000. UTC §414(a); Alaska Stat. §13.36.365 (a). The Alaska statute, but not the UTC, allows the trust instrument to provide otherwise.

1. Material Purpose

Traditional Law. Trusts that contain a "material purpose," precluding their premature termination or modification, are sometimes called indestructible trusts. Under traditional law, the types of trusts that are deemed to contain a material purpose are (1) postponement-of-enjoyment trusts, (2) spendthrift trusts, and (3) support and discretionary trusts.

1. *Postponement-of-Enjoyment Trusts.* In a postponement-of-enjoyment trust, such as in *Claflin* (and *Saunders*), the settlor wants the beneficiary to have the trust property and its income, but not until the beneficiary reaches a specified age, a certain period of time has elapsed, or a certain date. The settlor's purpose would be defeated if the beneficiary were permitted to obtain the trust property earlier. Consider the following example.

Example 11.2: G died, devising property in trust, to pay the income to A until A reaches 35 and to pay the principal to A when A reaches that age; but if A dies before reaching 35, to pay the principal to B upon A's death.

Even though A (age 28) and B desire to terminate the trust, they cannot do so.

2. *Spendthrift Trusts.* According to the Restatement 2d of Trusts and substantial case authority, spendthrift trusts are indestructible. See Restatement 2d of Trusts §337 comment *l*; Scott and Ascher on Trusts §34.1.2 (6th ed. 2023).

3. *Support and Discretionary Trusts.* According to the Restatement 2d of Trusts and substantial case authority, support and discretionary trusts are indestructible. See Restatement 2d of Trusts §337 comments m & n; cases cited in Scott and Ascher on Trusts §34.1.4 (6th ed. 2023).

Question

If these categories of trusts are indestructible, what is left? What kind of a trust does not have a "material purpose," such that it can be terminated early, or modified, by the beneficiaries under *Claflin*? See the Restatement 3d of Trusts §65 comment d; Restatement 2d of Trusts §337 comment f.

Relaxation of the Material Purpose Requirement. The Restatement 3d of Trusts §65 substantially relaxes the material purpose requirement by providing that the court may authorize termination "if it determines that the reason(s) for termination... outweigh the material purpose."[33] Comment d goes on to state that "[m]aterial purposes are not readily to be inferred. A finding of such a purpose generally requires some showing of a particular concern or objective on the part of the settlor, such as concern with regard to a beneficiary's management skills, judgment, or level of maturity." Other comments spell out some of the specific implications of this balancing approach.

Spendthrift and Discretionary Trusts. Comment e states that "[s]pendthrift restrictions are not sufficient in and of themselves to establish, or to create a presumption of, a material purpose that would prevent termination by consent of all of the beneficiaries. This is also true, in many contexts, of discretionary provisions."[34]

(The Restatement 3d continues the view that a postponement-of-enjoyment trust has a material purpose. See Restatement 3d of Trusts §65 comment d, illus. 5 & 6.)

---

33. An Alaska statute, enacted in 2000, provides a similar rule. See Alaska Stat. §13.36.360(a).

34. The Uniform Trust Code originally provided that "[a] spendthrift provision in the terms of the trust is not presumed to constitute a material purpose of the trust." UTC §411(c). In 2004, however, the Uniform Law Commission bracketed this subsection as optional on the ground that several states enacting the UTC had declined to adopt it.

Question

Can trust drafters foil the proposed relaxation of the *Claflin* rules by adding boilerplate language to spendthrift clauses asserting concern for the management skills of the beneficiaries? For example, suppose a trust instrument contains the following modified version of a spendthrift clause:

> Because I have concern about the management skills of the beneficiaries of this trust, I direct that no interest of any beneficiary in the income or principal of this trust shall be assignable in anticipation of payment or be liable in any way for the beneficiary's debts or obligations and shall not be subject to attachment.

What result?

Trust Directors and Premature Termination. Estate planners have adapted the trust director to serve a variety of functions. The trust director may be given the power to "modify, reform, terminate, or decant a trust." Uniform Directed Trust Act §6 comment.

Permissible Duration of Indestructible Trusts. Typically there is no direct legal limit on the duration of a trust. (The Rule Against Perpetuities, which we shall study in Chapter 17, typically uses a proxy: a limit on the remote vesting of contingent future interests.) There probably is a limit on the time during which a trust may be made indestructible. The cases are far from conclusive as to just what time limit will be imposed, but writers have usually assumed that it will be the period of the Rule Against Perpetuities, in the jurisdictions where that Rule applies. See Restatement 2d of Trusts §62 comment o; Restatement 2d of Property §2.1.

A trust meant to be indestructible for a longer period is valid, but subject to termination at the suit of the beneficiaries, either from the inception of the trust (as some writers assert) or, more probably, and as set forth in the Restatements, at the expiration of the permissible period. In 1959, California enacted a statute stating that a "trust provision, express or implied, that the trust may not be terminated is ineffective insofar as it purports to be applicable after" the permissible perpetuity period. Cal. Prob. Code §15413.

Modification Distinguished from Termination. Is the material purpose requirement applied in the same manner in cases where all the beneficiaries seek a proposed modification under the *Claflin* doctrine (i.e., by consent of all the beneficiaries) as it is in cases of proposed termination? The Restatement 3d of Trusts §65 comment f provides the following answer:

> *f. Material purpose and modification.* Although a trust may have a material purpose that would preclude complete or even partial termination of the trust, a particular modification agreed to by the beneficiaries might not be inconsistent with any material purpose of the trust. In such a case, all of the beneficiaries could join together to modify the terms of the trust to that extent. Thus, where modification is involved,... the material-purpose inquiry focuses on the particular amendment sought by the beneficiaries.

For example, a proposed modification might change the trustee or create a simple, inexpensive procedure for appointing successor trustees, or it might create or change procedures for removing and replacing trustees. Modifications of these types may well improve the administration of a trust and be more efficient and more satisfactory to the beneficiaries without interfering with a material purpose of the trust. On the other hand, repeated modifications to change trustees or even a particular change of trustee, or an amendment of provisions relating to the trusteeship, might have the effect of materially undermining the contemplated qualities or independence of trustees. A given change might even have the effect of shifting effective control of the trust in such a way as to be inconsistent with a protective management purpose or other material purpose of the trust. Thus, changes of trustees or in trustee provisions are to be particularly but sympathetically scrutinized for possible conflict with a material trust purpose.

2. Beneficiaries' Consent

Premature termination of a trust requires the consent of all of the beneficiaries. This is the sole requirement under English law. Under prevailing American law, it is a requirement additional to the absence of a material purpose.

Problems and Notes

1. G, a widow, died, survived by her 55-year-old daughter, A; her 52-year-old son, B; A's 25-year-old child, X; and B's 22-year-old child, Y. G's will devised the residue of her estate in trust, without a spendthrift restraint. At common law (see Note 3, below), whose consent is necessary to terminate G's trust, if the dispositive terms of the trust provided:

(a) Income to A for life, remainder in principal to X?

(b) Income to A for life, remainder in principal to X if X survives A?

(c) Income to A for life, remainder in principal to A's children?

Compare Bassett's Estate, 190 A.2d 415, 417 (N.H. 1963) ("This state rejects the 'notion' there is a conclusive presumption that a man or woman is always capable of bearing children regardless of age, physical condition and medical opinion to the contrary."); Restatement 2d of Trusts §340 comment e[35] ("If the unascertained beneficiaries are the children of a designated woman, and the woman is beyond the age of child bearing or otherwise physically incapable of bearing children, the court may terminate the trust."); and Cal. Prob. Code §15406 with Clark v. Citizens & Southern Nat'l Bank, 257 S.E.2d 244, 246 (Ga. 1979) ("There is a conclusive presumption of Georgia law that the possibility of issue is not extinct in a female until death.... Even if this were not the law in Georgia, the class would be subject to reopening upon the adoption of a child or children by the daughter Elizabeth.").

(d) Income to B for life, remainder in principal to B's children?

(e) Income to A for life, remainder in principal to A's descendants who survive

---

35. The Restatement 3d of Trusts §65 does not address the issue.

A, by representation; if none, to A's heirs?

2. Would you reach a different answer in any of the cases in Problem 1 if G's trust were an irrevocable inter vivos trust and if G were alive and gave her consent to the trust's termination?

3. *Effect of UPC §2-707.* By creating a substitute gift to descendants of remainder beneficiaries who fail to survive the distribution date, UPC §2-707 would change the identity of the beneficiaries whose consent is necessary to terminate a trust. Professor Dukeminier argued that this "makes it more difficult to terminate trusts." Jesse Dukeminier, The Uniform Probate Code Upends the Law of Remainders, 94 Mich. L. Rev. 148, 159 (1995). Professor Waggoner responded by pointing out that "very few trusts can be terminated before the distribution date" because they contain a boilerplate spendthrift provision or because they grant discretionary powers or discretionary-support powers to the trustee. Furthermore, most trusts create future interests in classes that are still subject to open. In any event, "an easy solution to the trust termination problem... is to add a section resembling [Cal. Prob. Code §15405] that permits a guardian ad litem to consent to termination or modification on behalf of 'a beneficiary who lacks legal capacity, including a minor, or who is an unascertained or unborn person.'" Lawrence W. Waggoner, The Uniform Probate Code Extends Antilapse-type Protection to Poorly Drafted Trusts, 94 Mich. L. Rev. 2309, 2346-47 (1996).

4. G created a trust, directing the trustee to divide the income equally between A and B, and on A's death to pay half the principal to X and on B's death to pay the other half of the principal to Y. A and X want to terminate the trust; B and Y refuse to consent. Can A and X compel termination of half the trust? See Restatement 3d of Trusts §65 comment c: "a court may order a partial termination of the trust... in a manner that will not prejudice the interests of nonconsenting beneficiaries."

Settlor's Right as Sole Beneficiary to Terminate. In Phillips v. Lowe, 639 S.W.2d 782 (Ky. 1982), the court held that the settlor, who was the sole beneficiary of a trust, could terminate the trust, even though the trust instrument expressly declared that the trust was irrevocable. Accord, e.g., Woodruff v. Trust Co. of Georgia, 210 S.E.2d 321 (Ga. 1974); Johnson v. First Nat'l Bank, 386 So.2d 1112 (Miss. 1980); Restatement 2d of Trusts §339. See also the Restatement 3d of Trusts §65, which is consistent with but less explicit on this position.

It should go without saying that if the settlor is not the sole beneficiary, the settlor cannot unilaterally revoke, terminate, or modify an irrevocable trust. Note, however, that the mistake doctrine allows for such a trust to be rescinded or reformed to incorporate a power to revoke if it can be shown that the trust was created as the result of a "material mistake" or that the power was omitted by mistake. See Restatement 3d of Trusts §§62, 63 comment d; Restatement 3d of Property §12.1 comment i, illus. 7.

Consent on Behalf of Minors and Incapacitated Persons. Section 340(1) of the Restatement 2d of Trusts states that if one or more of the beneficiaries is under an incapacity, "the *others* cannot compel the termination of the trust." Is it possible, however, for the court or a conservator or guardian to consent to the trust's termination on behalf of the incapacitated beneficiary? Some courts have answered this question in the affirmative. See, e.g., Randall v. Randall, 60 F. Supp. 308 (S.D. Fla. 1944); Riedlin's Guardian v. Cobb, 1 S.W.2d 1071 (Ky. 1928); Flexner's Trust, 288 N.Y.S.2d 494, aff'd mem., 294 N.Y.S.2d 669 (App. Div. 1968). See also Restatement 3d of Trusts §65 comment b; UPC §§5-409, 5-425.

Consent on Behalf of Unborn or Unascertained Persons. To be contrasted with the problem of gaining consent on behalf of minors, incapacitated persons, or persons under a disability is the problem of unborn or unascertained beneficiaries. Can anyone consent on their behalf? The Restatement 3d of Trusts §65 comment b states, "The consent of potential beneficiaries who cannot consent for themselves... may be provided by guardians ad litem, by court appointed or other legally authorized representatives, or through representation by other beneficiaries under the doctrine of virtual representation."

Guardian ad Litem. A well-known case in which the court suggested that a guardian ad litem might be appointed to consent to trust termination on behalf of unascertained beneficiaries is Hatch v. Riggs Nat'l Bank, 361 F.2d 559 (D.C. Cir. 1966). The court stated:

> It is hornbook law that any trust, no matter how "irrevocable" by its terms, may be revoked with the consent of the settlor and all beneficiaries.
>
> The beneficiaries of the trust created by appellant are herself, as life tenant, and her heirs, as remaindermen....
>
> Although the question has not been previously discussed by this court we think basic principles of trust law are in accord with appointment of a guardian ad litem to represent interests of unborn or unascertained beneficiaries, for purpose of consent to modification or revocation of a trust....

Accord, UTC §305. See also Cal. Prob. Code §15405; Wis. Stat. §701.0305; N.C. Gen. Stat. §36C-3-305.

Virtual Representation. Another doctrine under which unborn or unascertained persons are bound by litigation is that of *virtual representation.* Under this doctrine, which is generally held to be available to courts without legislation, unborn or unascertained persons are held to have been represented by living parties to a suit if the latter have the same or similar interests as those of the later-born or later-ascertained beneficiaries, and if the respective classes of interests are not otherwise adverse to one another. See UTC §304; UPC §1-403. The Restatement 3d of Trusts §65 comment b suggests that virtual representation may be used for trust termination or modification purposes, although these are not the traditional purposes to which the doctrine has been put.

Legislation in several states also alleviates the problem, but in a variety of ways. In North Carolina, for example, the settlor is empowered to revoke provisions in favor of persons "not in esse or not determined until the happening of a future event," if the revocation is effected before "the happening of the contingency vesting the future estates" and if the trust instrument does not expressly provide otherwise. N.C. Gen. Stat. §39-6.

New York authorizes the settlor to revoke a trust with the consent of "all the persons beneficially interested...." N.Y. Est. Powers & Trusts Law §7-1.9. The phrase "persons beneficially interested" has been interpreted as excluding possible unborn beneficiaries. See, e.g., Smith v. Title Guarantee & Trust Co., 41 N.E.2d 72 (N.Y. 1942). Section 7-1.9 further provides that, for purposes of trust termination, a disposition in favor of a class of persons described only as heirs, next of kin, or distributees of the creator of the trust does not create a beneficial interest in such persons.

For a survey of the legislation on virtual representation, see Susan T. Bart & Lyman W. Welch, State Statutes on Virtual Representation: A New State Survey, 35 ACTEC J. 368 (2010).

Relaxation of the Unanimity Requirement. The Restatement 3d authorizes *partial* termination (e.g., invasion of principal for a life income beneficiary) without unanimous consent. Comment c to §65 states that "if a court is satisfied that the best interests of the beneficiaries as a whole would be served by a proposed termination or modification and if continuation of the trust is not required by [the material purpose requirement], a court may order a partial termination of the trust (or other arrangement that might involve bonding, insurance or impounding of some trust property) in a manner that will not prejudice the interests of nonconsenting beneficiaries." The Uniform Trust Code adopts a similar approach. See UTC §411(e).

EXTERNAL REFERENCES. Martin D. Begleiter, Serve the Cheerleader, Serve the World: An Analysis of Representation in Estate and Trust Proceedings and Under the Uniform Trust Code and Other Modern Trust Codes, 43 Real Prop., Tr. & Est L.J. 311 (2008); Edward C. Halbach, Jr., Uniform Acts, Restatements, and Trends in American Trust Law at Century's End, 88 Calif. L. Rev. 1877 (2000).

PART C. MODIFICATION (OR TERMINATION) BECAUSE OF UNANTICIPATED CIRCUMSTANCES

Primary Statutory Reference: *UTC §412*

If trust beneficiaries have a right to compel termination of the trust, they also have a right to compel modification of its provisions. But suppose modification on petition of the beneficiaries is impossible, perhaps because there are unborn or unascertained beneficiaries or because one or more of the living beneficiaries refuses to consent. Under the so-called "equitable deviation doctrine," the court still might modify or terminate the trust on the basis of unforeseen circumstances. The Restatement 3d of Trusts §66 and UTC §412(a) provide that a court may modify the administrative or beneficial terms of a trust if "because of circumstances not anticipated by the settlor," modification will further the purposes of the trust.[36] Furthermore, the trustee may deviate from the trust terms without prior court approval if the trustee reasonably believes that there is an emergency and if the trustee has no opportunity to apply for court approval before deviating.

1. Distributive Deviations

A trust beneficiary in need may seek to accelerate or increase his or her right to income or principal beyond that which is granted by the terms of the trust. Such deviations have been permitted in cases of single-beneficiary, postponement-of-enjoyment trusts—trusts, for example, in which the beneficiary is given income and principal upon attaining a certain age or at the end of some other period. See, e.g., Post v. Grand Rapids Trust Co., 238 N.W. 206 (Mich. 1931); Bennett v. Nashville Trust Co., 153 S.W. 840 (Tenn. 1913). The deviation in such cases, of course, amounts to a judicially declared power to invade principal for support.[37]

Where, on the other hand, there are other beneficiaries who will be adversely affected by such a deviation, as where the corpus is given to one or more persons other than the income beneficiary, the deviation will usually be denied. See, e.g., Van Deusen's Estate, 182 P.2d 565 (Cal. 1947); Staley v. Ligon, 210 A.2d 384 (Md. 1965); Matter of Rotermund, 61 Misc. 2d 324, 305 N.Y.S.2d 413 (Sur. Ct. 1969). Arguing that support of the income beneficiary was the settlor's primary purpose in establishing the trust has usually been to no avail. Justice Traynor's statement in *Van Deusen's Estate* is representative of dominant judicial philosophy on this point:

> If the courts could increase the payments under testamentary trusts without the consent of all the beneficiaries merely because the income therefrom is not what it was at the time the will was executed and because at one time or another the testator expressed the desire to provide adequately for the beneficiaries, there would be no stability to any testamentary trust in this state.

More recently, however, trusts are lasting longer and longer, trust income has declined in current financial market conditions, and inflation has made some older

---

36. To the same effect are Alaska Stat. §13.36.345(a) and Fla. Stat. §736.04113.

37. Contrast Pierowich v. Metropolitan Life Ins. Co., 275 N.W. 789 (Mich. 1937), where a mother, as guardian of the infant beneficiaries under a life-insurance contract, sought a decree for payment to them of sums from the insurance proceeds prior to the times specified in the insurance contract. In denying the petition, the court found that the arrangement created a contract, not a trust, and held that it was without power to modify the terms of a contract.

trusts that provide for a specific sum to be paid to the income beneficiary badly out of date. In response, the UTC and the Restatement 3d of Trusts, as well as the California Probate Code §15409, provide courts with the authority to adjust the distributive terms of a trust in cases of changed and unanticipated circumstances. The Restatement 3d of Trusts provides:

> *§66. Power of Court to Modify: Unanticipated Circumstances*
>
> (1) The court may modify an administrative or distributive provision of a trust, or direct or permit the trustee to deviate from an administrative or distributive provision, if because of circumstances not anticipated by the settlor the modification or deviation will further the purposes of the trust.
>
> (2) If a trustee knows or should know of circumstances that justify judicial action under Subsection (1) with respect to an administrative provision, and of the potential of those circumstances to cause substantial harm to the trust or its beneficiaries, the trustee has a duty to petition the court for appropriate modification of or deviation from the terms of the trust.

UTC §412(a) adopts a similar approach. How would Petition of Wolcott, below, be decided under either the Restatement 3d's approach or that of the UTC?

Petition of Wolcott
56 A.2d 641 (N.H. 1948)

[Francis E. Getty died in 1944, leaving a will executed in 1932 that devised $2,500 to his widow, Ada C. Getty, $5,000 each to his two sons, and the residue of his estate in trust. The income from the trust was to be paid to Ada during her lifetime, and on her death the principal was to be paid to his then-living issue or, if none, to his heirs. The will conferred on the trustees broad discretionary powers concerning investment and management of trust assets, including the power to allocate receipts between income and principal and the power "generally to do all things in relation to the trust fund which the testator could have done if living."

The trustees sought authority to invade principal for Ms. Getty in an amount not to exceed $4,000 per year, on proof of her needs resulting from her advanced age and illness. The income amounted to about $2,300 per year and her needs were estimated at $5,800 per year; the trust principal was valued at $107,000. All living issue—the couple's two sons and an 18-year-old grandson, who was represented by a guardian ad litem—consented to the deviation.]

DUNCAN, J.... Despite broad discretionary powers conferred upon the trustees, the will contains no provision for the use of principal for the benefit of the widow. On the other hand, such use is not specifically forbidden. It may fairly be assumed that the beneficiary's need of the principal was not anticipated because of a failure to foresee changes which have occurred since the testator's death, including shrinkage in investment returns, decline in purchasing power, and the expense occasioned by the widow's extreme infirmity. The powers conferred upon the trustees as to investments and the allocation of receipts to income are indicative of a purpose to provide the widow with a liberal income, unrestricted by technical rules. No purpose to transmit any specific residuary amount to the sons or any other issue is disclosed. Fairly construed, the will evidences as its primary purpose "ample and certain provision" for the testator's wife.

What is sought by the petition is not construction of any particular provision of the will but rather authority to deviate from the provisions by which principal would be retained intact during the widow's lifetime. No reliance is placed by the trustees upon their general power "to do all things in relation to the trust which the testator could have done if living." The power is at best obscure in meaning, and if construed independently of other provisions, would have doubtful validity. Clark v. Campbell, 82 N.H. 281, 133 A. 166, 45 A.L.R. 1433. Because of the emergency confronting the life beneficiary, the trustees seek authority to do what the testator presumably would have authorized had he foreseen the emergency.

Where a remainder succeeding a life estate may ultimately vest in persons as yet undetermined and perhaps unborn, courts of equity have at times hesitated or refused to sanction an invasion of principal for the benefit of the life tenant.... In one view, permission is sought to appropriate to the use of one beneficiary the property of others without the consent of all. But this view, in our opinion, may be deemed applicable only to the extent that the testator's disclosed intention affords it a foundation. Strictly applied, it may prevent accomplishment of the testator's primary purpose. As is said in 2 Scott, Trusts, §168, p. 855: "As a matter of strict logic it may be necessary to permit a child to suffer in order to protect the possible children which he may ultimately have, but it is difficult to believe that the settlor would ever desire such a result." Where the testator's desire may be gathered from the will, "strict logic" need not be controlling.

Traditionally, the courts of this jurisdiction have shown a signal regard for the intent of the testator..., at times at the expense of other recognized principles deemed less cogent in their application. Cf. Edgerly v. Barker, 66 N.H. 434, 31 A. 900, 28 L.R.A. 328. In order to prevent impairment of a testator's primary purpose, authority to deviate from the express terms of a gift has been granted in cases of emergency unforeseen by him, even though contingent remainder interests were incidentally affected....

In the will before us, the testator's purpose to furnish reasonable support for his wife is not expressed in words, but is nevertheless implicit in the disposition made of his estate. His direction that his wife should have the income was a means of executing his purpose, and is "properly to be read as subordinate to (his) paramount intention." In re Walker, [1901] 1 Ch. 879, 885. His intent to provide reasonable support to the widow being evident from the will, those whose interests are secondary to hers take subject to the execution of that intent. The remaindermen are deprived of no rights so long as rights which the life tenant was intended to have are not exceeded.

Because of circumstances not provided for by the will and obviously not anticipated by the testator, an emergency threatens accomplishment of his purpose by the means which he provided. Those whose interests are most immediate consent to the authorization sought by the trustees, and there is no objection by the guardian ad litem. If the consent or acquiescence of the parties is not binding upon unborn contingent remaindermen, still they are sufficiently represented by those having like interests to be bound by a decree.... In this situation a court of equity need not hesitate to exercise its undoubted power to permit a deviation from the literal provisions of the will. A means of accomplishing the testator's purpose is thereby furnished, which it may reasonably be inferred that he himself would have provided, had he been able to foresee the exigency....

The trustees are advised that principal not in excess of $4,000 a year may be used to supplement the income of the trust, for the purpose of providing the widow with reasonable support, if the trial court shall find in accordance with the uncontroverted allegations of the petition, and it shall appear that the widow has no other income. In view of the discretion vested in the trustees by the testator, there is no reason why they may not safely be left to determine the amount of principal necessary within the limit specified, due regard being given to considerations of what is prudent and reasonable, and best calculated to accomplish the testator's purposes as a whole.

If the requisite findings are made, a decree in accordance with this opinion may be entered by the Superior Court.

Case discharged.

All concurred.

Notes and Questions

1. *Questions.* In what way was the testator's purpose to furnish reasonable support for his widow "implicit in the disposition made of his estate"?

Suppose the testator had directed his personal representative to determine the actuarial value of an income interest for life in favor of a person of his widow's age in a fund of the value of his estate (minus the $12,500 pecuniary devises to his wife and sons), directing his executor to use that amount to purchase a straight-life annuity for her. Suppose further that his will had then devised the remaining part of his estate to a separate trust in which the income was to be accumulated during her lifetime and added to corpus, the corpus and accumulated income to be paid over at his wife's death to his then-living descendants or, if none, to his heirs. If the annuity payments later proved insufficient to meet his widow's needs, would the court have ordered the principal of the residuary trust to be invaded for her benefit?

2. *Legislation.* A few statutes authorize expansion of a beneficiary's benefits on a showing of need. See N.Y. Est. Powers & Trusts Law §7-1.6; Pa. Stat. tit. 20, §7740.2.

3. *Adjustment Between Income and Principal.* Another possible solution to the problem posed in cases like *Wolcott*, where trust income is inadequate to meet the income beneficiary's needs, is the trustee's power to make adjustments between income and principal. Recall the discussion of this topic in Chapter 10. The Uniform Fiduciary Income and Principal Act (UFIPA) also provides that the trustee shall "administer a trust... impartially, *except to the extent the terms of the trust... manifest an intent that the fiduciary shall or may favor one or more of the beneficiaries.*" UFIPA §201(a)(2) (emphasis added).

4. *State Supreme Court Cases Rejecting Modification.* A trio of state supreme court decisions in 2010, all rejecting modification, suggest that courts remain wary of distributive deviations. Two courts, interpreting state versions of UTC §412(a), declined to find the existence of "circumstances not anticipated by the settlor." See Trust D Under Will of Darby, 234 P.3d 793 (Kan. 2010); Ladysmith Rescue Squad Inc. v. Newlin, 694 S.E.2d 604 (Va. 2010). The third court found unanticipated circumstances but no substantial impairment of the trust's purpose. See Smith v. Hallum, 691 S.E.2d 848 (Ga. 2010).

2. Administrative Deviations

Requests for deviations from the administrative provisions of a trust are handled differently from requests for distributive deviations. The most common examples of administrative deviations that courts usually permit involve the power of trustees to sell or invest trust assets. These cases involve changes in circumstances which the settlor did not anticipate, and which would defeat or substantially impair the accomplishment of the purposes of the trust. Courts often say that the changed circumstances must produce an exigency or emergency, and it is not enough that a deviation would be beneficial to the beneficiaries. Obviously, this standard is one of degree, making prediction and generalization difficult, as the following materials indicate.

Matter of Pulitzer
249 N.Y.S. 87 (Sur. Ct. 1931), aff'd mem., 260 N.Y.S. 975 (App. Div. 1932)

FOLEY, S. This is a proceeding for... instructions and determination of the court as to the propriety, price, manner, and time of sale of a substantial portion of the assets of the Press Publishing Company, the stock of which constitutes a material part of the assets of the trust here involved.... A serious and imperative emergency is claimed to exist, whereby, if such a sale is not made, a valuable asset of the trust estate may be in great part or wholly lost to the trust, the life tenants, and remaindermen....

Joseph Pulitzer[38] died in the year 1911. He left a will and four codicils which were admitted to probate by this court on November 29, 1911. The provisions directly pertinent to the issues here are contained in the first codicil, which is dated March 23, 1909. By its terms he gave the shares of the capital stock of the Press Publishing Company, which were owned by him, and his shares of the Pulitzer Publishing Company, of St. Louis, in trust for the life of each of the two youngest of his sons, Joseph Pulitzer, Jr., and Herbert Pulitzer.... There were directions to pay the income in certain fractional shares to his three sons[39] and to certain other persons....

To distinguish it from the residuary trust, the particular trust here has been called the "Newspaper Trust." Its trustees are the testator's three sons, Ralph Pulitzer, Herbert Pulitzer, and Joseph Pulitzer, Jr. The Pulitzer Publishing Company publishes the St. Louis Post Dispatch. The Press Publishing Company publishes the New York World, the Sunday World, and the Evening World. The trustees of the so-called "Newspaper Trust" hold within the trust a very large majority of shares of the Press Publishing Company. The remaining shares are owned by the trustees individually. The paragraph particularly sought to be construed here, which deals with the powers of the trustees and the limitations thereon, is contained in article seventh of the codicil of March 23, 1909, and reads as follows:

> I further authorize and empower my Executors and Trustees to whom I have hereinbefore bequeathed my stock in the Pulitzer Publishing Company of St. Louis, at any time, and from time to time, to sell and dispose of said stock, or any part thereof, at public or private sale, at such prices and on such terms as they may think best, and to hold the proceeds of any stock sold in trust for the beneficiaries for whom such shares were held in lieu thereof, and upon the same trusts. This power of sale is not to be construed as in any respect

---

38. Joseph Pulitzer, a German immigrant to this country, became one of its wealthiest and most influential journalists. Almost overnight, he converted the *New York World*, the first modern daily newspaper, from a moribund sheet into the most widely-read daily newspaper in the world. The *World*'s fascinating story is told in George Juergens, Joseph Pulitzer and the *New York World* (1966).

Pulitzer himself was profoundly influenced by the Horatio Alger story of American life and greatly coveted wealth. His estate was a comparatively modest $18,525,116, much less than the thirty to eighty million dollar figure that many had guessed. See W. A. Swanberg, Pulitzer 413 (1967). The estate would have been larger but for the family's luxurious lifestyle. Ed.

39. In fact, the distribution plan made a flurry of newspaper headlines. Herbert, the youngest child, was given a six-tenths interest in the trust income, three times the size of his eldest brother Ralph's share, while Joseph, Jr., was given only a one-tenth interest. Pulitzer's partiality for Herbert was revealed also by the terms for appointment of trustees. Initially, four independent trustees were appointed, and two of which were to be replaced by Herbert when he reached 21 and by Joseph, Jr., when he reached 30. Ralph, who was 32 at the time of his father's death and had already made his mark in the newspaper business, was the only one of the brothers not given a trusteeship, a fact that led him to make a public statement indicating that the omission might mistakenly suggest "a lack of confidence in me on [my father's] part." In fact, in an unexecuted will prepared for him in 1911, Pulitzer did name Ralph as a trustee. It is also notable that neither of Pulitzer's two daughters were made trustees or received any interest in the newspaper trust, although they were given income interests in a $1.5 million trust. See Swanberg, cited in the preceding footnote, at 414. Ed.

mandatory, but purely discretionary. This power of sale, however, is limited to the said stock of the Pulitzer Publishing Company of St. Louis, and shall not be taken to authorize or empower the sale or disposition under any circumstances whatever, by the Trustees of any stock of the Press Publishing Company, publisher of "The World" newspaper. I particularly enjoin upon my sons and my descendants the duty of preserving, perfecting and perpetuating "The World" newspaper (to the maintenance and upbuilding of which I have sacrificed my health and strength) in the same spirit which I have striven to create and conduct it as a public institution, from motives higher than mere gain, it having been my desire that it should be at all times conducted in a spirit of independence and with a view to inculcating high standards and public spirit among the people and their official representatives, and it is my earnest wish that said newspaper shall hereafter be conducted upon the same principles.

There are fifteen remaindermen in existence. One of them is an adult; the other fourteen are infants. Because of a possible adversity of interest they are represented here by two separate special guardians. The adult life tenants and remaindermen join in requesting the relief sought by the trustees.

Counsel for the trustees contend that the express denial of a power of sale contained in the paragraph was modified and cut down, as a matter of testamentary intent, by Mr. Pulitzer in subsequent language.... There is some support to be found in the provisions of the will for these contentions. Indication of an intent to authorize a sale in certain emergencies is thus found in article 6 of the codicil dated May 11, 1910.

But I prefer to place my determination here upon broader grounds and upon the power of a court of equity, in emergencies, to protect the beneficiaries of a trust from serious loss, or a total destruction of a substantial asset of the corpus. The law, in the case of necessity, reads into the will an implied power of sale....

The same rule applies to emergencies in trusts not only where there is an absence of power of sale in a will, but also where there is a prohibition against sale. It has been satisfactorily established by the evidence before me that the continuance of the publication of the newspapers, which are the principal assets of the Press Publishing Company, will in all probability lead to a serious impairment or the destruction of a large part of the trust estate. The dominant purpose of Mr. Pulitzer must have been the maintenance of a fair income for his children and the ultimate reception of the unimpaired corpus by the remaindermen. Permanence of the trust and ultimate enjoyment by his grandchildren were intended. A man of his sagacity and business ability could not have intended that from mere vanity, the publication of the newspapers, with which his name and efforts had been associated, should be persisted in until the entire trust asset was destroyed or wrecked by bankruptcy or dissolution. His expectation was that his New York newspapers would flourish. Despite his optimism, he must have contemplated that they might become entirely unprofitable and their disposal would be required to avert a complete loss of the trust assets The power of a court of equity, with its jurisdiction over trusts, to save the beneficiaries in such a situation has been repeatedly sustained in New York and other jurisdictions....

The trustees here find themselves in a crisis where there is no self-help available to them. A judicial declaration is necessary, not only as to their general authority, but as to the effect of the words of Mr. Pulitzer contained in his will. The widest equity powers exist in the Surrogate's Court of this state by the grant of the legislative authority contained in section 40 of the Surrogate's Court Act. Matter of Raymond v. Davis' Estate, 248 N.Y. 67, 71, 161 N.E. 421.

I accordingly hold, in this phase of the decision, that the terms of the will and codicils do not prohibit the trustees from disposing of any assets of the Press Publishing Company, that the trustees have general power and authority to act in the conveyance of the assets proposed to be sold, and that this court, in the exercise of its equitable jurisdiction, should authorize them by an appropriate direction in the decree to exercise such general authority....

Notes and Question

1. *Sequel.* The decline in profitability of the *World* newspapers, which led the court to order their sale despite the express provision to the contrary in the will, postdated Joseph Pulitzer's death. After assuming control of the *World* newspapers, Pulitzer's sons changed the papers' style in an effort to appeal to a more educated readership. Circulation and advertising plummeted and, by 1928, all three newspapers were operating with deep deficits. In 1931, the papers were sold to the Scripps-Howard organization for $5 million. The story is told in W. A. Swanberg, Pulitzer 411-18 (1967).

2. *Legislation on the Trustee's Administrative Powers.* The UTC provides that the court may modify the administrative provisions of a trust "if continuation of the trust on its existing terms would be impracticable or wasteful or impair the trust's administration." UTC §412(b).[40] Although UTC §412(a) authorizes modification of distributive or administrative terms "in accordance with the settlor's probable intention," §412(b), which applies only to administrative deviation, does not include such a requirement. The comment states that §412(b) is an application of the UTC's broader principle, expressed in §404, that the trust must be for the benefit of the beneficiaries. The same principle is expressed in Restatement 3d of Trusts §27. How would *Pulitzer* have been resolved under §412(b)?

For discussions of *Pulitzer*, see Thomas P. Gallanis, The Trustee's Duty to Inform, 85 N.C. L. Rev. 1595, 1621-1623 (2007); John H. Langbein, Mandatory Rules in the Law of Trusts, 98 Nw. U. L. Rev. 1105, 1117-1119 (2004).

---

40. The Alaska statute provides substantially the same approach. See Alaska Stat. §13.36.345.

3. *Trust Decanting*

Primary Statutory References: *Uniform Trust Decanting Act*

"Decanting" is the term used to describe the distribution of property from one trust to another. As Anne Marie Levin and Todd A. Flubacher explain in their article, Put Decanting to Work to Give Breath to Trust Purpose, 38 Est. Plan. 3, 3 (January 2011):

> The word "decanting" provides a rich metaphor to help us understand exactly what decanting a trust is all about. The word "decant" literally means to pour a liquid from one vessel to another, leaving unwanted sediment in the first vessel. When we decant a trust, the liquid is the trust principal, the first vessel is the original trust instrument, the second vessel is the new trust instrument, and the unwanted sediment is the unwanted terms and conditions of the original trust instrument, or the lack of desirable terms and conditions in the original trust instrument. Depending on the particular circumstances, decanting may be the most effective and economical option to fix problematic trusts.

At common law, depending on the terms of the original trust, a trustee may have the power to make distributions of trust assets from one trust to another. If, for example, a trustee may make distributions not only to, but for the benefit of, a beneficiary, those distributions may be to another trust for the beneficiary's benefit. See, e.g., Phipps v. Palm Beach Trust Co., 196 So. 299 (Fla. 1940) (trustee's power to invade principal included the power to pay principal to another trust for the beneficiary); Morse v. Kraft, 992 N.E.2d 1021 (Mass. 2013) (trustee's power to distribute or apply income or principal "for the benefit" of the beneficiaries included the power to transfer the property to new trusts for the beneficiaries).

In 1992, New York became the first state to enact a decanting statute specifically empowering a trustee to pour the assets of an irrevocable trust into another trust. Today, decanting is authorized in more than half the states by statute. The statutes differ in their particulars, of course.

Why might decanting be desirable? Consider the reasons given by William R. Culp, Jr. and Briani Bennett Mellen in their article, Trust Decanting: An Overview and Introduction to Creative Planning Opportunities, 45 Real Prop., Tr. & Est. L.J. 1, 14 (2010):

> Trust decanting... can be used to improve trust administration or management, such as by combining multiple trusts to promote administrative convenience or reduce administrative costs. Decanting can be used to address a trustee's ability to delegate specific functions or decisions to a cotrustee, or to appoint a successor trustee or cotrustee for a limited purpose or a specified time. For example, the new trust could provide for the appointment of a fiduciary advisor to make investment decisions, thereby protecting a less sophisticated trustee from decisions regarding those investments. Decanting also may be used to clarify the governing law of a trust and ensure uniform requirements for trust administration, enforcement, or obligations if the trustee and beneficiaries reside in several

different states.

If the terms of the trust contain drafting errors that are not discovered until after the trust has become irrevocable, trust decanting can be used to correct the errors, whether administrative, substantive, or distributive, to reflect more accurately the settlor's intent.

...Trust decanting can be used to address the beneficiaries' changed circumstances after a trust has become irrevocable, such as creditor or marital issues, disparate accumulations of wealth, or disability.... For example, a trust set to terminate when the primary beneficiary reaches a certain age could be decanted to another trust that continues for the life of the beneficiary.

In 2015, the Uniform Law Commission approved a Uniform Trust Decanting Act. The chair of the drafting committee was Stanley Kent, a law commissioner from Colorado, and the reporter was Susan Bart of the ArentFox Schiff law firm in Chicago. Consider the following excerpts from the Act's prefatory note.

Uniform Trust Decanting Act
Prefatory Note (2015) (internal citations omitted)

The Uniform Trust Decanting Act is promulgated in the midst of a rising tide of state decanting statutes. These statutes represent one of several recent innovations in trust law that seek to make trusts more flexible so that the settlor's material purposes can best be carried out under current circumstances. A decanting statute provides flexibility by statutorily expanding discretion already granted to the trustee to permit the trustee to modify the trust either directly or by distributing its assets to another trust. While some trusts expressly grant the trustee or another person a power to modify or decant the trust, a statutory provision can better describe the power granted, impose limits on the power to protect the beneficiaries and the settlor's intent, protect against inadvertent tax consequences, provide procedural rules for exercising the power and provide for appropriate remedies. While decanting may be permitted in some situations under common law in some states, in many states it is unclear whether common law decanting is permitted, and if it is, the circumstances in which it is permitted and the parameters within which it may be exercised.

Need for Uniformity. Trusts may be governed by the laws of different states for purposes of validity, meaning and effect, and administration. The place of administration of a trust may move from state to state. It often may be difficult to determine the state in which a trust is administered if a trust has co-trustees domiciled in different states or has a corporate trustee that performs different trust functions in different states. As a result it may sometimes be unclear whether a particular state's decanting statute applies to a trust and sometimes more than one state's decanting statute may apply to a trust. A uniform statute can eliminate conflicts between different state statutes. It can also protect a trustee who decants under one state's statute when more than one state's statute might apply and protect a trustee who reasonably relies on a prior decanting....

What Trusts May Be Decanted. Generally, the Uniform Trust Decanting Act permits decanting of an irrevocable, express trust in which the terms of the trust grant the trustee or another fiduciary the discretionary power to make principal distributions. The act does not apply to revocable trusts unless they are revocable by the settlor only with the consent of the trustee or an adverse party. The act does not apply to wholly charitable trusts. With one exception, if no fiduciary has discretion to distribute principal, the act does not apply unless the court appoints a special fiduciary and authorizes the special fiduciary to exercise the decanting power. The exception is that a fiduciary who is responsible for making trust distributions may decant a trust to create a special-needs trust even if the fiduciary does not have discretion over principal if the decanting will further the purposes of the first trust.

Who May Decant. As discussed below, the decanting power is a fiduciary power, and thus must be entrusted to one of the fiduciaries of the first trust. The act entrusts the "authorized fiduciary" with the decanting power. The "authorized fiduciary" generally is the fiduciary who has discretion to distribute principal, although a more expansive definition is needed in the case of a special-needs trust. Generally, the authorized fiduciary will be the trustee. Where there is a divided trusteeship that gives the power to make or direct principal distributions to another fiduciary, such as a distribution director, such other fiduciary will be the authorized fiduciary.

Discretion Over Principal. Except in the case of special-needs trusts, the decanting power is granted only to an authorized fiduciary who by definition must have the discretion to distribute principal. The extent of the decanting authority depends upon the extent of the discretion granted to the trustee to distribute principal. When the authorized fiduciary has "limited distribution discretion" that is constrained by an ascertainable or reasonably definite standard, the interests of each beneficiary in the second trust must be substantially similar to such beneficiary's interests in the first trust. Thus when the authorized fiduciary has limited distributive discretion, an exercise of the decanting power generally can modify administrative, but not dispositive, trust provisions. When the authorized fiduciary has "expanded distributive discretion," the authorized fiduciary may exercise the decanting power to modify beneficial interests, subject to restrictions to protect interests that are current, noncontingent rights or vested remainder interests, to protect qualification for tax benefits and to protect charitable interests....

Fiduciary Power. The Uniform Trust Decanting Act does not impose any duty on the authorized fiduciary to exercise the decanting power, but if the authorized fiduciary does exercise that power, the power must be exercised in accordance with the fiduciary duties of the authorized fiduciary. A fiduciary must administer a trust in good faith, in accordance with its terms (subject to the decanting power) and purposes, and in the interests of the beneficiaries. An exercise of decanting power must be in accordance with the purposes of the first trust. The purpose of decanting is not to disregard the settlor's intent but to modify the trust to better effectuate the settlor's broader purposes or the settlor's probable intent if the settlor had anticipated the circumstances at the time of decanting.

Decanting Procedure. Initially, the power to decant was often considered a derivative of the power to make a discretionary distribution to a beneficiary. Under this construct the decanting power was exercised by making a distribution from one trust to another, and a second trust, separate and distinct from the first trust, was required.

The Uniform Trust Decanting Act views the decanting power as a power to modify the first trust, either by changing the terms of the first trust or by distributing property from the first trust to a second trust. While the act generally modulates the extent of the authorized fiduciary's power to decant according to the degree of discretion granted to the authorized fiduciary over principal, the power to decant is distinct from the power to distribute.

Thus the authorized fiduciary may exercise the decanting power by modifying the first trust, in which case the "second trust" is merely the modified first trust. The decanting instrument can, when appropriate, merely identify the specific provisions in the first trust that are to be modified and set forth the modified provisions, much like an amendment to a revocable trust. If the decanting power is exercised by modifying the terms of the first trust, the trustee could either treat the second trust as a new trust or treat the second trust as a continuation of the first trust. If the second trust is treated as a continuation of the first trust, there should be no need to transfer or retitle the trust property....

Notes

1. *Decanting and Tax Objectives*. Trust decanting is an increasingly popular technique to achieve one or more of the wide variety of objectives discussed in the preceding excerpt. One of these objectives can be to obtain favorable tax treatment at the state level or federal level—or both.

There is a procedure by which a taxpayer (or, typically, the taxpayer's lawyer) can obtain guidance from the IRS about the potential federal tax consequences of a proposed action or arrangement: a "private letter ruling" is obtained from the IRS. On January 3, 2011, however, the IRS declared that it will no longer issue private letter rulings on the tax consequences of trust decanting. See Rev. Proc. 2011-3, §§5.09, 5.16, 5.17. The current version is at Rev. Proc. 2023-3, §5.

2. *Decanting and the Duty of Impartiality*. A trustee's power to eliminate non-vested beneficial interests when decanting must be exercised in accordance with the trustee's duty of impartiality. See Hodges v. Johnson, 177 A.3d 86 (2017). As the *Hodges* court emphasized, however, "[t]he duty to act impartially does not mean that the trustee must treat the beneficiaries equally"; rather, the duty requires the trustee to treat the beneficiaries "equitably in light of the purposes and terms of the trust." Id. at 95, quoting the Comment to UTC §803.

3. *Decanting and a No-Contest Provision.* In Gowdy v. Cook, 455 P.3d 1201 (Wyo. 2020), the state supreme court held that a beneficiary's request to change the terms of a trust by decanting violated the trust intstrument's no-contest clause. That clause provided that an attempt "to void, nullify, *or set aside*" the trust *or any trust provision* triggered the forfeiture of the beneficiary's interest.

EXTERNAL REFERENCES. Stewart E. Sterk, Trust Decanting: A Critical Perspective, 38 Cardozo L. Rev. 1993 (2017); Robert H. Sitkoff, The Rise of Trust Decanting in the United States, 23 Tr. & Trustees 976 (2017).

PART D. COMPROMISE OF CONTROVERSIES

Primary Statutory References: *UTC §111*
UPC §§1-403, 3-1101, 3-1102

Adams v. Link
145 A.2d 753 (Conn. 1958)

KING, J. The defendants Link and the United States Trust Company of New York are the executors and trustees under the will and codicil of Mildred A. Kingsmill, late of Darien. Mrs. Kingsmill left, as her sole heirs at law, two brothers, Orson Adams, Jr., and Alvin P. Adams, and a sister, Ethel A. Martin. This action grows out of, although it is distinct from, an appeal by Orson Adams, Jr., and Alvin P. Adams, two of the three heirs at law, from the admission of the will and codicil to probate.

In the view which we take of the case, only the right to terminate the trust created in paragraph sixth of the will need be considered. This paragraph disposed of the residue by a trust. It provided for the payment of the net income for life, in monthly or quarterly installments at their written election, to Joan K. Pringle and Mayes M. Foeppel, neither of whom was an heir at law. At the death of the survivor, the trust was to terminate and distribution of the corpus was to be made to the New York Association for the Blind. In fact, Joan K. Pringle predeceased the testatrix, leaving Mayes M. Foeppel as the sole income beneficiary and entitled, under the terms of the trust, to the entire net income for life.

During the pendency of the appeal from probate, a so-called compromise agreement was entered into between Mayes M. Foeppel, party of the first part, the New York Association for the Blind, party of the second part, and the three heirs at law of the testatrix, parties of the third part. The agreement in effect provided that (1) the appeal from the admission of the will and codicil to probate would be withdrawn; (2) 15 per cent of the residuary estate, i.e. the trust corpus, would be paid outright to the three heirs at law in equal shares; (3) 37 per cent would be paid outright to the New York Association for the Blind; and (4) 48 per cent would be paid outright to Mayes M. Foeppel less a deduction of $15,000 which would be used to establish a new trust, the precise terms of which are not material. Basically, it was for the education of a son of Alvin P. Adams, and upon completion of his education the trust would terminate and any unused corpus and interest would be returned to Mayes M. Foeppel. The compromise agreement was by its express terms made subject to the approval of the Superior Court. The defendant executors and trustees refused to participate in the agreement or to carry it out. The present action, the plaintiffs in which include all parties to the agreement except the New York Association for the Blind, which was made a party defendant, seeks in effect (a) the approval of the agreement by the Superior Court, and (b) a decree compelling the defendant executors and trustees to carry it out. Since the provision for the New York Association for the Blind was a charitable gift, the attorney general was made a defendant to represent the public interest, under the provisions of § 212 of the General Statutes. The court refused to approve the agreement, and from this action the plaintiffs took this appeal....

The fundamental effect of the compromise agreement, if approved by the court, would be to abolish the trust....

Conditions precedent which should concur in order to warrant termination of a testamentary trust by judicial decree are (1) that all the parties in interest unite in seeking the termination, (2) that every reasonable ultimate purpose of the trust's creation and existence has been accomplished, and (3) that no fair and lawful restriction imposed by the testator will be nullified or disturbed by such a result....

The underlying rationale of our rule is the protection, if reasonably possible, of any reasonable, properly expressed, testamentary desire of a decedent. 3 Scott, Trusts (2d Ed.) §337.

It appears that all the interested beneficiaries have joined in the agreement under consideration. For the purposes of this case only, we will assume, without in any way deciding, that the plaintiffs are correct in their claim that the defendant executors and trustees have no standing to attack the compromise. This assumption is permissible because the compromise was in terms made contingent upon court approval, and this approval could not be compelled by any agreement of the trust beneficiaries among themselves. Thus we may assume, without deciding, that the first condition precedent under our rule is satisfied. The second and third conditions precedent have not, however, been satisfied. The obvious objectives of the testatrix were to provide (a) an assured income for life for Mayes M. Foeppel, and (b) at her death an intact corpus for the New York Association for the Blind. In carrying out these objectives, the testatrix took two important steps. In the first place, the management of the trust corpus was committed to trustees selected by her and in whose financial judgment she is presumed to have had confidence. Secondly, expenditure of any principal by the life beneficiary was precluded. Taken together, these two steps would tend to achieve, and in all reasonable probability would achieve, the testatrix' two basic objectives. To abolish the trust and turn over a fraction of the corpus outright to the life beneficiary would be to enable her in a moment to lose the protection of the practically assured life income provided by the testatrix. The two basic objectives of the trust's creation and existence were reasonable and commendable and cannot be fully accomplished prior to the death of the life beneficiary. Obviously, had the testatrix intended to entrust the life beneficiary with the handling of any part of the corpus, she would have so provided by a simple, outright gift.

The plaintiffs attempt to avoid the impact of our rule by two main claims. The first is that since the protection accorded the life beneficiary could be lost by her voluntary alienation of the income or by its involuntary alienation through attachment or seizure under an order in equity, the testatrix could not have intended to protect the beneficiary. This amounts in effect to a claim that only a spendthrift trust is protected from termination by agreement of all interested beneficiaries. The case against termination under our rule is of course even stronger where a spendthrift trust is involved. But the operation of our rule is not restricted to such trusts. The mere fact that the testatrix failed to provide the maximum possible protection for the life beneficiary by creating a spendthrift trust ... does not warrant a conclusion that she intended no protection at all, so that we can consider that the trust no longer has any purpose.

The plaintiffs also claim that whatever the rule may be in cases involving no will contest, a more liberal rule applies where, as here, the termination of the trust is a part of the settlement of such a contest. Some support for this position may be found in cases cited in 3 Scott, Trusts (2d Ed.) §337.6. The rationale of our rule as to the power to set aside or terminate a trust is not, however, such that its applicability would be affected by the mere fact that the motivation of a trust termination agreement is the compromise of a will contest. It is true that such contests are not infrequently compromised by agreements involving the transfer of legacies or devises, in whole or in part, by beneficiaries under the will. Where such gifts are alienable this is permissible, since no violence is done to the provisions of the will. But that is not this case. Here the provisions of the will itself are being drastically changed so as to abolish a trust contrary to our rule. This cannot be done. It follows that the court below was not in error in denying approval of the agreement. Indeed, it was the only decision which could properly have been made. This conclusion makes unnecessary the consideration of the other grounds of appeal.

There is no error.

In this opinion the other judges concurred.

Notes and Questions

1. *Questions.* Was Adams v. Link correctly decided under *Claflin*? Was the trust at issue a postponement-of-enjoyment trust, or was it a successive-beneficiary trust?

2. *State of the Authorities.* The traditional approach agrees with the holding of Adams v. Link. See Restatement 2d of Trusts §337 comment o. An important case to the contrary, however, was Budin v. Levy, 180 N.E.2d 74 (Mass. 1962), holding

sensibly that the validity of a judicial settlement agreement does not depend on satisfying the *Claflin* requirements. The Restatement 3d of Trusts §65 comment h accords with *Budin*.

On nonjudicial settlement agreements, see UTC §111(c).

3. *Uniform Probate Code.* Section 3-1101 of the UPC provides that a compromise of any controversy as to the admission of an instrument offered to formal probate as the testator's will is binding even though it may affect a trust or inalienable interest. Section 3-1102 details the procedure for securing court approval of a compromise agreement. Section 1-403 states that unborn or unascertained beneficiaries who are not otherwise represented in a proceeding are bound by court orders that bind other parties to the extent that their interests are adequately represented by other parties who have a "substantially identical interest" in the proceeding.

Chapter 12
Charitable Trusts

Charities, an old maxim goes, are a favorite of the law. If this is the case today, it was not always so. As Professor Friedman has observed, "In the early nineteenth century, charity was associated with privilege, with the dead hand, with established churches..., with massive wealth held in perpetuity. None of these was particularly popular." Lawrence M. Friedman, A History of American Law 185 (3d ed. 2005).

Today, the hostile attitude toward charities has largely dissipated. In fact, charitable trusts enjoy legal privileges. Some of the rules restricting private trusts are suspended for charitable trusts. Not all the restrictive rules are suspended, of course. Like a private trust, a charitable trust creates a fiduciary relationship with respect to property, requiring a trust res, an intent to create a trust, compliance with the Statute of Frauds or the Statute of Wills, as appropriate, and so on. But the requirement of definite beneficiaries does not apply to charitable trusts, nor does the Rule Against Perpetuities (if the trust includes only charitable interests) or associated rules relating to accumulations of income.[1] In addition, charitable trusts enjoy certain tax benefits not accorded to private trusts.

Validity of Charitable Trusts. Although the validity of charitable trusts is now universally recognized in the United States, the question was in doubt in the early part of our history. Because charitable trusts are created to accomplish charitable purposes, not to benefit definite beneficiaries, special machinery had to be developed for their enforcement. Such procedure was provided in England by the Statute of Charitable Uses, 43 Eliz. ch. 4 (1601). Some early American courts assumed that the authority to enforce charitable trusts originated with and depended upon the English statute. Trustees of Philadelphia Baptist Ass'n v. Hart's Ex'rs, 17 U.S. (4 Wheat.) 1 (1819), held that if that statute was not imported into the state as part of the common law, state legislation was needed for charitable trusts to be created in the jurisdiction. More rigorous historical work showed, however, that the English Court of Chancery had enforced charitable trusts long before the Statute of Charitable Uses and continued to do so after the enforcement procedure provided by that statute had been repealed. On this basis, charitable trusts came to be recognized—with or without supporting legislation—as legitimate vehicles for devoting wealth to charitable purposes.

---

1. Many charitable trusts are designed to last without time limit, by providing that only the income shall be used for the charitable purpose. A perpetual charitable trust facilitated by a warrant from William Penn in 1706 continues today. See Trustees of New Castle Common v. Gordy, 93 A.2d 509 (Del. Ch. 1952). The trust operates from offices located at 807 Frenchtown Road, New Castle, Delaware 19720.

Enforcement of Charitable Trusts. One of the central features of a charitable trust is that it need not have definite beneficiaries. The beneficiaries of a private trust, as we know, are the ones who have standing for its enforcement. Lacking definite beneficiaries, a charitable trust is principally enforceable by the state Attorney General. The Restatement 2d of Trusts provides:

> *§391. Who Can Enforce a Charitable Trust.* A suit can be maintained for the enforcement of a charitable trust by the Attorney General or other public officer, or by a co-trustee, or by a person who has a special interest in the enforcement of the charitable trust, but not by persons who have no special interest or by the settlor or his heirs, personal representatives or next of kin.

See also Restatement 3d of Trusts §94(2); Restatement of Charitable Nonprofit Organizations §5.01 & ch. 6.

The reference in the Restatement 2d of Trusts to "a person who has a special interest in the enforcement of the charitable trust" is intended to cover situations in which an individual derives a benefit from the trust that is not available to the public at large or has a unique stake in the proper enforcement of the trust. Trustees of charitable corporations and charitable trusts, for example, have been allowed to sue their co-trustees for breaches of trust. See, e.g., Holt v. College of Osteopathic Physicians & Surgeons, 394 P.2d 932 (Cal. 1964). Beneficiaries or potential beneficiaries of charitable trusts or charitable organizations rarely succeed in establishing "special interest" standing. See, e.g., Derblom v. Archdiocese of Hartford, 289 A.3d 1187, 1201 (Conn. 2023). For example, the cases generally hold that students do not have standing to sue the trustees of their colleges or universities. See, e.g., Russell v. Yale University, 737 A.2d 941 (Conn. App. 1999). For a rare case granting "special interest" standing, see Jones v. Grant, 344 So. 2d 1210 (Ala. 1977). The UTCode breaks new ground by providing in §405(c) that the settlor of a charitable trust also may enforce the terms of the trust. See below, Part C.

Charitable Organizations. A newly created charitable organization can be formed in a variety of ways, including that of a charitable trust or that of a charitable corporation. Existing charitable organizations, including the well-known public charities such as the American Cancer Society and the major charitable foundations such as the Ford Foundation, are usually (but not always) formed as corporations. Many of the rules and principles applicable to charitable trusts, including the cy pres doctrine, are applicable to charitable corporations or other organizations. See Restatement 2d of Trusts §348 comment f; §386 comment b; §399 comment o.

Charitable organizations and trusts hold an enormous amount of the nation's wealth. According to FoundationMark (www.foundationmark.com) at the end of 2021, foundations in the U.S. held more than $1.3 trillion in assets. The largest foundation was the Bill and Melinda Gates Foundation, with total assets of $53.9 billion.

Sound-Alike Names. There are hundreds of thousands of charities in the United States, some of which have similar names. For example, there is the Make-A-Wish Foundation, the Grant-A-Wish Foundation, the Children's Wish Foundation International, the Wishing Well Foundation, the Fulfill A Wish Foundation (now Kids Wish Network), and the Grant-A-Wish Network. And then there is the Guide Dogs for the Blind and the Guide Dog Foundation for the Blind, not to mention the American Heart Association and the American Heart Disease Prevention Foundation. See Reed Ableson, Some Charities Cash In by Playing the Name Game, N.Y. Times, Dec. 30, 1999, at A1.

Perpetual Use of the Donor's Name? Many donors name charitable trusts or foundations after themselves. Examples include the Leona M. and Harry B. Helmsley Charitable Trust (with assets in 2022 of approximately $8.2 billion) and the Bill and Melinda Gates Foundation. Should donors be able to attach their names in perpetuity to these tax-favored vehicles? For an argument that the naming rights should end after 50 years, see William A. Drennan, Surnamed Charitable Trusts: Immortality at Taxpayer Expense, 61 Ala. L. Rev. 225 (2010).

Ratings of and Financial Information about Charities. You can find out how a charity is rated, including what proportion of its contributions actually go to the charitable purpose, by checking with the Better Business Bureau (www.bbb.org) or Charity Watch (www. charitywatch.org). Financial and other information about a charity is available through GuideStar (www.guidestar.org)

Tax-Exempt Status. The income of charitable trusts and charitable corporations is generally exempt from federal income tax. See Internal Revenue Code §501.

Contributions to Existing Charitable Organizations. A gift or devise to an existing charitable organization is sometimes treated as having created a separate charitable trust with respect to that contribution, with the organization as the trustee. The idea that a charitable trust has been created is more likely if the donor imposed one or more restrictions on the gift or devise. A restriction can take a variety of forms. The donor may restrict the use of the property to one of the purposes for which the charitable organization has been formed; for example, the donor may restrict a donation to an educational institution to the school's scholarship fund. The donor may specify that only the income is to be used, not the principal. Whether or not the transaction is characterized as a trust, the rules and principles applicable to charitable trusts usually are applicable to charitable organizations. See Restatement 2d of Trusts §348 comment f; Restatement of Charitable Nonprofit Organizations §1.02 comment d.

PART A. CHARITABLE PURPOSES

Primary Statutory Reference: *UTC §405*

In this Part, we present cases in which trusts have been challenged on the ground that they are not charitable trusts because their purposes are not "charitable." In the leading English case of Commissioners for Special Purpose of the Income Tax v. Pemsel, [1891] App. Cas. 531, 583 (H.L.), Lord Macnaghten expressed the following understanding of charitable trusts:

> "Charity" in its legal sense comprises four principal divisions: trusts for the relief of poverty; trusts for the advancement of education; trusts for the advancement of religion; and trusts for other purposes beneficial to the community, not falling under any of the preceding heads. The trusts last referred to are not the less charitable in the eye of the law, because incidentally they benefit the rich as well as the poor, as indeed, every charity that deserves the name must do either directly or indirectly.

In this country, the Restatement 3d of Trusts §28 defines charitable purposes as including the relief of poverty; the advancement of education; the advancement of religion; the promotion of health; governmental or municipal purposes; and other purposes that are beneficial to the community. See also UTC §405(a); Restatement of Charitable Nonprofit Organizations §1.01(b). As you read the cases in this Part, consider why the trust would be invalid as a private trust if it fails to meet the charitable trust definition.

Tax Deductibility. For qualified gifts to charity, the Internal Revenue Code allows a limited deduction from income taxation and an unlimited deduction from gift taxation; and for qualified devises to charity, the Code allows an unlimited deduction from estate taxation. See IRC §§170, 642(c), 2055, 2522. The estate tax provision, set forth below, is nearly identical to the income and gift tax provisions:

§2055. *Transfers for public, charitable, and religious uses.*

(a) In general.—For purposes of the tax imposed by section 2001, the value of the taxable estate shall be determined by deducting from the value of the gross estate the amount of all bequests, legacies, devises, or transfers—

(1) to or for the use of the United States, any State, any political subdivision thereof, or the District of Columbia, for exclusively public purposes;

(2) to or for the use of any corporation organized and operated exclusively for religious, charitable, scientific, literary, or educational purposes, including the encouragement of art, or to foster national or international amateur sports competition (but only if no part of its activities involve the provision of athletic facilities or equipment), and the prevention of cruelty to children or animals, no part of the net earnings of which inures to the benefit of any private stockholder or individual, which is not disqualified for tax exemption under §501(c)(3) by reason of attempting to influence legislation, and which does not participate in, or intervene in (including the publishing or distributing of statements), any political campaign on behalf of (or in opposition to) any candidate for public office;

(3) to a trustee or trustees, or a fraternal society, order, or association operating under the lodge system, but only if such contributions or gifts are to be used by such trustee or trustees, or by such fraternal society, order, or association, exclusively for religious, charitable, scientific, literary, or educational purposes, or for the prevention of cruelty to children or animals, such trust, fraternal society, order, or association would not be disqualified for tax exemption under §501(c)(3) by reason of attempting to influence legislation, and such trustee or trustees, or such fraternal society, order, or association, does not participate in, or intervene in (including the publishing or distributing of statements), any political campaign on behalf of (or in opposition to) any candidate for public office; [or]

(4) to or for the use of any veterans' organization incorporated by Act of Congress, or of its departments or local chapters or posts, no part of the net earnings of which inures to the benefit of any private shareholder or individual....

Are the trust law and tax law definitions of charitable purposes identical? Rev. Rul. 71-447, 1971-2 C.B. 230, states:

Both the courts and the Internal Revenue Service have long recognized that the statutory requirements [of IRC section 501(c)(3)] of being "organized and operated exclusively for religious, charitable,... or educational purposes" was intended to express the basic common law concept.

See also Rev. Rul. 67-325, 1967-2 C.B. 113, declaring that the phrase "charitable purposes" in IRC §§170, 2055, and 2522 is used "in the generally accepted legal sense."

Foreign Beneficiaries. The fact that a charitable trust is for the benefit of a community outside the United States does not prevent the trust from being upheld as a charitable trust or disqualify it for the federal estate or gift tax charitable deduction. Restatement 2d of Trusts §374 comment i; Rev. Rul. 74-523, 1974-2 C.B. 304. For federal income tax purposes, a "contribution or gift *by a corporation* to a trust, chest, fund, or foundation" is deductible "only if it is to be used within the United States or any of its possessions...." IRC §170(c).

1. General Gifts to Charity

Suppose a testator devises property in trust "for such charitable purposes as my trustee shall select" or "to apply the income therefrom, in perpetuity, for the promotion of religion." According to Restatement 3d of Trusts §28 comment a, and most authority, both dispositions create charitable trusts. In Estate of Small, 58 N.W.2d 477 (Iowa 1953), the court upheld a trust created by the will of Dr. W.B. Small. To Dr. Small, divine guidance, though necessary, was not sufficient. His will retained a post-death veto power:

I direct that my said trustees or their successors shall distribute... income... for such purposes as they may feel is directed by God the Father, Jesus Christ the Son, and Holy Spirit, *and* as they believe would be acceptable to *me* and meet *my* approval were *I* able to

---

give it .... (Emphasis added.)

A charitable trust also is created if the testator simply devises property "to charity" or "to the poor." See Jordan's Estate, 197 A. 150 (Pa. 1938) (devise "to charity" upheld as a charitable trust); Restatement 3d of Trusts §28 comment a. In these cases, of course, the court must select a trustee or frame a scheme for the application of the devise to the intended purpose.

Devises for purposes not restricted to charitable purposes have generated considerable litigation. In the leading case of Morice v. Bishop of Durham, 32 Eng. Rep. 947 (Ch. 1805), Lord Chancellor Eldon held that a devise in trust "to dispose of the ultimate residue to such objects of benevolence and liberality as the Bishop of Durham in his own discretion shall most approve of" failed to create a charitable trust because the purposes were not limited to charity and failed to create a valid private trust because the beneficiaries were indefinite. A century and a half later, in Chichester Diocesan Fund v. Simpson, [1944] App. Cas. 341 (H.L.), the House of Lords applied the idea that "benevolence" is not restricted to "charity" in the case of a devise to the testator's executors to apply it "for such charitable institution or institutions or other charitable or benevolent object or objects in England as my acting executors or executor may in their or his absolute discretion select."

In this country, many courts have agreed with the English view that "benevolence," standing alone, potentially encompasses purposes broader than those that are "charitable."[2] Thus, many American courts have held that a devise "to be used for such benevolent purposes as the trustees shall select" does not create a charitable trust. See, e.g., Estate of Kradwell, 170 N.W.2d 773 (Wis. 1969); Adye v. Smith, 44 Conn. 60 (1876). Contra, e.g., Goodale v. Mooney, 60 N.H. 528 (1881). For discussion, see Restatement 3d of Trusts §28 comment a; Scott and Ascher on Trusts §39.4.1 (5th ed. 2009).

Can you think of a "benevolent" use of property or income that would not come within the definition of "charity"? Of a "charitable" use that would not come within the definition of "benevolent"? Which of these questions is more important for our purposes? Do you think the distinction between "benevolent" and "charitable" is widely understood by the lay public? By the average lawyer?

Problems

1. G's will devised property in trust, directing her trustee to apply the income therefrom, in perpetuity:

---

2. A New York statute provides that "[n]o disposition of property for religious, charitable, educational or benevolent purposes... is invalid by reason of the indefiniteness or uncertainty of the persons designated as beneficiaries." N.Y. Est. Powers & Trust Law §8-1.1(a). Similar statutes appear in about ten other states. See, e.g., Mich. Comp. Laws §554.351. Statutory citations are listed in Scott and Ascher on Trusts §39.4.1 (5th ed. 2009).

(a) for such "charitable and benevolent purposes" as my trustee shall select.

(b) for such "charitable or benevolent purposes" as my trustee shall select.

(c) for such "charitable or benevolent purpose" as my trustee shall select.

Which version presents the strongest case for validity as a charitable trust? See Restatement 3d of Trusts §28 comment a.

2. Would the case for validity in the above cases be strengthened if G's trust had been an inter vivos trust and if, during G's lifetime, the trustee had administered the trust for purposes clearly "charitable"? Would it matter whether the inter vivos trust was revocable or irrevocable? In Hight v. United States, 256 F.2d 795 (2d Cir. 1958), the court held that the word "benevolent" has "no fixed meaning which is self-defining." Relying in part on extrinsic evidence concerning the type of institution the testator had selected during life for her benefactions, the court upheld as charitable a devise for "such charitable, benevolent, religious or educational institutions as my executors hereinafter named may determine."

3. G's will devised property in trust "to such philanthropic causes as my trustee may select." Is the trust charitable? See the following case.

Wilson v. Flowers
277 A.2d 199 (N.J. 1971)

PROCTOR, J. This is a will construction case. Plaintiffs, trustees under the will of Joseph L.K. Snyder, filed a complaint in the Chancery Division seeking instructions regarding the validity of Article Sixth (C)(12) of the testator's residuary trust of his will which directs them, inter alia, to contribute 20% of the residue "to such *philanthropic* causes as my Trustees may select" (emphasis added).

Defendants are the next-of-kin of the testator, and the Attorney General of New Jersey. The latter did not participate in the litigation.

After a hearing, Judge Mintz held that the plaintiffs had established the testator's probable intent that the gifts to "philanthropic causes" be solely charitable in nature. Thus, the gifts were not void and did not pass by intestate succession. Judgment directed 1) that the plaintiffs "shall contribute solely to charitable purposes the income to be disposed under Article Sixth (C)(12) of" the will, 2) that "the dispositions .. do not violate the rule against perpetuities," and 3) that plaintiffs-trustees "in making contributions to philanthropic causes pursuant to Article Sixth (C)(12) of said will are restricted solely to charities which qualify as charities under [the federal estate tax and the state inheritance tax]."

The primary issue on this appeal is whether the testator, in using the term "philanthropic causes," intended to limit his bounty to charitable causes or whether he intended the term to have a broader meaning. If the trust is not limited to charitable purposes, it is void either for uncertainty or for a violation of the rule against perpetuities. Defendants contend that the trust is void and that it should pass to them by intestate succession....

Defendants contend that the word "philanthropic" is broader than the word "charitable" both in terms of the testator's intent so far as that intent can be gleaned from the four corners of the will and in terms of its generally accepted meaning.

Turning to the second point first, we have been cited to no New Jersey case construing the word "philanthropic." However, there are many cases construing the word "benevolent" which defendants contend is more restrictive than "philanthropic." The cases follow the English rule that "benevolent" is broader than "charitable" and that a trust for such purposes is therefore void.

Defendants urge that since New Jersey courts follow the English cases that hold "benevolent" is broader than "charitable," they must, a fortiori, follow the English cases that hold that "philanthropic" is broader than 'charitable." We cannot accept this argument. It is no longer clear that "philanthropic" by legal connotation is broader than "charitable" in its legal connotation. Bogert has stated:

At the present time it would seem that the intent of a donor who leaves property to be distributed for "benevolent" or "philanthropic" purposes is in most cases charitable. If the duration of the trust is indefinite or perpetual a trust to show mere liberality will be void and in addition it will be subject to heavy tax burdens. Few trustors will desire these results. Common usage has made these words synonyms for charity....

The word "philanthropic" would seem, in its liberal sense, to include all acts of friendliness to mankind, whether conducive to improvement of society or merely to enrichment and enjoyment. In some English cases the word has been construed in this sense, and the result has been that a trust for "philanthropic purposes" has been held non-charitable because it would permit the trustee to perform acts of mere friendliness and generosity, having no connection with the need of the recipients of the benefits and no regard for the effect of the bounty upon the "beneficiaries." This is, however, perhaps a rather bookish meaning of the word. Probably in common use it is taken to mean charity, and some tendency to give it that effect is observable, especially where it is linked with the word "charitable" or with admittedly charitable objects. Bogert, Trusts & Trustees, §370, p. 69, 70 (2d ed. 1964).

There are a number of cases which have rejected the English cases and have treated "philanthropic" as synonymous with "charitable."....

But defendants contend that even if philanthropic and charitable have come to mean the same thing, the manner in which the word "philanthropic" is used in the present case indicates a contrary intent. Testator's will directs that 20% of the residue of the estate be given, in trust, "to such philanthropic causes as my Trustees may select, special consideration, however, to be given to charitable, educational and scientific fields." Defendants argue that the "special consideration" clause evidences an intent that charitable, educational and scientific uses must merely be some of the philanthropic uses to which the funds may be given. Thus, they contend "philanthropic" is broader than "charitable" as the testator used it.

It is our duty to follow what we find to be the testator's probable intention. The commonly accepted meaning of words and their context is a strong indication of intent, but that is not the end of the matter. There are frequently other manifestations of intent. In the present case, if we were to accept defendants' argument, we would be left with the conclusion that the testator intended to die intestate. Yet as we noted in Fidelity Union Trust Co. v. Robert, 36 N.J. 561, 572, 178 A.2d 185, 191 (1962), there is a strong presumption that testators do not intend to die intestate, particularly where, as here, the gift is made out of the residuary estate.... This presumption is reinforced by the testator's mandate that his trust be perpetual. A perpetual trust for noncharitable purposes would be void, and it is unlikely that the testator intended that result.

There is another factor which indicates the testator intended "philanthropic" to be synonymous with "charitable." The other parts of his will demonstrate an interest in charitable causes. In sections (C)(1) through (C)(11), the testator disposed of 80% of the residuary to eleven specific admittedly charitable causes. Only (C)(12), the remaining section of his residuary trust, is challenged here. An overall feeling of charity pervades section (C) and that the testator should link 11 specific charitable causes with the term "philanthropic causes" is an indication that he intended his entire residuary estate to be devoted to charitable causes. See Bogert, supra at §370, p. 69, 70.

Of course, these general indications of intent do not answer defendants' argument that the juxtaposition of the language employed shows the testator intended "philanthropic" to be broader than "charitable." But there is direct evidence which answers the argument.

[The Court considered testimony by the scrivener of the will that he had used the word "philanthropic" synonymously with "charitable," and two memoranda by the testator containing expressions of charitable purposes in the making of his will,]

[I]t is apparent that the trial court properly admitted the testators' memoranda and the scrivener's testimony regarding the testator's statements to him and the origin of the disputed word "philanthropic." While "philanthropic" may be technically broader than "charitable," we think that it has come to mean the same thing in modern usage. However, even if it has not, it is ambiguous enough to be construed as such. Most words are susceptible of more than one meaning.... Whether the use of a word which admits of more than one meaning is a patent ambiguity in the technical sense is not important; rather, the significant point is that there is an ambiguity at all. And in deciding whether there is an ambiguity, a court should always admit extrinsic evidence including direct statements of intent since experience teaches that language is so poor an instrument for communication or expression that ordinarily all such evidence must be examined before a court can be satisfied of whether an ambiguity exists. We do not, of course, mean to imply that such evidence can be used to vary the terms of the will, but rather that it should be admitted first to show if there is an ambiguity and second, if one exists, to shed light on the testator's actual intent.

In light of the above, it appears clear to us that the testator intended "philanthropic" to have the legal equivalence of "charitable." And if there were any doubt, well established rules of construction would lead us to lean in favor of a construction which upheld the gift as charitable....

The judgment of the Chancery Division is affirmed.

———

Mixed-Purposes Trusts; Separability. There is nothing unusual about trusts partly for private purposes and partly for charitable purposes. For tax reasons (see below), charitable remainder trusts and charitable lead trusts are staples in the modern estate planner's inventory. A charitable remainder trust provides for certain payments to a private beneficiary or beneficiaries for life, remainder in principal to a specified charity or for charitable purposes. A charitable lead trust provides for income to be paid to a specified charity or for charitable purposes for a period of years, remainder in principal to a private beneficiary or beneficiaries.

The fact that such "split-interest" trusts have both charitable and private beneficiaries does not cause them to fail. The charitable portion is separable and upheld. The private portion also is upheld if the private beneficiaries are definite and ascertainable, as they almost always are in such cases. A split-interest trust, however, might fail in part if the remainder interest violates the Rule Against Perpetuities. A charitable remainder preceded by non-charitable interests is not exempt from the Rule Against Perpetuities. But our discussion of that matter is deferred until Chapter 17.

Accumulation of Income. In the case of private trusts, accumulations of income beyond the perpetuity period are strictly forbidden. See Chapter 17. Charitable trusts fall under a different rule, a rule of reasonableness. See Restatement 2d of Property §2.2. The standard by which reasonableness is to be determined was explored in James' Estate, 199 A.2d 275 (Pa. 1964). Frank James died in 1960, devising the residue of his estate (amounting to around $40,000) in trust, with elaborate provisions directing that a portion of the income be accumulated for 400 years, at which time the principal and accumulated income was to be paid over absolutely for the use of the Masonic Homes at Elizabethtown, Pennsylvania. The court held the direction for accumulation to be invalid, saying:

> The will of Frank James supplies no indication of purpose for the 400 year accumulation provision, nor does it, either by express language or by implication, reveal any particular plan or need for retaining accumulations over such an extended period of time....
>
> No case has been cited to us, nor have we been able to locate any authority, which appears to recognize the validity of a proposed gift whose enjoyment is delayed for a period of four centuries without apparent reason.

We hold, therefore, that the provisions for accumulation of income are unreasonable and void as being unnecessary, charitably purposeless and contrary to public policy....

Under the *James' Estate* analysis, would the following trust be valid?

G devised $1 million in trust, to accumulate the income until the principal and accumulated income reach the amount of the national debt, at which time the fund is to be paid to the federal government to pay off the country's creditors.

See Girard Trust Co. v. Russell, 179 F. 446 (3d Cir. 1910). Compare Trusts of Holdeen, 403 A.2d 978 (Pa. 1979) (invalidating accumulation provisions in five inter vivos trusts of modest initial sums under which income was to be accumulated for periods ranging from 500 to 1,000 years, after which time the funds were to be paid to the Commonwealth of Pennsylvania), with Frazier v. Merchants Nat'l Bank, 5 N.E.2d 550 (Mass. 1936) (upholding a testamentary trust of about $117,000, under which the trustee was directed to accumulate the income until the principal and accumulated income reached $1,000,000, whereupon income was to be paid perpetually to the Salem Hospital). See also Estate of Orphanos v. Commissioner, 67 T.C. 780 (1977) (allowing a federal estate tax charitable deduction for a testamentary trust that directed the trustee to accumulate the income until it and the original property reached a "sufficient amount ... to erect a hospitol [*sic*] in Kerasitsa, Greece...."); cf. Matter of Booker, 682 P.2d 320 (Wash. Ct. App. 1984).

When a provision for accumulation is found invalid, as in *James' Estate,* how is the trust fund to be administered? On this point, Restatement 2d of Trusts §401 comment k, states that if the court decides that under all the circumstances the period of accumulation is unreasonably long, it will direct that the property "be applied to the designated charitable purpose either immediately or at a time to be fixed by the court, and, if necessary, will apply the doctrine of cy pres in order to carry out the settlor's general charitable intention." In *James' Estate,* the court noted that the testator "did not point to capital improvements or to any other needs of the charitable institution which ordinarily could not be met by drawing on current funds," and ordered the income to be distributed to the charitable institution currently. See generally Scott and Ascher on Trusts §39.7.9 (5th ed. 2009). On tax penalties imposed on private non-operating charitable foundations for accumulating income, see IRC §4942.

2. Specified Purposes

Whether or not any particular trust has a charitable purpose depends on "whether at the time when the question arises and in the state in which it arises the purpose is one that might reasonably be held to be of community or social interest." Restatement 3d of Trusts §28 comment *l*. The community is automatically interested in the enforcement of charitable trusts for the benefit of charity in general, for the benefit of the community at large, or for governmental purposes. When a trust is for the benefit of a specified segment of the community, however, the community-interest requirement is met only if the trust purposes relate to the relief of poverty, the advancement of education or of religion, or the promotion of health. Thus, comment a to Restatement 2d of Trusts §375 explicitly states that when a trust is for any of the latter purposes, "the class of persons who are to benefit directly by the performance of the trust need not be as large as it must be where the trust is simply for the general benefit of the class...."

Shenandoah Valley National Bank v. Taylor
63 S.E.2d 786 (Va. 1951)

MILLER, J. Charles B. Henry, a resident of Winchester, Virginia, died testate on the 23rd day of April, 1949. His will dated April 21, 1949, was duly admitted to probate and the Shenandoah Valley National Bank of Winchester, the designated executor and trustee, qualified thereunder. Subject to two inconsequential provisions not material to this litigation, the testator's entire estate valued at $86,000, was left as follows:

> Second: All the rest, residue and remainder of my estate, real, personal, intangible and mixed, of whatsoever kind and wherever situate,... I give, bequeath and devise to the S henandoah Valley National Bank of Winchester, Virginia, in trust, to be known as the "Charles B. Henry and Fannie Belle Henry Fund", for the following uses and purposes:
>
> (a) My Trustee shall invest and reinvest my trust estate, shall collect the income therefrom and shall pay the net income as follows:
>
> (1) On the last school day of each calendar year before Easter my Trustee shall divide the net income into as many equal parts as there are children in the first, second and third grades of the John Kerr School of the City of Winchester, and shall pay one of such equal parts to each child in such grades, to be used by such child in the furtherance of his or her obtainment of an education.
>
> (2) On the last school day of each calendar year before Christmas my trustee shall divide the net income into as many equal parts as there are children in the first, second and third grades of the John Kerr School of the City of Winchester, and shall pay one of such equal parts to each child in such grades, to be used by such child in the furtherance of his or her obtainment of an education.

By paragraphs (3) and (4) it is provided that the names of the children in the three grades shall be determined each year from the school records, and payment of the income to them "shall be as nearly equal in amounts as it is practicable" to arrange. Paragraph (5) provides that if the John Kerr School is ever discontinued for any reason the payments shall be made to the children of the same grades of the school or schools that take its place, and the School Board of Winchester is to determine what school or schools are substituted for it....

The John Kerr School is a public school used by the local school board for primary grades and had an enrollment of 458 boys and girls so there will be that number of pupils or thereabouts who would share in the distribution of the income.

The testator left no children or near relatives. Those who would be his heirs and distributees in case of intestacy were first cousins and others more remotely related. One of these next of kin filed a suit against the executor and trustee, and others challenging the validity of the provisions of the will which undertook to create a charitable trust....

The sole question presented is: does the will create a valid charitable trust?

Construction of the challenged provisions is required and in this undertaking the testator's intent as disclosed by the words used in the will must be ascertained. If his dominant intent as expressed was charitable, the trust should be accorded efficacy and sustained. But on the other hand, if the testator's intent as expressed is merely benevolent, though the disposition of his property be meritorious and evince traits of generosity, the trust must nevertheless be declared invalid because it violates the rule against perpetuities....

Authoritative definitions of charitable trusts may be found in 4 Pomeroy's Equity Jurisprudence, 5th Ed., sec. 1020, and Restatement of the Law of Trusts, sec. 368, p. 1140. The latter gives a comprehensive classification definition. It is:

> Charitable purposes include:
> (a) the relief of poverty;
> (b) the advancement of education;
> (c) the advancement of religion;
> (d) the promotion of health;
> (e) governmental or municipal purposes; and
> (f) other purposes the accomplishment of which is beneficial to the community....

We now turn to the language of the will for from its context the testator's intent is to be derived.... In mandatory language the duty and the duty alone to make cash payments to each individual child just before Easter and Christmas is enjoined upon the trustee by the certain and explicit words that it "shall divide the net income ... and shall pay one of such equal shares to each child in such grades."

Without more, that language and the occasions specified for payment of the funds to the children being when their minds and interests would be far removed from studies or other school activities definitely indicate that no educational purpose was in the testator's mind. It is manifest that there was no intent or belief that the funds would be put to any use other than such as youthful impulse and desire might dictate. But in each instance immediately following the above-quoted language the sentence concludes with the words or phrase "to be used by such child in the furtherance of his or her obtainment of an education." It is significant that by this latter phrase the trustee is given no power, control or discretion over the funds so received by the child. Full and complete execution of the mandate and trust imposed upon the trustee accomplishes no educational purpose. Nothing toward the advancement of education is attained by the ultimate performance by the trustee of its full duty. It merely places the income irretrievably and forever beyond the range of the trust....

In our opinion, the words of the will import an intent to have the trustee pay to each child his allotted share. If that be true,—and it is directed to be done in no uncertain language—we know that the admonition to the children would be wholly impotent and of no avail....

If it be determined that the will fails to create a charitable trust for *educational purposes* (and our conclusion is that it is inoperative to create such a trust), it is earnestly insisted that the trust provided for is nevertheless charitable and valid. In this respect it is claimed that the two yearly payments to be made to the children just before Christmas and Easter produce "a desirable social effect" and are "promotive of public convenience and needs, and happiness and contentment" and thus the fund set up in the will constitutes a charitable trust. 2 Bogert on Trusts, sec. 361, p. 1090, and 3 Scott on Trusts, sec. 368, p. 1972....

Numerous cases that deal with and construe specific provisions of wills or other instruments are cited by appellant to uphold the contention that the provisions of this will, without reference to and deleting the phrase "to be used by such child in the furtherance of his or her obtainment of an education" meet the requirements of a charitable trust.... Upon examination of these decisions, it will be found that where a gift results in mere financial enrichment, a trust was sustained only when the court found and concluded from the entire context of the will that the ultimate intended recipients were poor or in necessitous circumstances.

A trust from which the income is to be paid at stated intervals to each member of a designated segment of the public, without regard to whether or not the recipients are poor or in need, is not for the relief of poverty, nor is it a social benefit to the community. It is a mere benevolence—a private trust—and may not be upheld as a charitable trust.... Payment to the children of their cash bequests on the two occasions specified would bring to them pleasure and happiness and no doubt cause them to remember or think of their benefactor with gratitude and thanksgiving. That was, we think, Charles B. Henry's intent. Laudable, generous and praiseworthy though it may be, it is not for the relief of the poor or needy, nor does it otherwise so benefit or advance the social interest of the community as to justify its continuance in perpetuity as a charitable trust....

No error is found in the decrees appealed from and they are affirmed.

Notes, Questions, and Problems

1. *Duration of Trusts for Noncharitable Purposes.* Under the court's construction, the trust in *Taylor* was a so-called honorary trust, that is, a non-charitable specific purpose trust. The Uniform Trust Code and the Uniform Probate Code provide that

the duration of an honorary trust is limited to 21 years. See UTC §409; UPC §2-907.[3]

2. *Scholarships and Awards.* The fact that only one or a small number of persons are to receive the benefits of a trust does not disqualify it from being a valid charitable trust, as long as the class of persons from whom the recipients are to be selected is sufficiently large. Thus, trusts awarding scholarships or awards are generally held to be charitable, even though there may be only one recipient. See, e.g., Estate of Carlson, 358 P.2d 669 (Kan. 1961) (upholding a devise in trust to the city of Sylvia, Kansas, to provide funds for the medical education of a young man from Sylvia Township, "upon his promise that he will return to the City of Sylvia, and remain there for the purpose of practicing his profession"); but see, e.g., Estate of Huebner, 15 P.2d 758 (Cal. Ct. App. 1932) (testamentary trust providing that the income be used "to help defray the expense of some girl or boy in music or art" held not to be charitable). See generally Scott and Ascher on Trusts §38.9.1 (5th ed. 2009).

Trusts to provide education for one's own relatives are non-charitable, but courts have sustained trusts to provide scholarships for needy students in which the settlor expresses a preference for his or her relatives. See, e.g., Estate of Sells v. Commissioner, 10 T.C. 692 (1948) (trust "to provide scholarship first to relatives or other boys or girls" qualified for the federal estate tax charitable deduction); but see, e.g., Griffen v. United States, 400 F.2d 612 (6th Cir. 1968) (trust stated that income was "to be used for the education of my grandchildren and for the education of deserving boys and girls... to obtain [a] college education in a Protestant Christian College.... It is my intention and desire to make my grandchildren the primary beneficiaries of this trust, and if at any time any grandchild of mine desires to avail himself or herself of the benefits of this trust, he or she shall be entitled to such benefits [not to exceed $750.00 in any one school year] even to the exclusion of all other persons." A state court held that the trust was charitable, but a federal court held that it did not qualify for the estate tax charitable deduction.). On qualification as a charitable trust under state law, see Restatement 3d of Trusts §28, Reporter's Note on comment h.

3. *Changing Law/Political Purposes/Illegal Purposes.* The Restatement 3d of Trusts §28 comment *l* states that

> [a] trust may be charitable although the accomplishment of the purpose for which the trust is created involves a change in existing law.... [A] trust to improve the structure and methods of government is charitable....

---

3. Section 2-907 is an optional provision, but its enactment is recommended in conjunction with the rest of the Uniform Probate Code.

The same comment provides, however, that trusts to promote the success of particular political parties are not charitable. Finally, concerning trusts for unpopular causes, comment a(2) states that "[i]f the general purposes for which a trust is created are such that they may be reasonably thought to promote the social interest of the community, the mere fact that a majority of the people or of the members of a court believe that the particular purpose of the settlor is unwise or not well adapted to its social objective does not prevent the trust from being charitable." Of course, trusts that induce or tend to induce the commission of a crime are invalid. See Restatement 3d of Trusts §28 comment *l*.

The distinctions reflected in the Restatement, while generally followed in the cases, make for many close questions. To start with a straightforward example, however, it should be clear that a trust to support the Socialist Party (or the Democratic Party, the Republican Party, or the Libertarian Party) and its candidates is not charitable. But what about a trust providing for payments "to persons, entities and causes advancing the principles of socialism and those causes related to socialism"? See Estate of Breeden, 208 Cal. App. 3d 981, 256 Cal. Rptr. 813 (1989). Or, a trust "to provide a place where the doctrines of socialism could be taught by example as well as by precept"? See Peth v. Spear, 115 P. 164 (Wash. 1911). In George v. Braddock, 18 A. 881 (N.J. 1889), the court held that a valid charitable trust had been created where the testator devised property in trust for the purpose of "'spreading the light' on social and political liberty and justice in these United States" by way of distributing the publications of Henry George, whose teachings included the doctrine "that no private, absolute ownership in land can rightfully exist." Is such a trust deductible for federal estate tax purposes? Leubuscher v. Commissioner, 54 F.2d 998 (2d Cir. 1932), held that it was.

What about a trust to provide for support and education "of such minor [Black] child or children, whose father or mother, or both, have been... imprisoned... as a result of the conviction of a crime or misdemeanor of a political nature"? The will gave examples of the types of crimes the testator had in mind, such as contempt convictions in connection with appearances before the House Un-American Activities Committee. See Estate of Robbins, 57 Cal.2d 718, 21 Cal. Rptr. 797, 371 P.2d 573 (1962).

What about a trust to oppose candidates for public office who favor decriminalization of the use of marijuana? Cf. People *ex rel.* Hartigan v. National Anti-Drug Coalition, 464 N.E.2d 690 (Ill. App. Ct. 1984).

4. *Influencing Legislation/Political Campaigns/Tax Aspects*. Having a purpose to influence legislation or to support or oppose candidates for public office may jeopardize the tax-exempt status of a charitable organization and jeopardize the deductibility of contributions thereto. Under IRC §501(c)(3), tax-exempt status is denied to certain charitable organizations if attempting to influence legislation

constitutes a "substantial part of the [organization's] activities"[4] or if the organization participates in or intervenes in "any political campaign on behalf of (or in opposition to) any candidate for public office."

Gifts and devises to an organization or a trust are deductible for income, estate, and gift tax purposes only if the recipient "is not disqualified for tax exemption under IRC §501(c)(3) by reason of attempting to influence legislation, and... does not participate in, or intervene in (including the publishing or distributing of statements), any political campaign on behalf of (or in opposition to) any candidate for public office." IRC §§170(c)(2)(D), 2055(a)(2), (a)(3), 2522(a)(2).

Does a bar association that rates candidates for both appointive and elective judgeships at the municipal, state, and federal level as either "approved," "not approved," or "approved as highly qualified" and that communicates its ratings to the public in the form of press releases and publishes them in a regular publication of the association that is sent out to the association's members and approximately 120 other subscribers, including libraries and law schools, qualify for tax-exempt status under IRC §501(c)(3)? Does it matter that the association evaluates judicial candidates on a nonpartisan basis? That the rating of judicial candidates is not a substantial part of its activities? See Association of the Bar of the City of New York v. Commissioner, 858 F.2d 876 (2d Cir. 1988).

5. *Unpopular Purposes.* According to Professor Scott, "a trust is not a valid charitable trust if [it is for the dissemination of beliefs or doctrines that] are so irrational that it cannot be said that their dissemination can be of any benefit to the community." Scott on Trusts §370.4 (3d ed. 1967). In addition, a trust for the accomplishment of a purpose that is against public policy is one for an illegal purpose and invalid. Restatement 3d of Trusts §29. On the other hand, a trust is not invalid merely because the beliefs or doctrines to be disseminated are unpopular or accepted by a minority of the population.

How does a court go about applying the distinction between views that are merely unpopular and those that are so irrational or absurd that their dissemination is of no benefit to the community whatsoever? Some cases are not so difficult. Trusts for the

---

4. IRC §501(h) permits certain organizations to elect to replace the "substantial part of the activities" test of IRC §501(c)(3) with limits defined in terms of expenditures for influencing legislation. Under IRC §4911, the basic permitted level of such expenditures (the "lobbying nontaxable amount") for a year is 20% of the first $500,000 of the organization's exempt purpose expenditures for the year, plus 15% of the second $500,000, plus 10% of the third $500,000, plus 5% of any additional expenditures. In no event, however, can this permitted level exceed $1,000,000 for any one year. Within these limits, a separate limitation is placed on "grass roots lobbying" (attempting to influence the general public on legislative matters); the "grass roots nontaxable amount" is one fourth of the "lobbying nontaxable amount." An electing organization that exceeds either the "lobbying nontaxable amount" or the "grass roots nontaxable amount" in a taxable year is subject to an excise tax but does not necessarily lose its tax-exempt status. Loss of tax-exempt status occurs only if the organization "normally" makes expenditures of 150% of either limitation. See IRC §501(h).

promotion of agnosticism have been held to create valid charitable trusts. See Estate of Connolly, 48 Cal. App. 3d 129, 121 Cal. Rptr. 325 (1975) (promotion of agnosticism serves an educational purpose; court did "not imply that the viewpoint of agnosticism is correct or incorrect," but noted that "[t]he sense of today is all too frequently the nonsense of tomorrow"). Trusts for the promotion of atheism have also been upheld as serving an educational function. See Scott and Ascher on Trusts §38.11 (5th ed. 2009). A trust for the promotion of racism certainly would not be upheld.

In Estate of Kidd, 479 P.2d 697 (Ariz. 1971), James Kidd's holographic will devised his entire estate, amounting to $175,000, "to go in a reserach [sic] or some scientific proof of a soul of the human body which leaves at death. I think in time their [sic] can be a Photograph of soul leaving the human at death." The court held that a charitable trust had been created, and that where as here only a charitable purpose is stated, "the court will either appoint a trustee to carry out the purpose or will approve a scheme to carry it out," citing Restatement 2d of Trusts §397 comment e. The devise was claimed by 102 claimants and the trial court awarded the funds to the Barrow Neurological Institute. On appeal by six other claimants, the award was rejected on the ground that the Institute was not engaged in any research of the kind sought by the testator. The court directed the trial court to select from among two persons and two organizations which of them "is most suitable to carry out the trust expressed in Kidd's will." Since the court was concerned only about who was qualified to carry on the research specified, the decision seems to require, not that a trustee would be appointed to administer the fund, but that the fund would be given directly to a qualified claimant who would be obligated to use it for the specified purpose. On remand, the trial court awarded the fund to the American Society for Psychical Research, which some several years later reported that it had spent the money without having succeeded in photographing the human soul.

EXTERNAL REFERENCE. Mary Kay Lundwall, Inconsistency and Uncertainty in the Charitable Purposes Doctrine, 41 Wayne L. Rev. 1341 (1995).

PART B. THE CY PRES DOCTRINE

Primary Statutory Reference: *UTC §413*

1. General Principles

The cy pres doctrine, unique to charitable trusts, is described in the Restatement 3d of Trusts §67 in this way:

> *§67. Failure of Designated Charitable Purpose: The Doctrine of Cy Pres.* Unless the terms of the trust provide otherwise, where property is placed in trust to be applied to a designated charitable purpose and it is or becomes unlawful, impossible or impracticable to carry out that purpose, or to the extent it is or becomes wasteful to apply all of the

property to the designated purpose, the charitable trust will not fail but the court will direct application of the property or appropriate portion thereof to a charitable purpose that reasonably approximates the designated purpose.

See also Restatement of Charitable Nonprofit Organizations §3.02; UTC §413(a).

This description departs from the traditional description of the cy pres doctrine in two important respects. First, these Restatements and the UTC add the term "wasteful" to the list of circumstances under which a charitable trust may be judicially modified. The traditional statement of the doctrine, expressed in the Restatement 2d of Trusts §399, describes the doctrine as applying when it becomes "impossible or impracticable or illegal to carry out [the trust's] particular purpose...." What, if any, difference does the addition of "wasteful" make? Consider this question in connection with the Estate of Buck case below.

Second, these Restatements and the UTC, unlike the traditional law of the Restatement 2d, *presume* a settlor's general charitable intent, which is a precondition for application of the cy pres doctrine.[5] The traditional law, expressed in the Restatement 2d of Trusts, did not make that presumption. Instead, courts had to find that "the settlor manifested a more general intention to devote the property to charitable purposes...." Restatement 2d of Trusts §399. The newer Restatements and the UTC, however, presume the settlor's general charitable intent, thereby enabling courts to apply cy pres without making such a finding.

However, note that there is a subtle but important difference between the Restatement 3d of Trusts, on the one hand, and the Restatement of Charitable Nonprofit Organizations and the UTC, on the other hand. The Restatement 3d of Trusts presumes a settlor's general charitable intent, but the presumption is rebuttable. See id., §67 comment b. In contrast, the Restatement of Charitable Nonprofit Organizations and the UTC make the presumption irrebuttable. Put differently, they simply eliminate the requirement of general charitable intent. In the words of the Comment to UTC §405(a):

> Subsection (a) modifies the doctrine of cy pres by eliminating the traditional requirement that a plaintiff seeking cy pres must show that the settlor had a general charitable intent when a particular charitable purpose becomes impossible or impracticable to achieve. Traditional law required that showing, which meat that courts were placed in the position of having to determine whether the settlor had a general charitable intent. If such an intent was found, the court could apply cy pres and authorize the use of the trust property for other charitable purposes. If such an intent was not found, the charitable trust failed....

---

5. UTC §413(b) also departs from traditional law by providing that an express gift over to a noncharitable beneficiary prevails over the power of the court to apply cy pres only if it would cause the trust property to revert to a living settlor or if fewer than 21 years have elapsed since the date of the trust's creation.

For a critique of UTC §413's presumption of general charitable intent, see Alberto B. Lopez, A Revaluation of Cy Pres Redux, 78 U. Cin. L. Rev. 1307 (2010).

Subsection (a) eliminates the requirement that a court find a general charitable intent because in the great majority of cases the settlor would prefer that the property be used for other charitable purposes, and courts almost invariably find that the settlor had a general charitable intent.... The Restatement of Charitable Nonprofit Organizations §3.02 embraces the approach of subsection (a) and does not require a court to find, in order to apply cy pres, that the settlor had a general charitable intent.

See also Restatement of Charitable Nonprofit Organizations §3.02.

Under the traditional law, without a presumption of a general charitable intent, how is a general charitable intent to be found in a given case? What is the court to look for? On these questions, consider the following excerpt from Howard Savings Institution v. Peep, 170 A.2d 39 (N.J. 1961):

> First, the term "general charitable intent" ordinarily used by courts articulating the [cy pres] doctrine does not require an intention to benefit charity generally. It requires only a charitable purpose which is broader than the particular purpose the effectuation of which is impossible, impracticable or illegal.... Second, the inquiry "did the settlor manifest a general charitable intent" is just another way of asking "would he have wanted the trust funds devoted to a like charitable purpose, or would he have wanted them withdrawn from charitable channels."... So stated, it can be seen that *cy pres* is an intent-enforcing doctrine. But it is well to keep in mind that it is a surmise rather than an actual intent which the courts enforce through application of the doctrine. Rarely does a settlor contemplate the possible nonfulfillment of his precise purpose. Therefore, the court must make an educated guess based on the trust instrument and relevant extrinsic evidence as to what he would have intended had he been aware of the contingency which has frustrated the exact effectuation of his expressed intent.

On occasion, the terms of the trust make it appear that the settlor *has* contemplated the failure of the trust's purposes. A specific provision that the trust should terminate in the event of a failure of its purpose is given effect. Cy pres is usually then denied, for the provision in the event of termination tends to negate the idea that the settlor had a more general charitable intent. Restatement 3d of Trusts §67 comment b.

Preliminary to the general-charitable-intent inquiry, of course, is a finding, under the traditional standard, that the trust's articulated purpose is or has become impossible, impracticable, or illegal. Failing this finding, cy pres will be denied regardless of a broader charitable intent. In thinking about how the court should go about deciding whether the trust has become impracticable, consider the next case, which attracted considerable attention in California and elsewhere.

Estate of Buck

Superior Court of Marin County, California, 1986
[Opinion reprinted from 21 U.S.F. L. Rev. 691 (1987)]

[In 1975, Beryl Buck, a resident of Marin County, California,[6] died a childless widow. Her will devised the residue of her estate to the San Francisco Foundation, a community trust administering charitable funds throughout the five-county San Francisco Bay Area. This devise became known as the "Buck Trust." The will directed that the residue

> shall always be held and used for exclusively non-profit charitable, religious or educational purposes in providing care for the needy in Marin County, California, and for other non-profit charitable, religious, or educational purposes in that county.

Ms. Buck's residuary estate consisted primarily of a block of shares in Belridge Oil Company stock. Belridge, which Buck's father-in-law had founded, was a privately-held company with substantial oil reserves in Southern California. The value of Ms. Buck's interest in the Belridge stock at the time she executed her will was $7 million, and it had not changed significantly by the time she died in 1975. In 1979, however, the value of the Belridge stock in the Buck Trust had shot up to $260 million as a result of a bidding war when Shell Oil bought Belridge. By 1984, when the trial began, the value of the stock had increased to over $400 million, and the trust was generating an annual income of $30 million.

In 1984, the Foundation, having concluded that it was "impractical and inexpedient to continue to expend all of the income from the Buck Trust solely within Marin County," sought judicial authorization to spend some portion of Buck Trust income in the other four counties of the Bay Area. Its petition for cy-pres rested upon the theory that the dramatic increase in the trust fund's value was a posthumous "surprise," a change in circumstances raising doubt whether Ms. Buck, had she anticipated its occurrence, would have limited the scope of her charitable objective to Marin County. The Foundation relied on the proposed testimony of Yale law professor John Simon. Professor Simon contended that charitable behavior by "major American philanthropists" is characterized by breadth of purpose, a desire to serve "a community that is broadly defined in terms of population size and socioeconomic class." His theory was that Ms. Buck should be viewed as a major American philanthropist and in the absence of any evidence explaining her departure from this "philanthropic standard," it is reasonable to assume that she would have wanted some of her money spent elsewhere in the Bay Area.[7] The trial court ruled

---

6. Marin County is located north of San Francisco, immediately across the Golden Gate Bridge. It has one of the highest per-capita incomes in the country. Known for its trend-setting ways, it is sometimes called the "hot tub capital of the world."

7. Professor Simon's theory is set out in John G. Simon, American Philanthropy and the Buck Trust, 21 U.S.F. L. Rev. 641 (1987).

that Simon's proposed testimony was inadmissible as evidence of the testator's intent.

Near the close of the respondent's case, the Foundation, strongly criticized by the Marin County authorities, the press, and the state Attorney General, offered to resign as trustee. All the parties except the Objector-Beneficiaries agreed to a settlement, with the trust to be administered by a new Marin-based community foundation. The Objector-Beneficiaries, forty-six individuals and charitable organizations in the other four Bay Area counties, refused to join in the settlement on the ground that it was a "sell-out" of the needy in the Bay Area. On July 31, 1986, the Foundation was permitted to resign, and the court dismissed its cy-pres petition. On August 15, 1986, the trial court issued a judgment against the Objector-Beneficiaries.][8]

THOMPSON, J....

A. *CY PRES* APPLIES ONLY WHERE THE PURPOSE OF A TRUST HAS BECOME ILLEGAL, IMPOSSIBLE OR PERMANENTLY IMPRACTICABLE OF PERFORMANCE.

...The Restatement (Second) of Trusts, section 399 at 297, describes the cy pres doctrine as follows:

> If property is given in trust to be applied to a particular charitable purpose and *it is or becomes impossible or impracticable or illegal to carry out the particular purpose,* and if the settlor manifested a more general intention to devote the property to charitable purposes, the trust will not fail but the court will direct the application of the property to some charitable purpose which falls within the general charitable intention of the settlor. (Emphasis added)....

In practice, cy pres has most often been applied in California in such cases—where the charitable trust purpose is or has become literally impossible to fulfill (it "cannot be accomplished")—or in cases where it has become "reasonably impossible of performance."

B. NEITHER INEFFICIENCY NOR INEFFECTIVE PHILANTHROPY CONSTITUTES IMPRACTICABILITY....

The Restatement (Second) of Trusts, (1959) section 399 comment q at 306, does not require a literal impossibility. Rather, it defines "impracticability" as follows:

> The doctrine of cy pres is applicable even though it is possible to carry out the particular purpose of the settlor, if to carry it out would *fail to accomplish the general charitable intention* of the settlor. In such case it is "impracticable" to carry out the particular purpose.... (Emphasis added).

Ineffective philanthropy, inefficiency and relative inefficiency, that is, inefficiency of trust expenditures in one location given greater relative needs or

---

8. This statement of facts is based on Ronald Hayes Malone et al., The Buck Trust Trial—A Litigator's Perspective, 21 U.S.F. L. Rev. 585 (1987).

benefits elsewhere, do not constitute impracticability.... Such situation is not the equivalent of impossibility; nor is there any threat that the operation of the trust will fail to fulfill the general charitable intention of the settlor....[9]

[P]olicy considerations fully justify the dominant tendency of courts to require a situation of illegality, impossibility or strict impracticability before they will vary the terms of a charitable trust through an application of cy pres.

The present and well-tested law that cy pres will be invoked to save a charitable bequest that has become impossible or impracticable of fulfillment where the testator has a general charitable intent provides an intermediate concept "between the well established rules of construction that a will is to be construed so as to effectuate the intent of the testator, and that a gift to charity should be effectuated whenever possible." Estate of Klinkner, 85 Cal.App.3d 942, 951 [(1978)]. Where both the testator's intent and the charitable gift can, in fact, be effectuated, i.e., the specified trust purpose has not become impossible or impracticable of performance, there is no justification for cy pres.

The cy pres doctrine should not be so distorted by the adoption of subjective, relative, and nebulous standards such as "inefficiency" or "ineffective philanthropy" to the extent that it becomes a facile vehicle for charitable trustees to vary the terms of a trust simply because they believe that they can spend the trust income better or more wisely elsewhere, or as in this case, prefer to do so. There is no basis in law for the application of standards such as "efficiency" or "effectiveness" to modify a trust, nor is there any authority that would elevate these standards to the level of impracticability.

---

9. To the extent that concepts of effective philanthropy or efficiency relate to achieving the greatest benefit for the cost incurred they should not form the basis for modifying a donor's wishes. No law requires a testator to make a gift which the trustees deem efficient or to constitute effective philanthropy. Moreover, calculating "benefit" involves inherently subjective determinations; thus, what is "effective" or "efficient" will vary, depending on the interests and concerns of the person or persons making the determination. Cy pres does not authorize a court to vary the terms of a bequest merely because the variation will accommodate the desire of the trustee.

To the extent that the term efficiency embraces the concept of relative need, it is not an appropriate basis for modifying the terms of a testamentary trust. (The Foundation itself has acknowledged this, and indicated that such a concept "is neither what Mrs. Buck's will contemplates, nor a term which has an readily ascertainable meaning." (San Francisco Foundation's Statement Regarding Attorney General's Supplemental Response to Second Annual Report, judicially noticed on February 6, 1986.)) If it were otherwise, all charitable gifts, and the fundamental basis of philanthropy would be threatened, as there may always be more compelling "needs" to fill than the gift chosen by the testator. Gifts to Harvard or Stanford University, for example, could fail simply because institutions elsewhere are more needy. Similarly, needs in the Bay Area cannot be equated with the grueling poverty of India or the soul-wrenching famine in Ethiopia. Moreover, a standard of relative need would interpose governmental regulation on philanthropy because courts would be required to consider questions of comparable equity, social utility, or benefit, perhaps even wisdom, and ultimately substitute their judgments or those of the trustees for those of the donors.

C. CY PRES MAY NOT BE INVOKED UPON THE BELIEF THAT THE MODIFIED SCHEME WOULD BE MORE DESIRABLE OR WOULD CONSTITUTE A BETTER USE OF THE INCOME. Where the income of a charitable trust can be used for the purpose specified by the testator, cy pres may not be invoked on the grounds that a different use of the income would be more useful or desirable....

Courts have also held that terms of a charitable trust may not be modified on the grounds that a different use would be more beneficial to the community or advantageous to the charity....

Thus, cy pres may not be invoked on the grounds that it would be more "fair," "equitable" or "efficient" to spend the Trust funds in a manner different from that specified by the testator.

D. CY PRES DOES NOT AUTHORIZE THE COURT TO VARY THE TERMS OF A TRUST MERELY BECAUSE THE VARIATION WILL MEET THE DESIRE AND SUIT THE CONVENIENCE OF THE TRUSTEE. Nor is cy pres warranted to alleviate the strain or burden a trust has placed on a trustee organization and as stated by Martin Paley [Director of the San Francisco Foundation], to "modify the nature of the Buck Trust to conform to and become compatible with the values and procedures of the Foundation as a whole."

> [T]he cy pres doctrine does not authorize or permit a court to vary the terms of a bequest and to that extent defeat the intention of the testator merely because the *variation will meet the desire and suit the convenience of the trustee.* Connecticut College v. United States (1960) 276 F.2d 491, 497. (Emphasis added).

Rather, "[e]ither impossibility or impracticability of literal compliance with the donor's plan is indispensably necessary if cy pres is applied." Id....

The Foundation accepted the Buck Trust fully cognizant of the increased value of its assets and of the administrative burden such a large trust would impose on a relatively small community foundation. That, in fact, it has caused an administrative burden on the Foundation and is perceived to be a threat to the integrity of the Foundation as a whole does not warrant varying the terms of Mrs. Buck's bequest....

Cy Pres may not be applied to modify the terms of the Buck Trust....

Notes and Questions

1. *Aftermath.* The trial court's decision in *Buck* was not appealed. The trial court ordered the creation of the Marin Community Foundation to administer the Buck Trust. The court also appointed a special master to supervise the foundation. The court order required that the trustee expend twenty percent of the trust income annually on major projects located "in Marin County,... the benefits of which will inure not only to Marin County but all humankind." See Douglas J. Maloney, The Aftermath, 21 U.S.F. L. Rev. 681, 687 (1987). GuideStar reports that the Marin

Community Foundation had assets in excess of $963 million in 2022. See www.guidestar.org.

2. *"Waste" as a Basis for Cy Pres?* UTC §413, the Restatement 3d of Trusts §67, and the Restatement of Charitable Nonprofit Organizations §3.02 provide that a court may invoke cy pres when a charitable trust's specific purpose has become "wasteful." Would the circumstances in the Buck Trust dispute have met that standard? As you ponder the meaning of "waste," consider the following paragraph.

3. *Cy Pres as to Surplus Funds.* If the articulated purposes of the trust have not become impossible, impracticable, or illegal, but the income or principal exceeds that which is necessary for their accomplishment, the cy pres power may be applied as to the excess. In Thatcher v. City of St. Louis, 76 S.W.2d 677 (Mo. 1934), for example, a testamentary trust was established in 1851 by Judge Bryan Mullanphy, when St. Louis was the gateway to the West, for the articulated purpose of furnishing "relief to all poor immigrants and travelers coming to St. Louis on their way, bona fide, to settle in the West." Over time, other westward routes were opened up, and other historical events intervened to make St. Louis no longer the bottleneck for westward travel. Consequently, the trust's income became more than sufficient for the trust's articulated purposes. The court found that Judge Mullanphy's primary intent "was to alleviate a local condition in his home city of St. Louis, which grew out of the mass movement of a great population into the new western lands," rather than "to build up the West by aiding in its settlement." On the strength of this finding, the court applied its cy pres power as to the excess income, directing that it be applied to "furnishing relief to poor immigrants and travelers generally in the City of St. Louis in need and distress, and found to be worthy of assistance." This result accords with Restatement 3d of Trusts §67 comment c(1), which states in pertinent part: "Another type of case appropriate to the application of cy pres... is a situation in which the amount of property held in the trust exceeds what is needed for the particular charitable purpose to such an extent that the continued expenditure of all the funds for that purpose, although possible to do, would be wasteful." As the Restatement explains, "[t]he term 'wasteful' is used here neither in the sense of common-law waste nor to suggest that a lesser standard of merely 'better use' will suffice." Id. See also Restatement of Charitable Nonprofit Organizations §3.02 comment d.

4. *Devises to Non-Existent Charities.* There has been a fair amount of litigation involving devises to charitable institutions that existed when the will was drafted but ceased to exist at the time of the testator's death. The first question facing courts in these cases is whether the devise lapses. In In re Estate of Lind, 734 N.E.2d 47 (Ill. App. 2000), the court held that a devise to "Northwestern University Dental School" did not lapse where, although a dental school existed at the time of execution, it was thereafter abolished. The court concluded that the devise should go to the university for the benefit of the dental school, thereby making it subject to cy pres. Contra,

Crisp Area YMCA v. Nationsbank, 526 S.E.2d 63 (Ga. 2000) (cy pres held not to apply).

5. *Cy Pres Under UPMIFA*. In 2006, the Uniform Law Commission promulgated a revised version of the Uniform Management of Institutional Funds Act (UMIFA), now called the Uniform Prudent Management of Institutional Funds Act (UPMIFA). These acts govern the management of funds held by charitable institutions, such as universities. UPMIFA has been enacted in every state except Pennsylvania. Section 6(c) of UPMIFA tracks the cy pres standard of the UTC:

> If a particular charitable purpose or a restriction contained in a gift instrument on the use of an institutional fund becomes unlawful, impracticable, impossible to achieve, or wasteful, the court, upon application of an institution, may modify the purpose of the fund or the restriction on the use of the fund in a manner consistent with the charitable purposes expressed in the gift instrument.

6. *Gift Over as Blocking Cy Pres Modification?* A familiar rule of charitable trust law is that upon failure of the initial charitable gift, the existence of a gift over precludes cy pres because the gift over shows a specific alternative intent inconsistent with the application of cy pres. In some instances, however, courts have applied cy pres despite the presence of a gift over. See Restatement of Charitable Nonprofit Organizations §3.02 comment f. See also Ronald Chester, Cy Pres or Gift Over?: The Search for Coherence in Judicial Reform of Failed Charitable Trusts, 23 Suffolk U. L. Rev. 41 (1989). Consider the following case.

Home for Incurables of Baltimore City v. University of Maryland Medical System Corp.
797 A.2d 746 (Md. 2002)

ELDRIDGE, J. ...Dr. Coggins died on January 21, 1963. In his last will, dated December 27, 1962, after making a bequest of tangible personal property and a number of other bequests, Dr. Coggins gave the residue of his estate to the Mercantile Safe Deposit & Trust Company ("Mercantile") to be held by it as Trustee under "ITEM 5" of the will. The trust provided for monthly payments to four income beneficiaries until the death of the last of them. The last of these annuitants was Dr. Coggins's widow who died on September 10, 1998.

Paragraph (f) of ITEM 5 of the will stated that, upon the death of the survivor of the four annuitants,

> the trust shall terminate and the assets thereof as then constituted together with all unpaid income shall be paid over free of trust unto the KESWICK HOME, formerly Home for Incurables of Baltimore City, with the request that said Home use the estate and property thus passing to it for the acquisition or construction of a new building to provide additional housing accommodations to be known as the "Coggins Building," to house white patients who need physical rehabilitation. If not acceptable to the Keswick Home, then this bequest shall go to the University of Maryland Hospital to be used for physical rehabilitation....

The issues raised and the arguments made by the parties in this Court are basically the same as those advanced in the Circuit Court. We find it unnecessary, however, to address every argument made by the parties. Instead, we shall assume, *arguendo,* that Dr. Coggins intended the racial restriction to be a condition for Keswick to have the bequest, that Keswick's inability to comply with the illegal condition means that Keswick has not "accepted" the gift within the meaning of the will, and that judicial enforcement of the racially discriminatory condition, by awarding the proceeds to University Hospital, will not violate the United States Constitution, federal statutes, or the Maryland Constitution. Nonetheless, we shall hold that, under our cases dealing with illegal conditions in wills as well as the *cy pres* doctrine, the bequest should be awarded to Keswick.

This Court has long held that where a bequest is conditioned upon the commission of an illegal act or an act which is legally impossible of fulfillment, the condition is invalid on the ground of public policy. Under these circumstances, the condition will not be enforced by awarding the bequest to an alternative beneficiary; instead, the illegal condition will be excised....

There are a few cases elsewhere which do support University Hospital's position regarding *cy pres* statutes. They hold that, where there is an illegal discriminatory condition attached to a charitable bequest, and a reversionary clause or provision for a gift over if the condition is not complied with, there is no general charitable intention and the *cy pres* doctrine does not permit a court to save the primary bequest by excising the illegal condition....

As acknowledged by University Hospital, no Maryland appellate case has held that a charitable bequest with an illegal condition will not be saved under the *cy pres* doctrine when the will contains an express reversionary clause or gift over. The Maryland cases dealing with the *cy pres* doctrine have not involved *illegal* bequests. Rather, they have involved charitable bequests which could not be carried out for other reasons. Even in this situation, however, where the testator's intent is not contrary to law and public policy, the Maryland cases have not adopted the absolute rule contended for by University Hospital. Instead, the presence or absence of a gift over is merely one factor among many in determining whether the testator had a general charitable intent and whether the *cy pres* doctrine should be applied to save the charitable bequest at issue....

The illegal racially discriminatory condition in Dr. Coggins's will violates Maryland public policy.... Consequently the provisions of the will should be administered as if the word "white" was not contained in the bequest to the Keswick Home.

Questions

Did the court reach the right result? How would this case have been decided under UTC §413?

2. Discriminatory Trusts

Over the years, trusts containing terms that discriminate on the basis of race, gender, religion, or other factors have generated considerable cy pres litigation. Such trusts may be held unenforceable under federal or state law.

Where the trust is challenged on constitutional grounds, the initial question is whether state action exists.[10] A famous case on this question is Evans v. Newton, 382 U.S. 296 (1966). That case involved the will of Senator Augustus O. Bacon of Georgia, who died in 1914 devising land and an endowment fund to the City of Macon as trustee to hold the land in perpetuity as a park and pleasure ground, to be called Baconsfield, for "white women, white girls, white boys and white children of the City of Macon," with discretion in the trustees to admit "white men of the City of Macon, and white persons of other communities." Senator Bacon's will added:

> I am... without hesitation in the opinion that... the two races should be forever separate and that they should not have pleasure or recreation grounds to be used or enjoyed, together and in common.

In 1963, several Black residents sought admission to the park. Members of the Board of Managers sought to prevent desegregation of the park by having the probate court appoint new private trustees. The city resigned as trustee and new trustees were appointed. The United States Supreme Court rejected this attempt to sustain the park on a whites-only basis. The court found that the park had for many years been an integral part of the city's activities, that it was maintained by the city as a park for white persons only, and enjoyed tax exemption. The mere change in trustees, the court said, could not be assumed to have transferred the park from the public to the private sector.

When a court finds that a discriminatory restriction is unlawful, the question then becomes whether the court should exercise its cy pres power and continue the trust without the discriminatory provision or terminate the trust. Courts usually modify such trusts, reasoning that the settlor would have intended the trust to continue without the discriminatory provision. A notable counter-example is the sequel to *Evans v. Newton*. Following the Supreme Court's decision in that case, a Georgia trial court held that the cy pres doctrine was inapplicable because the racial restriction was so basic to Senator Bacon's purpose that he would have preferred termination to integration. On appeal, the Supreme Court of Georgia affirmed. In Evans v. Abney, 396 U.S. 435 (1970), the Supreme Court reviewed and affirmed the Georgia decision.

---

10. For an argument that racial and gender restrictions in charitable trusts are unconstitutional even if the trustee is a private individual, see James W. Colliton, Race and Sex Discrimination in Charitable Trusts, 12 Cornell J.L. & Pub. Pol. 275 (2003).

In Trammell v. Elliott, 199 S.E.2d 194 (Ga. 1973), the Georgia court modified a public university scholarship in favor of "qualified poor white boys and girls" to delete the racial restriction, distinguishing *Evans v. Abney* on the ground that there was no evidence that the testator's charitable intent was limited to the discriminatory term.

Gender and Religious Restrictions/Trust and Property Law. Restatement 3d of Trusts §28 comment f states:

> Like other trusts, charitable trusts are subject to the rule of §29 that trust purposes and provisions must not be unlawful or contrary to public policy.
>
> It is particularly common, however, for provisions to be included... limiting the direct benefits or eligibility to persons of a particular national origin, religion, gender, sexual orientation, age group, political affiliation, or other characteristics or background....
>
> Provisions of these types in charitable trusts are not valid if they involve *invidious* discrimination....
>
> It is not always possible to state with certainty what constitutes an "invidious" form of discrimination for these purposes.... For example, trust-law policies regarding restrictions on gender, sexual orientation, or age are especially sensitive to *context*, as the scope of more general statutory and constitutional protections evolve in these matters....
>
> When a scholarship or other form of assistance or opportunity is to be awarded on a basis that... explicitly excludes potential beneficiaries on the basis of membership in a particular... religious group, the restriction is ordinarily invidious and therefore unenforceable....
>
> This does not mean that a criterion such as gender, religion, or national origin may not be used in a charitable trust when it is a reasonable element of a settlor's charitable motivation.

Estate of Wilson
452 N.E.2d 1228 (N.Y. 1983)

[This case consolidated appeals from lower court judgments in two cases, Estate of Wilson and Estate of Johnson.

Clark W. Wilson devised the residue of his estate to the Key Bank in Central New York, in trust, to apply the income

> to defraying the education and other expenses of the first year at college of five (5) young men [from] Canastota High School, three (3) of whom who shall have attained the highest grades in science and two (2) of whom shall have attained the highest grades in chemistry, as may be certified by the Superintendent of Schools for the Canastota Central School District.

Edwin Irving Johnson devised the residue of his estate to the Board of Education of the Croton-Harmon Union Free School District, in trust, to apply the income

> for scholarships or grants for bright and deserving young men who have graduated from the High School of [the Croton-Harmon Union Free] School District, and whose parents

are financially unable to send them to college, and who shall be selected by the Board of Education of such School District with the assistance of the Principal of such High School.

Complaints were filed in both cases with the Civil Rights Office of the United States Department of Education. The allegation was that participation in the selection process by the school districts would violate Title IX of the Education Amendments of 1972, 20 U.S.C. §1681 et seq., which prohibits gender discrimination in federally financed education programs. The Department of Education notified each school district of its intent to conduct an investigation into the complaints. During the pendency of these investigations, the Canastota Central School District agreed to refrain from again providing names of students to the trustee of the Wilson Trust, and the executor of the Johnson will, the president of the Croton-Harmon Union Free board of education, and the state Attorney General agreed that the Johnson Trust would be administered on a sex-neutral basis, as if Johnson's Trust had used the word "persons" instead of "men."

In the *Wilson* case, the trustee brought an action in Surrogate's Court for a determination of the effect and validity of the above-quoted provision in the Wilson Trust. In *Johnson*, the state Attorney General brought an action in Surrogate's Court for construction of the above-quoted provision in the Johnson Trust.

The Surrogate in *Wilson* held that the school district's participation in the selection process was not unlawful, and ordered the trustee to continue administering the trust. On appeal, the Appellate Division held that the administration of the trust according to its literal terms was rendered impossible by the fact that the school district was under no legal obligation to supply the names of qualified male candidates. The Appellate Division therefore exercised its cy pres power by striking the clause requiring the district's certification; candidates were permitted to apply directly to the trustee.

The Surrogate in *Johnson* held that the administration of the trust according to its literal terms was rendered impossible by the school district's unwillingness to do so. Declining to reform the trust in accordance with the agreement reached among the parties, the Surrogate ordered the school district replaced as trustee with a private trustee who would give effect to the trust as written. On appeal, the Appellate Division held that the Surrogate's substitution of trustees constituted state action and a denial of equal protection of the laws in violation of the fourteenth amendment; the Appellate Division, in exercise of its cy pres power, ordered the gender restriction eliminated from the trust.

Appeals to the Court of Appeals followed in both cases.]

COOKE, C.J. These appeals present the question whether the equal protection clause of the Fourteenth Amendment is violated when a court permits the administration of private charitable trusts according to the testators' intent to finance the education of male and not female students. When a court applies trust law that neither encourages, nor affirmatively promotes, nor compels private discrimination but allows parties to engage in private selection in the devise or bequest of their property, that choice will not be attributable to the State and subjected to the Fourteenth Amendment's strictures.

I. The factual patterns in each of these matters are different, but the underlying legal issues are the same. In each there is imposed a decedent's intention to create a testamentary trust under which the class of beneficiaries are members of one sex....

II.... There can be no question that these trusts, established for the promotion of education, are for a charitable purpose within the meaning of the law.... Charitable trusts are encouraged and favored by the law.... [U]nlike other trusts, a charitable trust will not necessarily fail when the settlor's specific charitable purpose or direction can no longer be accomplished....

The court, of course, cannot invoke its cy pres power without first determining that the testator's specific charitable purpose is no longer capable of being performed by the trust. In establishing these trusts, the testators expressly and unequivocally intended that they provide for the educational expenses of male students. It cannot be said that the accomplishment of the testators' specific expression of charitable intent is "impossible or impracticable." So long as the subject high schools graduate boys with the requisite qualifications, the testators' specific charitable intent can be fulfilled.

Nor are the trusts' particular limitation of beneficiaries by gender invalid and incapable of being accomplished as violative of public policy. It is true that the eradication in this State of gender-based discrimination is an important public policy. Indeed, the Legislature has barred gender-based discrimination in education (see Education Law, §3201-a), employment (see Labor Law, §§194, 197, 220-e; General Business Law, §187), housing, credit, and many other areas (see Executive Law, §296).... The restrictions in these trusts run contrary to this policy favoring equal opportunity and treatment of men and women. A provision in a charitable trust, however, that is central to the testator's or settlor's charitable purpose, and is not illegal, should not be invalidated on public policy grounds unless that provision, if given effect, would substantially mitigate the general charitable effect of the gift (see 4 Scott, Trusts [3d ed.], §399.4).

Proscribing the enforcement of gender restrictions in private charitable trusts would operate with equal force towards trusts whose benefits are bestowed exclusively on women. "Reduction of the disparity in economic condition between men and women caused by the long history of discrimination against women has been recognized as ... an important governmental objective" (Califano v. Webster, 430 U.S. 313, 317). There can be little doubt that important efforts in effecting this type of social change can be and are performed through private philanthropy (see, generally, Commission on Private Philanthropy and Public Needs, Giving in America: Toward a Stronger Voluntary Sector [1975]). And, the private funding of programs for the advancement of women is substantial and growing (see Bernstein,

Funding for Women's Higher Education: Looking Backward and Ahead, Grant Magazine, vol. 4, No. 4, pp. 225-229; Ford Foundation, Financial Support of Women's Programs in the 1970s [1979]; Yarrow, Feminist Philanthropy Comes Into Its Own, NY Times, May 21, 1983, p. 7, col. 2). Indeed, one compilation of financial assistance offered primarily or exclusively to women lists 854 sources of funding (see Schlac[h]ter, Directory of Financial Aids for Women [2d ed., 1982]; see, also, Note, Sex Restricted Scholarships and the Charitable Trust, 59 Iowa L. Rev. 1000, 1000-1001, & nn. 10, 11). Current thinking in private philanthropic institutions advocates that funding offered by such institutions and the opportunities within the institutions themselves be directly responsive to the needs of particular groups (see Ford Foundation, op. cit., at pp. 41–44; Fleming, Foundations and Affirmative Action, 4 Foundation News No. 4, at pp. 14-17; Griffen, Funding for Women's Programs, 6 Grantsmanship Center News, No. 2, at pp. 34–45). It is evident, therefore, that the focusing of private philanthropy on certain classes within society may be consistent with public policy. Consequently, that the restrictions in the trusts before this court may run contrary to public efforts promoting equality of opportunity for women does not justify imposing a per se rule that gender restrictions in private charitable trusts violate public policy.

Finally, this is not an instance in which the restriction of the trusts serves to frustrate a paramount charitable purpose.... [T]he trusts subject to these appeals were not intended to directly benefit the school districts. Although the testators sought the school districts' participation, this was incidental to their primary intent of financing part of the college education of boys who attended the schools. Consequently, severance of the school districts' role in the trusts' administration will not frustrate any part of the testators' charitable purposes. Inasmuch as the specific charitable intent of the testators is not inherently "impossible or impracticable" of being achieved by the trusts, there is no occasion to exercise cy pres power.

Although not inherently so, these trusts are currently incapable of being administered as originally intended because of the school districts' unwillingness to co-operate. These impediments, however, may be remedied by an exercise of a court's general equitable power over all trusts to permit a deviation from the administrative terms of a trust and to appoint a successor trustee.

A testamentary trust will not fail for want of a trustee.... Accordingly, the proper means of continuing the Johnson Trust would be to replace the school district with someone able and willing to administer the trust according to its terms.

When an impasse is reached in the administration of a trust due to an incidental requirement of its terms, a court may effect, or permit the trustee to effect, a deviation from the trust's literal terms. This power differs from a court's cy pres power in that "[t]hrough exercise of its deviation power the court alters or amends administrative provisions in the trust instrument but does not alter the purpose of the charitable trust or change its dispositive provisions". The Wilson Trust provision that the school district certify a list of students is an incidental part of the trust's administrative requirements, which no longer can be satisfied in light of the district's refusal to co-operate. The same result intended by the testator may be accomplished by permitting the students to apply directly to the trustee. Therefore, a deviation from the Wilson Trust's administrative terms by eliminating the certification requirement would be the appropriate method of continuing that trust's administration....

III. It is argued before this court that the judicial facilitation of the continued administration of gender-restrictive charitable trusts violates the equal protection clause of the Fourteenth Amendment (see U.S. Const., 14th Amdt., §1). The strictures of the equal protection clause are invoked when the State engages in invidious discrimination. Indeed, the State itself cannot, consistent with the Fourteenth Amendment, award scholarships that are gender restrictive.

The Fourteenth Amendment, however, "erects no shield against merely private conduct, however discriminatory or wrongful." (Shelly v. Kraemer, 334 U.S. 1). Private discrimination may violate equal protection of the law when accompanied by State participation in, facilitation of, and, in some cases, acquiescence in the discrimination. Although there is no conclusive test to determine when State involvement in private discrimination will violate the Fourteenth Amendment, the general standard that has evolved is whether "the conduct allegedly causing the deprivation of a federal right [is] fairly attributable to the state" (Lugar v. Edmondson Oil Co., 457 U.S. 922, 937). Therefore, it is a question of "state responsibility" and "[o]nly by sifting facts and weighing circumstances can the... involvement of the State in private conduct be attributed its true significance" (Burton v. Wilmington Parking Auth., 365 U.S. 715, 722)....

The State generally may not be held responsible for private discrimination solely on the basis that it permits the discrimination to occur. Nor is the State under an affirmative obligation to prevent purely private discrimination. Therefore, when the State regulates private dealings it may be responsible for private discrimination occurring in the regulated field only when enforcement of its regulation has the effect of compelling the private discrimination....

A court's application of its equitable power to permit the continued administration of the trusts involved in these appeals falls outside the ambit of the Fourteenth Amendment. Although the field of trusts is regulated by the State, the Legislature's failure to forbid private discriminatory trusts does not cause such trusts, when they arise, to be attributable to the State. It naturally follows that, when a court applies this trust law and determines that it permits the continued existence of private discriminatory trusts, the Fourteenth Amendment is not implicated.

In the present appeals, the coercive power of the State has never been enlisted to enforce private discrimination. Upon finding that requisite formalities of creating a trust had been met, the courts below determined the testator's intent, and applied the relevant law permitting those intentions to be privately carried out. The court's power compelled no discrimination. That discrimination had been sealed in the private execution of the wills. Recourse to the courts was had here only for the purpose of facilitating the administration of the trusts, not for enforcement of their discriminatory dispositive provisions.

This is not to say that a court's exercise of its power over trusts can never invoke the scrutiny of the Fourteenth Amendment. This court holds only that a trust's discriminatory terms are not fairly attributable to the State when a court applies trust principles that permit private discrimination but do not encourage, affirmatively promote, or compel it.

The testators' intention to involve the State in the administration of these trusts does not alter this result, notwithstanding that the effect of the courts' action respecting the trusts was to eliminate this involvement. The courts' power to replace a trustee who is unwilling to act as in Johnson or to permit a deviation from an incidental administrative term in the trust as in Wilson is a part of the law permitting this private conduct and extends to all trusts regardless of their purposes. It compels no discrimination. Moreover, the minimal State participation in the trusts' administration prior to the time that they reached the courts for the constructions under review did not cause the trusts to take on an indelible public character.

In sum, the Fourteenth Amendment does not require the State to exercise the full extent of its power to eradicate private discrimination. It is only when the State itself discriminates, compels another to discriminate, or allows another to assume one of its functions and discriminate that such discrimination will implicate the amendment.

Accordingly, in Matter of Wilson, the order of the Appellate Division should be affirmed, with costs payable out of the estate to all parties appearing separately and filing separate briefs.

In Matter of Johnson, the order of the Appellate Division should be reversed, with costs payable out of the estate to all parties appearing separately and filing separate briefs and the decree of the Surrogate's Court, Westchester County, reinstated.

MEYER, J. (concurring in Matter of Wilson and dissenting in Matter of Johnson). I would affirm in both cases. Although the Constitution does not proscribe private bias, it does proscribe affirmative State action in furtherance of bias.

In Matter of Wilson the trust is private and the only involvement of a public official (the superintendent of schools) is his certification of a student's class standing, information which is, in any event, available to any student applying to the trustee for a scholarship. There is, therefore, no State action.

In Matter of Johnson, however, the trustee is the board of education, a public body. The establishment of a public trust for a discriminatory purpose is constitutionally improper, as Presiding Justice Mollen has fully spelled out in his opinion. For the State to legitimize that impropriety by replacement of the trustee is unconstitutional State action. The only permissible corrective court action is, as the Appellate Division held, excision of the discriminatory limitation....

Notes and Questions

1. What if the devise in *Wilson* had been for scholarships for "five young *women*"? Could public trustees have administered the trust under those terms? See Trustees of University of Delaware v. Gebelein, 420 A.2d 1191 (Del. Ch. 1980). What if the scholarships had been designated for "five deserving Protestant, Gentile boys"? See Howard Savings Institution v. Peep, 170 A.2d 39 (N.J. 1961).

2. Is a scholarship program for Black students administered by a public institution constitutional? In Podberesky v. Kirwan, 38 F.3d 147 (4th Cir. 1994), cert. denied, 514 U.S. 1128 (1995), a white student challenged the constitutional validity of a University of Maryland scholarship program for which only Black students were eligible. The court held that the scholarships were invalid under the Equal Protection Clause because they were not justified as a measure to counteract present effects of past discrimination.

More recently, in Students for Fair Admissions v. President and Fellows of Harvard College, 143 S.Ct. 2141 (2023), the Supreme Court struck down race-conscious admissions policies at Harvard and the University of North Carolina.

3. In Doe v. Kamehameha Schools/Bernice Pauahi Bishop Estate, 416 F.3d 1025 (9th Cir. 2005), a three-judge panel of the Ninth Circuit Court of Appeals ruled that the way in which a charitable trust was administered was discriminatory because it barred individuals from a non-preferred race from receiving benefits. The case involved Hawaii's Kamehameha Schools, which were established in 1887 through a charitable devise from Princess Bernice Pauahi Bishop, the last direct descendant of King Kamehameha I. The schools are private and non-sectarian. Although Princess Bishop's will did not impose admissions restrictions, the schools' policy has been to give preference to students who are of native Hawaiian ancestry. The race-conscious admissions policy was challenged under 42 U.S.C. §1981, which prohibits discrimination in the making and enforcement of contracts. The panel held that the admissions policy did violate the statute. It stated that "the challenged program [did not] constitute[] a valid affirmative action plan supplying a legitimate nondiscriminatory reason for the Schools' racially exclusionary admissions policy." Id. at 1042. This decision was subsequently reversed by the Ninth Circuit sitting en banc. See 470 F.3d 827 (9th Cir. 2006). We discuss the Bishop Estate Trust further in Part C below.

4. *Construction.* Modern trust forms often contain a definitions article. It is not unusual to find in that definitions article a boilerplate clause such as the following:

> *Gender and Form.* The use of any gender herein shall be deemed to be or include the other gender and the use of the singular herein shall be deemed to be or include the plural, and *vice versa*, wherever appropriate.

Had such a clause been included in Clark Wilson's will, would a court have been justified in construing "men" to mean "men or women"?

PART C. SUPERVISION OF CHARITABLE TRUSTS

Primary Statutory References: *UTC §405(c)*
                              Model Protection of Charitable Assets Act (2011)

Richard A. Posner, Economic Analysis of Law
547 (7th ed. 2007)

Even where no unforeseen contingencies materialize, perpetual charitable gifts raise an economic issue that echoes the concern with the separation of ownership and control in the modern business corporation. A charitable foundation that enjoys a substantial income, in perpetuity, from its original endowment does not compete in any product market or in the capital markets and has no stockholders or other owners. Its board of trustees is self-perpetuating and is accountable to no one for the performance of the enterprise. (Although state attorneys general have legal authority over the administration of charitable trusts, it is largely formal.) And as neither the trustees nor the staff have the kind of property right in the foundation's assets or income that would give them a strong incentive to maximize value, the carrot is missing along with the stick.

The incentives to efficient management of foundation assets could be strengthened by a rule requiring charitable foundations to distribute every gift received, principal and income, including the original endowment, within a specified period of years. The foundation would not be required to wind up its operations within the period; it could continue indefinitely. But it would have to receive new gifts in order to avoid exhausting all of its funds. Since donors are unlikely to give money to an enterprise known to be slack, the necessity of returning periodically to the market for charitable donations would give trustees and managers of charitable foundations an incentive they now lack to conduct a tight operation. Foundations—mostly religious and educational—that market their services or depend on continuing charitable support, and are therefore already subject to some competitive constraints, could be exempt from the exhaustion rule.

The objections to the suggested rule are that it is unnecessary—donors are already free to limit the duration of their charitable bequests—and that it might therefore (why therefore?) reduce the incentives to make charitable gifts. A counterargument is that many perpetual foundations were established at a time when the foundation was a novel institution. A person creating one at that time may not have been able to foresee the problem of inefficient and unresponsive management that might plague a perpetual foundation as a result of the peculiar set of constraints (or rather lack of constraints) under which they operate.

Notes

1. *Supervision of Charitable Trusts and Foundations.* There is a substantial body of evidence to support Judge Posner's view that closer supervision of charitable

trusts is needed. By general recognition, the state Attorney General has common-law power to seek judicial enforcement of such trusts, but the power is only sporadically exercised.

2. *Acts Promulgated by the Uniform Law Commission.* In 1954, the Uniform Supervision of Trustees for Charitable Purposes Act was promulgated by the Uniform Law Commission. The Act requires, among other things, that trustees file a copy of the trust and periodic reports with the Attorney General. The Act was adopted only in four states, California, Illinois, Michigan, and Oregon. Some other states, although still only a minority, also have enacted statutes designed to correct the misuse or non-use of charitable trust funds. Statutes are collected in Scott and Ascher on Trusts §37.3.10 (6th ed. 2023).

In 2011, the Uniform Law Commission promulgated the Model Protection of Charitable Assets Act. The purpose of the Act is explained in this excerpt from the Act's prefatory note:

> The Model Protection of Charitable Assets Act articulates and confirms the role of the state Attorney General in protecting charitable assets. The Attorney General's existing authority is broad and this Act does not limit or narrow that authority. In some states, however, the scope of the authority is unclear. In the great majority of states, the Act will provide a helpful statutory articulation of that authority.
>
> The Act adopts registration, reporting, and notice requirements that will enable the Attorney General to fulfill the responsibility of that office to represent the public interest by protecting charitable assets. The requirements are designed so as not to overburden either the Attorneys General or those with the duty to report....

The prefatory note also explains why the Act has been designated a Model Act rather than a Uniform Act:

> Because some states have substantial statutes in this area of the law, while others have little or no statutory authority with respect to the protection of charitable assets, the prospect of uniformity in statutory language is limited. The approach of this Act is to create a model, all or part of which would be useful to all of the states....

3. *The Bishop Estate Trust.* A particularly egregious example of the need for closer supervision of charitable trusts and foundations involves a charitable trust established under the will of Hawaiian Princess Bernice Pauahi Bishop. The Bishop Estate Trust had over $6 billion in assets and only one beneficiary, the Kamehameha Schools, a 3,200-student school for native Hawaiian children.

Princess Bishop's will directed that members of the state (then pre-state) supreme court should select the trust's five trustees. Over time, the trustees were all well-connected with the Hawaiian political establishment.

The scandal broke in 1997, when a major Honolulu newspaper published an article titled "Broken Trust," a scathing indictment of the Bishop Trust's management practices and the trustees.

Once the scandal broke, the state Attorney General and a court-appointed special master launched investigations into the trustees' management. The master's report disclosed repeated accounting and investment irregularities. The report further found that the trustees had compromised their fiduciary duties by investing trust assets in investments in which they had personal interests. There was no effort to diversify investments, and the master found that the actual return rate on the trustees' investments was 1 percent. Two of the trustees were also indicted for fraudulent use of trust assets. And the Internal Revenue Service, which had been investigating charges of self-dealing and other conflicts of interest, threatened to revoke the trust's tax-exempt status unless all of the trustees were removed. (The Attorney General and the special master had recommended that four of the five trustees be removed.)

In May 1999, one trustee resigned, and the probate court ordered the removal of the others. See Todd S. Purdum, For $6 Billion Hawaii Legacy, A New Day, N.Y. Times, May 15, 1999, at A1. The IRS assessed nearly $5 million in sanctions against each of the ousted trustees for having accepted excessive compensation. The state Attorney General sued them for over $50 million in damages.

The probate court created a new process for selecting the trustees. A panel of seven committee members, selected by the court, provided a short list of candidates from which the court would make the final selection. The court also turned over the daily operation of the estate to qualified professionals and capped the trustees' compensation at $97,500. The Attorney General, the new and former trustees, and the lawyers for the former trustees entered into a settlement that ended the litigation. Under the terms of the settlement, the former trustees neither returned any of their compensation nor paid any of the surcharges that had been assessed against them. The lawyers for the former trustees were allowed to keep all their fees. All criminal charges were dropped.

The saga is the subject of Samuel P. King & Randall W. Roth, Broken Trust: Greed, Mismanagement, and Political Manipulation at America's Largest Charitable Trust (2006). See also Symposium, The Bishop Estate Controversy, 21 U. Haw. L. Rev. 353-714 (1999).

Standing of Donors to Enforce Charitable Trusts and Gifts. As we noted at the beginning of this chapter, the state Attorney General and persons with a "special interest" in a charitable trust have standing to enforce the terms of the trust. Under traditional trust law, however, the settlor does not have standing. See Restatement 2d of Trusts §391. The same is true of donors of charitable gifts, including charitable foundations. See Courtenay C. and Lucy Patten Davis Foundation v. Colorado State University Research Foundation, 320 P.3d 1115 (Wyo. 2014).

The tide may be turning against the traditional rule. The UTC authorizes the settlor of a charitable trust to initiate proceedings to enforce the terms of the trust. See UTC §405(c). Accord, Restatement 3d of Trusts §95. See also Wis. Stat.

§701.0405 (standing granted to the "settlor of a charitable trust or his or her designees, whether identified within or without the terms of the trust"). But see Restatement of Charitable Nonprofit Organizations §6.03, which recognizes donor standing only if provided for "according to the documents governing the assets" or "under applicable law."

Smithers v. St. Luke's-Roosevelt Hospital Center
723 N.Y.S.2d 426 (App. Div. 2001)

ELLERIN, J.

The issue before us is whether the estate of the donor of a charitable gift has standing to sue the donee to enforce the terms of the gift. We conclude that in the circumstances here present plaintiff estate does have the necessary standing.

A recitation of the factual allegations in the complaint, which must be deemed true on this application to dismiss is instructive. Plaintiff Adele Smithers is the widow of R. Brinkley Smithers, a recovered alcoholic who devoted the last 40 years of his life to the treatment and understanding of the disease of alcoholism. In 1971 Smithers announced his intention to make a gift to defendant St. Luke's-Roosevelt Hospital Center (the "Hospital") of $10 million over time for the establishment of an alcoholism treatment center (the "Gift"). In his June 16, 1971 letter to the Hospital creating the Gift, Smithers stated, "Money from the $10 million grant will be supplied as needed. It is understood, however, that the detailed project plans and staff appointments must have my approval."

According to the complaint, the Hospital agreed to use the Gift to expand its treatment of alcoholism to include, following five days of detoxification in the hospital, "rehabilitation in a free-standing, controlled, uplifting and non-hospital environment," that is, a "therapeutic community" removed from the hospital setting. With $1 million from the first installment of the Gift, the Hospital purchased a building at 56 East 93rd Street in Manhattan to house the rehabilitation program, and in 1973 the Smithers Alcoholism Treatment and Training Center opened there.

Smithers thereafter remained involved in the management and affairs of the Smithers Center. At times, according to the complaint, the Hospital sought to avoid its obligations under the terms of the Gift, and its relationship with Smithers was an uneasy one. On July 31, 1978, Smithers wrote that the Hospital had "not lived up to my letter of intent," and that "[u]nder the circumstances no funds or stock will be forthcoming from me." Only slightly more than half of the Gift had been made at that time.

In 1981 the president of the Hospital, Gary Gambuti, commenced discussions with Smithers in an effort to induce him to complete the Gift. In a November 5, 1981, letter, Smithers informed Gambuti that he had no objection to the sale of the building. Smithers noted in the letter that when the Smithers rehabilitation facility was set up there was practically no place in the New York area for an alcoholic to undergo rehabilitation after detoxification, but now there are a number of facilities, most of which "have the advantage of being at least a few miles out of town—so there is more chance of outdoor recreation." According to Mrs. Smithers, her husband had no intention of completing the Gift, but agreed to the sale of the building to keep the Smithers Center afloat. In any event, Gambuti, in response, assured Smithers of the Hospital's continuing interest in the Smithers Alcoholism Program and its commitment to expanding its entire alcoholism treatment program. He wrote that he saw no reason to sell the building until a plan for this program had been proposed, and that he would appreciate receiving Smithers's comments and suggestions before the plan was finalized. He expressed his hope that Smithers would be willing "to sit down with us and review our proposals for the future expansion in alcoholism."...

Over the next two years, Gambuti repeatedly assured Smithers that the Hospital would strictly adhere to the terms of the Gift and carry out Smithers's intent in making it. Only when Smithers was completely satisfied of the Hospital's intentions did he agree to complete the Gift, which he accomplished in an October 24, 1983 letter, stating:

> Thanks to the cooperation of the officers and staff of the Smithers Center and St. Luke's Roosevelt Hospital Center (the "Hospital"), the Smithers Center is now in splendid shape, and I feel that the time has come for me to complete the funding of the project. (In this letter I will refer to all aspects of the existing alcoholism program, including in-patient, out-patient and rehabilitation services, and any future extension thereof, collectively as the "Smithers Center").
>
> ...
>
> This final contribution is subject to the following restrictions and is to be used exclusively for the following purposes.
>
> First, it is my intention that my final contribution be set aside as an endowment fund, (the "Smithers Endowment Fund"). The income is to be used exclusively for the support of the Smithers Center, to the extent necessary for current operations, and any unused income remaining at the end of each calendar year is to be accumulated and added to principal. Principal of the Smithers Endowment Fund is not to be expended for any purpose except for remodeling or rebuilding the administration section and out-patient floor at the Building on 58th Street, and for construction, repairs or improvements with respect to any other building space at any time used directly in connection with the Smithers Center. Such capital expenditures should be considered as secondary to the endowment function and should in no event exceed in the aggregate one half of the initial value of the Smithers Endowment Fund....

Beneath Smithers's signature is the following paragraph signed and dated by Gambuti:

> The contribution of the number of shares of IBM Stock referred to above by R. Brinkley Smithers is gratefully accepted, *subject to the restrictions set forth in this letter,* in full satisfaction of any outstanding pledge or other obligation. (Emphasis added.)

The existing rehabilitation services, which Smithers included in his definition of the Smithers Center and which the Hospital's acceptance of the Gift encompassed, were housed in the free-standing Smithers building and, according to the complaint, were intended always to be housed in *a* free-standing facility.

In late 1992, the Hospital asked Mrs. Smithers to organize a "Silver Anniversary Gala," in honor of her husband and herself, to raise funds for restoration of the building and for a scholarship program for Smithers Center patients in need of financial assistance. From 1992 to March 1995, she and, until his death in January 1994, Smithers successfully solicited millions of dollars' worth of donated goods and services for a total restoration of the building and organized the fundraiser, scheduled for April 1995. Then, in March 1995, just over a year after Smithers's death, the Hospital announced that it planned to move the Smithers Center into a hospital ward and sell the East 93rd Street building. The Hospital directed Mrs. Smithers, a month and a half before the fundraiser was scheduled to be held, to cancel the event.

The Hospital's announced intentions aroused Mrs. Smithers's suspicions. First, relocating the patients in a hospital ward would violate the Hospital's obligation to run the Smithers Center in a free-standing facility physically separate from the Hospital. Second, the Hospital's claim that it had to sell the building to become more competitive was inconsistent with its assurances to her husband and her through the years that the Smithers Center was operating at a profit. Mrs. Smithers notified the Hospital of her objections to the proposed relocation of the program and demanded an accounting of the Smithers Center's finances.

The Hospital at first resisted disclosing its financial records, but Mrs. Smithers persisted, and in May 1995 the Hospital disclosed that it had been misappropriating monies from the Endowment Fund since before Smithers's death, transferring such monies to its general fund where they were used for purposes unrelated to the Smithers Center. Mrs. Smithers notified the Attorney General, who investigated the Hospital's plan to sell the building and discovered that the Hospital had transferred restricted assets from the Smithers Endowment Fund to its general fund in what it called "loans." The Attorney General demanded the return of these assets and in August 1995 the Hospital returned nearly $5 million to the Smithers Endowment Fund, although it did not restore the income lost on those funds during the intervening years.

In the next three years, Mrs. Smithers tried to negotiate a resolution with the Hospital. The Attorney General participated in the negotiations, seeking, according to an affidavit in support of his motion to dismiss the complaint, "to effectuate a settlement that would resolve the plaintiff's concerns and benefit the Smithers Alcoholism Program." When the negotiations proved unsuccessful, the Attorney General, according to the affidavit, "proceeded to conclude his investigation... and to resolve those issues identified during the course of the investigation." On April 21, 1998, the Attorney General, having received a letter from an attorney writing on behalf of Mrs. Smithers, wrote to counsel for the Hospital advising that he would not object to the sale of the East 93rd Street building "so long as the Hospital can demonstrate [ ] to our satisfaction," *inter alia,* that the Hospital's plan for the Smithers program and the Smithers Center would continue "in accordance with the donor's gift," that the Hospital would disclose to the Attorney General any changes to the Smithers program budget resulting from "the proposed relocation of the inpatient rehabilitation unit from the East 93rd Street building to the Hospital," and that safeguards had been put into place to prevent future commingling of restricted funds. The letter stated that the Attorney General would require an assurance that no such commingling of funds would occur in the future.

In July 1998, the Attorney General entered into an Assurance... with the Hospital. Under the terms of this assurance the Hospital agreed to make no more transfers or loans from Gift funds for any purpose other than the benefit of the Smithers Center and to return to the Gift fund $1 million from the proceeds of any sale of the building. The Attorney General did not require the Hospital to return the entire proceeds of such a sale, because he found that, contrary to Mrs. Smithers's contention, the terms of the Gift did not preclude the Hospital from selling the building.

Two months later, Mrs. Smithers commenced this suit to enforce the conditions of the Gift and to obtain an accounting by the Hospital of its handling of the Endowment Fund and property dedicated to the Smithers Center....

Mrs. Smithers sought an injunction to permanently enjoin the Hospital from selling the building and relocating the Smithers Center without court approval, for specific performance by the Hospital of the terms of the Gift, e.g., perpetual maintenance of a free-standing rehabilitation unit and return to the Gift funds of all proceeds of any sale or rental of the building, for return of all income lost on the funds misappropriated by the Hospital from the Gift funds, for imposition of a constructive trust, for an accounting, and for a judicial declaration concerning the terms and conditions under which the Gift fund is to be administered....

On appeal, the Attorney General's office, having reevaluated the matter "under the direction of the newly elected Attorney General," reversed its position and urged this Court to remand for a hearing on the merits to determine whether or not the building was subject to gift restrictions. If it were, then all proceeds of the sale would be subject to the same restrictions and could not be used for the Hospital's general purposes. ...

While this appeal was pending, the Attorney General and the Hospital reached another agreement. This agreement raised some issues for the first time, but it brought the position of the Attorney General and the Hospital on other issues into accord with Mrs. Smithers's position....

...Mrs. Smithers did not bring this action on her own behalf or on behalf of beneficiaries of the Smithers Center. She brought it as the court-appointed special administratrix of the estate of her late husband to enforce his rights under his agreement with the Hospital through specific performance of that agreement. Therefore, the general rule barring beneficiaries from suing charitable corporations has no application to Mrs. Smithers. Moreover, the desire to prevent vexatious litigation by "irresponsible parties who do not have a tangible stake in the matter and have not conducted appropriate investigations" has no application to Mrs. Smithers either. Without possibility of pecuniary gain for himself or herself, only a plaintiff with a genuine interest in enforcing the terms of a gift will trouble to investigate and bring this type of action. Indeed, it was Mrs. Smithers's accountants who discovered and informed the Attorney General of the Hospital's misdirection of Gift funds, and it was only after Mrs. Smithers brought her suit that the Attorney General acted to prevent the Hospital from diverting the entire proceeds of the sale of the building away from the Gift fund and into its general fund. The Attorney General, following his initial investigation of the Hospital's administration of the Gift, acquiesced in the Hospital's sale of the building, its diversion of the appreciation realized on the sale, and its relocation of the rehabilitation unit, even as he ostensibly was demanding that the Hospital continue to act "in accordance with the donor's gift" (*see* April 21, 1998 letter, *supra*). Absent Mrs. Smithers's vigilance, the Attorney General would have resolved the matter between himself and the Hospital in that manner and without seeking permission of any court.

The donor of a charitable gift is in a better position than the Attorney General to be vigilant and, if he or she is so inclined, to enforce his or her own intent....

Moreover, the circumstances of this case demonstrate the need for co-existent standing for the Attorney General and the donor. The Attorney General's office was notified of the Hospital's misappropriation of funds by Mrs. Smithers, whose accountants performed the preliminary review of the Hospital's financial records, and it learned of the Hospital's closing of the detox unit—a breach, according to the Attorney General, of a specific representation— from Mrs. Smithers's papers in this action. Indeed, there is no substitute for a donor, who has a "special, personal interest in the enforcement of the gift restriction"....

Mrs. Smithers, appointed the Special Administratrix of Smithers's estate for the purpose of pursuing claims by the estate against the Hospital in connection with its administration of the Smithers Center, therefore has standing to sue the Hospital for enforcement of the Gift terms....

FRIEDMAN, J., dissenting.... In considering the subject of standing, I begin with the observation that, when a charitable gift is made, without any provision for a reversion of the gift to the donor or his heirs, the interest of the donor and his heirs is permanently excluded. Accordingly, in the absence of a right of reverter, the right to seek enforcement of the terms of a charitable gift is restricted to the Attorney General....

In holding that standing is generally restricted to the Attorney General, our courts have pointed out that a limited standing rule is necessary to protect charitable institutions from "vexatious litigation" by parties who do not have a tangible stake in the outcome of the litigation. While the majority believes that this concern does not apply to Mrs. Smithers because her motives are altruistic (and I agree that they are), the limited standing rule enunciated by our Court of Appeals is a prophylactic one that does not permit a case-by-case inquiry into the subjective motivations of the party commencing the action. Rather, it focuses on the actual interest of the party and here Mrs. Smithers has herself conceded "that [she] ha[s] absolutely nothing to gain personally as a result of this lawsuit."...

The principal focus of the majority's analysis centers upon the question of whether Mr. Smithers had standing to commence an action. As to this question, I agree with the majority that... he did since he seems to have retained the right to make appointments to key staff positions. This observation, however, is irrelevant to the question presented on this appeal. Here, we are not required to determine whether Mr. Smithers would have had standing, but whether his estate has standing.

With regard to this issue, and applying the rules of standing noted above, it is uncontroverted that the estate was not the donor of the gift. Thus, even if pure donor standing were recognized (as the majority concludes), this could not be a basis for granting standing to Mr. Smithers's estate. Next, to the extent that Mr. Smithers may have had standing based upon his right to exercise discretionary control over the gift, i.e., via the right to appoint key staffing positions, that right was personal to him, abated upon his death, and did not devolve to his estate. Hence, as plaintiff concedes that the estate has no right to exercise control over the gift, this may not be a basis of standing. Finally, since it is uncontroverted that the estate does not have a right of reverter in the gift or, in fact, any right to control the gift by way of appointment to staff positions or otherwise, it follows that there is no retained interest that could support a claim of standing. In view of this, I fail to perceive the legal basis for the majority's grant of standing to plaintiff....

In the end, the majority holds that a donor's estate has standing to commence an enforcement action against a charitable institution to which the donor contributed.... [P]rimary responsibility in this area is reposed in the Attorney General, and there is no authority supporting the majority's position that a donor's estate, in the absence of some continuing right in relation to the gift, has standing to enforce the terms of the gift....

Notes and Questions

1. *Donor Standing.* On the controversial question of donor standing, who has the better argument: the majority or the dissent? For a discussion of *Smithers* and UTC §405(c), see Ronald Chester, Grantor Standing to Enforce Charitable Transfers Under Section 405(c) of the Uniform Trust Code and Related Law: How Important

Is It and How Extensive Should It Be?, 37 Real Prop., Prob. & Tr. J. 611 (2003). See also the articles cited at the end of this chapter.

2. *UPMIFA*. Observe that donor standing is not provided for in the Uniform Prudent Management of Institutional Funds Act, known as UPMIFA. Why should the rule on donor standing regarding a restricted gift to a nonprofit organization be different from the rule on donor standing applicable to a charitable trust? At least one state supreme court has held that the two categories are different. See Courtenay C. and Lucy Patten Davis Foundation v. Colorado State University Research Foundation, 320 P.3d 1115 (Wyo. 2014) (holding that UTC §405(c) applies only to a charitable trust, not to a charitable gift).

3. *Donor Standing Assignable?* If a donor has standing to enforce the terms of a charitable trust, should the law permit the donor to assign his or her standing to others? For an argument that the answer should be a "qualified 'yes,'" see Joshua C. Tate, Should Charitable Trust Enforcement Rights Be Assignable?, 85 Chi.-Kent L. Rev. 1045 (2010).

———

Community Accountability? Closely related to the question of who may enforce a charitable trust is a further question: Is a charitable trust accountable to the communities affected by the trustees' decisions?

This question was posed in a highly-publicized case involving the Hershey Trust, the charitable trust which owns most of Hershey Foods Corporation. The trustees of the trust, whose beneficiary is the Milton Hershey School for poor and underprivileged children, announced plans to accept bids for all of its shares of Hershey Foods stock. By mid-2002, the trust's holdings in Hershey Foods had dropped from 80 percent of the trust's assets to 52 percent. In 2002, the trust's board adopted a resolution "to explore any and all options to unlock the value of their investment in Hershey Foods, including the sale of the company." The announcement touched off a community-wide rebellion of union workers, business leaders, and local officials, all of whom feared that an outside takeover of Hershey Foods would result in layoffs and other cost-saving measures by the successful bidder. As community opposition grew, state political figures, including the governor, expressed their disapproval of the trust's plan. The state Attorney General (who was running for governor) gradually shifted his position until he eventually petitioned the local court having jurisdiction over the trust for an order restraining the trust from selling its block of shares in Hershey Foods stock, arguing that the community would suffer irreparable harm if a sale were reached. The lower court granted the order. On appeal, the Commonwealth Court confirmed the injunction. See In re Milton Hershey School Trust, 807 A.2d 324 (Pa. Comm. Ct. 2002). The Commonwealth Court appended with approval the lower court's memorandum opinion.

In that opinion the lower court defined the interests of the trust as including not only those of the trust's designated beneficiary (the school) but the community as well. See id. at 329. The court reiterated its view that "the beneficiary of charitable trusts is the general public to whom the social and economic benefits of the trusts accrue," accepting the Attorney General's argument that under its *parens patriae* power, the Attorney General "has the authority to inquire whether an exercise of the trustee's power, even if authorized under the trust instrument, is inimical to the public interest." Id. at 330.

Following the Commonwealth Court's decision, the trust's board voted to discontinue the sale. It then moved to end all judicial proceedings in the matter, a petition the Attorney General opposed on the ground that a future sale remained possible. The lower court dissolved its earlier injunction. In an acerbic opinion, Judge Morgan pointedly stated that the trust's board had become detached from Milton Hershey's philanthropic scheme and that it needed to be reconstituted. Taking the cue, the Attorney General and board members met with Judge Morgan to discuss reorganizing both the trust's board and the school's board. Under the reorganization, the trust's board was reduced by six seats, and the school's board was reduced by seven. The CEO of Hershey Foods was added to both boards. All members who had voted for the sale were removed from the boards.

The Hershey saga did not end there. Instead, the dispute shifted to the legislature. Despite intense opposition from the business community and warnings from economic and trust experts, the Pennsylvania legislature enacted a statute, dubbed the "Hershey bill," that amended the state's version of the prudent investor rule. (Recall the discussion of the prudent investor rule in Chapter 10.) The amended statute, in relevant part, requires that a

> fiduciary shall consider,... in the case of a charitable trust, the special relationship of the asset and its economic impact as a principal business enterprise on the community in which the beneficiary of the trust is located and the special value of the integration of the beneficiary's activities with the community where that asset is located;....

20 Pa. Cons. Stat. §7203(c)(6). Is this wise? For a discussion of the Hershey Trust case, particularly the Attorney General's aggressive role in the controversy, see Mark Sidel, The Struggle for Hershey: Community Accountability and the Law in Modern American Philanthropy, 65 U. Pitt. L. Rev. 1 (2003). See also Jonathan Klick & Robert H. Sitkoff, Agency Costs, Charitable Trusts, and Corporate Control: Evidence from Hershey's Kiss-Off, 108 Colum. L. Rev. 749 (2008).

EXTERNAL REFERENCES. Edward C. Halbach, Jr., Standing to Enforce Trusts: Renewing and Expanding Professor Gaubatz's 1984 Discussion of Settlor Enforcement, 62 U. Miami L. Rev. 713 (2008); Reid Kress Weisbord, Reservations About Donor Standing: Should the Law Allow Charitable Donors to Reserve the Right to Enforce a Gift Restriction?, 42 Real Prop., Prob. & Tr. J. 245 (2007).

PART TWO
AN ADVANCED TWO-CREDIT COURSE

Chapter 13

Mistakes in Donative Documents

Restatement 3d of Property

§10.1 Donor's Intention Determines the Meaning of a Donative Document and Is Given Effect to the Maximum Extent Allowed by Law

The controlling consideration in determining the meaning of a donative document is the donor's intention. The donor's intention is given effect to the maximum extent allowed by law.

———

Nearly every authority would agree with the Restatement's general proposition that the controlling consideration in determining the meaning of a donative document is the donor's intention, and that the donor's intention should be given effect to the maximum extent allowed by law. This Chapter, however, is about instances in which there is evidence suggesting that the written terms of a donative document, usually a will, vary from actual intention. This type of evidence is inherently suspect, especially when the heart of it consists, as it often does, of testimony regarding predeath statements of intention allegedly made by the testator—so-called direct declarations of intent. After death, the testator cannot corroborate or deny the truthfulness of such evidence. The main protection against fabricated or mistaken evidence is the will itself. After all, the will is a document executed in accordance with statutory formalities that have as their underlying purposes the protection of the testator against fraud and undue influence (the so-called protective function), the providing of reliable written evidence of intent (the evidentiary function), the protection of the testator against effectuation of casual or unconsidered declarations of intent (the cautionary function), and the assurance that documents executed in accordance with the prescribed formalities will control the devolution of the property on death (the channeling function).

And yet, evidence offered against a will's literal meaning is sometimes correct. Mistake in translating intention into legally effective language is a frequent occurrence. Clerical error and lawyer incompetence make mistakes a phenomenon that is not limited to self-drawn wills.

The dilemma of how the law should respond to allegations of mistake (and uncertainty about the meaning of language) is the subject of the materials in this Chapter. Most of the cases deal with wills. A few, however, deal with other donative transfers, such as trusts. The first case we present involving a pour-over devise, in fact, concerns the question whether a particular trust arrangement was nontestamentary or testamentary.[1] The question was decisive to the outcome of *Brinker v. Wobaco Trust Ltd.*, because, as the opinion makes clear, the conventional view is that, upon a proper showing of mistake, nontestamentary instruments can be reformed, but that wills cannot be. For nontestamentary instruments, courts have used their equity powers to prevent unjust enrichment by correcting well-proven mistakes—clear and convincing evidence is the standard used. If the mistake were not corrected, the mistaken beneficiary would be unjustly enriched at the expense of the intended beneficiary. Why won't courts reform wills?

EXTERNAL REFERENCES. Joseph W. deFuria, Jr., Mistakes in Wills Resulting from Scriveners' Errors: The Argument for Reformation, 40 Cath. U. L. Rev. 1 (1990); Mary Louise Fellows, In Search of Donative Intent, 73 Iowa L. Rev. 611 (1988); Clifton B. Kruse, Jr., Reformation of Wills: The Implication of Restatement (Third) of Property (Donative Transfers) on Flawed but Unambiguous Testaments, 25 ACTEC Notes 299 (2000); John H. Langbein & Lawrence W. Waggoner, Curing Execution Errors and Mistaken Terms in Wills, University of Michigan Law School Working Paper Series (no. 207), available at http://ssrn.com/abstract=1653438 (2010); John H. Langbein & Lawrence W. Waggoner, Reformation of Wills on the Ground of Mistake: Change of Direction in American Law?, 130 U. Pa. L. Rev. 521 (1982).

PART A. REFORMING DONATIVE DOCUMENTS (OTHER THAN WILLS)

"The Moving Finger writes; and, having writ,
Moves on: nor all thy Piety nor Wit
Shall lure it back to cancel half a Line...."
– The Rubaiyat of Omar Khayyam

Brinker v. Wobaco Trust Ltd.
610 S.W.2d 160 (Tex. Civ. App. 1980)

[Norman and Maureen Brinker, husband and wife, had two children, Cynthia and Brenda. Before Maureen's death in 1969, Maureen and Norman established an inter vivos trust, called the "Norman E. Brinker Family Trust." The trust instrument named Norman as the "settlor" and named Maureen and a bank, collectively, as the "trustee." The trust was to be principally funded by the proceeds of life insurance on Norman's life, but since Norman was still living at the time of the lawsuit no proceeds had yet become payable. Maureen's will, however, appointed Norman as trustee of her residuary estate and directed that after a certain period it should pour

---

1. For discussion of pour-over devises, see Chapters 7 and 9.

over into the inter vivos trust, where it should "be held or disposed of in accordance with the provisions of Article IV" thereof. Article IV of the trust provided that income and ultimately principal be paid to "the issue of settlor." In 1970, after Maureen's death, Norman created two other separate trusts for the benefit of Cynthia and Brenda. These trusts named Norman as "settlor," and provided that if the principal beneficiary dies without issue, the trust assets are to be paid to the "settlor's issue then living."

In 1971, Norman married Magrit; this marriage produced two children, Christina and Mark. In 1973, Norman conferred with his attorney and decided on a plan to bestow some of Maureen's residuary estate upon the children of this second marriage; to that end he transferred assets of Maureen's residuary estate to another trust he had set up through a banking corporation in the Bahamas. After his second marriage ended in divorce in 1977, Norman had second thoughts and told Cynthia and Brenda what he had done.

Cynthia and Brenda then brought suit to impose a constructive trust on the assets removed from Maureen's estate and to construe or reform the Norman E. Brinker Family Trusts and the two 1970 trusts. The suit asked that Christina and Mark, the children born of their father's second marriage, be excluded as beneficiaries of these trusts. In a bench trial, the court refused to admit evidence seeking to establish Norman's and Maureen's intention in creating the trusts or to show that in the drafting of the trust instruments a mistake had been made that would warrant reformation of the instruments to reflect the true intention.]

CORNELIUS, C.J.... On a bill of exceptions, appellants [Cynthia and Brenda] produced evidence that Maureen and Norman Brinker intended for the trusts to benefit only the issue born of their marriage to each other, and that if the term "issue of settlor" as used in the trust indentures meant the issue of Norman Brinker by any other union, a mistake had been made in the drafting of the trust indentures which warranted reformation of the instruments.

The evidence consisted of the testimony of Norman Brinker and Mr. Robert Taylor, a tax lawyer who prepared both the trust indentures and Maureen's will. The evidence may be generally summarized as follows: Mr. Brinker testified that he and Maureen primarily wanted to be certain that whatever assets went into the trust would go for the benefit of their two children at that time, i.e., Cynthia and Brenda. He said they knew Maureen could not have any other children and that they intended for the trust to be just for Cynthia and Brenda. He further testified that neither he nor Maureen was familiar with trusts or wills or legal terminology, and that they depended entirely on their lawyer to correctly put into the trust instruments what they wanted done; that neither he nor Maureen chose to use the word "settlor" or even knew what it meant; that the word was never mentioned or discussed with their lawyer or the bank; and that although they read the trust instruments before executing them they did not understand them, and in effect told their lawyer, "You are the lawyer; we don't understand this, did you do what we asked you to do?", and upon the lawyer's assurance that he had, they completed the transaction.

Mr. Taylor testified in detail. He testified that the Brinkers instructed him to prepare the family trust; in the discussion it was mentioned that Maureen could not have any more children; he understood that they wanted only Cynthia and Brenda to share in that trust; and that was the way he intended to draw the instruments and thought he had done so. When asked if either Norman or Maureen said anything about wanting to include children who might be born of other marriages, he answered "No, just the opposite", although he admitted that they did not specifically tell him to cut out all afterborn children. He further testified that if the trust indentures were written so as to include other children as beneficiaries, he had made a mistake in drafting the trust instruments.

Upon being questioned about Norman alone being named settlor, Mr. Taylor stated that he considered Maureen to be a co-settlor, and had intended to designate her as such in the same manner as he had designated her and the bank as co-trustee, and that was the reason he had her execute the trust indenture along with Norman. He also recalled that Maureen discussed with him the possible remarriage of her husband and that she shared "the normal concern of a wife that her husband, if something happened to her, might remarry and reiterated that she wanted her property to go to Cindy and Brenda." On cross-examination appellees brought out concessions from Mr. Taylor that the trusts did benefit Cynthia and Brenda, which literally complied with the directions he received from Norman and Maureen, and that the Brinker Family Trust indenture did not contain typographical errors, but contained the actual words he dictated. On the suggestion that many corrections would be necessary to change the trust indenture to designate Maureen as co-settlor, Mr. Taylor disagreed and said he intended to so designate her and then use the singular of the word "settlor" to refer to both Maureen and Norman as he had done with the singular word "trustee" to refer to Maureen and the bank. Other features of the drafting and signing of the trust indentures were pointed out which could be construed to impeach Mr. Taylor's testimony that a mistake in the drafting had been made.

The foregoing summary demonstrates that a fact issue was made on the question of mistake in the drafting of the trust indenture to correctly express the parties' intention. The evidence raising such issue should have been admitted on appellants' plea for reformation.

If, by mistake, an instrument as written fails to express the true intention or agreement of the parties, equity will grant reformation of the instrument so as to make it correctly express the agreement actually made. The rule applies to express inter vivos trusts as well as to other written instruments. The mistake may be shown by parol evidence. And although a mutual mistake of the parties is required in most instances, if a settlor of a trust receives no consideration for the creation of the trust, a unilateral mistake on his part is sufficient. It is immaterial whether the mistake be one of fact or law. Any mistake of the scrivener which could defeat the true intention may be corrected in equity by reformation, whether the mistake is one of fact or law. The fact that the written instrument is couched in unambiguous language, or that the parties knew what words were used and were aware of their ordinary meaning, or that they were negligent in failing to discover the mistake before signing the instrument, will not preclude relief by reformation....

Appellees contend, however, that because the residuary trust in Mrs. Brinker's will eventually will pour over into the Brinker Family Trust, and Mrs. Brinker's will has now been probated, the Brinker Family Trust, so far as the pour over assets are concerned, has become testamentary and consequently it cannot be reformed. We disagree.

It is true that a testamentary disposition is not subject to reformation. But we hold that the Brinker Family Trust did not become testamentary by reason of Mrs. Brinker's residuary trust pour over.

Prior to the drafting of the Uniform Testamentary Additions to Trusts Act [see Chapters 7 and 9], there were two legal doctrines concerning the validity and nature of testamentary additions to inter vivos trusts. One was the doctrine of incorporation by reference, which held that the terms of the inter vivos trust became incorporated into the will by reference and became a part of it, thus rendering the trust testamentary insofar as the gift was concerned.... The other was the doctrine of independent significance, which held that the trust did not become a part of the will, but that the testamentary bequest or devise simply was added to and augmented the trust corpus to be administered as a part of the trust according to its provisions. Under that doctrine the trust provisions concerning disposition of the gift did not become testamentary.... The Uniform Testamentary Additions to Trusts Act was designed to validate testamentary additions to trusts even though such trusts were amendable, and to prevent the trust provisions affecting such gift from becoming testamentary. The Act provides in part as follows:

> ...the property so devised or bequeathed (a) *shall not be deemed to be held under a testamentary trust of the testator but shall become a part of the trust to which it is given and (b) shall be administered and disposed of in accordance with the provisions of the instrument...* setting forth the terms of the trust.... (Emphasis supplied.)

Texas adopted the Uniform Act in 1961.... Although the Texas version does not specifically provide that such a gift will not be deemed to be held under a testamentary trust, in other respects it is essentially the same as the Uniform Act, and it specifically provides that the gift "... shall be added to the corpus of such trust to be administered as a part thereof and shall thereafter be governed by the terms and provisions of the instrument establishing such trust...." We hold that the intention of the Texas Act was that the trust provisions would not become testamentary by reason of such a gift, but that the gift would simply augment the corpus of the trust and become a part of it.

Appellees assert that a reformation of the Family Trust would violate that portion of [the Texas version of the Uniform Act] which provides that a gift to a trust will be governed by the trust instrument *and any written amendments or modifications made before the death of the testator.* It is argued that to reform the Family Trust would be the equivalent of amending or modifying it after the death of Maureen Brinker. We cannot agree.

To amend or modify an agreement means to change it.... Reformation does not change the agreement; it enforces the agreement. It orders a change in the drafted instrument so that it will correctly express what has been the real agreement from its inception.

The excluded evidence on the issue of reformation is before us in the bill of exceptions, but as indicated in our summary of that evidence it is not so conclusive that it determines the issue as a matter of law and allows us to render a judgment. There is positive evidence of mistake; yet there are circumstances which bear upon the credibility and accuracy of the testimony which might lead reasonable minds to reject it. A fact issue has been created which requires resolution by a trier of fact. The judgment will therefore be reversed and remanded for a new trial.

Note

Reformation of Will Substitute. In Estate of Robinson v. Robinson, 720 So.2d 540 (Fla. Dist. Ct. App. 1998), the court confronted an argument that a revocable inter vivos trust could not be reformed because it was in substance a will. The court rejected the argument, saying that "we hold that a trust with testamentary aspects may be reformed after the death of the settlor for a unilateral drafting mistake so long as the reformation is not contrary to the interest of the settlor."

Mahoney v. Grainger
186 N.E. 86 (Mass. 1933)

RUGG, C.J. This is an appeal from a decree of a probate court denying a petition for distribution of a legacy under the will of Helen A. Sullivan among her first cousins who are contended to be her heirs at law. The residuary clause was as follows:

> All the rest and residue of my estate, both real and personal property, I give, demise [sic] and bequeath to my heirs at law living at the time of my decease, absolutely; to be divided among them equally, share and share alike; provided, however, that the real property which I own at my decease shall not be sold or disposed of until five (5) years after my decease, unless there is not sufficient personal property at the time of my decease to pay my specific legatees; in which case said real property may be sold. The income from said real property during said five (5) years is to be distributed among my heirs at law as I have directed.

The trial judge made a report of the material facts in substance as follows: The sole heir at law of the testatrix at the time of her death was her maternal aunt, Frances Hawkes Greene, who is still living and who was named in the petition for probate of her will. The will was duly proved and allowed on October 8, 1931, and letters testamentary issued accordingly. The testatrix was a single woman about sixty-four years of age, and had been a school teacher. She always maintained her own home but her relations with her aunt who was her sole heir and with several first cousins were cordial and friendly. In her will she gave general legacies in considerable sums to two of her first cousins. About ten days before her death the testatrix sent for an attorney who found her sick but intelligent about the subjects of their conversation. She told the attorney she wanted to make a will. She gave him instructions as to general pecuniary legacies. In response to the questions "Whom do you want to leave the rest of your property to? Who are your nearest relations?" she replied "I've got about twenty-five first cousins... let them share it equally." The attorney then drafted the will and read it to the testatrix and it was executed by her.

The trial judge ruled that statements of the testatrix

were admissible only in so far as they tended to give evidence of the material circumstances surrounding the testatrix at the time of the execution of the will; that the words heirs at law were words in common use, susceptible of application to one or many; that when applied to the special circumstances of this case that the testatrix had but one heir, notwithstanding the added words "to be divided among them equally, share and share alike," there was no latent ambiguity or equivocation in the will itself which would permit the introduction of the statements of the testatrix to prove her testamentary intention.

Certain first cousins have appealed from the decree dismissing the petition for distribution to them.

There is no doubt as to the meaning of the words "heirs at law living at the time of my decease" as used in the will. Confessedly they refer alone to the aunt of the testatrix and do not include her cousins.

A will duly executed and allowed by the court must under the statute of wills be accepted as the final expression of the intent of the person executing it. The fact that it was not in conformity to the instructions given to the draftsman who prepared it or that he made a mistake does not authorize a court to reform or alter it or remold it by amendments. The will must be construed as it came from the hands of the testatrix. Mistakes in the drafting of the will may be of significance in some circumstances in a trial as to the due execution and allowance of the alleged testamentary instrument. Proof that the legatee actually designated was not the particular person intended by the one executing the will cannot be received to aid in the interpretation of a will. When the instrument has been proved and allowed as a will oral testimony as to the meaning and purpose of a testator in using language must be rigidly excluded.

It is only where testamentary language is not clear in its application to facts that evidence may be introduced as to the circumstances under which the testator used that language in order to throw light upon its meaning. Where no doubt exists as to the property bequeathed or the identity of the beneficiary there is no room for extrinsic evidence; the will must stand as written.

In the case at bar there is no doubt as to the heirs at law of the testatrix. The aunt alone falls within that description. The cousins are excluded. The circumstance that the plural word "heirs" was used does not prevent one individual from taking the entire gift.

Decree affirmed.

Notes

1. *Malpractice Liability?* Is an attorney liable in malpractice for failing to confirm a client's statement regarding the identity of the client's heirs? The court held no in Leak-Gilbert v. Fahle, 55 P.3d 1054 (Okla. 2002).

2. *Plain-Meaning Rule.* The rule applied in *Mahoney* is sometimes known as the "plain-meaning" rule. When the meaning of the will is "plain," no deviation can be permitted. Accord Gustafson v. Svenson, 366 N.E.2d 761 (Mass. 1977) (holding that devises to testators' brother or "his heirs per stirpes" found in the wills of two sisters is unambiguous and rejecting extrinsic evidence of attorney that testators did not intend that their brother's wife should share in their estate). The following passage is a familiar statement of the plain-meaning rule:

> Where there is nothing in the context of a will from which it is apparent that a testator has used the words in which he has expressed himself in any other than their strict and primary sense, and where his words so interpreted are sensible with reference to extrinsic circumstances, it is an inflexible rule of construction, that the words of the will shall be interpreted in their strict and primary sense, and in no other, although they may be capable of some popular or secondary interpretation, and although the most conclusive evidence of intention to use them in such popular or secondary sense be tendered. [James Wigram, An Examination of the Rules of Law, Respecting the Admission of Extrinsic Evidence in Aid of the Interpretation of Wills 18 (5th ed. 1914).]

Closely linked to the plain-meaning rule is another rule—the no-extrinsic-evidence rule. If equity will not entertain suits to reform wills, no purpose would be served by allowing the introduction of extrinsic evidence to contradict clear and unambiguous terms in a will.

3. *Continental Legal Tradition.* The Anglo-American approach to construction questions is in sharp contrast to the continental legal tradition. As explained by Erich Schanze:

> Broadly stated, the Anglo-American tradition emphasizes objective, literal interpretation of statutory texts and private declarations of intention. Extrinsic or subjective factors are admissible only in a limited number of exceptions. In contrast, Continental legal systems tend to be generous in ascertaining purposes and intentions of legislative and private texts.

The radically different styles of construction are associated with a different philosophy of legislating and drafting. The scrutiny of legal definitions and the length of documents in the Anglo-American context are still a source of amazement for many civil lawyers. Likewise, the brevity of similar texts on the Continent must appear cryptic for a common lawyer. The diverging position is most notable in the interpretation of testaments .... [Erich Schanze, Interpretation of Wills—An Essay Critical and Comparative, in Comparative and Historical Essays in Scots Law 104 (D. L. Carey Miller and D. W. Meyers eds. 1992).]

PART B. RESOLVING AMBIGUITIES IN WILLS AND OTHER DONATIVE DOCUMENTS

Costello: All I'm trying to find out is what's the guy's name on first base.
Abbott: No. What is on second base.
Costello: I'm not asking you who's on second.
Abbott: Who's on first.
Costello: One base at a time!
  – Bud Abbott and Lou Costello, from their most famous comedy routine

Although courts will not "reform" wills, they will resolve ambiguities in wills in accordance with the testator's intention as proved by extrinsic evidence. An "ambiguity" is defined in the Restatement as "an uncertainty in meaning that is revealed by the text or by extrinsic evidence other than direct evidence of intention contradicting the plain meaning of the text." Restatement 3d of Property §11.1. The Restatement declares that an ambiguity "is resolved by construing the text of the donative document in accordance with the donor's intention, to the extent that the donor's intention is established by a preponderance of the evidence." Id. §11.2.

The Restatement provides that "all relevant evidence, whether direct or circumstantial, may be considered. Thus, the text of the donative document and relevant extrinsic evidence may both be considered" for purposes of determining a donor's intent. Id. §10.2. The Restatement includes a list of some types of ambiguities that should be resolved by determining the donor's intent through the use of extrinsic evidence. That list includes: (1) the text or extrinsic evidence (other than direct evidence contradicting the plain meaning of the text) reveals a mistaken description of persons or property; (2) the text reveals an apparent mistaken inclusion or omission; or (3) extrinsic evidence (other than direct evidence contradicting the plain meaning of the text) reveals that the donor's personal usage differs from the ordinary meaning of a term used in the text. Id. §11.2. The material that follows examines these types of ambiguities and the remedies the courts have provided to cure defective expressions of donative intent.

1. Ambiguous Descriptions of Persons or Property

Arnheiter v. Arnheiter
125 A.2d 914 (N.J. Ch. 1956)

SULLIVAN, J.S.C. Burnette K. Guterl died on December 31, 1953, leaving a last will and testament which has been admitted to probate by the Surrogate of Essex County. By paragraph 2 of said will her executrix was directed "to sell my undivided one-half interest of premises known as No. 304 Harrison Avenue, Harrison, New Jersey," and use the proceeds of sale to establish trusts for each of decedent's two nieces.

This suit comes about because the decedent did not own or have any interest in 304 Harrison Avenue either at her death or at the time her will was executed. At the hearing it was established that the decedent, at the time her will was executed and also at the time of her death, owned an undivided one-half interest in 317 Harrison Avenue, Harrison, New Jersey, and that this was the only property on Harrison Avenue that she had any interest in.

Plaintiff-executrix has applied to this court to correct an obvious mistake and to change the street number in paragraph "2" of the will to read "No. 317 Harrison Avenue" instead of "No. 304 Harrison Avenue." Relief cannot be granted to the plaintiff in the precise manner sought. It matters not that an obvious mistake in the form of a misdescription is proved. A court has no power to correct or reform a will or change any of the language therein by substituting or adding words. The will of a decedent executed pursuant to statute is what it is and no court can add to it.

Plaintiff, however, is not without recourse. In the construction of wills and other instruments there is a principle *"falsa demonstratio non nocet"* (mere erroneous description does not vitiate), which applies directly to the difficulty at hand.

> Where a description of a thing or person consists of several particulars and all of them do not fit any one person or thing, less essential particulars may be rejected provided the remainder of the description clearly fits. This is known as the doctrine of falsa demonstratio non nocet. [Clapp, 5 N.J. Practice, section 114, page 274.]

A leading case involving the application of the above maxim to facts similar to our own is Patch v. White, 117 U.S. 210 (1886). There, the testator bequeathed to his brother land which he described as belonging to himself and as containing improvements, the lot being "numbered six, in square four hundred and three." He did not own the lot so numbered but did own lot number 3, in square 406, which was improved. The lot numbered 6 in square 403 had no improvements. The court applied the principle of *falsa demonstratio non nocet,* and by disregarding or rejecting the words "six" and "three" in the description, concluded that the lot owned by the decedent passed to his brother under this provision of the will.

Turning to the problem at hand and to the description of the property as set forth in paragraph 2 of the will, we find the street number "304" to be erroneous because decedent did not own that property. If we disregard or reject that item of description, the will then directs the executrix "to sell my undivided one-half interest of premises known as Harrison Avenue, Harrison, New Jersey." Since it has been established that the decedent, at the time of her death and also when she executed her will, had an interest in only one piece of property on Harrison Avenue, Harrison, New Jersey; that her interest was an undivided one-half interest; that the property in question is 317 Harrison Avenue; and that decedent made no other specific provision in her will relating to 317 Harrison Avenue, we are led inevitably to the conclusion that even without a street number, the rest of the description in paragraph 2 of the will is sufficient to identify the property passing thereunder as 317 Harrison Avenue.

Judgment will be entered construing decedent's will as aforesaid.

Notes, Questions, and Problems

1. *Remedying Ambiguities. Arnheiter* not only illustrates the admissibility of extrinsic evidence in cases of ambiguity but also introduces one of the remedial techniques employed in such cases—the deletion of the erroneous parts of a mistaken description, so that what is left accurately describes the testator's intention. As the court noted, the leading case for this approach is Patch v. White, 117 U.S. 210 (1886), but the decision in that case was not reached without a struggle. Four justices dissented. They asserted that the court "is not construing the will of the testator; it is making a will for him." Id. at 227.

This statement from the dissenting opinion raises a challenging question: If courts have no power to reform wills by substituting or adding words, by what authority do they have the power to delete words?

The opposite question also has been raised: If courts have the power to delete words from wills, why do they not have the power to substitute or add words to them? The Restatement 3d of Property §11.2 comment c rejects the view that the only technique for resolving an ambiguity is deleting the erroneous portions of the description. The Restatement declares that the remedy should forthrightly correct the misdescription:

> Once an ambiguity is revealed, it is well accepted that extrinsic evidence may be considered in resolving the ambiguity. When the donor's intention is then proved by a preponderance of the evidence, the final step, correcting the mistaken expression, should follow as a matter of remedy, and should not be unnecessarily hindered by an artificial line between deleting and adding.

2. *Problems on Ambiguity.* Applying the conventional distinction between ambiguous and unambiguous descriptions of persons or property, would extrinsic evidence be admissible in the following cases? Could the misdescriptions be remedied by the technique employed in *Arnheiter* and *Patch*?

(a) Nathaniel Tucker knew about the work of the American Seaman's Friend Society in New York City and intended to devise a part of his estate to this society. The lawyer who prepared his will only knew about one association for the benefit of seamen, the Seaman's Aid Society of Boston. Nathaniel knew nothing of this society, but the lawyer persuaded him that the society he had in mind went by the name "Seaman's Aid Society of Boston," and this is the way the will was written. See Tucker v. Seaman's Aid Soc'y, 48 Mass. (7 Metc.) 188 (1843). For other cases raising a similar question, see In re Girard Trust Corn Exchange Bank, 208 A.2d 857 (Pa. 1965) (inter vivos deed of trust); Vadman v. American Cancer Soc'y, 615 P.2d 500 (Wash. Ct. App. 1980); National Soc'y for the Prevention of Cruelty to Children v. Scottish Nat'l Soc'y for the Prevention of Cruelty to Children, [1915] App. Cas. 207 (H.L.). See also Estate of Hillyer, 664 So.2d 361 (Fla. Dist. Ct. App. 1995) (reversing the lower court for admitting any extrinsic evidence regarding the testator's contrary intent because the disposition of the property was unambiguous).

Many charities have sound-alike names. See Chapter 12.

(b) The testator's will devised certain property "to my well-beloved nephews John and William Willard." The testator had two sets of relatives by the names of John and William Willard—grandnephews and grandsons. Evidence was sought to be introduced that the grandnephews were strangers to the testator, never visited him, and never resided near him. The grandsons, however, lived near the testator. The testator was very intimate and friendly with them and repeatedly declared that he had bought the devised property for his grandsons. The lawyer who drew the will sought to testify that the testator directed that the property in question should be given to the grandsons, but by mistake the lawyer wrote "nephews" instead. See Willard v. Darrah, 68 S.W. 1023 (Mo. 1902). For another case raising a similar question, see Siegley v. Simpson, 131 P. 479 (Wash. 1913) in which the testator made a devise to "my friend Richard H. Simpson." Extrinsic evidence showed that Hamilton Ross Simpson, whom the testator called "Bill" or "Rotary Bill," was the testator's "friend" and that Richard H. Simpson was merely a remote acquaintance.

3. *Significance of Language of Ownership.* Of what significance was it that the devise in *Arnheiter* contained explicit language of ownership: "*my* undivided one-half interest of premises known as No. 304 Harrison Avenue"? (The devise in *Patch* also said that the devised property "belongs to me.") Is it reasonable to infer, in the absence of express language of ownership, that the will refers to property owned by the testator? In Lynch's Estate, 75 P. 1086 (Cal. 1904), Lynch devised to his nephew Dennis "that certain lot... in Tulare County, State of California, and described as follows, to wit: the S. 1/2 of the N.W. 1/4 of Sec. 1, T. 21, R. 27 E." Lynch never owned this tract but he did own the west half of the southwest quarter of the same section. The court held that the intended devise was ineffective. The court was willing to disregard the "false description," leaving the will as though it read "the 1/2 of the 1/4 of Sec. 1" etc., but in its opinion this left the description too uncertain to be given effect:

There are four quarter sections within the section, each of which can be divided into halves in four different ways, so that there are sixteen descriptions of land to which this language could apply with equal certainty.

Compare *Lynch* with Whitehouse v. Whitehouse, 113 N.W. 759 (Iowa 1907). The will devised "the north half of the northwest quarter of section 29, township 80, range 25, Polk County, Iowa." The testator owned only the north half of the northeast quarter of the same section. The court held that extrinsic evidence was admissible to show to which of the north quarters the description should be applied after omitting the word "west." "[T]he presumption should prevail," the court stated, "that the testator is undertaking in his will, without saying so in express terms, to dispose of property which he believed belonged to him, rather than to belong to another." Accord Restatement 3d of Property §11.2 comment i illus. 5. See also Metropolitan Life Ins. Co. v. Johnson, 297 F.3d 558 (7th Cir. 2002), reproduced in Chapter 7, where the court held that a life insurance change-of-beneficiary form validly changed the beneficiary of the insured life insurance plan despite the fact that the insured checked the wrong life insurance box; the court noted that the insured was only enrolled in one life insurance plan, and he must have meant to refer to the plan in which he was enrolled.

———

Patent and Latent Ambiguities. According to the Restatement 3d of Property, a *patent ambiguity* "is an ambiguity that is apparent from the text of the donative document." A *latent ambiguity* "is an ambiguity that is not apparent merely from reading the text of the donative document but becomes apparent from extrinsic evidence.... [D]irect evidence of intention contradicting the plain meaning of the text does not establish a latent ambiguity." Restatement 3d of Property §11.1 comments b, c. *Arnheiter* and *Patch* present examples of latent ambiguities.

A common statement found in court opinions and other legal authority is that extrinsic evidence can be used to resolve a *latent* ambiguity but not a *patent* ambiguity. The distinction between latent and patent ambiguities was given currency by Sir Francis Bacon in his Maxims of the Law, in which he said that a patent ambiguity "is never holpen by averrement... because the law will not couple and mingle matter of specialty, which is of the higher account, with matter of averrement, which is of inferiour account." Francis Bacon, Elements of Common Law 82 (1639), reprinted in Francis Bacon, Law Tracts 99 (1737), and 7 Francis Bacon's Works 385 (1870).

American scholars of evidence law long ago repudiated Bacon's distinction. In his great Preliminary Treatise on Evidence 424 (1898), James Bradley Thayer described Bacon's distinction as an "unprofitable subtlety," and Dean Wigmore likewise condemned the distinction as resting on a "play upon words." 9 John H. Wigmore,

Evidence 226, 239 (3d ed. 1940).[2] That the distinction has any important influence on decisions today is doubtful, but it cannot be wholly ignored if for no other reason than that courts occasionally still talk in such terms. See, e.g., Estate of Schultheis, 747 A.2d 918 (Pa. Super. Ct. 2000). The Restatement 3d of Property provides that "no legal consequences attach to the distinction" between latent and patent ambiguities. Restatement 3d of Property §11.1 comment a. See also University of Southern Indiana v. Baker, 843 N.E.2d 528 (Ind. 2006) (observing that the distinction between latent and patent ambiguities "no longer serves any useful purpose").

Admissibility of Evidence of Direct Declarations of Intent. In general, then, extrinsic evidence is available as an aid to construction and to resolve an ambiguity whether latent or patent. See, e.g., First Union Nat'l Bank of Florida v. Frumkin, 659 So.2d 463 (Fla. Dist. Ct. App. 1995) (involving the patent ambiguity of an inconsistency between two testamentary trust provisions regarding the trustee's discretionary power to invade principal on behalf of a beneficiary); Maurice F. Jones Trust v. Barnett Banks Trust Co., 637 N.E.2d 1301 (Ind. Ct. App. 1994) (concerning the latent ambiguity of whether the phrase "which I am legally obligated to pay" applied to that portion of the federal estate taxes resulting from inclusion of a QTIP trust created by the testator's husband). But there is one general prohibition on the type of evidence that may be used. Traditionally, testimony about the testator's statements as to what language in the will was intended to mean is not admissible—testimony as to "declarations of intention," as Wigmore called it. 9 Wigmore at 229.

According to Wigmore, this limitation rests upon the "rule which prohibits setting up any extrinsic utterance to compete with and overthrow the words of a document." He recognized that such declarations could be used not for this purpose but rather for that of interpreting the words of the document, yet concluded: "There being two conceivable purposes for which it could be used, the one proper, the [other] improper, it is excluded because of the risk that the latter would dominate and that the temptation to abuse would be too strong." Id. at 229-30.

Equivocations. Despite the traditional inadmissibility of the testator's direct declarations of intent, there is one instance where it is well established that such evidence will be received, that is, where there is an *equivocation*. An equivocation exists when the words of the will apply equally to two persons or things.

The Commonwealth courts have been somewhat more insistent than the American courts that the words fit the two persons or things more or less equally. In addition, they have tended to limit the equivocation exception to a situation in which the

---

2. Wigmore had in mind the argument, repeated by the United States Supreme Court in Patch v. White, 117 U.S. 210, 217 (1886), that "as a latent ambiguity is only disclosed by extrinsic evidence, it may be removed by extrinsic evidence."

words are a fairly exact description of the two persons or things. An example of this narrow reading of the exception comes from an Ontario case, In re Gray, [1934] Ont. W.N. 17. The testator had one brother whose full name was "John Gray" and another whose full name was "Norman Farquharson Gray." His will left a part of the residue of his estate in equal shares to his brothers and sisters, with a proviso that the share of his brother "John Norman Gray" was to be placed in trust so that he was to have only a life estate instead of an absolute interest. The court rejected evidence of statements by the testator that this special provision was to apply to Norman. "In this case," the court said, "the name 'John Norman' cannot be said to be equally applicable in all its parts to each of the brothers... although the name so used in the will is in part correctly applicable to each of these brothers." Lacking competent evidence of which of the two brothers was meant, the court held that this part of the will was void because of uncertainty.

For a time it was suggested that the equivocation exception was limited to latent ambiguities. Older cases should have put this artificial distinction to rest. See, e.g., Doe d. George Gord v. Needs, 2 Mees. & W. 129, 150 Eng. Rep. 698 (Ex. 1836) (resolving patent ambiguity by testator's declarations of intention). The distinction, however, keeps reappearing in cases. See, e.g., Virginia Nat'l Bank v. United States, 443 F.2d 1030, 1034 (4th Cir. 1971) (treating an equivocation as a patent ambiguity and not allowing into evidence the testator's direct declaration of intent but allowing into evidence advice given to the testator pertaining to the testator's overall tax objectives); Breckner v. Prestwood, 600 S.W.2d 52, 56 (Mo. Ct. App. 1980) (admitting direct declarations of intent for latent but not patent ambiguities); see also Lehr v. Collier, 909 S.W.2d 717 (Mo. Ct. App. 1995) (allowing reformation of lifetime trust but holding that patent ambiguity precluded admission of direct declarations of intent).

Other cases have abandoned restrictions on the admissibility of a testator's direct declarations. For example, consider the case of Estate of Smith, 580 P.2d 754 (Ariz. Ct. App. 1978). In that case, Hazel Smith's will devised "my money and coin collection to Todd Fehlhaber and Sue Fehlhaber in equal shares, or to the survivor thereof." Included in Smith's estate were a collection of thirty-six coins and six two-dollar bills found in her safe deposit box and appraised at $49, and various bank accounts and certificates of deposit valued at close to $107,000. The residuary devisees sought to introduce an affidavit of the attorney who drew the will that related the testator's directions to the attorney. The affidavit indicated that the testator wanted the collection of coins and bills to go to Todd and Sue and that she wanted the rest of her assets, including the certificates of deposit and savings accounts, to go to the named residuary devisees. The lower court admitted this affidavit into evidence. The court of appeals affirmed, saying:

> We agree there was an ambiguity in the instant will and it was a patent one. The term "money" when used in wills is essentially ambiguous.... The word may have any meaning which the testamentary intent, as manifested by the will read in the light of proper evidence,

imparts to it.... Once having established an ambiguity, parol evidence is admissible for the purpose of explaining it.... The language used here admits of two constructions.... It was therefore proper to resort to extrinsic proof, including the statement of the attorney who drew up the will.

The Restatement of Property considerably broadened the definition of equivocation to be a description "indifferently applicable to two or more persons or objects." Restatement of Property §242 comment j. This definition would seem to apply to nearly all ambiguous descriptions of persons or property, either latent or patent. The Restatement 3d of Property abandons the restriction completely and provides that evidence of the testator's direct declarations of intent may be considered in resolving ambiguities of any type, latent or patent. See Restatement 3d of Property §10.2 comment f; §11.2 comment d.

Potential Evidentiary Bars to the Admissibility of the Testator's Statements. In addition to the traditional rule against admitting direct declarations of intent, other evidentiary rules may bar admission of the testator's statements. The Restatement 3d of Property §10.2 comment h provides that "[t]o the extent appropriate, the rules of evidence should be construed to allow direct evidence of the donor's intention, whether the evidence concerns utterances or events occurring before or after execution of the donative document."

Dead Man's Acts. In Estate of Thomas, 327 A.2d 31 (Pa. 1974), the court disposed of the so-called Dead Man's Act as an obstacle to the admission of the testator's statements, saying:

> Appellant contends finally that the Orphans' Court committed a clear violation of the Dean Man's Statute... in permitting the appellee and his wife to testify as to appellee's conversations with the decedent with reference to the shares of stock and the savings account mentioned in Paragraph Eighth and to decedent's intent to benefit him.[3] This contention is without merit. Where opposing parties in a controversy involving merely the testamentary distribution of property present their claims under the will, either party is competent under language of the Statute to testify as to prior conversations with the testator regardless of any individual interest possessed by them in the testator's property.

But see Estate of Malnar, 243 N.W.2d 435 (Wis. 1976) (applying Dead Man's

---

3. The Dead Man's Statute provides in pertinent part:

    Nor, where any party to a thing or contract in action is dead, or has been adjudged a lunatic and his right thereto or therein has passed, either by his own act or by the act of the law, to a party on the record who represents his interest in the subject in controversy, shall any surviving or remaining party to such thing or contract, or any other person whose interest shall be adverse to the said right of such deceased or lunatic party, be a competent witness to any matter occurring before the death of said party or the adjudication of his lunacy... unless the issue or inquiry be devisavit vel non, or be any other issue or inquiry respecting the property of a deceased owner, and the controversy be between parties respectively claiming such property by devolution on the death of such owner, in which case all persons shall be fully competent witnesses.

[Footnote by the court. Ed.]

Statute); Estate of Christen, 239 N.W.2d 528 (Wis. 1976) (holding that incompetency of legatee under prior will to testify as to conversations with the decedent does not extend to the spouse of the legatee). See generally Report, Dead Man Statutes: Their Purposes, Effect and Future, 7 Real Prop. Prob. & Trust J. 343 (1972). Rule 601 of the Uniform Rules of Evidence (1974, amended 2011) provides that "[e]very person is competent to be a witness unless these rules provide otherwise...." The 1974 Official Comment to Rule 601 states that "[t]his repeals the 'deadman's statute.'"

Hearsay Rule. The hearsay rule is not an obstacle to the admission of a testator's statements made before the will was executed. Such statements come within the exception to the rule for declarations showing a state of mind. As to postexecution statements, however, there is a split of authority, some courts holding their admission barred by the hearsay rule, others holding their admission not barred by that rule. 6 Wigmore, supra, §§1734-40. Rule 803 of the Uniform Rules of Evidence (1974, amended 2014) provides that the testator's statements relating to "the validity or terms of the declarant's will" are not barred by the hearsay rule.

Attorney-client privilege. The following analysis of the attorney-client privilege appears in Stevens v. Thurston, 289 A.2d 398 (N.H. 1972):

Defendants as contestants moved to discover the contents of the file of the attorney who drafted the will.... The Trial Court denied [the] motion and reserved and transferred defendants' exceptions.

It appears from the reserved case that the denial of the motion for discovery was based solely on the attorney-client privilege. We recognize and enforce the common-law rule that confidential communications between a client and attorney are privileged and protected from inquiry in the absence of a waiver by the client.... We have also held that the privilege continues after the death of the client in actions against the estate and may be waived by the representatives of the decedent....

This appeal from the probate of the will, however,... is not an adverse proceeding against the estate..., but a contest between parties claiming through the testator. If the defendants are successful, they, rather than the plaintiff, will be the representatives of the testator. Here the privilege is being asserted not for the protection of the testator or his estate but for the protection of a claimant to his estate. The authorities uniformly hold that in this situation all reason for assertion of the privilege disappears and that the protection of the testator lies in the admission of all relevant evidence that will aid in the determination of his true will.... Defendants' exception to the denial of their motion for discovery is sustained.

The distinction drawn by *Stevens* is well accepted. See, e.g., Fletcher v. Alameda County Superior Court, 52 Cal. Rptr. 2d 65 (Ct. App. 1996). It is embodied in §81 of the Restatement (Third) of the Law Governing Lawyers ("The attorney-client privilege does not apply to a communication from or to a decedent relevant to an issue between parties who claim an interest through the same deceased client, either by testate or intestate succession or by an inter vivos transaction."), and in §10.2 comment f of the Restatement 3d of Property.

Moseley v. Goodman

195 S.W. 590 (Tenn. 1917)

NEIL, C.J. E.J. Halley died on October 19, 1910, leaving the following will:

I, E.J. Halley, of a sound mind, will make this my last will and testament. I bequeath to the following people mound set of the names, E.O. Kolley, $500.00, Mr. R.G. Ramsey, $500.00, Miss Elizabeth Berry $500.00. I give to A. Goodman and Armstrong $10,000 a piece, Ed. Hurlburt $5000. Jack Brennan $5000. George Becktall $20,000, Mrs. Moseley $20,000. Mrs. Moseley's housekeeper $20,000, W.M. Palmer $20,000. Mrs. Mergle, Sr., $20,000, Ed. Mergle, $20,000, Theadore Mergle $10,000, the balance of my real estate I give to the St. Peter's Orphan Asylum.

The controversy arises over the legacy: "Mrs. Moseley $20,000, Mrs. Moseley's housekeeper $20,000." That is to say, while the legacy to Mrs. Moseley is the only one directly involved here, it is necessary to consider the legacy to the housekeeper in connection with it, so far as the word "housekeeper" is descriptive of the Mrs. Moseley, intended, as the one who had a housekeeper....

The facts disclosed by the record, by the overwhelming weight of the evidence, are as follows:

The testator was for many years engaged with his mother in business on Main street, in the city of Memphis, in the sale of liquors, tobacco, and cigars. He and his mother bought, through a series of years, cigars from Mr. F.S. Trimble, the husband of Mrs. Lillian E. Trimble. Mr. Trimble was the city salesman for one R.L. Moseley, and, as such, for several years, sold cigars to testator and his mother. Testator generally addressed him as "Moseley," it seems, because he sold the Moseley cigars, and the Moseley sign was very prominently displayed at the front of the building where Trimble worked. It does not appear that testator dealt personally with R. L. Moseley himself at all. Mrs. Trimble, during the same period, bought goods about once a month from testator and his mother, and the testator called her "Mrs. Moseley," and admired her character very greatly. He spoke of her to others as a fine woman. The mother of testator died about January, 1910, and he then fell into the habit of drinking, and became quite dissipated. He made a foreign tour with one Harper, he himself paying all the expenses. His mother had left him about $230,000. He claimed, when he came back, that he had spent $6,000 on this trip. He drank a great deal while he was traveling, and came back in a bad state of health. After his mother died, and before he started on the foreign tour, he engaged a room at an apartment house known as "The Monarch," which was owned, or leased, by Mr. Trimble. Mrs. Trimble had charge of it as manager. When testator started on his foreign tour he gave up his room, but immediately on his return he secured the same or another room at "The Monarch," Mrs. Trimble being still the manager. He still drank heavily and was ill. He stayed at "The Monarch" two or three weeks, and was then removed to the hospital, and died within a day or two thereafter, having made the will Monday night and died Wednesday morning.

Mrs. Trimble, at the time testator returned to "The Monarch," had, as her housekeeper for that institution, Mrs. Anna Lang. Both Mrs. Trimble and Mrs. Lang gave the testator very devoted attention, such attention as a sick man needs, serving night and day. Mrs. Trimble brought him milk and soup and other delicacies. Mrs. Lang ministered to him very assiduously and with great kindness in the way of sponging him and doing other things for his comfort. He appeared to be very grateful for these attentions. He generally called Mrs. Trimble Mrs. Moseley, though occasionally he called her Mrs. Trimble. There is evidence to the effect that he always called her Mrs. Moseley. The witness Rothschild deposed to this fact. He testified that on one occasion, when he was in the room of testator, the latter was talking about Mrs. Moseley quite a good deal, and he asked him who he was referring to, and he said: "Mrs. Trimble; I always call her Mrs. Moseley." He always spoke of Mrs. Lang as "housekeeper," or "the good woman."

It does not appear that he knew Mrs. Lenoir Moseley. It does appear that he knew her husband, R.L. Moseley. Mrs. Moseley herself testified that she did not know Mr. Halley at all. She endeavors to connect herself with the legacy not only by the fact that her name was Mrs. Moseley, but by the further fact that her sister, Miss Jessie Dunlap, was her housekeeper at her private home. It is in proof that the testator incidentally met Miss Dunlap on one occasion at "The Monarch."... [T]here is no real evidence that Halley knew that Miss Dunlap was housekeeper to the complainant. However, in our further treatment of the case we shall assume that he did have such information.

If the testimony was competent to the effect that the testator always or generally spoke of Mrs. Trimble as Mrs. Moseley, or generally called her Mrs. Moseley, there was ample evidence to sustain the verdict [in favor of Mrs. Trimble], and that point is not questioned. However, it is said that the evidence was not competent; that when it was proven that there was in existence a Mrs. Moseley, whose legal name was such, this satisfied the language of the will, and the testimony above referred to concerning Mrs. Trimble's being called Mrs. Moseley by the testator could not be used to raise a latent ambiguity. We are of the opinion that this view is erroneous.

The general principle is well stated in Ayres v. Weed, 16 Conn. 290, as follows:

> If a person is commonly called and known by a name which does not properly belong to him, but which properly belongs to another, it cannot with propriety be said that that name, although a false one, is not in fact descriptive of the former, unless we go so far as to say that a person is not described by the name by which he is known. That would clearly be a case where two different persons would be described by the same name, and where, therefore, parol evidence might be introduced to remove the doubt as to which of them was intended. That the name given to a person is a nickname does not render it the less a description of him, although, indeed, a less correct one, that if his true name were used; and it is well settled that if a legacy is given, or a devise made, to a person by his nickname, parol evidence is admissible to show that the testator usually called him by that name, in order to show that he was intended; much more would it be admissible to show that he was

generally known in the community by that name.

Now, there is no evidence in this record that Mrs. Trimble was generally known by the name of Mrs. Moseley; but it was sufficient to indicate the meaning of the testator if it be shown, as it is shown here, that he was accustomed to call her by that name....

[A] devise to a person by any name, however different the name used in the will from the true name of the person, is good, provided it is shown that the name used was one by which the testator was accustomed to designate the person, and such showing may be made by parol proof....

Counsel for the complainant insist that if the court should hold that Mrs. Trimble was the person intended, and so should affirm the judgment of the chancellor and the Court of Civil Appeals decreeing the legacy to her, that would be nothing short of striking the name of Mrs. Moseley from the will, and inserting in its place that of Mrs. Trimble, and so writing a new will for the testator. This argument is clearly fallacious. We look to the evidence merely to ascertain what individual the testator had in mind when he wrote the term "Mrs. Moseley." The evidence recited, if competent, must convince any one, as it did the jury, that he meant Mrs. Trimble, because "Mrs. Moseley" was the name by which he called her, and because of his long acquaintanceship with her, the esteem in which he had long held her, and the kindnesses on account of which he was indebted to her, and because of his associating with her the person whom he always called "the housekeeper," Mrs. Anna Lang....

Judgment will therefore be entered here affirming the judgment of the Court of Civil Appeals, with costs.

Note and Questions

1. *The Personal-Usage Doctrine. Moseley* illustrates an established exception to the no-extrinsic-evidence rule: the "personal usage" doctrine. See Restatement 3d of Property § 11.2(b)(3) comments r to u ("When the donor's personal usage differs from the ordinary meaning of a term used in the text, the document contains a latent ambiguity"); Restatement of Property § 242 comment d.

2. *Questions.* Could the personal-usage doctrine have been used in Mahoney v. Granger or in Tucker v. Seaman's Aid Soc'y?

2. Mistakes in the Inducement

Primary Statutory Reference: *UPC §2-302*

Gifford v. Dyer
2 R.I. 99 (1852)

This was an appeal from a decree of the Court of Probate of Little Compton, proving and approving the last will and testament of Abigail Irish. The will was dated December 4, 1850, and the testatrix died December 6, 1850. After several bequests of small sums to the children of Robin Gifford and to others, she gives and bequeaths the rest and residue of her property, one half to John Dyer, who was her brother-in-law, and the other half to her two nephews, Jesse and Alexander Dyer. Robin Gifford, the only child of the testatrix, was not mentioned in the will. It appeared in evidence, that at the date of the will, Robin Gifford had been absent from home, leaving a family, for a period of ten years, unheard from; that all the neighbors considered him dead, and that his estate had been administered upon as of a person deceased. The scrivener who drew the will, testified as follows:

> After I had read the will to her, she asked if it would make any difference if she did not mention her son. I asked if she considered him living. She said she supposed he had been dead for years; she said, if it would make any difference she would put his name in, for they will break the will if they can. I think that was the expression she used. I think she said what she had given her grandchildren was in lieu of what he would have, but am not positive. I think her son left in 1841, and was not heard of to my knowledge. She was speaking of a home at Mr. Dyer's and said, what she had given him would pay him well. She said her grandchildren had not been to see her while she was sick.

It appeared that the testatrix had resided with John Dyer for some time previous to her death....

GREENE, C.J. delivered the opinion of the court. It is very apparent in the present case, that the testatrix would have made the same will, had she known her son was living. She did not intend to give him anything, if living.

But if this were not apparent and she had made the will under a mistake as to the supposed death of her son, this could not be shown *dehors* the will. The mistake must appear on the face of the will, and it must also appear what would have been the will of the testatrix but for the mistake. Thus, where the testator revokes a legacy, upon the mistaken supposition that the legatee is dead, and this appears on the face of the instrument of revocation, such revocation was held void. Campbell v. French, 3 Vesey, 321.[4]

---

4. Campbell v. French is a case cited in Chapter 5 on Dependent Relative Revocation, under the topic "Revocation Based on a Mistake of Fact or Law." Ed.

Notes

1. *State of the Authorities.* Most of the decisions follow the view reflected in *Gifford.* See, e.g., Clapp v. Fullerton, 34 N.Y. 190 (1866); Arnold's Estate, 107 N.Y.S.2d 356 (Sur. Ct. 1951), aff'd, 122 N.Y.S.2d 804 (App. Div.), appeal denied, 124 N.Y.S.2d 343 (App. Div. 1953); Bowerman v. Burris, 197 S.W. 490 (Tenn. 1917); Carpenter v. Tinney, 420 S.W.2d 241 (Tex. Civ. App. 1967).

In line with the principle announced in *Gifford*, courts have given effect to a will that omitted or gave a nominal amount to a natural object of the testator's bounty, even though the will itself recited a reason for the action that was in fact false. Relief was denied because the will did not state what the testator would have done had he or she not been mistaken. See, e.g., Le Flore v. Handlin, 240 S.W. 712 (Ark. 1922) (will devised only $100 to one son because he "enjoyed a larger share of his father's estate than either of my two other sons," when in fact that son only received from his father's estate two horses worth about $12.50 each); Riley v. Casey, 170 N.W. 742 (Iowa 1919); Woelk's Estate, 296 P. 359 (Kan. 1931); Shumway's Will, 246 N.Y.S. 178 (Sur. Ct. 1930); Bedlow's Will, 22 N.Y.S. 290 (Sup. Ct. 1893).

2. *Children Omitted Because Thought Dead; Uniform Probate Code.* UPC §2-302(c) creates one exception to the general rule that mistakes in the inducement cannot be corrected. If a testator fails to provide for a child living at the time a testator executes a will solely because the testator mistakenly believes the child to be dead, the child receives a share of the testator's estate as if the child were an omitted afterborn child. See Chapter 8.

Children can be omitted from a parent's will because thought dead in a variety of settings. According to the National Crime Information Center, over 65 percent of the persons reported missing in 2022 were under 18 years of age. See le.fbi.gov/informational-tools/ncic.

3. *Relief for Fraud in the Inducement.* As noted in Chapter 4, courts traditionally will not relieve a mistake that induced the testator to make a devise. They will provide, however, a remedy for fraud in the inducement. An appropriate remedy may include invalidating all or part of the will or imposing a constructive trust remedy to prevent unjust enrichment. A constructive trust is imposed even on innocent devisees or heirs to assure that those persons who the testator would have intended to share in the estate had the fraud not occurred receive their intended shares.

3. Mistaken Omissions

The Restatement 3d of Property provides that a donative document is ambiguous if "the text reveals an apparent mistaken... omission." Restatement 3d of Property §11.2(b)(2). The Restatement 3d also provides that "extrinsic evidence may be considered to establish the content of the mistakenly... omitted language," and that if the content of a mistaken omission is established by extrinsic evidence, the omitted language may be inserted into the document. See Restatement 3d of Property

§11.2(b)(2) comments n to q.

In the following case, does the text of Lois Burnett's will reveal an apparent mistaken omission?

Burnett v. First Commercial Trust Co.
939 S.W.2d 827 (Ark. 1997)

ARNOLD, C.J. This is a case involving a testamentary trust. The issue is whether the will containing the trust is ambiguous in its disposition of the testatrix's property. We hold that the will is not ambiguous, and that the chancellor erred in receiving parol evidence on the question of the testatrix's intent. We therefore reverse and remand.

The testatrix, Lois E. Burnett, died on June 10, 1994. At the time of her death, her family consisted of her brother, James Burnett, her nephew, William Spencer, Jr., and Spencer's six children. Mrs. Burnett's will provided for her funeral expenses and made several small, specific bequests. The will then disposed of the remainder of her estate as follows:

> I give, devise, and bequeath all the rest and residue of my estate, whether real, personal, or mixed, and of whatever kind or nature, wheresoever located and whenever acquired to Arkansas Bank and Trust [now First Commercial Trust Company] in Trust for my friend, Flournoy Adkins, during his lifetime.

> The terms of said trust being as follows:

> 1. Flournoy Adkins is to receive my automobile at the time of my death for his use and benefit.
> 2. Flournoy Adkins has the right and use of my home located as follows:
> [description of the property].
> Upon the death of Flournoy Adkins, the Trustee shall distribute the above described land as follows: one-half interest to my nephew, William Spencer, Jr., and one-half interest to his six children... in equal shares, share and share alike.

As can be seen, the will instructs the trustee that the realty contained in the trust corpus is to be distributed upon the death of Flournoy Adkins. However, it makes no provision for the distribution of the *personalty* contained in the trust corpus. The distinction is important. At the time of Mrs. Burnett's death, the real property in the trust was valued at $25,000.00; the personal property was valued at $194,702.14.

On May 3, 1995, First Commercial brought an action for declaratory judgment seeking instructions on how to distribute the personalty in the trust upon Flournoy Adkins's death. First Commercial claimed that the trust's failure to expressly provide for such distribution was the result of a clerical error. The complaint asked that the personalty be distributed in the same manner as the realty: one-half to William Spencer, Jr., and one-half to the Spencer children. James Burnett, who had received no bequest in the will, answered the complaint. He contended that any part of the trust corpus lacking specific directions for distribution should pass through the laws of intestate succession. The chancellor found that the silence of the will regarding the distribution of the personalty created an ambiguity. He thus allowed the use of parol evidence to explain the omission.

Bruce Garrett, the attorney who prepared Mrs. Burnett's will, testified that Mrs. Burnett came to him in 1992 to change her will. Garrett testified that the will's failure to provide for the disposition of the trust's personal property was the result of a clerical error. The provision which read, "upon the death of Flournoy Adkins, the Trustee shall distribute the above described *land* "should have read,"shall distribute the above described *land and personalty*." Garrett further testified that Mrs. Burnett had decided to cut James out of the will and to provide for her friend, Flournoy Adkins. The previous will, which Mrs. Burnett executed in 1990, had bequeathed the bulk of her estate to James Burnett and William Spencer, Jr. A copy of Mrs. Burnett's old will reflecting the deletions, additions, and handwritten notes of Garrett and his secretary, was introduced into evidence. The exhibit shows that the provisions which were made for James Burnett in 1990 were marked through. A witness who was experienced in the use of shorthand testified that some of the secretary's notes on the will could be translated as directing the personal property to be distributed to the residual beneficiaries upon Adkins's death.

The chancellor, after hearing the evidence, found that the testatrix intended to bequeath all trust property, including personal property, to William Spencer, Jr., and his six children, upon the death of Flournoy Adkins. Jeanne Burnett, as special administratrix of her late husband's estate, brings this appeal.

Ordinarily, the intention of the testator is to be gathered from the four corners of the instrument itself. Extrinsic evidence may be received on the issue of the testator's intent, but only where the terms of the will are ambiguous. The language of Mrs. Burnett's will unequivocally expresses the intention that, upon the death of Flournoy Adkins, the land contained in the trust shall be distributed. No mention is made of her substantial personal estate. The question we must answer is whether Mrs. Burnett's failure to dispose of her entire estate creates an ambiguity. An ambiguity has been defined as an indistinctness or uncertainty of meaning of an expression used in a written instrument. Such a definition contemplates the need for interpretation of terms actually used in the will. As such, it does not encompass the situation in which a testatrix does not dispose of a portion of her estate. We have recognized that oral evidence should not be used to supply terms in a writing which are wholly absent.

In a similar case from Texas, In re Estate of Hunt, 908 S.W.2d 483 (Tex. App. 1995), a testatrix failed to completely dispose of a remainder interest in a trust. The court said the following:

> It is true that Marguerite Hunt failed to completely dispose of her estate in the Will. It is also true that upon reading the entire will it is reasonable to presume that it was Marguerite Hunt's intention to award the remainder interest in the Delph Trust to the Salvation Army.

But she did not say so. And we are prohibited from speculating as to what Marguerite Hunt would have done had she completed her will. A court may not rewrite a will or add provisions under the guise of construction of the language of the will in order to reflect some presumed intention of the testatrix. Even though there is a strong presumption against intestacy, the presumption does not arise when the testatrix fails, through design or otherwise, to make a complete disposition of her property. (Citations omitted).

Our own case law has espoused much the same philosophy—that the paramount objective in interpreting a will is the intention of the testator as expressed in the language of the will, and that it is presumed that a testatrix knows the contents of the will she executes. Chlanda v. Estate of Fuller, 326 Ark. 551, 932 S.W.2d 760 (1996); Heirs of Mills v. Wylie, 250 Ark. 703, 466 S.W.2d 937 (1971). The *Heirs of Mills* case is particularly enlightening. There, Mr. Mills's will contained a number of contingency provisions, including a provision that bequeathed most of his estate to a nephew and a sister-in-law, should Mills and his wife die in a "common disaster". However, the will failed to provide for the situation in which Mrs. Mills might predecease her husband. In fact, she did predecease him. Mr. Mills's heirs (who were not provided for in his will) filed suit, contending that, since the will made no bequest in the event Mrs. Mills predeceased her husband, Mr. Mills's estate should pass through the laws of intestate succession. In holding that the will contained no ambiguity, we said the following:

> actually our holding in this case may not be in accord with the actual intention of the testator—existing in his mind—but certainly it is in accord with long established law that the court's finding shall be based on the intention of the testator—*as expressed by the language of the will.*

Id. at 704, 466 S.W.2d at 938.

First Commercial argues that our acceptance of the appellant's argument will result in a partial intestacy. In response to a similar contention, we said the following in Chlanda v. Estate of Fuller, supra:

> It is correct to state that there is a presumption in the rules of construction that 'a person who takes the time and effort to make a will does not desire partial intestacy'. Kidd v. Sparks, 276 Ark. 85, 633 S.W.2d 13 (1982). However, a probate court should not resort to the rules of construction unless the intent of the testator, as shown by his express words, is in doubt.

326 Ark. at 555, 932 S.W.2d at 763.

The express language of Mrs. Burnett's testamentary disposition reflects the unambiguous intention that, upon the death of Flournoy Adkins, the land, and no other property contained in the trust corpus, shall pass under the will. We must therefore reverse and remand this case with instructions to enter orders consistent with this opinion.

REVERSED AND REMANDED.

GLAZE and THORNTON, JJ., dissent.

THORNTON, J., dissenting.... I would affirm the order of the Chancellor.

While there are numerous granting clauses in the will, all of the internally inconsistent provisions are contained in Section III of the will. Section III B reads as follows:

> B. Provided, however, in the event my friend, Flournoy Adkins, should predecease me, co-decease with me, or in the event that we should die at the same time or as a result of a common accident or catastrophe, then and in that event, I give, devise, and bequeath all the rest and residue of my estate as follows: one-half (½) to my nephew, William Spencer, Jr., and one-half (½) to my nephew's six children, Billy Spencer, Jasen Spencer, Adam Spencer, Mary Fagan, Ann Griffen, and Elizabeth Forbes, in equal shares, share and share alike.

In the event Flournoy Adkins survives Ms. Burnett's death, Section III A. establishes a trust for his benefit during his lifetime, with the following provision:

> A. I give, devise, and bequeath all the rest and residue of my estate, whether real, personal, or mixed, and of whatever kind or nature, wheresoever located and whenever acquired to Arkansas Bank and Trust as Trustee in Trust for my friend, Flournoy Adkins, during his lifetime.

Within these two provisions, there is no ambiguity. Ms. Burnett's estate goes to her nephew and his children if Mr. Adkins does not survive her, but if he does survive her, he is to have a life interest in all the property placed into trust.

However, the instrument contains an ambiguity in directing the trustee's distribution of the estate following Mr. Adkins's death. From the four corners of the instrument, it is apparent that Ms. Burnett intended for all of her property to be distributed in accordance with her will, and that following her death and the death of her friend, Flournoy Adkins, the property was to be distributed to her nephew and his children. Unfortunately, ambiguity arises because the instructions to the trustee fail to clearly specify that "personal" property should be distributed to *anyone* upon Mr. Adkins's death, providing only that upon the termination of the trust for the benefit of Mr. Adkins, the "land" shall be distributed to the nephew and his children.

Chancellor Switzer correctly finds that placing all the property in the trust, without addressing the distribution of personal property, creates an ambiguity. He states that "there is a conflict and repugnance between the provisions such as to require judicial interpretation."

As we consider whether a potential flaw in the establishment of the trust gives rise to an ambiguity requiring judicial interpretation, we should be reminded of these principles:

1) The testatrix did not want to die intestate, but intended all property to pass under her will. Whenever possible, wills should be interpreted so as to give effect to

the intent of the testator and avoid a partial intestacy.

2) Here, it is not necessary to look beyond the four corners of Section III to determine that an ambiguity exists requiring interpretation. We should remember that we are addressing an ambiguity in a trust provision established by the will, which also provides in the same section for the distribution of all the estate to her nephew and his children upon Mr. Adkins's death, if that occurs before the death of the testatrix. If the ambiguity is not resolved, the trust will fail. We are not called upon to reform the will, but to interpret ambiguous instructions to trustees managing a trust clearly established by the will in order to resolve the conflict and repugnance between provisions of section III of the instrument itself.

In the circumstances of this case, it was appropriate for the Chancellor to consider evidence to resolve the ambiguity and to determine what interpretation effectuates the testatrix's intent in the establishment of the trust....

Appellant relies upon our decision in Mills' Heirs v. Wylie, 250 Ark. 703, 466 S.W.2d 937 (1971), in which we cited Smith v. Smith, 229 Ark. 579, 317 S.W.2d 275 (1958), as follows:

> It is well settled law in this state, so well settled as to require no citation of authority, that where there is no ambiguity, or no conflict or repugnance between the provisions of the will, judicial interpretation or construction is not required.

Id. at 707, 466 S.W.2d at 940. In *Mills' Heirs*, we also state the rule that "where the meaning of the language is *not ambiguous*, testimony as to the testator's intention is 'inadmissible' ..." and then concluded: "Since we find that there was no ambiguity, there is no necessity to discuss the testimony." Id. at 708, 466 S.W.2d at 940 (emphasis added).

Unlike the will in *Mills' Heirs*, which had no internal inconsistencies, here we have an internally inconsistent testamentary trust, the ambiguous language of which would devise and bequeath the testatrix's property to her nephew and his children if her friend predecease her, but provided no instruction to the trustee as to the disposition of her personal property after her friend's death, should he survive her. This internal ambiguity requires that evidence of the testatrix's intent be admitted to resolve the conflict between provisions of the instrument.

I believe that the instrument must be looked at as a whole; that from the four corners of the instrument, it is apparent that an ambiguity exists; that evidence of the testatrix's intent was required to resolve the ambiguity; and that the Chancellor's rulings and order should be sustained. I would affirm the decision.

GLAZE, J., joins in this dissent.

Notes and Question

1. *Inserting Omitted Language into Wills by Construction.* Seemingly in conflict with the no-reformation rule are cases in which courts have inserted language

mistakenly omitted from wills. Where courts have added the missing language, they have explained their decisions on the theory that they are engaging in a process called "construction." The term "construction" in these cases is being used in the specialized sense of constructing the omitted language by implication from the language that is contained in the will rather than supplying it from extrinsic evidence. The construction theory has produced some curious results. In a pair of cases decided by the same court on the same day, for example, missing language was inserted in one but not the other.

In Dorson's Estate, 196 N.Y.S.2d 344 (Sur. Ct. 1959), the testator's will divided the residue of his estate into two trusts, Funds A and B. The testator's widow was the initial income beneficiary of both funds; when her interest terminated, each fund was to be divided into three parts, one part for each of the testator's three children. His daughter Marjorie was the beneficiary of Part 2 of both Fund A and B. Part 2 of Fund A provided for the income to be paid to Marjorie until she reached 35, at which time she was to receive one-third of the corpus; the income from the remaining two-thirds of corpus was to be paid to her until she reached 40, at which time one-half of the remaining corpus was to be paid to her until she reached 45, whereupon she was to receive the entire remaining corpus. Part 2 of Fund B contained identical language, except that the language directing that one-half of the remaining corpus be paid to Marjorie at age 40 was omitted. The court inserted that language into Fund B, saying that "[t]he testator's general dispositive scheme is clearly discernible from a reading of the will...." See also In re Bieley, 695 N.E.2d 1119 (N.Y. 1998) (using doctrine of gift by implication thereby avoiding question of whether court should admit evidence of scrivener's error); McCauley v. Alexander, 543 S.W.2d 699 (Tex. Civ. App. 1976) (inserting the word "estate," which appeared in the third paragraph of the will, into a devise in the second paragraph of the will, which named the devisee but failed to state what property was devised).

In Estate of Calabi, 196 N.Y.S.2d 443 (Sur. Ct. 1959), the testator's will, drafted by counsel, divided the residue of his estate into four trusts. Trusts C and D were to receive one-twelfth each of the residue. For Trusts A and B, the will spelled out the trust terms and identified the beneficiaries but the will omitted the terms and beneficiaries for Trusts C and D. The one-sixth of the residue not expressly disposed of was held to pass by intestacy to the testator's heirs, notwithstanding an allegation that Trusts C and D were intended to be for the benefit of the testator's grandchildren until each reached the age of 24. The court noted that no supporting evidence of this allegation was submitted, but it went on to say that "if such supporting evidence were available it would not be admissible." See also Farmers & Merchants Bank v. Farmers & Merchants Bank, 216 S.E.2d 769 (W. Va. 1975) (holding inadmissible the lawyer's testimony that the intended amount was $35,000 and that it was inadvertently omitted by the lawyer's typist with regard to a devise that named the devisee but failed to state the amount of the devise).

Would extrinsic evidence supporting the allegation, if offered in *Calabi,* have been inherently less reliable a basis for correcting the mistake than the basis for relief that the court used in *Dorson?*

2. *Inserting Omitted Language into Inter Vivos Trusts.* In contrast with the attitude toward reformation reflected in *Burnett* and *Calabi,* courts have openly reformed revocable trusts on the basis of extrinsic evidence of mistakenly omitted language, even after the settlor's death. A striking example of this incongruity between the law of wills and the law of inter vivos donative documents is Berman v. Sandler, 399 N.E.2d 17 (Mass. 1980). Ellen Sandler created a revocable and amendable inter vivos trust. Later, her attorney found that the first paragraph of section 1 of Article Third of the trust jeopardized the qualification of the trust for the federal estate tax marital deduction. The attorney drafted a document amending the trust. The amending document, which Sandler signed, directed that section 1 of Article Third be deleted and that certain new language be substituted for it. After Sandler's death, it was discovered that the amendment deleted section 1 in its entirety rather than the first paragraph thereof, as intended. In a suit for reformation brought by the trustee the court ordered the insertion into the amending document of the mistakenly omitted phrase "the first paragraph of." The court stated:

> It is settled that a written instrument, including a trust, will be reformed on grounds of mistake upon "full, clear, and decisive proof" of the mistake.... Since a settlor usually receives no consideration for the creation of a trust, a unilateral mistake on the part of the settlor is ordinarily sufficient to warrant reformation.... The additional fact that the settlor in the case at bar has died should not foreclose relief,... so long as the evidence of mistake meets the requisite standard of proof.... The overwhelming weight of the evidence... clearly and decisively points to a scrivener's error as the source of the mistake.... Accordingly, judgment shall enter in the court below reforming the trust amendment so as to delete only the first paragraph of the first section of Article Third and to retain the remainder of section 1 as it appears in the original trust agreement.

For a post-death application of the reformation doctrine to correct a mistaken omission of a trustee power to invade the corpus of an inter vivos trust for the benefit of the income beneficiary, see Estate of Tuthill, 754 A.2d 272 (D.C. 2000). The result in *Tuthill* is to be contrasted with the earlier refusal by the same court in Knupp v. District of Columbia, 578 A.2d 702 (D.C. 1990), to correct a mistaken omission of the residuary clause in a will.

4. Mistaken Inclusions

The Restatement 3d of Property provides that a donative document is ambiguous if "the text reveals an apparent mistaken inclusion...." Restatement 3d of Property §11.2(b)(2). The Restatement 3d also provides that "extrinsic evidence may be considered to establish the content of the mistakenly included... language," and that if the content of a mistaken inclusion is established by extrinsic evidence, the included language may be removed from the document. See Restatement 3d of Property §11.2(b)(2) comments n to q.

Connecticut Junior Republic v. Sharon Hospital
448 A.2d 190 (Conn. 1982)

HEALEY, J. The sole issue presented in this case is whether extrinsic evidence of a mistake by a scrivener of a testamentary instrument is admissible in a proceeding to determine the validity of the testamentary instrument. On October 3, 1979, Richards Haskell Emerson, a resident of Lakeville, died at the age of seventy-nine. He had never married and left several cousins as his closest heirs at law. Emerson left a will dated May 19, 1960, and two codicils dated December 4, 1969 (first codicil) and October 24, 1975 (second codicil), all of which were offered for probate by the named executor, the Third National Bank of Hampden County, Springfield, Massachusetts.

The Probate Court for the district of Salisbury admitted the will and codicils on February 19, 1980, after a hearing on the application for probate. This appeal rises out of the court's decision to admit portions of the second codicil which the plaintiffs contend were inserted by mistake of the scrivener and therefore do not embody the dispositions intended by the testator.

Contained in the decedent's will are three articles which set up trusts for the distribution of part of the decedent's estate and designate, as remaindermen, seven named charitable organizations (1960 charities), the defendants in this case. In the first codicil to his will, the decedent deleted the seven 1960 charities and substituted another group of eleven charitable organizations (1969 charities) as remaindermen, which are the plaintiffs in this case. There was only one charity named in both the will and the first codicil.

Subsequently, in 1975, the decedent instructed the trust officer of the Third National Bank of Hampden County to make changes in his will, as amended by the first codicil, so as to qualify the trusts as charitable annuity trusts under the Tax Reform Act of 1969, so that the charitable remainder interests would be allowable as federal estate tax deductions. The trust officer, thereafter, similarly instructed the decedent's attorney. The attorney, however, in drafting the second codicil, not only made the requested changes but also mistakenly reinstated the 1960 charities, which had originally been named in the will, as beneficiaries under two of the three articles of the will which are relevant to this case.[5] The decedent, who had never requested or authorized this change, signed the second codicil apparently without realizing the change in beneficiaries.

At the hearing on the application for the admission of the will and the two codicils, the Probate Court heard evidence on the matter and ruled that Connecticut

---

5. The remaining article relevant to this case continued to provide for the eleven 1969 charities.

law does not permit the introduction of extrinsic evidence on the issue of mistake, and found that in the absence of such evidence the presumption of the validity of a testamentary instrument mandated the admission of the entire second codicil to probate.[6] On appeal to the Superior Court, the defendants moved to strike the plaintiffs' reasons of appeal. Practice Book § 194. The Superior Court granted the defendants' motion and held that extrinsic evidence is not admissible to prove that the second codicil, which uses unambiguous language, contained a mistake due to a scrivener's error and, therefore, should not be admitted to probate. The defendants next joined in the executor's motion for summary judgment which was granted by agreement of the parties. From this judgment, the plaintiffs have appealed to this court.

The plaintiffs claim that the lower court erred (1) in failing to find a distinction between a "will construction" proceeding and a proceeding to "admit a will to probate"; (2) in failing to hold that Connecticut cases support the admissibility of extrinsic evidence to prove that material has been mistakenly inserted into a testamentary instrument....

I. The plaintiffs' first argument states that since the issue in this case is the validity of the second codicil and not its meaning, extrinsic evidence should be admissible to prove the scrivener's error. Specifically, they claim that courts which have considered the question have made a distinction between proceedings to admit a will to probate and will construction proceedings, holding or recognizing that extrinsic evidence showing a scrivener's error is admissible in the former but not in the latter proceeding, absent an ambiguity. See Annot., 90 A.L.R.2d 924, 931. Because of the scrivener's error, the plaintiffs claim that the mistake in reinstating the 1960 charities into the second codicil should have been allowed to have been proven by extrinsic evidence and should not have been admitted to probate. The lower court rejected this argument....

In Connecticut, our cases have not, to this point, distinguished between the two types of proceedings.... [W]e believe that the better course is to recognize that the same evidentiary rules apply to both types of proceedings.

II. We now turn to the major issue presented by this case. The trial court held that "parol evidence may not be admitted in the instant case to show that the scrivener erred in drafting the codicil or that the testator mistakenly signed it. Connecticut law

---

6. The Probate Court made this holding in spite of finding the following:

   Substantial and convincing evidence was offered to establish that the testator had directed that the second codicil to his will be prepared only for the purpose of qualifying the charitable bequests under Paragraphs Seventh and Eighth of the will and first codicil as charitable remainder annuity trusts eligible for an estate tax charitable deduction in the decedent's estate; and that by scrivener's error the "1960 charities" were substituted for the "1969 charities" in the 1975 codicil; and that the proposed 1975 codicil was presented to the testator in a context of innocent misrepresentation of its contents resulting in mistake in the instrument as executed with respect as to which charitable beneficiaries the testator intended to benefit.

docs not allow extrinsic evidence of a testator's intent to be admitted in cases dealing with either will construction or cases challenging the probate of an instrument. While there is an exception to this rule when there is ambiguity on the face of the will or codicil itself, this exception is not applicable in the instant case." We agree with the trial court....

[The plaintiffs] seek to introduce evidence that the testator's true intent was not to divide his estate among the combined eighteen charitable institutions as appears on the face of the will and codicils, but that his true intent, which was allegedly communicated to the scrivener, was to replace the eleven charitable institutions named in the first codicil with the seven charitable institutions originally named in his will. It is clear that whether this is a "will construction" proceeding or a proceeding to "admit a will to probate," where the claimants seek to introduce extrinsic evidence of a scrivener's error resulting in a disposition of property allegedly contrary to the testator's intention, as expressed to the scrivener, such evidence, absent an ambiguity, is not admissible because "'if such testimony is to be admitted, we do away [with] part at least of the beneficial effect of the statute of frauds, and leave every will exposed to litigation, on a claim of a different intent.'" *Stearns v. Stearns*, supra, 103 Conn. 224-25, 130 A. 112. See Comstock v. Hadlyme Ecclesiastical Society, 8 Conn. 254, 265-66 (1830);[7] Rapp v. Reehling, 124 Ind. 36, 23 N.E. 777 (1889). "Claimed errors in the drafting of a will, either by the testator or his scrivener, do not permit the introduction of extrinsic evidence." McFarland v. Chase Manhattan Bank, N.A., 32 Conn.Sup. 20, 37, 337 A.2d 1 (1973), aff'd, 168 Conn. 411, 362 A.2d 834 (1975). We find that this is the relevant public policy as expressed through our cases; therefore, we will not additionally discuss the plaintiffs' fourth claim of error set out above.

We would, however, properly make these observations. It is beyond cavil that

---

7. Our holding today is limited to the case where a mistake due to a scrivener's error with no resulting ambiguity is alleged. It is clear that there are certain types of "mistakes" which would merit the introduction of extrinsic evidence as proof thereof. In re Gluckman's Will, 87 N.J.Eq. 638, 641, 101 A. 295 (1917), the court stated:

Where a testator, in addition to complete testamentary mental capacity, is in full enjoyment of average physical and educational faculties, it would seem that in the absence of fraud or of undue influence, a mistake, in order to defeat probate of his entire will, must in substance or effect really amount to one of identity of the instrument executed; as, for instance, where two sisters, in one case, or a husband and wife, in another, prepared their respective wills for simultaneous execution, and through pure error one executed the other's, and vice versa. Anon., 14 Jur. 402 [1850]; Re Hunt, L.R. 3 P. & D. 250 [1875]; Nelson v. McDonald, 61 Hun. 406, 16 N.Y.Supp. 273 [1891]. Short of this, however, or of something amounting in effect to the same thing, it is against sound public policy to permit a pure mistake to defeat the duly solemnized and completely competent testamentary act. It is more important that the probate of the wills of dead people be effectively shielded from the attacks of a multitude of fictitious mistakes than that it be purged of wills containing a few real ones. The latter a testator may, by due care, avoid in his lifetime. Against the former he would be helpless....

[For a similar argument, see Richard W. Power, Wills: A Primer of Interpretation and Construction, 51 Iowa L. Rev. 75, 103-06 (1965). Ed.]

"[p]rinciples of law which serve one generation well may, by reason of changing conditions, disserve a later one...." Herald Publishing Co. v. Bill, 142 Conn. 53, 62, 111 A.2d 4 (1955). "Experience can and often does demonstrate that a rule, once believed sound, needs modification to serve justice better. . . ." Herald Publishing Co. v. Bill, supra. The principle of law, which we reiterate today, has been viable for many years and we have not been given nor do we glean any persuasive reason that justice, experience or logic requires it be changed....

There is no error.

In this opinion ARMENTANO and SPONZO, JJ., concurred.

PETERS, A.J., dissenting. In order to bring into focus my disagreement with the majority opinion, I want first to note where I am in total accord with that opinion. Like the majority, I note that the only issue is whether extrinsic evidence of a mistake by a scrivener is admissible in a proceeding to determine the validity of a testamentary instrument. I would add, however, that the issue is even narrower than stated by the majority since the present aim of the proponents of the evidence of mistake is only to delete provisions from, rather than add provisions to, the disputed testamentary disposition. Like the majority, I note that the issue comes to us in the procedural context of a motion to strike, so that we must accept as accurate, for the purposes of this appeal, the allegations that the attorney who drafted the testator's second codicil erroneously included therein a change of beneficiaries that the decedent had neither requested nor authorized. Furthermore, I would add that the Probate Court expressly found that substantial and convincing evidence had been offered in support of the proposition that innocent misrepresentation of the contents of the will had resulted in a mistake in the instrument as executed. Like the majority, I too would find insufficient evidence of ambiguity in the will itself to warrant recourse to extrinsic evidence that would not otherwise be admissible.

We are left, then, with the question which I would answer differently than does the majority. Must the true intent of the testator be thwarted when, because of the mistake of a scrivener, he has formally subscribed to a written bequest that substantially misstates his testamentary intention? For all practical purposes, this is a question of first impression in this state, certainly in this state in this century. I would permit extrinsic evidence of a scrivener's error to be introduced in litigation concerned with the admissibility of a disputed will to probate.

I take as a point of departure the established proposition that a will cannot validly be probated if it was executed by a testator in reliance on erroneous beliefs induced by fraud, duress, or undue influence.... [T]he testamentary process is distorted by the interference of a third person who misleads the testator into making a testamentary disposition that would not otherwise have occurred. There is similar distortion when a will is executed in reliance on erroneous beliefs induced by the innocent error, by the innocent misrepresentation, of the scrivener of a will. I can see no reason of logic or of policy to treat the mistake case differently from the fraud or undue influence case. In each instance, extrinsic evidence is required to demonstrate that a will, despite its formally proper execution, substantially misrepresents the true intent of the testator.

The majority would disallow extrinsic evidence of a scrivener's error for two principal reasons: the existing Connecticut case law, and the risk of subverting the policy of the Statute of Wills. I find neither reason persuasive.

The existing case law is, as the majority opinion acknowledges, of ancient vintage. I agree that antiquity does not automatically disqualify common law precedents that continue to serve modern needs. But I find our case law less persuasive than does the majority.

The principal case is Comstock v. Hadlyme Ecclesiastical Society, 8 Conn. 254 (1830), because it, like this case, deals with the question of admission of a will to probate. *Comstock* seems to me to be distinguishable because there the proponents of extrinsic evidence of mistake were seeking to reform the will by *adding* new provisions to its contents. The case before us would result, if the extrinsic evidence were considered, in the *deletion* of unintended testamentary bequests, surely a less problematical confrontation with the policy of the Statute of Wills....

That brings us to considerations arising out of the policy of the Statute of Wills. General Statutes §45-161. The risk of subversion of the intent of a testator, who cannot personally defend his testamentary bequest, is without doubt a serious concern. Balanced against that concern is the risk of blindly enforcing a testamentary disposition that substantially misstates the testator's true intent. We have long ago resolved this balance in favor of admitting extrinsic evidence when the testator's intent is undermined by fraud, undue influence or incapacity. Had the decedent's lawyer deliberately and fraudulently altered the second codicil, the relevant extrinsic evidence would unquestionably have been admitted. Under the modern law of misrepresentation, innocent misrepresentation is treated as generally equivalent to fraud in terms of its legal consequences. To allow the admissibility of extrinsic evidence to turn on the scrivener's fraudulent intent or lack thereof is to distort the purpose of a Probate Court. Its proper business is to determine what instrument, if any, the decedent properly executed as his will. Gray, "Striking Words Out of a Will," 26 Harv.L.Rev. 212, 217 (1913). The guilt or negligence of third parties is only incidentally relevant to such a determination, since the effect on the testator's mind of either fraud or mistake is subjectively the same. The Statute of Wills does not compel enforcement of testamentary dispositions that a testator never intended to make.

Objection to the admission of extrinsic evidence in this case must therefore find support outside the direct commandments of the Statute of Wills. Two such objections have been advanced. One objection relies on the effect of the will's formal execution as a validation by the testator of the contested provision. The second points to the juridical risk of spurious will contests.

The first objection, raised by the defendants at oral argument and in their brief, states that whatever error the scrivener may have made was validated and ratified by the testator's act in signing his will. Neither American law in general, nor the case law of this state, has ever assigned so conclusive an effect to the reading and subsequent execution of a will. While signing the will creates a strong presumption that the will accurately represents the intentions of the testator, that presumption is a rebuttable one.

The second objection is a fear that allowing extrinsic evidence of mistake will give rise to a proliferation of groundless will contests. There is no doubt that our increasingly fact-based jurisprudence serves to expose many apparently final dispositions to the juridical risk of unjustified judicial intervention. In the law of contracts, where the parol evidence rule has undergone considerable erosion, this risk has not been found to be unmanageable. In the law of wills, the risk is limited by the narrowness of the exception that this case would warrant. I would today do no more than permit the opponent of a will to introduce extrinsic evidence of the error of a scrivener, and would require proof of such an extrinsic error to be established by clear and convincing evidence.

In sum, I see no greater risk of juridical error in the case of a scrivener's error than in the case of fraud or undue influence. I find it difficult to draw a clear line of demarcation between a scrivener's mistake and an innocent misrepresentation. I believe that the true interests of a testator are better protected by admitting rather than suppressing evidence of substantial third party interference with the formulation of a testamentary disposition. Wills that do not reflect the true intent of the testator should be refused probate.

In this opinion SHEA, J., concurred.

Notes and Question

1. *Justice Peters's Dissent Becomes Law*. In Erickson v. Erickson, 716 A.2d 92 (Conn. 1998), the Supreme Court of Connecticut concluded "the reasons given by the dissent in [*Connecticut Junior Republic*] are persuasive" and overruled *Connecticut Junior Republic*. *Erickson*, which is discussed in Chapter 5, involved a statute that revoked a will upon marriage unless the will provided for the contingency of marriage. The court held that

> If a scrivener's error has misled the testator into executing a will on the belief that it will be valid notwithstanding the testator's subsequent marriage, extrinsic evidence of that error is admissible to establish the intent of the testator that his or her will be valid notwithstanding the subsequent marriage. Furthermore, if those two facts, namely, the scrivener's error and its effect on the testator's intent, are established by clear and convincing evidence, they will be sufficient to establish that 'provision has been made in such will for such contingency,' within the meaning of §45a-257(a) [the statute resulting in revocation of the will upon marriage].

The *Erickson* doctrine was applied in Estate of Getman, 15 Quinnipiac Prob. L.J. 257 (2000), where the court corrected a drafting error in a will. The testator's will dated September 29, 1999 referred to an inter vivos trust "created this date." On the basis of clear and convincing evidence, the court changed that reference an inter vivos trust "created May 9, 1999."

2. *English Practice: Partial Denial of Probate.* Under some circumstances, English practice goes so far as to deny probate of particular words of a will that were included by mistake. E.g., Re Reynette-James, [1975] 3 All E.R. 1037; Re Phelan, [1972] L.R. Fam. 33; Re Morris, [1971] L.R. Prob. 62; Goods of Boehm, [1891] L.R. Prob. 247 (1891).

3. *Ratification of the Mistake by Signing the Will?* In *Connecticut Junior Republic*, part of the argument advanced by the proponents of the second codicil was that "whatever error the scrivener may have made was validated and ratified by the testator's act in signing his will." Does Justice Peters in her dissent provide an adequate response to this argument? See Estate of Smelser, 818 P.2d 822 (Kan. Ct. App. 1991) (refusing to probate a part of a codicil that mistakenly revoked a devise based in part on fact that there was no "affirmative evidence" that the testator actually knew the codicil revoked the devise when she executed it). Accord Restatement 3d of Property §12.1 comment *l*.

4. *Malpractice Action Against Drafting Attorney.* After losing the case in the Connecticut Supreme Court, the disappointed charitable remainder beneficiaries brought a malpractice action in a Massachusetts court against the Massachusetts drafting attorney, Paul S. Doherty. Although the trial court in the malpractice case found that the drafting attorney had "inadvertently substituted the original charities for the first codicil charities," the trial court found that the testator, Richards Haskell Emerson, had ratified the reversion to the original charitable beneficiaries. The court's finding was based not merely on the fact that the testator had signed the second codicil, but on additional evidence. The additional evidence consisted of:

(1) evidence that Emerson was "an avid reader and an intelligent and meticulous man who paid careful attention to his personal and financial affairs,"

(2) evidence that Emerson had a forty-five minute meeting with Sagar McDonald, a senior vice-president of the trust company, before executing the second codicil, during which McDonald read aloud the second codicil, while Emerson followed a copy, that Emerson's questions "focused on the effects of the new trust arrangements on the life interests he had created," and that "Emerson made no comment about the names of the charitable remaindermen," and

(3) a deposition of Harvey Moses, a long-time friend of Emerson who died before the trial, in which Moses said that Emerson had told him that he, Emerson, had "reverted or returned or gone back to his original list of charities."

The trial court's judgment in favor of the drafting attorney was affirmed in Connecticut Junior Republic v. Doherty, 478 N.E.2d 735 (Mass. App. Ct. 1985).

PART C. A REFORMATION DOCTRINE FOR WILLS

Primary Statutory References: *UPC §§2-805, 2-806; UTC §§415, 416*

1. General Reformation Doctrine

Restatement 3d of Property

§12.1. Reforming Donative Documents to Correct Mistakes

A donative document, though unambiguous, may be reformed to conform the text to the donor's intention if it is established by clear and convincing evidence (1) that a mistake of fact or law, whether in expression or inducement, affected specific terms of the document; and (2) what the donor's intention was. In determining whether these elements have been established by clear and convincing evidence, direct evidence of intention contradicting the plain meaning of the text as well as other evidence of intention may be considered.

———

In this Part, we examine modern mistake cases, the Restatement 3d of Property, and recently promulgated uniform law, all supporting a reformation doctrine for wills similar to the one long in place for instruments pertaining to lifetime donative transfers.

The no-reformation-of-wills and no-extrinsic-evidence rules have not been universally acclaimed or followed. For example, Dean Wigmore objected to the no-extrinsic-evidence rule.[8] He contended that "[t]he ordinary standard, or 'plain meaning,' is simply the meaning of the people who did *not* write the document." He further stated, "The fallacy [of the conventional view] consists in assuming that there is or ever can be *some one real* or absolute meaning. In truth, there can be only *some person's* meaning; and that person, whose meaning the law is seeking, is the writer of the document...." 9 John H. Wigmore, Evidence 190-92 (3d ed. 1940). See also Restatement of Property § 242 comment c (largely rejecting the plain-meaning rule);

---

8. The role of the plain-meaning rule is an issue in statutory interpretation. See Antonin Scalia, A Matter of Interpretation: Federal Courts and the Law (1997); Cass R. Sunstein, Must Formalism Be Defended Empirically?, 66 U. Chi. L. Rev. 636 (1999). The process of interpreting statutes is distinguishable from the process of interpreting donative documents. First, determining the intent of a single donor by looking to the written document as well as extrinsic evidence is quite different from determining the intent of legislators based on the statutory language and legislative history. Second, unlike legislators who have the power to amend or clarify statutes if they disagree with a court's interpretation, the donors, who in many instances are dead, cannot amend or clarify their instruments if their intent is inadequately or mistakenly expressed. Therefore, the implications regarding the plain-meaning rule are not the same when the rule is applied to interpretation of donative documents as when it is applied to statutory interpretation. The two situations are usefully treated as distinct from each other. See Restatement 3d of Property §12.1, Reporter's Note 5.

James B. Thayer, A Preliminary Treatise on Evidence at the Common Law 423-25, 471-73 (1898) (critiquing the plain-meaning rule).

Courts have occasionally departed from the conventional rules. In Estate of Gibbs, 111 N.W.2d 413 (Wis. 1961), for example, the court openly substituted a correct term for a mistaken term despite finding no ambiguity. Gibbs's will devised one percent of his estate "to Robert J. Krause, now of 4708 North 46th Street, Milwaukee, Wisconsin." At Gibbs's death, and presumably when the will was executed, there was a Robert J. Krause who lived at the 46th Street address. For this reason, the court said, "there is no ambiguity." Nevertheless, the court held that extrinsic evidence could be introduced to the effect that Gibbs never knew Robert J. Krause of 46th Street, but that he did know and intended to benefit one Robert *W.* Krause, an employee and friend of Gibbs's for some thirty years. The court explained:

> [D]etails of identification, particularly such matters as middle initials, street addresses, and the like, which are highly susceptible to mistake, particularly in metropolitan areas, should not be accorded such sanctity as to frustrate an otherwise clearly demonstrable intent. Where such details of identification are involved, courts should receive evidence tending to show that a mistake has been made and should disregard the details when the proof establishes to the highest degree of certainty that a mistake was, in fact, made.

See also Wilson v. First Florida Bank, 498 So.2d 1289 (Fla. Dist. Ct. App. 1986) (after holding the will to be ambiguous and admitting the attorney's testimony, along with other corroborating extrinsic evidence, the court found that the testator intended the devise to the university to be of the residue of his estate under a will in which the testator made a series of devises of tangible personal property and specified amounts of money, and then stated "To the University of Georgia, Financial Aid Department... in trust... to establish a Scholarship Fund...."); Estate of Ikuta, 639 P.2d 400, 405-06 (Haw. 1981) (court replaced the word "old[e]st" with the word "youngest," saying, "[t]he purpose of the policy against reformation of a will is to prevent distortion of the testator's intent"); Estate of Lohr, 497 N.W.2d 730 (Wis. Ct. App. 1993) (after finding of an ambiguity in the will language and proof of a drafting error, court inserted under the rubric of construction, "[i]n the event my spouse shall not predecease me and shall be living THIRTY (30) Days after the date of my death" in place of "[i]n the event my spouse shall predecease me or shall not be living THIRTY (30) Days after the date of my death").

Compare and contrast the following two cases.

Flannery v. McNamara
738 N.E.2d 739 (Mass. 2000)

IRELAND, J. The plaintiffs, Helen M. Flannery and Margaret M. Moran (Flannerys), filed a complaint against the defendants, Paul J. McNamara, administrator of the estate of William H. White, Jr. (decedent), and the decedent's heirs, the Daleys and the Whites (heirs), seeking declaratory relief and reformation of the decedent's will. The Flannerys alleged that they, and not the decedent's heirs, are the rightful beneficiaries under the will. The heirs filed motions to dismiss the complaint, pursuant to Mass.R.Civ.P. 12(b)(6), 365 Mass. 754 (1974), for failure to state a claim on which relief can be granted. By agreement of the parties, the judge subsequently treated the rule 12(b)(6) motions as motions for summary judgment, under Mass.R.Civ.P. 56(e), 365 Mass. 824 (1974).

The judge granted the heirs' motions for summary judgment, ruling that, because the will was unambiguous on its face, extrinsic evidence of the decedent's alleged intent was inadmissible. Moreover, she held that, because the will did not provide for disposition of the decedent's property in the event his wife predeceased him, his property passed to the heirs by way of intestacy.

Subsequently, the Flannerys appealed from the Probate Court's grant of summary judgment for the heirs. We granted their application for direct appellate review. The Flannerys argue that the Probate Court judge erred by holding inadmissible extrinsic evidence that might persuade the court to (1) construe; or (2) reform a poorly drawn will, albeit unambiguous on its face, to reflect the decedent's intent, thereby avoiding unjust enrichment.

This appeal presents the question whether we should overrule (1) the so-called "plain meaning" rule, that prohibits the admission of extrinsic evidence to construe unambiguous wills; and (2) the rule prohibiting the reformation of wills. We decline to do so, and thus, affirm the Probate Court's decision.

1. *Statement of Facts.* On September 30, 1995, the decedent died in Arlington. The decedent's will, dated January 20, 1973, left his entire estate to his wife, Katherine M. White (Katherine). The relevant part of the will provides that:

> "I give, devise, and bequeath all of the property of which I die possessed real, personal, and mixed of nature and wheresoever located to my beloved wife, Katherine M. White."

The decedent's will failed to name a contingent beneficiary and it did not contain a residuary clause.

Katherine died October 14, 1993, survived by the decedent and her two sisters, the Flannerys. The couple had no children. McNamara, the decedent's attorney, repeatedly advised the decedent to let him review the will, but the decedent never showed the will to McNamara. The decedent died survived by his intestate heirs who were discovered through a genealogical search. The heirs are the decedent's first cousins, once removed.

The Flannerys make the following allegations. For almost five decades, they had a close relationship with the decedent. Moreover, after Katherine's death, the decedent relied heavily on the Flannerys for advice and assistance with daily matters. After the decedent died, he was buried in the Flannerys' family plot. On several occasions, the decedent told members of the Flannerys' family that his Arlington residence and its contents "will be [theirs] some day." Additionally, the decedent informed McNamara that he understood that, if Katherine were to predecease him, his will provided for his property to go to the Flannerys. In contrast, the decedent did not have a close relationship with the heirs.

After the decedent died in 1995, McNamara was appointed administrator of the decedent's estate. He received the decedent's will for probate and was preparing to distribute the estate to the heirs by way of intestate succession, when the Flannerys filed for declaratory relief and reformation of the will on November 25, 1997.

2. *Discussion.* The Flannerys claim that, although the decedent's will made no mention of them, he intended to pass his estate to them in the event that Katherine predeceased him. Specifically, the Flannerys contend that the portion of the will that reads, "all... to my beloved wife, Katherine M. White," should be either construed or reformed to read, "all... to my beloved wife, Katherine M. White, if she survives me, but if not, then to her sisters who survive me," namely, the Flannerys. We disagree.

a. *Construction.* "The fundamental object in the construction of a will is to ascertain the testator's intention from the whole instrument, attributing due weight to all its language, considered in light of the circumstances known to the testator at the time of its execution, and to give effect to that intent unless some positive rule of law forbids." Putnam v. Putnam, 366 Mass. 261, 266, 316 N.E.2d 729 (1974).

Here, the Flannerys assert that the decedent intended to name them as the beneficiaries of his estate in the event that his wife predeceased him. To prove this, the Flannerys seek to introduce extrinsic evidence of their relationship with the decedent and the decedent's statements concerning his intent.

Under current Massachusetts law, however, "[i]f a will is not ambiguous, extrinsic evidence to explain its terms is inadmissible... even where the language involved has a legal consequence either not likely to have been understood by the testator... or contrary to his intention expressed orally" (citations omitted). Putnam v. Putnam, *supra*. See Gustafson v. Svenson, 373 Mass. 273, 275, 366 N.E.2d 761 (1977) (extrinsic evidence of testatrices' alleged intent inadmissible where will, in particular the phrase "his heirs per stirpes," unambiguous). Thus, extrinsic evidence of the decedent's alleged intent is only admissible if his will is ambiguous. See Mahoney v. Grainger, 283 Mass. 189, 192, 186 N.E. 86 (1933) ("It is only where the testamentary language is not clear in its application to the facts that evidence may be introduced as to the circumstances under which the testator used that language in order to throw light upon its meaning").... The will before us is not ambiguous.

First, the decedent's will contains no patent ambiguities. A patent ambiguity is one created by obvious conflicts in the language of the will itself. The decedent's will unequivocally states "all... to my beloved wife, Katherine M. White." No conflict or inconsistency arises from such clear and plain language.

Second, the will contains no latent ambiguities. A latent ambiguity emerges when the words of a will appear to be unambiguous on their face, but certain extrinsic facts render their meaning uncertain. There are two types of latent ambiguities. "The first type occurs when a will clearly describes a person or thing, and two or more persons or things exactly fit that description. The second type of latent ambiguity exists when no person or thing exactly fits the description, but two or more persons or things partially fit." Phipps v. Barbera, [498 N.E.2d 411 (Mass. Ct. App. 1986)]. Neither type of ambiguity exists here. Indeed, there is only one person fitting the description of "my beloved wife, Katherine M. White," namely, the decedent's wife, Katherine. Moreover, Katherine alone fit that description exactly. Neither the fact that she predeceased the decedent, nor the absence of a residuary clause or a contingent beneficiary provision makes the will ambiguous. Long before the decedent's execution of his will in 1973, it was settled law that, when a beneficiary predeceases the testator, the legacy lapses and falls into residue if there is one; otherwise it must pass as intestate property. As such, the will contains no latent ambiguity.

The Flannerys, however, argue that extrinsic evidence is admissible to create a latent ambiguity. The Flannerys seek to show, through extrinsic evidence, that the decedent had a "personal usage" of the will's language that differed from its plain, commonly accepted usage, and that the will should be construed consistently with this usage. They specifically want to demonstrate that the plain language of the will, "to my beloved wife," was actually intended and understood by the decedent to mean, "to my wife if she survives me, but if not, then to her sisters who survive me."

Generally, we have flatly rejected the idea that extrinsic evidence may be used to create an ambiguity where the language of the will is otherwise plain and unambiguous. Indeed, "[i]t is not an aid to interpretation to resort to testimony as to what may have been in the testator's mind in order to create an ambiguity not evident from the language of the will." Pagliarulo v. National Shawmut Bank [233 N.E.2d 213 (Mass. 1968)]. Furthermore, we have traditionally rejected this type of "personal usage" argument proffered by the Flannerys. See Gustafson v. Svenson, supra (extrinsic evidence inadmissible when offered to prove testatrices intended the term "heirs," as used in their wills, not to include specific individual who qualified legally as heir)....

b. *Reformation*. Reformation of wills is presently prohibited in Massachusetts. The traditional rule with respect to reformation has been stated as follows:

> "Courts have no power to reform wills. Hypothetical or imaginary mistakes of testators cannot be corrected. Omissions can not be supplied. Language cannot be modified to meet unforeseen changes in conditions. The only means for ascertaining the intent of the testator are the words written and the acts done by him."

Sanderson v. Norcross, 242 Mass. 43, 46, 136 N.E. 170 (1922). Moreover, "[t]he fact that [the will] was not in conformity to the instructions given to the draftsman who prepared it or that he made a mistake does not authorize a court to reform or alter it or remould it by amendments." Mahoney v. Grainger, 283 Mass. 189, 191, 186 N.E. 86 (1933).

Nevertheless, the Flannerys urge us to reject this basic tenet....

However, the reformation of a will, which would dispose of estate property based on unattested testamentary language, would violate the Statute of Wills. Strong policy reasons also militate against the requested reformation. To allow for reformation in this case would open the floodgates of litigation and lead to untold confusion in the probate of wills. It would essentially invite disgruntled individuals excluded from a will to demonstrate extrinsic evidence of the decedent's "intent" to include them. The number of groundless will contests could soar. We disagree that employing "full, clear and decisive proof" as the standard for reformation of wills would suffice to remedy such problems. Judicial resources are simply too scarce to squander on such consequences....

3. *Conclusion.* For the reasons stated, the decedent's will can neither be construed nor reformed to read, "all... to my beloved wife, Katherine M. White, if she survives me, but if not, then to her sisters who survive me," in lieu of what the will plainly states on its face: "all... to my beloved wife, Katherine M. White." The order of the Probate Court granting the defendants' motions for summary judgment is affirmed, and a declaratory judgment shall issue.

So ordered.

[The concurring opinion of GREANEY, J. is omitted.]

Note

The Massachusetts Supreme Court affirmed its adherence to *Flannery* in Pellegrini v. Breitenbach, 926 N.E.2d 544 (2010). Massachusetts adopted the Uniform Probate Code, effective July 2012, but not Sections 2-805 or 2-806 on reformation.

Estate of Herceg
193 Misc.2d 201, 747 N.Y.S.2d 901 (Sur. Ct. 2002)

EUGENE E. PECKHAM, S. The residuary clause of the will of Eugenia Herceg, dated December 2, 1999, which was admitted to probate on August 16, 2001, reads as follows:

"All the rest, residue and remainder of the property which I may own at the time of my death, real and personal, and wheresoever the same may be situate."

There is no more. The name of the intended beneficiary of the residuary is missing. As a practical matter, the residuary clause amounts to only 10% of the estate, since the will made pre-residuary bequests of 90% of the net estate.

Colomba Pastorino, as Executrix of the will, has petitioned for construction of the will by reading the residuary clause to be the same as decedent's prior will dated June 18, 1997. The residuary clause of the 1997 will provided:

"All the rest, residue and remainder of the property which I may own at the time of my death, real and personal, and wheresoever the same may be situate... I give, devise and bequeath to my nephew, Sergio Pastorino, per stirpes. In the event that my nephew, Sergio Pastorino, does not survive me, his share shall go to his wife, Colomba Pastorino."

In fact, Sergio Pastorino died on November 25, 2000, without issue and Eugenia Herceg died on November 30, 2000. The persons who would take the decedent's estate in intestacy are a niece, Josephine D'Angelo, and a great nephew, Sergio Rossello. Josephine D'Angelo has filed a consent to the relief requested in the petition for construction. Sergio Rossello defaulted in appearing on the return day of the proceeding.

Daniel Gorman, the attorney draftsman of the will, has filed an affidavit stating that when the 1997 will was redrafted in 1999, using computer software "some lines from the residuary clause were accidentally deleted." Obviously a mistake has been made. The question presented is whether the mistake can be corrected. For the reasons set forth below, we hold that the testator intended the residuary beneficiary to be Colomba Pastorino, wife of decedent's nephew and that her name should be inserted into the will.

The difficulty in this case is that there is a line of cases holding that where the name of the beneficiary is missing it cannot be supplied by construction or reformation of the will.... In other words, the Court cannot supply missing names to correct a mistake, whether of the draftsperson of the will or the testator. There is also another line of cases that hold that extrinsic evidence cannot be admitted unless there is an ambiguity in the will.... If extrinsic evidence is not admitted, the prior wills of testatrix cannot be considered, nor the affidavit of the attorney draftsman.

Of course, the paramount objective in interpreting a will is to determine the intention of the testator from a reading of the whole will. Furthermore, the testator is presumed to intend to avoid intestacy otherwise he or she would not have bothered to make a will. Even more "The presumption against intestacy is particularly weighty where the subject of the gift is the residuary estate."

Thus we have a conflict between two long-standing policies of the Law of Wills. On the one hand the court is not supposed to supply what the testator has not, through extrinsic evidence or otherwise. On the other hand, the primary objective is to ascertain the intention of the testator in order to avoid intestacy. If we follow the first line of precedent, the fact that no one is named in the residuary clause of Eugenia Herceg's will would mean no residuary beneficiary exists and the residue passes by intestacy to her heirs at law. The second line of precedent would lead to the conclusion that any thing possible should be done to avoid intestacy and carry out the testator's intent which would mean considering the extrinsic evidence pointing to Colomba Pastorino as the intended residuary beneficiary after the death of her husband, Sergio Pastorino....

Actually, the law has started to move away from the rigid rule [that the name of the beneficiary cannot be supplied by construction or reformation] and toward the principle of considering all available evidence, including any available extrinsic evidence, to effectuate the intent of the testator. [T]he Restatement [Third] of the Law of Property ([Wills and Other] Donative Transfers) §12.1 provides: "A donative document, though unambiguous, may be reformed to conform the text to the donor's intention if the following are established by clear and convincing evidence: (1) that a mistake of fact or law, whether in expression or inducement, affected specific terms of the document; and (2) what the donor's intention was."

> "There would be no restriction as to the kind of evidence that could be considered for this purpose; the oral statements of the testator and the attorney who drafted the instrument would be admissible. The theory of this approach is that the testator's intention is better served and unjust enrichment of unintended legatees prevented, while the fraud-preventing purpose of the Statute of Wills is accomplished by requiring clear and convincing proof of the necessary elements." Gibbs & Ordover. "Correcting Mistakes in Wills & Trusts", N.Y.L.J., 8/6/98, p. 3, col. 2.

Thus the Restatement provides for considering any evidence of testator's intent, but raising the standard of proof from a preponderance of the evidence to clear and convincing evidence.

In actuality, the New York courts have already moved in this direction. In Matter of Snide, 52 N.Y.2d 193, 437 N.Y.S.2d 63, 418 N.E.2d 656 (1981) the decedent and his wife each signed the other's will. The Court of Appeals held that the decedent's will should be admitted to probate with the mistake corrected by reading both wills together and substituting the wife's name into the decedent's will wherever necessary, as if the decedent had signed the correct will.

Other cases have held that language missing from a will due to typographical or other error can be supplied to carry out the testator's intent.... Matter of Hahn, N.Y.L.J. 11/7/97 p. 32, col. 1 (Surr. Ct. Nassau County). In *Hahn*, the court stated "It is well established that when errors in draftsmanship have occurred, courts may add, excise, modify or transpose language or provisions to harmonize it with and to effectuate the testator's intent."...

Similarly, a number of cases have held that where the name of the beneficiary is wrong and extrinsic evidence establishes who was really intended to be the beneficiary, the court will order the correction. In Matter of Tracey, N.Y.L.J., 3/11/96 p. 33, col. 1 (Surr. Ct. Suffolk County), the attorney draftsperson submitted an affirmation that through scrivener's error the name of decedent's sister-in-law, Adelaide Berard, was included in the will and not that of the intended beneficiary, the decedent's niece, Adelaide Battipede. The court construed the will accordingly. Likewise, in Matter of Righi, N.Y.L.J. 7/22/96 (Surr. Ct. Suffolk County), a bequest to a sister, Anne Cavanagh, was substituted for the beneficiary actually named in the will, a niece, Catherine Cavanagh. Accord, Matter of Migden, N.Y.L.J. 5/23/95 p. 27, col. 4 (Surr. Ct. Bronx County).

It is a significant step beyond the cases just cited to say that not only can omitted language be added and the name of a beneficiary be corrected, but also that the name left out of the will can be added to the provisions of the will. Nevertheless, it seems logical to this court to choose the path of considering all available evidence as recommended by the Restatement in order to achieve the dominant purpose of carrying out the intention of the testator.

In this case, the court is persuaded that the evidence is clear and convincing that Colomba Pastorino is the intended beneficiary of the residuary of the estate of Eugenia Herceg. As stated above, the previous 1997 will provides for the residuary to pass to decedent's nephew, Sergio Pastorino, if he survives me, and if not to his wife, Colomba Pastorino. Additionally, two other prior wills dated October 1, 1992 and August 6, 1990, contain an identical residuary clause. This supports the contention of the petition that the identical residuary clause was intended to be included in the 1999 will admitted to probate.

Equally convincing is the fact that Colomba Pastorino was named the alternate executrix in the will admitted to probate in the event of the death of her husband. The testatrix had sufficient confidence in Colomba to name her as executrix in the event, which actually happened, of her husband, Sergio, predeceasing the testatrix. This demonstrates that Colomba had not fallen out of favor with the testatrix and been deliberately removed from the residuary. The consent by Josephine D'Angelo, the niece of the testatrix, and one of the persons who would take in intestacy confirms this saying "I acknowledge that the omission of the name of the residuary was a typographical error, and my aunt continued to have Sergio Pastorino, or his wife, Colomba Pastorino, if he was deceased, as the residuary beneficiary." Further confirmation comes from the attorney-draftsperson's affidavit which states " Mrs. Herceg's express intention was to continue the remainder of her property distribution as it was in the previous will." This conclusion is buttressed by the presumption against intestacy.... Mrs. Herceg disposed of 90% of her estate in various percentage bequests.... [A]lmost any construction is justified to avoid the unusual result of testatrix dying intestate as to the 10% of her estate remaining for the residuary. It is equally illogical to think the attorney-draftsman put into the will the standard language for a residuary disposition and then deliberately left out the name of the beneficiary. Rather what makes sense is to construe the will to add the missing provision by inserting the names of the residuary beneficiaries from the prior will....

Accordingly, the residuary clause, Paragraph Eighth, of the will of Eugenia Herceg is construed to insert the name of Colomba Pastorino as the beneficiary (her husband, Sergio Pastorino, having predeceased).

Note

In a case that may become a milestone in the movement to allow the reformation of a will even if the will is unambiguous, the California Supreme Court adopted the Restatement 3d's approach to reformation in Estate of Duke 352 P.3d 863, 879 (2015), stating:

> ...we are persuaded that authorizing the reformation of wills... serves the paramount purpose of the law governing wills without compromising the policies underlying the statutory scheme and the common law rules. If a mistake in expression and the testator's actual and specific intent at the time the will was drafted are established by clear and convincing evidence, no policy underlying the statute of wills supports a rule that would ignore the testator's intent and unjustly enrich those who would inherit as a result of a mistake.

—————

Commonwealth Reformation Legislation. In the United Kingdom, §20 of the Administration of Justice Act of 1982 provides that "[i]f a court is satisfied that a will is so expressed that it fails to carry out the testator's intentions, in consequence (a) of a clerical error; or (b) of a failure to understand his instructions, it may order that the will shall be rectified so as to carry out his intentions...."[9]

The New South Wales Wills, Probate and Administration (Amendment) Act of 1989 in §29A(1) adopted a broader authorization for courts to reform wills. The statute provided that "[i]f the court is satisfied that a will is so expressed that it fails to carry out the testator's intentions, it may order that the will be rectified so as to carry out the testator's intentions." This provision was amended by the New South Wales Succession Act 2006 §27(1) to provide that the "Court may make an order to rectify a will to carry out the intentions of the testator, if the Court is satisfied that the will does not carry out the testator's intentions because: (a) a clerical error was made, or (b) the will does not give effect to the testator's instructions."

The Tasmania Wills Act 1992, §47 also gave the court broad authorization to reform wills if "the Court is satisfied that there can be no reasonable doubt" that the testator made an error in expressing testamentary intention. This provision was amended by the Tasmania Wills Act 2008 §42(1) to provide that the "Court may make an order to rectify a will to carry out the intentions of the testator if the Court is satisfied beyond reasonable doubt that the will does not carry out the testator's intentions because (a) a clerical error was made; or (b) the will does not give effect to the testator's instructions."

---

9. For a review of English rectification cases, see R. Kerridge & A.H.R. Brierley, Mistakes in Wills: Rectify and Be Damned, 62 Camb. L.J. 750 (2003).

The Australian Capital Territory Wills Act §12A goes further. The Act authorizes reformation:

[i]f [the court is] satisfied that—

(a) any of the following apply in relation to circumstances or events (whether they existed or happened before, at or after the execution of the will):

(i) the circumstances or events were not known to, or anticipated by, the testator;

(ii) the effects of the circumstances or events were not fully appreciated by the testator;

(iii) the circumstances or events arose or happened at or after the death of the testator; and

(b) because of the circumstances or events, the application of the provisions of the will according to their tenor would fail to give effect to the probable intention of the testator if the testator had known of, anticipated or fully appreciated their effects.

Reformation in Specific Contexts. It is widely recognized that courts have general equity power to reform charitable trusts, whether created by will or otherwise, if the specific charitable purpose becomes impracticable. See Chapter 12.

Legislation and judicial authority exists in a number of states authorizing courts to reform dispositive provisions created by will or otherwise that violate the Rule Against Perpetuities. See Chapter 17.

Reformation under the Uniform Probate Code. How would *Flannery* and *Herceg* be decided under the current version of the UPC?

EXTERNAL REFERENCES. John H. Langbein & Lawrence W. Waggoner, Curing Execution Errors and Mistaken Terms in Wills, University of Michigan Law School Working Paper Series (no. 207), available at http://ssrn.com/abstract=1653438 (2010); John H. Langbein & Lawrence W. Waggoner, Reformation of Wills on the Ground of Mistake: Change of Direction in American Law?, 130 U. Pa. L. Rev. 521 (1982).

2. Reformation or Modification to Achieve Tax Objectives

Restatement 3d of Property
§12.2. Modifying Donative Documents to Achieve Donor's Tax Objectives

A donative document may be modified, in a manner that does not violate the donor's probable intention, to achieve the donor's tax objectives.

———

Courts have been willing to reform wills when the reformation is necessary to achieve certain tax benefits. Despite the traditional no-reformation rule for wills, state courts are inclined to reform split-interest charitable trusts, created by will or otherwise, to conform them to the federal tax requirements for an estate or gift tax charitable deduction. See, e.g., Estate of Burdon-Miller, 456 A.2d 1266 (Me. 1983). IRC §2055(e)(3) provides that a charitable deduction shall be allowed for the charitable interest in a split-interest trust "in respect of any qualified reformation." "Qualified reformation" is defined as "a change of a governing instrument by reformation, amendment, construction, or otherwise which changes a reformable interest into a qualified interest but only if... such change is effective as of the date of the decedent's death." For examples of rulings in which the Internal Revenue Service found that reformation entitled an estate to a charitable deduction, see, e.g., Priv. Ltr. Rul. 200027014 (July 7, 2000); Priv. Ltr. Rul. 9844008 (July 30, 1998). Many states have enacted statutes that authorize modification of split-interest charitable trusts, either by the trustee or by the court, to qualify them for a federal tax deduction. See Restatement 3d of Property §12.2 statutory note.

Courts also have reformed a will to give a better federal tax result by splitting a single QTIP ("qualified terminable interest property") trust into three separate QTIP trusts, one of which would be a generation-skipping transfer tax (GSTT) exempt trust with an "inclusion ratio" of 0. For background on QTIP trusts or the GSTT, see Chapter 19. See also Treas. Reg. §26.2654-1(b) (recognizing a division of a single trust into separate trusts for purposes of the generation-skipping tax if certain conditions are met). In Will of Choate, 533 N.Y.S.2d 272, 275 (Sur. Ct. 1988), the court emphasized that "[a]ll interested persons under the present single QTIP trust would remain entitled to precisely the same interest as he or she would have if the will were not construed as proposed," and noted further that "[t]his court has the power to construe and reform testator's will if the will, as written, does not carry out his intention, provided such reformation does not attempt to alter tax consequences retroactively or to change in any respect the dispositive provisions of his will." Accord First Agricultural Bank v. Coxe, 550 N.E.2d 875 (Mass. 1990); see also Shawmut Bank v. Buckley, 665 N.E.2d 29 (Mass. 1996) (authorizing excision of certain terms to prevent potential adverse tax consequences to surviving spouse regarding the nonmarital deduction trust created by the decedent).

Another type of reformation that courts frequently have used to achieve the decedent's tax objectives is to divide a QTIP marital deduction trust into two trusts in order to allow the decedent's executor to make the so-called *reverse QTIP* election under IRC §2652(a)(3). See, e.g., Estate of Branigan, 609 A.2d 431 (N.J. 1992); see also In re Quigan, N.Y.L.J., Nov. 17, 1994, at 34 (in reforming the will to assure the effectiveness of a credit shelter trust, the court said that, "[h]aving discerned the intent of the testatrix, the court may reform the will by modifying, adding, or deleting language to give effect to decedent's testamentary plan and to avoid any inadvertent, adverse tax consequences of the language actually used").

Courts have reformed wills to achieve tax objectives either to correct drafting errors or to achieve tax savings resulting from tax law changes that occurred between execution of a will and death. But see Estate of Dunlop, 617 N.Y.S.2d 119 (Sur. Ct. 1994). In *Dunlop* the executor petitioned the court to reform the testator's will to create five separate trusts so that, through the use of certain elections, the GSTT exemption could be utilized in both the decedent and the surviving spouse's estates. The court refused to reform the will because the adverse tax consequences did not result from unforeseen changes in the tax law but because the testator and the attorney-drafter were not aware of applicable law.

> This court finds that there is no presumption that the Will of the decedent, which never mentions or even alludes to the generation-skipping tax, sets forth an intent to minimize such tax in the estate of his surviving spouse.
>
> The result reached by this Court may seem harsh. Perhaps it is.... It is inappropriate, however, for this Court to be the mechanism to create a new estate plan for the testator and his widow. If such were the duty of this Court, what would be the limit to its functions in that regard? Would the Court always be bound to reform each and every Will of every testator so as to achieve maximum tax benefits, no matter what the Will stated? If that were the case, the courts would be overwhelmed with such requests for reformation, and the rule of law respecting testamentary dispositions would be undermined.
>
> It is one thing to seek reformation where an important tax law, or other statute, has been changed to adversely affect a carefully drawn estate plan. To permit such reformation, in every case, because the testator or his draftsman was uninformed or overlooked something, is beyond the power of the Court and is unwarranted.

A Washington statute provides that "[i]f a governing instrument contains a marital deduction gift, the governing instrument shall be construed to comply with the marital deduction provisions of the Internal Revenue Code in every respect." Wash. Rev. Code § 11.108.020(1).

The Restatement 3d of Property §12.2, which authorizes modification of donative instruments, including wills, to achieve the donor's tax objectives, only permits modification if it is in done in "a manner that does not violate the donor's probable intention." In Estate of Burkett, N.Y.L.J., Nov. 7, 1997, at 27 (Sur. Ct.), the court refused to modify a trust agreement because it would not effectuate the testator's intent.

Carlson v. Sweeney, Dabagia, Donoghue, Thorne, Janes & Pagos
895 N.E.2d 1191 (Ind. 2008)

RUCKER, JUSTICE. Arising in the context of a legal malpractice action, this case involves the reformation of trust provisions in two wills to comport with the testators' intent to avoid adverse federal estate tax consequences. We hold the trusts were properly reformed to include ascertainable standards in accordance with the Internal Revenue Code.

Facts and Procedural History. In 1988, Norman R. Carlson, Sr., and his wife Hilda Carlson (referred to collectively as "Testators") hired the Indiana law firm of

Sweeney, Dabagia, Donoghue, Thorne, Janes & Pagos ("Law Firm") to prepare their wills. Among other things, Testators instructed Law Firm to draft the wills in a way that upon the deaths of their son Norman R. Carlson, Jr., and daughter in-law Margaret Ann Carlson property passing from them would not be subject to federal estate or state inheritance tax. In essence Testators intended that their grandchildren would avoid federal and state estate tax liability. Law Firm prepared separate wills purporting to accomplish this end. In part each will left some property to the other spouse, if surviving, and put the residue into a trust, with the First Citizens Bank as Trustee. Among other things the Trustee was instructed that upon the death of the last of Norman, Jr., and Margaret, any remaining balance in the trust was to be distributed to two named grandchildren, Beth Carlson and David Carlson.... Relevant to this litigation the wills directed the Trustee to pay Margaret and Norman, Jr., "such sums from principal as the Trustee deems necessary or advisable from time to time *for either of their medical care, comfortable maintenance and welfare*, considering the income of either from all sources known to the Trustee." (emphasis added).

Norman, Sr., died in June 1992, and his wife Hilda died shortly thereafter in August 1992. Both wills were admitted to probate. Thereafter in 1994 Norman, Jr., hired a Texas attorney to assist with management of the trust. In counsel's opinion the language of the trust provisions in the wills subjected the property to federal estate taxes. Specifically, there were no "ascertainable standards" for the distribution of the trust principal. Thus the trust created a general power of appointment under Internal Revenue Service ("I.R.S.") Treasury Regulations, and property held under a general power of appointment is taxable upon the death of one holding the power. I.R.C. §2041(a)(2)(b)(1).[10]

At the request of Norman, Jr., his wife Margaret, and their two children Beth and David (referred to collectively as "Beneficiaries") on July 27, 1994, Law Firm filed in the LaPorte Superior Court a "Petition to Reform Testamentary Trust" with respect to Norman, Sr.'s will. The trial court granted the petition on August 4, 1994, and entered an order that the will be reformed to read: "The Trustee may also pay to my said son, Norman R. Carlson, Jr. and/or his said wife, Margaret Ann Carlson, such sums from principal as the Trustee deems necessary from time to time *for either of their health and maintenance*, considering the income of either from all sources

---

10. A general power of appointment is defined as a power that is exercisable in favor of the decedent, his estate, his creditors, or the creditors of the estate. See I.R.C. §2041(b)(1). However, a power to consume or appropriate property for the benefit of the decedent that is limited by an "ascertainable standard relating to the health, education, support, or maintenance of the decedent" is not deemed a general power of appointment. I.R.C. §2041(b)(1)(A). According to a federal regulation, "A power to use property for the comfort, welfare, or happiness of the holder of the power is not limited by the requisite standard...." Treas. Reg. §20.2041-1(c)(2).

known to the Trustee." (emphasis added).[11].... No challenge was made to the trial court's findings and no appeal was taken from its order of reformation.

Thereafter on June 2, 1999, Beneficiaries filed a complaint against Law Firm alleging malpractice in the preparation of Norman, Sr.'s and Hilda's wills....

Discussion. At the heart of this litigation is a federal court's recognition vel non of a state court's determination concerning the reformation of a will or trust. Although federal law dictates how a decedent's estate will be taxed, state law controls in determining the nature of the legal interest the taxpayer had in the property or income sought to be reached by the statute. The United States Supreme Court has made clear that neither the I.R.S. nor the federal courts are bound by a state trial court's decision.... Comm'r of Internal Revenue v. Estate of Bosch, 387 U.S. 456 (1967). Rather, "the State's highest court is the best authority on its own law." Id. at 465.

Essentially, in the last analysis this Court will determine whether, how, and to what extent a trial court's reformation of a will or trust comports with Indiana law. Whether a federal court deems itself bound by such a determination is a question of federal law—a matter about which we express no opinion....

Reformation Under Indiana Law.... [W]e conclude the trial court properly reformed the trust provision in the original wills to include language establishing an ascertainable standard thereby complying with I.R.S. Treasury Regulation §20.2041-1(c)(2). As reformed the wills are consistent with the original intent of the Testators of avoiding adverse federal estate and state inheritance taxes.

A written instrument, including a trust, may be reformed on grounds of mistake upon "clear and convincing evidence" not only of the mistake, but also of the original intent of the parties. Restatement (Third) of Trusts §62 comment b (2003). We point out however, the doctrine of reformation for mistake with regard to trusts differs from instruments such as contracts in one important respect. In contract law, reformation will not be granted unless the parties' mistake is mutual.... But mutuality of mistake is not always required where trusts are concerned. Because a settlor usually receives no consideration for the creation of a trust, a unilateral mistake on the part of the settlor is ordinarily sufficient to warrant reformation. 4A. Scott, Trusts §333.4 (4th ed. 1987); Restatement supra, §62 cmt. a....

We are of the view that a slightly modified rule is appropriate for a testamentary trust. Indiana Code section 30-4-3-25 provides, "Upon petition by an interested party, the court may rescind or reform a trust according to the same general rules applying to rescission or reformation of non-trust transfers of property." This provision

---

11. A similar petition was filed September 21, 1994 concerning Hilda's will, and a similar order was issued September 22, 1994. Throughout this opinion any reference to Norman, Sr.'s will or trust applies equally to Hilda's will or trust and vice versa.

mirrors Restatement (Third) of Trusts §62 (2003).[12] And the Restatement's comment b is instructive:

> Even if the will or other instrument creating a donative testamentary or inter vivos trust is unambiguous, the terms of the trust may be reformed by the court to conform the text to the intention of the settlor if the following are established by clear and convincing evidence: (1) that a *mistake of fact or law*, whether in expression or inducement, affected the specific terms of the document; and (2) what the settlor's intention was. [Restatement, supra, §62 cmt. b (emphasis added); accord Restatement (Third) of Property, §12.1 (2003).]

We adopt the Restatement view on this subject. As a practical matter most trust instruments are drafted by counsel, and the language in the instrument is the testator's only by adoption. In essence the testator informs counsel what she wants to accomplish and relies on counsel to carry out her wishes. If counsel makes a mistake in drafting and fails in this effort, then the testator's intent has not been realized. And this is so whether the mistake is one of fact or one of law. It appears to us that reformation is appropriate under such circumstances. See John H. Langbein & Lawrence W. Waggoner, Reformation of Wills on the Ground of Mistake: Change of Direction in American Law, 130 U. Pa. L.Rev. 521, 582-83 (1982) (commenting that there is no principled distinction between a lawyer's mistake involving the "misapprehension of the meaning of a term" [mistake of law] and "misrender[ing] a name or a sum" [mistake of fact]. "In either case the lawyer's mistake prevented the will from expressing an intent that the testator formed and communicated, and which a well-proven reformation case can correct.").

In this case the record is clear that as originally drafted, the trust provision in the Testators' wills did not accomplish that which was intended: to ensure that property passing to Norman Carlson, Jr., and his wife Margaret A. Carlson would not be subject to federal estate or state inheritance tax upon their deaths. The trust provision failed in this regard because it did not establish an "ascertainable standard" for the distribution of trust principal thereby creating a general power of appointment under I.R.S. Treasury Regulations. To remedy this unintended result, the trial court reformed the first paragraph of Section 2, Item III of the wills by inserting an ascertainable standard governing trustee distribution of principal to Testators and deleting the problematic language that could be construed as liberal discretionary distributions. Inclusion of an ascertainable standard will effectively negate a general power of appointment, see I.R.C. §2041(b)(1)(A), and thereby conform the trust to the Testators' original intent.

---

12. The Restatement of Trusts reads, "A trust may be rescinded or reformed upon the same grounds as those upon which a transfer of property not in trust may be rescinded or reformed." Restatement, supra, §62.

We reach three conclusions: (1) the record shows by clear and convincing evidence there was a mistake in the trust language of the original wills; (2) the record shows by clear and convincing evidence the Testators' true intent as exhaustively discussed above; and (3) the trusts were reformed consistent with Indiana law.

Reformation and Summary Judgment. This case is before us in a rather unusual procedural posture. It should be remembered that Beneficiaries sued Law Firm in part for damages flowing from alleged negligence in drafting the original wills. The trial court granted summary judgment in favor of Law Firm based on the reformed wills declaring in part, "[t]he effect of this Order is to dismiss any claim by Plaintiffs against Defendants for adverse federal income taxation resulting from the drafting of the subject testamentary instruments." The underlying thrust of the trial court's judgment and order is that the trust language in the wills has now been reformed to comply with I.R.S. regulations and there will be no adverse federal estate consequences. Thus Beneficiaries have not and will not suffer damages. According to the trial court, "the Internal Revenue Service must accept the reformation as controlling given the fact situation in this case."

There are at least two problems with the trial court's position. First, as the Beneficiaries point out and the Court of Appeals observed, "[T]he Carlsons have already expended time and money dealing with the Wills; if the Lawyers' work with regard to the Wills is determined to be negligent, these costs may be considered damages flowing from the Wills regardless of whether the IRS assesses a tax penalty." Carlson, 868 N.E.2d at 22 n. 12. We agree. Summary judgment in favor of Law Firm on this point was error. Second, as for the I.R.S., it is clear that the agency as well as the federal courts are bound by this Court's determination that the Testators' wills were properly reformed in accordance with the laws of this State. Bosch, 387 U.S. at 456. It is also clear that the reformed wills include the "ascertainable standard" language that comports with I.R.C. §2041(b)(1)(A). What is less clear, however, is what reaction the federal authorities will have to all of this. More precisely is there some reason the I.R.S. may find to avoid the effect of the reformation in spite of this Court's opinion? We have no way to know one way or the other, and decline to speculate.[13] Because there is a dispute of material fact on this issue, summary judgment in favor of Law Firm was inappropriate on this point as well.

Conclusion. We affirm in part the judgment of the trial court. This cause is remanded for further proceedings.

---

13. Apparently the parties may request a Private Letter Ruling (PLR) from the IRS to resolve the question we pose. Rev. Proc. 2008-1, 2008-1 I.R.B 16. And we anticipate they will do so.

Note and Questions

1. *Note on IRC §2041.* Section 2041 of the Internal Revenue Code subjects to federal estate taxation the value of all property "with respect to which the decedent has at the time of his death a general power of appointment created after October 21, 1942...." However, §2041 also provides that "[a] power to consume, invade, or appropriate property for the benefit of the decedent which is limited by an ascertainable standard relating to the health, education, support, or maintenance of the decedent shall not be deemed a general power of appointment."

2. *Who Held the Power of Appointment?* As mentioned in Note 1 above, IRC §2041 applies when "the *decedent* has at the time of his death a general power of appointment..." (emphasis supplied). Under the terms of the Carlsons' wills, the power of appointment was held by the trustee. So why was IRC §2041 an issue? The answer is that the wills also contained a provision (not mentioned by the Indiana Supreme Court in this opinion) empowering "a majority of the beneficiaries of the current income" to remove the trustee and appoint any other individual or corporation as trustee. The ability of Norman Jr. and Margaret to replace the trustee with a new trustee who might be related (or subordinate) to them could have been sufficient to impute to them the trustee's powers, including the power of appointment. See Rev. Rul. 95-58; Estate of Wall v. Commissioner, 101 T.C. 300 (1993); Estate of Vak v. Commissioner, 973 F.2d 1409 (8th Cir. 1992).

3. *Questions.* Why did the court use §12.1 of the Restatement 3d of Property, rather than §12.2? How would *Carlson* have been decided under the current UPC?

PART D. ATTORNEY LIABILITY FOR MISTAKE

"The minute you read something that you can't understand,
you can be almost sure it was drawn up by a lawyer."
  – *Will Rogers*

Would liability for malpractice or for breach of a third-party beneficiary contract be better solutions to the problem of attorney mistake than the adoption of a reformation doctrine? If a reformation remedy were to become available, would there still be room for liability even in cases where the reformation remedy was successfully invoked? Consider the following discussion of these questions in Langbein & Waggoner, Reformation of Wills on the Ground of Mistake, above, at 588-90:

> Because the error in many mistake cases is sufficiently egregious that a victim might be able to invoke the malpractice liability of the lawyer-draftsman if relief for mistake were denied, the argument can be made that the malpractice remedy makes relief for mistake unnecessary. The intended beneficiary whose devise has been frustrated by the lawyer's mistake can be remitted to his malpractice remedy against the offending draftsman. We think that there are a variety of responses to this contention.

Initially, we note that there is a range of mistake cases that fall outside the scope of malpractice relief, including homedrawn wills and those lawyer-drafted wills where for whatever reason the mistake does not rise to the level of malpractice. Furthermore, in a considerable fraction of lawyer malpractice cases, the draftsman may be wholly or partially judgment-proof, as when he is long since deceased,[14] or when he is uninsured or underinsured. In one region of the country for which a specialist insurance broker has supplied recent data on malpractice coverage to the American Bar Association's Standing Committee on Lawyers' Professional Liability, 51% of the policies in force have $100,000/$300,000 limits, well below the value of significant numbers of testate estates. For devises of unique property, for example, Blackacre or the family bible, relief in damages would not be an adequate substitute.

The malpractice solution is also objectionable because it would channel mistake cases into the tort system. When translated into a tort claim and discounted for the litigation expenses and counsel fees, and for the unpredictability and delay incident to the jury-dominated tort system, a devise frustrated by mistake would be worth but a fraction of the value in the testator's estate.

More fundamentally, the change in theory from devise to tort raises a serious problem of unjust enrichment. Whereas most forms of malpractice inflict deadweight loss that can only be put right by compensation, in these testamentary mistake cases a benefit is being transferred from the intended beneficiary to a mistaken devisee. That devisee is a volunteer lacking any claim of entitlement or justified reliance. The malpractice solution would leave the benefit where it fortuitously fell, thereby creating a needless loss to be charged against the draftsman (or his insurer). So long as the draftsman's error was innocent (which is what distinguishes mistake from fraud), there is no reason to exaggerate his liability in this way. If, on the other hand, the lawyer were charged with the malpractice but subrogated to the tort plaintiff's mistake claim, the mistake doctrine would simply be recognized in a circular and more litigious fashion.

We do not mean to say that negligent draftsmen will be immune from malpractice liability in testamentary mistake cases. When the malpractice causes true loss, that loss should be compensable. One such item of compensable loss may be the reasonable litigation expenses of the parties to the reformation (or other) proceeding occasioned by the mistake. We can also imagine circumstances in which a mistake might come to light after distribution and dissipation of the mistakenly devised property; here the change of position of the mistaken devisee would constitute justified reliance and require that the intended beneficiary be remitted to his malpractice remedy.

Finally, we point once more to the experience under the many existing doctrines that provide partial relief in the field of testamentary mistake. There has been no suggestion in the "mere construction" and other cases [set forth supra Part B] that malpractice should be regarded as an alternative to direct relief.

Professors Langbein and Waggoner argue that a reformation remedy is a better means of promoting justice than a malpractice remedy. In the malpractice case that

---

14. A malpractice claim against an attorney may survive the attorney's death. McStowe v. Bornstein, 377 Mass. 804, 388 N.E.2d 674 (1979).

follows, consider whether judicial reformation or malpractice liability is the better means of remedying the lawyer's mistake.

Ogle v. Fuiten
466 N.E.2d 224 (Ill. 1984)

GOLDENHERSH, J. Plaintiffs, James Elvin Ogle and Leland W. Ogle, initiated this action in the circuit court of Sangamon County against defendants, Lorraine Fuiten, as executrix of the estate of William F. Fuiten, and Robert G. Heckenkamp, who, under the name of Heckenkamp and Fuiten, had been associated with William F. Fuiten in the practice of law. In a two-count complaint plaintiffs alleged that William F. Fuiten had negligently drafted wills for Oscar H. Smith and Alma I. Smith, respectively an uncle and aunt of plaintiffs, and alternatively, that Fuiten failed to properly perform his contract with the Smiths to fulfill their testamentary intentions, and in so doing, failed to benefit the plaintiffs. Defendants moved to dismiss for failure to state a cause of action. The circuit court allowed the motion, and plaintiffs appealed. The appellate court reversed and remanded, and we allowed defendants' petition for leave to appeal.

The appellate court summarized the allegations contained in the complaint as follows:

> Count I essentially alleges: (1) Testators employed defendant Fuiten and the law firm of Heckenkamp and Fuiten to prepare wills in accordance with the testators' intentions; (2) the wills were prepared; (3) neither testator intended their property to devolve by the law of intestate succession; (4) it was their intention that their property be left to plaintiffs if neither testator survived the other by 30 days; (5) this contingency occurred; (6) Fuiten owed plaintiffs the duty of ascertaining the testators' intentions in all foreseeable events and to draft wills which would effectuate these intentions; (7) Fuiten breached this duty and negligently drafted the subject wills; and (8) plaintiffs suffered damage as a direct result of this breach.

> Count II essentially alleges the first five allegations noted above and additionally alleges: (6) the purpose of the employment of Fuiten and the firm was to draft wills not only for the benefit of testators, but for the benefit of these plaintiffs; (7) Fuiten and the firm were paid the agreed consideration under the employment agreement; (8) Fuiten and the firm knew plaintiffs were intended beneficiaries of the wills and the employment agreement; (9) Fuiten and the firm had agreed to draft wills leaving the property to plaintiffs in the event neither testator survived the other by 30 days; (10) Fuiten breached this agreement in that the wills failed to fulfill the testators' intentions; and (11) plaintiffs suffered foreseeable, direct damage as a consequence of this breach.

The wills of Oscar H. Smith and Alma I. Smith contained the following provisions:

> SECOND: I give, devise and bequeath all of my estate, real, personal and mixed wheresoever situated to my wife, ALMA I. SMITH, if she [my husband, OSCAR H.

SMITH, if he] shall survive me within thirty (30) days from the date of my death.

THIRD: I direct that if my wife, ALMA I. SMITH, [my husband, OSCAR H. SMITH] and I die in or from a common disaster that my estate be equally divided between my nephews, JAMES ELVIN OGLE, and LELAND OGLE, share and share alike.

These wills were construed in In re Estate of Smith (1979), 68 Ill.App.3d 30, 24 Ill.Dec. 451, 385 N.E.2d 363, and it was held that because Oscar Smith died suddenly of a stroke on April 10, 1977, and his wife, Alma, died 15 days later from a lingering cancer illness, and neither will contained any other dispositive provisions, their estates passed by intestacy to persons other than plaintiffs.

Because the judgment appealed from was entered upon allowance of defendants' motion to dismiss, all facts properly pleaded in the complaint must be taken as true. A cause of action should not be dismissed on the pleadings unless it clearly appears that no set of facts can be proved which will entitle plaintiffs to recover.

Conceding that under Pelham v. Griesheimer (1982), 92 Ill.2d 13, 64 Ill.Dec. 544, 440 N.E.2d 96, privity is not a prerequisite to an action by a nonclient against an attorney, defendants argue that the complaint fails to allege a duty owed plaintiffs. They argue that the only duty owed by defendants was to provide each testator "with a valid testamentary instrument that disposes of the testators' property at his death in the manner expressly stated in his will." They argue that to permit persons unnamed in the will, or persons named with a precondition which fails to occur, to bring an action against the attorney "creates an unlimited and unknown class of potential plaintiffs." They contend, too, that in order to recover from an attorney, a nonclient must allege and prove "that the primary purpose and intent of the attorney-client relationship itself was to benefit or influence the third party." Defendants argue that under this "intent to directly benefit" test, plaintiffs' cause fails because the testators' intent, as defined in the will-construction action, shows that plaintiffs were to benefit only under certain circumstances which did not occur. Thus, defendants contend, the intent of the testators to benefit plaintiffs is not, as required by *Pelham*, "clearly evident."

Also citing *Pelham*, plaintiffs contend that they have alleged facts which show that the testators, in obtaining the services of the defendants in the preparations of the wills, intended to "directly benefit" plaintiffs and that, as held by the appellate court, they have stated a cause of action in both counts of the complaint....

Defendants argue that to state a cause of action plaintiffs should be required to show, from the express terms of the will, that the plaintiff was an intended beneficiary of the relationship between the defendant attorney and the testator. They argue that this would protect against a flood of litigation. Defendants have cited no authority which has applied the rule which they espouse, and we find no basis in the cases which we have examined for imposing such a requirement.

We agree with the appellate court that "the allegations of count I sufficiently state the traditional elements of negligence in tort and count II sufficiently states the traditional elements of a third-party beneficiary/breach of contract theory." We note parenthetically that, unlike *Pelham*, the defendants' representation of the testators here was of a nonadversarial nature and consisted only of the drafting of the wills which plaintiffs alleged were for their benefit as intended beneficiaries. See Pelham v. Griesheimer (1982), 92 Ill.2d 13, 22, 64 Ill.Dec. 544, 440 N.E.2d 96.

Defendants contend that this action is an impermissible collateral attack upon the judicial determination of the validity of the testators' wills. Defendants' argument appears to be that because the wills were held valid, the question of the testators' intent has been settled, and plaintiffs may not now state a cause of action based on the allegation that the wills do not reflect the true intent of the testators.

In support of their position defendants cite Robinson v. First State Bank (1983), 97 Ill.2d 174, 73 Ill.Dec. 428, 454 N.E.2d 288, and attempt to analogize the claim in Robinson that the testator's attorney, through tortious interference, had prevented the plaintiffs from receiving their inheritance to the allegations here that the testators' attorney, because of negligence or breach of contract, had prevented plaintiffs from receiving the testators' estates. In *Robinson*, holding that the action, in effect, was a tardy will contest, this court affirmed the circuit court's dismissal of the action for tortious interference. Defendants argue that the present action necessarily assumes that the wills are invalid, without having been contested by plaintiffs on that ground within the statutory time.

We find *Robinson* distinguishable in that the basis for the plaintiffs' complaint was that the testator had been subject to the undue influence of her attorney. Claims of undue influence are properly raised in a will-contest action. In the present case, however, the basis for the plaintiffs' complaint is that, because of the attorney's negligence, the testators' true intent is not reflected in the wills. Thus, while the plaintiffs in *Robinson* had the opportunity to pursue their claims in a will-contest action, plaintiffs here had no similar opportunity to do so.

We note further that if plaintiffs here are successful in their action, the orderly disposition of the testators' property is not disrupted, and the provisions of the wills, and the probate administration, remain unaffected. On these facts, the present action is not a collateral attack on the wills....

For the foregoing reasons, the judgment of the appellate court is affirmed.

Notes

1. *The Privity Problem. Ogle* illustrates the modern trend to abrogate the privity requirement and allow malpractice actions in tort, contract, or both by the intended beneficiaries for mistakes in wills. See Restatement 3d of the Law Governing Lawyers §51 comment f illustrations 2, 3. A small number of jurisdictions, however, continue to dismiss cases for lack of privity. See, e.g., Baker v. Wood, Ris & Hames

P.C., 364 P.3d 872 (Colo. 2016); Noble v. Bruce, 709 A.2d 1264 (Md. 1998); Landrigan v. Nelson, 420 N.W.2d 313 (Neb. 1988); Barcelo v. Elliott, 923 S.W.2d 575 (Tex. 1996). But for Texas law, see also Belt v. Oppenheimer, Blend, Harrison & Tate, Inc., 192 S.W.3d 780 (Tex. 2006) (reaffirming *Barcelo* but holding as a matter of first impression that the executors of the testator's estate may bring a malpractice action against attorneys who had provided estate planning services to the testator); Smith v. O'Donnell, 288 S.W.3d 417 (Tex. 2009) (following *Belt*). For Nebraska law, see the case of Perez v. Stern, 777 N.W.2d 545 (Neb. 2010), requiringprivity except in the limited instance where the attorney owes an independent duty to the plaintiff. See also Estate of Schneider v. Finmann, 933 N.E.2d 718, 720 (N.Y. 2010), holding that "privity, or a relationship sufficiently approaching privity, exists between the personal representative of an estate and the [decedent's] estate planning attorney."

Other courts have adopted an intermediate position regarding the privity question, holding that a cause of action is available only to plaintiffs who can show that they were intended third-party beneficiaries of the contract between the lawyer and the testator. See, e.g., Hale v. Groce, 744 P.2d 1289 (Or. 1987); Guy v. Liederbach, 459 A.2d 744 (Pa. 1983).

Yet another group of cases has limited malpractice claims to those beneficiaries identified in the will. See, e.g., Mieras v. DeBona, 550 N.W.2d 202 (Mich. 1996). These cases reflect the courts' traditional hesitation to find testamentary intent beyond the four corners of the will. Rather than relying on the doctrine of privity, §51 of the Restatement 3d of the Law Governing Lawyers responds to this concern by requiring the plaintiff to prove testator's intent by clear and convincing evidence. See id. comment f, illustration 3; accord Pivnick v. Beck, 762 A.2d 653 (N.J. 2000).

For a case holding that the beneficiary of a *trust* cannot sue the trustee's attorney, see Audette v. Poulin, 127 A.3d 908 (R.I. 2015).

2. *Collateral Estoppel.* Courts have generally rejected the defendant's argument in *Ogle* that a malpractice action is an impermissible collateral attack upon the probate court's ruling on the validity of the testator's will. The courts have recognized that a consequence of the no-reformation-of-wills rule is that will construction proceedings do not necessarily lead to determination of a testator's intent. For example, consider Simpson v. Calivas, 650 A.2d 318, 323-24 (N.H. 1994), in which an alleged intended beneficiary sued the drafting attorney after the probate court had found that the will should be construed to exclude the plaintiff.

> The principal task of the probate court is to determine the testator's intent.... In this effort, the probate court is always permitted to consider the "surrounding circumstances" of the testator, and where the terms of a will are ambiguous, as here, extrinsic evidence may be admitted to the extent that it does not contradict the express terms of the will. Direct declarations of a testator's intent, however, are generally inadmissible in all probate proceedings. The defendant argues that even though his notes of his meeting with the decedent recorded the decedent's direct declarations of intent, they could have been

admissible as an exception to the general rule had there been a proper proffer. We need not reach the issue of whether the defendant's notes fall within an exception to the general rule because even assuming admissibility and therefore an identity of evidence, there remain distinct issues. Quite simply, the task of the probate court is a limited one: to determine the intent of the testator as expressed in the language of the will. Obviously, the hope is that the application of rules of construction and consideration of extrinsic evidence (where authorized) will produce a finding of expressed intent that corresponds to actual intent. Further, the likelihood of such convergence presumably increases as the probate court considers more extrinsic evidence; however, even with access to all extrinsic evidence, there is no requirement or guarantee that the testator's intent as construed will match the testator's actual intent....

 Inasmuch as the mandate of the probate court is simply to determine and give effect to the intent of the testator as expressed in the language of the will, a finding of actual intent is not necessary to that judgment. Accordingly, even an explicit finding of actual intent by a probate court cannot be the basis for collateral estoppel.

But see Pivnick v. Beck, above, in which the court held that collateral estoppel barred the plaintiff in a situation where extrinsic evidence was admissible in earlier probate proceeding to show that the trust did not reflect the settlor/testator's intent and the plaintiff had failed to meet the required clear and convincing evidentiary standard of proof.

EXTERNAL REFERENCES. Martin D. Begleiter, First Let's Sue All the Lawyers—What Will We Get: Damages for Estate Planning Malpractice, 51 Hastings L.J. 325 (2000); Martin D. Begleiter, Article II of the Uniform Probate Code and the Malpractice Revolution, 59 Tenn. L. Rev. 101 (1991); Martin D. Begleiter, Attorney Malpractice in Estate Planning—You've Got to Know When to Hold Up, Know When to Fold Up, 38 U. Kan. L. Rev. 193 (1990); Gerald P. Johnston, Legal Malpractice in Estate Planning—Perilous Times Ahead for the Practitioner, 67 Iowa L. Rev. 629 (1982).

Chapter 14

Powers of Appointment

"The power of appointment is the most efficient dispositive device that the ingenuity of Anglo-American lawyers has ever worked out."
– W. Barton Leach

PART A. INTRODUCTION TO POWERS

Primary Statutory Reference: *Uniform Powers of Appointment Act §102 (hereinafter "Uniform Act")*

The power of appointment is a core device in modern estate planning practice. Powers of appointment are routinely included in trusts for tax reasons and for reasons of adding flexibility to the arrangement.

The law of powers of appointment traditionally has been case law, rather than statute law, with many U.S. jurisdictions having little or no case law on point. To clarify and codify the law of powers of appointment, and to help make it uniform across the country, the Uniform Law Commission—relying heavily on the Restatement 3d of Property—promulgated the Uniform Powers of Appointment Act ("Uniform Act") in 2013.

Power of Appointment Defined. A power of appointment is generally defined as the authority, acting in a nonfiduciary capacity, to designate recipients of beneficial ownership interests in, or powers of appointment over, the appointive property. See Uniform Act §102(13). An owner, of course, has this authority with respect to his or her property. By creating a power of appointment, the owner typically confers this authority on someone else.

The property or property interest subject to a power of appointment is called the *appointive property.* The property interest subject to appointment need not be an absolute-ownership interest. In fact, powers of appointment frequently authorize appointment of only a remainder interest in the appointive property, as in the following example.

Example 14.1: G transferred property in trust, as follows: income to A for life, remainder to those of A's descendants who survive A as A may by will appoint or, in default of appointment, to X Charity.

A subsequently died, leaving a will exercising the power of appointment in favor of A's adult child, B.

Parties. The parties connected to a power of appointment are identified by a special terminology. The *donor* is the person who created (or reserved) the power of appointment—G in the above example. The *powerholder* (in older terminology, the *donee*) is the person upon whom the power of appointment was conferred—A in the above example.

The *permissible appointees* (in older terminology, the *objects*) are the persons in whose favor the power can be exercised—A's descendants in the above example. The donor determines the permissible appointees by expressly designating them in the instrument creating the power. If the donor does not expressly designate permissible appointees, the powerholder is free in almost all states to appoint in favor of anyone in the world, including the powerholder, the powerholder's estate, the powerholder's creditors, or the creditors of the powerholder's estate.

The *appointee* is the person to whom an appointment is made—B in the above example. The appointment makes the appointee the owner of the appointed property interest.

The *taker in default of appointment* (or simply, *taker in default*) is the person who takes the appointive property under the gift-in-default clause, to the extent the power is not effectively exercised—X Charity in the above example. The taker in default has a property interest that is subject to the power of appointment. Upon A's death, X Charity's property interest was divested in favor of the appointee, B.

In all cases, there is a donor, a powerholder, appointive property, and someone in whose favor an appointment can be made. The powerholder is under no duty to exercise a power of appointment[1] and, therefore, appointees might not always exist. Also, the donor should, but need not, include a gift-in-default clause designating takers in default.

A power of appointment is personal to the powerholder. If the powerholder dies without exercising the power, the power expires. Upon the powerholder's death, an unexercised power is not and cannot be passed to the powerholder's successors in interest. See Uniform Act §202.

1. Different Kinds of Powers of Appointment

Primary Statutory Reference: *Uniform Act §203*

Powers of appointment are differentiated in many ways. Two of the most important distinctions are (1) between presently exercisable and testamentary powers, and (2) between general and nongeneral powers. Both of these distinctions relate to the scope of the powerholder's authority. An extremely important,

---

1. The *nonmandatory* nature of a power of appointment is distinguishable from the *mandatory* type of power studied in Chapter 9.

overarching principle, set forth in Uniform Act §203 and followed in almost all states, is that the scope of the powerholder's authority is presumptively unlimited—that is, the powerholder's authority regarding appointees and the time and manner of appointment is limited only to the extent the instrument creating the power effectively expresses an intent to impose limits.

Presently Exercisable Powers/Testamentary Powers. When the terms of a power provide that the powerholder can exercise the power only in the powerholder's will, the power is *testamentary*. When the powerholder can exercise a power at the time in question, the power is *presently exercisable*. A presently exercisable power is usually exercisable *either* in an inter vivos instrument or in the powerholder's will.

A power that is exercisable by the powerholder's "last unrevoked instrument in writing signed and delivered to the trustee" is a presently exercisable power. Such a power is often used instead of a testamentary power so that the trustee need not be concerned about whether the powerholder's will is probated.[2] A more elaborate clause found in some form-books authorizes exercise of the power "in the last written instrument that the powerholder executes and delivers to the trustee during the powerholder's lifetime, or, failing any such instrument, in the powerholder's will."[3]

Occasionally, the powerholder can exercise a power only in an inter vivos instrument. This type of power is sometimes described as a power exercisable by deed alone, although technically speaking the power can be exercised by any instrument or act that is formally sufficient under applicable law to accomplish an inter vivos transfer. A testamentary exercise of a power to appoint a remainder interest is rarely prohibited, but some powers, such as a power to revoke or amend a trust, or to invade the corpus of a trust, are generally thought to be inherently restricted to inter vivos exercises.

General Powers/Nongeneral Powers.[4] A *general* power is one that is exercisable in favor of the powerholder, the powerholder's estate, or the creditors of either. See Uniform Act §102(6); IRC §§2041(b), 2514(c). In accordance with the overarching presumption of unlimited authority, the *absence* of express language excluding the

---

2. Lumbard v. Farmers State Bank, 812 N.E.2d 196 (Ind Ct. App. 2004), held that an unprobated will effectively exercised a general testamentary power of appointment. But see In re Estate of Scott, 77P.3d 906 (Colo. App. 2003), requiring that the will be probated.

3. Modified from Richard W, Nenno, Delaware Dynasty Trusts, Total Return Trusts, and Asset Protection Trusts 183 & 202 (2006).

4. Under an older terminology, adopted by the first Restatement of Property §320 but abandoned by the Restatement 2d of Property, the Restatement 3d of Property, and the Uniform Act, there were three types of powers. *General* powers were exercisable wholly in favor of the powerholder or the powerholder's estate. *Special* (or limited) powers were exercisable only in favor of persons, not including the powerholder, who constitute a group not unreasonably large. All other powers were *hybrid* powers.

powerholder, the powerholder's estate, or the creditors of either, indicates a general power.[5] See Uniform Act §203.

A *nongeneral* power is one in which the powerholder, the powerholder's estate, and the creditors of either are excluded as permissible appointees. A power of appointment is also nongeneral if the powerholder's exercise of the power is subject to the consent or joinder of an adverse party. Uniform Act §205.

The following examples illustrate the overarching presumption of unlimited authority:

Example 14.2: G transferred real property "to A for life, remainder to such person or persons as A may appoint; in default of appointment, remainder to B."

A's power is a presently exercisable general power. It is presently exercisable because the donor, G, did not expressly restrict the exercise of the power either to a will or to an inter vivos instrument. The power is general because the donor did not forbid A from exercising the power in A's own favor.[6]

Example 14.3: G transferred real property "to A for life, remainder to such of A's descendants as A may by will appoint; in default of appointment, remainder to B."

A's power is a nongeneral testamentary power. It is testamentary because of the donor's insertion of the phrase "by will." Thus, any purported inter vivos exercise of this power by A would be invalid. A's power is nongeneral because A is authorized to appoint only among A's descendants, a group that does not include A.[7]

Example 14.4: G transferred real property "to A for life, remainder to such person or persons except A, A's estate, A's creditors, or the creditors of A's estate, as A may by will appoint; in default of appointment, remainder to B."

In accordance with the categories of the Uniform Act and the Restatement 3d, A's power is in the same category as A's power in the preceding example—a nongeneral testamentary power.[8]

It has become common for the settlor of a trust to empower the trustee or a trust director to change a powerholder's general power into a nongeneral power or to

---

5. In at least one state, however, Maryland, the powerholder is authorized to appoint to the powerholder, the powerholder's estate, the powerholder's creditors, or the creditors of the powerholder's estate only if there is express language affirmatively authorizing such an appointment. See, e.g., Frank v. Frank, 253 A.2d 377 (Md. 1969).

6. In Maryland, however, the absence of such a restriction is not sufficient to authorize the powerholder to appoint to himself or herself; the language would have to say something like: "remainder to such person or persons, *including A or A's estate*, as A shall appoint." See note 5.

7. This power would be classified as a *special* power under the older nomenclature because the permissible appointees are reasonable in number.

8. The older nomenclature would classify this as a *hybrid* power, not a special power, because the donor did not identify permissible appointees that are reasonable in number.

change a powerholder's nongeneral power into a general power. Under this type of arrangement, the powerholder's "power is either general or nongeneral depending on the scope of the powerholder's power at any particular time." Comment to Uniform Act §102. The purpose of granting the trustee or trust director this authority is to adjust to changes in the tax law. As the tax law stands today, the applicable federal estate tax rate is often lower than the rate of the federal generation-skipping tax (GSTT). Consequently, a general power is often more advantageous than a nongeneral power if the nongeneral power would cause the trust property at the powerholder's death to be subject to the GSTT.

Example 14.5: G transferred property in trust, directing the trustee to pay the income "to A (G's daughter) for life, remainder in corpus to such of A's descendants as A may by will appoint." The terms of the trust provide that the trustee may at any time and from time to time expand the class of permissible appointees of A's power to include the creditors of A's estate or, having done so, to remove the creditors of A's estate from the class of permissible appointees. When the trust was created, A's power was a nongeneral power. Later, the trustee exercised the authority to add A's estate creditors as permissible appointees. As a result, A's nongeneral power became a general power. Later still, the trustee exercises the authority to remove A's estate creditors as permissible appointees. A's general power has now become a nongeneral power.

Problems

Hyacinth transferred property in trust "to my dear husband, Richard, for life, remainder to such person or persons as my brilliant son, Sheridan, may appoint, otherwise to my loyal neighbor, Elizabeth."

1. Classify the power of appointment created by Hyacinth.

2. Can the power be exercised by will?

3. What happens if the power is not exercised?

2. Powers Collateral, In Gross, or Appendant

Another way that powers of appointment are differentiated is on the basis of the powerholder's property interest, if any, in the appointive property. There are three categories: collateral powers, powers in gross, and powers appendant.

A power is *collateral* if the powerholder has *no* property interest in the appointive property.

A power is *in gross* if the powerholder has a property interest in the appointive property that cannot be affected by the exercise of the power. A power of appointment over the remainder interest held by the life tenant or the life income-beneficiary of a trust is a power in gross.

A power is *appendant* if the powerholder has a property interest in the appointive property that can be affected by the exercise of the power. In other words, the power of appointment purports to authorize the powerholder to divest the powerholder's own property interest and confer it on someone else through an exercise of the power. If the powerholder owns an equitable property interest that is subject to a spendthrift limitation, on which recall Chapter 11, should the power be treated as a power appendant?

Any purported exercise of a power appendant in favor of another carries with it the powerholder's owned property or property interest, either as a transfer of the owned property or property interest or as the subject of the exercise of the power of appointment. Conversely, any purported transfer of the owned property or property interest terminates the power over that property or property interest.

Example 14.6: G transferred real property "to such persons as A may appoint, and until and in default of appointment, to A and her heirs."

If A executes an instrument purporting to exercise the power, the instrument is construed as a transfer of A's owned interest. See Restatement 3d of Property §17.3 comment g. If A executes and delivers a deed conveying the property or an interest therein to another, A thereafter has no power to divest the grantee's property interest by a purported exercise of A's power.

Example 14.7: G transferred property in trust: income to A for life, remainder in corpus to B. A is empowered by the trust instrument to direct the trustee to transfer all or any part of the trust corpus to any one or more of A's descendants as A by deed or will directs.

If A directs the trustee to pay out part or all of the trust corpus to a permissible appointee of the nongeneral power, the transaction is treated as a transfer of A's remaining income interest in the assets and an exercise of A's nongeneral power over the remainder interest.[9]

Problems

Mr. Grace transferred property in trust to Mrs. Slocombe for life, remainder:

1. "to such of Mrs. Slocombe's male co-workers as Miss Brahms shall select"

2. "to such of Mrs. Slocombe's co-workers as Mrs. Slocombe shall by will select"

3. "to Miss Brahms. However, Mrs. Slocombe may at any time direct the trustee to pay the trust corpus outright to Mr. Humphries."

In each of the three cases, classify the power.

3. Invalid Powers

Powers that Violate the Rule Against Perpetuities. Powers of appointment (other than general powers presently exercisable) are subject to the Rule Against Perpetuities. A power that violates the Rule is invalid and cannot be validly

---

9. The consequence of invalidating the power with respect to the income interest has important federal gift tax consequences. The exercise of the nongeneral power over the remainder is nontaxable, see IRC §2514; but the transfer of the remaining portion of the income interest is a taxable gift.

exercised. The question of whether a power is invalid under the Rule is discussed in Chapter 17.

Powers Without Any Ascertainable Permissible Appointee. A power of appointment is invalid if it has no identifiable permissible appointees. A power of appointment has no identifiable permissible appointees, and hence the power is invalid, if the permissible appointees are described in a way that makes it impossible to identify any person who fits the donor's description of the permissible appointees. See the Comment to Uniform Act §201; Restatement 3d of Property §18.1 comment i. So long as the powerholder can appoint to at least one person who fits the donor's description, the courts uphold the power. The fact that the description makes it impossible to know all the permissible appointees of the power is not relevant.[10]

4. Creation of a Power of Appointment

Primary Statutory References: *Uniform Act §§201-205*

A power of appointment is created "by a transfer that manifests an intent to create a power of appointment." Restatement 3d of Property §18.1; see also Uniform Act §201(a). "The term 'transfer' includes a declaration by an owner of property that the owner holds the property as trustee." Comment to Uniform Act §201. The intent can be manifested by the donor either expressly or by implication. No particular language is necessary; the words "power of appointment" or "appoint" need not be used.

Example 14.8: G transfers "to A for life, remainder, if A dies intestate, to B in fee." This might be construed as implying a general power in A to appoint by will. See Simes & Smith on Future Interests §892.

Different courts have construed recurring ambiguous dispositive patterns differently and have reached results that are difficult to reconcile. When, for example, property is devised to a devisee "to be disposed of in [the devisee's] discretion," or words of similar import, a court might adopt one of three interpretations. One is that the devisee takes an absolute-ownership interest on the theory that the added language is without legal effect. The language is treated as either precatory or surplusage—merely describing that which any owner of property has power to do as an incident of that ownership.[11] A second interpretation does not

---

10. This test for evaluating a donor's description of permissible appointees of a power of appointment is significantly less demanding than the traditional test for evaluating mandatory powers in the United States. See Chapter 9.

11. *Example*: (1) G's will devises the residue of her estate "to A to dispose of as A sees fit."
(2) G's will states: "In case of my death, notify A to dispose of my belongings as A sees fit."
Although Cases (1) and (2) differ in that in Case (2) there is no language of gift to A, decisions can be found that treat both cases alike. In Cameron v. Parish, 57 N.E. 547 (Ind. 1900) (like Case (1)), and Weiss v. Broadway Nat'l Bank, 322 S.W.2d 427 (Tenn. 1959) (like Case (2)), the courts held that A

regard the language as mere surplusage but as negating ownership and creating only a power of appointment in the devisee. Under this construction, a further question is whether the power is general or nongeneral. The answer has depended on the devisee's relationship to the testator and on whether the testator has indicated by some additional language that the property should be disposed of within a certain class of permissible appointees.[12] A third interpretation treats the language as creating a *mandatory* power that is invalid if the class of permissible appointees is not definite and ascertainable. See Chapter 9. This interpretation is likely only if the devisee is an independent fiduciary.[13]

Another recurring and perplexing dispositive pattern is the devise to someone for life, remainder to the life tenant's "executors and administrators" or some similar phrase, such as "executors, administrators, and assigns," "heirs, devisees, and legatees," or "estate." Courts have had great difficulty in deciding the import of this type of devise.[14] Some courts hold that the life tenant takes a general power of appointment. See, e.g., Keeter v. United States, 461 F.2d 714 (5th Cir. 1972); Estate of Rosecrans, 480 P.2d 296 (Cal. 1971); Powell's Estate, 207 A.2d 857 (Pa. 1965). Other courts hold that a life tenant takes a remainder interest. See, e.g., Newlin v. Girard Trust Co., 174 A. 479 (N.J. Ch. 1934). One court, Will of Grady, 235 S.E.2d 425 (N.C. Ct. App. 1977), held that a remainder in favor of the life tenant's "estate" created either (1) a general testamentary power of appointment in the life tenant with a gift in default in favor of the life tenant's heirs or (2) a remainder in the life

---

took an absolute-ownership interest. In Kuttler's Estate, 325 P.2d 624 (Cal. Ct. App. 1958) (like Case (2)), and Dormer's Estate, 35 A.2d 299 (Pa. 1944) (like Case (1), except that A was G's executor), the courts held that A took a power of appointment. The differing views have obvious differences in result when A dies after G without attempting to dispose of the property.

12. *Example*: (1) G's will devises the residue of his estate "to A, my wife, to dispose of among such of my children as she sees fit."
(2) G's will devises the residue of his estate "to A, my sister, with the request that she dispose of some of the property to my blood relatives."
In McClure's Will, 32 N.E. 758 (N.Y. 1892), a case like Case (1), where A was G's second wife and not the mother of his children, the court held that A took a life estate and a nongeneral power of appointment over the remainder interest. In Flynn v. Flynn, 469 S.W.2d 886 (Ky. 1971), a case like Case (2), the court held that A took an absolute-ownership interest and that the language requesting A (who was a blood relative of G's) to dispose of some of the property among G's blood relatives was merely precatory.

13. *Example*: G's will devises the residue of her estate "to my executor, E, to distribute among such of my friends as E shall select."
In the much-criticized case of Clark v. Campbell, see Chapter 9, the court held that E's power was a *mandatory* power and invalid because the class of permissible appointees (G's "friends") was an indefinite class. UTC §402(c), the Restatement 3d of Trusts §46, and the Restatement 3d of Property §18.1 comment f provide that this type of disposition confers on E a *nonmandatory-discretionary-power of appointment*. E's power would be valid under this construction.

14. A possibility that probably can be eliminated is that the life tenant's executors take a beneficial interest or a general power of appointment.

tenant's heirs with no power of appointment in the life tenant. It went on to hold that, either way, the Rule in Shelley's Case applied to give the life tenant the remainder interest, which then merged with the life estate to give the life tenant absolute ownership!

If the remainder to the life tenant's "executors and administrators" is conditioned on some event, such as "income to A for life, and if A dies with issue, to A's executors and administrators," other possible constructions arise. Bredin v. Wilmington Trust Co., 216 A.2d 685 (Del. Ch. 1965), held that an implied remainder interest in favor of A's issue was created. In re Clark, 274 A.D. 49, 80 N.Y.S.2d 1 (1948), held that the life tenant took a general power of appointment over the remainder interest. Another possibility would be to hold that A took a *nongeneral* power. Yet another would be that A received a legal remainder in fee (to go with A's life estate) on condition that A leaves issue.

The Uniform Act recognizes the ambiguity that poorly drafted instruments can create (as seen above) and defers to the process of construction outlined in Chapters 10, 11, and 12 of the Restatement 3d of Property and more specifically to Restatement 3d of Property §18.1 comments b-g. See the Comment to Uniform Act §201.

PART B. WHO REALLY OWNS THE APPOINTIVE PROPERTY?—CREDITORS, SPOUSES, TAXES

As a technical matter, there is no doubt that the powerholder of a power of appointment is not recognized as the owner of the appointive property. The conventional distinction between beneficial ownership and a power is stated in Restatement 3d of Property §17.1 comment c:

> The beneficial owner of an interest in property ordinarily has the power to transfer ownership interests in or confer powers of appointment over that property to or on others by probate or nonprobate transfer.... By contrast, a power of appointment traditionally confers the authority to designate recipients of beneficial ownership interests in or powers of appointment over property that the [powerholder] does not own.

Upon exercise of a power of appointment, the *doctrine of relation back* provides that the appointed property passes directly from the donor to the appointee. The powerholder's appointment is deemed to relate back to and become part of the *donor's* original instrument. The powerholder is viewed as akin to the donor's agent, as it were; an appointment retroactively fills in the blanks in the original instrument.

Example 14.9: G transferred property in trust: income to A for life, remainder to such of A's descendants as A may appoint. A makes an inter vivos appointment to A's child, C. Under the doctrine of relation back, A's appointment is viewed as changing G's original disposition to read: "income to A for life, remainder to C."

Technical ownership aside, when it comes to federal taxation and the rights of the powerholder's surviving spouse and creditors, the law does not always follow the relation-back doctrine. The likelihood that the powerholder will be treated as the owner of the appointive property is greater in the case of a reserved power, as distinguished from a power conferred on the powerholder by another.

1. Powers Conferred on the Powerholder by Another

Primary Statutory References: *Uniform Act §§502, 504*
                                                          UPC §§2-205, 6-102

Gilman v. Bell
99 Ill. 144 (1881)

[Solomon Bell devised real property to Ellen Bell, the wife of his son, Robert, for Robert's lifetime, with the remainder passing at Robert's death to his heirs, all subject to a power in Robert to appoint to himself or any other person during his lifetime. Gilman, a judgment creditor of Robert's, sought to reach the real property.]

WALKER, J.... [I]t is insisted that, conceding it to be a mere naked power of appointment in favor of himself, in favor of creditors he should be compelled by a court of equity to appoint, or be treated as the owner, and the property subjected to the payment of his debts. The doctrine has been long established in the English courts, that the courts of equity will not aid creditors in case there is a non-execution of the power. But where there is a defective execution, the court will supply the defective execution of the power in favor of a purchaser, creditor, wife or child....

...Nor are the distinctions entirely without reason. No title or interest in the thing vests in the [powerholder]... until he exercises the power. It is virtually an offer to him of the estate or fund, that he may receive or reject at will, and like any other offer to donate property to a person, no title can vest until he accepts the offer, nor can a court of equity compel him to accept the property or fund against his will, even for the benefit of creditors.... Until accepted, the person to whom the offer is made has not, nor can he have, the slightest interest or title to the property. So the [powerholder]... only receives the naked power to make the property or fund his own. And when he exercises the power, he thereby consents to receive it, and the title thereby vests in him, although it may pass out of him eo instanti, to the appointee....

We are of opinion that appellee has no interest in this property, and that no relief can be granted, and the demurrer was properly sustained to the bill, and the decree of the court below must be affirmed.

Notes

1. *Majority View.* The majority view at common law is that the powerholder of a power, conferred on the powerholder by another, is treated as the beneficial owner of the appointive property only if (1) the power is general *and* (2) the powerholder exercises the power. No distinction is made between a testamentary and presently exercisable power. Creditors of a powerholder of a *non*general power, on the other hand, cannot reach the appointive assets even if the power was effectively exercised. The theory is that the donor who creates a nongeneral power did not intend to benefit the powerholder.

Explaining the distinction between the exercise and non-exercise of a general power for purposes of creditor access, one court stated:

> When a donor gives to another the power of appointment over property, the [powerholder]... does not thereby become the owner of the property. Rather, the appointee of the power [meaning, the powerholder], in its exercise, acts as a "mere conduit or agent for the donor." The [powerholder], having received from the owner of the property instructions as to how the power may be utilized, possesses nothing but the authority to do an act which the owner might lawfully perform.

Univ. Nat'l Bank v. Rhoadarmer, 827 P.2d 561 (Colo. App. 1991).

When the powerholder of a general power exercises the power *by will*, the view that the appointed property is treated as if it were owned by the powerholder means that the creditors of the powerholder's estate can reach the appointed property for the payment of their claims. See, e.g., Clapp v. Ingraham, 126 Mass. 200 (1879). The rule prevails even if this is contrary to the expressed wishes of the donor of the power. See, e.g., State Street Trust Co. v. Kissel, 19 N.E.2d 25 (Mass. 1939).

The exercise of the power by will does not confer actual beneficial ownership of the appointive assets on the powerholder for all purposes. The assets do not ordinarily become part of the powerholder's probate estate. Thus, in terms of priority, the powerholder's own estate assets are ordinarily used first to pay estate debts, so that the appointive assets are used only to the extent the powerholder's probate estate is insufficient.

2. *Effective Exercise Required?* Under the majority view at common law, the powerholder's creditors can reach the appointive assets only to the extent the powerholder's exercise was an *effective* exercise. A few states, however, follow the view that even an ineffective exercise entitles the powerholder's creditors to reach the appointive assets. See, e.g., Estate of Breault, 211 N.E.2d 424 (Ill. App. Ct. 1965). Moreover, even in states adhering to the majority view, an ineffective exercise can sometimes "capture" the appointive assets for the powerholder's estate, in which case the appointive assets become part of the powerholder's probate estate for all purposes, including creditors' rights. For an explanation of the "capture doctrine," see below at p. 797.

3. *Preferences Among Creditors*. When the powerholder of a general power is authorized to and makes an inter vivos appointment, treating the appointed assets as if they were owned by the powerholder does not automatically mean that the powerholder's creditors can subject the appointed assets to the payment of their claims. If the appointment is in favor of a *creditor*, the powerholder's other, unsatisfied creditors can reach the appointed assets only by having the appointment avoided as a "preference" in bankruptcy proceedings. Apart from bankruptcy, the powerholder can choose to pay one creditor rather than another with his or her owned assets, and the same is true with respect to appointive assets. If the appointment is in favor of a *volunteer* (i.e., the appointment is gratuitous), the powerholder's creditors can reach the appointed assets only if the transfer is the equivalent of a fraudulent transfer under applicable state law.[15]

4. *Minority Views*. In a minority of jurisdictions, the powerholder of a general power, conferred on him or her by another, is *not* treated as the owner of the appointive property even if the power is exercised. See, e.g., St. Matthews Bank v. DeCharette, 83 S.W.2d 471 (Ky. 1935). Of course, if the powerholder exercises the power in favor of himself or herself or his or her estate, the appointed property becomes owned in the technical sense, and creditors even in states adhering to the minority view would be able to subject the assets to the payment of their claims to the same extent as other property owned beneficially by the powerholder.

In at least one state, an exercise of a general power in a so-called blending clause is treated as the equivalent of an appointment in favor of the powerholder's estate for this purpose. See Stannert's Estate, 15 A.2d 360 (Pa. 1940). A blending clause is one that combines owned and appointive assets together, such as:

> All the residue of my estate, *including property over which I [may] have a power of appointment,* I give to....

A minority of states has enacted legislation that affects the rights of the powerholder's creditors. The legislation is not uniform. Some of the legislation expands the rights of the powerholder's creditors and some contracts them. The following is a sampling of the legislation.

> *Michigan* legislation expands the rights of the creditors of the powerholder of an *unexercised* general power. During the powerholder's lifetime, the powerholder's creditors can subject the appointive property to the payment of their claims if the power is presently

---

15. In many states, the applicable state law on fraudulent transfers derives from the Uniform Fraudulent Transfers Act (1984) or the newer Uniform Voidable Transactions Act (2014). Under §4(a) of the Uniform Voidable Transactions Act, a transfer is in fraud of present or future creditors if it was made "with actual intent to hinder, delay, or defraud" or "without receiving a reasonably equivalent value in exchange for the transfer" and the debtor "(i) was engaged or was about to engage in a business or a transaction for which the remaining assets of the debtor were unreasonably small in relation to the business or transaction; or (ii) intended to incur... debts beyond the debtor's ability to pay as they became due."

exercisable. (If the powerholder has actually made an inter vivos exercise of the power, the rules explained above with respect to inter vivos exercises presumably would be applied.) At the powerholder's death, the powerholder's creditors can subject the appointive property to the payment of their claims. In both instances, however, the appointive property is available only to the extent that the powerholder 's owned property is insufficient to meet the debts. See Mich. Comp. Laws §556.123.

New York legislation expands the rights of the powerholder's creditors in some particulars but restricts them in others. The legislation adopts the same rules as the Michigan legislation, but limits their application to general powers presently exercisable. As to general testamentary powers, the powerholder's estate creditors can subject the appointive property to the payment of their claims only if the powerholder, as donor, reserved the power in himself or herself; as to general testamentary powers conferred on the powerholder by another, the powerholder's estate creditors cannot reach the appointive property even when the powerholder's will *exercises* the power. See N.Y. Est. Powers & Trusts Law §§10-7.1 et seq.

5. *Position of the Uniform Act.* The Uniform Act takes the following position: if the power is conferred by another, the rights of the powerholder's creditors depend on whether the power is general or nongeneral. If the power is general, the appointive property is subject to a claim of (1) a creditor of the powerholder, to the extent the powerholder's property is insufficient, if the power is presently exercisable (whether or not actually exercised), and (2) a creditor of the powerholder's estate, to the extent the estate is insufficient, subject to the right of a decedent to direct the source from which liabilities are paid. See Uniform Act §502. If the power is nongeneral, the general rule is that creditors have no rights in the appointive property. See Uniform Act §504(a).

For purposes of creditors' rights, the Uniform Act treats a general power of appointment as a nongeneral power if the power is "subject to an ascertainable standard relating to an individual's health, education, or maintenance...." Uniform Act §502(b).

6. *Federal Bankruptcy Law.* The federal bankruptcy code implies that a general power presently exercisable passes to the powerholder's trustee in bankruptcy. A nongeneral power and a general testamentary power clearly do not. See 11 U.S.C. §541(b).

7. *Uniform Probate Code on Creditors' Rights in Nonprobate Transfers.* UPC §6-102, granting estate creditors a right to satisfaction out of nonprobate transfers, does not apply to powers conferred on the powerholder by another.

———

Having considered the rights of creditors, we now consider the ownership of property subject to a power conferred on the powerholder by another with respect, first, to the surviving spouse's elective share and, second, to the federal tax laws.

Elective Share. At common law, the surviving spouse of a powerholder receives less protection than the powerholder's creditors. As long as the power is not a reserved power, the powerholder's surviving spouse ordinarily cannot reach the appointive property (against the wishes of the powerholder), whether the power is general or nongeneral, presently exercisable or testamentary, exercised or unexercised. The explanation offered by the courts is that the surviving spouse's elective share claim is against the powerholder's probate estate and the appointive assets are not a part of the probate estate because they are not owned beneficially by the powerholder.

A relevant consideration, perhaps, is the context that generates a surviving spouse's claim to an elective share in assets subject to a general power conferred on the powerholder by another. One reason for conferring a general power on another is to qualify a trust for the federal estate or gift tax marital deduction. The powerholder of a general power, conferred on the powerholder by another, thus may be the remarried surviving spouse of the donor of the power (in which case the appointive property was originally owned by the donor) and the takers in default would be either the children of the marriage between the donor and powerholder or the donor's children by a prior marriage.

Example 14.10: G's will devised the residue of his estate into a marital deduction trust: income "to W, my wife, for life, then to such person or persons, including W's estate, as W may by will appoint; in default of appointment, remainder to my descendants who survive W, such descendants to take by representation, and if none of my descendants survives W, then in default of appointment, to X Charity." W subsequently remarries. At W's death, her will exercises her general testamentary power in favor of the children of her marriage to G. W is survived by her second husband, H. H elects to renounce W's will and claim a statutory elective share in W's estate.

The appointive property is not included in the assets in W's estate to which H's elective share attaches. The same result has been reached even in cases where W's appointment was in a blending clause or where W's appointment was in favor of her own estate. See Kates' Estate, 128 A. 97 (Pa. 1925) (rule of this case codified in 20 Pa. Cons. Stat. §2203, but restricted to general powers conferred on the powerholder by another); Restatement 3d of Property §23.1 (property subject to a general testamentary power subject to elective share rights only if the power was reserved by the donor, but not if conferred on the powerholder by another).

Uniform Probate Code §2-205(1)(A) broke new ground by including in the decedent's-nonprobate-transfers-to-others component of the augmented estate "property over which the decedent alone, immediately before death, held a presently exercisable general power of appointment," regardless of when or by whom that power was created. This is essentially the same rule adopted in the Restatement 3d of Property § 23.1(1) (omitting the requirement that the powerholder hold the power "alone"). Should the UPC (or the Restatement) have gone even further and included property subject to a general *testamentary* power conferred on the powerholder by another? Is the powerholder's relationship to such property as close to ownership as it is to property subject to a presently exercisable general power?

Non-UPC legislation in a few states makes property subject to a general power of appointment, conferred on the powerholder by another, available to the elective share of the powerholder's surviving spouse but only if the decedent's will exercised the power or manifested an intent to do so. See, e.g., Mich. Comp. Laws §556.116.

Federal Tax Laws. If the power was conferred on the powerholder by another, the federal tax laws treat the powerholder of a *general* power of appointment as the owner of the appointive property.

It is important to understand, however, that the federal estate and gift tax laws do not consider powers to be general if the power is limited by an ascertainable standard relating to the health, education, support, or maintenance ("HEMS") of the powerholder. See IRC §§2041(b)(1)(A), 2514(c)(1). The Uniform Act adopts this position for purposes of creditors' rights. See Uniform Act §502(b).

In addition, the federal estate and gift tax laws draw a distinction for certain purposes between general powers created after October 21, 1942 (called "post-42 powers") and powers created on or before October 21, 1942 (called "pre-42 powers").

For estate tax purposes, the value of property subject to a post-42 general power of appointment held by the powerholder at death, and conferred on the powerholder by another, is taxed in the powerholder's estate regardless of whether the power is exercised. As for pre-42 powers, the value of the appointive property is taxed in the powerholder's estate only if the power is exercised. See IRC §2041.

For gift tax purposes, an inter vivos exercise of a general power of appointment, conferred on the powerholder by another, is subject to the federal gift tax regardless of when the power was created. A release of a post-42, but not a pre-42, general power of appointment, conferred on the powerholder by another, is subject to the federal gift tax. See IRC §2514(a), (b).

For income tax purposes, the powerholder of a general power of appointment, conferred on the powerholder by another and presently exercisable by the powerholder alone, may be taxed on the income generated by the appointive property. See IRC §678(a).

For federal income, estate, and gift tax purposes, the powerholder of a *nongeneral* power, conferred on the powerholder by another, is not treated as the owner of the appointive property.

No federal gift tax consequences occur upon the inter vivos exercise (or release) of a nongeneral power. No federal estate tax consequences occur from holding a nongeneral power at death or from making a testamentary exercise of a nongeneral power. The powerholder of a nongeneral power is not taxed on income generated from the appointive property.

Nongeneral powers are implicated by the federal generation-skipping transfer tax. In general, that tax applies whenever property passes to a younger generation of family members without suffering estate or gift taxation in the next oldest generation.

Example 14.11: G's will devises the residue of G's estate into a trust: income to G's daughter A for life, remainder in corpus to such of A's children as A by will appoints; in default of appointment, to A's children in equal shares. At A's death, her will appoints 50% of the corpus of the trust to one of her children, and the other 50% to be equally divided between her other two children.

Under the federal estate tax, the property is taxed in G's estate and in the estates of A's appointees (G's grandchildren), if they still own the property when they die. The estate tax does not, however, tax the property in A's estate because A's power was a nongeneral power—the estate tax "skips" A's generation. Under the generation-skipping transfer tax, the trust property might no longer go untaxed when A dies.[16]

Tax Consequences—Why Create a General Power? Apart from the generation-skipping tax, which contains rather liberal exemptions, the considerations discussed so far seem to point in the direction of conferring only nongeneral powers on powerholders. And it is not only the tax considerations that seem to point in this direction. Conferring a nongeneral power virtually guarantees the appointive property's freedom from the claims of the powerholder's creditors and surviving spouse.

The reason why general powers are created is *not* that a general power confers such a greater benefit on the powerholder that the donor considers its creation to be worth the extra tax and other costs to the powerholder. At least, this is true if the choice is between conferring a general *testamentary* power or conferring a nongeneral power.[17] The powerholder of a nongeneral power can be given substantially the same degree of flexibility as the powerholder of a general testamentary power. The exclusion of the powerholder, the powerholder's estate, and the creditors of either from the list of permissible appointees is an insignificant reduction in the flexibility granted to the powerholder because powerholders seldom desire to appoint to their own estates. The scope of permissible appointees of a

---

16. The part of the property that is taxed is the fractional part, if any, that exceeded the transferor's GSTT exemption when the trust was created. See IRC §2631.

17. General powers presently exercisable are seldom created anyway, except for powers granted to the income beneficiary of a trust to invade the corpus of the trust. Even powers to invade corpus are not considered general powers for estate or gift tax purposes if their exercise is explicitly governed by an ascertainable standard relating to the health, education, support, or maintenance of the powerholder or if they can be exercised only in conjunction with the donor of the power or a person having a substantial interest in the appointive property that is adverse to the power's exercise in favor of the powerholder.

nongeneral power can be so broad as to include virtually every person to whom the powerholder would want to appoint.

In addition, in many circumstances, the donor may consider it highly desirable to limit the permissible appointees. The donor who confers a power of appointment on his or her surviving spouse may anticipate remarriage, or his or her surviving spouse may have children by a prior marriage. The donor may, therefore, limit the appointees to assure that the donor's property is not diverted from his or her children or other family members.

Why, then, are general powers created? One reason is that there are certain tax *benefits* that can be obtained by conferring on the powerholder a general power. Among these are to qualify the transfer for either the federal estate or gift tax marital deduction or the federal gift tax annual exclusion. Another benefit can be to obtain a step-up in income tax basis at the decedent's death. See Chapter 19.

Federal Estate and Gift Tax Marital Deduction. A trust qualifies for the federal estate or gift tax marital deduction if the terms of the trust grant the transferor's spouse the right to all the income from the trust for life, payable annually or at more frequent intervals, and a power of appointment over the remainder interest, exercisable by the spouse alone and in all events and in favor of the spouse or the spouse's estate. IRC §§2056(b)(5); 2523(e). Until 1981, such a trust—called a power of appointment trust—was the most popular device for creating a trust that qualified for the marital deduction.

The Economic Recovery Tax Act of 1981 added a new subsection to the marital deduction sections that authorizes the use of a "qualified terminable interest property trust"—called a QTIP trust—under which the spouse is granted the right to the income from the trust for life, payable annually or at more frequent intervals; if properly elected, the trust can qualify even if the donor's spouse is given a nongeneral testamentary power of appointment over the remainder interest or no power of appointment at all.

QTIP trusts have become a popular marital deduction device, cutting down even further the incidence of the creation of general powers of appointment.

Federal Gift Tax Annual Exclusion. Under IRC §2503(c), a trust for a minor qualifies for the federal gift tax annual exclusion if, among other requirements, the minor is given a general power of appointment over the remainder interest should the minor die before attaining the age of 21 years; a nongeneral power disqualifies the trust for the gift tax exclusion under this section. A "Crummey" power, named after the case of Crummey v. Commissioner, 397 F.2d 82 (9th Cir. 1968), is another device for qualifying for the annual gift tax exclusion; a Crummey power is a general power conferred on the powerholder by the donor of a trust that authorizes the powerholder to withdraw from the corpus all or a specified portion of subsequent contributions into the trust, usually made by the donor annually.

Federal Income Tax Step-Up in Basis. IRC §1014 grants a step-up in income tax basis—to the fair market value at the decedent's death—with respect to property acquired from a decedent or passed from a decedent. For example, if an asset was purchased by the decedent while alive for $500,000 and is worth $1 million at the decedent's death, the person receiving the asset at the decedent's death would receive it with a basis of $1 million for income tax purposes. This basis step-up is generally limited to assets that the decedent owned or that the decedent was *treated as* owning for estate tax purposes. See IRC §1014(b). One way to trigger the step-up in basis for assets that the decedent did not own outright is to give the decedent a (typically, testamentary) general power of appointment over the asset. This is often done in trusts to achieve a step-up in basis at the death of a trust beneficiary, who may have no taxable estate—due to the increase of the federal estate tax exemption, see Chapter 19—but whose death can be an occasion for a step-up in income tax basis. See Turney P. Berry, Sarah S. Butters & Thomas P. Gallanis, Powers of Appointment in the Current Planning Environment, in 49th Annual Hecklering Institute on Estate Planning ¶1301(B) (2015); Griffin H. Bridgers, Basis Step-Up Planning: A Double-Edged Sword, Prob. & Prop. 24 (Jul./Aug. 2018).

Problems

1. Groucho transferred property in trust "to my brother Harpo for life, remainder to such of my brother Chico's descendants as my brother Zeppo may appoint, otherwise to my brother Gummo." Once Groucho transfers the property in trust, who owns it? What happens if Zeppo exercises the power in favor of Chico's son, Chico Jr.? Who is the transferee, and who is the transferor?

2. Groucho wants to transfer property in trust to Harpo for life, with the remainder to pass to such persons as Zeppo may appoint. Groucho does not want Zeppo to be treated as the owner of the property. What kind of power of appointment would you suggest that Groucho give Zeppo? Why?

2. Reserved Powers

Primary Statutory References: *Uniform Act §501; UPC §§2-205, 6-102*

Bank of Dallas v. Republic Nat'l Bank of Dallas
540 S.W.2d 499 (Tex. App. 1976)

McDONALD, J. The issues to be decided are: 1) can the income, and/or 2) the corpus, of an irrevocable spendthrift trust, created by the settlor for the settlor and her children's benefit, be reached by garnishment for a debt of the settlor....

Patricia Murray Fewell as Settlor, on January 28, 1971, transferred certain properties to the trustee for the "use and benefit of herself and of her children," and thereafter amended such Trust.

The Trust as amended provides in Article 1(a):

Distributions. The trustee shall pay to the Settlor for her uncontrolled use and benefit, all of the net income of the trust during her lifetime. Whenever the trustee determines that the income of the Settlor from all sources known to the trustee is not sufficient for her reasonable support, comfort, and health and for the reasonable support and education of Settlor's descendants, the trustee may in its discretion pay to, or use for the benefit of, Settlor or one or more of Settlor's descendants so much of the principal as the trustee determines to be required for those purposes.

Article 11(b) provides that upon the death of the settlor the trustee shall distribute or hold the then remaining principal and undistributed income as the settlor may have appointed by will. If the settlor has not exercised her power to appoint by will, then upon her death any property remaining in the trust shall be apportioned into separate, equal trust, "one for each then living child of Settlor and one for the then living issue collectively, of each deceased child of Settlor."

Article II Sec. 2.3 provides in part that if upon death of the Settlor she has no living descendants, any undisposed portion of the trust shall be distributed to her brother and sister.

Article III Sec. 3.2 contains a spendthrift provision containing customary spendthrift language and... "nor shall such income or corpus or any portion of same be subject to execution, garnishment... or other legal proceeding of any character... to the payment of such beneficiary's debts...."

Appellants contend [that] [t]he trial court erred in holding that no part of the corpus, transferred by Patricia Murray Fewell as Settlor to the Patricia Murray Trust, under which she receives all of the income from all corpus for her lifetime, and under which she holds a general power of appointment exercisable at her death by will, is garnishable.

Appellees contend: (1) The trial court correctly held that the corpus of the trust was not subject to garnishment; and by crosspoint contend: (2) The trial court erred in holding that the income was subject to garnishment.

The courts of Texas recognize the validity of spendthrift trusts created by a Settlor for others, and no part of the spendthrift trust estate can be taken on execution or garnishment by creditors of the beneficiary....

But the rule is otherwise in cases where the settlor creates a spendthrift trust, and makes himself the beneficiary thereof. And where a settlor creates a trust for his own benefit, and inserts a spendthrift clause, it is void as far as then existing or future creditors are concerned, and they can reach his interest under the trust by garnishment....

As to the corpus the issue is more complex, as Mrs. Fewell is not the sole beneficiary. The trust provides that the trustee may exercise its discretion to invade principal under certain circumstances "for the benefit of Settlor" or "one or more of

Settlor's descendants."

Also the settlor's children have a remainder, though the settlor can defeat such interest by exercising her general powers of appointment under Article II(b).

Section 156c Restatement, Trusts & Trustees 2d, p. 326 states: "Reservation of general power to appoint principal. If the settlor reserves for his own benefit not only a life interest, but also a general power to appoint the remainder by deed or will, his creditors can reach the principal of the trust as well as the income;" and section 156d, at page 327 states: "Trust for settlor's support. Where the settlor creates a trust for his own support,... it can be reached by his creditors. They can compel the trustee to pay to them the maximum amount which he could pay to the settlor-beneficiary or apply for his benefit."

And Section 156e states: "Discretionary trust for the settlor. Where by the terms of the trust a trustee is to pay the settlor or apply for his benefit as much of the income or principal as the trustee may in his discretion determine,... creditors can reach the maximum amount which the trustee could pay to him or apply for his benefit."

Applying the foregoing rules of law to the facts, we hold the interest of Mrs. Fewell in the trust is such that the corpus may be reached by her creditors....

The judgment is affirmed in part; and reversed and remanded in part, with instruction to the trial court to render judgment against the trustee for the amount due on appellants' judgment.

Notes

If a reserved power of appointment, even a nongeneral power, was created in a transfer that was in fraud of creditors, the appointive assets can be subjected to the payment of the donor-powerholder's debts. Uniform Act §§501(b), 504(b); Restatement 3d of Property §22.1 comment b.

Even if the transfer was not in fraud of creditors, the appointive assets are subject to the claims of the donor-powerholder's creditors if the reserved power is a general power. It makes no difference whether the debt was incurred by the donor-powerholder before or after the transfer. See Uniform Act §501(d); Restatement 3d of Property §7.2 comment b, §22.2 comment a; Restatement 3d of Trusts §25 comment e; UPC §6-102.

Example 14.12: G transfers real property "to G for life, then to such person or persons, including G or G's estate, as G may appoint by deed or by will, and in default of appointment to A and her heirs." Creditors of G can subject not only G's owned life estate to the payment of their claims, but the remainder interest also. On G's death, the claims against G's estate can be satisfied out of the property to the same extent as if G owned the property at G's death and had devised the property to A by will.

Until recently, an anomaly existed with respect to a reserved power to revoke, such as that contained in a revocable inter vivos trust. The first Restatement of Property §318(2) and comment i excluded powers to revoke from the definition of a power of appointment, making the rule that a reserved power of appointment subjects the appointive assets to the claims of the donor-powerholder's creditors inapplicable. Thus it was generally held that the trust assets of a revocable trust were exempt from the claims of the settlor's creditors. See, e.g., Restatement 2d of Trusts §330 comment o. Several states now have statutes to the contrary, see, e.g., Mich. Comp. Laws §556.128, and recent decisions have also held to the contrary. See, e.g., State Street Bank & Trust Co. v. Reiser, 389 N.E.2d 768 (Mass. App. Ct. 1979). See Chapter 7.

The Restatement 3d of Property and the Uniform Act resolve this problem by including the power to revoke in the definition of the term "power of appointment." See Restatement 3d of Property §17.1 comment e; Uniform Act §102(13) and the accompanying Comment. This change in nomenclature resolves the anomaly: It extends the rule that the donor-powerholder's creditors can reach assets subject to a reserved general power of appointment to powers to revoke in revocable trusts.[18]

———

Elective Share. In the chapter on the elective share, we already considered the rights of the donor-powerholder's surviving spouse in assets over which the donor-powerholder retained a power to revoke or another type of power of appointment. See Chapter 8; Restatement 3d of Property §9.1 comment j.

UPC §2-205(1)(A) includes in the decedent's-nonprobate-transfers-to-others component of the augmented estate, to which the decedent's surviving spouse has a right to an elective share, "property over which the decedent alone, immediately before death, held a presently exercisable general power of appointment," regardless of when or by whom that power was created. Section 2-205(2)(B) includes property subject to a power, "exercisable by the decedent alone or in conjunction with any other person, or exercisable by a nonadverse party, to or for the benefit of the decedent, creditors of the decedent, the decedent's estate, or creditors of the decedent's estate" but only if that power was created by the decedent during the decedent's marriage to the surviving spouse. See Chapter 8.

The above provisions replaced provisions of the former UPC under which the "augmented estate" merely included the value of property transferred by the decedent *during the marriage* "to the extent that the decedent retained at the time of his death a power, either alone or in conjunction with any other person, to revoke or to consume, invade or dispose of the principal for his own benefit."

---

18. The court in Sullivan v. Burkin, see Chapter 8, considered a power to revoke to be a power of appointment.

Non-UPC legislation in a few states makes property subject to a reserved general power available to the elective share of the donor-powerholder's surviving spouse, but only if the donor-powerholder's will exercised the power or manifested an intent to do so. See, e.g., Mich. Comp. Laws §556.116.

Federal Tax Laws. For reserved powers, the federal tax laws basically treat the transferor as still owning the appointive property, whether the reserved power is general or nongeneral.

Federal Estate Tax. If the decedent holds at the time of his or her death, or releases within three years of his or her death, a reserved power over income or corpus of property transferred inter vivos, the value of the property is taxed in the decedent's estate. See IRC §§2035, 2036(a)(2), 2038.

Federal Gift Tax. An inter vivos transfer is not subject to the federal gift tax, to the extent that the transferor reserves a power of appointment over the transferred property, whether the reserved power is a general power (such as a power to revoke the trust) or a nongeneral power (such as a power to amend the trust in any way except for the transferor's benefit). The theory is that the reserved power renders the gift incomplete because the transferor has not parted with sufficient dominion or control over the property. See Treas. Reg. §25.2511-2.

Federal Income Tax. The transferor of an inter vivos transfer in which a general or, subject to certain statutory exceptions, a nongeneral power is reserved continues to be taxed on the income generated by the appointive property. The transferor may also be taxed on the income in cases where a power exercisable in his or her own favor, in favor of his or her spouse, or solely in favor of others, is conferred on a "nonadverse party" such as an independent trustee. See IRC §§674, 676, 677.

Example 14.13: G transferred property in trust: income to G for life, remainder in corpus to X. G retained the power to revoke the trust at any time.

G's transfer of the remainder interest to X was not a taxable gift because of G's reserved general power over the entire trust corpus.

G will continue until his death to be taxed on both the ordinary income generated by the property and also on capital gains (or losses) realized by the trust.

When G dies, the full value of the trust corpus will be taxed in G's estate.

Problem

Mrs. Peel transferred property in trust: income to herself for life, with the remainder to her good friend, Mr. Steed. She retained the power to revoke the trust at any time and in any manner. Does Mrs. Peel have a power of appointment? If yes, what are its consequences for Mrs. Peel's obligations to creditors, her surviving spouse, and the IRS?

PART C. EXERCISING A POWER OF APPOINTMENT

Primary Statutory References: *Uniform Act §§301-304*
UPC §§2-608, -701, -703, -704

   Capacity of the Powerholder. An effective appointment can only be made by a powerholder who has the requisite capacity. The capacity needed to make an effective appointment is the same capacity needed to make an effective transfer of the property if it were owned by the powerholder. See Restatement 3d of Property §19.8(a).

   Compliance With Formalities. An appointment must satisfy the formal requirements that would be applicable to a transfer of the property if it were owned by the powerholder. A testamentary appointment, for example, must be contained in a validly executed will.

   Intent to Exercise. A powerholder must manifest an intent to exercise a power in order for the power to be exercised. See Uniform Act §301(2)(A); Restatement 3d of Property §19.1(1). The recommended method for exercising a power of appointment is by a *specific-exercise clause*:

   I hereby exercise the power of appointment conferred upon me by my mother's will of [date] as follows: I appoint [fill in details of appointment].

   Unfortunately, the recommended method is not always used. Instead, some lawyers (and forms) use a blending clause with a blanket exercise.

   A *blending clause* purports to blend the appointive property with the powerholder's own property.

   A *blanket exercise* occurs when the powerholder purports to exercise "any" power of appointment the powerholder "has" or "may have."

   The exercise portion of a blending clause can take the form of a specific exercise or a blanket exercise. For example, a clause providing "All the residue of my estate, including the property over which I have a power of appointment under my mother's will, I devise as follows" is a blending clause with a specific exercise. A clause providing "All the residue of my estate, including any property over which I may have a power of appointment, I devise as follows" is a blending clause with a blanket exercise. Use of the latter is poor drafting.

   In the absence of an express exercise of a power, an intent by the powerholder to exercise the power can be implied. In the leading case of Blagge v. Miles, 1 Story 426, 3 F. Cas. 559 (C.C.D. Mass. 1841) (No. 1479), the court described circumstances giving rise to an implied exercise:

   Three classes of cases have been held to be sufficient demonstrations of an intended execution of a power: (1) Where there has been some reference in the will, or other instrument, to the power; (2) or a reference to the property, which is the subject, on which it is to be executed; (3) or, where the provision in the will or other instrument, executed by the [powerholder]..., would otherwise be ineffectual, or a mere nullity; in other words, it would have no operation, except as an execution of the power.[19]

The majority view at common law is that a garden-variety residuary clause (such as "All the residue of my estate, I give to..." or "All of my estate, I give to...") or other clause referring generally to "my estate" or "my property" does not exercise a general or nongeneral power of appointment, unless other facts establish intent.

A minority of jurisdictions follows the so-called *Massachusetts view*, that rebuttably presumes that a garden-variety residuary clause was intended to exercise a general power of appointment even though the clause makes no reference to powers.[20] These states recognize the tendency of powerholders to view general powers as equivalent to ownership. See, e.g., Amory v. Meredith, 89 Mass. (7 Allen) 397 (1863). Some jurisdictions have adopted the minority ("Massachusetts") view by legislation, and occasionally that view has been extended to nongeneral powers in cases in which the residuary legatees were permissible appointees of the nongeneral power.

Under Uniform Act §302(b), a residuary clause manifests a powerholder's intent to exercise a power *only* if the power is a general power exercisable in favor of the powerholder's estate and there is no effective gift-in-default clause. In 2014, UPC §2-608 was amended to conform to these Uniform Act provisions.

This rule recognizes the fact that most general powers are created in trusts that include a well thought-out gift-in-default clause. The minority ("Massachusetts") view defeats that gift-in-default clause, but the Uniform Act-UPC view does not.

If there is no effective gift-in-default clause, the Uniform Act and UPC presume the residuary clause exercises the general power. The alternative would be that the appointive property would return to the donor's estate and require that it be reopened if, as is likely, the donor predeceased the powerholder.

Conflict of Laws. The traditional view is that the law of the *donor*'s domicile governs issues concerning the powerholder's intent to exercise a power. See, e.g., Beals v. State Street Bank & Trust Co., 326 N.E.2d 896 (Mass. 1975); Bank of New York v. Black, 139 A.2d 393 (N.J. 1958); Matter of Estate of Rossi, 634 N.Y.S.2d 372 (Sur. Ct. 1995). But there is an emerging modern view that matters of exercise should be governed by the law of the *powerholder*'s domicile. See, e.g., White v.

---

19. The Restatement 3d of Property §§19.3, 19.5 adopted the *Blagge* principles.

20. The Massachusetts view did not apply to nongeneral powers of appointment. See Fiduciary Trust Co. v. First Nat'l Bank, 181 N.E.2d 6 (Mass. 1962).

In 1978, Massachusetts itself rejected the "Massachusetts view" by adopting a statute similar to the pre-1990 version of UPC §2-610, which codified the majority common-law view. Massachusetts has since adopted the pre-2014 version of UPC §2-608. See Mass. Gen. Laws ch. 190B, §2-608.

United States, 680 F.2d 1156 (7th Cir. 1982) (law of powerholder's domicile governs); Estate of McMullin, 417 A.2d 152 (Pa. 1980). See also Restatement 2d Conflict of Laws §275 (1971) ("Whether a power to appoint by will interests in movables is exercised by a general bequest not mentioning the power is determined by the law governing the construction of the [powerholder's] will (see §264), unless the donor manifested a different intention.").

The Uniform Act and the Restatement 3d of Property align with the modern view. See Uniform Act §103(2); Restatement 3d of Property §19.1 comment e. The rationale is that acts of the powerholder should be governed by the law of the powerholder's domicile because that is the law the powerholder (or the powerholder's lawyer) is likely to know.

EXTERNAL REFERENCES. See Restatement 2d of Conflict of Laws §§281-82 (1971); See also Sheldon F. Kurtz, Powers of Appointment Under the 1990 Uniform Probate Code: What Was Done—What Remains to be Done, 55 Alb. L. Rev. 1151, 1172-1182 (1992); Harrison F. Durand & Charles L. Herterich, Conflict of Laws and the Exercise of Powers of Appointment, 42 Cornell L. Q. 185 (1957).

————

Specific-Reference Requirements. In creating powers of appointment, it sometimes happens that the donor provides that the power can be exercised only by language that specifically refers to the power. Specific-reference requirements were a pre-1942 invention to prevent an inadvertent exercise of a general power and thereby avoid federal transfer taxes that applied only if the general power was exercised. See above at p. 769. For the proposition that a garden-variety residuary clause in the powerholder's will does not satisfy a specific-reference requirement, see Schwartz v. Baybank Merrimack Valley, N.A., Trustee, below. Does a blending clause with a blanket exercise satisfy a specific-reference requirement?

Schwartz v. Baybank Merrimack Valley, N.A., Trustee
456 N.E.2d 1141 (Mass. App. 1983)

GREANEY, J. This case involves a testamentary power of appointment, the terms of which called for its exercise by specific reference to the power in the [powerholder's] will. A judge of a Probate Court concluded, after trial, that the power had not been exercised by the residuary clause of the [powerholder's] will which neither referred to the power nor purported to exercise any power of appointment. We conclude that the judge's decision was correct and affirm his judgment.

The facts are drawn from the judge's findings. On April 1, 1957, Mary F. Cox executed a will which provided that the residue of her estate be held in trust for the benefit of her daughter Dorothy Cox during Dorothy's lifetime. Upon Dorothy's death, the trustee of Mary's trust was directed to pay the trust principal to such person or persons, including the executor of Dorothy's will, as Dorothy "shall appoint by her will specifically referring to the power herein given to her." If Dorothy failed to exercise her general power of appointment, the trust principal was to be paid to the New England Deaconess Hospital. Mary's will was admitted to probate on August 5, 1968, and, on July 17, 1970, BayBank Merrimack Valley, N.A. (BayBank), was appointed to succeed the original trustee under the will.

On May 6, 1977, Dorothy Cox executed a will, prepared by the plaintiff Maurice Schwartz, an attorney. The will, insofar as relevant, gave to a friend a life estate in her home and its contents, created a trust to maintain the home, and left specific cash bequests to a niece and a nephew and three charities. The residuary clause of Dorothy's will read as follows: "The said residue of my estate will be held in trust by my said Trustee ... to pay the income thereof, to my... niece, LOUISA GILBERT, during her lifetime. Upon her death, said residue and any accrued income thereof, shall go to... BEAVER COLLEGE, of Glenside, Pennsylvania, outright, and said Trust will terminate." Dorothy died on January 4, 1980, never having married and leaving no issue. Her will was allowed and, on March 26, 1980, Mr. Schwartz was appointed as her executor and trustee. Dorothy had insufficient assets at the time of her death to fund all the bequests in her will. In addition, Mr. Schwartz, the sole witness at trial, testified as to the circumstances attendant upon his drafting of the will. He indicated that he had asked Dorothy about her assets and the funding of legacies, and that she had made reference to money in BayBank which could be used to pay the legacies. He also testified that he did not ask to see Mary's will before he prepared Dorothy's will, that he first became aware of Mary's trust after Dorothy's death, and that Dorothy never requested that her will exercise her power of appointment. Finally, Mr. Schwartz testified that Dorothy received substantial sums from another trust created by her father and administered by The First National Bank of Boston as trustee, that Dorothy knew that the residue of the estates of both her parents were managed by trustees, that she received income from both trusts of about $20,000 annually, and that Dorothy had a checking account at a BayBank office.

1. The facts require examination in light of several general principles pertaining to the exercise of powers of appointment and two Massachusetts decisions.

Generally, when the donor of a power of appointment prescribes a specific formality for the exercise of the power, there will be no effective appointment in the absence of the [powerholder's] compliance with the formalities dictated by the donor. National Shawmut Bank v. Joy, 315 Mass. 457, 462, 53 N.E.2d 113 (1944).

Restatement (Second) of Property §18.2 (T.D. No. 6, 1983).[21] This rule, however, is not absolute. Failure to satisfy the formal requirements imposed by a donor will not cause the appointment to fail if the [powerholder's] action reasonably approximates the prescribed manner of appointment, especially where the appointee is a member of a favored class. Restatement (Second) of Property, supra, §18.3.[22] 5 American Law of Property §23.44 (1952). See Shine v. Monahan, 354 Mass. 680, 682, 241 N.E.2d 854 (1968). A donor's requirement of specific reference ordinarily negates any presumption that a general residuary clause may exercise the power and mandates, for effective exercise of the power, an affirmative act by the [powerholder] at least approximating the indicated formality.

The reasons behind these rules are simple enough to discern. The donor of the power presumptively intends by the specific reference requirement that the [powerholder] (a) focus on the consequence of the appointive act and consider the donor's wish with respect to the trust remainder if there is a default in exercise of the power, and (b) make an unambiguous written statement expressing a wish to exercise the power. With proper compliance, the specific reference device provides for the reasoned disposition of property by means of written and proven instruments which help to establish an unimpeachable record of title and serve to discourage unnecessary litigation.

These principles underlie two decisions of the Supreme Judicial Court within the last fifteen years which, while not directly on point, instructively discuss the subject of successful exercise of powers of appointment.

In Shine v. Monahan, 354 Mass. 680, 241 N.E.2d 854 (1968), the donor of an inter-vivos trust required that a general power of appointment be exercised "by specific reference in her [powerholder's] will to the full power hereby created." The [powerholder's] will provided for the distribution of "[a]ll the rest, residue and remainder of my property, including all property of which I have a power of appointment by virtue [of] any will or testament or inter-vivos trust executed by my husband [the donor]." An effective exercise of the power was found, under the principles of approximation, because the donor's purpose (to prevent inadvertent exercise of the power) had been satisfied by the [powerholder's] deliberate references to all powers of appointment given by her husband, the donor. Not to be

---

21. The tentative draft carries forward without material change the formulation of the rule set out in Restatement of Property §346 (1940).

22. These principles are also carried forward from the earlier Restatement of Property §347 comment a (1940), and are grounded on the maxim that "equity will aid the defective execution of a power." Favored class status is extended by the Restatement to (a) a natural object of the [powerholder's] affection, (b) a person with whom the [powerholder] has had a relationship akin to that with one who would be a natural object of the [powerholder's] bounty, (c) a creditor of the powerholder, (d) a charity, (e) a person who has paid value for the appointment, or (f) some other person favored by a court applying equitable principles. See Restatement (Second) of Property, supra, §18.3(2).

overlooked in the decision, is the court's careful distinction from the case before it of situations, as in National Shawmut Bank v. Joy, supra, where the donor required a specific reference and the [powerholder] simply referred in general terms to any power of appointment the [powerholder] might possess. 354 Mass. at 683, 241 N.E.2d 854.

In McKelvy v. Terry, 370 Mass. 328, 346 N.E.2d 912 (1976), the donor conferred on the [powerholder] a limited testamentary power of appointment to be exercised "by reference [in the powerholder's will] to the limited power of appointment herein given to him." The [powerholder's] will provided for distribution of "[a]ll of the residue of my estate, including lapsed legacies and devises (and also including any property over which I may have a power of appointment under any instrument, it being my intention to exercise all such powers which I may have at my death)." The court found this residuary provision to be a sufficient exercise of the power, commenting (at 332) that "the meaning or design of the relevant clause of the [powerholder's] will sufficiently matches any requirement of the [donor's] trust instrument. That instrument calls for a 'reference' to the power, not a specific reference, and we think... that the residuary clause of the will is an adequate reference although it is inclusive of any power created by any instrument in the [powerholder's] favor" (emphasis supplied). Referring to Shine v. Monahan, the court said (at 333): "We thought that there need not be exact compliance with the formality indicated by the donor where the approximation would satisfy his basic purpose. Less indulgence may be needed in the present case because the donor did not in terms require a specific reference." These excerpts from the *McKelvy* case imply the special nature of a specific reference requirement and emphasize that compliance with such a requirement cannot be easily circumvented. These principles and decisions provide the guidelines necessary to dispose of this case. The general testamentary power of appointment granted to Dorothy by Mary's will expressly required that it be exercised by Dorothy's will "specifically referring to the power." The critical inquiry is "not whether [the powerholder] intended to appoint but rather whether [the powerholder] manifested her intent in the manner prescribed by [the] donor, i.e., by making specific reference 'in her will' to the power granted by [the] donor's will" (emphasis original). Holzbach v. United Virginia Bank, 216 Va. 482, 485-486, 219 S.E.2d 868 (1975). See also Restatement (Second) of Property, supra, §17.1. Unlike the situations in the *Shine* and *McKelvy* cases, the residuary clause of Dorothy's will made no reference at all to any power. Lacking any attempt at compliance with the requirement of specific reference, there is simply no testamentary framework which will allow application of a rule of approximation. We conclude that Dorothy's will fails to exercise the power of appointment given to her by her mother.[23]

2. Some brief comment is in order on the plaintiff's several arguments seeking to avoid the conclusion that there has been a default in the exercise of the power.

(a) The plaintiff's reliance on the decision in Amory v. Meredith, 7 Allen 397 (1863), is misplaced. The rule in *Amory* provides that a general testamentary power of appointment will be deemed to have been exercised by a general residuary clause in the [powerholder's] will, unless a contrary intention is demonstrated. The rule does not apply where the donor requires that the power be exercised by means of specific reference.[24] See McKelvy v. Terry, 370 Mass. at 331-332, 346 N.E.2d 912. See also National Shawmut Bank v. Joy, 315 Mass. at 462, 53 N.E.2d 113.

(b) The fact that Dorothy's will includes several pecuniary bequests which in total may have exceeded her assets at the time of death does not, in these circumstances, imply that the power has been exercised by implication. See Boston Safe Deposit and Trust Co. v. Prindle, 290 Mass. 577, 584, 195 N.E. 793 (1935).

(c) The plaintiff's argument that property subject to a [powerholder's] general power is actually the [powerholder's] property is misplaced. Mary's will clearly did not grant a general power of appointment exercisable without restriction. We find the plaintiff's assertion to the contrary both untenable on the facts and unsupported by any authority dealing with a requirement of specific reference.[25]

---

23. This conclusion receives solid support in decisions of other States which have considered specific reference clauses in contexts like the one before us. See Estate of Eddy, 184 Cal. Rptr. 521, 526 (Cal. App. 1982); Estate of Smith, 585 P.2d 319, 321 (Colo. App. 1978); Talcott v. Talcott, 423 So.2d 951, 955-956 (Fla. App. 1982); Leidy Chemicals Foundation, Inc. v. First Natl. Bank, 351 A.2d 129, 132 (Md. 1976); Estate of Gilchrest, 408 N.Y.S.2d 684, 685 (N.Y. Sur.Ct. 1978); Estate of Schede, 231 A.2d 135, 137 (Pa. 1967); First Natl. Bank v. Walker, 607 S.W.2d 469, 474-475 (Tenn. 1980); Holzbach v. United Virginia Bank, supra.

24. The rule in *Amory* was superseded by what is now G.L. c. 191, §1A(4), inserted by St.1976, c. 515, §4, and made applicable to all wills executed on or after January 1, 1978. That statute provided and (as appearing in St.1977, c. 637, §1) still provides: "No general residuary clause in a will and no will making general disposition of all of the testator's property shall exercise a power of appointment created by another instrument which does not specify a specific method of exercise unless reference is made to powers of appointment or there is some other indication of intention to exercise the power." Since Dorothy executed her will on May 6, 1977, G.L. c. 191, §1A(4), would appear to have no application to this case. Nevertheless, it is worth noting that the statute pays attention to references in the instrument which require a specific method of exercise. The statute indicates that such references are not to be brushed aside on vague assertions of the [powerholder's] true intentions.

25. The relevant decisions in the Commonwealth apparently indicate that the property over which a [powerholder] has a general power becomes the [powerholder's] property only after the [powerholder] has actually exercised the power. For example, it has consistently been held that "where a person has a general power of appointment and exercises it the appointed property becomes available to his creditors. This is upon the theory that he could have appointed it to himself or his executors or otherwise could have devoted it to the payment of his debts, and therefore that the creditors have an equitable right to reach it." Prescott v. Wordell, 319 Mass. 118, 120, 65 N.E.2d 19 (1946), and cases cited. See e.g., Curtis v. Commissioner of Corps. & Taxn., 340 Mass. 169, 171, 163 N.E.2d 151 (1959);

(d) While the testimony of Mr. Schwartz may have been properly admitted to show the circumstances attendant upon the execution of Dorothy's will, see 2 Newhall, Settlement of Estates § 361 at 470 (1958), the pertinent texts of the wills of Mary and Dorothy, when laid side by side and read together, manifest no ambiguity. Extrinsic evidence is not admissible to contradict or control unambiguous language in a will. See Gustafson v. Svenson, 373 Mass. 273, 275, 366 N.E.2d 761 (1977); Gove v. Hammond, 385 Mass. 1001-1002, 430 N.E.2d 822 (1982). Nor is it admissible to correct an inadvertent omission by Dorothy or a mistake by the attorney who drafted the will. See *Gustafson* and *Gove,* supra. Finally, extrinsic evidence, in the absence of an ambiguity, is not admissible to show Dorothy's intent, even if the result is the failure of the intended gift. Ibid. See also First Natl. Bank v. Shawmut Bank of Boston, 378 Mass. 137, 144, 389 N.E.2d 1002 (1979). See generally, Liacos, Handbook of Massachusetts Evidence at 390-392 (5th ed. 1981 & Supp.1983).

Judgment affirmed.

Uniform Powers of Appointment Act §304

A powerholder's substantial compliance with a formal requirement of appointment imposed by the donor, including a requirement that the instrument exercising the power of appointment make reference or specific reference to the power, is sufficient if:

(1) the powerholder knows of and intends to exercise the power; and

(2) the powerholder's manner of attempted exercise of the power does not impair a material purpose of the donor in imposing the requirement.

Estate of Hamilton
593 N.Y.S.2d 372 (N.Y. App. Div. 1993)

CREW, J. Appeal from a decree of the Surrogate's Court... entered December 13, 1991, which, *inter alia,* adjudged that Anita G. Hamilton failed to exercise in her last will and testament the general power of appointment which was granted to her by the last will and testament of decedent.

On February 26, 1989 Milton W. Hamilton (hereinafter decedent) died, survived by his spouse, Anita G. Hamilton (hereinafter Hamilton), his daughters, respondents Mary H. McLaughlin, Gwendolyn H. Stevens, and his stepson, respondent John H. Ricketson. Paragraph fourth of decedent's last will and testament, executed on April 5, 1982, directed that the residuary of decedent's estate be divided into two funds, Fund A and Fund B. Fund A was a marital deduction trust and Fund B was a bequest to McLaughlin and Stevens. Paragraph fourth further provided that upon Hamilton's

---

State Street Bank & Trust Co. v. Reiser, 7 Mass.App.Ct. 633, 637, 389 N.E.2d 768 (1979). See also 2 Newhall, Settlement of Estates § 369 (1958).

death, the principal remaining in Fund A was to be "paid, transferred or distributed... in such manner... as [Hamilton] may by her last Will and Testament direct and appoint"; decedent specified, however, that this power of appointment was "exercisable only by specific reference to said power in [Hamilton's] last Will and Testament". In the event that Hamilton failed to effectively exercise the power of appointment, the assets remaining in Fund A would pass to McLaughlin and Stevens.

Hamilton died 15 days after decedent, leaving a last will and testament dated December 22, 1967. Paragraph second of Hamilton's will provided as follows:

> By this paragraph of my Last Will and Testament, I do specifically exercise the power of appointment given to me by *paragraph "Sixth" of the Last Will and Testament of my husband... dated the 26th day of August, 1966,* in favor of my son, JOHN HENRY RICKETSON... or to his issue him surviving, to the extent of seven-eighths (⅞ths) of the fund over which I have the power of appointment, and I give, devise and bequeath to SUE M. RICKETSON, wife of my son, one-eighth (⅛th) of the fund over which I have the power of appointment under *the said Last Will and Testament of my husband....* By these provisions, I do specifically exercise the power of appointment given to me by the Will of my said husband (emphasis supplied).

Decedent's and Hamilton's respective wills were subsequently admitted to probate.

Petitioner thereafter commenced this accounting proceeding seeking, *inter alia,* a determination as to whether Hamilton had effectively exercised the power of appointment granted her in decedent's 1982 will. Surrogate's Court concluded, *inter alia,* that although Hamilton had validly exercised the power of appointment given her in decedent's 1966 will, that will was revoked by subsequent wills executed by decedent in 1975 and 1982. Accordingly, Surrogate's Court decreed that Hamilton did not satisfy the "specific reference" requirement contained in decedent's 1982 will and, therefore, the remainder of the trust would pass to McLaughlin and Stevens. This appeal by Ricketson followed.

We affirm. [N.Y. Est. Powers & Trusts Law] 10-6.1 sets forth the rules governing the exercise of a power of appointment and provides, in pertinent part, that "[i]f the donor has expressly directed that no instrument shall be effective to exercise the power unless it contains a specific reference to the power, an instrument not containing such reference does not validly exercise the power"....

...The only power referenced by Hamilton in her will was the power of appointment granted her under decedent's 1966 will which, as noted previously, had been revoked by decedent's subsequent execution of a new will in 1975 and again in 1982, in which decedent clearly manifested his intent to revoke all prior wills and codicils. Thus, Hamilton's sole reference was to a power that had ceased to exist.

The remaining issues do not merit extended discussion. While it is true that decedent granted a power of appointment to Hamilton in his subsequent wills, we cannot infer from Hamilton's exercise of the appointive power conferred under decedent's 1966 will that she similarly intended to exercise any such power existing under decedent's 1982 will. In any event, Hamilton's intent in this regard is irrelevant for decedent "made it crystal clear" that the power of appointment granted by his 1982 will was exercisable only by Hamilton's specific reference thereto in her last will and testament. We similarly reject Ricketson's assertion that Hamilton's exercise of the power of appointment conferred by decedent's 1966 will "reasonably approximates" the manner in which decedent directed the power be exercised under his 1982 will....

ORDERED that the decree is affirmed, without costs.

MIKOLL, J.P., and YESAWICH, MAHONEY and HARVEY, JJ., concur.

Questions

1. *Reference Too Specific?* Would the result have been different if the powerholder's will had not referred to the donor's will by date and paragraph?

In Smith v. Brannan, 954 P.2d 1259 (Or. Ct. App. 1998), the donor and powerholder, who were husband and wife, executed wills in 1978. The donor's 1978 will created a marital deduction trust, granting his wife a right to the income for life and a general testamentary power of appointment over the remainder interest "by specific reference to this provision of my will." The powerholder's 1978 will purported to exercise her power of appointment granted to her "under Paragraph VI, A, of the Last Will and Testament of my husband... dated the 14th day of December, 1978." Subsequently, the powerholder was diagnosed with Alzheimer's disease, and the parties agreed that she lacked mental capacity to execute a new will. The donor, however, executed a 1988 will, which made some changes in his 1978 will, but repeated the language of the marital-deduction trust contained in his 1978 will. The court held that the powerholder's purported exercise of her power of appointment was ineffective because it failed to satisfy the donor's requirement of "specific reference to this provision of my [1988] will."

2. *Pre-2014 Uniform Probate Code.* In In re Strobel, 717 P.2d 892, 898 (Ariz. 1968), the court said that "[t]he presumptive purpose of [a specific reference] requirement is to ensure a considered and intentional, rather than an inadvertent exercise of the power." The *Strobel* presumption was codified in the pre-2014 version of UPC §2-704. Would the result in *Hamilton* have been different if the case had been controlled by that provision of the Uniform Probate Code?

3. *Uniform Powers of Appointment Act.* Would the result in *Hamilton* have been different if the case had been controlled by the Uniform Act? In 2014, UPC §2-704 was amended to conform to Uniform Act §304.

PART D. EFFECTIVENESS OF THE POWERHOLDER'S APPOINTMENT

Primary Statutory References: *Uniform Act §§305-314, 401-407*
UPC §2-603

Deceased Appointee. An exercise of a power of appointment in favor of a deceased person is ineffective, except as saved by an antilapse statute. See Uniform Act §306; Restatement 3d of Property §5.5 comment *l*, §19.12.

Testamentary Appointments—Applicability of Antilapse Statutes. Antilapse statutes in non-UPC states are commonly silent as to their application to the exercise of a power of appointment. (The Restatement 3d of Property recommends that such statutes should be "construed to apply to such an exercise, unless the applicable statute expressly excludes appointments." Restatement 3d of Property §19.12 comment b.) These statutes usually are held to apply to the testamentary exercise of a *general* power in favor of a deceased appointee, as long as the deceased appointee is in the protected relationship to the powerholder. As to a *nongeneral* power, the authority that exists suggests that the statute does not apply unless the deceased appointee is in the protected relationship to the powerholder *and* the substituted takers specified in the antilapse statute were permissible appointees of the power.[26]

The UPC antilapse statute expressly applies to the exercise of a power of appointment, by defining the term "devisee" as including "an appointee under a power of appointment exercised by the testator's will" if the appointee is a "grandparent, a descendant of a grandparent, or a stepchild[27] of either the testator or the donor of a power...." UPC §2-603(a)(6), (b).

UPC §2-603 and Restatement 3d of Property §5.5 comment *l* provide that the substitute gift is not defeated merely because the substitute takers are not permissible appointees of the power. The UPC expressly states that "a surviving descendant of a deceased appointee of a power of appointment can be substituted for the appointee under this section, whether or not the descendant is an object of the power." UPC §2-603(b)(5). Accord Restatement 3d of Property §19.12 comment e.

1. Permissible and Impermissible Appointments

Permissibility of Appointment Not Creating an Absolute-Ownership Interest—Appointment in Trust. The powerholder of a *general* power can validly

---

26. An appointee need not accept an appointment. A disclaimer relates back and operates as a nonacceptance and, therefore, an appointee who disclaims is treated as if he or she predeceased the appointment, and an antilapse statute may apply.

27. "Stepchild" is defined as a "child of the surviving, deceased, or former spouse of the testator or of the donor of a power of appointment, and not of the testator or donor." UPC §2-603(a)(7).

create limited or future interests in his or her appointees, in trust or otherwise, just as if the powerholder were the owner of the appointive property. Even an explicit prohibition of this type of an appointment in the language creating the power is ineffective, because it would be useless to try to enforce it. The powerholder could appoint to himself or herself or to his or her estate outright and then convey or devise the owned property as he or she chose. See Uniform Act §305; Restatement 3d of Property §19.13.

In the absence of a contrary intent manifested in the language creating the power, the powerholder of a *nongeneral* power can validly create limited or future interests in the permissible appointees of the power, in trust or otherwise. See, e.g., Loring v. Karri-Davies, 357 N.E.2d 11 (Mass. 1976) (prospectively overruling Hooper v. Hooper, 89 N.E. 161 (Mass. 1909)). A manifested prohibition of this type of an appointment, however, is effective. See Uniform Act §305.

Permissibility of Appointment Creating a New Power. The powerholder of a *general* power can confer a new power of appointment on his or her appointee. See Uniform Act §305(a); Restatement 3d of Property §19.13.

With respect to a *nongeneral* power, the better view is that the powerholder of a nongeneral power can create a general power in a permissible appointee. See Uniform Act §305(c)(2); Restatement 3d of Property §19.14. The fact that the powerholder of the appointed general power can exercise it in favor of impermissible appointees of the original power is irrelevant because, had the powerholder of the original power appointed outright to the permissible appointee, the permissible appointee would be free to transfer the property, by gift or otherwise, to an impermissible appointee of the original power. Conferring a general power on a permissible appointee is the equivalent of appointing outright to the permissible appointee.

A few courts have held to the contrary, however. These courts take the view that the ability of the powerholder of the appointed general power to exercise it in favor of impermissible appointees of the original power precludes the powerholder of the nongeneral power from conferring a general power on a permissible appointee. See Thayer v. Rivers, 60 N.E. 796 (Mass. 1901).

The powerholder of a nongeneral power can create a nongeneral power in any person so long as the permissible appointees of the appointed nongeneral power do not include anyone who is not a permissible appointee of the first nongeneral power. See Uniform Act §305(c)(3); Restatement 3d of Property §19.14.

Example 14.14: G's will devised real property to A for life, remainder to such of A's descendants as A may appoint. At his death, A exercised his nongeneral power by appointing to his child B for life, remainder to such of B's descendants as B shall appoint. A and B were living at G's death.

A's appointment is valid because all the permissible appointees of the nongeneral power conferred on B by A's appointment were permissible appointees of A's nongeneral power. If

A had purported to confer on B a power exercisable in favor of B's spouse and descendants as B shall appoint, that part of A's appointment creating the power in B would have been ineffective under traditional law.

What is the justification for limiting who can be permissible appointees of the appointed nongeneral power? See the Restatement 3d of Property §19.14 comment g(3).

In 2018, the Uniform Act was amended to authorize a powerholder of a nongeneral power to create a new nongeneral power in a permissible appointee to appoint to "one or more persons if the permissible appointees of the new nongeneral power include the permissible appointees of the original nongeneral power." See Uniform Act §305(b)(4). According to the accompanying Comment, the provision was added "in order to provide additional flexibility to the holder of a nongeneral power."

Problems

1. Rhett purchased the property known as Tara for his wife, Scarlett. Rather than convey Tara to her outright, he conferred upon Scarlett a general power of appointment to give Tara "to whomever she wishes, including herself, as long as the recipient is given a fee simple absolute. I do not authorize Scarlett to create any future interests in Tara." Not one to obey Rhett's orders, Scarlett exercised the power to give her good friend, Ashley, a life estate in Tara, with the remainder interest to be held by Ashley's descendants who survive him, by representation. Has Scarlett effectively exercised her power of appointment? What if Scarlett's power had been nongeneral?

2. Sherlock's will left his entire estate "to such persons as my good friend, John, may appoint." John exercised his power of appointment to create a general power of appointment in Sherlock's brother, Mycroft. Has John effectively exercised his power of appointment? What if John's power had been nongeneral?

3. Assume instead that Sherlock's will gave John the power to appoint the property "to such members of the Diogenes Club as John sees fit." Sherlock's older brother, Mycroft, is a member of the Diogenes Club, but John is not. May John create a nongeneral power of appointment in Mycroft to appoint to anyone in the world other than Mycroft, Mycroft's creditors, Mycroft's estate, and the creditors of Mycroft's estate?

Estate of Kohler
344 A.2d 469 (Pa. 1975)

Eagen, J. This is an appeal from a final decree entered by the Orphans' Court Division of the Court of Common Pleas of Montgomery County sustaining preliminary objections to a petition to reopen an adjudication.

The facts are not in dispute.

Martin Luther Kohler died August 20, 1916, leaving a will which created a trust. According to the terms of the will, income from the trust was to be paid to his two surviving daughters, Ruth K. Bates and Else K. Campbell, during their respective lifetimes. The will provided further:

> Upon the death of either of my said daughters then I direct the share of such daughter to be paid to her issue per stirpes as such issue shall arrive at the age of twenty-five years, or that the same be paid to such issue in such manner and in such sums as my said daughters shall by their respective wills direct.

Else K. Campbell died testate. Her will directed that the balance of the residue of her estate, including the power of appointment granted to her by the will of her father, Martin Luther Kohler, was to be divided into four equal shares. One share was bequeathed "to my son, Robert F. Campbell, if he survives me. Should my said son, Robert F. Campbell, predecease me, then his share shall fall into my residuary estate and shall thus increase the shares of the other residuary legatees."

Robert F. Campbell predeceased his mother, Else K. Campbell.

The Fidelity Bank, trustee of the Kohler trust, filed a final account and a petition for adjudication following the death of Else K. Campbell. No notice was given to the children of Robert F. Campbell, and the distribution suggested by the Fidelity Bank made no award to them. On December 6, 1973, the Orphans' Court Division of the Court of Common Pleas of Montgomery County rendered an adjudication confirming the account of, and approving the distribution proposed by the Fidelity Bank.

The children of Robert F. Campbell filed a petition to reopen the adjudication naming as respondents the Fidelity Bank, and the six beneficiaries among whom distribution was awarded by the adjudication. Preliminary objections were filed by the Fidelity Bank. Dismissal of the petition was sought on the ground that the children of Robert F. Campbell lacked standing to file the petition since they were not parties in interest in the trust. The court sustained Fidelity's preliminary objections. The children of Robert F. Campbell then filed this appeal.

The issue presented on this appeal is whether the will of Martin Luther Kohler created an *exclusive* power of appointment in Else K. Campbell or, more specifically, did the will give Else K. Campbell the power to exclude her son's issue from participation in the trust. The appellants contend it did not and maintain that there is nothing in the will of Martin Luther Kohler giving Else K. Campbell 'the right to distribute her share of the estate to 'such of her issue' as she might by will appoint"....

[T]he appellants argue that the language of the Kohler will, properly interpreted, provides for a gift to Else K. Campbell's issue per stirpes with power in her merely to vary the time and method of distribution. This argument is premised solely upon an interpretation of the words "such issue".....

Specifically, appellants contend that the term "such issue" in the clause "or that the same be paid to such issue" has as its antecedent the phrase "issue per stirpes" as used previously in the clause "I direct the share of such daughter to be paid to her issue per stirpes." From this it follows, they assert, that the testator did not intend that either daughter have the power to exclude any of their respective issue from a distributive share of the trust.

Appellants would have us read the disputed language as presenting the following alternatives:

> Upon the death of either of my said daughters, then I direct the share of such daughter to be paid to her issue per stirpes (1) as such issue shall arrive at the age of twenty-five years, or (2) that the same be paid to such issue in such manner and in such sums as my said daughters shall by their respective wills direct.

Such an interpretation, we believe, would render superfluous the words "that the same be paid to such issue." If the power in the daughters to vary the time *for distribution* of the shares of payment were intended merely as an alternative to distribution at the age of twenty-five, there would be no apparent reason to have repeated the words "or the same be paid to such issue."

Given the structure of the language actually used, we feel a much more natural interpretation is the following:

> Upon the death of either of my said daughters then I direct (1) the share of such daughter to be paid to her issue per stirpes as such issue shall arrive at the age of twenty-five years, or (2) that the same be paid to such issue in such manner and such sums as my said daughters shall by their respective wills direct.

With this interpretation no words are superfluous, and the alternatives expressed as noun clauses with identical subjects are in parallel construction. Since wills are to be construed so as to give effect to every word employed by the testator, we deem the latter interpretation preferable.

In addition, appellants' interpretation would have us interpret the term "such issue" to mean "said issue." However, the fact that the testator in the introductory phrases of the contested sentence used the adjective "said" to refer back to his previously mentioned daughters indicates that if he did, in fact, intend to have the term "such issue" refer to an antecedent, he would more likely have used the term "said issue."

In view of the interpretation we adopt, there can be little doubt that the testator intended the power of appointment to be exclusive. A power to appoint to 'such' of the class as the [powerholder] may select was long ago held to be an exclusive power, permitting the [powerholder] to select one or more of the class, to the exclusion of others....

In addition, we have already observed that no particular words are necessary to create a power of appointment.

Decree affirmed. Each side to pay own costs.

ROBERTS, J. (dissenting). I dissent. In my view the language of the will creating the testamentary trust here was intended only to empower the first life tenants to alter the timing and manner of distribution to their issue and not to confer the power entirely to exclude some of their issue from the class of beneficiaries. I would, therefore, vacate the decree and remand for the entry of a decree permitting distribution to appellants herein.

MANDERINO, J., joins in this dissent.

Notes

1. *Exclusionary and Nonexclusionary Powers Defined.* An *exclusionary power* is one "exercisable in favor of any one or more of the permissible appointees to the exclusion of the other permissible appointees." Uniform Act §102(5). In contrast, a *nonexclusionary power* is one "in which the powerholder cannot make an appointment that excludes any permissible appointee, or one or more designated permissible appointees, from a share of the appointive property." Comment to Uniform Act §102.

An example of clear language creating an *exclusionary power* would be a power to appoint "to any one or more of the powerholder's children." An example of clear language creating a *nonexclusionary power* would be a power to appoint "to all and every one of the powerholder's children."

2. *Construction of Ambiguous Language.* When the language is ambiguous, some courts presume the power is nonexclusionary. See, e.g., Hopkins v. Dimock, 48 A.2d 204 (N.J. Ch. 1946). The first Restatement of Property §360 adopted the contrary constructional preference, in favor of the power being exclusionary. Accord Restatement 3d of Property §17.5 comment f; Uniform Act §203(2).

3. *Doctrine of Illusory Appointments.* Under the *doctrine of illusory appointments,* each permissible appointee of a nonexclusionary power must receive a "reasonable benefit" rather than merely a "nominal sum" from the appointive assets. See Restatement 3d of Property §17.5 comment j.

Estate of duPont
379 A.2d 570 (Pa. 1977)

ROBERTS, J. Philip F. duPont died testate in 1928, leaving one-third of the residue of his estate to the Fidelity-Philadelphia Trust Company in trust for the benefit of his daughter, Mrs. Frances duPont Rust. In his will, Mr. duPont created in Mrs. Rust a special testamentary power of appointment over the one-third share of the residue. The will provides that Fidelity-Philadelphia is upon her death to transfer, assign, and pay over the principal of her share of (Mr. duPont's) residuary estate unto such of her children and issue of deceased children, and in such proportions as she may by her Last Will and Testament or any writing in the nature thereof direct, limit and appoint (emphasis added).

Mrs. Rust died in 1975. In her will, Mrs. Rust appointed a part of this share to appellants William Shore, Harry Devine, and Girard Trust Bank in trust for the benefit of her surviving daughter Carroll (Mr. duPont's granddaughter) for life and then for the benefit of the issue of Carroll (Mr. duPont's great grandchildren). Mrs. Rust gave appellants the discretion to make periodic payments from principal to Carroll's issue.

Upon Mrs. Rust's death, Fidelity-Philadelphia filed an account in the Orphans' Court Division of the Court of Common Pleas of Chester County. The auditing judge reviewed the objection to Mrs. Rust's exercise of her special power of appointment and concluded that Mrs. Rust exceeded the bounds of her special power by appointing part of the residue for the benefit of the issue of Mrs. Rust's surviving daughter Carroll. Objections to the adjudication of the auditing judge were dismissed by the orphans' court. In this appeal, appellants contend that Mr. duPont authorized Mrs. Rust to appoint to Carroll's issue while Carroll is still living. We do not agree. We agree with the holding of the orphans' court that Mrs. Rust exceeded her special power and therefore affirm.

The orphans' court interpreted "children and issue of deceased children" to include those persons who are either living "children" of Mrs. Rust or "issue of deceased children" of Mrs. Rust at the time of her death. The court concluded that the potential beneficiaries of the special power are confined to those persons within the precise class defined in Mr. duPont's will, and that Mrs. Rust could not alter or expand that group. Hence, the court held invalid the appointment in trust for the benefit of the issue of Mrs. Rust's surviving daughter Carroll because Carroll's issue were not "issue of deceased children" of Mrs. Rust at Mrs. Rust's death.

"The [powerholder]... is simply a trustee for the donor to carry into effect the authority conferred by the power. In exercising the power, he must observe strictly its provisions and limitations." Rogers' Estate, 218 Pa. 431, 433, 67 A. 762, 762 (1907); Schede Estate, 426 Pa. 93, 231 A.2d 135 (1967). For her exercise of the special power to be effective, Mrs. Rust had to exercise that power within the limits of her authority. Schede Estate, supra; Restatement of Property §351 (1940); 5 American Law of Property §23.52 (Casner ed. 1952).

To validate Mrs. Rust's appointment to Mr. duPont's great grandchildren while their mother Carroll is still living would be to ignore the express language of Mr. duPont's will. Mr. duPont's testamentary plan is explicit: the language "children and issue of deceased children" gives Mrs. Rust the power to benefit her living "children" (Mr. duPont's grandchildren). This language provides in the alternative that if any of those children predecease Mrs. Rust, and if those deceased children are survived by issue, those "issue of deceased children" (Mr. duPont's great grandchildren) should be eligible beneficiaries. Such a scheme is a reasonable method of avoiding the potentially harsh exclusion of the great grandchildren of Mr. duPont whose parent happened to predecease Mrs. Rust. By including "issue of deceased children" as permissible beneficiaries, Mr. duPont allowed Mrs. Rust to appoint to such issue in place of their parent who predeceased Mrs. Rust.

Mr. duPont, in granting Mrs. Rust the power, "upon her death," to benefit "(her) children and issue of (her) deceased children... in such proportions" as she should choose, decided that living children of Mrs. Rust are best qualified to see to the needs of their issue; only the issue of deceased children were to be provided for by Mrs. Rust directly. While Mr. duPont authorized Mrs. Rust to have the power to appoint "in such proportions" as she saw fit, he did not authorize the expansion or alteration of the class of permissible beneficiaries so as to encompass issue of living children. We find such an attempt to be in excess of the limits of Mrs. Rust's powers and therefore hold it invalid.

Mrs. Rust attempted to circumvent Mr. duPont's limitation to appoint only to "issue of *deceased* children" by delegating to appellants the authority to make appointments from principal to Carroll's issue after Carroll's death. Mrs. Rust authorized appellants to exercise at Carroll's death the discretion of Mr. duPont conferred exclusively upon Mrs. Rust to decide how the principal should be apportioned among members of the class of beneficiaries. However, Mr. duPont authorized Mrs. Rust to appoint "by her Last Will and Testament or any writing in the nature thereof." This language reflects an intent that Mrs. Rust exercise her appointment power at the time of her death. The testamentary nature of her special power is inconsistent with her attempt to postpone the choice of beneficiaries beyond the time of her death.

Appellants, at oral argument, contended that the decision of the orphans' court will burden Carroll's issue with harsh tax consequences. That concern does not relieve a court from the duty of discerning the testator's intent as it is expressed in the will and the overall testamentary plan.

> As to the obviation of taxes, it is incontestable that almost every settlor and testator desires to minimize his tax burden to the greatest extent possible. However, courts cannot be placed in the position of estate planners, charged with the task of reinterpreting deeds of trust and testamentary dispositions so as to generate the most favorable possible tax consequences for the estate. Rather courts are obliged to construe the settlor's or testator's intent as evidenced by the language of the instrument itself, the overall scheme of distributions, and the surrounding circumstances.

Estate of Benson, 447 Pa. 62, 72, 285 A.2d 101, 106 (1971).

Decree affirmed. Each party to pay own costs.

POMEROY and NIX, JJ., concur in the result.

Notes

1. *Appointment in Favor of an Impermissible Appointee.* A direct appointment in favor of a person who is not a permissible appointee of a nongeneral power is obviously ineffective. See Uniform Act §307(a); Restatement 3d of Property §19.15. In Vetrick v. Keating, 877 So.2d 54 (Fla. Ct. App. 2004), Vincent created a revocable inter vivos trust, giving his wife Marjorie a power of appointment over the remainder interest following her income interest. The terms of the power provided: "My Spouse, Marjorie, shall have the limited power to appoint to my children, all or any part of the trust at the time of my spouse's death in a valid Will making specific reference to the power of appointment herein conferred upon my spouse." Marjorie's will exercised her power as follows:

> Upon my death, the remaining net trust assets of said Family Trust shall be divided into separate shares, per stirpes, with respect to my husband's then living descendants. Such shares shall be administered as follows:
>
> A. The share held for SUSAN, TIMOTHY, MICHAEL, KEVIN, and BRIAN or their then-living descendants per stirpes, shall be distributed outright, free of trust.
>
> B. The share held for JUDITH shall be held in further trust and administered by the trustees hereinafter named as follows:
>
> The trustees shall distribute to JUDITH all of the net income therefrom at least quarterly. In addition, the trustees may distribute all or any part of the trust principal to or for the benefit of JUDITH and her descendants as the trustee considers advisable for her or their health, education, maintenance and support, with no duty to equalize such payments among eligible beneficiaries. Any undistributed income shall be added to the principal.
>
> Any trust principal remaining at JUDITH's death shall be distributed outright, free of trust, to her then living descendants, per stirpes, or if none to my then living descendant per stirpes; provided, however, that any property thereby distributable to a person who is the income beneficiary or an eligible income beneficiary of a trust under this Agreement shall instead be added to the principal of such trust.
>
> I appoint my financial advisor, JEFFREY KEATING, and my daughter JUDITH as co-trustees of this trust. If JEFFREY is unable to serve for any reason, he shall have the power to appoint a disinterested trustee to serve in his place, or if he does not do so, my brother-in-law, TIMOTHY D. O'Hara of Chicago Illinois shall appoint a disinterested trustee. It is my express intent that at no time shall JUDITH serve as sole trustee....

To what extent was Marjorie's exercise invalid?

2. *Indirect Appointments to Impermissible Appointee.* An appointment in favor of a permissible appointee is ineffective—a so-called *fraud on the power*—if the powerholder's purpose was to benefit an impermissible appointee. See Uniform Act §307(b); Restatement 3d of Property §19.16.

Example 14.15: G devised the residue of her estate in trust: income to her husband, H, for life, remainder in corpus to such of G's children by a former marriage as H should by will appoint. On H's subsequent death, H appointed the trust corpus to A, who was one of G's children by her former marriage. Evidence showed, however, that A had agreed, in consideration of the appointment, to transfer half of the appointive assets to X, H's child of a former marriage.

H's appointment is invalid because his effort to benefit the impermissible appointee, X, constitutes a fraud on his nongeneral power.

3. *Powerholder's "Estate" As the Permissible Appointee.* Suppose that a donor creates a power exercisable in favor of the powerholder's "estate" and the powerholder's will, making specific reference to the power, exercises the power by making direct devises of the appointive property. Is the exercise valid? In Matter of Estate of Rossi, 634 N.Y.S.2d 372 (Sur. Ct. 1995), the court held it was, reasoning that the powerholder of a general power "should be allowed to accomplish by the single act of unrestricted appointment what he could do by an appointment to himself and a later disposition of the assets so appointed...." Id. at 374 (citing Restatement 2d of Property §19.1 comment a).

4. *Effectiveness of Appointment to Takers in Default.* There is disagreement in the case law about the effectiveness of an appointment to someone who would receive the same property anyway as a taker in default. Some cases hold that such an appointment is ineffective, because an exercise in conformity with the taker in default's interest is a nullity. Uniform Act §313 agrees: "If a powerholder makes an appointment to a taker in default of appointment and the appointee would have taken the property under a gift-in-default clause had the property not been appointed, the power of appointment is deemed not to have been exercised and the appointee takes under the clause." Accord Restatement 3d of Property §19.25.

The capacity in which the person takes, as appointee or taker in default, is of no great concern to the person taking, as long as he or she takes. The significance of whether the appointment is effective or not lies elsewhere. The question usually arises in cases of general powers and the claims of the powerholder's creditors, usually the powerholder's estate creditors. By the majority common-law view, an ineffective appointment of a general power does not allow creditors to reach the appointive assets. It takes an effective appointment to subject the appointive assets to the claims of the powerholder's creditors. See above at p. 765. The issue of whether an appointment to default takers is an exercise of a power may also have tax implications if the powerholder had a pre-1942 general power.

2. Failures to Appoint; Ineffective Appointments

Basic Rule. If the powerholder fails to exercise the power, the appointive property passes under the donor's gift-in-default clause to the takers in default. See Uniform Act §§310(1), 311(1); Restatement 3d of Property §17.2(f). If there is no gift-in-default clause, or to the extent the clause is ineffective, what happens to the appointive property depends on whether the power is general or nongeneral.

General Power—Failure to Exercise. If a general power is unexercised (and there is no gift-in-default clause, or to the extent the clause is ineffective), the Uniform Act provides that, if the powerholder merely failed to exercise the power, the appointive property passes (1) to the powerholder if living and a permissible appointee, or (2) if the powerholder is an impermissible appointee or deceased, to the powerholder's estate if the estate is a permissible appointee. However, if the powerholder released the power or if there is no taker under the earlier provisions, the appointive property reverts to the donor or the donor's successor in interest. Uniform Act §310(2); accord Restatement 3d of Property §19.22. This contrasts with the earlier rule of the Restatement 2d of Property, which had provided that (if there is no gift-in-default clause, or to the extent the clause is ineffective) the appointive property reverts to the donor or the donor's successor in interest. See Restatement 2d of Property §24.1.

Recall that a likely powerholder of a general power is the donor's surviving spouse, in which case the power will be a power to appoint the remainder interest in a marital deduction trust. If the donor's estate was well planned, there will be a gift-in-default clause. If the powerholder does not wish to disturb the gift-in-default clause, the powerholder should not only refrain from exercising the general power but should affirmatively declare this intention in the powerholder's will by a clause such as:

> I hereby refrain from exercising the power of appointment conferred on me by my spouse's will of [date].

General Power—Ineffective Exercise—The "Capture Doctrine." There is a special rule governing the *ineffective* exercise (as opposed to *failure* to exercise) of a general power. The traditional result is that (if there is no gift-in-default clause, or to the extent the clause is ineffective) the appointive property reverts to the donor or the donor's successor in interest. If, however, the powerholder's appointment manifests an intent to assume control of the property for all purposes, and not merely for the limited purpose of giving effect to the expressed appointment, some cases—principally from Illinois and Massachusetts—apply a "capture doctrine," which means that the appointive property goes to the powerholder's estate rather than to the takers in default or to the donor or the donor's successor in interest.[28] Some courts have used the theory that the powerholder's ineffective appointment constitutes an implied appointment in favor of the powerholder's own estate.

The powerholder's intent to assume control of the property for all purposes is manifested by: (1) a blending clause, see, e.g., Fiduciary Trust Co. v. Mishou, 75 N.E.2d 3 (Mass. 1947); (2) a residuary clause that presumptively demonstrates an

---

28. The capture doctrine is not recognized in Virginia. See Sovran Bank v. Axelrad, 1991 WL 834837 (Va. Cir. Ct. 1991). Decisions in other jurisdictions in which the doctrine was neither mentioned nor applied in cases in which the facts would have caused the doctrine to apply include In re Hellinger's Estate, 83 N.Y.S.2d 10 (Sur. Ct. 1948); Boyd's Estate, 49 A. 297 (Pa. 1901).

intent to exercise the power pursuant to a statute or rule of common law; (3) a residuary clause that demonstrates an intent to exercise the power because the powerholder's estate is insufficient to satisfy the powerholder's bequests; or (4) in the view of some but not all courts, an appointment in trust. Compare Talbot v. Riggs, 191 N.E. 360 (Mass. 1934) (capture doctrine applied because powerholder's ineffective appointment was in trust), with Northern Trust Co. v. Porter, 13 N.E.2d 487 (Ill. 1938) (capture doctrine not applied even though powerholder's ineffective appointment was in trust).

Donors often attempt to protect their gift-in-default clauses against the capture doctrine. A clause in frequent use introduces the gift-in-default clause with the phrase:

> To the extent the powerholder does not effectively exercise this power of appointment,....

Since one of the theories used to justify an application of the capture doctrine is that, in the circumstances, the import of the powerholder's ineffective express appointment is an effective implied appointment in favor of his or her own estate, this type of clause may not give the donor the desired protection. Greater protection would be afforded by a slight rewording:

> To the extent the powerholder does not expressly exercise this power of appointment effectively,....

The Uniform Act and the Restatement 3d of Property adopt a "modern variation" of the capture doctrine. The ineffective exercise of a general power results in the appointive property passing under the gift-in-default clause or, to the extent the clause is nonexistent or ineffective, to the powerholder (or the powerholder's estate) if a permissible appointee; if not, the appointive property reverts to the donor or the donor's successor in interest. See Uniform Act §309; Restatement 3d of Property §19.21. Neither the Uniform Act nor the Restatement 3d conducts an inquiry into whether the powerholder manifested an intention to assume control over the property for all purposes.

Effective January 1, 2020, Illinois adopted the Uniform Act including its variation of the capture doctrine. See 760 Ill. Comp. Stat. §3/1318.

Nongeneral Powers. If the powerholder fails to exercise a nongeneral power of appointment, or makes an ineffective exercise thereof, the appointive property passes under the gift-in-default clause to the takers in default. If there are no takers in default, or to the extent the gift-in-default clause is ineffective, the appointive property passes to the permissible appointees of the power *if* the permissible appointees are a defined and limited class (such as the powerholder's "children" or "issue"). See Uniform Act §311(2); Restatement 3d of Property §19.23.

Two different theories are employed to reach this result. Some courts take the view that the powerholder of a nongeneral power with a defined and limited class of permissible appointees has a duty to exercise the power, i.e., that the power is a power in trust (also called a mandatory power). The court will not permit the permissible appointees of the power to suffer by the negligence of the powerholder in failing to appoint or making an ineffective appointment, "but fastens upon the property a trust for their benefit." See, e.g., Daniel v. Brown, 159 S.E. 209 (Va. 1931).

Other courts imply a gift in default in favor of the permissible appointees of the nongeneral power. See, e.g., Loring v. Marshall, 484 N.E.2d 1315 (Mass. 1985); Polen v. Baird, 25 S.E.2d 767 (W. Va. 1943).

Example 14.16: The permissible appointees of A's nongeneral power are A's children; there is no express gift in default.

If A dies without exercising the power, or makes an ineffective appointment, the appointive assets will go to A's children who survive A (and substituted takers for a deceased child, if an antilapse statute applies). Both the power-in-trust theory and the implied-gift-in-default theory lead to this result. If, however, there are no permissible appointees to which the property can pass, the appointive assets revert back to the donor or the donor's successor in interest.

Example 14.17: The permissible appointees of A's nongeneral power are anyone in the world except A, A's estate, A's creditors, and the creditors of A's estate.

If A dies without exercising the power, or makes an ineffective appointment, the appointive assets revert to the donor or the donor's successor in interest. The power is not a power in trust and there is no implied gift in default because the permissible appointees of A's power are not a defined and limited class.

The Uniform Act and the Restatement 3d of Property adopt the implied-gift-in-default theory. See Uniform Act §311(2); Restatement 3d of Property §19.23(b).

If the permissible appointees do not constitute a defined and limited class, the appointive property reverts to the donor or the donor's successor in interest.

3. Contracts to Appoint

Presently Exercisable Powers. A contract by the powerholder of a presently exercisable power of appointment to make a specified appointment in the future is enforceable if neither the contract nor the promised appointment confers a benefit on a impermissible appointee. See Uniform Act §405; Restatement 3d of Property §21.1.

If the presently exercisable power is a general power, it follows that a contract to appoint is enforceable, regardless of on whom the benefits are conferred.

If the presently exercisable power is a nongeneral power, a contract to appoint is likely to confer a benefit on a impermissible appointee. If so, the contract is unenforceable, but the promisee, if his or her conduct was not consciously wrongful, is entitled to restitution of the value of the consideration paid for the promise.

Example 14.18: A was the powerholder of a nongeneral power to appoint among her nephews and nieces. In exchange for consideration of $10,000, A contracted with one of her nephews, X, to appoint all the property to X, to the exclusion of A's other nieces and nephews.

Even though X is a permissible appointee of the power, the contract is unenforceable because the contract benefitted A, the promisor-powerholder. A was not a permissible appointee of the power.

If the powerholder does not breach the unenforceable contract, but instead abides by it, the powerholder's appointment may be ineffective on the ground that it constitutes a fraud on the nongeneral power.

Testamentary Powers. A contract to appoint a testamentary power, whether general or nongeneral, violates the donor's intent in limiting the exercise of the power to a testamentary exercise. Thus a contract to appoint a testamentary power is unenforceable. The promisee may, however, be entitled to restitution of the value of the consideration paid for the promise. See Restatement 3d of Property §21.2.

If the powerholder does not breach the unenforceable contract, but instead abides by it, the powerholder's appointment is valid if the power was a general power. See, e.g., Rogers' Estate, 6 N.Y.S.2d 255 (Sur. Ct. 1938). If the power was a nongeneral power, if the promisee-appointee was a permissible appointee of the power, and if the promisor-powerholder received consideration for the promise, it would seem that the appointment should be ineffective as a fraud on the power and that the promisee should then be able to obtain restitution from the promisor-powerholder (or his or her estate) of the value of the consideration paid for the promise. See, e.g., Pitman v. Pitman, 50 N.E.2d 69 (Mass. 1943). Restatement 3d of Property §21.2 comment c, however, suggests that the appointment is effective, but also suggests that, to prevent the impermissible appointee-powerholder-promisor from receiving a benefit, the promisee-appointee should be entitled to receive restitution of the value of the consideration paid for the promise.

4. Releases of Powers

Uniform Act §402 and the Restatement 3d of Property §§20.1 and 20.2 declare that all powers of appointment, general and nongeneral, testamentary and presently exercisable, are releasable in whole or in part, unless the donor has effectively manifested an intent that the power not be releasable. Several states have enacted legislation that is basically or wholly in accord with this proposition.

If the donor of a *general* power expressly provides that the power cannot be released, the donor's intention may not be effective. The restriction must be examined under the rules governing restraints on alienation. See Uniform Act §402 and the accompanying Comment; Restatement 3d of Property §§20.1 comments c and d.

An express provision prohibiting the release of a *nongeneral* power is probably valid. See Restatement 3d of Property §20.2.

The release of a general power of appointment, if permissible, causes the appointive property to pass under the gift-in-default clause or, if none or to the extent the clause is ineffective, to revert to the donor or the donor's successor in interest. See Uniform Act §310; Restatement 3d of Property §19.22.

The release of a nongeneral power of appointment, if permissible, causes the appointive property to pass under the gift-in-default clause or, if none or to the extent the clause is ineffective, to the permissible appointees if they are a defined and limited class (under an implied-gift-in-default theory) or, if the permissible appointees are not a defined and limited class, to revert to the donor or the donor's successor in interest. See Uniform Act §310; Restatement 3d of Property §19.23.

The methods a powerholder may use to release a power of appointment are explained in the Comment to Section 403 of the Uniform Act:

> A powerholder may release the power of appointment by substantial compliance with the method specified in the terms of the instrument creating the power or any other method manifesting clear and convincing evidence of the powerholder's intent. Only if the method specified in the terms of the creating instrument is made exclusive is use of the other methods prohibited. Even then, a failure to comply with a technical requirement, such as required notarization, may be excused as long as compliance with the method specified in the terms of the creating instrument is otherwise substantial.

Chapter 15

Estates and Future Interests

"This appeal involves a remainder interest, long one of the law professor's favorite instruments of torture."
  – Justice Michael J. Streit, Iowa Supreme Court,
    in Will of Uchtorff, *693 N.W.2d 790 (2005)*

Having studied the role of powers of appointment in the fashioning of trusts, we now turn to the subject of future interests. If powers of appointment are staples in modern estate planning practice, future interests are nothing short of indispensable. Future interests are intrinsic to trusts: It is nearly impossible to create a trust without creating one or more future interests.

The study of future interests was at one time dominated by the study of classification because many important legal consequences turned on classification. Today, some important legal consequences still turn on classification, especially in connection with the Rule Against Perpetuities. Additionally, you need to become familiar with the terms associated with classification to understand the legal literature and communicate to others in practice. This explains why we study classification in this Chapter.

PART A. CLASSIFICATION: POSSESSORY ESTATES AND FUTURE INTERESTS[1]

Classification means fixing the proper label or labels to a possessory estate or future interest. "Possessory estate" means an ownership interest in property granting the owner the current right to possession or enjoyment. "Future interest" means an ownership interest in property where the right to possession or enjoyment is deferred until some time in the future; the future possession or enjoyment may be certain to occur or may be uncertain to occur.

The hierarchy of possessory estates and future interests is a refined, artificial structure that took centuries to develop fully. If it had been designed in one fell swoop, the flexibility it provides estate planners and clients of today could readily be achieved with a system of much greater simplicity. Indeed, the American Law

---

1. For a fuller treatment than presented here, see Thomas F. Bergin & Paul C. Haskell, Preface to Estates in Land and Future Interests (2d ed. 1984); Lewis M. Simes, Handbook on the Law of Future Interests (2d ed. 1966); Thomas P. Gallanis, Estates, Future Interests, and Powers of Appointment in a Nutshell (6th ed. 2018).

Institute has approved a simplified system of possessory estates and future interests in the final volume of the Restatement 3d of Property. See Lawrence W. Waggoner, The American Law Institute Proposes Simplifying the Doctrine of Estates, University of Michigan Working Paper Series (no. 198), available at ssrn.com (abstract 1612878, 2010).

In this chapter, we cover *both* the traditional and the new simplified systems.

The complexity and artificiality in the traditional system evolved, step by step over a fairly long period of time, from the struggles of competing interest groups. The owners of the great English landed estates, assisted by ingenious lawyers, sought to avoid the estate taxes of the day and to safeguard their estates through the generations. As one loophole was plugged in favor of exacting the tax or promoting freer alienability and control for the recipients of the property, the ingenious lawyers found another. The result was that great distinctions were drawn on the basis of the words used in creating dispositions. Through classification, different ways of saying the same thing were accorded different legal consequences. Form controlled over substance. In classification, form still controls over substance. Form controls legal consequences less than before, however, because the legal consequences flowing from classification are fewer today than in the past.

As we study the traditional system, bear in mind also that the system of classification, which was originally developed mainly for legal interests in land, has been transposed today to the classification of the beneficial interests in the modern trust. See Olin L. Browder, Jr., Trusts and the Doctrine of Estates, 72 Mich. L. Rev. 1509 (1974).

1. *The* Numerus Clausus *Principle*

Johnson v. Whiton
34 N.E. 542 (Mass. 1893)

HOLMES, J. This is an action to recover a deposit paid under an agreement to purchase land. The land in question passed under the seventh clause of the will of Royal Whiton to his five grandchildren, and a deed executed by them was tendered to the plaintiff, but was refused, on the ground that one of the grandchildren, Sarah A. Whiton, could not convey a fee simple absolute, and this action is brought to try the question. The clause of the will referred to is as follows: "After the decease of all my children, I give, devise, and bequeath to my granddaughter Sarah A. Whiton and her heirs on her father's side one-third part of all my estate, both real and personal, and to my other grandchildren and their heirs, respectively, the remainder, to be divided in equal parts between them."

We see no room for doubt that the legal title passed by the foregoing clause. We think it equally plain that the words "and her heirs on her father's side" are words of limitation, and not words of purchase. The only serious question is whether the effect of them was to give Sarah A. Whiton only a qualified fee, and whether, by reason of the qualification, she is unable to convey a fee simple. We do not think that it would be profitable to follow the decisions to be found in Preston on Estates, p. 449 et seq., and Challis on Real Property, c. 19. By the old law, to take land by descent a man must be of the blood of the first purchaser, (Co. Litt. 12a; 2 Bl. Comm. 220;) and by St. 3 & 4 Wm. IV. c. 106, §2, descent is traced from the purchaser. For instance, if the land had been acquired in fee simple by Sarah A. Whiton's father, it could only have descended from her to her heirs on her father's side. It was no great stretch to allow a limitation in the first instance to Sarah of a fee with the same descendible quality that it would have had in the case supposed. Challis, Real. Prop. 216, 222, 224; Co. Littl. 220b; Blake v. Hynes, L.R. 11 Ir. 284; 1 Prest.Est. 474. See St. 22 & 23 Vict. c. 35, §19. Especially is this true if, as Mr. Challis argues, the grantee under such a limitation could convey a fee simple, just as he or she could have done if the estate actually had descended from the father. But our statute of descent looks no further than the person himself who died seised of or entitled to the estate. Pub. St. c. 125. The analogy which lies at the foundation of the argument for the possibility of such limitations is wanting. A man cannot create a new kind of inheritance. Co. Litt. 27; Com. Dig. "Estates by Grant," A, 6. These and other authorities show, too, that, except in the case of a grant by the king, if the words "on her father's side" do not effect the purpose intended, they are to be rejected, leaving the estate a fee simple, which was Mr. Washburn's opinion. 1 Washb. Real. Prop. 61. Certainly, it would seem that in this commonwealth an estate descending only to heirs on the father's side was a new kind of inheritance.

What we have to consider, however, is not the question of descent, but that of alienability; and that question brings a further consideration into view. It would be most unfortunate and unexpected if it should be discovered at this late day that it was possible to impose such a qualification upon a fee, and to put it out of the power of the owners to give a clear title for generations. In the more familiar case of an estate tail, the legislature has acted, and the statute has been carried to the furthest verge by construction. Pub.St. c. 120, §15; Coombs v. Anderson, 138 Mass. 376. It is not too much to say that it would be plainly contrary to the policy of the law of Massachusetts to deny the power of Sarah A. Whiton to convey an unqualified fee.

Judgment for defendant.

Note and Questions

Our legal system permits the ownership of property to be fragmented between possessory estates and future interests. Derived from the English common law, this fragmentation of ownership is an ingenious concept. However, it raises an obvious question: Can the fragmentation take only previously-defined forms or can owners subdivide the interests in any form they wish? The longstanding answer, as we learn from *Johnson*, is that the fragmentation can occur only in a fixed number of defined forms.This is known as the principle of the *numerus clausus* (Latin for "closed number").

The *numerus clausus* principle is well-established, but what is its rationale? The scholarly literature on this point is not abundant. For an often-cited analysis, see Thomas W. Merrill & Henry E. Smith, Optimal Standardization in the Law of Property: The *Numerus Clausus* Principle, 110 Yale L.J. 1 (2000). But are Merrill & Smith persuasive? Should rights in property be more standardized than rights in contract? See Joshua Fairfield, The Cost of Consent: Optimal Standardization in the Law of Contract, 58 Emory L.J. 1401 (2009).

The effect of the *numerus clausus* principle is to limit the forms of fragmentation. This has a beneficial by-product in the classroom: students need only learn a fixed number of possessory estates and future interests, and how to recognize them.

We begin with the possessory estates.

2. The Possessory Estates

Quantum of Estates. According to the hierarchy of estates, the possessory estates are ordered by "quantum." In descending order of quantum, the groupings are: (1) fee simple estate (all fee simple estates are of the same quantum); (2) fee tail; (3) life estate; (4) term of years; (5) estate from period to period; (6) estate at will; and (7) estate at sufferance.[2]

The Estates in Fee Simple. In the traditional system of classification, there are four fee simple estates: the estate in fee simple absolute and three fee simple defeasible estates.

The estate in *fee simple absolute* is an estate in land that is not subject to termination; it is unlimited in duration. (The personal property counterpart of the fee simple absolute is called absolute or outright ownership.) A fee simple absolute is never followed by a future interest.

Example 15.1: G conveyed real property "to A and his heirs." A has a fee simple absolute; no future interest follows it.

The words "and his heirs" are "words of limitation," meaning words defining the estate granted to A, not "words of purchase," meaning words granting an interest in the property to A's heirs. (At common law, a conveyance "to A" gave A only an interest for life. The additional words "and his heirs" were needed in order to convey to A a fee simple inter vivos.) The words "and his heirs" were never required in wills and today are not typically required in inter vivos conveyances.

---

2. An estate from period to period is "an estate which will continue for successive periods of a year, or successive periods of a fraction of a year, unless it is terminated." Restatement of Property §20. An estate at will is "an estate which is terminable at the will of the transferor and also at the will of the transferee and which has no other designated period of duration." Id. at §21. An estate at sufferance is "an interest in land which exists when a person who had a possessory interest in land by virtue of an effective conveyance, wrongfully continues in the possession of the land after the termination of such interest, but without asserting a claim to a superior title." Id. at §22. These estates are not important in the law of wills and other donative transfers. See Restatement 3d of Property §24.1 comment b.

The *defeasible fee simple* estates are subject to termination upon the happening of an event specified in the grant. There are three defeasible fee simple estates in the traditional system of classification: (1) the fee simple determinable, (2) the fee simple subject to a condition subsequent, and (3) the fee simple subject to an executory limitation. Distinguishing each of these estates requires an understanding of the concept of defeasance.

Defeasance means loss of ownership—in other words, that the holder of the possessory estate will lose that estate upon the happening of an event stipulated in the grant. A possessory estate subject to defeasance is either subject to a *limitation* or to a *condition subsequent*.

Possessory estates subject to a "limitation" are said to terminate *naturally* or *by their own terms*. The language in the grant signifying a limitation are words such as "during," "until," "while," "as long as," "so long as," "for so long as," or simply "for [a designated period]," followed by words such as "at," "upon," or "then." The limitation is called a *special* limitation if it describes an event not certain to occur.

Possessory estates subject to a "condition subsequent" are said to terminate by being *cut short* or *divested* upon the happening of the stipulated event. The language in the grant signifying a condition subsequent are words such as "on condition that" or "provided that," followed by words such as "but if" or "and if." (In some grants, only the "but if" or "and if" language will appear.)

With this background in mind, let us turn to the three kinds of defeasible fee simple estates within the traditional system. They are, again: (1) the fee simple determinable, (2) the fee simple subject to a condition subsequent, and (3) the fee simple subject to an executory limitation.

The *fee simple determinable* is a fee estate subject to a *special limitation,* which means that it automatically terminates if the specified event happens; the specified event is any event not certain to occur.

Example 15.2: G transferred real property "to A and her heirs *as long as* A does not allow liquor to be sold on the premises; upon A's allowing liquor to be sold on the premises, the property is to revert to me." A has an estate in *fee simple determinable*.

Example 15.3: G transferred real property "to A and her heirs *as long as* A does not allow liquor to be sold on the premises; and upon A's allowing liquor to be sold on the premises, the property is to go to B."[3] A has an estate in *fee simple determinable*.

The future interest following the estate in fee simple determinable is either reversionary or nonreversionary (for the meaning of these terms, see below at p. 810). We shall see that if the future interest following the fee simple determinable

---

3. The limitation regarding selling liquor applies only to A and not to A's successors in interest. Therefore, the executory interest to B is valid under the Rule Against Perpetuities because it must vest or fail within A's lifetime.

is reversionary, the future interest is called a possibility of reverter; if the future interest following the fee simple determinable is nonreversionary, the future interest is called an executory interest.

The *fee simple subject to a condition subsequent* is a fee estate subject to *divestment* in favor of a reversionary future interest called a right of entry (also called a power of termination). The happening of the specified event does not automatically divest the estate; rather, it empowers the grantor (or the grantor's successor in interest) to divest the estate by exercising the right of entry.

Example 15.4: G transferred real property "to A and his heirs *on condition that* A not allow liquor to be sold on the premises, *and if* A allows liquor to be sold on the premises, then the grantor is to have the right to re-enter and take possession of the premises." A has an estate in *fee simple subject to a condition subsequent.*

The *fee simple subject to an executory limitation* is a fee estate subject to *divestment* in favor of a nonreversionary future interest called an executory interest. The happening of the specified event divests the estate.

Example 15.5: G transferred real property "to A and her heirs, *but if* A allows liquor to be sold on the premises, then to B." A has an estate in *fee simple subject to an executory limitation.*

So far, we have described the traditional system. The Restatement 3d of Property eliminates the distinction among the three fee simple defeasible estates, collapsing the three categories into one category called the "fee simple defeasible." As defined in the Restatement 3d of Property, the estate in fee simple defeasible "is a present interest that terminates upon the happening of a stated event that might or might not occur." Restatement 3d of Property §24.3. As we shall see in the materials below on future interests, the Restatement 3d of Property also simplifies the distinctions among the three future interests following a defeasible fee—the possibility of reverter, the right of entry, the executory interest—by labeling each future interest either a "reversion" or a "remainder."

Particular Estates. Having studied the fee simple estates, we now turn to the particular estates. The term *particular estate* is a term of art denoting any possessory estate that is less than a fee simple—a fee tail, a life estate, a term of years, and so on.

Fee Tail. The estate in fee tail—created by language such as "to A and the heirs of his body"—is subject to termination if and when the line of the tenant in tail's issue fails. That is, the estate terminates upon the death of the tenant in tail's last living descendant.

The fee tail estate has an interesting history,[4] but its present is no longer very

---

4. See Restatement of Property Ch. 5; Bergin & Haskell, note 1 above, at 28-34.

important and its future even less so. In almost all states, the fee tail estate is abolished. Language purporting to create a fee tail has different consequences in different states. The most predominant results are that it creates a fee simple absolute in A or that it creates a life estate in A, with a remainder in fee in A's issue. The Restatement 3d of Property articulates the position of the American Law Institute in proclaiming that "[t]he fee tail estate is not recognized in American law." See Restatement 3d of Property §24.4 (explaining that a disposition "to A and the heirs of A's body" creates a fee simple absolute in A; a disposition "to A for life, then to the heirs of A's body" creates a life estate in A followed by a remainder in A's issue who would take from A under the applicable intestacy statute).

Life Estates and Terms of Years. Life estates and terms of years are estates that are subject to a *limitation;*[5] they expire naturally (by their own terms) on the death of the measuring life or the expiration of the term.

The phrases *equitable life estate* or *equitable term* are sometimes used to describe the interest of a trust beneficiary who has the right to the income from a trust for the beneficiary's lifetime or for a term. Equitable terms are most frequently encountered in charitable lead trusts, but they are also used in trusts that give the right to the income to a family member until that family member reaches a specified age.

Life estates and terms of years are by definition defeasible estates. They end at death or at the expiration of the term, respectively. Both, however, can be made *prematurely* defeasible. This occurs when either a special limitation or a condition subsequent is added to the grant.

Example 15.6: G transferred real property "to A for life or until A remarries." In the traditional system of classification, A's estate is called a *life estate subject to a special limitation* or a *determinable life estate.* In the simplified system of the Restatement 3d of Property, A's estate is a *defeasible life estate.*

Example 15.7: (1) G transferred real property "to A for life, remainder to B; but if A remarries, to B immediately." In the traditional system of classification, A's estate is called a *life estate subject to an executory limitation.* In the simplified system of the Restatement 3d of Property, A's estate is a *defeasible life estate.*

(2) G transferred real property "to A for life on condition that A not remarry; and if A remarries, G is to have the right to re-enter and take possession of the premises." In the traditional system of classification, A's estate is called a *life estate subject to a condition subsequent.* In the simplified system of the Restatement 3d of Property, A's estate is a *defeasible life estate.*

The duration of a life estate is often measured by the life of the one in possession ("to A for life"). But alternatively it can be measured by the life of another ("to A

---

5. "To A *for* life;" "to A *so long as* A lives;" "to A *until* A's death;" "to A *during* A's lifetime;" "to A *for* 10 years."

for the life of B"). In the traditional system of classification, this latter type of estate is called a *life estate pur autre vie*, using the "law French" of the courts of common law in England. The Restatement 3d of Property translates the law French into English: a *life estate for the life of another*.

Example 15.8: G transferred real property "to A for the life of B." Later, A died, survived by B. A's will devised A's entire estate to X. A, then X, has a life estate *pur autre vie* or life estate *for the life of another*—for the life of B.

Problems

Classify the possessory estates created in the following transfers under the traditional system of classification and under the simplified system of the Restatement 3d of Property:

1. G transferred real property "to A forever."

2. G transferred real property "to X Charity as long as the property is used for charitable purposes."

3. G transferred real property "to A and his natural heirs."

4. G transferred real property "to A as long as B continues to reside in Chicago."

3. Future Interests: Basic Division Between Reversionary and Nonreversionary Interests

We now turn from the classification of possessory estates to the classification of future interests.

The first step in the process of classification of a future interest is to decide whether the future interest is a reversionary interest or a nonreversionary interest. Reversionary interests are interests retained by (or created in) the transferor *when the interest was created.* Nonreversionary interests are interests *created in* a transferee (someone other than the transferor).

Once made, a classification based on the reversionary/nonreversionary distinction is not altered by subsequent transfers of the interest from one person to another.[6] So, a reversionary interest does not become a nonreversionary interest by virtue of a subsequent transfer of that interest from the transferor to a transferee. And, conversely, a nonreversionary interest does not become reversionary if it

---

6. Restatement 3d of Property §25.2 comment g observes: "Strict application of this section's black letter suggests the continuation of the rule that subsequent transfers do not cause the initial classifications to change. However, because no property-law consequence turns on whether a future interest is labeled as a reversion or a remainder..., it makes no difference which label is applied when there is a subsequent transfer." But see Restatement 3d of Property §25.2 Reporter's Note (observing that "[c]ertain concepts in tax law do depend on the distinction" between reversions and remainders, citing, among other IRC sections, §§673, 2037, and 2042).

subsequently comes into the hands of the transferor. It makes no difference whether the subsequent transfer is inter vivos, testamentary, or the result of intestate succession.

Problems

Classify the future interests in the following problems as reversionary or nonreversionary.

1. G conveyed real property "to A for life."

(a) Later, G conveyed all her interest in that property to B.

(b) Instead of conveying her interest to B, G later died with a will that did not mention the real property but contained a residuary clause devising all her property not otherwise disposed of to B. G was survived by A and B.

(c) In problem 1(b), G died intestate. G was survived by A and by her sole heir, B.

2. G's will devised real property to A for life. The will contained no residuary clause, so the residue of G's estate passed by intestacy to her sole heir, B.

3. Clause 3 of G's will devised real property "to A for life." Clause 105 of G's will devised the residue of G's estate to B.

4. G's will devised real property "to A for life, and upon A's death, the property is to go to B."

4. The Reversionary Future Interests

Under the traditional system of classification, if a future interest is reversionary it is a "reversion," a "possibility of reverter," or a "right of entry."

Reversions. Reversions are future interests retained by the transferor (or the transferor's successors in interest) when the transferor conveys an estate or estates of *less* quantum than the transferor had originally. The most common example is that of an owner of property in fee simple absolute who transfers out a particular estate (a possessory estate other than a fee simple).

Example 15.9: G conveyed real property "to A for life." G retained a reversionary interest, and the traditional system of classification calls that reversionary interest a *reversion*.

Possibilities of Reverter. Possibilities of reverter are future interests retained by the transferor (or the transferor's successors in interest) when the transferor transfers an estate of the *same* quantum as the transferor had originally. The most common example is that of an owner of property in fee simple absolute who transfers out a fee simple determinable.

Example 15.10: G conveyed real property "to A and his heirs as long as A does not allow liquor to be sold on the premises[, and upon A's allowing liquor to be sold on the premises, the property is to revert to the grantor]." G retained a reversionary interest, and the traditional system of classification calls that reversionary interest a *possibility of reverter*.

The words contained in the brackets in the preceding example are not necessary to create a possibility of reverter. Possibilities of reverter need not be expressly stated because, like reversions, they constitute an undisposed-of interest remaining in the transferor. See Simes & Smith on Future Interests §286. In practice, however, it is common expressly to state the possibility of reverter, and a small minority of decisions has held (erroneously) that, without the bracketed words, A takes a fee simple absolute. See, e.g., In re Copps Chapel Methodist Episcopal Church, 166 N.E. 218 (Ohio 1929).

Rights of Entry. Rights of entry—also called powers of termination[7]—are future interests created in the transferor (or the transferor's successors in interest) when the transferor transfers an estate subject to a condition subsequent (i.e., subject to divestment). (Whether the quantum of the estate is the same as or lesser than that of the transferor's original estate is unimportant.) The most common example is that of an owner of property in fee simple absolute who transfers a fee simple subject to a condition subsequent and who expressly creates the right to re-enter and retake the premises if and when the condition is broken.

Example 15.11: G transferred real property "to A and her heirs on condition that A not allow liquor to be sold on the premises, but if A allows liquor to be sold on the premises, the grantor is to have the right to re-enter and take possession of the premises." G retained (more accurately, created in himself) a reversionary interest, and the traditional system of classification calls it a *right of entry*.

A right of entry does not take effect in possession automatically when the condition is broken. If A allows liquor to be sold on the premises, A's action gives G a right to elect to take a possessory interest if G so chooses. See, e.g., Maletis, Inc. v. Schmitt Forge, Inc., 870 P.2d 865 (Or. Ct. App.), review denied, 881 P.2d 142 (Or. 1994) (classifying the reversionary interest in an easement as a right of entry and then finding that a letter indicating that the easement was extinguished served as sufficient notice of intent to terminate the easement).

Restatement 3d of Property. The Restatement 3d of Property eliminates the distinctions among the reversionary interests. See Restatement 3d of Property §25.2. All reversionary interests are called "reversions." What, then, of the historic distinction between the automatic nature of the possibility of reverter and the elective nature of the right of entry? Section 25.2 comment d of the Restatement 3d of Property explains:

---

7. *Power of termination* is the term used in the Restatement of Property §155. The Restatement 2d of Property used the older term, *right of entry.*

The principal distinction between a possibility of reverter and a right of entry was that the holder of a right of entry had to exercise the right to take possession of the property if and when the specified terminating event happened, whereas the holder of a possibility of reverter became automatically entitled to take possession if and when the specified terminating event happened. The different means of enforcement, however, turned out to be elusive in practical effect. The early common-law rule was that a right of entry could be exercised only by a physical entry on the land. In most states now, the commencement of an action to regain possession satisfies the requirement of an election to divest the possessory estate, and the holder of a possibility of reverter often must initiate a similar action in order to enforce his or her "automatic" interest. In addition, after the stipulated event has occurred, the time allowable under the law of many states for bringing an action to enforce a possibility of reverter is the same as that for making an election under a right of entry. The statute of limitations in several states begins running upon the occurrence of the specified event against both a possibility of reverter and a right of entry; in other states the statute has been so interpreted; and in still others, the statute is open to such an interpretation. The two interests are thus in alignment on the question of adverse possession. Finally, although the statute of limitations in some states is held not to begin running until an election under a right of entry has been effected, the courts, drawing an analogy to the equitable doctrine of laches, have required that an election be made within a "reasonable time" after the breach of the condition; and there is authority that the period of the statute of limitations constitutes a "reasonable time.".…

In the end, functional considerations no longer justify continuing to divide reversionary estates into the historic categories.

5. The Nonreversionary Future Interests

Under the traditional system of classification, if a future interest is nonreversionary, it is either a "remainder" or an "executory interest."

Remainders. A remainder is a future interest created in a transferee that becomes possessory if at all upon the *natural termination* of the preceding estate. The preceding estate (1) must have been created simultaneously with the creation of the future interest and (2) must be a particular estate. (Recall that a particular estate is a term of art denoting any possessory estate less than a fee simple. See above at p. 808.)

Example 15.12: G transferred real property "to A for life, and upon A's death, to B." The traditional system of classification calls B's interest a remainder.

Executory Interests. An executory interest is a future interest created in a transferee that becomes possessory if at all by *cutting short* or *divesting* the preceding estate. The preceding estate (1) need not have been created simultaneously with the creation of the future interest and (2) can be a fee simple or a particular estate.

Example 15.13: G transferred real property "to A and his heirs on condition that A not allow liquor to be sold on the premises, but if A allows liquor to be sold on the premises, the property is to go to B." The traditional system of classification calls B's interest an executory interest.

Special Case—Executory Interest Succeeds Fee Simple Determinable. In one special case, an executory interest does not "cut short" or "divest" the preceding estate but takes effect on its "natural termination." Since a remainder cannot follow a fee simple, a nonreversionary interest following a fee simple must be an executory interest, even when the fee simple is subject to a special limitation.

Example 15.14: G transferred real property "to A and her heirs as long as A does not allow liquor to be sold on the premises, and upon A's allowing liquor to be sold on the premises, the property is to go to B." The traditional system of classification calls B's interest an executory interest.

Springing and Shifting Executory Interests. The traditional system of classification divided executory interests into two categories—springing and shifting. *Shifting* executory interests potentially divest an estate conferred by the grantor on a transferee. *Springing* executory interests potentially divest an estate retained by the grantor.

Example 15.15: (1) G transferred real property "to A and his heirs, but if A allows liquor to be sold on the premises, to B." The traditional system of classification calls B's executory interest a *shifting executory interest.*

(2) G transferred real property "to B, to take effect in possession on B's marriage." The traditional system of classification calls B's executory interest a *springing executory interest.*

Restatement 3d of Property. The simplified system in the Restatement 3d of Property eliminates the distinctions among the nonreversionary interests. All nonreversionary interests are called "remainders." Section 25.2 of the Restatement 3d of Property states: "A future interest is either a reversion or a remainder. A future interest is a reversion if it was retained by the transferor. A future interest is a remainder if it was created in a transferee."

Should the Restatement 3d Have Eliminated the Distinction Between Reversions and Remainders? The reporter of the Restatement 3d of Property, Professor Lawrence Waggoner, considered whether to eliminate the distinction between reversions and remainders. The Restatement recognizes that, under the new system, "[n]o legal consequences in property law attach to the choice of labels, because there is no longer any persuasive reason for continuing to recognize the distinction between reversionary and nonreversionary interests." Restatement 3d of Property §25.2 comment e. However, the distinction is retained in the Restatement in order to comport with the customary vocabulary of the legal profession and with other Restatements and uniform laws:

The reason for categorizing future interests as either reversions or remainders is that the legal profession, especially in describing future interests created in a trust, is accustomed to referring to a future interest retained by the transferor as a "reversion" and a future interest created in a transferee as a "remainder." In addition, the Restatement Third of Trusts refers to a resulting trust as a "reversionary equitable interest" (see Restatement Third, Trusts §7), and the Restatement Third of Trusts and the Restatement Third of Restitution and Unjust Enrichment variously refer to property as "reverting" or "reverting back" to the transferor or the transferor's estate or successors in interest in certain cases. Finally, various uniform statutes, such as the Uniform Trust Code and the Uniform Principal and Income Act, refer to the future interest in trust principal as a "remainder."

Restatement 3d of Property §25.2 comment e. See also Restatement 3d of Property §25.2 Reporter's Note (observing that "[c]ertain concepts in tax law do depend on the distinction" between reversions and remainders, citing, among other IRC sections, §§673, 2037, and 2042).

Problems

Under the traditional and simplified systems of classification, classify the possessory estates and future interests in the following transfers:

1. G transferred real property "to X Charity as long as the land is used for charitable purposes."

2. G transferred real property "to X Charity, but if the land ceases to be used for charitable purposes, to B."

6. Vested and Contingent Future Interests

Future interests are subject to a further level of classification—classification in terms of vesting. Under the traditional system of classification, there are four categories here: indefeasibly vested, vested subject to (complete) defeasance, vested subject to open (partial defeasance), and contingent (nonvested).

For future reference, it may be noted that UPC §2-707 adopts a rule of construction that all future interests in trust are contingent upon the beneficiary surviving the distribution date. This is a subject we take up in Chapter 16.

Indefeasibly Vested. An indefeasibly vested future interest is one that is not subject to any conditions or limitations. In other words, the future interest must be certain to become a possessory fee simple *absolute* at some time in the future. See Restatement of Property §157 comment f.

Example 15.16: G transferred real property "to A for life, remainder to B." The traditional system of classification calls B's remainder *indefeasibly vested*. The remainder is certain to become possessory because A is bound to die. When A dies, B's remainder will become a possessory fee simple absolute.

Note in this example that B might not be alive when A dies. Except as otherwise provided by statute,[8] B's interest is not subject to a condition of survival of A. Therefore, the possibility of B's death before A's death has no bearing on the classification of B's interest. If B dies before A, B's indefeasibly vested remainder will pass at B's death to B's successors in interest—B's devisee or, if B dies intestate, B's heirs. See Chapter 16 for discussion of survival conditions.

Example 15.17: G conveyed real property "to A for life." The traditional system of classification calls G's reversion *indefeasibly vested*. The comments made in the above example regarding B's remainder apply to G's reversion in this example.

Example 15.18: G conveyed real property "to A for life, remainder to B for ten years." The traditional system of classification calls G's reversion *indefeasibly vested*. It is certain to become possessory ten years after A's death and will at that time become a fee simple absolute.

B's remainder is not indefeasibly vested. Although it is certain to become possessory upon A's death (a certain event), it will not become a fee simple absolute then. B's remainder is vested subject to defeasance after ten years. The comments made in Example 15.16 regarding survival apply equally here.

Vested Subject to Defeasance. Under the traditional system of classification, a future interest that is vested subject to defeasance is one that is subject to one or more conditions subsequent or to one or more limitations. The precise terminology of vesting will depend on whether the interest is subject to conditions subsequent or, on the other hand, to limitations.

If the future interest is subject to one or more *conditions subsequent*, the interest is *vested subject to divestment*. Only remainders and reversions can be vested subject to divestment. Note, however, that there is an important difference between remainders and reversions. Remainders are vested subject to divestment only when they are subject to a condition subsequent. (As we shall shortly see, remainders subject to a condition precedent are contingent.) In contrast, reversions are vested subject to divestment whenever they are subject to a condition, regardless of whether the condition is precedent or subsequent. The reason for this difference is that, by definition under the traditional system, reversions can never be contingent. *Reversions under the traditional system are always vested.*

Example 15.19: G transferred real property "to A for life, remainder to B, but if B fails to survive A, to C." The traditional system of classification calls B's remainder *vested subject to divestment* because the condition of survival attached to B's remainder is stated in condition subsequent form—"to B, but if."

C's executory interest is subject to the condition that B not survive A. This condition is stated in the form of a condition precedent—"if ... to C." C's executory interest is contingent.

---

8. UPC §2-707 would not apply on these facts because B's future interest is not in trust.

G retained no reversion.

Example 15.20: G conveyed real property "to A for life, remainder to B if B survives A, but if not, to return to me." B's remainder is subject to a condition of survival of A, but this time the condition is stated in the form of a condition precedent—"to B if." B's remainder is therefore contingent, not vested subject to divestment.

G's reversion is subject to the condition that B not survive A, and so G's reversion cannot be indefeasibly vested. This condition is stated in the form of a condition precedent. Nevertheless, the rule in the traditional system that reversions are always vested overrides all other rules and, therefore, G's reversion is called *vested subject to divestment.*

This analysis also applies if the phrase "but if not, to return to me" is omitted.

Example 15.21: G conveyed real property "to A for life, remainder to B if B survives A, but if not, to C." B's remainder is subject to a condition of survival of A that is stated in the form of a condition precedent—"to B if." B's remainder is therefore contingent, not vested subject to divestment.

C's remainder is subject to the condition that B not survive A. The condition is stated in the form of a condition precedent ("if [B does not survive A], to C") and, therefore, C's remainder is contingent, not vested subject to divestment.

Under the traditional system of classification, G retains a technical reversion. The particular estate in A is followed by contingent remainders in B and C. One might think that this would exhaust all the possibilities: the property will pass at A's death either to B or to C. However, the traditional system of future interests recognized an archaic rule of substantive law called the rule of the destructibility of contingent remainders. Given the theoretical possibility, under this rule, that the contingent remainders could be destroyed, the traditional system of classification provides that G retains a technical reversion. The reversion is said to be merely "technical," because except for the rule of the destructibility of contingent remainders, the reversion has no practical consequence. This technical reversion is vested subject to divestment because it cannot be indefeasibly vested and because it must be vested (recall the traditional rule that reversions are always vested).

A future interest that is subject to one or more *limitations* is called *vested subject to limitational defeasance.*

Example 15.22: G transferred real property "to A for life, then to B for life, then to C." In the traditional system of classification, B's remainder is called *vested subject to limitational defeasance.* It is sometimes referred to simply as a vested remainder for life. Note that B must survive A for B's interest to become possessory. This implicit requirement of survival is not regarded as a "condition" of survival.

C's interest is a remainder because B's interest is subject to a limitation and because it is an estate less than a fee simple. It is an indefeasibly vested remainder because it is subject to no condition or limitation.

Example 15.23: G conveyed real property "to A for life, then to return to me for life, then to C." This is the same as the example above, except that the future interest subject to limitational defeasance is a reversion in G rather than a remainder in B.

Example 15.24: G transferred real property "to A for life, then to B for 10 years, then to C." B's remainder is vested subject to limitational defeasance. In this case, the time of B's death is irrelevant. If B dies while A is still alive, B's remainder will pass to B's devisees or if B died intestate to B's heirs. If B dies after A's death but before the 10th anniversary thereof, the remaining portion of B's 10-year term will pass to B's devisees or if B died intestate to B's heirs.

Vested Subject to Open. Under the traditional system of classification, a nonreversionary future interest is vested subject to open when it is subject to no conditions precedent and when it is in favor of a class that contains at least one living member and that is still "open," *i.e.*, where it is possible for additional persons to become class members (typically through birth or adoption). Other and older labels for this type of interest are (1) *vested subject to partial divestment*, or (2) *vested in quality but not in quantity*. These terms are descriptive of the phenomenon that each time a new member is added to the class the shares of the existing class members are reduced (partially divested). Whichever label is used, it is important to note that the existing class members are the ones who are regarded as having a vested remainder. The interests of the unborn or unadopted class members are contingent on being born or adopted. They are executory interests because upon birth or adoption they partially divest the interests or shares of the living class members.

Example 15.25: G transferred real property "to A for life, remainder to A's children." When the transfer was made, A had two children, X and Y. Under the traditional system of classification, X has a *vested* remainder *subject to open* in an undivided half of the property. Y has a *vested* remainder *subject to open* in the other undivided half.

Suppose a third child, Z, is born after the transfer occurred. Upon Z's birth, Z's executory interest becomes a vested remainder subject to open in an undivided third of the property, and X's and Y's interests are each reduced (or partially divested) to vested remainders subject to open in an undivided third.

Reversionary interests are never subject to open at their inception because they are, by definition, retained by the transferor or the transferor's successors in interest when created. Even if a reversionary interest was originally "retained by" the transferor's successors in interest, which might be a group of people, such as the transferor's heirs, it is not a class subject to open because the membership of this group of takers is determined at the transferor's death.

After their inception, however, reversionary future interests might be transferred to a class that contains at least one living member and that is subject to open. If the reversionary future interest is a possibility of reverter or a right of entry, a transfer to a class would still not make either one of them *vested* subject to open because these interests are regarded as contingent.[9] A reversion, however, is always vested, and if it was subsequently transferred, it would become vested subject to open.

Example 15.26: G conveyed real property "to A for life." G later died (while A was alive), devising the indefeasibly vested reversion to A's children. Two children of A were living at G's death. These two children receive vested reversions subject to open and A's unborn children receive springing executory interests.

Example 15.27: Same as above except that A had no children at G's death. The situation at G's death would probably be viewed as follows: G carved springing executory interests (in favor of A's unborn children) out of the indefeasibly vested reversion. The indefeasibly vested reversion would thus become vested subject to divestment, and would pass to G's residuary devisee or G's heirs, depending on the situation.

Contingent. Under the traditional system of classification, a future interest is contingent (nonvested)[10] if it is subject to a *condition precedent.* A condition precedent may be explicit or implicit. An explicit condition precedent exists where the language of the disposition declares that the interest is to become possessory *if* some event occurs. Implicit conditions precedent exist when the future interest is in favor of unborn or unascertained persons.

Remainders can be contingent but need not be. Executory interests are nearly always contingent.[11] Reversions cannot be contingent but possibilities of reverter and rights of entry are regarded as contingent.

Example 15.28: G conveyed real property "to A for life, remainder to B if B survives A." Under the traditional system of classification, B's remainder is *contingent* because the condition of surviving A is stated in the form of a condition precedent—"to B if."

---

9. Although possibilities of reverter and rights of entry are classified as contingent, they are not subject to the Rule Against Perpetuities. This anomaly was noted by John Chipman Gray in his classic treatise. Gray agreed that possibilities of reverter were, and should be, exempt from the Rule, and so he maintained that there was "no practical object" in labeling them as contingent. John Chipman Gray, The Rule Against Perpetuities 107 (4th ed. 1942). Conversely, Gray argued that rights of entry, as truly contingent interests, should be subject to the Rule. Id. at 336.

10. The traditional term is *contingent,* but the Restatement 2d of Property adopted the term *nonvested.*

11. The typical executory interest is subject to a condition precedent and is classified as contingent (nonvested). In rare cases, an executory interest is created that is unconditional. An example would be if G conveyed real property "to B, to take effect in possession 25 years from now." Another example would be if G conveyed real property "to B, to take effect in possession at my death." It is assumed in each case that the possessory interest retained by G is a fee simple interest, not a term of 25 years or a life estate. This means that B's future interest cannot be a remainder and, therefore, it must be an executory interest. If it were a remainder, it would be classified as indefeasibly vested. The courts have been reluctant to call this type of an executory interest vested. Its classification has been perplexing because it is an executory interest. Nevertheless, it is generally assumed that, like vested interests in general, this type of an executory interest is not subject to the Rule Against Perpetuities. See Chapter 17.

G's reversion appears to be subject to the condition precedent that B not survive A, but G's reversion is vested subject to divestment because of the rule that reversions are always vested. This means that B's remainder in this situation acts like an executory interest because it potentially divests G's reversion. Nevertheless, it is a remainder because its predominant feature is that it takes effect in possession, if at all, on the natural termination of A's life estate.

Example 15.29: G transferred real property "to A for life, remainder to A's children." When the transfer was made, A had no children. Under the traditional system of classification, A's unborn children have *contingent* remainders. Their remainders, unlike B's remainder in the example above, are implicitly contingent on being born or adopted, but are not contingent on surviving A.

Example 15.30: G transferred real property "to A for life, remainder to A's heirs." Under the traditional system of classification, the remainder in favor of A's heirs is *contingent* because it is in favor of unascertained persons. The persons who are A's heirs cannot be ascertained until A's death.

Nevertheless, any person who would be an heir of A if A were to die immediately is called an heir apparent or an heir expectant. The heirs expectant are regarded as having contingent remainders during A's lifetime rather than mere expectancies. Thus it is sometimes said that they take by purchase rather than by succession. Their remainders are of course implicitly contingent on their actually becoming A's heirs when A dies.

Example 15.31: G transferred real property "to A for life, remainder to B, but if B fails to survive A, to C." The condition that B survive A is a condition subsequent as to B's remainder ("to B, but if"), making it, under the traditional system of classification, *vested subject to divestment.* C's executory interest is subject to the condition precedent that B not survive A and, therefore, is contingent.

Example 15.32: (1) G transferred real property "to A and her heirs on condition that A never allow liquor to be sold on the premises, but if A allows liquor to be sold on the premises, the property is to go to B."

(2) G transferred real property "to A and her heirs as long as A never allows liquor to be sold on the premises, and upon A's allowing liquor to be sold on the premises, the property is to go to B."

B's executory interest in both cases is subject to the condition that A allow liquor to be sold on the premises. In both cases, the condition is in condition precedent form and, therefore, under the traditional system of classification B's executory interest is *contingent.*

Example 15.33: (1) G conveyed real property "to A and his heirs on condition that A never allow liquor to be sold on the premises, but if A allows liquor to be sold on the premises, the grantor shall have the right to re-enter and take possession of the premises."

(2) G conveyed real property "to A and his heirs as long as A never allows liquor to be sold on the premises, and upon A's allowing liquor to be sold on the premises, the premises are to revert to the grantor."

G's right of entry in the first case and G's possibility of reverter in the second case would appear to be subject to the condition precedent that A allow liquor to be sold on the premises. Most traditional authorities do in fact classify these interests as contingent. See Am. L. Prop. §§4.6, 4.12; Simes & Smith on Future Interests §§281, 1238. The Restatement of Property §154 comment e, at 531, classifies possibilities of reverter as contingent but does not classify rights of entry in terms of vesting. It is believed that both interests are properly classified as contingent.

Future Interests in Sets. Some rules of thumb can be helpful in mastering the traditional system of classification when future interests occur in sets. When a set of nonreversionary future interests succeeds a life estate or a term of years, the first future interest will always be a remainder. The other or subsequent future interest(s), however, may be either remainders or executory interests. In determining which they are, the following rules apply:

Rule 1: If the first future interest is a contingent (nonvested) remainder, the other nonreversionary future interests will also be contingent (nonvested) remainders.

Rule 2: If the first future interest is a vested remainder subject to divestment, the other nonreversionary future interests will be executory interests.

Problems

Under the traditional system of classification, classify the possessory estates and future interests in the following transfers:

1. G transferred real property "to A for life, remainder to B if B survives A, but if not, to C."

2. G transferred real property "to A for life, remainder to B if B survives A, but if not, to C if C survives A."

3. G transferred real property "to A for life, remainder to B, but if B fails to survive A, to C."

4. G transferred real property "to A for life, remainder to B, but if B fails to survive A, to C if C survives A."

Restatement 3d of Property. The simplified system of classification in the Restatement 3d of Property reduces the four categories of vesting to two: "vested" and "contingent." A future interest is *vested* "if it is certain to take effect in possession or enjoyment." A future interest is *contingent* "if it might not take effect in possession or enjoyment." Restatement 3d of Property §25.3.

Accordingly, future interests that, under the traditional system, were indefeasibly vested are now called "vested." Future interests that, under the traditional system, were vested subject to defeasance or contingent are now called "contingent."

The Restatement 3d explains that a future interest that is "vested" or "contingent" can be "subject to open" if it is in favor of a class that is open to future entrants. See Restatement 3d of Property §25.3 comment f.

Note that the archaic rule of the destructibility of contingent remainders (discussed above in Example 15.21) is "not recognized as part of American law" according to the Restatement 3d of Property §25.5.

Problems

Go through the previous set of problems and classify the possessory estates and future interests using the simplified system of classification in the Restatement 3d of Property.

TABLE SUMMARIZING THE SIMPLIFIED SYSTEM OF THE RESTATEMENT 3D

Present Interest	Future Interest
Fee simple absolute (Absolute ownership)	None
Fee simple defeasible	Reversion (Vested or Contingent) Remainder (Vested or Contingent)
Life estate	Reversion (Vested or Contingent) Remainder (Vested or Contingent)
Term of years	Reversion (Vested or Contingent) Remainder (Vested or Contingent)

7. The Law Favors the Vesting of Estates

Traditionally, vested future interests are preferred to contingent future interests. Restatement of Property §243 comment i. Explicit recognition of this idea was colorfully stated in Roberts v. Roberts, 2 Bulst. 123, 80 Eng. Rep. 1002 (K.B. 1613), where it was declared that "the law always delights in vesting of estates, and contingencies are odious in the law, and are the causes of troubles, and vesting and settling of estates, the cause of repose and certainty." The law delights "in preventing of contingencies, which are dangerous...."

The source of the preference for vested future interests is complex, but it is commonly claimed that the desire to avoid certain common-law rules, such as the rule of the destructibility of contingent remainders and the Rule Against Perpetuities, to promote alienability, to promote completeness of the disposition, and to promote equality of distribution among different lines of descent all played important roles.

The Restatement 3d of Property, having abolished the destructibility rule and having reformed the system of classification and the Rule Against Perpetuities (on the latter, see Chapter 17), declines to endorse a preference for vested, as opposed to contingent, future interests. See Restatement 3d of Property §§11.3, 15.4 comment d, 25.3 comment d.

Perhaps the best way to describe the traditional preference for vested future interests is that the courts will construe a provision as not imposing a condition precedent if they can do so without contradicting the express language of the instrument, *i.e.*, where there is sufficient ambiguity in the language to permit what might be called an even choice.

Edwards v. Hammond
3 Lev. 132, 83 Eng. Rep. 614 (C.P. 1683)

Ejectment upon *not guilty*, and special verdict, the case was. A copyholder of land, burrough English, surrendered to the use of himself for life, and *after to the use of his eldest son and his heirs, if he live to the age of 21 years: provided, and upon condition, that if he die before 21, that then it shall remain to the surrenderer and his heirs.* The surrenderer died, the youngest son entered; and the eldest son being 17 brought an *ejectment*; and the sole question was, whether the devise to the eldest son be upon condition *precedent*, or if the condition be *subsequent? scil.* [an abbreviation of the Latin word *scilicet*, which means "that is to say"] that the estate in fee shall vest immediately upon the death of the father, to be divested if he die before 21. For the defendant it was argued, that the condition was *precedent*, and that the estate should descend to the youngest son in the mean time, or at least shall be in contingency and *in abeyance* 'till the first son shall attain to one and twenty; and so the eldest son has no title now, being no more than 17. On the other side it was argued, and so agreed by the Court; that though by the first words this may seem to be a condition *precedent*, yet, taking all the words together, this was not a condition *precedent*, but a present devise to the eldest son, subject to and defeasible by this condition subsequent, *scil.* his not attaining the age of 21....

Notes and Question

1. *Background of Edwards v. Hammond.* The transferor in the *Edwards* case, the surrenderer, was described as a "copyholder of land, burrough English." Copyholders were free men holding land by unfree tenure. The freehold and seisin of the copyholder's estate resided in his lord. The copyholder's evidence of title was his copy of the roll of the court of the manor; the court's roll served as a form of land registry. The rules governing the landholding of a copyholder were not uniform, but were to be found in the custom of the manor concerned. Borough English was a custom whereby the youngest son, not the eldest son, inherited lands subject to the custom. See A. W. B. Simpson, A History of Land Law 14 (2d ed. 1986).

The surrenderer in *Edwards*, engaging in a will substitute of the day, was trying to reverse this rule of inheritance by transferring (surrendering) his copyhold to his lord who would, upon the surrenderer's death, admit the grantee. The surrender would have been registered on the court rolls by the steward of the manor. The surrender did not completely cut out the surrenderer's youngest son, for by virtue of the custom of borough English, applicable in this case, the surrenderer's youngest son was his heir and, as such, was scheduled to take the land if the eldest son failed to reach twenty-one. Apparently, however, when the surrenderer died, the youngest son was admitted immediately; at least, he entered. This precipitated the action of ejectment, which was brought by the surrenderer's seventeen-year-old eldest son.

A contingent remainder in a copyhold was not subject to the common-law rule of destructibility of contingent remainders. Since copyholds were not freeholds, the seisin remained throughout in the lord of the manor.

2. *Consequences of Classification.* In *Edwards,* the direct result of holding that the remainder was vested subject to divestment was that the surrenderer's seventeen-year-old eldest son was immediately entitled to possession of the land. If the court had held that the remainder was contingent, the eldest son's right to possession would have been delayed until his twenty-first birthday, the youngest son having the right to possession in the meantime.

3. *The Mystique of Classification.* As you read the next case, Guilliams v. Koonsman, notice that the court also discussed at some length the proper classification of the future interests. Consider what consequence, if any, turns on how those future interests are classified. Is the *Guilliams* case an example of what Professor Waggoner called the "classificatory mystique"—the notion indulged by some courts that classifying the interests solves what is in fact a straightforward problem of construing the meaning of the dispositive language? See Lawrence W. Waggoner, Reformulating the Structure of Estates: A Proposal for Legislative Action, 85 Harv. L. Rev. 729, 732 (1972).

Guilliams v. Koonsman
279 S.W.2d 579 (Tex. 1955)

CALVERT, J. Our main problem involves the construction of the fourth paragraph of the will of J. J. Koonsman, deceased, which reads as follows:

> I give and devise to my son, Alvin Koonsman, all of my undivided interest in all of the remainder of my real property situated in Scurry County, Texas, which I may own at the time of my death, and to his child or children if any survive him, and in the event of Alvin's death without issue surviving him, then to my son and daughter, Jesse J. Koonsman and Mrs. Cora Guilliams, share and share alike, and to their heirs and assigns forever....

The only evidence in the record before us, other than the will itself and the probate proceedings in connection therewith, is the testimony of Alvin Koonsman that J. J. Koonsman, the testator, died March 6, 1942, and that he (Alvin) has only one child, John Billy Koonsman, born October 15, 1942. From this testimony it appears that John Billy was in esse for the purpose of taking under the will on the date it became effective, that is, the date of J. J. Koonsman's death.

What is the meaning of the words "and to his child or children if any survive him" following the devise to Alvin? We have been cited to and have found no case squarely in point. If the words "if any survive him" had been omitted and we were to follow the weight of authority, heretofore noted, we would be compelled to hold that Alvin and his son, John Billy, took the first estate created as cotenants. But those words were not omitted, and we ascribe to them a two-fold effect: first, they limited the interest of Alvin Koonsman to a life estate, and secondly, they operated to make the remainder to be taken by the child or children of Alvin contingent rather than vested.

The words "if any survive him," qualifying the devise to the children of Alvin, clearly indicate that his children were not to take as cotenants with Alvin but were to take in succession to him, with the result that the devise to Alvin is limited to a life estate. No particular form of words is necessary to the creation of a life estate.

> It has been said that where the construction of a will devising property to one and his children is doubtful, the courts lean toward giving the parent a life estate, and that even a slight indication of an intention that the children shall not take jointly with the parent will give a life estate to the parent with a remainder to the children. 33 Am. Jur. 474.

The conclusion that the remainder in the child or children is contingent rather than vested is also impelled by the words "if any survive him." Survival is made a condition precedent to the vesting of the remainder rather than a condition of defeasance. While it has been said that "The law favors the vesting of estates at the earliest possible period, and will not construe a remainder as contingent where it can reasonably be taken as vested," Caples v. Ward, 107 Tex. 341, 179 S.W. 856, 858, nevertheless, when the will makes survival a condition precedent to the vesting of the remainder, it must be held to be contingent.... The rule for determining whether a remainder is vested or contingent is thus stated by Gray in his work on The Rule Against Perpetuities:

> If the conditional element is incorporated into the description of, or into the gift to the remainder-man, then the remainder is contingent; but if, after words giving a vested interest, a clause is added divesting it, the remainder is vested.

3d Ed., §108(3), page 85. The rule as thus stated has been approved and adopted by the courts of this state. Here the condition of survival is incorporated into the gift to Alvin Koonsman's child or children.

There remains to be determined the nature of the estate devised to Jesse J. Koonsman and Mrs. Cora Guilliams by the fourth paragraph of the will. They are to take the fee "in the event of Alvin's death without issue surviving him." Their estate must be held to be a contingent remainder also. It is to take effect upon Alvin's death, but only if he dies "without issue surviving him." It is an alternative contingent remainder....

The judgments of the trial court and Court of Civil Appeals are reformed to...decree that the true meaning and effect of the fourth paragraph of the will is that the plaintiff, Alvin Koonsman, is therein and thereby given an estate for life in the property therein described, with a remainder in fee to the child or children of Alvin Koonsman, conditioned upon their surviving him, and an alternative remainder in fee to Jesse J. Koonsman and Mrs. Cora Guilliams, or their heirs and assigns, conditioned on the death of Alvin Koonsman without a child or children surviving him, and as so reformed the judgments of those courts are affirmed.

Notes and Questions

1. *Rule in Wild's Case.* A disposition to a named individual and his or her "children" (or "issue"), or a similar class gift term, is ambiguous. Wild's Case, 6 Coke 16b (K.B. 1599), promulgated what has come to be known as the Rule in Wild's Case. The rule applied only to a devise of land and provided that if the parent had no children at the date of the devise, the parent would take a fee tail estate; but, if the parent then had children, the parent and the children would take concurrently as joint tenants. The rule was repudiated in the Restatement 3d of Property §14.2 comment f.

Under the Restatement 3d, the presumptive meaning of a disposition to a named individual and his or her "children" or "issue," or a similar class-gift term, is that it creates successive rather than concurrent enjoyment. Hence, the presumptive meaning of a disposition "to A and his children" or "to A and her issue" is that A takes a life interest and A's children or issue take the remainder interest.

2. *Reconcilable?* Can you reconcile *Edwards* and *Guilliams*? *Guilliams* is supported by the Restatement of Property §278, but a few courts have held that a disposition such as that in *Guilliams* creates a vested remainder subject to divestment. See, e.g., Safe Deposit & Trust Co. of Baltimore v. Bouse, 29 A.2d 906 (Md. 1943). Do you think the testator *intends* different consequences by choosing condition precedent, condition subsequent, or even-choice language in describing contingencies? Do you think the testator's attorney might choose one form of conditional language rather than another for the purpose of accomplishing a particular legal result?

3. *Remainders for Life.* In addition to the rule of *Edwards*, another manifestation of the preference for vested interests is the rule that remainders for life are classified as vested subject to defeasance (subject to a limitation, not a condition precedent or subsequent). The remainder for life can be viewed as presenting an even choice to the courts because they could have classified it as contingent (on surviving the primary life tenant).

Consider, now, Example 15.34:

Example 15.34: G transferred real property "to A for life, then to B for life if B survives A, then to C."

This example presents a further problem because this remainder for life is expressly conditioned on survival of the primary life tenant. Does the inclusion of the phrase "if B survives A" remove this case from the even-choice category, and force a court to hold that B's remainder is contingent? A small number of courts have held that it does. Most courts, however, have held that B's remainder is vested despite the conditional language, suggesting that the preference for vesting is strong. See Simes & Smith on Future Interests §142. Does the majority view override an obvious attempt by a drafter to rebut the preference for vested interests? Is the classification of remainders for life as vested rather than contingent likely to make any practical or legal difference? What type of interest does C take in the above example?

4. *Remainders Subject to a Power.* Frequently someone will be given a power of some sort to divert the property to someone other than the taker of the remainder. In these cases, the remainder is subject to a condition, but the condition is not clearly stated as a condition precedent. The preference for vested estates can, therefore, be viewed as tipping the scale in favor of treating the condition as a condition subsequent.

Example 15.35: G transferred real property "to A for life, empowering A to sell, consume, or otherwise dispose of the property or any part thereof as may be necessary for A's support and maintenance; at A's death the property or such part thereof as may remain unexpended is to go to B." B's remainder is vested subject to divestment in whole or in part by the exercise of the power by A.

The same result would be reached in the case of a remainder interest in a trust where the settlor retained a power to revoke the trust or where the settlor conferred upon someone else (typically the trustee or the income beneficiary) a power to invade the corpus on behalf of the income beneficiary.

Example 15.36: G transferred real property "to A for life, remainder to such persons as A shall by will appoint, and in default of appointment, to B." B's remainder is vested subject to divestment by the exercise of the power by A. It could be argued in this case that the language expressly imposes a condition precedent (that A will not exercise the power) on B's remainder. Nevertheless, the idea that remainders subject to a power are vested subject to divestment is so well established that B's remainder is not regarded as contingent, even here.

5. *Remainder Subject to a Charge or a Lien.* Transferors occasionally appear to condition a remainder interest on the payment of a sum of money to a designated person. Most courts have held that the remainder is vested and that the taker is entitled to possession on the termination of the prior interest but subject to a charge or a lien on the property in the designated amount. See, e.g., Miller v. Miller, 247 N.W.2d 445 (Neb. 1976); Estate of Marra, N.Y.L.J., May 6, 1987, at 14 (Sur. Ct.). But see Allison v. Wilson, 411 S.E.2d 433 (S.C. 1991) (held that the testator intended that the requirement of a payment to the life tenant's spouse created a contingent remainder). This construction is consistent with the general preference for vested interests.

Example 15.37: G transferred real property "to A for life, remainder to B if B pays C $5,000 within one year of A's death." B had not paid C the $5,000 on the first anniversary of A's death. Under the majority view, if B does not pay the $5,000 to C within a reasonable time, C can enforce his charge or lien in that amount against the property. Had the court held B's remainder to have been contingent on B's having paid the money, B would not be entitled to the property and C would not receive the money.

Problems

Under the traditional and simplified systems of classification, classify the future interests in the following problems:

1. A was childless when G made the following two transfers:

(a) G transferred real property "to A for life, then to such of A's children as survive A, but if none survives A, to C."

(b) G transferred real property "to A for life, then to A's children, but if none of A's children survives A, to C."

2. After G's transfer took place, a child (X) was born to A. Does this event alter the classifications of the future interests in G's dispositions in Problem 1(a) and Problem 1(b)? If so, how?

3. After X was born, A had another child, Y. Years later, X died, survived by A and Y. Then A died, survived by Y. Who becomes entitled to the property at the time of A's death under Problem 1(a)? Problem 1(b)?

4. In the following two cases, B dies while A is still alive. Classify the future interests at the point of their creation and at the point of B's death.

(a) G transferred real property "to A for life, remainder to B, but if B fails to survive A, to C." (It is sometimes said that an executory interest cannot vest until it vests in possession. Is the statement correct?)

(b) G transferred real property "to A for life, remainder to B if B survives A, but if not, to C."

5. G transferred real property "to A for life, remainder to B if B lives to attain the age of 21." The rule of the destructibility of contingent remainders has been abolished by statute in the jurisdiction.[12] Classify the future interests at the point of their creation and at the following points:

(a) B reaches 21 while A is still alive.

(b) A dies; B is then alive but under 21.

---

12. The destructibility rule provides that a legal contingent remainder in real property is destroyed if it does not vest by the time the preceding freehold estate terminates.

PART B. SELECTED CONSEQUENCES OF CLASSIFICATION

The classification of possessory estates and future interests is less important than it once was. This is partly because some of the rules that turned on classification have been widely abolished—and partly because some of those rules applied only to *legal* future interests in *real property,* which are less often created today. Ironically, the reduced importance of classification has played a role in keeping the traditional, and complex, system of classification in force, by reducing the pressure to reexamine and reformulate it.

At the same time, the importance of certain aspects of classification has not disappeared altogether. This Part examines some of the rules that turn on classification.

Before we begin, however, it is worth mentioning two rules that we will *not* examine. At one time, two rules that turned on the difference between remainders and executory interests—the rule of the destructibility of contingent remainders[13] and the Rule in Shelley's Case[14]—were widely followed in the United States. These two rules are feudal relics, have no business being part of our law, and have been abolished in many states. We no longer spend time studying these two rules in this part of the course.

We now turn to consider the consequences of classification that still matter.

1. Alienability of Future Interests

Voluntary Alienability at Death. Future interests that, under the traditional system, would be classified as reversions, remainders, and executory interests are descendible and devisable. If the future interest is either contingent or vested subject to defeasance, it is, of course, descendible and devisable only if the owner's death does not cause the interest to be extinguished.

Example 15.38: G transferred real property "to A for life, remainder to B, but if B fails to survive A, to C." C died, then B, then A. C's executory interest is contingent on B not surviving A, but it is not contingent on C surviving A. Consequently, C's executory interest was not extinguished by C's death before A, and it is descendible and devisable. B's vested remainder subject to divestment was, however, extinguished by his death before A, and so B's remainder is neither descendible nor devisable.

---

13. See the preceding footnote.

14. The Rule in Shelley's Case provides that a remainder interest in real property which is either in favor of the life tenant's heirs or in favor of the life tenant's heirs of the body, and which is of the same quality as that of the life estate, is held by the life tenant.

Voluntary Alienability Inter Vivos. At common law, reversions and vested remainders (even if defeasible) are alienable inter vivos, but contingent remainders and executory interests are not. Contingent remainders were likened to an expectancy—not an interest, but the possibility of an interest arising in the future. When executory interests were later recognized, they were regarded as sufficiently analogous to contingent remainders to warrant the same treatment.

Despite the inalienability of contingent remainders and executory interests, the common law recognizes two ways by which such "inalienable" interests can *in effect* be transferred inter vivos, and equity recognizes still another. (It may be noted that these three methods of transferring inalienable future interests are also available for transferring nonexistent interests, such as expectancies.)

> *Contract to Convey.* A purported transfer, if for adequate consideration, is treated in equity as a contract to convey. The contract becomes specifically enforceable if and when all conditions precedent are satisfied so as to give the transferor an alienable interest.

> *Estoppel by Deed.* Even without adequate consideration—indeed, without any consideration at all—when a purported transfer is made by a deed that contains a covenant of warranty, the title inures at law by estoppel to the grantee if and when the conditions precedent are later satisfied.

> *Release.* At law, an inalienable future interest can be released to the holder of the interest that would be defeated by the satisfaction of the conditions precedent attached to the released interest. For example, in the case of a disposition "to A for life, remainder to B, but if B fails to survive A, to C," a release of C's executory interest to B would be enforceable at law. Releases do not have to be contained in a warranty deed, nor is consideration necessary. A writing under seal was, however, required at common law, but today where the significance of seals is abolished, an instrument capable of transferring an interest in land would probably be sufficient.

In modern times, contingent remainders and executory interests are no longer thought of as mere possibilities of receiving an interest in the future. Rather, they are thought of as property interests in which the right to possession is postponed and uncertain. See Restatement of Property §157 comment w. Even so, the states take various approaches to the inalienability rule.

In about seven states, the common-law rule of inalienability is still followed. In these states, the equitable contract to convey, the estoppel by deed, and the release methods of transferring inalienable interests are also recognized. Therefore, the inalienability rule followed in these states boils down to this: Purported transfers for inadequate consideration by quitclaim deed to someone other than a person in whose favor the interest could have been released are ineffective. See, e.g., Goodwine State Bank v. Mullins, 625 N.E.2d 1056 (Ill. App. Ct. 1993), appeal denied, 633 N.E.2d 4 (Ill. 1994).

By statute or case law in a few states, remainders and executory interests that are contingent as to person (interests in favor of unborn or unascertained persons) are still inalienable, but those that are contingent as to event are alienable.

Example 15.39: G transferred real property "to A for life, remainder to B if B survives A; if not, to B's heirs." B's remainder is contingent as to event, and under this approach it would be alienable. However, the remainder in favor of B's heirs is inalienable under this rule because it is contingent as to person.

In the vast majority of states, mostly by statute but also in some instances by judicial decision, all contingent future interests are alienable—even those that are contingent as to person. But how can a future interest contingent as to person be alienable? The answer is that these interests are alienable in theory rather than in practice. While the law typically authorizes a specially appointed fiduciary called a guardian ad litem to represent the interests of unborn or unascertained persons *in litigation*, it is uncommon to find that this fiduciary can be appointed to join in a *transfer* of the property interests on behalf of these persons.

Example 15.40: G transferred real property "to A for life, remainder to A's children." If A is childless, no one is authorized to transfer the remainder interest on behalf of A's unborn children. If A has living children, they can, of course, transfer their interests. A is alive, and, therefore, there is a possibility of additional children being born. No one is authorized to transfer the executory interests on their behalf. Thus, the most that A's living children can transfer is a remainder that is subject to open (partial divestment).

What, then, does it mean to say that in the vast majority of jurisdictions even future interests that are contingent as to person are alienable? The proposition refers to future interests that are in favor of unascertained persons, rather than to those that are in favor of unborn persons as in the example above.

Example 15.41: G transferred real property "to A for life, remainder to B's heirs." B is alive, but if B died now, B's sole heir would be B's daughter, C. In states in which future interests that are contingent as to person are said to be alienable, B's heir apparent (C) would be regarded as having a transferable interest, not merely an expectancy, in the subject matter of G's disposition. See Am. L. Prop. §4.67. If C should transfer her interest, her transferee would, however, receive an interest that is contingent on C's turning out to be B's real heir. See Restatement of Property §162 comment c. It is thus clear that no one, not even C, can transfer the remainder interest that follows A's life estate. The remainder interest, in other words, is still not truly alienable, C's ability to transfer her interest notwithstanding. (The notion that C has a property interest in the subject matter of the above disposition should not be confused with the notion that C—as B's heir apparent—has merely an expectancy in B's own property.)

As part of its modernization and simplification of the law of future interests, the Restatement 3d of Property provides in §25.2 comment f:

All future interests are alienable and are also devisable and inheritable if the owner's death does not terminate the interest, unless the transferor has imposed a valid restraint on alienation. The validity of restraints on the alienation of future interests held in trust is considered in the Restatement Third, Trusts ch. 12 (§§57 to 60). The validity of restraints on the alienation of legal future interests is considered in Restatement Second, Property (Donative Transfers) ch. 4 (§§4.1 to 4.3).

Involuntary Alienability—Creditors' Rights. Statutes in the various states provide creditors with the right to impound assets of their debtors prior to judgment and the right after judgment to subject assets to sale for its satisfaction. These statutes purport to specify the type of assets that are subject to these procedures, but the statutory language is usually so general that it is within the power of the courts to determine the extent to which the debtor's future interests can be affected.

The general principle followed by the courts under statutes is that if the future interest is voluntarily alienable, it is also subject to the claims of creditors. Indefeasibly vested remainders and reversions, since they are everywhere voluntarily alienable, are automatically available to creditors in the satisfaction of their claims. The same is true of remainders and reversions that are vested subject to defeasance.

Contingent remainders and executory interests, in states where they are not voluntarily alienable, are not subject to the claims of creditors. The fact that the equitable contract to convey, estoppel by deed, and release methods are available in these states does not change the result. Conversely, in states where contingent remainders and executory interests are voluntarily alienable—the vast majority of states—most courts routinely hold interests to be subject to creditors' claims. See, e.g., Everson v. Everson, 400 A.2d 887 (Pa. Super. Ct. 1979), aff'd as modified, 431 A.2d 889 (Pa. 1981). See also Restatement of Property §§166, 167.

When the owner of a future interest dies, the interest may be transmitted by will even if it was not alienable inter vivos. It may be argued that the decedent's creditors should be satisfied at this time from these assets, for otherwise they will be deprived of all chance of payment. There appears to be little law on the subject. Some statutes governing the payment of claims against decedents' estates resolve the problem by equating the creditors' rights to property that the decedent could have alienated inter vivos. Text writers and the Restatement of Property §169 have indicated the same result would probably be reached in situations in which the controlling statute is not so explicit.

In federal bankruptcy proceedings, the rights of creditors are far reaching. The bankrupt's estate includes "all legal or equitable interests" in property owned by the debtor as of the commencement of the case. 11 U.S.C. §541(a)(1). This language is broad enough to include all types of future interests, even those that are immune from the claims of creditors under state law.

EXTERNAL REFERENCES. Thomas P. Gallanis, The Future of Future Interests, 60 Wash. & Lee L. Rev. 513 (2003); Edward C. Halbach, Jr., Creditors' Rights in Future Interests, 43 Minn. L. Rev. 217 (1958).

2. Acceleration of Future Interests— Disclaimers and Other Causes

Primary Statutory Reference: *UPC §2-1106(b)(4)*

When property is given by way of a succession of present and future interests, a prior interest may fail in its inception for a variety of reasons. The question this Section addresses is what effect a failure of the prior interest has upon succeeding interests.

Restatement of Property

§233. Renunciation—Acceleration Prevented While Succeeding Interest Continues Subject to Unfulfilled Condition Precedent. When an attempted prior interest fails because it is renounced by the person to whom it is limited, a succeeding interest is not accelerated so long as a condition precedent to such succeeding interest continues unfulfilled.

Linkous v. Candler
508 S.E.2d 657 (Ga. 1998)

THOMPSON, J. Does the language of the trust agreement in this case indicate an intent to prohibit acceleration of the trust? Because such an intent need not be express, but can be implied from the four corners of the agreement, Wetherbee v. First State Bank & Trust Co., 266 Ga. 364, 365, 466 S.E.2d 835 (1996), we hold that the trust agreement does indeed prohibit acceleration, and that the superior court erred in ruling otherwise.

On June 3, 1961, while in the midst of a pending divorce, C. Howard Candler, Jr. and Ruth O. Candler created an irrevocable trust in full settlement of Howard Candler's support obligations to Ruth Candler. Trust Company of Georgia (now SunTrust Bank) was named as trustee. The trust provided that Ruth Candler was to have a life estate in the net income of the trust assets and that, upon Ruth Candler's death, the net income of the trust was to be distributed among the then living children of Howard and Ruth Candler. The trust also provided for a per stirpes distribution to the issue of any child of Howard and Ruth Candler who pre-deceased Ruth Candler. Upon the death of the "last survivor" of Howard and Ruth Candler's children, the trust was to be divided equally among the "then living" grandchildren of Howard and Ruth Candler with the issue of any then deceased grandchild taking per stirpes its deceased parent's share.

At the time the trust was created, Howard and Ruth Candler had four living children: C.H. Candler III; Samuel O. Candler; Ruth C. Lovett; and Flora G. Candler Fuller. Howard Candler died in 1988, and Ruth Candler died on September 2, 1996. Ruth Candler was survived by three of her children: C.H. Candler III; Samuel O. Candler; and Flora G. Candler Fuller. (Ruth C. Lovett died before either one of her parents in 1964, leaving three children.)

On March 4, 1997 the surviving children of Howard and Ruth Candler filed a petition requesting the superior court to construe the 1961 trust agreement and give direction to the trustee with regard to its obligations under the agreement. The petition named the trustee, all 13 of the grandchildren of Howard and Ruth Candler, and "all otherwise unrepresented descendants, born and unborn" as respondents. The court appointed William J. Linkous, Jr., as guardian ad litem, to protect the interests of the unrepresented descendants of Howard and Ruth Candler. Thereafter, petitioners filed a written instrument, pursuant to OCGA §53-2-115[15] seeking renunciation, release, and termination in full of their interests in the trust.

In a final order entered on September 17, 1997, the court ordered the trustee to distribute the trust to Howard and Ruth Candler's 13 grandchildren. The court reached that decision after concluding (1) that there was no language in the trust agreement which indicated an intent to prohibit acceleration; and (2) that petitioners' renunciation of their interests in the trust produced the same result as if they had predeceased Ruth Candler.

The guardian ad litem appeals. Relying upon Wetherbee v. First State Bank & Trust Co., supra, he asserts that the trust agreement indicates an intent on the part of Howard and Ruth Candler to prohibit acceleration of the trust. We agree.

The common law indicates that a remainder interest can be accelerated upon the renunciation of a preceding life interest, unless the terms and circumstances of the donative instrument manifest a contrary intent.[16] Restatement (First) of Property 659 §231 (1936). Jurisdictions have differed on what constitutes a "contrary intent." Therefore, the question must be whether, under Georgia law, the trust at issue manifests a contrary intent with respect to acceleration of the remainder interests.

In *Wetherbee*, Mr. Wetherbee created a trust for the maintenance and support of his wife for life. Upon his wife's death, a specified percentage of the trust was to be placed into a trust for each of his then living sons for their support for life. Upon the termination of the trust created for each son, the remainder was to go to his surviving wife and descendants. After Mr. Wetherbee died, his sons renounced their interests

---

15. This former Code section is no longer effective as of January 1, 1998, but only to the extent that no vested rights are impaired.

16. This common law principle was codified at OCGA §53-2-115(c): "Unless the decedent... has otherwise indicated by [the terms of] his or her will, the interest renounced and any future interest which is to take effect... after the termination of the interest renounced shall pass as if the person renouncing had predeceased the decedent." [For the current version of this provision, see Ga. Code §53-1-20. Ed.]

in the trust. When Mrs. Wetherbee died, the remaindermen sought to accelerate their interests. The Court observed that "the principle of acceleration of remainders is limited to those cases wherein the testator has not 'otherwise indicated' a contrary intent." *Wetherbee*, supra at 365, 466 S.E.2d 835. The Court then found a contrary intent because the testator had provided that the holder of the future interest must survive the holder of the renounced interest. In so doing, the court stated that the indication of the testator's contrary intent need not be express, but may be implied from the provisions and language of the trust.

Wetherbee controls the outcome of this case. Just as the instrument in *Wetherbee* provided that the holder of the remainder (the wife and descendants) must survive the holder of the renounced life interest (the sons), so too the instrument in this case provides that the grandchildren must survive their parents in order to take their interests in the trust. Accordingly, just as the instrument in *Wetherbee* indicated an intent to prohibit acceleration, so too the instrument in this case must be viewed as indicating an intent to prohibit acceleration.

Although other jurisdictions might take an approach which differs from *Wetherbee*, see generally Anno., 7 A.L.R.4th 1084 (1981), it cannot be said that Georgia lies outside the mainstream in this regard. Many jurisdictions hold, as does Georgia, that a substitutionary gift in a will indicates a contrary intent on the part of the testator with respect to acceleration of the remainder interests. See, e.g., Trenton Banking Co. v. Hawley, 7 N.J.Super. 301, 70 A.2d 896 (1950) (the gift of the remainder was made to a class that would have to stay open until the death of the life beneficiary); Bass v. Moore, 229 N.C. 211, 49 S.E.2d 391 (1948) (the remaindermen's right of enjoyment was contingent upon whether they survived the life beneficiary); Compton v. Rixey's Ex'rs., 124 Va. 548, 98 S.E. 651 (1919) (acceleration of remainder would be contrary to intent of testator); and Cool v. Cool, 54 Ind. 225 (1876) (no acceleration of the remainder when widow holder of life estate elected to take against the will). This rationale is logical, for if a class of remaindermen cannot be ascertained until the death of the life beneficiary, then acceleration must not have been contemplated by the testator.

The class of remaindermen in the Candler trust is subject to open by the birth of more grandchildren. In addition, it is subject to change by the death of a grandchild, entitling that grandchild's issue to take its share. This contingency does not expire until the death of the last of Howard and Ruth Candler's children. Therefore, the remaindermen cannot be ascertained until the last child of Howard and Ruth Candler has died. To hold otherwise would be contrary to the intent of the Candlers and would deprive potential class members of their share of the trust.

Judgment reversed.

Problems, Notes, and Questions

1. G died devising $100,000 in trust: "income to my daughter, A, for life,

remainder in corpus to such of A's children as survive A; if none, to my younger brother, B." The residue of G's estate was devised to G's husband, C. What should happen, at common law, to the $100,000 trust in the following alternative circumstances? See Restatement of Property, vol. 1, app. at 48-79.

(a) A predeceased G. G was survived by A's two children, X and Y.

(b) A survived G, but disclaimed her income interest. At G's death, A was married and 42 years old. A's two children, X and Y, were 17-year old twins who have just received letters of acceptance from a prestigious university where the costs of tuition and other charges amount to about $50,000 per year. Although A has not passed the menopause, she certifies that the last thing on her wish list is another child.

(c) In problem 1(b), would it make any difference if G's devise had taken the following form: "income to my daughter, A, for life, remainder in corpus to A's children, but if none of A's children survives A, to my younger brother, B"?

(d) Suppose G's devise had stated: "income to my daughter, A, for life, remainder in corpus to A's then-living children; if none, to my younger brother, B." Section 233 comment c of the Restatement of Property states:

> *Comment c. Construction problem as to existence of condition precedent.* The rule stated in [§233] applies only when the language of a limitation is construed to create a succeeding interest subject to a condition precedent which remains unfulfilled at the time when the creating conveyance becomes operative.... In resolving this preliminary problem of construction, the criterion is whether the terms and circumstances of the limitation manifest an intent to benefit persons living at the termination of the preceding interest or at the death of the person to whom such preceding interest was limited.

In Thomsen v. Thomsen, 166 P.2d 417 (Okla. 1946), the court said:

> The doctrine of acceleration is, according to the great weight of authority, a rule of interpretation and is to be applied so as to effect and not defeat the testator's intent.... [T]he doctrine... proceeds upon the supposition that although the ultimate devise is in terms not to take effect in possession until the death of the life tenant, yet in point of fact it is to be read as a limitation of the remainder to take effect in every event which removes the prior estate out of the way and is applied in promotion of the presumed intention of the testator, and not to defeat his intention.

(e) Assume the remainder, if stated as in Problem 1(c), can be accelerated because it is subject to a condition subsequent. Would B's interest and the interests of A's unborn and unadopted children somehow remain subject to open and to the condition subsequent of surviving their mother, A? See Restatement of Property §231 comments h & i (declaring that the accelerated remainder becomes indefeasible).

2. *Disclaimer Statutes.* Disclaimers, and their consequences on succeeding interests, are now widely regulated by statute. See Chapter 2. If the *Linkous* case had been governed by UPC §2-1106(b)(4), would there have been a different outcome? How would UPC §2-1106(b)(4) change your answers to Problem 1?

3. *Pate v. Ford.* In Pate v. Ford, 376 S.E.2d 775 (S.C. 1989), William W. Pate, Sr., died in 1979, leaving an estate valued at approximately $1.6 million. Aletha F. Pate, William's wife, died in 1983, leaving an estate valued at approximately $6.78 million. William's will devised the residue of his estate in trust, with the income going to Aletha for life. At her death, the corpus was to be divided into three equal shares. Aletha's will provided that, if William did not survive her, her estate shall also be divided into three equal shares, to be disposed of under identical terms as those contained in William's will.

Two of the three one-third shares were to continue in trust, one to pay the income to the couple's son, Billy, for life, and the other to pay the income to the couple's other son, Wallace, for life. The provisions for distribution of the corpus were identical:

> On Billy's death, [his one-third] trust shall terminate and ... my Trustee shall distribute the assets of the trust in equal shares per stirpes to my natural born grandchildren.
>
> On Wallace's death, [his one-third] trust shall terminate and ... my Trustee shall distribute the assets of the trust in equal shares per stirpes to my natural born grandchildren.

Wallace has five children. Billy has been thrice married, but has never had any children; Billy's wife is now 32 years old.

Wallace filed a disclaimer of his income interest in his one-third share. Under UPC §2-1106(b)(4), does the remainder interest following Wallace's income interest accelerate?

———

EXTERNAL REFERENCES. Thomas P. Gallanis, The Future of Future Interests, 60 Wash. & Lee L. Rev. 513 (2003); Patricia J. Roberts, The Acceleration of Remainders—Manipulating the Identity of the Remaindermen, 42 S.C. L. Rev. 295 (1991).

Sellick v. Sellick
173 N.W. 609 (Mich. 1919)

FELLOWS, J. This case involves the construction of the will of William J. Sellick, late of Paw Paw, Van Buren county, and the effect as between certain of the legatees of the election of the widow to take [a forced share] under the statute. Mr. Sellick left real estate inventoried at $8,500 and personal property inventoried at upwards of $176,000. He left a widow, Caroline Sellick, and one son, William R. Sellick, the plaintiff, now grown to manhood, who was the child of a former wife. He also left collateral kindred, including the defendants Arthur F. Sellick, a nephew, and Gertrude Sellick, a niece. To his collateral kindred other than defendants he gave varying sums aggregating $15,000. By the second clause of his will he gave to each of the defendants $5,000. The first clause of his will is as follows:

> I give, devise and bequeath to my wife, Caroline Sellick, twenty-five thousand dollars ($25,000), to be used and enjoyed by her during her life and at her death to be equally divided between my nephew, Arthur F. Sellick, and my niece, Gertrude Sellick.

The residue of his estate he gave to his son, the plaintiff. The widow elected to take [a forced share] under the statute. The trial judge construed the first clause of the will, when taken in connection with the second clause, which gave each defendant $5,000, and the residuary clause, as giving the widow absolutely $25,000, and accordingly held that the defendants took nothing under such clause. This rendered unnecessary the determination of the other questions involved. From a decree in accordance with these views the defendants appeal, and it is here urged by their counsel that the first clause of the will gave the widow a life estate, with remainder over to them; that by the election of the widow to take under the statute her life estate is at an end, and that, applying the doctrine of acceleration of remainders, they are now entitled to said sum of $25,000. On the other hand, it is insisted by counsel for the appellee that...we should not apply the doctrine of acceleration of remainders, but that such life estate, given to the widow by the will, should be sequestered to reimburse the plaintiff in part for the depletion of his bequest occasioned by the payment out of it of the sums necessary to make up the widow's statutory share. In short, that he is known in the law as a disappointed legatee, and that the doctrine of acceleration of remainders should not be adopted at the expense of disappointed legatees....

It must be conceded at the outset that the decisions of the court of last resort of the state of Pennsylvania sustain the contention of defendants' counsel unequivocally. Is the rule laid down by the Pennsylvania court supported by the weight of authority and by equitable principles? Should the doctrine of acceleration of remainders be applied where by its application the remainderman gets more than the will gave to him and legatees either specific or residuary get less? To these questions we shall now direct our attention.

This court has recognized the doctrine of acceleration of remainders upon the termination of the life estate of the widow by her election to take under the statute. Schulz's Estate, 113 Mich. 592, 71 N. W. 1079. But that was a case where none of the legatees were in any way harmed by the application of the doctrine. By the election of the widow to take under the statute their bequests were proportionately diminished, and by the acceleration of their remainders they were proportionately reimbursed....

In the case of Jones v. Knappen, 63 Vt. 391 (22 Atl. 630, 14 L. R. a. 293), the court had before it a case quite similar to the instant case. We quote from the syllabus:

> The election of the widow, who is made life tenant of her husband's property, to take against his will does not accelerate the time for distribution so that it may be made during her lifetime; where the remainder is to be divided between specific and residuary devisees and the result of her election would work inequity by diminishing the residuary, and leaving the specific devisees to be paid in full.

In this case the court quotes the following from Woerner on Administration, 119:

> The rejection by the widow of the provisions made for her by will, generally results in the diminution or contravention of devises and legacies to other parties. The rule in such case is that the devise or legacy which the widow rejects is to be applied in compensation of those whom her election disappoints

—and then says:

> The controlling, and, we think, the more reasonable principle announced in most of these cases is the one expressed by Woerner, supra, viz. to use the renounced devises and legacies given by the will to the widow to compensate, as far as may be, the devises and legacies diminished by such renunciation. When the remaindermen are affected pro rata by such renunciation, acceleration of the enjoyment of their devises or legacies, diminished proportionally, will equitably compensate them, so far as possible for such diminution. But in this case acceleration of enjoyment would increase the specific pecuniary legacies, to the detriment of the residuary legatees, whose shares only are diminished by the renunciation. Applying the principle stated, the life use of the property given by the will to the widow, and renounced by her, should be used to compensate the residuary legatees, the next of kin of the testator and of his wife....

We are persuaded that under the great weight of authority the contention of plaintiff's counsel in this regard must prevail. While the doctrine of acceleration of the time of taking effect of the remainder upon the termination of the life estate by act other than the death of the life tenant (i. e., by the election of the widow to take under the statute) must be recognized and applied in proper cases, such doctrine should not be applied where by the election a portion only of the legacies are diminished in order to make up the amount required by the statute to satisfy the widow's statutory rights. And that this should be true whether the legacy diminished be a specific or a residuary one. Under such circumstances the disappointed legatee may in a court of equity compel the sequestration of the legacy to the refractory legatee for the purpose of diminishing the amount of his disappointment.

Manifestly this is in consonance with equitable principles. In the instant case the residuary fund given to the plaintiff has been diminished by many thousand dollars in order to discharge the claim of the widow resulting from her election. To adopt defendants' claim would give to them the $25,000 many years before the time fixed by the testator for its payment. They would not only receive the amount given them by the will, but they would also receive the widow's life estate renounced by her to the disadvantage of the plaintiff. Equitable principles do not require that this should be done.

We are asked to fix the present worth of the widow's life use of the $25,000 with a view of finally closing the estate and disposing of all matters at once. The parties interested are all of age, and may make such adjustment as they may desire, but we do not feel empowered to fix the present worth of the widow's use and direct its present payment. We see no occasion, however, to longer hold the estate open. A trustee may be appointed to handle this fund of $25,000. He shall annually pay the income thereon to the plaintiff during the life of the widow, and upon her death pay the corpus to defendants in equal shares.

It follows that the decree must be reversed, and one here entered in conformity with this opinion. The defendants will recover costs of this court. Neither party will recover costs of the circuit court.

———

EXTERNAL REFERENCE. Restatement of Property §§234-35.

3. *Failure of a Future Interest—Effect*

A future interest can fail for a variety of reasons. The beneficiary might predecease the testator or predecease a subsequent time to which survival is required by the terms of the disposition; the future interest might be disclaimed; it might violate the Rule Against Perpetuities; and so on.

In general, a future interest that fails, regardless of the reason, is treated as if it had not been created. A particular problem exists, however, if the failed future interest is an executory interest.

Proprietors of the Church in Brattle Square v. Grant
69 Mass. (3 Gray) 142 (1855)
[Lydia Hancock, John Hancock's aunt, died in 1777, leaving a will that provided:

I give and bequeath unto...the Church of Christ in Brattle Street in Boston ... all that brick dwelling-house and land situated in Queen Street ... to hold the same ... upon [the] express condition and limitation ... that the minister or eldest minister of said church shall constantly reside and dwell in said house, during such time as he is minister of said church; and in case the same is not improved for this use only, I then declare this bequest to be void and of no force, and order that said house and land then [go] to my nephew, John Hancock, Esquire, and to his heirs forever.

The residue of her estate was also devised to John Hancock, who survived her, but died fifteen years later, in 1793.

Some seventy-five or so years after Lydia Hancock's death, the Proprietors of the Church brought a bill in equity, alleging that the conditions had been continuously satisfied and that a sale of the estate had now become necessary to carry out the intent of the devise.

The court held that Lydia Hancock's will created a fee simple subject to an executory limitation in favor of the deacons of the Church; and an executory interest (executory devise) in favor of John Hancock and his heirs. The court further held that John Hancock's executory interest violated the Rule Against Perpetuities (an English invention) and was invalid. (Obviously, the Declaration of Independence had not freed the new American state of all English influence!)

The final question was how the invalidity of John Hancock's executory interest affected the church's fee simple interest.]

BIGELOW, J.... Upon this point we understand the rule to be, that if a limitation over is void by reason of its remoteness, it places all prior gifts in the same situation as if the devise over had been wholly omitted. Therefore a gift of the fee or the entire interest, subject to an executory limitation which is too remote, takes effect as if it had been originally limited free from any divesting gift. The general principle applicable to such cases is, that when a subsequent condition or limitation is void by reason of its being impossible, repugnant or contrary to law, the estate becomes vested in the first taker, discharged of the condition or limitation over, according to the terms in which it was granted or devised; if for life, then it takes effect as a life estate; if in fee, then as a fee simple absolute. The reason on which this rule is said to rest is, that when a party has granted or devised an estate, he shall not be allowed to fetter or defeat it, by annexing thereto impossible, illegal or repugnant conditions or limitations.

Such indeed is the necessary result which follows from the manner in which executory devises came into being and were engrafted on the stock of the common law. Originally,... no estate could be limited over after a limitation in fee simple, and in such case the estate became absolute in the first taker. This rule was afterwards relaxed in cases of devises, for the purpose of effectuating the intent of testators, so far as to render such gifts valid by way of executory devise, when confined within the limits prescribed to guard against perpetuities.

The result, therefore, to which we have arrived on the whole case is, that the gift over to John Hancock is an executory devise, void for remoteness; and that the estate, upon breach of the prescribed condition, would not pass to John Hancock and his heirs, by virtue of the residuary clause, nor would it vest in the heirs at law of the testatrix. But being an estate in fee in the deacons and their successors, and the gift over being void, as contrary to the policy of the law, by reason of violating the rule against perpetuities, the title became absolute, as a vested remainder in fee, after the decease of the mother of the testatrix, in the deacons and their successors, and they hold it in fee simple, free from the divesting limitation.

Notes

1. *Possibility of Reverter.* In First Universalist Society v. Boland, 29 N.E. 524 (Mass. 1892), Clark conveyed real property by deed to the First Universalist Society as follows:

> so long as said real estate shall by said society or its assigns be devoted to the uses, interests, and support of [specified] doctrines of the Christian religion; and when said real estate shall by said society or its assigns be diverted from the uses, interests and support aforesaid to any other interests, uses, or purposes than as aforesaid, then the title of said society or its assigns in the same shall forever cease, and be forever vested in the following named persons....

The court held that Clark's conveyance created a fee simple determinable in the Society, and an executory interest in the persons named to take in the case of a diversion from the specified uses. The court further held that the executory interest violated the Rule Against Perpetuities and was invalid.

The court then turned to the question of the effect of that invalidity on the state of the title:

> Since the estate of the plaintiff may determine, and since there is no valid limitation over, it follows that there is a possibility of reverter in the original grantor, Clark. This is similar to, though not quite identical with, the possibility of reverter which remains in the grantor of land upon a condition subsequent. The exact nature and incidents of this right need not now be discussed, but it represents whatever is not conveyed by the deed, and it is the possibility that the land may revert to the grantor or his heirs when the granted estate determines. Clark's possibility of reverter is not invalid for remoteness. It has been expressly held by this court that such possibility of reverter...is not within the rule against perpetuities. Tobey v. Moore, 130 Mass. 448; French v. Old South Soc., 166 Mass. 479. If there is any distinction in this respect between such possibility of reverter and that which arises upon the determination of a qualified fee, it would seem to be in favor of the latter: but they should be governed by the same rule. If one is not held void for remoteness, the other should not be. The very many cases cited in Gray, Prop. §§305-312, show conclusively that the general understanding of courts and of the profession in America has been that the rule as to remoteness does not apply, though the learned author thinks this view erroneous in principle.... [T]he plaintiff's title must be deemed imperfect, and the entry must be, bill dismissed.

2. *State of the Authorities.* The distinction drawn by the *Grant* and *Boland* decisions has been generally followed. For more modern cases following *Grant*, see Betts v. Snyder, 19 A.2d 82 (Pa. 1941); Standard Knitting Mills, Inc. v. Allen, 424 S.W.2d 796 (Tenn. 1967). For a case in accord with *Boland*, see City of Klamath Falls v. Bell, 490 P.2d 515 (Or. Ct. App. 1971). See William H. Agnor, A Tale of Two Cases, 17 Vand. L. Rev. 1427 (1964).

The Restatement 2d of Property §1.5 comments b & c assert a different position, by suggesting that it might be appropriate to hold that the invalidity of an executory interest following a fee simple determinable as well as a fee simple subject to an executory limitation renders the fee interest absolute. This position was previously urged in Lawrence W. Waggoner, Reformulating the Structure of Estates: A Proposal for Legislative Action, 85 Harv. L. Rev. 729, 737-38, 757 (1972). The Restatement 3d of Property §24.3 facilitates this result by eliminating the subcategories within the estate in fee simple defeasible.

4. The Rule Against Perpetuities as a Consequence of Classification

Before going on to Chapter 16 on construction, we should like to note one final consequence of classification: the Rule Against Perpetuities. Classification is crucial in determining whether an interest is subject to the common-law Rule Against Perpetuities and to many statutory modifications of the Rule. As conventionally understood, the Rule applies to contingent future interests, but not to future interests that are vested.

Once the Rule is determined to be applicable, the next inquiry is whether the particular contingent future interest violates the Rule. This question is considered in Chapter 17.

Chapter 16

Construction

No greater challenge exists in estate planning practice than expressing your client's intent without ambiguity. An ability to write clearly is not the only skill necessary. Another is the ability to anticipate, and hence clearly to provide for, the entire range of possible future events that can affect a disposition. Both of these skills can be acquired.

A first step in learning to draft without ambiguity is to examine mistakes that have been made in the past. Too often, the cases in this Chapter bring into question the meaning of documents drafted by your predecessors at the bar. We have already seen evidence of this problem in Chapter 13. Whether the document was drafted by a lawyer or not, however, nearly every construction case that we have studied and that we are about to study represents someone's drafting failure.

Drafting failures tend to recur in patterns. With respect to future interests, the primary subject of this Chapter, the same mistakes are made over and over again. Once you know what they are, you will find that drafting to avoid these mistakes is surprisingly easy.

PART A. EXPRESS AND IMPLIED CONDITIONS OF SURVIVAL

Primary Statutory References: *UPC §§2-701, 2-707*

One of the recurring problems in future interests law concerns survival: Is a future interest extinguished (terminated) if its holder dies after the creation of the interest but before the time of possession or enjoyment or before reaching a specified age? This is a question of construction, of discerning the transferor's intent—not a question of lapse or of classification.

Lapse Distinguished. As we learned in Chapter 6, the rule of lapse requires a devisee under a *will* to survive the *testator*. The rule of lapse is based on the proposition that a property interest cannot be *transferred* to a deceased person. Thus, a devise to a person who predeceases the testator lapses, notwithstanding any contrary intent on the testator's part. The rule of lapse is mandatory, not constructional. See Restatement 3d of Property §15.2.

The rule of lapse, however, does not require a beneficiary of a future interest to be alive at the distribution date—the time when a future interest becomes possessory. The distribution date arises *after*, sometimes long after, the time when the future interest was *transferred* to its recipient. To illustrate, take the simple case of "to A for life, remainder to B." Suppose that this disposition was created in G's will. The common-law rule of lapse requires both A and B to be alive when G dies because that is the time when both A and B receive their interests. Once the hurdle of surviving G is satisfied, there is no further requirement implicit in the common law necessitating B's survival of A. Consequently, an interest is not subject to a condition of survival merely because it is a *future* interest. If a condition of survival exists, it derives from a finding of the transferor's intention on the point. The survival question is therefore a question of construction, distinguishable from the rule of lapse.

1. Basic Common-Law Rule: Conditions of Survival Not Implied

Before proceeding to a discussion of the basic constructional question of survival, we digress briefly to set the matter of survival into perspective. Future interests are normally granted to persons in one or more generations *younger* than that of the income beneficiary. If the income interest is granted to the grantor's surviving spouse, the remainder interest is likely to be granted to the couple's children or descendants; if the income interest is granted to a child of the grantor, the remainder interest is likely to be granted to the child's children or descendants. It is unusual, in other words, to grant an income interest to the grantor's grandchild and follow it with a remainder interest to the grantor's parents.

Consequently, when the beneficiary of a future interest predeceases the time of possession or enjoyment, it is an unusual event, an event typically caused by the beneficiary's *premature* death. When the unusual happens, however, and a beneficiary dies before the distribution date, the first place to look to see if that event was anticipated and provided for is in the governing instrument. If the governing instrument *expressly* imposes a condition of survival—as, for example, in the disposition "to A for life, remainder to B *if B survives A*"— then survival, of course, is required. Conversely, if the governing instrument *expressly* states that no condition of survival is imposed—as, for example, in the disposition "to A for life, remainder to B *whether or not B survives A*"—then B need not survive A.

What happens if the governing instrument *expresses* neither intention—as, for example, in the disposition "to A for life, remainder to B"?

> *The basic rule of construction at common law is that a condition of survival is not implied.*

Several rationales are offered in support of this rule and in favor of the product of this rule—transmissible future interests. The rule, it is said, (1) furthers the constructional preference for complete dispositions of property, (2) furthers the constructional preference for equality of distribution among the different lines of descent, and (3) is supported by the constructional preferences for vested over contingent interests, for vesting at the earliest possible time, and for indefeasible vesting at the earliest possible time. See Restatement of Property §243 comments.

While it may be true that the constructional preferences set forth in (3) played an important role in fashioning the rule against implied conditions of survival, one should not equate the two questions—classification and construction.

> *Whether a future interest is subject to a requirement of survival is a question of construction. Whether a future interest is vested or contingent is a question of classification.*

A vested future interest can be subject to a requirement of survival (as is B's interest in "to A for life, remainder to B, but if B fails to survive A, to C"). A contingent future interest can be subject to conditions unrelated to survival (as is C's interest in "to A for life, remainder to B, but if B fails to survive A, to C").

The basic rule of construction against implying conditions of survival applies to individual and class gifts.

Example 16.1: G's will devised real property "to A for life, remainder to B." Both A and B survived G. Later, B predeceased A.

B's property interest is not defeated by his death before A. Upon B's death, his remainder interest passes to his successors in interest. There is no implicit condition that B survive A, even though B's remainder is a future interest.

Example 16.2: G's will devised real property "to A for life, remainder in equal shares to B and C." A, B, and C survived G.

The rule of construction against implying conditions of survival applies to gifts to more than one individual. Consequently, if either B or C (or both) predeceases A, the predeceased taker's half passes at death through his or her estate to his or her successors in interest.

Example 16.3: G's will devised real property "to A for life, remainder to A's children." At G's death, A and A's daughter, X, were living. During A's lifetime, a son, Y, was born to A. Both X and Y predeceased A. The rule of construction against implying conditions of survival applies to single-generation class gifts. Restatement 3d of Property §§15.4, 26.3. Consequently, X's interest passed on her death to her successors in interest, and Y's interest passed on his death to his successors in interest.

EXTERNAL REFERENCES. John L. Garvey, Drafting Wills and Trusts: Anticipating the Birth and Death of Possible Beneficiaries, 71 Or. L. Rev. 47 (1992); Edward C. Halbach, Jr. & Lawrence W. Waggoner, The UPC's New Survivorship and Antilapse Provisions, 55 Alb. L. Rev. 1091 (1992); Edward C. Halbach, Jr., Issues About Issue: Some Recurrent Class Gift Problems, 48 Mo. L. Rev. 333, 361-70 (1983); Edward C. Halbach, Jr., Future Interests: Express and Implied Conditions of Survival (pts. 1 & 2), 49 Calif. L. Rev. 297, 431 (1961).

The Discredited (?) Divide-and-Pay-Over Rule. Once upon a time, some courts recognized a rule called the divide-and-pay-over rule. The rule was this: If the only language of a disposition directs that property be divided and paid over at a future time, survival of that time is required. A trust disposition triggering this rule would be, income "to A for life, then on A's death the trustee is to divide the corpus and pay it over to A's children."

The Restatement of Property rejects this rule:

> *§260. Direction to Divide and Pay Over at a Future Date.* In a limitation purporting to create a remainder or an executory interest, the fact that the only words of gift to the intended taker thereof consist of a direction to divide and pay over, or to convert, divide and pay over, at the end of the created prior interests or at some other future date is not a material factor in determining the existence of a requirement of survival to the date of distribution.

Today, in most states, the divide-and-pay-over rule has either been overtly repudiated or appears to have fallen into disuse or never to have been followed. See Restatement 3d of Property §26.3 comment i; Restatement of Property §260; Am. L. Prop. §21.21. Yet, the rule has not been eradicated entirely.[1] The Supreme Court of Illinois found it applicable as a "rule... of construction to aid courts in determining whether a gift to a class is a vested or contingent remainder." The court said: "Early vesting frequently frustrates intentions by casting property to strangers.... [E]arly vesting of remainders should no longer be followed in this State without question." Harris Trust & Savings Bank v. Beach, 513 N.E.2d 833, 838-39, 841 (Ill. 1987). The Illinois Supreme Court's opinion did not mention the rejection of the rule by the Restatement, cases in other jurisdictions, or scholarly commentary about the rule. The court did, however, pay attention to scholarly commentary demonstrating that the rule of early vesting frequently frustrates the donor's intention. See, e.g., Daniel M. Schuyler, Drafting, Tax, and Other Consequences of the Rule of Early Vesting, 46 Ill. L. Rev. 407, 437 (1951) ("Sometimes the rule of early vesting has the effect of defeating what any sensible person would assume to be the intention of a testator."); Edward H. Rabin, The Law Favors the Vesting of Estates, Why?, 65 Colum. L. Rev. 467, 479 (1965) ("[Passing] property to a dead person's estate... is undesirable because it raises the possibility that persons whom the testator had no intention of benefitting will become his *de facto* beneficiaries.").

Conditions Unrelated to Survival. We have seen that, at common law, a future interest to which no express conditions are attached is not subject to an implied condition of survival. But what if the future interest is subject to one or more *express*

---

1. In Will of Corwith, 622 N.Y.S.2d 424 (Sur. Ct. 1995), one of the parties to the proceeding for construction of a testamentary trust urged the court to apply the divide-and-pay-over rule. The court recognized that the rule had often been criticized, but refused to consider its continuing viability because it held that the future interest was contingent on survival of the life tenant on other grounds.

conditions *unrelated* to survival? Do these express conditions automatically subject the future interest to an *implied* condition of survival? That is the question posed in the cases below.

Bomberger's Estate
32 A.2d 729 (Pa. 1943)

[The testator's will devised $50,000 in trust, income to his niece, Mrs. Lilly Aughinbaugh, for life, corpus on Lilly's death to Lilly's children. The will continued:

> Should [niece Lilly]... die without leaving a child or children, I order and direct that the bequest shall be equally divided among my nephews and nieces..., then living, the child or children of nieces who may be deceased to have the share their mother would have been entitled to if living.

Lilly died childless. All of the testator's nieces and nephews predeceased Lilly. Charles, one of the nephews, had two children, both of whom survived Lilly. The other nephews died childless. Ada, one of the nieces, had eight children: seven of them survived Lilly, but one, John, died during Ada's lifetime. Annie, the other niece, had one child, Rachel, who survived Annie but predeceased Lilly.]

STEARNE, J.... The language which testator used did not impose the same contingency of survivorship upon the substitutionary gift to child or children of deceased nieces that it did upon the nephews and nieces. For a nephew or niece to take required that he or she be alive when Mrs. Aughinbaugh died without issue. However, if a niece left child or children, their interest was vested. They took in precisely the same manner as if their mother, a niece, had been living at the date of the death of Mrs. Aughinbaugh. There is nothing in the substitutionary gift which expressly states that children of deceased nieces must survive Mrs. Aughinbaugh.... The condition of survival to a fixed time is never implied. Such condition must appear plainly, manifestly and indisputably.

"When a condition of survival to the time of distribution has been annexed to the gifts to the first takers, but not to the gifts to the substituted beneficiaries, the condition is not to be implied with respect to the latter": President Judge Van Dusen Carpenter's Estate, 42 Pa. Dist. & Co. R. 367-369....

Costs to be paid from the fund.

Lawson v. Lawson
148 S.E.2d 546 (N.C. 1966)

[The testator's will devised land to his daughter Opal Lawson Long for her life, and at her death "to her children, if any, in fee simple; if none, to [Opal's] whole brothers and sisters... in fee simple." Fifteen years after the testator's death, Opal died without children. Four of Opal's six whole brothers and sisters survived Opal.

Two of Opal's whole brothers survived the testator but predeceased Opal; each left descendants surviving Opal.]

SHARP, J.... Respondents contend that at the death of the testator, J. Rad Lawson, the six whole brothers and sisters of the life tenant, all of whom were then living, took a vested remainder in the land, and that they, as children of the two whole brothers who predeceased Opal Lawson Long, inherited their interest. The law, however, is otherwise.

This case presents a typical example of a contingent remainder.

> A devises to B for life, remainder to his children but if he dies without leaving children remainder over, both the remainders are contingent; but if B afterwards marries and has a child, the remainder becomes vested in that child, subject to open and let in unborn children, and the remainders over are gone forever. The remainder becomes a vested remainder in fee in the child as soon as the child is born, and does not wait for the parent's death, and if the child dies in the lifetime of the parent, the vested estate in remainder descends to his heirs. 4 Kent's Commentaries, p. 284 quoted in Blanchard v. Ward, 244 N.C. 142, 146, 92 S.E.2d 776, 779.

In Watson v. Smith, 110 N.C. 6, 14 S.E. 649, testator devised land to J for life, and at J's death to such child or children of his that might then be living, but should he die without issue, then to G, W, H, and O in fee. The Court held that the limitation to G, W, H, and O, was a contingent remainder. "Alternative remainders limited upon a single precedent estate are always contingent. Such remainders are created by a limitation to one for life, with remainder in fee to his children, issue, or heirs, and, in default of such children, issue, or heirs, to another or others...." 33 Am. Jur., Life Estates, Remainders, etc. §148 (1941)....

Clearly the interests of the whole brothers and sisters was [sic] contingent and could not vest before the death of the life tenant, for not until then could it be determined that she would leave no issue surviving. "Where those who are to take in remainder cannot be determined until the happening of a stated event, the remainder is contingent. Only those who can answer the roll immediately upon the happening of the event acquire any estate in the properties granted." Strickland v. Jackson, 259 N.C. 81, 84, 130 S.E.2d 22, 25. Respondents' parents, having predeceased the life tenant, could not answer the roll call at her death.

The judgment of the court below is Affirmed.

Notes and Questions

1. *State of the Authorities.* The decision in *Bomberger* reflects the great majority view on the question posed by *Bomberger* and *Lawson*, and the view enunciated in Restatement of Property §261; Restatement 3d of Property §15.4 comment e, illustration 2, and §26.3 comment f. See, e.g., Estate of Ferry, 361 P.2d 900 (Cal. 1961); Rosenthal v. First Nat'l Bank, 239 N.E.2d 826 (Ill. 1968); Bogart's Will, 308 N.Y.S.2d 594 (Sur. Ct. 1970); Peters v. Allison, 814 N.E.2d 568 (Ohio Ct. App.

2004); Am. L. Prop. § 21.25; Simes & Smith on Future Interests §594.

A few courts have adopted the *Lawson* analysis and have imposed a condition of survival on interests that were subject to conditions unrelated to survival. See, e.g., Rushing v. Mann, 910 S.W.2d 672 (Ark. 1995); Jones v. Holland, 77 S.E.2d 202 (S.C. 1953); see also Schau v. Cecil, 136 N.W.2d 515 (Iowa 1965), superseded by statute as stated in Davies v. Radford, 433 N.W.2d 704 (Iowa 1988). *Schau* and *Davies,* along with Estate of Ruhland, 452 N.W.2d 417 (Iowa 1990), which raised similar issues, are explained and critiqued in N. William Hines, Implied Conditions of Personal Survivorship in Iowa Future Interests Law, 75 Iowa L. Rev. 941 (1990).

Professor Patricia J. Roberts, in Class Gifts in North Carolina—When Do We "Call the Roll"?, 21 Wake Forest L. Rev. 1 (1985), noted that the *Lawson* decision seems to have been implicitly overruled by White v. Alexander, 224 S.E.2d 617 (N.C. 1976). In *White*, G devised property to S for life, "and if he shall die without heirs of his body... to my heirs." S died without heirs of his body, causing the gift to G's heirs to take effect. The class of G's heirs was determined at G's death. Although some of the members of that class predeceased S, the Supreme Court of North Carolina refused to imply a requirement of survival as to their interests. Unfortunately, *White* did not expressly overrule *Lawson*. Indeed, the opinion in *White* did not even mention *Lawson*!

2. *Classification and Construction.* Did the court in *Lawson* confuse classification and construction?

———

Restricted and Unrestricted Conditions of Survival. Restricted conditions of survival are said to flow from language phrased in so-called *supplanting* form.

Example 16.4: "To A for life, then to B, but if B predeceases A leaving issue, then to such issue." B died without issue before A's death. B's interest is not extinguished. See, e.g., *Krooss*, below; Restatement 3d of Property §26.5 illustration 2.

Unrestricted conditions of survival are said to flow from language phrased in *alternative* form.

Example 16.5: "To A for life, then to B or B's issue." B died without issue before A's death. B's interest is extinguished. See, e.g., *Robertson*, below; Restatement 3d of Property §26.5 illustration 1.

Note that these are rules of construction, also known as default rules. They apply "[u]nless the language or circumstances establish that the transferor had a different intention." Restatement 3d of Property §26.5.

Example 16.6: "To A for life, then to A's brothers and sisters, but if a brother or sister fails to survive A leaving issue, to such issue." Several of A's brothers and sisters survived A, but one brother, B, died without issue before A's death. B's interest is extinguished and passes to the brothers and sisters who survived A. The gift is in the form of a class gift ("to A's brothers and sisters") and, together with the provision for substitution of issue, the use of class-gift language establishes that the transferor intended B's interest to pass to the surviving brothers and sisters on these facts. See Restatement 3d of Property §26.5 illustration 3.

What do you think of the distinction between supplanting and alternative language? Is it sensible? Do the two different expressions indicate that the transferors intended the different results accorded by the law?

In re Krooss
99 N.E.2d 222, 47 A.L.R.2d 894 (N.Y. 1951)

FULD, J. Herman Krooss died in 1932. He was survived by his wife Eliese and his two children, a son, John Krooss, and a married daughter, Florence Maue. By his will, he gave his residuary estate, real and personal, to his wife, "to have and to hold the same for and during the term of her natural life," with the power to use any part of it for her support and maintenance that she deemed necessary; no trust was created. The will further provided:

> Upon the death of my beloved wife, Eliese Krooss, I then give, devise and bequeath all the rest, residue and remainder of my estate, as well real as personal, and wheresoever situate, to my beloved children, John H. Krooss and Florence Maue, nee Krooss, share and share alike, to and for their own use absolutely and forever.
>
> In the event that either of my children aforesaid should die prior to the death of my beloved wife, Eliese Krooss, leaving descendants, then it is my wish and I so direct that such descendants shall take the share their parent would have taken if then living, share and share alike, to and for their own use absolutely and forever.

Florence Maue died, without having had descendants, in 1947, three years before the life beneficiary Eliese. Some months after Eliese's death, Florence's husband, as executor of his wife's estate, instituted the present proceeding in the Surrogate's Court of Bronx County to compel John Krooss, as executor under Eliese's will and as administrator c. t. a. of Herman Krooss' estate, to render and settle his respective accounts. In order to determine whether the executors of Florence's estate had status to prosecute the proceeding, the surrogate was required, initially, to construe Herman's will. He decided that the interest given to Florence was vested at the testator's death, subject to be divested only in the event of her predeceasing her mother leaving descendants, that it passed under her will, and that her husband, as executor, was entitled to bring the action.[2] The Appellate Division modified that

---

2. In her will, Florence left her residuary estate in trust to her husband and to her brother John, as trustees, to pay the net income therefrom to the husband for life; on his death, the principal was to be distributed between Florence's two nephews, the children of her brother John, if living, and to their issue per stirpes if either should die before the termination of the trust.

determination. Disagreeing with the surrogate's interpretation, the Appellate Division construed the will as imposing upon each of the remaindermen a condition that he or she survive the life beneficiary; Florence having died without children before Eliese, that condition was not met, and, concluded the court, as to Florence's share in the remainder, Krooss died intestate.

The law has long favored a construction of language in deed and will that accomplishes the vesting of estates; such a result is preferred because, among other things, it enables property to be freely transferred at the earliest possible date. Accordingly, the courts are intent upon restricting defeating events to the exact circumstances specified.

The will under consideration is simple in language and simple in plan. The testator gave his widow a life estate and a power to use the principal if it proved necessary for her maintenance and support. What remained after her death he gave "absolutely and forever" in equal shares to his two children, Florence and John. Had the will stopped at that point, there would be no question that the remainders were vested. And, since that is so, additional language will not be read as qualifying or cutting down the estate unless that language is as clear and decisive as that which created the vested remainder. The further language used by the testator in this case demonstrates, not that he was rendering the vesting of the estates in his children conditional upon survival of the life beneficiary, but that he was willing to have those estates divested only upon the combined occurrences of two further events. He explicitly provided, if either of his children died before his wife, "leaving descendants," then "such descendants shall take the share the parent would have taken if then living". If the words used mean what they say, then, divestiture of the remainder estates depended upon the happening of two plainly expressed and stipulated conditions: (1) the child, Florence or John, must die before the life beneficiary, and (2) the child so dying must leave descendants. Only if both of those conditions came to pass was the remainder—by apt and unequivocal language already vested in Florence and John—to be divested and bestowed instead upon the descendants of him or her who might have died.

When a will contains language that has acquired, through judicial decision, a definite and established significance, the testator is taken to have employed that language in that sense and with that meaning in mind. . . .

Over the years, the courts have uniformly held that language such as that used by the testator here, or language substantially identical, creates a vested remainder in fee subject to be divested by the remainderman's failing to survive the life beneficiary, *if, but only if,* such remainderman leaves issue or descendants surviving....

Leading commentators after reviewing the cases, have expressed themselves in similar fashion. (See 2 Powell on Real Property (1950), §§330-331, pp. 728-737; 2 Redfield on Law of Wills (1866), §65, pp. 648-649; 3 Restatement, Property, §254 comment a illustration 1, particularly Example II, pp. 1284-1286.) Thus, Professor Richard R. Powell of Columbia University Law School and Reporter on Property for the American Law Institute, in his recent work on the Law of Real Property, considers the subject at some length and sums up the law in this way (op. cit., §330, pp. 729-730):

> Supplanting limitations differ, in that some provide a taker who is to become the substitute whenever the prior taker fails to survive, while others provide a taker who is to become the substitute only under some circumstances. In cases of the second type, the constructional preference for early indefeasibility causes the requirement of survival to be strictly construed, and to operate only under the exact circumstances stipulated.... Similarly, in a gift "to my wife B for life, then to my children and the issue of those of my children who may be dead leaving children," the interest of a child of the testator who dies without surviving issue is indefeasible.

Turning to the will before us, we find that, at the expiration of the wife's life estate, the testator "then" gave the remainder to his children "absolutely and forever." The use of the word "then" as an "adverb of time" must be, as it long has been, construed to relate solely "to the time of enjoyment of the estate, and not to the time of its vesting in interest." Hence, the sole combination of events which could divest the "absolute" gift to the daughter Florence was her death before her mother, "leaving descendants". Only one of the specified conditions was fulfilled; although Florence did predecease her mother, she did not leave descendants. Consequently, her absolute gift remained vested and was not defeated. Not only the language employed, but the omission of any "words of survival" to indicate an intent that Florence's brother was to take if Florence died without children, illumines the testator's design to give his daughter a vested remainder....

The order of the Appellate Division should be reversed and the decree of the Surrogate's Court affirmed, with costs in this court and in the Appellate Division to all parties, appearing separately and filing separate briefs, payable out of the estate....

Note and Questions

1. *Restricted Condition of Survival Stated as a Condition Precedent*. Would the meaning of Herman Krooss's will have been litigated if the restricted condition of survival had been stated in the form of a condition precedent?

As a general rule, clarity of expression is promoted by stating conditions in precedent form. Conditions stated in subsequent form tend to be lazily formulated and incomplete. Although it takes greater effort and discipline to state conditions in precedent form, the end product is usually worth the effort.

How might the devise to Florence be restated using conditions precedent?

2. *Class Gift*. If Herman Krooss's will had created a class gift in favor of his children, rather than a gift of half to John and half to Florence, there is precedent for the view that Florence's share would have gone to John. See Restatement 2d of

Property §27.3 comment e; Martino v. Martino, 35 S.W.3d 252 (Tex. Ct. App. 2000); Turner v. Adams, 855 S.W.2d 735 (Tex. Ct. App. 1993).

Robertson v. Robertson
48 N.E.2d 29 (Mass. 1943)

FIELD, C.J. This petition for partition of certain real estate, in Hudson, was brought in the Probate Court by Ralph A. Robertson and comes before us upon an appeal by Essie Pope, one of the respondents, from a decree of that court for partition.

The case arises upon the following facts which appear in the report of material facts made by the judge: Lillian G. Pope, late of Hudson, died July 12, 1931, leaving a will that has been duly allowed, which contained the following provisions:

> Fourth;—To my daughter, Grace M. Morse and her husband, Alvah W. Morse, the use, income and enjoyment of my homestead estate situated at No. 11 Felton Street, in said Hudson for the term of their natural lives or of the life of the survivor. [Grace and Alvah, or the survivor, were given a power to sell the premises.] In case that at the death of the survivor of said Grace M. Morse and said Alvah W. Morse said homestead has not then been sold then it is to go to [sic] one half part to my said son, Ernest F. Pope, one quarter part of [sic] my said daughter, Ella B. Robertson and one quarter part to my said grandson, Ralph A. Robertson, or to the issue of any that may then be dead by the right of representation.

> Fifth;—All the rest and residue of my estate to my children, Ella B. Robertson, Grace M. Morse and my grandchild, Ralph A. Robertson, in equal shares, or to the issue of any who may be dead by the right of representation.

The testatrix left surviving her a son, Ernest F. Pope, married to Essie Pope, a daughter Grace M. Morse, married to Alvah W. Morse, a daughter Ella B. Robertson, and a grandson, Ralph A. Robertson, who, it may be guessed, was the son of Ella B. Robertson although the fact does not appear. The son, Ernest F. Pope, died January 26, 1940, leaving a widow, Essie Pope, and no issue. The daughter Grace M. Morse died June 26, 1940, leaving no issue. Her husband, Alvah W. Morse, had predeceased her. At the time of the death of Grace M. Morse the premises described in the will of the testatrix as her "homestead estate" had not been sold. The record does not disclose what, if any, property the testatrix owned at the time of her death other than the "homestead estate."

Ralph A. Robertson, the grandson of the testatrix, brought the present petition for partition of the "homestead estate," referred to in the fourth clause of the will, and upon this petition a decree was entered that partition of the "homestead estate" be made between the petitioner, Ralph A. Robertson, and Ella B. Robertson in equal shares, and a commissioner was appointed to make such partition. The basis of this decree was that Ella B. Robertson and Ralph A. Robertson each took one quarter part of the "homestead estate" under the fourth clause of the will, but that the devise by that clause of one half part thereof to Ernest F. Pope failed by reason of his death before the death of his sister Grace M. Morse, and therefore was disposed of by the fifth or residuary clause of the will in equal shares to Ella B. Robertson, Ralph A. Robertson, and Grace M. Morse, each of whom took under said clause one sixth part of the "homestead estate," and that the one sixth part of the "homestead estate" that passed to Grace M. Morse went "by purchase from the heirs and legatees under" her will in equal shares to Ella B. Robertson and Ralph A. Robertson, so that each of them took by such transfer one twelfth part of the "homestead estate," with the result that in the aggregate Ella B. Robertson and Ralph A. Robertson each was entitled to one half part of the "homestead estate." Essie Pope, the widow of Ernest F. Pope, appealed from this decree, and contends, in substance, that the one half part of the "homestead estate" devised to her husband by the fourth clause of the will did not fail so that this part fell into the residue of the estate, but rather that it was the property of his estate in which she, as his widow, is entitled to share. The record does not show, however, to what extent she, as his widow, was entitled to share in his estate....

We think that the decree of the Probate Court was based upon the correct interpretation of the will, that Ernest F. Pope took only a contingent remainder in one half part of the "homestead estate," with the result that, since the contingency upon which it depended did not happen, the appellant, Essie Pope, the widow of Ernest F. Pope, is not entitled to share in the partition of the "homestead estate."...

The fact that the gift to Ernest F. Pope by the provision of the fourth clause here quoted was subject to being defeated by an exercise of the power of sale... did not render the gift to him contingent. A remainder after a life estate is none the less vested because subject to being defeated by the exercise of a power of sale if, apart from the existence of the power, it would be a vested remainder. In these circumstances such a remainder is a vested remainder subject to being divested by the exercise of the power rather than a contingent remainder.... And in our opinion the conditional language with reference to the gift in default of sale under the power, "In case that at the death of the survivor of said Grace M. Morse and said Alvah W. Morse said homestead has not then been sold," does not of itself preclude this result so far as the effect of the existence of the power to sell is concerned. If the remainder in one half part of the "homestead estate" given to Ernest F. Pope was contingent rather than vested, it is for reasons other than the existence of the power of sale....

We think that the language of the fourth clause of the will as a whole read in the light of the other provisions of the will discloses an intention on the part of the testatrix to postpone the acquisition by her son, Ernest F. Pope, of a vested interest in one half part of the "homestead estate" until the happening of a future event, that is, the death of the survivor of the life tenants, so that he must be deemed to have taken only a contingent interest—an interest contingent upon his surviving the life tenants, a contingency that did not happen....

[T]he gift to the "issue" of Ernest F. Pope was not a gift by way of substitution in the sense of a supplanting gift. See for the distinction between an "alternative limitation" and a "supplanting limitation" Am. Law Inst. Restatement: Property, §253 comment c. The gift to the "issue" of Ernest F. Pope ascertained as of the time of distribution, the time of the death of the surviving life tenant, is as direct a gift as the gift to Ernest F. Pope. The language of the will fixes the same time for these gifts to take effect, the time of the death of the surviving life tenant. One half part of the "homestead estate" is "then... to go" to Ernest F. Pope or to his "issue," and the gifts are expressly made in the alternative by reason of the use of the conjunction "or" connecting them. The canon of construction stated in Am. Law Inst. Restatement: Property, §252, relating to an "alternative limitation employing the word 'or'," is as follows:

> In a limitation purporting to create a remainder or an executory interest, in "B or his children," or in "B or his issue," or in "B or his descendants," or by other language of similar import, the alternative form tends to establish as to the interest of B that (a) a requirement of survival to the end of all preceding interests exists; and (b) such survival is a condition precedent of such interest.

This canon of construction is clearly applicable to the language of the will here involved. And in the light of the other considerations herein stated we think that it must be followed with the result that, by reason of the death of Ernest F. Pope before the death of the surviving life tenant, the gift of an interest in one half part of the "homestead estate" to him never vested in him....

The conclusion here reached may seem to rest upon a somewhat technical analysis of the language used by the testatrix. It is, however, to be assumed that this language was used by her advisedly to express her intention, and we "have to go upon slight differences." Lee v. Welch, 163 Mass. 312, 314, 39 N.E. 1112, 1113. If the testatrix had added the words "if he was then living" to the gift of an interest in one half part of the "homestead estate" to Ernest F. Pope, there could be no doubt of the correctness of the conclusion here reached. But it would be even more technical to rest a different conclusion upon the omission of these words when the same intention of the testatrix is shown by other language used by her.... The conclusion here reached that the vesting of this interest was intended to be postponed until the death of the surviving life tenant is not in conflict with any intention of the testatrix disclosed by her will.

Decree affirmed.

Notes and Questions

1. *Conditions Precedent.* How might the dispositive language in *Robertson* be restated using conditions precedent?

2. *Restricted Condition.* Do you think Herman Krooss's intention in *Krooss* was so much different from Lillian Pope's intention in *Robertson*? Why did the court in

Robertson not consider whether Lillian would have preferred that the primary beneficiaries' interests fail only if they died leaving issue?

Do you think that the testator's intention in Will of Corwith, 622 N.Y.S.2d 424 (Sur. Ct. 1995), was substantially different from Herman's? In *Corwith*, the testator, Charles F. Corwith, died in 1981, leaving a will creating marital and nonmarital trusts in its residuary provisions. The issue regarding the survival condition concerned the nonmarital trust in which the testator, after providing for his wife during her life, directed that the trust property be distributed in the following manner.

> Upon the death of my wife, GRACE, if she survives me,... to pay over, transfer and assign two-thirds (2/3) of part B of my residuary estate, in equal portions, to (1) My aforesaid nephew, CHARLES L. CORWITH: (2) my aforesaid niece, ELAINE McDUFFIE: (3) My aforesaid nephew, VINCENT C. MARTLING; and (4) My aforesaid niece, NANCY MALINOWSKI, and one-third (1/3) of part B of my residuary estate, in equal portions, to [named charities]. If any of the aforesaid nieces or nephews do not survive to be entitled to a share of the trust or residue, then such share shall go to his or her issue, per stirpes.

The testator was survived by his wife but she had since died. The testator's nephew, Charles L. Corwith, survived the testator but died without issue during the life of the testator's wife. The nephew's estate, relying on *Krooss*, argued that the testator intended to impose only a restricted condition of survival—death before the life tenant *with* issue. The court disagreed, holding that the survival language in *Krooss* was "clearly distinguishable." It held that Charles's interest was a remainder subject to a condition precedent of surviving the testator's wife. The result was that Charles's interest failed and passed by intestacy to the testator's wife, as the testator's sole heir. Do you think that the survival language in *Corwith* is clearly distinguishable from the survival language in *Krooss*?

3. *Remainders Subject to a Power.* In holding that a remainder interest is not contingent on survival of the life tenant by reason of its being subject to a power, the court in the *Robertson* case was well within existing authority. See, e.g., Restatement of Property §261 illus. 1. A few courts have held to the contrary, however. See, e.g., Jarrett v. McReynolds, 183 S.E.2d 343 (Va. 1971).

4. *Remainder "to B or his heirs."* Does a remainder "to B or his heirs" present the same or different problems as a remainder "to B or his issue"? The Restatement of Property §37 comment *l* states that a devise of a future interest "to B or his heirs" "normally is construed to create an estate in fee simple absolute in [B], if [B] is alive when the limited estate becomes a present interest and in [B]'s heirs if [B] is then dead." This is the result reached in Rowett v. McFarland, 394 N.W.2d 298 (S.D. 1986), and in Landmark Communications, Inc. v. Sovran Bank, 387 S.E.2d 484 (Va. 1990). But the Restatement also holds out the possibility that such a devise could be construed as creating an indefeasibly vested remainder in B, as if the devise had been "to B *and* his heirs."

2. Special Case of Multiple-Generation Class Gifts—Class Gifts in Favor of "Issue" or "Descendants"

Primary Statutory References: *UPC §§2-708, 2-709*

Remainder interests in trusts are commonly given to a class composed of the transferor's or the income beneficiary's "descendants" or "issue." A distinguishing characteristic of these class gifts is that potentially the takers reside in more than one generation. As with most other types of future interests, the recommended form for these class gifts imposes an express condition of survival to the time of possession or enjoyment. As Weller v. Sokol, below, demonstrates, a requirement of survival commonly is implied for multiple-generation class gifts, even in the absence of one expressly stated. See Restatement 3d of Property §15.3; Restatement 2d of Property §28.2; Restatement of Property §249 comment i, §296 comment g. This result is, of course, contrary to the rules of construction concerning future interests in favor of individuals and in favor of single-generation classes, such as "children," "grandchildren," "nieces and nephews," and so on. Why are class gifts in favor of "descendants" or "issue" treated differently?

A related question in the case of multiple-generation class gifts is the form of distribution among the takers. In Weller v. Sokol, below, a per-stirpes form of distribution was specified in the governing instrument. In cases in which the governing instrument does not specify a form of distribution, the English rule favored a per capita form of distribution.[3] The English preference has now largely disappeared in the United States. Generally speaking, the preferred form of distribution in this country is representational. See Edward C. Halbach, Jr., Issues About Issue: Some Recurrent Class Gift Problems, 48 Mo. L. Rev. 333, 350-55 (1983).

Contrast UPC §§2-708 and 2-709 with the positions taken in the Restatements of Property:

> *Restatement 3d of Property §14.4 comment c, Form of representation....* If the donative document does not specify a form of representation, the property is divided in accordance with the form of representation adopted in the intestacy law of the domicile of the designated ancestor.

---

3. The historical meaning of a per capita form of distribution was that every member of the class takes an equal share, even those with living intervening ancestors. To illustrate, suppose G establishes a trust for A for life, remainder in corpus to A's descendants. If A had two children, one of whom had one child and the other of whom had two children, each child and grandchild would take a one-fifth share under a per capita form of distribution. No condition of survivorship of A would be implied. See Restatement 2d of Property § 28.2 comment d, illus. 5. The Restatement 3d of Property § 14.4 comment d, however, points out that the preferred construction today is that "per capita" invokes the system of representation known as per capita with representation (as illustrated in Chapter 2).

Restatement 2d of Property §28.2. Class Gift to "Issue" or "Descendants". If a gift is made to a class described as the "issue" or "descendants" of a designated person, or by a similar multigenerational class gift term, in the absence of additional language or circumstances that indicate otherwise,

(1) A class member must survive to the date of distribution in order to share in the gift; and

(2) such class member in order to share in the gift must have no living ancestor who is a class member; and

(3) the initial division into shares will be on the basis of the number of class members, whether alive or deceased, in the first generation below the designated person.

Restatement of Property §303. Distribution—Class Described as "Issue of B," or as "Descendants of B," or as "Family of B." (1) When a conveyance creates a class gift by a limitation in favor of a group described as the "issue of B," or as the "descendants of B," ... then, unless a contrary intent of the conveyor is found from additional language or circumstances, distribution is made to such members of the class as would take, and in such shares as they would receive, under the applicable law of intestate succession if B had died intestate on the date of the final ascertainment of the membership in the class, owning the subject matter of the class gift.

Although the specifics of intestate distribution among an intestate's descendants take different forms, all such forms are representational in overall approach. See Chapter 2. That is to say, a descendant takes only if no intervening ancestor of that descendant is alive. Any representational form of distribution, regardless of which type, would justify the rule adopted in Weller v. Sokol on the question of implying a condition of survival.

Weller v. Sokol
318 A.2d 193 (Md. 1974)

SINGLEY, J. This case combines a number of appeals from a decree of the Circuit Court of Baltimore City which construed the will of the late Arthur Nattans (Arthur Nattans I). While the appeal was originally taken to the Court of Special Appeals, we granted certiorari in order that it could be docketed in this Court.

Although the factual background and particularly the family pedigree are difficult to keep in mind, the case presents two relatively simple issues:

(i) When a will directs a distribution on the death of the testator's last surviving child among "issue and descendants" per stirpes of children of the testator who have died leaving issue surviving, where are the stocks or stirpes to be found?

(ii) Is distribution to be made only to issue and descendants living at the time of distribution?

The chancellor (Ross, J.) determined that the stocks, or stirpes, were to be found among the children of the testator, and not among the grandchildren who were the first takers of an absolute interest, and that distribution was to be made only to descendants living at the time of distribution. For reasons to be developed, we shall affirm.

Arthur Nattans I died domiciled in Baltimore on 17 April 1905, survived by his widow, Jennie Nattans; by three children of a prior marriage; Emily N. Herbert, Addie N. Bachrach, and Samuel A. Nattans, and by five children of his second marriage: Rita Nattans (later Myers), Ralph Nattans, Edith Nattans (later Hecht), Hortense Nattans (later Solomon), and Arthur Nattans (Arthur Nattans II).

The provisions of the Nattans will, executed on 3 October 1903, with which we shall here be concerned are contained in Items Sixth and Tenth. By Item Sixth, 396 shares of stock of Read Drug and Chemical Company of Baltimore City (Read's) owned by Mr. Nattans were bequeathed to trustees to pay the income from specified numbers of shares to the Nattans children, as follows:

Emily N. Herbert . . . . . . 40 shares
Addie N. Bachrach . . . . . . 29 shares
Samuel A. Nattans . . . . . . 29 shares
Rita Nattans (Myers) . . . . . . 60 shares
Ralph Nattans . . . . . . 40 shares
Edith Nattans (Hecht) . . . . . . 60 shares
Hortense Nattans (Solomon) . . . . . . 60 shares
Arthur Nattans II . . . . . . 40 shares

Item Tenth provided:

> "*Tenth.* In the event of the death of any of my children above named, during the continuance of this trust, without leaving issue him or her surviving, the income herein given to the child so dying, without issue living at his or her death, shall be divided equally among his or her surviving brothers and sisters annually during the continuance of this trust. And in case of the death of any one of my said children during the continuance of said trust, leaving issue him or her surviving, the income of the share of the one so dying shall go to and become the property of his or her child, if only one, or children, if more than one, equally, share and share alike. Upon the death of the last survivor of all my said eight children this trust shall cease, and thereupon the entire trust property, shall be divided by my said trustees, or their successors in the trust, among the issue and descendants of such of my children as may have died leaving lawful issue him or her surviving *per stirpes and not per capita.* And the said trustees, and their successors in the trust, are authorized and directed to make, execute and deliver all such deeds and instruments of conveyance or assignment as may be necessary to make said division." (Emphasis in original.)

In Ryan v. Herbert, 186 Md. 453, 47 A.2d 360 (1946), our predecessors had occasion to review a declaratory decree which had construed the provisions of Item Tenth relating to devolution of income prior to the termination of the trust. That decree, which was affirmed on appeal, had directed that on the death of a child of Arthur Nattans I prior to the termination of the trust, leaving any issue whatsoever surviving, such issue took a vested interest in the income to which the dying child had been entitled, subject only to defeasance by the termination of the trust.

As a result, when Harold Herbert and Arthur N. Bachrach, grandsons of Arthur Nattans I, died prior to the termination of the trust without leaving descendants surviving, the income which each had been receiving was paid to his respective estate. No consideration was given to the devolution of the corpus at time of termination beyond a recognition that it would certainly pass in proportions which differed from the shares of income, and that it might well pass to persons other than those who had received income from the trust under the determination reached in Ryan....

To us, however, the most compelling argument springs from the very nature of a stirpital distribution. The "issue and descendants" of the children of Arthur Nattans I could not be determined until the termination of the trust. See Restatement of Property, § 296 comment g, §§ 303(1), 304, 311(1). At that time neither Harold Herbert nor Arthur N. Bachrach was alive. While their right to receive income was found to be vested in Ryan, their right to participate in the corpus, under the terms of the will, was implicitly conditioned on survival until distribution....

Decree affirmed, costs to be paid from the assets of the trust estate.

Note

1. *Multiple-Generation Class Gifts.* As the text above Weller v. Sokol indicates, the Restatement 3d of Property §15.3 supports the rule of *Weller* that a requirement of survival is implied for multiple-generation class gifts, even in the absence of one expressly stated.

2. *Single-Generation Class Gifts.* What about single-generation class gifts? See Restatement 3d of Property §15.4 below.

Restatement 3d of Property

§15.4 Postponed Class Gift—Beneficiary of Single-Generation Class Gift Fails to Survive Distribution Date

Unless the language or circumstances establish that the transferor had a different intention, or unless an applicable statute provides otherwise, a beneficiary of a postponed single-generation class gift who fails to survive the distribution date or any other future time or event is not excluded from the class. The deceased class member's share passes through his or her estate.

....

[Comment] c. Rationale of the rule of this section—traditional doctrine. The traditional rule of construction with respect to a single-generation class gift is that a condition of survival of the distribution date or of any other future time or event is not implied. Accordingly, the share of a deceased class member passes through his or her estate. Section 15.4 adheres to the traditional rule, because it is the rule best

suited within the confines of the common-law tradition to approximate the likely preference of the transferor, supported by the constructional preference for the construction that does not disinherit a line of descent.... A rule better suited to the transferor's purposes would not only recognize an implied condition of survival, but also an implied substitute gift to the descendants of a deceased class member who survive the distribution date. The traditional technique of the common law, however, is to effectuate intent by construction, and not by the creation of substitutionary shares not expressed by the transferor. There are judicial decisions in which the court found an implied gift on the basis of the facts and circumstances of an individual case. For example, in the case of a disposition "to A for life, and if A dies without issue, to B," courts have found an implied gift to A's issue if A dies with issue. But courts have not presumed to create a substitute gift in all cases, as the antilapse statutes have been able to command.

[Comment] d. Historical rationale no longer convincing. The traditional rule had its origin in the constructional preference for vested interests and its corollary, the constructional preference for vesting at the earliest possible moment. Although the origin of the preference for early vesting is somewhat obscure, it is generally thought to be based on the desire to avoid the now-defunct rule of destructibility of contingent remainders and the once overly harsh but now widely liberalized or abolished Rule Against Perpetuities. Neither the constructional preference for vested interests nor for vesting at the earliest possible time is endorsed in this Restatement....

[Comment] e. Modern rationale—"trickle-down" theory. The strongest justification for the rule of this section is "that it enables the deceased class member to pass his share to his issue, thereby keeping the benefits of the gift equal among the descendant lines." Restatement Second, Property (Donative Transfers) §27.3 comment a. This is sometimes known as the "trickle-down" theory. Under this theory, the share of a deceased class member will descend through the class member's estate and, when the trust is dissolved at some later time, might end up benefiting the deceased class member's descendants. The traditional rule produces the best chance within the common-law tradition of protecting a descending line that has one or more living members on the distribution date.

It would probably be within the traditional technique of the common law to construe single-generation class gifts as presumptively being subject to an implied condition of survival of the distribution date, as is already done with respect to multiple-generation class gifts.... By itself, however, an implied condition of survival of the distribution date would make it impossible for the trickle-down theory to work. Unless a court is willing to couple a survival requirement with a blanket presumption creating a substitute gift to the descendants of a deceased class member, merely implying a condition of survival of the distribution date in all cases would extinguish the possibility of benefit to the deceased class member's descendants. Another possible approach would be to restrict the rule of construction against implying a condition of survival to instances in which the deceased beneficiary left descendants who survived the distribution date. That approach, while recommended to courts for adoption, is not adopted in this Restatement because of lack of judicial or legislative authority.

The principal weakness of the traditional rule is this: although the share of a deceased class member might end up in the hands of the deceased class member's descendants, it might not. The deceased class member might die without issue. The deceased class member might die intestate, in which case there might be multiple heirs, one or more of whom also predecease the distribution date. On the distribution date, the deceased class member's share can easily pass to complete strangers. To be sure, a class member who survives the distribution date can also pass his or her share to complete strangers, but at least the class member who survives the distribution date has the right to enjoy his or her share personally.

Another weakness of the traditional rule is the administrative cost of identifying the owner or owners of the interest on the distribution date. Identifying the current owners requires tracing the nonpossessory future interest through the estate of any class member who died before the distribution date and perhaps tracing fractional shares of the interest through the estates of the class member's successors in interest if any of them have also died before the distribution date.

Consequently, the traditional rule is a crude and costly means of protecting the deceased class member's descendants from disinheritance, but probably is the only means of doing so within the traditional technique of the common law....

[Comment] i. Antilapse-type statutes. A few states have enacted legislation that extends antilapse-type coverage to postponed single-generation class gifts. Most of these statutes are based on §2-707 of the Uniform Probate Code, which only applies to future interests created in a trust. These statutes provide a more direct and efficient means of protecting equality among different lines of descent than the rule of this section. Under UPC §2-707, a beneficiary of a single-generation class gift who fails to survive the distribution date is excluded from the class, but the beneficiary's descendants who survive the distribution date, if any, take by representation in the beneficiary's place. To prevent the statute from being intent-defeating, the substitution of descendants only applies if the trust document fails to create an alternative future interest that is entitled to take effect in possession or enjoyment or if the evidence establishes that the settlor had a contrary intention (a clause expressing a contrary intention would be one that provided that "if any class member predeceases the distribution date, the class member's share is not to pass to the deceased class member's descendants"). In effect, this provision applies the antilapse statute applicable to wills and will substitutes (see §5.5) as if the transferor were a testator who died on the distribution date. Section 2-706 of the UPC applies the same approach to beneficiary designations under life insurance policies and similar arrangements.

UPC §2-707 self-adjusts to different situations by including all lines with living descendants at the distribution date and excluding all lines without living descendants at the distribution date....

The Restatement Second of Property (Donative Transfers) endorsed the approach of such statutes by stating that "it would be a better overall result to provide a substitute taker for the deceased class member and avoid involvement of the class member's share in his or her estate." Restatement Second, Property (Donative Transfers) §27.3 comment b. The Restatement Second also took the position that "[t]he policy of these statutes commends itself to decisional law." Restatement Second, Property (Donative Transfers) §27.3, comment i. A court that is willing to adopt this antilapse-type approach judicially should prefer it to the rule of this section.

Notes

1. *Equitable Deviation: Judicial Modification of a Trust Because of Unanticipated Circumstances.* The Restatement 3d of Trusts §66 provides that a court may modify a distributive provision of a trust if, "because of circumstances not anticipated by the settlor," the modification "will further the purposes of the trust." This doctrine is known as the equitable deviation doctrine. (Recall the discussion in Chapter 11.) Comment b, illustration 5, of the Restatement 3d of Trusts applies the equitable deviation doctrine to a trust in which one of the beneficiaries dies prematurely:

> 5. S, who outlived her husband and her only child, left her estate in three shares, one for each of her three grandchildren. Each share was to be held in trust for the grandchild's support and education, with the property to be distributed to the grandchild "if and when he or she attains age 25." Two of the grandchildren had reached age 25 by the time of S's death and thus took their shares outright; the other grandchild, G, was 18 when S died and has now died at age 23, leaving a widow and two very young children. Under the applicable rule of construction, G's interest fails as a result of his failure to survive until the time of distribution. Thus, unless modified, S's will has made an incomplete disposition of this share of her estate, and therefore this trust share will pass by resulting trust (see §§7 and 8) to S's heirs at law—that is, upon S's partial intestacy, this reversionary interest will belong equally (one-third each) to the three grandchildren. This would result ultimately in a one-ninth share of S's estate being available to G's family while the other grandchildren end up with, essentially, four-ninths of S's estate apiece (one-third via their respective trusts and one-ninth by resulting trust). These consequences of a failure of the remainder of G's trust share would produce a striking distortion of an overall testamentary trust plan that, on its face, appears to contemplate equal treatment of S's three lines of descent. Because of the unanticipated circumstances in this case and S's failure to make provision for them, the rule of this section allows the court to modify the terms of the trust if it concludes that S's probable intention and the trust purpose would be better served by doing so.

2. *Statutory Reform.* Pennsylvania and Tennessee have statutes imposing a general survival requirement for class gifts. See Pa. Cons. Stat. tit. 20, §2514(5); Tenn. Code §32-3-104. Illinois has a statute that imposes a survival requirement on future interests created by will given to the testator's descendants. 755 Ill. Comp. Stat. 5/4-11. Iowa has enacted a statute imposing a survival requirement on all future interests in trust, but with numerous exceptions. See Iowa Code §633A.4701, below.

California amended §6146 of its probate code in 1983 to require survival of the point of possession or enjoyment, but the amendment was ambiguous and the legislature repealed it in 1984 before it became effective.[4]

Iowa Code

§633A.4701. Survivorship with respect to future interests under terms of trust—substitute takers.

1. Unless otherwise specifically stated by the terms of the trust, the interest of each beneficiary is contingent on the beneficiary surviving until the date on which the beneficiary becomes entitled to possession or enjoyment of the beneficiary's interest in the trust.[5]

2. If a beneficiary dies prior to becoming entitled to possession or enjoyment of the beneficiary's interest and the terms of the trust provide for an alternate beneficiary who is living on the date the interest becomes possessory, the alternate beneficiary succeeds to the interest in accordance with the terms of the trust.

3. If a beneficiary dies prior to becoming entitled to possession or enjoyment of the beneficiary's interest and no alternate beneficiary is named in the trust, and the beneficiary has issue who are living on the date the interest becomes possessory, the issue of the beneficiary who are living on such date shall take the interest of the beneficiary.

4. If both a beneficiary of an interest and any alternate beneficiary of that interest named in the trust die prior to the interest becoming possessory, and the beneficiary has no issue who are living on the date the interest becomes possessory, the issue of the alternate beneficiary who are living on such date shall take the interest of the beneficiary.

5. If both the beneficiary of an interest and any alternate beneficiary of that interest named in the trust die prior to the interest becoming possessory, and neither the beneficiary nor the alternate beneficiary has issue who are living on the date the

---

4. For the current version of California law, see Cal. Prob. Code §§21109 and 21110, neither of which requires survival until the time of possession or enjoyment.

5. In Will of Uchtorff, 693 N.W.2d 790 (Iowa 2005), the court held that the statute was not applicable to a remainder interest to the testator's son. The language creating the remainder interest described it "as an indefeasibly vested interest in fee." That language, the court held, expressed a contrary intention. Ed.

interest becomes possessory, the beneficiary's interest shall be distributed to the takers of the settlor's residuary estate, or, if the trust is the sole taker of the settlor's residuary estate, in accordance with section 633A.2106 [providing for a resulting trust to the transferor's estate].

6. If both the beneficiary of an interest and any alternate beneficiary of that interest named in the trust die prior to the interest becoming possessory, and both the beneficiary and the alternate beneficiary have issue who are living on the date the interest becomes possessory, the issue of the beneficiary succeed to the interest of the beneficiary. The issue of the alternate beneficiary shall not succeed to any part of the interest of the beneficiary.

7. For the purposes of this section, persons appointed under a power of appointment shall be considered beneficiaries under this section and takers in default of appointment designated by the instrument creating the power of appointment shall be considered alternate beneficiaries under this section.

8. Subsections 2, 3, 4, 5, 6, and 7 do not apply to any interest subject to an express condition of survivorship imposed by the terms of the trust. For the purposes of this section, words of survivorship including, but not limited to, "my surviving children", "if a person survives" a named period, and terms of like import, shall be construed to create an express condition of survivorship. Words of survivorship include language requiring survival to the distribution date or to any earlier or unspecified time, whether those words are expressed in condition precedent, condition subsequent, or any other form.

9. For the purposes of this section, a term of the trust requiring that a beneficiary survive a person whose death does not make the beneficiary entitled to possession or enjoyment of the beneficiary's interest in the trust shall not be considered as "otherwise specifically stated by the terms of the trust" nor as an "express condition of survivorship imposed by the trust".

10. If an interest to which this section applies is given to a class, other than a class described as "issue", "descendants", "heirs of the body", "heirs", "next of kin", "relatives", "family", or a class described by language of similar import, the members of the class who are living on the date on which the class becomes entitled to possession or enjoyment of the interest shall be considered as alternate beneficiaries under this section. However, neither the residuary beneficiaries under the settlor's will nor the settlor's heirs shall be considered as alternate beneficiaries for the purposes of this section.

Problem

1. How would the Iowa statute apply to a trust providing for the income to go to the settlor's child A for life, remainder in corpus to A's children who survive A; if none, to the settlor's brother B. A had one child, X, who predeceased A. X left a child who survived A. B predeceased A. B left a child who survived A.

2. How would the Iowa statute apply to a trust providing for the income to go to the settlor's child A for life, remainder in corpus to A's children. A had two children, X and Y. X survived A. Y predeceased A, leaving issue who survived A.

3. How would UPC §2-707 apply to the trusts in Problems 1 and 2?

EXTERNAL REFERENCES. Section 2-707 has provoked debate. For the arguments in favor of § 2-707, see Edward C. Halbach, Jr., Uniform Acts, Restatements and Other Trends in American Trust Law at Century's End, 88 Calif. L. Rev. 1877, 1902-04 (2000); Lawrence W. Waggoner, The Uniform Probate Code Extends Antilapse-Type Protection to Poorly Drafted Trusts, 94 Mich. L. Rev. 2309 (1996); Edward C. Halbach Jr. and Lawrence W. Waggoner, The UPC's New Survivorship and Antilapse Provisions, 55 Alb. L. Rev. 1091 (1992). For critiques of § 2-707, see David M. Becker, Uniform Probate Code Section 2-707 and the Experienced Estate Planner: Unexpected Disasters and How to Avoid Them, 47 UCLA L. Rev. 339 (1999); Laura E. Cunningham, The Hazards of Tinkering with the Common Law of Future Interests: The California Experience, 48 Hastings L.J. 667 (1997); Jesse Dukeminier, The Uniform Probate Code Upends the Law of Remainders, 94 Mich. L. Rev. 148 (1995).

———

"Construction" of Single-Generation Class Gift to Include Descendants of Deceased Class Members. An alternative means of producing the same result as UPC §2-707 is to construe a single-generation class gift as if it were a multiple-generation class gift. The general rule of construction is that a class gift to a single-generation class only includes members of the designated generation. Thus, the Restatement 3d of Property §14.1 provides:

> Unless the language or circumstances establish that the transferor had a different intention... the term "children" means descendants in the first generation, and does not include grandchildren or more remote descendants.

Comment g, however, notes that "[t]he rule of this section is a rule of construction, [so] it yields to a finding that additional language or circumstances establish that the transferor had a different intention." Comment g cites four instances in which it is justifiable to find a different intention: where "children" is coupled with words of representation; where "children" and "issue" (or "children" and "descendants") are used interchangeably; where the disposition would fail unless "children" is construed to mean "issue"; and where to do so is more consistent with the transferor's overall dispositive plan. The next case, Cox v. Forristall, found a different intention based on the transferor's overall dispositive plan.

Cox v. Forristall
640 P.2d 878 (Kan. Ct. App. 1982)

MEYER, Judge.... The will of B. T. Freeman devised a life estate in the farm to his daughters Miranda Catherine Freeman and Alice Freeman. The will provided that in the event of marriage of either life tenant, the life interest in the farm would remain in the other tenant. Further, the will provided:

> And the life interest of both of my said daughters having terminated by marriage, the said farm shall become and be the property of my children, share and share alike, namely: Miranda Catherine Freeman, Alice Freeman, Bonnie Freeman Forrestall (sic), Nellie Freeman Hanson, Annie Freeman Cherryholmes, Grace Freeman, Frances Freeman, Enda (sic) Freeman, Sarah Freeman, Delilah Freeman Stackley, and Albert Freeman. In the event of the death of either of my said children above named prior to the expiration of the life interest of my said daughters, Miranda Catherine and Alice, the share of such child or children so dying shall descend to, become and be the property of the then living issue of their body, and in the event of their dying without issue, the share of such child or children so dying shall descend to, become and be the property of my children then living, share and share alike.

[B. T. Freeman was survived by eleven children, including Miranda and Alice. Miranda died in 1951. Alice died in 1980. Neither Miranda nor Alice ever married, and both died without issue. Only one of B. T. Freeman's eleven children, Delilah, survived Alice. Frances, Edna, and Sarah died during Alice's lifetime without issue. The other five, Bonnie, Nellie, Annie, Grace, and Albert, died during Alice's lifetime with issue (who survived Alice).]

The [trial] court interpreted the will so that the word "children" as used in the clause "my children then living" also includes, per stirpes, the grandchildren of B. T. Freeman if they are children of a deceased child of B. T. Freeman who died prior to the termination of the life estates established in the will....

The basic argument is over what happened to the shares of the children who died without issue. Appellant maintains that upon the death of each child who died without issue, their remainder interest passed to B. T. Freeman's other children who were living at the time of the death of said child, thus preventing that share from passing to the issue of B. T. Freeman's children who had died prior to the children dying without issue....

The Supreme Court, in Estate of Lester, 191 Kan. 83, 87, 379 P.2d 275 (1963), stated:

> [O]ther things being equal, there is a presumption against any intention on the part of a testator to disinherit his legal heirs who are favored by the policy of the law and may not be disinherited by mere conjecture. When a testator intends to disinherit those who would take under the statutes of descent he must indicate that intention clearly by plain words, express devise to others, or necessary implication. By "necessary" implication is meant one which results from so strong a probability as to the testator's meaning that an intent contrary to that imputed cannot be supposed. The presumption against disinheritance is

recognized especially in the absence of unfriendly relations existing between the testator and his descendants. [Citations omitted.]

Appellant's interpretation states that as each child dies without issue, that share passes to the remaining children of B. T. Freeman who are alive at the time of the death of said child.

The trial court's interpretation looks to who is living at the termination of the life estate and passes the shares of the children dying without issue to the remaining children and grandchildren of B. T. Freeman living at the termination of said life estate. This divides the shares equally among the remaining interests whereas appellant's interpretation gives the last to die the biggest shares. Under appellant's interpretation, the issue of the earliest of B. T. Freeman's children to die lose part of the inheritance; if any of those children subsequently die without issue, the inheritance bypasses them and passes only to those children of B. T. Freeman who are alive.

The provision regarding the passage of the shares of children without issue is ambiguous in two respects.

First, the phrase "children then living" is ambiguous because it is not clear when "then" refers to; viz., whether one looks to the time of the successive deaths of each child without an heir, or at the death of the last life tenant.

Secondly, under the previous phrase, the share of each of B. T. Freeman's children is to pass to their issue if they die prior to the expiration of the life interest. It is difficult to harmonize the two phrases unless "children" is interpreted to mean children and grandchildren.

We have found two cases in Kansas where the word "children" was held to include "grandchildren." In Estate of Works, 168 Kan. 539, 213 P.2d 998 (1950), a will devised real estate to the testator's five children. The will further provided:

"The above bequests and gifts of my real estate are made to my children heretofore named upon the condition that they and each of them shall hold the same during their lifetime, and at the death of any one of them the real estate herein bequeathed and devised shall descend to their legitimate children. And in case any one or more of the children above named, should die without legitimate issue, then the share above given and devised to such childless devisee shall descend to and become the property of their brothers and sisters, children of mine who shall survive, share and share alike."

In *Works*, when the testator died, all of his children were living. At the time of the testator's death, his son Charles had two living children, Warren and Clark. Clark, however, predeceased his father Charles, but had three children, Charles, Paul and Mary Ella. The issue was whether Warren, the one living child of Charles, received the entire remainder in the land, or whether Warren took only one-half of the remainder and the three children of Clark took the other half. The court held that Warren took one-half and the three children of Clark took the other half, even though Clark predeceased Charles, the son of the testator.

The court stated:

> "Although the word 'children' is not ordinarily construed to include grandchildren, it is properly construed to include grandchildren when the context, or the surrounding facts and circumstances, in case of ambiguity, make it clear that the grantor so intended.
>
> "If there appears to be a doubt or uncertainty as to the grantor's intention in using the word 'children' there is a reasonable presumption against disinheritance of a grandchild whose parent is dead." 168 Kan. at 543-4, 213 P.2d 998, citing from Bennett v. Humphreys, 159 Kan. 416, Syl. PP 6, 7, 155 P.2d 431 (1945).

In Bennett v. Humphreys, 159 Kan. 416, 417, 155 P.2d 431 (1945), land was deeded to John Bell Bennett. The deed stated, in part:

> It is part of consideration of this deed that John Bell Bennett cannot sell this property during his life time and at his death is to be divided equally among his children.

At the time of the death of the life tenant, John Bennett, there was only one child living. However, another child had predeceased the life tenant, leaving a grandchild. The court held that the grandchild and the child took equally, citing the above rule.

Since certain terms of decedent's last will are ambiguous, it seems clear to us that the trial court attempted an interpretation of that will which it felt would reflect the intent of the decedent.... [W]e conclude the trial court was correct.

AFFIRMED.

Note

For another case construing a single-generation class gift to include the descendants of a deceased class member, see Edwards v. Bender, 25 So. 1010 (Ala. 1899). Unlike the dispositive language in *Cox*, the dispositive language in *Edwards* did not contain an express requirement of survival. The testator's will devised a tract of land to his daughter Nancy for life, remainder to Nancy's "children," without an express requirement of survival. Nancy had five children. Four of the five survived her, but one predeceased her, leaving a child, Eula, who survived her. The court held that the word "children" "may be extended to include grandchildren, when such intent appears from the whole instrument, or where otherwise the devise would fail." Although the devise would not otherwise fail (because four of Nancy's five children survived her), the court found it "evident" that the testator's intention, "though not expressly stated," was that "the issue of her children as might die before [the life tenant] should take the share which such deceased child would have taken." The court based this conclusion on the fact that the will contained a gift over in case Nancy died without issue. Nancy, of course, did not die without issue; she was survived by four of her five children.

EXTERNAL REFERENCES. Lawrence W. Waggoner, The Uniform Probate Code Extends Antilapse-Type Protection to Poorly Drafted Trusts, 94 Mich. L. Rev. 2309, 2318-2321 (1996); Annot., Word "Child" or "Children" in Will as Including Grandchild or Grandchildren, 30 A.L.R.4th 319 (1984).

3. Avoiding Ambiguity in Express Conditions of Survival

The routine procedure in estate planning practice is to impose express conditions of survival on the beneficiaries of future interests. This is done for basically the same reasons that prompt proposals for a statute imposing a survival requirement when the governing instrument fails to do so by its own terms. A future interest that passes through a beneficiary's estate is awkward, expensive, and subject to taxation under IRC §2033. In addition, the absence of an express requirement of survival may lead to litigation concerning whether one is to be implied, litigation that may occur decades after the beneficiary's death.

The major advantage of the rule against implying conditions of survival—preserving a share of the estate for descending lines in which an ancestor predeceases the time of distribution—is easily accomplished by accompanying an express condition of survival with multiple-generation class gifts—future interests in favor of "issue" or "descendants."

If carelessly drafted, however, express conditions of survival can themselves be ambiguous and lead to litigation about their meaning.

Problem

At 9:15 p.m., a tax partner in your firm came into your office, just as you were about to leave for the day. She asked you to examine a 38-page draft she prepared for an irrevocable inter vivos life insurance trust. Her client is scheduled to arrive at her office at 9:00 a.m. tomorrow morning to sign the trust.

The tax partner explained to you that the trust is a great device for this client because the client's life insurance policy that will be assigned to the trust has a face value of $25 million and a present value of $5 million. For purposes of the federal generation-skipping transfer tax, the trust will therefore have an "inclusion ratio" of 0, meaning that even though the corpus of the trust will far exceed the client's GSTT exemption under IRC §2631, no generation-skipping transfer tax will ever be incurred. You acted as if you knew what the tax partner was talking about. She left to go home. You stayed.

You began reading through the trust. You noticed that the draft provides that after the settlor's death the trustee is to collect the proceeds of the life insurance policy, invest them, and pay the income therefrom to the settlor's son, Arnold, for life. So far, so good, you thought. Then you came to the provisions for the distribution of the corpus of the trust "upon Arnold's death." These provisions state:

(a)   To the surviving descendants of Arnold, by representation; or

(b)   If Arnold shall leave no surviving descendants, then to the surviving descendants of the Settlor, by representation; or

(c)   If the Settlor shall then have no surviving descendants, but he is survived by any of the descendants of his brother, to the descendants of his brother, by representation; or

(d)   If the Settlor is not survived by any of his descendants or by any of the descendants of his brother, to the surviving descendants of his father, by representation; or

(e)   If the Settlor is not then survived by any of the descendants of his father, to the Settlor's surviving heirs at law.

Finish the story. It is now 1:00 a.m.

Boone County National Bank v. Edson
760 S.W.2d 108 (Mo. 1988)

WELLIVER, J. Boone County National Bank brought this action to construe a will. They sought direction as to the proper distribution of a trust estate created by the will. Boone County National Bank is the trustee of a trust established by the Last Will and Testament of Margaret Poindexter Tello (Testatrix). The Boone County Circuit Court found the will clear and unambiguous....

Appellants [Kathie E. Kalmowitz, Judith D. Edson, and Carol E. Thompson] appealed claiming the will, as written, contains a mistake creating an ambiguity. The Court of Appeals, Western District concluded that the will is ambiguous and reversed the judgment. No party disputes the awarding of costs and attorney fees to be paid out of the trust estate.... We affirm the trial court.

I. The Testatrix had her attorney write the will in question in 1960. The Testatrix died in 1971 and the will was probated.

The residuary clause of the will created a trust for the support of Lois Tello, Testatrix' daughter. The terms of the trust directed the trustee to pay the income of the trust to Lois and authorized the trustee to invade the corpus of the trust as necessary to properly maintain, support and educate Lois. The will provided for termination of the trust on the death of Lois.

The conditions and directions for distribution of the remaining trust corpus and any undistributed income are set out in paragraph III-G of the will. It provides as follows:

> This trust shall terminate upon the death of my said daughter. At such time my Trustee is directed to pay over all of the remaining corpus of the trust, together with any undistributed income, to the child or children of my said daughter, if she dies with children her surviving, to be divided among her said children in equal shares per stirpes and not per capita. In the event that my said daughter dies without children her surviving, I give, devise and bequeath all of the remaining corpus and undistributed income to my sisters, Jessie P.

Moore, of Harlowton, Montana, and Dorothy Edson, of Harlowton, Montana, in equal shares. In the event that my sister, Jessie P. Moore, predeceases me, I desire that her share go to my other sister, Dorothy Edson. In the event that the said Dorothy Edson predeceases me, I give, devise and bequeath her share to her granddaughters, Carol Jane Edson, Kathie Margaret Edson, and Judith Dorothy Edson, or to their survivor, in equal shares.

For convenience and clarity, a diagram of the family relationships follows:

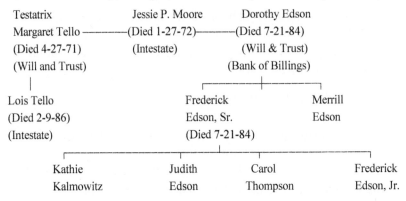

The question presented to us is whether or not the language used in the dispositive provision is ambiguous—that is, did Testatrix intend to use the pronoun "me" in the last two sentences of paragraph III-G or to use the pronoun "her" or the name "Lois."

The Testatrix died in 1971. She was survived by both of her sisters, Jessie P. Moore and Dorothy Edson, and Lois. Jessie P. Moore died intestate in 1972 leaving no spouse or children. Dorothy Edson died testate in 1984 prior to the death of Lois. Dorothy had two sons, Frederick Edson, Sr. (deceased) and Merrill Edson (respondent herein). Frederick was survived by four children, Frederick M. Edson, Jr., and appellants Kathie E. Kalmowitz, Judith D. Edson, and Carol E. Thompson.

Dorothy Edson, by her will, left all of her residuary estate to respondent First Interstate Bank in trust for the benefit of her four grandchildren. She specifically excluded her son, Merrill.

Lois Tello died intestate in 1986 and the trust for her benefit terminated. She was not survived by a spouse or any children.

The deposition of the drafting attorney was taken and offered and was ruled by the trial court to be inadmissable in this proceeding. Relying solely on his memory and not on notes or written memorandums, the attorney testified that it was his memory that the Testatrix intended that either "her" or the name "Lois" should have been used instead of the pronoun "me." He also testified that after the will was typed, it was given to Testatrix to carefully be read before signing.

II. The opposing parties each filed motions for summary judgment after discovery. Each motion incorporated by reference the deposition testimony of the attorney who drafted Testatrix' will....

If the last two sentences of paragraph III-G were construed to read the pronoun "her" or the name "Lois" instead of the pronoun "me," the entire trust corpus would be distributed to appellants Kathie E. Kalmowitz, Judith D. Edson, and Carol E. Thompson, in equal shares.

Our scope of review is established by Murphy v. Carron, 536 S.W.2d 30, 32 (Mo. banc 1976). The judgment must be sustained unless there is no substantial evidence to support it, unless it is against the weight of the evidence, unless it erroneously declares the law or unless it erroneously applies the law.

III. Appellants contend that the trial court erred in overruling their motion for summary judgment. Appellants virtually assume that it was the Testatrix' intent to use the pronoun "her" or the name "Lois", either of which would tie distribution of the assets to the death of Lois instead of the death of the Testatrix. Having so assumed, appellants find the ambiguity which they assert requires construction of the will, and, they then argue that proper construction requires that the court substitute either the pronoun "her" or the name "Lois" in lieu of the pronoun "me" in the last two sentences of paragraph III-G.

One of our rights most sacredly guarded by the law is our right to dispose of our property after death by a will prepared and executed prior to death. To assure the integrity of the instrument, we require formal and verified execution of the instrument. To assure all who would make wills that their intent can and will be carried out following their death, of necessity, we must impose the most strict rules of construction. This we believe the Missouri Courts have done throughout the history of our state....

If a will expresses the intention of the testatrix in clear and unequivocal language, there can be no occasion for construction of the instrument. The courts will not rewrite a will under the guise of construction.

In no case may words be transposed, supplied, substituted or otherwise omitted where the meaning is plain and unambiguous, and any alteration of the language originally employed would create a meaning different from that which it naturally had when the will was written.

The court cannot give the language used a different meaning for the purpose of carrying into effect a conjecture or hypothesis of the testatrix' intention, by supplying or rejecting words.

A. Appellants contend that the trial court misconstrued the will when it failed to substitute the intended pronoun to correct a mistake made by the draftsman. In construing a will, a court cannot correct a mistake made by the draftsman, unless the mistake appears on the face of the instrument, and unless it also appears what would have been the will if the mistake had not occurred. See Annotation, Effect of mistake of draftsman (other than testator) in drawing will, 90 A.L.R.2d 924 (1963). A mistake must be apparent on the face of the will, otherwise there can be no relief. Goode v. Goode, 22 Mo. 518, 524 (1856). Change "this doctrine, and you may as well repeal the statute requiring wills to be in writing, at once. Witnesses will then make wills and not testators." Id. We find the language used is clear and unambiguous on its face, and there is no justification for correcting possible draftsman's mistake. The trial court properly excluded the deposition of the drafting attorney.

B. The Testatrix provided for her daughter by establishing a trust for her care and support. It is clear from reading the will that Testatrix' intent was to provide for Lois. It also is clear the trust was to terminate upon Lois' death. It also is clear the Testatrix wanted the trust corpus to go to Lois' surviving children, if any, but to Testatrix' sisters if no children survived Lois.

Nothing in the will sheds light on whether Testatrix wanted further distribution tied to her death or that of her daughter, except the clear and unambiguous words which she used to tie further distribution to her own death. We can speculate that most people might have done it the other way, or that taxwise it would have been cheaper to do it the other way, but there is nothing on the face of the instrument to show an intent that it go other than by the words used, the words which she read before signing and the words which she signed.

The clear unambiguous words of the instrument mandate that the trial court be affirmed in all respects.

AFFIRMED.

In re Gustafson
547 N.E.2d 1152 (N.Y. 1989)

BELLACOSA, J. In concluding that appellants are not entitled to inherit under the relevant gift provision of this disputed will, we reaffirm two basic principles governing the adjudication of decedents' estates by courts: our primary function is to effectuate the testator's intent and the words used to express that intent are to be given their ordinary and natural meaning.

Testator executed his will in 1955 and it was admitted to probate in 1959. At issue is clause (c) of paragraph FIFTH, which bequeaths part of the residuary [trust] to the "surviving child or children" of testator's brother Leonard, who predeceased the trust's life tenant, testator's widow, Elsie. A "surviving child" of Leonard, Jacqueline, is respondent before us and claims entitlement to the whole of that residuary portion. Appellants are the widow and children of Leonard's other child, Daniel (Jacqueline's brother), who, like his father, predeceased the life tenant. Daniel's children, as appellants, strive to take under paragraph FIFTH'S gift provision and urge the courts to construe the word "children" to include grandchildren so that the collateral descendants of the testator, i.e., the grandnephews and grandnieces, can partake of the testamentary plan. Since they are faced with the fundamental proposition that the word "children" will be given its ordinary and natural meaning unless the will as a whole shows an unmistakable intent that different or remoter persons or classes should be included, they argue that the one-time use of the word "issue" in a different, inoperative clause of the will creates ambiguity and warrants forsaking the general rule of construction. Daniel's widow, as separate appellant, seeks to inherit on an argument that his inchoate share vested in him prior to the death of the life tenant, Elsie, [and passed to her by intestacy from Daniel].

We affirm the order of the Appellate Division, 145 A.D.2d 979, 536 N.Y.S.2d 351, [which awarded all of Leonard's share to Jacqueline, and none of it to Daniel's widow or children,] because a construction which would substitute for the testator's chosen word a broader, judicially applied definition is unwarranted and would be unsettling to the law of descent and distribution. Further, the relevant vesting date can be only the death of the life tenant.

Carl V.E. Gustafson was 59 years old, married and childless when he died in 1959. He disposed of virtually his entire estate through two trusts of equal size with an integrated, complementary residuary plan....

This case and appeal revolve around the trust created in paragraph FIFTH of the will, in which Elsie, testator's widow, held a life estate. Upon her death, testator's will directed the corpus of this trust be paid as follows:

(a) One-half to my brother, E. Leonard Gustafson.

(b) One-half to my brother, Roy L. Gustafson.

(c) If a brother predeceases Elsie Warren Gustafson, then his share of this Trust shall be paid over to his surviving child or children, share and share alike.

(d) If one of my brothers shall predecease Elsie Warren Gustafson, without issue surviving, then his part of this Trust shall be paid over to his surviving brother.

Roy survived Elsie and took his share pursuant to clause (b)....

At issue then is only the portion that would have been Leonard's one-[half] residuary share under clause (a), which, because of Leonard's predeceasing Elsie, must pass through clause (c). Leonard's son, Daniel, having also predeceased Elsie, leaves a widow and children who now seek to take a share of the residuary through this clause, though they are not "surviving child or children."

Courts construing donative instruments are governed by a threshold axiom: a testator's intent, as ascertained "from the words used in the will... according to their everyday and ordinary meaning", reigns supreme.... In Matter of Villalonga, 6 N.Y.2d 477, 484, 190 N.Y.S.2d 372, 160 N.E.2d 850, the natural and ordinary meaning of the word at issue here was held and applied as follows: "'[c]hildren' means immediate offspring, and we reiterate the rule of the [Matter of] Schaufele [252 N.Y. 65, 67, 168 N.E. 831] case that it will never be held to include grandchildren 'unless the will as a whole shows that unmistakable intent.'" (Emphasis added.) The will before us cannot clear that high hurdle.

The order of testator's priorities is straightforwardly expressed in paragraph FIFTH. First, he provided for his widow as long as she lived. Then, upon her death, his brothers would benefit (para FIFTH [a], [b]). If his brother(s) predeceased his widow, then the focus of testator's beneficial intent shifted to the "surviving child or children" of his brother(s) (para FIFTH [c]), a generation proximate to himself. The final subdivision of this paragraph provides that if a brother dies "without issue surviving", the surviving brother takes all. Thus, if neither issue nor children survived one brother, the other brother (or his children or his issue) would take to prevent a lapse. Accordingly, from the four corners of the will's relevant gift provision, assigning to each word its ordinary meaning, the testamentary scheme is reasonably discernible. Carl Gustafson wanted to benefit: (1) his widow while she lived; (2) his brothers who survived his widow; and (3) if a brother did not survive his widow, then the brother's child(ren) who did so survive. Those preferences of the testator as to the order and distribution of his property are not "incoherent", "inequitable", "inconsistent" or "anomalous", but even if they were, testators are privileged to act in any way they see fit to displace the State's otherwise mandated, homogenous distribution by intestacy, so long as they are compos mentis. Courts, on the other hand, are not privileged to put contrary or even additional words into a testator's actual written expression in order retrospectively to effectuate their own notions of "fair" or "equitable" distribution of estates.

Prowitt v. Rodman, 37 N.Y. 41, does not support a different result. There, an exception to the plain meaning of "children" was allowed because "the testator intended that the remote descendants should be takers... *if there should be a failure of the immediate offspring of [the trust life tenant]*" (id., at 54 [emphasis added]; see also, Matter of Welles, 9 N.Y.2d 277, 280, 213 N.Y.S.2d 441, 173 N.E.2d 876 ["It seems to us that the only possible occasion justifying a more inclusive meaning (of 'children') would be to avoid failure of the estate."]). There is no failure of an estate here, which is the only justification for the exception to the paramount plain meaning rule of construction.

Nor is this case about the testator's intention to disinherit unknown, collateral descendants two generations removed from him. The law of decedents' affairs recognizes no rule requiring a testator to manifest an intent to disinherit in such circumstances. Rather, our rules relate to the testator's intent to bestow a gift and to whom. In that respect, he was plain, precise and orderly, and appellants' claim to a gift in this trust remainder by implication would wrongly extend the plainly expressed and universally understood words. Our ruling, therefore, is natural, not "narrow", and a faithful application of the holding of the governing precedent, not an "extension" of it. Simply put, children means children in the judicial construction of this will....

We must also address the vesting date with respect to the remainder of the trust at issue. The death of the testator's life tenant, his widow, controls. Rather than "happenstance", this is the common measuring device for the orderly transferences of decedents' assets, a rule providing specificity, not serendipity. The vesting date here is arrived at by an application of well-settled principles of the law of future interests. The language of paragraph FIFTH (c) created a requirement of survival. When the first devisee or legatee takes a life estate, words of survivorship tend to "'establish the time of the termination of all preceding interests as the time to which survival is required'" (Matter of Gautier, 3 N.Y.2d 502, 509, 169 N.Y.S.2d 4, 146 N.E.2d 771, quoting Restatement of Property §251, at 1266). Here, the preceding interest terminated only upon the death of testator's widow, Elsie, in 1986. Daniel's predecease in 1981 is irrelevant in this respect and precludes his heirs from asserting that any entitlements inchoately vested in him before Elsie's death to accrue later to their benefit.

As we have consistently held, the plain meaning of the testamentary language itself is the surest path to the judicial discernment of a testator's donative intent. Expanding the application of exceptions to that sound general proposition would soon swallow the rule and render less secure the effectuation of testator's relied upon, expressed intentions. Indeed, to create a new exception out of something called "paramount intent", different from the intent clearly expressed on the face of a will and in its only relevant donative provision, would be seriously unsettling because it would sacrifice predictability, an especially crucial element in the field of decedents' estates where "settled rules are necessary and necessarily relied upon...."

Accordingly, the order of the Appellate Division should be affirmed, with costs to all parties filing briefs payable out of the residuary trust at issue.

HANCOCK, J. (dissenting). I would modify the order of the Appellate Division and hold that the term "children" in paragraph FIFTH (c) of the will includes grandchildren and, therefore, that Leonard's share must be divided equally between his son Daniel's surviving children, collectively, and his daughter, Jacqueline.

In my view, construing "children" narrowly here and, thereby, disinheriting the lineal descendants of one of the testator's brothers is unwarranted and represents a distinct—and unfortunate—extension of the "unmistakable intent" rule. In Matter of Villalonga, 6 N.Y.2d 477, 190 N.Y.S.2d 372, 160 N.E.2d 850, where we applied that rule and declined to read "children" broadly, we emphasized that: (1) the will there was "a simple one... and not afflicted with the weakness of ambiguity" (id., at 481, 190 N.Y.S.2d 372, 160 N.E.2d 850), (2) "[t]here [was] no interchangeable use made of the terms 'children' and 'issue' " (id., at 481, 190 N.Y.S.2d 372, 160 N.E.2d 850), and (3) "[n]or [did] the general distributive scheme disclose a testamentary purpose to benefit children of predeceased immediate offspring together with surviving immediate offspring" (id.). Those very factors—the absence of which led our court to construe "children" narrowly in *Villalonga*—are present in this case.

The will here is ambiguous. The ambiguity arises, in part, from the interchangeable use of the terms "children" and "issue" in paragraph FIFTH. Also, the use of "issue" in paragraph FIFTH (d) manifests a clear intention to benefit a predeceasing brother's surviving lineal descendants—not just the brother's immediate offspring as a narrow reading of "children" in paragraph FIFTH (c) suggests. Moreover, the intent of the testator as indicated by the language and structure of the entire will seems straightforward: to make gifts to his brothers or their respective family lines, treating them equally. Indeed, there is nothing in the testamentary scheme to suggest that the testator wanted to disinherit the family of his brother's son (Daniel's family), in favor of that brother's other child (Jacqueline), on the seemingly unrelated and meaningless contingency of his brother's son predeceasing his widow.

Significantly, the *Villalonga* court itself reaffirmed the well-established exception to the rule it applied, *viz.*, that where uncertainty exists, "children" should be given a broad construction to avoid an inequitable result (id., at 482-483, 190 N.Y.S.2d 372, 160 N.E.2d 850). Quoting Matter of Paton, 111 N.Y. 480, 486, 18 N.E. 625, our court reiterated that, "[o]f course, if the language employed 'is equally susceptible of one or another interpretation, we should, on every principle of right, and within the spirit of the authorities, give it that which is most equitable and consonant with the dictates of justice'" 6 N.Y.2d, at 484, 190 N.Y.S.2d 372, 160 N.E.2d 850 [emphasis added]. Accordingly, we should construe "children" in paragraph FIFTH (c) as "issue" and, thereby, avoid an incoherent interpretation of paragraph FIFTH (c) and (d) and, at the same time, avoid the patent inequity which otherwise results.

The majority's attempt to reconcile paragraph FIFTH (c) and (d) avoids neither problem. Nor does it withstand scrutiny. Paragraph FIFTH (d) cannot fairly be read—as the majority contends—as providing that, "if neither issue nor children survived one brother, the other brother (or his children or his issue) would take to prevent a lapse." Plainly, the language of paragraph FIFTH (d) does not so provide. It does no more than give the share of the estate in question to the "surviving brother" if the other dies "without issue surviving". There is no language in paragraph FIFTH (d) itself that directs or permits "issue" (or "children") to take. Only paragraph FIFTH (c) can be read as providing for that, and then, only if "children", as used by the testator, is construed to mean "issue".

Indeed, the majority's contention, that paragraph FIFTH (d) permits a devise to a brother's "issue" under certain circumstances, plainly undercuts their position and supports the view taken here. Their contention necessarily recognizes the basic point that "issue" (i.e., children of deceased children) were intended to be beneficiaries in some situations. But because, as noted, such a disposition cannot be effected under paragraph FIFTH (d), it follows that it can only be made under paragraph FIFTH (c)—i.e., by construing "children" in paragraph FIFTH (c) broadly as permitting "issue" to take.

Similarly, other provisions in the will either make little sense or run counter to the testator's over-all design if "children" is narrowly construed. For example, the distribution under paragraph SIXTH, providing for the direct gifts to the testator's two brothers, would have failed if one of them had died with grandchildren or other issue, but with no surviving immediate offspring. And the very same would be true for paragraph EIGHTH—which was explicitly intended to cover any bequest elsewhere in the will that might fail. Under that paragraph, as under paragraphs FIFTH and SIXTH, if "children" is read narrowly, there would be no provision for the very real contingency of a brother dying with no surviving sons or daughters, but with grandchildren or other lineal descendants still alive. Thus, paragraph EIGHTH, intended to avoid intestacy, would actually have permitted intestacy if read strictly.

I would resolve the ambiguities, and avoid the otherwise resulting inconsistencies and anomalies in the will, by broadly construing "children" to mean "issue". Such a construction would, in my view, yield the most reasonable and fair result—i.e., permitting Leonard's son's family (Daniel's family) as well as Leonard's daughter (Jacqueline) to share in the estate—and, thereby, avoid the certainly unintended inequity of depriving Daniel's children on the mere happenstance that their father died before their great uncle's widow. Finally, construing "children" broadly would, thus, give effect to the testator's paramount intent.

WACHTLER, C.J.,[6] and ALEXANDER and TITONE, JJ., concur with BELLACOSA, J.

HANCOCK, J., dissents in part and votes to modify in a separate opinion in which SIMONS and KAYE, JJ., concur.

Order affirmed, etc.

Notes and Questions

1. *Restatement of Property.* The court in *Gustafson* relied in part on the first Restatement of Property for the proposition that words of survival relate to the time of termination of all preceding interests—the death in 1986 of Carl Gustafson's widow, Elsie. Accord Restatement 3d of Property §15.3 comment f, §15.4 comment g. The first Restatement provides:

> *§251. Time to Which Survival Is Required by Added Word, Phrase or Clause.* In a limitation purporting to create a remainder or an executory interest, a description of the intended takers as persons "who survive," or who are "living," or by other language of the same import, but which fails to designate the time to which such takers must survive, tends to establish the time of the termination of all preceding interests as the time to which survival is required.

---

6. Sol Wachtler was appointed Chief Judge in 1985. In the early 1990s, he was arrested and convicted of harassing his ex-lover, Joy Silverman, a married woman seventeen years his junior. He knew her as the stepdaughter of his wife's uncle, but their relationship became intimate after he became trustee of a trust for her benefit established by the will of his wife's uncle. Wachtler tells the story of his downfall and life in prison in Sol Wachtler, *After the Madness: A Judge's Own Prison Memoir* (1997). Ed.

Comment e to this section states that this constructional preference "is a strong one," but also notes that it is opposed "by the preference for early indefeasibility." Consequently, when the preference is "reinforced by a special context indicating survival of a testator as the only survival intended, the tendency stated in this Section is overcome."

2. *Survival of the Time of Substitution?* The dissenting judge in *Gustafson*, Judge Hancock, expressed concern about the outcome of the case, as decided by the majority. Judge Hancock thought that "disinheriting the lineal descendants of one of the testator's brothers is unwarranted and represents a distinct—and unfortunate—*extension* of the 'unmistakable intent' rule." To prevent the disinheritance of Daniel's family, Judge Hancock unsuccessfully argued that "children" should be construed to mean "issue."

Is there another means of preventing the disinheritance of Daniel's family, which Judge Hancock did not mention and possibly did not notice? Note the order of deaths as between Daniel and his father, Leonard. Daniel died in 1981. Leonard died in 1978. Colman's Will, 33 N.W.2d 237 (Wis. 1948), is precedent for construing the word "surviving" in clause (c) as relating to Leonard's death rather than to Elsie's death.

Suppose that G's will created a trust, income to her husband, H, for life, remainder in corpus to the couple's children, but if any of the children predeceases H, that child's share to go to that child's surviving children. G and H had two children, A and B. A survived H. B predeceased H, leaving two children (X and Y) living at B's death. X predeceased H; Y survived H. In *Colman*, the court said:

> The general rule is that when a vested interest is divested by a condition subsequent, such interest immediately vests in the substitutionary legatees unless the will expressly provides otherwise....Consequently then, as under the will involved herein, the substitutionary legatees are children not of the testator nor of the life tenant, but of a third person, the class is determined and the bequest vests in such class on the death of their parent, or ancestor if taking per stirpes....When the interest of the parent vests in the children as a class the interest of any child then living is not divested by the death of such child prior to the termination of the life estate.... The law favors a vested rather than a contingent estate; and an absolute rather than a defeasible estate; and a vesting at the earliest possible period.

3. *Survival of the Testator.* Comment e to Restatement §251, above in Note 1, states that the preference for early indefeasibility, if reinforced by a special context, can overcome the presumption that words of survival relate to the termination of all preceding interests. In such a case, words of survival can be found to relate to the death of the testator.

A case adopting this construction is Nass's Estate, 182 A. 401, 114 A.L.R. 1 (Pa. 1936). George Nass, Sr., died in 1895, leaving a will that disposed of his residuary estate in trust, the income from which was given to his wife for life. On the death of his wife, the trust was to be divided into four equal parts. One part was given to his son, George, absolutely. A half of each of the remaining three parts was given absolutely to each of his daughters, Mary, Amanda, and Julia. The other halves of the remaining three parts were continued in trust, with the income to be paid equally to each of the daughters for life. Upon the death of each daughter, the portion of the principal from which she had been receiving income was to go that daughter's child or children. Nass's will continued:

> In case of the decease of my said Daughters or either of them without leaving lawful issue then and in such case I give devise and bequeath the said part or share hereinbefore given, devised and bequeathed to the said Executors In Trust unto my surviving child or children absolutely and forever.

Nass's wife died in 1915. Mary, one of the daughters, died in 1913 leaving a child who survived Mary (and presumably Nass's wife, also). George died in 1924, leaving issue. Amanda died in 1934, leaving a husband but no children. Julia, the only child still living, claimed the one-eighth share of the principal from which Amanda had been receiving the income. The court rejected Julia's claim, saying:

> Our rule of construction applied to survivorship has been held to refer to the time of death of the testator unless a contrary intent appears in the will. The rule is not without sound reason, for its general effect is to distribute the property among all of testator's descendants rather than to shunt it off into one line where it may pass out of the family. It is apparent that in this case any other construction would work an inequality which would not carry out what was presumably testator's scheme. He intended to treat, not only his own children alike, but his children's children, and no other thought appears in the will. He intended an equal division of his estate among his issue, and the repeated use of the word "equal" throughout his will is a clear demonstration of this fact. "Where the will shows an intention that the descendants of deceased children shall take, and an evident intention of equality of distribution is manifested, the word "survivors" has been held to apply to the death of the testator." Page on Wills (2d Ed.) p. 1562. If testator's intent be considered otherwise, it results in giving the entire fund to one child, Julia, whose life has been prolonged beyond the lives of the other children, and would tend to prefer her and her heirs over the heirs of other children.... Nor is the fact that the person to whom the prior estate is given, though his death is to precede the ultimate limitation, is himself a party entitled to share, sufficient to show an unequivocal intention that he was not to take upon the happening of the contingency.

4. *Single- vs. Multiple-Generation Class Gift.* Does the Restatement's preference for construing ambiguous words of survival as relating to the termination of all preceding interests make more sense when the future interest is to a multiple-generation class such as "issue" or "descendants" than when the future interest is to a single-generation class such as "children" or "nieces and nephews"?

5. *Uniform Probate Code.* If *Gustafson* (above), *Colman* (above in Note 2), and *Nass* (above in Note 3) had been governed by UPC §2-707, what result?

Problem

In Smith v. Cockrill, 196 S.E. 681 (Va. 1938), Benjamin F. McConchie's will devised certain real property to his daughter, Sarah, for life, remainder in fee simple to the testator's two other children, Mary and James. The will continued:

> But should Mary... or James... die before Sarah..., then his or her one-half... is to go to their children to be divided equally amongst their children that may be living at the death of Sarah.... And if either Mary... or James... should die before Sarah... without issue, then their one-half interest is to go to my surviving child in fee simple.

First Mary died, then James. James died intestate, apparently without ever having married; he never had any children. Mary was survived by her son, Max. Max also predeceased Sarah, leaving five children, all of whom survived Sarah. It is not clear whether Max survived James. Sarah left the residue of her estate to Rosa E. Smith.

The court held that Max's five children were entitled to the property at Sarah's death:

> [Benjamin McConchie] wanted to keep it in the family, so to speak....
>
> We have, therefore, arrived at the conclusion that after the death of Mary..., her interest passed to her son, Max..., and upon his death and the death of the life tenant, Sarah... to his children...; and that upon the death of James... his share likewise passed to [Max's five children], they taking the share which Mary... would have been entitled to. Rosa E. Smith takes no share of the realty under the will of Sarah.

Does the court's conclusion deserve to be supported with any greater rigor than this? *Can* it be supported with any greater rigor than this? If the case had been governed by UPC §2-707, what result?

Assuming the outcome reached by the court carried out Benjamin McConchies's intent, how could the disposition have been drafted so that no litigation would have been required to determine its meaning? How about "to Sarah for life, then to my descendants who survive Sarah, by representation;[7] if none of my descendants survives Sarah, to...."?

4. Age Specifications

Dispositions in trust frequently link a beneficiary's right to income or to possession or enjoyment of principal to reaching a specified age. According to a 1999 survey of the wealthiest one percent of Americans (then defined as those with a net worth of $3 million or more or whose annual income was $225,000 or more) commissioned by the U.S. Trust Company:

---

7. The will should also include a definition of the term "by representation." Cf. UPC §2-709.

Raising a financially responsible, hard-working child could be made more difficult if that child were to be given a large inheritance or trust assets at too young an age. Just over half the parents (55%) worry about making wise inheritance decisions with regard to their children. More of the affluents (58%) believed the wiser thing to do was stipulate an age when the inheritance could be received, rather than pass on an inheritance to the child upon the death of the respondent (33%). On average, this stipulated age was 28 years old.

Other steps they have taken include establishing trusts for their children. Eight of 10 respondents have or plan to set up trusts for their heirs. On average, those surveyed who have set up trusts for their children do not intend for their children to gain control of the trust assets until they are 28 years old.

As the following materials demonstrate, age specifications must be drafted with great care. If carelessly drafted, ambiguities in an age specification will probably be resolved by application of various rules of construction that sometimes conflict in a given case. The analysis is likely to begin with the rules of construction laid down in an ancient English case called Clobberie's Case, 2 Vent. 342, 86 Eng. Rep. 476 (Ch. 1677). The full report in this case appears as follows:

> In one *Clobberie's* case it was held, that where one bequeathed a sum of money to a woman, at her age of 21 years, or day of marriage, to be paid unto her with interest, and she died before either, that the money should go to her executor; and was so decreed by my Lord Chancellor Finch.
>
> But he said, if money were bequeathed to one at his age of 21 years; if he dies before that age, the money is lost.
>
> On the other side, if money be given to one, to be paid at the age of 21 years; there, if the party dies before, it shall go to the executors.

The staying power of the constructional rules established in *Clobberie's Case* has been remarkable. See Restatement 2d of Property §27.3:

> *Comment f. Age requirement specified....* The language of the disposition that indicates the age requirement is not a condition but is only a description of the time to which distribution is delayed is when the gift is to the class members "to be paid to each class member at 21" or "when they attain 21 with income in the meantime." If the gift is to the class members "who attain 21," the age requirement is clearly a condition.

In re Parker
L.R. 16 Ch. Div. 44 (1880)

[The testator, Mary Elizabeth Parker, died in 1863, leaving a will that devised the residue of her estate in trust, the terms of which were described by the court as follows:

> upon trust to pay the dividends, interest, and income thereof, or such part thereof as my said trustees for the time being shall from time to time deem expedient, in and towards the maintenance and education of my children until my said children shall attain their respective ages of 21 years; and from and immediately after their attaining their respective

ages of twenty-one years, then upon trust to pay, assign, and transfer the said stocks, funds, and securities to my said children in equal shares, if more than one, and if but one, then to such one child; and as to each daughter's share, whether original or accruing, upon trust to settle the same," for the benefit of herself and her children. And the testatrix declared "that it shall be lawful for the trustees or trustee for the time being of this my will to assign, transfer, or dispose of any component part, not exceeding one half of the presumptive share of any of my children for the preferment or advancing in life, or preparing for business, or on the marriage of any such child (being daughters) notwithstanding their minorities.

The testator was survived by her two sons and a daughter. One of the sons died in 1873, under the age of 21. The daughter and the other son both reached 21.]

JESSEL, M.R.... In my opinion, when a legacy is payable at a certain age, but is, in terms, contingent, the legacy becomes vested when there is a direction to pay the interest in the meantime to the person to whom the legacy is given; and not the less so when there is superadded a direction that the trustees "shall pay the whole or such part of the interest as they shall think fit." But I am not aware of any case where, the gift being of an entire fund payable to a class of persons equally on their attaining a certain age, a direction to apply the income of the whole fund in the meantime for their maintenance has been held to create a vested interest in a member of the class who does not attain that age.

The words here are plain. The trust is of residue: "to pay the dividends, interest, or income thereof, or such part thereof as my said trustees for the time being shall from time to time deem expedient, in or towards the maintenance and education of my children, until my said children shall attain their respective ages of twenty-one years"; so that there is nothing here giving an aliquot share of income to any individual child; the direction being to pay the income of the whole fund in such shares as the trustees shall think fit. I do not think you can infer anything from the direction for the settlement of the daughters' shares.

Then follows a gift of the whole fund to the children equally on attaining twenty-one. I should have felt no difficulty if it had not been for the advancement clause, which speaks of the "presumptive share of any of my children," but I do not think that clause is sufficient to alter the effect of the preceding part of the will.

That being so, I hold that the infant did not take a vested interest in his one-third share of the residue.

Clay v. Security Trust Co.
252 S.W.2d 906 (Ky. 1952)

DUNCAN, J. This Declaratory Judgment action seeks a construction of the last will and testament of James T. Clay who died a resident of Fayette County in February, 1932....

The will under consideration is as follows:....

Third All the balance of my estate of whatsoever nature and kind I give to my sister Laura Clay Macey, which is to be held by my Trustee hereinafter named during her life, and the income therefrom is to be paid to her in monthly installments. I desire my Trustee to consult with my said sister in making change of investments of the said fund. At the death of my said sister, Laura Clay Macey, I direct my Trustee to hold the said estate until my nephew John Ireland Macey, the only child of Laura Clay Macey, arrives at the age of thirty-five years, and direct that the income shall be paid to him in monthly installments until the said fund is turned over to him.

At the time of testator's death he was survived by his sister, Laura Clay Macey, two half-brothers, Matthew D. Clay and Neal McClure Clay, and his nephew, John I. Macey (John Ireland Macey), the son of Laura Clay Macey. John I. Macey predeceased his mother, Laura Clay Macey and died in 1944 before he attained the age of 35. Laura Clay Macey died on February 8, 1951....

The question in the case is whether the remainder interest given to John I. Macey in the third clause of the will was a vested or contingent remainder. Appellees contend and the lower court found that the interest was a vested one and that the fund in question should be paid to the devisee under the will of John I. Macey. Appellants contend that the interest was contingent upon Macey attaining the age of 35 and that inasmuch as he died prior to his 35th year, the fund descends under the laws of descent and distribution and is payable to the heirs of James T. Clay....

One of the rules of construction of almost universal application is the presumption against partial intestacy. The rule is that where a will is susceptible of two constructions, the law favors that one which disposes of the entire estate. The presumption is even stronger where the will contains a residuary clause.

Another rule of equally general application is that which favors the early vesting of estates. All doubts will be resolved in favor of the construction which accomplishes an early vesting unless a contrary intention clearly appears.

Two other rules of particular applicability to the problem here presented are the following: (1) the absence of a gift or limitation over in the event of failure to attain a specified age is regarded as indicating an intention on the part of the testator that the gift should vest immediately; (2) a gift of the substance to which futurity is apparently annexed is not considered contingent upon the attainment of a specified age where there is a gift of the intermediate use.

In the case of Danforth v. Talbot's Adm'r, 46 Ky. 623, 7 B. Mon. 623, the court had before it for a construction a will the applicable portions of which were as follows:

7th. On the decease of my said wife, the above described farm, &x., &c., shall become the property of my son Cyrus, when arrived at the age of twenty-six years, (excepting the reservation in favor of Ann R.;) but after providing for the support and comfort of his mother, he may be entitled to all the profits arising from the same, except the reserved rights of his sister, Ann R.

In that case the court in a well-reasoned opinion held that the estate devised to Cyrus Talbot was not contingent upon his attaining the age of 26, but that the devise had the effect of merely postponing the time of enjoyment. There it was said:

> And although the event referred to, that is, the arrival of the son at the age of twenty-six, must, when abstractly and precisely considered, be regarded as uncertain and contingent, must it be assumed to have been so regarded by the testator? He evidently did not regard it as contingent. He speaks of it as a thing certainly to happen. He does not even say, "if" he shall arrive, &c., but "when" arrived at the age of twenty-six years; and he makes no devise over upon the event not happening, as he would almost certainly have done if he had regarded the happening of the event as uncertain, or its not happening as a contingency which would give a different direction to the estate....

In the same case the court recognized and applied the rules of construction noted herein which arise from the omission of a devise over upon Cyrus not attaining the age of 26 and the right given him under the will to the intermediate use prior to the time of full enjoyment.

We recognize that the opinion in that case was written more than one hundred years ago. However, that fact does not militate against the weight which should be accorded it if it is sound and the reasons supporting it are valid....

For the reasons indicated, we are of the opinion that the construction adopted by the Chancellor was proper and the judgment is affirmed.

Restatement 3d of Property

§26.6 Age Specification: Implied Condition of Survival

Unless the language or circumstances establish that the transferor had a different intention, a future interest that is distributable upon reaching a specified age is conditioned on the beneficiary's living to that age.

....

[Comment] c. Historical note. An old English case, *Clobberie's Case*, 2 Vent. 342, 86 Eng. Rep. 476 (Ch. 1677), has been the principal source for the rules of construction regarding a future interest distributable to a beneficiary upon reaching a specified age. Although *Clobberie's Case* has continued to influence the law into modern times, the rules laid down by that case turn on small differences in wording....

[Comment] e. Contrary intent—language of present gift with possession postponed. The rule of this section is a rule of construction that yields if the language or circumstances establish that the donor had a different intention. Language providing that the share is "to be paid at" a specified age is treated as a factor but not necessarily a controlling factor suggesting that there is no condition of survival to the specified age.

[Comment] f. Contrary intent—intermediate income. A provision directing that income from the beneficiary's presumptive share be paid to the beneficiary while the beneficiary is under the specified age is taken as a strong but not necessarily a controlling factor that there is no condition of survival to the specified age.

Notes and Questions

1. *Restatement 3d of Property.* How does the Restatement 3d of Property (above) treat the rules from *Clobberie's Case*?

2. *Drafting Age Specifications.* Normally, it will be desirable expressly to require survival of the specified age and to provide for alternative takers in the event of a failure to survive. In one situation, however, there may be reason expressly to negate a requirement of survival. This arises when the donor wishes to qualify an inter vivos gift in trust to a minor child for the annual gift tax exclusion allowed by IRC §2503(c).

To qualify for the exclusion under IRC §2503(c), the property must "pass to the donee on his attaining the age of 21 years, and in the event the donee dies before attaining the age of 21 years, be payable to the estate of the donee or as he may appoint under a general power of appointment...." The custom in estate planning practice is to use the power of appointment option. But if that option is not chosen, then the governing instrument should clearly state that the death of the donee before reaching 21 does not extinguish the donee's interest. How would you draft the trust to accomplish this result? Should the instrument say "whether or not the donee lives to age 21," or should it track §2503(c) and say "if the donee dies under 21, then the property is to be paid to the donee's estate"? See Olin L. Browder, Trusts and the Doctrine of Estates, 72 Mich. L. Rev. 1509, 1522-28 (1974); John O. Fox, Estate: A Word to be Used Cautiously, If at All, 81 Harv. L. Rev. 992 (1968); Annot., 10 A.L.R.3d 483.

3. *Will of Princess Diana.* The 1993 will of Princess Diana, who died in an automobile accident in Paris in 1997, disposed of the residue of her approximately $35 million estate in the following provision. Was this provision well drafted?

> 5. SUBJECT to the payment or discharge of my funeral testamentary and administration expenses and debts and other liabilities I GIVE all my property and assets of every kind and wherever situate to my Executors and Trustees Upon trust either to retain (if they think fit without being liable for loss) all or any part in the same state as they are at the time of my death or to sell whatever and wherever they decide with power when they consider it proper to invest trust monies and to vary investments in accordance with the powers contained in the Schedule to this my Will and to hold the same UPON TRUST for such of them my children PRINCE WILLIAM and PRINCE HENRY as are living three months after my death and attain the age of twenty five years if more than one in equal shares PROVIDED THAT if either child of mine dies before me or within three months after my death and issue of that child are living three months after my death and attain the age of twenty one years such issue shall take by substitution if more than one in equal shares per

stirpes the share that the deceased child of mine would have taken had he been living three months after my death but so that no issue shall take whose parent is then living and so capable of taking.

5. *Gifts Over on Death or on Death Without Issue*

Possessory Interests. G's will devised real property as follows:

(a) To A and his heirs, but if A should die, to B.

(b) To A and his heirs, but if A should die without issue, to B.

G died and then A died without issue. B is still alive. Who is entitled to the property, B or A's successors in interest?

In Case (a), the usual construction is that the property goes through A's estate to A's successors in interest.[8] See Restatement 3d of Property §26.7; Restatement of Property §263.

In Case (b), the usual construction is that A's interest is divested in favor of B.[9] See Restatement 3d of Property §26.8; Restatement of Property §267. But see, e.g., Friedman v. Marshall, 876 S.W.2d 745 (Mo. Ct. App. 1994), where the court construed a devise of a possessory interest subject to a condition of death without issue to apply to death *before the testator* without issue.

Woods' Estate
149 A.2d 865 (N.H. 1959)

.... Elizabeth A. Luce ... died in 1954. Clara E. Woods died December 30, 1956, and the administratrix was appointed January 5, 1957. Among the assets inventoried in the Woods estate was an undivided one-half interest in certain real estate in Keene.

This property was formerly owned by Mrs. Luce. In her will, after leaving $100.00 to her husband in lieu of all his rights in her estate, she provided that

> all the rest, residue and remainder of my property, whether real or personal, and wherever situated, I give, bequeath and devise in equal shares to my daughter, Jessie Evelyn Starkey, of said Keene, and my sister, Clara E. Woods, of said Keene. In case of the death of either the said Jessie Evelyn Starkey or the said Clara E. Woods, I give, bequeath and devise the share of such decedent to the survivor.

The administratrix of the Woods estate, Evelyn S. Deming, formerly Jessie Evelyn Starkey, claims that as daughter of Mrs. Luce she takes all her mother's real estate

---

8. In Case (a), of course, it makes no difference whether A died with or without issue.

9. The same result would be reached if B survived G but predeceased A; A's interest would be divested in favor of B's successors in interest. See, e.g., Hays v. Cole, 73 So.2d 258 (Miss. 1954).

to the exclusion of Clara's heirs. In her petition, she asks us to answer the following questions: "(1) Did the said Clara E. Woods inherit in fee an undivided one-half interest in said real estate under the will of the late Elizabeth A. Starkey Luce? (2) In the event the foregoing question is answered in the negative, should the inventory be amended to exclude said one-half interest in said real estate from the estate of Clara E. Woods?"

BLANDIN, J. The basic question presented is whether Clara E. Woods took a vested interest in fee under the will of her sister, Elizabeth A. Luce, in certain real estate, so that upon her death it descended to Clara's heirs, Florence Cram and Doris Cocco, or whether it passed to Mrs. Luce's only daughter, Evelyn S. Deming. The answer depends on what the testatrix meant when, after bequeathing all the remainder of her estate in equal shares to her daughter and sister, she added the words: "In case of the death of either... I give, bequeath and devise the share of such decedent to the survivor." Although as administratrix of Mrs. Woods' estate, Mrs. Deming inventoried a "½ interest in Land and buildings" in the disputed real property, she presently claims this was error and that she takes it all as survivor under Mrs. Luce's will.

It is axiomatic that the law favors the early vesting of interests in the interest of certainty, the avoidance of complications, and the expeditious settlement of estates. Furthermore, the common meaning attributed to words of survivorship is that they refer to the death of the devisee in the lifetime of the testatrix. The practical difficulties of applying the construction urged by the administratrix, especially with reference to the disposition of personal estate, are obvious and militate against her claim. Furthermore, the words appear in themselves significant. Since death is certain, there seems no point in using the words "In case" unless they were intended to refer to the death of either of the devisees before that of the testatrix.

We are not unmindful of the administratrix's argument that Mrs. Luce's main concern was her sister, Clara, and her daughter, the administratrix, and that since she did not mention her brother, Samuel Luce, and another sister, Florence Cram, it must have been her intent that neither they nor their children should share in her estate. We agree that her real interest was in her daughter and her sister Clara, but had she been desirous of arranging matters so that no child of her brother or Mrs. Cram should take under her will, she could easily have done so.

In the case of Mulvanity v. Nute, 95 N.H. 526, 68 A.2d 536, cited by the administratrix, the will unequivocally expressed an intention that a joint tenancy be created. The testator gave certain property to his son and sister as "Joint Tenants" and stated that "upon the decease of one the title to vest in the survivor." 95 N.H. at page 527, 68 A.2d at page 536. He expressed the desire that his son and sister have the right to occupy the premises during their lifetime. The Court held that a joint tenancy in fee was created. It added that in order to establish the unusual estate of a life estate with remainder to the survivor, which is what the administratrix claims was created by Mrs. Luce's will, "clear and unambiguous language" would have to be used. Id. at page 528, 68 A.2d at page 537. See also RSA 477:18. We find no such language in this will indicating an intent to set up such an uncommon estate, but rather it expresses a reasonably plain purpose to make a gift in fee to two persons with the survivor taking all if, but only if, one of them died before the testatrix.

In all the circumstances, we believe the testatrix, when she said "In case of the death of either," referred to death in her lifetime. Since this did not occur, it follows that Clara E. Woods took an undivided one-half interest in fee in the disputed real property which was properly inventoried as part of her estate.

Case remanded.

———

Future Interests. G's will created a trust, the terms of which were:

(a) Income to LT for life, remainder in corpus to A, but if A should die, to B.

(b) Income to LT for life, remainder in corpus to A, but if A should die without issue, to B.

G died, then A died without issue, and then LT died. B is still alive. Who is entitled to the property, B or A's successors in interest? The usual construction in both cases is that A's interest is divested in favor of B.[10] See Restatement 3d of Property §§26.7, 26.8; Restatement of Property §§264, 269.

G died and then LT died. A is still alive. Did A's survival of LT render A's interest absolute, or does A's interest continue to be defeasible? The majority construction in both cases is that A's survival of LT rendered A's interest absolute. See Restatement 3d of Property §§26.7, 26.8; Restatement of Property §§264, 269. There is, however, division in the cases on the point, especially regarding Case (b). See Annot., 26 A.L.R.3d 407.

Definite versus Indefinite Failure of Issue. A further question exists in connection with the dispositions containing a gift over on death without issue. To reintroduce those dispositions, suppose that G disposed of property in her will as follows:

(a) To A and her heirs, but if A should die without issue, to B.

(b) To L for life, remainder to A, but if A should die without issue, to B.

After G's death, A died survived by issue. In Case (b), L was still alive when A died.

Does A's death survived by issue render her interest absolute, or does her interest continue to be defeasible? The preferred and usual construction is that A's death survived by issue who survive the distribution date renders her interest absolute. See Restatement 3d of Property §26.8 comment b; Restatement of Property §266. This

———

10. In Case (a), of course, it makes no difference whether A died with or without issue.

construction, called a "definite failure of issue" construction, is codified in several states. See, e.g., Cal. Prob. Code §21112.

An older construction, now nearly universally abandoned, is called an "indefinite failure of issue" construction. Under this construction, which is the English construction carried over from the fee tail estate, A can still "die without issue" after her death. A's "death without issue" occurs if and when her last living descendant dies.

Accrued Shares. G devised a tract of land "to my three sons, A, B, and C; but if any son dies without leaving issue surviving him, the portion devised to such son shall go to my said sons then living."

After G's death, A died without issue; then B died without issue, leaving a will that devised his entire estate to his widow, W. Does C now own the entire tract of land? What happens if C dies without issue? What if C dies *with* issue? Compare Restatement of Property §271 (applying the principle of the accrued share) and §272 comment c (declining, if C dies with issue, to imply a remainder in C's issue) with Restatement 3d of Property §26.9 comment b (implying, if C dies with issue, a remainder in C's issue) and comment f (rejecting the principle of the accrued share).

PART B. SPECIAL PROBLEMS OF CLASS GIFTS

Class gifts are extremely useful in estate planning practice, especially multiple-generation class gifts, such as to issue, descendants, or heirs. We are already knowledgeable about many of the features that distinguish class gifts from individual gifts.

In Chapter 6, we studied the definition of a class gift—how to differentiate a class gift ("to my children") from individual gifts ("to my three children, C1, C2, and C3"; "to my three children"; "to my children, C1, C2, and C3"). Chapter 6 also examined the effect of the death of a potential class member before the testator's death and the applicability of anti-lapse statutes in such cases.

Chapter 2 introduced us to the different forms of representation in multiple-generation class gifts—per stirpes, per capita with representation, and per capita at each generation. In addition, Chapter 3 examined the status of adopted children, nonmarital children, and children of assisted reproduction or de facto parentage.

In Part A of this chapter, we studied the effect of a contingency unrelated to survival on a future interest in favor of a single-generation class, and we saw that a condition of survival is thought to be implicit in a multiple-generation class gift in which a representational form of distribution is called for.

What is left?

1. Increase in Class Membership: Class Closing and the Rule of Convenience

Primary Statutory Reference: *UPC §2-705*

A unique feature of most class gifts (other than class gifts to heirs) is the ability of new entrants to join the class. Each new entrant increases the number of potential takers and partially divests the shares of the existing class members.

A class is subject to increase—subject to open—as long as it is possible for new entrants to come into the class. The ability of a class to increase ends—the class "closes"—at the *earlier* of two events: (1) the natural (or physiological) closing of the class; or (2) the artificial (or premature) closing brought about by the application of the so-called *rule of convenience.*

Natural (or Physiological) Class Closing. The natural closing of a class occurs when births (or, if adopted members are within the class description, adoptions) become physiologically impossible. A class gift in favor of a transferor's grandchildren physiologically closes upon the death of the transferor's last living child. A grandchild who is in gestation on the date the class closes is regarded as in being on the closing date.

The physiological closing of a class is traditionally predicated on the assumption that death terminates the possibility of having children. Medical developments have shown that the traditional assumption may not always be true. With frozen sperm, ova, and embryos on the contemporary scene, the possibility of having children can exist for years after death. See Chapter 3. Should a child produced after death be included as a class member? The Restatement 3d of Property §15.1 comment j provides:

> *j. Child produced posthumously by assisted reproduction.* In cases in which the distribution date is the deceased parent's death, a child produced posthumously by assisted reproduction is treated as in being at the decedent's death for purposes of the class-closing rules, if the child was born or in utero within a reasonable time after the decedent's death.... Determining whether birth or pregnancy occurred within a reasonable time after the decedent's death requires a balancing of the interest in final settlement of trusts and estates and allowing the surviving spouse or domestic partner time to grieve before making a decision whether to go forward with an assisted-reproduction procedure, and how soon after death an attempt was made to produce a pregnancy through assisted reproduction, whether successful or not....
>
> In cases in which the distribution date arises after the deceased parent's death, a child produced posthumously by assisted reproduction is in being on the date when the child is in utero for purposes of the class-closing rules, just as is any other child.

See also UPC §2-705(e)(2) (treating a posthumous child as living on the distribution date if that date is the deceased parent's death and the child lives at least 120 hours after birth and was in utero not later than 36 months after the deceased parent's death or born not later than 45 months after the deceased parent's death).

Of course, in the vast majority of cases, no frozen sperm, ova, or embryos capable of producing a post-death child exist, and the traditional assumption about the parent's death marking the closing of the class prevails and works well.

Artificial (or Premature) Class Closing: The Rule of Convenience. A class may close earlier than its physiological closing. When this happens, the class has been closed artificially or prematurely. Artificial or premature closing is governed by the rule of convenience.

The Restatement 3d of Property §15.1 states the rule of convenience as follows:

§15.1 When Class Closes—Rule of Convenience

Unless the language or circumstances establish that the transferor had a different intention, a class gift that has not yet closed physiologically closes to future entrants on the distribution date if a beneficiary of the class gift is then entitled to distribution.

The rule of convenience is a rule of construction, not a rule of law. It yields to a contrary intent. In practice, however, a contrary intent can seldom be shown, and consequently the rule of convenience typically prevails.

Once a class has been closed by the rule of convenience, subsequently conceived or adopted persons are not entitled to participate in the class gift, even though they otherwise fit the class label. New entrants come into a class only if they are conceived[11] or adopted[12] while the class is still open.

As the Restatement indicates, the rule of convenience holds that a class closes when a class member becomes entitled to distribution of a share. This rule is founded on two basic premises. First is the premise that the use of only a group or

---

11. As indicated above, a child in gestation when a class closes is regarded as in being at that time. In administering this principle, there is precedent suggesting a rebuttable presumption that the date of conception was nine months before the date of birth. See, e.g., Equitable Trust Co. v. McComb, 168 A. 203, 207 (Del. Ch. 1933); Wells' Will, 221 N.Y.S. 714, 724 (Sur. 1927). To enter the class, the child must be born alive and probably must be born viable. See, e.g., Ebbs v. Smith, 394 N.E.2d 1034 (Ohio C.P. 1979); Recent Developments, Torts—Wrongful Death—Unborn Child—The Estate of an Unborn Child Has a Cause of Action for Wrongful Death—O'Neill v. Morse, 70 Mich. L. Rev. 729, 735 (1972); Restatement 3d of Property §15.1 comment h.

12. With respect to an adopted child, the date of adoption, not the date of conception, is the significant date for inclusion in the class. See, e.g., Estate of Markowitz, 312 A.2d 901, 903 (N.J. Essex County Ct. 1973) ("Born when?... Regardless of the time when an adopted child is physically born, he or she does not come into existence as a child of the adoptive parent [in the sense that the law equates the relationship of a biological child with that of an adopted child] until the effective date of the order of adoption."); but see Restatement 3d of Property §15.1 comment i ("By analogy to a child in gestation, a child who is in the process of being adopted is regarded for class-gift purposes as an adopted child during the period the adoption is in process." To be included in the class, the adoption must be "concluded within a reasonable time" after the closing of the class.)

class description indicates that *all* persons who fit the description—whenever born (or adopted)—were intended to share in the gift. In other words, the starting point is that the class was not intended to close until it closes naturally. Second, because of inherent difficulties or "inconveniences" in allowing participation by persons born (or adopted) after distribution, it is believed that the transferor, if the transferor had contemplated these difficulties, would have intended to exclude these persons. That is, although the basic intent of the transferor is to keep the class open until it closes naturally, if inconveniences will arise from doing so, the transferor would prefer for the class to be closed prematurely or unnaturally, so that the inconveniences will be avoided.

The inconvenience of a class being kept open after distribution is that the distributees would not take an indefeasible interest. Instead, they would receive a considerably less useful defeasible one. Taking an interest that is subject to being partially divested upon the birth (or adoption) of additional class members would render the property less marketable and, if personal property, would require some device such as the posting of security to protect the interests of unborn (or unadopted) members of the class.

Immediate Class Gifts. When at least one member of the class is in existence, an immediate gift closes at the date the gift becomes effective.

Example 16.7: G devised real property "to my grandchildren." When G executed his will, his only son A had a child (X). Subsequently, but before G's death, a second child (Y) was born. G was survived by his son A and by his two grandchildren, X and Y. No grandchildren were in gestation at G's death.

Under the rule of convenience, the class closes at G's death even though A is still alive and is therefore deemed to be capable of having more children. X and Y each take an undivided interest in one-half of the property in fee simple absolute. In other words, their interests are not subject to partial divestment in favor of any later born (or later adopted) child of A.

Suppose that at G's death, A's wife was pregnant, and that G's third grandchild (Z) was born viable. Z would be considered to have been "in being" at G's death, and consequently Z would participate in the class gift. So, X, Y, and Z would each take an undivided one-third possessory interest in the property in fee simple absolute.

There is an exception to the rule that an immediate class gift by will closes at the testator's death. If there is *no* class member then "in being," (an empty class) the class does not close prematurely, but remains open until it closes naturally.

Example 16.8: G devised real property "to my grandchildren." At G's death, her son A was still alive, but A had no living children and none was then in gestation.

The rule of convenience does not close the class at G's death. The class remains open until the death of A. *All* afterborn grandchildren, if any, are entitled to participate.

Note, however, that if a child of A's had been in gestation at G's death, and if that child had been subsequently born viable, then the rule of convenience would have closed the class on G's death, resulting in that child having taken the whole property in fee simple absolute.

Specific-Sum Class Gifts. When a class gift grants a specific sum to each member of the class, as opposed to the more traditional type of class gift in which a proportional share of a fund or item of property is granted to each class member, the class closes when the gift becomes effective, whether or not any class member is then alive. If no class member is then alive, the class gift fails.

———

Problem

G's will created a trust, income to G's grandchildren until the death of G's last living grandchild, remainder in corpus to X Charity. When G died, grandchild GC1 and grandchild GC2 were living. Subsequently, grandchild GC3 was conceived and born, then grandchild GC4. To what portion of the income, if any, are the after-born grandchildren entitled?

It may help you in thinking about this problem to note that the Restatement 3d of Property §15.1 comment p describes the income payments as a "series of successive postponed class gifts."

Postponed Class Gifts. The basic principle of the rule of convenience is that a class closes when a distribution of the property must be made. Having applied this principle to immediate class gifts, we now turn our attention to class gifts in which distribution is postponed.

Problems

When do the classes close in the following cases?

1. G devised real property "to A for life, remainder to B's children." G was survived by A, B, and B's child (C1). A second child (C2) was born to B during A's lifetime. B's third child (C3) was conceived and born after A's death. B survived A.

2. In Problem 1, suppose that by the time of A's death, no children had been born to B and that none was then in gestation.

3. G devised property in trust, income to G's grandchildren, corpus to be equally divided among G's grandchildren when the youngest grandchild attains age 21. When G executed her will, her first grandchild (GC1) had just been born. Subsequently, another grandchild (GC2) was born. G then died. After G's death, the following events happened, in the order stated: GC1 became 21; another grandchild (GC3) was conceived and born; GC2 became 21; a fourth grandchild (GC4) was conceived and born; GC3 became 21; GC4 became 21.

No further grandchildren had been born or were in gestation on GC4's 21st birthday, but G's children were still living. G's youngest child, E, was a male, age 43; he was contemplating marriage to his 34-year-old female friend, F.

The Restatement 3d of Property §15.1 comment o provides:

> A class gift that is distributable when the youngest member of the class reaches a specified age is ambiguous. There are two plausible constructions. One is that the class closes when no living class member is under the specified age. The other is that the class closes when the youngest member of the class whenever born reaches that age. The former construction is preferred unless the facts and circumstances make it likely that another class member will subsequently be born or adopted.

See also Lux v. Lux, below.

Lux v. Lux
288 A.2d 701 (R.I. 1972)

KELLEHER, J. [Philomena Lux left the residue of her estate "to my grandchildren, share and share alike." Her will further provided:

> 3. Any real estate included in said residue shall be maintained for the benefit of said grandchildren... until the youngest of said grandchildren has reached twenty-one years of age.

Philomena was survived by one son, Anthony John Lux, Jr., age thirty, and his five children, whose ages ranged from two to eight. The youngest grandchild was born after the will was executed but before Philomena's death.

The court held that clause 3 created a trust for the benefit of the grandchildren, the corpus of which was to be distributed when the youngest grandchild reaches 21; the class of grandchildren should remain open until then. Next, the court turned to the meaning of the term "youngest," saying:]

There are four possible distribution dates depending on the meaning of "youngest." Distribution might be made when the youngest member of the class in being when the will was executed attains twenty-one; or when the youngest in being when the will takes effect becomes twenty-one; or when the youngest of all living class members in being at any one time attains twenty-one even though it is physically possible for others to be born; or when the youngest whenever it is born attains twenty-one. This last alternative poses a question. Should we delay distribution here and keep the class open until the possibility that Philomena's son can become a father becomes extinct? We think not.

We are conscious of the presumption in the law that a man or a woman is capable of having children so long as life lasts. A construction suit, however, has for its ultimate goal the ascertainment of the average testator's probable intent if he was aware of the problems that lead to this type of litigation. It is our belief that the average testator, when faced with the problem presented by the record before us, would endorse the view expressed in Restatement, Property §295 comment k at 1594 (1940), where in urging the adoption of the rule that calls for the closing of the class when the youngest living member reaches the age when distribution could be made, states:

> When all existent members of the class have attained the stated age, considerations of convenience ... require that distribution shall then be made and that the property shall not be further kept from full utilization to await the uncertain and often highly improbable conception of further members of the group. The infrequency with which a parent has further children after all of his living children have attained maturity, makes this application of the rule of convenience justifiable and causes it to frustrate the unexpressed desires of a conveyor in few, if any, cases.

We hold, therefore, that distribution of the trust corpus shall be made at any time when the youngest of the then living grandchildren has attained the age of twenty-one. When this milestone is reached, there is no longer any necessity to maintain the trust to await the possible conception of additional members of the class....

Problems

When do the classes close in the following cases?

1. G bequeathed $90,000 to be divided equally among those of G's grandchildren who reach the age of 21. (This type of bequest probably would be in trust, and it might provide either for the accumulation of the income until distribution, or for its payment to the grandchildren as it is earned.)

(a) One of G's grandchildren had reached 21 before G's death. Does the class close when that grandchild reached 21 or when G died?

(b) None of G's grandchildren had reached 21 before G's death. Subsequently, the first grandchild (GC1) reached 21; there were two other grandchildren (GC2 and GC3) then alive. Thereafter, GC2 died under 21. Then GC3 reached 21. When did this class close? Who are the ultimate takers and what are their shares?

(c) The income from the trust was to be accumulated and added to the corpus; each grandchild was to receive a proportionate part of the corpus upon reaching 21. G was survived by a daughter, age 30, and a son, age 24, both unmarried and childless. Shortly after G's death, the son married a college classmate and the daughter married a widower, age 45, who had two children by his previous marriage. The ages of the widower's two children were 19 and 21. G's son and his bride were childless, but planned on having a family. G's daughter adopted her husband's children. Is the class closed yet? See Silberman's Will, 242 N.E.2d 736 (N.Y. 1968);[13] Nowels Estate, 339 N.W.2d 861 (Mich. Ct. App. 1983); Restatement 3d of Property §15.1 comment m; Cal. Prob. Code §21115(b); UPC §2-705.

---

13. Discussed in Samuel M. Fetters, The Determination of Maximum Membership in Class Gifts in Relation to Adopted Children, Silberman's Will Examined, 21 Syracuse L. Rev. 1 (1969).

2. G bequeathed $90,000 in trust to pay the income to A for life, then to distribute the corpus equally among those of G's nieces and nephews who reach 21. (Again, the income after A's death, but before distribution of the corpus, might be either accumulated or paid out.)

(a) Prior to A's death, one of G's nieces reached 21. Does the class close when that niece reached 21 or when A died?

(b) None of G's nieces or nephews had attained 21 by the time of A's death. Subsequently, one of the nephews, X, reached 21. Two months after X's 21st birthday, a niece was born. Another niece was born fourteen months after X's 21st birthday. Is either of these nieces included in the class?

3. G devised land "to my grandchildren, but if any grandchild should die before attaining 21, his or her share to go to my then surviving grandchildren." G was survived by children and grandchildren. All of the grandchildren were under 21. Additional grandchildren were born after G's death. How many class gifts are created here? When do they close? See Restatement 3d of Property §15.1 comment n.

2. Class Gifts to Heirs or Next of Kin

Primary Statutory References: *UPC §§2-701, 2-711*

The terms "heirs" and "next of kin" have primary meanings that are fixed by statute. Historically, and technically, the two terms have different meanings. *Heirs* are identified by the statute of descent—the term refers to those to whom a decedent's *real property* descends on the decedent's death intestate. *Next of kin* are identified by the statute of distribution—the term refers to those to whom a decedent's *personal property* is distributed upon the decedent's death intestate. A few states still provide for different patterns of takers for real and personal property, but most states, by far, have consolidated the two patterns into a single statute, called a statute of descent and distribution. Consequently, in the vast majority of states, the pattern of intestate succession is the same for real and personal property.

The term "heirs" or "next of kin" is sometimes used in a nontechnical sense, to mean children or issue. This usually arises when one or the other term is used interchangeably with children or issue, such as in the disposition "to A for life, remainder to A's heirs, but if A dies without issue, to B." See, e.g., Connor v. Biard, 232 S.W. 885 (Tex. Civ. App. 1921); Restatement 3d of Property §16.1 comment m. By statute in Georgia, all "limitations over" to "heirs" presumptively mean children and the descendants of deceased children. See Ga. Code §44-6-23, interpreted in Dodson v. Trust Co. of Georgia, 117 S.E.2d 331 (Ga. 1960). See also N.C. Gen. Stat. §41-6.

Suppose a future interest is given to the "representatives" of a deceased person. Does the term "representatives" mean "issue"? Or, does it mean "heirs"? In Boston

Safe Deposit & Tr. Co. v. Wilbur, 728 N.E.2d 264 (Mass. 2000), the court held that the term meant "heirs."[14]

When the term "heirs" or "next of kin" is used in a technical sense, the class gift so created is not subject to open. Once the takers are determined, by application of the relevant intestacy statute, new entrants cannot later join the class.

Restatement 3d of Property

§16.1 Class Gift to "Heirs"—Presumptive Meaning

Unless the language or circumstances establish that the transferor had a different intention, the term "heirs" (or a like term), in a class gift to the "heirs" (or to a class described by a like term) of a designated person, means the persons who would succeed to the designated person's intestate estate if the designated person died intestate on the distribution date owning only the subject matter of the gift.

Dodge Testamentary Trust

330 N.W.2d 72 (Mich. Ct. App. 1982)

BEASLEY, P.J. This appeal is taken by various interested parties from an order of the Wayne County Probate Court directing distribution of the trust corpus of a testamentary trust arising under the will of John F. Dodge, deceased. The order was entered pursuant to a thorough and carefully drawn opinion prepared by Judge Willis F. Ward of the Wayne County Probate Court,[15] in which he made findings of fact, conclusions of law and determination of claims.

John F. Dodge, an early and highly successful automobile manufacturer, died testate on January 14, 1920.[16] His will, which was dated April 4, 1918, was admitted

---

14. The court used the term "statutory distributees" instead of "heirs," but the meaning is the same.

15. In the mid-1930s, the late Judge Willis Ward played football for the University of Michigan (and was President Gerald Ford's roommate for away games). In a highly controversial decision protested by Ford and other members of the team, Ward was not allowed to play in a game held in Ann Arbor against Georgia Tech because he was African American and Georgia Tech would not play the game if Ward competed. In the following spring, Ward successfully competed for the University of Michigan in the famous Big Ten track meet in which Jesse Owens set five world records. Owens went on to triumph at the 1936 Berlin Olympics, but Ward decided not to try out for the U.S. team. He said later that after the Georgia Tech incident, "I didn't even think of the Olympics.... That incident, and Hitler in Germany, killed my desire to excel." David S. Pollock, The Benching of Willis Ward, Ann Arbor Observer, Oct. 1996, at 31. Ed.

16. John F. Dodge died in New York, while on a trip with Horace Dodge, his brother and co-founder of the Dodge Brothers machine shop, which later produced the Dodge automobile. The Dodge brothers were on a trip to the National Automobile Show, where Dodge cars were on display. John was a victim of the influenza pandemic that began in 1918, an influenza epidemic that swept the globe and killed an estimated 675,000 Americans. Horace also contracted influenza, as did John's wife Matilda, who upon learning of John's illness took the first train to New York to be at his bedside. Matilda was so sick that she was unable to attend her husband's funeral back in Detroit. Horace died in Palm Beach later that

to probate in the Wayne County Probate Court. In his will, John F. Dodge created a residuary trust which [set forth comprehensive and lengthy provisions governing the distribution of the income among the testator's widow and four of his six children and their "issue." With respect to the corpus of the trust, Paragraph 20:14(h) of the will provided:]

> [U]pon the death of all of my said children, Winifred Dodge Gray, Isabella Cleves Dodge, Frances Matilda Dodge and Daniel George Dodge, then I direct my said trustees to convey my said estate to the heirs of my said children, Winifred Dodge Gray, Isabella Cleves Dodge, Frances Matilda Dodge and Daniel George Dodge, in such proportion as by law such heirs shall be entitled to receive same.
>
> The provisions I have made in this Will for my son John Duval Dodge, have been made after careful thought and deliberation on my part, un-influenced by any person or persons whomsoever, and I believe these provisions to be the most wise I can make for my said son, John Duval Dodge. I make this explanation in order that it may be known that I have given careful thought to the claims of my said son, John Duval Dodge, and in order that neither my wife, nor any of my children may be accused of having influenced me in reference to the provisions that I have herein made in regard to my said son.

John F. Dodge left surviving him his widow, Matilda R. Dodge (Wilson), and six children, John Duval Dodge, Winifred Dodge Gray (Seyburn), Isabella Cleves Dodge (Sloane), Frances Matilda Dodge (Van Lennep), Daniel George Dodge, and Anna Margaret Dodge. The first three children were born of testator's marriage to Ivy Dodge, who died in 1900, and the second three were born of his marriage to Matilda R. Dodge (Wilson). His widow, Matilda, remarried in 1925 to Alfred Wilson, and they adopted two children, Richard S. Wilson and Barbara Wilson (Eccles). Matilda, who died in 1967, is perhaps best known for her generous bequests which have become the site of Oakland University and the various Meadowbrook cultural events.

Winifred Dodge Gray (Seyburn) was the first-born offspring of John F. Dodge and the last to die in 1980. Her death in 1980 operated to terminate the residuary trust created under the will. Winifred Dodge Gray (Seyburn) had two children as issue of the Gray marriage, Winifred Gray Seyburn Cheston, born in 1917, and Suzanne Gray Seyburn Meyer, born in 1920. Winifred Dodge Gray (Seyburn) also had two children as issue of the Seyburn marriage, Edith Seyburn Quintana, born in 1923, and Isabel Seyburn Harte, born in 1924. These four children of Winifred Dodge Gray (Seyburn) survive.

Isabella Cleves Dodge (Sloane) died March 9, 1962, without issue, while a resident of Florida.

---

year of a relapse. See Jean Maddern Pitrone, Tangled Web: Legacy of Auto Pioneer John F. Dodge 94-98 (1989). Ed.

John Duval Dodge, who was substantially disinherited in his father's will, died in 1942, leaving a widow, Dora Dodge, who died in 1950, and a daughter, Mary Ann Dodge (Danaher), who survives.[17]

Anna Margaret Dodge was born June 14, 1919, subsequent to execution of her father's will in 1918. She died intestate on April 13, 1924.

Daniel George Dodge died August 15, 1938, leaving surviving him his widow, Annie Laurine Dodge (Van Etten), and his mother, Matilda R. Dodge (Wilson).

Frances Matilda Dodge (Van Lennep) died in 1971, survived by her husband, Frederick L. Van Lennep, whom she had married in 1949. Also, she left surviving her three children, Judith Frances Johnson (McClung), born in 1941 as issue of Frances' first marriage to James P. Johnson, Jr., whom she divorced in 1948, Fredericka Van Lennep (Caldwell), born in 1951, and John Francis Van Lennep, born in 1952, all of which children survive.

Not mentioned in the will was testator's infant daughter, Anna Margaret Dodge, she having been born June 14, 1919, a year after execution of the will. She took as a pretermitted heir, i.e., the same share she would have received if the testator died intestate. However, she died intestate at age five in 1924, and the devolution of her property was affirmed in Dodge's Estate, 242 Mich. 156, 218 N.W. 798 (1928).

John Duval Dodge attacked the validity of his father's will, which case was settled under a then newly-enacted statute authorizing such settlements, which statute was enacted largely as a result of this subject situation.[18] Subsequently, in 1939, John Duval Dodge renewed his will contest and attempted to set aside the settlement agreement. The decision of the circuit court upholding the settlement agreement and rejecting the claim that the will and trust were invalid was affirmed in Dodge v. Detroit Trust Co., 300 Mich. 575, 2 N.W.2d 509 (1942).

In the within proceedings, a guardian ad litem was appointed to represent all unknown claimants to the trust and, after extensive discovery procedures, he reported that there were not any additional interested parties. On this appeal, we consolidate seven separate appeals (files), in some of which there are cross-appeals.

---

17. John Duval Dodge was reportedly a rebellious son, who was expelled from boarding school more than once for truancy. When, at age nineteen, he secretly married eighteen-year-old Marie O'Connor, and when word of the marriage was reported in a newspaper, John F. Dodge instructed his lawyer to draw up a new will, essentially disinheriting John Duval. See Jean Maddern Pitrone, supra note 16, at 58, 77-78, 84-85. Ed.

18. The testator's will gave his son, John Duval Dodge, only a monthly stipend of $150 for life so that he "would never be a public charge." The testator's widow, Matilda, wanted to settle her stepson's suit, but state law did not then permit out-of-court settlements. At her direction, her attorneys pressured the state legislature to change the law to allow such settlements. The result was the "Dodge Law" to which the court alluded. Once the statute became effective, John Duval's suit was settled for $1.6 million. See Jean Maddern Pitrone, supra note 16, at 100, 111. Ed.

We have reviewed at least 30 briefs which have been filed, varying in length from five pages to more than 80 pages.

At the outset, we hold that since the probate court order, which is the subject of all these appeals, affects the rights of the parties with finality, it is a final order, directly appealable to this Court.

In his splendid opinion, the probate judge discussed four issues of law and made detailed rulings cited to authority. First, he dealt with the meaning of the word "heirs" as used in paragraph 20:14(h) of the last will and testament of John F. Dodge, deceased. The issue arises because, in the termination provision of the testamentary trust, the testator said:

> ...then I direct my said trustees to convey my said estate to the heirs of my said children, Winifred Dodge Gray, Isabella Cleves Dodge, Frances Matilda Dodge and Daniel George Dodge, in such proportion as by law such heirs shall be entitled to receive same.

The question is whether the word "heirs" was used in the will in its technical sense to denote those persons who inherit under the intestacy laws or whether "heirs" as used in the will was intended to designate only the "issue" or "children" of testator's children.

The cardinal rule of law and the predominant rule in the construction and interpretation of testamentary instruments is that the intent of the testator governs if it is lawful and if it can be discovered. This legal proposition finds support in many cases. Unless the will is ambiguous on its face, the testator's intention is derived from the language of the will....

We are satisfied that, in 1918 when the will of John F. Dodge was drawn and signed, the word "heirs" was a technical term with a well and clearly defined meaning, namely, those designated by the statutes of intestate succession to receive one's estate on death and that "heirs" included the spouse of the decedent.[19]

We note that the attorney drawing John F. Dodge's will appears to have been able and experienced in the practice of probate law. He was not a mere tyro, unfamiliar with common and accepted usage in legal circles of words used in the descent and distribution of property upon death.[20]

Thus, we ascribe to the word "heirs", as used in the subject will, its technical meaning as it existed in 1918 when the will was drafted and executed. We decline to conclude that the draftsman of the will made a "mistake" when he used in the will two different words, "issue" and "heirs". On the contrary, we believe that the attorney drawing the will used these two different words in their known, technical

---

19. Brooks v. Parks, [185 N.W. 573 (Mich. 1915)]; Shumway's Estate, 194 Mich. 245, 160 N.W. 595 (1916); Menard v. Campbell, 180 Mich. 583, 147 N.W. 556 (1914).

20. 61 Supreme Court Records and Briefs, pp. 346-361 (October Term, 1941).

legal sense with the intention that the trust corpus descend differently than the trust income....

The second issue decided by the probate court was when should the remainder (corpus) interests of the heirs of the testator's named children vest. Should it be the time of each child's death, or should it be later at the termination of the trust upon the death of the last surviving child?

Unless a testator clearly and unambiguously states to the contrary, vesting of contingent remainders shall be determined as of the date of death of the ancestor. We decline to hold that testator's will in this case clearly and unambiguously established the time of vesting at the date of the termination of the trust. Consequently, we conclude that the date of death of the ancestor is the time of vesting of the contingent remainder interests in this trust....

In the within case, it is contended that the following circumstances suggest that the deceased would have preferred to postpone vesting until termination of the trust: (1) the deceased's express desire to postpone vesting beyond the date of his own death; (2) the indications that the deceased would not have wanted John Duval Dodge to take as an heir of the named life tenants; and (3) the potential for greater federal estate taxation under a theory of successive vesting. These speculations, while interesting, do not justify departure from the established rule favoring early vesting....

The third issue discussed and decided by the probate court was whether the word "heirs", as used in the testator's will, should be defined according to the statutes of distribution in effect at the time of the death of each named life income beneficiary, rather than according to the statute of descent in effect at the testator's death. The probate court held that the statutes of distribution in effect at the date of death of the immediate ancestor should be applied in determining the heirs of the children named in the testator's will and in determining the share to which each such heir was entitled. The probate court recited three reasons for this conclusion.

First, the court said that the testator expressed a clear wish in his will that the heirs of his children should take "in such proportion as by law such heirs shall be entitled to receive same". The probate court interpreted this phrase to mean that the testator did not intend that the law at the time of his death would govern determinations to be made many years into the unpredictable future.

Second, the probate court noted that the trust corpus presently in question consists entirely of personal property. No evidence was presented to refute this or to establish that real estate ever was intended to be included in the trust.

Third, the probate court seemed to believe that, since it had already decided that "heirs" is to be defined by reference to the statute in existence at the date of death of the immediate ancestor, it would create a dilemma if it held that the statute was modified by the statute in effect at the date of the execution of the will....

The significance of this issue is that the statute of descent in effect at the time of the testator's death, 1917 P.A. 341; 1915 CL 11795,[21] left nothing to the husband of an intestate woman who died leaving issue to inherit her real estate. However, the statute of descent was amended by 1931 P.A. 79; 1929 CL 13440[22] to allow one-third of any real estate to descend to the surviving husband and the remaining two-thirds to go to the woman's issue. Furthermore, the statute of distribution gave the husband one-third of the woman's personal property.[23]

Thus, if the probate court applied the statute of distribution or the amended statute of descent to determine the "heirs" of the testator's daughter Frances, then it would properly find her surviving husband, Frederick L. Van Lennep, to be entitled to a one-third share of the quarter of trust corpus reserved for her (Frances's) heirs.

On the other hand, if the probate court should have applied the statute of descent in effect at the time of the deceased's death, then Van Lennep was not entitled to take at all, and the entire quarter of the corpus passing to Frances's heirs would go to her children, including appellant, Judith Johnson McClung.

Therefore, in order for appellant McClung to prevail, she must prevail in both of the following propositions: first, that the deceased intended the statutes in effect at the date of his (testator's) death to apply to the determination of his children's heirs, and, second, that he intended the statute of descent, rather than the statute of distribution, to apply.

We reject both of these contentions. The language of the will reveals a clear intention to apply future intestacy laws, rather than those in effect at the time the will was drafted. The will provides specifically that the heirs of the testator's four named children should take "in proportion as by law such heirs *shall* be entitled to receive same". Furthermore, since the vesting of the heirs' interests should occur upon the death of each of the four named children, the application of any statutes

---

21. 1915 CL 11795, provides in part:

If such intestate shall die under the age of twenty-one years, and not having been married, all the estate that came to such intestate by inheritance from a parent, which has not been lawfully disposed of, shall descend to the other children and the issue of deceased children of the same parent, if there be such children or issue, and if such persons are in the same degree of kindred to said intestate they shall take equally, otherwise they shall take by right of representation.

22. 1929 CL 13440, provides in part:

If the intestate shall leave a husband or widow and no issue, one-half of the estate of such intestate shall descend to such husband or widow....

If the intestate shall leave a husband or wife and no issue, nor father, mother, brother nor sister, and there be no child of brother or sister, the estate of such intestate shall descend to the husband or wife of such intestate, as the case may be.

23. 1915 P.A. 314; 1915 CL 13913, provides in part:

In any other case the residue, if any, of the personal estate shall be distributed in the same proportion and to the same persons, and for the same purposes, as prescribed for the descent and disposition of the real estate.

other than those in effect on the dates of the four named children's respective deaths would be inconsistent and would create a kind of legal dilemma....

The fourth issue considered and determined by the probate court was whether the statutes of the State of Michigan or of the state of domicile of the ancestor determine the "heirs". The issue, which presents a close and difficult question, relates to Isabella Cleves Dodge (Sloane), who died in 1962 while a resident of the State of Florida.

The significance of which state's law controls results from the fact that, in 1962, Florida law[24] provided that collateral kindred of the half blood would inherit only half as much as those of the whole blood while Michigan law[25] provided that heirs of the half blood in these circumstances would take equally with heirs of the whole blood. Thus, under Florida law the heirs of Isabella Cleves Dodge (Sloane) would take as follows: two-fifths to Winifred Dodge Seyburn, two-fifths to Mary Ann Dodge Danaher, and one-fifth to Frances Dodge Van Lennep, the latter being a half-sister because Isabella and Frances had different mothers. Under Michigan law, Winifred Dodge Seyburn, Mary Ann Dodge Danaher and Frances Dodge Van Lennep would each take one-third.

.... Since Isabella Dodge Sloane died in 1962 domiciled in Florida, it is claimed that technically her heirs should be decided under Florida law....

In this case, the testator, John F. Dodge, created a testamentary trust which provided for payment of trust income to four named children, the oldest of whom was under 25 at the time of execution of the will. By its terms, the trust terminated upon the death of the last survivor of the four named children. We assume that the testator contemplated that the trust would continue for many years and that there was nothing in the circumstances to indicate where each named child would die.

The Dodge will does not expressly say that in determining residuary heirs of the four named children, resort should be had to the state of domicile at the time of death of the deceased child. Neither does the Dodge will expressly say that residuary heirs of the four named children should be determined under Michigan law. Under these circumstances, we believe [Sewart Estate, 70 N.W.2d 732 (Mich. 1955)] is controlling.

In 52 A.L.R.2d 482, 495, *Sewart* is described as illustrative of the general rule that in the absence of anything to indicate a contrary intention on the part of the testator, the "heirs" are ascertained by reference to the law of the testator's domicile.

In *Sewart*, the Court said, among other things:

> In passing on controversies of this nature courts have repeatedly recognized that the maker of the will was presumably familiar with the laws of his own State and ordinarily

---

24. 1945 Fla.Laws 731.24.

25. 1948 CL 702.84.

without specific information as to statutes in force in other States. Such situation may not be ignored in the construction of the language of a will.[26]

In *Sewart*, the Court also stated:

A decision of the supreme court of Kansas in Keith v Eaton, 58 Kan 732; 51 P 271 (1897), is also in point.... In holding that the will must be construed in accordance with the law of the domicile of the testator, it was said...:

In the absence of a contrary meaning, to be gathered from the circumstances surrounding a testator or from the instrument as a whole, the sense of the words used by him is to be ascertained in the light of the law of his domicile. Presumptively, he is more familiar with that law than with the law of other jurisdictions. That is the law which is constantly with him, controlling his actions and defining his rights, and more naturally than any other law would be present to his mind in the drafting of an instrument dispository of his property.[27]

We... find that, in accordance with *Sewart*, the intention of the testator was that the heirs of his four named children be determined under the laws of the State of Michigan. This intention is controlling.

In summary, giving effect to our rulings concerning these four issues discussed by the probate court, we hold that: (1) "heirs" as used in paragraph 20:14(h) of the will means those persons designated by statute to whom the law would give that class of property under the laws of intestate succession; (2) the contingent remainder interest of such "heirs" in the trust corpus vested at the date of death of the respective four named children of the testator; (3) the word "heirs" is defined as of the date of death of each of the four named children of the testator; and (4) in determining the "heirs" of each of the four named children of the testator, we look to the laws of the State of Michigan....   AFFIRMED.

Notes and Questions

1. *Quality of Legal Services.* If nothing else, the will of John F. Dodge disproves the theory that the wealthy need not worry about the quality of legal services. Every litigated question could and should have been anticipated and unambiguously provided for in the will. A lawyer's job is to anticipate such questions, bring them to the client's attention for decision, and effectuate the client's intention without ambiguity.

2. *Uniform Probate Code; Restatement 3d of Property.* If UPC §§2-701 and 2-711 or Restatement 3d of Property §16.1 (reproduced above the *Dodge* case) had

---

26. 342 Mich. 497, 70 N.W.2d 732.

27. 342 Mich. 499-500, 70 N.W.2d 732.

governed John F. Dodge's trust, would the case have been litigated? Would the outcome have differed?

3. *Controlling Statute.* In drafting a class gift to a designated person's heirs, the statute to be applied to determine the takers should be expressly identified in the governing instrument. See UPC §2-703; Restatement 3d of Property §16.1 comment g. Failing an express identification, the *Dodge* case held that the controlling statute is: (1) the statute of distribution (2) of the testator's domicile (3) in existence when the designated person died.   Using the intestacy statute of the testator's domicile is in line with predominant authority, but the Restatement 3d of Property §16.1 follows the Restatement of Property §305 in taking the position that the takers should be governed by the statute that would be used to determine the designated person's actual takers if the designated person had died intestate, owning the subject matter of the gift.

Using the statute in existence at the designated person's death is also the predominant view. See Restatement 3d of Property §16.1 comment g. There is some authority, however, for the view that the statute to be used is the one in existence when the transfer occurred. See Samuel M. Fetters, Future Interests, 23 Syracuse L. Rev. 219, 224-25 (1972), for a discussion of New York cases to this effect.

4. *No Condition of Survival.* Once the takers are determined, class gifts to heirs follow the normal rule that no condition of survival is imposed unless one is expressly stated. In so holding, the *Dodge* case is consistent with existing authority. As is the case with respect to other types of class gifts (see Lawson v. Lawson, p. 849), there is a minority view that a class gift to heirs that is contingent on an event unrelated to survival is also subject to a condition of survival. See, e.g., Continental Illinois Nat'l Bank & Tr. Co. v. Eliel, 161 N.E.2d 107 (Ill. 1959). But see Hofing v. Willis, 201 N.E.2d 852 (Ill. 1964).

5. *Spouse as an Heir.* Although a person's spouse was not an heir under the common-law canons of descent, modern intestacy statutes include the spouse as an heir. Consequently, as the *Dodge* case illustrates, the designated person's spouse is entitled to participate in a class gift to the designated person's heirs, in the absence of a manifested intent to the contrary on the part of the transferor. See Thomas v. Higginbotham, 318 S.W.2d 234 (Mo. 1958); Restatement 3d of Property §16.1 comment h.

6. *Can the State Be an "Heir"?* If, at the time the heirs are to be ascertained, the only claimant is the state by virtue of its right to escheat, §2-711 of the UPC and the Restatement 3d of Property §16.1 comment i take the position that the state takes.

3. Inter Vivos Transfers to the Grantor's Heirs:
The Doctrine of Worthier Title

Primary Statutory Reference: *UPC §2-710*

Problem

After substantial revision, an irrevocable inter vivos life insurance trust provided that after the Settlor's death and the life insurance proceeds are collected and invested by the trustee, the income is to be paid to the Settlor's son, Arnold, for life. See p. 872. Upon Arnold's death, the corpus of the trust is to be distributed as follows:

(a) To the descendants of Arnold who survive Arnold, to be divided among them by representation; or

(b) If Arnold is not survived by any descendants of his own, then to the descendants of the Settlor who survive Arnold, to be divided among them by representation; or

(c) If Arnold is not survived by any descendants of the Settlor, then to the descendants of the Settlor's brother [name of brother] who survive Arnold, to be divided among them by representation; or

(d) If Arnold is not survived by any descendants of the settlor's brother [name of brother], then to the descendants of the Settlor's father [name of father] who survive Arnold, to be divided among them by representation; or

(e) If Arnold is not survived by any descendants of the Settlor's father, then to Arnold's heirs at law.

(f) If the Settlor is not survived by his son, Arnold, then upon the Settlor's death the corpus of the trust is to be distributed to the Settlor's heirs at law.

In the light of the *Dodge* case, it might occur to you that subparagraphs (e) and (f) still need work. Apart from the general need to clarify the term "heirs at law," would it ever have occurred to you that subparagraph (f) was drafted by the settlor's lawyers with the *actual* intention that it constitute a *reversion* in the settlor himself, so that in the unlikely event that subparagraph (f) becomes effective the corpus of the trust would go to the settlor's residuary legatees named in the settlor's will?

One of the tax purposes of this irrevocable inter vivos life insurance trust is to avoid the inclusion of the policy proceeds in the settlor's gross estate. Would that purpose be jeopardized in this case if subparagraph (f) is interpreted as a reversion in the settlor rather than a remainder in the settlor's heirs? See IRC §2042(2) (providing that the decedent's gross estate for federal estate tax purposes includes the value of a life insurance policy "with respect to which the decedent possessed at his death any of the incidents of ownership," a term defined to include a reversionary interest "exceed[ing] 5 percent of the value of the policy").

Doctor v. Hughes
122 N.E. 221 (N.Y. 1919)

CARDOZO, J. The action is brought by judgment creditors to subject what is alleged to be an interest in real property to the lien of a judgment.

In January, 1899, James J. Hanigan conveyed to a trustee a house and lot in the city of New York. The conveyance was in trust to pay from the rents and profits to the use of the grantor the yearly sum of $1,500. The payments might, however, exceed that sum in the discretion of the trustee. Direction was also made for the payment of some debts, and for the payment of two mortgages, then liens upon the property. The trustee was empowered to mortgage, in order to pay existing liens, or to carry into effect the other provisions of the deed. He was also empowered to sell. Upon the death of the grantor, he was to "convey the said premises (if not sold) to the heirs at law of the party of the first part." In case of a sale, he was to pay to the heirs at law "the balance of the avails of sale remaining unexpended." He was authorized at any time, if he so desired, to reconvey the premises to the grantor, and thus terminate the trust.

At the trial of this action, the grantor was still alive. His sole descendants were two daughters. By deed executed in June, 1902, one of the daughters, Mrs. Hughes, conveyed to her husband all her interest in this real estate. Judgment against Mr. and Mrs. Hughes for upwards of $4,000 was afterwards recovered by the plaintiffs. The question to be determined is whether either judgment debtor has any interest in the land. The Special Term held that there passed to Mr. Hughes under the conveyance from his wife an estate in remainder which was subject to the claims of creditors. The Appellate Division held that the creator of the trust did not intend to give a remainder to any one; that his heirs at law, if they receive anything on his death, will take by descent, and not by purchase; and hence that there is nothing that creditors can seize.

We reach the same conclusion. The direction to the trustee is the superfluous expression of a duty imposed by law. "Where an express trust is created, every legal estate and interest not embraced in the trust, and not otherwise disposed of, shall remain in or revert to, the person creating the trust or his heirs." Real Property Law, §102. (Consol. Laws, c. 50). What is left is not a remainder (Real Property Law, §38), but a reversion (Real Property Law, §39). To such a situation neither the rule in Shelley's Case (1 Coke Rep. 104), nor the statute abrogating the rule (Real Property Law, §54), applies. The heirs mentioned in this deed are not "the heirs... of a person to whom a life estate in the same premises is given." Real Property Law, §54. The life estate belongs to the trustee. The heirs are the heirs of the grantor.... The question is whether there is any remainder at all. In the solution of that problem, the distinction is vital between gifts to the heirs of the holder of a particular estate, and gifts or attempted gifts to the heirs of the grantor. "A man cannot, either by conveyance at the common law, by limitation of uses, or devise, make his right heir a purchaser." Pilus v. Milford, 1674, 1 Vent. 372; Read v. Erington, 1594, Cro. Eliz.

322; Bingham's Case, 2 Co. Rep. 91a., 91b; Cholmondaley v. Maxey, 12 East, 589, 603, 604. "It is a positive rule of our law." Hargrave's Law Tracts (1787) p. 571....

At common law, therefore, and under common-law conveyances, this direction to transfer the estate to the heirs of the grantor would indubitably have been equivalent to the reservation of a reversion. In England, the rule has been changed by statute. The Inheritance Act of 1833 provides (3 & 4 Wm. IV, c. 106, §3) that—

> When any land shall have been limited by any assurance ... to the person or to the heirs of the person who shall thereby have conveyed the same land, such person shall be considered to have acquired the same as a purchaser by virtue of such assurance, and shall not be considered to be entitled thereto as his former estate or part thereof.

But in the absence of modifying statute, the rule persists to-day, at least as a rule of construction, if not as one of property.... The reservation of a reversion is not inconsistent with the creation of a trust to continue until the death of the reversioner. We do not say that the ancient rule survives as an absolute prohibition limiting the power of a grantor. At the outset, probably ..., it was a rule, not of construction, but of property. But it was never applied in all its rigor to executory trusts,... and deeds, like wills, must be so construed as to effectuate the purpose of the grantor (Real Property Law, §240, subd. 3). There may be times, therefore, when a reference to the heirs of the grantor will be regarded as the gift of a remainder, and will vest title in the heirs presumptive as upon a gift to the heirs of others. But at least the ancient rule survives to this extent: That, to transform into a remainder what would ordinarily be a reversion, the intention to work the transformation must be clearly expressed. Here there is no clear expression of such a purpose. No doubt there are circumstances on which it is possible to build an argument.... Nothing in the surrounding circumstances suggests a purpose to vary the course of descent or distribution as it would be regulated by law. If that is so, the courts are not to be controlled by mere inaccuracies of expression. Such slips of speech might be significant if we were construing an admitted remainder. They do not turn into a remainder what would otherwise be a reversion. There is no adequate disclosure of a purpose in the mind of this grantor to vest his presumptive heirs with rights which it would be beyond his power to defeat. No one is heir to the living, and seldom do the living mean to forego the power of disposition during life by the direction that upon death there shall be a transfer to their heirs. This grant by its terms was subject to destruction at the will of the trustee. We think it was also subject to destruction, as against the heirs at law, at the will of the grantor. They had an expectancy, but no estate.

The judgment should be affirmed, with costs....

Note

Post-Doctor v. Hughes Case Authority. In Burchell's Estate, 87 N.E.2d 293 (N.Y. 1949), the terms of an irrevocable inter vivos trust of real property were that the income was to be paid to the grantor for her life. Upon her death, the principal of the trust estate was to go to such persons as the grantor appoints by will; in default of appointment, to the grantor's next of kin as in intestacy.

In an opinion written by Judge Bromley, the court held that the gift in default created a remainder interest in the grantor's heirs, not a reversion in the grantor:

> Confusion as to the nature of an estate when that estate is limited to heirs of the grantor arises because of the existence in our modern jurisprudence of remnants of the ancient doctrine of worthier title (46 Harv. L. Rev. 993). Prior to our decision in Doctor v. Hughes (225 N.Y. 305...), a conveyance by a grantor with a limitation over to his heirs was said to be governed by that doctrine, under which a limitation over to a grantor's heirs resulted in an automatic reversion in the grantor and nullified the limitation over....

> It is clear from the cases in this State since Doctor v. Hughes..., as admirably analyzed in Richardson v. Richardson [81 N.E.2d 54 (N.Y. 1948)], that, despite the language in that opinion that a reversion exists unless there is clear evidence to the contrary, the rule has been less limited in application. Where a clear intent exists, there is no problem in construing the instrument, since the doctrine no longer exists as a rule of property. But where the grantor's intent is not expressed in unmistakable language, the rule comes into play. Then we look to the instrument for those indicia deemed significant in arriving at the intent of the grantor. In the first of the line of cases following Doctor v. Hughes (supra), (Whittemore v. Equitable Trust Co., 250 N.Y. 298), we applied the rule of construction in the manner indicated in the second interpretation above. We discovered the intent of the grantor from other factors, as shown by the instrument, in order to give full effect to the words of limitation.

> While we have not yet adopted a rule, either by statute or judicial construction, under which language limiting an interest to heirs is unequivocally given its full effect, the presumption which exists from the use of the common-law doctrine as a rule of construction has lost much of its force since Doctor v. Hughes (supra). Evidence of intent need not be overwhelming in order to allow the remainder to stand. Whether the rule should be abrogated completely is a matter for the Legislature.

> The instant cases furnish sufficient additional indications of the settlor's intent to justify our giving effect to the language of the instrument limiting an estate to the grantor's heirs. Not the least among those indications was the reservation of a testamentary power of appointment as the sole control over the subsequent disposition of the corpus of the trust estate.... The fact that the trust agreement reserved a power of appointment is evidence that the settlor believed she had created an interest in the property on the part of others and reserved the power in order to defeat that interest or to postpone until a later date the naming of specific takers. Where we have held that a reversion was intended although a testamentary power of appointment was reserved, the instruments have provided that the trust principal would revert to the grantor upon some contingency or that the grantor retained control over the principal.

> In analyzing an instrument and attempting to explore the almost ephemeral qualities which go to prove the necessary intent, many single factors may be considered. Some considered significant in one case may be deemed minimal in another, since their effect may be counteracted by the presence of other factors. It is impossible to set up absolute

criteria to serve as a measuring standard for all cases. In the last analysis, the ultimate determination rests on the particular instrument under consideration, aided by the rule which has grown out of the old common-law doctrine and developed over a long line of cases as a rule which allows the language of the instrument creating a remainder to take effect provided some additional evidence pointing the intent of the grantor is present to buttress the language which would create the remainder.

Notes and Questions

1. *Hatch v. Riggs; Post-Hatch Case Authority.* In Hatch v. Riggs National Bank, 361 F.2d 559 (D.C. Cir. 1966), the court held that "the doctrine of worthier title is no part of the law of trusts in the District of Columbia." Since 1966, when the *Hatch* case was decided, there has been only one state supreme court authority recognizing the validity of the doctrine. See All Persons v. Buie, 386 So.2d 1109 (Miss. 1980).

2. *Legislative Abolition of the Doctrine of Worthier Title.* The New York court in *Burchell* seemed to favor complete abrogation of the doctrine of worthier title but declined to take that step because the court thought abrogation was a matter exclusively for the legislature. The New York legislature stepped in and abolished the doctrine in 1966. Over twenty-five other states also have abrogating legislation—including Alaska, Arizona, Arkansas, California, Colorado, Florida, Hawaii, Illinois,[28] Indiana, Kentucky, Massachusetts, Michigan, Minnesota, Missouri, Montana, New Mexico, North Carolina, North Dakota, Pennsylvania, South Dakota, Tennessee, Texas, Utah, Virginia, Washington, West Virginia, Wisconsin, and Wyoming. A statute in Georgia makes application of the doctrine unlikely, by declaring that the word "heirs" is presumed to mean children, unless a contrary intention appears. Ga. Code §44-6-23.

Section 2-710 of the UPC and §16.3 of the Restatement 3d of Property abolish the doctrine.[29]

3. *Analysis of the Doctrine.* The Restatement 3d of Property §16.3 comment a criticizes the transformation of the worthier title doctrine into a rule of construction:

> In shifting the doctrine to a rule of construction, Judge Cardozo may have desired to soften the old rule of law by allowing it to yield to the grantor's contrary intention. But shifting a mandatory rule of law to a rule of construction is not a natural evolutionary step in legal development. Rules of law and rules of construction stem from entirely different

28. But see Stewart v. Merchants Nat'l Bank, 278 N.E.2d 10 (Ill. App. Ct. 1972), where the court seems to have held that the statute only abrogates the doctrine of worthier title as a rule of law, not as a rule of construction. See Note, The Doctrine of Worthier Title as a Rule of Construction in Illinois, 67 Nw. U. L. Rev. 773 (1973). Harris Trust & Savings Bank v. Beach, 513 N.E.2d 833 (Ill. 1987), however, referred to Illinois' "1955 statutory abolition of the doctrine."

29. The states of Alaska, Arizona, Colorado, Hawaii, Idaho, Massachusetts, Michigan, Montana, New Mexico, North Dakota, South Dakota, and Utah abolished the doctrine of worthier title as part of their enactment of Article II of the 1990 version of the UPC.

premises. Rules of law are intent-defeating; rules of construction are intent-effecting. Defeating intention is only justified to vindicate goals of public policy. The function of a rule of law is to prohibit individual choice deemed unduly harmful to society.... Rules of construction, on the other hand, operate in areas in which society as a whole is indifferent to the result. The only public policy goal that rules of construction vindicate is giving effect to private intention in areas of societal indifference. Rules of construction seek to facilitate this intent-effecting goal by providing a presumptive meaning—one designed to accord with common intention—to words that have failed to express the actual intention of the parties clearly....

When the policy basis of a rule of law disappears, as it has with respect to the worthier-title doctrine, the normal course is for the legislature to abrogate the rule (as Parliament did in 1833) or for the courts to attempt to limit its mischief, or ultimately to abrogate the rule. Shifting the worthier-title doctrine from a rule of law to one of construction is not a normal step in the evolutionary process of law, and it has done more harm than good.

4. *Drafting Procedures to Avoid the Doctrine.* Consider again subparagraph (f) of the irrevocable life insurance trust found in the problem on p. 910. Remember, the federal government has considerable revenue to gain if the doctrine of worthier title is applied.[30] If it is applied, and if the life insurance proceeds are included in the settlor's gross estate, the possibility exists of attorney liability in malpractice. See generally Gerald P. Johnston, Legal Malpractice in Estate Planning—Perilous Times Ahead for the Practitioner, 67 Iowa L. Rev. 629 (1982).

Assuming that the settlor's lawyer notices the worthier title problem before the irrevocable (and unamendable) trust is signed, the better course is to redraft subparagraph (f) so that it leaves no doubt that it creates a remainder interest in the settlor's heirs. In a world in which the phrase "remainder to my heirs" presumptively means "reversion in myself," how can the settlor's lawyer make it beyond dispute that subparagraph (f) means what it says? Should subparagraph (f) be redrafted to say "to my heirs at law, and I really mean it—no kidding!"? A more lawyerly way of saying it might be:

> ... to my heirs at law, such persons to take as purchasers, my intention being to create a remainder interest in favor of my heirs at law; I do not intend to retain a reversion in myself.

Suppose the worthier title problem in subparagraph (f) was not noticed until *after* the trust was signed and the $6 million life insurance policy was irrevocably assigned to the trustee. Could the settlor's lawyer successfully petition for reformation of subparagraph (f), to add language making it clear that a remainder was intended? See Palmer on Restitution ch. 18; John H. Langbein & Lawrence W.

---

30. On the tax consequences in general of application of the doctrine of worthier title, see Stanley M. Johanson, Reversions, Remainders, and the Doctrine of Worthier Title, 45 Tex. L. Rev. 1, 16-27 (1966).

Waggoner, Reformation of Wills on the Ground of Mistake: Change of Direction in American Law?, 130 U. Pa. L. Rev. 521, 524-28 (1982). Would this reformation be controlling for federal tax purposes? Would it make any difference if the reformation occurred before or after the settlor's death? See Rev. Rul. 73-142, 1973-1 C.B. 405 (the decree, which was finalized before the decedent's death, was controlling because it effectively extinguished the power that would have brought the value of the trust corpus within the provisions of IRC §§2036 and 2038).

5. *Testamentary Branch of the Doctrine.* At common law, the worthier title doctrine had two branches—the inter vivos branch and the testamentary branch. The above materials relate solely to the inter vivos branch, which as its name implies, applies only to inter vivos transfers.

The testamentary branch provided that a *devise* of *land* to the testator's heirs was a nullity if the interest devised to them was identical to the interest they would take in intestacy. Like the inter vivos branch, this was a rule of law, not of construction. See Joseph W. Morris, The Wills Branch of the Worthier Title Doctrine, 54 Mich. L. Rev. 451 (1956). No decision in this country has prolonged the existence of the testamentary branch by holding that it "persists today, at least as a rule of construction, if not as one of property." The Restatement 3d of Property §16.3 comment c declares the testamentary branch not to exist as either a rule of law or of construction. In two states in which no abrogating legislation exists, the rule was abolished by court decision (City Nat'l Bank v. Andrews, 355 S.2d 341 (Ala. 1978); In re Campbell, 319 N.W.2d 275 (Iowa 1982); Estate of Kern, 274 N.W.2d 325 (Iowa 1979)) and it is doubtful that it remains in effect anywhere today.[31]

6. *Continuation of the Inter Vivos Branch as a Rule of Law?* In a few states that have not enacted abrogating legislation, older cases exist applying the inter vivos branch of the worthier title doctrine as a rule of law, not of construction. Whether these decisions would be followed today is unclear.

PART C. INCOMPLETE DISPOSITIONS

Theoretically, the calculus of estates does not admit of a disposition that is incomplete: A transferor is considered to have retained by way of a reversionary interest any interest not expressly transferred. For example, in the simple disposition "to A for life," it would be assumed that a reversion in the transferor takes effect upon the death of the life tenant. As we shall see, however, courts sometimes find that a disposition creates a future interest by implication. This process is commonly illustrated by the disposition "to A for life, remainder to B if A dies without issue."

---

31. But see Estate of Grulke, 546 N.W.2d 626 (Iowa Ct. App. 1996) (court applied worthier title doctrine to a devise in a will executed in 1973 because the *Kern* decision, decided in 1979, applied prospectively only).

If A dies with issue, this disposition has been found to contain an implied remainder interest in their favor. See Restatement of Property §272.

1. Implication of Interests in Principal

McKinney v. Mosteller, 365 S.E.2d 612 (N.C. 1988), provides a striking example of a court adhering to a formal and rigid analysis of dispository language. The court refused to acknowledge a drafting mistake or to rectify it. G's will devised the residue of his estate as follows:

> If my wife, W, survives me, then in trust to pay the income to W for life, remainder in corpus to A and B.

W predeceased G. G's sole heir was C. The court held that C was entitled to the residue of G's estate, not A and B. The court explained:

> [A] gift by implication is not favored in the law and cannot rest upon mere conjecture....
>
> The residuary beneficiaries argue strongly that it is clear that they were to be the secondary object of the testator's bounty. Even assuming that extrinsic evidence supports that contention, we are commanded to gather the intent of the testator from the four corners of his will, and such intent should be given effect unless contrary to some rule of law or at variance with public policy. The effect that we give to the testator's will is neither offensive to public policy nor contrary to any rule of law. As gleaned from the will itself, the intent of the testator is manifest and unequivocal, that is, the residue is to pass to the named beneficiaries under the residuary clause of the will only if the testator's wife survives him. She did not. Therefore, the residue passes to the heirs at law in accordance with the laws of intestacy as enacted by the legislature....

In Hilton v. Kinsey, 185 F.2d 885 (D.C. Cir. 1950), James H. Hilton died in 1919, devising his estate in trust, income to his children, J. Franklin Hilton and Catharine Hilton, for life; a cross remainder in the income was provided to the survivor for life. As to the corpus, the will stated:

> In case my son, J. Franklin Hilton, or my daughter, Catharine S. Hilton, should have any [children], such [children], if of J. Franklin Hilton, shall be entitled to his [share] after his death, and if my daughter, Catharine S. Hilton, should have any [children], said [children] shall be entitled to her [share] after her death.... Should [they] have no children, then the money of the estate [should be paid to specified charities].

J. Franklin died in 1941, without children; Catharine died in 1947, survived by her daughter, Mary.

The court held that Mary, not the charities or the testator's heirs, was entitled to the half of the corpus from which J. Franklin had been receiving the income prior to his death:

[W]hen the general plan of the testator for the disposition of his property is considered ... it is clear that ... the children of J. Franklin and Catharine, if any, were to be the ultimate beneficiaries of the residuary estate. Under similar circumstances it has been held that although testator's plan is incompletely expressed, it may be implied from the contents of the will as a whole and a cross-remainder of the corpus read into the will. In Boston Safe-Deposit & Trust Co. v. Coffin, [152 Mass. 95, 25 N.E. 30,] the testator, as to one portion of his estate, made the following disposition: The income to grandchildren A, B, and C for life; upon the death of A, or B, or C without issue, the income to be divided among the survivors; upon the death of A, or B, or C with issue, that issue to take the portion of the estate of which the grandchild had enjoyed the interest and income; if A, B, and C all die without issue, the principal to go to the other children of the testator. Both A and B predeceased C, dying without issue. C enjoyed the entire income until his death. He died with issue. It was argued that the issue of C was entitled to the original amount from which C received the income, namely, one-third of the corpus, the remaining two-thirds passing by intestacy. The court rejected this contention, holding that there was an implied cross-remainder of the two-thirds to the issue of C, and, accordingly, that C's children took the entire corpus.

There is a striking similarity between that case and the present one. Franklin predeceased Catharine. Subsequent to his death she was clearly entitled to, and actually received for a period of six years until her death, the income from the entire corpus of the estate. Prior to her death her interest in the estate was not the life income from half the corpus, but the income from the whole. And the gift to the children was to be not a half, but the whole interest of the parent. Therefore, we hold that the provision for a cross-remainder as to the income between the parents had the effect of increasing the share of the children of one should the other die without children.

Warner v. Warner
237 F.2d 561 (D.C. Cir. 1956)

BURGER, C.J. This is an appeal from a decision of the District Court instructing a trustee, on his petition for instructions, as to the distribution of the corpus of a trust created by the will of Brainard Warner, Sr. The pertinent trust provisions are as follows:

All the rest, residue and remainder of my estate,... I give,... unto The Washington Loan and Trust Company,... in trust ...; third, to divide the remainder of the net income from this trust estate among my wife, Mary H. Warner and my nine children in equal shares, such payments to commence as soon as practicable after my decease and to continue for and during the term of the life of my said wife.[32] On the death of my said wife, I direct my said trustee to divide the entire residuum of my estate into nine (9) equal parts paying one part

---

32. By the time of testator's death in 1916 one child, Southard Parker Warner, had predeceased him, unmarried and without issue.

thereof unto each of my said children.[33] In the event of the death of any of said children before the decease of my said wife, with issue him or her surviving, then such issue shall take the share of its deceased parent in the income and on the death of my wife the share of the deceased parent in the principal, but if there be no such issue, then the share of the deceased child in the income shall be paid to the survivor or survivors of my said wife and children as the case may be, share and share alike until the death of my said wife, when the final division shall take place.

Five of testator's nine children survived him and the life tenant; one child predeceased testator without issue; three children survived testator but predeceased the life tenant, one leaving issue and two leaving no issue. Plaintiff joined as parties defendant the five surviving children, the three children of the child who died before the life tenant and with issue, and the two sole beneficiaries[34] of the estates of the two children who survived testator but predeceased the life tenant without issue. The plaintiff-trustee asked for instructions on the following questions:

1. Did the testator intend that the interest of those children who survived him and died without issue before the death of the life tenant pass under their respective wills to the distributees thereunder, or

2. Did the testator intend that the interests of those children who survived him and died without issue before the death of the life tenant be divested on death and follow the provision for the payment of income and vest per stirpes in the surviving children or the issue of a deceased child and be distributed accordingly?

The District Court ruled that an examination of the entire will revealed that testator intended to provide primarily both income and principal for his children and their issue, thereby retaining his estate in the "blood line." The Court stated it was "satisfied that the testator intended to divest the share of the child dying without issue in the principal as well as the income, and the proper construction is that there are cross-remainders both as to the income and principal to surviving children, although the will, being ineptly drawn, fails to include the word 'principal'." In other words the trial court has read the will as though it contained provisions for final division of principal in substantially the same terms as testator used with respect to income.

Jennie M. Warner appealed from this decision, contending that her husband, Andrew Parker Warner, having survived the testator, received a vested remainder which could be divested *only* if he died *with issue* and since Andrew died without

---

33. The wife died in 1954 and during the period from the death of the testator until the death of the wife, three more of his children had died as follows: (a) Brainard H. Warner, Jr., who died leaving issue who still survive; (b) Rebecca P. Warner, who died testate and without issue; and (c) Andrew Parker Warner, who died testate and without issue.

34. Jennie M. Warner, widow of Andrew Parker Warner, and Anna Parker Warner, sister of Rebecca P. Warner.

issue, Jennie, sole beneficiary under his will, was entitled to his share of the principal. Thus, the issues before us are:

(a) Did Andrew acquire a vested remainder in the principal?

(b) If so, what provision of the will, if any, operates to *divest* Andrew's remainder?

As to the first issue, there is little dispute. The law favors early vesting unless testator manifests a contrary intent. Since Andrew Parker Warner was in being at the death of the testator and had an immediate right to possession upon the expiration of his mother's life tenancy, his remainder interest became vested at the death of the testator.

The second question, then, is what provision of the will, if any, divested Andrew's remainder interest in the principal. Divestiture is not accomplished by the provision that "In the event of the death of any of said children before the decease of my said wife, with issue him or her surviving, then such issue shall take the share of its deceased parent ... in the principal." A provision, such as this, that the children of deceased remaindermen shall take their parents' share is not sufficient to prevent the remainder from being vested; divestiture occurs only upon death leaving issue—there is no divestiture by death alone without issue.

If divestiture of Andrew's share of the principal is to be accomplished, it must be by implication based on the fact that the will provides for divestment of the interest *in income* of those children dying without issue. Appellees contended, and the District Court held, that since the testator provided for the divestiture of the *income interests* of children dying without issue and set up cross-remainders of such interests in the survivors of his wife and children, similar cross-remainders must be implied as to the interest in principal of children dying without issue, even though the will does not so state....

We cannot agree with the District Court that an examination of the entire will demonstrates testator intended to retain his estate in the blood line and that the will was "ineptly drawn." Standing alone, the fact that testator explicitly provided for the divestiture of the *income* interest of children dying without issue is not the kind of evidence of testator's intent on which courts should rely to divest such children's vested remainder in the *principal*. Furthermore, while it is true that the testator provided for the divestment of a deceased parent's share of the *principal* when the parent was survived by issue, this provision alone does not establish that testator wanted all his property to remain in the blood line. If such *were* testator's intent he would more likely have made entirely different provisions—e.g., he might have set up a trust, with his wife and nine children as income beneficiaries, and the trust to terminate when the last one of this group died; at that time the issue of the nine children would take their parents' share of the corpus plus one-ninth of the wife's share; there would be appropriate provisions for the issue of a deceased parent taking the parent's share of the income and cross-remainders of income interests of those parents dying without issue; it would also be provided that the share of principal of a child dying without issue would go to the issue of the other children. Such a provision would have assured that the estate was kept in the blood line for a longer period of time than was possible under the disposition testator did make. For under the will as *written* any child who survived the wife received the corpus absolutely and could dispose of it in any way he chose—he could leave it in toto to his spouse, charities, etc., by testamentary or inter vivos grants, thus taking it out of the blood line completely. This, it seems to us, tends substantially to neutralize if not entirely negate the "blood line" argument.[35] Contrary to the conclusion of the court below, we feel the will *does not* show an intent to keep the estate in the blood line.

An analysis of the controlling provisions of the will also suggests it was not "ineptly drawn" and that, on the contrary, the will uses the pertinent terms artfully. Testator, with discriminating use of the terms "income" and "principal," specifically provided that issue shall take the share of a deceased parent in the *income* and on death of the life tenant a share in the *principal*. He next provided for a cross-remainder of the *income* interest of a child who predeceased the life tenant without issue and then refers to the "final division." The crucial words he used are all words of art contained in a single sentence and we find it difficult to assume that a testator who was presumably trained and experienced in probate and trust work[36] would make such specific provisions, employing the words "income" and "principal", and intend something *other* than what he said. We are impressed by the fact that if testator *intended* to say what he did in fact say, he chose the simplest way of doing so, even to the point of a terseness which gave rise to the seeming need for judicial instruction. To find for appellees we must rule that, assuming testator meant just what he said, he should have explicitly stated, "Furthermore, there are to be no cross-remainders of principal." We cannot expect testators to rebut, in this fashion, possible interpretations of their words.

To sustain the trial court's holding we must at least do one of two things:

(a) *read out* of the will the words "in the income." or

(b) *read into* the will a whole new clause dealing with "the final division" of *principal* in the event of the death of any of testator's children without issue.

The trial court felt that the testator merely omitted the word "principal." However, the problem is more than a matter of simply supplying the words "and principal" to the phrase dealing with disposition of income. The "income provision" concerns the wife and surviving children and *only* during the life of the wife. The problem of

---

35. That testator was not concerned that all his property stay in the "blood line" is further evidenced by the fact that he bequeathed $6000 to each of his nine children absolutely, to be paid when they became 21.

36. Testator was president of the Washington Loan and Trust Company, Washington, D.C., for some years prior to making this will.

"principal" disposition commences only on the death of the wife and would apply (on the trial court's theory) only to the children then surviving or, if deceased, to their issue. The suggestion that the simple insertion of the words "and principal" after "in the income" solves all over-looks the fact that the first problem involves the wife *and* the children and the second involves only the children and their issue *after* the wife's death.

It seems to us to be beyond the powers of judicial interpretation to say that the last inclusion of the phrase "in the income" was inadvertent or that the testator intended, but omitted to provide, that the principal be disposed of in a pattern similar to the disposition of the income. We must conclude that the will is "ineptly drawn" only if we start with the premise that the testator intended to confine his bounty to "blood relatives" and to eliminate "in-laws."[37] We can find nothing in the will which supports such a premise....

It is where the words of an instrument as written produce no rational result whatever that courts, faced with an obligation to resolve the problem by decision, can and do interpret the instrument to produce a result which they regard as consistent with the whole. But where the words as written produce a result which is not irrational or inconsistent with the evident intent of the instrument then courts should refrain from reading controlling words into or out of the instrument. That this may lead to a partial intestacy is not sufficient to warrant rewriting this will on the basis of the scant evidence we have as to testator's unexpressed intent, since the document can be rationally interpreted and applied without adding or excising words.

Therefore, we hold that this instrument gave testator's children vested remainders in the principal subject to being divested only on death with issue and that the interests of Rebecca P. Warner and Andrew Parker Warner were transmissible by their respective wills to their distributees, Anna Parker Warner and Jennie M. Warner. Since the parties have never explicitly considered the question of the effect of this ruling on Southard's 1/9th share and the trial court did not reach or rule on this point, we shall remand the case for further proceedings not inconsistent with this opinion.

Reversed and remanded.

Estate of Thall
219 N.E.2d 397 (N.Y. 1966)

FULD, J. Solomon Thall died in September, 1943, survived by his wife, a sister and issue of a deceased brother. By a will executed in 1941, he left his residuary estate in trust for the life of his wife with the income to be shared by her and by the

---

37. As we pointed out above, all parties concede that if testator's son survived the life tenant, the 1/9th share could be given to "in-laws" or any others selected by the son.

testator's sister Sophie Levitsky and Sophie's two sons, Emanuel Landis and Ben Ami Landis. Upon the death of the widow, the corpus of the trust, after payment of certain legacies, was to go to Sophie, Emanuel and Ben Ami, "share and share alike". There then follow these clauses pertaining to the corpus:

> In the event that my sister Sophie Levitsky shall predecease me or surviving me shall predecease my said wife, I give and bequeath her share to her sons Emanuel Landis and Ben Ami Landis, share and share alike.
>
> Should either Emanuel Landis or Ben Ami Landis predecease me or predecease my said wife, I give and bequeath the share of the one so dying to his surviving child or children, and if more than one, share and share alike.
>
> If either of my said nephews Emanuel Landis or Ben Ami Landis should predecease me or surviving me shall predecease my said wife without leaving any child or children him surviving, I direct that his share shall be paid to his surviving brother.

The testator's widow is still alive. Ben Ami Landis died in 1956 survived by his daughter Barbara Ann. Sophie Levitsky died in 1961, and Emanuel Landis died without issue in 1962.

The will makes no provision for disposition of the income provided for Sophie and her two sons in the event which actually occurred, the death of all of them before that of the testator's widow, and this hiatus renders a construction of the will necessary at this time. The will likewise fails to provide for disposition of the corpus under the circumstance which in fact came to pass, namely, the death of one of Sophie's sons without issue *after* the death of the other son who was survived by a child.

The Surrogate decided that both the net income (after deduction of the widow's interest) and the entire corpus (excluding certain specific bequests) should be equally divided, one half to Ben Ami's daughter, Barbara Ann, and one half to those persons who were the testator's distributees on the date of his death. On appeal, the Appellate Division modified the Surrogate's decree by providing (1) that all of the net *income* was payable to the testator's distributees and (2) that, upon the death of the testator's widow, the entire corpus should be paid to Barbara Ann Landis. In our view, Barbara Ann is entitled to all of that portion of the net income not payable to the widow and, upon the latter's death, is to receive the whole of the corpus, except for the specific bequests.

The first rule of testamentary construction, of course, is that a will be interpreted to reflect the actual intention of the testator and the second that this intention be ascertained from a reading of the document as a whole. If a "general scheme" be found, it is the duty of the courts to carry out the testator's purpose, notwithstanding that "general rules of interpretation" might point to a different result.

Corollary to these broad principles is the doctrine that a court may "give effect to an intention or purpose, indicated *by implication*, where the express language of the entire will manifests such an intention or purpose" and the testator has simply neglected to provide for the exact contingency which occurred. As the Appellate Division wrote [Matter of Selner's Estate,] (261 App.Div. [618,] at pp. 620-621, 26 N.Y.S. [783] at p. 786, supra),

> If... the property or estate claimed to be bequeathed or devised by implication, in a contingency which has occurred, has been made the subject of an express bequest or devise in another contingency, which did not occur, then effect may be given to such bequest or devise by implication, in the contingency which did occur, if a reading of the entire will makes manifest that such was the intention of the testator.

In the case before us, the testator's intent, as manifested in his will, is plain. Outside of assuring his wife a minimum income during her lifetime, his paramount concern was for his sister and her two sons. His widow and his collateral relatives were left no part of the bulk of his estate. Indeed, in his bequests to the latter, token $1,000 gifts, he repeated more than once his direction that their legacies were to lapse if they predeceased him—or his widow, in the case of gifts from the trust corpus. Quite different were the provisions of the testator's will for his sister and her sons. In addition to receiving that portion of the trust income not bequeathed to his wife, they were to have the entire trust corpus—except for small gifts to collaterals—upon the wife's death. The testator's interest in his sister and her sons also appears in other parts of his will, for instance, in his bequests of personal property to them.

In disposing of his residuary estate, it is evident that the testator inadvertently neglected to foresee every eventuality. As indicated, he provided that Sophie's share, if she predeceased his widow, was to be divided between Emanuel and Ben Ami; that, if either Emanuel or Ben Ami predeceased the widow, the share of the one so dying was to pass to his surviving children, unless he died without issue, in which event his share was to be paid to his surviving brother. Manifestly, the testator expected that Sophie would die before her sons and that each of the sons thereafter dying would be survived by either a child or a brother. However, he failed to anticipate—what actually came to pass—that the second of the sons would die without issue, survived not by his brother but by the latter's child. Quite obviously, what the testator most desired was that his estate should ultimately go to, and remain within, a particular branch of his family. He could not have intended the descendants of Sophie to be deprived of any portion of his estate by the happenstance that the son (of hers) who was without children died *after*, rather than *before*, the son who left offspring. In short, since the testator desired his sister's descendants to take, there is a necessary "implication" that he did not intend any interest of a grandchild of hers to be defeated by the deaths of Emanuel and Ben Ami, as it were, in the wrong order.

Quite dissimilar are the cases in which the court has decreed an intestacy where the intent of the testator is not sufficiently clear to permit a bequest or devise by implication. [In Matter of Jay's Will, 1 N.Y.2d 897, 154 N.Y.S.2d 649, 136 N.E.2d

720,] for instance, the testator left his residuary estate to his wife for life and upon her death to his issue and, if she died without issue, to his mother or sister or the "survivor". We held that the death of the mother and sister prior to the testator's widow resulted in intestacy. In that case, however, unlike the present, there was no manifest intention by the testator to preserve for a particular branch of his family the interests of the remaindermen who might predecease the life tenant.

It is our conclusion, then, that upon the death of the testator's widow the corpus of the trust, except for specific bequests, is to be turned over to Barbara Ann Landis. It is also our conclusion that she is presently entitled, by reason of section 63 of the Real Property Law, Consol.Laws, c. 50, to the income other than the portion payable to the widow. That section provides that,

> When, in consequence of a valid limitation of a future estate, there is a suspension of the power of alienation, or of the ownership, during the continuance of which the rents and profits are undisposed of, and no valid direction for their accumulation is given, such rents and profits shall belong to the persons presumptively entitled to the next eventual estate.

It is clear that Barbara Ann Landis is the person "presumptively entitled to the next eventual estate", and, consequently, all of the income not otherwise disposed of belongs to her.

We have considered the other arguments advanced by the several parties and agree with the Appellate Division's resolution of them.

The order of the Appellate Division should be modified as herein indicated, with costs to all parties filing briefs payable out of the income of the trust in the same manner as the Surrogate's decree directs the payment of counsel fees and allowances, and, as so modified, affirmed.

Notes and Questions

1. *Death in the "Wrong Order."* In stating that the testator "did not intend any interest of a grandchild of [Sophie's] to be defeated by the deaths of Emanuel and Ben Ami, as it were, in the wrong order," the court seemed to be under the impression that if Emanuel's death without issue had occurred before, rather than after, Ben Ami's death, Emanuel's share of the corpus would have gone to Ben Ami's issue, Barbara Ann. Does the language of the will support the court's assumption? Compare Restatement of Property §271 (accepting the principle of the accrued share) with Restatement 3d of Property §26.9 comment f (rejecting the principle of the accrued share).

2. *Comparison With Krooss.* Judge Fuld, who wrote the opinion of the court in *Thall*, also wrote the opinion of the court in In re Krooss, p. 852. *Krooss* was not cited or discussed in *Thall*. Is *Krooss* relevant to the disposition of Emanuel's share of the corpus? Are *Krooss* and *Thall* reconcilable?

3. *Income to the Persons Entitled to the Next Eventual Estate.* With respect to the trust income, the court invoked §63 of the New York Real Property Law,[38] which directs that undisposed-of income belongs "to the persons presumptively entitled to the next eventual estate." The application of this section, however, is dependent on the instrument not disposing of the income. Did the instrument dispose of the income? See Olin L. Browder, Jr., Trusts and the Doctrine of Estates, 72 Mich. L. Rev. 1509, 1560-61 (1974).

2. Incomplete or Ambiguous Dispositions of Income

Dewire[39] v. Haveles[40]
534 N.E.2d 782 (Mass. 1989)

WILKINS, Justice. This petition for a declaration of rights seeks answers to questions arising from an artlessly drafted will....

Thomas A. Dewire died in January, 1941, survived by his widow, his son Thomas, Jr., and three grandchildren (Thomas, III, Paula, and Deborah, all children of Thomas, Jr.). His will placed substantially all his estate in a residuary trust. The income of the trust was payable to his widow for life and, on her death, the income was payable to his son Thomas, Jr., the widow of Thomas, Jr., and Thomas Jr.'s children.[41] After the testator's death, Thomas, Jr., had three more children by a second wife. Thomas, Jr., died on May 28, 1978, a widower, survived by all six of his children. Thomas, III, who had served as trustee since 1978, died on March 19, 1987, leaving a widow and one child, Jennifer. Among the questions presented, and the most important one for present purposes, is to whom the one-sixth share of the trust income, once payable to Thomas, III, is now payable.

---

38. This section now appears, in somewhat modified form, as N.Y. Est. Powers & Trusts Law §9-2.3.

39. Sheila Dewire, executrix of the estate of Thomas A. Dewire, III, and mother of Jennifer.

40. Paula Dewire Haveles, Deborah Dewire, Stephen Dewire, Andrew Dewire, and Constance Dewire. Paula Dewire Haveles is the current trustee of the testamentary trust under the will of her grandfather, Thomas A. Dewire.

41. The language of the will directing this distribution appears in article third of the will and reads as follows:

Third: To my wife, Mabel G. Dewire, I give, devise and bequeath all the rest, residue and remainder of all the estate of which I shall die seized, for and during the term of her natural life, and upon her decease to my son, Thomas A. Dewire, Jr., and his heirs and assigns, but in trust nevertheless upon the following trusts and for the following purposes:

A. To hold, direct, manage and conserve the trust estate, so given, for the benefit of himself, his wife and children in the manner following, that is to say:

To expend out of the net income so much as may be necessary for the proper care, maintenance of himself and wife conformable to their station in life, and for the care maintenance and education of his children born to him in his lifetime, in such manner as in his judgment and discretion shall seem proper, and his judgment and discretion shall be final.

In his will, the testator stated: "It is my will, except as hereinabove provided, that my grandchildren, under guidance and discretion of my Trustee, shall share equally in the net income of my said estate." At another point, he referred to the trust income being "divided equally amongst my grandchildren."...

There is no explicit provision in the will concerning the distribution of income on the death of a grandchild while the gift of income to grandchildren continues....

Our task is to discern the testator's intention concerning the distribution of a grandchild's share of the trust income on his death. As a practical matter, in cases of this sort, where there is no express intention, we must resort to reasonable inferences in the particular circumstances which on occasion shade into rules of construction that are applied when no intention at all can be inferred on the issue. In this case, the reasonable inference as to the testator's intention is that Jennifer should take her father's share in the income.

Certain points are not in serious controversy and are relatively easy to resolve. The gift of net income to the testator's grandchildren, divided equally or to be shared equally, is a class gift.... The class includes all six grandchildren, three of whom were born before and three of whom were born after the testator's death.... Because there is a gift over at the end of the class gift, the testator intended the class gift to his grandchildren only to be a gift of a life interest in the income of the trust. The general rule is that, in the absence of a contrary intent expressed in the will or a controlling statute stating otherwise, members of a class are joint tenants with rights of survivorship.

This last stated principle becomes important in deciding whether Jennifer, the child of the deceased grandson, takes her deceased father's share in the trust income or whether the remaining class members, the other five grandchildren, take that income share equally by right of survivorship. Jennifer argues, under the general rule, that the will manifests an intent contrary to a class gift with rights of survivorship. We agree with this conclusion. Thus we need not decide, as Jennifer further argues, whether the rule of construction presuming a right of survivorship in class members should be rejected in the circumstances and replaced by a rule based on principles similar to those expressed in the antilapse statute.[42]....

---

42. The Massachusetts antilapse statute applies only to testamentary gifts to a child or other relation of a testator who predeceased the testator leaving issue surviving the testator and to class gifts to children or other relations where one or more class member predeceased the testator (even if the class member had died before the will was executed). G.L. c. 191, §22. The rule of construction of §22 is that the issue of a deceased relation take his share by right of representation "unless a different disposition is made or required by the will."

In this case, no class member predeceased the testator and, therefore, §22 does not explicitly aid Jennifer. The policy underlying §22 might fairly be seen as supporting, as a rule of construction (absent a contrary intent), the substitution of a class member's surviving issue for a deceased class member if the class is made up of children or other relations of the testator. See Bigelow v. Clap, 166 Mass. 88, 91, 43 N.E. 1037 (1896). It has been suggested that "[t]he policy of [antilapse] statutes [dealing with

The testator provided that the trust should terminate twenty-one years after the death of his last grandchild. It is unlikely that the testator intended that trust income should be accumulated for twenty-one years, and we would tend to avoid such a construction. Certainly, we should not presume that he intended an intestacy as to that twenty-one year period. He must have expected that someone would receive distributions of income during those years.[43] The only logical recipients of that income would be the issue (by right of representation) of deceased grandchildren, the same group of people who would take the trust assets on termination of the trust (assuming no violation of the rule against perpetuities). If these people were intended to receive income during the last twenty-one years of the trust as well as the trust assets on its termination, it is logical that they should also receive income during the term of the class gift if their ancestor (one of the grandchildren) should die. Such a pattern treats each grandchild and his issue equally throughout the intended term of the trust. Where, among other things, every other provision in the will concerning the distribution of trust income and principal (after the death of the testator and his wife) points to equal treatment of the testator's issue per stirpes, there is a sufficient contrary intent shown to overcome the rule of construction that the class gift of income to grandchildren is given to them as joint tenants with the right of survivorship....

Judgment shall be entered declaring that... Jennifer Ann Dewire in her lifetime is entitled to one-sixth of the net income of the trust during the period of the class gift of income, that is, until the death of the last grandchild (and a proportionate share of the income of any grandchild who dies leaving no issue)....

So Ordered.

Notes and Questions

1. *Position of the American Law Institute.* The Restatement 3d of Trusts §49 comment c(3) supports the *Dewire* case by providing:

c(3).... Multiple life beneficiaries: income share(s) not expressly disposed of.... Where the income of a trust is payable to two or more life beneficiaries with a gift over on the

---

the death of a class member after the testator's death] commends itself to decisional law." Restatement (Second) of Property, Donative Transfers §27.3 comment i (Tent. Draft No. 9, 1986). If the antilapse statute protects the interests of the issue of a relation who predeceases a testator, there is good reason why we should adopt, as a rule of construction, the same principle as to a relation of a testator who survives the testator but dies before an interest comes into possession. In the case of a class gift of income from a trust, the interest could be viewed as coming into possession on each income distribution date.

[G.L. c. 191, §22 is now replaced by G.L. c. 190B, §2-603. Ed.]

43. At one point in his will, the testator says that the trust income is payable "to [Thomas, Jr.] and his children and their heirs at law."

death of the survivor, and an income beneficiary dies, the disposition of the income share [that] the deceased beneficiary had been receiving depends on the terms of the trust. Where the terms of the trust make no express provision for the situation, the normal inference is that the settlor intended the income share to be paid to the issue (if any) of the deceased income beneficiary in the typical case in which the remainder is to pass to the descendants of the beneficiaries upon the survivor's death.

This provision of the Restatement 3d is discussed by the Reporter in Edward C. Halbach, Jr., Uniform Acts, Restatements, and Trends in American Trust Law at Century's End, 88 Calif. L. Rev. 1877, 1906 (2000). *Dewire* also is supported by the Restatement 3d of Property §26.9 comment e(1):

> *e(1). Gap when trust principal distributable on death of last living income beneficiary.* A gap potentially arises if the terms of the trust direct that the trust principal is to be distributed on the death of the last living income beneficiary, and if the terms of the trust make no express provision for the distribution of the share of income that a deceased income beneficiary other than the last living income beneficiary had been receiving.
>
> If the income beneficiary's income interest is not limited to the beneficiary's lifetime, no gap arises because the income beneficiary's interest is a life estate for the life of the last living income beneficiary (a life estate pur autre vie)....
>
> A gap arises if the income beneficiary's income interest is limited to the beneficiary's lifetime. The traditional rule of construction is that the gap is filled by an implied cross remainder to the living income beneficiary or beneficiaries.... An exception, however, arises if the remainder in trust principal is to pass to the issue of the beneficiaries upon the survivor's death. In such a case, filling the gap by implying an income interest in favor of the deceased beneficiary's issue from time to time living would be more consistent with the transferor's overall plan of disposition....

2. *UPC §2-707.* Would UPC §2-707 produce the result reached by the court in *Dewire*? Professor Waggoner argues that it would. See Lawrence W. Waggoner, The Uniform Probate Code Extends Antilapse-Type Protection to Poorly Drafted Trusts, 94 Mich. L. Rev. 2309, 2332-33 (1996).

3. *Question.* Suppose that G devised property in trust, to "pay one-third of the income to my son, A, for life, one-third to my daughter, B, for life, and one-third to my son, C, for life; upon the death of the survivor of my children, the trust principal is to be distributed to my then-living descendants, by representation; if none, to X Charity." A died first, survived by descendants. Then B died without surviving descendants. Under the Restatement 3d, who would take B's share of the income? See Restatement 3d of Property §26.9 illus. 5.

EXTERNAL REFERENCES. Olin L. Browder, Trusts and the Doctrine of Estates, 72 Mich. L. Rev. 1509, 1542-75 (1974); Edward C. Halbach, Jr., Issues About Issue: Some Recurrent Class Gift Problems, 48 Mo. L. Rev. 333, 355-57 (1983).

Chapter 17

The Rule Against Perpetuities and Related Rules

We now make an abrupt shift from matters of construction, the purposes of which are to carry out intent, to rules of law that defeat intent for reasons of overriding social policy. Specifically, the main subject of this chapter is the Rule Against Perpetuities. The Rule Against Perpetuities was originally designed to prevent the dead hand from indirectly curtailing the alienability of property for too long a period—in perpetuity. The indirect curtailment of alienability was said to arise from attaching contingencies to future interests in property.

A rule that developed over time into the rule known as the Rule Against Perpetuities was initiated in the much-celebrated Duke of Norfolk's Case, 3 Ch. Cas. 1, 22 Eng. Rep. 931 (1682). The so-called *modern* Rule Against Perpetuities was formulated by Professor John Chipman Gray in the second edition of his book, The Rule Against Perpetuities (2d ed. 1906):

> *No [contingent property] interest is good unless it must vest, if at all, not later than 21 years after some life in being at the creation of the interest.*[1]

Nothing resembling this mechanically precise "rule" was stated by the judge in the Duke of Norfolk's Case, the Lord Chancellor, the First Earl of Nottingham. His pronouncements about prohibiting perpetuities appear to be mere musings:

> But what Time? And where are the Bounds of that Contingency? You may limit, it seems, upon a Contingency to happen in a Life: What if it be limited, if such a one die without Issue within twenty-one Years, or 100 Years, or while Westminster-Hall stands? Where will you stop, if you do not stop here? I will tell you where I will stop: I will stop wherever any visible Inconvenience doth appear....

Despite the appearance of imprecision, even casualness, of the Lord Chancellor's statement, the Duke of Norfolk's Case was an exceedingly important case at the time. But not in the way that might first be imagined: The decision apparently served less as a judicial warning that perpetuities would not be tolerated than as an approval of conveyancers' practices current at the time. The future interest challenged in the Duke of Norfolk's Case was an executory interest. Although Pells v. Brown, Cro. Jac. 590, 79 Eng. Rep. 504 (K.B. 1620), had earlier held that the destructibility rule was inapplicable to executory interests, the *Pells* decision was a sudden and

---

1. This formulation was carried forward, word for word, in subsequent editions of his book. See Gray on Perpetuities §201.

unexpected departure from prior law. Also, a later decision, Purefoy v. Rogers, 2 Wm. Saund. 380, 85 Eng. Rep. 1181 (K.B. 1670), cast some doubt on the continuing validity of *Pells*, by holding that a contingent remainder could not avoid destruction by changing into an executory interest. The Duke of Norfolk's Case assured the practicing bar that *Pells* remained solid law.

Gradually, over the 150 or so years following the Duke of Norfolk's Case, the pronouncement that a contingency limited to "happen in a Life" was valid, but beyond that, an invalidity would arise "wherever any visible Inconvenience doth appear," grew step by step into the Rule Against Perpetuities stated by Professor Gray. The period of a life was enlarged to multiple lives, which in effect is but a single life, the choice being postponed to turn upon which of several is the survivor. Scatterwood v. Edge, 1 Salk. 229, 91 Eng. Rep. 203 (K.B. 1697). To this period was added the period of an actual minority of a beneficiary, and also an actual period of gestation. Some considerable time later, in Cadell v. Palmer, 1 Cl. & F. 372, 6 Eng. Rep. 956 (H.L. 1833), the minority period was disengaged from an actual minority and allowed as a 21-year period in gross.

Although Professor Gray's book solidified the common-law Rule Against Perpetuities, stunting its further evolution throughout much of the twentieth century, the Rule Against Perpetuities again is undergoing change. We analyze these changes later in this chapter.

EXTERNAL REFERENCES. On the Duke of Norfolk's Case, see George L. Haskins, Extending the Grasp of the Dead Hand: Reflections on the Origins of the Rule Against Perpetuities, 126 U. Pa. L. Rev. 19 (1977); George L. Haskins, "Inconvenience" and the Rule For Perpetuities, 48 Mo. L. Rev. 451 (1983). On Professor Gray's influence, see Stephen A. Siegel, John Chipman Gray, Legal Formalism, and the Transformation of Perpetuities Law, 36 U. Miami L. Rev. 439 (1982). On the mechanics of the Rule, see W. Barton Leach, Perpetuities in a Nutshell, 51 Harv. L. Rev. 638 (1938); W. Barton Leach, The Nutshell Revisited, 78 Harv. L. Rev. 973 (1965).

PART A. MECHANICS OF THE COMMON-LAW RULE AGAINST PERPETUITIES

Interests to Which the Rule Applies. At common law, the Rule Against Perpetuities applies to future interests in property, whether legal or equitable, but only if they are contingent (nonvested). Classification of the interests in a disposition is, therefore, a preliminary but crucial step to solving perpetuity questions. Specifically, the Rule applies to contingent remainders and to executory interests, both of which are contingent future interests. The Rule does not apply to vested remainders, not even to those that are vested subject to defeasance; nor does the

Rule apply to reversions, which are always vested.[2] The other two reversionary future interests—possibilities of reverter and rights of entry—also are considered exempt from the Rule Against Perpetuities.

Class gifts are subject to the Rule, and in fact are treated specially. The early English decision of Leake v. Robinson, 2 Mer. 363, 35 Eng. Rep. 979 (Ch. 1817), laid down the proposition that *if the interest of any potential class member might vest too remotely, the entire class gift is invalid.* This is the so-called "all-or-nothing rule," by which it is meant that a class gift is either *completely* valid or *completely* invalid. It is not permissible to treat the interest of each class member separately and say that some class members have valid interests and other class members have invalid interests. More extensive consideration of the special case of class gifts is presented in Part H, later in this chapter.

The "Perpetuity Period." The common-law perpetuity period is defined as a life in being plus 21 years. The period can be extended by one or more periods of gestation, *but only when an actual pregnancy makes the extension necessary.*[3] The period of gestation is not a formal part of the perpetuity period. See Cadell v. Palmer, 1 Cl. & F. 372 (H.L. 1883).

The life in being, often called the *measuring life*, must be the life of a person "in being at the creation of the interest." This means that the person whose life is the measuring life must be alive or in gestation when the perpetuity period begins to run. The measuring life must also be a human life—the life of a corporation, an animal, or a plant cannot be used. But there are no other formal restrictions. Theoretically, anyone in the world who was alive or in gestation when the interest was created can be the measuring life. As a practical matter, though, it is not that complex when one gets down to the business of identifying the measuring life in actual cases.

Although the 21-year part of the perpetuity period is described by Gray as coming *after* the death of the person who is the measuring life, and we often refer to it as the *tack-on* 21-year period, the 21-year part need not be preceded by a measuring life; it can stand on its own. A testamentary transfer "to such of my grandchildren as are living on the 21st anniversary of my death" would be valid without a measuring life.

While authority on the question is sparse, it seems to be agreed that the 21-year part cannot come first, followed by a life that is in being 21 years *after* the creation of the interest. This is a consequence of the requirement that the measuring life must be in being *at* the creation of the interest.

---

2. "A vested interest is not subject to the Rule against Perpetuities." Gray on Perpetuities §205.

3. UPC §2-901(d) (USRAP §1(d)) takes a different approach. It provides: "In determining whether a nonvested property interest [is valid under the common-law Rule], the possibility that a child will be born to an individual after the individual's death is disregarded."

Example 17.1: G devised property in trust "to pay the income to G's children for 21 years, then to pay the income to such of G's grandchildren as may then be living for life, and on the death of the survivor to pay the corpus of the trust to G's descendants then living by representation."

If G is survived by one or more children, the remainder interest in the corpus of the trust violates the Rule and is invalid.

1. The Requirement of Initial Certainty

Requirement of Initial Certainty. Implicit in Professor Gray's formulation is the *requirement of initial certainty*, which is that *a contingent future interest is invalid if, at the creation of the interest, there exists any possible chain of post-creation events that would permit the interest to remain contingent beyond a life in being plus 21 years.*

Measuring Life. The "life in being" is traditionally called the "measuring life." This term might suggest that one must identify a particular person as the measuring life and *then* test the interest to determine whether or not the interest might remain contingent beyond 21 years following such person's death. This is *not* the procedure, however. It is wrong to speak as if there is a measuring life for all interests, whether valid or invalid. For a life in being to be a "measuring life," the person must satisfy the requirement of initial certainty, which means that *there must be a causal connection between the person's death and the vesting or termination[4] of the interest no later than 21 years thereafter.*

Only *valid* dispositions have a measuring life. An invalid interest is invalid because there is *no* measuring life that makes it valid. This is what is meant when it is said that invalidity under the common-law Rule depends upon the existence, as of the interest's creation, of an invalidating chain of possible post-creation events. *The search for a "measuring life," therefore, turns out to be a search for a "validating life."*

In Truth, There Is No "Perpetuity Period" at Common Law. The requirement of initial certainty is a mechanism for testing the validity of an interest *in advance* of its actual vesting or termination. With the decision made in advance, the common law has no need to mark off a "perpetuity period" in the case of invalid interests.[5]

---

4. An interest terminates when vesting becomes impossible. In the following example, B's interest terminates if and when B predeceases A: "to A for life, remainder to B if B survives A."

5. See Lawrence W. Waggoner, Perpetuities: A Perspective on Wait-and-See, 85 Colum. L. Rev. 1714, 1714-17 (1985); Lawrence W. Waggoner, Perpetuity Reform, 81 Mich. L. Rev. 1718, 1720-24 (1983). Professor Dukeminier disputes this. Jesse Dukeminier, A Modern Guide to Perpetuities, 74 Calif. L. Rev. 1867, 1868-76 (1986); Jesse Dukeminier, Perpetuities: The Measuring Lives, 85 Colum. L. Rev. 1648, 1649-54 (1985). The dispute is in reality a by-product of a different controversy concerning the wait-and-see method of perpetuity reform (see below Part E); it has no bearing on the solution of perpetuity problems under the common-law Rule, a point that corroborates the position that

Here is why: A "perpetuity period" would be necessary only if *actual* post-creation events were to be taken into account. But the common-law Rule does not permit actual post-creation events to be considered.

2. How to Search for a Validating Life

Goal of the Search: To Find One Person for Whom There Is No Invalidating Chain of Possible Post-creation Events. The Official Comment to §1 of the Uniform Statutory Rule Against Perpetuities (USRAP) sets forth the following guidance for solving a perpetuities problem:

> The process for determining whether a validating life exists is to postulate the death of each individual connected in some way to the transaction, and ask the question: Is there with respect to this individual an invalidating chain of possible [post-creation] events? If one individual can be found for whom the answer is No, that individual can serve as the validating life. As to that individual there will be the requisite causal connection between his or her death and the questioned interest's vesting or terminating no later than 21 years thereafter.

Note that the converse is also true: If no person can be found for whom there is no invalidating chain of possible post-creation events, there is no validating life; an interest for which there is no validating life is invalid.

Only Insiders Need to Be Considered. In searching for a validating life, there is no formal rule forbidding the testing of anyone in the world to see if that person has the causal connection demanded by the requirement of initial certainty. There is, for example, no law against testing your favorite movie star or rock star in each case, if you want to do that. But experience has shown that no outsider will pass the test.

What we mean to say is that you can safely limit the persons you test to insiders—those who are connected in some way to the transaction. Only insiders have a chance of supplying the requisite causal connection demanded by the requirement of initial certainty. The insiders to be tested vary from case to case, but would always include the transferor, the beneficiaries of the disposition, including but not restricted to the taker or takers of the challenged interest, the holder and permissible appointees of a power of appointment, persons related to the foregoing—for example by blood or adoption, especially in the ascending and descending lines—and anyone else who has any connection to the transaction. If there is any doubt about a particular person, no harm is done by subjecting that person to the test. Usually it takes no more than an instant to resolve whether or not a person arguably on the fringe of the transaction has the requisite causal connection demanded by the requirement of initial certainty.

---

there is no "perpetuity period" as such at common law.

There is, however, no point in even considering the life of a complete outsider who is clearly unconnected to the transaction—a person selected at random from the world at large. Outsiders in that category have already been tested and found *always* to be wanting. No outsider can possibly fulfill the requirement of initial certainty, because any outsider can die immediately after the creation of the interest without having any effect whatsoever on the time when the interest will vest or terminate. Take, for example, the simple disposition "to A for life, remainder to such of A's children as live to age 21." Is the dean of your law school a possible validating life? Of course not. The timing of the dean's death has no causal connection to the time when the last of A's children will live to age 21.

Survivor of a Group. In appropriate cases, the validating life need not be individuated. Rather, if we view the situation as of the date of the interest's creation, the life can be an unidentified member of a group of individuals. It is common in these cases to say that the members of the group are the validating *lives*. This is acceptable, as long as it is recognized that the true meaning of the statement is that the validating *life* is the life of the member of the group who turns out to live the longest. As the court said in Scatterwood v. Edge, 1 Salk. 229, 91 Eng. Rep. 203 (K.B. 1697), "for let the lives be never so many, there must be a survivor, and so it is but the length of that life; for [Justice] Twisden [in Love v. Wyndham, 1 Mod. 50, 54 Eng. Rep. 724, 726 (K.B. 1669)] used to say, the candles were all lighted at once."

Beneficiary of the Interest as the Validating Life. A well established but sometimes overlooked point is that the beneficiary of an interest might be the validating life for his or her own interest. See, e.g., Rand v. Bank of California, 388 P.2d 437 (Or. 1964). This point is especially useful in cases in which an interest is contingent on the beneficiary's reaching an age in excess of 21 or is contingent on the beneficiary's survival of a particular point in time that is or may be in excess of 21 years after the interest was created or after the death of a person in being at the date of creation.

Problems

Consider the validity of the remainder interest in the following cases:

1. G devised property "to A for life, remainder to B."

2. G devised property "to A for life, remainder to B if B survives A."

3. G devised property "to A for life, remainder to A's children."

Problems

All the contingent property interests in the following cases satisfy the requirement of initial certainty and are therefore valid. Using the above text as a guide, identify the validating life for each interest.

1. G devised property "to A for life, remainder to such of A's children as live to age 21." G was survived by his son (A), his daughter (B), A's wife (W), and A's two children (X and Y).

2. Take the same facts as in Problem 1, but change the disposition to read "to B for life, remainder to such of A's children as live to age 21."

3. G devised property "to such of my grandchildren as live to age 21." Some of G's children are living at G's death.

4. G devised property "to such of A's children as live to age 25." A predeceased G. At G's death, A had three living children, all of whom were younger than 25.

5. G devised property "to such of A's children as are living on the 25th anniversary of my death." A predeceased G. At G's death, A had three living children.

———

Multiple Interests. Dispositions of property sometimes create more than one interest that is subject to the Rule. When this happens, the validity of each interest must be tested separately. A validating life that validates one interest might or might not validate the other interests. Consequently, one must search for a validating life for each interest.

Problems

1. G devised property "to A for life, then to A's children for their lives, and on the death of each of them to the survivor or survivors of them for life, and on the death of the survivor of them, to B and her heirs."

Do any of the interests created in this disposition violate the common-law Rule Against Perpetuities?[6] Suppose the remainder interest to B had been contingent on survival of A's last surviving child—that is, suppose it had said "to B if B is then living"?

2. All but one of the future interests in the following cases fail the requirement of initial certainty and are therefore invalid. Explain why there is no validating life in each case. Which future interest is valid and why?

(a)(1) G devised real property "to A and her heirs as long as liquor is not sold on the premises, and upon liquor being sold on the premises, the property is to go to B;" or

(2) G devised real property "to A and her heirs on condition that no liquor be sold on the premises, but if liquor is sold on the premises, the property is to go to B."

In both cases, G was survived by A and B.

---

6. See Hochberg v. Proctor, 805 N.E.2d 979, 989 (Mass. 2004); Dodge v. Bennett, 215 Mass. 545, 102 N.E. 916 (1913); Gray on Perpetuities §207.

(b) G devised property in trust, directing the trustee to pay the net income therefrom "to A for life, then to A's children for the life of the survivor, and upon the death of A's last surviving child, to pay the corpus of the trust to A's grandchildren." G was survived by A and A's two children, X and Y.

———

Interests That Must Vest or Terminate Within 21 Years. As noted above, there is no need to search for a validating life for interests that are certain to vest or terminate within 21 years after their creation; the 21-year part of the period validates such interests.

In Green v. Green, 221 N.E.2d 388 (Ohio P. Ct. 1966), an action for a declaratory judgment was brought to construe the will of Roy C. Green, who died on July 24, 1955. Roy was survived by his only child Richard, his sister Helen, Richard's wife Elsie, and their three children, William, Judith, and Betsy. William was born on February 1, 1941, Judith on May 21, 1942, and Betsy on July 28, 1947. Roy's will established a trust that provided:

> (6) The trust shall terminate upon the last to happen of the following counts:
>
> (a) The death of my son, Richard C. Green.
>
> (b) The death or remarriage of Elsie L. Green.
>
> (c) The day the youngest living child of my son, Richard C. Green, in being on the date of my death, attains twenty-five (25) years of age.
>
> (d) The death of my sister, Helen Green.
>
> Upon the termination of the trust, the Trustee shall assign, transfer, convey and deliver all of the property then comprising the trust to the lineal descendants of my son, Richard C. Green, per stirpes.

To a contention that the interest in the corpus violated the Rule Against Perpetuities, the court responded:

> Where a trust is to terminate at the time when a designated person attains a specified age, courts have construed this to mean that if the person dies before attaining the required age, the trust terminates immediately upon his death. Fishberg's Will, 158 Misc. 3, 285 N.Y.S. 303 (Sur. Ct. 1936); Sammis v. Sammis, 14 R.I. 123 (1883); Butler v. Butler, 40 R.I. 425, 101 A. 115 (1917).
>
> Other courts have held that the trust terminates when the designated person would have attained the specified age had he lived that long. Clark's Estate, 13 N.J. Misc. 393, 178 A. 574 (Orphans' Court 1935); Stein v. United States National Bank of Portland, 165 Or. 518, 108 P.2d 1016 (1941).
>
> Basically, the court is trying to find the intention of the testator, and this is reflected in the authorities cited.
>
> Fortunately, we need not analyze the cases to see whether they can be reconciled, nor need we choose between the two views, for under either view the trust in the present case

will terminate, the class will close, and the remainders will vest within twenty-one years after lives in being at the date of the testator's death....

What feature of the case allowed the court to declare the interests valid without choosing "between the two views"?

3. Time of Creation

Primary Statutory References: *UPC §2-902 (USRAP §2)*

The time when a property interest is created is important because it fixes the time when the validating life must be "in being." It also is important because it demarks the facts that can be taken into account in determining the validity of an interest. Under the common-law Rule, an interest is valid only if at the time when the interest is created, with the facts *then existing* taken into account, the interest is certain to vest or terminate within a life in being plus 21 years. The facts that *actually* occur from that time forward, with one exception concerning interests created by the exercise of certain powers of appointment (see below Part H), are irrelevant; all that counts is what *might* happen.

Property interests created by will are created when the testator dies, not when the testator signs the will. Thus the validating life for testamentary transfers must be a person who was alive (or in gestation) when the testator died, and the facts that can be taken into account in determining the validity of an interest created by will are those existing at the testator's death.

Property interests created by inter vivos transfers are created when the transfers become effective for purposes of property law generally. This ordinarily would be the date of delivery of the deed or the funding of the trust. Thus the validating life for inter vivos transfers must be a person who was alive (or in gestation) when the transfer became effective, and the facts that can be taken into account in determining the validity of an interest created by inter vivos transfer are those existing at that time.

The Postponement Principle. For purposes of the Rule Against Perpetuities, the time of creation of a property interest is postponed in certain cases. One of the leading decisions on the postponement principle is Cook v. Horn, 104 S.E.2d 461 (Ga. 1958). In the course of its opinion, the court explained the principle in these terms:

> While there is a scarcity of authority on this question, and none that we have found in Georgia, the prevailing opinion by both the courts of other jurisdictions and recognized text writers is that, when a settlor has the power during his lifetime to revoke or destroy the trust estate for his own exclusive personal benefit, the question whether interests, or any of them, created by an instrument or deed of trust are void because in violation of the rule against perpetuities, is to be determined as of the date of the settlor's death and not as of the date

the instrument is executed and delivered. See Ryan v. Ward, 192 Md. 342, 64 A.2d 258, 7 A.L.R.2d 1078; Mifflin's Appeal, 121 Pa. 205, 15 A. 525, 1 L.R.A. 453; Goesele v. Bimeler, 14 How. 589, 14 L.Ed. 554; Manufacturers Life Insurance Company v. von Hamm-Young Co., 34 Haw. 288; Pulitzer v. Livingston, 89 Me. 359, 36 A. 635; City Bank Farmers Trust Company v. Cannon, 291 N.Y. 125, 51 N.E.2d 674, 157 A.L.R. 1424; Equitable Trust Co. v. Pratt, 117 Misc. 708, 193 N.Y.S. 152, affirmed on opinion below 206 App. Div. 689, 199 N.Y.S. 921; Gray, Rule Against Perpetuities, (4th Ed.) 510, par. 524; 45 Harv. L. Rev. 896; 51 Harv. L. Rev. 638; 86 Univ. of Pa. L. Rev. 221; Restatement of Property, §373, comments (c), (d), and Ryan v. Ward, 192 Md. 342, 64 A.2d 258, 7 A.L.R.2d 1078.

While none of these authorities is binding upon this court, the conclusion reached by them is in accord with the aim of and reason for the rule against perpetuities, which is to prevent the tying up of property for an unreasonable length of time and to prohibit unreasonable restraint upon the alienation of property. So long as the settlor of an inter vivos trust has the absolute right to revoke or terminate the trust for his own exclusive personal benefit, there is no tying up of property and no restraint upon the alienability of the property in the trust fund, and thus no reason to include this time during which the trust is so destructible in determining whether a limitation is violative of the rule against perpetuities. Restatement, Property, sec. 373 states:

> The period of time during which an interest is destructible, pursuant to the uncontrolled volition, and for the exclusive personal benefit of the person having such a power of destruction is not included in determining whether the limitation is invalid under the rule against perpetuities.

We conclude that this rule is a sound one, which does no violence to the rule against perpetuities, but is in complete accord with its aim and purpose.

Does the postponement principle extend to cases other than revocable trusts? Case authority on this question is sparse, if not nonexistent, but the commentators believe that it does. See Simes & Smith on Future Interests §1252. The Restatement of Property §373 also declares the principle to be broader: For purposes of the Rule Against Perpetuities, the creation of an interest is postponed so long as the interest "is destructible, pursuant to the uncontrolled volition, and for the exclusive personal benefit, of the person having such a power of destruction."

Under this statement of the principle, the power need not be a power to revoke and it need not be held by the settlor or transferor. An *unqualified* and *currently exercisable* power held by *any* person *acting alone* to become the beneficial owner of the questioned interest is sufficient. Accord Restatement 2d of Property §1.2; UPC §2-902(b) (USRAP §2(b)).

An example of a power that should cause a postponement of the time of creation of the remainder interest under the postponement principle would be a presently exercisable general power of appointment over the remainder interest. Another example would be a power, held by any person who could act alone, to invade the corpus of a trust.

Be sure to notice an important consequence of the idea that a power need not be held by the settlor to postpone the time of creation: It makes postponement available even in cases of testamentary transfers.

Example 17.2: G devised property in trust, directing the trustee to pay the income "to A for life, remainder to such persons as A shall appoint; in default of appointment, the property to remain in trust to pay the income to A's children for the life of the survivor, and upon the death of A's last surviving child, to divide the corpus equally among A's grandchildren." A survived G.

If the perpetuity period commences running on G's death, the remainder interest in favor of A's grandchildren is invalid. But if the Restatement view is followed, thus postponing the running of the period to the expiration (at A's death, assuming that A does not relinquish the power before death) of A's presently exercisable general power, the interest is valid. The substance of this transaction is the equivalent of G's having devised the property to A in fee simple absolute and of A's having in turn devised the property at his death in accordance with G's gift in default clause. The Restatement view ought therefore to be followed. Note, however, that if G had conferred on A a *nongeneral* power or a general *testamentary* power, the perpetuity period clearly would commence running on G's death, causing the grandchildren's interest to be invalid. For more discussion of powers of appointment, see Part H below.

Problem

In Year One, G created an irrevocable inter vivos trust, funding it with $20,000 cash. In Year Five, when the value of the trust corpus had risen to $30,000, G added $10,000 cash to the trust. G died in Year Ten. G's will poured the residue of his estate into the trust. G's residuary estate consisted of Blackacre (worth $20,000) and securities (worth $80,000). At G's death (but before the pour-over), the value of the trust corpus had risen to $50,000. When are the interests in trust "created" for the purpose of determining whether or not they are valid under the Rule Against Perpetuities? Cf. UPC §2-902(c) (USRAP §2(c)).

———

The Rule of Convenience. As noted, in determining whether a contingent property interest is valid or invalid, the facts existing at the creation of the interest are to be taken into account. This refers not only to the facts as such, but also to the rules of law or construction that those facts trigger. A rule of construction that figures prominently in many perpetuity cases is the rule of convenience (discussed earlier, in Chapter 16).

Problems

Determine the validity of the property interests in the following cases:

1. G devised property in trust, directing the trustee to pay the net income therefrom "to A for life, then to A's children for the life of the survivor, and upon

the death of A's last surviving child, to pay the corpus of the trust to A's grandchildren." A predeceased G. G was survived by A's two children, C1 and C2.

2. G devised real property "to such of A's children as live to age 25." At G's death, A (who was then alive) had three living children, all of whom were under 25.

3. In Problem 2, suppose that A's eldest child had reached 25 by the time of G's death.

4. G devised real property "to A for life, then to such of A's children as live to age 25." A survived G. By the time of G's death, A's eldest child had reached 25.

4. Constructional Preference for Validity

Gray stated that a will or deed is to be construed without regard to the Rule Against Perpetuities, and then the Rule is to be "remorselessly" applied to the provisions so construed. Gray on Perpetuities §629. Some cases have adopted this view. See, for example, Colorado Nat'l Bank v. McCabe, 353 P.2d 385 (Colo. 1960); Continental Illinois Nat'l Bank & Trust Co. v. Llewellyn, 214 N.E.2d 471 (Ill. App. Ct. 1966).

Most courts, we believe, would now be inclined to adopt the position of the Restatement of Property §375, which is that when an instrument is ambiguous—that is, when it is fairly susceptible to two or more constructions, one of which produces a Rule violation and the other of which does not—the construction that does not produce a Rule violation should be adopted. Cases supporting this view include First Nat'l Bank of Atlanta v. Jenkins, 345 S.E.2d 829 (Ga. 1986); Southern Bank & Trust Co. v. Brown, 246 S.E.2d 598 (S.C. 1978); Davis v. Rossi, 34 S.W.2d 8 (Mo. 1930).

Does Rust v. Rust, which follows, also represent an application of the constructional preference for validity?

Rust v. Rust
211 S.W.2d 262 (Tex. Civ. App.), aff'd, 214 S.W.2d 462 (Tex. 1948)

McCLENDON, C.J. Suit to construe the will of John Y. Rust, Jr. The controlling question is whether the provisions of the will disposing of the residuary estate violates Art. I, Sec. 26, Texas Constitution, Vernon's Ann.St., condemning perpetuities. The trial court upheld all provisions of the will, rendered judgment accordingly, and defendant Mrs. Margene Welch Rust, surviving wife of testator, has appealed in her individual capacity, and as guardian of the estate of Margene A. Rust (a minor), the only child of herself and testator.

The pertinent portions of the will (after a $1,000 legacy to Mrs. Rust) read:

Four. All the remainder of my property of every kind and character, real, personal, mixed or choses in action of which I may die seized or possessed and wheresoever situated, I will, give, devise and bequeath in trust to my executors and trustees hereinafter named and to the survivor thereof and the substitute trustee hereinafter named to hold, manage, use and control for the use and benefit of my daughter, Margene A. Rust.

The property here left for the use and benefit of my daughter, Margene, shall be held in trust by my trustees, the survivor thereof and the substitute trustee until the 17th day of October, 1967, upon which date the trust shall terminate and the property here left in trust shall vest in fee simple in my daughter, Margene A. Rust, free of any restrictions whatsoever.

If my daughter, Margene A. Rust, dies before October 17, 1967, the date upon which the trust herein created terminates, and leaves surviving her issue of her body, then such issue of her body shall become the beneficiary or beneficiaries of this trust and upon the date of its termination the fee simple title to all the property here left in trust shall vest share and share alike in such issue of her body then surviving.

If my daughter, Margene A. Rust, dies before October 17, 1967, the date upon which the trust herein created terminates and does not leave surviving her any issue of her body, then upon her death, all of the property here left in trust shall pass in fee simple share and share alike unto my then living brothers and sister with the child or children of any brother or sister who then may be deceased, taking the share of the parent per stirpes....

Testator's two brothers George Foster and Armistead Dudley Rust were named independent executors without bond. They, and the survivor of them, were also named as trustees; a bank in San Angelo was named substitute trustee....

John Y. Rust, Jr., died May 6, 1942. His will was probated May 26, 1942, and his executors promptly qualified and took charge of his estate. His only heirs at law were his surviving wife and daughter. His father, John Y. Rust, Sr., was living. His mother, Agnes B. Rust, died in 1941. The only other children of his father and mother were the two brothers and a sister, Sarah Agnes Rust Gordon. George Foster Rust was married to Minnie Rust. They had no children. Armistead Dudley Rust was married to Sarah J. Rust. They had one child, Nancy Rust, a minor. Mrs. Gordon's husband was Charles R. Gordon. Their only child was a daughter, Jean, married to Charles R. Rainey. Her only child was a three-month old son.

Testator's estate consisted principally of a ¼ undivided interest in ranch lands—20,394.9 acres in Kimble County, known as Bear Creek Ranch, and 20,895.1 acres in Tom Green County, known as Campbell Ranch. His interest therein was appraised at $116,284.44. The rest of his estate was personalty, appraised at $10,533.05. His total indebtedness was listed at $81,547.75, $73,520.75 of which was in a note to his father for advances to cover excessive living expenses, secured by trust deed upon his interest in the two ranch properties. Net value of his estate was appraised at $45,289.94. The other 3/4 interest in these ranches was owned by his brothers and sister. We give these details regarding his family and estate for whatever light they may shed upon a proper interpretation of the will.

The executors have paid Mrs. Rust's legacy; have renewed the trust deed (now held by a bank); and together with the other joint owners have executed two oil and gas leases upon the ranch properties.

The suit was brought by the two brothers, as executors and trustees, as well as individually, joined in by all the other contingent beneficiaries under the will and the owner of the mineral leases, against Margene W. Rust, individually and as guardian of Margene A. Rust, and against the latter individually. In view of a possible conflict of interest between Margene W. Rust and her ward, the court appointed a guardian ad litem for the latter, who sought to uphold the will, and appears here as an appellee in support of the judgment....

Since, on May 6, 1942 (the date of testator's death) it was within the range of possibilities that Margene A. Rust (born October 17, 1932) might die before October 17, 1946, (21 years prior to the termination of the trust period) and leave a surviving child, the controlling issue is whether, on the one hand, her interest in the property constituted a vested (base) fee subject to defeasance in case of her death prior to October 17, 1967, or, on the other hand, no title would vest in her unless and until she was living on that date. Stated differently, the issue is whether (a) her living until October 17, 1946, constitutes a condition precedent to the vesting of any title in her (appellants' contention), or (b) her death prior to that date constitutes a condition subsequent divesting the title vested in her as of the date of her father's death....

It is, of course, essential to immediate vesting (possession or enjoyment being postponed) that the person to take be presently in existence and of certain identity. See 2 A.L.I. Rest. Property, §157, com. q. And it is also well established that the fact that the legal title is vested in trustees, with full discretion as to the application of the income or corpus to the uses of the beneficiary during the trust period, does not militate against the immediate vesting of the beneficial (equitable) title in the beneficiary....

Furthermore, if the beneficial title vested in Margene A. Rust, "it is immaterial that full possession and enjoyment of the property is postponed beyond the period of a life or lives in being and 21 years thereafter with the ordinary period of gestation added." Anderson v. Menefee [Tex. Civ. App., 174 S.W. 907]....

Applying these rules to the bequest to Margene A. Rust, clearly and without substantial doubt, we think, the fee title to the residuary estate vested in her immediately upon the death of her father, defeasible upon the condition subsequent of her death prior to October 17, 1967, and subject to the trust provisions.

The first paragraph of clause Four, standing alone, would vest a fee simple absolute title in her, subject to the trust, since in so many words it unconditionally vests the legal title in the trustees for her "use and benefit." The second paragraph puts a time limit for the duration of the trust, upon expiration of which her title is to be "free of any restrictions whatsoever." The language, "the trust shall terminate and the property... shall vest in fee simple in" her, "free of any restrictions whatsoever," is not reasonably susceptible of the construction that her title had not theretofore vested but was to vest initially as of that date. The words, "free of any restrictions whatsoever," can have no other meaning than that her title should thenceforth be free of the restrictions imposed by the trust, otherwise they would be pure surplusage. The vesting at that time was to be free of these restrictions. Even without this last clause, the language employed is that usually found in instruments creating remainders universally held to be vested, and not contingent. A devise by A to B for life with remainder at his death to C creates a vested remainder in C upon the death of A, subject to B's life estate. The use of "at his death" or words of similar import denote the time when the right of possession and enjoyment of the estate begins, and not the time when the estate in remainder vests.

The third and fourth paragraphs are clearly conditional clauses of defeasance, and as such conditions subsequent. The remaining paragraphs merely detail the powers and duties of the trustees. We find nothing in the language of the will, "read as an entirety and in the light of the circumstances of its formulation," which would call for a construction other than that the contingency of the daughter's dying before October 17, 1967, constituted a condition subsequent divesting her title, and that her living until then was not a condition precedent to its vesting....

The fourth clause vests the fee simple title in the named contingent remaindermen immediately upon the death of the daughter prior to October 17, 1967, without bodily issue. Under no possible contingency could this paragraph create a perpetuity.

The third is the only paragraph which presents any constructional doubt. A doubt which we resolve in favor of a vested remainder upon the death of the daughter prior to October 17, 1967, leaving bodily issue, for reasons we now discuss.

The general plan of the testator seems clear. His primary solicitude was for his daughter, his only child. His principal estate was in extensive ranch property, held in undivided interests, and heavily incumbered. To preserve the estate to his daughter would necessitate wise business management over an extended period of years. He fixed this period as terminating on the daughter's 35th birthday. For obvious reasons he intrusted this management to his two brothers, who owned ⅔ of the remaining interest in the property. The only limitations imposed upon the daughter's otherwise complete fee simple title to the property were (1) the trust provisions which merely postponed her possession and untrammeled enjoyment of the property, and (2) defeasance of her title upon the contingency of her death during the trust period.

His secondary solicitude, should this contingency eventuate, was for his daughter's "bodily heirs", if any, giving them the identical status with reference to the property as that of his daughter. He substitutes them as beneficiaries of the trust and vests complete title at the end of the trust period. The same considerations favoring immediate vesting in the bodily issue and continuing the trust exist in this contingency as originally as to the daughter's title. The considerations as to the trust provisions would not apply in the contingency of the daughter's death without bodily issue.

The only doubt cast upon this immediate vesting is the use of the word "then" before the last word "surviving." In addition to the presumption of early vesting of title, and the general scheme of the testator, there are other considerations which favor construing "then" as referring to the death of the daughter and not the termination of the trust. "Issue of her body," we think, were clearly used in the sense of "children." This appears from use of the words, "share and share alike." As said by the great Oran M. Roberts, in the leading case of Hancock v. Butler, 21 Tex. 804:

> It is presumed it would be difficult to find one case where a man had expressly given his property, to all his descendants, to take per capita—children, grandchildren, great-grandchildren, etc. The general sense of American mind, as exhibited in deeds, wills, and in statutes of descent and distribution, is that it is proper to give property to children, grandchildren, etc., they taking per stirpes.

The possibility of the daughter having any grandchild, the child of a deceased child, prior to 1967, was exceedingly remote.

Another applicable presumption is that against intestacy. "A construction which would render the decedent intestate as to any part of his estate is not favored." 44 Tex. Jur., p. 707, §148. In case of the death of the daughter before October 17, 1967, leaving a surviving child or children, all of whom including any descendants should die prior to that date, there would be no one to take under the will, if the title had not previously vested in the daughter's "bodily heirs." The only other limitation over (par. 4) was contingent exclusively upon the daughter's dying before October 17, 1967, without leaving any "issue of her body."

Additionally, it is well settled that: "...the rule against perpetuities is a rule of property and not one of construction; and where the instrument is capable of two constructions, "one of which would give effect to the whole... and the other result in defeating (it)..., in whole or in part, preference will be accorded to the construction which will uphold" it. 41 Am.Jur., p. 58, §12....

If, however, we be mistaken in this construction, and the limitation over to the bodily heirs of the daughter is void as creating a perpetuity, the other provisions of the will would not thereby be affected. In that case the title of the daughter would be defeasible only in case of her death before October 17, 1967, without leaving any heir of her body. A.L.I. Rest. Property, §229, com. e. Under this construction the surviving bodily heirs of the daughter would take the same title from her by inheritance that they would under the will, construed as valid, subject only to the contingency that the daughter should make no different disposition by will, or otherwise part with her title....

The trial court's judgment is affirmed.

5. Consequences of Invalidity

When an interest is invalid because it violates the common-law Rule Against Perpetuities, the invalid interest is stricken from the disposition. Unless the doctrine of infectious invalidity applies, see below, the other interests created by the disposition (assuming that none of them violates the Rule) take effect as if the invalid interest had never been created.

Example 17.3: G devised real property "to A for life, then to A's children for the life of the survivor, and upon the death of A's last surviving child, to A's grandchildren." G devised her residuary estate to her husband, H.

Due to the invalidity of the remainder to A's grandchildren, the disposition reads as if *that* remainder interest had never been created: "to A for life, then to A's children for the life of the survivor." Since G's devise did not validly dispose of all interests in the parcel of real property, the undisposed-of interest passes under G's residuary clause to H. This testamentary transfer of the remainder interest to H is deemed to have occurred at G's death. Thus when A's last surviving child dies, the property goes to H (or H's successor in interest).

Note that if G's original devise had been in her residuary clause, the undisposed-of interest would have been intestate property and would have passed at G's death to her heirs at law.

Example 17.4: G devised real property "to A for life, then for life to such of A's children as reach 25, then to B."

The remainder for life to A's children is invalid. The effect of striking it is not to create a gap that must be filled by the residuary clause. Rather it is to accelerate B's remainder: The devise now reads "to A for life, then to B."

In preparation for reading the *Brown* decision, below, consider again the *Grant* and *Boland* cases in Chapter 15.

Brown v. Independent Baptist Church
91 N.E.2d 922 (Mass. 1950)

QUA, C.J. The object of this suit in equity, originally brought in this court, is to determine the ownership of a parcel of land in Woburn and the persons entitled to share in the proceeds of its sale by a receiver.

Sarah Converse died seised of the land on July 19, 1849, leaving a will in which she specifically devised it

> to the Independent Baptist Church of Woburn, to be holden and enjoyed by them so long as they shall maintain and promulgate their present religious belief and faith and shall continue a Church; and if the said Church shall be dissolved, or if its religious sentiments shall be changed or abandoned, then my will is that this real estate shall go to my legatees hereinafter named, to be divided in equal portions between them. And my will further is, that if my beloved husband, Jesse Converse, shall survive me, that then this devise to the aforesaid Independent Church of Woburn, shall not take effect till from and after his

decease; and that so long as he shall live he may enjoy and use the said real estate, and take the rents and profits thereof to his own use.

Then followed ten money legacies in varying amounts to different named persons, after which there was a residuary clause in these words,

The rest and residue of my estate I give and bequeath to my legatees above named, saving and except therefrom the Independent Baptist Church; this devise to take effect from and after the decease of my husband; I do hereby direct and will that he shall have the use and this rest and residue during his life.

The husband of the testatrix died in 1864. The church named by the testatrix ceased to "continue a church" on October 19, 1939.

The parties apparently are in agreement, and the single justice ruled, that the estate of the church in the land was a determinable fee. We concur. The estate was a fee, since it might last forever, but it was not an absolute fee, since it might (and did) "automatically expire upon the occurrence of a stated event." Restatement: Property, §44. It is also conceded, and was ruled, that the specific executory devise over to the persons "hereinafter named" as legatees was void for remoteness. The reason is... that the determinable fee might not come to an end until long after any life or lives in being and twenty-one years, and in theory at least might never come to an end, and for an indefinite period no clear title to the entire estate could be given.

Since the limitation over failed, it next becomes our duty to consider what became of the possibility of reverter which under our decisions remained after the failure of the limitation. First Universalist Society of North Adams v. Boland, 155 Mass. 171, 175, 29 N.E. 524, 15 L.R.A. 231 [in Chapter 15]; Restatement: Property, §228, illustration 2, and Appendix to Volume II, at pages 35-36, including note 2. A possibility of reverter seems, by the better authority, to be assignable inter vivos (Restatement: Property, §159) and must be at least as readily devisable as the other similar reversionary interest known as a right of entry for condition broken, which is devisable, though not assignable. It follows that the possibility of reverter passed under the residuary clause of the will to the same persons designated in the invalid executory devise. It is of no consequence that the persons designated in the two provisions were the same. The same result must be reached as if they were different.

The single justice ruled that the residuary clause was void for remoteness, apparently for the same reason that rendered the executory devise void. With this we cannot agree, since we consider it settled that the rule against perpetuities does not apply to reversionary interests of this general type, including possibilities of reverter. Proprietors of the Church in Brattle Square v. Grant, 3 Gray, 142, 148, 63 Am. Dec. 725 [in Chapter 15]; First Universalist Society of North Adams v. Boland, 155 Mass. 171, 175-176, 29 N.E. 524, 15 L.R.A. 231 [in Chapter 15]; Restatement: Property, §372. See Gray, Rule Against Perpetuities, 4th Ed., §§41, 312, 313. For a full understanding of the situation here presented it is necessary to keep in mind the fundamental difference in character between the attempted executory devise to the legatees later named in the will and the residuary gift to the same persons. The executory devise was in form and substance an attempt to limit or create a new future interest which might not arise or vest in anyone until long after the permissible period. It was obviously not intended to pass such a residuum of the testatrix's existing estate as a possibility of reverter, and indeed if the executory devise had been valid according to its terms the whole estate would have passed from the testatrix and no possibility of reverter could have been left to her or her devisees. The residuary devise, on the other hand, was in terms and purpose exactly adapted to carry any interest which might otherwise remain in the testatrix, whether or not she had it in mind or knew it would exist.

We cannot accept the contention made in behalf of Mrs. Converse's heirs that the words of the residuary clause "saving and except therefrom the Independent Baptist Church" were meant to exclude from the operation of that clause any possible rights in the land previously given to the church. We construe these words as intended merely to render the will consistent by excluding the church which also had been "above named" from the list of "legatees" who were to take the residue.

The interlocutory decree entered December 16, 1947, is reversed, and a new decree is to be entered providing that the land in question or the proceeds of any sale thereof by the receiver shall go to the persons named as legatees in the will, other than the Independent Baptist Church of Woburn, or their successors in interest. Further proceedings are to be in accord with the new decree. Costs and expenses are to be at the discretion of the single justice.

So ordered.

Question and Problem

1. *Criticism of Brown.* The *Brown* decision has been criticized on the ground that the testator "did not die twice." Lewis M. Simes, Is the Rule Against Perpetuities Doomed?, 52 Mich. L. Rev. 179 n.4 (1953). What is Simes's point?

2. *Problem.* G devised real property "to A for life, remainder to A's children, but if none of A's children reaches 25, to B." G was survived by A, who had two children, X and Y, neither of whom had reached 25 at G's death. What is the consequence of the invalidity of B's executory interest?

———

Infectious Invalidity. Under the *doctrine of infectious invalidity*, a court has the discretionary authority to invalidate one or more otherwise valid interests created by the disposition, or even invalidate the entire will. The question turns on whether the general dispositive scheme of the transferor would be better carried out by eliminating only the invalid interest or by eliminating other interests as well.

This is a question that must be answered on a case by case basis. Several items are relevant to the question, including who takes the stricken interests in place of those designated to take by the transferor. Some jurisdictions have become noted for a greater willingness to apply infectious invalidity than others. See Simes & Smith on Future Interests §1262; Am. L. Prop. §24.48 et seq.; Restatement of Property §402.

Problem

G was survived by two children, A and B, and by B's child, X, who was then five years old. G's will divided his property in half, devising one half to A outright and the other half in trust "to B for life, then remainder in corpus to such of B's children who reach the age of 30." What result under the Rule Against Perpetuities?

6. Separability

When an interest is expressly subject to alternative contingencies, the courts treat the situation as if two interests were created in the same person or class, so that the invalidity of one of the interests does not invalidate the other. This principle was established in Longhead v. Phelps, 2 Wm. Bl. 704, 96 Eng. Rep. 414 (K.B. 1770), and has been followed in this country. See Simes & Smith on Future Interests §1257; Am. L. Prop. §24.54; Restatement of Property §376.

To illustrate, suppose property is devised "to B if X-event or Y-event happens." B in effect has two interests, one contingent on X-event happening and the other contingent on Y-event happening. If X-event might occur too remotely, the consequence of separating B's interest into two is that only one of them, the one contingent on X-event, is invalid. B still has a valid interest—the one contingent on the occurrence of Y-event. Another way of viewing it is to say that the invalid contingency is stricken or excised. Thus the devise is altered to read "to B if Y-event happens." The following example further illustrates this approach.

Example 17.5: G devised real property "to A for life, then to such of A's children as survive her and reach 25, but if none of A's children survives her or if none of A's children who survives her reaches 25, then to B."

B takes only if none of A's children survives A; his interest that is contingent on that event is valid. If one or more of A's children survives A, B cannot take even if none of them lives to 25. B's interest that is contingent on none of A's surviving children reaching 25 is invalid. The language "or if none of A's children who survive him reaches 25" is in effect stricken from the devise.

The interest of A's children is invalid and replaced by a reversion.

The principle of separability is applicable only when the transferor has *expressly* stated the contingencies in the alternative. Where alternative contingencies are merely implicit, no separation will be recognized. See Proctor v. Bishop of Bath and Wells, 2 H. Bl. 358, 126 Eng. Rep. 594 (C.P. 1794).

Example 17.6: G devised real property "to A for life, then to such of A's children as survive him and reach 25, but if none of A's children does so, then to B."

B has only one interest, and it is invalid. B cannot take even if none of A's children survives A.

PART B. TECHNICAL VIOLATIONS OF THE COMMON-LAW RULE

Observe that the requirement of initial certainty makes validity dependent on the full array of *possible* post-creation events, not on the events that *actually* happen. In the world of the common-law Rule, every chain of possible post-creation events that can be imagined, no matter how fanciful, is taken seriously—even those that have become impossible by the time of the lawsuit. As stated by Sir Lloyd Kenyon, the Master of the Rolls, in the immensely influential case of Jee v. Audley, 1 Cox 324, 29 Eng. Rep. 1186 (Ch. 1787):

> Another thing pressed upon me, is to decide on the events which have happened; but I cannot do this without overturning very many cases. The single question before me is, not whether the limitation is good in the events which have happened, but whether it was good in its creation; and if it were not, I cannot make it so.

Translation: A *single* chain of imagined events that can postpone vesting (or termination) beyond a life in being plus 21 years spoils the transferor's disposition.

In consequence of the requirement of initial certainty, validity is withheld from interests that are likely to, and in fact would (if given the chance), vest well within the period of a life in being plus 21 years. Reasonable dispositions can be rendered invalid because of exceedingly remote possibilities, such as women who have passed the menopause giving birth to (or adopting) additional children, married individuals in their middle or late years later remarrying persons who were born after the transfers, or the probate of estates taking more than 21 years to complete. Professor Leach called these, respectively, the fertile octogenarian, the unborn widow (we call this case the afterborn spouse), and the administrative contingency. See W. Barton Leach, Perpetuities in a Nutshell, 51 Harv. L. Rev. 638, 643-44 (1938).[7] On its face, each disposition seems quite reasonable, violating the common-law Rule on technical grounds only.

---

7. See also W. Barton Leach, Perpetuities in Perspective: Ending the Rule's Reign of Terror, 65 Harv. L. Rev. 721 (1952); W. Barton Leach, Perpetuities: Staying the Slaughter of the Innocents, 68 L.Q. Rev. 35 (1952).

1. The Case of the Fertile "Octogenarian"[8]

Fertile-Octogenarian Example. G died at age 75, survived by his 55-year-old daughter A, who had passed the menopause, and by A's adult children, C1 (age 35) and C2 (age 30). G's will devised property in trust, income "to A for life, then to A's children for the life of the survivor, and upon the death of A's last surviving child, corpus to A's grandchildren."

In thinking about the full array of possible post-creation events, consider the one that seems most likely: A has no more children, and the remainder in the corpus of the trust vests on the death of either C1 or C2, who were "in being" at the creation of the trust.

Among the array of "possible" post-creation events exists one that is extremely unlikely: A could become pregnant and have a third child[9]—or A could adopt a third child—and that third child could outlive by more than 21 years A, C1, C2, and anybody else one can think of who is in being and has any connection to this transaction. Under this chain of events, the interest in the corpus in favor of A's grandchildren vests beyond a life in being plus 21 years.

Jee v. Audley. Jee v. Audley, the early and famous English decision quoted earlier, laid down for perpetuity law the conclusive presumption of lifetime fertility. Again, we quote the words of the judge in that case, Sir Lloyd Kenyon, the Master of the Rolls:

> I am desired to do in this case something which I do not feel myself at liberty to do, namely to suppose it impossible for persons in so advanced an age as John and Elizabeth Jee [both age 70] to have children; but if this can be done in one case it may in another, and it is a very dangerous experiment, and introductive of the greatest inconvenience to give a latitude to such sort of conjecture.

The conclusive presumption of Jee v. Audley has stuck and, due to reported advances in reproductive technology, is perhaps justified: A is conclusively presumed capable of bearing children until she dies. Consequently, the grandchildren's remainder interest in the corpus of G's trust is invalid.

For a real example, see Associated Press, India: Mother Claims to Be Oldest, N.Y. Times, Dec. 10, 2008, at A12 (reporting the birth of a child to a woman reputed to be 70 years old).

Two American common-law decisions, Will of Lattouf, 208 A.2d 411 (N.J. Super. Ct. App. Div. 1965), and Bassett's Estate, 190 A.2d 415 (N.H. 1963), have squarely rejected Jee v. Audley and held in a perpetuity case that the presumption is

---

8. The term "octogenarian" is not to be taken literally; it refers to persons who are infertile, young or old, male or female.

9. Advances in reproductive technology have made this possible.

rebuttable (in *Lattouf*, due to a hysterectomy, and in *Bassett's Estate*, on the basis of undisputed medical testimony), not conclusive. The Restatement of Property §377 squarely supports the conclusive presumption, and there are many perpetuity cases, recent as well as not so recent, that have adhered to it. See, e.g., Abram v. Wilson, 220 N.E.2d 739, 742 (Ohio P. Ct. 1966) ("Obviously ... it is clearly possible for the testator's 75-year-old brother to have children...."); Turner v. Turner, 196 S.E.2d 498, 501 (S.C. 1973) ("The possibility of childbirth is never extinct."[10])

The *Lattouf* case is discussed in Lawrence W. Waggoner, *In re Lattouf's Will* and the Presumption of Lifetime Fertility in Perpetuity Law, 20 San Diego L. Rev. 763 (1983).

Possibility of Adoption. Professor Leach was an outspoken critic of the conclusive presumption of lifetime fertility, and wrote extensively in favor of making it rebuttable, as the *Lattouf* court did. See, e.g., W. Barton Leach, Perpetuities: New Hampshire Defertilizes the Octogenarians, 77 Harv. L. Rev. 279 (1963); W. Barton Leach & Owen Davies Tudor, The Common Law Rule Against Perpetuities, in Am. L. Prop. §24.22. Professor Leach argued that perpetuity law should get into step with two other areas of the law in which the presumption was rebuttable—trust termination cases[11] and charitable deduction cases under the federal tax laws.[12] What has happened, however, is that the law in these two areas has more recently moved in the direction of perpetuity law, rather than the other way around. The reason is the same for all three areas: Although it might be possible in a particular case, such as *Lattouf*, to establish that the birth of biological children is impossible,[13] it can almost never be established that it is impossible for a woman or man to have additional children by adoption. See Clark v. Citizens & S. Nat'l Bank, 257 S.E.2d 244 (Ga. 1979) (possibility of adoption would not allow the presumption to be rebutted even it were rebuttable in trust termination cases); Rev. Rul. 74-410, 1974-2 C.B. 187 (possibility of a 60-year-old woman adopting one or more children is not so remote as to be negligible; charitable deduction denied); Rev. Rul. 71-442, 1971-2 C.B. 336 (possibility of a 56-year-old man adopting a child is not so remote as to be negligible; charitable deduction denied); Tech. Adv. Mem. 8010011 (Nov. 30, 1979) (possibility of 60-year-old man adopting a child is not so remote as to be negligible; charitable deduction denied despite medical evidence that man's age and physical condition were such that his ability to father a child was "near zero").

---

10. In 1987, South Carolina became the first state to enact the USRAP, under which a disposition such as the one in *Turner* would most likely not be invalid.

11. See Scott on Trusts §340.1.

12. See Lawrence W. Waggoner, Perpetuity Reform, 81 Mich. L. Rev. 1718, 1730 n.28 (1983).

13. Advances in reproductive technology cast doubt even on this proposition.

Constructional Preference for Validity. If shifting the presumption of lifetime fertility to a rebuttable presumption holds out little hope for overcoming invalidity in cases in which future children are extremely unlikely (though not strictly impossible), another approach seems more promising. This approach is to apply the constructional preference for validity and hold that the possibility of future children was so remote that the transferor never contemplated it and so did not intend to include such children in the class gift even if—against the odds—one or more ultimately materializes. So construed, the requirement of initial certainty is met, and the interest is valid.[14] See, e.g., Bankers Trust Co. v. Pearson, 99 A.2d 224 (Conn. 1953) (testator was held to have meant children in being when he spoke of the children of his brother, age 55, and sisters, ages 52 and 57); Joyner v. Duncan, 264 S.E.2d 76 (N.C. 1980) (testator was held to have meant children in being when he spoke of the children of his 47-year-old son). Since the relevant time for determining the intent of a testator is the time of execution of the will—not the time of death—this construction ordinarily is available to a court only if at the time the testator executed the will there was reason to expect that the person in question would not have additional children.

Surprisingly, the Supreme Judicial Court of Massachusetts has seemed unwilling to adopt such a construction even in apparently appropriate cases. See Second Bank-State St. Trust Co. v. Second Bank-State St. Trust Co., 140 N.E.2d 201 (Mass. 1957); Sears v. Coolidge, 108 N.E.2d 563 (Mass. 1952). In neither case did the court articulate reasons for denying the construction. It may be significant that other ways of upholding the gifts were found,[15] which allows us to speculate that the construction might have been adopted had another validating method not been available. Is there a different explanation? Although facts known to the testators suggested that they never contemplated the possibility of the birth or adoption of additional children, the court might have sensed that these facts, by themselves, do not show that the testators arrived at a specific intent to exclude such children in the unlikely event of their birth or adoption. If this is the explanation for the refusal to apply the construction in the *Second Bank-State St. Trust Co.* or *Sears* cases, it is not entirely persuasive, however: If the testators had been apprised of the fact that the children's inclusion would cause an invalidity, it is all but certain that they *would* have arrived at a specific intent to exclude them. The application of the

---

14. This procedure has been rejected outright in England on the ground that class gifts are unambiguous and therefore extrinsic evidence is inadmissible for the purpose sought. See Ward v. Van der Loeff, [1924] App. Cas. 653 (Visc. Cave); cf. Estate of Kalouse, 282 N.W.2d 98 (Iowa 1979). The Restatement of Property §377 comment c, which supports the procedure, answers this point by asserting that it is proper in this situation to utilize the Rule itself as a basis for finding an ambiguity. Cf. Simes & Smith on Future Interests §1289.

15. In the *Second Bank-State St. Trust Co.* case, the court saved the gift under the subclass doctrine; in the *Sears* case, the court saved the gift under the second-look doctrine. On these doctrines, see Part H below.

constructional preference for validity therefore seems justified in those two cases and cases like them.

The Case of the "Precocious Toddler"*[16]—*Young Children and the Presumption of Fertility. If an elderly person or a person whose physical condition prevents the birth of children is conclusively presumed to be able to have children, are children who have not yet reached puberty subject to the same conclusive presumption? Cases raising this problem are rare. The best known is Re Gaite's Will Trusts, [1949] 1 All Eng. Rep. 459 (Ch.), the facts of which form the basis of Example 17.7, below.

Example 17.7: G devised property in trust, directing the trustee to pay the net income "to A for life, corpus to such of A's grandchildren living at my death or born within five years thereafter who shall attain the age of 21 years." G was survived by A (a 65-year-old widow) and by A's two children and one grandchild.

If a child under the age of 5 is conclusively presumed to be capable of having a child, the remainder in favor of A's grandchildren who reach 21 is invalid. Although any grandchild of A's born to A's two children who were living at G's death will either reach 21 or die before reaching that age no later than 21 years after the death of the survivor of these two children (who were "in being" at G's death), the conclusive presumption if applicable would say that it is possible that A will conceive and bear a child who will in turn conceive a child, all within five years of G's death. Such grandchild therefore might reach 21 more than 21 years after the death of the survivor of A and A's two children and one grandchild who were living when G died.

There have been American cases in which a child shortly after (probable) puberty was conclusively presumed capable of having children. An example is Rust v. Rust, above. This presumption may, of course, be justified. See Hilda L. Keane, A Case of Maternity at Seven Years of Age, Brit. Med. J., Sept. 23, 1933, at 567.

———

Age Contingencies Exceeding 21. G's will devised $100,000 in trust, "income to my son B for life, remainder to such of B's children as reach 30; if none reaches 30, to B's descendants who survive B, by representation; if none, to X Charity." Appropriate provisions for the distribution of the income are made if one or more of B's children is still under 30 when B dies. If G died at age 75, and if B was age 50 when G died, how likely is it that one or more of B's children will not reach 30 within 21 years after B's death?

In the world of the common-law Rule, G's disposition flunks the requirement of initial certainty. At common law, it is assumed that B can have another child after G's death and that this afterborn child can outlive B and any of B's children who

---

16. Professor Leach's term, again: He cornered the market!

were living when G died. There is no validating life—no one beyond 21 years of whose death the afterborn grandchild's interest *cannot* remain contingent. Under the all-or-nothing rule for class gifts, that possibility makes the interest of *all* the class members invalid—including the interest of B's children who were "in being" at G's death. In addition, the alternative remainders in favor of B's descendants and in favor of X Charity are invalid because there is no validating life for either of them.

Age Contingencies Not Exceeding 21—The Fertile Decedent and the Child En Ventre Sa Frigidaire![17] G devised $100,000 in trust, "income to my son B for life, remainder to such of B's children as reach 21; if none reaches 21, to B's descendants who survive B, by representation; if none, to X Charity." Appropriate provisions for the distribution of the income are made if one or more of B's children is still under the age of 21 when B dies.

G's residuary devisees challenge the validity of G's disposition. They argue that the requirement of initial certainty is not met because it is possible that when B dies he will leave sperm on deposit in a sperm bank, and that after B's death B's widow—who could be someone not "in being" at G's death—will become pregnant with that sperm and give birth to a child of B's; B's postdeath child cannot reach 21 within 21 years after B's death and will not *necessarily* reach 21 within 21 years after the death of anyone else you might put forward. G's residuary devisees argue that there is no validating life and the remainder interests after B's life estate are invalid.

Do the remainder interests flunk the requirement of initial certainty? How would you answer the argument advanced by G's residuary devisees? For a legislative solution to this problem, see the Uniform Statutory Rule Against Perpetuities (USRAP) §1(d) and its UPC counterpart, UPC §2-901(d).

2. The Case of the Afterborn Spouse

Pound v. Shorter
377 S.E.2d 854 (Ga. 1989)

WELTNER, J. When Elizabeth Shorter died in 1929, her will created a trust that provided for her one unmarried son as follows:

> In trust further, should my son die, either before or after my death, leaving neither child, nor children of a deceased wife surviving him, but leaving a wife surviving him, to pay over the annual net income arising each year from said trust property, in quarterly installments each year, to the wife of my said son, during her life, and upon the death of the wife of my said son, to thereupon pay over, deliver and convey, in fee simple, the corpus

---

17. Professor Leach's term: See W. Barton Leach, Perpetuities in the Atomic Age: The Sperm Bank and the Fertile Decedent, 48 A.B.A.J. 942 (1962).

of said trust property to the children and descendants of children of my brother... and sister....

The son married in 1953 and died in 1987, survived by his widow. He left no descendants. After his death, the trustee bank filed a petition to determine the validity of the trust item. The trial court found that the item created a perpetuity and decreed that the trust be terminated and that the son's widow have fee ownership. Fifty-two lineal descendants of Elizabeth Shorter appeal.

1. The Rule against Perpetuities, adopted first by the legislature in 1863, provides:

> Limitations of estates may extend through any number of lives in being at the time when the limitations commence, and 21 years, and the usual period of gestation added thereafter. The law terms a limitation beyond that period a perpetuity and forbids its creation. When an attempt is made to create a perpetuity, the law will give effect to the limitations which are not too remote and will declare the other limitations void, thereby vesting the fee in the last taker under the legal limitations. OCGA §44-6-1.

2. We have undertaken a study of both the rule against perpetuities and an alternative approach, commonly called "wait and see." Fifteen states have adopted some form of the "wait-and-see" approach and all have done so through legislation. We conclude:

(1) that the traditional rule against perpetuities has been effective so far in Georgia, judging by the few cases brought to invalidate grants, and the even fewer invalidations; and

(2) that the alternative "wait-and-see" approach has many problems, including initial uncertainty (which is avoided by the traditional rule) and the necessity for selecting a method by which to determine the length of the waiting period.[18]

3. We are not convinced that the goals of certainty and early vesting will be served by adopting the alternative, and accordingly decline to do so.

4. As the will encompasses the possibilities that the son might marry a woman who was unborn in 1929 (a life *not* "in being") and then predecease her, it violated the rule against perpetuities.

Judgment affirmed.

All the Justices concur.

---

18. The problems may be summarized as follows: (1) there is actually no severe problem of grants being invalidated due to a violation of the rule against perpetuities; (2) technical violations of the rule can be avoided by competent drafting, so only unwary counsel is trapped by the rule; (3) there is a big problem of expense and inconvenience during the waiting period; (4) there is an increase in litigation due to the alternative doctrine; (5) much of the testator's estate is diverted to lawyers' fees; (6) most alternative statutes provide for cy pres litigation at the end of the waiting period if the interest has neither vested nor failed, and that litigation is difficult and expensive due to the passage of time; and (7) the alternative does not simplify the perpetuities law. Ira Mark Bloom, Perpetuities Refinement: There is an Alternative, 62 Wash. L. Rev. 23 (1987).

Notes

1. *Reality*. Not disclosed but known by the court was the fact that Mildred Shorter, the son's widow, was in being in 1929 when Elizabeth Shorter died.[19] In direct response to the *Pound* decision, the Georgia legislature the following year enacted the USRAP, which adopts the wait-and-see method of perpetuity reform.

2. *State of the Authorities*. In accord with Pound v. Shorter are Easton v. Hall, 154 N.E. 216 (Ill. 1926); Chenoweth v. Bullitt, 6 S.W.2d 1061 (Ky. Ct. App. 1928); Restatement of Property §370 comment k, illus. 3.

3. *No Violation If Devisees Can Be Their Own Validating Lives*. The possibility of an afterborn spouse does not always create a perpetuity violation. In an appropriate case, the devisees of the remainder interest following the spouse's death are their own validating lives. This would be the case if the contingent remainder were in favor of named individuals (Y and Z perhaps) or a class that was closed at G's death (for example, the children of G's predeceased daughter, A).

Furthermore, if the remainder was not contingent on survival, the fact that it was still subject to open at G's death would not invalidate it if the class could not increase beyond lives in being. For example, in the absence of a condition precedent of survival, a remainder in favor of G's grandchildren would be valid in the above example. See Lanier v. Lanier, 126 S.E.2d 776 (Ga. 1962). But one in favor of G's great-grandchildren would be invalid.

4. *Constructional Preference for Validity*. Even when no other validating lives can be located, the principle of construction favoring validity can often be used to avoid the afterborn-spouse problem. When the language of the instrument fairly allows, some courts have construed G's reference to a child's spouse as referring only to the person to whom the child was married when the will was executed or when G died. See Willis v. Hendry, 20 A.2d 375 (Conn. 1941) (G's will referred to "the wife of my said son"); Friend's Will, 28 N.E.2d 377 (N.Y. 1940) (G's will referred to "the widow of my said son Sol"). This procedure, however, is not always available to courts, as the *Pound* case demonstrates.

3. The Case of the Administrative Contingency

This technical violation can occur where a disposition involves the performance by a fiduciary (an executor, a trustee) of some administrative function, the completion of which might, but is extremely unlikely to, take more than 21 years.

---

19. This is not to suggest that there never are "afterborn spouses." Pablo Casals, the famous cellist, was around 80 when he married his 20-year old student Martita. Of the marriage, Casals wrote: "I was aware at the time that some people noted a certain discrepancy in our ages—a bridegroom of course is not usually thirty years older than his father-in-law." Pablo Casals, Joys and Sorrows 277 (1970).

Typical examples are the completion of the probate of a will, the settlement of an estate, the payment of debts or taxes, the sale of estate assets, or the delivery of trust corpus on the termination of a trust.

Administrative Contingency Example. G died at age 75, devising real property "to such of my grandchildren, born before or after my death, as may be living upon final distribution of my estate." G is survived by her children (A and B) and her four grandchildren.

The grandchildren's interest is invalid, by the majority view. Though unlikely, there is a possibility that the final distribution of G's estate will not occur within 21 years after G's death.[20] This possibility eliminates validating the interest on the basis of the 21-year part of the period. In addition, there are no lives in being that can validate it. As always, not only are afterborn grandchildren presumed, but also presumed is the possibility that final distribution of G's estate will occur when such afterborn grandchildren have outlived by more than 21 years the deaths of A, B, and G's four grandchildren who were living at G's death.

As the above example illustrates, the term "administrative contingency" is somewhat misleading. It does not refer to the possibility that the administrative task will never be completed. If it did, all interests that are to take effect in possession upon the completion of an administrative task would be contingent and invalid. But in fact, such gifts are upheld. See cases collected in Am. L. Prop. §24.23 n.2. Rather, it is accepted as certain that the task will be completed, presumably because of the fiduciary's legal obligation to do so;[21] the uncertainty is that the task might not be completed within the perpetuity period. Thus, the administrative contingency problem commonly arises because the interest is contingent on survival of the administrative function. These dispositions have the completely rational objective of preventing the actual distribution of property to the estate of a dead person, thereby avoiding unnecessary expenses of administration and possible double estate taxation.[22]

---

20. There have been rare instances of distribution of an estate being delayed for a very long time. See, e.g., Richards v. Tolbert, 208 S.E.2d 486 (Ga. 1974) (57 years between death and probate of the will); Hostetter v. Estate of Hostetter, 394 N.E.2d 77 (Ill. App. Ct. 1979) (25 years); Haddock v. Boston & Me. R.R., 15 N.E. 495 (Mass. 1888) (63 years); Garrett's Estate, 94 A.2d 357 (1953), cert. denied, 345 U.S. 996 (1953) (22 years).

21. But see Miller v. Weston, 189 P. 610 (Colo. 1920) (en banc), where the court held that a devise to A "on the admission of this will to probate" is contingent on the probate of the will and invalid because probate "may never happen." The court was unwilling to accept probate as a certainty even if "probate is required by law to be made." In effect, the perpetuity requirement of initial certainty did not allow the possibility of the law's being disobeyed to be ignored!

22. Concerns about double estate taxation, under the federal estate tax at least, may be somewhat overdrawn. The reason is that IRC §2013 provides for a credit against the estate tax of a second decedent in the amount of the estate tax imposed on the estate of the prior decedent. If the two decedents die within two years of one another, the amount of the credit is 100 percent of the prior

Survival of a Period That Might Exceed 21 Years. At bottom, the administrative contingency problem is often one of survival of a period of time that might exceed 21 years. Interests that are contingent on survival of a period that might exceed 21 years, however, are not always invalid. They will be valid if the devisees can themselves be the validating lives, which requires that the questioned interest either be in favor of one or more individual takers or a class that is closed at the testator's death.

Example 17.8: G devised real property "to such of my children as may be living upon final distribution of my estate." G is survived by children.

The children's interests are valid. Since no children will be born to G after her death, her children are their own validating lives.

Class Subject to Open for More Than 21 Years. When the interest is in favor of a class that is not closed at the testator's death, the administrative contingency problem can arise even if there is no condition of survival.

Example 17.9: G devised real property "to such of my great-grandchildren, born before or after my death, as may be living upon final distribution of my estate." G is survived by children and grandchildren.

The interest would be invalid even if the phrase "as may be living" were omitted. A great-grandchild could be conceived and born before the completion of the probate of G's estate and more than 21 years after the death of the survivor of G's children and those of G's grandchildren that were living at G's death. Note, however, that the invalidity here is due to the fact that the class of great-grandchildren could not only increase after the testator's death, but also increase after the death of lives in being at his death.

If the class cannot increase after lives in being, the absence of a condition of survival will save a gift in favor of a class even though it is not closed at the testator's death. To illustrate this point, suppose the gift in Example 17.9 were in favor of G's grandchildren. Now suppose that the phrase "as may be living" were omitted. This would make the grandchildren's interest valid because no new members could join the class after the death of the survivor of G's children, all of whom were, of course, "in being" at G's death.

The Fiduciary's Obligation. A minority of courts has devised an escape from the administrative contingency problem. Since the administrative function is to be performed by a fiduciary, the procedure is to hold that the fiduciary's obligation is not only to complete the task, but to do so within a reasonable time, and to hold further that a reasonable time is something less than 21 years. See Belfield v. Booth,

---

decedent's estate tax attributable to the inclusion of the transferred property. The credit is 80 percent of this amount if the second decedent dies between two and four years after the death of the prior decedent, 60 percent if the second death occurs between four and six years, 40 percent for deaths between six and eight years, and 20 percent for deaths between eight and ten years.

27 A. 585 (Conn. 1893); Asche v. Asche, 216 A.2d 272 (Del. 1966); Brandenburg v. Thorndike, 28 N.E. 575 (Mass. 1885); cf. Estate of Taylor, 428 P.2d 301 (Cal. 1967) (vesting occurs at time distribution *should* have been made). There is a difficulty with this minority view: Although there may be an obligation to complete fiduciary tasks expeditiously, it is a fiction to say that there is *always* a violation of a fiduciary duty when the settlement of an estate takes more than 21 years. While rare, there can be cases where protracted and successive litigation over a multitude of issues legitimately ties up an estate for a very long time. Even on a case-by-case basis, it would seem to be impossible to conclude with the certainty required by the Rule that no such delay will properly arise.

Constructional Preference for Validity. Depending on the language employed, the principle of construction favoring validity may be available as a method of avoiding invalidity. For example, if a condition of survival is ambiguous on the point, it would probably be construed to relate to the death of the testator or of the life tenant rather than to the completion of the administrative task, such as the final distribution of the estate.[23] Indeed, this construction has on occasion been adopted even when the language unambiguously related to the estate's final distribution.[24]

Despite precedents supporting one or the other of these two salvage devices, the administrative contingency problem has not been solved. Most courts would probably still conclude that devises, such as G's in the first example given above, violate the Rule and are therefore invalid.[25]

---

23. See First Nat'l Bank v. Jenkins, 345 S.E.2d 829 (Ga. 1986) (the testator's will provided that "upon the death of [the life tenant], and after [paying hospital and medical expenses incurred by the life tenant during his life time and at his death paying for his funeral and grave marker], my trustee is directed to divide all the remaining trust property [among various beneficiaries] then living;" held, the remainder interests vested at the life tenant's death, with "only possession or actual payment ... delayed until his estate is settled, including payments for funeral expenses and the grave marker."); Restatement of Property §374 comment f.

24. See Malone v. Herndon, 168 P.2d 272 (Okla. 1945), where a will providing that on the death of the life tenant leaving issue surviving him, the "trust estate shall be paid over, delivered and conveyed to such issue living at the time of said payment, delivery and conveyance" was construed to require survivorship of the life tenant.

25. See Prime v. Hyne, 67 Cal. Rptr. 170 (Ct. App. 1968), for an example of a decision that rejected the notion that the fiduciary's duty guarantees that an estate will be distributed within 21 years of the decedent's death.

PART C. PERPETUITY-SAVING CLAUSES—THE PRACTITIONER'S FRIEND

The common-law Rule Against Perpetuities is less fearsome to practicing estate planning lawyers than it is to law students and law graduates studying for the bar examination. This is not because estate planning lawyers have found that the Rule becomes more understandable with experience, but because they have discovered a secret: They need not be greatly concerned about the technicalities of the Rule because they use perpetuity-saving clauses.

Formulated and used properly, perpetuity-saving clauses mean that lawyers need not ever fear that the trusts or other property arrangements they draft will violate the common-law Rule. In addition, unless the trust or other property arrangement is unreasonable—for example, unless it is to continue beyond the death of the last living member of the transferor's youngest descendant living when the trust or other arrangement was created—the practicing lawyer need not fear that the perpetuity-saving clause will have any practical effect other than to save the disposition from a Rule violation. Trusts are routinely created that would violate the Rule, were it not for the perpetuity-saving clause; essentially a technicality, a perpetuity-saving clause is nevertheless essential in such trusts.

Perpetuity-saving clauses are comprised of two components: the *perpetuity-period component* and the *gift-over component*. The perpetuity-period component establishes a period of time measured by the life of the survivor of a group of designated persons in being at the time of the transfer plus 21 years.[26] The gift-over component expressly creates a gift over that is guaranteed to vest at the termination of the period established in the perpetuity-period component but only if the interests in the trust or other arrangement have neither vested nor terminated earlier in accordance with their primary terms.

It is important to note that regardless of what group of persons is designated in the perpetuity-period component, the survivor of the group is not necessarily the person who would be the validating life for the questioned interest in the absence of the saving clause. Without the saving clause, the questioned interest might in fact have been invalid because of the existence of an invalidating chain of possible post-creation events with respect to every person who might be proposed as a validating

---

26. Under the Restatement 2d of Property §1.3 comment a, a saving clause would be invalid if "the number of individuals specified as the measuring lives... is so large that it would be an impossible administrative burden to locate them initially, let alone determine the death of the survivor...." See also USRAP §1 comment, part B. Some law firms unwisely use clauses linked to the descendants of a famous person. An associate at a New York law firm mentioned to us in 2011 that the trusts drafted by his firm (used to?) contain the following: "In no event shall the trust continue beyond the expiration of 21 years from the death of the last survivor of the descendants of Joseph P. Kennedy, the late Ambassador of the United States to the Court of St. James, living on the date hereof"!

life. The persons designated in the saving clause, however, become validating lives for all interests in the trust or other property arrangement. The saving clause confers on the last surviving member of the group the requisite causal connection demanded by the requirement of initial certainty. See Norton v. Georgia R.R. Bank & Trust, 322 S.E.2d 870 (Ga. 1984) (upholding the validity of a traditional perpetuity-saving clause).

In most cases, the saving clause does more than avoid a violation of the common-law Rule; it also, in a sense, overinsures the client's disposition against the possibility that the gift over will ever take effect. The period of time established by the perpetuity-period component of the clause provides a margin of safety. Almost always, the length of time is sufficient to exceed—usually by a substantial margin—the time when the interests in the trust or other arrangement actually vest (or terminate) by their own terms. The clause, therefore, is usually a formality that validates the disposition without affecting the substance of the disposition at all.

Prototype Clause. We present below two types of trusts as prototypical of trusts that are actually created in practice; we also give you a sample of a type of saving clause frequently used. Were it not for the inclusion of a perpetuity-saving clause, the remainder interests in both trusts would flunk the requirement of initial certainty and be invalid. (The first type of trust is more frequently created than the second, but the second type is also used in practice.)

Assume that G dies at age 75, G is survived by G's children (A and B) and four grandchildren.

Example 17.10: Corpus to Grandchildren Contingent on Reaching an Age Exceeding 21. G devised property in trust, income in equal shares to G's children for the life of the survivor, then in equal shares to G's grandchildren, remainder in corpus to G's grandchildren who reach age 30; if none reaches 30, to G's descendants who survive G's last surviving child, by representation; if none, to X Charity.

Example 17.11: Corpus to Descendants Contingent on Surviving Last Living Grandchild. G devised property in trust, income in equal shares to G's children for the life of the survivor, then in equal shares to G's grandchildren for the life of the survivor, and on the death of G's last living grandchild, corpus to G's descendants then living, by representation; if none, to X Charity.

G's lawyer inserted a perpetuity-saving clause in both dispositions. Specifically, the saving clause selected by G's lawyer says:

> The trust hereby created shall terminate in any event not later than 21 years after the death of the last survivor of the beneficiaries of this trust and their descendants who are in being at the time this instrument becomes effective, and unless sooner terminated by the terms hereof, the trustee shall, at the termination of such period, make distribution to the persons then entitled to the income of this trust, and in the same shares and proportions as they are so entitled.

Malpractice Liability. Would G's lawyer be liable in malpractice if the lawyer had failed to insert a perpetuity-saving clause in the above dispositions? In the technical violation cases studied earlier, would a lawyer drafting an irrevocable inter vivos trust be liable in malpractice if the lawyer inserts a perpetuity saving clause that gears the perpetuity-period component to a group of persons living at the settlor's death?

Lucas v. Hamm
364 P.2d 685 (Cal. 1961), cert. denied, 368 U.S. 987 (1962)

[After the death of the testator, the attorney who drew the will, in his capacity as counsel of record for the executors, advised the residuary devisees in writing that the residuary trust provision was invalid. The devisees subsequently entered into a settlement agreement with the testator's blood relatives under which the devisees received $75,000 less than they would have received had the trust provision been valid.

In an action for damages brought by the devisees against the drafting attorney, the trial court dismissed the complaint for lack of privity, and the plaintiffs appealed.]

GIBSON, C.J.... [The court held that lack of privity does not insulate an attorney who negligently draws a will from liability in tort to the devisees who lose their testamentary rights because of the attorney's negligence, nor does it insulate the attorney from liability in contract to such devisees as third party beneficiaries if the attorney fails properly to fulfill his or her obligations under the contract with the testator. See Chapter 13. The court then took up the question whether the attorney had been negligent or had breached the contract.]

The complaint, as we have seen, alleges that defendant drafted the will in such a manner that the trust was invalid because it violated the rules relating to perpetuities and restraints on alienation. These closely akin subjects have long perplexed the courts and the bar. Professor Gray, a leading authority in the field, stated: "There is something in the subject which seems to facilitate error. Perhaps it is because the mode of reasoning is unlike that with which lawyers are most familiar.... A long list might be formed of the demonstrable blunders with regard to its questions made by eminent men, blunders which they themselves have been sometimes the first to acknowledge; and there are few lawyers of any practice in drawing wills and settlements who have not at some time either fallen into the net which the Rule spreads for the unwary, or at least shuddered to think how narrowly they have escaped it." Gray, The Rule Against Perpetuities (4th ed. 1942) p. xi; see also Leach, Perpetuities Legislation (1954) 67 Harv. L. Rev. 1349 (describing the rule as a "technicality-ridden legal nightmare" and a "dangerous instrumentality in the hands of most members of the bar"). Of the California law on perpetuities and restraints it has been said that few, if any, areas of the law have been fraught with more confusion or concealed more traps for the unwary draftsman; that members of the bar, probate courts, and title insurance companies make errors in these matters; that the code provisions adopted in 1872 created a situation worse than if the matter had been left to the common law, and that the legislation adopted in 1951 (under which the will involved here was drawn), despite the best of intentions, added further complexities. (See 38 Cal. Jur. 2d 443; Coil, Perpetuities and Restraints; A Needed Reform (1955) 30 State Bar J. 87, 88-90.)

In view of the state of the law relating to perpetuities and restraints on alienation and the nature of the error, if any, assertedly made by defendant in preparing the instrument, it would not be proper to hold that defendant failed to use such skill, prudence, and diligence as lawyers of ordinary skill and capacity commonly exercise. The provision of the will quoted in the complaint, namely, that the trust was to terminate five years after the order of the probate court distributing the property to the trustee, could cause the trust to be invalid only because of the remote possibility that the order of distribution would be delayed for a period longer than a life in being at the creation of the interest plus 16 years (the 21-year statutory period less the five years specified in the will). Although it has been held that a possibility of this type could result in invalidity of a bequest (Estate of Johnston, 47 Cal. 2d 265, 269-270, 303 P.2d 1; Estate of Campbell, 28 Cal. App. 2d 102, 103 et seq., 82 P.2d 22), the possible occurrence of such a delay was so remote and unlikely that an attorney of ordinary skill acting under the same circumstances might well have "fallen into the net which the Rule spreads for the unwary" and failed to recognize the danger. We need not decide whether the trust provision of the will was actually invalid or whether, as defendant asserts, the complaint fails to allege facts necessary to enable such a determination, because we have concluded that in any event an error of the type relied on by plaintiffs does not show negligence or breach of contract on the part of defendant. . . .

The judgment is affirmed.

Notes

1. *Criticism.* R. E. Megarry, in 81 L.Q. Rev. 478, 481 (1965), commented on the *Lucas* decision:

> An Englishman's comment on the decision must perforce observe a proper restraint. Doubtless the Supreme Court of California is the best judge of the standard of competence which is to be expected of California lawyers of ordinary skill and capacity. Let it be accepted that [it] is highly unlikely that it would take longer than the perpetuity period for the estate to be distributed. The question then becomes whether an ordinary lawyer who undertakes to draft a will should be expected to know that a gift will be void for perpetuity if there is any possibility, however unlikely, that the perpetuity period will be exceeded. This part of the rule is so fundamental, and so highly stressed by all the books and teachers, that he who does not know it must be expected to know little or nothing of the rest of the rule. The standard of competence in California thus seems to be that it is not negligent for lawyers to draft wills knowing little or nothing of the rule against perpetuities, and without consulting anyone skilled in the rule (a point mentioned by the Court of Appeal but ignored in the judgment of the Supreme Court). If the rule against perpetuities is in this category,

what other fundamentals of the law are there of which the California attorney may be ignorant without culpability? How does California translate and apply *spondet peritiam artis?* However bright the future of Lucas v. Hamm may be in England on the score of privity, it is to be hoped that on the standard of professional competence it will prove to be a slur on the profession which, like the mule, will display neither pride of ancestry nor hope of posterity.

2. *Continuing Validity of Lucas?* In Wright v. Williams, 121 Cal. Rptr. 194, 199 n.2 (Ct. App. 1975), the court said: "There is reason to doubt that the ultimate conclusion of Lucas v. Hamm is valid in today's state of the art. Draftsmanship to avoid the rule against perpetuities seems no longer esoteric." See also Millwright v. Romer, 322 N.W.2d 30 (Iowa 1982).

3. *Model Rules of Professional Conduct,* Rule 1.1: "A lawyer shall provide competent representation to a client. A lawyer shall not: (a) handle a legal matter which the lawyer knows or should know that the lawyer is not competent to handle, without associating with a lawyer who is competent to handle it; (b) handle a legal matter without preparation adequate in the circumstances; or (c) neglect a legal matter entrusted to the lawyer."

EXTERNAL REFERENCE. Gerald P. Johnston, Legal Malpractice in Estate Planning—Perilous Times Ahead for the Practitioner, 67 Iowa L. Rev. 629 (1982).

PART D. MODERN POLICY OF THE RULE AGAINST PERPETUITIES

Lewis M. Simes, The Policy Against Perpetuities[27]
103 U. Pa. L. Rev. 707 (1955)

What public policy actuates this rule? If we are to content ourselves with the terse and sometimes superficial pronouncements on the subject scattered through the books, the policy of the Rule has never been in doubt. Ever since it first emerged in the *Duke of Norfolk's Case,* it has been declared to be a rule in furtherance of the alienability of property.... [I]f it were not for this Rule, property would be unproductive and society would have less income.

But why should a future interest make property inalienable, and why does inalienability make property unproductive? In answering these questions we must recall that the Rule against Perpetuities developed as a rule restricting future interests in specific land. Viewed thus, the rationale of the Rule is not difficult to perceive. In order to make a profit from land, one must have a type of ownership which insures enjoyment forever or for a fixed and determinable period of time.

---

27. Also published in Lewis M. Simes, Public Policy and the Dead Hand (1955).

People who purchase land, whether for profit or for their own use and enjoyment, are not likely to buy unless they can secure either a fee simple absolute or a lease for a fixed term of years....

Now, if the policy of the Rule against Perpetuities is to make property productive, just how far is this policy advanced in the application of the Rule today? Is property still taken out of commerce by remote contingent future interests? *I believe it is no exaggeration to say that, at the present time, due to changes both in the nature of capital investments and in the law, the proposition that contingent future interests make property unproductive is rarely true in the United States and almost never true in England.* I should like to discuss at some length my reasons for this belief.

In the first place, the future interest with which the Rule against Perpetuities is concerned is nearly always an equitable interest in a trust. The modern trust instrument, if well drawn, will contain broad powers of sale and reinvestment. While the beneficiary who has an equitable estate subject to a future interest may have difficulty in selling his property, that does not make it unproductive. As a practical matter, the trustee will have an absolute legal estate which he can sell, and will be empowered to reinvest the proceeds. While at one time in the history of the law, in the absence of express authorization in the trust instrument, the trustee's powers of reinvestments were extremely limited, today the rapidly extending "prudent man rule" gives the trustee a wide field of selection in making trust investments productive.

Moreover, not only is the trustee empowered by the terms of any well-drawn trust instrument to sell and reinvest in productive property; the law requires him to do so. One of the duties imposed by law upon trustees is to use reasonable care in making the trust property productive.

Suppose, however, that the trust instrument is not well drawn, and no express powers of alienation are given to the trustee. Still the trust property is not necessarily taken out of commerce. The law recognizes that, when circumstances change in a matter unforeseen by the settlor, the trustee may secure permission of the court to sell....

Statutes in several states have gone even further in permitting the trustee to sell and reinvest in the absence of a power to do so expressed in the trust instrument....

Of course, it must be recognized that, so far as the common law is concerned, it is perfectly clear that the existence of a power in a trustee to sell and reinvest does not take the case out of the Rule against Perpetuities. Though courts have rarely discussed the position...when they have done so, they have generally dismissed the matter without adequate rationalization.

There is a second reason why future interests do not make property unproductive. Not only is there commonly a power of sale in a trustee where future interests arise in American family settlements; the subject matter of the trust is commonly corporate shares and government or corporate bonds. In the case of corporate shares, the economic value is neither in the interest owned by the beneficiary of the trust, nor is it in the shares in the hand of the trustees. It is the property of the corporation. Certainly that is freely alienable....

There is, moreover, a third situation where, according to American law, the existence of future interests does not render property unproductive. Let us assume that somewhat unusual case where the trust device is not used, and legal future interests in land are created. A devises a particular piece of land to B for life, remainder to B's issue who survive him, in fee simple. Beginning with the case of Bofl v. Fisher,[28] decided in 1850, the American courts have developed a doctrine to this effect: where land is affected with a future interest, a court of equity has power to order a sale and to set up a trust in the proceeds, when this is necessary for the preservation of all interests in the land....

If alienability for purposes of productivity is not the justification of the modern Rule against Perpetuities, then what is the public policy which justifies it?

Before suggesting what I believe to be the true answer, I should like to take a moment to mention two other explanations of the Rule which are sometimes made. First, it is said that the Rule is designed to prevent an undue concentration of wealth in the hands of a few. Professor Leach has indicated that the Rule is intended to remove the "threat to the public welfare from family dynasties built either on great landed estates or on great capital wealth." But, as he points out, that threat is rather effectively removed by our income and estate taxes. I am disposed to agree with him. Indeed, I feel that undue concentration of wealth is an evil which can best be combated by tax legislation, rather than by perpetuity rules.

A second reason sometimes given for the Rule is as follows: it is socially undesirable for some members of society to have assured incomes and be protected from the economic struggle for existence; the principle of survival of the fittest should apply, so that those who are unable to maintain themselves in the economic struggle for existence should not survive. The American Law Institute, without giving its blessing to this particular rationale, states it as follows: "It is obvious that limitations unalterably effective over a long period of time would hamper the normal operation of the competitive struggle. Persons less fit, less keen in the social struggle, might be thereby enabled to retain property disproportionate to their skills in the competitive struggle." Several answers may be made to this argument. The Rule against Perpetuities does permit economic provision for the unfit for one generation, indeed for one generation and during the minority of the next. It would seem almost as bad to permit this sort of thing for the first generation as for succeeding generations. If it be answered that there is a social objection to the continuation of a line of weaklings, the answer is that a restriction on the tying up

---

28. 3 Rich. Eq. 1 (S.C. 1850). [See also Am. L. Prop. §§4.98-.99; Simes & Smith on Future Interests §§1941-46; Lewis M. Simes & Clarence B. Taylor, Improvement of Conveyancing by Legislation 235-38 (1960); Restatement of Property §179. Ed.]

of property does not eliminate that objection. Modern society, with its elaborate welfare machinery, is not organized on a theory of survival of the fittest, but of survival of the weak. Moreover, if human experience means anything, we may well conclude that the progeny of weaklings are likely to be more numerous in a state of poverty than in a state of wealth.

Thus I believe that neither of these explanations for the Rule is adequate. There are in my opinion, however, two other bases for the social policy of the Rule, the force of which can scarcely be denied.

First, the Rule against Perpetuities strikes a fair balance between the desires of members of the present generation, and similar desires of succeeding generations, to do what they wish with the property which they enjoy. It is almost axiomatic that one of the most common human wants is the desire to distribute one's property at death without restriction in whatever manner he desires. Indeed, we can go farther and say that there is a policy in favor of permitting people to create future interests by will, as well as present interests, because that also accords with human desires. The difficulty here is that, if we give free rein to the desires of one generation to create future interests, the members of succeeding generations will receive the property in a restricted state. They will thus be unable to create all the future interests they wish. Perhaps, they may not even be able to devise it at all. Hence, to come most nearly to satisfying the desires of peoples of all generations, we must strike a fair balance between unrestricted testamentary disposition of property by the present generation and unrestricted disposition by future generations. In a sense this is a policy of alienability, but it is not alienability for productivity. It is alienability to enable people to do what they please at death with the property which they enjoy in life. As Kohler says in his treatise on the philosophy of law: "The far-reaching hand of a testator who would enforce his will in distant future generations destroys the liberty of other individuals, and presumes to make rules for distant times."

But, in my opinion, a second and even more important reason for the Rule is this: it is socially desirable that the wealth of the world be controlled by its living members and not by the dead. I know of no better statement of that doctrine than the language of Thomas Jefferson, contained in a letter to James Madison, when he said: "The earth belongs always to the living generation. They may manage it then, and what proceeds from it, as they please, during their usufruct." Sidgwick, in his *Elements of Politics*, also discusses the problem in the following words: " ...it rather follows from the fundamental assumption of individualism, that any such posthumous restraint on the use of bequeathed wealth will tend to make it less useful to the living, as it will interfere with their freedom in dealing with it. Individualism, in short, is in a dilemma.... Of this difficulty there is, I think, no general theoretical solution: it can only be reduced by some practical compromise."

EXTERNAL REFERENCE. For a critique of Professor Simes's argument, see Thomas P. Gallanis, The Rule Against Perpetuities and the Law Commission's Flawed Philosophy, 59 Camb. L. J. 284 (2000).

———

The Know-and-See Theory. Professor Simes said that the Rule "strikes a fair balance between the desires of members of the present generation, and similar desires of succeeding generations, to do what they wish with the property which they enjoy." Where, specifically, is that "fair balance" to be drawn?

Hobhouse suggested a know-and-see theory: "A clear, obvious, natural line is drawn for us between those persons and events which the Settlor knows and sees, and those which he cannot know or see." Sir A. Hobhouse, The Dead Hand 188 (1880).

Leach and Tudor expanded on the know-and-see test:

> The Rule against Perpetuities came into being as a means of preventing inordinate family pride from tying up the soil of England in a manner which would produce undesirable economic and social consequences. In establishing the balance between private right and public interest the courts arrived at a solution which permitted the following: ...In a will a man of property could provide for all of those in his family whom he personally knew and the first generation after them upon attaining majority.

W. Barton Leach & Owen Davies Tudor, The Common Law Rule Against Perpetuities, in Am. L. Prop. § 24.16, at 51. The authors went on to muse that it might have been better if the tack-on, 21-year part of the period were not a period in gross, but instead were treated like the period of gestation—allowed only if needed to take account of an actual minority. The fact is, however, that it is now beyond dispute that the tack-on, 21-year part of the period is a period in gross; that point was settled long ago in Cadell v. Palmer, 1 Cl. & F. 372, 6 Eng. Rep. 956 (1833).

Professor Waggoner has suggested a further refinement of the theory:

> [T]he [know-and-see] standard [arguably means] that donors should be allowed to exert control through the youngest generation of descendants they knew and saw, or at least one or more but not necessarily all of whom they knew and saw....

Lawrence W. Waggoner, The Uniform Statutory Rule Against Perpetuities, 21 Real Prop. Prob. & Tr. J. 569, 587 (1986).

Question

In the modern age, what need is there for the Rule Against Perpetuities?

PART E. PERPETUITY REFORM: DISCRETE REPAIR, EQUITABLE MODIFICATION, AND WAIT-AND-SEE

Before the perpetual-trust movement gained momentum (see below Part F), reform of the common-law Rule was in full throttle. The goal of the reform movement was to preserve the policy of the common-law Rule but blunt its nonpurposive applications—cases in which it would strike down all or part of a perfectly reasonable trust or other disposition.

The need for perpetuity reform was not in much doubt, but controversy persisted about the method. Three basic methods were advanced: (1) *discrete statutory repair* of the fertile octogenarian, afterborn spouse, and administrative contingency problem areas, along with reduction of age contingencies to 21; (2) *equitable modification*; and (3) *wait-and-see*, with deferred reformation (reformation only if an interest remains contingent at the expiration of the permissible vesting period).

In the 1990s, the third method—wait-and-see with deferred reformation—had become the dominant method, and may make a comeback if Congress acts to remove the perpetual-trust incentive. The Uniform Statutory Rule Against Perpetuities (USRAP), which is incorporated into the Uniform Probate Code as Part 9 of Article II, was enacted in more than half of the states plus the District of Columbia, and still is in full effect in 11 states—California, Indiana, Kansas, Massachusetts, Minnesota, Montana, New Mexico, North Dakota, Oregon, South Carolina, and West Virginia.

Alabama, Alaska, Arizona, Arkansas, Colorado, Connecticut, the District of Columbia, Florida, Georgia, Hawaii, Maine, Michigan, Nebraska, Nevada, North Carolina, Tennessee, Utah, Virginia, and Washington were also among the USRAP enacting states, but they have since gone over to the perpetual-trust camp either by repealing their version of the USRAP or by modifying it to allow perpetual or long-lasting trusts.

1. Discrete Repair and Equitable Modification

Discrete Statutory Repair. The discrete-statutory-repair method is now in effect in only one jurisdiction—New York.[29] The New York statute requires any age contingency to be reduced to 21 if it would otherwise violate the common-law Rule. The statute also creates a presumption that a reference to "spouse" refers to a person

---

29. See N.Y. Est. Powers & Trusts Law §§9-1.2, -1.3. Illinois had a specific-statutory-repair statute until 2020 (see Ill. Rev. Stat. ch. 765, §305/4(c) (repealed), but it was of little importance after Illinois allowed perpetual trusts by permitting a trust document to opt out of the Rule. Until 1988, the discrete-statutory-repair method also was in effect in Florida (see Fla. Stat. §689.22(5)(a)-(d) (repealed)); it was repealed when Florida enacted the USRAP. Until 1991, California had a statute aimed at the afterborn spouse category, but not the other technical-violation categories (see Cal. Civ. Code §715.7 (repealed)); this provision was repealed when California enacted the USRAP.

in being at the creation of the interest; that an administrative contingency is limited to 21 years; and that a male age 14 or over can have a child and that a female between ages 12 and 55 can have a child. Finally, the statute allows the presumption of lifetime fertility to be rebutted, and provides that the possibility of adoption is to be disregarded.

Equitable Modification. In the prominent case of Berry v. Union Nat'l Bank, 262 S.E.2d 766 (W. Va. 1980), the court used its equity powers to reduce the duration of a 25-year trust to 21 years.[30]

In decisions antedating *Berry,* the courts in Hawaii, Mississippi, and New Hampshire had also used their equity powers to modify an otherwise invalid trust. See In re Chun Quan Yee Hop, 469 P.2d 183 (Haw. 1970) (period in gross lowered from 30 to 21); Carter v. Berry, 140 So.2d 843 (Miss. 1962) (age contingency lowered from 25 to 21); Edgerly v. Barker, 31 A. 900 (N.H. 1891) (age contingency lowered from 40 to 21).[31]

Legislation in a few states authorizes or directs the courts to reform defective instruments. See, e.g., Tex. Prop. Code §5.043.

Although these judicial decisions and statutes authorize or direct reformation of the defective instrument in a way that comes as close as possible to the transferor's intent without violating the common-law Rule, the cases have all been of a similar type to *Berry,* and in each case the courts have reformed the disposition by lowering the period in gross or age contingency to 21.

A method of reformation more faithful to the transferor's intention would have been to insert a saving clause into the governing instrument. See Olin L. Browder, Construction, Reformation, and the Rule Against Perpetuities, 62 Mich. L. Rev. 1 (1963); Lawrence W. Waggoner, Perpetuity Reform, 81 Mich. L. Rev. 1718 (1983); John H. Langbein & Lawrence W. Waggoner, Reformation of Wills on the Ground of Mistake: Change of Direction in American Law?, 130 U. Pa. L. Rev. 521 (1982).

The Supreme Court of New Hampshire came close to adopting this method of reformation in Richardson Trust, 634 A.2d 1005 (N.H. 1993). The trust in essence provided that income was to be distributed to the testator's issue and, upon a failure of issue, the income was to be distributed to a named charity. The probate court ruled, and the supreme court affirmed, relying on *Edgerly,* that the income should be distributed to the testator's issue until either no issue remain or the "trust violates the rule against perpetuities," at which time the principal should be distributed in accordance with the intestate succession statute.

---

30. In 1992, West Virginia enacted the USRAP, effectively displacing *Berry* for post-effective-date transfers.

31. Hawaii and Mississippi later enacted the USRAP; New Hampshire later allowed perpetual trusts.

The Supreme Court of Mississippi adopted this method of reformation but revealed a degree of misunderstanding by also purporting to adopt the wait-and-see method of perpetuity reform without seeming to realize that immediate reformation and wait-and-see are mutually inconsistent methods of perpetuity reform. In Estate of Anderson v. Deposit Guaranty Nat'l Bank, 541 So.2d 423 (Miss. 1989), the court upheld the testamentary trust, which was to last for 25 years from the date of admission of the will to probate, the income to be used for the education of the descendants of the testator's father, and the corpus at the end of the 25-year period to be paid over to testator's nephew, Howard Davis, or if Howard was not then living, to the heirs of Howard's body. The court used its equity power to insert a saving clause, but also adopted wait and see.

In another case, Merrill v. Wimmer, 481 N.E.2d 1294 (Ind. 1985), the Supreme Court of Indiana held that judicial reformation to correct a perpetuity violation is forbidden by reason of the fact that in Indiana the common-law Rule was then codified. Do you agree that codification of the common-law Rule precludes the reformation method of perpetuity reform?[32]

Reformation Authorized by the USRAP. Although the USRAP adopts the wait-and-see method of perpetuity reform, reformation also plays an important role. Section 3 establishes a deferred-reformation rule by directing a court to reform a disposition if, after exhaustion of the permissible-vesting period, it violates the Statutory Rule Against Perpetuities. More significant for our purpose here, however, is §5 of the USRAP. Under that section, the wait-and-see rule adopted by the USRAP applies only prospectively; as to pre-existing interests, §5(b) authorizes immediate reformation. In line with the law review articles listed above, *Richardson,* and *Anderson,* the Official Comment to §5(b) urges courts to consider reforming a pre-existing perpetuity violation by judicially inserting an appropriate saving clause rather than by lowering an age contingency or period in gross to 21. The comment notes that a saving clause would probably have been used at the drafting stage of the disposition had it been drafted competently. In addition, the comment notes that the period of time marked off by the perpetuity-period component of an appropriate saving clause ordinarily would be more than sufficient to give the contingencies attached to the contingent interest to work themselves out to a final resolution under the terms set forth by the transferor. See Abrams v. Templeton, 465 S.E.2d 117 (S.C. Ct. App. 1995) (inserting a saving clause that required, rather than merely authorized, a court to reform a pre-enactment trust containing invalid interests).

---

32. "[T]he reformation method... does not alter the [common-law] Rule at all. The Rule is left intact, and the disposition is altered to conform to it." Waggoner, Perpetuity Reform, 81 Mich. L. Rev. 1718, 1755-56 (1983). In any event, Indiana subsequently enacted the USRAP, which specifically authorizes reformation of pre-effective date interests.

2. Wait-and-See/Deferred Reformation

Primary Statutory References: *UPC §§2-901, 2-903 (USRAP §§1, 3)*

Under the common-law Rule, validity or invalidity turns on the full array of possible post-creation events. In its early stages, the perpetuity-reform movement focused on the technical-violation categories. Because the post-creation chains of possible events that invalidate those interests are unlikely to happen, it was natural to propose that the requirement of initial certainty be abandoned in favor of taking actual post-creation events into account. Instead of invalidating an interest because of what *might* happen, waiting to see what *does* happen seems to be more sensible. Known as the wait-and-see method of perpetuity reform, this approach was promulgated by the two preeminent national organizations concerned with law reform in trusts and estates—the American Law Institute and the National Conference of Commissioners on Uniform State Laws.

Neither the ALI's Restatement 2d of Property (1983) nor the NCCUSL's USRAP (1990) alters what may be called the *validating* side of the common-law Rule. Dispositions that would have been valid under the common-law Rule remain valid. Practitioners under either wait-and-see regime can and should continue to use a traditional perpetuity-saving clause. The wait-and-see element is applied only to interests that fall prey to the *invalidating* side of the common-law Rule. Interests that would be invalid at common law are saved from *initial invalidity*. To prevent the unjust enrichment of unintended takers caused by a drafter's mistake in failing to insert an appropriate perpetuity-saving clause, otherwise invalid interests are, as it were, given a second chance: These interests are valid if they actually vest within the permissible-vesting period and become invalid only if they remain in existence but still contingent at the expiration of that period.

Academics fussed with one another over how the permissible-vesting period was to be measured. The conventional assumption was that the permissible-vesting period had to be measured by reference to so-called measuring lives who are in being at the creation of the interest: The permissible-vesting period under this assumption expires 21 years after the death of the last surviving measuring life. Academic controversies raged over who the measuring lives should be and how the law should identify them.

Saving-Clause Principle of Wait-and-See. It now seems understood that wait-and-see is nothing more mysterious than a perpetuity-saving clause injected by the law when the governing instrument fails to include one. In effect, the perpetuity-period component of a standard saving clause constitutes a privately established wait-and-see rule. The permissible-vesting period under wait-and-see is, or should be, the equivalent of the perpetuity-period component of a well-conceived saving clause.

The saving clause is rounded out by providing the near-equivalent of a gift-over component via a provision for judicial reformation of a disposition in case the interest is still in existence and contingent when the permissible-vesting period expires.

Title in Abeyance. One of the early objections to wait-and-see should be mentioned at this point. It was once widely argued and still occasionally is argued that wait-and-see can cause harm because it puts the validity of property interests in abeyance—no one can determine whether an interest is valid or not. This argument has been shown to be false. Keep in mind that the wait-and-see element is applied only to interests that would be invalid were it not for wait-and-see. These otherwise invalid interests are always contingent future interests. It is now well understood that wait-and-see does nothing more than subject that type of future interest to an *additional* contingency. For the interest to vest, the original contingencies must be satisfied within a certain period of time. If that period of time—the permissible-vesting period—is easily determined, then the additional contingency causes no more uncertainty in the state of the title than would have been the case had it been explicitly placed in the governing instrument itself. It should also be noted that only the status of the affected future interest in the trust or other property arrangement is deferred. In the interim, the other interests, such as the interests of current income beneficiaries, are carried out in the normal course without obstruction.

The Permissible-Vesting Period. As indicated above, the greatest controversy has been over how to measure the permissible-vesting period. This is the subject to which we now turn. The problem arises because the common-law Rule contained no mechanism for measuring an actual period of time to wait to see if an otherwise invalid interest vests or terminates in "due time." The only mechanism the common law provided is the requirement of initial certainty, which, as noted earlier in this chapter, is a mechanism for testing the validity of an interest at the point of its creation. The decision is made at the point of creation, with post-creation events disregarded and, therefore, the common law had no cause to measure a "perpetuity period" during which post-creation events are allowed to be taken into account. At common law, there either is a validating life or there is no validating life. There is no validating life for invalid interests, hence there is no common-law "perpetuity period" to wait out. A permissible-vesting period is necessary only under the wait-and-see method of perpetuity reform.

Restatement 2d of Property (1983). In adopting the wait-and-see method of perpetuity reform, the Restatement 2d of Property used a predetermined list of measuring lives. Under §1.3(2) of the Restatement 2d of Property, the permissible-vesting period expires 21 years after the death of the survivor of:

> (a) The transferor if the period of the rule begins to run in the transferor's lifetime; and
>
> (b) Those individuals alive when the period of the rule begins to run, if reasonable in number, who have beneficial interests vested or contingent in the property in which the

non-vested interest in question exists and the parents and grandparents alive when the period of the rule begins to run of all beneficiaries of the property in which the non-vested interest exists, and

    (c) The donee of a nonfiduciary power of appointment alive when the period of the rule begins to run if the exercise of such power could affect the non-vested interest in question.

If a property interest is still in existence but nonvested at the expiration of the permissible-vesting period, §1.5 provides that "the transferred property shall be disposed of in the manner which most closely effectuates the transferor's manifested plan of distribution and which is within the limits of the rule against perpetuities."[33]

The Restatement 2d's version of wait-and-see has not been directly adopted by any common-law court,[34] nor has it been legislatively enacted by any state. A statute enacted in Iowa, however, was influenced by the Restatement 2d; the Iowa statute designates as the measuring lives the beneficiaries and "the grandparents of all such beneficiaries and the issue of such grandparents...." Iowa Code §558.68(2)(b)(2) (enacted in 1983). See Estate of Keenan, 519 N.W.2d 373 (Iowa 1994) (reformed the trust after finding that it would be certain to violate the wait-and-see period).

Uniform Statutory Rule Against Perpetuities. The National Conference of Commissioners on Uniform State Laws promulgated the USRAP in 1986, amended it modestly in 1990,[35] and brought it into the Uniform Probate Code. The general contour of the USRAP is similar to that of the Restatement 2d of Property. The validating side of the common-law Rule is retained, but the invalidating side is replaced with wait-and-see and deferred-reformation elements. The major departure from the Restatement approach is that the USRAP uses a flat 90-year permissible-vesting period under its wait-and-see element rather than a period ending 21 years after the death of the survivor of a predetermined list of measuring lives.

---

33. Professor Dukeminier assailed the Restatement's predetermined list by arguing that it "does not faithfully adhere to any principle at all," is drafted so ambiguously that its words "are like quicksilver" that "slip and slide and elude our grasp," and "may take years of learned analysis and litigation to solve its sphinxine riddles." Jesse Dukeminier, Perpetuities: The Measuring Lives, 85 Colum. L. Rev. 1648 (1985).

34. It has received favorable comment in a few cases, however. See Hansen v. Stroecker, 699 P.2d 871, 874-75 (Alaska 1985) ("We are persuaded [by the Restatement 2d and other authorities] that the wait-and-see approach should be adopted as the common law rule against perpetuities in Alaska.") Alaska subsequently enacted the USRAP, and now allows perpetual or near-perpetual trusts.

    See also Dewire v. Haveles, 534 N.E.2d 782 (Mass. 1989) (the court suggested that it might follow the Restatement 2d; note, however, that Massachusetts subsequently enacted the USRAP); Nantt v. Pucket Energy Co., 382 N.W.2d 655 (N.D. 1986) (citing the Restatement 2d of Property, the court said that the wait-and-see rule "is a basic common sense approach to 'perpetuities' today"; note, however, that North Dakota subsequently enacted the USRAP).

    But see Pound v. Shorter, above at p. 956 (without mentioning the Restatement 2d, the court rejected wait-and-see as a common-law concept; note, however, that Georgia subsequently enacted the USRAP and now allows 360-year trusts).

35. The 1990 amendment added subsection (e) to §1 (UPC §2-901(e)).

Rationale of the 90-Year Permissible-Vesting Period. The most striking feature of the USRAP is its use of a flat period of 90 years as the permissible-vesting period. Its rationale was explained by Professor Waggoner, the drafter of the USRAP:

> [T]he philosophy behind the 90-year period was to fix a period of time that approximates the average period of time that would traditionally be allowed by the wait-and-see doctrine. There was no intention to use the flat-period-of-years method as a means of lengthening the [permissible vesting] period beyond its traditional boundaries. The fact that the traditional period roughly averages out to a longish-sounding 90 years is a reflection of a quite different phenomenon: the dramatic increase in longevity that society as a whole has experienced in the course of the twentieth century. Seen in this light, the 90-year period is an evolutionary step in the development of the wait-and-see doctrine.

Lawrence W. Waggoner, The Uniform Statutory Rule Against Perpetuities: The Rationale of the 90-Year Waiting Period, 73 Cornell L. Rev. 157 (1988).

Acceptance of the 90-Year Period under the Federal Generation-Skipping Transfer Tax. In general terms, trusts that were irrevocable on September 25, 1985, are exempt from the federal generation-skipping transfer tax. See Tax Reform Act of 1986, Pub. L. 99-514, §1433(b)(2). These trusts are called "grandfathered trusts." Under Treasury Regulations, "grandfathered trusts" can become ungrandfathered if a nongeneral power of appointment is exercised in a manner that postpones the vesting of an interest beyond the perpetuity period. See Treas. Reg. §26.2601-1(b)(1)(v)(B)(2), (D) ex. 6-7. Acting in ignorance of the 90-year period of the USRAP, the original version of this regulation defined the perpetuity period solely in terms of a life in being plus 21 years. After the 90-year period of the USRAP was brought to the attention of Treasury Department officials, the Department amended the regulation to accommodate the USRAP's 90-year period.

Deferred Reformation—the Approach of the USRAP. Section 3 of the USRAP directs a court, upon the petition of an interested person, to reform a disposition within the limits of the 90-year permissible-vesting period, in the manner deemed by the court most closely to approximate the transferor's manifested plan of distribution, in any one of three circumstances. The "interested person" who would frequently bring the reformation suit would be the trustee.

Seldom will this section become operative. Of the fraction of trusts and other property arrangements that are incompetently drafted, and thus fail to meet the requirement of initial validity under the codified version of the validating side of the common-law Rule, almost all of them will have terminated by their own terms long before any of the circumstances requisite to reformation under §3 arise.

If the right to reformation does arise, it will be found easier than perhaps anticipated to determine how best to reform the disposition.[36] The court is given two reformation criteria: (i) the transferor's manifested plan of distribution, and (ii) the 90-year permissible-vesting period. Because governing instruments are where transferors manifest their plans of distribution, the imaginary horrible of courts being forced to probe the minds of long-dead transferors will not materialize.

The theory of §3 is to defer the right to reformation until reformation becomes truly necessary. Thus, the basic rule of §3(1) is that the right to reformation does not arise until a contingent property interest or a power of appointment becomes invalid; under §1, this does not occur until the expiration of the 90-year permissible-vesting period. By confining perpetuity litigation to those few cases in which the permissible-vesting period actually is exceeded, perpetuity litigation is limited to purposive cases. In contrast to the equitable deviation approach of Berry v. Union Nat'l Bank, above p. 972, which encourages nonpurposive or wasteful perpetuity litigation, the USRAP's 90-year wait-and-see and deferred-reformation approach adopts a judicial hands-off policy. See Lawrence W. Waggoner, The Uniform Statutory Rule Against Perpetuities: Oregon Joins Up, 26 Willamette L. Rev. 259 (1990).

The deferred-reformation approach has additional advantages beyond working more efficiently by greatly minimizing the number of reformation suits. In the few cases in which perpetuity reformation becomes necessary, the deferred-reformation approach minimizes the risk of judicial error by postponing judicial intervention until the time when more information about family circumstances existing at the time of distribution of the trust corpus is known. In addition, any concern that deferring the right to reformation deprives the courts of valuable extrinsic evidence that would be available under the equitable deviation approach is groundless. Under the equitable deviation rule, exemplified by the *Berry* case, the courts have not relied on extrinsic evidence of the transferor's intent. The reason is obvious: The transferors never entertained the possibility that the governing instruments contained perpetuity violations in the first place. Hence, the transferors never formed an intent regarding what they would have wanted had they been informed of the violations. As expected, therefore, the courts operating under the equitable-deviation rule have not determined the transferor's intent by reference to extrinsic evidence but by reference to the governing instrument. Deferring the right to reformation until after the permissible-vesting period has run its course does not deprive the courts of valuable extrinsic evidence. See Mary Louise Fellows, Testing Perpetuity Reforms: A Study of Perpetuity Cases 1984-89, 25 Real Prop. Prob. & Tr. J. 597 (1991).

---

36. Note that reformation under §3 is mandatory, not subject to the discretion of the court. Consequently, as noted in the comment to §3, the common-law doctrine of infectious invalidity is superseded by the USRAP.

The deferred-reformation approach also is consistent with the saving-clause principle embraced by the USRAP. Deferring the right to reformation until the permissible-vesting period expires is the only way to grant every reasonable opportunity for the donor's disposition to work itself out without premature interference. One of the reasons why the USRAP specifically rejects the idea of granting a right to reformation at any time on a showing of a violation of the common-law Rule is that the experience under these statutorily or judicially established equitable-deviation principles has not been satisfactory. As in *Berry*, the courts have lowered periods in gross or age contingencies to 21. This is a step that amounts to an unwarranted distortion of the donor's intention, a distortion that is avoided by deferring the right to reformation until the contingencies as originally written by the donor have been given a chance to be fulfilled.

To be sure, if the courts use the equitable-deviation approach to insert a perpetuity-saving clause rather than to lower a period in gross or an age contingency to 21, as in Richardson Trust, above at p. 972, and Estate of Anderson v. Deposit Guaranty Nat'l Bank, above at p. 973, the frustration of the donor's intention is avoided, but this comes at the expense of a reformation suit. The insertion-of-a-saving-clause approach is therefore less efficient than wait-and-see with deferred reformation. The period of time produced by a judicially inserted perpetuity-saving clause would be about the same in length as that which is automatically granted by the USRAP without front-end litigation. The more efficient course is to defer the right to reformation until after the permissible-vesting period has run its course. Deferring the right to reformation reduces the necessity and cost of litigation because, as noted, the contingencies attached to most future interests that would otherwise have fallen victim of the common-law Rule will be resolved well within the permissible-vesting period. Litigation to reform an offending disposition will seldom become necessary. The Restatement 2d is in accord with this approach. Reformation is provided for in the Restatement 2d only if the contingent property interest becomes invalid after waiting out the permissible-vesting period. See Restatement 2d of Property §1.5.

At the same time, the USRAP is not inflexible, for it grants the right to reformation before the expiration of the 90-year permissible-vesting period when it becomes necessary to do so or when there is no point in waiting that period out. Subsection (2), which pertains to class gifts that are not yet but still might become invalid under the wait-and-see element, grants a right to reformation whenever the share of any class member is entitled to take effect in possession or enjoyment. Were it not for this subsection, a great inconvenience and possibly injustice could arise, for class members whose shares have vested within the period might otherwise have to wait out the remaining part of the 90 years before obtaining their shares. Reformation under this subsection will seldom be needed, however, because of the common practice of structuring trusts to split into separate shares or separate trusts at the death of each income beneficiary, one separate share or separate trust for each of the income beneficiary's then-living descendants; when this pattern is followed, the circumstances described in subsection (2) will not arise.

Subsection (3) also grants the right to reformation before the 90-year permissible-vesting period expires. The circumstance giving rise to the right to reformation under subsection (3) occurs if a contingent property interest can vest but not before the 90-year period has expired. Though unlikely, such a case can theoretically arise. If it does, the interest—unless it terminates by its own terms earlier—is bound to become invalid under §1 eventually. There is no point in deferring the right to reformation until the inevitable happens. The USRAP provides for early reformation in such a case, just in case it arises.

Problems

Consider how G's disposition might appropriately be reformed under the USRAP in the following cases.

1. G devised property in trust, directing the trustee to pay the income "to A for life, then to A's children for the life of the survivor, then to A's grandchildren for the life of the survivor, and on the death of A's last surviving grandchild, the corpus of the trust is to be divided among A's then-living descendants by representation; if none, to" a specified charity. G was survived by her child (A) and by A's two minor children (X and Y). After G's death, another child (Z) was born to A. Subsequently, A died, survived by her children (X, Y, and Z) and by three grandchildren (M, N, and O). X, Y, and Z died within the 90-year period following G's death, but some of A's grandchildren were still living at the expiration of the 90-year period.

2. G devised property in trust, directing the trustee to pay the income "to A for life, then to A's children"; the corpus of the trust is to be equally divided among A's children who reach the age of 30. G was survived by A, by A's spouse (H), and by A's two children (X and Y), both of whom were under the age of 30 when G died. After G's death, another child (Z) was born to A. Although unlikely, suppose that at A's death (prior to the expiration of the 90-year period), Z's age was such that he could be alive but under the age of 30 on the 90th anniversary of G's death. Suppose further that at A's death X and Y were over the age of 30.

––––––

EXTERNAL REFERENCES. The USRAP sparked a lively and sometimes bitter academic debate. See e.g., Ira M. Bloom, Perpetuities Refinement: There Is an Alternative, 62 Wash. L. Rev. 23 (1987) (arguing that the USRAP is unnecessary because of infrequency of appellate-level perpetuity cases; author proposes own version of perpetuity-reform statute); Jesse Dukeminier, The Uniform Statutory Rule Against Perpetuities: Ninety Years in Limbo, 34 UCLA L. Rev. 1023 (1987) (labeling the USRAP "an extraordinarily risky venture" (at 1024), "so bizarre that the mind boggles" (at 1025), "Waggoner's phantom ship" (at 1068), an idea that gives "a bizarre turn to perpetuities reform" (at 1069), and an act that "is deserving of oblivion" (at 1079)); Mary Louise Fellows, Testing Perpetuity Reforms: A Study of Perpetuity Cases 1984-89, 25 Real Prop. Prob & Tr. J. 597 (1991) (testing the various types of perpetuity reform measures and concluding, on the basis of empirical evidence, that the USRAP is the best opportunity offered to date for a uniform perpetuity law that efficiently and effectively achieves a fair balance between present and future property owners); Thomas P. Gallanis, The Future of Future Interests, 60 Wash. & Lee L. Rev. 513 (2003) (arguing that "a direct durational limit on future interests is far preferable to a rule against the remoteness of vesting," and proposing a Uniform Future Interests Act); Paul G. Haskell, A Proposal for a Simple and Socially Effective Rule Against Perpetuities, 66 N.C. L. Rev. 545 (1988) (arguing for replacement of both the validating and invalidating sides of the common-law Rule with a statutory rule requiring vesting in possession no later than 125 years after creation); Amy Morris Hess, Freeing Property Owners from the RAP Trap: Tennessee Adopts the Uniform Statutory Rule Against Perpetuities, 62 Tenn. L. Rev. 267 (1995) (arguing that if the common-law Rule is to remain part of the law of Tennessee, then the USRAP is "a highly desirable and long overdue reform"); Ronald C. Link & Kimberly A. Licata, Perpetuities Reform in North Carolina: The Uniform Statutory Rule Against Perpetuities, Nondonative Transfers, and Honorary Trusts, 74 N.C. L. Rev. 1783 (1996) (explaining the USRAP and demonstrating through North Carolina cases how it will "greatly simplify" the law); John D. Moore, Comment, The Uniform Statutory Rule Against Perpetuities: Taming the "Technicality-Ridden Legal Nightmare," 95 W. Va. L. Rev. 193 (1992) (reviewing pre-USRAP perpetuities law in West Virginia, analyzing the USRAP, and comparing the USRAP to other alternative reforms).

PART F. THE PERPETUAL-TRUST MOVEMENT

A few states had abolished (or had never adopted) the common-law Rule Against Perpetuities before 1986—including Wisconsin, South Dakota, and Idaho—but transferors had little desire to take advantage of the absence of the Rule in those states in order to establish perpetual trusts for their descendants from time to time living forever. See Max M. Schanzenbach & Robert H. Sitkoff, Perpetuities or Taxes: Explaining the Rise of the Perpetual Trust, 27 Cardozo L. Rev. 2465 (2006). After all, a transferor's genetic overlap with his or her descendants is cut in half at each succeeding generation. Specifically, a transferor's genetic overlap with his or her children is 50%, with his or her grandchildren is 25%, with his or her great-grandchildren is 12.5%.[37] With four-generation families becoming more and more

---

37. The 50% genetic overlap between a transferor and his or her children is precise; the genetic overlap between a transferor and his or her more remote descendants is an average. See John H. Beckstrom, Sociobiology and Intestate Wealth Transfers, 76 Nw. U. L. Rev. 216, 232 (1981).

common due to increased longevity, an aging transferor might live long enough to know and see some or all of his or her great-grandchildren, but as infants, not as adults. Seldom did a transferor think beyond great-grandchildren and contemplate benefiting more remote generations. The great-grandchildren of the transferor's great-grandchildren—the transferor's great-great-great-great-grandchildren—are six generations removed from the transferor: They will be born about 100 years after the transferor's death and have a genetic overlap with the transferor of a mere 1.5625%.[38] The transferor will be one of their 64 great-great-great-great-grandparents!

The federal generation-skipping transfer tax (GSTT) helped to change all that. Restated in 1986, the GSTT spurred a growing movement for states to abolish the Rule Against Perpetuities in order to allow perpetual trusts. The number of states abolishing the Rule in the years after 1986 has grown rapidly. Why is this so, given that the GSTT imposes high taxes on trusts that persist through more than one generation? The answer is that the GSTT also contains a large exemption—in 2024, $13.61 million per donor.

In fashioning the GSTT exemption, Congress made a mistake: It relied on state perpetuity law to control the length of GSTT-exempt trusts. This mistake put the duration of GSTT-exempt trusts in the hands of the states, whose interest is more in generating trust business for its institutional trustees than in protecting the federal fisc. Hence was born a movement to abolish the Rule Against Perpetuities, or at least to modify it to permit trusts of hundreds of years. The movement began slowly, but accelerated as local lawyers and banking institutions in state after state learned of the potential for attracting trust business that the GSTT-exempt perpetual trust provided.

Despite the growing GSTT-exempt perpetual-trust movement, Congress has been complacent. Congress has not acted to curb the duration of the GSTT exemption—not yet, anyway. The way it works now is that, once a trust qualifies for the GSTT exemption, the exemption continues as long as the property remains in the trust. A GSTT-exempt trust remains GSTT-exempt, no matter how long the trust lasts and no matter how much its value increases beyond the GSTT-exempt amount. Do perpetual trusts remind you of the ancient but now widely abolished fee tail estate? They should.

Perpetual-Trust States. Twenty-three jurisdictions now allow perpetual trusts by statute: Alaska, Arkansas, Delaware (trusts of personal property), the District of Columbia, Hawaii, Idaho, Illinois, Kentucky, Maine, Maryland, Michigan (trusts of personal property), Missouri, Nebraska, New Hampshire, New Jersey, North

---

38. At the 14th generation below the transferor, the genetic overlap is about 0.0061%, which—due to our common origins—is about the same overlap one has to any randomly selected member of the population. See John H. Beckstrom, above note 37, at 233, citing Richard Dawkins, The Selfish Gene 100 (1976).

Carolina, Ohio, Oklahoma, Pennsylvania, Rhode Island, South Dakota, Virginia (trusts of personal property), and Wisconsin. However, of these, Arkansas, North Carolina, and Oklahoma also have constitutional prohibitions on perpetuities.

Multiple-centuries trust states: Sixteen jurisdictions now allow trusts to last for a century or more: Alabama (360 years), Alaska (1,000 years for the exercise or termination of a nongeneral power of appointment), Arizona (500 years), Colorado (1,000 years), Connecticut (800 years), Delaware (110 years for trusts of real property), Florida (1,000 years), Georgia (360 years), Michigan (360 years for trusts of real property), Mississippi (360 years), Nevada (365 years), Tennessee (360 years), Texas (300 years), Utah (1,000) years, Washington (150 years), and Wyoming (1,000 years). See also the U.K. Perpetuities and Accumulations Act 2009 (125 years).

Opt-Out States: Nine of the perpetual-trust or near-perpetual-trust jurisdictions transform the Rule Against Perpetuities into a default rule. Settlors can opt out, but they have to do so expressly. The opt-out jurisdictions are the District of Columbia, Illinois, Maine, Maryland, Nebraska, New Hampshire, Ohio, Virginia, and Wyoming. Would the failure of a lawyer to insert an opt-out clause constitute malpractice?

The function of a default rule (rule of construction) is to carry out intent. The Rule Against Perpetuities is a mandatory rule of law that defeats intent on grounds of public policy. Changing an intent-defeating rule into a default rule is dumbfounding. See Restatement 3d of Property §16.3 comment a, discussed in Chapter 16.

Has Allowance of Perpetual Trusts Brought Trust Business into States Allowing Them? An empirical study, using annual reports of institutional trustees to federal banking authorities, found that roughly $100 billion in trust assets had flowed into states allowing perpetual trusts. But the perpetual-trust states that attracted the most trust business were those states—Delaware, Illinois, and South Dakota—that *also* do not tax trust income produced by funds originating from out of state. See Robert H. Sitkoff & Max Schanzenbach, Jurisdictional Competition for Trust Funds: An Empirical Analysis of Perpetuities and Taxes, 115 Yale L.J. 356 (2005). And there is a caution about the $100 billion figure: that figure does *not* represent the value of perpetual trusts. It appears that settlors create perpetual trusts up to the GSTT exemption limit and also move the bulk of their wealth into non-perpetual trusts with the same trustee. The data did not allow the authors to distinguish between perpetual trusts and non-perpetual trusts.

Sample Dispositive Provisions of a Perpetual Trust. Richard Nenno, the Managing Director and Trust Counsel of the Wilmington Trust Company, gives the following sample dispositive provisions for an irrevocable inter vivos perpetual trust of personal property established under Delaware law:[39]

---

39. Richard W. Nenno, Delaware Trusts 2009 225-227 (2009).

<u>SECTION 1: DISTRIBUTION</u>

A. <u>Division of Assets</u>. Trustee shall divide assets contributed to this trust, from time to time, into shares for Trustor's then living issue, per stirpes, and administer and distribute such shares according to the provisions of Subsection B of this Section 1. Any share set aside for an issue of Trustor for whose benefit a share is then held in trust under the provisions of Subsection B shall be distributed to the Trustee of such share, to be added to its principal and disposed of as a part of it.

B. <u>Shares Held for Issue</u>. Trustee shall hold each share set aside for an issue of Trustor in further trust for such issue, referred to hereafter in this Subsection B as the "beneficiary."

(1) <u>During the Beneficiary's Life</u>. During the beneficiary's life, Trustee may, from time to time, distribute to the beneficiary and his or her issue all, some, or none of the net income and/or principal as Trustee, it its sole discretion, deems appropriate, after taking account of all other sources of funds available to them. Trustee shall accumulate any net income not so distributed and add it to principal, to be disposed of as a part of it. No such distribution shall be deemed to be an advancement, and no such distribution shall be made that would discharge the beneficiary's legal obligations to support any of such issue.

(2) <u>On the Death of the Beneficiary</u>. On the death of the beneficiary, Trustee shall distribute so much of the beneficiary's share as is then held hereunder, free from this trust, to such of Trustor's issue (other than the beneficiary) and the spouses of such issue (including the beneficiary's spouse), in such manner and amounts, and on such terms, whether in trust or otherwise, as is effectively appointed by specific reference hereto in the last written instrument which the beneficiary executes and delivers to Trustee during his or her lifetime, or, failing any such instrument, in his or her Will. However, the beneficiary may not appoint any more than an income interest to his or her spouse or to a spouse of any other issue of Trustor. Before the beneficiary exercises this limited power of appointment, he or she should consider Section 2041(a)(3) of the [Internal Revenue] Code and 25 Delaware Code Section 501, as amended, or any corresponding Delaware statute enacted after the date of this agreement.

On the death of the beneficiary, Trustee shall divide the balance of the beneficiary's share, to the extent not effectively appointed, into further shares for his or her then living issue, per stirpes, but if no such issue is then living, then for the then living issue, per stirpes, of the closest ascendant of the beneficiary who was an issue of Trustor and who has then living issue, but if no such issue is then living, then for Trustor's then living issue, per stirpes. Trustee shall hold each share set aside pursuant to the preceding sentence in further trust under the provisions of this Subsection B. Any share set aside for an issue of Trustor for whose benefit a share is then held in trust under the provisions of this Subsection B shall be distributed to the trustee of such share, to be added to its principal and disposed of as a part of it.

C. <u>Perpetuities Savings Clause</u>. Notwithstanding the foregoing provisions, unless sooner terminated in the manner previously provided, each trust held hereunder shall end in its entirety or with respect to certain of its assets on the date required by the Delaware rule against perpetuities. Thereupon, Trustee shall distribute the principal of such trust or such assets, as the case may be, free of trust, to the beneficiary for whom the trust was set aside.

D. <u>Failure of Issue</u>. If at any time Trustee holds any portion of the principal of the trust fund not disposed of effectively under the previous provisions, then, at such time, Trustee shall distribute such principal, free from trust, to such then living person or persons as are then determined to be Trustor's distributees by the application of the intestacy laws of the State of Delaware governing the distribution of intestate personal property then in effect, as though Trustor had died at that particular time, intestate, a resident of the State of Delaware and owning such property then so distributable.

Geometric Explosion of Descendant-Beneficiaries. Government statistics indicate that the average married couple has about two children. If we assume that two children and four grandchildren are living at the settlor's death, that the interval between generations is 25 years, that three generations of descendants are living at any particular time, and that the settlor and each member of the senior descendant generation dies at age 75, the following projections can be made. The average settlor will have about 450 descendants (who are beneficiaries of the trust) 150 years after the trust is created,[40] over 7,000 beneficiaries 250 years after the trust is created,[41] and about 114,500 beneficiaries 350 years after the trust is created.[42] Four hundred and fifty years after the trust is created, the number of living beneficiaries could rise to 1.8 million.[43] According to a study by the New England Historic Genealogical Society, President Barack Obama shares a common ancestor with former President George W. Bush (Samuel Hinckley, who died in Barnstable, Massachusetts in 1662) and with former Vice President Richard Cheney (Maureen Duvall, who died in Maryland in 1694).[44]

---

40. The youngest beneficiaries of the trust would then be in the 8th generation below the settlor. The genetic overlap between the settlor and that generation is 0.39%.

In Jesse Dukeminier & James E. Krier, The Rise of the Perpetual Trust, 50 U.C.L.A. L. Rev. 1303, 1339 (2003), the authors greatly underestimate the growth of the number of beneficiaries. They say that there will only be 16 beneficiaries after 100 years. Like our projection in the text above, they assume two children per family. Under that assumption, the only way that such a trust could only have 16 beneficiaries after 100 years—we assume they mean 100 years after the settlor's death—would be if they only count the senior generation. Actually, three or more generations of descendants are likely to be living at the same time, *all* of whom are permissible recipients of income and/or corpus, which makes them beneficiaries of the trust. See Subsection B(1) of the Wilmington Trust form above. Consequently, 100 years after the settlor's death, there are likely to be at least 16 living members of the senior generation, 32 living members of the middle generation, and 64 living members of the junior generation—112 beneficiaries in all.

41. The youngest beneficiaries of the trust would then be in the 12th generation below the settlor. The genetic overlap between the settlor and that generation is 0.02%.

42. The youngest beneficiaries of the trust would then be in the 16th generation below the settlor. The genetic overlap between the settlor and that generation is 0.015%.

43. The youngest beneficiaries of the trust would then be in the 20th generation below the settlor. The genetic overlap between the settlor and that generation is 0.00009%.

44. See www.americanancestors.org.

Capital Appreciation. Will the explosive growth of beneficiaries outpace the growth of the trust portfolio? The likely answer is yes. Over time, the inflation-adjusted appreciation of stocks occurs primarily from reinvestment of dividends, not from price appreciation. See Jeremy J. Siegel, The Future for Investors 126 (2005). Assuming that all of a trust's income is distributed, Professor Siegel's research shows an inflation-adjusted annual compound growth rate of the underlying corpus of a portfolio composed wholly of stocks of only 4.25%. No prudent trustee, however, would put all of the trust's assets into stocks. A more likely asset mix might be 60% stocks and 40% bonds. If the bonds are held to maturity, they will be a considerable drag on the growth rate of the corpus. The annual trustee fees taken out of the corpus also will constitute a drag on the potential capital appreciation of the trust portfolio.

For an article arguing that "[t]he impact of inflation, rising expectations, and, in most cases, a growing pool of living descendants will soon outstrip the ability of... [a dynasty] trust to provide for descendants in the lifestyle to which they are likely to have become accustomed," see William J. Turnier & Jeffrey L. Harrison, A Malthusian Analysis of the So-Called Dynasty Trust, 28 Va. Tax. Rev. 779 (2009).

Are Perpetual Trusts Good Policy? Consider the following argument that perpetual trusts are not against public policy:

> Many states now allow people to create private trusts of unlimited duration. Is it unjust or poor social policy to allow settlors to benefit future people without time limits on trusts? Although perpetual trusts may be self-indulgent impositions on posterity, no leading theory of distributive justice seems to bar their creation. So long as trustees are empowered to sell and determine the use of trust property, utilitarian and other consequentialist theories suggest that the availability of perpetual trusts offers more social advantages than drawbacks, though some would subject trust accumulations or distributions to redistributive taxes aimed at helping the less fortunate. Not surprisingly, libertarian theories would give donors the freedom to create temporally unlimited trusts as well. Less obviously, liberal egalitarian theories probably should permit people to create perpetual trusts, provided that trust property remains alienable by trustees and that certain benefits are taxed so that the less lucky may share in the good fortune of trust beneficiaries.

Eric Rakowski, The Future Reach of the Disembodied Will, 4 Pol., Phil. & Econ. 91 (2005).

The American Law Institute disagrees. See Part G, below.

EXTERNAL REFERENCES ON PERPETUAL TRUSTS. Lawrence W. Waggoner, Congress Promotes Perpetual Trusts: Why?, University of Michigan Law School Working Paper Series (no. 349), available at http://ssrn.com/abstract=2326524 (2013); Lawrence W. Waggoner, From Here to Eternity: The Folly of Perpetual Trusts, University of Michigan Law School Working Paper Series (no. 259), available at http://ssrn.com/abstract=1975117 (2012); Michael Vincent, Computer-Managed

Perpetual Trusts, 51 Jurimetrics 399 (2011); Robert H. Sitkoff & Max Schanzenbach, Jurisdictional Competition for Trust Funds: An Empirical Analysis of Perpetuities and Taxes, 115 Yale L.J. 356 (2005); Joshua Tate, Perpetual Trusts and the Settlor's Intent, 53 U. Kan. L. Rev. 595 (2005); Stewart E. Sterk, Jurisdictional Competition to Abolish the Rule Against Perpetuities: R.I.P. for the R.A.P., 24 Cardozo L. Rev. 2097 (2003); Jesse Dukeminier & James E. Krier, The Rise of the Perpetual Trust, 50 UCLA L. Rev. 1303 (2003).

PART G. THE RESTATEMENT THIRD OF PROPERTY

In 2011, the American Law Institute published the final chapters of the Restatement 3d of Property, including Chapter 27 on the Rule Against Perpetuities. Chapter 27 contains two innovations.

First, Chapter 27 firmly states, as the official position of the American Law Institute, that the movement to allow perpetual or multiple-centuries trusts is ill advised:

> It is the considered judgment of the American Law Institute that the recent statutory movement allowing the creation of perpetual or near-perpetual trusts is ill advised. The movement to abrogate the Rule Against Perpetuities has not been based on the merits of removing the Rule's curb on excessive dead-hand control. The policy issues associated with allowing perpetual or near-perpetual trusts has not been seriously discussed in the state legislatures. The driving force has been the effort to compete for the trust industry (financial services) business from other states.
>
> A rule that curbs excessive dead-hand control is deeply rooted in this nation's history and tradition, and for good reason. A 360-year trust created in the year 2010 could endure until the year 2370 and have over 100,000 beneficiaries. A 1000-year trust created in 2010 could terminate in the year 3010 and have millions of beneficiaries. No transferor has enough wisdom to make sound dispositions of property across such vast intervals and for beneficiaries so remote and so numerous. A 1000-year or 360-year trust created in 2010 might incorporate what are currently considered to be flexible provisions for a trust that could last that far into the future. To put that claim into perspective, consider the devices for controlling family wealth through subsequent generations that were available 360 or more years ago, in the year 1650 or earlier. Such devices, drafted before the invention of the typewriter, first took the form of the unbarrable entail and, after the entail became barrable, the strict settlement. These devices became archaic long ago. If that which was considered sophisticated 360 or more years ago is considered primitive today, there is reason to suspect that that which is considered sophisticated today will be considered primitive 360 or more years from now.

Restatement 3d of Property ch. 27, Introductory Note.

Second, Chapter 27 of the Restatement 3d of Property reformulates the Rule Against Perpetuities. The Rule is no longer a rule against the remote vesting of contingent future interests, measured by lives in being. Instead, the Rule concerns the time of the interest's termination. The Rule provides that a trust or other donative disposition of property is subject to judicial modification to the extent that the trust or other disposition does not terminate on or before the expiration of the perpetuity period. The perpetuity period is limited to the lives of individuals no more than two generations younger than the transferor.

For the idea of changing the Rule to require termination on or before the expiration of a perpetuity period, see Daniel M. Schuyler, Should the Rule Against Perpetuities Discard Its Vest?, 56 Mich. L. Rev. 683 (1958); Thomas P. Gallanis, The Future of Future Interests, 60 Wash. & Lee. L. Rev. 513, 559-60 (2003).

Below are excerpts from the Restatement 3d.

Restatement 3d of Property

§27.1 Statement of the Rule Against Perpetuities

(a) A trust or other donative disposition of property is subject to judicial modification under §27.2 to the extent that the trust or other disposition does not terminate on or before the expiration of the perpetuity period, except that if, upon the expiration of the perpetuity period, the share of a beneficiary is distributable upon reaching a specified age and the beneficiary is then younger than the earlier of the specified age or the age of 30, the beneficiary's share may, without judicial modification, be retained in trust until the beneficiary reaches or dies before reaching the earlier of the specified age or the age of 30.

(b) The perpetuity period expires at the death of the last living measuring life. The measuring lives are as follows:

(1) Except as otherwise provided in paragraph (2), the measuring lives constitute a group composed of the following individuals: the transferor, the beneficiaries of the disposition who are related to the transferor and no more than two generations younger than the transferor, and the beneficiaries of the disposition who are unrelated to the transferor and no more than the equivalent of two generations younger than the transferor.

(2) In the case of a trust or other property arrangement for the sole current benefit of a named individual who is more than two generations younger than the transferor or more than the equivalent of two generations younger than the transferor, the measuring life is the named individual.

....

[Comment] b. Generations-based perpetuity period: rationale....

A generations-based perpetuity period is more responsive to the purposes of the Rule than one based on lives in being, because the generational approach produces a period that self-adjusts to the individual trust and family circumstances and hence imposes a more tailored outer limit on dead-hand control....

[Comment] e(2). Adopted child. With one exception (see below), an adoptee is assigned to the generation immediately below the adoptive parent's generation....

The one exception... arises in the case in which, before the adoption, the adoptee was a descendant of the transferor or a descendant of an ancestor of the transferor. In that case, the adoption does not cause the adoptee to be reassigned to a higher generation than his or her previous assignment....

[Comment] e(3). Child of assisted reproduction. A child of assisted reproduction is assigned to the generation immediately below the child's parent....

[Comment] e(4). Spouse or domestic partner. A spouse or domestic partner or surviving spouse or surviving domestic partner of the transferor or of a relative of the transferor is treated as related to the transferor and is assigned to the same generation as his or her spouse or domestic partner.... Divorce, dissolution of the partnership, or death does not cause the former spouse or domestic partner to be removed from the list of measuring lives, unless the divorce, dissolution, or death causes the former spouse or former domestic partner to cease being a beneficiary.

[Comment] f. Beneficiaries who are unrelated to the transferor who can be subsection (b)(1) measuring lives.... This Restatement follows the federal generation-skipping transfer tax (GST tax) to determine whether an unrelated beneficiary is no more than the equivalent of two generations younger than the transferor. Currently, the GST tax assigns an unrelated beneficiary on the basis of the age difference between the beneficiary and the transferor. IRC §2651(d) provides that such an individual is "assigned to a generation on the basis of the date of such individual's birth with—(1) an individual born not more than 12½ years after the date of the birth of the transferor assigned to the transferor's generation, (2) an individual born more than 12½ years but not more than 37½ years after the date of the birth of the transferor assigned to the first generation younger than the transferor, and (3) similar rules for a new generation every 25 years."...

§27.2 Judicial Modification

Upon the petition of an interested person, the court shall modify a disposition that is subject to judicial modification under §27.1(a). The form of the modification must be in a manner that most closely approximates the transferor's manifested plan of distribution and is within the perpetuity period provided in §27.1(b).

Problems

Analyze the following dispositions under the common-law Rule Against Perpetuities and under the Rule as reformulated in the Restatement 3d of Property.

1. G died, leaving a will that devised property in trust, directing the trustee to pay the income "to my son S for life, then to S's children from time to time living for the life of the survivor, and on the death of S's last surviving child, to distribute the trust

principal to S's then living descendants." G was survived by S and by S's two children, X and Y. After G's death, S had another child, Z. S, X, and Y are now dead, survived by Z.

2. G died, leaving a will that devised property in trust, directing the trustee to pay the income "to my nephew N for life, then to N's surviving spouse for life, and upon the death of N's surviving spouse, to pay the trust principal to N's then living descendants by representation." G was survived by N and by N's wife, W1. Thirty years after G's death, W1 died, and then N married W2. Then N and W2 had a daughter, X. Later, N died, survived by W2 and X. Later still, W2 died, survived by X.

3. G died, leaving a will that devised property in trust, directing the trustee to pay the income "to my daughter D for life, then to D's children from time to time living for the life of the survivor, and on the death of D's last surviving child, to distribute the trust principal to D's grandchildren who reach the age of 30." At G's death, D had one child, C1. After G's death, D had a second child, C2. Then D died, followed later by C1, who died without issue. C2 has now died, survived by a daughter, GC1, who is age 15.

4. G died, leaving a will that devised property in trust, directing the trustee to distribute the income at the trustee's discretion among G's descendants from time to time living. The terms of the trust require the trust to terminate when G no longer has any living descendants. On termination of the trust, the trustee is directed to distribute the trust principal to a specified charity. At G's death, G had two adult children, C1 and C2, four adult grandchildren, GC1, GC2, GC3, and GC4, and two minor great-grandchildren, GGC1 and GGC2. No grandchildren of G were born or adopted after G's death. G's grandchildren died in numerical order—GC1, then GC2, then GC3, and then GC4. At GC4's death (at age 88), G had 50 living descendants: eight great-grandchildren, 16 great-great-grandchildren, and 26 great-great-great grandchildren.

EXTERNAL REFERENCES. Lawrence W. Waggoner, The Case for Curtailing Dead-Hand Control: The American Law Institute Declares the Perpetual-Trust Movement Ill Advised, University of Michigan Law School Working Paper Series (no. 199), available at http://ssrn.com/abstract=1614934 (2010); Lawrence W. Waggoner, The American Law Institute Proposes a New Approach to Perpetuities: Limiting the Dead Hand to Two Younger Generations, University of Michigan Law School Working Paper Series (no. 200), available at http://ssrn.com/abstract=1614936 (2010).

PART H. THE RULE AGAINST PERPETUITIES: SPECIAL APPLICATIONS AND EXCLUSIONS

1. Class Gifts

a. General Rule: "All or Nothing"

Under the traditional Rule Against Perpetuities, a class gift stands or falls as a whole. This all-or-nothing rule, usually attributed to Leake v. Robinson, 2 Mer. 363, 35 Eng. Rep. 979 (Ch. 1817), is commonly stated as follows:

> *If the interest of any potential class member might vest "too remotely," the entire class gift is invalid.*

The following three examples illustrate the all-or-nothing rule: Example 17.12 illustrates a class gift that is invalid because it is subject to decrease "too long," Example 17.13 illustrates a class gift that is invalid because it is subject to increase "too long," and Example 17.14 illustrates a class gift that is invalid because it is subject to both increase and decrease "too long."

Example 17.12: G devised real property "to my son A for life, then to such of A's children as reach age 25." G was survived by A and by A's two children, V and X. V had reached 25 at G's death, but X was under 25.

The class gift in favor of A's children is invalid. There is no validating life because the membership of the class might decrease, though not increase, beyond 21 years after the death of A, V, X, and anyone else who was in being at G's death.

Example 17.13: G devised property in trust, directing the trustee to pay the net income therefrom "to my daughter A for life, then to A's children for the life of the survivor, and upon the death of A's last surviving child to pay the corpus of the trust to A's grandchildren." G was survived by A and by A's two children, V and X.

The remainder interest in the corpus in favor of A's grandchildren is invalid. There is no validating life because the membership of the class might increase, though not decrease, beyond 21 years after the death of A, V, X, and any one else who was in being at G's death you might care to propose.

Example 17.14: Same facts and disposition as the above example, except that the remainder upon the death of A's last surviving child was in favor of "A's then-living grandchildren."

The remainder interest in the corpus in favor of A's grandchildren is invalid. The class might increase "too long" and, due to the addition of the condition precedent of survival of A's last surviving child, it might also decrease "too long."

Class Gifts under Wait-and-See. The above discussion relates to the treatment of class gifts under the common-law Rule Against Perpetuities, under which the

Ch. 17. The Rule Against Perpetuities and Related Rules

requirement of initial certainty still reigns. As for the all-or-nothing rule itself, perpetuity reformers have not seen fit to change it. The rule is not reversed in the USRAP, for example. The sting of the all-or-nothing rule, however, is substantially eliminated by the application of the wait-and-see element. See USRAP §1 comment Part G.

Consider how the above examples would be treated under the wait-and-see element of USRAP (UPC §2-901(a)(2)). If you posit G's death at around age 75, you will see that it is extremely unlikely that the class gift in Example 17.12 will decrease beyond the 90-year permissible-vesting period after G's death. You will also see that the class gift in Example 17.13 is unlikely to increase beyond the 90-year period, and the class gift in Example 17.14 is unlikely to increase or decrease beyond that period. Should the unlikely happen in any of these cases, G's disposition would become subject to reformation under USRAP §3 (UPC §2-903), the application of which is explained and illustrated in the official comment to §3.

Class Gifts under the Restatement 3d of Property. The Reporter's Notes to the Restatement 3d of Property observe: "Because the Rule as adopted in this Restatement focuses on when a trust or other donative disposition of property terminates, and no longer focuses on the validity or invalidity of individual future interests, the all-or-nothing rule [of class gifts] and the specific-sum and sub-class subsidiary doctrines [discussed below] are no longer relevant." Restatement 3d §27.1, Reporter's Note 9.

b. Gifts to Subclasses; Specific-Sum Class Gifts

Two types of class gifts are exempt from the all-or-nothing rule: (1) specific-sum class gifts and (2) gifts to sub-classes. These special types of class gifts are exempt because the underlying rationale of the all-or-nothing rule does not apply to them. In both cases, the interest of each taker (or group of takers) is *expressly* separated by the transferor, and the share of each taker (or group of takers) is, or is certain to become within a life in being plus 21 years, unaffected by the total number of takers (or the total number of groups of takers).

The significance of exempting these two types of class gifts from the all-or-nothing rule is that each class member's or sub-class's interest can be judged separately. Thus, under the common-law Rule, some class members or sub-classes can have valid interests even though other class members or sub-classes have invalid interests. Under the USRAP, the class members or sub-classes that would have valid interests under the common-law Rule are valid and the class members or sub-classes that would have invalid interests under the common-law Rule are valid if they vest within 90 years.

Specific-Sum Class Gifts. The all-or-nothing rule does not apply to specific-sum class gifts—class gifts that give a specific sum of money to each class member. Specific-sum class gifts are to be distinguished from conventional class gifts, under which a sum of money or item of property is to be divided proportionally among however many members of the class there turn out to be. See Restatement 3d of Property §13.1 comment *l*. The specific-sum exemption was established in Storrs v. Benbow, 43 Eng. Rep. 153 (Ch. 1853), and has been followed in this country. See Restatement of Property §385; Simes & Smith on Future Interests §1266.

Example 17.15: G bequeathed "$10,000 to each child of my son, A, born before or after my death, who lives to age 25." G was survived by A and by A's two children, X and Y. X but not Y had already reached 25 at G's death.

If the phrase "born before or after my death" had been omitted, the rule of convenience would close the class at G's death, and the entire gift would have been valid even if the all-or-nothing rule applied. The inclusion of the "before-or-after" phrase, however, means that G intended to include afterborn children.

At common law, the interests of the afterborn children are invalid, but the interests of X and Y are valid because they were living at G's death. The interest of X, the child who already had reached 25 on G's death, is valid because it is vested. The interest of Y, the other child, is valid because Y himself is his own validating life.

Under the USRAP, as at common law, the interests of X and Y are valid. The USRAP also saves the interests of all of A's children, born (or adopted) before or after G's death, who reach 25 within the 90-year period following G's death, which would undoubtedly include all of A's children who reach 25. Should any of A's children be alive and under 25 at the expiration of 90 years (a very unlikely possibility), the interest of that child can be reformed to make it vest at the 90-year mark.

Under the generations-based Rule of the Restatement 3d of Property §27.1, all of the devises are valid. See Restatement 3d of Property §27.1, Reporter's Note 9.

The rationale for separate treatment was explained by the Lord Chancellor in Storrs v. Benbow:

> It would be a mistake to compare [specific-sum class gifts] with [conventional class gifts], for the difficulty which [arises with respect to conventional class gifts] as to giving it to some and not giving it to others does not apply here. The question of whether or not the... after-born [children] shall or shall not take, has no bearing at all upon the question of whether... an existing [child] takes: the legacy given to him cannot be bad because there is a legacy given under a similar description to a person who would not be able to take because the gift would be too remote.

The justification for separate treatment emerging from this quotation is that: (1) the interest of each child was *expressly* separated from the interests of the other children; and (2) no child had a contingent interest in the share of any other child.

Gifts to Sub-Classes. For similar reasons, the all-or-nothing rule does not apply to gifts to sub-classes. This exemption is sometimes labeled the *doctrine of vertical separability*. In order for this exemption to apply, two requirements must be met: (1) the takers must be described as a group of sub-classes; and (2) the share going to each sub-class must be certain to be finalized within a life in being plus 21 years. The sub-class exemption is derived from Cattlin v. Brown, 68 Eng. Rep. 1319 (Ch. 1853), and is followed in this country. See, e.g., Estate of Coates, 652 A.2d 331 (Pa. 1994); Restatement of Property §389.

Example 17.16: G devised property in trust, directing the trustee to pay the income "to my son A for life, then in equal shares to A's children for their respective lives; on the death of each child, the proportionate share of corpus of the one so dying shall go to the children of such child." G was survived by A and by A's two children, X and Y. After G's death, another child (Z) was born to A. A has now died survived by X, Y, and Z.

Both of the requirements of the sub-class rule are met. The takers are described as a group of sub-classes rather than as a single class: "children of the child so dying," as opposed to "grandchildren." The share going to each sub-class is certain to be finalized within a life in being plus 21 years: As of A's death, who is a life "in being," it is certain to be known how many children she had surviving her; since in fact there were three surviving children, each sub-class's share is one-third of the corpus, neither more nor less.

At common law, the remainder in X's children and the remainder in Y's children are valid. X is the validating life for the one, Y for the other. The remainder in Z's children, however, is invalid. Z was not a life "in being," and he could have children more than 21 years after the deaths of A, X, and Y.

In a case like this, where there was an afterborn child (Z), a court might apply the doctrine of infectious invalidity to invalidate the remainders in the children of X and Y. To do so would probably better carry out G's overall intent. See Estate of Morton, 312 A.2d 26 (Pa. 1973); Restatement of Property §389 comment f.

Under the USRAP, as at common law, the remainders in X's children and in Y's children are valid. The USRAP almost certainly saves the remainder in Z's children also. If Z dies within the 90-year period following G's death, which is very likely, the remainder in Z's children is valid. Even if Z outlives the 90-year period, the interest of Z's children can be reformed to close the class and vest the interest in Z's children who are living at the 90-year mark.

Under the generations-based Rule of the Restatement 3d of Property §27.1, all of the class gifts are valid. See Restatement 3d of Property §27.1, Reporter's Note 9.

The rationale for separate treatment of the share of each sub-class is the same as that which supports the specific-sum exemption. The basis in Cattlin v. Brown for distinguishing Leake v. Robinson was stated by the Vice-Chancellor as follows:

[This case] is in reality the case of Storrs v. Benbow, substituting a given share for a given sum of money... [It] is free from the difficulty which [arose in Leake v. Robinson].... [N]o person out of the prescribed limits [i.e., beyond a life in being plus 21 years] could possibly take the whole of [X's] or [Y's] share, and the exact amount of each share is finally ascertained within the legal limits; and from the time that it is so ascertained no party without the legal period can possibly acquire the least interest in it, so as to divest or diminish it; nor can any party whose interest is so ascertained within the period... acquire any interest in the shares of such other parties so as to augment it.

In other words, the interests of the members of each sub-class were *expressly* separated from the interests of the members of the other sub-classes; and, no sub-class had a contingent interest in the share of any other sub-class that might vest beyond a life in being plus 21 years.

Example 17.16, above, is a typical sub-class case: possession was to occur as each child died. This feature—possession of a proportionate share of corpus occurring as each income beneficiary dies—is characteristic of a sub-class case. Such a disposition falls rather naturally into compliance with the first requirement of the sub-class rule: The takers are virtually forced into being described as a group of sub-classes. And, as long as the preceding income interests are valid—i.e. they are created in a class that cannot increase or decrease beyond a life in being plus 21 years—and as long as the amount of corpus going to each sub-class is certain to be finalized within a life in being plus 21 years, then the second requirement will also be met.

2. Powers of Appointment

Primary Statutory References: *UPC §§2-901(b), (c) (USRAP §§1(b), (c))*

If a power of appointment violates the Rule Against Perpetuities, the power is invalid, and the disposition takes effect as if the power had never been created. If the power itself is valid, some or all of the interests created by its exercise may violate the Rule and be invalid.

a. General Powers Presently Exercisable

Validity of the Power at Common Law. Under the common-law Rule, a general power that is presently exercisable is treated as the equivalent of a *vested* property interest and therefore is not subject to the Rule Against Perpetuities.

If the exercisability of a general power is subject to a condition precedent, the power is treated as the equivalent of a *contingent* property interest for purposes of the common-law Rule. Although a mouthful, this type of power might be called a *general power not presently exercisable because of a condition precedent.* This is the term used in USRAP §1(b) (UPC §2-901(b)). The term signifies that once the condition precedent is satisfied, the power becomes presently exercisable. (Note that a power of appointment expires on the powerholder's death. A deferral of a power's exercisability until a future time (even a time certain), therefore, imposes a condition precedent on the power's exercisability—the condition precedent being that the powerholder must be alive at that future time.)

A general power not presently exercisable because of a condition precedent must satisfy the requirement of initial certainty. This requires a certainty, when the power is created, that the *condition precedent* to its exercise will be resolved one way or the other no later than 21 years after the death of an individual then alive.

Consequently, although (as we shall see) neither a nongeneral power nor a testamentary power can be conferred on an unborn person (unless some special restriction is imposed on it forbidding its exercise beyond a life in being plus 21 years), an unborn person can be the recipient of a valid general power that becomes presently exercisable upon the powerholder's birth. To be valid, the powerholder's birth must be certain to occur, if at all, within a life in being plus 21 years.

Example 17.17: G devised real property "to my son A for life, then to A's first born child for life, then to such persons as A's first born child shall appoint." G is survived by A, who is childless.

The general power conferred on A's first born child is valid. The condition precedent—that A have a child—is certain to be resolved one way or the other within A's lifetime; A is the validating life. If, however, the relevant language had been "then to such persons as A's first born child shall appoint after reaching the age of 25," the additional contingency of reaching 25 would have invalidated the general power, at common law.

Validity of the Power under Wait-and-See. Under the USRAP, the validity of powers of appointment is governed by §§1(b) and (c).[45] Under §1(b)(1), a general power of appointment not exercisable because of a condition precedent is initially valid if it satisfies the requirement of initial certainty. If the requirement of initial certainty is not satisfied, the power is not automatically invalid but instead is subject to the wait-and-see element contained in §1(b)(2). The power is valid if the condition precedent actually occurs within the 90-year period; if it does not, the disposition is subject to reformation under §3.

Validity of the Power under the Restatement 3d of Property. Under the terminology of §27.1 of the Restatement 3d of Property, the holder of a power of appointment—whether general or nongeneral, presently exercisable or testamentary—is a "beneficiary" of a "donative disposition of property." See Restatement 3d of Property §27.1 comment d(2). Accordingly, the power of appointment is subject to judicial modification under §27.2 if it does not terminate on or before the expiration of the generations-based perpetuity period in §27.1(b).

We now turn from the validity of the power itself to the validity of the *exercise* of the power.

Validity of the Exercise at Common Law. In determining the validity of an exercise of a general power presently exercisable, the power is treated as the equivalent of ownership of the property subject to the power. Accordingly, the powerholder is considered to have created the appointed interests. An exercise is treated as if the powerholder first exercised the power in his or her own favor and then created the appointed interests out of the owned property. Consequently the appointed interests are created, for purposes of the common-law Rule, when the

---

45. A general power presently exercisable is not subject to the USRAP.

exercise of the power becomes effective, with the possibility of postponement in certain cases under the principles outlined above at pp. 939-940.

Example 17.18: G was the life income beneficiary of a trust and the holder of a presently exercisable general power over the succeeding remainder interest. G exercised the power by deed, directing the trustee after her death to pay the income to G's children in equal shares for the life of the survivor, and upon the death of her last surviving child to pay the corpus of the trust to her grandchildren.

The validity of the appointed interests depends on whether or not G's appointment was irrevocable. If it was irrevocable, the remainder interest in favor of G's grandchildren is invalid. The appointed interests were created when the deed was delivered or otherwise became effective. If G reserved a power to revoke her appointment, the remainder interest is valid. The appointed interests are created at G's death.

Validity of the Exercise under Wait-and-See. The only change under the USRAP is that an exercise that would have been invalid at common law is not initially invalid but instead is subject to the wait-and-see element of the USRAP. The 90-year period applies in determining the validity of appointed interests that would have been invalid at common law.

Validity of the Exercise under the Restatement 3d of Property. Following the approach at common law, the Restatement 3d of Property treats the powerholder who exercises a general power presently exerciseable as the "transferor." See Restatement 3d of Property §27.1 comment j(1). Under the Restatement 3d, then, the trust or other donative disposition created by the exercise of the general power presently exercisable is subject to judicial modification under §27.2 if the trust or other donative disposition does not terminate on or before the expiration of the generations-based perpetuity period in §27.1(b).

b. Nongeneral Powers and Testamentary Powers

Validity of the Power at Common Law. A nongeneral power (whether testamentary or presently exercisable) or a general testamentary power is invalid under the common-law Rule Against Perpetuities if, when the power is created, it is possible for the power to be *exercised* later than 21 years after the death of an individual then alive.

Example 17.19: (1) G devised real property "to my daughter A for life, then to A's first born child for life, then to such persons as A's first born child shall by will appoint;" or

(2) G devised real property "to my daughter A for life, then to A's first born child for life, then to such of A's grandchildren as A's first born child shall appoint."

G is survived by A, who is childless.

The power of appointment conferred on A's first born child—a general testamentary power in Case (1), a nongeneral power presently exercisable in Case (2)—is invalid. The latest possible time of exercise is at the death of A's first born child, who cannot be the validating life because that child was not "in being" at the creation of the power.

The lesson is that a nongeneral or testamentary power conferred on an unborn person is invalid.

Validity of the Power under Wait-and-See. A nongeneral power (whether testamentary or presently exercisable) or a general testamentary power is invalid under the USRAP unless (i) when the power was created, it is certain to be irrevocably exercised or otherwise to terminate no later than 21 years after the death of an individual then alive, or (ii) the power is irrevocably exercised or otherwise terminates within 90 years after its creation.

Validity of the Power under the Restatement 3d of Property. Under the terminology of §27.1 of the Restatement 3d of Property, the holder of a power of appointment—whether general or nongeneral, presently exercisable or testamentary—is a "beneficiary" of a "donative disposition of property." See Restatement 3d of Property §27.1 comment d(2). Accordingly, the power of appointment is subject to judicial modification under §27.2 if it does not terminate on or before the expiration of the generations-based perpetuity period in §27.1(b).

Problems

G devised property in trust, directing the trustee to pay the income "to my daughter D for life, then in equal shares to D's children for their respective lives; on the death of each child, the proportionate share of corpus of the one so dying shall go to such persons as the one so dying shall by will appoint." G was survived by D and D's two children, X and Y. After G's death, another child (Z) was born to D.

1. Are the powers conferred on D's children valid under the common-law Rule? See Restatement of Property §390 comment f; Am. L. Prop. §24.32; J.H.C. Morris & W. Barton Leach, The Rule Against Perpetuities 141-42 (2d ed. 1962). Cf. Slark v. Dakyns, L.R. 10 Ch. App. 35 (C.A. 1874). But see Camden Safe Deposit & Trust Co. v. Scott, 189 A. 653 (N.J. 1937); Re Phillips, 11 D.L.R. 500 (Ont. 1913).

2. How would the situation be treated under the USRAP? Assume that Z was born five years after G's death and that Z died at age 75, leaving a will that purported to exercise Z's power of appointment. See USRAP §1 comment part H, ex. 25.

3. How would the situation be treated under the Rule as reformulated in the Restatement 3d of Property?

———

Fiduciary Powers. A distributive power held by a fiduciary is a nongeneral power of appointment for purposes of the Rule Against Perpetuities. Distributive fiduciary powers include a trustee's power to invade the corpus of the trust for the benefit of the income beneficiary or a trustee's power to accumulate the income or pay it out or to spray it among a group of beneficiaries.

A purely administrative fiduciary power is not subject to the Rule Against Perpetuities.

Problem

G devised property in trust, directing the trustee to pay the income to G's son S for life, then to S's children for the life of the survivor, and on the death of S's last surviving child to pay the corpus to B. The trustee is granted the discretionary power to sell and reinvest the trust assets and to invade the corpus of the trust on behalf of the income beneficiary or beneficiaries. G was survived by S and by S's two children, X and Y.

Consider the validity of the trustee's fiduciary powers, first under the common-law Rule, then under the USRAP, and finally under the Rule as reformulated in the Restatement 3d of Property.

———

Validity of the Exercise—Nongeneral and Testamentary Powers. If a nongeneral or testamentary power passes the appropriate test for validity as set forth above, it can validly be exercised. Whether or not such a power has *in fact* been validly exercised is the next question.

For the most part, the Rule Against Perpetuities applies to appointed interests (and appointed powers) in the same way it applies to interests (and powers) created by an owner of property. At common law, the requirement of initial certainty applies. Under the USRAP, interests (or powers) that do not satisfy the requirement of initial certainty and are therefore not validated by §1(a)(1) (or, in the case of appointed powers, §§1(b)(1) or 1(c)(1)), are entitled to a 90-year period to determine their validity. See USRAP §1(a)(2), (b)(2), (c)(2) (UPC § 2-901(a)(2), (b)(2), (c)(2)). Under the Rule as reformulated in the Restatement 3d of Property, the donor of the nongeneral or testamentary power is treated as the "transferor" of the trust or other donative disposition created by the exercise of the power. (If the trust or other donative disposition was created by a nongeneral or testamentary power that was itself created by the exercise of a nongeneral or testamentary power, the "transferor" is the donor of the first power.) See Restatement 3d of Property §27.1 comment j(3). The generations-based Rule of the Restatement 3d of Property §27.1 then applies.

Problem

Consider the validity of the powers in the following case, first under the common-law Rule, then under USRAP, and finally under the Rule as reformulated in the Restatement 3d of Property.

G's will devised property in trust, directing the trustee to pay the income to G's son S for life, then to such of S's descendants as S may by will appoint. S died with a will exercising the power of appointment by providing that the trust is to continue beyond S's death, paying the income to S's child X for X's lifetime, then to deliver the trust principal to such person or persons, including X or X's estate, as X may appoint, and in default of appointment to X's descendants who survive X, by representation.

Estate of Bird
225 Cal. App. 2d 196 (1964)

STONE, J. Jeannette Miller Bird and Geoffrey Andrew Bird, her husband, executed their wills simultaneously February 17, 1961.

Jeannette died June 16, 1961, and her will, which was admitted to probate, provided, insofar as here pertinent: "2. This trust shall exist and continue for and during the life of my said husband, GEOFFREY ANDREW BIRD, and shall cease and terminate upon his death. I give and grant to my husband the exclusive power to dispose of the corpus, and undistributed income, under the terms of his Last Will and Testament...."

Geoffrey Bird died just three months later, September 16, 1961. He exercised the power of appointment created by Jeannette's will, by the following provisions in his will:

FIFTH: I will, devise and bequeath to CITIZENS NATIONAL BANK, in trust, all of the rest, residue and remainder of my property of every nature, kind and description, including the property and assets which are included in the Marital Deduction Trust as set forth in my wife's Will, and I do now specifically exercise my power of testamentary disposition by including such assets in this trust.

(a) Said property is to be held by the Trustee for the following purposes:

1. The net income shall be distributed in monthly or other convenient installments to or for the benefit of my said children in equal shares for life....

3. This trust shall terminate on the death of the last survivor of my children and my grandchildren living at the time of my death, and the entire corpus and undistributed net income shall go and be distributed to the children of my grandchildren per capita.

Counsel for both appellant and respondent agree that the matter is one of first impression in California, and they pose two questions: First, whether the period prescribed by the rule against perpetuities... is determined as of the time the power was created, that is, at Jeannette's death, or at Geoffrey's death when the power was exercised. Second, if the time the power is created governs, is the determination made according to the facts existing at the time of creation of the power, or are the circumstances existing at the time the power is exercised, controlling? We hold that the period is counted from the time the power of appointment is created, but that the facts and circumstances are considered as of the time of its exercise. This holding disposes of both questions raised....

Simes and Smith, in their work, The Law of Future Interests, section 1276, page 214, tell us that the common law rule is:

...in determining the validity of an appointment under a special power or a general testamentary power, though the period is counted from the creation of the power, facts and circumstances are considered as of the time of its exercise....

The Restatement of Property adopted the common law rule applicable to general testamentary powers of appointment.... The rule is expressed in section 392 as follows:

> ...an appointment under either a general testamentary power or a special power is invalid, because of the rule against perpetuities, only to the extent that its limitations, (a) construed in the light of the circumstances existent when the power is exercised, but (b) measured, for the purpose of applying the rule against perpetuities, from the time when the power was created, violate that rule.

In commenting upon the rationale of the rule, the Restatement points out that:

> The element of the stated rule embodied in Clause (a), mitigates the destructive effect of the doctrine of "relation back." In applying the rule against perpetuities to the limitations of an attempted appointment made under either a general testamentary power or a special power, no useful end would be served by finding an invalidity because of some possible uncertainty, present when the power was created, but actually and definitively excluded by the course of events which has already occurred and which is known at the time of the exercise of the power. By the part of the rule embodied in Clause (a) the fiction of "relation back" is prevented from having destructive effects greater than those required for the reasonable effectuation of the underlying social policy of the rule against perpetuities.

This is in accord with the liberal approach toward the rule against perpetuities taken by the California Supreme Court in the recent case of Wong v. Di Grazia, 60 A.C. 505, [35 Cal.Rptr. 241, 386 P.2d 817]....

The facts of this case demonstrate the reasonableness of the common law rule embodied in section 392 of the Restatement of Property, supra. By reason of the proximate deaths of Jeannette and Geoffrey, only three months elapsed between creation of the power and its exercise. There was no factual change during that short interval. The lives in being at the time the power was exercised were in being when the power was created, so that the power of appointment did not, in fact, violate the rule against perpetuities. To defeat the purposes and the wishes of Jeannette and Geoffrey because a violation of the rule against perpetuities was theoretically possible, but in fact did not occur, seems to us to be unnecessarily restrictive. It is the sort of rigid mechanistic application of the rule which the Supreme Court decried in Wong v. Di Grazia, supra.

In any event, we find Civil Code section 715.2 and the common law rule to which it refers, controlling. Applying his test, there was no violation of the rule against perpetuities at the time the power of appointment was created, when considered in the light of the facts and circumstances as of the time the power of appointment was exercised.

The judgment is reversed.

Notes and Questions

1. *Supporting Authority.* Taking a "second look" at the facts existing at the date of the exercise of a nongeneral or testamentary power is a well established procedure. See Restatement of Property §392; Am. L. Prop. §24.35.

2. *Second Look for Gifts in Default.* Can a second look at the facts also be taken in determining the validity of a gift in default in cases in which the power is not exercised? Am. L. Prop. §24.36, written by W. Barton Leach and Owen Davies Tudor, supports a second look for gifts in default. Shortly after this treatise was published, this position was adopted in apparently the first American case to consider the question, Sears v. Coolidge, 108 N.E.2d 563 (Mass. 1952). Four years later, Simes & Smith on Future Interests §1276 came out against the decision in *Sears.* Not long after, however, a Canadian court upheld a gift in default by applying the second-look doctrine. See Re Edwards, 20 D.L.R.2d 755 (Ont. 1959). Later, the Pennsylvania court did the same thing but did so without discussing the issue, except to assert that it was "the better view." See In re Frank, 389 A.2d 536 (Pa. 1978). The authority of this decision is undercut by the fact that the Pennsylvania wait-and-see statute was applicable to the case and required the same result, and the court so noted.

Problems

G devised property in trust, income to his daughter D for life, remainder in corpus to such persons as D shall by will appoint. D's will appointed the property in a further trust, the terms of which were that the income was to go to D's children in equal shares for their lives; on each child's death, the share of corpus proportionate to the child's share of income was to go to the child's then-living descendants, by representation.

Consider the validity of D's appointment under the common-law Rule, under the USRAP, and under the Rule as reformulated in the Restatement 3d of Property in the following circumstances:

1. D died, survived by her two children, X and Y, both of whom were also in being at G's death.

2. D died, survived by her two children, X and Y; X was in being at G's death but Y was born after G's death.

———

Amerige v. Attorney General
88 N.E.2d 126 (Mass. 1949)

[Timothy Leeds left property by will in trust for his brother, James Leeds, for life and then for such persons as James should by will appoint.

James by will expressly blended his own property with that over which he had the power conferred by Timothy, and gave a part of the combined estates in trust for the benefit of his daughter, Mary Elizabeth Williams, for life and then for such persons as she should by will appoint.

Mary Elizabeth by her will also blended her own estate with that over which she had the power conferred by James and left the residue thereof in trust for her two children for life, then to his or her issue, but in default of issue to hold for the life of the survivor, then to his or her issue, but if then there should be no issue of either, to certain charities.

The court held that Mary Elizabeth's appointment violated the common-law Rule Against Perpetuities to the extent it included property from the estate of Timothy.

Among others, James was survived by his daughter Mary Elizabeth, who was also living at Timothy's death, and by Mary Elizabeth's two children, Mary and Edward, neither of whom was living at Timothy's death.]

SPALDING, J. This is a petition for instructions by the trustees under the will of Mary Elizabeth Williams, late of Hopkinton. The case was heard in the Probate Court on a statement of agreed facts and was reserved and reported to this court without decision....

The charities... advance the argument that none of the property appointed by Mary Elizabeth Williams is derived from property of Timothy. They invoke the principle that where the donee of a general power of appointment disposes of owned and appointive property as a single fund the appointive property is allocated to the various dispositions of such fund in such manner as to give the maximum effect to such dispositions. That principle is recognized by our decisions, Stone v. Forbes, 189 Mass. 163, 170-171; Minot v. Paine, 230 Mass. 514, 525, and by the American Law Institute in § 363 of the Restatement of Property. Thus, it is argued, James Leeds dealt with his own and the appointive property as a single fund and to give the maximum effect to his dispositions the debts, expenses, legacies and residuary gifts must be charged against the appointive property and if this is done that property is exhausted and there is no property of Timothy remaining which Mary Elizabeth Williams could appoint. But that principle is not applicable here. In the case at bar there were successive donees of the power created by Timothy, James Leeds and Mary Elizabeth Williams. The appointments which violate the rule against perpetuities were made by Mary Elizabeth Williams, the second donee. None of the appointments made by James is invalid and no contention is made to the contrary. In all of the cases we have seen where the principle of allocation has been applied the valid and invalid dispositions have been made by the same person in the same will. To give the maximum effect to such dispositions under the principle of allocation the law is attempting to carry out the presumed intent of the testator. The doctrine ought not to be applied in the case of successive donees where the dispositions of the first donee are valid and those of the second invalid. It cannot reasonably be said that James contemplated that Mary Elizabeth Williams would exercise the power improperly with the result that he must be presumed to have intended that his dispositions be charged against the appointive property.

The case is remanded to the Probate Court for further proceedings in conformance with this opinion....

Note

The Restatement 2d of Property §22.1 comment f takes a position contrary to *Amerige*, providing that selective allocation in James's estate would have been appropriate in order to validate Mary Elizabeth's appointment. Accord Restatement 3d of Property §19.19 comment h.

3. Charitable Gifts

With one exception, future interests given to charities are subject to the Rule Against Perpetuities. The Rule applies to charitable interests in the same way it applies to future interests given to private parties. At common law, if there is a condition precedent attached to the interest, and if there is no validating life, the charitable interest fails.

Example 17.20: G devised real property "to A for life, then to such of A's children as reach 25, but if none of A's children reaches 25, to X Charity."

The remainder in favor of X Charity is invalid. So is the remainder in favor of A's children. Under the wait-and-see modification of the common-law Rule, these interests would not be initially invalid, but would be given a chance to vest or terminate on their own terms within the allowable waiting period.

Constructional Preference at Common Law for Vested Charitable Interests. Charitable interests, like private interests, are not subject to the common-law Rule (and to the USRAP) if they are vested. There is a pronounced tendency in the decisions to construe charitable interests as vested if the language of the instrument permits this classification. Many charitable gifts, which if contingent would have been invalid, have been saved by this device.

Charitable Interests Excluded if Preceded by Another Charitable Interest. As noted above, there is one formal exception to the principle that charitable future interests receive no preferential treatment under the Rule. A future interest held by a charity is excluded from the application of the Rule if the interest was preceded by an interest that also is held by a charity. See Restatement 2d of Property §1.6 (common law); USRAP §4(5) (UPC §2-904(5)); Restatement 3d of Property §27.3(2), (5).

The rationale for this exclusion is that, because the law allows a perpetual tying up of property for a single charity, it ought to do so when the transferor provides for a shift from one charity to another, even though the shift might occur beyond the perpetuity period.

Example 17.21: G devised real property "to the X School District so long as the premises are used for school purposes, and upon the cessation of such use, to Y City."

The future interest in favor of Y City is valid.

4. Contracts

Owing to its roots as a means by which to curb remotely vesting future interests that made *property* inalienable, especially indestructible executory interests, the Rule Against Perpetuities is inapplicable to legal relationships that do not create property interests. Contracts—even long-term contracts—are generally exempt. It has been held that optional modes of settlement for the payment of life insurance proceeds cannot violate the Rule, nor can annuity contracts, even though future payments may be subject to uncertainties that might not be resolved within a life in being plus 21 years. Doyle v. Massachusetts Mutual Life Ins. Co., 377 F.2d 19 (6th Cir. 1967); Holmes v. John Hancock Mutual Life Ins. Co., 41 N.E.2d 909 (N.Y. 1942); Restatement of Property §401.

5. Commercial Transactions

As noted above, legal relationships that do not create property interests are not subject to the Rule Against Perpetuities. Although this exempts most contracts from the Rule, some contractual arrangements do create contingent future interests under our classificatory scheme of estates, and hence have been held subject to the Rule. Examples include options in gross, rights of first refusal, leases to commence in the future, and certain deeds concerning oil, gas, or mineral interests.

The Rule Against Perpetuities would seem to be a wholly inappropriate instrument of social policy to use as a control over these arrangements. The period of the Rule—a life in being plus 21 years—may be suitable as a limit on gratuitous transfers of property, but it is not suitable for bargained-for exchanges. (The Rule Against Perpetuities argument usually is raised by the party seeking to avoid performance of the contract.)

In recognition of the point that the life-in-being-plus-21-year period has no relevance to commercial transactions, the USRAP broke new ground by excluding all commercial transactions from the Rule Against Perpetuities. See USRAP §4(1) (UPC §2-904(1)). The drafting committee of the USRAP took notice of the fact that some of these commercial transactions do restrain the alienability of property but thought that their control was not, strictly speaking, a Rule Against Perpetuities question and hence was beyond the scope of the project. Note that these transactions are subject to the common-law rules regarding unreasonable restraints on alienation and, in some cases, marketable title acts. Some states also have statutory provisions limiting the duration of certain commercial transactions to a flat period of years. See, for example, Mass. Gen. Laws ch. 184A, §5 (30 years).

Restatement 3d of Property

§27.3 Exclusions from the Rule Against Perpetuities

The Rule Against Perpetuities does not apply to:

(1) commercial transactions, except that the Rule does apply to a trust or other disposition of property arising out of (a) a premarital or postmarital agreement, (b) a separation or divorce settlement, (c) a spouse's election, (d) any other arrangement arising out of a prospective, existing, or previous marital relationship between the parties, (e) a contract to make or not to revoke a will or trust, (f) a contract to exercise or not to exercise a power of appointment, (g) a transfer in satisfaction of a duty of support, or (h) a reciprocal transfer;

....

[Comment] b. ...[C]ommercial transactions excluded: rationale. Paragraph (1) excludes (with certain enumerated exceptions) commercial transactions, even commercial transactions that create a contingent property interest. The reason is that the perpetuity period—whether that period is measure by a life in being plus 21 years or by two younger generations—is only appropriate for measuring the allowable duration of family-oriented trusts and other donative dispositions of property.

6. Possibilities of Reverter and Rights of Entry

At common law, possibilities of reverter and rights of entry (also known as rights of re-entry, rights of entry for condition broken, and powers of termination) are generally exempt from the Rule Against Perpetuities. Their nonreversionary counterpart—the executory interest that follows either a fee simple determinable or a fee simple subject to an executory limitation—*is* subject to the Rule.

By statute in some states, possibilities of reverter and rights of entry expire if they do not vest within a specified period of years. See, for example, 765 Ill. Comp. Stat. §330/4 (40 years).

The USRAP does not apply to possibilities of reverter and rights of entry. Still, the Official Comment to USRAP §4 urges states enacting the USRAP to consider enacting a provision limiting the duration of these interests to a certain period of years, such as 30, if the state has not already done so.

The Restatement 3d reformulates the Rule so that it applies to all future interests, whether formerly classified as "vested" or "contingent." See Restatement 3d of Property §27.1 comment a.

PART I. A DIVERGENT "RULE AGAINST PERPETUITIES"—PROHIBITION OF THE SUSPENSION OF THE POWER OF ALIENATION

The rule we have been thinking of as the Rule Against Perpetuities is, in its traditional form, a rule against remotely vesting future interests. Prior to the turn of the twentieth century, it was not altogether clear that that rule was *the* rule against perpetuities. A divergent form of the rule existed, called the rule against the suspension of the power of alienation (the antisuspension rule). In Avern v. Lloyd, L.R. 5 Eq. 383 (1868), the court held that if living persons, acting together, can convey a fee, the disposition cannot be invalid regardless of the time of possible vesting; validity merely required that the power of alienation not be suspended beyond a life in being plus 21 years. To illustrate the difference, consider these dispositions, which would violate the rule against remotely vesting future interests:

Example 17.22: G conveys land "to A and his heirs, but if the land ever ceases to be used for residential purposes, to B and her heirs."

Because A and B can join together and convey a fee in the land, the power of alienation is not suspended, and the disposition is valid.

Example 17.23: G conveys land "to A and her heirs, but if the land ever ceases to be used for residential purposes, to B and his heirs if B is then living; if not, to B's heirs at law."

Because B's heirs at law (an unascertained class) have an interest in the land, A and B cannot join together and convey a fee in the land. However, B's heirs at law will be ascertained no later than at the death of B, a life in being, so this disposition also is valid under the suspension rule.

Professor John Chipman Gray, in his book on the Rule Against Perpetuities that was first published in 1886, argued strongly that the antisuspension rule was not *the* rule against perpetuities—the rule against perpetuities was the rule against remotely vesting future interests. Gray won the battle, for the *Avern* decision was disapproved in In re Hargreaves, 43 Ch. Div. 401 (C.A. 1890), and henceforth the rule against remotely vesting future interests became *the* Rule Against Perpetuities in both the United States and England.

Nevertheless, in the United States, statutory support for the antisuspension rule was already in place, and therefore that rule was not obliterated altogether; in fact, even today, this is the rule in a few states, as we shall see.

The source of the legislative antisuspension rule was the New York property reform legislation of 1830. That legislation, including its antisuspension provision, spread to a number of other states (in some instances with significant modifications). Experience with the antisuspension provision, however, was not a happy one. The original New York legislation was quite restrictive; it allowed no tack-on 21-year period, and it allowed the power of alienation to be suspended only "during the continuance of not more than two lives in being," not multiple lives.

The quantity of litigation in New York, produced by the necessity for construction of the original statute and efforts to avoid the severity of the perpetuities period it imposed, reflects against the practicability of the legislative doctrine. It has long been the consensus of opinion that the New York effort at perpetuities reform was misguided. As indicated below, a retreat is in full progress, which takes the form either of a reenactment of the common-law Rule in some states that had copied the New York legislation, or in amendments, as in New York itself, which have substantially the same effect.

The current New York legislation is set forth below. You will note that the current statute codifies both the common-law Rule Against Perpetuities and a much-liberalized version of the antisuspension rule, under which the common-law period of multiple lives plus a 21-year tack-on period is allowed. In effect, the antisuspension rule has been rendered nearly meaningless, since almost any disposition that violates the antisuspension rule also violates the common-law Rule.

New York Estates, Powers & Trusts Law

§9-1.1. Rule against perpetuities.

(a) (1) The absolute power of alienation is suspended when there are no persons in being by whom an absolute fee or estate in possession can be conveyed or transferred.

(2) Every present or future estate shall be void in its creation which shall suspend the absolute power of alienation by any limitation or condition for a longer period than lives in being at the creation of the estate and a term of not more than twenty-one years. Lives in being shall include a child conceived before the creation of the estate but born thereafter. In no case shall the lives measuring the permissible period be so designated or so numerous as to make proof of their end unreasonably difficult.

(b) No estate in property shall be valid unless it must vest, if at all, not later than twenty-one years after one or more lives in being at the creation of the estate and any period of gestation involved. In no case shall lives measuring the permissible period of vesting be so designated or so numerous as to make proof of their end unreasonably difficult.

Suspension Legislation In Other States. As noted above, the original New York legislation spread to other states, in some instances with only minor amendments, in other instances with rather significant changes. The principal difference in this regard was between those states that adopted the "two-lives" period for suspension (Arizona, Michigan, Minnesota, and Wisconsin) and those that substituted a "multiple-lives" period like that under the common-law Rule (California, Idaho, Indiana, Montana, North Dakota, Oklahoma, and South Dakota).

The antisuspension rule has been repealed or in effect abrogated in all the above states except Idaho (suspension must be restricted to lives in being plus 25 years, modified by a provision allowing reformation of dispositions that violate the suspension rule and a provision declaring that there is no suspension if the trustee has a power of sale), South Dakota (suspension must be restricted to lives in being plus 30 years, modified by a wait-and-see element and a provision declaring that there is no suspension if the trustee has a power of sale), and Wisconsin (suspension must be restricted to lives in being plus 30 years, modified by a provision declaring that there is no suspension if the trustee has a power of sale). These three states have the antisuspension rule as their only restriction on perpetuities. In these states, in other words, the Rule Against Perpetuities does not exist. A similar approach—replacing the Rule Against Perpetuities with an antisuspension rule—was adopted in 2010 in Kentucky. See Ky. Rev. Stat. §381.225 (suspension must be restricted to lives in being plus 21 years, modified by a provision declaring that there is no suspension if the trustee has a power of sale).

EXTERNAL REFERENCES. See Restatement 2d of Property, Statutory Note to §1.1; Am. L. Prop. chs. 6 & 7; Simes & Smith on Future Interests ch. 41.

PART J. USE OF THE PERPETUITY PERIOD TO CONTROL TRUST INDESTRUCTIBILITY AND INCOME ACCUMULATION

The type of vesting required by the common-law Rule Against Perpetuities (and USRAP) is vesting *in interest*, not vesting *in possession*. Consequently, these Rules do not directly limit the *duration* of a trust. A trust can, theoretically, endure beyond the 21-year period following the death of the validating life or, if the wait-and-see modification has been adopted and applies, beyond the permissible-vesting period. In effect, however, because of the application of a related rule, the continuance of a trust beyond the perpetuity period can occur only by inaction of the beneficiaries. And, should the beneficiaries allow the trust to continue, another related rule requires the trustee to disgorge the trust's income; no income can therefore be accumulated for future distribution.

1. Permissible Duration of Indestructibility of Trusts

The beneficiaries of a trust can join together to compel the trust's termination and the distribution of its assets, unless the trust is an indestructible trust. An indestructible trust is a trust in which the settlor has expressly or impliedly restrained its premature termination. See Chapter 11.

Restatement 2d of Property

§2.1. Duration of Trust. A trust created in a donative transfer, which has not terminated within the period of the rule against perpetuities as applied to such trust, shall continue until the trust terminates in accordance with its terms, except that a trust, other than a charitable trust, may be terminated at any time after the period of the rule against perpetuities expires by a written agreement of all of the beneficiaries of the trust delivered to the trustee, which agreement informs the trustee that the trust is terminated and gives the trustee directions as to the distribution of the trust property.

_____

Duration of Indestructibility under the USRAP. Under the USRAP, the applicable perpetuity period is 90 years with respect to trusts whose validity is governed by the wait-and-see element of § 1(a)(2), (b)(2), or (c)(2). See USRAP §1 comment part G.

Duration of Trusts or Other Donative Dispositions under the Restatement 3d of Property. As we have seen in this chapter, the Restatement 3d of Property reformulates the Rule Against Perpetuities from a rule against the remote vesting of contingent future interests into a rule requiring termination of trusts or other donative dispositions of property on or before the expiration of the perpetuity period.

EXTERNAL REFERENCES. Restatement 3d of Property ch. 27; Restatement 2d of Trusts §62 comment o; Restatement 2d of Property §2.1, Reporter's Note; Gray on Perpetuities §121; Scott on Trusts §62.10(2); Simes & Smith on Future Interests §§1391-93.

2. Accumulations of Income

Restatement 2d of Property

§2.2 Accumulation of Trust Income.

(1) An accumulation of trust income under a noncharitable trust created in a donative transfer is valid until the period of the rule against perpetuities expires with respect to such trust and any accumulation thereafter is invalid.

(2) An accumulation of trust income under a charitable trust created in a donative transfer is valid to the extent the accumulation is reasonable in the light of the purposes, facts and circumstances of the particular trust.

(3) The trust income released by an invalid accumulation shall be paid to such recipients and in such shares and in such manner as most closely effectuates the transferor's manifested plan of distribution.

(4) An accumulation of trust income occurs when part or all of the current income of the trust can be and is retained in the trust, or can be and is so applied by the

trustee as to increase the fund subject to the trust, and such retention or application is not found to be merely in the course of judicious management of the trust.

Comment:

a. Historical Note: Prior to the death of Peter Thellusson in July, 1797, directions or authorizations to accumulate income were seldom involved in litigation. Probably they were seldom made. Certainly such provisions were not frequently made so as to call for an accumulation of long duration. Thus, the necessity for any rule specifically regulating their creation had not arisen. The will of Peter Thellusson raised the problem in a dramatic manner. He had devised the major part of his very large estate to his eldest male lineal descendant to be ascertained at the end of a period measured by nine lives in being and had directed that the income of his assets should be accumulated from the time of his death to the time of the ascertainment of such ultimate taker. This will was held valid by the House of Lords in Thellusson v. Woodford [11 Ves.Jr. 112, 32 Eng. Rep. 1030 (1805)][46] and the opinions rendered by the lower and higher courts in this case laid the foundation for what has since been the rule against accumulations. In the House of Lords it was declared that "a testator can direct the rents and profits to be accumulated for that period during which he may direct that the title shall not vest, and the property shall remain unalienable." In England, the presentation of this case in the lower courts had led to the enactment of a statute [39 and 40 Geo. III c. 98 (1800)] considerably more restrictive than the rule affirmed in the Thellusson case. The subsequent English decisions are largely based on the modifications introduced by this statute. In most of the jurisdictions in the United States the law concerning accumulations is still found only in court decisions. The statutory ingredient in the American law of accumulations is set forth in the Statutory Note to §2.2. Since the statutes deal only with some aspects of the problem, such as the permissible period, the allowable exceptions to the statute's applicability, and the disposition of released income, a large part of the law of accumulations is nonstatutory.

b. Tax considerations. The widespread use of accumulation trusts has been encouraged by the federal income tax advantage of having trust income taxed to the trust as a separate income tax entity in years when the tax rate applicable to the trust was lower than the tax rate applicable to trust beneficiaries to whom the income might be distributed. Also, income accumulated in the trust could be made available to future generations without a federal gift tax or federal estate tax being imposed on the current generation of beneficiaries under the trust. The development of the so-called throwback rule and the extension of its reach by the Tax Reform Act of 1969, with some modifications thereof in the Tax Reform Act of 1976, have undermined the utilization of accumulation trusts to effect significantly, in the long run, federal income tax savings. The introduction in the Tax Reform Act of 1976 of a generation-

---

46. Students of legal history are referred to Patrick Polden, Peter Thellusson's Will of 1797 and its Consequences on Chancery Law (2002). Ed.

skipping tax has curtailed to some extent the avoidance of federal gift and estate taxes as the beneficial enjoyment of the trust property moves from one generation of trust beneficiaries to another. Nevertheless, trusts under which the trustee has discretion to pay out or accumulate trust income continue to have substantial attractions for use in estate planning.

c. Tax accounting income contrasted with trust accounting income. Income from a tax accounting standpoint is a broader concept than income from a trust accounting standpoint. Realized capital gain is income from a tax accounting standpoint, but is principal from a trust accounting standpoint. Income in respect of a decedent collected by a trust becomes principal of the trust, but is income for tax purposes. There can be an accumulation of income for the purposes of this section only if income from a trust accounting standpoint is retained in the trust.

d. Discretionary accumulations compared with mandatory accumulations. Most accumulation trusts give the trustee discretion to accumulate the income or pay it out to some trust beneficiary. The discretion will usually relate not only to current income, but also to income accumulated in past years. A mandatory accumulation trust does not provide the desirable flexibility to meet changing conditions that may affect the needs of the beneficiaries. Its use is most appropriate when the trust fund has to be built up to some larger amount to effectuate the purpose the trust is designed to accomplish.

e. Undesirable social consequences provided by accumulations of trust income. Accumulations of trust income do not keep the trust income from use in the economy because such income will be invested in some manner and not taken completely out of circulation. The fiduciary restrictions on trust investments, however, mean that there is not the same freedom of the use of such income in the economy in the hands of the trustee as there would be in the hands of the trust beneficiary.

Accumulations of trust income tend to build up the control of increased amounts of wealth in fewer and fewer people. However, the impact of the higher income tax rates slows down substantially the build-up process referred to.

Accumulations do tend to perpetuate the policies of the transferor who may have established the trust and, as in the case of the rule against perpetuities in relation to vesting, some limit on the period of time such policies should remain in control is desirable.

———

EXTERNAL REFERENCE. Robert H. Sitkoff, The Lurking Rule Against Accumulations of Income, 100 Nw. U. L. Rev. 501 (2006).

PART K. RELATED RULES OF SOCIAL POLICY—VALIDITY OF RESTRAINTS ON PERSONAL CONDUCT

In addition to the Rule Against Perpetuities and other rules relating to the duration of the indestructibility of trusts and the duration of accumulations of income, there are a variety of other rules that limit the dead hand. These rules prevent transferors of property from conditioning their largesse on certain types of personal conduct of the beneficiaries. We quote below this series of rules, as set forth in the Restatement 2d of Property.

Restatement 2d of Property

§5.1. Basis for Determining Validity of Restraints on Personal Conduct. Unless contrary to public policy or violative of some rule of law, a provision in a donative transfer which is designed to prevent the acquisition or retention of an interest in property in the event of any failure on the part of the transferee to comply with a restraint on personal conduct is valid.

§5.2 Effect of Impossibility of Performance. Impossibility of performance of the terms of a provision in a donative transfer, otherwise valid under the general rule stated in §5.1, excuses lack of performance if, and only if, this result is the appropriately ascertained intent of the person imposing the restraint.

§6.1 Restraints on Any First Marriage.

(1) Except as stated in subsection (2), an otherwise effective restriction in a donative transfer which is designed to prevent the acquisition or retention of an interest in property by the transferee in the event of any first marriage of the transferee is invalid. If the restriction is invalid, the donative transfer takes effect as though the restriction had not been imposed.

(2) If the dominant motive of the transferor is to provide support until marriage, the restraint is normally valid.

§6.2 Restraints on Some First Marriages. An otherwise effective restriction in a donative transfer designed to prevent the acquisition or retention of an interest in the event of some, but not all, first marriages of the transferee is valid if, and only if, under the circumstances, the restraint does not unreasonably limit the transferee's opportunity to marry. If the restriction is invalid, the donative transfer takes effect as though the restriction had not been imposed.

§6.3 Restraints on Remarriage. An otherwise effective restriction in a donative transfer which is designed to prevent the acquisition or retention of an interest in property by the transferee in the event of the remarriage of the transferee is valid only if:

(1) The transferee was the spouse of the transferor, or

(2) The restraint is reasonable under all the circumstances.

§7.1 Provisions Encouraging Separation or Divorce. An otherwise effective restriction in a donative transfer which is designed to permit the acquisition or retention of an interest in property by the transferee only in the event of a separation or divorce from the transferee's spouse is invalid, unless the dominant motive of the transferor is to provide support in the event of separation or divorce, in which case the restraint is valid.

§7.2 Provisions Detrimentally Affecting Family Relationship. An otherwise effective provision in a donative transfer which is designed to permit the acquisition or retention of an interest in property only in the event of either the continuance of an existing separation or the creation of a future separation of a family relationship, other than that of husband and wife, is invalid where the dominant motive of the transferor was to promote such a separation.

§8.1 Provisions Concerning Religion. An otherwise effective provision in a donative transfer which is designed to prevent the acquisition or retention of property on account of adherence to or rejection of certain religious beliefs or practices on the part of the transferee is valid.

§8.2 Restraints Against Personal Habits. An otherwise effective provision in a donative transfer which is designed to prevent the acquisition or retention of an interest in property on account of the transferee acquiring or persisting in specified personal habits is valid.

§8.3 Restraints Concerning Education or Occupation. An otherwise effective provision in a donative transfer which is designed to prevent the acquisition or retention of an interest in property on account of a failure on the part of the beneficiary to acquire or continue an education or occupation is valid.

§9.1 Restraints on Contests. An otherwise effective provision in a will or other donative transfer, which is designed to prevent the acquisition or retention of an interest in property in the event there is a contest of the validity of the document transferring the interest or an attack on a particular provision of the document, is valid, unless there was probable cause for making the contest or attack.

§9.2 Restraints on Attacks on Fiduciaries. An otherwise effective provision in a will or other donative transfer, which is designed to prevent the acquisition or retention of an interest in property in the event the propriety of the performance of the fiduciary with respect to the administration of the transferred property is questioned in a legal proceeding, is valid, unless the beneficiary had probable cause for questioning the fiduciary's performance.

§10.1 Restraints on Enforcing Obligations of Transferor or Transferor's Estate. An otherwise effective provision in a will or other donative transfer, which is designed to prevent the acquisition or retention of an interest in property if there is an attempt to enforce an independent obligation of the transferor or the transferor's estate, is valid.

§10.2 Restraints on Asserting Right to Other Property Owned or Disposed of by Transferor. An otherwise effective provision in a will or other donative transfer which imposes a condition precedent to the interest of a beneficiary that the transfer, if accepted, is in lieu of an interest in other property owned or disposed of by the transferor, is valid.

PART THREE
ADDITIONAL TOPICS

Chapter 18

Elder Law: Planning for the Aged and the Disabled

One of the fastest growing areas of legal practice has been Elder Law. The term "Elder Law" refers to a broad range of legal issues facing older persons and their families and friends. These include housing and employment discrimination on the basis of age; financial aspects of medical care, such as eligibility for Medicare and Medicaid; Social Security; and pension and other employee benefits. In this Chapter, we focus on two aspects of Elder Law that most directly concern the estate planner: (1) preservation and management of assets and (2) health-care decision-making. We also look at the problems of planning for disabled persons, including children.

The reasons for the rapid growth of Elder Law as a field of legal specialization are readily apparent. The number and percentage of elderly individuals in the United States have grown rapidly. Increasing age raises more concerns about health and how health care is paid for. These concerns require planning for both property and personal care. Older Americans are wealthier than ever, but the cost of medical care also has increased dramatically. Elderly persons today are faced with greater questions about how they will dispose of their accumulated wealth in their remaining years. They and their families also are faced with even more difficult and painful decisions about how much health care should be provided for them and who should be given the authority to make those decisions. These matters pose special challenges to the estate planner who represents an elderly client.

INTERNET REFERENCES. Valuable web sites in the area of Elder Law include the sites maintained by Justice in Aging (formerly known as the National Senior Citizens Law Center) at justiceinaging.org, AARP (formerly known as the American Association of Retired Persons) at www.aarp.org, the National Academy of Elder Law Attorneys at www.naela.org, and the American Bar Association's Commission on Law and Aging at americanbar.org/groups/law_aging/. For relevant governmental sites, the best starting point is the federal Administration on Aging (which is now part of the Administration for Community Living) at www.acl.gov.

PART A. DEMOGRAPHIC AND SOCIAL BACKGROUND

There is little doubt that the elderly population is increasing rapidly in this country. Some demographic figures tell the story. The U.S. population age 65 and older increased from 40.5 million in 2010 to 55.7 million in 2020 and is projected to grow to 94.7 million in 2060.[1] The U.S. population age *85 and older* is projected to grow from 6.7 million in 2020 to 14.4 million in 2040.[2]

The economic status of the elderly has improved noticeably in recent decades. In 1960, with 20 percent of their population classified as poor, the elderly were the poorest age group in American society.[3] Yet by 2020, the poverty rate for persons 65 and older was only 9 percent.[4]

While the economic status of the elderly has risen, so has the demand for, and the cost of, health care. Americans are not the healthiest people on the planet, as data from the Central Intelligence Agency's World Factbook makes clear. According to the data, the United States ranks behind 47 other countries in life expectancy. Still, Americans' longevity as well as the susceptibility to disease and disability increase the need for health care in this country, particularly custodial and long-term forms of care. These are especially expensive forms of health care, explaining why the elderly in the U.S. account for more than one-third of all of the nation's health care expenditures (37 percent in 2020) even though they constitute only 17 percent (in 2020) of the population.[5] The upshot of these developments is growing anxiety over what has been called the "graying of America." Judge Richard A. Posner succinctly articulated this concern:

> Although as yet there appears to be no correlation, after other causes are corrected for, between the average age of a nation's population and the nation's per capita expenditures on health care, the combination of increasing medical costs due primarily to advances in medical technology with a rapid increase in the number of elderly people portends a significant increase in aggregate medical expenditures unless the demands for health care of younger people are to be scanted. Already persons age 65 and older, although less than 13 percent of the population, account for more than a third of all expenditures on health care in the United States. And this ignores the cost, as yet largely nonmonetary because borne by family members in the form of personal services rather than cash outlays, of the home care that many elderly people require. [T]his cost is real—is not just a matter of children's bounteous and unstinting desire to care for their aged parents.[6]

---

1. Administration for Community Living, 2021 Profile of Older Americans, at 4-5 (2022).

2. Id. at 5.

3. Thomas S. Ulen, The Law and Economics of the Elderly, 4 Elder L.J. 99, 109 (1996).

4. Administration for Community Living, 2021 Profile of Older Americans, at 12 (2022).

5. National Health Expenditure Data are available at www.cms.gov. The population percentage is available at 2021 Profile of Older Americans, above note 1, at 3.

6. Richard A. Posner, Aging and Old Age 36 (1995).

The costs of the most common forms of care—home care and nursing home care—are not covered by Medicare. These costs must be paid by the elderly themselves or their families. (Medicaid does cover part of cost of nursing home care for the indigent.) Home health care costs approximately $25-40 per hour, and nursing homes can charge more than $100,000 per year for a private room. Long-term care insurance policies are available for these expenses, but they, too, are expensive.

An increasingly popular form of custodial care for the elderly is the "assisted-living" facility. These facilities are residential complexes providing help for elderly residents with ordinary tasks such as dining and housecleaning as well as offering organized social activities. Staff attend to the residents' practical nursing needs, and medical personnel are available for emergency care. Generally, they are less costly and offer residents more independence and privacy than nursing homes. Most assisted living is privately financed with little or no Medicare or Medicaid contributions.

All of these trends help to explain the growth in Elder Law. We now turn to two aspects of Elder Law of central concern to the estate planner: (1) the management and preservation of the client's assets and (2) health-care decisionmaking.

PART B. MANAGEMENT AND PRESERVATION OF ASSETS

In this Part, we examine devices and strategies for the management and preservation of the client's assets. We begin with the durable power of attorney for property.

1. Durable Powers of Attorney for Property

Primary Statutory Reference:
UPC Article 5B
(Uniform Power of Attorney Act)

A power of attorney creates an agency relationship between the maker of the power (the principal) and the attorney-in-fact (the agent). Under the traditional law of agency, the authority of the attorney-in-fact is terminated automatically upon the principal's death or incapacity. See Restatement 2d of Agency §§120, 122 (1958); but see Restatement 3d of Agency §3.11 comment b (2006) (rejecting the traditional view).

The original UPC brought forth a much-desired change in power-of-attorney law by authorizing durable powers of attorney. As opposed to an ordinary power of attorney, a *durable* power of attorney continues to be valid even if the principal loses capacity. In addition, the UPC provided that death of the principal does not automatically terminate the agent's authority. Under the UPC, written powers of attorney, durable or otherwise, continue to be valid after the principal's death; actions taken by the attorney-in-fact in good faith under the power are authorized until the attorney-in-fact gains actual knowledge of the principal's death.

All fifty states and the District of Columbia now have legislation authorizing the creation of durable powers of attorney for property.

In 2006, the Uniform Law Commission promulgated a revised statute on durable powers of attorney for property. This statute is the Uniform Power of Attorney Act (UPOAA). In 2010, the UPOAA was incorporated into the UPC as Article 5B, replacing the UPC's prior provisions on these powers of attorney.

The UPOAA provides an optional statutory form for a durable power of attorney for property. The form is reproduced below.

Uniform Power of Attorney Act §301
(Statutory Form Power of Attorney)

Important Information

This power of attorney authorizes another person (your agent) to make decisions concerning your property for you (the principal). Your agent will be able to make decisions and act with respect to your property (including your money) whether or not you are able to act for yourself. The meaning of authority over subjects listed on this form is explained in the Uniform Power of Attorney Act [insert citation].

This power of attorney does not authorize the agent to make health-care decisions for you. You should select someone you trust to serve as your agent. Unless you specify otherwise, generally the agent's authority will continue until you die or revoke the power of attorney or the agent resigns or is unable to act for you.

Your agent is entitled to reasonable compensation unless you state otherwise in the Special Instructions.

This form provides for designation of one agent. If you wish to name more than one agent you may name a coagent in the Special Instructions. Coagents are not required to act together unless you include that requirement in the Special Instructions.

If your agent is unable or unwilling to act for you, your power of attorney will end unless you have named a successor agent. You may also name a second successor agent.

This power of attorney becomes effective immediately unless you state otherwise in the Special Instructions.

If you have questions about the power of attorney or the authority you are granting to your agent, you should seek legal advice before signing this form.

Designation of Agent

I _____ name

    (Name of Principal)

the following person as my agent:

Name of Agent: _____

Agent's Address: _____

Agent's Telephone Number:_____

Designation of Successor Agent(s) (Optional)

    If my agent is unable or unwilling to act for me, I name as my successor agent:

Name of Successor Agent:_____

Successor Agent's Address: _____

Successor Agent's Telephone Number:_____

    If my successor agent is unable or unwilling to act for me, I name as my second successor agent:

Name of Second Successor Agent: _____

Second Successor Agent's Address: _____

Second Successor Agent's Telephone Number: _____

Grant of General Authority

    I grant my agent and any successor agent general authority to act for me with respect to the following subjects as defined in the Uniform Power of Attorney Act [insert citation]:

(INITIAL each subject you want to include in the agent's general authority. If you wish to grant general authority over all of the subjects you may initial "All Preceding Subjects" instead of initialing each subject.)

(___) Real Property

(___) Tangible Personal Property

(___) Stocks and Bonds

(___) Commodities and Options

(___) Banks and Other Financial Institutions

(___) Operation of Entity or Business

(___) Insurance and Annuities

(___) Estates, Trusts, and Other Beneficial Interests

(___) Claims and Litigation

(___) Personal and Family Maintenance

(___) Benefits from Governmental Programs or Civil or Military Service

(___) Retirement Plans

(___) Taxes

(___) All Preceding Subjects

Grant of Specific Authority (Optional)

My agent MAY NOT do any of the following specific acts for me UNLESS I have INITIALED the specific authority listed below:

(CAUTION: Granting any of the following will give your agent the authority to take actions that could significantly reduce your property or change how your property is distributed at your death. INITIAL ONLY the specific authority you WANT to give your agent.)

(___) Create, amend, revoke, or terminate an inter vivos trust

(___) Make a gift, subject to the limitations of the Uniform Power of Attorney Act [insert citation to Section 217 of the act] and any special instructions in this power of attorney

(___) Create or change rights of survivorship

(___) Create or change a beneficiary designation

(___) Authorize another person to exercise the authority granted under this power of attorney

(___) Waive the principal's right to be a beneficiary of a joint and survivor annuity, including a survivor benefit under a retirement plan

(___) Exercise fiduciary powers that the principal has authority to delegate

[(___) Disclaim or refuse an interest in property, including a power of appointment]

Limitation on Agent's Authority

An agent that is not my ancestor, spouse, or descendant MAY NOT use my property to benefit the agent or a person to whom the agent owes an obligation of support unless I have included that authority in the Special Instructions.

Special Instructions (Optional)

You may give special instructions on the following lines:

_____

_____

_____

Effective Date

This power of attorney is effective immediately unless I have stated otherwise in the Special Instructions.

Nomination of [Conservator or Guardian] (Optional)

If it becomes necessary for a court to appoint a [conservator or guardian] of my estate or [guardian] of my person, I nominate the following person(s) for appointment:

Name of Nominee for [conservator or guardian] of my estate:

_____

Nominee's Address: _____

Nominee's Telephone Number:_____

Name of Nominee for [guardian] of my person: _____

Nominee's Address: _____

Nominee's Telephone Number: _____

Reliance on This Power of Attorney

    Any person, including my agent, may rely upon the validity of this power of attorney or a copy of it unless that person knows it has terminated or is invalid.

Signature and Acknowledgment

_____   _____

Your Signature   Date

_____

Your Name Printed

_____

_____

Your Address

_____

Your Telephone Number

State of_____

[County] of_____

This document was acknowledged before me on _____,

                            (Date)

by_____.

    (Name of Principal)

_____   (Seal, if any)

Signature of Notary

My commission expires: _____

[This document prepared by:

_____

_____]

Important Information for Agent

Agent's Duties

When you accept the authority granted under this power of attorney, a special legal relationship is created between you and the principal. This relationship imposes upon you legal duties that continue until you resign or the power of attorney is terminated or revoked. You must:

(1) do what you know the principal reasonably expects you to do with the principal's property or, if you do not know the principal's expectations, act in the principal's best interest;

(2) act in good faith;

(3) do nothing beyond the authority granted in this power of attorney; and

(4) disclose your identity as an agent whenever you act for the principal by writing or printing the name of the principal and signing your own name as "agent" in the following manner: (Principal's Name) by (Your Signature) as Agent.

Unless the Special Instructions in this power of attorney state otherwise, you must also:

(1) act loyally for the principal's benefit;

(2) avoid conflicts that would impair your ability to act in the principal's best interest;

(3) act with care, competence, and diligence;

(4) keep a record of all receipts, disbursements, and transactions made on behalf of the principal;

(5) cooperate with any person that has authority to make health-care decisions for the principal to do what you know the principal reasonably expects or, if you do not know the principal's expectations, to act in the principal's best interest; and

(6) attempt to preserve the principal's estate plan if you know the plan and preserving the plan is consistent with the principal's best interest.

Termination of Agent's Authority

You must stop acting on behalf of the principal if you learn of any event that terminates this power of attorney or your authority under this power of attorney. Events that terminate a power of attorney or your authority to act under a power of attorney include:

(1) death of the principal

(2) the principal's revocation of the power of attorney or your authority;

(3) the occurrence of a termination event stated in the power of attorney;

(4) the purpose of the power of attorney is fully accomplished; or

(5) if you are married to the principal, a legal action is filed with a court to end your marriage, or for your legal separation, unless the Special Instructions in this

power of attorney state that such an action will not terminate your authority.

Liability of Agent

The meaning of the authority granted to you is defined in the Uniform Power of Attorney Act [insert citation]. If you violate the Uniform Power of Attorney Act [insert citation] or act outside the authority granted, you may be liable for any damages caused by your violation.

If there is anything about this document or your duties that you do not understand, you should seek legal advice.

Questions

1. Why does the form distinguish between powers granted pursuant to a general grant of authority and powers granted pursuant to a specific grant of authority? For powers in the latter category, why are they not in the former category?

2. Are there ways in which the form could be improved?

———

Durable powers of attorney for property, including statutory-form powers, often authorize supplemental funding of inter vivos trusts. Trusts, usually revocable trusts with discretionary provisions, provide a better tool for the management of the property of an incapacitated person than a formal guardianship or conservatorship. Moreover, trusts are more likely to be honored by transfer agents and other third parties than powers of attorney.[7] A technique often used is for a settlor, while fully competent, to create a so-called standby trust—a trust funded with nominal assets such as $100 or $1,000. In conjunction with the trust's creation, the settlor executes a durable power of attorney authorizing the attorney-in-fact (who might be the trustee of the trust) to transfer all or a specified portion of the settlor's assets into the trust if the settlor later loses physical or mental capacity. This technique allows the settlor to retain control of his or her assets while the settlor is still able to manage them, but also to have an arrangement in place by which the assets can be responsibly managed on the settlor's behalf should that become necessary.

EXTERNAL REFERENCES. Linda Whitton, The Uniform Power of Attorney Act: Striking a Balance Between Autonomy and Protection, 1 Phoenix L. Rev. 343 (2008); Linda Whitton, Navigating the Uniform Power of Attorney Act, 3 NAELA J. 1 (2007); Karen Boxx, The Durable Power of Attorney's Place in the Family of Fiduciary Relationships, 36 Ga. L. Rev. 1 (2001).

---

7. On liability for failing to honor a power of attorney under the Uniform Power of Attorney Act (UPOAA), see UPOAA §120, 121 (UPC §§5B-120, 5B-121).

2. Custodial Trusts

Primary Statutory Reference: *Uniform Custodial Trust Act*

In 1987, the Uniform Law Commission took another step to facilitate the management of property on behalf of adult beneficiaries, whether incapacitated or not. The Uniform Custodial Trust Act (UCTA), enacted so far in nineteen states and the District of Columbia, establishes a statutory trust that can be invoked by transferring property to another person "as custodial trustee for (name of beneficiary, who can be the transferor) under the [enacting state] Uniform Custodial Trust Act." The UCTA is designed to provide a statutory standby trust similar to the custodial arrangement for minors established by the Uniform Transfers to Minors Act. The terms of the custodial trust, set forth in the statute itself, provide among other things that if the beneficiary is incapacitated the custodial trustee shall expend so much or all of the custodial trust property as the custodial trustee considers advisable for the use and benefit of the beneficiary. The statute also facilitates a pour-over into a trust designed to coordinate management and distribution of other assets by providing, in §17(a)(3)(i), that the assets remaining in a custodial trust at the beneficiary's death are to be transferred "as last directed in a writing signed by the deceased beneficiary while not incapacitated and received by the custodial trustee during the life of the deceased beneficiary...."

3. Planning for Long-Term Care

Traditionally, individuals have had to pay for long-term care out of their own assets or those of their families. As the cost of such care has risen, the elderly and their families have looked for various alternative means of financing long-term residential care. In this Part, we look at some of the main devices used to help defray these costs, and their estate planning implications.

a. Qualifying for Medicare or Medicaid

Medicare and Medicaid are the two major governmental programs that provide health-care benefits to the elderly. Medicare is a federal health insurance program for qualified elderly and disabled persons. Medicaid is a joint federal-state program intended to provide benefits to specific categories of poor people, including the elderly. Both programs offer assistance in paying for long-term care but only in limited circumstances.

Medicare. Medicare coverage is limited to persons age 65 or older who qualify for Social Security benefits on the basis of their lifetime earnings record. There are two main parts to the Medicare program. Part A, known as Hospital Insurance, covers inpatient hospital care; skilled nursing care in a medical institution, nursing facility, or private home; and hospice care. Part B, known as Supplemental Medical

Insurance, primarily covers expenses for physician care. Unlike Part A, it is optional, and it requires payment of premiums and larger deductibles. (Medicare also has Part C, the Medicare Advantage Plan (like an HMO or PPO plan); and Part D, prescription drug coverage.)

Medicare covers long-term care but only in exceptional circumstances and only to a limited extent. It provides full coverage for skilled nursing care in a skilled nursing care facility during a period of illness but only up to a limited period of time, after which the patient must pay increasingly large per diem deductibles. It also pays for skilled nursing services, as well as physical and speech therapy, provided in the patient's own home, but only if the patient is homebound and the services are provided under a plan of treatment prescribed by a physician. The term "skilled nursing care" refers to services ordered by a physician and provided by professional personnel such as registered nurses and licensed practical nurses. It does not include long-term custodial care, such as dressing, bathing, or administering medications; services like Meals-on-Wheels; or adult day care. Courts have demonstrated a reluctance to characterize services as "skilled," rather "custodial." In Friedman v. Secretary of the Department of Health and Human Services, 819 F.2d 42 (2d Cir. 1987), for example, the court affirmed the government's denial of Medicare benefits to a hospital patient who was admitted to the intensive care unit for treatment of head injuries and who also suffered from Parkinson's disease and inflammation of the veins. After treating him, his doctors concluded that he no longer required skilled medical care, but his family decided that it was best for him to stay in the hospital rather than being transferred to a custodial care facility. The government denied Medicare payments for the time after the first custodial care option became available, despite the fact that the patient received medical treatment for his Parkinson's condition and inflammation of the veins while he remained in the hospital. The safe course of action is to assume that most long-term care will not be covered by Medicare.

Medicaid. The primary federal program for assistance for nursing home care is Medicaid. Medicaid differs from Medicare in two important respects. First, while Medicare is exclusively a federal program, Medicaid funding and administration are jointly state and federal. Wide variations exist in state benefits and eligibility requirements. Second, unlike Medicare, which covers certain medical needs regardless of the beneficiary's financial status, Medicaid is limited to low-income persons with few assets.

The income and asset limitations rules are complex. In general, however, states follow four principles. First, the applicant must apply for all sources of income for which he or she is eligible, including pension and retirement benefits, annuities, and the like. Second, the individual must assign to the state any third-party payment or other medical support to which he or she is entitled. Third, the income and assets of family members other than the spouse are not taken into account. Fourth, family members other than the spouse are not held responsible for reimbursing the state for the costs of medical care provided to a Medicaid beneficiary. For married couples, the rules governing the non-applicant spouse's income and assets are varied and complex. With respect to income, only the applicant's income is generally considered where the applicant is institutionalized and the spouse is not. With respect to assets, only some of the non-institutionalized spouse's assets are exempt; others are taken into consideration.

Individuals who want to qualify for Medicaid to pay for long-term care do not have to deprive themselves of all assets. Only so-called "non-exempt" assets are counted under state eligibility rules. Significant exempt assets that the applicant may retain, or even use non-exempt assets to acquire, typically include the principal residence, at least up to a certain value of home equity[8]; household goods and personal items up to a stated maximum (such as $2,000); a wedding ring; a vehicle; burial plots; and a stated amount of money to be used for funeral expenses. These exemption rules create opportunities for careful estate planning that maintain assets for Medicaid-qualifying clients. Such planning must be done very carefully, however; otherwise, exempt assets may lose their exempt status.

In the not too distant past, two techniques were especially common in Medicaid planning for the elderly: transfers of assets to the children and others, and Medicaid trusts. The availability of both of these techniques was limited considerably by the federal Omnibus Budget Reconciliation Act of 1993 (known as OBRA 93). Asset transfers were limited further by the Deficit Reduction Act of 2005 (known as DRA 05).

Asset Transfers. It was common, especially among the middle class, for elderly persons to transfer assets to their relatives to qualify for Medicaid without becoming destitute. Not atypically, the donor and donee reached a tacit agreement that the donee would use some or all of the transferred assets to care for the donor. See Esther B. Fein, Welfare for Middle-Class Elderly? In Final Years, Many Transfer Assets to Qualify for Medicaid, N.Y. Times, Sept. 25, 1994, at A39.

Federal law, however, imposes restrictions on asset transfers as a means of qualifying for Medicaid. It creates a period of ineligibility for persons who transfer non-exempt assets or their personal residence[9] for less than fair market value within a certain period prior to applying to Medicaid for institutionalized care. Under DRA 05, the look-back period is 60 months (up from 36 months under OBRA 93), and the ineligibility period begins on the date of the person's Medicaid application or the

---

8. Before 2006, the principal residence typically was exempt regardless of its value. The Deficit Reduction Act of 2005 provided that persons with more than $500,000 in home equity are ineligible for Medicaid nursing home care. The act allowed states to increase the safe harbor to $750,000. Homes occupied by a spouse or a minor or disabled child remain fully exempt. Beginning in 2011, the $500,000 and $750,000 have been indexed for inflation.

9. A transfer of the principal residence to certain persons (e.g., a spouse, a disabled child) are exempt from penalty.

date of the transfer, whichever is later. For a discussion of DRA 05 and its implications for Medicaid policy, see Catherine Reif, A Penny Saved Can Be a Penalty Earned: Nursing Homes, Medicaid Planning, the Deficit Reduction Act of 2005, and the Problem of Transferring Assets, 34 N.Y.U. Rev. L. & Soc. Change 339 (2010).

The federal Health Insurance Portability and Accountability Act of 1996, which took effect January 1, 1997, made it a crime to "knowingly and willfully dispose[] of assets (including any transfer in trust) in order for an individual to become eligible for medical assistance under a State [Medicaid] plan..., if disposing of the assets results in the imposition of a period of ineligibility for such assistance under section 1917(c)."[10] Violators were subject to fines of up to $25,000 or imprisonment for up to five years, or both.

The harshness of this criminal penalty provoked many organizations to label it the "Granny Goes to Jail Act" and to call for its repeal. But rather than repeal the law altogether, Congress enacted §4734 of the Balanced Budget Act of 1997.[11] Under this section, it was no longer a crime to dispose of certain assets in order to qualify for Medicaid; instead, it was a crime to *counsel or assist* anyone in disposing of certain assets in order to qualify for Medicaid. Now it was Granny's lawyer who was in danger of going to jail.

New York State Bar Association v. Reno
999 F.Supp. 710 (N.D.N.Y. 1998)

MCAVOY, CHIEF JUDGE. Plaintiff, the New York State Bar Association ("NYSBA"), seeks to enjoin the Attorney General of the United States from enforcing section 4734 of the Balanced Budget Act of 1997, which was incorporated into section 217 of the Health Insurance Portability and Accountability Act of 1996, 42 U.S.C. §1320a-7b(a). Plaintiff asserts that section 4734 violates the First and Fifth Amendments to the United States Constitution.

I. BACKGROUND

A. Statutory Background

Before Congress enacted section 217 of the Health Insurance Portability and Accountability Act of 1996, certain transfers of assets up to 36 months prior to an application for Medicaid benefits and certain transfers to trusts up to 60 months prior to application, could result in a period of ineligibility for Medicaid benefits. 42 U.S.C. § 1396p(c). In enacting section 217, Congress left the ineligibility period intact, but added certain criminal penalties. Essentially, section 217 made it a crime to dispose of assets in order to become eligible for Medicaid benefits if the

---

10. P.L. 104-191, §217, amending 42 U.S.C. §1320a-7b(a).

11. P.L. 105-33, §4734, amending 42 U.S.C. §1320a-7b(b).

disposition of assets "resulted in the imposition of a period of ineligibility." §1320a-7b(a)(6) (sometimes referred to as the "Granny Goes to Jail Act"). Violators were subject to fines of up to $25,000 or imprisonment for up to 5 years, or both. Id.

A number of organizations lobbied for the repeal of section 217, including the NYSBA. Rather than repeal the Granny Goes to Jail Act, Congress amended section 217 by enacting section 4734 of the Balanced Budget Act of 1997. Section 4734, which became effective August 5, 1997, struck the former language and added a provision making it illegal to counsel or assist an individual to dispose of certain assets to qualify for Medicaid:

> Criminal penalties for acts involving Federal health care programs
>
> (a) Making or causing to be made false statements or representations
>
> Whoever—....
>
> (6) for a fee knowingly and willfully counsels or assists an individual to dispose of assets (including by any transfer in trust) in order for the individual to become eligible for medical assistance under a State plan under subchapter XIX of this chapter, if disposing of the assets results in the imposition of a period of ineligibility for such assistance under section 1396p(c) of this title, shall...(ii) in the case of such a statement, representation, concealment, failure, conversion, or provision of counsel or assistance by any other person, be guilty of a misdemeanor and upon conviction thereof fined not more than $10,000 or imprisoned for not more than one year, or both.

42 U.S.C. §1320a-7b(a).

While section 4734 was in conference, the Congressional Research Service ("CRS") prepared a memorandum, dated July 11, 1997, analyzing the legal and constitutional issues raised by the proposed language of section 4734. CRS expressed concern that the language would infringe the First Amendment, noting: "To the extent that the provision would prohibit counseling about legal activities, a court would seem likely to declare it unconstitutional."

Congress nevertheless passed the provision without modification, and the President signed section 4734 into law.

B. Procedural Background

Plaintiff filed the instant motion for a preliminary injunction on January 27, 1998. After a number of extensions and adjournments, Defendant now states that it will neither defend the constitutionality of 42 U.S.C. §1320a-7b(a)(6) nor enforce its criminal provisions. On March 11, 1998, Attorney General Janet Reno notified the United States House of Representatives and the United States Senate that the Department of Justice would not enforce the aforementioned criminal provisions. Not surprisingly, Defendant now argues that a preliminary injunction is no longer needed.

In response, NYSBA filed opposition arguing that its members' free speech rights are still being chilled. Essentially, NYSBA argues that section 4734 is unconstitutional for the following reasons: (1) it violates the First Amendment because it unconstitutionally restricts free speech; (2) it violates the First Amendment because it is overly broad; and (3) it violates the Fifth Amendment because it is vague.

II. DISCUSSION

A. Standing

[The court concluded that the NYSBA did have standing to bring this action.] B. Preliminary Injunction

In this circuit the standard for obtaining a preliminary injunction is well established. In order to obtain a preliminary injunction the movant must make an affirmative showing of: (1) irreparable harm; and either (2) likelihood of success on the merits; or (3) sufficiently serious questions going to the merits to make them a fair ground for litigation and a balance of hardships tipping decidedly in favor of the movant. See, e.g., Covino v. Patrissi, 967 F.2d 73, 77 (2d Cir. 1992); Resolution Trust Corp. v. Elman, 949 F.2d 624, 626 (2d Cir. 1991); Jackson Dairy, Inc. v. H.P. Hood & Sons, Inc., 596 F.2d 70, 72 (2d Cir. 1979). However, "where the moving party seeks to stay governmental action taken in the public interest pursuant to a statutory or regulatory scheme, the district court ... should not grant the injunction unless the moving party establishes, along with irreparable injury, a likelihood that he will succeed on the merits of his claim." Plaza Health Laboratories, Inc. v. Perales, 878 F.2d 577, 580 (2d Cir. 1989); see also Union Carbide Agricultural Products Co. v. Costle, 632 F.2d 1014, 1018 (2d Cir. 1980).

i. Irreparable Harm

As this Court recently noted, "[c]ourts in this circuit have repeatedly stated that '[p]erhaps the single most important prerequisite for the issuance of a preliminary injunction is a demonstration that if it is not granted the applicant is likely to suffer irreparable harm before a decision on the merits can be rendered.'" Nakatomi Investments v. City of Schenectady, 949 F. Supp. 988, 990 (N.D.N.Y. 1997) (quoting Borey v. National Union Fire Ins. Co., 934 F.2d 30, 34 (2d Cir. 1991)). Irreparable injury, moreover, means injury for which a monetary award cannot be adequate compensation. Jackson Dairy, 596 F.2d at 72 (citing Studebaker Corp. v. Gittlin, 360 F.2d 692, 698 (2d Cir. 1966), Foundry Srvs. Inc., v. Beneflux Corp., 206 F.2d 214, 216 (2d Cir. 1948)).

Turning to the first prong of this test, if the government's enforcement of section 4734 will deprive Plaintiff of its First Amendment rights, this constitutes per se irreparable injury to Plaintiff. Elrod v. Burns, 427 U.S. 347, 49 L. Ed. 2d 547, 96 S. Ct. 2673 (1976). In *Elrod v. Burns*, the Supreme Court instructed that "[t]he loss of First Amendment freedoms, for even minimal periods of time, unquestionably constitutes irreparable injury." 427 U.S. at 373; see also Paulsen v. County of Nassau, 925 F.2d 65, 68 (2d Cir. 1991) (stating that even a temporary abridgment of the First Amendment right to free expression constitutes irreparable injury).

Here, the Attorney General states that the Department of Justice will not enforce section 1320a-7b(a)(6)'s criminal provisions. The Attorney General argues that NYSBA members face no threat of criminal sanction. As a result, Plaintiff will not suffer any irreparable harm, thus obviating Plaintiff's need for injunctive relief. Defendant's argument, however, misses the point....

Here, the parties have staked out starkly opposing positions on the issue of whether a threat of enforcement presently exists. The Attorney General assures the Court that she will not enforce section 4734. Plaintiff responds that the Attorney General's statements do not eliminate the threat of future enforcement, and... may not represent the position of the President of the United States–who has been silent regarding ... enforcement.

Fortunately, the Court need not resolve this issue definitively because the Court finds that Plaintiff will suffer injury irrespective of the imminent enforcement of section 4734.

Governmental infringement of the First Amendment does not exist merely in the imposition of criminal sanctions. As the Supreme Court noted in *Elrod*, the First Amendment is implicated whenever free speech is "either threatened or in fact being impaired at the time the relief [is] sought." Elrod, 96 S. Ct. At 2689....

The irreparable harm that exists here is the potential for self- censorship among NYSBA members. NYSBA members have an ethical obligation as attorneys to respect and uphold the law. In fact, Plaintiff's affidavits state that section 4734 actually has resulted in NYSBA members refraining from providing certain counsel and assistance to clients. Furthermore, Defendant provides no assurance that NYSBA members will not be prosecuted on some future date or that state Medicaid fraud units will also not enforce section 4734.

Accordingly, inasmuch as section 4734 remains part of the laws of the United States, which NYSBA members are ethically bound to uphold, the limitation on free speech found in section 4734 constitutes irreparable injury to Plaintiff. Thus, Plaintiff has satisfied the first of the two elements required for a preliminary injunction.

ii. Likelihood of Success

The second element requires the Court to determine whether Plaintiff is likely to succeed on the merits of its constitutional challenge. As this Court stated in *Nakatomi Investments*, "it has long been axiomatic that once a party shows that a regulation deprives them of a protected First Amendment interest, the burden shifts to the Government to justify the infringement." 949 F. Supp. at 990 (citing Members of City Council v. Taxpayers for Vincent, 466 U.S. 789, 803 n.22, 80 L. Ed. 2d 772, 104 S. Ct. 2118 (1984), City of Los Angeles v. Preferred Communications, Inc., 476 U.S. 488, 496, 90 L. Ed. 2d 480, 106 S. Ct. 2034 (1986)).

At this time, however, it does not appear that the government contests the unconstitutionality of section 4734. Therefore, the Court must find that Plaintiff will likely succeed on the merits of its claims.

III. CONCLUSION

For the foregoing reasons, Plaintiff's Motion for a Preliminary Injunction is GRANTED. It is hereby ORDERED that pending final judgment, the United States, its agents, servants, employees, attorneys, and all persons in active concert and participation with Defendant are enjoined from commencing, maintaining, or otherwise taking action to enforce 42 U.S.C. §1320a-7b(a)(6).

IT IS SO ORDERED.

———

Medicaid Trusts. The Medicaid-qualifying device that was Congress's biggest target in enacting OBRA 93 was the so-called "Medicaid qualifying trust" (MQT). These were irrevocable inter vivos trusts created by a Medicaid applicant or beneficiary (or spouse) giving the trustee the power to apply income and/or principal for the benefit of the grantor or spouse. Prior to enactment of the federal Medicaid Qualifying Trusts rules of 1986, these self-settled trusts did qualify for Medicaid because under conventional trust law the discretionary character of the trust made the beneficiary's interest immune from creditor claims. Under the 1986 MQT law (which was actually a misnomer, as it *dis*qualified such trusts), the income and principal of this type of trust were considered available to the settlor-beneficiary to the full extent that the trustee *could* pay them to the beneficiary. Trusts created by a third party for the applicant (or spouse) were treated more favorably. Only the income and/or principal actually paid to the applicant (or spouse) counted as available to the beneficiary.

Seeking further to tighten perceived abuses of Medicaid, Congress repealed the 1986 MQT rules and substituted a highly complex and somewhat ambiguous set of rules. OBRA 93, which applies to trusts created after August 10, 1993, tightens the rules for MQTs in two important ways. First, it expands the definition of "trusts" to include any arrangement that is "similar to a trust."[12] Second, the statute defines a self-settled trust, whose assets will be deemed to be available to the applicant, as any inter vivos trust created by the applicant, his or her spouse, a person (including a court) with legal authority to act on behalf of the applicant (or spouse), or a person acting at the applicant's (or spouse's) direction or request, where the trusts assets were provided by the applicant (or spouse). This expansive definition includes trusts created by a guardian, conservator, or attorney-in-fact acting under a power of attorney. If the trust is revocable by the applicant, its principal is considered an

---

12. 42 U.S.C. §1396p(d)(6). The Health Care Financing Administration, which is the federal agency overseeing the Medicaid program, has defined "similar to a trust" to include "escrow accounts, investment accounts, pension funds, and other similar devices managed by an individual or entity with fiduciary obligations." HCFA State Medicaid Manual §3259.1(A)(2).

available asset, and income paid to the applicant is considered available to the applicant. For irrevocable trusts, income and principal will be deemed available to the applicant to the extent that they *may* be paid to or applied for the benefit of the applicant. This means that the assets and income of a self-settled discretionary trust in which the trustee has complete discretion to pay principal and income to the applicant will count fully as available to the Medicaid applicant. Actual use of income and/or principal from the trust for any other purpose triggers the asset-transfer rules outlined above.[13]

There are three major exceptions to these rules. First, a trust for a disabled person under age 65 which contains that person's assets and is created by that person's parent, grandparent, legal guardian, or a court, will be exempt if the state will receive all the property remaining in the trust, up to the amount paid as Medicaid assistance, when the disabled person dies. Second, a trust for a disabled person (regardless of age) will be exempt if it meets several conditions. It must be created by a non-profit organization that maintains a separate account for each beneficiary, and the beneficiary's account must be established solely for his or her benefit by his or her parent, grandparent, guardian, or a court. Remaining assets at the beneficiary's death must be paid to the state up to the amount paid as Medicaid benefits. Third, trusts created for the applicant's benefit are exempt where they are composed only of his or her pension, Social Security, or other income, if at the beneficiary's death the state will be reimbursed for the amount of Medicaid assistance.

Trusts created by a third person for the applicant's benefit are treated differently. Income and principal from such trusts are considered available to the applicant when they are "actually available" and when the applicant has "a legal interest in a liquidated sum and has the legal ability to make such sum available for support and maintenance." 45 C.F.R. §233.20(a)(3)(ii)(D). Under this language, there is a crucial distinction between a discretionary trust, on the one hand, and a mandatory or support trust, on the other. Only the latter pose problems for Medicaid eligibility.

Medicaid Estate Recovery. If a person receives Medicaid payments or services, the state may be required or permitted to seek to recover the cost from the person's estate. The state is *required* to recoup payments for institutionalized care, and (with respect to recipients 55 or older) payments for nursing home care and certain other specified services. States are *permitted* to seek reimbursement for all other Medicaid

---

13. OBRA 93 left open several interpretative issues. One of these concerned the status of income-only trusts, that is, irrevocable self-settled trusts from which only income can be paid to the applicant. On December 23, 1993, the HCFA issued a statement clarifying the law on this point. According to the HCFA, if no portion of the corpus can be distributed to the applicant, then no portion of the corpus will be deemed available to the applicant. For discussion, see Ira Stewart Wiesner, OBRA '93 and Medicaid: Asset Transfer, Trust Availability, and Estate Recovery Statutory Analysis in Context, 47 Soc. Sec. Rep. Ser. 757, 774-775 (1995).

services. The recovery is deferred until the death of the person's surviving spouse, if any, and until the person has no child under age 21 or permanently disabled. The "estate" for purposes of recovery is defined by state law, and could be limited to the decedent's probate estate or could extend to assets passing through nonprobate transfers.

b. Other Financing Strategies

For the vast majority of elderly persons, Medicare and Medicaid are inadequate solutions to the problem of financing custodial and long-term skilled care. As already noted, Medicare does not cover long-term custodial care, nor does it cover skilled care in a skilled nursing facility beyond a limited time (currently 100 days for each "spell of illness"). With respect to the services that it does cover, it has a substantial copayment element for participants. Medicaid *is* available to pay the costs of long-term custodial care but only for the indigent. Most elderly persons, then, need other means to finance such care. Here we look briefly at the primary financing devices available to the middle-class elderly person who can rely on neither personal wealth nor government benefits to defray all or even most of the costs of long-term care.

Insurance. Perhaps the most obvious available means of financing the high cost of health care is private insurance. Two types of insurance should be mentioned, so-called "Medigap" insurance and long-term care insurance. A third arrangement involving insurance, also discussed below, is an accelerated benefit settlement.

Medigap Insurance. Medigap insurance is only a limited financing device that does not answer the problem for those who need or will need long-term care. As its name suggests, it is designed to cover the gaps created by Medicare's deductibles and copayment obligations. Since 1992, federal law has standardized Medigap insurance policies, so that persons may choose one of ten different packages with varying degrees of coverage. Even at its most comprehensive level, however, Medigap insurance does not fill all of the gaps in Medicare's coverage. By far, the most important of these remaining gaps are custodial care and long-term institutionalized skilled care.

Long-Term Care Insurance. For elderly persons who do not qualify for Medicaid, most of the costs of long-term care are paid through a second form of private insurance, long-term care insurance. Unlike Medigap insurance, long-term care insurance policies are not standardized, and there are considerable differences among the policies that various insurers offer. Policies usually cover skilled care in a skilled nursing facility and intermediate care. Most elderly residents of nursing homes require custodial care rather than skilled medical care. It is important to be clear, then, whether a policy covers institutionalized custodial care. For some elderly persons, however, custodial care need not require that they be institutionalized. Home health care services, such as visits by nurses, physical therapists, or home health aides, are not always covered by long-term care insurance, so, again, it is important to clarify whether the policy includes this form of care.

There are several problems with long-term care insurance. First, nearly all policies have financial limitations. Long-term care insurance does not pay all costs but only up to a fixed daily amount. The duration of coverage also is fixed, and longer periods of coverage carry with them higher premiums. Second, policies exclude preexisting conditions and conditions that appear within the first six months of coverage. Third, and most important, long-term care insurance is very expensive. The older the insured person is, the higher the cost. People in their 60s and 70s can expect to pay thousands of dollars per year in premiums. Thus, despite the fact that long-term care insurance is growing, it is not a complete answer to the problem of financing care for the elderly.

Accelerated Life Insurance Benefits. A third method of using insurance to finance health care is through accelerated benefits on existing life insurance policies. Under an accelerated benefits rider, the insurer pays the policyowner a percentage of the death benefit before the insured's death. The typical rider states that payments will be made only to persons expected to die within six months to a year. Consequently, this arrangement is less a means of paying for long-term care than it is for the terminally ill, such as cancer victims, to liquidate their existing life insurance policies.

An advantageous feature of accelerated death benefits is that they are not included as taxable income for federal income tax purposes if three requirements are met. First, the payment can only be made to a person who is terminally ill. Second, the amount paid must equal the amount deducted from the policy's final death benefit minus a discount which can be no greater than the interest rate the insurer charges on policy loans. Third, the cash surrender value remaining after payment must be proportional to the amount of the remaining death benefit.

Insurance companies began to offer accelerated death benefits only in 1990, largely in response to the growing interest in viatical settlements. Under a viatical settlement (so called because of the ancient Roman practice of *viaticum,* in which officials received money and supplies before departing on risky journeys to the far-flung corners of the Roman empire), a financial intermediary purchases an existing life insurance policy from a terminally ill person and pays a portion of the policy's face amount in return for being named the beneficiary. A viatical settlement is necessary where the policy itself does not contain an accelerated benefits rider. Because their discount rate usually is greater than that allowed under federal tax law, viatical settlements may not receive the favorable tax treatment given to most accelerated death benefits. On the other hand, not many life insurance policies include accelerated benefits riders.

Home Equity Conversion. Many elderly persons lack sufficient liquid assets either to fund a trust for medical and custodial care or to buy long-term care insurance. They may well find themselves in the position of being "cash poor and house rich." For older Americans who are home owners, the house is typically their most valuable asset. They likely have paid off the mortgage, and the house's market value may have appreciated significantly since the owner first bought it. Home equity conversion allows an elderly homeowner in this position to use home equity as an income-producing asset without selling the house. If the person requires custodial care but is medically able to continue living at home, home equity conversion may be an effective means of financing long-term care.

Perhaps the most popular form of home equity conversion is the reverse mortgage. The reverse mortgage is a lending arrangement in which the borrower receives either a line of credit or periodic payments in exchange for a security interest on his or her house. The amount of the loan increases over time as more payments are made and interest is added to the principal loan amount. The amount of the loan is calculated on the basis of the house's appraised value, its expected appreciation, and the owner-borrower's life expectancy. The borrower does not have to repay the loan until he or she dies or sells the house, and the proceeds from sale are usually used to repay the loan. The mortgage is called "reverse" because, unlike the conventional "forward" mortgage, the principal amount is highest at the end, not the beginning, and interest is backloaded.

The terms and costs of reverse mortgages vary considerably depending upon the program under which the mortgage is offered, the duration of the loan, the borrower's age, and other factors. Eligibility requirements usually restrict borrowers to persons 62 and older owning a single-family dwelling or FHA-approved condominium. There are, however, no minimum or maximum income or asset limits.

4. Planning for the Disabled

Parents and other relatives who have disabled children face a similar planning dilemma to that confronting the elderly. They want to provide for the needs of such children without impairing the child's eligibility for public assistance benefits. Trusts for disabled children are a common strategy that parents use for this purpose. To what extent will a disabled child's income and/or principal interest in a trust affect public assistance eligibility, and to what extent are trusts for disabled children liable for claims by the state? The *Myers* case which follows illustrates the standard judicial analysis of these questions. To provide some background for the problem, we first include the following excerpt.

Randall D. Van Dolson, Medicaid Eligibility Rules and Trusts for Disabled Children
133 Tr. & Est. 51, 51-52, 55 (1994)

A significant planning goal of a parent with a disabled child is to provide for the supplemental needs of the child following the parent's death without affecting the child's eligibility for need-based governmental support programs such as Supplemental Security Income ("SSI") and Medicaid. For many parents of moderate wealth, such programs are an important financial resource without which the family's other resources, during the lifetime of the parents or following their deaths, would be rapidly depleted. Since such programs provide support for persons who are, in effect, destitute, assets owned by or available to a disabled child must be spent-down to pay the cost of care and services which otherwise would be provided by the government. Only after the assets have been depleted will the child be eligible for government assistance.

...Since such programs provide little more than bare necessities, many parents view the child's best interest to be served by a strategy which supplements, but does not supplant, available government assistance.

Such a strategy should not be viewed as contrary to public policy or interest. Supplemental assistance enables a disabled child to enjoy a quality of life not available within the constraints of government support programs. Unless able to provide for the child's supplemental needs, many parents would not provide for the child at all. Government assistance would continue to provide basic support, but the child's quality of life would not be enhanced....

The Medicaid program, administered by the states and jointly financed by federal and state funds, provides medical assistance, including institutionalization, to certain disabled persons whose available income and resources are limited. In those states where Medicaid will pay the cost of independent housing, the benefits over the lifetime of a disabled child who lives in a community setting are substantial. Resources affect Medicaid eligibility if actually available or to the extent an individual has the ability to make them available....

Before June 1, 1986, an individual could transfer assets to an irrevocable trust which authorized the trustee to distribute income and principal to the individual. Because the trust funds could be distributed to or used for the benefit of the individual only in the discretion of the trustee, the trust was not considered an available resource for Medicaid eligibility purposes and upon expiration of the appropriate transfer penalty period the individual could qualify for Medicaid benefits. Often the transfer was to a friendly trustee, an arrangement which, in effect, might not significantly curtail the individual's control of and benefit from the transferred property.

The Medicaid Qualifying Trust ("MQT") rules, effective June 1, 1986, were enacted to curb the perceived abuse associated with such self-created trusts. Under the MQT rules the assets of an irrevocable trust established other than by Will by an individual or an individual's spouse were considered available to the full extent of the trustee's authority to make distributions of income and/or principal to the individual. If discretion were limited to income, the principal of the trust was disregarded as a resource in determining eligibility.

The MQT rules did not affect discretionary trusts established by a parent for a disabled child and funded with the parent's, not the child's, assets....

Section 13611 of OBRA-93 [42 U.S.C.§1396p]... repeals the Medicaid Qualifying Trust provisions.... While the [OBRA 93] rules affect self-created trusts traditionally used to qualify persons who are disabled by the aging process for Medicaid benefits, they should not affect the eligibility of an adult disabled child who is a beneficiary of a discretionary spendthrift trust created by a parent and funded with the parent's assets.

Myers v. Department of Social and Rehabilitation Services
866 P.2d 1052 (Kan. 1994)

HOLMES, C.J. The Kansas Department of Social and Rehabilitation Services (SRS) appeals from a judgment of the district court holding Darrell E. Myers, Jr., was the beneficiary of a discretionary trust and that the assets of the trust could not be considered as resources available to Myers in determining whether he was eligible for medical assistance. The Court of Appeals affirmed the judgment of the district court in an unpublished decision decided May 28, 1993. We granted the petition for review of SRS and now affirm the Court of Appeals and the district court.

The facts are not in dispute. In 1981, Caroline H. Myers executed her will, which provided for a trust for the care, support, and maintenance of her son, Darrell E. Myers, Jr. She bequeathed the sum of $110,000 to the trust. Upon her son's death, the principal and any undistributed income were to be distributed to Caroline's daughter and granddaughter, or the survivor thereof. Caroline H. Myers died in 1989. The trust was funded on November 20, 1989.

Darrell E. Myers, Jr., had been receiving public medical assistance from the State prior to the death of Mrs. Myers and the funding of the trust in 1989. Myers had apparently suffered from severe mental and physical disabilities for several years although the record does not indicate when he began receiving public assistance. In July of 1990, SRS terminated Myers' medical assistance when he failed to return an annual eligibility review form. Myers reapplied for assistance in November of 1990, but SRS denied the application, claiming Myers had resources which exceeded the eligibility level established by SRS regulations. The denial notice stated that assets held in trust for Myers were considered available to meet his medical needs.

After several reapplications and denials, Myers appealed the SRS decision of October 25, 1991, denying him medical assistance. The decision of SRS was affirmed by the administrative hearing officer on January 6, 1992, and his decision was affirmed by the State Appeals Committee on March 24, 1992.

In April of 1992, Myers filed a petition for judicial review. The district court, after reviewing the record and hearing arguments of counsel, issued its judgment finding the trust established in Caroline H. Myers' will to be a discretionary trust. Because neither the principal nor income were available to Myers, SRS could not consider the trust assets in determining Myers eligibility for public medical assistance. SRS timely appealed the district court's decision, which was affirmed by the Court of Appeals.

The issue before us on review is whether the district court and Court of Appeals erred in determining that the Myers trust is a discretionary trust in which the assets are considered unavailable to Myers for the purpose of determining his eligibility for public medical assistance. The question on appeal is the meaning and intent of the trust language set forth in Caroline H. Myers' will. Our decision will control whether SRS may consider the trust principal and income "available" for purposes of determining Myers' eligibility for public medical assistance.

The will of Caroline H. Myers provides in pertinent part:

> In the event my husband does not survive me then all the rest, residue remainder of my property, of which I shall die seized or possessed, shall be divided and set apart by my Executors into the following shares:
>
> 1) The sum of one hundred and ten thousand ($110,000.00) dollars in trust to my trustee hereinafter named on the terms and conditions hereinafter stated *for the lifetime use and benefit of my son, Darrell E. Meyers [sic], Jr....*
>
> A) In the event my son predeceases me I direct my Executor to divide his bequest equally and distribute it to my daughter and granddaughter or the survivors of them. In the event my granddaughter predeceases me, I direct my Executor to distribute her bequest to my daughter. In the event my daughter predeceases me, I direct my Executor to distribute her share to my granddaughter.
>
> B) *During my son's lifetime, my trustee shall hold, manage, invest and reinvest, collect the income there from* [sic] *any* [sic] *pay over so much or all the net income and principal to my son as my trustee deems advisable for his care, support, maintenance, emergencies and welfare.* At my son's death I direct this trust for his benefit be terminated and the principal and any undistributed net income be distributed in accordance with paragraph A above.
>
> *FIRST*: I hereby name and appoint the Overland Park State Bank and Trust Company of Overland Park, Kansas as my trustee.
>
> *SECOND*: The principal of the trust hereinabove created and the interest resulting herefore [sic] while in the hands of the Trustee shall not be subject to any conveyance, transfer or assignment, or be pledged as security for any debt by the beneficiary, and the same shall not be subject to any claim by and [sic] creditor of the beneficiary through legal process or otherwise. (Emphasis added.)

K.S.A. 1992 Supp. 39-708c (b) grants the Secretary of SRS the power and duty to determine general policies and to adopt rules and regulations relating to the forms of social welfare administered by SRS. K.S.A. 1992 Supp. 39-709(e) provides that medical assistance shall be granted to residents whose income and resources do not exceed the levels prescribed by the Secretary. K.A.R. 30-6-106 sets forth the general rules for consideration of resources and reads in relevant part:

> (c)(1) Resources shall be considered available both when actually available and when the applicant or recipient has the legal ability to make them available.[14] A resource shall be considered unavailable when there is a legal impediment that precludes the disposal of the resource. The applicant or recipient shall pursue reasonable steps to overcome the legal impediment unless it is determined that the cost of pursuing legal action would be more than the applicant or recipient would gain, or the likelihood of succeeding in the legal action would be unfavorable to the applicant or recipient.

Pursuant to K.A.R. 30-6-107, an individual having non-exempt resources in excess of $2,000 is not eligible for public medical assistance.

The sole issue before this court is the interpretation, as a matter of law, of the meaning and intent of the language used by Caroline H. Myers in the trust provisions of her will. Both parties confine their arguments primarily to the language which reads:

> During my son's lifetime, my trustee shall hold, manage, invest and reinvest, collect the income there from [*sic*] any [*sic*] pay over so much or all the net income and principal to my son as my trustee deems advisable for his care, support, maintenance, emergencies and welfare.

....SRS contends that the Myers trust is a support trust which requires the trustee to inquire into the basic support needs of the beneficiary and provide for those needs. As such, SRS argues the trust is an available resource within the meaning of K.A.R. 30-6-106(c)(1).

Myers, on the other hand, argues that the language of the trust is unambiguous in its creation of a discretionary trust. Thus, the trust language gives the trustee full discretion to decide whether payments from the trust income or principal are advisable. Because the trustee has complete authority to withhold all trust assets, the trust is not an available resource for Myers. Additionally, the trustee of the Myers trust, although not a party to this action, maintains that pursuant to the terms of the trust, the trustee has a responsibility to the remaindermen as well as to Myers.

The Court of Appeals, in affirming the district court's ruling that the Myers trust was discretionary and not an available resource of the beneficiary, relied primarily on this Court's recent decision in *State ex rel. Secretary of SRS v. Jackson*, 249 Kan.

---

14. This language is similar to that used in the federal Medicaid regulation (45 C.F.R. §233.20(a)(3)(ii)(D)). Ed.

635, 822 P.2d 1033 (1991) (*Jackson II*).

Both parties cite *Jackson II* as authority for their respective positions. In *Jackson II*, this court was similarly called upon to decide whether trust funds were an available resource for purposes of determining eligibility for public medical assistance. Carrie Jackson was the beneficiary of a trust fund created by her grandfather. During the period she was receiving nominal support from the trust, Jackson was also receiving public assistance benefits. The State contended that the trust fund providing support for Jackson was an available resource to her and was seeking reimbursement from Jackson, pursuant to K.S.A. 39-719b, for public assistance benefits paid to her in an amount in excess of $35,000.

In *State ex rel. Secretary of SRS v. Jackson*, 15 Kan. App. 2d 126, 803 P.2d 1045 (1990) (*Jackson I*), the Court of Appeals determined that the trust was purely discretionary in nature, and thus the trust assets were not an available resource to Jackson. However, in *Jackson II*, this court modified the Court of Appeals' ruling, concluding that the language in the trust instrument treated the trust income differently from the trust principal. The Jackson trust read in relevant part:

> (A) During the lifetime of Carrie Conner Jackson, the Trustees, in their uncontrolled discretion, shall pay to Carrie Conner Jackson the net income of the Trust. In addition, the Trustees may pay to Carrie Conner Jackson, from the principal of the Trust from time to time, such amount or amounts as the Trustees in their uncontrolled discretion, may determine is necessary for the purposes of her health, education, support and maintenance. 249 Kan. at 641.

In construing the language of the trust instrument, this Court reasoned:

> Stripped down, the provision states the Trustees shall pay the net income and, in addition, may pay from the principal. The payment of the net income is not tied to any determination of need as are payments from the principal....

> True, the term "in their uncontrolled discretion" is used in the provisions relating to the payment of income and principal, but its usage in payment of income provisions is inconsistent with the "shall pay" language except perhaps as to the form of the payment.... "Shall pay" so interpreted results in the payment of income not being a discretionary trust provision. 249 Kan. at 641-42.

The court concluded that the income of the trust was a resource available to Jackson but that the principal was not.

Although in *Jackson II* this court relied primarily upon the usage and meaning of the two terms "shall" and may," the court also raised legitimate social policy concerns in stating that "public assistance funds are ever in short supply, and public policy demands they be restricted to those without resources of their own." 249 Kan. at 644. While reliance on such public policy is appropriate in an applicable case, nothing in *Jackson II* indicates or implies that such policy overrides the intent of a testator or settlor if a discretionary trust is established.

SRS maintains that *Jackson II* is controlling of this case. Specifically, SRS argues that the phrase "as my trustee deems advisable" in the Myers trust is inconsistent with the language of "shall pay." SRS contends that under the holding in *Jackson II*, the "shall pay" language should control, limiting the trustee's discretion to how and when payments are to be made. SRS maintains that the language in the Myers will creates a support trust, requiring the trustee to inquire into and provide for the basic support needs of the beneficiary.

In reaching its conclusions, SRS reads the questioned language of the will as if the words "shall" and "pay" must be read together without consideration of the subsequent language "as my trustee deems advisable." We are not convinced such conclusion is justified when all the language is read and considered together.

Myers' reliance on *Jackson II* is based upon obvious differences in not only the language of the Jackson and Myers trusts but also the manner in which similar language in the two documents was used. Both trusts use discretionary language, "as my trustee deems advisable" here, and as the trustee "may determine is necessary' in the Jackson trust. Also, both trusts use the nondiscretionary term "shall" and in addition the Jackson trust used the word "may" in referring to payments from principal. Unfortunately, here the similarities end. Unlike the Jackson trust, the Myers language regarding income and principal is contained in the same sentence. Also, the nondiscretionary language, "shall", and the discretionary language "as my trustee deems advisable", occur in the same sentence. Thus, unlike the Jackson trust, the payment of both income and principal is tied to a determination of need and to the discretionary language "as my trustee deems advisable." ....

We now turn again to the specific language and intent of the Myers trust. In examining the language in the will of Caroline H. Myers it appears that she established the trust primarily for the care and support of her son. Specifically, the instrument states, "my trustee shall hold, manage, invest and reinvest, collect the income there from [*sic*] any [*sic*] pay over so much or all the net income and principal to my son as my trustee deems advisable for his care, support, maintenance, emergencies and welfare."

SRS contends that the word "shall" applies equally to the management of the trust, and the direction to pay, as well as to the language establishing the purposes for which the trust funds are to be paid. However, as Myers maintains, it is arguable that the word "shall" only applies to holding, managing, investing and reinvesting, and the collection of income; and that the balance of the sentence gives the trustee complete discretion to determine whether funds are to be paid out for Myers' support and maintenance.

The trial court in determining that the Myers will established a discretionary trust concluded:

> The trust created pursuant to the Will of Caroline H. Myers, in which Darrell E. Myers, Jr. is the beneficiary, is a discretionary trust. The trust provides that the trustee "shall ... pay

over so much or all the net income and principal as (it) deems advisable" for the care, support, maintenance, emergencies and welfare of Mr. Myers. It is clear that the trustee has discretion as to what, if any, of the trust funds are to be paid to or for the benefit of Mr. Myers. The Court is not persuaded by the argument of Respondent that the word "shall" mandates the trustee to make payments to Mr. Myers. Once the trustee decides, in its discretion, to release funds to Mr. Myers, it is at that point that it "shall" make the payment; until such discretionary determination is made, however, the trustee is under no duty to pay any portion of the net income or principal to Mr. Myers. The trustee is given the discretion to pay over "so much or all" of the trust funds to Mr. Myers, which clearly indicates that the trustee is under no duty to pay a specific sum or any sum at all. It is therefore the conclusion of the Court that the trust established by Caroline H. Myers is a discretionary trust and not an "available resource" that can be used to determine eligibility for state assistance, until such trust funds are actually paid to and received by Darrell E. Myers, Jr.

We agree with the trial court's reasoning. The Myers trust directs the trustee to pay out so much of the income and principal as, in the trustees' discretion, it deems advisable for Myers' support. We conclude this language creates a discretionary trust. The nondiscretionary language of "shall" pertains primarily to the management functions of the trust and does not control or override the discretionary language of "as my trustee deems advisable," which pertains to whether payment of net income or principal will be made at all and, if so, the amount and purpose of any such payment. Neither the beneficiary nor any creditor can compel the trustee to pay any trust income or principal to the beneficiary, and SRS may not consider the trust assets to be resources available to Myers in determining whether Myers qualifies for medical assistance.

Our determination would appear to be consistent with the intent of Caroline H. Myers. In her will she directs the trustee at the death of her son to distribute "the principal and any undistributed net income" to the remaindermen. This language indicates that Caroline H. Myers did not presume that the trust principal would necessarily be exhausted. The record reveals that Myers was receiving public assistance prior to the death of his mother and she undoubtedly was aware of such assistance. At the time of this action, Myers was a resident of Johnson County Residential Care Facility. The record indicates that in 1991, the daily charge for Myers' care was $75 and there was additional monthly expense of approximately $600 for prescription medications. At that rate of expense, the trust fund would be exhausted in less than three and one-half years. We do not believe that exhausting the trust funds in this manner would be consistent with the purpose of the Myers trust.

At the time of Caroline H. Myers' death, her son was 50 years of age. The Myers trust was established to assist in the care and support of Myers during his "lifetime." This purpose cannot be met by a complete exhaustion of the trust assets in a short period of time or if complete discretionary authority was not placed in the trustee. Because the Myers trust is discretionary in nature, the trustee is allowed complete and uncontrolled discretion to allocate trust funds if and when it deems advisable. Only if it can be demonstrated that the trustee is abusing its discretion by acting arbitrarily, dishonestly, or improperly may the trustee be required to distribute funds. See *Jennings v. Murdock*, 220 Kan. 182, 201, 553 P.2d 846 (1976).

The judgment of the Court of Appeals affirming the judgment of the district court is affirmed. The judgment of the district court is affirmed.

Notes and Question

1. *Liability of Trusts to State Agencies Providing Care to the Disabled.* There has been considerable litigation concerning an issue closely related to the Medicaid eligibility question posed by *Myers*: the right of a state to reimbursement from a trust for the care of an institutionalized beneficiary. In the case of self-settled trusts, courts generally have applied the conventional trust law rules governing creditors rights in self-settled trusts and allowed the state to reach as much of the trust estate as could have been paid to the settlor. See State v. Hawes, 564 N.Y.S.2d 637 (App. Div. 1991).

Where, as is usually the case, the trust is created by a third person, the standard analysis has been the same as that used in *Myers*: the trust's liability depends on whether the trust is a discretionary trust or a support trust. If it is a discretionary trust, then the state's claim is denied on the ground that the beneficiary lacks an ascertainable interest in income or principal that is subject to creditor claims. See, e.g., Miller v. Department of Mental Health, 442 N.W.2d 617 (Mich. 1989); First Nat'l Bank v. Dep't of Health & Mental Hygiene, 399 A.2d 891 (Md. 1979).

Most trust instruments combine trustee discretion with a support purpose, creating what has been called a "discretionary support trust." (Recall the discussion in Chapter 11.) The results of the cases in which the courts have analyzed whether such trusts are support or discretionary trusts have been rather unpredictable. The hybrid character of these trusts has led some courts to focus instead on whether the settlor intended the trust to support the institutionalized beneficiary or merely to supplement other sources of support, including government assistance. If the court finds that the settlor intended to create a supplemental needs trust, then the state's claim has usually been denied. See, e.g., Lang v. Dept. of Public Welfare, 528 A.2d 1335 (Pa. 1987); In re Estate of Escher, 407 N.Y.S.2d 106 (Surr. Ct. 1978), *aff'd*, 426 N.Y.S.2d 1008 (App. Div. 1980), *aff'd sub nom.* In re Gross, 420 N.E.2d 91 (N.Y. 1981). *Question:* How would the trust instrument in the *Myers* case have fared under this approach?

The differences in the approaches that courts have taken to this question should lead the practitioner to be especially cautious in drafting the trust instrument. For guidance, see Rebecca C. Morgan, Robert B. Fleming Jr. & Bryn Poland, Third-Party and Self-Created Trusts: A Modern Look (2023).

2. *Statutory Approval of Supplemental Needs Trusts.* In many states, statutes expressly authorize the use of supplemental needs trusts ("SNTs") for persons with disabilities. These statutes, however, carefully define the terms and scope of permissible trusts. The New York statute, for example, defines such trusts as discretionary trusts created "for the benefit of a person with a severe and chronic or persistent disability." The statute shelters the income and principal of such trusts from providers of government health-care benefits where the trust instrument "clearly evidences the creator's intent to supplement, not supplant, impair or diminish, government benefits or assistance for which the beneficiary may otherwise be eligible or which the beneficiary may be receiving...." Upon the beneficiary's death, the state is entitled to full reimbursement from the trust principal for the total amount of medical benefits provided to the trust beneficiary. See generally N.Y. EPTL §7-1.12.

A Minnesota statute takes a different approach. It declares void as against public policy trust provisions that purport to convert the beneficiary's income or principal interest from an available to a non-available resource if the beneficiary is found eligible for or receives public assistance for medical care. It then declares valid under public policy a "supplemental needs trust," defined as a trust intended "to provide for the reasonable living expenses and other basic needs of a person with a disability when benefits from publicly funded benefit programs are not sufficient to provide adequately for those needs." Minn. Stat. §501C.1205(2)(d).

3. *Statutory Discretionary-Support Trusts Under the Uniform Custodial Trust Act and the Uniform Probate Code.* Under §9(b) of the Uniform Custodial Trust Act, the custodial trustee for an incapacitated beneficiary is authorized to make expenditures for support "without regard to other support, income, or property of the beneficiary." Note that, in providing a statutory discretionary-support trust for an incapacitated surviving spouse on whose behalf an elective share is taken, the Uniform Probate Code incorporates the Uniform Custodial Trust Act. In doing so, however, the UPC makes certain adjustments to the Custodial Trust Act, including an adjustment to §9(b). Under UPC §2-212(c)(2), the custodial trustee is *required* to take "other support, income, and property of the [incapacitated surviving spouse]" into account in making expenditures for support; enacting states, however, are given a choice as to whether the items to be taken into account include or do not include "benefits of medical or other forms of assistance from any state or federal government or governmental agency for which the [incapacitated surviving spouse] must qualify on the basis of need."

PART C. MAKING HEALTH-CARE DECISIONS

1. Advance Health-Care Directives

Primary Statutory Reference: *Uniform Health-Care Decisions Act (2023)*

Advance health-care directives are written instructions concerning the level of medical care to be given a person in the event of incapacity. The two most important types of such directives are "living wills" and durable health-care powers of attorney. Use of both of these instruments has grown dramatically in recent decades, as the rising cost of medical care and growing sophistication of medical technology are leading more Americans to try prevent what they regard as the excessive prolonging of life. The two instruments are often confused with each other, and it is important to understand the differences between them.

Living Wills. Probably the better known of the two types of health-care directives, the living will is a legal document by which an individual gives treatment instructions in the event that he or she becomes either terminally ill or is in a persistent vegetative state. It details what forms of medical care the patient wants and under what circumstances he or she wants life-sustaining treatment either administered or, more commonly, terminated.

Nearly all states now recognize living wills by statute. The statutes vary considerably in their details, but they have two factors in common. First, the statutes provide that a living will is effective only in circumstances of the individual's incapacity. Second, the statutes permit the living will to be used to terminate life-sustaining treatment in the event of the declarant's terminal illness or persistent vegetative state. Living wills are not designed to be total health-care decisional instruments. If an individual has a chance of recovery, the living will is not effective. Virtually no statute permits a living will to authorize termination of life-sustaining treatment where the patient is neither terminally ill nor in a persistent vegetative state. Some statutes define the meaning of the terms "terminal" and "persistent vegetative state" clearly, while others leave them undefined.

The statutory formalities required for execution of a living will also vary. Most statutes require a living will to be witnessed; a few also require notarization. Witnesses are usually required to be disinterested, and in some states hospital personnel are forbidden from serving as witnesses. Many states have statutory model forms, and a few states require the use of such forms.

Living will instructions are effective only if they are communicated to medical care providers, and hospitals now almost routinely provide living wills or other advance health-care directives to their patients. Under the federal Patient Self-Determination Act of 1990 (P.L. No. 101-508, § 4751, 104 Stat. 1388), hospitals and nursing homes are required to inform patients, upon admission, of their right to refuse medical treatment.

While state law in nearly all states provides legal immunity to medical care providers who follow living will instructions, only a few states provide penalties for failure to obey them. Some evidence indicates that living wills are honored more in the breach than in the observance. See Jane Brody, Putting Muscle Behind End-of-Life Wishes, N.Y. Times, Feb. 24, 2009, at D7; Denise Grady, At Life's End, Many Patients Are Denied Peaceful Passing, N.Y. Times, May 29, 2000, at A1.

Sample Living Will[15]

I, _____, declare that if I become unable to make my own health care decisions, as determined by my attending physician, such decisions, including those to accept or refuse any treatment, service or procedure used to diagnose, treat or care for me, and to withhold or withdraw life-sustaining measures, shall be made in accordance with my wishes which follow.

I do not want my life prolonged by life-sustaining measures, but want to be allowed to die naturally and to be given all care necessary to make me comfortable and to relieve pain:

1. If I am diagnosed as having an incurable and irreversible terminal condition; or

2. If I am diagnosed as being permanently unconscious or in a persistent vegetative state; or

3. If I am diagnosed as having an incurable and irreversible condition which is not terminal but which causes me to experience severe and progressive physical or mental deterioration and loss of capacities I value, so that the burdens of continued life (with treatment) are greater than the benefits I experience.

In the circumstances described, (a) artificially provided fluids and nutrition, such as by feeding tube or intravenous infusion, should be withheld or withdrawn, (b) if I should suffer cardiac or respiratory arrest, cardiopulmonary resuscitation should not be provided and (c) any other medicine or medical procedures that may be available to prolong my life should not be used.

Any invalid or unenforceable direction shall not affect my other directions.

This document shall not limit the powers given to any existing or future health care agent designated by me.

I understand the purpose and effect of this document and sign it after careful deliberation, this ___ day of _____, 19__.

                         _____(L.S.)

---

15. This form is reprinted from U.S. Trust Company, Practical Drafting—Trust and Will Provisions. This form is described by the publisher as a "common law" document and as having been prepared on the assumption that applicable state law recognizes its validity and imposes no requirements on its use; should such restrictions or requirements exist, the form must be modified.

Residing at: _____

Each of the undersigned declares that the person who signed this document did so in his or her presence; that said person is personally known to him or her and appears to be of sound mind and acting willingly and free from duress or undue influence; and that he or she is 18 years of age or older and is not designated as the persons's health care proxy.

_____ residing at _____

_____ residing at _____

Durable Health-Care Powers of Attorney. The other main type of advance health-care directive is the durable health-care power of attorney, sometimes called a "health-care proxy." Unlike a living will, the durable power names a surrogate decisionmaker who has authority to act in the event the principal becomes incapacitated. All fifty states and the District of Columbia have statutes authorizing durable health-care powers.

Durable health-care powers have several advantages over living wills. Durable powers can be general or detailed, depending on what the principal wants. By using a third party, they enhance the flexibility needed to cover a wide variety of circumstances. Some state statutes limit the powers that can be delegated to a surrogate, so it is important in drafting a durable power to check whether the statute permits all the powers that the principal wants the agent to have. Where the agent is given broad powers, he or she can act in circumstances in which the principal's wishes are not specifically known.

As with living wills, the statutes permitting durable health-care powers vary in their details. Most of them, however, provide fewer formalities of execution than those usually required for living wills. While most do require witnessing, for example, only a few require notarization. Still, the recommended practice is to have a durable power both witnessed and notarized.

The Uniform Law Commissioners approved the original Uniform Health-Care Decisions Act in 1993 and approved a new Uniform Health-Care Decisions Act in 2023. Both Acts authorize use of durable health-care powers and living wills. If a patient fails to execute a health-care power, both Acts identify persons who may serve as surrogates if they are reasonably available.

The limitations of health-care decisional instruments are discussed in Thomas P. Gallanis, Write and Wrong: Rethinking the Way We Communicate Health-Care Decisions, 31 Conn. L. Rev. 1015 (1999); David Orentlicher, The Limitations of Legislation, 53 Md. L. Rev. 1255 (1994); Patricia D. White, Appointing a Proxy Under the Best of Circumstances, 1992 Utah L. Rev. 849 (1992).

Section 11 of the new Uniform Health-Care Decisions Act has an optional form, which is reproduced on the following pages.

ADVANCE HEALTH-CARE DIRECTIVE
HOW YOU CAN USE THIS FORM

You can use this form if you wish to name someone to make health-care decisions for you in case you cannot make decisions for yourself. This is called giving the person a power of attorney for health care. This person is called your Agent.

You can also use this form to state your wishes, preferences, and goals for health care, and to say if you want to be an organ donor after you die.

YOUR NAME AND DATE OF BIRTH

Name:

Date of birth:

PART A: NAMING AN AGENT

This part lets you name someone else to make health-care decisions for you. You may leave any item blank.

1. NAMING AN AGENT

I want the following person to make health-care decisions for me if I cannot make decisions for myself:

Name:

Optional contact information (it is helpful to include information such as address, phone, and email):

2. NAMING AN ALTERNATE AGENT

I want the following person to make health-care decisions for me if I cannot and my Agent is not able or available to make them for me:

Name:

Optional contact information (it is helpful to include information such as address, phone, and email):

3. LIMITING YOUR AGENT'S AUTHORITY

I give my Agent the power to make all health-care decisions for me if I cannot make those decisions for myself, except the following:

(If you do not add a limitation here, your Agent will be able make all health-care decisions that an Agent is permitted to make under state law.)

PART B: HEALTH-CARE INSTRUCTIONS

This part lets you state your priorities for health care and to state types of health care you do and do not want.

1. INSTRUCTIONS ABOUT LIFE-SUSTAINING TREATMENT

This section gives you the opportunity to say how you want your Agent to act while making decisions for you. You may mark or initial each choice. You also may leave any choice blank.

Treatment. Medical treatment needed to keep me alive but not needed for comfort or any other purpose should (mark or initial all that apply):

(_____) Always be given to me. (If you mark or initial this choice, you should not mark or initial other choices in this "treatment" section.).

(_____) Not be given to me if I have a condition that is not curable and is expected tocause my death soon, even if treated.

(_____) Not be given to me if I am unconscious and I am not expected to be conscious again.

(_____) Not be given to me if I have a medical condition from which I am not expected to recover that prevents me from communicating with people I care about, caring for myself, and recognizing family and friends.

(_____) Other (write what you want or do not want):

Food and liquids. If I can't swallow and staying alive requires me to get food or liquids through a tube or other means for the rest of my life, then food or liquids should (mark or initial all that apply):

(_____) Always be given to me. (If you mark or initial this choice, you should not mark or initial other choices in this "food and liquids" section).

(_____) Not be given to me if I have a condition that is not curable and is expected tocause me to die soon, even if treated.

(_____) Not be given to me if I am unconscious and am not expected to be conscious again.

(_____) Not be given to me if I have a medical condition from which I am not expected to recover that prevents me from communicating with people I care about, caring for myself, and recognizing family and friends.

(_____) Other (write what you want or do not want):

Pain relief. If I am in significant pain, care that will keep me comfortable but is likely to shorten my life should (mark or initial all that apply):

(_____) Always be given to me. (If you mark or initial this choice, you should not mark or initial other choices in this "pain relief" section.)

(_____) Never be given to me. (If you mark or initial this choice, you should not mark or initial other choices in this "pain relief" section.

(_____) Be given to me if I have a condition that is not curable and is expected to cause me to die soon, even if treated.

(_____) Be given to me if I am unconscious and am not expected to be conscious again.

(_____) Be given to me if I have a medical condition from which I am not expected to recover that prevents me from communicating with people I care about, caring for myself, and recognizing family and friends.

(_____) Other (write what you want or do not want):

2. MY PRIORITIES

You can use this section to indicate what is important to you, and what is not important to you. This information can help your Agent make decisions for you if you cannot. It also helps others understand your preferences.

You may mark or initial each choice. You also may leave any choice blank.

Staying alive as long as possible even if I have substantial physical limitations is:

(____) Very important

(____) Somewhat important

(____) Not important

Staying alive as long as possible even if I have substantial mental limitations is:

(____) Very important

(____) Somewhat important

(____) Not important

Being free from significant pain is:

(____) Very important

(____) Somewhat important

(____) Not important

Being independent is:

(____) Very important

(____) Somewhat important

(____) Not important

Having my Agent talk with my family before making decisions about my care is:

(____) Very important

(____) Somewhat important

(____) Not important

Having my Agent talk with my friends before making decisions about my care is:

(____) Very important

(____) Somewhat important

(____) Not important

3. OTHER INSTRUCTIONS

You can write in this section more information about your goals, values, and preferences for treatment, including care you want or do not want. You can also use this section to name anyone who you do not want to make decisions for you under any conditions.

PART C: OPTIONAL SPECIAL POWERS AND GUIDANCE

This part lets you give your Agent additional powers, and to provide more guidance about your wishes. You may mark or initial each choice. You also may leave any choice blank.

1. OPTIONAL SPECIAL POWERS

My Agent can do the following things ONLY if I have marked or initialed them below:

(____) Admit me as a voluntary patient to a facility for mental health treatment for up to _____ days (write in the number of days you want like 7, 14, 30 or another number).

(If I do not mark or initial this choice, my Agent MAY NOT admit me as a voluntary patient to this type of facility.)

(____) Place me in a nursing home for more than [100] days even if my needs can be met somewhere else, I am not terminally ill, and I object.

(If I do not mark or initial this choice, my Agent MAY NOT do this.)

2. ACCESS TO MY HEALTH INFORMATION

My Agent may obtain, examine, and share information about my health needs and health care if I am not able to make decisions for myself. If I mark or initial below, my Agent may also do that at any time my Agent thinks it will help me.

(____) I give my Agent permission to obtain, examine, and share information about my health needs and health care whenever my Agent thinks it will help me.

3. FLEXIBILITY FOR MY AGENT

Mark or initial below if you want to give your Agent flexibility in following instructions you provide in this form. If you do not, your Agent must follow the instructions even if your Agent thinks something else would be better for you.

(____) I give my Agent permission to be flexible in applying these instructions if my Agent thinks it would be in my best interest based on what my Agent knows about me.

4. NOMINATION OF GUARDIAN

You can say who you would want as your guardian if you needed one. A guardian is a person appointed by a court to make decisions for someone who cannot make decisions. Filling this out does NOT mean you want or need a guardian.

If a court appoints a guardian to make personal decisions for me, I want the court to choose:

(____) My Agent named in this form. If my Agent cannot be a guardian, I want the Alternate Agent named in this form.

(____) Other (write who you would want and their contact information):

PART D: ORGAN DONATION

This part lets you donate your organs after you die. You may leave any item blank.

1. DONATION

You may mark or initial only one choice.

(____) I donate my organs, tissues, and other body parts after I die, even if it requires maintaining treatments that conflict with other instructions I have put in this form, EXCEPT for those I list below (list any body parts you do NOT want to donate):

(____) I do not want my organs, tissues, or body parts donated to anybody for any reason. (If you mark or initial this choice, you should skip the "purpose of donation" section.)

2. PURPOSE OF DONATION

You may mark or initial all that apply. (If you do not mark or initial any of the purposes below, your donation can be used for all of them.)

Organs, tissues, or body parts that I donate may be used for:

(____) Transplant

(____) Therapy

(____) Research

(____) Education

(____) All of the above

PART E: SIGNATURES

YOUR SIGNATURE

Sign your name:

Today's date:

City/Town/Village and State (optional):

SIGNATURE OF A WITNESS

You need a witness if you are using this form to name an Agent. The witness must be an adult and cannot be the person you are naming as Agent or the Agent's spouse[, domestic partner,] or someone the Agent lives with as a couple. If you live or are receiving care in a nursing home, the witness cannot be an employee or contractor of the home or someone who owns or runs the home.

Name of Witness:

Signature of Witness:

(Only sign as a witness if you think the person signing above is doing it voluntarily.)

Date witness signed:

PART F: INFORMATION FOR AGENTS

1. If this form names you as an Agent, you can make decisions about health care for the person who named you when the person cannot make their own.

2. If you make a decision for the person, follow any instructions the person gave, including any in this form.

3. If you do not know what the person would want, make the decision that you think is in the person's best interest. To figure out what is in the person's best interest, consider the person's values, preferences, and goals if you know them or can learn them. Some of these preferences may be in this form. You should also consider any behavior or communication from the person that indicates what the person currently wants.

4. If this form names you as an Agent, you can also get and share the person's health information. But unless the person has said so in this form, you can get or share this information only when the person cannot make decisions about the person's health care.

———

Empirical studies have indicated that the use of living wills and durable health-care powers has increased in the wake of the United States Supreme Court's decision in the *Cruzan* case that follows.

Cruzan v. Director, Missouri Department of Health
497 U.S. 261 (1990)

REHNQUIST, C.J. Petitioner Nancy Beth Cruzan was rendered incompetent as a result of severe injuries sustained during an automobile accident. Copetitioners Lester and Joyce Cruzan, Nancy's parents and coguardians, sought a court order directing the withdrawal of their daughter's artificial feeding and hydration equipment after it became apparent that she had virtually no chance of recovering her cognitive faculties. The Supreme Court of Missouri held that because there was no clear and convincing evidence of Nancy's desire to have life sustaining treatment withdrawn under such circumstances, her parents lacked authority to effectuate such a request. We granted certiorari, and now affirm.

On the night of January 11, 1983, Nancy Cruzan lost control of her car as she traveled down Elm Road in Jasper County, Missouri. The vehicle overturned, and Cruzan was discovered lying face down in a ditch without detectable respiratory or cardiac function. Paramedics were able to restore her breathing and heartbeat at the accident site, and she was transported to a hospital in an unconscious state. An attending neurosurgeon diagnosed her as having sustained probable cerebral contusions compounded by significant anoxia (lack of oxygen). The Missouri trial court in this case found that permanent brain damage generally results after 6 minutes in an anoxic state; it was estimated that Cruzan was deprived of oxygen from 12 to 14 minutes. She remained in a coma for approximately three weeks and then progressed to an unconscious state in which she was able to orally ingest some nutrition. In order to ease feeding and further the recovery, surgeons implanted a gastrostomy feeding and hydration tube in Cruzan with the consent of her then husband. Subsequent rehabilitative efforts proved unavailing. She now lies in a Missouri state hospital in what is commonly referred to as a persistent vegetative state: generally, a condition in which a person exhibits motor reflexes but evinces no indications of significant cognitive function. The State of Missouri is bearing the cost of her care.

After it had become apparent that Nancy Cruzan had virtually no chance of regaining her mental faculties, her parents asked hospital employees to terminate the artificial nutrition and hydration procedures. All agree that such a removal would cause her death. The employees refused to honor the request without court approval. The parents then sought and received authorization from the state trial court for termination. The court found that a person in Nancy's condition had a fundamental right under the State and Federal Constitutions to refuse or direct the withdrawal of "death prolonging procedures." The court also found that Nancy's "expressed thoughts at age twenty-five in somewhat serious conversation with a housemate friend that if sick or injured she would not wish to continue her life unless she could live at least halfway normally suggests that given her present condition she would not wish to continue on with her nutrition and hydration."

The Supreme Court of Missouri reversed by a divided vote. The court recognized a right to refuse treatment embodied in the common-law doctrine of informed consent, but expressed skepticism about the application of that doctrine in the circumstances of this case. Cruzan v. Harmon, 760 S. W. 2d 408, 416-417 (1988) (en banc). The court also declined to read a broad right of privacy into the State Constitution which would "support the right of a person to refuse medical treatment in every circumstance," and expressed doubt as to whether such a right existed under the United States Constitution. Id., at 417-418. It then decided that the Missouri Living Will statute embodied a state policy strongly favoring the preservation of life. The court found that Cruzan's statements to her roommate regarding her desire to live or die under certain conditions were "unreliable for the purpose of determining her intent," id., at 424, "and thus insufficient to support the co-guardians['] claim to exercise substituted judgment on Nancy's behalf." Id., at 426. It rejected the argument that Cruzan's parents were entitled to order the termination of her medical treatment, concluding that "no person can assume that choice for an incompetent in the absence of the formalities required under Missouri's Living Will statutes or the clear and convincing, inherently reliable evidence absent here." Id., at 425. The court also expressed its view that "[b]road policy questions bearing on life and death are more properly addressed by representative assemblies" than judicial bodies. Id., at 426.

We granted certiorari to consider the question whether Cruzan has a right under the United States Constitution which would require the hospital to withdraw life-sustaining treatment from her under these circumstances....

As [various state] cases demonstrate, the common-law doctrine of informed consent is viewed as generally encompassing the right of a competent individual to refuse medical treatment.... State courts have available to them for decision a number of sources—state constitutions, statutes, and common law—which are not available to us. In this Court, the question is simply and starkly whether the United States Constitution prohibits Missouri from choosing the rule of decision which it did. This is the first case in which we have been squarely presented with the issue whether the United States Constitution grants what is in common parlance referred to as a "right to die."...

The Fourteenth Amendment provides that no State shall "deprive any person of life, liberty, or property, without due process of law." The principle that a competent person has a constitutionally protected liberty interest in refusing unwanted medical treatment may be inferred from our prior decisions.... But determining that a person has a "liberty interest" under the Due Process Clause does not end the inquiry;[16] "whether respondent's constitutional rights have been violated must be determined by balancing his liberty interests against the relevant state interests." Youngberg v. Romeo, 457 U.S. 307, 321 (1982)....

Petitioners insist that under the general holdings of our cases, the forced administration of life-sustaining medical treatment, and even of artificially delivered food and water essential to life, would implicate a competent person's liberty interest. Although we think the logic of the cases discussed above would embrace such a liberty interest, the dramatic consequences involved in refusal of such treatment would inform the inquiry as to whether the deprivation of that interest is constitutionally permissible. But for purposes of this case, we assume that the United States Constitution would grant a competent person a constitutionally protected right to refuse lifesaving hydration and nutrition.

Petitioners go on to assert that an incompetent person should possess the same right in this respect as is possessed by a competent person.... The difficulty with petitioners' claim is that in a sense it begs the question: An incompetent person is not able to make an informed and voluntary choice to exercise a hypothetical right to refuse treatment or any other right. Such a "right" must be exercised for her, if at all, by some sort of surrogate. Here, Missouri has in effect recognized that under certain circumstances a surrogate may act for the patient in electing to have hydration and nutrition withdrawn in such a way as to cause death, but it has

---

16. Although many state courts have held that a right to refuse treatment is encompassed by a generalized constitutional right of privacy, we have never so held. We believe this issue is more properly analyzed in terms of a Fourteenth Amendment liberty interest. See Bowers v. Hardwick, 478 U.S. 186, 194-195 (1986).

established a procedural safeguard to assure that the action of the surrogate conforms as best it may to the wishes expressed by the patient while competent. Missouri requires that evidence of the incompetent's wishes as to the withdrawal of treatment be proved by clear and convincing evidence. The question, then, is whether the United States Constitution forbids the establishment of this procedural requirement by the State. We hold that it does not.

Whether or not Missouri's clear and convincing evidence requirement comports with the United States Constitution depends in part on what interests the State may properly seek to protect in this situation. Missouri relies on its interest in the protection and preservation of human life, and there can be no gainsaying this interest. As a general matter, the States—indeed, all civilized nations—demonstrate their commitment to life by treating homicide as a serious crime. Moreover, the majority of States in this country have laws imposing criminal penalties on one who assists another to commit suicide. We do not think a State is required to remain neutral in the face of an informed and voluntary decision by a physically able adult to starve to death.

But in the context presented here, a State has more particular interests at stake. The choice between life and death is a deeply personal decision of obvious and overwhelming finality. We believe Missouri may legitimately seek to safeguard the personal element of this choice through the imposition of heightened evidentiary requirements. It cannot be disputed that the Due Process Clause protects an interest in life as well as an interest in refusing life-sustaining medical treatment. Not all incompetent patients will have loved ones available to serve as surrogate decisionmakers. And even where family members are present, "[t]here will, of course, be some unfortunate situations in which family members will not act to protect a patient." In re Jobes, 108 N.J. 394, 419, 529 A.2d 434, 447 (1987). A State is entitled to guard against potential abuses in such situations. Similarly, a State is entitled to consider that a judicial proceeding to make a determination regarding an incompetent's wishes may very well not be an adversarial one, with the added guarantee of accurate fact finding that the adversary process brings with it. Finally, we think a State may properly decline to make judgments about the "quality" of life that a particular individual may enjoy, and simply assert an unqualified interest in the preservation of human life to be weighed against the constitutionally protected interests of the individual.

In our view, Missouri has permissibly sought to advance these interests through the adoption of a "clear and convincing" standard of proof to govern such proceedings.... The more stringent the burden of proof a party must bear, the more that party bears the risk of an erroneous decision. We believe that Missouri may permissibly place an increased risk of an erroneous decision on those seeking to terminate an incompetent individual's life-sustaining treatment. An erroneous decision not to terminate results in a maintenance of the status quo; the possibility of subsequent developments such as advancements in medical science, the discovery of new evidence regarding the patient's intent, changes in the law, or simply the unexpected death of the patient despite the administration of life-sustaining treatment at least create the potential that a wrong decision will eventually be corrected or its impact mitigated. An erroneous decision to withdraw life-sustaining treatment, however, is not susceptible of correction....

The Supreme Court of Missouri held that in this case the testimony adduced at trial did not amount to clear and convincing proof of the patient's desire to have hydration and nutrition withdrawn.... The testimony adduced at trial consisted primarily of Nancy Cruzan's statements made to a housemate about a year before her accident that she would not want to live should she face life as a "vegetable," and other observations to the same effect. The observations did not deal in terms with withdrawal of medical treatment or of hydration and nutrition. We cannot say that the Supreme Court of Missouri committed constitutional error in reaching the conclusion that it did.

Petitioners alternatively contend that Missouri must accept the "substituted judgment" of close family members even in the absence of substantial proof that their views reflect the views of the patient.... But we do not think the Due Process Clause requires the State to repose judgment on these matters with anyone but the patient herself. Close family members may have a strong feeling—a feeling not at all ignoble or unworthy, but not entirely disinterested, either—that they do not wish to witness the continuation of the life of a loved one which they regard as hopeless, meaningless, and even degrading. But there is no automatic assurance that the view of close family members will necessarily be the same as the patient's would have been had she been confronted with the prospect of her situation while competent. All of the reasons previously discussed for allowing Missouri to require clear and convincing evidence of the patient's wishes lead us to conclude that the State may choose to defer only to those wishes, rather than confide the decision to close family members.

The judgment of the Supreme Court of Missouri is affirmed.

SCALIA, J., concurring. [W]hile I agree with the Court's analysis today, and therefore join in its opinion, I would have preferred that we announce, clearly and promptly, that the federal courts have no business in this field; that American law has always accorded the State the power to prevent, by force if necessary, suicide—including suicide by refusing to take appropriate measures necessary to preserve one's life; that the point at which life becomes "worthless," and the point at which the means necessary to preserve it become "extraordinary" or "inappropriate," are neither set forth in the Constitution nor known to the nine Justices of this Court any better than they are known to nine people picked at random from the Kansas City telephone directory; and hence, that even when it is demonstrated by clear and convincing evidence that a patient no longer wishes certain measures to be taken to preserve his or her life, it is up to the citizens of Missouri to decide, through their elected representatives, whether that wish will be honored. It is quite impossible (because the Constitution says nothing about the matter) that those citizens will decide upon a line less lawful than the one we would choose; and it is unlikely (because we know no more about "life and death" than they do) that they will decide upon a line less reasonable....

BRENNAN, J., with whom MARSHALL, J., and BLACKMUN, J., join, dissenting. [B]ecause I believe that Nancy Cruzan has a fundamental right to be free of unwanted artificial nutrition and hydration, which right is not outweighed by any interests of the State, and because I find that the improperly biased procedural obstacles imposed by the Missouri Supreme Court impermissibly burden that right, I respectfully dissent. Nancy Cruzan is entitled to choose to die with dignity...

The right to be free from medical attention without consent, to determine what shall be done with one's own body, is deeply rooted in this Nation's traditions, as the majority acknowledges. This right has long been "firmly entrenched in American tort law" and is securely grounded in the earliest common law. Ante, at 269. See also Mills v. Rogers, 457 U.S. 291, 294, n.4 (1982) ("[T]he right to refuse any medical treatment emerged from the doctrines of trespass and battery, which were applied to unauthorized touchings by a physician"). "Anglo-American law starts with the premise of thorough-going self determination. It follows that each man is considered to be master of his own body, and he may, if he be of sound mind, expressly prohibit the performance of lifesaving surgery, or other medical treatment." Natanson v. Kline, 186 Kan. 393, 406-407, 350 P.2d 1093, 1104 (1960). "The inviolability of the person" has been held as "sacred" and "carefully guarded" as any common-law right. Union Pacific R. Co. v. Botsford, 141 U.S. 250, 251-252 (1891). Thus, freedom from unwanted medical attention is unquestionably among those principles "so rooted in the traditions and conscience of our people as to be ranked as fundamental." Snyder v. Massachusetts, 291 U.S. 97, 105 (1934)....

Although the right to be free of unwanted medical intervention, like other constitutionally protected interests, may not be absolute, no state interest could outweigh the rights of an individual in Nancy Cruzan's position. Whatever a State's possible interests in mandating life-support treatment under other circumstances, there is no good to be obtained here by Missouri's insistence that Nancy Cruzan remain on life-support systems if it is indeed her wish not to do so. Missouri does not claim, nor could it, that society as a whole will be benefited by Nancy's receiving medical treatment.... The only state interest asserted here is a general interest in the preservation of life. But the State has no legitimate general interest in someone's life, completely abstracted from the interest of the person living that life, that could outweigh the person's choice to avoid medical treatment.... Thus, the State's general interest in life must accede to Nancy Cruzan's particularized and intense interest in self-determination in her choice of medical treatment. There is simply nothing legitimately within the State's purview to be gained by superseding her decision....

This is not to say that the State has no legitimate interests to assert here. As the majority recognizes,... Missouri has a parens patriae interest in providing Nancy Cruzan, now incompetent, with as accurate as possible a determination of how she would exercise her rights under these circumstances. Second, if and when it is determined that Nancy Cruzan would want to continue treatment, the State may legitimately assert an interest in providing that treatment. But until Nancy's wishes have been determined, the only state interest that may be asserted is an interest in safeguarding the accuracy of that determination.

Accuracy, therefore, must be our touchstone. Missouri may constitutionally impose only those procedural requirements that serve to enhance the accuracy of a determination of Nancy Cruzan's wishes or are at least consistent with an accurate determination. The Missouri "safeguard" that the Court upholds today does not meet that standard. The determination needed in this context is whether the incompetent person would choose to live in a persistent vegetative state on life support or to avoid this medical treatment. Missouri's rule of decision imposes a markedly asymmetrical evidentiary burden. Only evidence of specific statements of treatment choice made by the patient when competent is admissible to support a finding that the patient, now in a persistent vegetative state, would wish to avoid further medical treatment. Moreover, this evidence must be clear and convincing. No proof is required to support a finding that the incompetent person would wish to continue treatment.

....An erroneous decision to terminate life support is irrevocable, says the majority, while an erroneous decision not to terminate "results in a maintenance of the status quo." But, from the point of view of the patient, an erroneous decision in either direction is irrevocable. An erroneous decision to terminate artificial nutrition and hydration, to be sure, will lead to failure of that last remnant of physiological life, the brain stem, and result in complete brain death. An erroneous decision not to terminate life support, however, robs a patient of the very qualities protected by the right to avoid unwanted medical treatment. His own degraded existence is perpetuated; his family's suffering is protracted; the memory he leaves behind becomes more and more distorted.

Even a later decision to grant him his wish cannot undo the intervening harm. But a later decision is unlikely in any event. "[T]he discovery of new evidence," to which the majority refers, is more hypothetical than plausible. The majority also misconceives the relevance of the possibility of "advancements in medical science," by treating it as a reason to force someone to continue medical treatment against his will. The possibility of a medical miracle is indeed part of the calculus, but it is a part of the patient's calculus. If current research suggests that some hope for cure or even moderate improvement is possible within the lifespan projected, this is a factor that should be and would be accorded significant weight in assessing what the patient himself would choose.

Even more than its heightened evidentiary standard, the Missouri court's categorical exclusion of relevant evidence dispenses with any semblance of accurate fact finding. The court adverted to no evidence supporting its decision, but held that no clear and convincing, inherently reliable evidence had been presented to show that Nancy would want to avoid further treatment. In doing so, the court failed to consider statements Nancy had made to family members and a close friend. The court also failed to consider testimony from Nancy's mother and sister that they were certain that Nancy would want to discontinue artificial nutrition and hydration, even after the court found that Nancy's family was loving and without malignant motive. The court also failed to consider the conclusions of the guardian ad litem, appointed by the trial court, that there was clear and convincing evidence that Nancy would want to discontinue medical treatment and that this was in her best interests. The court did not specifically define what kind of evidence it would consider clear and convincing, but its general discussion suggests that only a living will or equivalently formal directive from the patient when competent would meet this standard.

Too few people execute living wills or equivalently formal directives for such an evidentiary rule to ensure adequately that the wishes of incompetent persons will be honored. While it might be a wise social policy to encourage people to furnish such instructions, no general conclusion about a patient's choice can be drawn from the absence of formalities. The probability of becoming irreversibly vegetative is so low that many people may not feel an urgency to marshal formal evidence of their preferences. Some may not wish to dwell on their own physical deterioration and mortality. Even someone with a resolute determination to avoid life support under circumstances such as Nancy's would still need to know that such things as living wills exist and how to execute one. Often legal help would be necessary, especially given the majority's apparent willingness to permit States to insist that a person's wishes are not truly known unless the particular medical treatment is specified.

As a California appellate court observed: "The lack of generalized public awareness of the statutory scheme and the typically human characteristics of procrastination and reluctance to contemplate the need for such arrangements however makes this a tool which will all too often go unused by those who might desire it." Barber v. Superior Court, 147 Cal. App. 3d 1006, 1015, 195 Cal. Rptr. 484, 489 (1983). When a person tells family or close friends that she does not want her life sustained artificially, she is "express[ing] her wishes in the only terms familiar to her, and... as clearly as a lay person should be asked to express them. To require more is unrealistic, and for all practical purposes, it precludes the right of patients to forego life-sustaining treatment." In re O'Connor, 72 N.Y.2d 517, 551, 531 N.E.2d 607, 626 (1988) (Simons, J., dissenting). When Missouri enacted a living will statute, it specifically provided that the absence of a living will does not warrant a presumption that a patient wishes continued medical treatment. Thus, apparently not even Missouri's own legislature believes that a person who does not execute a living will fails to do so because he wishes continuous medical treatment under all circumstances.

The testimony of close friends and family members, on the other hand, may often be the best evidence available of what the patient's choice would be. It is they with whom the patient most likely will have discussed such questions and they who know the patient best. "Family members have a unique knowledge of the patient which is vital to any decision on his or her behalf." Newman, Treatment Refusals for the Critically and Terminally Ill: Proposed Rules for the Family, the Physician, and the State, 3 N.Y.L.S. Human Rights Annual 35, 46 (1985). The Missouri court's decision to ignore this whole category of testimony is also at odds with the practices of other States.

The Missouri court's disdain for Nancy's statements in serious conversations not long before her accident, for the opinions of Nancy's family and friends as to her values, beliefs and certain choice, and even for the opinion of an outside objective factfinder appointed by the State evinces a disdain for Nancy Cruzan's own right to choose. The rules by which an incompetent person's wishes are determined must represent every effort to determine those wishes. The rule that the Missouri court adopted and that this Court upholds, however, skews the result away from a determination that as accurately as possible reflects the individual's own preferences and beliefs. It is a rule that transforms human beings into passive subjects of medical technology....

I respectfully dissent.

MARSHALL, J., and BLACKMUN, J., concur.

[The concurring opinion of Justice O'Connor and the dissenting opinion of Justice Stevens are omitted.]

Notes and Questions

1. *Sequel to the Cruzan Case.* Nancy Cruzan died at age 33 on December 26, 1990, twelve days after her feeding tube was removed by order of a Missouri probate court. She had been in a vegetative state for eight years. Although Nancy Cruzan had not signed a living will or a durable health-care power of attorney, the probate court found that there was clear and convincing evidence she would have wanted to die; the finding was based on testimony of former co-workers as to conversations in which she stated that she would never want to live "like a vegetable."

On August 17, 1996, at age 62, Nancy Cruzan's father, Lester ("Joe") Cruzan, apparently committed suicide by hanging himself. According to the New York Times, he had "expressed uncertainty about whether the right action had been taken" regarding his daughter. See N.Y. Times, Aug. 19, 1996, at B12.

2. Would it be better as a matter of public policy for states to reverse the current presumption that the patient would want life-sustaining treatment and adopt a default rule of death? Consider the following excerpt.

James Lindgren, Death By Default
56 Law & Contemp. Problems 185, 227–230 (1993)

[T]he states of New York and Missouri [which have adopted a clear-and-convincing evidence requirement] have put the rights of the state above the rights of the individual. Other states and much of the medical profession also start with a default rule of life in desperate end-of-life situations. Under the usual standards for default rules in law and economics, life as the default rule here makes no sense. Usually, a default rule is the one that the party would have chosen if she could speak. In end-of-life situations it usually isn't. Or a default rule promotes efficiency in the form of wealth maximization. Most assuredly, it doesn't here. Or it promotes efficiency in the form of happiness, welfare, or general utility. Either welfare analysis is theoretically impossible here or, if it isn't, a rough utilitarian approach would lead to a default rule of death (at least where the family agrees). Under all three ways of analyzing default rules, the current default rule in *Cruzan* and *O'Connor* fails....

The default rule should switch wherever patient preferences switch. Thus, one must determine when most would prefer to have at least some treatments withdrawn. According to national public opinion polls, it appears that there are at least eight such overlapping situations:

(1) patients on life support who have no hope of recovery;

(2) patients in a coma with no brain activity being kept alive by a feeding tube;

(3) patients who are terminally ill or in irreversible coma, supported by life support systems, including food and water;

(4) patients with an illness that makes them totally dependent on a family member or other person for all their care (a situation in which they would not want their doctors "to do everything possible to save" life);

(5) patients with a disease with no hope of improvement suffering a great deal of physical pain;

(6) patients in a coma with no hope of recovery but no pain;

(7) hopelessly ill or comatose patients on life support if their families request the withdrawal of support; and

(8) permanently unconscious patients receiving food and water.

The study of medical directives and further polling of doctors, nursing home residents, the elderly, and retirees reveals more situations in which at least some treatments should be withheld:

(9) patients with a terminal illness which has progressed and caused their heart to stop beating;

(10) mentally incompetent patients with a terminal illness which has progressed and caused their heart to stop beating;

(11) permanently unconscious patients in a persistent vegetative state unable to

eat normally, needing artificial feedings;

(12) nursing home patients, no matter what the level of cognitive functioning at the time of treatment, needing resuscitation, amputation, or tube feeding (either temporary or permanent);

(13) nursing home residents about to die of natural causes needing drugs, fluids, food by tubes, breathing machines, or heart massage; and

(14) terminally ill retirees needing CPR, a resuscitator, a nasogastric feeding tube, or intravenous fluids.

.... Medical care is supposed to be based on the informed consent of the patient. Unconsented treatment is supposed to be a battery. Yet under the influence of the *O'Connor* and *Cruzan* decisions, unconsented treatment has been made legally acceptable in a few jurisdictions. Some courts seem to be confused about what they're doing. They're willing to follow a patient's wishes when they're "clear and convincing," but ignore them if they aren't. Perhaps that would make sense if the default rule were set to reflect most people's wishes toward withdrawing life-sustaining treatment in desperate end-of-life situations. Then we would be saying: Unless we have proof that this terminally ill patient is different from other terminally ill patients, we will treat this patient as others would like to be treated and withdraw life support. But with life as the default rule, we are frustrating the intent of most patients subject to that rule.

———

Health-Care Decisionmaking in the Absence of a Formal Advance Directive. The *Cruzan* decision is a narrow though important one. All that the Court held there was that a state may impose a clear-and-convincing standard of proof of the patient's wishes. This leaves states free to adopt less stringent approaches to health-care decisionmaking, including deferring to informal directives from a patient or to the recommendation of a surrogate where the patient has not expressed his or her preferences.

Courts have followed several different approaches. Where the patient failed to leave written instructions but had made prior oral statements about life-sustaining treatment, several courts follow what has been called the "limited-objective" standard. In an important case applying this approach, In re Conroy, 486 A.2d 1209 (N.J. 1985), the court said that life-sustaining treatment could be withheld even though the patient had made no clear statement regarding her desires, so long as there was some trustworthy evidence that she would have refused treatment. Under the Missouri statute that the Court in *Cruzan* validated, such evidence would be insufficient.

Where the patient had made no prior statements, or had made only ambiguous statements, or was incompetent, most courts have allowed a third party, such as a guardian or the patient's family, to authorize termination of life-sustaining treatment.

These courts have followed either of two approaches: the substituted-judgment approach or the best-interests approach. Under the substituted-judgment approach, a court-appointed guardian, family member, or other proxy is supposed to stand in the patient's shoes and determine what the patient would have wanted under the circumstances. Under the best-interests approach, the proxy is supposed to take into account the patient's condition and likelihood that the recommended treatment will succeed.

The 1993 and 2023 versions of the Uniform Health-Care Decisions Act enable default surrogates to make medical decisions for patients lacking health-care directives. Under both Acts, these decisions must be made in accordance with the patient's wishes, if known, or else in accordance with the patient's best interests. The Acts do not require clear and convincing evidence. It is worth noting, however, that the California Supreme Court held that, under a statute based upon the 1993 Act, a guardian (appointed by the court, not by the patient, and thus not necessarily having special knowledge of the patient's wishes) would have to support with clear and convincing evidence a decision to remove artificial nutrition and hydration from a patient in the limited case where the patient, although incapacitated, was not comatose, terminally ill, or in a persistent vegetative state. See Wendland v. Wendland, 28 P.3d 151 (Cal. 2001).

Moving the focus away from the patient, some commentators have suggested that the best approach would be to follow the wishes of the patient's family. These commentators argue that family members have interests distinct from the patient's and that these interests often are among the most important factors in situations where a decision must be made whether to terminate life-sustaining treatment. See Leslie Pickering Francis, The Roles of the Family in Making Health Care Decisions for Incompetent Patients, 1992 Utah L. Rev. 861 (1992); Nancy K. Rhoden, Litigating Life and Death, 102 Harv. L. Rev. 375 (1988).

For a discussion of the legal standards used to decide when a court-appointed surrogate should intervene in making decisions for an elderly person, see Jan Ellen Rein, Preserving Dignity and Self-Determination of the Elderly in the Face of Competing Interests and Grim Alternatives: A Proposal for Statutory Refocus and Reform, 60 Geo. Wash. L. Rev. 1818 (1992).

EXTERNAL REFERENCES. Lawrence A. Frolik & Linda S. Whitton, The UPC Substituted Judgment/Best Interest Standard for Guardian Decisions: A Proposal for Reform, 45 U. Mich. J. L. Ref. 739 (2012); Linda S. Whitton & Lawrence A. Frolik, Surrogate Decision-Making Standards for Guardians: Theory and Reality, 2012 Utah L. Rev. 1491 (2012).

2. Organ Donations

Primary Statutory Reference: *Revised Uniform Anatomical Gift Act*

Henry Hansmann, The Economics and Ethics
of Markets for Human Organs
14 J. of Health Politics, Policy & Law 57, 58-59 (1989)

Historically, the common law did not provide anyone with a clear property right in a human corpse, and thus did not give anyone the authority to transfer a cadaver or any of its parts for any purpose by gift or sale....[17] Thus when transplants first became feasible, there was no mechanism whereby individuals could designate that their organs could be used for transplants upon death. To rectify this situation, the Uniform Anatomical Gift Act (UAGA) was promulgated in 1968 and adopted in some form in every state by 1973[18] .... The UAGA explicitly gives individuals the right to designate prior to death whether their bodies or organs are to be donated for transplants. In cases where a decedent's wishes are not known, the act gives the next of kin the right to designate whether or not organs are to be donated.

The UAGA deals expressly only with donations of organs; it is silent on the subject of sales. According to the chairman of the committee that drafted the UAGA, it was intended neither to encourage nor to discourage remuneration: "...it is possible, of course, that abuses may occur if payment could customarily be demanded, but every payment is not necessarily unethical.... Until the matter of payment becomes a problem of some dimensions, the matter should be left to the decency of intelligent human beings."...

In the 1960s (prior to the adoption of the UAGA) some states adopted statutes explicitly prohibiting the sale of human bodies and organs. Most of these states repealed such statutes when they adopted the UAGA. It is unclear whether these repeals were simply the result of a program of repealing all relevant statutes predating the UAGA or whether they reflected a judgment that the prohibitions on sales were either overridden by the UAGA or, conversely, made redundant by it. In any event, Delaware evidently did not hold the latter view, since it added an explicit prohibition on sales to its version of the UAGA.

The status of the sale of organs for transplantation therefore remained uncertain until Congress adopted the National Organ Transplant ACT (NOTA) in 1984. NOTA was essentially an effort to enhance the system of voluntary provision of transplantable organs contemplated by the UAGA. Its principal provisions

---

17. This does not mean that sales or gifts were illegal, but only contracts for sale or deeds of gift were not enforceable at law.

18. A revised version of the Uniform Anatomical Gift Act was promulgated in 1987. The revised act simplifies the process of organ donations by eliminating the witnessing requirement. Ed.

established federal financial support for local nonprofit organ procurement organizations and for a national organ procurement and transplantation network to assist in matching organ donors and recipients. However, NOTA also effectively outlawed commercial markets in transplantable organs by making it a federal crime "for any person to knowingly acquire, receive, or otherwise transfer any human organ for valuable consideration for use in human transplantation if the transfer affects interstate commerce."[19] Several states have subsequently supplemented this act with separate statutes of their own outlawing the sale or purchase of human organs. As a consequence, any effort to establish a market for organs today would require the repeal or amendment of legislation at both the federal and state levels.

Neither the federal nor the state legislation outlawing markets for organs were accompanied by careful policy analysis justifying the ban. NOTA did, however, establish the federal Task Force on Organ Procurement and Transplantation to inquire further into the policy issues raised by transplants. But when the task force submitted its report in 1986 it affirmed NOTA's ban on commercialization of organ transplantation without further analysis, simply offering the conclusory observation that "society's moral values militate against regarding the body as a commodity" and suggesting that such a ban is appropriate to "encourage altruism".... The task force also proceeded to encourage individual states to adopt their own prohibitions on the commercial sale of organs because NOTA, limited as it is to sales affecting interstate commerce, might not be entirely effective in suppressing such sales.

———

The Revised Uniform Anatomical Gift Act. The Uniform Law Commission promulgated new versions of the Uniform Anatomical Gift Act in 1987 and again in 2006. The current version is known as the Revised Uniform Anatomical Gift Act. The purposes of the Revised Act are explained in the Act's Prefatory Note:

> This Revised Uniform Anatomical Gift Act ("UAGA") is promulgated by the National Conference of Commissioners on Uniform State Laws ("NCCUSL") to address in part the critical organ shortage by providing additional ways for making organ, eye, and tissue donations. The original UAGA was promulgated by NCCUSL in 1968 and promptly enacted by all states. In 1987, the UAGA was revised and updated, but only 26 states adopted that version. Since 1987, many states have adopted non-uniform amendments to their anatomical gift acts. The law among the various states is no longer uniform and harmonious, and the diversity of law is an impediment to transplantation....
>
> This revision retains the basic policy of the 1968 and 1987 anatomical gift acts by retaining and strengthening the "opt-in" system that honors the free choice of an individual to donate the individual's organ (a process known in the organ transplant community as "first person consent" or "donor designation"). This revision also preserves the right of

---

19. 42 U.S.C. §274e (1982). The act specifies that its prohibition does not extend to payments made to cover costs incurred in the process of transplanting the organ.

other persons to make an anatomical gift of a decedent's organs if the decedent had not made a gift during life. And, it strengthens the right of an individual not to donate the individual's organs by signing a refusal that also bars others from making a gift of the individual's organs after the individual's death. This revision:

1. Honors the choice of an individual to be or not to be a donor and strengthens the language barring others from overriding a donor's decision to make an anatomical gift (Section 8);

2. Facilitates donations by expanding the list of those who may make an anatomical gift for another individual during that individual's lifetime to include health-care agents and, under certain circumstances, parents or guardians (Section 4);

3. Empowers a minor eligible under other law to apply for a driver's license to be a donor (Section 4);

4. Facilitates donations from a deceased individual who made no lifetime choice by adding to the list of persons who can make a gift of the deceased individual's body or parts the following persons: the person who was acting as the decedent's agent under a power of attorney for health care at the time of the decedent's death, the decedent's adult grandchildren, and an adult who exhibited special care and concern for the decedent (Section 9) and defines the meaning of "reasonably available" which is relevant to who can make an anatomical gift of a decedent's body or parts (Section 2(23));

5. Permits an anatomical gift by any member of a class where there is more than one person in the class so long as no objections by other class members are known and, if an objection is known, permits a majority of the members of the class who are reasonably available to make the gift without having to take account of a known objection by any class member who is not reasonably available (Section 9);

6. Creates numerous default rules for the interpretation of a document of gift that lacks specificity regarding either the persons to receive the gift or the purposes of the gift or both (Section 11);

7. Encourages and establishes standards for donor registries (Section 20);

8. Enables procurement organizations to gain access to documents of gifts in donor registries, medical records, and the records of a state motor vehicle department (Sections 14 and 20);

9. Resolves the tension between a health-care directive requesting the withholding or withdrawal of life support systems and anatomical gifts by permitting measures necessary to ensure the medical suitability of organs for intended transplantation or therapy to be administered (Sections 14 and 21);

10. Clarifies and expands the rules relating to cooperation and coordination between procurement organizations and coroners or medical examiners (Sections 22 and 23);

11. Recognizes anatomical gifts made under the laws of other jurisdictions (Section 19); and

12. Updates the [act] to allow for electronic records and signatures (Section 25).

———

A Legal Market for Human Organs? Despite these steps, there remains a wide gap between the demand and the supply of human organs available for transplantation. In November 2023, the number of people on the United Network for Organ Sharing waiting list for organ transplants was over 103,000.[20] It is likely that the actual number of people who would benefit from organ transplants is much higher. Yet the number of transplants performed is only a fraction of the demand. In 2022, 42,889 transplants were performed.[21]

One problem is the lack of public awareness of the process of making organ donations. Lawyers bear some of the responsibility for this. Few lawyers are knowledgeable about the law of organ transfers. Most lawyers do not raise the issue with their clients. Oversight and ignorance, then, may account for most people's failure to leave directions regarding donation of their organs, rather than the intention not to donate.

However, it seems unlikely that education alone will close the gap between the supply and demand for human organs. The prohibition against compensating donors or their families also is an important cause of the problem. The United Network for Organ Sharing and the National Kidney Foundation have urged Congress to amend NOTA to permit payments for the donor's burial expenses, but Congress thus far has failed to act.

Several scholars have urged that the ban on selling human organs be lifted for the purpose of permitting more transplants. Some organs, such as kidneys, can be obtained from living donors, and it would be relatively simple to structure a compensation system for them. With respect to cadaveric organs, the market might be structured as a futures market. The donor would receive a current payment in exchange for the buyer's right to harvest the organ if the donor dies under circumstances in which a transplant is feasible.

Several different objections have been raised to the idea of allowing human organs to be bought and sold in an open market. One is that compensation would drive out voluntarism; that is, individuals who otherwise would be willing to donate organs out of a sense of altruism would be less willing to do so if they could be compensated. If this effect were widespread, then compensation would not significantly increase the supply of human organs for transplantation.

Another objection, one that relates only to markets for organs from living donors, is that organ-selling would exploit the poor and the ill-informed for the benefit of the rich. The poor, it is argued, are likely to be the main group of sellers, and the sale of an organ such as a kidney increases the risk of death. One possible response is that the existence of a market for kidneys would especially benefit the poor, as purchasers, since they are disproportionately represented among those who suffer

20. Data obtained from the website of the United Network for Organ Sharing, unos.org.

21. Id.

from kidney failure. Another, more general response is that prohibiting the poor from selling their kidneys or other organs in order to protect them represents a perverse form of paternalism. The legitimate concern with improvident sales, the argument continues, can easily be met through regulation rather than through total prohibition.

A third objection frequently raised in discussions about sales of human organs comes under the aegis of commodification. The commercial sale of human organs, it is argued, should be prohibited because it would commodify them. Why commodification is objectionable is not always made clear, but one reason sometimes given is that commodifying certain goods is morally objectionable because it would injure human dignity. Certain goods are special in the sense that they are inextricably connected with human dignity and personality. Allowing these goods to be freely bought and sold would transform their character in ways that undermine their moral function. Which goods count in this special class is, of course, a highly contentious question, but some scholars have argued that human organs are among those goods. On the question of commodification generally, see Margaret Jane Radin, Market-Inalienability, 100 Harv. L. Rev. 1849 (1987).

EXTERNAL REFERENCES. Michele Goodwin, Empires of the Flesh: Organ and Tissue Taboos, 60 Ala. L. Rev. 1219 (2009); Michele Goodwin, Altruism's Limits: Law, Capacity, and Organ Commodification, 56 Rutgers L. Rev. 305 (2004); Henry Hansmann, The Economics and Ethics of Markets for Human Organs, 14 J. of Health Politics, Policy & Law 57 (1989); Lori B. Andrews, My Body, My Property, 16 Hastings Center Rep. 28 (1986); Arthur Caplan, Ethical and Policy Issues in the Procurement of Cadaver Organs for Transplantation, 314 New Eng. J. Med. 981 (1984).

Chapter 19

Federal Transfer Taxation

The system of federal transfer taxation is composed of three major components: (1) the federal gift tax, (2) the federal estate tax, and (3) the federal generation-skipping transfer tax (known as the "GSTT").

Each of these components has been dramatically affected by four pieces of twenty-first century legislation. The Economic Growth and Tax Relief Reconciliation Act of 2001 ("EGTRRA") provided for lower transfer tax rates and higher exemptions during the years from 2002 through 2009, then entirely repealed the estate tax and the GSTT for the year 2010—but only for 2010. Section 901 of EGTRRA stated that "[a]ll provisions of, and amendments made by, this Act shall not apply after December 31, 2010." In other words, EGTRRA provided that, effective January 1, 2011, the federal transfer tax system would revert to the higher rates and lower exemptions that existed prior to EGTRRA—unless Congress acted. Congress did act, but barely in time. The Tax Relief, Unemployment Insurance Reauthorization, and Job Creation Act of 2010 ("Tax Relief Act" or "Tax Relief Act of 2010") was signed into law on December 17, 2010. Under its provisions, lower rates and even higher exemptions were in effect for the years 2010, 2011, and 2012. But the Tax Relief Act applied only to those years and thus was only a temporary measure. On January 1, 2013, barely in time, Congress approved the American Taxpayer Relief Act of 2012 ("Taxpayer Relief Act" or "Taxpayer Relief Act of 2012"), which stabilized the transfer tax system on terms similar to the substantive provisions of the Tax Relief Act of 2010. Then in 2017, Congress enacted legislation known as the "Tax Cuts and Jobs Act" though this name was deleted from the final bill; this legislation was signed by the President on December 22, 2017, with many provisions becoming effective only days later, on January 1, 2018. This 2017 Tax Act contained extensive reform provisions, but many of these will sunset starting on January 1, 2026. Of course, the calls for permanent reform and repeal continue, especially for repeal of the estate tax.

The federal transfer tax system was complex even before these four Acts, and the continuing uncertainty about the system's future makes the job of the estate planner even more difficult. The goal of this Chapter is to present an overview; it does not include the details that would be discussed in a course in Federal Transfer Taxation.

Federal law subjects the gratuitous transfer of property—probate and nonprobate transfers—to an excise tax, which is usually imposed on the donor or the donor's estate. This excise tax can be derived from any of three taxes that make up the transfer tax component of the federal tax system: the federal gift tax, the federal estate tax, and the federal generation-skipping transfer tax.

PART A. THE FEDERAL TRANSFER TAX SYSTEM

1. The Cumulative Estate and Gift Tax System

The federal estate and gift taxes use progressive rather than flat tax rates. Under a progressive system, the total taxes on gratuitous transfers of $30 million are supposed to be more than double the taxes on gratuitous transfers of $15 million. To have integrity, a progressive transfer tax system therefore must be cumulative. That is to say, the tax on the latest round of taxable transfers, whether occurring at death or during life, must take account of all of the taxpayer's prior taxable transfers.

Until 1976, however, the progressivity of the system was compromised by the fact that the federal estate and gift taxes operated independently rather than cumulatively. The federal estate tax was enacted in 1916; the federal gift tax was enacted in 1932. Each tax had its own exemption and progressive rate schedule, but progressivity was compartmentalized. Although the gift tax was cumulative within itself, the estate tax rate applicable to a decedent's taxable estate was not based on the cumulative total of lifetime taxable gifts plus the taxable estate, but only on the taxable estate. A $30 million taxable estate incurred the same estate tax whether the decedent had made no lifetime taxable gifts or lifetime taxable gifts of, say, $10 million.

All this changed with the enactment of the Tax Reform Act of 1976. This act joined the estate and gift taxes into a unified transfer tax structure with a single exemption, in the form of a credit, and a single rate schedule under which the rate applicable to a decedent's taxable estate was based on the cumulative total of the decedent's lifetime taxable gifts and taxable estate. Under this unified system, deathtime transfers are treated as continuations of lifetime gift-giving.

EGTRRA reintroduced bifurcation in the transfer tax system in two significant ways. First, it created different exemption amounts for the estate tax and the gift tax. Under EGTRRA, the effective exemption amount for *estate* taxes increased from $675,000 in 2001 to $1 million in 2002 and further increased to $3.5 million by 2009. The effective exemption amount for *gift* taxes, however, increased to $1 million in 2002 but did not increase further; it remained at that level through 2010. Use of the credit during life meant that it was not available at death and, therefore, it was still in some sense a unified credit—but it was no longer unified regarding the amount.

Second, for the year 2010, EGTRRA repealed the estate tax but left the gift tax in effect, continuing its $1 million exemption amount in the form of a credit and subjecting gifts to a maximum rate of 35 percent.

The Tax Relief Act of 2010 reinstated uniformity for 2011 and 2012. The estate tax was revived, and the exemption amounts for the estate tax and the gift tax were the same. The unified-credit exemption amount for 2011 was $5 million. For gifts made (or decedents dying) in 2012, the $5 million was inflation-adjusted to $5.12

million. The gift tax and estate tax *rates* also were re-unified for 2011 and 2012, with a top rate of 35 percent.

The Taxpayer Relief Act of 2012 provided for permanent estate and gift taxes with a unified-credit exemption of $5 million adjusted in subsequent years for inflation, with a top estate and gift tax *rate* of 40 percent.

The 2017 Tax Act doubled the unified-credit exemption for 2018 through 2025—for 2024, the inflation-adjusted[1] amount is $13.61 million. The top estate and gift tax *rate* is kept at 40 percent.

2. The Federal Gift Tax

The federal gift tax now in effect dates back to 1932, when it was enacted as an excise tax on lifetime gifts of property. The 1932 gift tax was intended not only to supplement the estate tax by exacting a cost for making inter vivos gifts that reduce the donor's taxable estate, but also to supplement the income tax by exacting a cost for making inter vivos gifts that reduce the donor's taxable income. The 1932 gift tax was preceded by a gift tax that was enacted in 1924 but repealed in 1926. Progressivity under the 1924 gift tax was undermined by the fact that the tax was computed on an annual basis, without regard to gifts made in prior years. Unlike its predecessor, the 1932 gift tax is computed on a cumulative basis. Although donors must report taxable gifts and pay gift taxes on an annual basis, the statute determines tax rates applicable to a gift by reference to the total amount of taxable lifetime gifts made by donors, rather than by reference only to taxable gifts made in a given year. The cumulative aspect of the gift tax system works in a manner similar to the cumulative aspect of the transfer tax system as a whole, described above.

Overview of the Gift Tax. The first step in the determination of a donor's gift tax consequences for a taxable period is to identify the donor's transactions during that period that constitute "gifts" for gift tax purposes and to value the donated property. Although a donor's transfer of cash without consideration to her son, S, on S's birthday will almost certainly constitute a gift, there are many less obvious circumstances in which gifts for gift tax purposes can arise. For example, a gift can include forgiving a loan to a family member, deliberately allowing the statute of limitations to run on the loan, or making the loan at a below-market rate of interest. See IRC §7872.

The second step is to ascertain what amounts of the "gifts" made by the donor during the taxable period are "*taxable* gifts." IRC §2503(b) excludes from taxation

---

1. The 2017 Tax Act changed the index for inflation from the Consumer Price Index (CPI) to the so-called "chained CPI." The chained CPI is likely to rise at a slower pace than the CPI because the chained CPI takes into account the ability of consumers to react to rising prices by purchasing lower-priced substitute goods. The 2017 Tax Act makes permanent the use of the chained CPI as the relevant index; this aspect of the 2017 Tax Act does not sunset.

gifts made by a donor during a calendar year to the same donee up to an inflation-adjusted amount: $18,000 in 2024.[2] This exclusion is frequently referred to as the *annual exclusion*. The annual exclusion, in general, is only available for gifts that do not constitute "future interests." Thus, G can make cash gifts of $18,000 each to all fifteen of his grandchildren this year, next year, and each year thereafter without incurring any gift taxation. Indeed, G will not even be required to file a gift tax return. A gift by G of a remainder interest in Greenkacre, however, will not qualify for the annual exclusion because it is a gift of a future interest.

The third step is to subtract from the amount of gifts made during a taxable period (as reduced by the annual exclusion) any allowable deductions, such as the marital deduction or the charitable deduction, which are discussed on pp. 1089-1092. The difference between the total value of a donor's gifts and the allowed exclusions and deductions is the amount of the donor's *taxable gifts*. The applicable tax rate is then applied to the taxable gifts.

Taxable Lifetime Transfers. If a donor reserves a power to revoke a transfer, the transfer is not subject to gift taxation. In gift tax terminology, the gift is called *incomplete*, and the donor continues to be treated as owner of the transferred property for gift tax purposes. See Treas. Reg. §25.2511-2(c). If a donor transfers property but retains certain nonbeneficial powers, the gift tax law continues to treat the gift as incomplete and the donor as owner. Although the donor relinquishes the right to enjoy personally the property or the income it produces, the donor retains the power to decide who can enjoy the property or its income. Retaining the right to choose who will enjoy the property can be sufficient under the gift tax law to ignore the transfer. See Treas. Reg. §25.2511-2(b), (c).

Powers of Appointment. IRC §2514(b) provides that if a powerholder of a general power of appointment exercises or releases that power, a gift occurs. As defined in IRC §2514(c), a general power of appointment is any power that the powerholder can exercise in favor of the powerholder, the powerholder's estate, the powerholder's creditors, or the creditors of the powerholder's estate. The definition excludes, however, a power to consume the property or to invade the trust property if that power is limited by an ascertainable standard relating to the "health, education, support, or maintenance" of the powerholder. See IRC §2514(c)(1). The definition also excludes a power that can be exercised only in conjunction with the donor of the power or an adverse party. See IRC §2514(c)(3). See Chapter 14 for further discussion of powers of appointment.

One exception to the rule, that the release of a general power is a gift, concerns a lapse of a general power of appointment with respect to an amount that does not exceed the greater of $5,000 or 5 percent of the aggregate value of the property

---

2. The annual exclusion amount is indexed for inflation occurring after 1997. In 2024, the inflation-adjusted exclusion amount is $18,000.

subject to the power at the time of the lapse. See IRC §2514(e). Trusts are often structured to take advantage of this so-called *5 and 5* exception.

Example 19.1: G established a trust giving A an income interest for life and a power to invade the corpus up to $5,000 or 5 percent, whichever is greater, of the aggregate value of the trust each year during A's life, and also giving B the right to the remaining trust corpus at A's death. Of course, if A invades the corpus up to the maximum amount allowed each year, no gift tax consequences occur except to the extent A subsequently makes a gift of the amount A received from the invasions. If A, however, does not invade the corpus but allows the power to lapse in any year, that lapse, but for IRC §2514(e), would have resulted in a gift of the remainder interest to B.

The 5 and 5 power allows a donor to give a powerholder access to the trust corpus without putting the powerholder in a position of having to suffer gift taxation upon forgoing withdrawals.

Minimizing Transfer Tax Liability. The advantages of having donative transfers taxed during life rather than at death ought to be taken into account by estate planners as they develop strategies to assist their clients. Five features of the gift tax encourage lifetime giving.

Tax exclusive tax base. Because the donor, and not the donee, is liable for the gift tax, the gift tax itself is not included in the amount of the gift for gift tax purposes. In contrast, the decedent's estate is liable for the estate tax and, therefore, the estate tax is included in the amount of the estate for estate tax purposes. The difference in treatment of the two transfer taxes creates an incentive for making lifetime gifts. In other words, the incentive arises from the fact that the gift tax is *tax exclusive*, but the estate tax is *tax inclusive*. A comparison of Examples 19.2 and 19.3, below, demonstrates the tax savings available from making a lifetime gift.

Example 19.2 (lifetime transfer): G makes a gift to A of $100. The gift tax rate is 30 percent. G pays the government a gift tax of $30 and A receives the gift of $100.

Example 19.3 (deathtime transfer): G dies owning $130 that she devises to B. The estate tax rate is 30 percent. G's estate pays the government an estate tax of $39 and B receives the remaining $91 ($130 - 39).

These examples show that, to the extent a donor makes gifts exceeding the unified-credit-equivalent amount, every dollar of gift tax paid is removed from the donor's taxable estate free of estate tax.

Annual exclusion. The first $18,000 (as of 2024, as a result of the Internal Revenue Code's inflation adjustment provision) of gifts made to each donee during the year are not included in the donor's taxable gifts. See IRC §2503(b). Although the original purpose of the annual exclusion was to relieve taxpayers of the need to report—and the government of the need to monitor—holiday and birthday gifts, the introduction of an amount as high as $18,000 has made it a major tax-minimization tool. An annual gift plan to children, grandchildren, and other donees can result in the tax-free removal of a significant amount of wealth from the donor's taxable estate.

The annual exclusion is only available with regard to gifts of present interests. If a donor transfers money or other property absolutely, the annual exclusion is, of course, available. It is also available if a donor gives a donee the right to the possession or enjoyment of or the income from the property for life or for a term of years as long as the right to possession or income begins immediately.

IRC §2503(c) makes an exception to the present-interest rule for a gift to a minor. The donor can make a gift in trust giving a trustee the discretion to distribute or accumulate the income from the property as long as the property and any accumulated income is distributed when the minor attains 21. If the minor dies before attaining 21, IRC §2503(c) requires the trust to provide that the property and any accumulated income be paid to the minor's estate or as the minor directs under a general power of appointment.

Gift splitting. The benefits of the annual exclusion ($18,000 in 2024) are further enhanced by the fact that the Code gives the donor and the donor's spouse the right to elect to treat gifts as having been made one-half by the donor and one-half by the donor's spouse. See IRC §2513. This gift-splitting rule allows a married couple to transfer twice the exclusion amount ($36,000 in 2024) per year to a donee tax-free.

Tuition-and-medical-expense exclusion. Yet another advantage of lifetime giving is found in IRC §2503(e), which excludes from gift taxation any property or money that a donor pays directly to an educational organization for tuition on behalf of a donee or directly to any organization or individual who provides medical care to a donee. Before IRC §2503(e) was enacted, payments for tuition and medical expenses might not have been taxable if the state law viewed them as discharging the donor's support obligation. See Kathleen C. Horan, Postmajority Support for College Education—A Legally Enforceable Obligation in Divorce Proceedings?, 20 Fam. L.Q. 589 (1987). IRC §2503(e) goes far beyond support obligation payments, however, because it applies to tuition and medical payments made on behalf of any donee.

Valuation techniques. In general, property subject to a gift tax is valued at its fair market value at the time of the gift. See IRC §2512(a). Fair market value is defined as "the price at which... [the] property would change hands between a willing buyer and a willing seller, neither being under any compulsion to buy or to sell, and both having reasonable knowledge of relevant facts." Treas. Reg. §25.2512-1. Donors use this general valuation rule to reduce their total transfer taxes by dividing up property during life and making gifts of the fragmented interests through family limited partnerships or otherwise.

Problems

1. G agrees to perform services for A for $1,000. G directs A to pay the $1,000 to B. What are the gift tax consequences, if any? See IRC §§2501(a)(1), 2503(b), 2511(a); Treas. Reg. §25.2511-1(c)(1), (h)(2).

2. G deposits $1,000 in a joint bank account for herself and B. What are the gift tax consequences, if any? See IRC §2511(a); Treas. Reg. §25.2511-1(h)(4), -2(c).

3. G transfers $100,000 worth of securities in trust, directing the trustee to pay the income earned on the principal to A until A attains the age of 35 and, upon A attaining the age of 35, to distribute the trust principal to A. What are the gift tax consequences if G retains the right to direct the trustee to accumulate the income and to distribute it at the time the trust terminates? See IRC §§2511(a), 2503(b); Treas. Reg. §§25.2511-2(d); 25.2503-3(b), (c).

3. The Federal Estate Tax

The federal estate tax was enacted in 1916 as an excise tax on the transfer of property at death. The tax is measured by the deathtime value of the property transferred. The core provision of the estate tax is IRC §2033, which makes the decedent's probate estate subject to tax. From the beginning, however, Congress recognized that measures had to be taken to subject will substitutes to estate taxation; otherwise, will substitutes could be used as tax avoidance devices to achieve, in effect, tax-free probate transfers. Most of the statutory provisions of the estate tax are devoted to the purpose of taxing will substitutes, such as life insurance, joint tenancies and joint accounts, pension death benefits, revocable trusts, and even irrevocable trusts with a retained life estate.

The architecture of the federal estate tax calls for two steps to calculate the *taxable estate*. The first step is to determine the property that is included in the decedent's *gross estate* and the valuation thereof. The second step is to determine the taxable estate by subtracting from the gross estate the deductions permitted.

a. The Gross Estate

The decedent's gross estate includes the value of the decedent's probate estate, specified will substitutes, property over which the decedent held a general power of appointment, and certain transfers (QTIPs, discussed below at p. 1091) for which a marital deduction was previously allowed.

Probate Property. Under IRC §2033, the decedent's gross estate includes "the value of all property to the extent of the interest therein of the decedent at the time of his death." This statutory language describes the decedent's probate estate: the property that passes at the decedent's death by will or by intestacy. This includes the value of any real estate owned by the decedent in fee simple absolute and the value of any undivided portion of real estate owned as a tenant in common. The value of any transmissible remainder interest owned by the decedent at death would also be included.

Example 19.4: H created a trust, directing the trustee to pay the income earned on the principal to H's wife, W, for life, and at W's death to distribute the trust's principal to their daughter, D. D owns a transmissible remainder interest. If D fails to survive W, D's remainder interest is part of D's probate estate and is part of her gross estate for federal estate tax purposes under IRC §2033. However, if the trust imposed a condition that D survive W, and in fact D failed to survive W, then the remainder interest would terminate and its value would not be included either in D's probate estate or her gross estate.[3]

An income interest that expires on the death of the income beneficiary is not included in the income beneficiary's probate or gross estates.

Example 19.5: G created a trust, directing the trustee to pay the income earned on the principal to G for life, and at G's death to distribute the trust principal to G's descendants who survive G, by representation; if none, to X Charity. Because G's income interest expires on G's death, it is not included in G's gross estate under IRC §2033.

Lifetime Gifts Within Three Years of Death. The values of certain types of gifts are included in the decedent's gross estate simply because the decedent died within the three-year period following the gift. The focus is on gifts of life insurance policies within three years of death. Such a gift causes the full value of the proceeds to be included in the decedent's gross estate. See IRC §2035(a)(2). The rule also applies to transfers or relinquishments of retained interests or powers within three years of death. See IRC §2035(a). An exception is made for distributions from trusts that were revocable by the decedent. Instead, the distributions are treated as if the decedent had made the transfers directly. See IRC §2035(e).

Another feature of the three-year rule is IRC §2035(b), which provides that the decedent's gross estate includes the amount of any gift tax paid by the decedent on gifts made by the decedent (or the decedent's spouse) during the three-year period ending on the date of the decedent's death. This provision eliminates the tax-exclusive advantage of making lifetime taxable gifts in those circumstances in which the decedent has enjoyed the property until shortly before death.

Retained Property Interests. If a donor makes a lifetime gift of property but retains certain described interests in that property, the estate tax provides that the gross estate includes the value of that property. By not parting with complete ownership of the property, the donor is treated as owning the property at death for estate tax purposes.

---

3. UPC §2-707 adopts a rule of construction that imposes a condition of survivorship on the beneficiary of a future interest under the terms of a trust. (Recall the discussion in Chapter 16.) Therefore, even if the trust does not explicitly impose a condition that G survive the income beneficiary, UPC §2-707 would require survivorship unless the settlor demonstrated a contrary intention.

Retention of an income interest. IRC §2036(a)(1) provides that if a donor gratuitously transfers a remainder interest in property, in trust or otherwise, while retaining possession or enjoyment or the right to the income for life, then the value of the transferred property at the donor's death is included in the gross estate.[4]

If the donor transfers the retained life estate in the property before death, IRC §2036(a)(1) is no longer applicable. If, however, the donor transfers the retained life estate within three years of death, IRC §2035(a) operates to include the property valued at the time of the donor's death, and IRC §2035(b) operates to include the amount of any gift tax paid with regard to the transfer of the life estate.[5]

Retention of a reversionary interest. If a donor makes a gift of possession of, or the income from, property for the donee's life or a term of years, IRC §2033 will include the value of the reversionary interest that the donor retained in the gross estate. Gifts of income interests with retained reversions are unusual after 1986 when Congress amended the income tax law to provide that the donor will be taxed on all income from trusts in which the donor retains a significant reversionary interest. See IRC §673(a).

IRC §2037 addresses transfers in which the donor retains a reversionary interest that terminates at the donor's death.

Example 19.6: G establishes a trust and directs the trustee to pay the income earned on the principal to A for A's life and at A's death to distribute the trust's principal to G if G is alive or to B if G is dead.

For IRC §2037 to apply, three requirements must be met: (1) the donor must have made a transfer of an interest in which possession or enjoyment of the property can, through ownership of the interest, be obtained only by surviving the donor; (2) the donor retained a reversionary interest in the property; and (3) the value of the reversionary interest immediately before the donor's death exceeds 5 percent of the value of the property.[6] Neither the income tax nor the transfer tax laws create

---

4. The period that possession or income must be retained for IRC §2036(a)(1) to apply is "for... [the decedent's] life or for any period not ascertainable without reference to his death or for any period that does not in fact end before his death...."

5. IRC §2035(a) applies regardless of whether the donor transfers the life estate by gift or sells it for full and adequate consideration. The exception of IRC §2035(d), having to do with "bona fide sale[s]," is inapplicable. See United States v. Allen, 293 F.2d 916 (10th Cir.), cert. denied, 368 U.S. 944 (1961) (deciding under an earlier version of IRC §2035 that full and adequate consideration for this purpose means an amount equal to the value of the entire property that would be includable under IRC §2036(a)(1)).

6. The first federal estate tax statute contained a version of IRC §2037. For transfers made before October 8, 1949, only reversionary interests that arise "by the express terms of the instrument of transfer" are taken into account. See IRC §2037(a)(2). For transfers made on or after October 8, 1949, IRC §2037 applies even though the reversionary interest is not expressly retained and arises only by operation of law.

incentives for a donor to establish trusts of this kind. Donors create irrevocable trusts reserving reversionary interests typically to meet family or business needs and not for the purpose of achieving tax savings. If the donor transfers the retained reversionary interest before death, IRC §2037 does not apply. If the transfer occurs within three years of death, however, IRC §2035(a) includes the transferred property in the donor's gross estate.

Retained Powers; Revocable Trusts. If a donor reserves a power to revoke a transfer, the donor is treated as owner of the transferred property for estate tax purposes. See IRC §2038(a)(1). The donor also is treated as owner for gift tax purposes. Typically donors establish revocable trusts retaining a right to possession or income from property along with a power to revoke. These trusts assist donors in asset management and they avoid probate and its potential costs, but they produce no tax savings. See the discussion of revocable trusts in Chapter 7.

If a donor transfers property but retains certain nonbeneficial powers, the estate tax law continues to treat the donor as owner.[7] Although the donor relinquishes the right to enjoy personally the property or the income it produces, the donor retains the power to decide who can enjoy the property or its income. Retaining the right to choose who will enjoy the property or its income is sufficient for the estate tax law to ignore the transfer.[8] See IRC §§2036(a)(2), 2038(a)(1).

If the donor relinquishes the retained powers before death, IRC §§2036 and 2038 generally do not apply. If the transfer occurs within three years of death, however, IRC §2035(a) includes the transferred property in the donor's gross estate. But see IRC §2035(e), discussed above at p. 1082, pertaining to revocable trusts.

Powers of Appointment. The gross estate also may include property over which the decedent has a power of appointment created by another person. These are distinguished from *reserved* powers, which are powers that the donor has retained in property that the donor has otherwise transferred by gift. IRC §2041(a)(2) provides that if, at death, the decedent held a general power of appointment, the gross estate includes the value of the appointive property.[9] A general power of

---

7. See generally IRC §§2036, 2038.

8. Sometimes a transfer is subject to the operation of both IRC §§2036 and 2038. In those cases, the Internal Revenue Service (IRS) will rely on IRC §2036 because it results in the inclusion of the entire value of the property in the decedent's gross estate. In that way, the IRS avoids the limitation of IRC §2038, which requires that the gross estate include only that portion of the property over which the decedent had retained a power to alter, amend, revoke, or terminate.

9. The Revenue Act of 1916, in which the modern estate tax originated, contained no provision specifically dealing with powers of appointment. United States v. Field, 255 U.S. 257 (1921), held that, under this original enactment, the gross estate did not include the value of property subject to an exercised general power of appointment. Congress had since enacted a specific provision in the Revenue Act of 1918 to tax property subject to an exercised general power of appointment. Amendments in 1942 and 1951 provide that the value of property subject to general powers created

appointment is defined in the same manner as it is defined in IRC §2514(c) for gift tax purposes. See IRC §2041(b)(1). Donors give general powers of appointment in order to achieve multiple objectives, including to qualify the gifts for the annual exclusion or the marital deduction or to avoid the generation-skipping transfer tax. Powerholders who receive nongeneral powers of appointment will not have the appointive property included in their gross estates. Thus, powerholders who die holding powers to appoint property to their lineal descendants or even to anyone except themselves, their creditors, their estates, or the creditors of their estates will not have that property included in their gross estates. Similarly, powerholders who die holding powers to consume property for health or education purposes will not have that property included in their gross estates. Although the benefits of these liberal rules have been diminished by the introduction of the generation-skipping transfer tax, powers of appointment continue to play important roles in estate planning as attorneys minimize taxes and achieve their clients' distribution schemes.

If the exercise or release of the power is of such a nature that if it were a transfer of property owned by the powerholder the property would be includable in the powerholder's gross estate under IRC §§2035 to 2038, the property over which the power is exercised or released should be included in the powerholder's gross estate. See Treas. Reg. §20.2041-3(d).

Example 19.7: G establishes a trust and gives B an income interest for life as well as a general power to appoint the remainder interest. B subsequently appoints the remainder interest during life to C while retaining the income interest for life. IRC §§2041(a)(2) and 2036(a)(1) require that the entire value of the trust corpus be included in B's gross estate at B's death. If B wants to remove this property from his gross estate, he must make a lifetime gift of his income interest as well as make a lifetime appointment of the remainder interest.

One exception to the estate taxation rules concerns a lapse of a general power to appoint that does not exceed the greater of $5,000 or 5 percent of the aggregate value of the trust at the time of the lapse. See IRC §2041(b)(2). But for IRC §2041(b)(2), §2041(a)(2) and §§2035 through 2038 would operate to include in the powerholder's gross estate that portion of the trust corpus over which the powerholder had invasion rights. The 5 and 5 power is useful because it allows a donor to give a powerholder access to the trust corpus, but that access does not result in estate taxation to the powerholder.

Jointly Held Property. Jointly held property refers to property held in joint tenancy with right of survivorship, property held in tenancy by the entirety, joint bank and stock accounts, and jointly held U.S. Savings Bonds. A tenancy by the entirety can be owned only by persons who are married to each other. Joint ownership with the right of survivorship is popular, especially for people who have

---

after October 21, 1942, is includable in the decedent's gross estate regardless of whether the power is exercised.

small estates, because it effectively avoids probate.

IRC §2040 establishes two rules for determining the amount of jointly held property included in the decedent's gross estate: (1) a fractional-interest rule and (2) a percentage-of-consideration rule.

The fractional-interest rule applies in two situations. First, if the decedent received a jointly held interest as a gift or devise from a person who did not also become a joint tenant, then IRC §2040(a) includes a fractional share of the property equal to the decedent's fractional cotenancy interest in the decedent's gross estate. Essentially, the survivorship rights are ignored and the decedent's interest is treated as if it were an interest held in a tenancy in common.

The second situation in which the fractional-interest rule applies is when a married couple owns jointly held property. IRC §2040(b) includes one-half of the value of the property in the estate of the first spouse to die regardless of how much the decedent spouse contributed to its purchase. The spouses' relative amounts of contribution to the purchase of the jointly held property are also irrelevant for gift tax purposes. See IRC §2523, which provides that a gift of property between spouses made in a qualified manner is nontaxable. IRC §2056(a), which provides that a decedent can deduct the value of property included in the gross estate that passes to the surviving spouse in a qualified manner, in combination with IRC §2040(b), has the effect of excluding from taxation any portion of the jointly held property until the surviving spouse makes a lifetime gift or dies.

The percentage-of-consideration rule found in IRC §2040(a) applies for all jointly held property owned by unmarried tenants who acquire the property by purchase. This rule plays an important role for domestic partners who own property jointly with right of survivorship and for others who, to avoid probate and to facilitate financial and personal living arrangements, take property in joint tenancy with right of survivorship. The percentage-of-consideration rule operates to withhold tax advantages from the donor who provided the consideration for the joint property. IRC §2040(a) creates a presumption that the decedent provided all the consideration for the jointly held property. The decedent's estate has the burden of proving the amount of consideration, if any, that the surviving cotenant or cotenants provided. The amount of jointly held property included in the decedent's gross estate is determined by multiplying the property's value by the percentage of consideration the decedent is deemed to have provided.

Life Insurance. A life insurance contract on the life of the decedent and paid for by the decedent is a nonprobate transfer as long as the beneficiary of the insurance proceeds is someone other than the decedent's estate and the proceeds are not available to the creditors of the decedent's estate. IRC §2042(2) provides that the insurance proceeds are included in the gross estate if at the decedent's death the decedent retained an "incident of ownership." Incidents of ownership are defined in Treas. Reg. §20.2042-1(c)(2) to mean "the right of the insured or his estate to the economic benefits of the policy." It includes the power to change the beneficiary, to surrender or cancel the policy, to assign the policy, to revoke an assignment, to pledge the policy for a loan, or to obtain from the insurer a loan against the surrender value of the policy. Therefore, the only way that a decedent can keep insurance proceeds out of the gross estate is to make a lifetime gift of the policy, to relinquish all rights over the policy during life, and to assure that the proceeds are not paid to the estate or available to pay creditors of the estate. For further discussion of life insurance, see Chapter 7.

Annuities. If a decedent purchased an annuity contract that provided for periodic payments for life, the annuity contract would not be part of the decedent's probate or gross estate. This type of annuity, called a nonrefund-single-life annuity, does not lead to any gratuitous transfer but instead is fully exhausted at the decedent's death. (Of course, if the decedent owns any part of the payments at death, they will be included in the decedent's probate and gross estates.)

A second type of annuity contract is one where the decedent purchases a single-life annuity that pays a refund of a portion of the cost upon the decedent's premature death. If the refund is paid to the decedent's estate, it is included in the gross estate under IRC §2033. If the refund is paid to a designated beneficiary, it is included in the gross estate under IRC §2039.

A third type of annuity contract is one where the decedent purchases a joint-and-survivor annuity by which the insurance company obligates itself to make payments to the decedent and to the decedent's designated beneficiary during their joint lives and, upon the death of either, to make payments to the survivor for life. If the decedent dies first, IRC §2039 includes the value of the survivor's right to future payments in the decedent's gross estate.

A fourth type of annuity contract is one where the decedent purchases a self-and-survivor annuity by which the insurance company obligates itself to make payments only to the decedent and to make payments to the designated beneficiary only after the decedent's death. If the decedent dies first, IRC §2039 includes the value of the survivor's right to future payments in the decedent's gross estate. The purchase of either a joint-and-survivor annuity or a self-and-survivor annuity is a gift for gift tax purposes.

IRC §2039 is an important provision because it applies to benefits under employee retirement and pension plans and individual retirement accounts.[10] As a result of federal income tax policy encouraging savings through pension plans, for many middle- and upper middle-class clients, pension wealth is likely to be their largest asset.

---

10. IRC §2039(b) provides that "any contribution by the decedent's employer or former employer to the purchase price of such contract... shall be considered to be contributed by the decedent if made by reason of his employment."

Problems

1. G made a gift of $117,000 to A in 2023, having never before made a taxable gift. G died in 2024. (The gift tax annual exclusion for 2023 was $17,000.) What are the estate tax consequences of G having made the gift? See IRC §§2001, 2035, 2502(a), 2503(b), 2505(a).

2. In 1995, G transferred $200,000 worth of securities in trust, directing the trustee to pay the income earned from the principal to A for A's life and at A's death to distribute the trust principal to B. A was also given the noncumulative right to withdraw 5 percent of the principal each year from the trust. At A's death in 2011, the trust principal had a value of $300,000. What are the estate tax consequences of A dying in 2011 having been a beneficiary of the trust? See IRC §§2033, 2041(a)(2), (b)(2).

b. *The Deductions for Expenses, Debts, and Losses*

Various deductions in the Internal Revenue Code serve to reduce the gross estate to the taxable estate.[11] These deductions are the marital deduction, the charitable deduction, the deduction for funeral and administration expenses, bona fide claims against the decedent's estate, and the deduction for certain losses during administration. There is no deduction for the estate tax payable to the federal government; hence the estate tax is tax inclusive.

Deductions for Debts, Expenses, and Losses. IRC §2053 grants a deduction for the decedent's allowable funeral expenses and, subject to certain limitations, the expenses of administering property included in the decedent's gross estate. Some administration expenses also constitute allowable income tax deductions, and the executor must elect whether to deduct the expenses as either estate tax or income tax deductions.[12] IRC §2053 also allows a deduction for outstanding bona fide debts of the decedent, but if a debt is based on a promise or agreement, the deduction is limited to the extent that the liability was undertaken for an adequate and full consideration in money or money's worth. Mortgage obligations of the decedent, which were incurred in a bona fide manner for adequate and full consideration in money or money's worth, are either deductible or constitute a reduction in the value of the property subject to the mortgage, depending upon whether the decedent was personally liable for the payment of the underlying debt.

IRC §2054 permits the deduction of casualty and theft losses incurred during the administration of the estate, provided that the loss is not reflected in the valuation

---

11. Admittedly, the importance of these deductions is somewhat reduced for years 2018 through 2025 because of the high unified-credit exemption.

12. See IRC §642(g). Generally, the personal representative will make the election based on whether an income tax or estate tax deduction will result in the greatest tax savings. Recall the case of Estate of Bixby in Chapter 10, which we read on the subject of the duty of impartiality.

of the property where the alternate valuation date, which is allowed by IRC §2032, was elected.

Marital and Charitable Deductions. Because the estate tax and gift tax allow similar deductions for marital and charitable devises or gifts, these deductions are considered together, below.

4. The Estate and Gift Tax Marital Deduction

The federal estate and gift taxes allow a married donor to transfer property to the donor's spouse without suffering taxation if the property is transferred in a qualified manner. When Congress originally enacted the marital deduction in 1948, the rationale of the marital deduction was to grant married citizens of common-law states tax treatment similar to that enjoyed by married couples residing in community property states. The estate tax deduction was limited to 50 percent of the decedent's adjusted gross estate and the gift tax deduction was limited to 50 percent of the value of the property transferred from one spouse to the other. In 1981, Congress removed all quantitative limitations on transfers between spouses and thereby abandoned the community property model. Current law treats a married couple as the taxable unit for transfers between spouses. This means that transfers between spouses generally are ignored and that an estate or gift tax is assessed only when property is transferred outside the marital unit.

The community property model continues to play a role in the operation of the transfer tax marital deduction. The rules defining a qualified devise or gift, which were designed to mimic the kind of property a community property spouse would own, remain applicable.[13] The removal of the quantitative limitations in 1981, however, was also accompanied by the introduction of another type of devise or gift that would qualify for the marital deduction—qualified terminable interest property (QTIP)—which does not require the surviving spouse to receive significant ownership rights. See IRC §§2056(b)(7), 2523(f). Estate planning tools, such as trusts and powers of appointment, are used frequently to meet the qualification requirements.

If a donor transfers property to the donor's spouse in absolute ownership, the marital deduction is available. For example, if the married couple holds property in joint tenancy and one of the spouses dies, one-half of the property's value is included in the gross estate under IRC §2040(b). That half qualifies for the marital deduction under IRC §2056.

If a donor transfers, at death or during life, only an income interest to the donor's spouse that expires (say, in twenty years), IRC §§2056(b)(1) and 2523(b)(1) deny

---

13. See Lily Kahng, Fiction in Tax, in Taxing America 25 (Karen B. Brown & Mary Louise Fellows eds., 1997), discussing the legislative history of the marital deduction.

a marital deduction for the value of the term of years. Donors may, however, enjoy a marital deduction if they transfer copyrights or patents to their spouses, even though these property rights expire. The reason is that, unlike for the term of years, the donors have not retained or donatively transferred to third persons any interests in the copyrights or patents that would take effect upon the termination of the copyrights or patents. A terminable interest passing to the spouse is not deductible only if: (1) an interest in that same property was retained by the donor or donatively transferred to a third person and (2) the donor or the third person would take possession of the property after the interest transferred to the spouse terminated or failed.

There are several exceptions to the nondeductible-terminable-interest rule. The exceptions have one thing in common: the interests passing to the spouse will result in gift or estate taxation when that spouse transfers them during life or at death. By adopting qualification rules that assure transfer taxation will occur when the donee-spouse ultimately transfers the property during life or at death, the marital deduction operates only for the purpose of deferring property from transfer taxation until the death of the donee-spouse. The marital deduction does not exempt property from taxation; it just postpones taxation until the death of both spouses.

The two most popular of the terminable-interest exceptions have been the *life estate/general power of appointment* and the *QTIP*. See IRC §§2056(b)(5), (7), 2523(e), (f). Planners typically find that the requirements can be met efficiently through trusts. Planners also find that they can infuse the disposition with the flexibility their clients want by using a trust with various types of powers of appointment and fiduciary powers.

Life Estate/General Power of Appointment. IRC §§2056(b)(5) and 2523(e) provide that donors can enjoy the marital deduction if they give their spouses income interests for life along with powers to appoint the property alone to any person and in all events. IRC §2033 assures that any unconsumed income will be subject to the estate tax. IRC §2041 assures that the trust corpus will be subject to the estate tax. Similarly, if the spouse makes a gift of the life estate and makes a lifetime appointment of the remainder interest, then IRC §§2511 and 2514 will operate together to tax the fee.

For the income interest to qualify, the spouse must have an absolute right to be paid the current income at least annually. Regulations make clear that property placed in the trust must be property that produces a current income stream or, at least, that the spouse has the right to compel the trustee to convert any nonincome-producing property into property that will produce a fair current return. See Treas. Reg. §§20.2056(b)-5(f)(5), 25.2523(e)-1(f)(4).

For the power to qualify, it must be unrestricted, except that IRC §§2056(b)(5) and 2523(e) provide that a general power only exercisable by will is sufficient. Although the trustee cannot have a power to appoint any part of the property to any person other than the surviving spouse, the trustee can be given additional fiduciary powers to distribute the trust principal to the spouse. Nothing in the statutory requirements precludes a donor from supplementing the spouse's right to a lifetime income interest and general testamentary power with a lifetime power to appoint to a class of beneficiaries, such as the donor's lineal descendants. The exercise of this nongeneral power during life will result in a gift tax, because its exercise operates as a release of the general testamentary power. See IRC §2514(b).

QTIP ("Qualified Terminable Interest Property").[14] IRC §§2056(b)(7) and 2523(f) provide that a donor can obtain a marital deduction by transferring a life estate in property to the spouse. For the life estate to qualify for the marital deduction, the donor (for gift tax purposes) or the donor's executor (for estate tax purposes) must elect to have the life estate treated as a qualified terminable interest, and no person, not even the spouse, can have a power to appoint any part of the property to any person other than the surviving spouse during the spouse's life.

To assure that this property does not escape taxation in the donor's and the spouse's respective estates, Congress enacted IRC §§2044 and 2519. IRC §2519 treats any disposition of any portion of the life estate as a transfer of the entire remainder interest and thereby assures that the remainder interest is subject to gift taxation. IRC §2044 includes the value of the property at the spouse's death in the spouse's gross estate, unless IRC §2519 applied previously. The effect of these two sections is to assure that property that enjoys a marital deduction in one spouse's estate is taxed in the other spouse's estate.

The life estate requirements parallel those found under IRC §2056(b)(5), having to do with the life estate/general power of appointment exception. Just as under IRC §2056(b)(5), the trustee can have a power to distribute principal to the spouse during the spouse's life. Unlike under IRC §2056(b)(5), however, the spouse cannot have a lifetime power to appoint to anyone other than the spouse. In other words, donors can enjoy the marital deduction if they make a transfer of property in trust giving their spouses current income interests for life to be paid out annually and powers to appoint to the couple's lineal descendants by will and make the election as directed. Donors cannot enjoy the marital deduction, however, if the powers to appoint to lineal descendants are exercisable during the donee-spouses' lifetimes.

Estate Trust. Donors also may enjoy the marital deduction by placing property in trust and giving the trustees discretion to distribute income or principal to their spouses. These trusts qualify for the marital deduction as long as a donor also provides that, at the spouse's death, any accumulated income and principal remaining must be distributed to the spouse's estate. The property placed in the trust

---

14. The generation-skipping transfer tax has encouraged use of the QTIP over an income interest/general power of appointment trust. The generation-skipping transfer tax makes it more feasible for both spouses to make maximum use of the generation-skipping transfer tax exemption through use of the QTIP. See IRC §2652(a)(3).

is deductible under IRC §§2056 and 2523 because no person other than the spouse received an interest in the property from the donor. Before 1987, this so-called estate trust was attractive because it permitted the trustee to accumulate income at the then lower trust income tax rates. After the Tax Reform Act of 1986 and subsequent tax law changes, that advantage generally has been eliminated. Now an estate trust generally is popular only for donors who own assets that do not produce current income and who do not want to give the power to the trustee or to the spouse to convert the assets to income-producing property.

5. *The Estate and Gift Tax Charitable Deduction*

The federal transfer tax system encourages charitable giving. A donor can avoid estate and gift taxes for property transferred to a qualifying charitable organization. See IRC §§2055, 2522. There is no limit on amount deductible.

Charitable deductions are available not only for direct transfers to a charity, but also if the donor establishes a trust giving a charity either an income interest (a charitable lead trust) or a remainder interest (a charitable remainder trust).

IRC §2056(b)(8), which was added by the Economic Recovery Tax Act of 1981, provides that a marital deduction is allowable for certain charitable remainder trusts as long as the trust has no noncharitable beneficiaries other than the surviving spouse. The full value of this type of trust is deductible by virtue of IRC §§2055 and 2056 by the decedent spouse's estate. The surviving spouse receives only an income interest and therefore no portion of the trust property is included in the surviving spouse's estate at death.

6. *The Federal Generation-Skipping Transfer Tax*

The federal generation-skipping transfer tax ("GSTT") was enacted in 1986 as an excise tax on gratuitous transfers that *skip* a generation. The tax was introduced in 1976, but the 1976 version was repealed retroactively and replaced in 1986 by the current version. Congress believed that for a transfer tax to approach equity among families, it must apply to each family with approximately the same frequency. To this end, Congress designed the GSTT to assure generally that a tax is paid whenever property skips a generation or passes through a generation in a form that would allow it to escape gift or estate taxation in the *skipped* generation. In the terminology of the GSTT, a generation-skipping transfer occurs when property passes to a *skip person*.

Skip Person; Transferor; Interest. The GSTT uses a special terminology. Key interlocking definitions are:

"Skip person"—either (1) a natural person assigned to a generation that is two or more generations below the generation assignment of the "transferor" or (2) a trust in which all "interests" are held by skip persons or in which no person holds an "interest" and at no time may a distribution, upon termination or otherwise, be made from the trust to a nonskip person. See IRC §2613. The general rule for determining skip persons is subject to a predeceased-parent exception. See IRC §2651(e). If an individual is a descendant of the transferor and that individual's parent who was also a descendant of the transferor is dead at the time a transfer subject to a gift or estate tax occurs, then that individual is assigned to one generation higher than that individual would otherwise be assigned. Collateral heirs are also eligible for the predeceased-parent exception, but only if, at the time of the transfer, the transferor does not have any living lineal descendants.

"Transferor"—the person who made the transfer insofar as the federal estate or gift tax is concerned, i.e., the decedent if the transfer was subject to the estate tax; the donor if the transfer was subject to the gift tax. See IRC §2652(a).

"Interest"—A person has an "interest in property held in trust" if the person (1) has the right (other than a future right) to receive income or corpus from the trust, (2) is a permissible current recipient of income or corpus from the trust and is not a qualified charity, or (3) is a qualified charity and the trust is a qualified charitable remainder annuity or unitrust or a pooled income fund.[15] See IRC §2652(c).

The GSTT Exemption and Computation of the Tax. Like the federal estate and gift taxes, the generation-skipping transfer tax (GSTT) is targeted at the wealthy. IRC §2631 provides each transferor a *GSTT exemption.* The exemption amount was $1 million in 1986. The Taxpayer Relief Act of 1997 provided that the exemption amount be adjusted for inflation. After 2003, EGTRRA provided that the exemption amount be the same as the unified credit effective exemption amount for estate taxes, so that in 2004 the GSTT exemption was $1.5 million and increased to $3.5 million in 2009. The Tax Relief Act of 2010 established a GSTT exemption of $5 million and a GSTT rate of 35 percent for 2011 and 2012. The Taxpayer Relief Act of 2012 established a GSTT exemption of $5 million (indexed for inflation in subsequent years) and a GSTT rate of 40 percent. The 2017 Tax Act doubled the exemption for 2018 through 2025—in 2024, the inflation-adjusted amount[16] is $13.61 million—and kept the GSTT rate at 40 percent.

The mechanism by which the GSTT exemption operates is through the use of an *inclusion ratio*, which gives the fraction of a transfer or a trust that is subject to the generation-skipping transfer tax. In the case of *direct skips* (defined below), the inclusion ratio is:

$$1 - \frac{\text{amount of GSTT exemption allocated to the skip}}{\text{value of the property transferred in the skip}}$$

---

15. Charitable remainder annuity trusts and unitrusts are described in Chapter 12.

16. See note 1 above on the change from the CPI to the chained CPI.

In cases of *taxable terminations* and *taxable distributions* (defined below), the inclusion ratio is:

$$1 \quad - \quad \frac{\text{amount of GSTT exemption allocated to the trust}}{\text{value of the property transferred to the trust}}$$

An inclusion ratio of 1 means that the entire amount of a taxable-event transfer (see below) is subject to the generation-skipping transfer tax, an inclusion ratio of 0 means that none of a taxable-event transfer is subject to the tax, and an inclusion ratio of something more than 0 but less than 1 means that that fraction of a taxable-event transfer is subject to the tax. The tax benefits of the GSTT exemption encourage wealthy donors to establish long-term trusts that last as long as perpetuity law permits. Recall the discussion in Chapter 17.

Taxable Events. The GSTT applies to three types of generation-skipping transfers: direct skips, taxable terminations, and taxable distributions. See IRC §2611.

Direct skips. A direct skip is a transfer that is subject to either the gift or estate tax and is made to a skip person. See IRC §2612(c). To the extent that a gift qualifies for the annual exclusion or the tuition-or-medical-expense exclusion, the gift is not subject to the generation-skipping transfer tax. See IRC §§2611(b)(1), 2642(c)(3). The generation-skipping transfer tax on a direct skip is computed on a tax-exclusive basis, but the transferor's payment of the tax is treated as a taxable gift. See IRC §2515. Liability for payment of the tax is on the transferor or, if the direct skip came from a trust, on the trustee. See IRC §2603(a)(2), (a)(3).

Example 19.8: G makes an outright taxable gift to her grandchild, X, bypassing her child, A (X's parent). The gift is a direct skip for which the inclusion ratio is 1. The gift is therefore subject to both the gift tax and the generation-skipping transfer tax. In addition, G will pay a gift tax on the amount of generation-skipping transfer tax paid. This provision has the effect of treating a transfer from G to X the same as a transfer from G to A, who in turn uses the transferred property to make a gift to X.[17]

Taxable terminations. A taxable termination is the termination (by death, lapse of time, release of power, or otherwise) of an interest in property held in a trust, unless immediately after such termination, a nonskip person has an interest in the property or unless at no time after the termination may a distribution (including a distribution upon termination) be made from the trust to a skip person. See IRC §2612(a). The GSTT on a taxable termination is computed on a tax inclusive basis. Liability for payment of the tax is on the trustee, and hence payable from the corpus of the trust. See IRC §2603(a)(2).

---

17. In Example 19.8, under the predeceased-parent exception, G's gift to X would not be a direct skip if A were dead when G made the gift. See IRC §2651(e).

Example 19.9: G transfers property to a trust directing the trustee to pay income annually to her child, A, for life and at A's death to distribute the corpus to A's descendants. The trust has an inclusion ratio of 1. G will incur a gift tax when she establishes the trust. A dies, survived by his child, X. Because immediately after the termination of A's income interest, the trust corpus passes to a skip person, the termination of A's interest is a taxable termination and the trust will be liable to pay a generation-skipping transfer tax based on the highest estate and gift tax rate in effect for the year the termination takes place on the value of the property, determined at the death of A, that is held in trust when A dies.[18]

Taxable distributions. A taxable distribution is any distribution from a trust to a skip person other than a taxable termination or a direct skip. See IRC §2612(b). The generation-skipping transfer tax on a taxable distribution is computed on a tax-inclusive basis as a result of IRC § 2603(a)(1) placing tax liability for payment of the tax on the transferee.

Example 19.10: G transfers property to a trust, authorizing the trustee to distribute income and/or corpus to G's descendants. The trust has an inclusion ratio of 1. The trustee distributes $100,000 of the corpus to G's child, A, and $100,000 to G's grandchild, X. The distribution to A is not a taxable distribution because A is not a skip person. The distribution to X is a taxable distribution, taxed at the highest estate and gift tax rate in effect for the year that the distribution takes place. The transferee, X, is liable for the tax (IRC § 2603(a)(1)); if the trustee pays the tax out of the trust, the amount of the tax paid is itself a taxable distribution (IRC §2621(b)).

The generation-skipping transfer tax is thought to be essential for the transfer tax system as a whole to apply in a progressive manner. As the examples show, it prevents the wealthy from avoiding taxation by giving a significant percentage of their wealth to very young or unborn beneficiaries rather than to older beneficiaries. The tax advantage that the generation-skipping transfer tax prevents is not that the older beneficiaries, were it not for the tax, would have been taxed sooner and the younger beneficiaries would have been taxed later. The generation-skipping transfer tax prevents the older beneficiaries from not having been taxed at all.

7. Portability

Under the federal estate tax as traditionally formulated, the unified-credit exemption amount—$675,000 in 2001, $5 million in 2011—was personal to the decedent. Any unused portion of the exemption amount could not be shared with another taxpayer, not even with the decedent's surviving spouse. For this reason, an estate planning technique often used by married couples was the so-called "bypass" or "credit shelter" trust: a trust funded at the death of the first spouse to die, up to

---

18. The predeceased-parent exception does not apply in this example because A was alive at the time G made the transfer into the trust that resulted in a taxable gift. See IRC §2651(e).

the applicable exclusion amount, with only the remaining assets passing to the surviving spouse in a manner qualifying for the marital deduction. (If the decedent's entire estate had qualified for the marital deduction, the decedent's exemption amount would have been wasted.)

The Tax Relief Act of 2010 introduced the concept of "portability" between spouses of the estate tax exemption amount. The surviving spouse can elect to take advantage of the unused portion of the estate tax exemption amount of the predeceased spouse (or the most recent predeceased spouse, if more than one). Consider the following example.

Example 19.11: H and W are a married couple. H has made no lifetime gifts and dies in 2011 with a gross estate of $10 million. H's will names W as his sole beneficiary. H is not liable for estate tax, because the entire $10 million qualifies for the marital deduction. In a system without "portability," when W dies, W will have only W's own estate tax exemption amount ($5 million in 2011, but indexed for inflation thereafter). With "portability," W can use W's own exemption amount plus H's unused exemption amount.

The portability provisions of the Tax Relief Act of 2010 applied to the estates of decedents dying after December 31, 2010, and the provisions were scheduled to end ("sunset") on January 1, 2013. The Taxpayer Relief Act of 2012, enacted by Congress on January 1, 2013, made portability permanent.

Note that portability does not apply to the GSTT exemption.

———

EXTERNAL REFERENCES. Paul L. Caron, The Costs of Estate Tax Dithering, 43 Creighton L. Rev. 637 (2010); Symposium on Wealth Transfer Taxation, 63 Tax L. Rev. (2009); Mark S. Bekerman, What Portability Means to Trust and Estate Professionals, 23 Prob. & Prop. 39 (Sept./Oct. 2009).

PART B. FEDERAL TAXATION AND STATE LAW

Primary Statutory References: *UPC §2-806, UTC §416*

The assessment of federal income and transfer taxes depends upon the property owner's economic rights and obligations. Economic rights and obligations, with exceptions such as U.S. Savings Bonds, patents, and copyrights, are created and protected by state law. Although state law's characterization or labeling of property interests is not controlling on the federal government's power to tax, state law's determination of a person's economic rights and obligations typically is controlling. Part B describes the role that state law plays in the federal tax law and how the federal authorities determine that state law.

If the tax dispute turns on state law and the taxpayer has not adjudicated the particular issue in state court, the Internal Revenue Service (IRS) and the federal courts determine state law in accordance with the *Erie* doctrine. The *Erie* doctrine provides that federal courts must apply state law as announced by state legislation or the state's highest court. See Erie Railroad Co. v. Tompkins, 304 U.S. 64 (1938). If the legislature or the highest court has failed to address the particular issue, then the federal authorities must apply what they find to be state law after giving proper regard to relevant rulings by a state's lower court decisions.

If the taxpayer has adjudicated the state law question in a state court before having had a final federal determination of the taxpayer's tax liability, is the state court's ruling regarding the taxpayer's economic interests and obligations a binding determination of the state law for purposes of determining federal tax liability?

Commissioner v. Estate of Bosch
387 U.S. 456 (1967)

CLARK, J. These two federal estate tax cases present a common issue for our determination: Whether a federal court or agency in a federal estate tax controversy is conclusively bound by a state trial court adjudication of property rights or characterization of property interests when the United States is not made a party to such proceeding.

In No. 673, Commissioner of Internal Revenue v. Estate of Bosch, 363 F. 2d 1009, the Court of Appeals for the Second Circuit held that since the state trial court had "authoritatively determined" the rights of the parties, it was not required to delve into the correctness of that state court decree. In No. 240, Second National Bank of New Haven, Executor v. United States, 351 F.2d 489, another panel of the same Circuit held that the "decrees of the Connecticut Probate Court... under no circumstances can be construed as binding" on a federal court in subsequent litigation involving federal revenue laws. Whether these cases conflict in principle or not, which is disputed here, there does exist a widespread conflict among the circuits over the question and we granted certiorari to resolve it.... We hold that where the federal estate tax liability turns upon the character of a property interest held and transferred by the decedent under state law, federal authorities are not bound by the determination made of such property interest by a state trial court....

(a) No. 673, Commissioner v. Estate of Bosch. In 1930, decedent, a resident of New York, created a revocable trust which, as amended in 1931, provided that the income from the corpus was to be paid to his wife during her lifetime. The instrument also gave her a general [testamentary] power of appointment, in default of which it provided that half of the corpus was to go to his heirs and the remaining half was to go to those of his wife. In 1951 the wife executed an instrument purporting to release the general power of appointment and convert it into a special power. Upon decedent's death in 1957, respondent, in paying federal estate taxes, claimed a marital deduction for the value of the widow's trust. The Commissioner determined, however, that the trust corpus did not qualify for the deduction under [IRC] §2056(b)(5)... and levied a deficiency. Respondent then filed a petition for

redetermination in the Tax Court. The ultimate outcome of the controversy hinged on whether the release executed by Mrs. Bosch in 1951 was invalid—as she claimed it to be—in which case she would have enjoyed a general power of appointment at her husband's death and the trust would therefore qualify for the marital deduction. While the Tax Court proceeding was pending, the respondent filed a petition in the Supreme Court of New York for settlement of the trustee's account; it also sought a determination as to the validity of the release under state law. The Tax Court, with the Commissioner's consent, abstained from making its decision pending the outcome of the state court action. The state court found the release to be a nullity; the Tax Court then accepted the state court judgment as being an "authoritative exposition of New York law and adjudication of the property rights involved,"... and permitted the deduction. On appeal, a divided Court of Appeals affirmed. It held that "[t]he issue is... not whether the federal court is 'bound by' the decision of the state tribunal, but whether or not a state tribunal has authoritatively determined the rights under state law of a party to the federal action." The court concluded that the "New York judgment, rendered by a court which had jurisdiction over parties and subject matter, authoritatively settled the rights of the parties, not only for New York, but also for purposes of the application to those rights of the relevant provisions of federal tax law."... It declared that since the state court had held the wife to have a general power of appointment under its law, the corpus of the trust qualified for the marital deduction. We do not agree and reverse....

The problem of what effect must be given a state trial court decree where the matter decided there is determinative of federal estate tax consequences has long burdened the Bar and the courts. This Court has not addressed itself to the problem for nearly a third of a century.[19] In Freuler v. Helvering, 291 U.S. 35 (1934), this Court, declining to find collusion between the parties on the record as presented there, held that a prior *in personam* judgment in the state court to which the United States was not made a party, "[o]bviously... had not the effect of *res judicata*, and could not furnish the basis for invocation of the full faith and credit clause...." At 43. In *Freuler*'s wake, at least three positions have emerged among the circuits. The first of these holds that

> ...if the question at issue is fairly presented to the state court for its independent decision and is so decided by the court the resulting judgment if binding upon the parties under the state law is conclusive as to their property rights in the federal tax case.... Gallagher v. Smith, 223 F. 2d 218, 225.

The opposite view is expressed in Faulkerson's Estate v. United States, 301 F.2d 231. This view seems to approach that of Erie R. Co. v. Tompkins, 304 U.S. 64

---

19. It may be claimed that Blair v. Commissioner, 300 U.S. 5 (1937), dealt with the problem presently before us but that case involved the question of the effect of a property right determination by a state appellate court.

(1938), in that the federal court will consider itself bound by the state court decree only after independent examination of the state law as determined by the highest court of the State. The Government urges that an intermediate position be adopted; it suggests that a state trial court adjudication is binding in such cases only when the judgment is the result of an adversary proceeding in the state court....

We look at the problem differently. First, the Commissioner was not made a party to either of the state proceedings here and neither had the effect of *res judicata*...; nor did the principle of collateral estoppel apply. It can hardly be denied that both state proceedings were brought for the purpose of directly affecting federal estate tax liability. Next, it must be remembered that it was a federal taxing statute that the Congress enacted and upon which we are here passing. Therefore, in construing it, we must look to the legislative history surrounding it. We find that the report of the Senate Finance Committee recommending enactment of the marital deduction used very guarded language in referring to the very question involved here. It said that "proper regard," not finality, "should be given to interpretations of the will" by state courts and then only when entered by a court "in a bona fide adversary proceeding."... We cannot say that the authors of this directive intended that the decrees of state trial courts were to be conclusive and binding on the computation of the federal estate tax as levied by the Congress. If the Congress had intended state trial court determinations to have that effect on the federal actions, it certainly would have said so—which it did not do. On the contrary, we believe it intended the marital deduction to be strictly construed and applied. Not only did it indicate that only "proper regard" was to be accorded state decrees but it placed specific limitations on the allowance of the deduction as set out in [IRC] §§2056 (b), (c), and (d). These restrictive limitations clearly indicate the great care that Congress exercised in the drawing of the Act and indicate also a definite concern with the elimination of loopholes and escape hatches that might jeopardize the federal revenue. This also is in keeping with the long-established policy of the Congress, as expressed in the Rules of Decision Act, 28 U.S.C. §1652. There it is provided that in the absence of federal requirements such as the Constitution or Acts of Congress, the "laws of the several states... shall be regarded as rules of decision in civil actions in the courts of the United States, in cases where they apply." This Court has held that judicial decisions are "laws of the... state" within the section. Moreover, even in diversity cases this Court has further held that while the decrees of "lower state courts" should be "attributed some weight... the decision [is] not controlling..." where the highest court of the State has not spoken on the point. And in West v. A.T.&T. Co., 311 U.S. 223 (1940), this Court further held that "an intermediate appellate state court... is a datum for ascertaining state law which is not to be disregarded by a federal court *unless it is convinced by other persuasive data that the highest court of the state would decide otherwise.*"... (Emphasis supplied.) Thus, under some conditions, federal authority may not be bound even by an intermediate state appellate court ruling. It follows here then, that when the application of a federal statute is involved, the decision of a state trial court as to an underlying issue of state law should *a fortiori* not be controlling. This is but an application of the rule of Erie R. Co. v. Tompkins, supra, where state law as announced by the highest court of the State is to be followed. This is not a diversity case but the same principle may be applied for the same reasons, *viz.*, the underlying substantive rule involved is based on state law and the State's highest court is the best authority on its own law. If there be no decision by that court then federal authorities must apply what they find to be the state law after giving "proper regard" to relevant rulings of other courts of the State. In this respect, it may be said to be, in effect, sitting as a state court.

We believe that this would avoid much of the uncertainty that would result from the "non-adversary" approach and at the same time would be fair to the taxpayer and protect the federal revenue as well.

The judgment in No. 240 is therefore affirmed while that in No. 673 is reversed and remanded for further proceedings not inconsistent with this opinion.

It is so ordered.

[The dissenting opinions of DOUGLAS, FORTAS, and HARLAN, JJ., are omitted.]

Notes and Questions

1. *The Aftermath of Bosch.* Did the *Bosch* court avoid the uncertainty that concerned it? Professor Verbit summarizes post-*Bosch* decisions as follows:

> [F]ederal courts have taken the following attitude towards state lower court decisions under the guise of following the rule of *Bosch*: (1) that lower state court rulings are entitled to no weight and are therefore not admissible in federal tax proceedings, (2) that lower state court decisions are relevant evidence even though the product of non-adversary proceedings, (3) that lower state court decisions are to be "followed" if they correctly applied state law, and (4) that the existence of the state court decision should be noted but the federal court will thereafter decide the case as if the state court decision did not exist.

Gilbert P. Verbit, State Court Decisions in Federal Transfer Tax Litigation: *Bosch* Revisited, 23 Real Prop. Prob. & Tr. J. 407, 445-46 (1988). See also F. Ladson Boyle, When It's Broke—Fix It: Reforming Irrevocable Trusts to Change Tax Consequences, 53 Tax Law. 821 (2000) (demonstrating that the tax consequences of reformation remain uncertain in some, but not all, areas of dispute that arise between taxpayers and the Service); Paul L. Caron, The Role of State Court Decisions in Federal Tax Litigation: *Bosch*, *Erie*, and Beyond, 71 Or. L. Rev. 781, 784 (1992) (conducting a survey of post-*Bosch* cases and rulings that "reveals a quarter century of disarray caused by a misreading of the *Erie* underpinnings of the 'proper regard' standard").

2. *"Collusive" Decisions or Reformation of a Mistake?* Why is it wrong to accept the results of a collusive decision? Are there situations in which the federal government should be indifferent about whether a state decision determining

property rights is collusive? If the issue is accomplishing the decedent's intent and if a state court determines what the decedent's intent was, why should a federal court disregard that holding? Professors Langbein and Waggoner have argued:

> The Treasury occupies the position of an unintended beneficiary in these cases.... When the mistake arises in a lawyer-drafted instrument, as is usually the case, the Treasury's posture is particularly unattractive. The Treasury benefits through third-party negligence—a species of wrong-doing—at the expense of the innocent intended beneficiaries.

John H. Langbein & Lawrence W. Waggoner, Reformation of Wills on the Ground of Mistake: Change of Direction in American Law?, 130 U. Pa. L. Rev. 521, 550 (1982).

Picking up on this point, Professor Verbit, in Verbit, above, at 461-62, advocates an abandonment of the *Bosch* rule and the adoption of a rule in which all final decisions of state courts would be binding in federal tax cases. His argument, at core, is an acknowledgment that the courts are deciding cases for the purpose of carrying out the donor's intent:

> Instead of viewing the actions of state judges as participation in a "Great Treasury Raid," it is equally possible to view the situation as one in which state courts construe and reform instruments to effect the testator's intent while the IRS is attempting to capitalize on every drafting error, however slight.... Contemporary estate planning is often tax-driven. To the extent that is the case, a legitimate question should be considered: Why deny a tax benefit to a taxpayer who has omitted a phrase or used one word too many if the evidence is that the taxpayer intended to qualify for the tax benefit? This is particularly compelling if an error is of essentially a technical nature and the taxpayer is really the innocent victim of a drafter's error.

The doctrine of reformation to correct mistakes in *unambiguous* documents, testamentary as well as nontestamentary, is becoming more widely accepted. Recall the discussion in Chapter 13. In particular, courts have reformed instruments to correct drafting errors that would otherwise result in detrimental tax results. The effect for federal tax purposes of these state court decisions, even those made by a state's highest court, however, is in doubt.

The official position of the IRS is that a state court order reforming a donative instrument does not have retroactive effect for tax purposes. See Rev. Rul. 93-79, 1993-2 C.B. 269; Tech. Adv. Mem. 83-46-008 (Aug. 4, 1983) (basing its holding on the statement in *Bosch* that a state decision must "determine property rights"); see also Rev. Rul. 73-142, 1973-1 C.B. 405 (holding that a lower state court decree will be controlling for federal estate tax purposes if the decree was issued before the taxing event, even if the proceeding was nonadversarial).

Notwithstanding the IRS's official position, there are many reported instances in which taxpayers have been able to obtain a Private Letter Ruling from the IRS recognizing the retroactive effect of a state court order of reformation. See, e.g.,

Priv. Ltr. Rul. 201837005 (Sept. 14, 2018); Priv. Ltr. Rul. 201737008 (September 15, 2017), Priv. Ltr. Rul. 201442042 (October 17, 2014). Private Letter Rulings, however, are not binding on other taxpayers and cannot be relied on as precedent.

Federal tax cases support the IRS's official position. Van Den Wymelenberg v. United States, 397 F.2d 443 (7th Cir.), cert. denied, 393 U.S. 953 (1968), concerned a trust that, through inadvertence, did not qualify for federal gift tax annual exclusions under IRC §2503(c). After the IRS disallowed the exclusion, the settlors executed a Corrected Trust Agreement to have the trust conform to the requirements of IRC §2503(c) with the intention that it have retroactive effect. The district court upheld the deficiencies assessed by the IRS and the Seventh Circuit affirmed, relying on concerns about collusion to support its decision:

> Taxpayers cite several Wisconsin state cases for the proposition that a written instrument which, through mistake, does not embody the intent of the parties may be reformed by the parties through voluntary execution of a corrected instrument. However, not even judicial reformation can operate to change the federal tax consequences of a completed transaction.
>
> As to the parties to the reformed instrument the reformation relates back to the date of the original instrument, but it does not affect the rights acquired by non-parties, including the Government. Were the law otherwise there would exist considerable opportunity for "collusive" state court actions having the sole purpose of reducing federal tax liabilities.

397 F.2d at 445. The claim that the government had nonparty rights is questionable. It neither changed its position in reliance on the prereformed instrument nor gave consideration for the taxes collected. The refusal to recognize the retroactive effect of a reformation based on the ground of collusive state court proceedings is also questionable. If the issue is distrust for state court decisions, the answer should not be that reformation has no retroactive effect. Rather the answer should be that the reformation issue be litigated or relitigated in the federal court applying state law with the IRS as a party. See Restatement 3d of Property §12.1 Reporter's Note 11. For other cases supporting the view that reformation by state courts has no retroactive effect for tax purposes, see Estate of Bennett v. Commissioner, 100 T.C. 42 (1993); Estate of La Meres v. Commissioner, 98 T.C. 294 (1992); Estate of Nicholson v. Commissioner, 94 T.C. 666 (1990). But see Estate of Starkey v. United States, 223 F.3d 694 (7th Cir. 2000) (finding that an ambiguity in the documents was appropriately resolved by a state appellate court in nonadversarial litigation to construe a gift to charity after the Service had denied the estate a charitable deduction and holding that the charitable deduction was warranted); Flitcroft v. Commissioner, 328 F.2d 449 (9th Cir. 1964) (pre–*Bosch* case accepting as controlling for income tax purposes a state court decree reforming a lifetime trust to make it irrevocable; Rev. Rul 93-79, above, indicates that it will not follow this case).

3. *Modification to Achieve Donor's Tax Objectives.* If between the time decedents execute their wills and their deaths the tax law changes, should courts be able to modify the wills so as to achieve tax savings? In Note 2 the argument for reformation was based on proof that a mistake occurred that resulted in the donative instrument failing to express decedent's original and particularized intent. If modification is appropriate in a situation of changed tax circumstances, it would have to be based on a determination of the donor's probable intention.

In Estate of Branigan, 609 A.2d 431 (N.J. 1992), the executors sought to modify decedent's will in two respects for the purpose of taking advantage of changes in the federal estate tax laws that occurred subsequent to the execution of the will and subsequent to the death of the testator. The first proposed modification was to divide the marital deduction trust into two trusts, which would permit the executor to take advantage of the "reverse QTIP" under IRC §2652(a)(3) for the purpose of obtaining the $1 million generation-skipping tax exemption. The second proposed modification was to convert the sons' nongeneral testamentary powers of appointment into general testamentary powers of appointment. This modification would reduce taxes by having the sons taxed under the federal estate tax with its lower rates rather than under the federal generation-skipping transfer tax. The court granted the first proposed modification but not the second:

> The doctrine of probable intent as it has evolved is sufficiently broad to accommodate plaintiffs' request to alter the trust funds for purposes of minimizing GSTT taxes. Indeed, the doctrine has been applied in contextual settings in which the imputation of the presumed intent to minimize taxes was necessary to prevent the frustration of the testator's overall testamentary plans. Similarly, this case presents evidence material to the testator's intention with respect to the significance of federal taxes as a factor in his testamentary plan. Considerable evidence supports the finding that decedent had specifically attempted to minimize QTIP taxes generated under the existing will....
>
> In addition to the extrinsic evidence supporting decedent's specific intent to minimize taxes, the doctrine of probable intent reasonably assumes, in its several possible applications, a widely-accepted intent on the part of most testators to save taxes....
>
> Moreover, in this case the imputation of an intent on the part of the testator to incorporate in his will those technical provisions essential to achieve tax savings is not hampered by any possibly conflicting purpose relating to other aspects of his will. [E]ffectuating an intent to save taxes in the matter before us does not entail the alteration of a substantive provision of decedent's will. Plaintiffs can secure part of the tax savings they seek under the current federal tax laws by dividing the single QTIP trust into two QTIP trusts. That division does not affect or change any substantive disposition or bequest under decedent's will. The beneficiary, purposes, and powers of the trusts will remain intact. Moreover, the splitting of the trust does not entail modification of a material or significant administrative provision or structural feature of the will. Rather, the modification constitutes only a technical alteration relating to an aspect of estate administration that does not otherwise appear to have any material bearing on the decedent's testamentary plan. The change of that administrative provision is designed

solely to conform the will to the existing federal tax scheme, an objective sought to be achieved by the testator.

We therefore conclude that plaintiffs' request to reform decedent's will to modify the existing provisions of trust funds in order to derive maximum benefits under the federal estate tax laws is reasonable.

.... The reasoning that enables us to sanction a change in the will with respect to certain of its structural and administrative features but not the substantive terms of trust bequests prevents us from authorizing the reformation of the will to alter the testator's sons' limited powers of appointment. We understand that very substantial federal taxes could be saved by that change. Moreover, the executors argue that that modification will revitalize the original intent of the testator by making the donee of the power the deemed transferor and tax the skip property at the son's own rates.... The modification, however, certainly would alter the dispository provisions of the will. Under that proposed scheme, the interests of the grandchildren whose fathers were living at the time of decedent's death could be affected by making their father's power of appointment general with the possibility they could lose their inheritance....

We cannot conclude that plaintiffs' desire to evade taxes at the cost of the dispository scheme and the possible disinheritance of some of the heirs effectuates the testamentary intent of the testator.

609 A.2d at 436-38.

The Restatement 3d of Property adopts a standard similar to the one found in *Branigan* for modifying donative documents to achieve the donor's tax objectives:

> *§12.2. Modifying Donative Documents to Achieve Donor's Tax Objectives.* A donative document may be modified, in a manner that does not violate the donor's probable intention, to achieve the donor's tax objectives.

Uniform Probate Code §2-806 and Uniform Trust Code §416 codify Restatement 3d §12.2. Whether the modifications will ultimately be successful in achieving tax savings in many situations, however, is in question. As indicated in Note 2, the IRS and federal tax cases have taken the position that state court reformation proceedings do not have retroactive effect for tax purposes.

———

EXTERNAL REFERENCES. Barry F. Spivey, Completed Transactions, Qualified Reformation and *Bosch*: When Does the IRS Care about State Law of Trust Reformation?, 26 ACTEC Notes 345 (2001); Paul L. Caron, The Federal Tax Implications of *Bush v. Gore*, 79 Wash. U. L.Q. 749 (2001); Paul L. Caron, The Federal Courts of Appeals' Use of State Court Decisions in Tax Cases: "Proper Regard" Means "No Regard," 46 Okla. L. Rev. 443 (1993); John H. Langbein & Lawrence W. Waggoner, Reformation of Wills on the Ground of Mistake: Change of Direction in American Law?, 130 U. Pa. L. Rev. 521, 550-54 (1982).

PART FOUR
LOOKING TO THE FUTURE

CHAPTER 20.   LOOKING TO THE FUTURE

Chapter 20

Looking to the Future

In this brief concluding Chapter, we look to the future. One of our aims here, as throughout this book, is to spark your interest in the field of trusts and estates, so that you might consider making it the focus of your legal career. A related aim is to get you thinking about where the field of estate planning may be headed.

Part A of the Chapter introduces you to sophisticated private entities for managing and increasing the assets of the very wealthiest families—namely, the family office and the private trust company—and to the policy questions such devices raise. Part B of the Chapter offers the reflections of an experienced academic and estate planner on the future of the field, with the suggestion that time-honored drafting and planning techniques should be re-examined to determine if they truly meet the desires of present and future generations.

PART A. SOPHISTICATED PLANNING FOR THE VERY WEALTHY: FAMILY OFFICES AND PRIVATE TRUST COMPANIES

Iris J. Goodwin, How the Rich Stay Rich: Using a Family Trust Company to Secure a Family Fortune
40 Seton Hall L. Rev. 467, 472-475, 478, 484-487,
498-500, 502, 504-505, 510-515 (2010)

Continuing to invest the family fortune after it has been transferred into trust has long held significant appeal for wealthy families and, for well over a century, family trust companies have been used as a means to this end. Family trust companies first appeared in the late nineteenth and early twentieth centuries. At the time, they were organized as state-chartered and state-regulated banks under the same laws and regulatory requirements that would govern any state-chartered trust company serving the public. In our era, a family trust company can still be organized this way, but recent changes in the law (at least in some states) make this unnecessary....

[I]t is now... possible to create an unregulated or a "lightly regulated" trust company if the entity is limited in its purpose to serving as trustee of trusts benefiting a group of related people. In one group of states, legislatures have responded with new and separate private trust company charters so that trust companies serving only a related group of people can be subject to "lighter" requirements than those imposed on trust companies serving the general public. In certain other states, liberalization of the law has occurred by simply allowing a limited-purpose corporation to act as a trust company under the general statutes of the state. Some states make available both options—light regulation or no regulation. Whichever scheme a family elects, these innovations at the state level have reduced formation and operation costs for these new entities....

The "lightly regulated" family trust company is still chartered by the state and subject to state supervision, though not on a level comparable to a bank or trust company serving the general public. The organizing documents must, however, limit the purpose of the entity to the provision of fiduciary services to members of a family or a group of related people and, further, prohibit the trust company from soliciting business from the public at large. Even a so-called "lightly regulated" family trust company will usually have to have a minimum number of directors (and perhaps one or more directors domiciled in the state), a minimum number of board meetings per year, a physical office in the state, and a minimum number of employees. Further, there must be in place a formalized risk-management discipline, which state regulators will periodically review; this discipline can include bylaws, a policy manual (setting forth, among other things, a committee structure and decision rules for those committees), annual reports, and appropriate record keeping. Capital requirements vary by state but are universally modest, with some states as low as $250,000 and others up to $2 million. Some states imposing lighter capital requirements, such as South Dakota and New Hampshire, also require a surety bond of $1 million....

Some states offer an even more permissive regime. In these states, a state-issued charter is not required to establish a family trust company, nor is the state required to exercise subsequent regulatory oversight. States that allow family trust companies to form without any regulation typically permit the family to create a limited-purpose corporation that then acts as a trust company under the general statutes of the state. The organizing documents—as was the case with the lightly regulated regime—must limit the purpose of the entity to the provision of fiduciary services to members of a family and, further, prohibit the trust company from soliciting business from the public at large. For entities organized under these regimes, there are usually no capital requirements. The simpler procedures required for organization, the absence of periodic examinations, and the absence of capital requirements allow a family trust company to be quickly and easily established and also make it less expensive to operate....

Because not every state allows a family to establish a modern family trust company, obviously the entity must be organized and operated in a state where the law has been liberalized, unless the entity is to be organized under one of the legal regimes governing those trust companies serving the public. The state in which the trust company is organized and operated is important for other reasons as well, however. The situs of the trust company will also supply the situs and governing law for any trusts established by the family where the trust company is named as trustee. If the family trust company is to be the masterstroke in a sophisticated estate plan, it is crucial that it be located in a state where the law is optimal for the realization of all aspects of the plan.... At this juncture, suffice it to note only that fortunately for the families undertaking these complex estate plans, many of the states that have liberalized their laws with respect to forming privately owned, family trust companies have also changed their laws governing the creation and administration of trusts....

To take a step back, the need to invest subject to a fiduciary standard would not arise but for the family fortune being in trust. If the members of the family held family assets outright, then each generation of the family as it came into its inheritance would be free to invest—and indeed to risk—the funds as it saw fit. Thus, the question is why a very wealthy family eager to minimize its transfer tax burden would transfer its property into trust?

The simple transfer-tax reason that wealthy families put their fortunes into trust is that only the initial transfer into trust—the transfer in fee simple from the donor to the trustee—is subject to transfer tax. And this is the case even though multiple, successive generations of the family subsequently benefit from the property as equitable owners. In contrast, if the family fortune were transferred outright from parent to child and then from child to grandchild and so on, each of the transfers (all in fee simple) would trigger a tax. Taken together, the multiple instances of taxation as property descended from one family member to another, generation to generation, would make for a great drain on the family fortune. But if the property is transferred into trust, it is not subject to transfer tax again until the trust terminates and the property goes outright to the beneficiaries (termed "remaindermen"). Only after the trust terminates, when those remaindermen—now holding the property outright and free of trust— transfer the property, will the property again be subject to transfer tax. And most significantly, if the property can stay in trust in perpetuity, the property is beyond the transfer tax regime forever....

The fact that to date the Rule Against Perpetuities remains intact in many states is no impediment to a wealthy family still living in a perpetuities jurisdiction. Wherever family members live, the family simply needs to name a trustee in a non-perpetuities jurisdiction who can administer the trust in that state. The need for a "nexus" with a non-perpetuities jurisdiction does, however, mean that, for a family planning to place a family trust company at the helm as trustee of a perpetual trust, the family needs to establish its trust company in a state that not only permits a modern family trust company but also has eliminated the Rule Against Perpetuities. Fortunately, for the family wanting to establish its own trust company and name that entity trustee of a perpetual trust, many of the states that have liberalized their laws with respect to forming privately owned, family trust companies have also changed their laws to eliminate the Rule Against Perpetuities....

The common law trust has existed for centuries, but only in recent decades has the law governing fiduciary investing done other than encourage trustees to conserve trust property. For many years, the trustee's primary duty was to avoid risk, including the risk inherent in investing assets for growth. And a case can be made that this risk-averse attitude comported with donors' expectations, especially in earlier eras when the asset placed in trust was almost certainly land and the only reason to transfer property to future generations in trust rather than outright was to avoid transfer tax. When the likely res ceased to be land and became a portfolio of marketable securities, however, donors and their beneficiaries began to rankle under a law that looked only to conserve assets at nominal value even while the purchasing power of those assets declined. Donors and beneficiaries alike noted that between inflation and trustees' commissions, assets placed in trust dwindled however modest the distributions to beneficiaries under the trust agreement....

About twenty years ago, however, the law governing the investment of trust assets began to change. Sophisticated studies examining financial markets in light of modern "portfolio theory" suggested that complaints of settlors and beneficiaries bespoke economic reality, especially once trusts were no longer invested in land but rather in marketable securities. The law responded with a new standard to govern the investment of trust funds. Thus, [the] Prudent Investor [Rule] supplanted [the] [p]rudent [m]an [rule].

As a theory of efficient markets, modern portfolio theory provided a new understanding of the risk inherent in investing (including investing in trust) and suggested a new methodology by which to manage it. At its core, efficient market theory teaches us that it is impossible to predict which securities will do better or worse. Simply stated, each security has risks. Even an investment (such as a U.S. Treasury bill) seeming to conserve trust principal at its face value is itself not without risk—if nothing else, the risk of inflation. All that can be done with respect to risk is to manage it....

As part and parcel of this reframing of the concept of prudent investing, the law also jettisoned the idea that some categories of investments are per se prudent and others imprudent in favor of directing trustees to develop a risk profile appropriate to the particular trust in question....

This new legal order is an invitation to trustees to invest assets in ways heretofore unimaginable for property placed in trust, especially in the case of a perpetual trust holding a great fortune. [The] Prudent Investor [Rule] recognized that the mix of investments and overall risk profile appropriate to a particular account must speak to the size of the account, the terms of the trust instrument, and the situations of beneficiaries. Because the size of account and the investment horizon now matter in determining the magnitude of risk appropriate to a trust portfolio, a family that transfers its considerable wealth into a perpetual trust can justify types of securities with magnitudes of risk (and potential returns) that could not be justified in a smaller trust or in one that would terminate sooner.

Academic commentators are well aware of the perpetual trust, but to date, they tend to view it primarily as a vehicle by which a family exploits the repeal of the

Rule Against Perpetuities by placing its property beyond the reach of the transfer tax regime for untold generations to come. In addition, this literature contains occasional references to the utility of the perpetual trust for asset protection purposes. These observations are correct, as far as they go. The real significance of the perpetual trust cannot be appreciated, however, until we discern how it can serve the family as a multigenerational investment vehicle. Only then can we see how the attributes of tax minimization and asset protection contribute to the determination of the overall risk profile appropriate to the account when portfolio theory governs the investment of trust property. It is here that the true value of tax minimization and asset protection lies....

In short, when applied to the res of a large perpetual trust, portfolio theory legitimates, and indeed encourages, an entrepreneurial mindset in a fiduciary that would have been unthinkable in earlier eras....

While establishing a family trust company might appear to be the final frontier in securing a fortune long into the future, more is required. If wealthy families are going to take unto themselves the role of fiduciary, in order to bring a sophisticated understanding of risk to bear on trusts designed as multi-generational investment vehicles, family members must be prepared to oversee the day-to-day management of an ongoing enterprise, not the least of which includes making state-of-the-art investment decisions. In creating a family trust company and making it trustee of family trusts, financial entropy will not be averted, and indeed much of the family's financial security is sure to be jeopardized, unless at least some family members are ready, willing, and able to undertake the considerable responsibility of managing the trust company. Further, given that the investment horizon here is multigenerational, this need for financial acumen and indeed personal discipline is also multigenerational. Ensuring that every generation has at least some family members prepared to bring facilitating attitudes about money, investing and risk to bear on the family fortune requires attention within the family to the cultivation of such attitudes from generation to generation. Absent sustained talent and discipline, the slow, steady, downward trajectory of the trust portfolios of an earlier era will soon in retrospect bespeak a golden era in the financial life of the family.

In the face of this need to attend to the intergenerational cultivation of attitudes about wealth and investing in addition to managerial expertise, there has grown up a considerable industry to guide the very rich in what might be termed "financial reproduction" or "financial parenting." The literature of this industry puts forward various techniques for the transmission of attitudes and perspectives calculated to foster prudence and indeed industriousness within the family. But at the end of the day, what this literature counsels is that the family that would preserve its fortune must become quite self-consciously identified with its wealth. And further, the family that would manage and indeed grow its wealth must effectively commit itself to maintaining this identity as a wealthy family across generations....

Given that these families are seeking to maintain their wealth far into the future, this education ultimately requires an institutional framework, a governance structure that will bring discipline to the development of this ethos and then allow for constructive reconsideration of it by subsequent generations. What is needed is "a long series of linked transitions" and a system of family governance that will "guide[] the joint decisions family members must make to successfully complete those transitions."

It is in this way that the Family Mission Statement found its way into the literature guiding the very wealthy in their efforts at financial reproduction. Adopted from the corporate world where such statements serve to bring specificity and focus to the interactions and endeavors of diverse protagonists, Family Mission Statements were first put forward for families of average means; the idea was to catalyze within the family a discussion of its basic values and then "codify" them into a constitution of sorts. This document is to unify families around fundamental principles that "get built right into the very structure and culture of the family." Like any constitution, the Family Mission Statement serves as a point of reference as the family moves forward. It can also be revisited and amended in light of fundamental changes in the family or the larger world.

Still embraced by many people of modest means as a tool of the broader endeavor of "social reproduction," the Family Mission Statement has nevertheless acquired a certain edge as wealth educators now proffer it to the very wealthy in pursuit of the narrower goal of "financial reproduction." Most basically, these families are advised that the process of developing such a statement provides a context in which a wealthy family can confront the origin and meaning of privilege in its own instance and, further, reinvent itself as a wealthy family from generation to generation. Interestingly, however, especially where the very rich are concerned, some of this literature draws parallels between the wealthy family seeking continued financial prosperity and the well-managed business enterprise. The claim is that the business enterprise provides an apt analogy because, like a business, the object of the family is "to organize [its] financial, intellectual, and human assets for the purpose of preserving and enhancing each of these in succeeding generations." One wealth adviser elaborates, "[T]he most important role in the management of an enterprise is arranging for orderly succession." And further on: "Families attempting long-term wealth preservation often don't understand that they are businesses and that the techniques of long-term succession planning practiced by all other businesses are available to them as well."

The wealthy family-as-business ceases to be a metaphor, however, and becomes a reality when this literature turns to consider the uses of the family trust company. While perhaps not appreciating the magnitude of the investment opportunity presented by these entities (especially under [the] Prudent Investor [Rule]), this literature still recognizes that the family trust company can serve the family in the mechanics of investing—for example, as a consolidation vehicle, allowing all family holdings to be managed in one place and subjected to a coordinated, long-term investment strategy. More interestingly, however, is the insight in this literature that the family trust company can serve as the primary institutional context for the essential tasks of "financial reproduction" in all its dimensions and across multiple generations. For a very wealthy family, myriad aspects of family life can be coordinated through the trust company. The trust company is a "family seat," a "repository for the family history" with a "perpetual life," a locus for governance of many types to take place, a meeting place where the wealthy family interacts and perpetuates its identify as a wealthy family. Most importantly for a family identified with its wealth, the family trust company provides a context in which successive generations can be tutored in long-term wealth preservation consistent with the family's particular ethos about money and investing, perhaps articulated in a Family Mission Statement. The family trust company presents a golden opportunity to put into play the attitudes and skills deemed instrumental to the family's historic financial success. As successive generations of a family manage their investment risk to secure their fortune long into the future, successive generations are also given opportunity to rediscover and indeed reaffirm their "differentness"—their privilege.

The suggestion that the family trust company can serve as a context within which a wealthy family can develop an ethos about money and investing—and ultimately an identity as a wealthy family—acquires great resonance when considered alongside the opportunities under the Prudent Investor statute to invest property in trust, especially where the portfolio is large enough and the time horizon extended. To realize the full potential of [the] Prudent Investor [Rule] as applicable to a large perpetual trust, a trustee needs a sophisticated understanding of risk and skills sufficient to choose investments consistent with the risk profile. If a family seeks to take this role through a family trust company, these aptitudes must somehow be present in every generation going forward. What the literature of financial reproduction makes clear, however, is that the development of these aptitudes in one generation and the transmission of them to another is (of necessity) about much more than investing. As older and younger generations of a family come together to play various roles in the management of the family fortune—and to exploit the opportunities available under [the] Prudent Investor [Rule] where a fortune is in trust—what is also happening is the transmission of an identity as a very wealthy and privileged family.

Notes and Questions

1. *Family Offices.* In traditional parlance, a family office is a private company that manages the assets of, and provides services for, one family. The services range from handling all investment, legal, and accounting matters to the management of real estate, the supervision of household staff, and the handling of travel arrangements for family members. As a rough rule of thumb, the minimum wealth to make a family office worthwhile is said to be $100 million, though in some instances a family

office can make sense for a family with assets below $100 million. See Russ Alan Prince, How Much Money is Required to Have a Single-Family Office?, Forbes, Oct. 4, 2013, at www.forbes.com. Some family offices have become "multifamily" offices, enabling families with assets below $100 million to join together and avail themselves of these services. See Robert Frank, How to Bank Like a Billionaire, Wall St. J., Jun. 10, 2004.

2. *Policy Questions.* What are the benefits—and costs—of allowing the very wealthy to use family offices to manage and increase wealth across generations? We first encountered questions of donative freedom and the reach of the dead hand in Chapter 1. Have your views about the pros and cons of inherited wealth changed in any way since you read that opening chapter? If so, how and why?

3. *Contrast: The Giving Pledge.* In contrast to the aim of maintaining and growing family wealth far into the future, consider the efforts by Bill and Melinda Gates and Warren Buffett to encourage billionaires to pledge to give the majority of their assets to charity. Among the more than two hundred forty who have signed the pledge are Michael Bloomberg, Barry Diller and Diane von Furstenberg, George Lucas and Mellody Hobson, Gordon and Betty Moore, T. Boone Pickens, David Rockefeller, David M. Rubenstein, Ted Turner, and Mark Zuckerberg and Priscilla Chan. A list of signatories is available at http://givingpledge.org.

4. *Wall Street Reform and Family Offices.* In 2010, the Dodd-Frank Wall Street Reform and Consumer Protection Act imposed a new system of regulatory oversight on investment advisers. Under prior law, and the Dodd-Frank Act, investment advisers must register with the Securities and Exchange Commission (SEC) and be subject to regulation, with the Dodd-Frank Act adding to the level of regulatory oversight. Under Section 203(b)(3) of the Investment Advisors Act of 1940, 15 U.S.C. §80b-2(b)(3), however, there had long been an exemption for advisers providing investment services to fewer than 15 clients, an exemption that covered most family offices. That exemption was eliminated by the Dodd-Frank Act, which instead exempted any "family office" as defined in a rule to be promulgated by the SEC. See 15 U.S.C. §80b-2(a)(11)(G). In June 2011, the SEC promulgated the final version of a rule (Rule 202(a)(11)(G)-1) defining a family office for purpose of the exemption. Under this rule, as further amended in September 2016, a "family office":

> (1) Has no clients other than family clients...
>
> (2) Is wholly owned by family clients and is exclusively controlled (directly or indirectly) by one or more family members and/or family entities; and
>
> (3) Does not hold itself out to the public as an investment adviser.

This definition of "family office" relies on the rule's definition of "family client." Under the rule, the definition of "family client" is linked to the rule's definition of "family member"—a term defined in a way that includes "spouses and spousal equivalents" but excludes other in-laws as well as family friends. After the rule was promulgated, experts estimated that only about 50% of the then-existing family offices would fit within the new exemption. The others would face the following choices: (1) limit services to family members as defined in the rule; (2) outsource all investment management functions; or (3) restructure the family office as a private trust company (see the following note). See Andrew Osterland, Dodd-Frank Deadline Looms for Family Offices, Investment News, Jan. 29, 2012.

5. *Private Trust Companies*. A private trust company is "an entity authorized to act as a fiduciary under state law, but prohibited from soliciting business from the general public." See Alan V. Ytterberg & James P. Weller, Managing Family Wealth Through a Private Trust Company, 36 ACTEC L.J. 623, 624 (2010). Under the Dodd-Frank Act, a private trust company licensed and regulated under state law is and continues to be exempt from SEC registration. See 15 U.S.C. §§80b-2(a)(2)(C), 80b-2(a)(11)(B). Thus, a family with a family office that no longer fits within the "family office" exemption may avoid SEC registration by establishing a private trust company under state law—a process that includes getting a charter or license from the state—and transferring to the private trust company the investment and management of the family's assets.

6. *Privacy versus Transparency*. In an effort to combat money laundering and other financial crimes, Congress enacted the Corporate Transparency Act (CTA) as §§6401-6403 of the National Defense Authorization Act for Fiscal Year 2021, Pub. L. No. 116-283 (H.R. 6395), 134 Stat. 338, 116th Cong. 2d Sess. The CTA became effective January 1, 2024. The CTA requires every "reporting company" to disclose their "beneficial owners" and certain additional information to the Financial Crimes Enforcement Network (FinCEN), which is a bureau of the U.S. Department of the Treasury. The definition of "reporting company" is broad, and generally covers any entity created by the filing of a document with the secretary of state of a U.S. state or similar office. This includes corporations, limited liability companies, limited partnerships, and the like. There are some statutory exceptions, but many family offices and private trust companies are expected to fall within the definition of a "reporting company." The definition of "beneficial owner"—whose name, birthdate, residential street address, and image of driver's license or passport must be provided to FinCEN—includes individuals who exercise "substantial control" over the reporting company, as well as individuals who own or control at least 25 percent of the ownership interests in the company. Willfully failing to submit the required information may result in civil penalties of up to $500 per day as well as criminal penalties including a fine of up to $10,000 and imprisonment for up to two years.

Question. Does this legislation achieve the right balance between privacy and transparency?

PART B. PLANNING FOR FUTURE GENERATIONS

We began the casebook, in Chapter 1, with excerpts from a Trachtman Lecture given by Roberta Cooper Ramo to the American College of Trust and Estate Counsel (ACTEC) in 1996. We complete the circle with excerpts, below, from a Trachtman Lecture delivered more than a decade later by Professor Jeffrey Pennell. In these excerpts, Professor Pennell invites estate planners to re-examine their assumptions about the techniques that will best serve the next generation(s) of clients.

Jeffrey N. Pennell, Estate Planning for the Next Generation(s) of Clients: It's Not Your Father's Buick, Anymore
34 ACTEC J. 2, 3-4, 10-14, 19 (2008)

I'm confident that Baby Boomer clients are very different than their G.I. generation parents, for whom most of our current estate planning boxes were developed and refined. Boomer attitudes about wealth; about the role and abilities of women; about marriage, divorce, remarriage, and family; about education; and about work, careers, retirement, and about inheritance are all (remarkably) different than that of their parents in the G.I. generation. And I suspect that Boomers may not resonate with planning options that estate planners developed for the G.I. generation. This remains to be seen, because Boomers are only starting to become serious about estate planning as they finally inherit wealth. Most Boomers have not yet become orphans, in the sense that over 75% still have not lost their mothers. And their need for estate planning is just beginning to become clear, as they reach an age at which alumni newsletters report classmates who have died of natural causes. My suggestion is that estate planners have not yet reconsidered the planning boxes that were developed for a prior generation of clients....

My observation is simply that the need for change is coming. Indeed, for that little we know, it may be upon us already. Either way, we have not really embraced it. My sense is that estate planners have not paid much attention to this demographic development. I'd like to explore that notion in a number of ways in this monograph. I say "It's Not Your Father's Buick, Anymore" because the estate planning vehicle that my father thought was appropriate or desirable is not what I expect today's generation of clients to embrace.

Another reality that informs this topic is that estate planners bring certain biases to their work. We all have presumptions, predilections, and prejudices that influence our representations, the recommendations that we make, and the documents that we draft. As proof, consider whether you believe that the "right" form of representation among descendants is the traditional common law per stirpes, or is it per capita or per capita at each generation? I'll bet that every estate planner has a personal sense about this, and it would surprise me if the typical planner's basic documents include a different form of representation than the one the drafter personally believes is best. Surely a good planner would change that preferred approach in a given situation, but

I wonder how many planners really delve into this topic and try to educate their clients about the differences in approach, or why one approach may be better for a client's situation than another. My point is only that we make implicit recommendations to clients by the drafting choices that we make and by the planning boxes that we present as basic solutions. So an important element in this discussion is knowing our presumptions, predilections, and prejudices, and the extent to which these are a function of our generation, upbringing (in general, and in the law practice), and sensitivity to client situations. And while my intent is to challenge you to consider the thesis, I encourage you to be circumspect about various specifics. Because I too am a merchant of various presumptions, predilections, and prejudices....

One of my primary concerns in the context of traditional marital deduction and nonmarital trust planning is the message that we send to surviving spouses about issues of trust, and the ability to deal with wealth. It has been my custom to ask audiences of estate planners the following question, about themselves: "Do you trust your surviving spouse to have control over marital deduction qualified wealth, to make gifts following your death"? The response usually is overwhelmingly "yes."... Then I ask whether these planners ask their clients the same question, and make it possible in the plan for the surviving spouse to take advantage of the incredible opportunities that are available for transfer tax minimization by making inter vivos transfers. The response usually is that hardly anyone empowers the surviving spouse in this manner....

More than any other element of traditional estate planning, I believe this presumed distrust—the lack of control over the marital bequest—reflects the thinking of the G.I. generation of men about their widows. The most frequently heard response is that the propertied spouse fears that the surviving spouse will remarry and disinherit their children in favor of that new spouse. As confirmed by statistics (and probably also undeniable in practice experience), the likelihood of a surviving *widower* remarrying after the death of his wife is much greater than the likelihood of a surviving *widow* remarrying....

I do not have a statistic that shows how often remarried spouses disinherit their own children by a former marriage in favor of a new spouse. But most estate planners of any experience will confirm that surviving remarried widows seldom engage in disinheritance planning, whereas surviving remarried widowers do so with much greater frequency. So, if control over the wealth of the first spouse to die is a problem, it ought to be the wife who articulates the concern, and then only if the husband is likely to be the survivor and has the smaller estate (meaning there is logic in using a marital deduction bequest), which was not a normal paradigm for planning purposes in the G.I. generation. Instead, in the more common but opposite situation, the statement of fear about remarriage probably is a manifestation of what the husband would do if he survived, rather than a legitimate fear of what the wife is likely to do if she survives and has the power to withdraw corpus to make gifts. Do you reflect these gender differences in your normal husband-wife planning? And how do you think Boomer [Generation] or Silent [Generation] Survivors—male or female—will resonate with the plan we traditionally recommend, with its message of distrust?...

Another illustration about changing paradigms that might be useful relates to a form of drafting that experience and a few empirical studies suggest is not very common. The typical estate plan anticipates a fund large enough to justify division of the family trust (typically after both spouses have died) into separate shares for lineal lines of descent—living children and descendants of deceased children. The alternative... anticipates a single "group trust" that will be held until some time after the death of the surviving spouse (or after the death of the settlor, if the trust is not to be held for the benefit of a surviving spouse).

In some circumstances the family trust will be held as a group trust but never divided into shares, either for immediate distribution or to be separately held until a child reaches an older age. A good illustration of when this might be appropriate is a family with many children whose ages are quite disparate, or with children all beyond the age at which an inheritance would be meaningful (and so the trust will be held into the next generation), or some combination of these factors.... The reflected reality is that separate shares may be uneconomical or unfair, because older children benefited from receiving their education and payments for other major expenses prior to the family wealth being divided into equal shares, while younger children will consume their separate shares to pay for similar items that arise after division. This is particularly relevant if the age spread among children is substantial.

A group trust also may be appropriate if some children have extraordinary needs, which ought to take priority above all else. And it might effect the desire of clients with a traditional or blended family to empower a trustee to continue providing for all in a way that reflects different needs and abilities without what might be perceived as the "unfairness" of creating equal shares for individuals who are anything but homogenous or "equal." Finally, it can avoid one group of children benefiting substantially more than others, just because their parent was the more wealthy spouse. With a changing paradigm of marriage, remarriage, and blended families, G.I. generation notions of division and separate inheritances may not make sense in some Silent and Boomer situations. Nevertheless, both empirical and apocryphal responses reveal the very suggestion here is very bold.

In this regard, it is impressive that, absent the special circumstance of a special needs child (who needs added protection) or a black sheep (who is being disinherited), the G.I. generation of parents were nearly unanimous in saying that they wanted to treat their children equally, albeit that isn't what they did when they were alive. Instead, most parents treat their children equitably—maybe communistically is a more accurate (albeit a more hot button term)—in providing for their children inter vivos. But they still think, and they say, that they intend to treat (and love) all their children equally at death. Why does being a good provider, in an appropriately equitable (not necessarily equal) manner, change when the client talks about their postmortem intent? My mentor was a very wise and vastly experienced and sensitive estate planner who used to say that an effective estate plan is an extension of the decedent's pocketbook. And if the observation is correct that most decedents don't make equalizing distributions when providing for children during life, it seems odd that this changes at death. What accounts for this dissonance—between what people do while alive and what they call for in their estate plan?...

My personal sense is that this may boil down to fiduciary selection: I suspect we would find sharing more acceptable if we believed that a trustee would be efficient and insightful in discriminating between legitimate need and ineptitude or lack of ambition. Unfortunately, experienced fiduciaries think that discretion like this is the devil.

...[W]e might give added thought to the notion of sharing in a less artificial manner than "equal" shares. In some situations a group trust until the last child dies might be appropriate. In other cases the client ultimately will want the children to be able to go their separate ways, and it may be unwise to make older children wait for distribution until their younger siblings have reached the age for distribution, because there is too wide a spread in their ages. In such a case an alternative compromise... permits each child to "peel-off" a share as the child reaches a specified age. In each of these cases, adapting our traditional planning boxes may be wise, because changing family dynamics make these options more important and acceptable. In all of these cases exploring creative solutions that are outside our traditions will pay dividends. Unfortunately, in my experience we have not shared wisdom in matters such as these nearly as much as we have collaborated in dealing with tax law or state law changes....

So much of our work has been overshadowed by the agenda that Congress has written for us, in the form of tax law change over the past 32 years (since 1976 to be sure, and maybe since 1969). To a lesser extent the same might be said about the uniform laws (although many who plan estates ignore those legislative developments as either irrelevant or as commanding no special response).

My purpose here is simply to suggest that mainstream estate planners will benefit from a focus that considers more than just the tax agenda, and to encourage consideration of whether planning and drafting has kept up. I don't intend to say that I know the right answers to so many of the questions, or even to know how a typical client would elect if given a choice. As a profession we have given others a free reign in dealing with some of these issues, perhaps with speckled success. And with respect to some others of these issues, as a profession we haven't even begun the conversation about what a new generation of clients would prefer. I hope we can do that.

Question and Final Problem

1. *Re-Examining Assumptions*. In Chapter 2, we mentioned, at p. 44, that some empirical evidence reveals a disjunction between the system of representation that many lawyers think that clients want (per stirpes) and the system of representation that many clients actually want (per capita at each generation). What other assumptions do you believe should be re-thought?

2. *Problem.* Imagine that you have been retained by the Uniform Law Commission as an independent expert in the law of trusts and estates. Identify one provision or set of provisions in the Uniform Probate Code or Uniform Trust Code that should be amended significantly. Avoid mere tinkering. Explain your choice, and draft the proposed amendment(s).

Index

References are to chapters and subdivisions thereof.